W9-CNC-648

Global Crises, Global Solutions
Second edition

The first edition of *Global Crises, Global Solutions* was nominated as one of the books of the year by *The Economist* in 2004. This new edition is entirely revised and updated but retains the format that made the first edition a bestseller and one of the most widely discussed policy books of recent times.

If we had more money to spend to help the world's poorest people, where could we spend it most effectively? Using a common framework of cost-benefit analysis, a team of leading economists, including five Nobel Prize winners, assess the attractiveness of a wide range of policy options for combating ten of the world's biggest problems: air pollution, conflicts, diseases, education, global warming, malnutrition and hunger, sanitation and clean water, subsidies and trade barriers, terrorism, women and development. The arguments are clearly presented and fully referenced so that readers are encouraged to make their own evaluation of the menu of policy options on offer. Whether you agree or disagree with the economists' conclusions, there is a wealth of data and ideas to discuss and debate!

BJØRN LOMBORG is Director of the Copenhagen Consensus Center and Adjunct Professor in the Department of Management, Politics and Philosophy at Copenhagen Business School. He is the author of the controversial bestseller, *The Skeptical Environmentalist* (Cambridge, 2001), and was named as one of the most globally influential people by *Time* magazine in 2004.

Global Crises, Global Solutions

SECOND EDITION

Edited by

BJØRN LOMBORG

CAMBRIDGE UNIVERSITY PRESS
Cambridge, New York, Melbourne, Madrid, Cape Town, Singapore, São Paulo, Delhi

Cambridge University Press
The Edinburgh Building, Cambridge CB2 8RU, UK

Published in the United States of America by Cambridge University Press, New York

www.cambridge.org
Information on this title: www.cambridge.org/9780521741224
© Cambridge University Press 2009

First published 2009

Printed in the United Kingdom at the University Press, Cambridge

A catalogue record for this publication is available from the British Library

ISBN 978-0-521-57121-8 hardback
ISBN 978-0-52174122-4 paperback

Contents

Figures

Tables

Contributors

Chapter authors

Harold Alderman is Lead Human Development Economist for the Africa Region at the World Bank. His main research interests are food policy and nutrition as well as the economics of education and of targeted poverty programs. His articles have appeared in journals such as *World Development, Journal of Nutrition, Economic Review, British Medical Journal*, and *Food Policy*.

Kym Anderson is Lead Economist in Trade Policy at the World Bank and Professor of Economics at the University of Adelaide. His research interests and publications are in the areas of international trade and development, agricultural economics, and environmental and resource economics. He has published more than 20 books and 200 journal articles and chapters in other books. He has been a consultant to numerous national and international bureaucracies, business organizations and corporations. His publications include *Agricultural Trade Liberalization: Implications for Indian Ocean Rim Countries* (Department of Foreign Affairs and Trade, 2002), *Reforming Trade Policy in Papua New Guinea and the Pacific Islands: What Roles for WTO and APEC?* (Institute for National Affairs, 2000), and *Lao Economic Reform and WTO Accession* (Institute of Southeast Asian Studies, 1999).

Daniel G. Arce is The Bidgood Chair of Economics and Finance at the University of Texas. His primary areas of research interest are in game theory, business ethics, collective action, conflict, corporate governance, global public goods, leadership, and (counter)terrorism.

His articles have appeared in journals such as *Economic Inquiry, British Journal of Political Science, Journal of International Development, Managerial and Decision Economics*, and *Journal of Conflict Resolution.*

Geoffrey J. Blanford is Program Manager for research on Global Climate Change Policy Costs and Benefits at the Electric Power Research Institute, California. The program conducts analysis of the economic and environmental implications of domestic and international climate policy proposals, with emphasis on the principles of efficient policy design, the role of technology, and the value of R&D. His areas of interest include development of the MERGE model for integrated assessment and its application to issues such as technology policy and international climate agreements.

David Bloom is Clarence James Gamble Professor of Economics and Demography at Harvard University. His research interests include labor economics, health, demography, and the environment. He has served as a consultant to the UNDP, the World Bank and WHO. His articles have been published in journals such as the *Journal of Monetary Economics, World Economics*, and *World Development.* He contributed to *Solving the Riddle of Globalization and Development* (with M. Agosin *et al.*, Routledge, 2007).

Lisa Chauvet is Research Fellow at IRD-DIAL (Institut de Recherche pour le Développement – Développement Institutions et Analyses de Long Terme). Her research interests are international aid and foreign direct investment, development macroeconomics, empirical analysis of economic growth, and political economy of civil wars.

Paul Collier is Professor and Director of the Centre for the Study of African Economies at Oxford University. His research interests are within the fields of governance in low-income countries, especially the political economy of democracy, economic growth in Africa, globalization and poverty, and the economics of civil war. His recent publications include *Trade and Economic Performance: Does Africa's Fragmentation Matter?* (Working Paper, 2008), *Climate Change and Africa* (with G. Conway and A. Venables, Working Paper, 2008), and *Post Conflict Monetary Reconstruction* (with C. Adams and V. Davies, World Bank Economic Review, 2008).

Jennifer Davis is Assistant Professor, Department of Civil and Environmental Engineering at Stanford University. Her areas of research are within sustainability, private-sector participation, institutional and organizational analysis, water, sanitation, and health. Her research has been published in journals such as *Environment and Resources*, *Water Policy*, *World Development*, and *International Development Planning Review*, and in *In Search of Good Governance: Experiments from South Asia's Water and Sanitation Sector* (with S. Tankha *et al.*, New Delhi: Water and Sanitation Program, 2002).

Walter Enders is Professor and Lee Bidgood Chair of Economics and Finance, University of Alabama. His areas of expertise are open-economy macroeconomics, time-series econometrics, and transnational terrorism. He has published numerous research articles in journals such as the *Review of Economics and Statistics*, *Quarterly Journal of Economics*, and the *Journal of International Economics*. He has also published articles in the *American Economic Review*, *Journal of Business and Economic Statistics*, and the *American Political Science Review*.

Paul Glewwe is Professor of Economics at the University of Minnesota. His research interests are economics of education, poverty and

inequality in developing countries, and applied econometrics. Besides teaching he has worked for the World Bank. His recent articles have appeared in the *Handbook of the Economics of Education*, *Economic Development and Cultural Change*, *Journal of Development Economics*, *Journal of Economic Literature*, and *World Bank Economic Review*. He has contributed to books including *Economic Growth, Poverty, and Household Welfare in Vietnam* (with N. Agrawal *et al.*, World Bank, 2004).

W. Michael Hanemann is Chancellor's Professor, Department of Agricultural and Resource Economics at the University of California. His area of research is in non-market valuation, environmental economics and policy, demand modelling for market research, and policy design. His articles have been published in *Natural Resources Journal*, *American Economics Review*, and *Journal of Law and Economics*.

Håvard Hegre is Associate Professor, Department of Political Science at the University of Oslo. His research interests are the dynamics of institutional change and conflict, environmental factors of civil war, human rights, governance, and conflict. His contributions include *Global Trends in Armed Conflict* (with H. Buhaug *et al.*, Norwegian Ministry of Foreign Affairs, 2007), and *Breaking the Conflict Trap: Civil War and Development Policy* (with P. Collier *et al.*, World Bank/Oxford University Press, 2003).

Sue Horton is Professor of Economics at Wilfrid Laurier University. Her areas of research are human resources, economics of health, nutrition, household time use, labor markets, and poverty in developing countries. She has worked in over 20 developing countries and has consulted for the World Bank, the Asian Development Bank, several UN agencies, and the International Development Research Centre. Her recent contributions include *Economics of nutritional investment* in *Nutrition and Health in Developing Countries* (R.D. Semba and M. Bloem, Humana Press, 2008) and *The Economics of Addressing Nutritional Anemia* (with H. Alderman) in *Nutritional Anemia*

(K. Kraemer and M. Zimmerman, Basel: Sight and Life Organization, 2007).

Guy Hutton is an economist focusing on the fields of health, air pollution, and water and sanitation. He has published widely on economic evaluation and financing of development interventions. He works for the World Bank Water and Sanitation Program in East Asia and the Pacific region. He has previously held posts at the Swiss Tropical Institute, London School of Hygiene and Tropical Medicine, and Oxford University.

Dean T. Jamison is Senior Fellow at the Fogarty International Center of the National Institutes of Health. He has worked for the World Bank as Senior Economist and Division Chief and for the WHO. His research interests are economy, management, effect of education on productivity in agriculture, and cost-effectiveness of interventions in education and health. His articles have featured in journals such as the *Journal of Health Economics* and *The Lancet*, and he contributed to *Priorities in Health* (World Bank, 2006).

Marc Jeuland is a PhD candidate in Environmental Management and Policy at the University of North Carolina – Chapel Hill. His research interests are in non-market valuation techniques, water resources planning and management, and the economic analysis of investments in the water and sanitation sector. His recent co-authored publications include *Private Demand for Cholera Vaccines in Beira, Mozambique* (in *Vaccine*, 25, 2007), *Re-visiting Socially Optimal Vaccine Subsidies: An Empirical Application in Kolkata, India* (*Journal of Policy Analysis and Management*, 2008), and *Sustaining the Benefits of Rural Water Supply Investments: Experience from Cochabamba and Chuquisaca, Bolivia* (Water Resources Research, 2008).

Prabhat Jha is Professor of Epistemology at the University of Toronto. His research interests include large-scale epidemiology studies of the major causes of death in developing countries, control of HIV transmission in developing countries, and tobacco control policy in developed and developing countries. He has

published articles in *Science* and the *National Medical Journal of India*. He also contributed to *Governments and the Economics of Tobacco Control* (World Bank, 1999).

Neha Khanna is Associate Professor at Binghamton University (State University of New York), where she holds joint appointments in the Economics Department and on the Environmental Studies Program. She has researched the world oil market and its implications for international security, the relationship between economic growth and environmental quality, climate change, and the efficacy of voluntary pollution-prevention programs. In addition, she is working on the impact of public policy measures on human health and on the sustainable extraction of ground water. She has recently written for journals such as *Economic Inquiry*, *Econometric Reviews*, and the *Journal of Environmental Economics and Management.*

Elizabeth King is Research Manager for Public Services of the Development Research Group at the World Bank. Her research interests are human capital, poverty, economic development, education reforms in developing countries, and gender inequality. Her articles have featured in journals such as the *Journal of Development Studies*, *Economic Development and Cultural Change*, and *American Economic Review*. She is also the author of *Promoting Gender Equality and Women's Empowerment* in *Confronting the Challenges of Gender Equality and Fragile State* (World Bank, 2007).

Stephan Klasen is Professor of Economics at Georg-August University in Göttingen. His research focuses on issues of poverty and inequality in developing countries. In addition, he has worked extensively on causes, measurement, and consequences of gender bias in mortality, education, and employment in developing countries. His recent works have been featured in journals such as *World Development* and *Journal of Economic Inequality.*

Bjørn Larsen is a freelance consultant to international and bilateral development agencies, research institutions, and consulting firms. His fields of interest include air pollution, water supply, sanitation and hygiene in developing countries, and environmental health risk linkages to child malnutrition and poverty. His recent publications include *Does urban air pollution control pay off in low-income countries?: A cost–benefit analysis in Greater Dakar, Senegal* (prepared for ECON/Roche/World Bank, 2007).

Peter F. Orazem is Professor of Economics at Iowa State University. His research interests are labor economics, transition and developing economies, and the economics of education. He has contributed to the *Southern Economic Journal, Economic Development and Cultural Change,* and *World Bank Economic Review.* His most recent contribution was *Schooling in Developing Countries: The Roles of Supply, Demand and Government Policy* (with Elizabeth King, in *Handbook of Development Economics,* Iowa State University, Department of Economics, Staff General Research Papers, 2008).

Harry Patrinos is Lead Education Economist at the World Bank. His research interests are school-based management, demand-side financing, and public–private partnerships. His recent publications are *Quality of Schooling, Returns to Schooling and the 1981 Vouchers Reform in Chile* (Working Paper, World Bank, 2008) and *Empowering parents to improve education: evidence from rural Mexico* (Working Paper, World Bank, 2008).

Maria Porter is Post-doctoral Fellow, Center for Demography and Economics of Aging at the University of Chicago. Her primary research interests are in the fields of development, population and household economics, and aging.

Richard G. Richels is Director of Global Climate Change Research at the Electric Power Research Institute in Palo Alto, California. His main area of research is economics of climate change.

Frank Rijsberman is Director of the Water and Sanitation Services at Google.org. His area of research is within water resource management. His articles have appeared in journals such as *Agricultural Water Management, Issues, Water Policy, Water Science and Technology,* and *Paddy and Water Environment.*

Juan Rivera is Professor of Nutrition at the School of Public Health in Mexico. His main areas of research focus on undernutrition, malnutrition, and obesity. He also researches the development and evaluation of programs and policies that raise the level of nutrition in the general population. He has published more than 130 scientific articles and chapters in books.

Claudia Sadoff is a Lead Economist with the World Bank, based in the Kathmandu Resident Mission. Her expertise is in water resources policies and institutions, cooperation and benefit sharing in international rivers, and the dynamics of water, wealth, and poverty. She is a member of the Global Water Partnership's Technical Committee and the World Economic Forum's Global Agenda Council on Water Security. Her recent publications include *Water Security – an Adaptation Imperative* (with D. Grey) in *Environment Matters* (The World Bank, 2008).

Todd Sandler is the Vibhooti Shukla Professor of Economics and Political Economy at the University of Texas. His research areas are international political economy, defense economics, terrorism, global and regional public goods, and environmental economics. He applies theoretical and empirical models of economics to the study of international political economy, defense, environmental issues, and public finance. He is particularly interested in the application of game theory (non-cooperative and cooperative) and microeconomics to issues in international relations. His publications include *Global Collective Action* (Cambridge University Press, 2004), *Regional Public Goods: Typologies, Provision, Financing, and Development Assistance* (Almqvist & Wicksell International, 2002), and *Economic Concepts for the Social Sciences* (Cambridge University Press, 2001).

Richard S.J. Tol is Professor of Economics of Climate Change at Vrije University in The Netherlands and Research Professor at the *Economic and Social Research Institute* in Dublin, Ireland. His main research interests are the application of economic, mathematical, and statistical techniques – such as time-series analysis, valuation, decision analysis, and game theory – and environmental problems, in particular climate change, natural disasters, and river basin management. His recent publications include *Economic Analysis of Land Use in Global Climate Change* (Routledge, 2008) and *Environmental Crisis: Science and Policy* (Springer, 2007).

Dale Whittington is Professor of Environmental Sciences and Engineering at the University of North Carolina. His research interests are cost–benefit analysis, environmental economics, and water resources policy. His research has appeared in journals such as *Environmental and Resource Economics* and *Water Policy*. He also wrote *Guidelines for Designing Energy Modules in Living Standard Measurement Surveys: Report to the World Bank* (2004).

L. Alan Winters is Professor of Economics at the University of Sussex. He has published more than 200 articles and 30 books in areas such as regional trading arrangements, non-tariff barriers, European Integration, transition economies' trade, international labor mobility, agricultural protection, trade and poverty, and the world trading system. His recent books include *The Temporary Movement of Workers to Provide Services* in *A Handbook of International Trade in Services* (ed. A. Mattoo, R.M. Stern, and G. Zanini, Oxford University Press, 2007) and his articles have appeared in journals such as *The World Economy*, *Journal of Economic Integration*, and *Social Science & Medicine*.

Gary W. Yohe is Woodhouse/Sysco Professor of Economics at Wesleyan University. His main research area is global climate change and risk management. His articles have featured in journals such as *Global Environmental Change* and *Environment and Development Economics*.

Alix Peterson Zwane serves as the Program Manager leading efforts to develop the health and water sub-program within the Inform and Empower Initiative at Google.org. Before that she was a member of the faculty in the Department of Agricultural and Resource Economics at UC Berkeley. She spent five years there where her research included topics such as the links between poverty and tropical deforestation, methods for creating incentives for private R&D on challenges unique to the tropics, and cost-effective and sustainable solutions to diarrheal diseases, with extensive field work in East Africa and Latin America. Her work has been published in technical and policy journals including the *Journal of Development Economics* and the *Journal of Environmental Economics and Management*.

Perspective paper authors

S. Brock Blomberg is Professor of Economics at Claremont Mckenna College. His research interests are macroeconomics, political economy, and international economics. His works include *A Gravity Model of Globalization, Democracy and Transnational Terrorism* in *Guns and Butter* (with P. Rosendorff and G. Hess (eds.)), and he has been published in journals such as *World Economy*, *Review of Economics and Statistics*, *Journal of Monetary Economics*, *Journal of Public Economy*, and *Journal of Conflict Resolution*.

David Canning is Professor of Economics and International Health at the Harvard School of Public Health. His fields of interest are economic growth, demographic changes, and health. He has contributed to journals such as *The Manchester School*, *Population and Development Review*, *Public Policy and Aging Report*, *Science*, and the *International Journal of Forecasting*.

Alan Deardorff is Professor of Economics and Public Policy at the Gerald R. Ford School of Public Policy. His primary area of interest is international trade and he has worked on analyses of anti-dumping laws, the safeguards clause of the GATT, and arguments for and against extending intellectual property protection to developing countries. His publications include *Terms of Trade: Glossary of International Economics* (World Scientific Publishers, 2006) and *Measurement of Nontariff Barriers* (with R. Stern, The University of Michigan Press, 1998).

Anil Deolalikar is Professor of Economics, University of California, Riverside. His areas of research are economic development, public policy, economic demography, and human capital in development. His recent publications are *Attaining the Millennium Development Goals in India: Reducing Infant Mortality, Child Malnutrition, Gender Disparities and Hunger-Poverty and Increasing School Enrollment and Completion?* (Oxford University Press, 2005), *Health Care and Family in Vietnam* in *Reconfiguring Families in Vietnam* (Stanford University Press, forthcoming), and *Human Development in India: Past Trends and Future Challenges* in *The Indian Economy at 60: Performance and Prospects* (R. Jha, Palgrave Macmillan, forthcoming).

Ibrahim A. Elbadawi is Lead Economist, Development Economic Research Group of the World Bank. His research interests include exchange rate economics, growth, aid effectiveness, democracy and development, and economics of civil wars. His research and policy experiences cover Africa and the Middle East. His recent publications are *Political Violence and Economic Growth* (with C. Bodea, World Bank, 2008), *Referendum, Response, and Consequences for Sudan: The Game Between Juba and Khartoum* (World Bank, 2008), and *Riots, Coups and Civil War: Revisiting the Greed and Grievance Debate* (with C. Bodea, World Bank, 2007).

Christopher Green is Professor of Economics at McGill University. His areas of specialization include industrial organization, public policies toward business, and environmental economics, in particular the economics of climate change. His articles have appeared in journals such

as *Nature, Energy Policy, Policy Options,* and *Energy Policy*.

Lawrence Haddad is Director of Institute of Development Studies at the University of Sussex. His main research interests are the intersection of poverty, food insecurity and malnutrition – including poverty dynamics, social capital, HIV/AIDS, social protection, agriculture and poverty, and women's empowerment. His publications include *Food and Nutrition Policies and Interventions* in *Human Nutrition* (ed. C.A. Geissler and H.J. Powers, Elsevier, 2005).

Michael D. Intriligator is Professor of Economics at UCLA. He is the author of more than 200 journal articles and other publications in the areas of economic theory and mathematical economics, econometrics, health economics, reform of the Russian economy, and strategy and arms control, which are his principal research fields. His articles have appeared in journals such as *American Behavioral Scientist, Business World and Conflict Management,* and *Peace Science*.

Victor Lavy is William Haber Chaired Professor of Economics at the Hebrew University of Jerusalem. His research interests are economic development, economics of education and human resources, evaluation of social programs and intervention. His articles have featured in journals such as *American Economic Review, Economic Journal, Journal of Public Economics* and *Scandinavian Journal of Economics.*

Ramanan Laxminarayan is Senior Fellow, Resources for the Future and consultant to the World Bank and WHO. His research deals with the integration of epidemiological models of infectious disease transmission and economic analysis of public health problems. His articles have featured in *Environment and Development Economics, The Lancet,* and *Health Affairs.* His recent publications include *Extending the Cure: Policy Responses to the Growing Threat of Antibiotic Resistance* (with A. Malani, Resources for the Future, Washington D.C., 2007).

Andrew Mack is Director of the Human Security Report Project at Simon Fraser University in Vancouver, Canada. His research interests are the political economy, civil war, and global security, and his articles have appeared in journals such as *World Politics, The Washington Quarterly, British Journal of International Studies, World Policy, Foreign Policy*, and *Comparative Politics*. In addition he has contributed to a wide range of books.

Anil Markandya is Professor of Economics at the University of Bath. He specializes in environmental and resource economics. He has worked on valuation of the environment, external costs of fuels, green accounting, economy-wide policies and the environment, climate change, ozone layer protection, and development of economic instruments for environmental protection. His recent publications include *Water Quality Issues in Developing Countries* (Columbia University Press, 2006), *Policy Failures as a Cause of Environmental Degradation* in *The Handbook of Environmental Economics* (Elsevier Science, 2005), and *Gains of Regional Cooperation: Environmental Problems and Solutions* in *Energy Resources, Governance and Welfare in the Caspian Sea Basin* (University of Seattle Press, 2005).

Reynaldo Martorell is Robert W. Woodruff Professor of International Nutrition at the Rollins School of Public Health, Atlanta, Georgia. His area of research is within the fields of maternal and child nutrition, child growth and development, emergence of obesity, and chronic diseases in developing countries. His articles have appeared in journals such as the *Journal of Nutrition, The Lancet, International Journal of Paediatrics, Food and Nutrition Bulletin*, and *Prevention and Chronic Disease*.

Lant Pritchett is Lead Socio-Economist at the World Bank. His research interests are within the fields of economic growth, education, governance/democracy, inequality, migration, and population. His publications include *Economic Growth in the 1990s: Learning from a Decade of Reforms* (World Bank, 2005), *Making Services Work for Poor People* (World Development Report, 2004), *Assessing Aid: What Works, What Doesn't and Why* (with D. Dollar, World Bank, 1998), and *Infrastructure for Development* (World Development Report, 1994).

Jitendra (Jitu) Shah is a Country Sector Coordinator for the Environment, Rural, and Social Sectors for Lao, Cambodia, Thailand, and Malaysia in the South East Asia Unit of the World Bank, based in Bangkok. His work at the World Bank has spanned environmental management of projects and programs on local, regional, and global scales. His recent publications include *Energy Futures and Urban Air Pollution: Challenges for China and the United States* (The National Academy Press, 2008) and he has written for publications such as the *Journal of Air Waste Management Association*.

Aysit Tansel is Professor of Economics at Middle East Technical University, Ankara. Her main areas of interest are labor economics with a focus on economics of education, empirical models of economic growth with emphasis on health and education, and educational inequalities and gender gap in education and economic growth, returns to education, private tutoring, economics of gender, labor force participation, and unemployment. Her publications include *Brain-Drain from Turkey: Survey Evidence of Student Non-Return* (with N.D. Güngör, Career Development International, 2003) and her articles have appeared in journals such as *Economics of Education Review, Journal of Development Economics*, and *Applied Economics*.

Anthony Venables is BP Professor of Economics at Oxford University. His area of research is international, spatial, development, and resource economics. His works include *Multinational Firms in the World Economy* (Princeton University Press, 2004) and his articles have been published in the *Journal of International Economics, World Economy, Journal of Transport Economics and Policy, Journal of Urban Economics*, and *Journal of Economic Geography*.

The Experts

Jagdish Bhagwati is University Professor at Columbia University and Senior Fellow in International Economics at the Council on Foreign Relations. He has been Economic Policy Adviser to Arthur Dunkel, Director General of GATT (1991–3), Special Adviser to the UN on Globalization, and External Adviser to the WTO. He has served on the Expert Group appointed by the Director General of the WTO on the Future of the WTO and the Advisory Committee to Secretary General Kofi Annan on the NEPAD process in Africa, and was also a member of the Eminent Persons Group under the chairmanship of President Fernando Henrique Cardoso on the future of UNCTAD. Five volumes of his scientific writings and two of his public policy essays have been published by MIT Press. The recipient of six Festschrifts in his honour, he has also received several prizes and honorary degrees, including awards from the governments of India (Padma Vibhushan) and Japan (Order of the Rising Sun, Gold and Silver Star). Professor Bhagwati's latest book, *In Defense of Globalization*, was published by Oxford University Press in 2004 to worldwide acclaim.

François Bourguignon is Director of the Paris School of Economics and the former Chief Economist of the World Bank. Bourguignon is a specialist in the economics of development, public policy, economic growth, income distribution and redistribution, inequality and poverty measurements, and has published more than 200 articles and several volumes. He has played a vital role in placing economic growth and its relationship with inequality and income distribution and poverty at the center of the World Bank's agenda. Bourguignon has founded and directed the Département et Laboratoire d'Economie Théorique et Appliquée (DELTA), a research unit in theoretical and applied economics. He is a Fellow of the Econometric Society, and was president of the European Economic Association for Population Economics. He received the silver medal for academic achieve-ments from the French National Centre of Scientific Research in 1999.

Finn E. Kydland is Henley Professor of Economics and Director of the Laboratory for Aggregate Economics and Finance at the University of California, Santa Barbara. Kydland has authored many publications on macroeconomics, economic growth, monetary economics and international economics. In 2004, Kydland shared the Nobel Memorial Prize in Economics with Edward C. Prescott for their research on business cycles and macroeconomic policy – specifically, the driving forces behind business cycles and the time consistency of economic policy. He is a Research Associate for the Federal Reserve Banks of Dallas, Cleveland and St. Louis, and a Senior Research Fellow at the IC2 Institute at the University of Texas at Austin. He is an Adjunct Professor at the Norwegian School of Economics and Business Administration, and has held visiting scholar and professor positions at, among other places, the Hoover Institution and the Universidad Torcuato di Tella in Buenos Aires, Argentina. He was elected a Fellow of the Econometric Society in 1992.

Robert Mundell is University Professor at Columbia University in New York. He has been an adviser to a number of international agencies and organizations including the United Nations, the IMF, the World Bank, the Government of Canada, governments in Latin America and Europe, the Federal Reserve Board and the US Treasury. The author of numerous works and articles on economic theory of international economics, he is known as the father of the theory of optimum currency areas; he formulated what became a standard international macroeconomics model; he was a pioneer of the theory of the monetary and fiscal policy mix; he reformulated the theory of inflation and interest; he was a co-developer of the monetary approach to the balance of payments; and he was an originator of supply-side economics. In 1999, he received the Nobel Memorial Prize in Economic Science. In 2001 he was appointed Companion of the

Order of Canada. In 2005 he received the Global Economics Award of the Kiel World Economics Institute, Germany and was appointed Knight Grand Cross of the Royal Order of Merit. He has received honorary degrees and professorships in several universities in North America, Europe and Asia.

Douglass C. North is Spencer T. Olin Professor in Arts and Sciences, Washington University in St. Louis. In 1992 he became the first economic historian ever to win one of the economics profession's most prestigious honours, the John R. Commons Award. He is a founder of Washington University's Center for New Institutional Social Sciences. In 1993, he shared the Nobel Memorial Prize in Economics with Robert Fogel. His research has focused on the formation of political and economic institutions and the consequences of these institutions on the performance of economies through time, including such areas as property rights, transaction costs, and the free-rider problem. He is recognised as one of the founders of the 'new institutional economics', and has done important work on the connection of the cognitive sciences to economic theory.

Thomas C. Schelling is Distinguished University Professor, University of Maryland. He was the recipient of the Frank E. Seidman Distinguished Award in Political Economy and the National Academy of Sciences award for Behavioural Research Relevant to the Prevention of Nuclear War. In 2005, he shared the Nobel Memorial Prize in Economics with Robert Aumann. He served in the Economic Cooperation Administration in Europe, and has held positions in the White House and Executive Office of the President, Yale University, the RAND Corporation, and the Department of Economics and Center for International Affairs at Harvard University. He has published on military strategy and arms control, energy and environmental policy, climate change, nuclear proliferation, terrorism, organ-

ised crime, foreign aid and international trade, conflict and bargaining theory, racial segregation and integration, the military draft, health policy, tobacco and drugs policy, and ethical issues in public policy and in business.

Vernon L. Smith is Professor of Economics and Law at George Mason University, a research scholar in the Interdisciplinary Center for Economic Science, and a Fellow of the Mercatus Center all in Arlington, Virginia. In 2002, he shared the Nobel Memorial Prize in Economics with Daniel Kahneman. He serves or has served on the board of editors of the *American Economic Review*, *The Cato Journal*, *Journal of Economic Behavior and Organization*, the *Journal of Risk and Uncertainty*, *Science*, *Economic Theory*, *Economic Design*, *Games and Economic Behavior*, and the *Journal of Economic Methodology*. He has laid the foundation for the field of experimental economics, developing an array of experimental methods, setting standards for what constitutes a reliable laboratory experiment in economics. His work has been instrumental in establishing experiments as an essential tool in empirical economic analysis.

Nancy L. Stokey is Frederick Henry Prince Professor at University of Chicago. She serves or has served as vice-president of the American Economic Association, co-editor of *Econometrica*, associate editor of the *Journal of Economic Growth* and has served as associate editor of *Games and Economic Behavior* and of the *Journal of Economic Theory*. An expert on economic theory and economic development, she examines the impact education and job training have had on the development of national economies. She has shown that economies continue to expand when workforces adopt more complex skills – moving, for instance, from manufacturing into high technology. She is a member of the National Academy of Sciences, a fellow of the American Academy of Arts and Sciences, and a fellow of the Econometric Society.

Acknowledgements

This book and the Copenhagen Consensus 2008 project are only possible because of the efforts of many people. I would like to thank the Copenhagen Business School and Denmark's Foreign Ministry for their support. I am grateful to Henrik Meyer, Tommy Petersen, Maria Jakobsen, Lotta Salling, Tobias Bang, Anita Overholt Nielsen, Ask Nielsen, Sara Tornqvist, Jesper Risom, and David Young for their dedication and hard work. I am particularly grateful to the authors and experts who came to Denmark for Copenhagen Consensus 2008 and whose work forms these pages. As always, I am overwhelmed by their enthusiasm and excellent, diligent research.

Abbreviations and Acronyms

ACP	Africa, Caribbean and Pacific		COI	cost-of-illness
ACT	artemisinin combination therapy		CoW	Correlates of War
AETG	advanced energy technology gap		COPD	chronic obstructive pulmonary disease
ALP	acquisition of life potential		CR	capital recovery
ALRI	acute lower respiratory infections		CRS	constant returns to scale
AMFm	Affordable Medicines Facility-malaria		CV	contingent valuation
			CVD	cardiovascular disease
AR4	Fourth Assessment Report (IPPC)		DALY	disability-adjusted life year
			DCPP	Disease Control Priorities Project
ARI	acute respiratory infection		DDA	Doha Development Agenda
ARV	antiretrovirals		DHS	demographic and health surveys
ATP	accelerated technology path		DOC	diesel oxidation catalysts
AU	African Union		DOTS	drugs with direct observation (TB)
BASICS	Basic Support for Institutionalizing Child Survival		DPF	diesel particulate filters
			DPKO	Department of Peacekeeping Operations
BAU	'business as usual'		DRC	Democratic Republic of Congo
B/C	benefit/cost		EDUCO	Educacion con Participacion de la Comunidad (community managed schools)
BCR	benefit–cost ratio			
CAR	Central African Republic			
C/B	cost-benefit			
CBA	cost-benefit analysis		EITI	Extractive Industries Transparency Initiative
CBRN	chemical, biological, radiological, or nuclear		EPA	Environmental Protection Agency
CCS	carbon capture and storage		EPI	Expanded Program on Immunization
CCT	conditional cash transfer			
CDC	Centers for Disease Control and Prevention		EPRI	Electric Power Research Institute
			EV	equivalent variation
CE	cost-effectiveness		FAO	Food and Agriculture Organization
CFR	case fatality rate			
CGE	computable general equilibrium		FARC	Fuerza Armadas Revolucionarias de Colombia
CIS	Commonwealth of Independent States			
			FDI	foreign direct investment
CLTS	community-led total sanitation		FTAA	Free Trade Area of the Americas
CMB	chemical mass balance		GAIN	Global Alliance for Improved Nutrition
CMH	Commission on Macroeconomics and Health			
			GATT	General Agreement on Tariffs and Trade
CNG	compressed natural gas			

xxv

GAVI	Global Alliance for Vaccines and Immunization	OPEC	Organization of Petroleum Exporting Countries
GCM	global climate model	ORS	oral rehydration salts
GDP	gross domestic product	OTH	over-the-horizon
GHG	greenhouse gas	PACES	Plan de Amplicación de
GM	genetically modified		Cobertura de la Educación
GNEP	Global Nuclear Energy Partnership		Secundaria
GNI	gross national income	PC	perfect competition
GWP	gross world product	PEM	protein-energy malnutrition
HAART	highly active antiretroviral therapy	PFLP	Popular Front for the Liberation of Palestine
HCV	human capital value	PHC	primary health center
I&M	inspection and maintenance	PIDI	Proyecto Integral de Desarrollo Infantil
ICRG	International Country Risk Guide	PM	particulate matter
ICT	information and communication technology	PKO	peacekeeping operation
		POU	point of use
IEG	International Energy Group	ppm	parts per million
IFF	International Finance Facility	ppmv	parts per million by volume
IMF	International Monetary Fund	PPP	polluter pays principle
IMR	infant mortality rate	PPP	purchasing power parity
INACG	International Nutritional Anemia Consultative Group	PRIO	International Peace Research Institute
IPCC	Intergovernmental Panel on Climate Change	PV	present value
		PWE	population weighted exposure
ITERATE	International Terrorism: Attributes of Terrorist Event	QALY	quality of life
		R&D	research and development
ITO	International Trade Organization	RR	relative risk ration
IVACG	Vitamin A Consultative Group	SD	standard deviation
IZINCG	International Zinc Nutrient Consultative Group	SDT	special and differential treatment
		SES	higher socioeconomic status
LDC	less developed country	SFU	solid fuel use
LPG	liquefied petroleum gas	SRES	Special Report on Emissions Scenarios
MDG	Millennium Development Goal		
MIPT	Memorial Institute for the Prevention of Terrorism	SSA	sub-Saharan Africa
		STD	sexually transmitted disease
MNE	multinational organisation	STI	sexually transmitted infection
MNF	multinational forces	SUZY	scaling up zinc for young children
NATO	North American Treaty Organization	TAU	'technology as usual'
		UCDP	Uppsala Conflict Data Program
NCD	non-communicable disease	UN	United Nations
NGO	non-governmental organisation	UNFCCC	UN Framework Convention on Climate Change
NPV	net present value		
OAU	Organisation for African Unity	UNICEF	UN Children's Fund
OECD	Organisation for Economic Cooperation and Development	UPE	universal primary education
		URI	upper respiratory infections
OLS	ordinary least squares	USEPA	US Environmental Protection Agency

VSL	value of a statistical life	WTO	World Trade Organization
VSLY	value of a statistical life year	WTP	willingness-to-pay
VOC	volatile organic compound	YLD	years lived with a disability
WA	weight-for-age	YLL	years of life lost
WHO	World Health Organization		

Introduction

BJØRN LOMBORG

This book is about doing what is rational instead of what is fashionable.

It is fashionable to declare that we want to tackle every major world problem. It is also a great thing to say. Unfortunately, it is not rational. We have limited resources. A dollar spent in one place cannot be spent elsewhere. But it is worse than that. When we say that we want to do everything, we are deceiving ourselves. A few big issues get the most air time, attention and money.

During this decade, there has been an incredibly intense focus on terrorism and global warming. Some surveys show these two threats scare people in rich countries more than any other problems that the world faces. Terrorism and global warming have not only dominated some sections of the media, but have attracted billions of dollars and used vast amounts of political capital.

Terrorism and climate change are both serious problems that deserve attention. But, as this book will show, there are many other threats that we hear less about, that also deserve our attention.

The Copenhagen Consensus exercise started as a simple but untested idea of applying economic principles to prioritize global opportunities. In 2004, the process was carried out for the very first time. The result was a prioritized list of opportunities to solve or ameliorate some of the world's greatest problems, compiled by some of the world's top economists. This attracted attention from all over the world. Denmark's government spent millions more on HIV/AIDS projects, which topped the economists' "to do" list.

Since 2004, the Copenhagen Consensus Center has carried out several similar "prioritizations." We are drawing on the experience of the Copenhagen Consensus prioritization with United Nations ambassadors in the USA in 2006, and on the Consulta de San José last year, where we did a Copenhagen Consensus prioritization for Latin America and the Caribbean. Basic principles of economics can be used to help any nation or organization to spend its money to achieve the most "good" possible.

Since 2004, of course, knowledge about the world's many problems has increased. New and smarter solutions have been proposed. That is why Copenhagen Consensus was always designed as a global project that would be updated every four years. This ensures that new, important challenges and solutions are included in the process and that research is updated.

We have learned from all of our past experiences that an informed ranking of solutions to the world's big problems is possible. We have learned that cost-benefit analyses (CBAs) do not lead to short-sighted solutions or a fixation on money. They lead to a focus on the best ways to approach the real problems of the world's poorest, most afflicted people. Time and again, the new research presented in this book shows we have the knowledge to do tremendous amounts of good in each of the biggest world challenges. The hurdle is often getting the right resources to the right place.

This book can give philanthropists or policymakers an assurance that the check they write out is going to achieve the most "good" possible. I hope it will help draw attention to solutions to the problems that we do not talk about.

Copenhagen Consensus 2008 started with one big question: If we had an extra $75 billion to put to good use, which problems would we solve first? To answer that question, we commissioned the research that is presented here.

Experts look at ten of the biggest issues facing the planet: Air pollution, conflict, diseases, education, global warming, malnutrition and hunger, sanitation and water, subsidies and trade barriers, terrorism, women and development.

Each challenge is significant:

- *Air pollution*: Air pollution causes 2.5 million deaths each year, the vast majority in the developing world.
- *Conflict*: Civil wars in small, poor countries cause untold suffering – a single conflict can cost $250 billion or more, takes many years to recover from and can block all other humanitarian interventions.
- *Disease*: Under the heading of "disease," the experts looked particularly at the plight of developing countries – they not only suffer much more than the industrialized world from diseases such as malaria, TB and HIV/AIDS, but also have to face an increasing burden of heart disease, cancer and other non-communicable diseases.
- *Education*: A lack of education commits many children to an impoverished future. Nearly a quarter of children in developing countries do not complete the fifth grade and, of these, 55 percent started school but dropped out: 26 million of today's four-year-olds will not complete five grades of schooling.
- *Global warming*: Global warming is by definition a global challenge, which could have a large number of important consequences such as increasing food and water insecurity, threatening ecosystem health and low-lying coastal populations while damaging the world economy.
- *Malnutrition and hunger*: Despite significant reductions in income poverty in recent years, under-nutrition remains widespread. One in four children under five – or 146 million children in the developing world – is underweight for his or her age; each year, under-nutrition contributes to the deaths of about 5.6 million children under the age of five.
- *Sanitation and water*: An astonishing 1.1 billion people lack good, clean water supplies, and 2.7 billion have no access to proper sanitation.
- *Subsidies and trade barriers*: Barriers to trade and migration have negative impacts that particularly affect the world's poorest people.
- *Terrorism*: this is a terrifying problem because it has no effective solution. Terrorist attacks are a cost-effective tactic of the weak against a more formidable opponent. Very cheap terrorist attacks can create significant anxiety and carnage.
- *Women and development*: Despite large strides in many countries, too many women continue to suffer discrimination, with negative impacts on the health and wellbeing of themselves and their children, as well as the broader economy.

We know that we could achieve good in any of the ten challenge areas. But with limited resources: Where can we do the most and least good? To answer that question, we need to focus on solutions, not problems.

This book presents some of the recommended solutions by specialist experts in each field. There is a range of fresh thinking and new approaches: You will find the first CBA of peacekeeping troops, by Paul Collier, for example (chapter 2). However, it is essential that we test and debate the experts' recommendations. That is why a second set of experts has carefully reviewed the research papers, and suggested other ways of viewing the problem.

The work presented in this book helps to undermine one of the many excuses that policymakers have used for not investing more in global aid and development projects. It provides sorely needed information about where money can achieve the most good.

As in previous Copenhagen Consensus exercises, in the Copenhagen Consensus 2008 project, an Expert Panel of eight economists – including five Nobel laureates – examined all of the research presented here. They engaged with all of the experts and came to their own conclusions about the merits of each suggested solution to each challenge. Seldom does such a high-powered group of world-class economists deal with such weighty issues.

I am often asked: Why economists? Many environmentalist campaigners would tell you that any extra money should be dedicated to battling climate change. That's certainly the global challenge we hear the most about. But an expert in air pollution will tell you that clearing the skies of killer smog should be a top priority. Someone who has spent his life studying conflict will tell you of the potential benefits from reducing the risks of civil war.

When it comes to setting economic priorities, the best people to turn to are economists: Experts in prioritization, they are the obvious people to provide a global overview. They put each challenge on an equal footing. The massive media hype about some problems is irrelevant to them. They focus on where limited funds could achieve the most good.

In choosing the best solutions to the world's biggest problems, the expert panel focused largely on the costs and benefits of different options. This is a transparent and practical way to show whether spending is worthwhile or not. It lets us avoid the fear and media hype that often dictate the way we see the world. Carefully examining where an investment would have the biggest rewards provides a principled basis upon which important decisions can be made. The Expert Panel discussed and debated all of the solutions to all of the challenges, in closed-door sessions designed to promote free debate. They weighed up each solution that you will find in this book, and compared it to the other options.

To provide another perspective on these problems and introduce fresh voices to the debate about prioritization, eighty students from twenty countries were invited to Denmark to analyze the research and come up with their own conclusions. The Copenhagen Consensus 2008 Youth Forum was a parallel meeting to the Expert Panel discussions, and the decision-makers of tomorrow enthusiastically embraced the difficult task of prioritizing between different solutions. The Youth Forum event was open to the general public and to journalists, to open up the decision-making process of the project. The Youth Forum and the Expert Panel produced their own prioritized lists, ranking solutions across all of the challenges. This highlights their view of the most (and least) cost-effective solutions.

It is vital, however, that these important issues are not just left to economists. That is why this book exists: I invite you to use this research to produce your own prioritized list of best and worst investments that the planet could make.

The easy thing – the fashionable thing – would be to say, "let's do everything." That is unrealistic. I hope that the quality of the research presented here will help you to form your own opinion on the best investments that all of us could make to help improve the planet.

PART I
The challenges

Air Pollution

BJØRN LARSEN, WITH GUY HUTTON AND
NEHA KHANNA

Introduction

Air pollution in its broadest sense refers to suspended particulate matter (PM: dust, fumes, mist, and smoke), gaseous pollutants, and odors (Kjellstrom *et al.* 2006). To this may be added heavy metals, chemicals and hazardous substances. A large proportion of air pollution worldwide is due to human activity, from combustion of fuels for transportation and industry, electric power generation, resource extraction and processing industries, and domestic cooking and heating, among others. Air pollution has many impacts, most importantly affecting human and animal health, buildings and materials, crops, and visibility.

In addressing the multiple burdens of air pollution, its related causes, and possible solutions, a broad distinction is necessary between *indoor* and *outdoor* air pollution:

- Human-induced *indoor air pollution* is to a large extent caused by household solid fuel use (SFU) for cooking and heating, usually involving open fires or traditional stoves in conditions of low combustion efficiency and poor ventilation. Indoor air pollution also originates from other "modern" indoor air pollutants associated with industrialization, with a variety of suspected health effects such as sick-building syndrome. However, from a global burden of disease point of view, these modern indoor air pollutants are relatively minor; this study therefore focuses on air pollution from SFU. Due to the close proximity and low or zero cost of solid fuels such as biomass in most rural areas, indoor air pollution is more of an issue in rural than in urban areas, although in many urban areas coal

and charcoal are common household energy sources. Indoor air pollution from SFU is particularly hazardous given that pollution concentrations often exceed WHO guidelines by a factor of 10–50. Indoor air pollution is also related to environmental tobacco smoke ("passive smoking") and exposure to chemicals and gases in indoor workplaces.

- Human-induced *outdoor air pollution* occurs mainly in or around cities and in industrial areas, and is caused by the combustion of petroleum products or coal by motor vehicles, industry, and power generation, and by industrial processes. Outdoor air pollution is fundamentally a problem of economic development, but also implies a corresponding under-development in terms of affording technological solutions that reduce pollution, availability of more energy-efficient public transport schemes, and enforcing regulations governing energy use and industrial emissions.

Rates of exposure to these two types of air pollution therefore vary greatly between rural and urban areas, and between developing regions, given variations in vehicle ownership and use, extent and location of industrial areas and power generation facilities, fuel availability, purchasing power, climate, and topology, among other things. Indoor sources also contribute to outdoor air pollution, particularly in developing countries; conversely, outdoor air pollution may contribute to pollution exposure in the indoor environment (Kjellstrom *et al.* 2006).

Over 3 billion people are exposed to household air pollution from solid fuels used for cooking and heating, and over 2 billion people are globally exposed to urban air pollution in more than 3,000 cities with a population over 100,000 inhabitants.[1] Epidemiologically, household SFU and urban air pollution differ in important respects. SFU disproportionately affects young children and adult females, while urban air pollution, according to current evidence and assessment methods, predominantly affects adults and especially the older population groups. There are also important differences in terms of solutions. Air pollution from SFU can be substantially reduced or practically eliminated by a few interventions such as installation of improved stoves with a chimney or a substitution of "clean" fuels such as liquefied petroleum gas (LPG), natural gas, or, potentially, biomass gasifier stoves. However, broad packages of interventions are often required to achieve any significant improvement in urban air quality.[2] Given these differences, this chapter discusses SFU and urban air pollution separately.

While there are many air pollutants, current assessment methods identify fine particulates (PM 2.5) as the pollutant with the largest global health effects. The focus of this chapter is therefore on particulates. Particulates are caused directly by combustion of fossil fuels and biomass, industrial processes, forest fires, burning of agricultural residues and waste, construction activities, and dust from roads, but also arise naturally from marine and land-based sources (e.g. dust from deserts). Particulates, or so-called "secondary particulates," are also formed from gaseous emissions such as nitrogen oxides and sulfur dioxide.

Household Air Pollution from Solid Fuels

The Challenge

An estimated 1.5 million deaths occur annually as a result of household air pollution from

SFU, mainly for cooking as well as winter heating. The total disease burden, including morbidity, is estimated at 36 million DALYs (WHO 2007).[3] These deaths and DALYs arise mainly from acute lower respiratory infections (ALRI) in young children and chronic obstructive pulmonary disease (COPD) in adults and, to a lesser extent, lung cancer. There is also moderate evidence of increased risk of asthma, cataracts, and tuberculosis (Desai et al. 2004; Smith et al. 2004). While urban air pollution is strongly associated with elevated risk of heart disease and mortality (Pope et al. 2002), no credible studies of such a link are available for SFU because of the longitudinal data requirements. It is however plausible that SFU is a contributor to heart disease and mortality and, if so, the health effects of SFU might currently be significantly underestimated.

By WHO region of the world, use of improved domestic fuels (e.g. LPG, kerosene) in rural areas varies from under 15 percent in Sub-Saharan Africa and South East Asia, to 33 percent in the Western Pacific developing region, and closer to 50 percent in Eastern Mediterranean and Latin American countries. The main types of unimproved fuels used in rural areas are firewood, dung, and other agricultural residues, followed by charcoal and coal/lignite (Rehfuess et al. 2006). Indoor air pollution from SFU is generalized throughout the developing world. However, the health effects depend on many factors, including type of solid fuel and stove, household member exposure to solid fuel smoke (e.g. household member activity patterns, indoor versus outdoor burning of fuels, cooking practices and proximity to stove, and smoke venting factors such as dwelling room size and height, windows and doors, construction material, chimney), and household member age and baseline health status and treatment of illness.

About 1.2 million or 80 percent of global deaths from SFU occur in thirteen countries. Eight of these countries are in Sub-Saharan Africa and five are in Asia. India and China alone account for over 50 percent of global deaths from SFU (figure 1.1).

Average prevalence of household SFU is over

---

[1] The World Bank provides air quality modeling results for these cities. They are therefore used here as an indicator of global population exposed to urban air pollution.
[2] An exception is elimination of lead (Pb) from gasoline, or control of localized pollution from industrial plant(s) or thermal power plant(s).
[3] Estimated using baseline health data for 2002 and most recent available data on prevalence of household SFU.

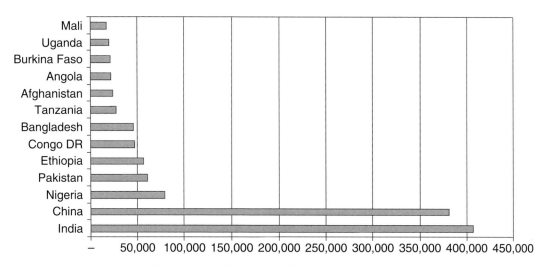

Figure 1.1 *Annual deaths from household SFU air pollution, 2002*
Source: *Produced by the author from national estimates by WHO (2007). Mortality estimates are adjusted by the author for Pakistan to reflect the most recent data in the prevalence of SFU.*

Table 1.1. Profile of thirteen countries with the highest mortality from SFU

	India	China	Other countries (11 with highest mortality from SFU)
Average SFU prevalence (most recent available)	82%	80%	> 90%
Deaths from SFU in 2002	407100	380700	421600
ALRI (% of deaths from SFU)	62%	5%	86%
COPD (% of deaths from SFU)	38%	90%	14%
LC (% of deaths from SFU)	0.1%	5%	0.01%
U5 child mortality rate in 2005	74	27	148
U5 child malnutrition (moderate and severe underweight)*	47%	8%	33%
GNI per capita in 2005	730	1740	480

Note: * Most recent data available from Unicef Global Database on Undernutrition.
Source: Author.

90 percent in these thirteen countries, ranging from 67 percent in Nigeria, 70 percent in Pakistan, some 80–82 percent in China and India, 89 percent in Bangladesh, and over 95 percent in eight of the other countries. With the exception of China, these countries are characterized by relatively high under-five child mortality rates, high malnutrition rates, and low national income levels (table 1.1).

Larsen (2007a) provides an estimate of mortality from indoor air pollution from household solid fuels in rural China. The central estimate of annual mortality is 460,000, assuming 50 percent of solid fuel stoves have a chimney and 355,000 if 100 percent of solid fuel stoves have a chimney, suggesting that mortality from SFU in China may be somewhat higher than presented in figure 1.1. The estimates are based on the

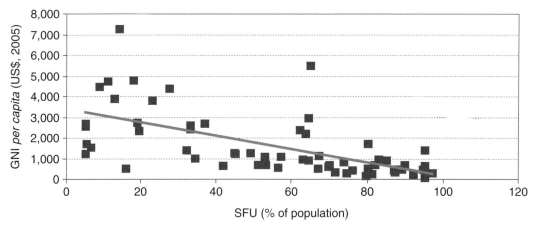

Figure 1.2 *Household SFU prevalence rates and GNI per capita*
Notes: GNI per capita is from WDI (2007). SFU is from WHO (2007).
Source: The author.

same health end-points as in Smith *et al.* (2004) and WHO (2007). A framework with multi-level risks is applied to reflect some of the diversity of solid fuels and stove and venting technologies commonly used in households in China. Seven indoor air pollution exposure and risk levels are applied: Households using predominantly biomass with or without chimney, a combination of biomass and coal with or without chimney, predominantly coal with or without chimney, and households using non-solid fuels (mainly LPG).

An important question is if countries will be able to grow themselves out of the SFU and associated health effects in the next few decades without any need for large-scale interventions. One argument is that prevalence of household SFU is strongly correlated with country income level, so that economic growth will solve the problem (figure 1.2). A second argument is that child mortality rates are declining, so under-five mortality from SFU will gradually decline (by reducing ALRI fatality rates) even without a reduction in SFU. A counter-argument is however that COPD mortality could possibly increase with aging populations even with a gradual decline in SFU. Each of these issues deserves attention and a set of simple projections is therefore presented in this chapter.

A linear regression analysis shows that an

increase of US $1,000 in gross national income (GNI) *per capita* is associated with a 20 percentage point decline in SFU prevalence. Let us assume that this cross-country relationship holds intertemporally for the thirteen countries that account for 80 percent of SFU mortality. In the eleven countries other than China and India in figure 1.1, it would take about fifty-five years to reduce SFU prevalence to 50–55 percent and seventy-five years to reduce SFU prevalence to 10 percent, at a *per capita* income growth of 3 percent per year. In China and India it would take ten–twenty years and twenty–thirty years, respectively, at current economic growth rates. However, SFU prevalence in China has not declined at a rate anywhere close to the rate suggested by the cross-country regression results, although a substantial substitution from fuel wood to coal has been observed in the last two decades. Fuel substitution has also been quite slow in India despite rapid economic growth in the last decade.

In most countries, a majority of deaths from SFU is from ALRI in children under five. There is a strong correlation between SFU deaths per population and under-five child mortality rates. COPD mortality is to some extent correlated with life expectancy and an aging population (figure 1.3).

ALRI mortality from SFU has most likely

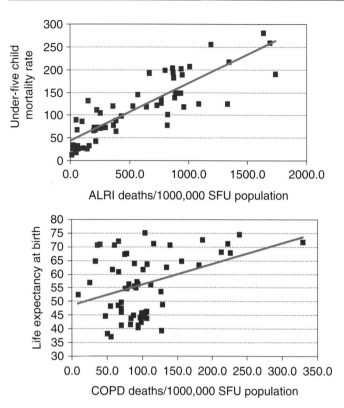

Figure 1.3 *Deaths from SFU in relation to child mortality rates and life expectancy*
Notes: Under-five child mortality rate and life expectancy at birth are for 2005 (World Bank 2007). ALRI and COPD deaths from SU =FU are from WHO (2007)> Countries with >= 1,000 deaths from SFU are included in the figure.
Source: The author.

declined in recent decades, and is likely to decline further even without a reduction in SFU or adoption of improved stoves. This comes about from a reduction in ALRI case fatality rates – through, for instance, improved case management and reduction in malnutrition rates – even in the event that incidence of morbidity does not decline.[4] In the countries with the highest SFU mortality (in the sample of thirteen countries), under-five child mortality rates have declined substantially since 1960 but appear to have stagnated in several of the Sub-Saharan countries. At rates of decline observed in the last two decades, it would take an average of thirty-five years in Bangladesh, India, and Pakistan for under-five child mortality rates to reach the current rate of 27 per 1,000 live births in China. It would take an average of seventy-five years in Ethiopia,

Uganda, and Tanzania.[5] If all-cause ALRI mortality declines at the same rate as under-five child mortality, and there is no change in SFU, then in fifty years annual ALRI mortality from SFU would be 250,000, or 40 percent of the current level in this group of thirteen countries.

COPD mortality occurs largely in older population groups. With aging of populations over time, COPD mortality from SFU could increase over the next fifty years. The share of population aged forty-five+ years is expected to nearly double in China and India and more than double

[4] See Fishman *et al.* (2004) for a discussion of child mortality risk in relation to malnutrition.
[5] This calculation is based on average under-five mortality rates and rates of decline in the groups of countries. Years required to reach the level of China will be different in each individual country.

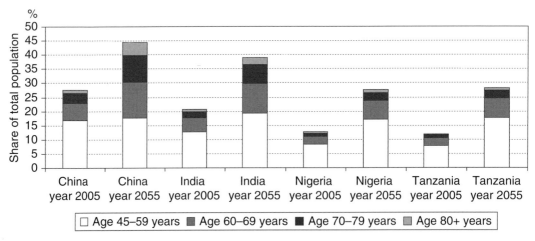

Figure 1.4 *Demographic projections, 2005–55*
Source: Prepared by the author using World Bank demographic projections.

Table 1.2. Projections of COPD deaths from SFU

SFU prevalence in 2055	COPD deaths: Ratio of deaths in yr 2055/yr 2005			
	China	India	Nigeria	Tanzania
0.6	2.67	2.52	4.10	2.77
0.5	2.23	2.10	3.42	2.31
0.4	1.78	1.68	2.74	1.85
0.3	1.34	1.26	2.05	1.39
0.2	0.89	0.84	1.37	0.92
0.1	0.45	0.42	0.68	0.46
0	0.00	0.00	0.00	0.00

Source: Author.

in Nigeria and Tanzania from 2005 to 2055. The fastest growth in China and India is expected to be for the population aged 60+ (figure 1.4).

To provide a simple projection of COPD mortality from SFU, consider a scenario in which age-specific COPD death rates (per 1,000 population in age group) are constant over time.[6] Using World Bank country demographic projections, we can apply the relative risks of COPD from SFU in Desai *et al.* (2004) to estimate COPD mortality by SFU prevalence rates in fifty years

---

[6] Age-specific COPD death rates are taken from Global Burden of Disease regional tables.

from now. The results are presented for China, India, Nigeria and Tanzania in table 1.2.

COPD mortality from SFU would be higher in 2055 than today in all four countries at SFU prevalence rates >25 percent in year 2055 (current SFU prevalence is 67 to 95+ percent). SFU needs to decline to <15 percent in Nigeria for COPD mortality to fall below today's level (table 1.3). The main drivers of these projections are aging of the population and population growth. But even COPD death rates (COPD deaths/population) would be higher than today unless SFU prevalence falls below 25–30 percent in China and Nigeria and below 35–40 percent in

Table 1.3. Indoor particulate (PM) concentrations from cooking stoves

	Open fire/Traditional stove	Improved stove	LPG	
24-hour PM 3.5	1930	330	–	Guatemala. Albalak *et al.* (2001).
24-hour PM 10	1210	520	140	Referenced in Albalak *et al.* (2001), adapted from Naeher *et al.* (2000).
24 hour PM 2.5	520	88	45	
24-hour PM 2.5	868	152	–	
PM 10	600–1000	300	50	Mexico. Saatkamp *et al.* (2000)

Source: Reproduced from Larsen (2005).

India and Tanzania. Assuming that SFU cross-country income elasticities are realistic, income growth alone would not alleviate any or much of COPD mortality from SFU.

The Solutions

There exists a range of solutions to lower exposure to indoor air pollution. This includes reducing the source of pollution and altering the living environment and user behavior. Source reduction involves improved cooking devices (with or without a flue attached), cleaner fuel, and reduced need for fire. Alterations to the living environment include improved ventilation and better kitchen design and stove placement. Altered user behavior includes fuel drying, stove and chimney maintenance, use of pot lids to conserve heat, and keeping children away from the smoke (Bruce *et al.* 2005).

While there are many options available for reducing exposure to indoor air pollution, there is limited evidence on their effectiveness in real-life conditions for modeling the cost-benefit of these options. These include behavioral dimensions such as location of cooking area (indoor vs. outdoor; separate indoor area) and location of young children in relation to cooking area (carrying babies while cooking; playing near cooking area). Benefits of these behavioral modification are however difficult to quantify and depend very much on particular circumstances. The solutions to household SFU air pollution that lend themselves to a cost-benefit analysis (CBA) thus fall into two categories: (a)

Table 1.4. WHO air quality guidelines

	Annual average (ug/m3)	24-hour average (ug/m3)
PM 2.5	10	25
PM 10	20	50

Source: NAE/NRC (2008).

improved stove technology; and (b) substitution of cleaner fuels. The focus of this chapter is therefore on technology and fuel choice.

Some results of indoor particulate (PM) concentrations measurements in relation to type of stove and fuel from Latin America are presented in table 1.3. The improved stoves, such as the *plancha*, produce PM 2.5 or PM 3.5 levels that are often only 20 percent of concentration levels from an open fire, and are even found to be less than 10 percent of that of an open fire in a study in Guatemala by McCracken and Smith (1998). The reduction in PM 2.5 seems to be even larger than reductions in PM 10. However the concentration levels of PM, even with an improved stove, are still substantially higher than found in most outdoor urban environments and many times higher than the WHO guidelines for ambient PM concentrations (table 1.4). It may also be noted that although the use of LPG eliminates PM from fuel sources, indoor PM may still be significant due to other sources of pollution.

While wood and to some extent charcoal are the most common solid fuels used in developing countries, China and Mongolia have high household prevalence of coal, especially for heating in open portable space heaters, some with and some

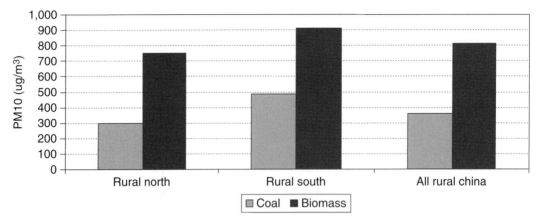

Figure 1.5 *Population weighted exposure to indoor particulates (PM 10)*
Source: Larsen (2007a), produced from data presented in Mestl et al. (2006).

without a chimney. Mestl *et al.* (2006), based on data from the China 2000 Population Census, report that about 60 percent of rural households used biomass as primary cooking fuel. Nearly 30 percent of rural households used coal as the primary fuel. Mestl *et al.* (2006) model annual average population weighted exposure (PWE) to indoor air pollution by using monitoring data reported in Sinton *et al.* (1995) and a few recent studies, the share of the population using solid fuels, and household member activity patterns.[7] PWE to PM 10 indoor air pollution is estimated at 360 ug/m³ for rural households using coal and 810 ug/m³ for rural households using biomass (figure 1.5).[8] Most of the monitoring studies of indoor PM 10 in Sinton *et al.* (1995) used by Mestl *et al.* (2006) are, however, from the late 1980s and early 1990s and may therefore not reflect current indoor PM levels.

In a recent study by the World Bank, for China CDC and other institutions in China, indoor air quality was monitored in select rural households in four of the poorest provinces. Three of these provinces are in northern China (Jin *et al.* 2005).

In this study, indoor PM 4 levels in households using predominantly biomass are roughly twice the level in households using predominantly coal (table 1.5). This is very similar to Mestl *et al.* (2006). Jin *et al.* (2005) do, however, report somewhat lower concentration levels in the rural North than found by Mestl *et al.* (2006). But when compared to provincial/county-level modeling results in Mestl *et al.* (2006), the results are of similar orders of magnitude.

Edwards *et al.* (2006) report indoor air quality monitoring in nearly 400 households in the three provinces of Hubei, Shaanxi, and Zhejiang in 2002–3. Great care was taken to select homes that reflected the diversity of fuels and stove technology and stove performance in China. PM 4 concentrations in 75 percent of kitchens and 73 percent of living rooms during the winter – and 48 percent of kitchens and 46 percent of living rooms during the summer – exceeded the national indoor air quality PM 10 standard of 150 ug/m³ for a twenty-four-hour average. If PM 10 had been measured, a greater percentage of homes would have exceeded the standard in both seasons.

Edwards *et al.* (2006) conclude that PM 4 concentrations are significantly lower in the homes with improved stoves (chimney) – 152 ug/m³ compared to 268 ug/m³ in homes with unimproved stoves (no chimney). The study is however not conclusive regarding PM concentrations

---

[7] Activity patterns: Mestl *et al.* (2006) estimate time spent per day for individuals in various age groups in several indoor microenvironments (kitchen, bedroom, living room, and indoors away from home) and outdoors.
[8] Actual indoor air PM 10 is, however, higher than these levels because PWE adjusts for time spent outdoors where pollution levels are lower.

Table 1.5. PM 4 concentrations in rural households in China (ug/m³)

Province	Gansu		Inner Mongolia	Ghizhou		Shaanxi	
Main cooking fuel	Biomass		Biomass	Coal		Coal and biomass	
Main heating fuel	Biomass		Biomass and coal	Coal		Coal	
Time period*	Mar	Dec	Dec	Mar	Dec	Mar	Dec
Location/							
Cooking room	518	661				187	223
Living/bedroom	351	457					
Living room						215	329
Bedroom				315	202	186	361
Cooking/living room				352	301		
Cooking/living/bedroom			719				

Note: * Time period of PM measurements was March and December.
Source: Reproduced from Jin *et al.* (2005).

associated with coal vs. biomass fuel, for similar types of stove technologies.

Ezzati and Kammen (2001, 2002) also present indoor PM concentration measurements for several types of charcoal stoves. PM concentrations are found to be substantially lower than concentrations from fuel wood stoves. Charcoal is often considered by households as an intermediate fuel on the energy ladder; while it certainly is not considered a clean fuel, it is often a preferred choice in many urban areas whenever available instead of fuel wood, before households can afford LPG or other clean alternatives.

In some Sub-Saharan countries the use of charcoal is relatively widespread especially in urban areas. Charcoal is used by 14–36 percent of households in declining order in Ghana, Congo Republic, Zambia, Madagascar, Tanzania, Uganda, Benin, and Kenya.[9] In most South and East Asian countries, charcoal is much less prevalent, with the exception of Thailand (19 percent: MICS 2006) and increasingly in Cambodia (9 percent: DHS 2005). In Latin America, more than 40 percent of households in Haiti use charcoal, but the prevalence is very low in most of the other countries in the region.

Figure 1.6 presents an energy efficiency ladder for stoves, and their typical costs, that are often cited in the research literature on fuel use and indoor air pollution (e.g. Baranzini and Goldemberg 1996; Luo and Hulscher 1999; Saatkamp *et al.* 2000). The stove efficiency ladder provides a generic perspective on potential energy savings from improved wood and charcoal stoves and kerosene, LPG, and electric stoves in comparison to traditional stoves. According to figure 1.6 improved wood and charcoal stoves are about 50 percent more efficient than traditional stoves, and LPG and electric stoves are twice as efficient than the improved wood and charcoal stoves.

Economic Estimates of Costs and Benefits

Benefit-cost ratios of intervention to control or prevent air pollution from household SFU will depend on what benefits and costs are included in the analysis and how non-market benefits and costs are valued. Health effects of air pollution are often a major concern and motivation for intervention. Which health effects to include, and how they are valued, are therefore an important consideration in an economic analysis. Large-scale household stove programs have also been motivated by natural resource considerations,

[9] From the most recently available Demographic and Health Surveys in Africa.

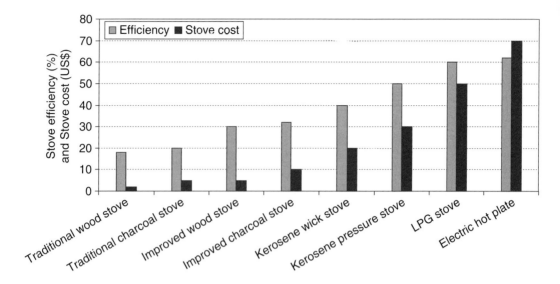

Figure 1.6 *Stove efficiency and capital costs*
Source: Larsen (2005).

for instance in China in the 1980s. The aim of that program was primarily improved energy efficiency, but PM concentrations were also lowered (Edwards *et al.* 2006). Benefits may include environmental improvements and time savings from reduced fuel collection in addition to health impacts.

Desai *et al.* (2004) provide a meta-analysis of health effects from household solid fuel air pollution. Health effects were categorized by level of evidence from the research literature. Relative risk ratios associated with solid fuel use, relative to clean fuels such as LPG, were derived for each health outcome (table 1.6).[10] The national and global mortality and DALY estimates presented by WHO (2007) reflect the relative risk ratios in Desai *et al.* (2004), limiting the health effects to ALRI in children under five, and COPD and lung cancer in adult women and men.

ALRI in children from SFU is important

for at least two reasons. ALRI is much more severe and involves more sick days than, for instance, acute upper respiratory infections (URI), and respiratory child mortality is almost exclusively from ALRI. However, in countries with lower child mortality rates, the cost of morbidity relative to mortality increases. This is, for instance, the situation in China and much of Latin America. Definition of morbidity health end-points and relevant age groups for inclusion in an economic analysis is therefore important, especially in these countries. While ALRI is a major concern, URI and other respiratory symptoms are far more frequent than ALRI.

Several studies in China have documented the increased risk of respiratory illness and symptoms from SFU (table 1.7). Ezzati and Kammen (2001) find in Kenya that SFU air pollution substantially increases the risk of acute respiratory infections in general and not only ALRI. This is the case for both children and adult females, although the sample size in their study was relatively small (table 1.8).[11] Quantifying the cost of these health end-points therefore seems to be important.

There are very few studies of the economic benefits and costs of interventions to reduce

[10] The relative risks largely reflect the use of unimproved wood and coal stoves without a chimney.

[11] Note: Desai *et al.* (2004) did not include Ezzati and Kammen (2001) in their meta-analysis because the risk ratios in Ezzati and Kammen did not easily convert to a simple dichotomous outcome (exposed or not exposed).

Table 1.6. Relative risk ratios from a meta-analysis of research literature

Evidence	Health outcome	Population group	Relative risk	Confidence Interval
Strong	ALRI	Children < 5	2.3	1.9–2.7
	COPD	Women >= 30	3.2	2.3–4.8
	Lung cancer*	Women >= 30	1.9	1.1–3.5
Moderate – I	COPD	Men >= 30	1.8	1.0–3.2
	Lung cancer*	Men >= 30	1.5	1.0–2.5
Moderate – II	Lung cancer**	Women >= 30	1.5	1.0–2.1
	Asthma	Children 5–14	1.6	1.0–2.5
	Asthma	All >= 15	1.2	1.0–1.5
	Cataracts	All >= 15	1.3	1.0–1.7
	Tuberculosis	All >= 15	1.5	1.0–2.4

Notes: * Exposure to coal smoke; ** Exposure to biomass smoke.
Source: Desai *et al.* (2004).

Table 1.7. Relative risk ratios from studies of indoor air pollution in China

Health outcome or end-point	Pollutant or fuel	Relative risk ratios*	Confidence interval (95%)	Notes	Reference
Bronchitis (acute)	Coal smoke (heating)	1.73[a]	1.42–2.12	Children in urban Chongqing, Guangzhou, Lanzhou, and Wuhan	Qian *et al.* (2004)
Cough with phlegm		2.12[a]	1.72–2.61		
Phlegm		1.33[a]	0.90–1.97		
Wheezing with colds	Coal smoke (cooking and/or heating)	1.57	1.07–2.29	Children (7th grade students) in urban, rural Wuhan	Salo *et al.* (2004)
Wheezing w/out colds		1.44	1.05–1.97		
Chronic cough	PM$_{10}$ and SO$_2$	0.83	0.31–2.24	Adult women in rural Anqing	Venners *et al.* (2001)
Chronic phlegm		1.52	0.52–4.45		
Wheezing		2.91[c]	1.18–7.18		
Shortness of breath		2.87[b]	1.46–5.64		
Wheezing	Wood and hay smoke	1.36[a]	1.14–1.61	Adults >14 in rural Anhui	Xu *et al.* (1996)
Wheezing	Coal	1.47[a]	1.09–1.98		

Notes: * Some of the studies reported odds ratios instead of relative risk ratios. The difference is however minimal for the prevalence or incidence rates of the health outcomes in the table. [a] No information about significance levels (P-values); [b] Statistically significant at 1 percent; [c] Statistically significant at 10 percent.
Source: Reproduced from Larsen (2007a).

household air pollution from fuel use. Four recent studies are reviewed in this chapter. Two of them are global studies estimating costs and benefits at the regional level; the other two are from Colombia and Peru.

Mehta and Shahpar (2004) present a cost-effectiveness analysis of household air pollution control interventions by WHO regions with significant SFU prevalence. Benefits are healthy years gained from reduced risk of ALRI in children and COPD in adult females and males based on regional data from WHO. An improved stove is assumed to reduce SFU pollution exposure and health effects by 75 percent. Per household

Table 1.8. Odds ratios of ARI from SFU air pollution exposure

PM 10 (ug/m3)	Children under 5 years	Age group 5–49 years
<200	1.0	1.0
200–500	2.42	3.01
500–1000	2.15	2.77
1000–2000	4.30	3.79
2000–3500	4.72	–
2000–4000	–	4.49
>3500	6.73	–
4000–7000	–	5.40
>7000	–	7.93

Source: Reproduced from Ezzati and Kammen (2001).

annualized cost of cooking systems range across regions from $40–90 for LPG, $10–20 for kerosene, and $3–24 for improved stove ($3–5 in Africa and Asia). The system cost for LPG and kerosene includes recurrent fuel cost. The program cost of interventions is included, but is a very small fraction of cooking system cost. All values are in purchasing power parity (PPP) international dollars. Non-health benefits such as fuel savings and/or time savings are not included.

Table 1.9 presents the results from Mehta and Shahpar (2004). Healthy years gained are converted here to US $1,000 and US $5,000 per year gained to produce benefit-cost (B/C) ratios. At US $1,000 per year gained, the B/C ratios are greater than 1.0 for improved stoves in Africa and SEAR D and for kerosene in WPRO B.[12] At US $5,000 per year gained, the B/C ratios are >1 also for improved stoves in SEAR B, for kerosene in all regions, and for LPG in WPRO B.

Hutton et al. (2006) conducted in collaboration with WHO a global CBA for each WHO region. Benefits are reduced mortality, and morbidity for ALRI in children and COPD and lung cancer in adult females and males, time savings from reduced cooking time and fuel collection,

time savings from reduced sick days, reduced solid fuel consumption, and local and global environmental benefits.

We discuss the two most promising scenarios presented in Hutton et al. (2006), namely an improved stove intervention and use of LPG instead of solid fuel. The improved stove intervention is a chimneyless rocket stove, assumed to reduce SFU health effects by 35 percent. Annualized unit stove cost is US $2.6–3.1. Annualized unit cost of the LPG stove and gas cylinder is US $9–18. LPG consumption is 0.3–0.9 kg per household per day. Annualized program cost per household is less than $1 in most regions.[13] Reduced mortality is valued at the human capital value (HCV) and morbidity is valued using the cost-of-illness (COI) approach. We therefore convert the health benefits to disability-adjusted life years (DALYs) for the purposes of this chapter.

Time savings are valued at 100 percent of wages for adults (approximated by GNI per capita) and 50 percent of GNI per capita for children. Rural households are assumed to purchase 25 percent of baseline fuel wood consumption. Urban households are assumed to purchase 75 percent of fuel wood consumption. Solid fuel savings from interventions are treated as a benefit. Local environmental effects are assessed as fewer trees cut down, while global environmental effects considered are lower CO_2 and CH_4 emissions, valued using current market values of emission reductions on the European carbon market.

Benefit-cost ratios are presented in table 1.10. The benefit-cost ratios do not include time benefit, solid fuel cost savings and environmental benefits in order to make results more comparable across studies. With health benefits valued at US $1,000 per DALY, the B/C ratios for an improved stove are >1 in the Africa regions, EMRO D (including Pakistan) and SEAR D (including India). The B/C ratios for LPG are >1 only in Africa. At US $5,000 per DALY, the B/C ratios for an improved stove are >1 in all regions except AMRO B. For LPG, the B/C ratios are >1 for Africa and SEAR D.

As observed from table 1.10, the B/C ratios for both interventions are significantly lower

---

[12] India is the largest country in SEAR D. China is the largest country in WPRO B.
[13] All annualized costs reflect a discount rate of 3 percent.

Table 1.9. B/C ratios of indoor air pollution control, by WHO regions, 2004 study

WHO regions	US $1000 per healthy year			US $5000 per healthy year		
	Improved stove	LPG	Kerosene	Improved stove	LPG	Kerosene
Afro D	2.01	0.16	1.00	10.1	0.8	5.0
Afro E	1.38	0.09	0.50	6.9	0.5	2.5
Amro B		0.07	0.41		0.4	2.1
Amro D	0.17	0.13	0.85	0.9	0.7	4.2
Emro D	0.13	0.09	0.56	0.6	0.5	2.8
Sear B	0.85	0.07	0.41	4.2	0.3	2.0
Sear D	1.63	0.14	0.72	8.1	0.7	3.6
Wpro B	0.03	0.71	3.89	0.2	3.5	19.4

Note: The regions of Amro A, Europe, and Emro B are not presented here. SFU is limited in these regions.
Source: Adapted from Mehta and Shahpar (2004).

Table 1.10. B/C ratios of indoor air pollution control, by WHO regions, 2006 study

WHO regions	US $1000 per DALY		US $5000 per DALY	
	Improved stove	LPG	Improved stove	LPG
Afro D	7.45	1.94	37.2	9.71
Afro E	5.00	1.48	25.0	7.38
Amro B	0.02	0.01	0.11	0.06
Amro D	0.42	0.12	2.11	0.59
Emro D	1.66	0.61	8.31	3.03
Sear B	0.45	0.08	2.23	0.39
Sear D	2.10	0.49	10.5	2.47
Wpro B	0.53	0.13	2.65	0.66

Note: The regions of Amro A, Europe, and Emro B are not presented here. SFU is limited in these regions.
Source: Adapted from Hutton et al. (2006).

in the AMRO regions, SEAR B and WPRO B (including China) than in the other regions. This is because the health benefits per beneficiary population are much lower (lower baseline ALRI mortality in children) than in Africa, EMRO D and SEAR D (table 1.11). The relatively low B/C ratios for WPRO B are also because of the modeling of delayed benefits in terms of COPD which generally develops from long-term exposure to SFU smoke.

Mehta and Shahpar (2004) and Hutton et al. (2006) have similar findings for the improved stove intervention across regions, with Hutton et al. (2006) finding somewhat higher B/C ratios.

For LPG, however, Hutton et al. (2006) find substantially higher B/C ratios for Africa, both compared to Mehta and Shahpar (2004) and to other regions. One important reason for this is the lower household consumption of LPG in Africa (table 1.11).

Larsen (2005) and Larsen and Strukova (2006) provide an economic analysis of indoor air pollution control interventions in rural Colombia and rural Peru, respectively. Health benefits include ALRI mortality in children, COPD mortality and morbidity in adult women, and ARI morbidity in children and adult women. Relative risk ratios used to estimate health benefits are from

Table 1.11. Benefits and costs of indoor air pollution control

	Africa		The Americas		E Med.	S + SE Asia		W Pac
Interventions and variables	AFR-D	AFR-E	AMR-B	AMR-D	EMR-D	SEAR-B	SEAR-D	WPR-B
1 Reduce by half those without modern cooking fuel by switching to LPG								
Beneficiary population (million)	185	171	71	18	97	118	378	318
Total deaths avoided (000)	108	91	1.1	1.9	24	10	110	72
DALYs avoided (000)	3571	3003	25	55	741	155	2931	828
Stove cost (US$ annualized per stove)	9.87	9.83	8.98	9.52	17.80	15.78	6.74	15.25
Program cost (US$ annualized per HH)	0.45	0.23	1.26	0.51	0.35	0.22	0.15	0.40
LPG consumption (kg/HH/day)	0.285	0.285	0.880	0.880	0.385	0.405	0.530	0.545
Total cost (US$ million)	1838	2033	2058	465	1225	1964	5928	6271
B/C ratio (DALY = US$1,000) health only	1.94	1.48	0.01	0.12	0.61	0.08	0.49	0.13
B/C ratio (DALY = US$5,000) health only	9.71	7.38	0.06	0.59	3.03	0.39	2.47	0.66
2 Reduce by half those without improved stove								
Beneficiary population (million)	102	111	111	23	115	78	365	418
Total deaths avoided (000)	38	32	0.4	0.7	9	3.4	38	25
DALYs avoided (000)	1251	1049	9	19	259	54	1025	289
Stove cost (US$ annualized per stove)	3.08	3.07	2.71	2.87	2.93	2.86	2.65	2.76
Program cost (US$ annualized per HH)	1.17	0.72	3.85	1.43	0.90	0.65	0.43	0.02
Total cost (US$ million)	168	210	415	46	156	122	487	546
B/C ratio (DALY = US$1,000) health only	7.45	5.00	0.02	0.42	1.66	0.45	2.10	0.53
B/C ratio (DALY = US$5,000) health only	37.23	24.98	0.11	2.11	8.31	2.23	10.52	2.65

Note: The regions of Amro A, Europe, and Emro B are not presented here. SFU is limited in these regions.
Source: Adapted from Hutton *et al.* (2006).

Desai *et al.* (2004). For ARI risk in adult women, the same relative risk as for children is applied. Risk of COPD for adult males is not included. An improved wood stove is assumed to reduce SFU health effects by 50 percent in both countries. LPG eliminates SFU health effects.

Both studies use a similar approach to valuation of health effects. Mortality is valued in two scenarios using a value of statistical life (VSL)

[14] VSL: Benefit transfer of US$2 million (Mrozek and Taylor 2002) adjusted in proportion to GDP *per capita* differentials between Colombia and Peru and high-income countries.

Table 1.12. Valuation of mortality (US $ per death)

	Colombia	Peru
VSL adults	127,200	148,600
HCV adults	11,300	13,400
HCV children	58,700	68,900

Sources: Larsen (2005); Larsen and Strukova (2006).

and the human capital value (HCV) for adults.[14] Child mortality is valued using HCV (table 1.12). Morbidity is valued using the COI approach. Time benefits are reduced fuel wood collection time, assuming that all fuel wood is collected by

Table 1.13. B/C ratios of indoor air pollution control interventions in rural Colombia

Benefits of interventions	Health only		Health and time benefits	
Valuation of mortality	HCV for children and adults	HCV for children; VSL for adults	HCV for children and adults	HCV for children; VSL for adults
B/C ratios				
Improved wood stove (from unimproved stove)	4.3	7.8	7.0	10.5
LPG (from unimproved stove)	1.2	2.2	2.3	3.3
LPG (from improved stove)	0.6	1.1	1.4	1.9
Source: Larsen (2005).				

Table 1.14. B/C ratios of indoor air pollution control interventions in rural Peru

Benefits of interventions	Health only		Health and time benefits	
Valuation of mortality	HCV for children and adults	HCV for children; VSL for adults	HCV for children and adults	HCV for children; VSL for adults
B/C ratios				
Improved wood stove (from unimproved stove)	5.4	6.8	7.8	9.2
LPG (from unimproved stove)	0.8	1.0	1.4	1.6
LPG (from improved stove)	0.4	0.5	0.8	0.9
Source: Larsen and Strukova (2006).				

the households, valued at 75 percent of average rural wage rates. It is assumed that switching to LPG would save the household 30 minutes per day, and using an improved stove would save 10 minutes per day.[15] The cost of an improved wood stove and LPG stove is US$60 each, annualized at a 10 percent discount rate. The cost of LPG is market price at typical household energy consumption for cooking. The intervention program cost is US$5 per household.

In Colombia, the largest monetized health benefits are reductions in ARI morbidity followed by COPD mortality. Reduction in COPD morbidity and ALRI mortality provides the smallest benefit. ALRI mortality in children is the smallest benefit because of the country's relatively low child mortality rate. In Peru, the largest monetized health benefits are ARI morbidity in children and adult women followed by ALRI mortality in children (valued at HCV).

The benefit-cost ratios are highest for installation of an improved wood stove, ranging from 4.3 to 10.5 in Colombia and 5.4 to 9.2 in Peru (tables 1.13 and 1.14). In Colombia, switching to LPG from an unimproved stove gives a B/C ratio of 1.2–3.3, while switching to LPG from an improved stove has a B/C ratio of >1.0 if adult mortality is valued at VSL. In Peru, the B/C ratio is only >1 for switching to LPG from an unimproved stove when adult mortality is valued at VSL or time benefits are included. The studies do not present health benefits in DALYs.

The estimated health benefits of indoor air pollution control in rural Colombia and Peru can be converted to DALYs.[16] We use the same

[15] The benefits of reduced fuel wood consumption would likely be larger than the assumed value of time benefits for households that purchase some or all of their fuel wood.
[16] The following conversions per case are used: Child mortality = 34 DALYs; COPD adult mortality = 6 DALYs; COPD morbidity = 2.25 DALYs; f morbidity in children under five =165/100,000 DALYs; ARI (acute respiratory infection) morbidity in female adults = 700/100,000 DALYs.

Table 1.15. B/C ratios of indoor air pollution control in rural Colombia and Peru

	Colombia	Peru	Colombia	Peru
	DALY = US $1,000		DALY = US $5,000	
Health benefits (only)				
Improved stove	1.50	1.87	7.50	9.35
LPG (from unimproved stove)	0.38	0.26	1.90	1.31
LPG (from improved stove)	0.19	0.13	0.95	0.65
Health and time savings benefits				
Improved stove	4.55	4.50	10.55	11.98
LPG (from unimproved stove)	1.54	0.81	3.05	1.86
LPG (from improved stove)	0.96	0.50	1.72	1.02

Sources: Benefits converted to DALYs from Larsen (2005); Larsen and Strukova (2006).

cost of improved wood stove and LPG stove (US$60 per stove), but now annualized over ten years at a 6 percent discount rate instead of a 10 percent rate. The intervention program cost remains US$5 per household.

At DALYs valued at US$1,000, the B/C ratios for improved stoves range from 1.5 to 1.9 while the B/C ratios for LPG are <<1 (table 1.15). At DALYs valued at US$5,000, the B/C ratios for using LPG instead of an unimproved stove is in the range of 1.3–1.9. However, the B/C ratio remains <1 for using LPG instead of an improved stove. The B/C ratios for LPG are significantly lower in Peru because of the substantially higher cost of LPG in Peru than in Colombia.

The B/C ratios increase significantly when time savings are included as a benefit. At DALYs valued at US$5,000, and time savings at 75 percent of rural wages, the B/C ratios for using LPG instead of an improved stove are >1 in both Colombia and Peru. However, the B/C ratio is <1 in Peru if time savings are valued at less than 75 percent.

Intervention program cost and annualized improved wood stove cost are of comparable magnitude. A lower or higher cost of either of these cost components will therefore have a significant effect on the B/C ratios. In the case of substituting to LPG, the intervention program costs and stove costs are only on the order of 10 percent of total cost, with the annual cost of

LPG being of the order of 90 percent. Changes in the price of LPG will therefore significantly affect the B/C ratios.

The relative risk of ALRI from household SFU presented in Desai *et al.* (2004), and used in all the CBA studies, is for morbidity. Only one study of ALRI mortality was identified in their literature review. The relative risks of ALRI morbidity are therefore applied to ALRI mortality to provide national and global estimates of the disease burden from SFU. However, case fatality rates from ALRI differ substantially across groups of children within countries. An important question is therefore how may the approach influence a CBA of interventions to control or prevent indoor air pollution and what are the potential implications in terms of strategic targeting of interventions.

Nutritional status is an important factor that influences ALRI mortality in children under five. Fishman *et al.* (2004) estimate that the relative risk of ALRI mortality in moderately and severely underweight children is 4–8 times higher than in non-underweight children from a review of studies in four African and six Asian countries (table 1.16).

We tabulated household fuel use by underweight status of children in the households from the most recent demographic and health surveys (DHS) in Cambodia, Ghana and Senegal. Figure 1.7 presents prevalence of fuel wood use by underweight status in these countries. Use

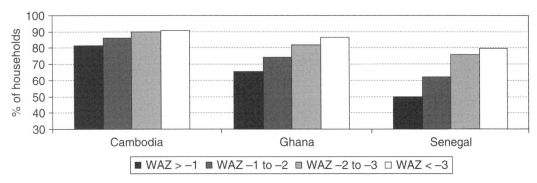

Figure 1.7 *Household use of fuel wood, by children's underweight status*
Note: Tabulated by the author.
Sources: Cambodia (DHS 2005); Ghana (DHS 2003); Senegal (DHS 2005).

Table 1.16. Relative risk of ALRI mortality, by child nutritional status

	Relative risk ratio (RR)
Severe underweight (WAZ <–3)	8.09
Moderate underweight (WAZ –2 to –3)	4.03
Mild underweight (WAZ –1 to –2)	2.01
Non-underweight (WAZ >–1)	1.00

Source: Fishman *et al.* (2004).

of fuel wood is far more prevalent in households with underweight children, especially in Senegal where the household energy transition has advanced furthest. The use of charcoal in Ghana, often considered an intermediate fuel on the household energy ladder and generally less polluting than fuel wood, is twice as prevalent in households with non-underweight children than in households with severely underweight children. In Cambodia, where households have started to switch away from fuel wood only in the last five years, a similar trend is emerging as in Ghana. In Senegal, the use of LPG is nearly three times more prevalent in households with non-underweight children than in households with moderately and severely underweight children.

To illustrate the potential effect of nutritional status on estimation of mortality from SFU and

benefit-cost ratios of interventions, we considered a situation typically representative of Sub-Saharan countries where at least 90 percent of households use solid fuels (table 1.17). Around 38 percent of children under five are mildly underweight and 32 percent are moderately or severely underweight. Only 10 percent of households use LPG, concentrated in households with non-underweight or mild underweight children. Applying the relative risks of ALRI in children in Desai *et al.* (2004) and Fishman *et al.* (2004), and substitution to LPG in households with children of different nutrition status, gives the benefit-cost ratios presented in figure 1.8. These B/C ratios are relative to a normalized B/C ratio = 1 in the approach that ignores nutritional status. The B/C ratio for severely underweight children is six times higher, and the B/C ratio for non-underweight children is 23 percent lower than a B/C ratio that ignores nutritional status.

Clearly, a careful analysis of SFU in relation to nutritional status is needed to establish the relative risks of ALRI mortality from SFU. However, the simple estimation above may suggest that the B/C ratios for interventions reaching households with a high propensity to have malnourished children may be several times higher than the B/C ratios reported in this chapter, not only for LPG but also for improved stoves.

Benefit-cost ratios from the four studies reviewed are summarized in table 1.18. "Low" is

Table 1.17. SFU in relation to children's nutritional status in a typical SSA country (percent of households)

	Weight-for-age (WA)				
	Non-underweight	Mild underweight	Moderate underweight	Severe underweight	Total
SFU	24%	34%	25%	7%	90%
LPG	6%	4%	0%	0%	10%
Total	30%	38%	25%	7%	100%

Note: SFU is an approximation to regional SFU prevalence.
Source: WA distribution is average for AFR D and E in Fishman *et al.* (2004).

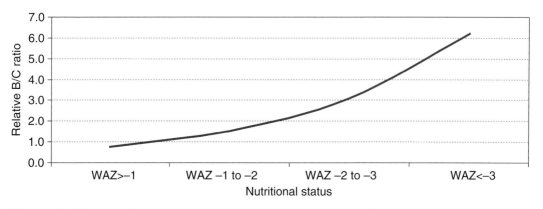

Figure 1.8 *B/C ratio of fuel substitution, relative to ignoring nutritional status*
Source: Estimated by the author.

from Mehta and Shahpar (2004), "high" is from Hutton *et al.* (2006), Colombia is from Larsen (2005) and Peru is from Larsen and Strukova (2006). Only health benefits are included in the B/C ratios to make the results more comparable. B/C ratios for an improved stove are presented for DALY= US $1,000, and LPG for DALY=US $5,000.

Both global studies find that B/C ratios >1 for improved stoves in the Africa regions and SEAR D. The B/C ratios <1 for WPRO B warrant further investigation, as one-third of all mortality from SFU is in this region (especially China). The findings for EMRO D is mixed, with the B/C in Hutton *et al.* (2006) being more than fifteen times higher than in Mehta and Shahpar (2004).

The low B/C ratios found for the AMRO regions in the two global studies are in contrast to the findings for Colombia and Peru. However the studies differ in important respects. The studies in Colombia and Peru assess benefits and costs in rural areas, where mortality rates are higher than in urban areas. Thus the benefits of interventions are estimated to be higher than in the global studies. The Colombia and Peru studies include ARI morbidity for adult women. This is 10–20 percent of DALYs and does therefore not explain the difference with the global studies and does not substantially affect B/C ratios. Further CBA analysis should therefore be undertaken in countries with relatively low child mortality rates, such as in AMRO and SEAR B.

The global studies are inconclusive for LPG, even at US $5,000 per DALY. However, Hutton *et al.* (2006) do find B/C ratios >>1 in the Africa regions, EMRO D and SEAR D, which together

Table 1.18. Summary of B/C ratios of indoor air pollution control

	Improved stoves		LPG	
	DALY = US$1,000		DALY = US$5,000	
	"low"	"high"	"low"	"high"
Afro D	2.0	7.5	0.8	9.71
Afro E	1.4	5.0	0.5	7.38
Amro B		0.02	0.4	0.06
Colombia (Amro B)	1.5		0.95–1.9	
Amro D	0.2	0.4	0.7	0.59
Peru (Amro D)	1.9		0.65–1.3	
Emro D	0.1	1.7	0.5	3.03
Sear B	0.9	0.5	0.3	0.39
Sear D	1.6	2.1	0.7	2.47
Wpro B	0.03	0.5	3.5	0.66

Note: Benefits are reduced health effects only. Time and fuel savings would increase the B/C ratios.

account for over 60 percent of mortality from SFU. Both global studies assessed the benefits and costs of going from currently used stoves to LPG. A majority of these stoves are unimproved in most regions. The B/C ratios may therefore be expected to be lower if an assessment was undertaken for going from improved stoves to LPG. This incremental analysis was done in the Colombia and Peru studies, with the B/C ratios of going from an unimproved stove to LPG being twice as high as when going from improved stoves to LPG – e.g. 1.9 vs. 0.95 in Colombia.

None of the studies evaluated the option of replacing fuel wood (and other unimproved biomass fuels) with charcoal. Charcoal is not considered a clean fuel like LPG, but is nevertheless a preferred option for many urban households. Based on a study by Ezzati and Kammen (2001) in Kenya, Gakidou et al. (2007) suggest that the relative risk of ALRI from charcoal is 1.3, in contrast to 2.3 from biomass and largely unimproved stoves (Desai et al. 2004). If so, then the health effects of charcoal may be lower than many improved wood stoves. For instance, preliminary results from intervention trials in Guatemala suggest that the excess risk of ALRI is lowered by 50 percent from improved stoves with a chimney.

The B/C ratios summarized in table 1.18 are likely to be conservative for many reasons. Country prevalence of SFU and child mortality rates is correlated within a region, such as in AMRO. Thus using regional averages would tend to under-estimate the health effects. Important benefits such as time and fuel savings are not included in the B/C ratios. Including these benefits, even at conservative unit values, will substantially increase the ratios.

As already discussed, targeting of interventions to households with high risk of mortality from SFU (e.g. households prone to have malnourished children) may provide substantially greater benefits than a more generic program. If such households are targeted with multiple interventions, a benefit-cost analysis should be undertaken within a multiple-risk framework in order to avoid over-estimation of benefits of each intervention. Gakidou et al. (2007) exemplifies an analysis of targeting high-risk households by contrasting a program targeting households with low socioeconomic status with a general program. Recent examples of benefit estimation (or cost of inaction) of environmental interventions (such as controlling indoor air pollution) in a multiple-risk framework are Gakidou et al. (2007), Larsen (2007), and a forthcoming report on the health effects and

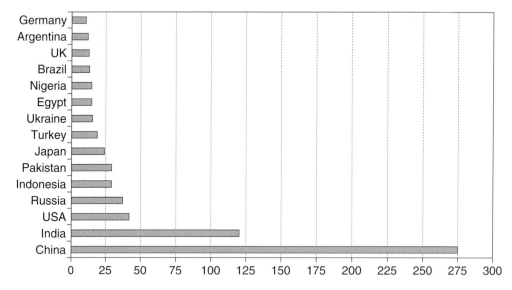

Figure 1.9 *Estimated deaths from urban PM, 2002*
Source: Adapted from WHO (2007).

costs of environmental risk factors including indirect effects through malnutrition (World Bank 2008a).

Urban Air Pollution

The Challenge

Particulate matter (PM) is the urban air pollutant that has most consistently been shown to have the largest health effects in studies around the world. It is especially finer particulates, usually measured as PM 10 and PM 2.5 that have the largest health effects. Ostro (2004) provides a review of studies of PM and health. Exposure to lead (Pb) is also a major concern. Lead has been eliminated from gasoline in a majority of countries in the world, but other sources of lead remain a localized issue. The focus of this chapter is on PM.

PM air pollution originating in the outdoor environment is estimated to contribute as much as 0.6–1.4 percent of the burden of disease in developing regions (WHO 2002). This excludes air pollution caused by major forest fires (e.g. Indonesia in 1997), and serious accidents caus-

ing release of organic chemical substances (such as Bhopal in 1984) or radioactive pollution (such as Chernobyl in 1986).

Nearly 50 percent of the world's population, or 3.2 billion people, lived in urban areas in 2006 (World Bank, 2007); as many as 2.3 billion lived in cities with a population over 100,000. The World Bank provides estimates of annual average PM 10 concentrations in these cities – over 3,000 cities in total. WHO estimates a total of 865,000 deaths in 2002 as a consequence of PM 10 in these cities (WHO 2007).

About 85 percent of deaths from PM in the urban environment occur in low-and middle-income countries, and more than 55 percent in Asia alone. The death rate from PM is also high in the middle-income countries of Europe and Central Asia, because of the high share of elderly and susceptibility to cardiopulmonary disease in this region (table 1.19). Fifteen countries account for 77 percent of global deaths (figure 1.9). China and India alone account for 45 percent of global deaths.

Estimated deaths in China of 275,000 is based on an urban population weighted PM 10 of 80 ug/m^3 (WHO 2007). However, a recent

Table 1.19. Estimated deaths from urban PM in world cities, 2002

	Million Population (in cities > 100000)	PM10 (Population weighted)	Deaths from PM (000)	Deaths from PM (% of total)
East Asia and Pacific*	645	80	327	38%
Europe and Central Asia*	190	36	111	13%
Latin America and Caribbean*	265	43	48	6%
Middle East and North Africa*	125	98	45	5%
South Asia*	250	100	160	18%
Sub-Saharan Africa*	140	71	42	5%
Europe (High-income countries)	155	26	56	6%
East Asia and Pacific (High-income countries)	145	34	32	4%
North America (High-income countries)	240	23	44	5%
Total	2155	60	865	100%

Note: *World Bank regions (low- and middle-income countries).
Sources: Population and PM10 are from World Bank. Deaths from PM are from WHO (2007).

study by the World Bank in collaboration with Chinese institutions estimates deaths from urban PM 10 in China at 395,000 (World Bank 2008b). The study is based on PM 10 concentrations in 660 cities with a total population of 580 million, using a log-linear risk function derived from data in Pope *et al.* (2002). PM 10 concentration monitoring data used in this study are significantly higher than the PM 10 concentrations used by WHO in its estimate of mortality.

There is increasing evidence that it is the very small particulates that cause the greatest health effects. Ambient standards have therefore started to shift to PM 2.5. The annual average ambient concentration standard for PM 2.5 in the USA is 15 ug/m^3 and WHO has a guideline of 10 ug/m^3. WHO has also tightened its guideline for annual PM 10 to 20 ug/m^3 (NAE/NRC 2008).

Over 55 percent of the urban population in China is exposed to ambient concentrations of PM 10 greater than 100 ug/m^3. Ambient PM 10 is particularly high in the inland northern half of China, where natural sources contribute substantially to PM concentrations (World Bank 2008b). Particulate size distribution analysis from Chinese studies indicates that PM 2.5 is

about half of PM 10, thus indicating that over 55 percent of the urban population in China is exposed to PM 2.5 exceeding 50 ug/m^3. This implies that about 300 million people in China are exposed to PM 2.5 and PM 10 ambient levels that are five times higher than WHO guidelines.

In the eight largest cities in India, each with a population greater than 3 million and a total population of about 70 million, four cities have annual PM 10 ambient concentrations exceeding 100 ug/m^3 (CAI-Asia 2006). The population-weighted average in these cities is over 90 ug/m^3. More than half of the population in these eight cities is thus exposed to PM 2.5 and PM 10 levels that are five times higher than WHO guidelines.

Table 1.20 presents annual average PM 10 ambient concentrations in mega-cities in the developing world for which regular monitoring data are available. The cities in Pakistan, Egypt, China, Bangladesh, and India have very high PM 10 levels. Major cities in Latin America, as well as in Thailand and the Philippines, have moderate levels of PM 10, with the exception of Lima and Santiago.

PM 10 and PM 2.5 concentrations in most

Table 1.20. Annual average PM 10 concentration in mega-cities in the developing world

City	Country	PM10 (ug/m3)	Source
Lahore	Pakistan	202	Year 2004 (Krupnick *et al.* 2006 and CAI-Asia 2006)
Karachi	Pakistan	194	Year 2004 (Krupnick *et al.* 2006 and CAI-Asia 2006)
Cairo	Egypt	170	Year 2004–2006 (EEAA 2007)
Beijing	China	145	Years 2003–2004 (CAI-Asia 2006)
Dhaka	Bangladesh	140	Years 2002–2006 (CAI-Asia 2006)
Delhi	India	130	Years 2003–2005 (CAI-Asia 2006)
Tianjin	China	120	Years 2003–2004 (CAI-Asia 2006)
Kolkata	India	110	Years 2003–2005 (CAI-Asia 2006)
Lima	Peru	101	Years 2001–2004 (Larsen and Strukova 2005)
Shanghai	China	100	Years 2003–2004 (CAI-Asia 2006)
Tehran	Iran	100	Year 2002 (World Bank 2005)
Jakarta	Indonesia	90	Years 2002–2004 (CAI-Asia 2006)
Santiago	Chile	82	Years 1997–2003 (Cifuentes *et al.* 2005)
Ho Chi Minh City	Vietnam	80	Years 2001–2005 (CAI-Asia 2006)
Mumbai	India	75	Years 2003–2005 (CAI-Asia 2006)
Bogotá	Colombia	62	Years 2001–2003 (Larsen 2004)
Mexico City	Mexico	60	Years 1997–2003 (Cifuentes *et al.* 2005)
Bangkok	Thailand	50	Years 2000–2005 (CAI-Asia 2006)
São Paulo	Brazil	49	Years 1997–2003 (Cifuentes *et al.* 2005)
Manila	Philippines	45	Years 2001–2003 (CAI-Asia 2006)

Source: Author.

Sub-Saharan cities are believed to be moderate. However, available monitoring data from this part of the world are severely limited.

The main health effects of fine particulates are cardiopulmonary mortality and respiratory related illness (Pope *et al.* 2002; Ostro 2004). It is therefore the older age groups that are most vulnerable to PM exposure. As urbanization continues in the coming decades, and the population becomes increasingly old, the health effects of outdoor PM pollution may therefore be expected to increase if PM concentrations levels do not decline significantly.

China's urban population was over 550 million in 2005, or about 40 percent of the total population. The urban population share is expected to reach 60 percent, or over 900 million, by 2030. India's urban population is expected to grow from 285 million in 2001 to 473 million in 2021 and 820 million in 2051 (CAI-Asia 2006).

Annual population growth in cities with a population over 100,000 is presented in table 1.21 for select large developing countries. The average growth was 3.2 percent per year during 1990 to 2004 and 2.8 percent from 2000 to 2004. By 2030, if growth slows to half the rate during 2000–4 by 2030, the population in these cities will have grown by 70 percent. Assuming no change in age and cause of death distribution, mortality from PM pollution may increase by the same rate. This may, however, be a conservative assumption as the population is expected to age significantly over this period of time.

Table 1.21. Annual population growth in cities with population over 100,000 in select large developing countries

	Annual growth 1990–2004	Annual growth 2000–2004
China	3.6%	3.1%
India	2.5%	2.2%
Indonesia	4.6%	4.1%
Pakistan	3.4%	3.5%
Turkey	2.6%	2.3%
Egypt	1.8%	2.1%
Nigeria	4.8%	4.2%
Brazil	2.3%	2.1%
Iran	2.7%	2.1%
Bangladesh	3.7%	3.5%
Mexico	1.8%	1.4%
Viet Nam	3.3%	2.8%
Weighted average	3.2%	2.8%

Source: Calculated from World Bank PM10 global database.

The Solutions

Reducing air pollution exposure is largely a technical issue, and includes removing pollution at its source and filtering pollution away from the source. These technical solutions are implemented in a policy environment that makes it illegal to use a polluting substance or process (e.g. bans on leaded gasoline or asbestos), increases the costs of polluting (the polluter pays principle, PPP), requires the use of pollution control and prevention technologies, mandates maximum allowable pollution loads, or increases information on or encourages best practices with regard to the use of less polluting technologies and substances.

Applying these policies is often more an economic than a technical issue. A CBA of the most effective options can therefore help promote policies for pollution control and prevention. It does however first require identification of the most significant sources of pollution and effective options to reduce pollution from these sources. We therefore start out with a review of so called PM source-apportionment studies, PM emission inventories, and projection of future emissions from major pollution sources in some of the countries with the highest death toll from outdoor air pollution.

Several PM 2.5 source-apportionment studies (table 1.22) have been conducted in Beijing, representing a city where natural-source contribution to PM 2.5 ambient concentrations is expected to be significant because of the semi-arid conditions in northern China. The five studies reviewed here find that primary particulates from coal combustion contribute 7–20 percent of ambient PM 2.5 concentrations, with a median of 15 percent. The contribution from coal is especially high in the winter. Vehicle emissions contribute 5–7 percent in three of the studies and over 25 percent in Zhang et al. (2007). The high contribution found by Zhang et al. (2007) could be associated with the monitoring sample site being near a major traffic area. Biomass burning contributes 5–15 percent with a mean of about 8 percent. Secondary particulate, mainly from sulfur dioxide and nitrogen oxides, is a major source of ambient PM 2.5, with a contribution in the range of 10–>30 percent.

Primary commercial energy consumption in China doubled from 1990 to 2005. The largest share of the increase in energy consumption came from coal, followed by petroleum products. Coal consumption was over 65 percent of total primary commercial energy consumption in 2005. Industry including power generation consumed over 70 percent of commercial primary energy in 2005, while transportation consumed less than 10 percent (NAE/NRC 2008).

As of March 2007 there were 148 million vehicles in China. Some 52 million were four+-wheelers (of which nearly 13 million were private cars) and 83 million were motorcycles. Car sales rose to over 5 million in 2006 (Reuters 2007). In 1999, 49 percent of four+-wheelers were trucks, 20 percent were buses, and 31 percent were cars. Cars are expected to constitute 70 percent of the fleet in 2030 (Blumberg et al. 2006). In perspective, there were a little over 5 million four+-wheelers in 1990. This figure is expected to grow to nearly 300 million by 2035.

Table 1.22. PM 2.5 source apportionment studies from Beijing

Method*	CMB Zhang *et al.* (2004)	CMB Zheng *et al.* (2005)	PMF Song *et al.* (2006)	PMF Zhang *et al.* (2007)	CMB Zhang *et al.* (2007)
Coal combustion	16.4%	7%	15.8%	13.8%	20%
Vehicle emissions	5.6%	7%	5.5%	28.5%	25%
Fugitive/road/soil/construction dust	21.4%	20%	7.0%	19.9%	19%
Biomass burning	4.5%	6%	10.1%	11.7%	15%
Industry			4.7%	4.8%	5%
Secondary particulates	9.6%	33%	31.0%	19.2%	15%
Organic matter	15.0%	11%			
Other		2%			
Unexplained	27.5%	14%	25.9%	2.2%	1%
Total	100.0%	100.0%	100.0%	100.0%	100.0%
Average measured PM2.5 (ug/m3)	122	101	93	142	142

Notes: *CMB = chemical mass balance; PMF = positive matrix factorization.
Sources: Adapted from NAE/NRC (2008); Zheng *et al.* (2005); Zhang *et al.* (2007).

Motorcycles are expected to grow to 140 million (CAI-Asia 2006).

With the projected growth in the vehicle fleet in China, vehicle emission contribution to PM 2.5 may be expected to grow substantially (especially secondary particulates). Blumberg *et al.* (2006) report that primary and secondary PM 2.5 emissions from vehicles are projected to grow seven-fold from 2005 to 2030 in major cities in China if vehicles and fuels only meet Euro 2 standards. Even if vehicles and fuels meet Euro 4 standards, PM 2.5 emissions will nearly double.

Chowdhury *et al.* (2007) provides PM 2.5 emission source apportionment for three major cities in India, based on site monitoring, particulate analysis and chemical mass balance (CMB). The analysis was conducted for each season. Annual averages for each city and an average for the three cities are presented in table 1.23. Overall, diesel and gasoline combustion contribute the largest share to PM 2.5 ambient concentrations (26 percent) followed by road dust (23 percent). Biomass burning (solid fuels, waste, etc.), secondary particulates and other unidentified sources are also significant. A majority of PM 2.5 from diesel and gasoline is from road vehicles. Diesel contributes substantially more

than gasoline, although PM 2.5 from gasoline (mainly from two- and three-wheelers) is very significant in Kolkata.

A PM emission inventory for urban Pune also indicates that vehicles, road dust and the burning of biomass for cooking are major contributors to PM 2.5 (table 1.24). In Pune, however, brick kilns are the largest identified source of PM 2.5. In addition, PM 2.5 from rural agricultural burning is as significant as all urban sources combined (Gaffney and Benjamin 2004). Only a share of these emissions contributes to the urban ambient concentrations of PM 2.5.

A study by GSSR (2004) indicates that as much as over 80 percent of PM emissions from vehicles in Pune are from two- and three-wheelers (table 1.25).

Motor vehicles in India increased from fewer than 2 million in 1971 to 67 million in 2003; two-wheelers accounted for over 70 percent of total vehicles in 2003. Total vehicles are projected to increase at a rate of 10 percent per year (assuming 8 percent GDP growth) and reach over 670 million in 2030, of which two-wheelers are expected to constitute 425 million (CAI-Asia 2006). This represents a nearly tenfold increase from 2003.

Table 1.23. PM 2.5 source apportionment studies in three major cities in India

	Delhi	Kolkata	Mumbai	Average three cities
Diesel	15.9%	20.7%	21.0%	19%
Gasoline	4.9%	13.7%	3.6%	7%
Road dust	24.5%	15.1%	28.9%	23%
Coal	7.1%	8.7%	3.7%	7%
Biomass burning	14.6%	14.6%	13.2%	14%
Secondary PM	15.1%	14.2%	18.3%	16%
Other mass (unidentified sources)	17.9%	12.9%	11.4%	14%
Total	100%	100%	100%	100%

Source: Adapted from Chowdhury *et al.* (2007).

Table 1.24. PM 2.5 emission inventory estimate for urban Pune, India

	PM2.5
Road dust	23%
Brick kilns	30%
On-road vehicles	19%
Construction activities	3%
Household cooking (wood, dung, etc.)	15%
Street sweeping	1%
Trash burning	3%
Industry and other	6%
Total	100%

Source: Author's estimate from PM 10 emission inventory in Gaffney and Benjamin (2004).

Table 1.26. Source contribution to ambient PM 2.5 in Dakar, Senegal

	Contribution to ambient PM 2.5 (central estimate)
Road vehicles	34%
Secondary particulates	23%
Fugitive emissions	22%
Solid waste burning	8%
Cement industry	8%
Power plants	3%
Other industry	<2%

Source: Larsen (2007c).

Table 1.25. PM emissions from vehicles in Pune, India

	PM emission shares	Vehicle activity shares
Passenger cars	2%	15%
Two-wheelers	56%	66%
Three-wheelers	33%	18%
Buses	7%	2%
Trucks	2%	
Total	100%	100%

Source: Adapted from GSSR (2004).

In Senegal where transportation is highly dieselized (78 percent diesel, 22 percent gasoline), one may expect that road vehicles will contribute significantly to urban air particulate pollution. Larsen (2007c) constructed an emissions inventory of contributions to PM 2.5 ambient concentrations in Dakar that includes an estimate of secondary particulates and fugitive emissions (road dust, dust from natural sources, etc.). The central estimate indicates that 34 percent of ambient concentrations of PM 2.5 is from road vehicles (primary particulates), followed by secondary particulates and fugitive emissions (table 1.26). Household cooking is not a contributor to PM in urban Dakar as LPG is the primary fuel in 95 percent of households.

Table 1.27. Source contribution to ambient PM 2.5 in Bogotà, Colombia

	Contribution to ambient PM 2.5 (central estimate)
Road vehicles	37%
Secondary particulates	30%
Stationary sources	17%
Fugitive emissions	15%
Forest fires/waste burning	1%

Source: Larsen (2005).

Road vehicles were also found to be major contributors to ambient PM 2.5 in Bogotá, where the contribution from fugitive emissions is less than in Dakar (Larsen 2005). The contribution from road vehicles is followed by secondary particulates, stationary sources, and fugitive emissions (table 1.27).

The large share of two-wheelers in the vehicle fleet is limited to Asia and three-wheelers are largely concentrated South Asia and to some extent in South-East Asia. In the rest of the developing world, the passenger car is the predominant motorized form of transportation. In a study of on-road vehicle distribution in six cities in developing countries, passenger cars constitute 72–87 percent of on-road vehicle activity with the exception of Pune, where two- and three-wheelers are dominant (table 1.28). In Lima and Pune, as much as 25 percent of passenger vehicles are diesel fueled.

A very large share of vehicles in developing countries have no or minimal emission control technology. This is especially the case for diesel vehicles, which then emit many times more particulates than gasoline vehicles. Globally, the diesel fuel share in transportation was 44 percent and the gasoline share was 56 percent in 2005. This does not include aviation, but is not limited to road vehicle transport (separate data are not readily available for road transport). Of the countries included in table 1.29, transport dieselization ranges from 17 percent in Nigeria to 85 percent in Pakistan and also shows wide variation within each of the regions. In countries

with relatively few passenger cars, the dieselization rate is high because of the dominance of trucks and buses, with a significant share of diesel combusted by long-haul trucks outside urban areas. However, passenger car dieselization is also relatively high in some countries, such as France, Senegal, and Peru.

As we have seen, vehicles are found to be a major source of particulate emissions and contributors to ambient PM in many developing countries. Projected growth in vehicle fleets also indicates that vehicle emissions will continue to be a major source of pollution in the absence of interventions. Vehicle emission control is therefore the focus of our review of cost-benefit studies.

Emission control, broadly speaking, involves measures that reduce emissions per passenger km travelled and reduces overall transport demand. This includes:

- Emission control devices on new and in-use vehicles (e.g. catalytic converters, diesel oxidation catalysts, diesel particulate traps)
- Cleaner fuels (e.g. low-sulfur gasoline and diesel, LPG/CNG)
- Inspection and maintenance (I&M) of in-use vehicles
- Engine modifications (e.g. 4-stroke vs. 2-stroke engines for two- and three-wheelers)
- New technology vehicles (e.g. electric, hybrid, fuel cells, solar)
- Smaller, less-polluting vehicles and non-polluting transport modes (e.g. bicycling, walking)
- Transport modal shifts from low- to high-occupancy transportation (e.g. buses, metros, subways, trains)
- Traffic management to improve vehicle flows (e.g. off-street parking, traffic light management, congestion charges, dedicated lanes for high-occupancy vehicles)
- Urban planning and reduced commuting to work
- Old-vehicle replacement programs (e.g. old high-usage vehicles, replacing three-wheelers with newer four-wheel taxis).

Most or all of these measures would need to be included in an effective package of interventions

Table 1.28. On-road vehicle distribution in six cities, worldwide

	Passenger vehicles	Two- and three-wheelers	Taxi	Buses	Trucks	Non-motorized	Passenger vehicles (diesel share)
Almaty	82.9%	0.1%	n/d	11.6%	4.7%	0.7%	5.8%
Lima	72.0%	1.0%	3.0%	18.0%	6.0%	0.0%	25.0%
Mexico City	79.0%	1.6%	11.0%	3.5%	5.1%	0.0%	0.6%
Nairobi	87.8%	1.7%	0.5%	3.8%	5.4%	0.8%	8.0%
Pune	12.0%	68.3%	0.3%	1.5%	1.4%	16.5%	25.4%
Santiago	78.9%	1.2%	7.9%	6.7%	5.3%	0.0%	3.1%

Source: Lents *et al.* (2004).

Table 1.29. Diesel fuel share in transportation, 2005

Country	Region	Diesel fuel share in transportation
Pakistan	Asia	85%
India	Asia	71%
China	Asia	51%
Indonesia	Asia	44%
Japan	Asia	39%
Thailand	Asia	27%
Senegal	SS Africa	78%
South Africa	SS Africa	39%
Nigeria	SS Africa	17%
France	Europe	74%
Germany	Europe	53%
UK	Europe	53%
Russia	Europe	34%
Peru	Latin America	74%
Chile	Latin America	61%
Mexico	Latin America	31%
Egypt	Middle East and North Africa	67%
Saudi Arabia	Middle East and North Africa	45%
Morocco	Middle East and North Africa	36%
United States	North America	27%

Source: From IEA, www.iea.org/Textbase/stats/prodresult. asp?PRODUCT=Oil.

to reduce urban pollution from transport. In the light of current transport situations in most developing countries, vehicle emission control devices, cleaner fuels, and I&M are essential measures. Controlling emissions from two- and three-wheelers is also essential in many Asian countries.

The European Union has implemented progressively more stringent emission limits for road vehicles since the mid-1990s. PM emission standards now in effect (Euro 4) for diesel passenger cars and light commercial vehicles are 75–80 percent more stringent than the Euro 1 standards approved in 1993–4, and the Euro 5–6 standards will be ten times more stringent than the standards today (table 1.30). PM standards for heavy-duty diesel engines are >90 percent more stringent than the Euro 1 standard (table 1.31).

The Euro standards also substantially reduce the maximum limit for NOx in both gasoline and diesel vehicles. A significant share of secondary particulates is from NOx emissions.

To achieve these emissions limits and for emission control devices to perform and operate properly, the sulfur content in the fuel must be limited. Lowering the sulfur in diesel also has its immediate benefits in terms of PM reduction. The maximum allowable sulfur content in vehicle diesel fuel in the European Union was 2,000 ppm in 1994, lower than the content in diesel used in many developing countries today. The maximum allowable content in gasoline and diesel was 500 ppm in 1996, and is now at 50 ppm. "Sulfur-free" diesel and gasoline fuels (≤10 ppm S) were available from 2005, and are mandatory from 2009 (table 1.32).

Table 1.30. EU diesel vehicle emission standards for PM (g/km)

	Passenger vehicles	Light commercial vehicles (by weight class 1–3)		
		LCV (I)	LCV (2)	LCV (3)
Euro 1 (1992/94)*	0.14	0.14	0.19	0.25
Euro 2 (1996/98)**	0.08	0.08	0.12	0.17
Euro 3 (2000/01)	0.05	0.05	0.07	0.1
Euro 4 (2005/06)	0.025	0.025	0.04	0.06
Euro 5 (2009/10)	0.005^a	0.005^a	0.005^a	0.005^a
Euro 6 (2014/15)	0.005^a	0.005^a	0.005^a	0.005^a

Notes: *The earlier year is for passenger vehicles. The later year is for light commercial vehicles.
** Applicable for IDI engines. Slightly less stringent limits apply for DI engines. ^{a} Proposed to be changed to 0.003 g/km using the PMP measurement procedure.
Source: Adapted from www.dieselnet.com.

Table 1.31. EU heavy-duty diesel engines' emission standards for PM (g/kWh)

Tier	Year	PM
Euro I	1992 <85 kW	0.612
	1992, >85 kW	0.36
Euro II	1996	0.25
	1998	0.15
Euro III	*1999.10, EEVs only*	*0.02*
	2000	0.1
		0.13*
Euro IV	2005	0.02
Euro V	2008	0.02

Notes: * For engines of less than 0.75 dm³ swept volume per cylinder and a rated power speed of more than 3000/min.
Source: Adapted from www.dieselnet.com.

Table 1.32. Maximum EU allowable sulfur content in vehicle gasoline and diesel fuel

	Year	Max sulfur content (ppm)
Euro 2	1996	500
Euro 3	2000	350
Euro 4	2005	50
Euro 5	2009	10

Source: www.dieselnet.com/standards/eu/ld.php.

Similar reductions in sulfur content have been implemented in, for instance, the USA, Japan and other high-income countries. An increasing number of developing countries are also moving to low-sulfur diesel and have plans to mandate ultra-low sulfur diesel. South Africa has been moving to 500 ppm sulfur in diesel and is planning to limit the sulfur content to 50 ppm in 2010. Botswana, Lesotho, Namibia and Swaziland are also using 500 ppm sulfur diesel imported from South Africa. Mexico, Bolivia, Chile and metropolitan areas of Brazil are using <500 ppm sulfur diesel. Many Asian developing countries have mandated 500 ppm

diesel fuel for diesel vehicles, including China, India, Malaysia, the Philippines, Thailand, and Vietnam and some of them are moving to 50 ppm sulfur diesel (ADB 2003; UNEP 2006).

There are, however, many countries that continue to use high-sulfur diesel. Pakistan, Indonesia, Russia, the Central Asian countries of the former Soviet Union, and many countries in Africa and Latin America are reported to use diesel with a sulfur content of >2,000 ppm. Many African and Middle Eastern countries are even using diesel with a sulfur content of >5,000 ppm (UNEP 2006).

Technical options to substantially reduce PM emissions from in-use diesel vehicles are available after low- and ultra-low sulfur diesel is made available in the market. Either of two technologies is used to retrofit in-use diesel vehicles – i.e. diesel oxidation catalysts (DOC) and diesel particulate filters (DPF). DOCs are effective with low-sulfur diesel (500 ppm) and DPFs are effective with ultra-low sulfur diesel (50 ppm). DOCs are found to reduce PM emissions in in-use vehicles by 20–50 percent, while DPFs quite consistently reduce PM by over 80–90 percent.

A report by UNEP (2006) summarizes the global experience with DOC and DPF. DOCs have been installed on over 50 million diesel passenger vehicles and more than 1.5 million buses and trucks worldwide. DPFs have been installed on over 1 million new diesel passenger vehicles in Europe. From 2008, all new on-road diesel vehicles in the USA and Canada must be equipped with a high-efficiency DPF. And from 2009, all new diesel cars and vans in the European Union will have to be equipped with DPF. Worldwide, over 200,000 heavy-duty vehicles have already been retrofitted with DPF.

DOCs and DPFs have been used for retrofitting of buses and trucks in many countries on a wider scale or in demonstration projects in Chile (Santiago), China (Beijing), Europe, Hong Kong, India (Pune), Japan, Mexico (Mexico City), Taiwan, Thailand (Bangkok), and the USA. These technologies are expected to be increasingly used in developing countries as they move to low- and ultra-low sulfur diesel fuel.

Economic Estimates of Costs and Benefits

Despite its importance, very few full CBAs have been conducted on measures to address outdoor air pollution. Most studies are single-country or single-city in nature, so no global estimates are possible. Existing studies cover several major industrialized countries or economic areas (e.g. the USA, Europe, Japan, Canada, and the UK) and some heavily polluted cities located in developing countries. Differences that may reduce the transferability of results to other settings include different economic levels, valuation of health benefits and different pollution levels and population exposure. In most studies, the economic gains measured are limited to reductions in premature deaths, lower health care costs and work days gained due to less morbidity. In only few studies were other economic benefits included, such as avoided damage to agriculture and ecosystems, or avoided damage to infrastructure and public buildings from corrosive pollutants.

Five recent studies of road vehicle emission control in developing countries are discussed here: Stevens et al. (2005) from Mexico City, Blumberg et al. (2006) from China, Larsen (2005) from Bogotá, Colombia, ECON (2006) from Lima, Peru, and Larsen (2007c) from Dakar, Senegal. These studies focus on particulate emission control from improved vehicle fuels and control technologies, and represent CBA in high-middle-income, low-middle-income, and low-income countries in three regions of the developing world.

All the studies use a VSL to monetize the benefits of reduction in mortality. Larsen (2005), ECON (2006) and Larsen (2007c) also use a HCV. The results from these five studies are discussed and presented here with the VSL approach to provide consistency across the studies. The VSL/GDP per capita ratio ranges from about 66 in the Colombia, Peru, and Senegal studies to 74 in China in 2005 and 89 in Mexico.[17] The Colombia, Peru, and Senegal studies use the COI approach for valuation of morbidity. The China study uses a combination of COI and willingness-to-pay (WTP). The Mexico study does not include morbidity benefits of emission reductions.

Older studies, such as Larsen (1994, 1997) from Iran and Morocco and Eskeland (1994) from Chile are not discussed because their control cost figures are now more than a decade old.

Stevens et al. (2005) evaluates the benefits and costs of in-use vehicle emission control from retrofitting diesel vehicles with particulate control technologies in Mexico City, using 2010 as the year of program implementation. Benefits are limited to reduced mortality from reductions in primary particulates and secondary particulates from hydrocarbon gases. Benefits of reduced morbidity are not included (morbidity is often

[17] In contrast, USEPA uses a VSL that is on the order of 200 times GDP per capita in the USA.

found to represent 20–30 percent of total health benefits, depending on valuation methods used). The analysis assumes that ultra-low sulfur diesel will be available by 2010, based on planned completion of phase-in by the year 2009.

Health benefits are estimated using emissions intake fractions and particulate concentration-response coefficients from the international literature. A median intake fraction of 80 per million was applied for primary particulates inside the urban area, and 20 per million for primary particulates outside the urban area of Mexico City. Median concentration response coefficients are from Pope *et al.* (2002) for cardiopulmonary and lung cancer mortality in adults (>30 years) and from Woodruff *et al.* (1997) for respiratory deaths in infants. VSL is used for valuation of mortality with a median value of US $660,000.

The benefits and costs of the particulate control technologies are evaluated for three types of vehicles: Urban transport buses circulating only within Mexico City; delivery trucks that remain within the city; and long-haul tractor trailers used throughout Mexico. The cost of the retrofit control devices in 2010 in the study ranges from US $1,400–1,800 for catalyzed DPF, US $2,000–2,600 for active regeneration DPF, and US $420–450 for DOC. These figures are estimated from published market prices in 2005, adjusted for high-volume production by 2010. Costs are annualized using a 6 percent discount rate over a period ranging from four years for the oldest vehicles to thirteen years for new trucks. Operation and maintenance costs (fuel penalty and filter cleaning) range from 20 to 35 percent of annualized capital cost for catalyzed DPF and active regeneration DPF, respectively, with no O&M for DOC.

Benefit-cost ratios (table 1.33) range from about 1 to over 25, are higher for older vehicles than newer vehicles, and are higher for buses and trucks than for tractor trailers (the latter vehicles used predominantly outside urban areas). The highest benefit-cost ratios are for DOC on older vehicles. The cost per 1,000 retrofitted vehicles is lowest for DOC but net benefits are higher for DPFs because of their higher particulate reduction efficiency.

Table 1.33. Median B/C ratios for diesel vehicle PM control retrofit in Mexico City

	Buses	Trucks	Tractor trailers
Older vehicles:			
DPF catalyzed	–	–	–
DPF active regeneration	11.8	5.5	3.1
DOC	27.5	9.4	6.7
Newer vehicles:			
DPF catalyzed	6.1	6.3	2.2
DPF active regeneration	3.5	3.7	1.2
DOC	12.5	7.6	3.0

Note: Benefit-cost ratios presented here are therefore approximations because benefits and costs reported in Stevens *et al.* (2005) are rounded off. Older vehicles refer to model year 1993 and older. Newer vehicles refer to model year 1994 or newer. Annual vehicle use is 45,000–62,000 km for buses, 29,000–40,000 km for trucks, and 87,000–120,000 km for tractor trailers (the range for each vehicle type reflects age of vehicles).
Source: Calculated from cost per statistical life saved in Stevens *et al.* (2005).

Blumberg *et al.* (2006) evaluates the benefits and costs of controlling road vehicle emissions in China from improved vehicle standards and low-sulfur gasoline and diesel for the period 2008–30. Quantified benefits are mainly reduced health effects from primary and secondary particulate emissions (PM), but also some benefits (2.1 percent of total benefits) from reduced ground level ozone, increased agricultural yields, reductions in material soiling and degradation of antiquities, and improved visibility (based on findings in Europe and the USA). Emissions of primary and secondary particulates (from NOx) are estimated for three scenarios: (a) baseline emissions based on Euro 2 standards and fuels (500 ppm sulfur content); (b) vehicles with Euro 4 standards by 2010 for light-duty vehicles and Euro 5 standards by 2012 for heavy-duty vehicles; and (c) vehicles with Euro 4 and 5 standards, ultra-low sulfur (50 ppm) gasoline and diesel by 2010, and 10 ppm gasoline and diesel for heavy-duty vehicles in 2012.

Blumberg *et al.* (2006) present net benefits of

Table 1.34. Benefits and costs of vehicle emission control in China

	Improved vehicle standards		Improved fuels (vehicle standards in place)		Improved vehicle standards and fuels	
Year	2015	2030	2015	2030	2015	2030
PM emission reductions (10,000 tons relative to baseline)	10	35	5	20	15	55
Benefits (US$ billion)	8.4	115	4.3	45	13	160
Benefit-cost ratios	4	24	2	14	3	20

Source: Blumberg *et al.* (2006).

emission reductions from 2008 to 2030. Benefit-cost ratios are presented for the years from 2015 to 2030. The ratios range from 2–4 in 2015 to 14–24 in 2030. Benefits increase by a multiple of 10–14 over this period. Three factors underlie this increase in benefits: (a) an increase in the exposed population; (b) an increase in emission reductions; and (c) an increase in the unit values of mortality and morbidity (table 1.34). Based on the data presented in Blumberg *et al.* (2006), we estimate that the increases in exposed population and emission reductions account for approximately 55–60 percent of the increase in benefits from 2015 to 2030, and that the increase in unit values of mortality and morbidity accounts for approximately 40–45 percent.

The benefits or mortality reductions appear to account for about 80 percent and morbidity reductions for about 20 percent of total benefits.[18] Benefit-cost ratios are therefore particularly sensitive to estimated mortality reduction and valuation of mortality. Health benefits (table 1.35) are estimated using emissions intake fractions and particulate concentration-response coefficients from the international literature. The intake fractions are 29 per million for primary PM and 0.64 per million for secondary PM (from NOx emissions) in fifty-nine cities with a 2002 population over 1 million (13–15 percent of China's population) and 4.5 per million for primary PM and 0.09 per million for secondary PM outside these cities. The concentration-response coefficient for mortality is a 0.41 percent increase in all-cause adult mortality (>30 years) per 1 ug/m3 PM taken from Pope *et al.* (2002). A VSL is used to monetize mortality benefits of emission

Table 1.35. Valuation of health benefits in China study

	2010	2015	2030
Valuation of mortality	160	250	850
Valuation of morbidity	140	190	450

Note: Values are indexed to 100 in 2005. Values are approximate from charts in Blumberg *et al.* (2006).

reduction. VSL for each year "*t*" from 2008 to 2030 is given by (1):

$$VSL_{2005} \, (cGDP_t \, / \, cGDP_{2005})^\varepsilon \qquad (1)$$

where $cGDP_t$ is GDP *per capita* in year "*t*" and ε is the income elasticity of WTP for mortality risk reduction. Blumberg *et al.* (2006) uses a VSL of US $127,400 in base year 2005. This is the mean value from several VSL studies in China. An income elasticity of 1.42 is applied to derive VSL for subsequent years. Blumberg *et al.* (2006) report that this elasticity is from a VSL study in Chongqing by Wang and Mullahy (2006). So in 2015, the VSL is about 55 percent higher than in 2010 and 87 percent higher than in 2008, based on projected GDP *per capita* growth rates. The VSL in 2030 is eight–nine times higher than in 2008. Unit values for morbidity increase at the rate of GDP *per capita*.

Incremental fuel costs (500 ppm to 50 ppm sulfur fuel) presented in Blumberg *et al.* (2006), based on modeling of the refinery sector in China, are about US $1.3 per barrel for diesel

---

[18] We estimate these benefit shares by estimating the reductions in health effects, based on the data presented in Blumberg *et al.* (2006).

and US$0.8 per barrel of gasoline. Incremental vehicle costs from Euro 2 to Euro 4 vehicles applied in Blumberg *et al.* (2006) are US$150, US$400, and US$1500 per light-duty gasoline vehicle, light-duty diesel vehicle, and heavy-duty diesel vehicle, respectively. Incremental cost of a Euro 5 heavy-duty diesel vehicle is an additional US$1000. A 20 percent reduction in incremental vehicle cost was applied for every doubling of new vehicle sales. A discount rate of 3 percent was applied to annualize incremental vehicle costs over a period of ten years for light-duty vehicles and fifteen years for heavy-duty vehicles.

While it is of interest to estimate benefits and costs over an extended period of time, it is also of policy relevance to estimate the benefit-cost ratio for the early years of policy implementation. We therefore use the data in Blumberg *et al.* (2006) to estimate the benefit-cost ratios for 2010 by using the VSL, morbidity unit values, and exposed population for this year. As costs of emission controls are not presented in Blumberg *et al.* (2006) for the year 2010, we apply unit control costs and emission reductions in 2015 to arrive at an approximate benefit-cost ratio for the income level in China in 2010. We then get a benefit-cost ratio of 2.4 for improved vehicle standards and a ratio of 1.2 for improved fuels. Blumberg *et al.* (2006) do not present benefit-cost ratios for gasoline and diesel vehicles and fuels separately, and these can not be easily derived from the data provided in the report.

Larsen (2007c) evaluates the benefits and costs of lowering the sulfur content in road transport diesel and retrofitting in-use diesel vehicles with particulate control technology in urban Dakar, Senegal. Benefit-cost ratios are presented for lowering of sulfur from >2,000 ppm to 500 ppm, and from 500 ppm to 50 ppm, as well as for DOC and DPF for several sizes of vehicles and annual usage. The benefits are limited to the health effects of primary particulate emissions reduc-

Table 1.36. B/C ratios of reducing sulfur in vehicle diesel fuel in Dakar, Senegal

Diesel (sulfur 500 ppm)	Light diesel vehicles	Diesel buses and trucks
Low-cost (US $ 1.0 per barrel)	3.2	3.7
Medium-cost (US $ 1.6 per barrel)	2.0	2.3
High-cost (US $ 3.0 per barrel)	1.1	1.3
Diesel (sulfur 50 ppm)		
Low-cost (US $ 2.1 per barrel)	2.0	2.4
Medium-cost (US $ 2.8 per barrel)	1.5	1.8
High-cost (US $ 3.0 per barrel)	1.4	1.7

Notes: Light-diesel vehicles used 90 percent in Greater Dakar. Diesel buses and trucks used 100 percent in Greater Dakar.
Source: Larsen (2007c).

tions. The benefits of reductions in secondary particulates from reduction in gaseous emissions are not included. The health benefits are estimated from modeled improvements in ambient air quality and concentration-health response coefficients from the international literature, of which cardiopulmonary and lung cancer mortality coefficients from Pope *et al.* (2002) are the most significant in terms of total health benefits.[19] The reduction in mortality accounts for 75 percent of total health benefits, based on a VSL of US $45,000 in year 2004.

The benefits and costs of lower-sulfur diesel are evaluated for light-diesel vehicles and for diesel buses and trucks primarily used within urban Greater Dakar. The incremental costs of 500 ppm sulfur diesel range from US $1–3 per barrel. The incremental cost of 50 ppm sulfur diesel (relative to 500 ppm diesel) range from US $2.1–3 per barrel. Benefit-cost ratios range from 1.1 to 3.7 for 500 ppm sulfur diesel and 1.4 to 2.4 for 50 ppm diesel, depending on assumptions of incremental cost of lower-sulfur diesel (table 1.36 and 1.37).

The benefits and costs of DOC and DPF for taxis and small and large buses used within urban Greater Dakar are evaluated for a range of annual vehicle usage and useful lifetime of the particulate control devices. The cost of DOC in the analysis is US $1,000 per vehicle.

[19] Improvements in ambient air quality from emission reductions are estimated based on the development of an all-source particulate emission inventory including area-wide sources and particulates from natural sources.

Table 1.37. B/C ratios for in-use diesel vehicle retrofit PM control in Dakar, Senegal

	DOC		DPF	
	Low-usage vehicles*	High-usage vehicles*	Low-usage vehicles*	High-usage vehicles*
Five-year useful life				
Buses (large)	0.89	1.77	0.38	0.76
Buses (small)	0.55	1.11	0.24	0.47
Taxis	–	–	0.67	1.34
Ten-year useful life				
Buses (large)	1.43	2.86	0.61	1.23
Buses (small)	0.89	1.79	0.38	0.77
Taxis	–	–	1.08	2.17

Note: * Low and high usage refers to 35,000 km and 70,000 km per year, respectively.
Source: Larsen (2007c).

The cost of DPF is US $850 for taxis and US $5,000 for buses. Costs are annualized by using a discount rate of 10 percent over the useful life of the devices, ranging from five to ten years in the analysis. Benefit-cost ratios are >1 for DOC on high-usage buses and taxis, and on low-usage buses if the useful life of the DOC approaches ten years. The benefit-cost ratios are >1 for DPF for high-usage taxis, and for high-usage buses if the useful life of the DPF approaches ten years.

The cost of DOC and DPF applied in this study is about twice the cost applied in Stevens *et al.* (2006). If cost reductions in the next few years are as assumed in Stevens *et al.* (2006), the benefit-cost ratios in Larsen (2007c) would be twice higher than presented here.

Larsen (2005) evaluates the benefits of lowering the sulfur content in road transport diesel from 1,000 ppm to 500 ppm and retrofitting in-use diesel vehicles with particulate control technology in Bogotá, Colombia (table 1.38). The benefits are limited to the health effects of primary particulate emissions reductions. The benefits of reductions in secondary particulates from reduction in gaseous emissions are not included. The health benefits are estimated from modeled improvements in ambient air quality and concentration-health response coefficients from the international literature, of which cardiopulmonary and lung cancer mortality coefficients from Pope *et al.* (2002) are the most

significant in terms of total health benefits.[20] The study applies a VSL of US $127,200.

The study does not provide benefit-cost ratios, but these can be derived by applying unit cost figures. We here apply the central estimate of cost in Larsen (2007c) for Dakar, Senegal. At an incremental cost of US$1.6 per barrel for 500 ppm sulfur diesel, the benefit-cost ratios range from 1.8 to 2.2 for light- and heavy-duty diesel vehicles. At a cost of US$5,000 for particulate control technology for heavy vehicles, the benefit-cost ratios for diesel buses are in the range of 3–5, and as high as 10–20 for heavy-duty diesel trucks. These ratios are for vehicles used within Bogotá. The ratios would be substantially lower for inter-urban vehicle use. The difference in benefit-cost ratios for retrofit particulate control technology on buses and heavy-duty trucks stems from differences in baseline emissions, annual usage, and emission reductions.

ECON (2006) evaluates a range of options to control particulate emissions from vehicles in Lima, Peru (table 1.39). Benefits and costs are monetized for lowering the sulfur content in diesel from >2,500 ppm to 50 ppm, retrofit particulate control for urban diesel buses, an I&M

---

[20] Improvements in ambient air quality from emission reductions are estimated based on the development of an all-source particulate emission inventory including area-wide sources and particulates from natural sources.

Table 1.38. B/C ratios for low-sulfur diesel and PM control technology in Bogotà, Colombia

	500 ppm diesel	Particulate control technology	
		Five-year useful life	Ten-year useful life
Light-duty diesel vehicles	1.8	–	–
Heavy-duty diesel trucks	2.2	10–13	16–20
Diesel buses	1.9	3	5

Note: Annual usage is 50,000 km per year for buses and 66,000 km per year for heavy trucks.
Source: Estimated based on benefit calculations in Larsen (2005).

Table 1.39. B/C for vehicle PM emission controls in Lima, Peru

	B/C ratios	Discount rate
50 ppm diesel (from >2500 ppm)	1.88	3%
	1.29	6%
Retrofit particulate control for diesel buses	5.66	3%
	2.87	6%
I&M program for diesel vehicles	5.36	
New CNG buses (compared to diesel buses using 50 ppm sulfur diesel)	0.44	3%
New CNG buses (compared to diesel buses high-sulfur diesel)	0.71	3%

Source: Adapted from ECON (2006).

program for diesel vehicles, and introduction of new buses using compressed natural gas (CNG) instead of new diesel buses. The benefits are health effects from reductions in primary and secondary particulates.

Improvements in ambient air quality from emission reductions are modeled following the approach in Larsen (2005). The health benefits from these improvements in ambient air quality are estimated based on Larsen and Strukova (2005), which use concentration-health response coefficients from the international literature of which cardiopulmonary and lung cancer mortality coefficients from Pope *et al.* (2002) are the most significant in terms of total health benefits. The study applies a VSL of US $148,600.

The benefit-cost ratios for ultra-low sulfur diesel (50 ppm) are in the range of 1.3–1.9, based on assessment of the cost of refinery upgrading in Peru using discount rates of 6 and 3 percent to annualize capital cost. A 20 percent reduction in primary particulate emissions is applied, which may be on the low side in light of the high sulfur in diesel in Peru (>2,500 ppm) at the time of the study. The benefit-cost ratios for retrofitting diesel buses with particulate control technologies are in the range of 2.9–5.7, using discount rates of 6 percent over five years of useful equipment life and 3 percent over ten years of useful equipment life. The equipment cost is assumed to be US $3,000 per vehicle, with a particulate

emission reduction efficiency of 90 percent. The benefit-cost ratio for an I&M program is 5.4, based on an estimated cost of US $4,100 per ton of PM reduction. The benefit-cost ratio for introducing CNG buses instead of diesel buses is found to be significantly <1 because of the high incremental cost of buses and investment requirements in refueling stations.

Some of the differences in benefit-cost ratios found in the five studies reviewed are due to variation in the VSL used for valuation of mortality benefits. The benefits can, however, be expressed as DALYs valued in monetary units. Equation (2) is used to convert benefit-cost ratios using VSL for valuation of mortality benefits (B/C$_{VSL}$) to benefit-cost ratios with benefits expressed in DALYs valued in monetary units (B/C$_{DALY}$):

$$B/C_{DALY} = B/C_{VSL} \times \beta \times YLL^* DALY\$/ [VSL^*(1 - \alpha)] \qquad (2)$$

where β is share of mortality benefits to total health benefits (mortality and morbidity); YLL is years of life lost per death; $DALY\$$ is US $1,000 or US $5,000; VSL is the value of statistical life applied in each study; and α is the share of life lost to disability (YLD) to total DALYs.

We reviewed Colombia, Peru, and Senegal studies conducted for the World Bank that were used to estimate benefits of emission reductions in Larsen (2005), ECON (2006), and Larsen (2007c), and found a β of about 0.75 and an α ranging from 0.43 in Senegal to 0.5 in Colombia, and 0.56 in Peru. Using the data presented in Blumberg *et al.* (2006), we also find a β of approximately 0.75. By applying DALY factors (DALYs per case of mortality and morbidity) from the Colombia, Peru, and Senegal studies to the estimated health effects in Blumberg *et al.* (2006), we find an α of 0.45 for China. For Mexico, we used $\beta = 0.75$ and $\alpha = 0.5$. We used $YLL = 8$ in (3.2). This reflects age-weighted years of life lost to premature death, discounted at 3 percent per year (the age-weighting and discounting is the standard calculation procedure of DALYs by WHO).

A summary of the most promising control measures in the five studies indicates that the B/C ratios are highest in Mexico when using VSL for valuation of mortality benefits. This is as expected given that the VSL applied in the Mexico study is four–five times higher than the value applied in China, Colombia, and Peru, and more than ten times higher than the value used in the Senegal study. When health benefits are converted to DALYs and valued at US $1,000 per DALY, the B/C ratios are consistently <1 and mostly <0.5.

At US $5,000 per DALY, the B/C ratios for low- (500 ppm) and ultra-low (50 ppm) sulfur diesel for vehicles used primarily in urban areas are >2 in Senegal. The ratios are <1 in Colombia and Peru, primarily because of the relatively low emission reductions assumed in those two studies. The China study uses emission intake fractions (health effects are in most studies assumed to be proportional to the intake fractions) that are much lower than used in the Mexico study and found in three major cities in China according to Blumberg *et al.* (2006). So if similar intake fractions were used in the China study as in the Mexico study, the B/C ratio would be >1 when DALYs are valued at US $5,000.

At US $5,000 per DALY, particulate control technologies are generally found to have a B/C ratio of >1 for high-usage buses, trucks, and taxis used in urban areas. The I&M for diesel vehicles, although only evaluated in one of the studies, is also found to have a high B/C ratio (table 1.40).

There are also benefit-cost analysis studies in low- and middle-income countries that look at pollution control in the industrial and power sector, fuel substitution, and energy efficiency. Some of the most recent studies are presented in table 1.41. Benefit-cost ratios are mostly in a range from <1 (lower bound) to 6, but are as high as over 100 in the case of Mexico, which in part is related to the applied VSL. Some examples of benefit-cost analysis studies in high-income countries are presented in table 1.42.

Implications and Outlook

In interpreting the results of the reviews in this chapter, it is important to keep in mind the multiple uncertainties of CBA in the field of indoor and outdoor air pollution. First, measuring the impact of air pollution on health is very complex since there are many different pollutants and their effects on health are difficult to discern. Hence, controlled trials in the medical scientific sense have been very few in the area of air pollution. Second, there exists significant uncertainty as to the improvement in ambient air quality and population exposure from individual interventions. Third, there is uncertainty as to the number of years of life saved from reduced adult mortality risk associated with improved air quality. The different methods and values used between the various studies thus makes it difficult to compare the results of studies reported in the literature.

While the control strategies for indoor and outdoor air quality improvement are largely unrelated, they share some similar basic approaches: (1) fuel switching, (2) technology emission control, and (3) fuel use efficiency. Each of these options offers different opportunities and drawbacks. General constraints to the implementation of air pollution control measures cover lack of political motivation

Table 1.40. Summary of B/C ratios for vehicle PM emission control

Country	Location	Intervention	B/C ratio VSL	B/C ratio US$1,000 per DALY	B/C ratio US$5,000 per DALY
China	59 cities	Euro 4, 5 vehicle technology	2.4	0.21	1.03
		50 ppm gasoline and diesel	1.2	0.10	0.51
Colombia	Bogotà	500 ppm diesel	1.9	0.18	0.90
		DPF for buses	5	0.47	2.36
Mexico	Mexico City	DOC (older buses)	27.5	0.67	3.33
		DOC (newer buses)	12.5	0.30	1.52
		DOC (older city delivery trucks)	9.4	0.23	1.14
		DOC (newer city delivery trucks)	7.6	0.18	0.92
		DPF active regeneration (older buses)	11.8	0.29	1.43
		DPF catalyzed (newer buses and city delivery trucks)	6.2	0.15	0.75
Peru	Peru	50 ppm diesel	1.9	0.18	0.88
	Lima	Retrofit PM control for buses	5.6	0.52	2.59
		I&M program for diesel vehicles	5.3	0.49	2.45
Senegal	Dakar	500 ppm diesel	2.1	0.49	2.46
		50 ppm diesel	1.7	0.40	1.99
		DOC for large buses (high-usage; ten-year life)	2.8	0.65	3.27
		DPF for taxis (high usage; ten-year life)	2.2	0.51	2.57

Source: Author.

Table 1.41. Examples of B/C studies of outdoor air pollution control in low- and middle-income countries

Study	Netalieva et al. (2005)	Mao et al. (2005)	Li et al. (2004)	Blackman et al. (2000)	Aunan et al. (1998)
Location	Kazakhstan	China (two cities)	Shanghai, China	Ciuded Juarez, Mexico	Hungary
Interventions	Emission reductions in the oil extraction industry	Beijing (B); Chongqing (C) substituting natural gas as for coal	Emissions control: (C1) power; (C2) industrial	PM emissions control from traditional wood fired brick kilns: A: use natural gas; B: improved kilns; C: relocation	Air pollution control in various sectors: Agriculture (A); Industry (B); Transportation; energy (C); Households (D); Services (E)
Benefits	Health	Health	Health, labor productivity	Health	Health
B/C ratios	5.7	B: 29% IRR C: 75% IRR	C1: 1.1 (0.5–2.9) C2: 2.8 (1.3–7.6)	A: 75 B: 107 C: 30	A: 3; B: 5; C: 6; D: 16; E: 17

Notes: B/C ratios = benefit-cost ratios; IRR = internal rate of return.

Table 1.42. Examples of B/C studies of outdoor air pollution control in high-income countries

Study	US Federal Regulations (USOBM 2005)	United States (USEPA 1999)	European Commission (Pye and Watkiss 2005)	UK Air Quality Strategy review (UKDEFRA 2006)	Canada (Pandey and Nathwani 2003)	Japan (Voorhees et al. 2000)	Japan (Kochi et al. 2001)
Location	US-wide	US-wide	Europe-wide	UK-wide	Canada	Tokyo	Japan-wide
Policies	National emissions standards for hazardous air pollutants	Clean Air Act five categories	Air quality targets for CO/Benzene, heavy metals, ozone, hydrocarbons	17 policies to achieve AQS: (reported here: meeting European standards, low and high intensity)	Pollution control program	NOx emission control	SO$_2$ emissions control: 1: 1968–73 2: 1974–83 3: 1984–93
Period	1994–2004	1990–2010	NA	Until 2020		1973–93	1968–93
Discount rate	7%	5%	2%–6%	HM Treasury rate			2.5%
Costs	Compliance & monitoring	R&D, capital, O&M	NA	Capital and recurrent			Capital, fuel conversion; running
Benefits	Health	Health, crop damage, visibility	Health; labor productivity	Health (1%, 3% and 6% hazard rates reported; optimistic 6% reported here)			Medical expenses, labor losses avoided, adjusted by WTP factor
B/C ratio	2.72–13.0	3.8	6.0	L: 1.5–3.8 H: 0.9-2.3	3.0	6.0	1. 5.39 2. 1.18 3. 0.41

Notes: NA = not available; B/C ratio = benefit-cost ratio; R&D = research and development; O&M = operations and maintenance; CO = carbon monoxide; AQS = air quality standards; NOx = nitrogen oxides; SO$_2$ = sulfur dioxide; WTP = willingness-to-pay.
Source: Author.

or competing political priorities, lack of economic (purchasing) power, lack of regulatory framework or regulation monitoring, and lack of access of the potential user to the necessary resources or technologies. And, importantly, households and the public in general may not be fully aware of the health effects of air pollution, so that effective demand for solutions is not present. Government and private sector activities should thus focus on addressing these barriers, according to their importance in each air pollution context.

A summary of interventions with the highest B/C ratios is presented in table 1.1. The B/C ratios for improved household cooking stoves are from Hutton et al. (2006) for the regions of Africa, EMRO D (including Pakistan and Afghanistan) and SEAR D (including India and Bangladesh). These are the regions with the largest number of estimated deaths from indoor air pollution, or 65 percent of global deaths. Full adoption of improved household cooking stoves in these regions could potentially save 340,000–680,000 lives per year, assuming a 35–70 percent reduction in health effects from the use of improved stoves.

The B/C ratio of improved stoves in the WPR B (including China) is well below 1 for DALYs valued at US $1,000, according to Hutton et al. (2006) when only health benefits are accounted for; 27 percent of global deaths from indoor air pollution are in this region, mainly arising from COPD in adults in China. Further benefit-cost analysis of interventions to control indoor air pollution is therefore warranted.

Three interventions to control urban air pollution from road vehicles are presented in table 1.1. The B/C ratios reflect the range for the technologies assessed in the studies reviewed, and are all below 1 for DALYs valued at US $1,000, but in the range of 0.9–3.3 for DALYs valued at US $5,000.

In light of the PM apportionment and PM emission inventory studies reviewed here, the interventions in table 1.1 may reduce global health effects of urban air pollution by 10–20 percent. This would correspond to saving 80,000–160,000 lives per year. In Asia, controlling pollution from two- and three-wheelers would also be an essential ingredient of improving urban air quality.

The findings from the studies reviewed here raise important questions as to valuation of the health benefits of indoor and outdoor air pollution control (table 1.43). A uniform valuation, such as cut-off point per DALY, might be a useful tool to inform the international community of what programs and in which countries development assistance can provide the largest benefits relative to costs. However, the population in the countries are themselves likely to bear most of the costs, such as the cost of improved stoves or LPG, and low-sulfur diesel and particulate control technology on vehicles. Individual countries may therefore be interested in knowing more about the benefits of these programs as perceived and experienced by its population, in terms of both child and adult health effects. In this respect, VSL is generally believed to better reflect individuals' valuation of mortality risk reduction than the relatively arbitrary value of a DALY. Monetized benefits will therefore to a significant extent vary across countries in relation to *per capita* income levels. More VSL studies are therefore needed in developing countries, at least to provide reasonably reliable benefit transfers to guide policy-makers.

A consideration that is often ignored or inadequately considered in benefit-cost analysis is the cost of programs or incentives to achieve impact and change on a large scale. Achieving adoption

Table 1.43. Summary of intervention B/C ratios

Interventions	B/C ratios (DALY = US $1,000)	B/C ratios (DALY = US $5,000)	Annual benefits (Reduction in mortality, 000 lives)
Improved cooking stoves	1.7–7.5	8–37	340–680
Low- and ultra-low sulfur diesel for urban road vehicles	0.2–0.5	0.9–2.5	80–160
Diesel vehicle particulate control technology	0.2–0.7	0.9–3.3	
I&M program for diesel vehicles	0.5	2.5	

Source: Author.

and sustained use and proper maintenance of improved stoves or switching to cleaner fuels for indoor air pollution control for a majority of the population is likely to require substantial awareness and promotion programs and follow-ups. The studies reviewed in this chapter assume a constant cost per household. It may however be that marginal costs of such programs to achieve demand for pollution control and full population coverage are increasing. Limited evidence from hand-washing promotion programs suggests a population response rate of 10–20 percent (Pinfold and Horan 1996; Saade *et al.* 2001; Borghi *et al.* 2002). The program cost data in these studies do seem to indicate a potentially rising marginal cost curve. For outdoor air pollution control the situation is somewhat different. Most importantly, governments need to be willing and have the capacity to implement and enforce regulations. This, however, does also require stakeholder participation (e.g. oil refineries, bus operators, consumers), which is more likely with public and stakeholder awareness of health effects and public demand for cleaner air as, in the end, consumers will bear most of the cost of air pollution control.

When evaluating the benefits and costs of controlling indoor and outdoor air pollution, several important linkages to other areas of the environment and health may be considered. This includes the greenhouse gas emission implications of fuel and technology choices. And, when assessing the health benefits of air pollution interventions, it would be preferable to do so in a multiple-risk framework to account for potentially simultaneous interventions to improve health. This would help avoid over-estimation of health benefits, as attributable fractions of the disease burden estimated from single risk factors are generally not additive. This issue is particularly relevant for indoor air pollution interventions in relation to measures to improve child nutritional status, disease treatment, and case management, as well as to improved water, sanitation, and hygiene. In terms of outdoor air pollution, Martins *et al.* (2004) find that the health effects of urban air pollution in São Paulo, Brazil, are largest in the lowest socioeconomic groups (several times higher than in the highest socioeconomic groups). Thus addressing effect modifiers may lower the health effects of air pollution.

The targeting of interventions for population groups most vulnerable to health effects and mortality from air pollution is also potentially important. For instance, Gakidou *et al.* (2007) estimate the global health benefits of targeting "poor" vs. "rich" households in the developing world in terms of improving child nutrition and providing clean water, sanitation, and fuels.

Bibliography

ADB, 2003: Cleaner fuels: policy guidelines for reducing vehicle emissions in Asia, Asian Development Bank, Manila

Albalak, R., Bruce, N., McCracken, J., Smith, K., and De Gallard, T., 2001: Indoor respirable particulate matter concentrations from an open fire, improved cook stove, and LPG/open fire combination in a rural Guatemalan community, *Environmental Sciences and Technology*, **45**(13): 2650–5

Aunan, K., Patzay, G., Asbjorn Aaheim, H., and Martin Seip, H., 1998: Health and environmental benefits from air pollution reductions in Hungary, *The Science of the Total Environment*, **212**: 245–68

Baranzini, A. and Goldenberg, J., 1996: Desertification, energy consumption,

and liquefied petroleum gas use, with an emphasis on Africa, *Energy for Sustainable Development*, **2**(5)

Blackman, A., Newbold, S., Shih, J., and Cook, J., 2000: The benefits and costs of informal sector pollution control: Mexican brick kilns, *Resources for the Future*, Washington, DC

Blumberg, K., He, K., Zhou, Y., Liu, H., and Yamaguchi, N., 2006: *Costs and benefits of reduced sulfur in China*, The International Council on Clean Transportation, December, www.theicct.org

Borghi, J., Guinness, L., Ouedraogo, J., and Curtis, V., 2002: Is hygiene promotion cost-effective? A case study in Burkina Faso, *Tropical Medicine and International Health*, **7**(11): 960–9

Bruce, N., Rehfuess, E., Mehta, S., Hutton, G., and Smith, K., 2005: Indoor air pollution, in D. Jamison, J. Breman, A. Measham, G. Alleyne, M. Claeson, D. Evans, P. Jha, A. Mills, and P. Musgrove (eds.), *Disease control priorities in developing countries*, Oxford University Press, New York

CAI-Asia, 2006: *Country synthesis report on urban air quality management. Individual reports for Bangladesh, People's Republic of China, India, Indonesia, Pakistan, Philippines, and Vietnam*, Asian Development Bank and the Clean Air Initiative for Asian Cities Center, Discussion draft, December

Cifuentes, L., Krupnick, A., O'Ryan, R., and Toman, M., 2005: Urban air quality and human health in Latin America and the Caribbean, Paper prepared for the Inter-American Development Bank, Washington, DC

Desai, M., Mehta, S., and Smith, K., 2004: Indoor smoke from solid fuels: assessing the environmental burden of disease at national and local levels, *Environmental Burden of Disease Series*, **4**, WHO, Geneva

ECON, 2006: Urban air pollution control in Peru, Paper prepared for the Peru Environmental Analysis, World Bank, ECON Analysis, Oslo

Edwards, R.D., Liu, Y., He, G., Yin, Z., Sinton, J., Peabody, J., and Smith K.R., 2006: Household CO and PM measured as part of a review of China's national improved stove program, *Indoor Air*, **17**(3): 189–2003

EEAA, 2007: Egypt state of environment report 2006, Egyptian Environmental Affairs

Agency, Ministry of State of Environmental Affairs, Arab Republic of Egypt

Eskeland, G., 1994: The net benefits of an air pollution control scenario for Santiago, in *Managing environmental problems: economic analysis of selected issues*, World Bank, Report 13061–CH

Ezzati, M. and Kammen, D., 2001: Quantifying the effects of exposure to indoor air pollution from biomass combustion on acute respiratory infections in developing countries, *Environmental Health Perspectives*, **109**(5): 481–8

Ezzati, M. and Kammen, D, 2002: The health impacts of exposure to indoor air pollution from solid fuels in developing countries: knowledge, gaps, and data needs, Discussion Paper, *02-24*, Resources For the Future, Washington, DC

Fishman, M.S., Caulfield, L.E., De Onis, M., Blossner, M., Hyder, A.A., Mullany, L., and Black, R.E., 2004: Childhood and maternal underweight, in M. Ezzati, A.D. Lopez, A. Rodgers, and C.J.L. Murray (eds.), *Comparative quantification of health risks: global and regional burden of disease attributable to selected major risk factors*, **1**, WHO, Geneva

Gaffney, P. and Benjamin, M., 2004: Pune, *India regional emissions inventory study*, USEPA and Ministry of Environment and Forests, New Delhi, India

Gakidou, E., Oza, S., Fuertes, C., Li, A., Lee, D., Sousa, A., Hogan, M., Vander Hoorn, S., and Ezzati, M., 2007: Improving child survival through environmental and nutritional interventions; the importance of targeting interventions toward the poor, *Journal of the American Medical Association*, **298**(16): 1876-87

GSSR, 2004: Pune vehicle activity study. Report by Global Sustainable Systems Research, updated February 16, International Sustainable Systems Research Center, www.issrc.org

Hutton G., Rehfuess, E., Tediosi, F., and Weiss S., 2006: *Global cost-benefit analysis of household energy and health interventions*, Department for the Protection of the Human Environment, WHO, Geneva

Jin, Y.L., Zhou, Z., He, G.L., Wei, H.Z., Liu, J., Liu, F., Tang, N., Ying, B., Liu, Y.C., Hu, G., Wang, H., Balakrishnan, K., Watson, K., Baris, E., and Ezzati M., 2005: Geographical, spatial, and temporal distributions of multiple indoor air pollutants in four Chinese provinces, *Environmental Science & Technology*, **39**(24): 9431–9

Kjellstrom, T., Lodh, M., McMichael, T., Ranmuthugala, G., Shrestha, R., and Kingsland, S., 2006: Air and water pollution: burden and strategies for control, in, D. Jamison, J. Breman, A. Measham, G. Alleyne, M. Claeson, D. Evans, P. Jha, A. Mills, and P. Musgrove (eds.), *Disease control priorities in developing countries*, Oxford University Press, New York

Kochi, I., Matsuoka, S., Memon, M.A., and Shirakawa, H., 2001: Cost benefit analysis of the sulfur dioxide emissions control policy in Japan, *Environmental Economics and Policy Studies*, **4**: 19–33

Krupnick, A., Larsen, B., and Strukova, E., 2006: *Cost of environmental degradation in Pakistan: an analysis of physical and monetary losses in environmental health and natural resources*, Report prepared for the World Bank, Washington, DC

Larsen, B., 1994: *Air pollution projections and costs and benefits of reductions in Iran*, Background paper for Iran Environmental Strategy Study, World Bank, Washington, DC

Larsen, B., 1997: *Air pollution, health, and cleaner fuels: a cost-benefit analysis for Casablanca/ Mohammedia*, Background paper for Morocco Environment Review, World Bank, Washington, DC

Larsen, B., 2004: *Cost of environmental damage in Colombia: a socio-economic and environmental health risk assessment*, Paper prepared for the Ministry of Environment, Housing and Land Development, Background paper for the Colombia Country Environmental Analysis: Colombia Mitigating Environmental Degradation to Foster Growth and Reduce Inequality, World Bank, Washington, DC

Larsen, B., 2005: *Cost-benefit analysis of environmental protection in Colombia*, Paper prepared for the Ministry of Environment, Housing and Land Development, Background paper for the Colombia Country Environmental Analysis: Colombia Mitigating Environmental Degradation to Foster Growth and Reduce Inequality, World Bank, Washington, DC

Larsen, B., 2007a: *Cost of indoor air pollution in China: rural estimates*, East Asia Department Paper, forthcoming, World Bank, Washington, DC

Larsen, B., 2007b: *Costs of environmental health risks in children u5 accounting for malnutrition in Ghana and Pakistan*, Draft background paper for the report *Environmental health and child survival: epidemiology, economics, experiences*, World Bank, Washington, DC

Larsen, B., 2007c: *A cost-benefit analysis of environmental health interventions in urban Greater Dakar, Senegal*, Paper prepared for the Senegal Country Environmental Analysis, World Bank, Washington, DC by ECON/Roche Canada

Larsen, B. and Strukova, E., 2005: Cost of environmental damage in Peru. Paper prepared for the Peru Country Environmental Analysis: Environmental Sustainability a Key to Poverty Reduction in Peru, World Bank, Washington, DC, June 2007

Larsen, B. and Strukova, E., 2006: *A cost-benefit analysis of improved water supply, sanitation and hygiene and indoor air pollution control in Peru*, Paper prepared for the Peru Country Environmental Analysis: Environmental Sustainability a Key to Poverty Reduction in Peru, June 2007

Lents, J., Davis, N., Osses, M., Nikkila, R., and Barth, M. 2004: Comparison of on-road vehicle profiles collected in seven cities worldwide, Presentation at Transport and Air Pollution, 13th International Scientific Symposium, September 13–15, NCAR, Boulder, CO

Li, J., Guttikunda, S., Carmichael, G., Streets, D., Chang Y.-S., and Fung, V., 2004: Quantifying the human health benefits of curbing air pollution in Shanghai, *Journal of Environmental Management*, **70**: 49–62

Luo, Z. and Hulscher, W., 1999: *Woodfuel emissions*, RWEDP, Bangkok, May

Mao, X., Guo, X., Chang, Y., and Peng, Y., 2005: Improving air quality in large cities by substituting natural gas for coal in China: changing idea and incentive policy implication, *Energy Policy*, **33**: 307–18

Martins, M.C.H., Fatigati, F., Vespoli, T., Martins, L., Pereira, L., Martins, M.A., Saldiva, P., and Braga, A., 2004: Influence of socioeconomic conditions on air pollution adverse health effects in elderly people: an analysis of six regions in São Paulo, Brazil, *Journal of Epidemiology and Community Health*, **58**: 41–6

McCracken, J. and Smith, K., 1998: Emissions and efficiency of improved woodburning cookstoves in Highland Guatemala, *Environment International*, **24**(7): 739–47

Mehta, S. and Shahpar, C., 2004: The health benefits of interventions to reduce indoor air pollution from solid fuel use: a cost-effectiveness analysis, *Energy for Sustainable Development*, **8**(3): 53–9

Mestl, H.E.S., Aunan, K., Seip, H.M., Wang, S., Zhao, Y., and Zhang, D., 2006: Urban and rural exposure to indoor air pollution from domestic biomass and coal burning across China, *Science of the Total Environment*, **377**(1): 12–26

Mrozek, J. and Taylor, L., 2002: What determines the value of life? A meta analysis, *Journal of Policy Analysis and Management*, **21**(2): 253–70

NAE/NRC, 2008: *Energy futures and urban air pollution challenges for China and the United States*, National Academy of Engineering and National Research Council, The National Academies Press, Washington, DC

Naeher, L.P., Leaderer, B.P., Smith, K.R., 2000: Particulate matter and carbon monoxide in highland Guatemala: indoor and outdoor levels from traditional and improved wood stoves and gas stoves, *Indoor Air*, **10**(3): 200–5

Netalieva, I., Wesseler, J., and Heijman, W., 2005: Health costs caused by oil extraction emissions and the benefits from abatement: the case of Kazakhstan, *Energy Policy*, **33**: 1169–77

Ostro, B., 2004: *Outdoor air pollution: assessing the environmental burden of disease at national and local levels*, WHO Environmental Burden of Disease Series, **5**, WHO, Geneva

Pandey, M. and Nathwani, J., 2003: Canada wide standard for particulate matter and ozone: cost-benefit analysis using a life quality index, *Risk Analysis*, **23**(1): 55–67

Pinfold, J. and Horan, N., 1996: Measuring the effect of a hygiene behaviour intervention by indicators of behaviour and diarrhoeal disease, *Transactions of the Royal Society of Tropical Medicine and Hygiene*, **90**: 101–6

Pope, C.A., III, Burnett, R.T., Thun, M.J. *et al.*, 2002: Lung cancer, cardiopulmonary mortality, and long-term exposure to fine particulate air pollution, *Journal of the American Medical Association*, **287**: 1132–41

Pye, S. and Watkiss, P., 2005: *Clean Air for Europe (CAFE) programme cost-benefit analysis. Baseline analysis 2000 to 2020*, Study conducted by AEA Technology Environment for the European Commission, DG Environment

Qian, Z., Zhang, J., Korn, L.R., Wei, F., and Chapman, R.S., 2004: Exposure–response relationships between lifetime exposure to residential coal smoke and respiratory symptoms and illnesses in Chinese children, *Journal of Exposure Analysis and Environmental Epidemiology*, **14**: S78–S84

Rehfuess, E., Mehta, S., and Prüss-Üstün, A., 2006: Assessing household solid fuel use: multiple implications for the millennium development goals, *Environmental Health Perspectives*, **114**(3): 373–8

Reuters, 2007: China motor vehicle fleet hits 148 million, Reuters, April 10

Saade, C., Bateman, M., and Bendahmane, D., 2001: The story of a successful public–private partnership in Central America: handwashing for diarrheal disease prevention, BASICS II, EHP, Unicef, USAID, and World Bank, Washington, DC

Saatkamp, B., Masera, O., and Kammen, D., 2000: Energy and health transitions in development: fuel use, stove technology, and morbidity in Jaracuaro, Mexico, *Energy for Sustainable Development*, **4**(2), August

Salo, P.M., Xia, J., Anderson Johnson, C., Li, Y., Kissling, G.E., Avol, E.L., Liu, C., and London, S.J., 2004: Respiratory symptoms in relation to residential coal burning and environmental tobacco smoke among early adolescents in Wuhan, China: a cross-sectional study, *Environmental Health: A Global Access Science Source*, **3**(1): 14

Sinton, J.E., Smith, K.R., Hansheng, H., and Junzhuo, L., 1995: Indoor air pollution database for China, http://whqlibdoc.who.int/hq/1995/WHO_EHG_95.8.pdf

Smith, K.R., Mehta, S., and Maeusezahl-Feuz, M., 2004: Indoor air pollution from household use of solid fuels, in M. Ezzati *et al.* (ed.), *Comparative quantification of health risks: global and regional burden of disease attributable to selected major risk factors*, WHO, Geneva

Stevens, G., Wilson, A., and Hammitt, J., 2005: A benefit-cost analysis of retrofitting diesel vehicles with particulate filters in the Mexico City Metropolitan Area, *Risk Analysis*, **25**(4): 883–99

Song, Y., Zhang, Y.H., Xie, S.D., Zeng, L.M., Zheng, M., Salmon, L.G., Shao, M., and Slanina, S., 2006: Source apportionment of PM 2.5 in Beijing by positive matrix factorization, *Atmospheric Environment*, **40**: 1526–37

UKDEFRA, 2006: *Economic analysis to inform the air quality strategy review consultation: third report of the interdepartmental group on costs and benefit*, Department for Environment, Food and Rural Affairs, April

UNEP, 2006: *Opening the door to cleaner vehicles in developing and transition countries: the role of lower sulphur fuels*, UNEP Partnership for Clean Fuels and Vehicles, Nairobi, Kenya, www.unep.org/pcfv/PDF/SulphurReport.pdf

USEPA, 1999: *The benefits and costs of the Clean Air Act: 1990 to 2010*, Environmental Protection Agency, November, www.epa.gov/oar/sect812

USOBM, 2005: *Validating Regulatory Analysis: 2005 report to congress on the costs and benefits of federal regulations and unfunded mandates on state, local and tribal entities. Office of Budget and Management*, December, www.whitehouse.gov/omb/inforeg/2005_cb/final_2005_cb_report.pdf

Venners, S.A., Wang, B., Ni, J., Jin, Y.G., Yang, J., Fang, Z., and Xu, X., 2001: Indoor air pollution and respiratory health in urban and rural China, *International Journal of Occupational and Environmental Health*, **7**: 173–81

Voorhees, A., Araki, S., Sakai, R., and Sato, H., 2000: An ex post cost-benefit analysis of the nitrogen dioxide air pollution program in Tokyo, *Journal of the Air and Waste Management Association*, **50**: 391–410

WHO, 2002: *World Health Report 2002*, WHO, Geneva

WHO, 2007: *Estimated deaths and DALYs attributable to selected environmental risk factors by WHO member state in 2002*, WHO, Geneva, www.who.int/quantifying_ehimpacts/countryprofilesebd.xls

Woodruff, T.J., Grillo, J., and Schoendorf, K.C., 1997: The relationship between selected causes of postneonatal infant mortality and particulate air pollution in the United States, *Environmental Health Perspectives*, **105**(6): 608–12

World Bank, 2005: *Islam Republic of Iran: cost assessment of environmental degradation*, Report **32043-IR**, World Bank, Washington, DC

World Bank, 2007: *World development indicators*, World Bank, Washington, DC

World Bank, 2008a: *Environmental health and child survival: epidemiology, economics, experiences*, Environment Department, World Bank, Washington, DC, forthcoming

World Bank, 2008b: *Cost of pollution in China: economic estimates of physical damages*, World Bank, Washington, DC, forthcoming

Xu, X., Niu, T., Christiani, D.C., Weiss, S.T., Chen, C., Zhou, Y., Fang, Z., Liang, W., and Zhang, F., 1996: Occupational and environmental risk factors for asthma in rural communities in China, *International Journal of Occupational Environmental Health*, **2**(3): 172–6

Zhang, W. *et al.*, 2007: Source apportionment for urban PM 10 and PM 2.5 in the Beijing area, *Chinese Science Bulletin*, **52**(5): 608–15

Zhang, Y.H., Zhu, X.L., Zeng, L.M. *et al.*, 2004. Source apportionment of fine-particle pollution in Beijing, in *Urbanization, energy, and air pollution in China*, National Academy of Engineering and National Research Council, The National Academies Press, Washington, DC: 139–53

Zheng, M. *et al.*, 2005: Seasonal trends in PM 2.5 source contributions in Beijing, China, *Atmospheric Environment*, **39**: 396–76

Alternative Perspective

Perspective Paper 1.1

JITENDRA SHAH*

Introduction

This Perspective paper reviews the Copenhagen Consensus 2008 Challenge paper on Air Pollution by Bjorn Larsen, Guy Hutton, and Neha Khanna. The Challenge paper (Larsen *et al.* 2008) addresses the impacts of air pollution in both indoor and outdoor environments; this Perspective paper is, however, limited to outdoor urban air pollution. The first section provides an introduction and overview of air pollution. The second section is a brief commentary on the Challenge paper and lists areas where our views agree or differ. The third section elaborates our views and outlines alternative or additional ways for achieving a more cost-effective and sustainable outcome regarding air pollution control, especially in developing countries.

Fast-growing economies have resulted in cities that record some of the highest levels of urban air pollution in the world (Chow *et al.* 2004; Molina and Molina 2004), especially in East and South Asia, as shown in figure 1.1.1 (CAI-Asia 2008).[1] These cities and regions also have the fastest-growing emitters of greenhouse gases (GHG), largely on account of China, India, and others, who are dependent on fossil fuel-based energy. According to the World Health Organization (WHO), thousands of people in Asia die prematurely each year because of poor air quality and millions of people are affected in their daily

[1] www.cleanairnet.org/caiasia/1412/channel.html.

lives. Other impacts besides health should also not be ignored completely – smog, tourism, agriculture productivity, property damage, and other impacts are important for some of these cities and need to be considered.

In Bangkok, Thailand, air quality has improved significantly since the mid-1990s, with reductions in lead, carbon monoxide, and particulates in urban areas, because of comprehensive and sustained setting of emissions standards and control measures. The total cost of exposure to PM_{10} in the six main cities of Thailand for excess deaths and bronchitis was estimated at $644 million annually in 2002 (World Bank 2002). While PM_{10} levels meet standards on average, they are exceeded frequently along transport corridors. These emissions come from diesel-powered buses, trucks, older 2-stroke tuk-tuks, motorcycles, vehicles, and cooking by vendors. The Government of Thailand is evaluating a comprehensive set of options to further reduce vehicular pollution – retrofitting older vehicles, inspection and maintenance for commercial and high-polluting vehicles, promotion of alternative and clean fuels, and transportation management.

Courts and environmental agencies in India have mandated tough measures in mega-cities such as Delhi and Mumbai. These cities have taken comprehensive action over the last few years. They have relocated industrial units; moved quickly to Euro III standards for vehicles; introduced CNG for buses, and three-

50

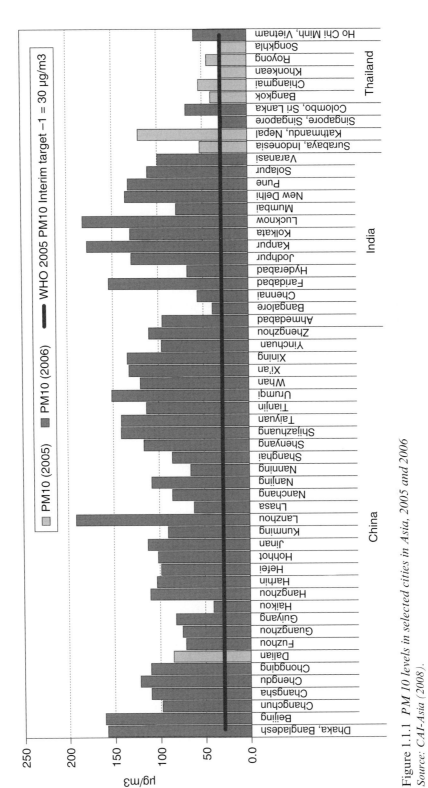

Figure 1.1.1 *PM 10 levels in selected cities in Asia, 2005 and 2006*
Source: *CAI-Asia (2008).*

wheelers; and open burning is banned. But PM_{10} levels in Delhi are increasing again after a few years of respite and NOx levels are on the rise (Roychowdhury 2008). Many in India, including the supreme courts, have argued that not everything can be reduced to economics or cost and benefit. The right to breathe clean air is considered a fundamental human right.

The World Bank and others have estimated the economic cost of air pollution in China to be in excess of 3.8 percent of its GDP (*China Daily*, November 19, 2007). Beijing, after being labeled one of the most polluted cities in the world, has made a lot of progress over the last decade. Despite spending over $17 billion on clean-up efforts, air quality remained a concern for residents and many athletes and visitors coming to the Olympics (Reuters, April 2, 2008, www.enn. com/). China is considering ceasing operation of a large number of industries around Beijing and restricting car use, thus slowing economic activity to try and improve air quality. If one adds the costs of air pollution control in other large cities in China, the total costs would probably far exceed $75 billion (the allocation assumed for the Copenhagen Consensus). Global public events such as the Olympic Games can be a unique opportunity for implementing politically difficult actions: Such events have an overwhelming impact on a city and environmental sustainability should be fully integrated in planning and infrastructure investments. However, not every city in Asia will have such momentous events and, hence, wider cost-effective and sustainable air quality management is needed.

In summary, many cities have been trying very hard to control air pollution and yet sustainable solutions for air quality management have been few and far between. Gains in Delhi, Bangkok, and other cities after a long battle may now be reversed in just a few years as rural–urban migration continues unabated. Regional cooperation is also needed, as most of the pollution often comes from neighboring cities and countries (e.g. Hong Kong, Beijing, Singapore, Kuala Lumpur). Everyone would probably agree that air pollution should be included in the top ten Copenhagen challenges: Because much of the air pollution impact is in developing cities and countries, it is extremely important to deal with this challenge in a cost-effective manner, when there are many other competing development priorities.

Commentary on the Challenge Paper

The Challenge paper covers the subject well and has many useful references, facts and figures, and food for thought. The outdoor air pollution is a result of economic development and requires good policies and technical interventions. The paper defines urban air pollution narrowly and focuses on PM and health impacts alone. A more holistic view of total pollutants (including carbon dioxide, which has now been ruled an air pollutant by the US Supreme Court, and which means the USEPA must control it) and their total effects is needed to make the B/C analysis more meaningful. If one wants to narrow the focus to one pollutant, however, PM 10 or PM 2.5 is the right pollutant because of the associated and estimated health impacts (Chow *et al.* 2006; Pope and Dockery 2006).

Air monitoring around the globe has shifted to PM 10 or PM 2.5. Over 2 billion people are exposed to outdoor pollution in cities (mostly in India and China) and thus much of the problem is now in the developing countries. To combat this pollution, a broad range of interventions is required and choices should be based on their cost effectiveness (Bachmann 2007; Chow *et al.* 2007). Conducting source apportionment studies is a good way to identify and quantify contributions from different sources so that control strategies can be focused. Annual emissions inventories, although necessary, are notoriously inaccurate, especially when emission factors from developed countries are applied (Guttikunda *et al.* 2008). Based on the analysis presented here, as well as what we have observed, for most countries and cities the major sources of PM 10 pollution are: vehicle emissions (gasoline and diesel), re-suspended road dust (fugitive and construction), coal and oil combustion (domestic and industrial), biomass burning (for cooking, heating, agricultural, and disposal), secondary sulfate and nitrate, uncontrolled industry (power plants, cements, etc.), and others (or unexplained). Emissions from shipping and associated goods movement are becoming more widely recognized as a major source in port areas.

The Challenge paper shifts the focus to low-sulfur fuel and its benefits for vehicular emissions control and the related benefit cost studies. Larsen *et al.* (2008) suggest that low-sulfur diesel fuel and vehicles with appropriate emissions control are the "silver bullets" that will substantially improve urban pollution levels. The analysis does not examine alternatives that might invest the same amount of money across a broad range of emissions reductions and have a much larger benefit to air quality, and more broadly to overall public health and quality of life. To focus on this one solution exclusively is not well supported or documented in the literature for developing or developed countries. Current EPA and Euro fuel and vehicle emission standards were adopted because, after more obvious, and cost-effective, emission reduction measures had been implemented, the low-hanging fruit had been picked. This is not the case in most developing countries. While it may be true for developed countries where vehicle emissions are dominant, for developing countries with low vehicle turnover, many other sources of air pollution, and weak capacity and institutions, the proposed focus is misplaced. If the toxicity of the vehicular pollution were included, this focus might be justified. However, without better supporting arguments and comparisons with benefits and cost of control options for other sources, the reason for focusing exclusively on emissions from vehicles seems unclear. Larsen *et al.* seem to ignore their own analysis presented earlier, where they document that the urban air pollution problem is in developing countries, such as India and China, where vehicular pollution is not the biggest contributing source to PM 10. It would be appropriate to look at pollution control options, and enforcement of their use, for major sources such as coal-fired power stations, including the role of low-sulfur diesel fuel. There is also much

to be gained from better appliances, fuels, and education in the domestic heating and cooking sectors. Vehicular emissions should be looked at in a more comprehensive manner, by evaluating other control options including public transport, demand management, emission standards, better enforcement of existing emissions standards (e.g. I&M), fiscal incentives for cleaner engines, methods to identify gross polluters, inspection and maintenance, retrofitting and re-powering, alternative fuels, and transportation management (Fulton *et al.* 2002; Matsumoto *et al.* 2007). Recent successful examples of achieving improved air quality by focusing on improved public transport (bus rapid transit) in Bogotá, Columbia shows that such measures may be much more appropriate, cost-effective, and sustainable and should be considered in a comprehensive strategy (Hidalgo 2005).

The Challenge paper acknowledges that economic benefit-cost studies are not available globally. Using the sketchy data available with assumptions based on a few studies, the authors apply their approach to Dakar, Senegal, without considering the realism of such application and looking at other sources. We agree with all the limitations, and the issue of multiple uncertainties, mentioned in the paper. Government capacity limitation to implement recommended action is mentioned but these limitations have not been adequately analyzed or reflected in the recommended focus on low-sulfur diesel fuel and vehicular emission controls in developing countries.

Approaches for Cost-Effective and Sustainable Air Quality Management

Our review suggests that low-sulfur diesel fuel (<50 or 15 ppm) and other technologically advanced solutions are needed to reduce vehicular emissions, and will have to be part of a comprehensive air pollution control strategy. Such options take a long lead time and should be part of overall urban planning. However, the benefit-cost or cost-effectiveness of low-sulfur diesel fuel needs to be compared with appropriate control options for other major sources. Focusing

Table 1.1.1. Examples of "no-regret" actions for air pollution control in cities

Policy initiatives	• Phase-in improved technology vehicles, and engines, through tighter standards • Remove fuel subsidies • Abolish burning of garbage and other biomass • Lower taxes on clean products
Institutional measures	• Identify and encourage champions for change • Formulate a Clean Air Group that includes industry, fuel providers and non-governmental organizations (NGOs)
Road, transport, and traffic management	• Make public transportation affordable or even free for downtown destinations • Train bus drivers on pollution and fuel use • Promote fuel efficiency for cars and industry • Establish one-way traffic with synchronized signals • Pave roads, including access roads
Awareness, media, educational, and social	• Publish and broadcast Air Quality Indices • Promote a regular media outlet for air quality stories to keep up interest • Offer environmental education in primary schools and agricultural extension services
Technical measures	• Eliminate refueling leaks, establish primary volatile organic compounds (VOCs) recovery, as a minimum • Reduce sulfur content of diesel fuel and gasoline to 500ppm or lower • Require new gasoline-powered vehicles to have operational catalytic converters • Mandate inspection and maintenance for commercial vehicles • Design and disseminate better stoves for coal briquettes, wood pellets, and other solid fuels • Focus on less polluting: better ventilated kitchens • Promote more efficient agricultural burning methods
Enforcement initiatives	• Identify and target gross polluters • Provide complaint phone or text message numbers for visual sighting of polluters

Note: Compiled from delegates at the 2004 International Air Quality Forum in Indianapolis, IN.
Source: Chow *et al.* (2004): 1226–35.

exclusively on low-sulfur diesel may not be the most cost-effective approach for many developing countries. Uncontrolled heavy industrial emissions, dirty coal-fired power stations, and non-traditional area sources such as burning (e.g. garbage, slash and burn, peat land fires, and rice paddies), construction, and re-suspended road dust which are important contributors to air pollution have higher benefit-cost ratios (World Bank 1997b). Similarly, some of the "no-regret actions" listed in table 1.1.1 may be implemented, as they too would have higher benefit-cost ratios. The low-sulfur fuel and vehicle emission control costs may also come down further in the future, and that may make them more attractive (Chow 2001; Lloyd and Cackette 2001).

Developing countries need good science and analysis that: (1) quantify which sources are the largest contributions to outdoor concentrations (not the same as the emissions inventory); (2)

evaluate the effectiveness and costs of a large number of emission reduction strategies; (3) rank the strategies by cost-benefit and political acceptability; (4) implement and enforce the strategies; and (5) periodically evaluate their effectiveness and adjust them for greater effect. All potential sources and major decision-making dimensions must be considered (financial, technical, economic, implementability, political viability, etc.). Public awareness and support for disciplined time-bound action, effective regulators, and above all political champions are needed for successful implementation! There is a tendency to recommend what has been applied and worked in developed countries without adequately recognizing the limitations and political economy in developing countries. In addition, technology has advanced since many of these policies were implemented in developed countries, and leapfrogging opportunities should

Marginal cost of emission reductions
($ per ton)

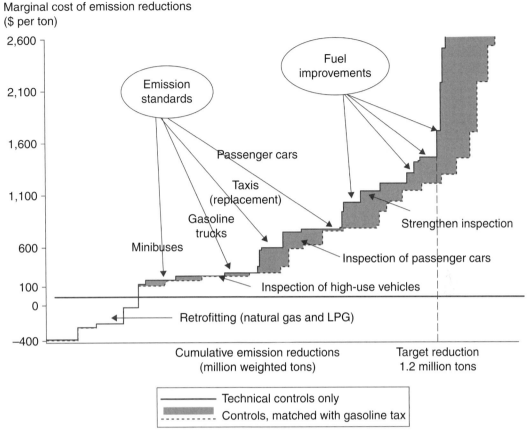

Figure 1.1.2 *Ranking of measures to reduce traffic emissions in Mexico City*
Note: Calculations based on –0.8 elasticity of demand for gasoline.
Source: Eskeland (1992).

be recognized. South–South cooperation may be more effective and convincing for policy-makers. Leapfrogging is a very good idea – but there are no "silver bullets" that will magically get rid of the pollution that has been building up for decades. It is important to recognize and address institutional capacity to make sure that the anticipated benefits of costly technologies really come to fruition.

Looking at control options from a technical viewpoint only may not deliver the expected benefits and for developing countries, non-technical issues, including capacity constraints and implementation difficulties, should be considered when developing air pollution control strategies. Champions are needed in developing

countries to promote innovative solutions that may sometimes be viewed as "too expensive" or anti-growth. We need to support these champions in making sure that the recommended actions are in fact the most cost-effective. These champions may lose credibility if valuable resources are expended to control sources while achieving no perceptible improvements in air quality.

The Incremental Cost of Abatement Curve is a useful analytical and presentational tool that can be derived directly from cost effectiveness analysis. Figure 1.1.2 gives details for an incremental cost curve developed for Mexico City. Under the cost-effectiveness analysis, the costs and benefits of three groups of abatement strategies for vehicular pollution were analyzed

(Eskeland 1992). The benefits were expressed in tons abated, but not valued in economic terms. The three groups of options analyzed were: (a) options that promote the use of cleaner fuels (e.g., natural gas retrofits and fuel improvements such as unleaded petrol); (b) options that promote the use of cleaner transport technologies (e.g., vapor recovery, tighter emission standards, and increased inspections of vehicles); and (c) options that reduce overall travel demand or shift demand to less-polluting travel modes (e.g. a gasoline tax). On the left side of the curve – natural gas retrofits and vapor recovery – are the technical options that offer the cheapest emissions abatement. (In fact, these two are "win–win" options, in that they pay for themselves financially, not only economically.) The middle part of the curve shows that inspections of vehicles and the imposition of emissions standards are the next most cost-effective options to be pursued. Finally, starting at emissions reduction of about 700,000 tons, the imposition of a gasoline tax improves the cost effectiveness of the purely technical options.

The great value of this incremental cost curve is that it explicitly and clearly shows the results of cost-effectiveness analysis. It is useful both analytically, to show priorities for action, as well as presentationally, to illustrate to decision-makers and the general public the underlying logic of the action plan. Such incremental costs of abatement curves should be developed for other major sources for development of comprehensive pollution control action plans by city planners and decision-makers. The Simple Interactive Model (SIM-air) discussed below includes such analysis and displays results that are easy to understand by policy-makers.

Institutional capacity-building for a better air quality management, including knowledge on sources, management options, and impacts, is vital. In the developing country cities, there is usually little in the way of an organized knowledge base or development or application of analytical tools that may help support air quality management. Most available tools are complex and data-intensive and there is a need for a new generation of simple interactive tools

that can be used in cities in the developing world that recognize their information and institutional challenges. The SIM-air is an easy-to-use Microsoft Excel based open source modeling tool to assist cities to collate local information and help making informed air quality management decisions (www.cleanairnet.org/cai/1403/article-59386.html; there is an application for the city of Bangkok @ www.pcd.go.th/info_serv/en_air_diesel.html#). Utilization of such an easy-to-use tool, that includes cost and benefits analysis, is recommended. SIM-air is utilized by researchers in many cities to demonstrate and apply an integrated analytical approach to air quality management. Modern information technology advances and increasing presence and networking in developing world cities offer a tremendous opportunity to develop simple tools to help city managers, regulators, the regulated, academia, and citizen groups to develop a coordinated knowledge base and analytical approaches to develop a shared stakeholder vision for the issues and options in integrated air quality management for a city. The tool includes typical management options and some are pre-programmed and linked to cost and health impacts (assumptions and linkages can be modified by the users). Example management options programmed in SIM-air include:

- CNG conversion of buses (percent x of fleet converted to CNG or clean fuel)
- Low-sulfur diesel (percent y reduction of sulfur levels in diesel)
- Energy efficiency in industry
- Shift industries from grid A to B
- Coal to LPG shift in domestic/area sources
- Scrappage (retirement of highly polluting vehicles, e.g. replacing motorcycles with 2-stroke engines with motorcycles with 4-stroke engines)
- Trucks using bypass (avoiding high-density areas such as downtown, schools, hospitals, etc. to reduce congestion)
- Encourage public transport (percent z cars off-road)

A holistic approach is recommended where the major sources of air pollution and their potential damages are considered. One can then, by using the least cost abatement curve, look at what are the costs and benefits of cleaning up each source.

Bibliography

Bachmann, J.D., 2007: 2007 Critical review – will the circle be unbroken: A history of the US National Ambient Air Quality Standards, *Journal of the Air Waste Management Association*, **57**(6): 652–97

CAI-Asia, 2008: *Clean Air Initiative for Asian cities*, Fourth Regional Dialogue of AQM Initiatives and Programs in Asia, 30–31 January, Bangkok

Chow, J.C., 2001: 2001 Critical review discussion – diesel engines: Environmental impact and control, *Journal of the Air Waste Management Association*, **51**(9): 1258–70

Chow, J.C., Watson, J.G., Shah, J.J., Kiang, C.S., Loh, C., Lev-On, M., Lents, J.M., Molina, M.J., and Molina, L.T., 2004: 2004 Critical review discussion – megacities and atmospheric pollution, *Journal of the Air Waste Management Association*, **54**(10): 1226–35

Chow, J.C., Watson, J.G., Mauderly, J.L., Costa, D.L., Wyzga, R.E., Vedal, S., Hidy, G.M., Altshuler, S.L., Marrack, D., Heuss, J.M., Wolff, G.T., Pope, C.A., III, and Dockery, D.W., 2006: 2006 Critical review discussion – health effects of fine particulate air pollution: Lines that connect, *Journal of the Air Waste Management Association*, **56**(10): 1368–80

Chow, J.C., Watson, J.G., Feldman, H.J., Nolan, J., Wallerstein, B.R., and Bachmann, J.D., 2007: 2007 Critical review discussion – will the circle be unbroken: A history of the US National Ambient Air Quality Standards, *Journal of the Air Waste Management Association*, **57**(10): 1151–63

Eskeland, G., 1992: Development and the environment, in *World Development Report 1992*, Oxford University Press, New York: 74

Fulton, L., Hardy, J., Schipper, L., and Golub, A., 2002: *Bus systems for the future: Achieving sustainable transport worldwide*, OECD/IEA Paris

Guttikunda, S., Wells, G.J., Johnson, T.M., Artaxo, P., Bond, T.C., Russell, A.G., Watson, J.G., and West, J., 2008: *Source apportionment of urban particulate matter for air quality management: Review of techniques and applications in developing countries*, World Bank, Washington, DC

Hidalgo, D., 2005: Comparación de alternativas de transporte público masivo – una aproximación conceptual, *Revista de Ingeniería*, May 21, www.transmilenio.gov.co

Larsen, B., Hutton, G., and Khanna. N., 2008: *Copenhagen Consensus 2008 Challenge paper on Air Pollution*, Copenhagen, see chapter 1 in this volume

Lloyd, A.C. and Cackette, T.A., 2001: Critical review – diesel engines: Environmental impact and control, *Journal of the Air Waste Management Association*, **51**(6): 809–47

Matsumoto, N., King, P.N., and Mori, H., 2007: Best practice on environmental policy in Asia and the Pacific, chapter 6 in *International Review for Environmental Strategies*, **7**(1): 93–112

Molina, M.J. and Molina, L.T., 2004: Critical review – Megacities and atmospheric pollution, *Journal of the Air Waste Management Association*, **54**(6): 644–80

Pope, C.A., III and Dockery, D.W., 2006: Critical review – health effects of fine particulate air pollution: Lines that connect, *Journal of the Air Waste Management Association*, **56**(6): 709–42

Roychowdhury, A., 2008: RAISING THE BAR: Beijing has pulled out the stops to clean its air before the Olympics, *Down to earth*, CSE, Delhi, February 15

World Bank, 1997a: Urban air quality management strategy, in J. Shah, T. Nagpal, and C. Brandon (eds.), *Asia: Guidebook*, World Bank: Washington, DC, www.cleanairnet.org/caiasia/

World Bank, 1997b: Shah, J. and Nagpal, T., Urban air quality management strategy in Asia: *Greater Mumbai, Technical Report*, **378**; *Manila, Technical Report*, **379**; *Kathmandu, Technical Report*, **380**; *Jakarta, Technical Report*, **381**, World Bank, Washington, DC, www.cleanairnet.org/caiasia/

World Bank, 2002: *Thailand Environment Monitor: Air Quality*, Bangkok Thailand, www.worldbank.org/TH

The Security Challenge in Conflict-Prone Countries

PAUL COLLIER, LISA CHAUVET, AND
HÅVARD HEGRE

Overview

Definition of the Challenge

Large-scale violent conflict takes several forms, and our focus is far from comprehensive. Recent media attention has been dominated by Iraq and it is important to acknowledge at the outset that this type of situation is not covered in our analysis. Iraq is in many respects highly atypical of modern conflict. It began as an international war, yet over time international conflict has tended to become far less common. Most warfare in low-income countries is internal. The situation in Iraq has indeed evolved into what is currently probably best described as an ongoing civil war. While our focus is indeed civil war, the interventions that we evaluate here are designed to prevent rather than arrest such wars. In the first Challenge paper on Conflicts for the Copenhagen Consensus, Collier and Hoeffler (2004c) also chose to focus on civil wars. However, within this remit they were more ambitious than the present chapter, including the "deep prevention" of civil war, the ending of on-going conflicts, and the prevention of the recurrence of violence in post-conflict situations. In this chapter, our ambition is more limited. We focus predominantly on the prevention of the recurrence of violence in post-conflict societies. This restricted focus enables us to consider post-conflict instruments in more depth, and it is also the core of the problem of violent conflict. Around half of all civil wars are post-conflict relapses. From this core we range a little more widely, taking in the prevention of coups d'états and some limited "deep prevention."

Benefits

Civil war is often horrific. Unlike the American Civil War of the nineteenth century, modern civil wars in low-income countries overwhelmingly affect the civilian population. They target the most vulnerable members of societies that are already the most impoverished on earth. Their consequences are often highly persistent: Child soldiers who have been taught to kill are not only appalling victims, they are a menace to their society for many years to come. It is inevitably difficult to place a meaningful value on the avoidance of such phenomena.

The benefits of a reduction in the global incidence of civil war are common to all successful deployments of instruments for conflict reduction. They accrue at three levels: National, regional, and global. The benefits at the national level are partly economic and partly social. As in Collier and Hoeffler (2004c) we build a lower-bound estimate based on the effects of civil war on economic growth. The mortality effects are more difficult, but we follow their estimate in terms of disability-adjusted life years (DALYs). Where we depart most radically from that previous study is in allowing for the possibility of a much wider range of costs. These are by their nature far less quantifiable than the direct consequences for GDP and mortality, but they are likely to be large. We therefore work with both the economic costs considered by Collier and Hoeffler (2004c), treating this as a lower bound, and a more speculative figure which we suggest may nevertheless better illustrate the center-of-the-range of likely full costs. We hope that subsequent research, perhaps drawing on pertinent analogies with other catastrophic phenomena, will begin to place better bounds on these effects.

Stabilizing Post-Conflict Situations

Within the challenge of reducing the global incidence of civil war, we focus on post-conflict situations. As noted above, post-conflict relapses into renewed violence account for around half of all global civil wars, and so they provide an opportunity for highly focused interventions. Further, since 2000 there have been many settlements of civil wars, some of which look fragile and would probably already have relapsed into violence but for international intervention, examples being the Democratic Republic of Congo (DRC), and Timor Leste, where as of 2008 1,000 Australian troops have been sent in response to violent unrest.

Discouraging Coups

A second opportunity is the drastic reduction of coups d'états. Coups have been getting less common but they still threaten many governments of low-income countries. Unfortunately, as we show, democracy does not provide protection against them so that the rapid spread of democracy in recent years has actually increased the danger that democratically elected governments will be overthrown by their own militaries. While coups do not have anything like the high costs of civil wars, they are usually undesirable, and we consider feasible ways in which, in the weakest societies, they could be discouraged.

Instruments

The major innovation of the present study is to focus on international military interventions as instruments for conflict reduction. Given the experience in Iraq, this is inevitably controversial. However, as we argue below, for precisely this reason it is important to have a dispassionate assessment of the instrument. Iraq is likely to be an extremely poor guide to the utility of military instruments. To benchmark the military instruments, we compare them to the post-conflict aid. Such aid is most probably the most effective use of aid for conflict reduction, though of course not necessarily the most effective use of aid overall. It is also politically far less controversial than military interventions. Hence, if post-conflict aid is as cost-effective in conflict reduction as the military interventions then the latter are redundant.

Benchmark Instrument: Post-Conflict Aid

Since Collier and Hoeffler (2004c), much new research has enabled a better-grounded estimate of the benefits of post-conflict aid for reducing the risks of conflict recurrence. We show that there is indeed now a good case that such aid significantly and substantially reduces the risk of further violence. However, once we subject the instrument to a cost-benefit analysis (CBA), its overall performance is good but not spectacular. Aid is unfortunately quite expensive relative to what it achieves unless huge values are placed upon the maintenance of peace. We then use this benchmark intervention to compare three much more politically controversial instruments of military intervention.

International Peacekeeping

UN peacekeeping interventions have increased enormously since the end of the Cold War and are now a massive claim on both money and manpower. Our study is the first attempt to provide a CBA of their deployment, and considering the scale and controversy surrounding this deployment of resources such an analysis is surely overdue. As with most first attempts, our estimates need to be treated with due caution. However, our figures suggest that international peacekeeping is highly cost-effective in securing peace.

Over-the-Horizon Security Guarantees

An important variant on international peacekeeping is the strategy of over-the-horizon guarantees. This is the strategy currently being adopted in Sierra Leone where an in-country military force of only eighty international troops is supported by a credible logistical commitment to fly troops in should they be needed. A similar, though less explicit arrangement appears to be in place between Timor Leste and Australia.

Caps on Military Spending

Our third military-related instrument is for a donor cap on military spending by governments of post-conflict societies. While this is evidently controversial, we show that because aid inadvertently leaks into such military spending, at present the lack of a cap inflates spending. More importantly, we show that in the post-conflict context military spending sharply increases the risk of further conflict so that discouraging it not only restores aid to its intended uses but directly reduces the risk of conflict. Such limits on spending are an example of a wider family of interventions aimed at reducing armaments in conflict-prone regions, another such instrument being limits on the arms trade. While there is indeed now some evidence that cheap guns increase the risk of violence in these societies, there is less evidence that instruments that try to limit armaments such as trade embargoes are actually effective. We have selected the spending cap as being the instrument that may be the most straightforward to implement effectively.

The Need for Security

The need for security from political violence is fundamental to human society. The great archaeological legacies of antiquity, such as the Great Wall of China, and the massive barrier constructed by the ancient Jutes against the Germanic tribes, stand as an enduring testimony to the overwhelming priority afforded to defence. This priority continued until very recently: For forty years the richest society on earth, America, devoted 10 percent of its national income to defence spending to meet the security threat from the Soviet Union. However, with the collapse of the Soviet Union, an era has ended. Political violence has not passed into history, but it now happens "elsewhere." Rich countries no longer fight each other, and they no longer fight themselves. Among the middle-income countries war has virtually disappeared. Even the big poor countries are now pretty safe: China and India have massive armies, but they have not used them against each other for over forty years.

But some places are still dangerous. Usually, the violence is internal: The country tears itself apart while the rest of the world watches.

Sometimes the violence draws others in, mostly the neighbours, and sometimes the local regional power. Occasionally the international powers intervene: To prevent internal mayhem, as in the Democratic Republic of the Congo, to expel an invader, as in Iraq 1, or to force regime change, as in Iraq 2. The uncomfortable fact is that a large group of impoverished little countries are structurally dangerous. Quite where the violence erupts is usually unpredictable, but its incidence is predictable. Just as the security problem for the previous generation was the containment of the Soviet Union, so for our generation the problem is the curtailment of violence in these societies. We begin with a review of global trends in armed conflict, based on recent research at the International Peace Research Institute of Oslo (PRIO) and the Uppsala Conflict Data Program, Uppsala University.

Global Trends in Armed Conflict

We rely upon the Uppsala Conflict Data Program (UCDP) definition of an armed conflict:

> a contested incompatibility that concerns government and/or territory over which the use of armed force between the military forces of two parties, of which at least one is the government of a state, has resulted in at least 25 battle-related deaths each year.

As noted in the Overview, intrastate (civil) conflict is the most common form of armed conflict, and this has been so since the end of the Second World War. Despite the current prominence of Iraq, interstate wars (fought between at least two countries) have been relatively rare events. Figure 2.1 shows the number of large and small conflicts that were active in every year since 1946. Until 1991, the number of armed conflicts trended upward but since then there has been a general trend towards peace. Correspondingly, the number of very large wars has diminished, but there are now more small wars. However, "small" may be deceptive. The measure used is battle-related deaths – a small war causes between 25 and 999 such deaths over a year. However, the increasing involvement of

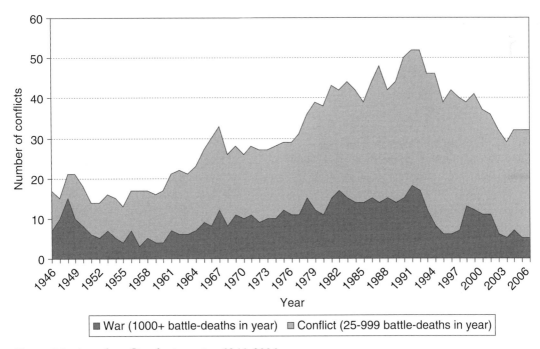

Figure 2.1 *Armed conflicts by intensity, 1946–2006*
Sources: Gleditch et al. (2002); Harbom and Wallensteen (2007).

civilians, and indeed the blurring of the distinction between civilians and combatants, implies that even "small" wars measured in battle deaths can have highly adverse consequences for the societies in which they occur.

Figure 2.2 shows that the geographic distribution of conflict has also changed. There has been a substantial decline in the number of conflicts fought in Europe and the Americas. Conflict in the Middle East has been relatively stable. In recent years most conflicts have been fought in Asia and Africa. Indeed, most conflicts are geographically grouped: Two ellipses, one stretching from Turkey to the Philippines and the other in the Great Lakes and Horn of Africa, illustrate the transnational nature of civil conflict.

While the total number of active conflicts has been fairly constant in recent years, this does not imply that new conflicts have not broken out: New conflicts have replaced the ones that have ended. Figure 2.3 shows for each year how many of the on-going conflicts were continuation of hostilities between the same actors, and how

many were entirely new. Nine of the thirty-two conflicts active in 2005 had been inactive in the previous year, and in 2006 there were a further four new active conflicts. All of these new conflicts in 2005 and 2006 were conflict relapses, further emphasizing the importance of our focus on post-conflict situations.

The increase in the number of conflicts up to 1992 was not due to an increase in new conflicts, but rather to a gradual accumulation: Few conflicts ended. It is this that has changed since 1992. The main reason for the encouraging reversal of trend is a considerable increase in successful termination of conflicts. It is thus timely to concentrate, as is done in this chapter, on interventions which attempt to prevent these many recent terminations from reigniting.

The Consequences of Violent Internal Conflict

One contribution of this chapter is to attempt to measure the cost of violent internal conflict. Since

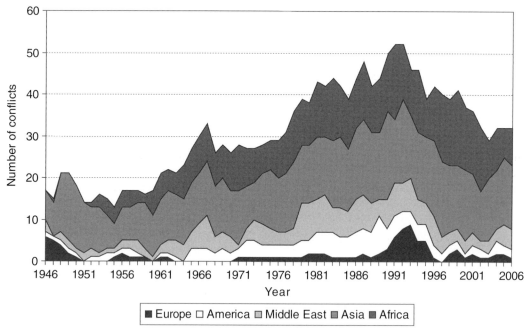

Figure 2.2 *Armed conflicts, by region, 1946–2006*
Sources: Gleditch et al. (2002); Harbom and Wallensteen (2007).

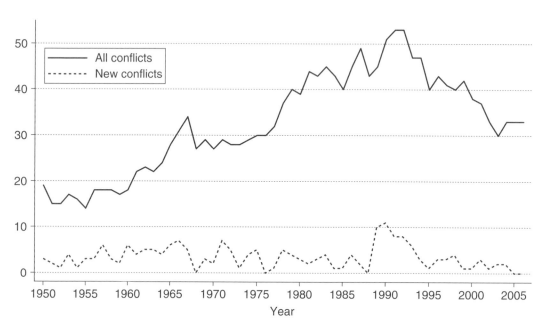

Figure 2.3 *Number of conflicts and of new conflicts, 1950–2006*
Sources: Gleditch et al. (2002): Harbom and Wallensteen (2007).

we focus on the prevention of repeat conflicts we consider the typical cost in a small, low-income country that has already had a war. Even if we include only the direct loss of income and ignore mortality and morbidity effects, the cost is around $43 billion. Including mortality and morbidity, the costs rise to close to $60 billion. However, these estimates, though large, grossly under-state the true cost because they make no allowance for five important considerations. These omissions reflect limitations of both our own work and of the economic methodologies currently available. It is therefore important that we should state them right at the outset of our study.

The first omission is that the people affected by violent internal conflict tend disproportionately to be among the poorest and most disadvantaged people in the world. This is because low income is itself a risk factor in political violence. Modern economic methodology indeed allows such considerations to be included in a global comparative analysis: In effect, a dollar added to the income of a person on very low income should be valued more highly than a dollar added to the income of a person at a higher level of income. Conventional economic estimates of the diminishing utility of income, derived from observed behavior towards risk, suggest that the required adjustment is large. However, it may be best made once different proposals are compared: In effect, the income level of the beneficiaries of each proposal should be taken into account. The income level of the beneficiaries of the maintenance of post-conflict peace is, however, likely to be lower than that from other proposals. Thus, comparisons based on the implicit assumption that they have the same income as the beneficiaries of other proposals should be revised accordingly. The income differential between the typical citizen in the countries of the "bottom billion" and a typical citizen of the other developing countries is already around 1:5 (Collier 2007).[1] Even within the "bottom billion" there is a wide range of incomes, with those countries that have recently been in conflict grouped right at the bottom. Further, interventions need to be guided not just by current poverty but by reasonable estimates of future poverty (Wood 2006). For exam-

ple, an intervention which this year permanently alleviates the poverty of 1,000 people in China is simply less valuable than an intervention with the same effect in the DRC, not because Chinese people should be less valued than the Congolese but because the prospects for the Chinese are manifestly more promising. As Wood (2006) argues, in some sense our interventions should have the objective of alleviating future misery, appropriately discounted. This makes successful interventions in environments that otherwise offer little hope much more valuable than those in societies that are already succeeding. He shows formally that within the Collier and Dollar (2002) analytic framework for optimal aid allocation, these dynamic considerations have large consequences: Far more aid should go towards the slowest-growing countries. Since 1980, the income of the typical citizen of the "bottom billion" has been diverging from the typical citizen of the next four billion by around 5 percent per year. As we show below, slow growth is itself a significant risk factor in violent conflict, so that the most violence-prone countries are systematically among the slowest growing.

The second omission is that because peace is fundamental to development, its absence frustrates all other potential interventions. For example, the vaccination of children or the reliable provision of anti-retroviral drugs is virtually impossible in wartime conditions. Sometimes this creates "weakest-link" problems in the provision of global public goods. For example, smallpox was eliminated globally in a country-by-country campaign which was evidently a race against time: Until it is eliminated everywhere there is a risk that it will break out again as a global disease. The last country on earth where it was eliminated was Somalia during the 1970s. Had it not been eliminated in Somalia before the society collapsed into civil war, smallpox would still be a global disease. From 1993 to 2007 the absence of security in Somalia made similar global health advances infeasible. The maintenance of peace is thus a logically prior investment that opens the possibility of all the other interventions. Conceptually, within the formal analysis of modern economics, the opened possibilities should be thought of as having an "option value." The concept of an option value was developed in financial economics to show that the true return on liquid assets was greater than merely the interest earned on them because they enabled other investment opportunities to be taken as they arose, but the idea generalizes to any action that is necessary for other possibilities. Hence, the discovery of other promising uses for global resources is more likely to enhance the case for investment in post-conflict peace than to compete with it: Few interventions are not dependent upon peace.

The third omission is that the costs of civil war are concentrated within a society. The "methodological individualism" inherent in economic analysis essentially treats the costs as being the same whether the losers are spatially and socially dispersed across a continent, or constitute a distinct political and social unit. Yet in some sense the collapse of a society is far more disturbing than were the same individuals to experience the same suffering as isolated individuals in other societies. In effect, a well-functioning nation and its society generate public goods both for its members and for the world that are disrupted if it implodes into sustained internal violence. A useful thought experiment that reveals this idea is to ask what would be lost if all the citizens of, say, Ghana, were to move to the USA and Europe. Each individual ex-Ghanaian might be happier yet the world might reasonably consider that it had lost something of value. Just as species of animals and plants are now recognized to have an "existence value," so do societies. The convulsions that have occurred in Somalia and Rwanda may well have gone beyond destroying the "existence value" of their societies. These societies were not erased from global consciousness, which is the counterfactual implied by existence value, but rather they became nightmares. An analogy here is the consequences of terrorism. The direct damage done by terrorist attacks is manifestly trivial relative to the resources devoted to countering them. Yet the deployment of large resources to counter-terrorist measures need not be mistaken if a value is assigned to the horror and revulsion which

people who are neither victims nor potential victims feel once an attack occurs.

The fourth omission is that the costs of internal conflict are highly persistent. This persistence raises two issues for quantification: Just how long do the adverse effects last, and how should the future be valued relative to the present? We base our cost estimates on the duration of a typical civil war being seven years and the recovery back to normal being around fourteen years. While these figures are based on evidence rather than being assumptions, we have deliberately been conservative in adopting figures at the lower end of the reasonable range. Even the duration of internal conflict is surprisingly difficult to estimate, and one distinguished study puts it at fifteen years as opposed to the seven we use here. Similarly, a new study on the path of exports after civil war finds that even after a quarter of a century following a large war, there is still no sign of recovery from the collapse that occurs during it. It has also been shown that the collapse in health conditions that occurs during war is highly persistent. The valuation of the future relative to the present is standard in economics, by means of discounting. However, as the Stern Report (2006) has argued in connection with the costs of climate change, the valuation of the future becomes more problematic when the effects are inter-generational and their magnitude large. Stern argues that in such circumstances it is appropriate to discount the future less heavily than is appropriate for short-horizon, marginal investments. Both of these qualifications apply to the costs of violent internal conflict. The degree to which the after-effects of a civil war are discounted is important for an overall measure of costs because some of the costs are two decades or more into the future. In our estimates for this study we have discounted future effects at 3 percent and 6 percent per year, but these may both be higher than is warranted once the effects highlighted by Stern are considered. Hence, due both to the potential for highly persistent costs, and to the case for a less severe discount on the future, we are likely to have under-estimated the cost of violence.

Our final omission is of three global spill-over

effects: Crime, disease, and terrorism. Large-scale political violence and the resulting breakdown of the state create territories that have a comparative advantage in international criminality. They provide safe havens both for criminals themselves and for their material activities such as the storage of illegal commodities, notably drugs. Some 95 percent of hard drug production is concentrated in civil war or post-conflict environments. They socialize young men into violence and provide powerful "push" incentives for them to emigrate to societies in which they are then liable to be predatory. We omit these costs from our core quantification partly because the link between violence and criminality is not 1:1: some peaceful societies can nevertheless be quasi-criminal states, as for example Guinea-Bissau. A second reason is that the costs are highly speculative because the counterfactual is unclear: to what extent would criminality merely shift and to what extent would it be curtailed? The third reason is that the cost of international criminality is enormous, so that any reasonable number would be both speculative and large. Civil wars also create the conditions for the spread of disease: The breakdown in public health systems and the mass movement of refugees. Some of this spread of disease affects neighbours, and can potentially also affect the entire world. One of the explanations for the origin of HIV/AIDS for which there is some evidence is that it originated during an African civil war. Again, we exclude the risk of such a pandemic from our core estimate of costs for the same reasons as crime: There is again no 1:1 connection, and since the damage of a pandemic is enormous our results would be dominated by a highly speculative number. Finally, civil wars appear to assist terrorism. Al Qaida based its training camps in Afghanistan because the absence of a recognized government was convenient. Similarly, the American government finally decided that leaving Somalia without a recognized government was too dangerous, once evidence built up that Al Qaida was relocating there. We exclude the risk that civil war will assist international terrorism: There is no 1:1 link, and we would again have a huge but speculative number driving our calculations.

Should all five of these factors simply be ignored when estimating the benefits of peace? It seems unreasonable to do so. If on average each factor implied that the true costs were double the number generated by neglecting it, then cumulatively the five would imply a 32-fold increase in the valuation of the cost of conflict! If the average adjustment was 50 percent, it would imply a 7.5-fold increase, and if it were only 20 percent a 2.5-fold increase. Can we make any judgment on the magnitude of the likely adjustment? The first omission – that conflict-affected people are the poorest and least hopeful people on earth – surely warrants a large adjustment. Both the evidence from estimates of typical utility functions and the simulations of Wood (2006) suggest that the required adjustment is more likely to involve doubling than alterations by a few percentage points. For the other factors there is even less guidance, but doubling would seem to be unwarranted. Were we, for example, to allow a 20 percent adjustment for each of the other four omissions, and to double our estimate as an adjustment to the first omission, the overall adjustment would be a 4.2-fold increase, implying a cost of the typical civil war of the order of $250 billion.

Evidently, the leap from the estimate of $60 billion to that of $250 billion is speculative. We therefore leave it to the reader to judge between them. The $60 billion estimate essentially treats a prolonged civil war as broadly analogous to an economic recession with some added illness. In our view the $250 billion figure better approximates to how ordinary people view civil war. It is, for example, more commensurate with the scale of resources the governments of developed countries are periodically willing to deploy to attempt to change political regimes for the better. In our subsequent analysis we will use the figure of $60 billion as being the likely lower bound, and that of $250 billion as an illustrative figure that is probably closer to the center of the range.

International Policy Options: Abstention vs. Intervention

What, if anything, should be done internationally to address this security problem? Some very able scholars argue that within these societies autonomous processes will correct it, so that external strategies are unnecessary (Weinstein 2005). Others argue to the same effect that external interventions are illegitimate, ineffective, or even counter-productive. However, benign neglect can itself backfire. When Somalia collapsed into anarchy in 1993 it was allowed to remain without a government for fourteen years. Only once there was evidence that Al Qaida had moved in to the resulting safe haven was international action organized to impose a new government. Perhaps, if Somalia had been left on its own for a century, it would have developed a viable government without external assistance. But, perhaps not: Little very recognizable as a national government had emerged in mainland Africa in the centuries prior to external intervention. Small, impoverished societies tend to be structurally insecure: Insecurity is a trap from which it is difficult to escape without assistance from beyond the society, although the intervention may come from neighbours, as in the end it did with Somalia, rather than from the developed world.

There are two reasons why external security intervention should be afforded a high priority: Compassion and self-interest. The argument from compassion is that the insecure societies are the poorest and most desperate environments on earth, and that the provision of security is fundamental both to personal wellbeing and to economic development. Without security, a society can hardly get started. The benefits of security provision are thus both particularly well targeted on the most needy societies, and have good prospects of being geared up by making other interventions feasible. The argument from compassion is complemented by the argument from self-interest. Insecurity spills over across borders. As we show, most of the costs of insecurity accrue to neighbours rather than to the society directly affected, and so neighbourhoods have both an interest and a right to be involved. And some of the costs spill over to rich societies. Broken societies are havens for illegality, whether this is trafficking in drugs or training of terrorists. The argument from self-interest

is compatible with the argument from compassion: Most commonly enlightened self-interest is a vital spur to effective solutions. However, on its own, the self-interest of the rich societies risks distorting our perception of effective solutions. The high profile of the terror risk facing rich countries has tended to crowd out the rather different security challenges facing failing societies. A discourse on international security that does not address these challenges is one-sided and less likely to gain acceptance. In fact, the security challenge facing rich countries is in large part a side-effect of the much larger security challenge facing failing societies. A sustained strategy of strengthening these societies against structural insecurity is likely to be more worthwhile than that of neglect interspersed with invasions if "they" appear to threaten "us."

Although the core of this chapter focuses on a few specific interventions we should stress that we do not see these as the only means of enhancing security in these societies. Rather, they are one part of a wide array of desirable interventions. Each gains both effectiveness and acceptability by being part of the whole. Precisely because the military interventions highlighted here are inevitably going to be regarded as controversial, we wish to make clear that we are not advocating military-only approaches. What would a comprehensive strategy of addressing structural insecurity look like? We can get some insights from the successful sustained security strategy of countering the threat posed by the Soviet Union. That threat was taken seriously and infused a wide array of policies. Not only was 10 percent of US income devoted to security for over forty years. The pre-war policy of isolationism was torn up: America created NATO, the system of mutual security guarantees, and placed over 100,000 troops in Europe. The serious response went well beyond security measures: America reversed its protectionist trade policy, integrating a fragile post-war Europe into its own powerhouse economy by dismantling trade barriers. Nor did getting serious stop with trade: America launched a giant aid program to Europe: Marshall Aid. American responses to the security challenge even extended to how its allies governed themselves. No viable strategy was neglected. Even with this massive response, it took over forty years of sustained effort. Is the challenge facing our generation greater or less than that? It is clearly less stark: The DRC is not pointing missiles at Washington. The amorphous nature of the threat is closer to the security challenge at the end of the First World War. As Macmillan (2006) notes, this was one reason why in 1919 the peacemakers failed to resolve the core security challenge. The amorphous nature of the current security risk has led to wild swings in Western response. Somalia was an instance of total neglect whereas Iraq 2 is at the opposite end of the spectrum: Pre-emptive total intervention. The lesson of how America saw off the threat from the Soviet Union is that for challenges of this scale to be "winnable" the major nations of the international community need to apply a consistent set of policies for a long time. Security and compassion are not rivals here, they can coalesce into a sense of common purpose.

The Quantitative Analysis of Security

This chapter does not provide a comprehensive menu of policies that might effectively address structural insecurity, but it provides a quantitative analysis of some salient possibilities. Quantitative analysis is vital in order to move discussion beyond political posturing. Inevitably, issues of security are difficult to get into a quantitative framework because they are about averting relatively low-probability events. Take the Cold War. Our instinct is to say that the immense expenditures on countering the threat posed by the Soviet Union proved to be well justified, but that sense depends upon a counterfactual: What would have happened without this expenditure, and in particular what probability to place upon the more dire among the possible scenarios. Compared to the security expenditure during the Cold War, the security expenditures considered in this chapter are far more amenable to quantification. This is because dire scenarios are not hypothetical: The forms of insecurity of concern to failing states occur with

sufficient frequency to be analyzable as statistical phenomena. We are thus able to quantify the factors that make societies more or less prone to these forms of political violence. Some of the factors that make a society prone to violence do not directly provide fruitful opportunities for policy intervention. For example, societies in countries with a lot of mountainous terrain face a much higher risk of rebellion, most probably because such terrain facilitates the organization of rebellion. Yet leveling mountains is not a sensible strategy. However, other risk factors are more amenable to policy, and these provide the foundation for estimating the costs and benefits of interventions that marginally reduce risks.

Marginal analysis may not seem very exciting, but it is the essence of policy analysis. Security is all about risks, and so the pay-offs to effective interventions are indeed going to be measured as reductions in risks. These changes in risk will then be multiplied by the consequences of counterfactual scenarios that become more and less likely. Analytically, our approach will be equivalent to the way the costs and benefits of any expenditure on risk reduction, such as safety belts in vehicles, are measured. The benefits of fitting the belt are the reduced chance of severe injury times some cost in terms of loss in the quality of life (QALY) should such an injury occur. These benefits then have to be weighed against the cost. Such calculations, involving both the estimation of changes in risk and the valuation of counterfactual scenarios, are a routine part of CBA. The application of this approach to the structural insecurity of failing states involves no departure of principle, but it indisputably gives rise to a culture shock among both political scientists and economists. Political scientists, who are familiar with thinking about the issues of failing states, often grow uncomfortable when faced with quantification. There is, of course, good reason for the concern that quantification necessarily sets aside the myriad of factors that cannot be quantified. Economists, for whom quantification is entirely normal, often grow uncomfortable for a different reason: Failing states are a phenomenon for which data are poor and so they worry that there is insufficient basis for quantitative analysis. Both of these concerns are reasonable. A CBA of security strategies should be seen as one approach that can help to supplement the way in which decisions are made rather than being the only basis for those decisions. Nevertheless, it can hardly be claimed that the record of decisions on insecurity interventions in failing states is so impressive that no such supplement is warranted. Purely qualitative analysis has its own catastrophic pitfalls. The precise numbers generated in this chapter are fragile, but where possible we indicate the likely range.

The key security challenges facing poor countries are civil wars and coups. Currently, the governments that face these risks respond to them by military spending. Both the risks and the response are highly costly. If there were cost-effective international interventions that would substantially reduce the risks of wars and coups, and reduce military spending, the pay-off to poor countries would be enormous. Yet even among the international interventions designed to help such countries, security has received less policy attention than the "photogenic" topics such as health and education. International security interventions, though numerous and expensive, have not been guided by CBA. Especially with the establishment in September 2005 of a permanent UN Peace-Building Commission, there is a real opportunity for more informed and coherent international action. There is the potential to build on recent advances in the quantitative study of security issues in poor countries, as exemplified by the contributions to the new *Handbook of Defence Economics* (Hartley and Sandler 2007).

We first estimate the costs of these phenomena in poor countries and then investigate four possible ways of ameliorating them: Increasing aid in post-conflict situations; imposing limits on the military spending of post-conflict governments; expanding peacekeeping forces; and guaranteeing security from "over-the-horizon." The results presented here are new rather than a repetition of the previous Challenge paper for the Copenhagen Consensus, although they build upon that work (Collier and Hoeffler 2004c).

Since that paper was written there have been substantial advances in the quantitative analysis of conflict, and of the efficacy of potential interventions. Specifically, there have been quantitative analyses of how military spending, aid, coups, the risk of war, and peacekeeping forces are inter-linked using more recent data. These new studies provide the foundation for estimates of the costs and benefits of the four proposed interventions. Since these are the first such estimates they have a dual function. Most directly, they can inform policy: Even ballpark figures of costs and benefits provide guidance as to the absolute and relative merits of interventions that have already sometimes been deployed. Beyond this direct effect, we hope that our estimates will open up a new area for future researchers so that over time this further research will reveal a credible range of answers.

The Scourges: Civil Wars and Coups

Structural insecurity has various manifestations, and we do not attempt to address them all. The major forms of insecurity are international wars, such as that between Ethiopia and Eritrea; civil wars, such as that within Sudan; pogroms perpetrated by the government against its own civilians, such as happened in Rwanda; community-level violence between different ethnic, religious, or political groups, such as occurred in Northern Nigeria; and coups d'états, such as occurred in Côte d'Ivoire. All these forms occur from time to time in the countries of "the bottom billion," while having receded into history in the developed societies. We will focus only on civil wars and coups. There are two reasons for this restriction of focus. First, each of these five phenomena is quite distinct and requires a separate analysis. It is inappropriate as far as quantitative and policy analysis are concerned either to amalgamate them into some amorphous aggregate of "insecurity," or to assume that what is true of one category will extend to the others. Our research has concentrated upon civil wars and coups, and it would require major further research to extend it to the other forms of violence. Second, while all these forms are periodically of importance, civil wars are unambiguously the most costly: They are highly disruptive and last a long time. Hence, this is the place to start. Coups are potentially of importance far beyond their direct disruption, because they either usher in or prolong military rule. Hence, the costs of coups are, at least in part, the obverse of the gains from democracy. Not all coups oust democratic governments, and some even lead to democracy. But on the whole, coups empower the military over civilian government. The fear of a coup can also generate costs: As we will see, governments sometimes increase military spending in order to pre-empt a coup attempt. Thus, coups are costly and the quantification of these various costs poses a challenging array of problems.

Civil Wars

For the purposes of undertaking a CBA of strategies to reduce the incidence of civil war, we need two components. One is the cost of the typical civil war, and the other is a quantitative analysis of the factors that cause civil war.

The Costs of Civil War

The full consequences of civil war are so various that it is not practical to quantify them all. We therefore focus on the salient costs while considering whether those factors we omit are likely to be so important as to nullify our analysis.

The most readily measurable costs are the economic damage done to the country during the war. Even this depends upon some hypothesized counterfactual of how the country's economy would have evolved in the absence of war. Such counterfactuals are generated from multi-country growth regressions. The approach is to introduce into such standard growth regressions a dummy variable that picks up the typical effect of civil war. This was the approach taken in Collier (1998), who estimated that civil war typically reduced a country's growth rate by around 2.2 percentage points for the duration of the conflict. Since that study, there have been various other estimates. One genuine difficulty is

whether to attribute some of the costs not to the war itself but to the damaging economic policies that governments commonly adopt during war: While these policies are usual in wartime they can also occur during peace and so potentially the pure costs of war could be seen as distinct from the costs of bad policies. Collier (1998) treats the costs of war-related policies as part of the costs of war and that will be our approach here. The figure of 2.2 percent remains around the centre of the range of estimates. Note that it implies that in most countries even during a civil war the economy keeps growing, so that simple before-and-after comparisons would radically under-state the costs. Since the typical civil war lasts around seven years, by its end the economy is typically around 15 percent poorer than it would have been with peace.

The next issue is what happens once the war is over. If the economy were to persist in being 15 percent poorer than it would have been then almost all the costs of war would occur after it was over. In fact, the typical post-conflict economy gradually recovers to its pre-war growth path. The recovery time has been estimated by Collier and Hoeffler (2004b) and by Elbadawi et al. (2008). As a rule of thumb, the recovery takes about twice as long as the war itself: Destruction is more rapid than reconstruction. Hence, for the typical economy, a civil war shrinks the economy for seven years by 2.2 percent per year relative to the counterfactual, followed by a recovery at around 1.1 percent for fourteen years. New research on more detailed aspects of post-conflict recovery broadly supports this pattern. For example, Martin and Mayer (2008) investigate the recovery in the share of exports in GDP, which unsurprisingly collapses during civil war. They find that for the majority of civil wars, namely those where the level of combat-related deaths is moderate, it takes around eighteen years to get back to normal. Similarly, Adam et al. (2008) investigate the recovery in the demand for domestic currency, which also declines during civil war as governments resort to desperate measures of financing which undermines confidence. They find that typically it takes up to two decades fully to restore confidence in the currency. This pattern of economic collapse during war followed by slow recovery creates a V-shaped path for income relative to the counterfactual. If both this path and the counterfactual path are depicted graphically, the difference between them is a triangle showing the losses due to the war. By discounting the area of this triangle we arrive at our first component of the cost of civil war: The net present value (NPV) of the cost of a war to the country affected.

However, countries have neighbors and in the modern global economy national economies are sufficiently inter-connected that wars are likely to create spill-over effects. Potentially, these effects could be positive. For example, the troubles in Zimbabwe have shifted tourist business for the Victoria Falls to the Zambian side of the river. However, the more likely effects are negative. We have estimated the effects to neighbors and find that they are indeed predominantly negative (Chauvet et al. 2006). The approach we used was again standard, although care has to be taken to distinguish those neighborhood effects that have nothing to do with war from war itself: For example, a neighborhood might be affected in common by a drought, as in Southern Africa during the mid-1990s. We find, unsurprisingly, that the costs to any particular neighbor are considerably less than the costs to the country itself. Typically, a country might lose around 0.9 percentage points off its growth rate if one of its neighbors is at war. However, the typical civil war country has three or more neighbors and further the economies of the neighboring countries are usually larger than that of the civil war country itself. This is because, as we will see, being small and poor are both risk factors. In our subsequent analysis we include only costs to immediate neighbors. However, this omits demonstrated adverse spill-over effects across a wider area. Murdoch and Sandler (2002) show that the adverse effects on growth permeate the entire sub-region, not just neighbors, perhaps due to reputation and trade effects. Even with the restriction to immediate neighbors, the numbers imply that the costs to the neighbors as a group are likely to be even larger than the costs

to the country at war. This has wide-ranging implications. Evidently, if most of the costs of a civil war accrue to neighbors then they have a strong interest in peace and may be seen as having legitimate rights in actions that encourage both conflict avoidance and the settlement of wars. Untrammelled national sovereignty may not be appropriate in these conditions.

While a rethinking of sovereignty evidently lies beyond the scope of the present chapter, the issue bears sufficiently on international strategies for limiting civil war that it warrants some discussion. The delineation of national sovereignty limits the set of strategies that are potentially available. Our key proposal, which is for a package of international interventions, rests on a view of what concept of sovereignty would be appropriate, and this in turn is based on the research reported here. Historically, the entire concept of national sovereignty arose out of the Thirty Years' War, largely because of a perception that whatever wrongs a government perpetrated on its own population they had little effect upon the wellbeing of other countries. At the time the concept was developed in the seventeenth century there were reasonable grounds for such a proposition: Economies and societies were not highly integrated. Nowadays, however, at least in the case of a civil war in a small country with many neighbors, the externalities are too large to be dismissed in this way. The United Nations has formulated a proposition known as the "responsibility to protect" which in effect suggests that the international community has the right to intervene to protect the citizens from their own government. Compared with that proposition, the notion that the neighbors of a country at risk of civil war have a right to protect their own citizens is surely modest. If the neighborhood externalities are approximately as large as the effects on the country itself, which is one of our results, then for sovereignty to be shared by the neighborhood would simply reflect a standard economic solution to the problem of how externalities should be internalized into the decision process.

While the costs of civil war are large and widespread, are they offset by gains to the society itself after the conflict is over? In particular, are there future political gains? Rebellion is often portrayed by its perpetrators as an investment in political liberation. At least implicitly, the costs are judged to be outweighed by the subsequent political benefits. Some civil wars, indeed, have such beneficial consequences that they surely outweigh the costs. However, the political legacy of civil war is on average depressing. Measured by political rights, the post-war period is usually worse than the pre-war one. Indeed, one troubling legacy that will particularly concern us is that the country becomes more rather than less prone to further civil war: Wars do not usually resolve political conflicts, but rather intensify them. It is thus hard to view civil wars as on average generating benefits anywhere commensurate with their costs. This may raise the question as to why, in that case, they occur. Are rebellions mistakes? In some cases, this indeed seems quite likely. For example, the terrible conflict raging in Western Sudan was triggered by a local rebellion. Regardless of the rights and wrongs of this rebellion, it is unthinkable that it has generated net benefits for the population on whose behalf the rebellion was ostensibly launched. In other cases, there may be a substantial divergence between those who launch the war and the mass of the population. Overwhelmingly, the costs of conflict accrue to those who have no influence over the decision to fight, including neighboring countries and those who are children at the time of the war. It is quite possible that the perpetrators of violence benefit from it, or have reasonable prospects of doing so, even if the overall net costs of conflict are enormous.

We now turn to the construction of an estimate for the cost of a civil war. Our starting point is the loss of growth to the country and its neighbors, as discussed above. Using the estimated reduction in growth of 2.2 percent, the average duration of conflict of seven years, and the gradual recovery post-conflict of 1.1 percent, we arrive at a present value of the cost of conflict to the country itself of 105 percent of one year's GDP, measured at the point of conflict onset. Similarly, the cost to each neighbor is 42 percent of one year's GDP.

In the study undertaken for the first Copenhagen Consensus on Conflicts (Collier and Hoeffler, 2004c), these numbers became the underpinnings of the estimate of the cost of conflict. For the present study we have access to better information. In particular, the data on post-conflict countries are greatly improved on those available four years ago. However, although there is now more evidence on the consequences of conflict, the growth effects used in that study continue to look reasonable. Our revision of those estimates is therefore confined to using new data on GDP, and on constructing GDP figures that pertain specifically to post-conflict countries and their neighbors. We thus multiply the percentage losses of GDP by the GDP of the typical post-conflict country at the onset of peace, and the typical sum of the GDP of the neighbors of post-conflict countries. The former cost, which is the cost to the country directly affected, is around $20 billion at PPP prices. The cost to neighbors is in aggregate around $23 billion. It is superficially surprising that the cost to neighbors is of the same order of magnitude as that to the country itself. However, despite the smaller proportionate impact upon their economies, the neighbors are more numerous, each country having several neighbors, and they are also typically larger and richer. Recall that conflict occurs disproportionately in small economies with very low incomes, so that it is to be expected these differences are systematic.

The combined cost of $43 billion is a little lower than the estimate of Collier and Hoeffler (2004c), which was for the expected cost of an initial civil war. The cost of war recurrence in post-conflict settings is lower than that estimate because the economies of post-conflict countries are systematically smaller than average. Collier and Hoeffler (2004c) then added an estimate for the costs of loss of life and DALYs. In our estimates we adopt two values for DALYs, namely $1,000 and $5,000. With a discount rate of 3 percent, these yield an additional cost of a civil war of $13 billion and $33 billion, respectively. We also estimate the figures using a 6 percent discount rate, yielding total war costs of $46 billion and $66 billion, respectively.

In addition to the loss of income and loss of life, civil wars divert expenditure into socially unproductive uses, notably military spending. During civil war military spending by the government increases by around 1.8 percentage points of GDP. This is evidently a lower bound since by its nature a civil war also involves military spending on the part of the rebel organization. Since there are usually no data on such spending this is not included. However, to give an indication of its likely scale, one middle-sized rebel group, the Tamil Tigers, are estimated to be spending around $350 million per year, almost exclusively on military activities. The typical civil war lasts for around seven years, so that the increase in military spending during the war amounts to around 10 percentage points of GDP allowing for discounting. Nor is this the end of the excess military spending resulting from civil war. During the post-conflict decade, domestic military spending typically remains high. Although it is reduced from its level during the war the reduction is typically only around a fifth of the war-induced increase. Hence, spending at around 1.5 percent of GDP in excess of normal during this decade is a further cost of around 8 percent. The total diversion of spending into military purposes resulting from the war is thus around 18 percent of a year's GDP, even if it is assumed that thereafter spending reverts to its initial level. Given our GDP figure of around $20 billion, this cost is around $3.6 billion.

Thus, the total cost of a typical civil war in a low-income country that has already experienced a war is around $58.6 billion. Over the entire period since 1960 there have been on average around two outbreaks of civil war each year, implying a running total cost of the order of $123 billion per year. To put this in perspective, the costs of civil wars are thus of the same order of magnitude as the global total of development aid. In recent years the number of outbreaks has been lower but, as discussed above, it is probably premature to see this as a new pattern.

Recall from the first section (p. 58) that these quantified costs omit other important considerations that are less readily quantified but may collectively make the quantified costs merely the tip of an iceberg. We suggested that for illustrative purposes a figure of $250 billion per war might be closer to the full costs and decided to work with both figures, the $59 billion figure being a lower bound.

The Causes of Civil War

Historians are still arguing about the cause of the First World War, and the typical civil war is likely to be no less complicated. Our aspirations in analyzing causality are more modest. We abstract completely from the immediate political antecedents to a civil war: The mistakes made by the government, the charisma of an opposition leader, the inflammatory statements and provocative actions on both sides. These are indeed in some sense the "causes" of the war. Instead, our focus is on the underlying conditions that make countries more or less prone to civil war. In some societies these conditions are so ripe that relatively small errors on the part of leaders ignite large-scale violence, whereas in others the conditions make civil war impossible regardless of what individual leaders do. Since 2001, several economists and political scientists have applied statistical analysis, usually logit regressions, to establish these underlying risk factors and the results have been published in reputable, peer-reviewed journals (Hegre et al. 2001; Fearon and Laitin 2003; Miguel et al. 2004; Collier and Hoeffler 2004a; Urdal 2006). These studies largely agree although around the margins there are, of course, many interesting differences and room for dispute. There are defensible alternative choices that can be made as to statistical method, data sources, the variables to be included, and the definitions of variables. In this chapter our analysis is based on the new work of Collier, Hoeffler, and Roemer (forthcoming; hereafter, CHR), which is a major update of Collier and Hoeffler (2004c), including a comprehensive coverage of wars and an array of robustness checks.

While in this chapter we need to know only about those risk factors that are potentially amenable to policy, it is nevertheless sensible to ground our analysis in a brief overview of the risk factors that this approach generates. This is especially the case since many people presume that they understand the causes of civil war simply from the accumulated accounts of them given in newspapers. Such accounts generally amplify the discourse of ethnic grievance disseminated by the parties to the conflict, each seeking to justify its actions to an international audience. Rebellion is usually justified by its perpetrators in terms both of historic wrongs and current atrocities. These claims often have sufficient basis in fact to be credible, but they fall far short of actually explaining the occurrence of the conflict.

We find that three economic characteristics make a country particularly prone to civil war: A low level of income, a low rate of growth, and a structure of income in which primary commodity exports constitute a substantial, but not overwhelming, proportion. Hence, those countries with all three of these characteristics – low-income, slow-growing, and dependent upon primary commodity exports – are decidedly at risk. In addition to these economic factors, social factors also matter. Societies that have a small population, those with many ethnic divisions, those that are mountainous, and those with a high proportion of youth, are at risk. "Small is dangerous" only in the sense that if the same territory is split up into more and more countries the overall risk that somewhere on the territory there will be a civil war goes up sharply. It is not the case that a small society literally has a higher risk than a big society. These are not the only factors that are important. Others that are pertinent for policy will be discussed in the next section.

CHR conclude from their results that the most reasonable interpretation of the risks of civil war is the "feasibility hypothesis." This is that in the relatively unusual conditions under which civil war is militarily and financially feasible there is a very high probability that it will occur, although the specific agenda of the rebel group (or often groups) is indeterminate.

The quantitative analysis of proneness to civil war, which can be thought of as a diagnosis, provides some basis for both prognosis and pre-scription. The latter is the focus of this chapter: What international interventions look to have promise as strategies to reduce the incidence of civil war, and how do their likely prospective benefits compare to their costs? This is the subject of the third part of the chapter, where we focus upon a particular set of strategies for reducing conflict, namely international military intervention. Our reason for this choice of focus is primarily that it is currently the policy area where popular opinion is most in need of being informed by fresh evidence. Clearly, the experience of Iraq 2 has massively reduced both the willingness of citizens of developed countries to countenance military intervention in developing countries, and reduced the legitimacy of such interventions in the eyes of the governments of developing countries. In effect, though for different reasons, international opinion resembles its state in the wake of the withdrawal from Somalia: Never intervene. Yet our research suggests that it is possible to delineate situations in which military intervention would be beneficial. Our contribution is thus intended in part to rehabilitate the concept of international military intervention from the highly particular circumstances of Iraq 2.

Even so, we wish to emphasize that we see such intervention very much as a "last-resort" solution. To date, much greater emphasis has been placed upon the prevention of violent conflict by means of creating the conditions for political legitimacy. In practice, this has meant the promotion of democracy. Clearly, if the establishment of democratic forms of government substantially reduces the risk of political violence then it is both a more attractive and a less costly solution than any military-based strategy. However, so attractive is the democratic approach that its efficacy has, perhaps, been assumed, or "derived" from some equally attractive foundation assumptions as to the basis for citizen loyalty to government. Nevertheless, that democracy reduces the incidence of political violence remains, in the end, a proposition the validity of which depends upon empirical evidence. The proposition has been tested in Hegre (2003) and Collier and Rohner

(2008). They find that systematically, across a wide range of measures of political violence, and across different structural models of the risk of civil war, democracy has an ambiguous effect. In particular, they find that below a threshold level of income democracy significantly increases the risk of violence whereas above the threshold it has the opposite effect. Thus, in low-income countries democracy seems not to be the key solution to political violence, and indeed seems likely to intensify the problem of maintaining peace. Collier and Rohner (2008) suggest that the explanation for these results may be that democracy has two opposing effects. Its legitimacy effect, whereby citizens accept the authority of an elected government, may be stronger in societies that are more educated or have other characteristics commonly associated with higher levels of income. Offsetting this, democracy makes government repression more difficult, and while this is in itself an attractive consequence of democracy, it might weaken a strategy of maintaining the peace that governments in low-income countries find particularly effective. This form of security, sometimes referred to as "the peace of the zoo," might nevertheless have some attractions if the alternative is civil war. There is some evidence that it is effective at least against some forms of political violence, and that democracy curtails resort to repression. However, these are not exhaustive explanations. Neither we nor Collier and Rohner (2008) mean to imply by these results that democracy is inappropriate for low-income countries. Rather, our argument is that the comfortable belief that the genuinely high security risks facing small, low-income countries with particular social and geographic characteristics can be resolved purely by political means is probably not well founded. The evidence points to the need for international interventions to address these security concerns.

Even if this is accepted it does not imply that international military intervention is an appropriate form of international assistance. Recent quantitative research suggests that two types of international intervention have promise: Economic and military. The key economic interventions are aid, supportive trade policies, and the promulgation of standards and codes pertinent for the specific characteristics of risk-prone countries such as the management of natural resource revenues. These were the main focus of our previous Copenhagen Consensus paper (Collier and Hoeffler 2004c), and we continue to regard them as important.

Prognosis

While prescription is our goal, prognosis is also pertinent. If other developments in the global economy and polity are in any case gradually reducing the incidence of civil war then the problem may not require the scarce commodity of global cooperation. Unfortunately, three major recent international developments have raised the risk of new outbreaks of civil war.

One development is the commodity booms and the consequent discovery of valuable resources in fragile states. Both the analysis of CHR and that of Fearon and Laitin (2003) suggest that this will tend to increase risks of violence. A recent example is the extraction of oil from Chad, which came on stream in 2004 and can credibly be linked to both rebellion and coup attempts in the following year. Oil discoveries are proliferating in "fragile" states, because high prices have boosted exploration and politically difficult territories are the major remaining unexploited areas. For example, in 2007 oil was discovered beneath the lake between Uganda and the DRC, an area that has already suffered substantial violence and where the border is ill defined. In addition to the consequences of new discoveries, there are also concerns over the long-term consequences of high commodity prices for economic development. If there is a "resource curse," then the damage done to the economy will itself increase the risk of conflict. Collier and Goderis (2007a, 2007b) use a cointegration approach to investigate the short- and long-run effects of high commodity prices on the growth of commodity exporters. They base their analysis on global data for the period 1970–2003. They find that for the first few years high commodity prices significantly boost the growth of constant price GDP, so that income is augmented both directly by terms of trade improvement and indirectly through the growth of output. However, after this initial boost most countries experience sustained and substantial economic contraction: There is indeed a powerful "resource curse." Simulating the present commodity booms in Africa, they project an eventual decline in constant price GDP relative to the counterfactual by around 25 percent. The decline is not inevitable but is contingent upon initial levels of governance. "Governance" is a slippery concept to measure, but they use data from the International Country Risk Guide (ICRG). An advantage of this measure is that it is a long-standing commercial service that, since companies continue to buy it, can be presumed to have some informational content. So measured, a commodity exporter with good governance, such as Norway, completely avoids the resource curse and grows as a result of the boom in both the short term and the long term. The critical level below which governance is not adequate to harness the long-term growth potential of commodity rents is unfortunately rather high – around that of Portugal in the mid-1980s. Most of the low-income countries currently experiencing commodity booms have standards of governance well below this level. Both the scale of the current commodity booms and these research results on the resource curse vindicate the proposal made in the previous Copenhagen Consensus paper on Conflicts (Collier and Hoeffler 2004c) to support the Extractive Industries Transparency Initiative (EITI), an international attempt to improve the standards of governance of resource revenues. While the proposal was not prioritized by the Expert Panel of judges, the international community subsequently indeed decisively scaled up EITI. In 2007 it turned what had begun as a small NGO campaign into an official international organization headquartered in Oslo. Our concern here, however, is not to revive this former proposal but simply to note the likely consequences of the commodity booms for the global incidence of conflict and hence guide the prioritization of conflict among the other competing claims on international resources.

The second development is the large number of recently negotiated peace settlements. While these are at least in the short term a triumph of international diplomacy research, both quantitative and qualitative, finds that negotiated settlements have historically faced a high risk of relapse (Walter 2001; Nilsson 2008). This implication of the recent spate of international settlements of disputes should, however, be qualified: While a pessimistic prognosis is entirely reasonable on the historical data, an alternative optimistic interpretation would be that the new international political will to prevent civil war has decisively changed behavior.

The third development is the proliferation of democracy across low-income states since the 1990s. Most low-income countries are now at least partially democratic. As already discussed, Collier and Rohner (2008) find that this seems likely to increase rather than reduce the incidence of civil war, and similar concerns about democracy in low-income countries is much more general in the political science literature. The specific results of Collier and Rohner (2008) are consistent with previous research by Hegre (2003), while other political scientists propose that the problem arises because intermediate levels of democracy ("anocracy") are more dangerous than autocracy. Collier, Hoeffler, and Soderbom (2008; hereafter, CHS) examine the consequences of elections in post-conflict situations for the continuing maintenance of peace. Their general analysis of post-conflict risks is discussed more fully in a subsequent section, so here we focus purely on this particular result. They find that post-conflict elections have systematic effects on risk, but they are not particularly encouraging. Although in the year prior to the election the risk of reversion to conflict falls sharply, in the year after the election it increases even more sharply, so that the net effect is risk-increasing. Recent research has also investigated whether elections in low-income countries with very poor economic policies and governance accelerate or retard the process of reform (Chauvet and Collier 2007, 2008). It finds that the overall effects are ambiguous, but that echoing the specifically conflict-related concerns about "anocracy," semi-democracy retards reform even relative to its slow pace under autocracy. There is also both micro and macro evidence that commodity booms and democracy interact adversely. Vicente (2006) compares São Tomé and Cap Verde, two similar islands off the West African coast, both formerly Portuguese. The discovery of oil in São Tomé creates a "natural experiment." Vicente (2006) shows that following the oil discovery government corruption rapidly increased in São Tomé relative to that in Cap Verde. Collier and Hoeffler (2008) investigate the macro-statistical interaction of democracy and natural resource rents using global data. They find that whereas in the absence of resource rents democracy improves economic performance, with large resource rents democracy substantially worsens it. In effect, instead of democracy disciplining the use of resource rents, the rents undermine the functioning of democracy. The critical level of resource rents above which democracy has adverse effects is around 8 percent of GDP, so that the current resource booms have lifted many low-income resource exporters well above this threshold.

These three major recent developments – the commodity boom, negotiated settlements, and democratization – are between them likely to change the global incidence of conflict. In the short term, the evidence on the ground is that there has been a change for the better, but it would probably be unreasonably optimistic to conclude from this that the problem of conflict was no longer a priority. As we have seen, on the whole the analytic literature suggests that each of these three developments is liable to increase the incidence of conflict rather than reduce it, although their short-term effects may be benign. CHR test whether recent favorable developments mark a significant sea-change in the incidence of global conflict. Their model of civil war investigates the entire period 1965–2004, and they introduce a dummy variable for the sub-period 2000–4 into their analysis of risk. They find that it is insignificant: Their results suggest that the improvements during the sub-period were explicable in terms of the variables

included in the model, rather than reflecting some omitted political development. This suggests that without more effective international intervention, internal violent conflict is likely to continue to be a substantial problem for low-income societies in coming decades and thus warrants our concern and attention.

Coups

There have been over 200 coup attempts just in Africa since the late 1970s. Coups continue to plague the region: for example, recent successful coups have occurred in Mauritania (2005) and the Central African Republic (CAR) (2003), a failed coup led to the present civil war in Côte d'Ivoire, and in 2006 there was another failed coup against the democratic government of Madagascar. The phenomenon has recently become researchable by quantitative techniques thanks to a comprehensive dataset compiled by McGowan (2003).

The Costs of Coups

Although coups are nothing like as costly as civil wars, they do generate costs in various forms.

One cost is the direct loss of income in the year of the coup due to the political disruption. Collier, Goderis, and Hoeffler (2006; hereafter, CGH) investigated these costs through a cointegration analysis of growth using global data from the period 1970–2003. CGH found that a coup significantly and substantially reduced growth in the year following the coup, by around 3 percentage points. It was not feasible to instrument for coups in this analysis and there is some potential risk of endogeneity: An exogenous growth collapse might indeed increase the risk of a coup. However, this effect would need to be very powerful to account for such a large apparent growth loss and the interpretation we place on the result here seems to us to be reasonable. CGH did not find the effects to be highly persistent: If the dependent variable was changed to growth over a decade a coup during the decade had no significant effect. Since the average coup would occur in the middle of the decade, this gives some guide to the likely evolution of the economy. In the first year following the coup (i.e. year 6) the economy would lose 3 percent relative to the counterfactual, but during years 7–10 it would fully recover this lost growth. Assuming the recovery to be linear and reached in year 10, on average over the four years following a coup GDP would be 1.5 percent below its counterfactual, implying a cumulative cost of around 6 percent of annual GDP.

A different cost of a coup is its consequences for military spending. There are two components to this cost. One, investigated by Collier and Hoeffler (2007a), is that a successful coup leads to a sharp increase in military spending. This is unsurprising: The coup leaders reward the army for its loyalty by expanding its budget. It is reasonable to think of this increase as a waste of public revenues. The increase is persistent: Military regimes tend to spend considerably more on the military than civilian regimes, even controlling for the risks of war and other factors which account for military spending. Were a coup to result in the maximum shift in regime type, from a fully democratic government to a severe autocracy, military spending would be persistently higher by around 2 percentage points of GDP. Coups never result in such sharp swings, although that in Burma may have come quite close depending on how the counterfactual evolution of the country is seen. Many coups simply replace one military dictator with another and so a more reasonable assessment of the persistent impact upon military spending is around 0.5 percentage points of GDP. If this loss persists for a decade, which is again within the reasonable range, then the cost after discounting would be around 4 percentage points of GDP. Note that this treats the excess military spending resulting from rule by the military as an indulgence. Since Collier and Hoeffler (2007c) estimate the effect on military spending controlling for the risk of conflict this is probably reasonable, although we should recognize the possibility that a higher level of military spending than that chosen by a civilian government could conceivably not be a social waste.

The other potential link between military spending and coups arises because where the risk of a coup is high governments try to reduce it by pre-emptively raising military spending. This is investigated in Collier and Hoeffler (2007a) who build a simultaneous model to disentangle the two-way causation between coups and military spending. They find that controlling for endogeneity, a high level of coup risk indeed significantly increases spending. However, the size of the effect is quite small and we omit it from our calculations.

Potentially, the risk of a coup has a chilling effect on economic performance, an effect that would be consistent with the adverse effects of "political instability" that are commonly found in the growth literature. However, CGH used the estimated coup risks generated by the above model to investigate the possibility and did not find coup risk to be significant in the growth process once the significant adverse effects of actual coups were included.

Like civil wars, coups could potentially be politically beneficial. Evidently, coup leaders routinely justify their actions in such terms. Besley and Kudamatsu (2007) have investigated what determines whether an autocratic government performs well or badly and has highlighted the importance of the ability to remove a leader in response to disaffection among the "selectariat." While it is indeed possible to find examples of coups which led to improved governance, this does not appear to be the general pattern. Collier and Hoeffler (2007a) find that a coup leads to a significantly higher risk of further coups. This is hardly surprising, since for the very process which attempts to legitimate a coup inadvertently legitimates a counter-coup. In unpublished work, Collier and Hoeffler also find that coups significantly increase the risk of civil war. This was, for example, the sequence in Côte d'Ivoire, until then "the jewel of Francophone Africa." On the basis of these statistical results there is some basis for concluding that coups, like civil wars, generally erode the political system. However, for our purposes we merely need to assume that the costs delineated above are not offset by political benefits to the society.

In summary, a successful coup d'état typically generates economic costs of the order of

10 percent of one year's GDP. In part, this is due to losses in output, and in part due to the diversion of output to useless military spending. For the typical small, coup-prone developing country, these costs amount to around $2 billion per successful coup. In Africa over the period 1956–2003 there were eighty-three successful coups, implying a cost of the order of $166 billion spread over the period, before discounting, or an annual average of around $4 billion. Costs of this order of magnitude are not large, measured on the scale of global concerns.

As with civil wars, before accepting this figure we should consider whether our quantification omits other important costs. The first omitted consideration in our quantification of civil wars was that the citizens of war-prone countries are the poorest and least hopeful on earth. As we shall see, this consideration carries over to coups because, like civil wars, they are more likely the lower is income and the slower is growth. In general, the other considerations that apply to civil wars do not carry over to coups: Their effects are not usually large and highly persistent, and they do not threaten the existence value of a society. They do, however, often have one further cost: Almost by definition a coup ushers in a military government. Sometimes the government that is replaced was itself a military government, but sometimes a coup indeed replaces a democratic regime by the military. As argued by Azam (1994), democracy should surely be seen as having some value over and above its consequences for macroeconomic performance. Hence, such coups are intrinsically undesirable. Should the international community attach any negative value to regime change from democratic to military rule? Manifestly, part of the justification for the hugely expensive intervention in Iraq was to induce regime change in the opposite direction and there was also a huge international effort to support the transition to democracy in Eastern Europe. Hence, the international community certainly behaves in a manner consistent with an assignment of some positive value to democracy as opposed to military rule. We thus have two large omitted considerations, the atypically poor

circumstances of coup-prone countries, and the non-economic costs generated by the replacement of democracy by military rule. Again, one approach is to ignore these considerations and treat the figure of $2 billion per coup as the lower bound. Alternatively, we can scale up this lower bound by an adjustment factor. We previously suggested that the order of magnitude adjustment for the fact that citizens of countries prone to civil war were particularly poor was to double the lower bound, and these arguments carry over to coups. What, if any, allowance should be made for the intrinsic value of democracy? Again, we propose that a reasonable adjustment is to double the estimate. This is because the economic costs of a coup are modest so that even doubling does not place a very high intrinsic value on democracy. As an example of how the transition between democracy and military dictatorship is now valued, consider Nigeria. When the military regime that had ruled Nigeria for fifteen years was replaced by President Obasanjo, the event was treated within Nigeria as a national triumph and globally as a giant step forward for Africa. Allowing for these two adjustments would produce a cost of a typical successful coup at around $8 billion, or an average cost to Africa over the period 1965–2003 of around $16 billion. One way of "truth-testing" this figure is to pose the direct question: "What would it have been worth, both to Africa itself and to the international community, for Africa to have been free of coups?" For us, the figure of $16 billion is at least within the sensible range of answers. A figure double this would imply that being coup-free would have been broadly commensurate with the entire international aid program to Africa, which seems excessive, whereas a figure half of it would begin to marginalize the problem that Africa's main form of political change has been military. As with civil wars, we thus have a reasonably hard lower bound figure, namely $4 billion per year, and a highly approximate attempt at a figure more representative of the centre of the range, $16 billion per year. As with civil wars, the reader is left with the choice between them.

Even if the cost of coups has been of the order

of $16 billion per year, the cost is not large relative to some other global problems. However, coups have one potentially interesting feature for the international community. Those governments subject to coup risk naturally consider the threat of a coup to be of vital concern. In Africa, setting aside death in office from natural causes, coups have been by far the most frequent reason for changes of regime, dwarfing the number of changes due to either elections or rebellions. Hence, governments have a strong interest in cooperating with strategies that significantly reduce this risk. We will suggest that this may open up interesting possibilities for packaging international interventions.

Causes of Coups

What makes a government particularly prone to a coup d'état? Collier and Hoeffler (2007a) find that low *per capita* income significantly and substantially increases risks. At the mean of other variables, halving income increases the risk by 35 percent. This has the important implication that exposure to coups is concentrated among the poorest countries. Growth also affects coup risk, but although the effect is statistically significant it is small. As noted, coups beget further coups. This result is not merely picking up a fixed effect since the heightened coup risk fades with time.

Since coups are political events it would seem likely that they are determined primarily by the political context. In particular, we might expect that autocratic regimes are more prone to coups than democratic regimes. Unfortunately, the data do not bear this out. Collier and Hoeffler (2007a) search for a significant break point along the range of the Polity IV classification of political regimes, the range being from −10 (severe autocracy) to +10 (impeccable democracy). They find that there is only one such break point, namely at −5, this demarcating highly repressive regimes as opposed to less repressive regimes. Unfortunately, far from the extreme autocracies facing a higher risk of coups, they face a markedly lower risk: Repression works. The effect is large, repression halving the risk

at the means of other variables. An implication of this is that governments cannot defend themselves from coups simply by democratizing: Democratic governments face higher risks.

Prognosis

Again we briefly turn to prognosis. How important are coups likely to be in the future? The higher risk due to democracy suggests that coups may continue to occur. However, unlike civil wars, there is a favorable time trend: Coups have gradually been going out of fashion. As noted, they have by no means disappeared. But their gradually declining incidence suggests that there may be a moment when "eradication" is possible, at least at the regional level.

Four Military-Related Instruments

To summarize so far, over the past forty years civil wars have on average cost a lower-bound estimate of around $117 billion per year, with a center-of-the-range illustrative estimate of around $500 billion per year; the corresponding costs for coups have been around a further $4 billion per year (lower bound) to $16 billion (illustrative center-of-the-range). These costs have fallen systematically upon the poorest and slowest-growing countries in the world: The "bottom billion." The costs considerably exceed the aid flows that these countries have received over this period: Even the lower bounds are broadly commensurate with total aid flows, but a considerable proportion of this aid has accrued to countries that are at income levels above this bottom group. The prognosis for coups is encouraging: They are becoming less common, most probably because they are increasingly seen as illegitimate by the international community. However, we should note that this very process implies that the cost of those coups that still occur is greater since the lost democracy is valued more highly. The prognosis for civil wars is more confused: The short-term evidence on the ground is encouraging, but three important longer-term influences are all adverse.

The case for concern about political violence is three-fold. Partly, as the above numbers show, the economic costs are substantial. Second, as our discussion in the Overview emphasized, the lower-bound numbers are probably far below the true costs. In particular, the costs are concentrated upon the poorest people on earth, and without secure peace it is difficult to help them in other ways. Further, global peace is increasingly seen by many people as having an intrinsic value over and above its measurable economic benefits. While it is important that such vague sentiments are not allowed to over-ride well-founded quantification, it may suggest that large-scale violence has some negative "existence value" that, while not infinite, is substantial. This was, indeed, to an extent the sentiment of the previous Copenhagen Consensus Expert Panel: They described the eradication of violent conflict as being of fundamental value, if only instruments could be found that were demonstrably effective.

We now turn from the objectives to the instruments. In the Copenhagen Consensus paper on Conflicts (Collier and Hoeffler 2004c), the main instruments considered were development aid and the promulgation of international standards for the governance of natural resource revenues. The Expert Panel was generally skeptical of the efficacy of aid. The promulgation of governance standards incurred very little cost and its benefits were at that time highly speculative, so that the strategy did not lend itself to the calculation of a cost-benefit ratio.

In the present chapter, we have narrowed the focus to two types of violent conflict that we see as preventable – namely, the recurrence of civil war in post-conflict situations, and the prevention of coups in countries that are at least partially democratic. We have also narrowed the range of instruments, focusing in particular upon various military strategies. Our focus on military strategies is partly because in one sense these are the most "natural" strategies with which to counter large-scale political violence. If civil wars and coups are to be discouraged, quite possibly force needs to be opposed by force. The other reason for our focus on military strategies is, as we have discussed, that the war in Iraq

and the immense attention that it has attracted have come to dominate thinking on military intervention. Yet the invasion of Iraq and the subsequent military engagement have both been highly peculiar. Although Iraq is often described as a post-conflict situation, it is not analogous to the post-conflict period following a civil war in a low-income country which is both the core phenomenon addressed in this chapter and the most common conflict risk, globally. The 2003 war in Iraq was manifestly not a civil war but an international war. The situation since April 2004 has had combat-related mortality rates arising out of organized internal violence against an incumbent government that are well above the threshold for classification as a civil war, albeit one that is partially internationalized. Hence, citizen opinion as to the likely efficacy of international military intervention has been powerfully shaped by an experience that is irrelevant to the core security problem of small, low-income societies. Whether or not such intervention is sometimes a useful, cost-effective instrument, is a matter for analysis. This chapter attempts such analysis. We are not concerned to advocate military intervention. However, the need for a dispassionate analysis of its potential efficacy seems to us to be much stronger now than at the planning stage of the first Copenhagen Consensus.

We are going to investigate three international strategies that focus on military provision. The first strategy is the attempt to change the size of the domestic military establishment chosen by a government; we will focus particularly on post-conflict governments. The second strategy is to provide military services internationally, generally but not exclusively as peacekeepers under the auspices of the United Nations. The third strategy is to offer guarantees of external military provision should circumstances require it.

International Curtailment of Domestic Military Spending

The level of military spending chosen by the government of a country facing a risk of a civil war or a coup d'état is sometimes either higher or lower than international actors would prefer. For example, in Uganda during the 1990s the major aid agencies tried to induce the government to reduce its military spending. Conversely, foreign governments sometimes provide either arms or finance to bolster a government's capacity to fight an insurrection, an example being US military support to the government of Colombia. These attempts at changing the level of spending chosen by a government raise two important questions: Is such a change desirable, and if so, is external influence effective? Here we consider the first of these questions. The efficacy of intervention is deferred until the next section.

Evidently, the case for curtailment or support must be made on a case-by-case basis, but does research give any guide as to the likely effect of military spending by a government on the risk of internal conflict? Since our interest is specifically in post-conflict situations, this is the context on which we focus. Military spending in low-income countries has been the subject of some substantial published quantitative studies (Dunne and Perlo-Freeman 2003; Collier and Hoeffler 2007c). They find that the level of military spending chosen by a government is systematically explicable in terms of the threats that it faces, the domestic pressure groups, and the ability of the government to finance public spending. Collier and Hoeffler (2007c) are able to show that governments indeed significantly and substantially increase their military spending in response to the risk of civil war, objectively measured. This is consistent with the pattern we discussed above when estimating the cost of a civil war: Post-conflict governments usually fail to reduce their military spending back to peacetime levels. Thus, the high level of post-conflict military spending is at least in part a response to the recognition that the post-conflict risk of conflict reversion is high.

In effect, post-conflict governments are operating on the hypothesis that high military spending in this situation is risk-reducing. While this is *a priori* plausible, it is no more than a hypothesis. Collier and Hoeffler (2007c) set out a counter-hypothesis, rooted in a game-theoretic analysis of why in post-conflict situations

military spending might have an unintended adverse effect. Their key point is to consider the decision as to whether to revert to violence from the perspective of those outside the post-conflict government. Typically, as part of the peace settlement, this group will have been given various undertakings as to post-conflict policies: In effect, they will have been promised some share in government revenues. Sometimes this will be highly explicit, as in the settlement of the conflict in southern Sudan, at other times it will be largely implicit. In either case, there is a potential time consistency problem. As the peace persists, the capacity of the rebel party to maintain its military forces gradually declines. The rebels may then reasonably fear that there will come a point at which the government revokes its commitments and uses its now-superior military force to crush its opponents. Fearing this, the rebels may decide to pre-empt this risk by returning to conflict. An example of such a sequence is the post-election shoot-out between the forces of the opposition and the government in the DRC in November 2006. In this instance, the rebels left the return to violence too late for success and their leader had to go into exile. Thus, the key rebel decision problem is to determine the intentions of the government: Will it renege on its commitments? The rebels thus face a "screening" problem of trying to distinguish genuine commitment from lies. In turn, if the government is indeed genuinely committed to maintaining its promises, it faces a problem of how to establish this fact, given that anything it says could also be said by a government that was trying to dupe the rebels, and that the environment is one of intense hatreds and suspicions. In other words, the genuinely committed government faces a "signaling problem": What action can it take that would reveal its type? As in the standard theory of signaling, such a government needs to find an action that, were it not genuinely committed, it would simply refuse to do. Only such an action cannot be imitated and so it reveals the government's true type. A substantial reduction in government military spending may well be such a signal. It has two advantages. One is that it directly bears upon rebel fears of rule by oppression. The other is that it is difficult to reverse: Once the military is scaled down it would take time to rebuild it. Hence, a deep cut in military spending might well signal that the government is committed to maintaining an inclusive style of government and so reassure opponents sufficiently that they do not return to violence.

In principle, either of these hypotheses could be correct. They are tested in Collier and Hoeffler (2006). The evident problem with such an investigation is that because military spending is endogenous to risk, an apparent relationship from military spending to risk is likely to be spurious. High levels of spending may appear to cause high levels of risk when in fact causality is the other way round. In order to control for endogeneity and establish a clear causal relationship, it is therefore necessary to instrument for military spending. Fortunately, because military spending is systematically predictable by a range of variables, it is possible to find valid instruments that strongly influence chosen levels of spending but do not influence the risk of civil war. Once military spending is instrumented, Collier and Hoeffler (2006) find that its effect on the risk of conflict is distinctive in post-conflict situations. Their key result is that in post-conflict situations, but only those situations, government military spending is significantly and substantially counter-productive. This is consistent with the prediction of the screening–signaling theory: It is only in the post-conflict situation that the opposition has an established military capacity which is in decline, and some explicit or implicit understanding with the government that helped to conclude the civil war.

If it is correct, this is evidently an important result. An implication would be that post-conflict government are operating on precisely the wrong theory of risk reduction and inadvertently aggravating rather than reducing it. In turn, it would suggest that international actors would in general be right to discourage spending to the extent that they have the scope to do so and so open the question of the efficacy of such interventions.

To investigate the robustness of the Collier and Hoeffler (2006) results we undertook an entirely fresh analysis, using both an improved methodology and expanded data. Whereas Collier and Hoeffler (2006) relied upon a logit analysis of risk during five-year periods, the subsequent paper on post-conflict risks by CHS switched to the more continuous approach of hazard functions. As discussed further below, in our re-analysis of the CHS model for the present study we therefore included domestic military spending, instrumented as in Collier and Hoeffler (2006) as an explanatory variable. This was potentially quite a severe test due both to the change in approach and the expansion of the dataset. In fact, domestic military spending, as instrumented, continued to be both statistically significant and adverse, substantially increasing the risk of further conflict.

We now use these results to quantify the costs of high post-conflict military spending by the government. The costs are normally measured simply at face value: That is, if the government spends $100 million extra on the military, this is typically seen by external actors as a waste that has an opportunity cost of $100 million. Our point here is to demonstrate that if both the present results and the Collier and Hoeffler (2006) results are approximately right, then this is a gross under-estimate of their true costs. For the typical post-conflict country an additional $100 million of military spending would increase the military budget by 0.5 percentage points of GDP. This in turn would increase the risk of conflict reversion by 2.56 percentage points. Applying our previous estimates of the costs of a civil war to the post-conflict country and to its neighbors, this additional risk incurs lower-bound costs of $1.5 billion, and center-of-the-range costs of around $6.3 billion. Thus, the government spending of $100 million generates additional costs of the order of $6.3 billion: The concealed and inadvertent costs are of the order of sixty times the apparent costs.

Thus, in post-conflict situations, domestic military spending has very high and largely inadvertent costs. This creates some basis for international actors to attempt to curtail it to the extent that they have instruments that are efficacious. We will investigate this in the next section.

While the "true" costs may seem very high, we have actually chosen not to include a further layer of costs which come from neighborhood "arms races." Collier and Hoeffler (2007c) establish that typically one influence upon military spending is the amount spent by neighbors, although the motive for emulation need not be that of a perceived threat. For example, it could simply be that the military in each country uses the spending increases of neighbors as an effective means of lobbying its ministry of finance. The resulting interdependence of military spending generates an arms race multiplier. In effect, the excessive military spending of post-conflict countries induces increases in the military spending of their neighbors that diverts public spending from productive uses. As long as these neighbors are not themselves post-conflict, there is no adverse effect on the risk of conflict: The aggravation of risk is confined to post-conflict situations. Nevertheless, in effect excess military spending by one country is a neighborhood public bad, in that it induces this expenditure diversion.

Expanding the Role of Peacekeeping Forces

International peacekeeping in post-conflict situations is now a major activity with a high political profile in both developed and developing countries. This is precisely the type of policy for which a quantitative analysis can add value to decisions because, in its absence, decisions are liable to be highly politicized. In particular, following the experience of post-conflict peacekeeping in Iraq, there is little appetite in developed countries for sending troops into post-conflict situations, and little belief in their likely success. Conversely, in part of Africa the Department of Peacekeeping Operations (DPKO) of the United Nations is increasingly seen as the "new IMF" – that is, a challenge to untrammelled domestic sovereignty. Yet Iraq may be a very misleading basis for understanding post-conflict peacekeeping. Recall that Iraq was not a peacekeeping operation following a civil war, but rather an international war that, after a brief interval, has triggered an ongoing civil war. Similarly, the notion of untrammelled national sovereignty in the face of high risks of further conflict may need to be challenged in view of the high costs that conflicts inflict upon neighborhoods.

Peacekeeping interventions have become very much more common since the end of the Cold War. Currently there are 100,000 uniformed personnel serving in UN peacekeeping operations in sixteen countries.

Guaranteeing Security from "Over the Horizon"

The supply of effective peacekeeping troops is limited. A simple way of economizing on them is to base them in their home countries but to provide "over-the-horizon" guarantees of rapid intervention should this be necessary. The initial British military intervention in Sierra Leone has evolved since 2000 into a variant which is potentially a particularly interesting security technology, namely an "over-the-horizon" guarantee. The British government has withdrawn all but a token military force in Sierra Leone, but has made a ten-year commitment to fly troops back into the country should there be any security need. Sierra Leone has continued to be peaceful under this guarantee, but evidently in any particular instance it is not possible to establish the likely counterfactual: Possibly peace would have been maintained even without any commitment.

The British over-the-horizon guarantee reinvents and refines a much older strategy of the French government, which, until the late 1990s provided a less explicit security safeguard for the whole of Francophone Africa. For over thirty years, from the early 1960s until the late 1990s, the French government provided security cover to Francophone governments in Africa that, while less than a guarantee, was nevertheless credible because it was backed by a chain of French military bases around the region.

The ending of the French policy can be clearly dated: It began with the onset of the genocide in Rwanda. French troops had been stationed in the country to protect the government, and this presence came dangerously close to propping up the regime as it began the genocide, only just being terminated in time to avoid accusations of complicity. Following this, French government policy was rethought, its first important manifestation being the reaction to the coup d'état in Côte d'Ivoire in December 1999. The "old guard" within the French government advised the president to use French military forces to put down the coup, as would previously have been standard. However, the president decided that this would be inconsistent with France's new policy and so decided not to authorize intervention. This marks the clear end to the French informal security quasi-guarantee.

The subsequent history of Côte d'Ivoire suggests that the French withdrawal of a security guarantee was very costly. The country descended into prolonged civil war that necessitated French military intervention to police a security zone between the warring sides. Paradoxically, the British government reinvention of the policy of a security guarantee occurred shortly after the French had abandoned it.

A priori, an international security guarantee may be either more or less effective than actually maintaining peacekeeping troops on the ground, country-by-country. An over-the-horizon guarantee has two major cost advantages over country-by-country peacekeeping. First, for most of the time most of the troops can be kept in their home country, which is far cheaper than maintaining them in-country. For example, the British have only eighty troops actually in Sierra Leone but could fly in a large force overnight and did so during the onset of Operation Palliser. Second, the same force can guarantee security in several different countries. Since these risks are unlikely to be called simultaneously, a pooled central force can provide a far larger potential presence when it is actually needed. This is, incidentally, consistent with the result discussed previously that the risk of civil war within a given geographic area is reduced

as the number of countries is reduced: There are security economies of scale. CHS find that it is the absolute scale of the force that matters, as opposed to troops per head of population, and so pooling can actually be more effective in deterring the recurrence of conflict than individual country-by-country forces that cannot be rapidly reinforced because neither the politics nor the logistics have been sorted out in advance. Thus, potentially, an over-the-horizon guarantee might be a considerably superior technology to conventional peacekeeping.

A CBA of Interventions to Reduce the Risk of Civil Wars and Coups

We now consider how military interventions and aid might be deployed in post-conflict situations so as to reduce risk, and how the costs of these interventions compare with the benefits. The analysis is complicated because several distinct interactions must be considered. We begin with aid provided in post-conflict situations. We choose this intervention for three reasons. First, compared to other forms of aid it is far more effective in reducing the risk of violent conflict. This qualification is important: Aid to post-conflict societies may or may not be more effective in poverty reduction than aid to other low-income societies. In general, it is likely to be the case that aid for the express purposes of poverty reduction is best highly targeted within a society. Similarly, aid to reduce mortality may best be targeted on activities such as the vaccination of infants. If, however, the objective is to reduce the risk of violent conflict, then post-conflict societies are the most appropriate focus because of their abnormally high risk of conflict. Recall that the typical post-conflict society has a risk of conflict reversion during the first decade of 40 percent. Other societies generally have risks far less than this. Nor is it possible to make actionable forecasts of differences in risks between such societies: The forecasts themselves would be highly uncertain and in any case could not be publicized to aid agencies. Further, as we will see, aid is more effective in the growth process post-conflict than in other situations. Thus, the case for as an instrument for security is at its most powerful in the post-conflict context. Our second reason for focusing on post-conflict aid is that it is the least controversial type of security intervention. In contrast, military intervention in any form is now highly controversial. Because of this, aid for post-conflict situations constitutes a useful benchmark. If it is more cost-effective than military interventions then it dominates them both in economic terms and politically. If it is less cost-effective then potentially there is a trade-off between effectiveness and political acceptability. Our third reason is that, as we will argue, aid can complement other interventions, forming a more effective package.

The Benchmark Intervention: The Instrument of Post-Conflict Aid

Post-conflict aid is the main non-military instrument of maintaining peace available to the international community. It was indeed the initial rationale for aid, being the founding purpose for the World Bank, which was initially going to be called the International Bank for Reconstruction. The potential importance of post-conflict aid is increased by the evidence that political interventions such as democratic elections do not appear to be effective solutions to the post-conflict security challenge.

Whether aid is effective in reducing the risk of conflict reversion depends upon three steps. First, aid should be effective in the post-conflict growth process. Second, growth should be effective in bringing down post-conflict risks. Third, there should be no offsetting effect of aid that directly increases the risk of conflict.

We previously considered the instrument of post-conflict aid in the first Copenhagen Consensus. We now summarize the results of that work and discuss how those results need to be qualified in the light of more recent work.

Aid and Growth Post-Conflict

The effect of aid on growth has become considerably more contested since the original Collier and Hoeffler paper (2004c). In general there is increased skepticism as to the efficacy of aid although there have also been some high-quality research papers that have found evidence that aid-for-growth is effective. A useful "meta-study" by Doucouliagos and Paldam (2006) reviews some seventy underlying studies of the effect of aid, and from this the modal study finds small but positive effects. However, few studies focus specifically on aid in the post-conflict context. There are good reasons to expect that aid might be less problematic in such situations. Unlike the normal aid relationship, there is no serious "moral hazard" problem. That is, no society is likely to be tempted into civil war by the prospect of post-conflict aid: The costs are simply too high relative to the likely returns. Further, the devastation of infrastructure during war opens obvious opportunities for high-return aid investments. For example, in Uganda the restoration of rural roads by World Bank projects shortly after the end of the civil war in the late 1980s is estimated to have had an annual rate of return of 40 percent.

At the time of the first Copenhagen Consensus the only quantitative study of aid in the post-conflict growth process was that of Collier and Hoeffler (2004b). The detailed results of that paper were summarized in Appendix 3 of their Copenhagen Consensus paper (2004c), and will not be repeated here. They found that during the first post-conflict decade growth is typically faster than normal. That is, there is some economic recovery. Indeed, this result has been fundamental to subsequent estimates of the cost of civil war because the recovery limits the post-conflict costs: Eventually the economy reverts to the level of economic activity without the conflict. While the result that there is a growth recovery massively reduces the estimated cost of a civil war, it is also the foundation for the evidence that post-conflict aid is effective. Collier and Hoeffler (2004c) find that the pace of post-conflict growth is determined partly by the quality of economic policies and governance, and partly by the volume of aid. In particular, they find that, compared with aid in societies that are not post-conflict, aid is considerably more effective in raising growth.

Although this chapter was reputably published, in view of the considerable skepticism relating to aid and the small sample available for that study it is important to consider whether there is further statistical evidence. Three studies specifically focused on aid and economic performance in post-conflict situations have subsequently been published. Elbadawi *et al.* (2008) incorporate effects of aid via the real exchange rate and use a much larger sample of post-conflict countries. Their focus on the real exchange rate reflects recent concerns that aid might inadvertently kill the growth process through generating "Dutch disease": Destroying the competitiveness of exports. An influential paper by Rajan and Subramanian (2005) provides some evidence for these concerns. Incorporating these real exchange rate effects, Elbadawi *et al.* (2008) indeed find that there is an adverse effect of aid via real appreciation. However, crucially for present purposes, they also find that this effect is much weaker in post-conflict situations so that aid is substantially and significantly more effective than normal. In part this may be because exporting is in any case likely to be limited in post-conflict economies. Typically the recovery of exports is confined to mineral extraction, which is not very sensitive to concerns about the real exchange rate. Adam, Collier, and Davies (2008; hereafter, ACD) focus on the consequences of conflict for inflationary financing. Unsurprisingly, they find that during civil wars governments resort to money-printing and heavy implicit taxation of the financial system. During civil war the typical government has its back to the wall and is desperate for revenue, even from sources that are so damaging in the long term that normally it would not adopt them. Further, these sources of finance may be the only options because, far more than in the case of international war, external sources of borrowing dry up. There is abundant evidence that inflation and severe financial repression are indeed both damaging to long-term growth. In effect, during conflict economic policy is in crisis mode. During the post-conflict period governments are faced with hard choices. There are large demands on spending, while tax revenues have been reduced

by both economic decline and the retreat of activity into subsistence. ACD (2008) show that, in the absence of aid, governments resolve this dilemma by persisting with inflationary financing, thereby delaying the recovery of confidence in the currency and the restoration of the financial system. ACD (2008) find that aid is used distinctively by governments in post-conflict situations: It resolves this dilemma and is used by governments to abandon the deficit financing strategy. Finally, Davies (forthcoming) investigates capital flight during and after civil war. Capital flight is a major macroeconomic phenomenon in the countries most prone to conflict. McIndoe (2007) updates the published estimates of capital flight by Collier, Hoeffler, and Pattillo (2001) and estimates that as of 2004 around 36 percent of Africa's private wealth was outside the region. Consistent with other studies, Davies finds that capital flight increases both during civil war and during the post-conflict period. His important contribution is to analyze what determines capital flight during the post-conflict period, and in particular to what extent this is distinctive. He finds that in the post-conflict period capital flight is significantly and substantially more sensitive to inflation than in other superficially similar but peaceful situations. Possibly the explanation for this heightened sensitivity is that asset holders are aware of the risks of conflict reversion and are looking for signals from their government of whether it is continuing to function in crisis mode or is taking a longer-term view. The government's choice of the inflation rate is thus a powerful, if inadvertent, signal of whether it is taking a long-term view. This result is important for present purposes because it evidently relates closely to that of ACD (2008) on the distinctively anti-inflationary effects of aid in post-conflict situations. In currently unpublished work, ACD combine these results and show that in the post-conflict context aid is substantially reinforced by the induced reduction in capital flight. This is a further macroeconomic reason why aid might have distinctively powerful growth effects in the post-conflict context.

Hence, in the post-conflict context, aid has an important, distinctive, and positive macroeconomic role which is not offset by the usual concerns about appreciation of the real exchange rate. While the evidence that aid raises growth in developing countries is generally somewhat weaker now than at the time of the first Copenhagen Consensus, the evidence that in the post-conflict context it raises growth has become stronger. Not only do supporting econometric results now exist, but the distinctive macroeconomic channels by which they might be explained are now much better understood. The coefficient on post-conflict aid estimated in Collier and Hoeffler (2004b) implies that the gain in the growth rate from additional aid worth 1 percentage point of GDP sustained over the decade would be around 0.5 percentage points, and in the light of subsequent evidence this still seems a reasonable figure.

Growth and Risk Post-Conflict

We now turn to the second factor that must hold before aid can be regarded as even potentially cost-effective as an instrument for reducing post-conflict risks. This is that growth must be shown to reduce risks.

At the time of the first Copenhagen Consensus the main evidence for this was the paper on the causes of conflict by Collier and Hoeffler (2004a). This had found general evidence that growth reduced risks, but the endogeneity problem inherent in the relationship was addressed only by means of a five-year lag. Since then, an important study specifically on growth and the risk of civil war has been published (Miguel et al. 2004). This uses the ingenious and robust instrument of rainfall shocks for growth, an approach that requires them to confine their analysis to Africa. They show that, so instrumented, growth significantly and powerfully reduces risk. The robustness of the general growth–risk relationship is further confirmed in the study by CHR (forthcoming) which, as discussed, is a major update of the Collier and Hoeffler (2004a) analysis, doubling the dataset so as to be comprehensive and applying many robustness checks.

The general relationship that faster growth reduces the risk of civil war is thus far more well founded than at the time of the former study. The next issue is whether there is any evidence relating specifically to the post-conflict context. After all, much of our argument rests on the distinctive features of this period and so it is entirely possible that the growth–risk relationship is different. For example, a pessimistic view would be that the post-conflict situation is typically so fragile that even though growth has the potential to benefit everyone, it might so disturb delicately balanced relationships that it opens up arenas for violent dispute.

At the time of the earlier Copenhagen Consensus paper there was only one study specifically on risks during the post-conflict decade, namely that of Bigombe et al. (2000). This simply introduced a post-conflict dummy variable into the Collier and Hoeffler (2004a) model, using the same data as their original paper. It found that growth was slightly but significantly more effective in reducing the risk of conflict during the first post-conflict decade than in normal situations. Clearly, this evidence was limited in that its derivation was so closely related to the more general Collier and Hoeffler result on the effect of growth on risk: To the extent that the general result could be doubted, so could this refinement.

Since the earlier Copenhagen Consensus paper there has been a substantial advance in the analysis of post-conflict risk as a result of the model in CHS (2008). As discussed further below, this paper takes a completely fresh approach to the data, analyzing sixty-eight post-conflict situations, and uses a methodology much better suited to the question of how post-conflict risk evolves, namely the estimation of hazard functions as opposed to five-year logits. That study found that growth both significantly and substantially reduced the risk of reversion to conflict. As discussed, in work for the present study, we have revised and re-estimated the CHS (2008) study, incorporating domestic military spending as an explanatory variable. The addition of this variable does not affect the significance of the growth variable but somewhat increases the size of the coefficient.

In addition to its direct contribution to risk reduction, faster growth cumulates to a higher level of income. Potentially, the level of income affects risk over and above its effect on the growth rate. Again, at the time of the earlier Copenhagen Consensus paper the main statistical evidence for a direct effect of the level of income came from the Collier and Hoeffler model. Since the evident endogeneity of income to conflict was addressed only by means of a lag, there were reasonable lingering concerns that the result was not robust. The proposition that low income causes an increased risk of conflict is now more widely accepted in the literature. It is also supported by the analysis in CHR (forthcoming), which addressed the potential endogeneity of income by instrumenting it using some standard geographic variables. CHR found that this increased the magnitude of the effect compared to using the lagged income variable. There is also now evidence for the effect of the level of income specifically in post-conflict situations. CHS (2008) include the level of income, lagged by two periods, in their analysis of post-conflict risks in addition to the lagged growth rate, and find it to be significant.

Hence, since the previous study for the Copenhagen Consensus, the evidence that growth reduces risk in post-conflict situations, both directly and indirectly via the level of income, has become considerably stronger. General endogeneity problems have been decisively addressed and the evidence specifically pertaining to the post-conflict situation is far more reliable.

CHS (2008) provide a useful simulation that gives a sense of the magnitude of the overall effect of growth on risk. They take a post-conflict country otherwise at the mean of characteristics for post-conflict societies and vary the ~*e cumulating the effects on the level ·~*v is stagnant the risk of ~ is 42.1 per-

percentage point of growth brings down the decade risk of reversion to conflict by around 1.5 percentage points.

Finally, we need to consider the possibility that while aid might raise growth, and growth might reduce risk, aid might inadvertently directly increase the risk of conflict thereby nullifying its favorable indirect effect via the growth process. At the time of the first Copenhagen Consensus there was some speculation that aid might have such adverse effects, there being a discussion around the concept that aid should aim to "do no harm." However, the only quantitative evidence was from Collier and Hoeffler (2002), which had introduced aid directly into their model of conflict risk. They found that, aid controlling for growth, aid had no significant effect on the risk of conflict. However, this study predated the advance made by Tavares (2003) so that aid was not instrumented. Since aid could be presumed to be allocated with some view of conflict risk, the results were potentially spurious. Since the innovation of Tavares and the first Copenhagen Consensus, Collier and Hoeffler have in unpublished work revisited this question, instrumenting aid, and find the same result: Aid does not have a significant effect on the risk of conflict. This result is not specific to post-conflict, but it is evidently a step towards reassurance that a post-conflict aid program would not inadvertently generate effects that undermined the intended benefits via growth.

Costs and Benefits

So far, we have shown that there is now quite strong evidence that post-conflict aid is effective in bringing down the risks of conflict recurrence. This does not imply that the intervention is cost-effective, but it is a necessary condition for cost-effectiveness. In most cases other possible global interventions are known to be effective, and so the only issue is whether their known ~*~ justify their costs. In effect, our analysis ~mply brought post-conflict aid up to ~.

ssembled the building blocks the costs and benefits of ~~ First, consider

growth rate, of income. If the society conflict reversion during the decade cent. If it sustains 10 percent growth through the decade, which some post-conflict societies such as Mozambique indeed manage to achieve, the risk falls to 26.9 percent. The reduction in risk comes roughly equally from the direct growth effect and the cumulating effect of a higher level of income. Hence, on average, each additional

benefits ~ so far, has s~ ~~ ~ this sta ~ting We ha ve no needed to' calcu, aid to post-~

late ~ nflict societies.

the costs. To achieve the above risk reduction in the risk of conflict recurrence of 1.5 percentage points over the post-conflict decade would require an additional 1 percentage point of growth sustained over the decade. This in turn could be achieved by aid worth 2 percentage points of GDP sustained for a decade. For the typical post-conflict society this would cost around $400 million per year, or $4 billion before discounting.

Now consider the benefits. Recall that our lower-bound estimate of the cost of conflict reversion is around $60 billion. At this lower bound the gross gain purely in terms of the reduction in the risk of recurrence of civil war of 1.5 percentage points is of the order of $900 million. Note that although the figure of $60 billion is discounted so as to be a present value in the year that the conflict might start, the reduced risk is spread over the entire decade, in effect being a flow of gains of around $90 million accruing annually through the decade. Hence, for this to be shown as present value at the beginning of the post-conflict decade this flow would itself need to be discounted. It is thus commensurate with the undiscounted figure for costs of $4 billion. Evidently, at this lower bound post-conflict aid is not cost-effective when the only gains that are counted are the security gains. When the lower-bound estimate is replaced by the center-of-the-range illustration of $250 billion, the gain rises to $4.25 billion and so modestly exceeds its costs. This, of course, depends upon estimates of benefits that are speculative. However, we should note that when we have presented the figures on the degree of effectiveness of aid in bringing down risks to the international donor community they are seen as constituting a powerful case for post-conflict aid. In effect, with these responses international donors are revealing a value on peace rather in excess of our illustration of $250 billion and there is no particular basis for seeing such a high valuation as misplaced.

There is, of course, a further reason to value post-conflict aid, namely that it also generates additional income during the decade and so alleviates poverty. The additional 1 percentage point of growth augments GDP during the decade by $10 billion before discounting and before valuing the benefits beyond that decade. Hence, again using the center-of-the-range illustration, the gross gains are around $13.8 billion from costs of $4 billion, implying a ratio of benefits to costs of around 3.5:1.

Post-conflict aid thus looks to be a good use for development aid, but not so spectacular that it would trump most other calls on scarce international public resources. To an extent donors are already taking this opportunity. However, although aid is provided in post-conflict settings it is not usually sustained. Over the entire course of the first post-conflict decade aid is no higher than were the society not post-conflict, while during the first couple of years of peace there is a flood of aid. Hence, aid typically tapers out just as it should be tapering in.

Military Intervention Opportunity – 1: A Conditionality Requirement Limiting Military Spending

One concern about aid is that it may inadvertently finance military spending. Donors do not permit their development assistance to be used for this purpose, but there are various ways in which aid might nevertheless have this effect. One is as a result of the well-understood concept of fungibility: Aid given ostensibly for one purpose releases government money that would otherwise have been used for this purpose and the money so released can be spent on anything. Another mechanism is that aid is foreign exchange and so augments the capacity of the economy to import. Typically governments levy substantial taxes on imports and so, indirectly, aid is taxed, the resulting revenue being available for the government to use for any purpose.

Typically, the governments of developing countries choose to spend about 10–20 percent of their revenues on the military. It would not, therefore, be surprising if through one or other of these routes aid augmented military spending by some such proportion. Collier and Hoeffler (2007c) investigated this empirically, by including aid as an explanatory variable in their analysis of the determinants of military spending. To allow for evident problems of endogeneity they instrumented aid, following the approach pioneered by Tavares (2003). This approach utilises the fact that a considerable proportion of aid provided by the bilateral aid agencies is determined partly by the domestic budget cycle within the aid-providing country, and partly by historic ties to particular recipient countries, both of which are independent of the current circumstances of recipients. With aid so instrumented, Collier and Hoeffler (2007c) indeed find that it significantly increases military spending, the proportion of aid that leaks into military spending being around 11 percent. Collier and Hoeffler (2007c) do not analyze whether aid in post-conflict situations leaks by a larger or smaller factor than in other contexts. In what follows, we will assume that the rate of leakage is average, namely 11 percent. This is probably a conservative assumption since we know that in post-conflict situations governments place a much higher priority on military spending than in normal peacetime situations, manifested by military spending being significantly higher.

This raises two issues, one being the true costs of these leakages viewed from the perspective of the donor, the other being whether any actions on the part of the donor could potentially reduce leakage.

One cost of the leakage is evidently the opportunity cost in terms of the intended uses of aid. If 11 percent of aid leaks into an activity which is unproductive, then all the beneficial effects of aid are attributable to the remaining 89 percent. Were it possible to prevent leakage, the amount of aid available for beneficial uses would thus be augmented by around 12 percent (11/89). Hence, just through this route, an effective conditionality clause combined with post-conflict aid would raise the benefits of post-conflict aid in the benchmark example from $13.8 billion to $15.5 billion, implying a ratio of costs to benefits of 1:4.

However, the main cost of the leakage is that in augmenting military spending it is inadvertently generating adverse effects since, as discussed, extra military spending in the post-conflict context is significantly counter-productive. Recall

that the adverse effects of military spending in post-conflict situations are between fifteen and sixty times its direct cost, depending upon whether lower-bound or center-of-range estimates are taken.

Take a typical post-conflict situation in which GDP is around $20 billion. Then the aid package of 2 percentage points of GDP considered above would amount to $400 million per year. Thus, an 11 percent leakage of aid into military spending would augment the military budget by around $44 million. This leakage would generate inadvertent costs in terms of a heightened risk of conflict of between $660 million and $2.6 billion. We should stress that this is not the net effect of post-conflict aid, since this adverse effect is already implicitly included in the net benefits estimated above. Nevertheless, it is a major negative effect. The contribution of aid to peace by means of faster growth is inadvertently partially offset by its tendency to undermine peace by augmenting the domestic military budget which, uniquely in post-conflict situations, aggravates the situation.

Supposing that the leakage could be prevented by effective conditionality, what would the benefits be? Obviously, the benefits of conditionality have to be assessed in combination with the aid itself: The conditionality simply augments the effectiveness of the aid. However, taking the center-of-the-range estimate, the benefits of the aid would increase from $15.5 billion to around $18.1 billion, thus raising the benefit-to-cost ratio to around 4.5:1.

This raises the evident question as to whether anything can be done to curtail the leakage of aid into military spending. There are various possible approaches, which may be reinforcing.

One is to improve the information available to post-conflict governments on the typical effects of high domestic military spending. Governments may be deluding themselves in believing that it resolves their security problem or – more realistically – ministers of finance who wish to constrain military spending lack persuasive evidence to counter pressures from the large and powerful military lobby that is inevitably resistant to reductions in its budget.

A second approach is for the donors to tighten conditions on the provision of aid. Any conditions must recognize the limits resulting from both the fungibility of project funding and the freedom attached to the alternative aid channel of budget support. It is infeasible to establish how their money is being spent. However, if the concern is that money should not go into military spending, then the donor has the analytically more feasible task of monitoring this part of the budget. In effect, the military spending of the post-conflict government would need to be subject to an explicit cap as a condition for the receipt of post-conflict aid. This in turn is liable to encounter two obstacles, one political, the other technical. The political obstacle is the argument that such a condition would breach the sovereignty of the post-conflict government. This argument can be countered by the reasonable position that the sovereignty of the government does not extend to the right to spend donor money on purposes that flout donor conditions agreed to by the government. The donor cap would be designed to prevent aid being diverted rather than to induce the government to spend less of its own money on the military. Indeed, if the government did not want to constrain its military spending, it would simply reject the aid. The technical obstacle to a budget cap is that it can be evaded by concealed misclassification of spending items. For example, it eventually came to light that following an attempt by the British aid agency DFID to curtail the military spending of the Ugandan government, some Ugandan military spending had been misclassified under the education budget. To overcome this technical obstacle would require a verified system of scrutiny of budget data, a function that could potentially be supplied by one of the international financial institutions. Again, governments that wished to avoid budgetary scrutiny could simply decline the aid.

A third approach is to address the security needs of post-conflict governments by effective provision of external peacekeeping, perhaps by means of an over-the-horizon guarantee, as in Sierra Leone.

These approaches complement each other and can potentially be packaged together. A commitment to the external provision of security from international actors would balance a commitment from the post-conflict government to limit its own military spending and to permit sufficient scrutiny of its budgetary system to make this commitment credible. These matching commitments reinforce each other: The effectiveness of external peacekeeping as measured by risk reduction would be substantially increased if domestic military spending were reduced. Conversely, the perceived need for military spending would be reduced if there were an international commitment to the maintenance of security. Finally, the credibility of that commitment would be enhanced by the fact that the government had, at the insistence of the international community, renounced its option of self-defence.

However, a package would need some authorizing environment that could orchestrate it. The package would have four components. One would be a commitment on the part of the donors to provide post-conflict aid. A second would be a commitment on the part of the Security Council to external military peacekeeping or an over-the-horizon guarantee. A third would be a commitment by the government to cap its military spending for the post-conflict decade, and to accept an international system of budgetary verification. A fourth would be the provision of such a system of verification. While no single entity is in a position directly to provide this package, there is now an entity that could negotiate and authorize its provision, namely the UN Peace-Building Commission. This reports both to the Security Council and the General Assembly and was established in 2005 precisely because it was recognized that there was a missing link in the international governance architecture.

Whether such a packaged approach would be politically feasible depends in particular upon the willingness of conflict-affected regions to accept it: The combined neighborhoods of conflict-affected countries constitute a large and influential group. Given that the main costs of conflict accrue to these neighborhoods, it would be in their interest to do so. It would also be in the interest of the developed countries that provide the finance both for post-conflict aid and for post-conflict peacekeeping. Their clear interest is that in combination this assistance should be far more successful than in the past.

Military Intervention Opportunity – 2: Peacekeeping in Post-Conflict Situations

We now turn to a CBA of international peacekeeping. The first and critical step is evidently to investigate whether peacekeeping is effective in reducing the risk of conflict.

The Effect of Peacekeeping on Risk

At the time of the first Copenhagen Consensus there was no quantitative study available to determine whether peacekeeping is effective in reducing post-conflict risk. Although chapter 3 by Collier and Hoeffler included peacekeeping as a possible intervention, the analysis was based entirely upon the particular case of Sierra Leone and the contribution of peacekeeping was inferred from the peace in that country that had prevailed while peacekeepers were present, compared with an imputed counterfactual risk of conflict generated from the Collier and Hoeffler (2004a) model. Evidently, this was not a very satisfactory basis for assessing the more general impact of peacekeeping. Since then, the analysis of peacekeeping has advanced considerably, with a major evaluation by Doyle and Sambanis (2006) and the CHS (2008) model of post-conflict risks which introduces peacekeeping as an explanatory variable.

Our analysis is based upon a re-estimation of the CHS (2008) model. That had a sample of sixty-eight post-conflict situations, this being a comprehensive set of countries with post-conflict experience and adequate data. We should note, however, that the very notion of "post-conflict" is controversial. Civil wars do not always have a clear ending. Some researchers, though not CHS, consider that a civil war has only ended once there has been no fighting for two years, so

that early relapses are not even analyzed. CHS then analyze the persistence of peace through a hazard function. Each year is treated separately, and the model focuses on the first ten years after the end of the civil war.

Before turning to the role of military spending, it is useful to get a broader sense of the model through its selection of other explanatory variables and its results. Variables are selected through a process of stepwise deletion of a wide range of variables that have been proposed by the pertinent literatures. Evidently, one such literature is the quantitative studies on the causes of civil war, although those studies use logit analysis as opposed to hazard functions, and do not focus in detail upon post-conflict situations. These studies do, however, show that post-conflict situations are distinctively risky for reasons other than fixed effects. Hence, the high rate of reversion to conflict is not simply because these countries are inherently at high risk even prior to their initial war (Collier and Hoeffler 2004a; CHR forthcoming). The other pertinent strand of literature is the largely qualitative studies of post-conflict situations.

CHS (2008) investigate temporal, economic, social, and political influences on risk reversion as well as the presence of peacekeeping forces. Their analysis of temporal effects produces the somewhat disappointing result that during the post-conflict decade there is no "safe period." It is known from the quantitative studies of general risks of civil war that the risk of reversion to conflict gradually diminishes over time. However, this risk reduction is slow, occurring decade-by-decade rather than year-by-year. During the first decade the risk indeed appears to decline, but the effect is not statistically significant nor is it substantial. The inference is that the entire first decade is at risk of further conflict. Recent delayed reversions to serious violence in Timor Leste and the DRC are consistent with the statistical pattern.

Consistent with the influences on the overall risk of civil war, CHS find that two economic variables significantly affect the risk of reversion: The level of income and its growth rate. We have already discussed these effects in our analysis of aid. Despite the high profile given to social factors such as ethnic divisions, CHS do not find ethnic or religious structure to be significant in post-conflict risks. The more general analysis of the risk of civil war does find such effects to be significant. However, the lack of a specifically post-conflict effect should make us wary of dismissing peacekeeping and economic interventions as "missing the essence of the problem." Just as ethnic and religious divisions between communities are usually treated as the "explanation" for conflict, the most prominent "solution" is assumed to be political, namely democracy and elections. Here the results of CHS (2008) are perhaps salutary. They find that in post-conflict societies democracies are considerably more at risk of reversion to conflict than are severe autocracies, and that post-conflict elections appear to shift risk rather than reduce it. Risk falls sharply in the year prior to an election but increases even more in the year following it. Presumably, in the year before an election all the major actors hope to win it, whereas after the election a loser emerges whose best chance of a continuing share in power may then be to revert to conflict. An example of just this sequence, which is indeed too recent to be included in the CHS analysis, is the DRC, whose election of October 2006 was followed by large-scale fighting between the government army and that of the losing opponent. In that situation it seems reasonable to attribute the eventual restoration of post-election peace at least in part to the presence of 17,000 international peacekeepers. If so, their presence has had a very substantial pay-off. In contrast, the $500 million spent by the international community on promoting the elections may not have been a particularly good investment in peace.

CHS were able to get comprehensive and detailed financial data from the United Nations on peacekeeping expenditures and so were able to introduce them as an explanatory variable in the analysis. An immediate problem is to address the potential endogeneity of the provision of peacekeeping. Clearly, there is some decision process that determines whether and how many peacekeepers are sent, and for

how long. The risk of conflict could impinge on these decisions in either direction: Troop provision could be directed to the situations judged to be most at risk or – if troop-providing countries seek to avoid danger – high-risk situations may systematically be avoided. Evidently, the appropriate way of addressing these concerns would be to find a good instrument for military deployment in post-conflict situations. Unfortunately, although CHS (2008) explore a number of potential instruments, they are not able to find one that is satisfactory. This is consistent with the major study by Doyle and Sambanis (2006), who conclude that the decision process by which troops are allocated is so complex, involving repeat-play bargaining between a large number of countries, that it is not possible to find a satisfactory instrument for the scale of deployment. CHS therefore investigate the likely bias from failing to instrument, by initially introducing the assignment of peacekeepers as a dummy variable rather than as a continuous variable measuring expenditure. The dummy variable is significant and positive, indicating either that the decision to send troops increases the risk of conflict reversion or, more credibly, that the United Nations decides to send troops to those situations which are systematically more at risk than average. This suggests that if there is an endogeneity problem it is most likely to bias any favorable effects of peacekeeping downwards: Troops are being sent where risks tend to be higher. Thus, a result which shows that troops reduce risk is under-stating the true benefits since the true counterfactual risk is higher than that being assumed by the model.

With this caveat, CHS indeed find that expenditure on post-conflict UN peacekeeping significantly reduces the risk of conflict reversion. The variable is significant at 2 percent. In addition to being statistically reasonably significant, the effect is quite substantial. However, CHS do not attempt to move from this result to a CBA of peacekeeping provision. This is the main specific value added of our analysis here.

For the purposes of the present study we re-analyzed the CHS (2008) model. Our primary extension of the model was to introduce domestic military spending – that is, military provision by the post-conflict government. This has already been discussed above. However, we should note here that while the effect of such spending on post-conflict risk had already been analyzed in the model of Collier and Hoeffler (2006) (including due allowance for endogeneity by means of instrumenting), this had not been integrated with an analysis of external peacekeeping. In effect, there were two published studies, one on peacekeeping and the other on domestic military spending, but no study that combined the two. The inclusion of domestic military spending which we undertook for the present study did not overturn any of the results already described. However the additional variable was itself statistically significant and, importantly for our present discussion, it approximately doubled the estimate of the effects of peacekeeping (while statistical significance was unaffected). These are the results on which we base our cost-benefit analysis.

We investigate the maintenance of a peacekeeping force at a constant scale for the entire post-conflict decade. Some international forces have indeed been maintained for such long periods, although shorter periods are more common. However, since CHS (2008) do not find that the first few years are significantly more dangerous, a long period of provision seems to be the right intervention to model. It would be possible to fine-tune provision, gradually scaling it down somewhat as risks fall – for example, due to economic recovery – and this would doubtless increase the ratio of benefits to costs. But again it would presuppose a degree of sophistication in the decision process that seems unwarranted.

The reduction in risk achieved by peacekeeping forces depends upon their scale of deployment. Compared with no deployment, an annual expenditure of $100 million reduces the cumulative ten-year risk very substantially, from around 38 percent to 16.5 percent. At $200 million per year, the risk falls further to around 12.8 percent, and at $500 million it is down to 9 percent.

The CBA of Peacekeeping

To convert this reduction in risk into a benefit commensurate with costs, we multiply the reduction in risk by the cost should a conflict occur. Recall that each percentage point of risk of conflict recurrent is valued at between $586 million at the lower bound and $2.5 billion at the center-of-the-range illustration. Hence, peacekeeping at the level of $100 million per year for the decade generates an undiscounted benefit of between $12.6 billion and $53.7 billion. Since the undiscounted cost is $1 billion, the ratio of costs to benefits is between around 1:13 and 1:54.

While the ratio of costs to benefits is a useful guide to action, it is not in fact the appropriate criterion by which to choose an intervention. For example, as will be evident from the above figures, peacekeeping forces appear to be subject to diminishing returns and so there is at least potentially some optimal scale of intervention. Optimality requires that the benefits should diminish relative to the costs so that at some stage they become equal at the margin.

As part of our re-analysis of the CHS (2008) model, we investigated the extent and nature of these diminishing returns. Such diminishing benefits can potentially come from three different ways. One, which we investigated, is whether the effect of peacekeeping is better described by a non-linear treatment of the explanatory variable, such as through the introduction of a quadratic. We could find no such effect. A second approach would have been to force diminishing returns by ranking all the post-conflict situations in their order of estimated expected pay-off to peacekeeping. We preferred not to adopt this approach since it presumed that the assignment of peacekeepers as between situations would be highly attuned to their relative benefits, when the evidence suggests that decision processes are not so characterized. The approach we took was to rely for diminishing returns on the curvature implicit in our modeling of risk: As risks are reduced, their further reduction becomes progressively more difficult. This is unlikely to be a mere artefact but the precise degree of curva-

The Security Challenge in Conflict-Prone Countries 95

ture is evidently not well estimated. Hence, the results are approximate.

By construction, the optimal scale of an intervention is that scale which should be chosen to maximize the benefits, abstracting from considerations of risk and the shadow price of resources. However, it is important to recognize that at this point the ratio of benefits to costs will not be at its maximum. The criterion of choosing the scale of an intervention by whether the ratio of benefits to costs is maximized is thus generally inappropriate. Rather, it is better to determine the optimal intervention as that at which the marginal benefit equals the marginal cost, and at that point evaluate the ratio of the benefits to the costs. This is not merely pedantic. In many types of intervention there are diminishing returns to the intervention, so that sub-optimal interventions have much higher ratios of benefits to costs. In some ways a better criterion for selection of an intervention is the estimated net pay-off over and above its costs. However, a high ratio of benefits to costs is evidently not irrelevant since it gives some reassurance that even if the numbers are quite inaccurate there is little danger of doing net harm.

We find that the optimal scale of peacekeeping forces is around $850 million. At this stage the risk of conflict reversion is reduced to only 7.3 percent, the last percentage point reduction (i.e. from 8.3 percent) costing $2.4 billion over the decade to achieve benefits of $2.5 billion (taking our center-of-the-range illustration). At this level, the risk of conflict has been reduced by a little over 30 percentage points and so has generated gross gains of around $75 billion (taking our center-of-the-range figure) compared to its cost of $8.5 billion. While this leads to a much less impressive ratio of costs-to-benefits of around 1:9, it leads to an enormous overall gain per post-conflict situation of around $63.5 billion.

While these numbers might seem astoundingly large, this is because of the nature of the phenomenon. If, for example, we take the current practical example of the DRC, the large UN force is costing around $1 billion per year, and so within the vicinity of what looks from our

figures to be appropriate. During the presence of these forces peace has been maintained, albeit with periodic outbreaks of considerable violence, one of which, as noted, followed the elections. A counterfactual with a high probability of relapse into large-scale violence is by no means unreasonable in this instance. Our analysis above estimates that in the typical case a deployment of peacekeepers at this scale would bring down the risk by 30 percentage points and this again seems entirely within the credible range for the DRC. Indeed, many commentators might regard the estimate as being overly conservative for the DRC, where the risk of large-scale violence in the absence of international peacekeepers might have been rather higher than the 38 percent of the peacekeeping benchmark. Similarly, our analysis supposes that a collapse into civil war in the DRC would incur global costs of the order of $250 billion. Again, although an accurate figure is impossible, this does not seem to be absurd once all the potential neighborhood and global repercussions are considered. If the international community could with certainty "buy" the difference between sustained peace and collapse in the DRC for around two years' worth of the global aid budget it would quite possibly choose to do so.

In summary, international peacekeeping looks to be a good intervention. If the intervention is kept to a modest scale it has a very high cost-benefit ratio, and if it is set at an optimal scale it delivers enormous overall net gains.

Military Intervention Opportunity – 3: Over-the-Horizon Guarantees

Now imagine that the instrument of a security guarantee could be elevated to a fully fledged international instrument, whether under the auspices of the United Nations or a regional entity such as the African Union. To avoid the problems encountered by the French in Rwanda, the security guarantee would have to be circumscribed by clear limits: For example, governments in the process of genocide could not expect to be propped up by international military intervention. Here we propose three possible criteria for eligibility for the provision of protection. The three are not exclusive.

The first is the automatic provision of powerful peacekeeping forces to protect governments that came to power through certified democratic elections from the threat of rebellion during their period of office. The second is a similar protection against the threat of a coup d'état. The third is for an over-the-horizon guarantee in post-conflict societies. While the initial maintenance of peace cannot credibly be done without troops on the ground, the British experience to date in Sierra Leone suggests that it may be possible to phase the bulk of international troops out after, say, five years, replacing them with a guarantee made credible by appropriate logistics for the second five-year period.

Supposing that this cover was attempted, would it be effective, what would be its benefits, and what would it cost? This is the remit of the present analysis.

The Over-the-Horizon Guarantee and the Risk of Conflict

The original Collier and Hoeffler study for the Copenhagen Consensus (2004c) briefly discussed over-the-horizon guarantees, but there was no basis for quantification other than to assume that the Sierra Leone intervention was the model for all such interventions. Since the time of that study a new model of the risk of conflict, namely that of CHR (forthcoming), has specifically estimated the impact of the French over-the-horizon guarantee. As discussed above, this was not an explicit guarantee, but it was well understood that French forces would be likely to intervene to support regimes in Francophone Africa and this was made credible logistically by a string of French military bases in the region. As discussed, the policy was operational from the time of independence of France's African colonies until the coup in Côte d'Ivoire of December 1999 revealed that as a result of the experience in Rwanda French policy had been rethought.

As with our assessment of peacekeeping, the first and critical step is to quantify the impact of the over-the-horizon guarantee on the risk of conflict. Because the French guarantee lasted for over thirty years and covered an entire group of countries it is amenable to statistical investigation. If the guarantee were effective we would expect these countries to have a significantly lower incidence of civil war than predicted by their other characteristics. This is tested by CHR (forthcoming). They introduce a dummy variable for the guarantee into a global analysis of the onset of civil war for the period 1965–2004. They find that the variable is significant and substantial: The risk of civil war in these countries during this period was only one-third what would otherwise have been expected. They then investigate whether the dummy could have other explanations: In particular, whether all Francophone countries are systematically less at risk regardless of their location, and whether Francophone African countries are less at risk regardless of the period. Each of these alternative hypotheses can be rejected in favor of the interpretation that it was only Francophone African countries during this period that were significantly less at risk. Of course, this does not preclude that there was some other feature of these countries that was distinctive during this period. Nevertheless, the external security commitment seems a likely explanation. After all, the French government was committing significant sums to maintaining this military capability. In aggregate the risk of a civil war breaking out in one or other of the thirteen countries of Francophone Africa was reduced by three-quarters, the annual risk for the countries combined falling from around 10.2 percent to around 2.6 percent.

The risk reduction achieved by the French security guarantee will form our estimate of the likely efficacy of an international guarantee. However, our purpose is not to arrive at a CBA of the French guarantee itself, but to use the effects of the guarantee as a guide to other contexts in which such guarantees might be used. Evidently, the French guarantee was effective and CHR (forthcoming) have quantified its contribution. However, in extrapolating from this result to post-conflict guarantees we face a choice. Such situations have far higher levels of risk than those prevailing in Francophone

Africa and we could potentially assume either that the reduction in risk is of the same absolute or proportionate amount. Whereas the decade-risk facing the typical Francophone country in this period was around 10% percent that facing the typical post-conflict country is around 40 percent. In effect, we must choose whether a guarantee provided in a post-conflict setting would bring the risk down by 7.6 percentage points, as in Francophone Africa, or by around 30 percentage points, which would be the same proportionate impact. Recall that a reduction of 30 percentage points would make the contribution commensurate with a large peacekeeping force in-country. We therefore prefer to choose the lower figure. Only in extrapolating the result to conflict prevention in low-income democracies, where underlying risk levels are broadly comparable to those in Francophone Africa, we will extrapolate by assuming that risks are reduced by three-quarters.

The CBA of a Guarantee

We will consider the benefits from a guarantee of forces broadly equivalent to the scale and credibility of commitment provided by France for thirty years, but provided internationally to countries which met the criteria specified above.

First, consider the guarantee to support democratic governments militarily should they be threatened by a rebellion. According to UCDP/PRIO data, in the past decade four democratic low-income countries have suffered outbreaks of civil war and we take this as the likely rate over the next decade. If an international guarantee could reduce this by three-quarters, as did the French guarantee, then three of these wars would be averted. The annual benefit would be in the range $18 billion (lower bound) to $75 billion (center-of-the-range).

We now attempt to get an equivalent benefit to the replacement of external peacekeepers in the second half of the first decade of post-conflict situations by a guarantee. Of course, at present, most peacekeepers are withdrawn before this period but on our analysis this is a mistake. The counterfactual depends not just on whether peacekeepers are present, but also on their scale and the scale of the withdrawal. We will construct the experiment so as to keep the level of risk in the post-conflict country constant. Thus, we assume that the over-the-horizon guarantee reduces risk by around 7 percentage points and release peacekeeping troops in-country up to the point where the withdrawal creates an offsetting increase in the risk of 7 percentage points. This clearly depends upon the size of forces. For example, if the initial forces were at the "optimal" level of $850 million, then they could be scaled back to merely $150 million while leaving the overall risk level unaffected. In practice, this "optimal" level will normally be excessive because it makes no allowance for aversion to risk. If the typical provision were $500 million then it could be scaled back to around $100 million. If provision were at $250 million it could be scaled back to $70 million.

The benefit of a centralized guarantee then depends upon how many situations to which it might apply. Normally, there are around six countries in the second half of the first decade post-conflict. Hence, the global gain in peacekeeping would range from $4.2 billion down to around $1.1 billion, depending upon the scale of peacekeeping. In order to simplify we will take the central figure based on a force of $500 million, implying a saving of $2.4 billion annually.

The third and final possible coverage of a guarantee would be against coups d'états in democracies. In many respects, this is the easiest task for a guarantee: Coups in small, low-income countries can usually be made unviable by an adequate and prompt scale of external intervention. For example, the African Union was able to put down the coup d'état in the democratic mini-state of São Tomé, Principe by the threat of military intervention from Nigeria, but it lacks the logistical power to reverse coups in larger countries. Unfortunately, there is no equivalent study to that of CHR (2008) in the external deterrence of coups. Recall that the annual cost of successful coups to Africa over the past forty years has been within the range of $4 billion–$16 billion. By no means all these coups threatened democracies and coups are getting less common, but recall that democracy does not provide protection against coups: even in 2006 there was a coup attempt against the democratic government of Madagascar which was fortunately unsuccessful. The best that we can do here is to assume that as with civil war a credible guarantee would reduce the risk by three-quarters, and that this would apply to the more democratic half of Africa's countries. This would imply savings within the range of $1.5 billion–$6 billion per year.

We now turn to the costs. The financial cost of the French over-the-horizon guarantee is not simple to determine. Partly, military budgets are invariably subject to a degree of secrecy and partly the counterfactual is obscure. However, for our estimate we relied upon an informal estimate from the French Treasury, which must be treated as subject to caveats. The estimate was that the cost was of the order of $1 billion per year. This is a high figure, equivalent to a super-force of peacekeepers in a single country, but this very scale presumably added to its credibility. Indeed, the guarantee force must evidently be at least as large as that needed in the largest envisaged operation. Since the French guarantee applied only to Francophone Africa, a more extensive guarantee such as we envisage would presumably be more expensive. In what follows we suppose that the cost of an international force would be double that of the French force, at $2 billion.

Combining the benefits with the costs, the pay-off to the guarantee depends upon whether the same force can cover all three risks. If it can, then the benefits are very large relative to the costs. The lower edge of the combined benefits is $19 billion per year and the center-of-the-range estimate is around $81 billion. Since the assumed cost is only $2 billion per year, the implied ratio of costs to benefits is 1:10–1:40:

Packaging interventions: Post-conflict aid + Military spending limits + Peacekeeping + Guarantees

As is apparent from our previous discussion, our four interventions complement each other. The effectiveness of post-conflict aid can be enhanced by limits on military spending. Those limits, and the curtailed military spending that they imply, can in turn be made more acceptable by the offer of credible external security provision. If this is provided in the form of an over-the-horizon guarantee, not only is it cheaper for those who provide it, but it is also less intrusive and so more acceptable for those who receive it. In particular, while a guarantee against coups does not of itself generate particularly large global gains, it generates huge gains for the governments who benefit from them: Coups are by far the biggest risk of regime change in low-income countries. Hence, such a guarantee might be sufficiently attractive to governments for them to be prepared to accept more limited military spending. Finally, the growth that substantial post-conflict aid would generate, and the strategy of phasing in over-the-horizon guarantees, provides the long-term credible "exit strategies" that are now essential before credible international military commitments are likely to be forthcoming. Thus, the package is more credible than any of its component parts viewed individually.

Further, each component of the package has clear precedents. Post-conflict aid is now standard, something that was not the case a decade ago. For example, the World Bank now has an explicit window for this need that lasts for the first seven post-conflict years. Military spending limits are applied by donors, but currently largely on an ad hoc basis. At the regional level, President Arias of Costa Rica is promoting an initiative for a coordinated mutual limitation on military spending, recognizing its properties as a regional public bad. Peacekeeping has grown enormously over the past decade, with DPKO the key agency within the UN system. Finally, over-the-horizon guarantees have been reintroduced by the British in Sierra Leone, and are being attempted by the African Union to guard against coups. Europe already has a "rapid reaction force" which has the potential to enforce these guarantees. What has been missing to date is the vision to combine these interventions. However, the creation of the UN Peace-Building Commission provides an entity which could potentially coordinate such a vision. The Commission did not exist at the time of the first Copenhagen Consensus and so there was no potential to coordinate such a package of instruments.

We therefore conclude with a "grand vision" of a security package that combines all four instruments. Since the linkages between the components are primarily political we have not attempted to quantify them. Hence, in terms of our estimated costs and benefits the package merely sums the components so that each can be accepted or rejected separately according to the threshold adopted. However, the package has political coherence and so it is worth also considering the four instruments together. We work with both our "center-of-the-range" illustration, and the lower-bound estimate that is around one-quarter of this pay-off.

Post-conflict aid would be increased by 2 percent of GDP for the entire post-conflict decade, and on average cover twelve countries each with a GDP of $20 billion. It would thus cost $4.8 billion a year and add around 1 percentage point to the growth rate of post-conflict countries during this period. Combined with the ceiling aimed at preventing the leakage of this aid into military spending, this would yield a pay-off of between around $12 billion (lower bound) and $21 billion (center-of-the-range).

Ceilings on military spending by post-conflict countries would aim to reduce such spending by 0.2 percentage points of GDP, this being the likely leakage from the additional aid. This would reduce spending by around $480 million per year in these countries, with a benefit in terms of reduced risk of conflict of the order of $7 billion (lower bound) and $28 billion (center-of-the-range).

Peacekeeping forces would be provided in post-conflict settings at a scale of around $500 million per year in the typical country, being scaled down through the use of over-the-horizon guarantees in the second five years. Until allowance is made for double counting due to the risk-reduction from the other components of the package, the ten-year risk per country would fall from around 38 percent to around 9 percent.

With twelve such countries the annual cost would be around $4 billion and the annual gain between around $21 billion (lower bound) and $84 billion (center-of-the-range).

Finally, an over-the-horizon guarantee would be provided at a cost of $2 billion per year. Again before allowing for double counting of risk reduction from other elements of the package, the gains from lower risks would be between around $17 billion (lower bound) and $70 billion (center-of-the-range) per year.

The combined cost of the package would be around $10.8 billion per year. The benefits, once double counting of security gains are eliminated, would be between around $57 billion (lower bound) and $192 billion (center-of-the-range). Decomposing this, using the center-of-the-range figures, it consists of security gains post-conflict of around $100 billion, increased GDP of around $11 billion, reduced coup risk of around $6 billion, and fewer wars in democracies of around $75 billion. The ratio of costs to benefits is thus within the wide range 1:5–1:19.

Conclusion

Peace is a precondition for social and economic development. Civil war is development in reverse. Peace is an implicit assumption of those other challenge strategies that involve activities in the poorest countries. Further, internal violent conflict, in both the form of civil wars and coups, is highly persistent: One manifestation of violence begets another. Such violence is concentrated among the poorest and least hopeful countries on earth. There is thus a powerful case for peace to be an objective for international intervention: It is both primary and well targeted. The evident caveat to prioritizing peace is whether the international community can do anything to further it. After the intervention in Iraq many people might reasonably feel that the unintended consequences of security interventions are such that intervention in any form is too risky.

In this chapter, we have attempted to show that there is now considerable evidence that a combination of post-conflict aid and the provi-

Table 2.1. A summary of costs and benefits

Opportunity	Costs of intervention (over ten years)	Benefits: Averted economic losses and DALYs over ten years	Benefits: More averted losses of war when million spending is lower	Benefits: Added growth due to aid	Benefits: Averting coups	Total benefits including all over ten years	BCR
Discount rate 3 percent, DALY cost $1,000: Cost of war is 58.6 billion							
Aid	4 billion	880 million		10 billion		10.9 billion	2.7
Conditionality	4 billion	880 million	650 million	11.7 billion		13.3 billion	3.3
Peacekeeping troops	1 billion	12.6 billion				12.6 billion	12.6
Optimal level of PKOs	8.5 billion	18.0 billion				18 billion	2.1
Over-the-horizon guarantees (costs and benefits calculated for six post-conflict countries)	$20 billion	$176 billion			15 billion	191 billion	9.6
Combined 500 million PKO and over-the-horizon guarantee (costs and benefits calculated for six post-conflict countries plus countries at coup risk)	$28 billion	$103.6 billion			15 billion	118.7 billion	4.2
Discount rate 6 percent, DALY cost $1,000: Cost of war is 49.8 billion							
Aid	4 billion	744 million		10 billion		10.7billion	2.7
Conditionality	4 billion	744 million	550 million	11.7 billion		13.2 billion	3.3
Peacekeeping troops	1 billion	10.7 billion				10.7 billion	10.7
Optimal level of PKOs	8.5 billion	15.3 billion				15.3 billion	1.8
Over-the-horizon guarantees (costs and benefits calculated for all six post-conflict countries)	$20 billion	$149 billion			15 billion	164 billion	8.2
Combined 500 million PKO and over-the-horizon guarantee (costs and benefits calculated for all six post-conflict countries plus countries at coup risk)	$28 billion	$86.1 billion			15 billion	101.1 billion	3.6
Discount rate 3 percent, DALY cost $5,000: Cost of war is 78.5 billion							
Aid	4 billion	1.2 billion		10 billion		11.2 billion	2.8
Conditionality	4 billion	1.2 billion	650 million	11.7 billion		13.3 billion	3.3
Peacekeeping troops	1 billion	16.9 billion				16.9 billion	16.9
Optimal level of PKOs	8.5 billion	24.1 billion				24.1 billion	2.8
Over-the-horizon guarantees (costs and benefits calculated for six post-conflict countries)	$20 billion	$234 billion			15 billion	249 billion	12.5
Combined 500 million PKO and over-the-horizon guarantee (costs and benefits calculated for all six post-conflict countries plus countries at coup risk)	$28 billion	$135.6 billion			15 billion	163.6 billion	5.8
Discount rate 6 percent, DALY cost $5,000: Cost of war is 69 billion							
Aid	4 billion	1.0 billion		10 billion		11.0 billion	2.8
Conditionality	4 billion	1.0 billion	550million	11.7 billion		13.3 billion	3.3
Peac-keeping troops	1 billion	14.8 billion				14.8 billion	14.8
Optimal level of PKOs	8.5 billion	21.2 billion				21.2 billion	2.5
Over-the-horizon guarantees (costs and benefits calculated for six post-conflict countries)	$20 billion	$207 billion			15 billion	227 billion	11.4

Table 2.1. (continued)

Opportunity	Costs of intervention (over ten years)	Benefits: Averted economic losses and DALYs over ten years	Benefits: More averted losses of war when million spending is lower	Benefits: Added growth due to aid	Benefits: Averting coups	Total benefits including all over ten years	BCR
Over-the-horizon guarantees (costs and benefits calculated for six post-conflict countries)	$20 billion	$207 billion			15 billion	227 billion	11.4
Combined 500 million PKO and over-the-horizon guarantee (costs and benefits calculated for all six post-conflict countries plus countries at coup risk)	$28 billion	$119 billion			15 billion	134 billion	4.8
Center-of-the-range cost estimate: Cost of war is 250 billion							
Aid	4 billion	3.8 billion		10 billion		13.8 billion	3.5
Conditionality	4 billion	3.8 billion	2.6 billion	11.7 billion		18.1 billion	4.5
Peacekeeping troops	1 billion	53.7 billion				53.7 billion	53.7
Optimal level of PKOs	8.5 billion	310 billion				310 billion	36.5
Over-the-horizon guarantees (costs and benefits calculated for six post-conflict countries)	20 billion	750 billion			60 billion	810 billion	40.5
Over-the-horizon guarantees (costs and benefits calculated for six post-conflict countries)	20 billion	762 billion			15 billion	762 billion	38.1
Combined 500 million PKO and over-the-horizon guarantee (costs and benefits calculated for six post-conflict countries plus countries at coup risk)	28 billion	432 billion			60 billion	492 billion	17.6
Over-the-horizon guarantees (costs and benefits calculated for six post-conflict countries plus countries at coup risk)	20 billion	$780 billion					39

sion of security through military interventions of various forms can fairly reliably and substantially bring risks down. Cumulatively this would radically lower the incidence of global conflict: That is, international intervention is effective.

The most difficult stage of our analysis has been to move from this demonstration of effectiveness to an analysis of cost-effectiveness. This is because assigning a value to the benefit of global peace is intrinsically problematic. We have therefore presented both a "lower-bound" figure which has some reasonable basis in quantitative analysis, and a "center-of-the-range" figure which is much more speculative but which we feel may better capture true sentiments.

Table 2.1 provides a summary of the costs and benefits of the various measures. We use discount rates of 3 percent and 6 percent. Depending on which of these measures is taken, the ratio of costs of our package to its benefits

varies from around 1:4 to 1:18. The individual components of the package range much more widely. Whether this is sufficient to warrant prioritization is a matter for the Expert Panel. However, it seems to us that the key step has been the demonstration of effectiveness. Peace is so fundamental that if interventions are effective and the absolute costs are not out of bounds, the interventions should be undertaken.

Bibliography

Adam, C., Collier, P., and Davies, V., 2008: Post-conflict monetary reconstruction, *World Bank Economic Review*, **22**(1): 87–112

Azam, J.-P., 1994: Democracy and development: a theoretical framework, *Public Choice*

Besley, T. and Kudamatsu, M., 2007: Making autocracy work, STICERD, London School of Economics, mimeo

Bigombe, B., Collier, P., and Sambanis, N., 2000: Policies for building post-conflict peace, *Journal of African Economies*, **9**(3)

Chauvet, L. and Collier, P., 2007: Elections in failing states, CSAE, Oxford, mimeo

Chauvet, L. and Collier, P., 2008: Preconditions for reform in failing states, *Journal of Conflict Management and Peace*

Chauvet, L., Collier, P., and Hoeffler, A., 2006: The cost of failing states and the limits to sovereignty, CSAE, mimeo

Collier, P., 1998: On the economic consequences of civil war, *Oxford Economic Papers*, 168–83

Collier, P., 2007: The *bottom billion: why the poorest countries are failing and what can be done about it*, Oxford University Press, New York[1]

Collier, P. and Dollar, D., 2002: Aid allocation and poverty reduction, *European Economic Review*, **46**(8): 1475–1500

Collier, P. and Goderis, B., 2007a: Prospects for commodity exporters: Hunky dory or humpty dumpty?, *World Economics*, **8**(2): 1–15

Collier, P. and Goderis, B., 2007b: Commodity prices and the resource curse: Resolving a conundrum, Department of Economics, Oxford University, mimeo

Collier, P., Goderis, B., and Hoeffler, A., 2006: Shocks and growth in low-income countries, Department of Economics, Oxford University, mimeo

Collier, P. and Hoeffler, A., 2002: Aid, policy and peace, *Journal of Defence Economics and Peace*, **13**(6): 435–50

Collier, P. and Hoeffler, A., 2004a: Greed and grievance in civil war, *Oxford Economic Papers*, **56**(4): 563–95

Collier, P. and Hoeffler, A., 2004b: Aid, policy and growth in post-conflict societies, *European Economic Review*, **48**: 1125–45

Collier, P. and Hoeffler, A., 2004c: Conflicts, chapter 3 in B. Lomborg (ed.), *Global crises: global solutions*, Cambridge University Press, Cambridge

Collier, P. and Hoeffler, A., 2006: Military spending in post-conflict societies, *Economics of Governance*, **7**(1): 89–107

Collier, P. and Hoeffler, A., 2007a: Coup risk and military spending, Department of Economics, Oxford University, mimeo

Collier, P. and Hoeffler, A., 2007b: Civil war, in Hartley and Sandler (eds.), *Handbook of defence economics*, North-Holland, Amsterdam

Collier, P. and Hoeffler, A., 2007c: Unintended consequences: Does aid increase military spending?, *Oxford Bulletin of Economics and Statistics*, **69**(1): 1–27

Collier, P. and Hoeffler, A., 2008: Testing the Neocon agenda: Democracy, resource rents and growth, *European Economic Review*, **53**(3): 293–308

Collier, P., Hoeffler, A., and Pattillo, C., 2001: Capital flight as a portfolio choice, *World Bank Economic Review*, **15**(1): 55–80

Collier, P., Hoeffler, A., and Rohner, D., forthcoming: Beyond greed and grievance: Feasibility and civil war, *Oxford Economic Papers*, **61**(1): 1–27

Collier, P., Hoeffler, A., and Soderbom, M., 2008: Post-conflict risks, *Journal of Peace Research*, **45**(4): 461–78

Collier, P. and Rohner, D., 2008: Conflict, democracy and development, *Journal of the European Economic Association*: 531–40

Davies, V., forthcoming: Capital flight and war, *World Bank Economic Review*

Doucouliagos, H. and Paldam, M., 2006: Aid effectiveness on accumulation: A meta-study, *Kyklos*, **59**: 227–54

Doyle, M. and Sambanis, N., 2006: *Making war and building peace*, Princeton University Press, Princeton

Dunne, P. and Perlo-Freeman, S., 2003: The demand for military spending in developing countries, *International Review of Applied Economics*, **17**(1): 23–48

Elbadawi, I., Kaltani, I.A., and Schmidt-Hebbel, K., 2008: Foreign aid, the real exchange rate, and growth in the aftermath of civil wars, *World Bank Economic Review*: 113–40

Fearon, J. and Laitin, D., 2003: Ethnicity, insurgency and civil war, *American Political Science Review*, **97**(1): 75–90

Gleditsch, N.P., Wallensteen, P., Eriksson, M., Sollenberg, M., and Strand, H., 2002: Armed

[1] Collier (2007) proposes the concept of the "bottom billion," composed of fifty-eight small, low-income countries in various development traps and with a combined population of around 1 billion people. These countries are distinctive in that they are both much poorer than other developing countries and diverging from them.

conflict 1946–2001: A new data set, *Journal of Peace Research*, **39**(5): 615–37

Harbom, L. and Wallensteen, H., 2007: Armed conflict, 1989–2006, *Journal of Peace Research*, **44**(5): 623–34

Hartley, K. and Sandler, T. (eds.) 2007: *Handbook of defence economics*, North-Holland, Amsterdam

Hegre, H., 2003: Disentangling democracy and development as determinants of armed conflict, Paper presented at the 44th Annual Convention of the International Studies Association, Portland, OR, February 26–March 1

Hegre, H., Ellingsen, T., Gates, S., and Gleditsch, N.P., 2001: Toward a democratic civil peace? Democracy, political change, and civil war, 1816–1992, *American Political Science Review*, **95**(1): 33–48

Macmillan, M., 2006: *The peacemakers*, John Murray, London

Martin, P. and Mayer, T., 2008, Civil wars and international trade, *Journal of the European Economic Association*: 541–50

McGowan, P.J., 2003: African military coups d'état, 1956–2003, *Journal of Modern African Studies*, **41**(3): 339–70

McIndoe, T., 2007: An analysis of capital flight, Oxford University, M.Phil. thesis

Miguel, E., Satyanath, S., and Sergenti, E., 2004: Economic shocks and civil conflict: an instrumental variables approach, *Journal of Political Economy*: 725–53

Murdoch, X and Sandler, T., 2002: Economic growth, civil wars and spatial spillovers, *Journal of Conflict Resolution*, **46**(1): 91–110

Nilsson, D., 2008: Partial peace. rebel groups inside and outside of civil war settlements, *Journal of Peace Research*, **45**(4): 479–95

Rajan, R.G. and Subramanian, A., 2005: What undermines aid's impact on growth?, IMF Working Paper, **126**

Tavares, X., 2003: Does foreign aid corrupt?, *Economic Letters*, **79**: 99–106

Urdal, H., 2006: A clash of generations? Youth bulges and political violence, *International Studies Quarterly*, **50**: 607–29

Vicente, P., 2006: Does oil corrupt? Evidence from a natural experiment in West Africa, CSAE, Oxford, mimeo

Walter, B.F., 2001: *Committing to peace*, Princeton University Press, Princeton

Weinstein, J., 2005: Autonomous recovery and international intervention in comparative perspective, Center for Global Development, Working Paper, **57**, Washington, DC

Wood, A., 2006: Looking ahead optimally, Queen Elizabeth House, Oxford, mimeo

Alternative Perspectives

Perspective Paper 2.1

IBRAHIM A. ELBADAWI*

Introduction

In their Challenge paper, Paul Collier, Lisa Chauvet, and Håvard Hegre (2007; hereafter, CCH) argue that the typically small low-income countries coming out of recent conflicts are likely to face enormous internal security risks from relapses into new civil wars or military coups. CCH cite recent evidence from the literature suggesting that post-conflict relapses account for 50 percent of the overall incidences of new civil wars. While they note that coups tend to be less frequent and less costly, they argue that they are, nevertheless, highly undesirable because they appear to be most effective in toppling nascent post-conflict democracies. CCH observe that currently governments that face these types of risk tend to respond by increasing military spending which, they argue, has failed to reduce

their security risks. Hence, both the risks and the response to them are costly.

CCH estimate the core costs of civil war and coups for a typical high-risk post-conflict country. These estimates are derived from simulating empirical models of the growth consequences of civil wars, coups, and the military expenditures associated with their underlying risks. The core costs, however, are likely to grossly under-state the true costs because they fail to account for five omissions.[1] To account for these omissions, the authors also estimate scaled-up "center-of-the-range" costs, which should be regarded as an informed, though speculative, assessment of the true general equilibrium costs of post-conflict risks. The estimates suggest that the costs involved are, indeed, very high:

- The core cost of a typical civil war amounts to $60 billion, while the full center-of-the-range estimates comes to a staggering $250 billion
- Over the past forty years, civil wars have exacted a core cost of about $123 billion per year, and a full cost of $500 billion a year
- Coups, on the other hand, have been associated with core and total costs of $4 and $16 billion a year, respectively

Having established the high costs of post-conflict risks, and hence the high *gross* benefits of dealing with these risks, CCH discuss the analytical basis for their proposed prescriptive security package and the benefit-cost ratios associated with it. They develop a diagnosis

* Paper prepared for the Roundtable Copenhagen Consensus 2008, Copenhagen, May 26–30, 2008. I would like to thank, without implication, Gary Milante for helpful comments. The views expressed in this paper do not necessarily reflect the official position of the World Bank, its Board of Directors, or affiliated institutions.
[1] These are that: the people affected by conflicts are disproportionately among the most impoverished in the world; the absence of peace frustrates all other potential development initiatives; the cost of civil wars is concentrated within a society; the cost of internal conflict is highly persistent; and, conflicts have global spill-over effects, including in terms of crime, disease, and terrorism.

based on the received literature, largely drawing on the empirical cross-country research by Collier and his research associates. The main thesis of this strand of the literature is that factors that influence "feasibility" of a rebellion, especially economic feasibility, are the main determinants of the risk of political violence. Therefore, high-risk countries are those with low income, slow growth, high dependence on commodity exports, and rough terrain. Moreover, a more recent extension of the original Collier and Hoeffler (2004a) model, which undertakes extensive robustness tests, also finds social characteristics to be robustly associated with high risk of civil war, including small population, large share of youth, and social fractionalization (Collier, Hoeffler, and Rohner 2008). However, the other fundamental finding of this literature is that political legitimacy, as accounted for by democracy, has no influence on the risk of civil war and that it tends to *increase* not *decrease* the risk of coups. While halving income, this literature suggests, increases the risk of coups by 35 percent, high repression (–5 or less in the Polity IV scale)[2] would increase such risk by 50 percent.

Based on their *diagnosis* of post-conflict risks, CCH's fundamental, if implicit, punch line appears to be that, aside from direct security measures, the only other viable response to post-conflict risks should be to directly address the problems of slow growth and lack of economic diversification. It can also be inferred from their diagnosis that political legitimacy, as desirable as it may be for its own intrinsic value, has no role in this process. Moreover, their *prognosis* of recent development is even more explicit with regard to the latter. CCH argue that high risks of civil wars and coups are more likely due to recent development associated with a combination of commodity booms in weakly governed poor countries (e.g. Collier and Goderis 2007a, 2007b); proliferation of democracy across low-income countries (Collier and Rohner 2008); and the large number of negotiated peace settlements, which tend to have a history of high risks of relapse. Furthermore, negotiated peace settlements also

include provisions for post-conflict elections, which have also been associated with high post-election risks, though they might lead to reduced risks prior to election time (Collier, Hoeffler, and Soderbom 2008).

Against the backdrop of their seemingly compelling diagnosis–prognosis analytics, CCH develop their ultimate contribution, which is the prescriptive package for addressing post-conflict risks. The proposed package is benchmarked on development aid, which was assessed to be highly effective (as the post-conflict aid effectiveness literature suggests)[3] but not spectacular. CCH estimate that an aid package for a typical post-conflict country of about $4 billion would generate an overall benefit of about $14.25 billion, which suggests a benefit-cost ratio of 3.5:1. To increase the benefit-cost ratios to high enough levels, necessary for a credible response, CCH propose augmenting development aid with a reciprocal package of three military-related instruments:

- Linking development aid to an agreement to limit military spending by the recipient country
- Addressing security needs of the recipient country through provision of "peacekeeping force" and/or "over-the-horizon" security guarantees
- Verification of commitment to the military expenditure cap by a supranational body with political legitimacy, such as the UN Peace-Building Commission

This paper provides an alternative opposing perspective on the risks faced by post-conflict and other low-income countries. Drawing from other work in the literature, the diagnosis developed will attempt to challenge the "feasibility hypothesis" and establish lack of political legitimacy as a cause of conflicts. Moreover, we shall argue that there is robust evidence from the

---

[2] Polity is a global index of the standard of democracy and ranges from –10 (strongly autocratic) to 10 (strongly democratic); for a detailed description of these indices and data, see: www.cidcm.umd.edu/inscr/polity/.

[3] See, for example, Collier and Hoeffler (2004b); Adam *et al.* (2008); Elbadawi *et al.* (2008).

growth literature linking democracy to growth sustainability, which has been the most difficult challenge facing low-income countries with fractionalized societies and high susceptibility to external shocks. Since high and sustained growth is critical for reducing post-conflict risks, democracy will be important even from a pure "feasibility hypothesis" hypothesis. We shall also discuss the role of the UN peacekeeping mandate in peacebuilding, a totally neglected issue in the CCH analysis. It will be argued that the nature of the mandate is critical for sustained peace in the longer run, following the departure of the peacekeeping force. This analysis also highlights the role of domestic institutions and how they can be positively influenced by an expanded "transformational" UN mandate.

The next section presents the alternative diagnosis on democracy and political legitimacy, while the third section discusses the issues regarding the nature of the UN mandate. The fourth section draws the implications of the alternative diagnosis for the proposed package and the cost-benefit calculus of CCH. The fifth section draws some conclusions.

An Alternative Diagnosis: Political Legitimacy Matters

Despite what appears to be compelling empirical evidence in support of the "feasibility hypothesis," there is hardly a consensus, partly because the evidence is at odds with a large body of theoretical literature.[4] Moreover, the more recent literature that underpins this hypothesis makes the untenable assumption that the civil war outcome can be neatly isolated from the overall

---

[4] Moreover, the "feasibility hypothesis" is also at odds with the conventional wisdom held by politicians and journalists; see Cederman and Girardin (2007) and the review of the culturalist perspective in Fearon and Laitin (2003).

[5] The empirical literature in this tradition includes Ellingsen (2000); Sambanis (2001, 2004); Collier and Hoeffler (2002); Reynal-Querol (2003); Cederman and Girardin (2007).

phenomenon of political violence[5] (Sambanis 2006 on terrorism is an exception). In his review of the main approaches and results of the study of civil war, Sambanis (2004, abstract) notes: "If we cannot understand why we get civil war instead of other forms of organized political violence, then we do not understand civil war at all." Sambanis goes on to write that: "For many countries caught in a conflict trap, civil war is a phase in the cycle of violence. By isolating civil war in quantitative studies, we choose to focus on an event rather than a process, and we discard a lot of useful information that explains how we end up having a civil war" (2004: 268). Perhaps the only paper in the recent empirical literature that explicitly accounts for this consideration is Bodea and Elbadawi (2007a), who embed the study of civil war in a more general analysis of varieties of violent conflicts within the borders of the state. Empirically, other possible manifestations of irregular and violent contestation of political power are coups and riots or low-intensity conflict. Bodea and Elbadawi (2007a) develop a theory of risk of political violence that shows that the combinations of low income (or major shocks to the economy) and low standards of democracy are likely to be associated with high probability of violence, regardless of the social characteristics of a society and for all types of political violence. Further they argue that because existing lines of identity and contestation will provide motivational and informational advantages to potential rebel leaders to grow a rebel organization, social fractionalization will be most likely associated with civil war. Also, fractionalization does not necessarily affect coup and low-intensity violence, because coups require other type of organizational advantages (insider presence in the police and military) and lower levels of violence tend to be more random and lack coherent organization.

Subscribing to this simple and, hopefully, intuitive theoretical framework, Bodea and Elbadawi (2007a) use a multinomial logit empirical specification, in which the manifestations of violence range from lower-intensity armed violence to coups and civil wars. If civil war is just one of the alternative expressions of violent contestation of political power, a multinomial model is more appropriate than the use of logit or probit models.[6] To investigate the determinants of conflict, they estimate a family of encompassing multinomial regressions using a global database from 1950 to 1999, accounting for three types of domestic violence (civil wars, coups, and other violent outcomes) as well as a host of "grievance" and "feasibility" variables commonly analyzed in the recent empirical literature. To test the effect of political regime on the risk of violent conflict the paper uses a typology of democracy based on the two components of the Polity IV score that deal with competitiveness of the political system at the leadership and mass level. Bodea and Elbadawi identify fully fledged democracies, partial non-factional democracies, partial factional democracies, partial autocracies, and full-blown autocratic regimes. Their findings show that credible democratic regimes granting full political rights may reduce the risk of civil war more efficiently than repressive autocracy. They also find that countries most vulnerable to conflict, from violent demonstrations to coups and civil war are partial *factional* democracies, while partial *non-factional* democracies are not more risky than autocracies.

These findings are important because they suggest that the high risks associated with democratic transitions in poor countries, including post-conflict low-income countries, is not because their democracies are unstable and anocratic but rather because they tend to be factional, where institutional openness and political participation are channeled through networks rooted in traditional, ethnic identities. So rather than "throwing the baby out with the bath tub," a more nuanced diagnosis should investigate approaches to promote non-factional democracy, because it cannot be riskier than full autocracy.

Another pertinent contribution is Bruckner and Ciccone (2007), who analyze the impact of economic growth on the risk of civil wars in Sub-Saharan Africa (SSA). Following an innovative approach due to Miguel, Satyanath,

and Sergenti (2004), who instrument economic growth using rainfall, Bruckner and Ciccone introduce international commodity prices as an additional instrument as well as control for political regime type. They find that low growth increases the likelihood of both onset and incidence of civil war in autocracies. However, in countries with democratic institutions there is no statistically significant effect. Based on their results Bruckner and Ciccone draw the following important conclusion: "Hence, our findings do not support the view that lower income growth raises the chance of civil war regardless of a country's institutional setup. Instead, they point to an interaction between economic and institutional causes of civil war" (2007: 13).

One more, and very important, contribution arguing for democracy as a risk-mitigating factor focuses on the regional dimensions of civil wars. Raleigh (2007) analyzes the effects of neighborhood characteristics on a state's risk of conflict and instability. Specifically, she asks the following vital questions: What is the interaction between neighboring conflict and political disorder? And, do democratic neighborhoods have different conflict trajectories from non-democratic neighborhoods and, if so, where and why? The empirical analysis of Raleigh's paper suggests that, especially for low-income countries, neighborhoods matter in that neighboring wars increase risks of civil war onset and that neighborhood political attributes can mitigate or aggravate country risks. In particular, it was found that "if a state is surrounded by stable, developed democracies the risk of conflict, regardless of income, never increases past 4%" (2007: 27). On the other hand, low-income countries in an autocratic or anocratic neighborhood will experience exceptionally high risk.

Finally, we briefly review the evidence on the indirect effect of democracy on risk through its impact on economic growth. In an extensive

---

[6] Also, a multinomial framework is more appropriate than a bivariate model of domestic conflict (civil war, coups, and armed violence lumped together) because it recognizes that different forms of conflict may have different determinants (O'Brien 2002; Reagan and Norton 2005).

study, Barro (1996) finds democracy to have significant positive but non-monotonic effects on growth. The growth-maximizing level of democracy (measured by the Freedom House index of political rights) suggested by Barro's regression comes out roughly equal to the levels prevailing in Malaysia and Mexico in 1994. Barro interprets his finding to suggest that at low levels of democracy (associated with extreme dictatorships) an increase in political rights "tends to enhance growth and investment because the benefit from limitations on government power is the key matter. But in places that have already achieved a moderate amount of democracy, a further increase in political rights impairs growth and investment because the dominant effect comes from the intensified concern with income distribution" (1996: 37).

However, most subsequent studies have failed to replicate Barro's result, as they do not find democracy (as well as autocracy, for that matter) to be robustly associated with long-term growth.[7] Nevertheless, given that civil liberties and political rights have intrinsic values of their own, it is still comforting to find that they at least do not constitute a trade off for long-term growth – i.e. they are not necessarily less effective in promoting growth than authoritarian regimes. Moreover, Rodrik (1999), who himself finds no systematic relationship between democracy and long-term growth, argues that

[7] For example, Rodrik (1999) finds no systematic relationship between democracy and long-term growth; while Helliwell (1994) finds that democracy spurs education and investment, but has no direct effect on growth when these two channels are controlled for. Tavares and Wacziarg (2001) estimate a system of simultaneous equations and find an indirect effect of democracy on growth through enhanced education, reduced inequality, and lower government consumption.

[8] See also Rodrik and Wacziarg (2005), who find democratic transitions to be robustly associated with short-term growth; they find this evidence to be particularly strong for socially fractionalized SSA and other low-income countries.

[9] Bodea and Elbadawi (2007b) estimate a dynamic panel model, which fully accounts for country heterogeneity and potential endogeneity, and controls for the impact of organized political violence and other growth controls, including democracy and social characteristics.

in fact democracies perform better than authoritarian regimes in other aspects of economic development.[8] In particular, Rodrik shows that long-run growth under democracies is more predictable; that democracies are more capable of handling adverse shocks; and that democracies pay higher wages, because they tend to promote more egalitarian social order. According to Rodrik (1999), democracies are better at handling shocks because shocks tend to exacerbate conflict among social groups, especially in societies that are fractionalized along class or identity lines. When institutions for mediating such conflicts are weak or do not exist, the economic costs of external shocks can be magnified due to policy reversals and adoption of growth-retarding short-run distributive policies. However, given that democracies provide the ultimate institutions of conflicts management, the social conflicts and the ensuing economic costs following external shocks should be lower under democracies than under authoritarian regimes.

Returning to the long-term growth effect of democracy, Bodea and Elbadawi (2007b) show that, akin to their political violence analysis, when democracy is disaggregated into well-functioning, non-factional, and factional partial democracies, a more nuanced story emerges. They find that,[9] relative to autocracy, full democracy as well as partial but non-factional democracy have had positive impacts on growth. They also find ethnic fractionalization to have a negative and direct effect on growth, though its effect is substantially ameliorated when inter-ethnic context is mediated by non-factional democracy, again even when it is only partial. They therefore argue that the growth impact of non-factional democracy is rather compelling because it does not only have a direct and positive effect on *per capita* income growth but also reduces the negative growth effect of ethnic fractionalization through an interaction term.

Taken together, the literature reviewed above suggests the following important findings. First, relative to full autocracy, fully functioning democracy reduces the risk of civil wars and other forms of political violence, while non-factional, even if partial, democracy has no direct impact. Second, because it is robustly associated with long-term growth, non-factional democracy indirectly contributes to reducing the risk of political violence. Third, though it may not be robustly associated with long-term growth, (aggregate) democracy is critical for growth sustainability, especially in socially fractionalized societies experiencing frequent external economic shocks, as is the case for many low-income post-conflict countries. Therefore, unlike the CCH diagnosis and their prospective prognosis, ours would suggest that the promotion of democracy, especially non-factional democracy, should be a legitimate risk-mitigation instrument and, therefore, a key component of the post-conflict peacebuilding strategy.

An Alternative Diagnosis: The UN Mandate and Sustainable Peace

An important strand of the post-conflict risk/peacebuilding literature focuses on the concept of "sustainable peace" which, according to the UN view, hinges on the "capacity of a sovereign state to resolve the natural conflicts to which all societies are prone by means other than war."[10] The empirical articulation of this view is the "participatory peace" concept, which involves an end to war, no significant residual violence, undivided sovereignty, and a minimum level of political openness (Doyle and Sambanis 2000, 2006).[11] This literature analyzes the nature of the mandate governing UN peacekeeping operations that might be required for achieving this ambitious concept, which is obviously much more demanding than the more basic one that simply requires the absence of war, or what Sambanis (2008) calls "negative peace." In this literature, the probability of peacebuilding success (such as participatory or negative peace) is specified as proportional to an area of the "peace" triangle, which is determined by three sets of factors: Degree of hostility in society, and the extent of local, and international competencies for peacebuilding. Greater hostility (ethno-religious war; high social fractionalization; no

peace treaty; many factions; long wars; and many deaths and displacements) and low local competencies (reflected by low indicators of socioeconomic development) make peacebuilding success less likely. Since most post-conflict societies are characterized by high degree of hostilities and low local competency, the peacebuilding space hinges on greater commitment by the international community.

Using a logistic regression model of "participatory" peacebuilding success that also controls for hostility and local competency variables, Sambanis (2008) finds a significant and positive marginal short-run impact of UN missions (regardless of the mandate). However, accounting for the mandate by distinguishing between *facilitative* (monitoring and reporting) and *transformational* (multidimensional, enforcement, and transitional administration) UN missions suggests that the nature of the mandate is crucial to success. With other variables held at their sample median, going from facilitative to transformational peacekeeping increases the probability of peacebuilding success by 36 percent. Moreover, the evidence also suggests that transformational UN missions are more robustly associated with participatory peace, and hence post-conflict democratization, than "economistic" factors, such as the level and growth rate of income *per capita*.

Another pertinent contribution of Sambanis' paper pertains to assessing the long-run impact of UN missions as a determinant of peace duration, simply defined as absence of war or "negative peace." Using a survival probability model, Sambanis finds that UN intervention reduces the risk of peace failure by 50 percent. However, in the long run, peacebuilding success is found to be more closely associated with local capacity

---

[10] This is the formal definition adopted by the UN Security Council, as quoted in Sambanis (2008: 3).

[11] Empirically, Sambanis (2008) codes participatory peace as a binary variable that takes the value of 1, if all of the Doyle–Sambanis conditions of "participatory peace" are met *two years after the departure of a UN peacekeeping mission*, or two years after the end of conflict when no UN operation was involved. The threshold of political openness used was 3.0 in the Polity IV score.

variables. While the effect of UN mission is less robust in the long run, hostility variables are non-significant. Therefore, fast-growing, rapidly diversifying, or high-income economies are far more likely to experience a longer peace duration, even when hostilities remain high.

This research suggests, therefore, that "transformational" UN peacekeeping operations are very effective in promoting a broad concept of peace that entails post-conflict democratization and building of a robust institutional capacity for mediating conflicts within the post-conflict society. Moreover, in the longer run, economic performance is the main determinant of post-conflict risk. Therefore, the ultimate long-term goal of peacebuilding should be to enable post-conflict societies to sustain a high level of economic performance, in terms of high *per capita* growth and economic diversification.

However, as the analysis above suggests, sustaining high growth requires post-conflict democratization that, in turn, hinges on the nature of the UN mandate. Therefore, despite the fact that high economic performance is the ultimate mitigation strategy against post-conflict risks, it is highly unlikely that such growth can be achieved without the support of a "transformational" UN operation in the immediate five–ten years following the end of conflict.

Another perspective emphasizing the importance of the emerging post-conflict political process for economic outcomes – and, hence, peace – is due to Keefer (2008). Keefer argues that because weakly credible leaders cannot persuade the majority of their citizenry to believe their promises, they are likely to undertake policies in the interest of the few specific groups that do believe them, which leads to under-provision of public goods, over-provision of private goods, and high levels of corruption. In such a distorted environment, Keefer argues, citizens are less likely to resist efforts to unseat the incumbent elites. This is one way through which lack of

political credibility can be a cause of conflict. Lack of political credibility also raises the risk of conflicts by weakening the resistance to an incipient counter-insurgency. Weakly credible leaders are incapable of mounting an effective counter-insurgency effort because they are also inept at making credible commitment to the counter-insurgents. Embedding empirical proxies for political credibility in a standard model of civil war onset, Keefer finds strong empirical support for his proposition.[12] The link between political credibility and provision of public goods, and hence growth, suggests that Keefer's research should have strong implications for peacebuilding as well. This is because Sambanis' finding on the dominance of income and economic growth, as determinants of successful peacebuilding in the long run, provides a link to the literature on the causes of civil wars, which has been shown to be driven by accumulated effects of low or negative growth. The contribution by Keefer is thus important because it goes to the deep institutional issue of what determines the provision of public goods, growth, and hence the risk of conflict in a society, as well as the prospects for sustained peace when war ends.

Implications for the Proposed Package

The alternative diagnoses of the last two sections suggest that high economic performance in post-conflict situations should be the ultimate mitigating strategy for post-conflict risks in the long run. This supports the fundamental insight behind CCH's benefit-cost calculus, which is anchored on the collapse of growth as a core input to cost and its revival as the benefit of peace. However, our analysis also suggests that both peace and post-conflict growth would require credible political processes that can transcend narrowly focused identity politics; and that sustainability of growth may also require post-conflict democratization. Moreover, these post-conflict institutions are not likely to materialize without broad-based "transformational" UN operations during the immediate period following the end of conflicts. In terms of the direct

---

[12] Keefer (2008) accounts for political credibility by "more continuous years of competitive elections" for the case of democracies, and in both democracies and autocracies by indicators of institutionalized or programmatic political parties.

influences on post-conflict risks, unlike those of CCH I argue that lack of political legitimacy can be a direct cause of civil wars and coups. However, in socially fractionalized societies, factional democracies can be as bad as autocracy. Finally, the regional dimension of conflicts is also strongly emphasized in the alternative diagnosis of this article. While a conflictive region can be a major source of instability for a member country, a democratic neighborhood can exert a potent mitigating influence in a country that might otherwise be ripe for conflict.

We are now ready to address the ultimate question of this opposing perspective to CCH: What implications will this have for the CCH package and its associated benefit-cost calculus?

First, UN peacekeeping operations should be of a "transformational" nature (in the Sambanis' sense, to enable them to assist with the ultimate goal of creating (or restoring) political legitimacy post-conflict, especially with regard to promoting stable inter-ethnic non-violent political contests. This consideration will have implications for the design of peace agreements as well as the benefit-cost calculus of UN PKO:

- The requirements of inclusive post-conflict political processes suggest that peace agreements should not be confined to the military protagonists in the civil war, such as the case of the two recent Sudanese peace agreements;[13] instead, even at the expense of complexity, peace agreements should avoid disenfranchising non-militarized stakeholders, such as political parties or local communities, who might have strong popular following
- The benefit-cost calculus should disaggregate cost of the UN PKO by mandate – because, though transformational PKO will be costlier, their benefits are likely to be spectacularly more significant if their impact on growth sustainability, through their potential role in promoting *non-factional* democratic transformation, is properly accounted for

Second, the design of PKO, "over-the-horizon" security guarantees as well as military spending conditionality should be sensitive to the underside risk of undermining the local legitimacy of the emerging post-conflict political order:

- The idea of hybrid PKO, involving a regional supranational entity, such as the African Union participation with the UN in the Darfur PKO, is a very worthwhile initiative in terms of augmenting international legitimacy, which is often times viewed (rightly or wrongly) as subject to unduly excessive Western influence
- The "over-the-horizon" security guarantees should be explicitly anchored on the buy-in by the concerned national and supranational political institutions; if anything, the largely successful British-led peace-keeping operation in Sierra Leone, including its "over-the-horizon" guarantee component, is partly attributed to its being subservient to the political process, while the struggling American-led one in Liberia has been insulated from parliamentary oversight[14]
- The "over-the-horizon" security guarantees should also be guided by coherent objectives that enjoy wide appeal, such as the one articulated by CCH regarding the provision of security guarantees against coups to post-conflict democracies, which also happen to have strong pan-African support
- Aid conditionality associated with military expenditure could also benefit from buy-in by regional supranational bodies, because supranational arrangements add further legitimacy as well as providing much-needed peer pressure on member countries, especially if donor countries could commit to limiting arms sales to troubled regions affected by risks of civil wars and coups

[13] These are the 2005 Comprehensive Peace Agreement between the National Congress Party (NCP)-led Government of the Sudan and the Sudanese People Liberation Movement (SPLM) that ended the longest civil war in Africa; and the dysfunctional Darfur Peace Agreement in 2007 between the Government of National Unity (led by the NCP and the SPLM) and one faction from the Darfur rebels. While the latter failed to stop the violence in Darfur, the former produced peace but uneasy coexistence between the two militarized parties.

[14] See McNamee *et al.* (2007) for a detailed analysis.

- Admittedly, supranational regional entities in poor regions, such as SSA, have not been very effective, which suggests that they would require substantial support in terms of equipment, training, and technical capabilities before they could become dependable partners in PKO, especially "transformational" PKO; while this will surely add to the cost estimates, it is also likely to have large benefits

Third, the very important, but relatively neglected, regional dimension of civil wars requires a major rethink of the security and developmental approaches to peacebuilding:

- Promoting regional democracy, again in the context of partnership with supranational regional bodies, should be an explicit agenda for the UN Peace-Building Commission and other Western donor countries
- To further strengthen this regional orientation, the capacity of these entities as agents for the promotion of regional cooperation, and deeper economic interdependence among member states, should be enhanced through technical and financial support – including through substantive partnerships with multilateral and bilateral development agencies on regional development initiatives on infrastructure, international water course, etc. . . .

The implications of our different reading of the relevant literature and the subsequent alternative diagnosis of the issues involved would therefore suggest significant modifications to CCH's proposed package, in terms of both modalities and the calculus of the benefit-costs ratios.

Conclusions

CCH (2007) propose an integrated security package to deal with post-conflict risks from civil war relapses and coups. Though coups are less frequent and less costly, they have rightly argued that they nevertheless remain a serious threat to nascent post-conflict democracies. CCH's proposed security package is composed of three military instruments: Making development aid conditional on mutually agreed and verifiable limits to military expenditure; peacekeeping operation following end of civil wars; and provision of "over-the-horizon" security guarantees, including protecting post-conflict democratically elected governments from coups. CCH's proposed package is benchmarked on development aid, which was assessed by the authors to have good but not spectacular benefit-cost ratios. Development aid would, therefore, need to be augmented by further and more direct security measures. Moreover, CCH demonstrate that military expenditure – the response of choice (or perhaps of necessity) by insecure post-conflict governments – has, if any thing, been associated with further risks and higher leakages of development aid. Therefore, both the risk and the response are costly to post-conflict governments. Hence, the proposed cap on military expenditure, CCH argue, would not only close off a major source of risk, but would also increase aid effectiveness. The other two security measures are direct risk-mitigating instruments that, CCH suggest, will be required to persuade post-conflict governments to agree to significant reductions in military expenditure.

CCH's estimate of the risk reduction associated with their proposed scale of peacekeeping and over-the-horizon guarantee operations is spectacular. Barring double counting, they suggest that the ten-year risk per country would fall from around 38 to just 9 percent. Taken together, their (center-of-the-range) estimate of total cost of the package comes to $10.8 billion per year, compared to a total benefit ranging from $57– $192 billion per year. The associated benefit-cost ratio of the package ranges from 1:5 to 1:19, which is much higher than the corresponding ratio for development aid alone.

CCH's proposed package is premised on the economic "feasibility" view of civil war risks, which suggests that the high risk of civil wars and coups is associated with low income, slow growth, and high dependence on commodity exports as core determinants. However, according to this strand of the literature, political legitimacy, as accounted for by democracy, has no direct influence on the risk of civil war and that it tends to increase not decrease the risk of coups. Moreover, CCH's prognosis suggests even higher risks in the future associated with the recent wave of democratization in low-income countries, especially in those experiencing commodity booms.

In this paper, I have provided an alternative diagnosis of the risks involved, based on a more inclusive reading of the received literature. This opposing perspective questions the validity of the "feasibility hypothesis," and provides evidence on the relevance of political legitimacy as a direct risk-mitigating factor. Moreover, democracy is also shown to be critical for growth sustainability, which unlike igniting growth for a few years, remains the most difficult challenge facing low-income countries with fractionalized societies and high susceptibility to external shocks. Since high and sustained growth is critical for reducing post-conflict risks, democracy will be important even from the perspective of a pure "feasibility" hypothesis. Another important argument for democracy as a risk-mitigating factor focuses on the regional dimensions of civil wars. This literature suggests that neighboring wars increases risks of civil war onset and that a stable democratic neighborhood significantly reduces country risks. Furthermore, and unlike, CCH, the opposing perspective of this article emphasizes the role of domestic political intuitions as the ultimate providers of public goods, growth, and security in the longer run. Naturally, this recognition would require accounting for the complexities involved in the building of credible polity in the typically socially fractionalized post-conflict societies. This, in turn, highlights the critical significance of "transformational" UN peace-keeping operations in promoting post-conflict democratization and institution-building.

Therefore, by prematurely dismissing political legitimacy as a risk-mitigating factor, the CCH package is, inherently, an externally driven proposal. Moreover, by ignoring the critical role of domestic institutions and the regional dimensions of conflicts and the risks generated by them, CCH's proposed package also fails to account for the importance of the nature of the UN mandate as well as the need to involve supranational entities as key partners in the peacebuilding process. As such, and despite CCH's emphasis on reciprocity, the proposed package is also blatantly West-centric. Accounting for the issues raised by the opposing perspective, I have discussed several adjustments to CCH's proposed package, aimed at enhancing the ownership of national political institutions in the peacebuilding process and promoting buy-in and partnership on the part of regional supranational bodies. The implications of these adjustments for the benefit-cost calculus will be substantial, though they are not likely to reverse the fundamental conclusions regarding the spectacular net global benefits of pursuing a pro-active peacebuilding agenda on the part of the international community.

Bibliography

Adam, C., Collier, P., and Davies, V., 2008: Postconflict monetary reconstruction, *World Bank Economic Review*, **22**(1): 87–112

Barro, R., 1996: Determinants of economic growth: A cross country empirical study, NBER Working Paper, **5698**, August

Bodea, C. and Elbadawi, I., 2007a: Riots, coups and civil war: Revisiting the greed and grievance debate, Post-Conflict Transition Policy Research Working Paper, **4397**, Development Economic Research Group, World Bank, Washington DC

Bodea, C. and Elbadawi, I., 2007b: Political violence and underdevelopment, Unpublished mimeo, presented at the Plenary Session of the AERC bi-annual Research Workshop, Nairobi, December 2006

Bruckner, M. and Ciccone, A., 2007: Growth, democracy and civil war, CEPR Discussion Paper, **6568**, November

Cederman, L.-E. and Girardin, L., 2007: Beyond fractionalization: Mapping ethnicity onto nationalist insurgencies, *American Political Science Review*, **101**(1): 173–86

Collier, P., Chauvet, L., and Hegre, H., 2007: The security challenge in conflict-prone countries,

A Challenge paper for the Copenhagen Consensus, September, see chapter 2 in this volume

Collier, P. and Goderis, B., 2007a: Prospects for commodity exports: Hunky dory or humpty dumpty?, *World Economics*, **8**(2): 1–15

Collier, P. and Goderis, B., 2007b: Commodity prices and the resource curse: Resolving a conundrum, Department of Economics, Oxford University, unpublished mimeo

Collier, P. and Hoeffler, A., 2002: On the incidence of civil war in Africa, *Journal of Conflict Resolution*, **46**(1): 13–28

Collier, P. and Hoeffler, A., 2004a: Greed, grievance and civil war, *Oxford Economic Papers*, **26**: 563–95

Collier, P. and Hoeffler, A., 2004b: Aid, policy and growth in post-conflict societies, *European Economic Review*, **48**(5): 1125–45

Collier, P., Hoeffler, A., and Rohner, D., 2007: Beyond greed and grievance: Feasibility and civil war, Department of Economics, Oxford University, unpublished mimeo

Collier, P., Hoeffler, A., and Soderbom, M., 2008: Post-conflict risks, *Journal of Peace Research*, **45**(4): 461–78

Collier, P. and Rohner, D., 2008: Conflict, democracy and development, *Journal of the European Economic Association*, **6**(2–3): 531–40

Doyle, M.W., and Sambanis, N., 2006: *Making war and building peace: United Nations peace operations*, Princeton University Press, Princeton

Doyle, M.W., and Sambanis, N., 2000: International peacebuilding: A theoretical and quantitative analysis, *American Political Science Review*, **94**(4): 779–801

Elbadawi, I.A., Kaltani, L., and Schmidt-Hebbel, K., 2008: Foreign aid, the real exchange rate, and growth in the aftermath of civil wars, *World Bank Economic Review*, **22**(1): 113–40

Ellingsen, T., 2000: Colorful community of ethnic witches' brew? Multiethnicity and domestic conflict during and after the Cold War, *Journal of Conflict Resolution*, **44**(2): 228–49

Fearon, J. and Laitin, D., 2003: Ethnicity, insurgency and civil war, *American Political Science Review*, **97**(1): 75–89

Helliwell, J., 1994: Empirical linkages between democracy and economic growth, *British Journal of Political Science*, **24**: 225–48

Keefer, P., 2008: Insurgency and credible commitment in autocracies and democracies, *World Bank Economic Review*, **22**(1): 33–61

McNamee, T., Mils, G., and Napier, M., 2007: Rebuilding Africa's fragile states, The Royal United Service Institute, London, www.rusi.org, unpublished mimeo

Miguel, E., Satyanath, S., and Sergenti, E., 2004: Economic shocks and civil conflicts: An instrumental variables approach, *Journal of Political Economy*, **112**(41): 725–53

O'Brien, S.P., 2002: Anticipating the good, the bad and the ugly, *Journal of Conflict Resolution*, **46**(6): 791–811

Raleigh, C., 2007: Civil war risk in democratic and non-democratic neighborhoods, Post-Conflict Transition Policy Research Working Paper, **4260**, Development Economic Research Group, World Bank, Washington, DC

Reagan, P.M. and Norton, D., 2005: Greed, grievance and mobilization in civil war, *Journal of Conflict Resolution*, **49**(3): 319–426

Reynal-Querol, M., 2003: Ethnicity, political systems and civil wars, *Journal of Conflict Resolution*, **46**(1): 29–54

Rodrik, D., 1999: Where did all the growth go? External shocks, social conflict, and growth collapses, *Journal of Economic Growth*, **4**(4): 385–412

Rodrik, D. and Wacziarg, R., 2005: Do democratic transitions produce bad economic outcomes?, *American Economic Review, Papers and Proceedings*, **95**(2): 50–5

Sambanis, N., 2001: Do ethnic and non-ethnic civil wars have the same causes? A theoretical and empirical inquiry, *Journal of Conflict Resolution*, **45**(3): 259–82

Sambanis, N., 2004: What is civil war? Conceptual and empirical complexities of an operational definition, *Journal of Conflict Resolution*, **48**(6): 814–58

Sambanis, N., 2006: Terrorism and civil war, in P. Keefer and N. Loayza (eds.), *Terrorism and Development*, Cambridge University Press, Cambridge

Sambanis, N., 2008: Short- and long-term effects of United Nations peace operations, *World Bank Economic Review*, **22**(1): 9–32

Tavares, J. and Wacziarg, R., 2001: How democracy affects growth, *European Economic Review*, **45**(8): 134178

Perspective Paper 2.2

ANDREW MACK

Introduction

Paul Collier, Lisa Chauvet, and Havard Hegre (hereafter, CCH) have produced an important, detailed and closely reasoned case for reducing the *recurrence* of political violence in post-conflict societies. Their paper focuses on this issue because – depending on definition and dataset – 40 percent or more of armed conflicts that stop, start again within a decade. The paper also examines the drivers of military coups, drawing on data from Sub-Saharan Africa (SSA), and asks what can be done to prevent them.

CCH's analysis proceeds first by determining the major risk factors for civil war and for military coups, of which in both cases low GDP *per capita* and (relatedly) low economic levels of economic growth are critically important. From this it follows that increasing GDP *per capita* via economic growth should be an effective strategy for reducing the incidence of both civil wars and military coups.

CCH's paper seeks to determine the efficacy of two broad policy approaches to stabilizing post-conflict situations – one emphasizing post-conflict economic assistance, the other military intervention – via three quite distinct policy instruments.

Post-Conflict Economic Assistance

CCH's case for post-conflict economic assistance is directly related to their analysis of the causes of armed conflict. It builds on the immensely influential earlier work of Collier and Anke Hoeffler, many of whose findings were replicated by the similarly influential work of James Fearon and David Laitin.[1]

The assumptions which underpin the policies that these scholars advocate are clear: Increasing economic growth reduces the risk of armed conflict, as does the higher level of income *per capita* that results from this growth. In post-conflict situations economic assistance increases growth and hence income, the combined effect of which reduces the risk that wars that have stopped will start again.

In this new study, CCH find that, with no economic growth, a typical post-conflict country has a 42 percent risk of returning to conflicts within ten years. With a 10 percent growth rate the risk declines to just 29 percent. Put another way (and assuming that the effect is linear) this means that, "each additional percentage point of growth brings down the decade risk of reversion to conflict by around 1.5 percentage point." For the typical post-conflict country this level of growth can be achieved by an annual provision of aid equivalent to 2 percentage points of GDP.

Given that development assistance increases economic growth in the post-conflict situation, and given that growth, plus the resulting higher income levels, reduces the risk of wars restarting, it follows that post-conflict economic assistance is not simply a development policy – it is also an important security strategy.

CCH's analysis of the cost-effectiveness of this approach, which echoes that of other studies, will be welcome news to donors and international organizations that are seeking to help countries falling back into conflict, but who

[1] P. Collier and A. Hoeffler, "Greed and grievance in civil war," *Oxford Economic Papers,* **56**(4), 2004, and J.D. Fearon and D.D. Laitin, "Ethnicity, insurgency, and civil war," *American Political Science Review*, **97**(1), February 2003.

Table 2.2.1: How war end, 1946–2005

Years	Victories Total number	Victories Number restarted in under 5 years	Victories % restarted in under 5 years	Negotiated Settlements Total number	Negotiated Settlements Number restarted in under 5 years	Negotiated Settlements % restarted in under 5 years	Other Total number	Other Number restarted in under 5 years	Other % restarted in under 5 years	Total Terminations Total number	Total Terminations Number restarted in under 5 years	Total Terminations % restarted in under 5 years
1946–49	13	1	7,7	3	0	0,0	7	0	0,0	23	1	4,3
1950–59	16	3	18,8	9	0	0,0	16	5	31,3	41	8	19,5
1960–69	23	2	8,7	11	1	9,1	16	3	18,8	50	6	12,0
1970–79	22	7	31,8	13	2	15,4	11	0	0,0	46	9	19,6
1980–89	20	3	15,0	8	1	12,5	26	15	57,7	54	19	35,2
1990–99	23	2	8,7	41	18	43,9	58	32	55,2	122	52	42,6
Total 1946–1999	117	18	15,4	85	22	25,9	134	55	41,0	336	95	28,3
2000–2005	5	1*	20,0	17	2*	11,8	21	14*	66,7	43	17*	39,5
Total 1946–2005	122	19	15,6	102	24	23,5	155	69	44,5	379	112	29,6

Source: UCDP/Human Security Report Project dataset, 2007
*includes terminations for which it is too early to determine failure rate on a 5 year threshold (ie. terminations 2002 or later)

have little idea of the relative efficacy of different policy options. However, the methodology CCH use to establish the *average* risk of conflicts restarting over a period of sixty years, obscures highly significant recent changes in the ways in

which conflicts come to an end. In the case of negotiated settlements, these changes are associated with dramatically reduced risks of wars recurring.[2]

Understanding these changes requires disaggregating the data on terminations into three basic categories as shown in table 2.2.1. (Note these data come from a different terminations dataset to that used by CCH, one that includes minor as well as major conflicts.) The three categories of terminations are: "Victories," "Negotiated settlements," and a category that, for want of a better word, Uppsala's Conflict Data Program calls "Other" – i.e., those conflicts that simply peter out without either a victory or a peace agreement, or where the battle death toll falls below the 25 deaths a year threshold.

As table 2.2.1 shows, in every decade from the 1940s to the 1980s there were many more victories than negotiated settlements. But in the 1990s, there was a dramatic change – there were almost twice as many negotiated settlements as victories.[3] In the new millennium, 2000–5, there were more than three times as many negotiated settlements as victories. Both the reduction in the number of victories and the increase in the

[2] Note: the conflict data used in table 2.2.1 come from the Uppsala/PRIO dataset that CCH use in their section on global conflict trends at the beginning of their paper. The Uppsala/PRIO conflict dataset contains more than 350 terminations – but a very large percentage of these are of conflicts that killed very few people and thus would not be expected to have much economic impact. CCH use the Correlates of War (CoW) dataset that contains only data on high-intensity wars. This is clearly more suitable for their purpose of determining the economic impact of armed conflict. The other difference between the two datasets is that CCH use a ten-year period to determine the risk of conflicts restarting, while the Uppsala terminations data in table 2.2.1 uses five years. We can't be *sure* that the trends in different types of termination revealed in table 2.2.1 will be the same for the smaller dataset that CCHS rely on, but since both are affected by the same external forces it is reasonable to assume that they will be similar.

[3] This section draws on the findings of the *Human Security Brief, 2007*, Human Security Report Project, Simon Fraser University, 2008. The terminations data comes from the Uppsala Conflict Data Program at Uppsala University in Sweden.

number of negotiated settlements reflect the sharp increase in what the UN calls "peacemaking" – the practice of seeking to end wars via negotiation rather than on the battlefield. As CCH note in their paper, a major downside of negotiated settlements has been that they were far more likely to restart than conflicts that ended in victories. The Uppsala terminations dataset shows that recently as the 1990s, 44 percent of negotiated settlements broke down within five years, compared with just 9 percent of conflicts that ended in victory.[4] This long-established pattern changed in the new millennium. Negotiated settlements now appear to be the most stable form of settlement, with just 12% percent breaking down in the first six years of the decade. This is almost certainly because they are now receiving far more support from the international community than was the case in the past. Over the equivalent period in the last decade (1990–5), almost 90 percent of negotiated settlements failed.

The least stable type of conflict termination is that which Uppsala designates as "Other." This type of termination is inherently prone to breakdown, for at least three reasons:

- It rarely attracts the international support typically received by conflicts that end in mediated settlements
- It does not involve a decisive defeat of one of the warring parties, as is the case in conflicts that end in victory; there are thus no material restraints that prevent either side to start fighting again
- Absent any sort of peace agreement, the disputes that drove the violence in the first place will likely remain unresolved

By the end of 2005, 67 percent of conflicts that had terminated in the "Other" category had already broken down.

Clearly it is the conflicts that end in the "Other" category that are the major problem with respect to wars restarting. Equally clearly there is an obvious policy measure that promises to reduce their number – namely, "peacemaking," a term that encompasses a variety of different, but related policy initiatives, including "good offices," conciliation, negotiation, conflict resolution, and third-party mediation. More peacemaking would mean more negotiated settlements. And since negotiated settlements are now receiving far more support than was previously the case, there is every reason to assume that any new agreements that resulted from increased peacemaking activities would be less prone to a resumption of fighting than the consistently unstable "Other" terminations.

The increased support to negotiated settlements includes the development aid that CCH stress, and which is critically important, but it also includes increased humanitarian assistance (up five-fold *per capita* since 1990), more and better managed DDR missions, security sector reform, the support of "Friends" and "Contact" groups – and, of course, peacekeeping.

There is huge scope for improvement in the international community's peacemaking capacity at minimal cost. The UN Department of Political Affairs is modestly increasing its mediation capacity, but the resources devoted to peacemaking – at the UN and elsewhere – remain trivially small compared to those devoted to peacekeeping and post-conflict reconstruction. Increased resources for peacemaking was a major recommendation of the Secretary-General's influential High-Level Panel on Threats Challenges and Change in 2004 and the Outcome Document accepted by member states of the United Nations at the 2005 UN Summit.

Despite the fact that increasing the resources devoted to peacemaking promises a high return on a very modest investment, despite compelling evidence from quantitative research by Barbara Walter[5] – which CCH themselves cite – that attests to the effectiveness of peacemaking, CCH have little to say about it. Talking of the propensity of negotiated settlements to restart they note that:

[4] The 1990s were an exceptional decade, however. Between 1946 and 1999, 15 percent of conflicts ending in victory restarted, compared with 26 percent of negotiated settlements.
[5] B.F. Walter, *Committing to peace*, Princeton University Press, Princeton, 2001.

while a pessimistic prognosis is entirely reasonable on the historical data, an alternative optimistic interpretation would be that the new international political will to prevent civil war has decisively changed behavior.

We believe that there is considerable evidence to support this latter claim, though the trend is too short lived to be confident that it will necessarily continue.

It is perhaps no accident that CCH pay so little attention to peacemaking. Mediation, which is what peacemaking is about, focuses on addressing, and seeking to resolve or reduce, grievances. CCH do not, however, believe that grievances are what drives armed conflict: Their focus (see below) is on reducing the *feasibility* of war. If grievances are important drivers of conflict then peacemaking initiatives that seek to address are not a cost-effective means of conflict reduction.

The claim that grievance is not an important driver of conflict is spelled out in detail in Collier and Hoeffler's (hereafter, CH) hugely influential "Greed versus grievance" paper published in 2004.[6] CH note that the grievances associated with intense political conflicts are ubiquitous – indeed, they are found in all societies – but civil wars are rare events. The implication is clear: If grievances really were a major driver of political violence, the world would be suffering far more armed conflicts.[7]

Because feelings of grievance are emotions, and because none of the datasets that CH relied on can measure emotions directly, they use "proxy" indicators for grievance that *can*

be measured. The use of proxies in this way is common practice in quantitative studies of armed conflict. CH took a large cross-national, time-series, dataset and used multiple regression analysis to determine if there were any significant associations between the grievance proxies and war onsets. There were none. From this, they conclude that grievance does not matter.

The dismissal of political and economic grievances as drivers of civil war is one of the most contentious findings to emerge from the quantitative research on armed conflicts. Critics of CH have argued that the proxy measures used are inappropriate, that a number of other assumptions are problematic, and that other quantitative studies, plus a mass of case study evidence, demonstrate that grievances are indeed important risk factors for armed conflict.

But there is a more profound reason for contesting the claim that grievances do not matter in explaining the onset of civil wars: One that cannot be rebutted by creating more appropriate proxy measures, better cross-national data, or using different statistical significance tests.[8] All the variables that CH rely on as proxies for grievance use *nationwide* data – this is also true of James Fearon and David Laitin's equally influential research. The proxies are intended to measure *average* levels of grievance for whole populations. *But whole populations do not start wars.* The outbreaks of conflict that the authors are seeking to explain involve, initially at least, only a tiny fraction of the population of the countries in question. It is the motivations and behavior of these latter individuals that matter in determining what drives civil war onsets, *not* the grievances of the rest of society.

So even if the proxy indicators on which CH rely on *were* appropriate measures of *societal* grievance, they would still tell us nothing about any grievances harbored by the relatively small number of individuals who actually start rebellions. As Fearon and Laitin point out, "civil war may only require a small number [of rebels] with intense grievances to get going."[9] CH appear to be making the same point at the end of their "Greed and grievance" article, when they note that, "the grievances that motivate rebels may

---

[6] Collier and Hoeffler, "Greed and grievance in civil war":
[7] This argument is, in itself, not particularly persuasive since clearly minor grievances will not lead to civil war, but particularly intense grievances may well do so.
[8] Collier concedes that he and his co-author "may not be measuring objective grievances well enough." See P. Collier, "Economic causes of civil conflict and their implications for policy," in C.A Crocker, F.O. Hampson and P. All, *Leashing the dogs of war: Conflict management in a divided world*, United States Institute of Peace Press, Washington, DC, 2007: 203.
[9] Fearon and Laitin, "Ethnicity, insurgency, and civil war": 76.

be substantially disconnected from the large social concerns of inequality, political rights, and ethnic or religious identity."[10]

There is a second reason why grievances matter – one of particular relevance to the risk of conflicts restarting. Wars increase poverty and weaken already fragile states still further – in other words, they exacerbate the very conditions that caused them to start in the first place. But warfare – and the atrocities that so often accompany it – also generates new grievances.

Both CH and Fearon and Laitin agree that this is the case. Indeed Collier argues more recently that if these grievances are not addressed the risk of new wars will increase: "The construction of sustainable peace in post-conflict societies *will have to address the subjective grievances of the parties to the conflict.*"[11] Fearon and Laitin make essentially the same point when they note that, although they find little evidence that civil war is predicted by broadly held grievances, "It seems quite clear that intense grievances *are produced by* civil war."[12]

It follows that seeking negotiated settlements, which almost by definition seek to address grievances, should be an important part of preventing wars that have stopped from restarting again.

Some of the measures that CCH, and CH before them, prescribe for reducing the risks of conflicts restarting – increasing economic growth, for example – may help to reduce grievances. But there are many other grievance-reducing strategies that they do not consider: Truth and reconciliation commissions, power-sharing and autonomy provisions for rebels that have been pursuing separatist agendas, for example.

Note that this critique of CH/CCH's rejection of grievance-based explanations of war onset is *not* a critique of their account of *some* of the determinants of conflict onsets, which focus on the *feasibility* of, and *opportunities* for, rebellion.[13] Here, the focus is not on the *motives* of the would-be rebels but on *the conditions that favor insurgency,* that make the creation of – mostly small – illegal, military organizations *feasible.*

According to opportunity/feasibility thesis, most wars take place in poor countries not because people are poor and consequently aggrieved, but because low *per capita* income means that governments will tend to be weak, and weak governments simply lack the capacity to detect and crush rebels, or buy off political opposition.[14] Poverty also affects the risk of war by reducing the opportunity costs of joining insurgent groups for marginalized young males living on the edge of subsistence.

One obvious implication of the CH and Fearon and Laitin findings is that conflict prevention, including stopping wars from restarting in post-conflict situations, should focus on reducing the *feasibility* of rebellion.[15]

This assumption leads logically to the stress that CCH place on economic growth and raising income levels. As incomes rise, the opportunity costs of joining rebellions for impoverished young males increase and the state gets stronger and thus better able to crush resistance or buy off challengers.

The stress on feasibility/opportunity as risk factors for rebellion is an extremely important contribution to the debate on the causes of war, but it complements, rather than contradicts, grievance-based explanations.

---

[10] Collier and Hoeffler, "Greed and grievance in civil war": 589.

[11] Collier, "Economic causes": 211, italics added.

[12] Fearon and Laitin, "Ethnicity, insurgency, and civil war": 88, italics in original.

[13] Collier, "Economic causes": 200.

[14] Income *per capita* is used as a measure of state capacity because there are no widely available direct measures. Fearon and Laitin are most closely associated with this interpretation of the significance of low *per capita* income.

[15] The economic theories of rebellion that CH cite are closely associated with economic theories of crime. Strategies of "opportunity reduction" that are related to these theories have a long and successful history in crime prevention. Here the aim is not so much to address the motives that drive individuals to commit criminal acts but rather to pursue changes that make crime less attractive. This is precisely the type of opportunity-reducing strategy that CH and Fearon and Laitin are advocating to make war less attractive to would-be rebels. See, R.V. Clarke and G.R. Newman, *Situational crime prevention*, Willan Publishing, Albany, NJ

Military Interventions: Peacekeeping and "Over-the-Horizon" Security Guarantees

CCH make a strong case for the utility of military-related interventions as means of reducing the risks of civil war and coups. They consider three mechanisms: Limits to the defense outlays of post-conflict governments, peacekeeping operations, and "over-the-horizon" security guarantees.

The fact that the number of peace operations has increased dramatically since the early 1990s is an important part of the reason for the net decline in the number of armed conflicts since the early 1990s. Since peace operations are deployed *after* wars stop, the claim that they may play a role in stopping them may seem somewhat odd. But peace operations contribute to peace in two ways. First, a commitment to deploy a peace operation is often a necessary condition to get warring parties in a civil war to agree to a peace settlement. Second, peace operations can play a critical role in preventing wars starting again.

The claim that peace operations reduce the risk that negotiated settlements will break down is well supported in the literature: Where CCH's prescriptions diverge from current peacemaking practice is in their suggestion for a new interventionary force. This "fully international instrument . . . under the auspices of the UN or a regional organization" would automatically provide forces to support democratically elected governments against threats of rebellion and coups d'états.

In a second departure from current practice, CCH argue for the creation of an "Over-the-horizon" positive security guarantee to the post-conflict country for a period after the peacekeeping force had been withdrawn. There would, in other words, be an international commitment to dispatch a military force to the country concerned in the event of renewed fighting. This, CCH argue, would be militarily efficacious

since it would also provide a deterrent against rebels seeking to restart wars. It would also be cost-effective because it is cheaper to keep troops at home than to deploy them overseas.

CCH use two examples to support the contention that highly professional armed forces and over-the-horizon guarantees can help prevent civil wars starting – or resuming. The first is the deployment of British forces in Sierra Leone, the second French post-colonial security policy in Francophone Africa. CCH are surely correct to point to the highly positive role of the British in Sierra Leone in maintaining the peace, but the assumption that this is a practice that will necessarily work elsewhere is questionable.

The model presupposes that a relatively small number of highly professional forces can achieve what the UN's more numerous, but often under-trained and under-equipped, forces cannot. In the case of Sierra Leone this was clearly true. UK forces stabilized the security situation then withdrew, leaving behind a skeletal force that could be rapidly reinforced if necessary: The over-the-horizon guarantee. But consider another case where Western armed forces were inserted into another African conflict zone with disastrous consequences. The US force that was engaged in the "Blackhawk Down" debacle in Somalia in October 2003 was every bit as professional as the British force in Sierra Leone, but the US intervention was a failure. Some eighteen Americans were killed in a firefight with Somali warlord forces and the USA pulled out. Context is critical. As Sambanis and Doyle point out in their classic recent study of peace operations: What works in one context may fail miserably in another.[16]

Well aware of the inappropriateness of generalizing from a single case, CCH sought cross-national quantitative data to support their peacekeeping + over-the-horizon security guarantee proposal. Comparing the incidence of wars in Francophone Africa with that in other African states, they find that "the French informal quasi-security guarantee" to France's former colonies, "backed by a chain of military bases around the region" was associated with a substantially lower risk of conflict than

---

[16] M.W. Doyle and N. Samabanis, *Making war and building peace: United Nations peace operations*, Princeton University Press, Princeton, 2006.

that experienced by Africa's non-Francophone states.

CCH do not, however, establish that it was the over-the-horizon guarantees that was the critical factor in lessening the incidence of conflict in Francophone Africa. France did not just have a military presence in Africa, it also had a huge, neo-colonial political apparatus run by the notorious Jacques Foccart and supported by a lavish foreign aid program. This politico-economic presence provides an equally, if not more, plausible explanation for the relative peacefulness of France's former African colonies than does the French military presence.

CCH suggest that part of the explanation for the violent political unrest in Côte d'Ivoire since 2003 is the *absence* of the French over-the-horizon guarantee. In fact, France retains a considerable military presence in the country, and there are French military deployments in Senegal, Côte d'Ivoire, Togo, Gabon, Chad, the CAR, and Djibouti – indeed, there are more than 5,000 French troops currently involved in peace operations in Africa.[17] Yet this continuing presence, plus direct French military involvement in Côte d'Ivoire, Chad, the CAR, and the DRC does not appear to have been very effective in stemming political violence in Francophone Africa.

Even if we accept the argument that, *in principle* an international or regional force, plus the over-the-horizon security guarantee for post-conflict situations, would contribute to a lessening of armed conflict, it does not follow that this is a politically feasible option for the international community to adopt.

In the case of Francophone Africa, the French quasi-security guarantee reflected perceived French national interests. The nations of the international community do not have a comparable common interest in providing the type of international force that CCH envisage. There are good military and logistical arguments for such an initiative, one that has been advocated for many years by proponents of a permanent UN Standing Rapid Deployment Force. A unified UN force would, in principle, suffer none of the debilitating problems that today's multina-

tional UN peace operations face. These include lack of inter-operability and radically different levels of training and equipment of the national armed forces that commit troops to UN peace-keeping missions, and desperately slow deployment times.

None of the proposals for such a UN force has ever come near to fruition. The USA opposes the idea in principle because it sees it as giving too much power to the United Nations; the G-77 countries reject it because they argue – correctly – that such a force would only ever be used against them.

The international force that CCH envisage is inspired by the type of forces that the UK committed to Sierra Leone. They would need, in other words, to be highly trained, well equipped, deployable within a very short time, and prepared for a peace enforcement – as against a peacekeeping – mission. Since Russia and China are non-starters for such missions, any such force would almost certainly have to come from the OECD countries. But therein lies the problem.

The industrialized nations do put their forces into conflict and post-conflict environments, but only where they perceive major political or geo-strategic interests at stake: Afghanistan (the USA and Europe), Lebanon (Europe), the Balkans (Europe), Timor Leste (Australia), etc. But, with few exceptions (France and the UK), they have been reluctant to deploy in Africa which, until recently, was the world's most conflict-prone region. Peacekeeping deployments to the region that is currently the most conflict-prone – South and Central Asia – are constrained for different reasons. Here the obstacle is not so much the reluctance of OECD countries to send troops (Afghanistan is *sui generis*), but the reluctance of regional states to accept them.

The CCH proposal has something in common with other initiatives to create multilateral military forces that are less radical than the UN force idea, but which still seek to help prevent or stop

---

[17] Andrew Hansen, "The French military in Africa," *Council on Foreign Relations Backgrounder*, Council on Foreign Relations, New York. February 8, 2008, www.cfr.org/publication/12578/#3.

conflicts – or to prevent them from restarting. These include the UN's Standby Arrangements System, the Standby High-Readiness Brigade, and the African Union's plans for a Rapid Response Force.

None of these has proven successful thus far. The most egregious failure came in 1994, when UN Secretary-General, Boutros Boutros Ghali pleaded with countries in the UN Standby Arrangements System to provide troops to stop the genocide in Rwanda. Not one government volunteered. The stand-by forces lived up to their name: They stood by while 800,000 Rwandans were butchered.

The Canadian "Responsibility to Protect" ("R2P") report, which was in large part a response to the failures to prevent genocide in Rwanda and Srebrenica, called for the international community to be prepared to act – with force, if necessary – to stop gross violations of human rights that national governments either could not, or would not, stop themselves. "R2P" was accepted, albeit in somewhat diluted form, at the UN Leaders Summit in 2005. The leaders assembled agreed that the international community would be:

> prepared to take collective action, in a timely and decisive manner, through the Security Council, in accordance with the Charter, including Chapter VII, *on a case-by-case basis* . . .. should peaceful means be inadequate and national authorities manifestly fail to protect their populations from genocide, war crimes, ethnic cleansing and crimes against humanity.[18]

Notwithstanding these sentiments, "war crimes, ethnic cleansing and crimes against humanity" continued to be perpetrated on the people of Darfur – and nothing happened. Today the

"international community" is even balking at providing desperately needed helicopters for the new UN/African Union force in Darfur.

The lack of any real international commitment to embrace "collective action" in response to war crimes and other gross violations of human rights is evident in the reference in the General Assembly declaration cited above to the Council responding to such cases on a "case-by-case basis." This classic let-out clause was deliberately inserted so that the Council would not be *required* to respond forcefully to gross violations of human rights. There is no way that the Council will ever accept CCH's proposal that there should be an "*automatic* provision of powerful peacekeeping forces to protect governments that came to power democratically from the threat of rebellion."

This does not mean that nothing can be done. And, somewhat ironically, France may prove to be the major player. Over the past decade, French policy in Africa has been evolving. The "special relationships" with repressive regimes such as Chad have not disappeared, but there is now a new emphasis on:

> military cooperation with international forces and African regional bodies. France's permanent bases are in the process of being "Europeanized" . . . as France invites other European countries to commit forces to the bases.[19]

The case of Operation Artemis, the largely successful, French-led, UN-mandated, EU mission to the DRC in 2003,[20] and the French/UK proposals for EU "battlegroups" for peace operations suggest that a modest version of the CCH proposal may evolve over time. But with each "rapid reaction" battlegroup having a force level of just 1,500, major peace enforcement operations would be ruled out, deployments would in no sense be automatic, and the composition of the battle groups would be multinational not truly international.

These sorts of proposal will likely gain some traction in the decade ahead. While they will not provide the same benefits as CCH's more ambitious proposal, they offer something that does

---

[18] *World Summit Outcome*, United Nations, General Assembly, United Nations, New York, October 25, 2005: 30, italics added, http://unpan1.un.org/intradoc/groups/public/documents/UN/UNPAN021752.pdf.

[19] Hansen, "The French military in Africa."

[20] K. Homan, "Operation Artemis in the Democratic Republic of Congo," Clingendael, Netherlands Institute of International Relations, 2007, www.clingendael.nl/publications/2007/20070531_cscp_chapter_homan.pdf.

not currently exist: The ability to deploy highly professional forces with minimum delay to post-conflict or other crisis zones to help maintain stability until the main UN peacekeeping force arrives.

Such a force could, in principle, also provide a modified version of the over-the-horizon security guarantee that CCH envisage – one that would come into effect in the aftermath of a peacekeeping operation. The critical advantage of the sort of force that the Europeans envisage is that it could deploy in a few weeks – getting a new UN-mandated peacekeeping mission approved and funded, persuading governments to contribute troops, and finally deploying them can take many months – sometimes longer.

Military Coups[21]

CCH argue that coups are important, "because they . . . usher in or prolong military rule" and because they reduce economic growth – which in turn increases the risk of future coups – and rebellions. From an analysis of military coups in Africa from 1956 to 2003, CCH argue that a successful coup d'état, "typically generates economic costs of the order of 10 percent of one year's GDP. In part this is due to losses in output, and in part due to the diversion of output to economically useless military spending." In a detailed 2005 paper on coups d'états Collier and Hoeffler argue that "A common core of economic factors underpins proneness to coups and rebellions: Low income and a lack of growth."[22] They also find that a past history of coups increases the risk of future coups. The finding that income and growth levels are critical determinants of coup-risk leads them to argue that "Africa looks more likely to be saved from the menace of coups if it could achieve economic growth than by further political reform."[23] In the long term the evidence certainly supports the claim that increasing economic growth will reduce the risk of coups. But it is a painfully slow process and cannot explain the 36 percent decline in the average number of coups per year in SSA between 1980 and 2006.

Figure 2.2.1 shows the average number of coups per year by decade from 1946 to 2006. The data come from the University of Heidelberg's *Conflict Barometer,* a different, but more up-to-data dataset from that drawn on by CH.

The most striking features of the trend data are, first, the complete absence of coups from 1946 to 1959, reflecting the fact that most of the region was under colonial rule in this period and, second, the decline in coup numbers since 1992 – a decline that parallels the sharp decrease in armed conflicts over the same period.

The downward trend in coups numbers described in figure 2.2.1 presents a puzzle for the CH/CCH explanation of the causes of coups. African economies stagnated in the 1980s and early 1990s. Only since the mid-1990s has the region managed an average rate of growth of around 5 percent. With a growth rate of 5 percent a year it would take more than fourteen years for a country to double its income, but this would reduce the risk of a coup by only 14.3 percent.[24] So there has to be another explanation for the decline in the number of coups. There is, but it is an explanation that owes more to political factors than economic change. Writing a decade ago, Halperin and Lomasney suggest that the answer may lie in a shift in global norms and political practices:

> In recent years, the international community has decisively intervened on a number of occasions, through sanctions and other means, to restore to power democratically elected officials who have been either prevented from taking office or removed from office by force.[25]

During the Cold War years, military coups tended to be treated by the international

---

[21] This section draws on the *Human Security Brief 2007*, Human Security Report Project, Simon Fraser University, 2008.
[22] P. Collier and A. Hoeffler, "Coup traps: why Does Africa have so many coups d'état?," CSAE, Oxford, August 2005, draft.
[23] Collier and Hoeffler, "Coup traps."
[24] Collier and Hoeffler, "Coup traps": 13.
[25] M.H. Halperin and K. Lomasney, "Guaranteeing democracy: A review of the record," *Journal of Democracy,* **9**(2) (1998): 134–47.

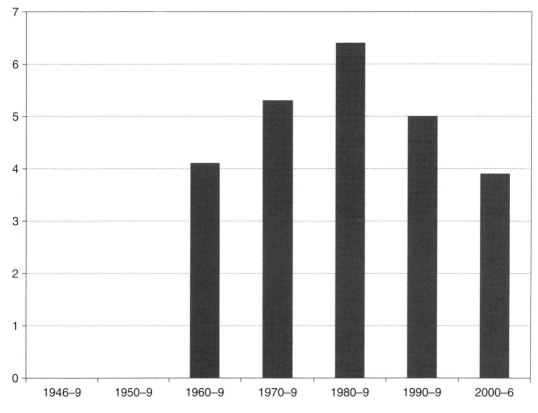

Figure 2.2.1 *Average number of coups per year in SSA, 1946–2006*

community, including regional institutions such as the Organization of African Unity (OAU), as issues that lay within the domestic jurisdiction of member states. The principle of non-interference in the internal affairs of member states was rarely challenged.

In SSA, the African Union, which was created in 2002 as the OAU's successor organization, has taken a very different stance. Article 30 of the African Union's *Constitutive Act of the Union* stipulates that, "Governments which shall come to power through unconstitutional means shall not be allowed to participate in the

activities of the Union." Since 2002, the African Union has intervened on several occasions in an effort to reverse coups and restore elected governments.[26]

Major donor states have also taken a strong – though not always consistent – line against coups, and they often have considerable leverage. Given that a major incentive for staging a coup is to gain control over the "rents" that development assistance provides, any perception that donors will deny victorious coup leaders this prize may serve as a deterrent to future military adventurism.

The USA, which is the world's largest single aid donor, is a major player here. Section 508 of the Foreign Assistance Act prohibits most forms of US economic and military assistance to countries whose elected head of state is deposed by a military coup. Since the end of the Cold War,

[26] P. Lyman, "Prepared Testimony Before the Senate Committee on Foreign Relations Subcommittee on African Affairs," United States Congress, Washington, DC, July 17 2007. www.cfr.org/publication/13950/, accessed February 19, 2007.

the USA has invoked section 508 against the CAR, Côte d'Ivoire, Comoros, Gambia, Guinea Bissau, and Niger. This upsurge of international activism provides a better explanation for the decline in the number of coups and attempted coups in Africa than do changes in income levels or economic growth. The threat of sanctions presents would-be coup leaders with *externally* generated disincentives to overthrow governments. By contrast CH's policy prescription focuses on reducing the risk of coups by promoting *internal* changes to the at-risk countries: Namely, maximizing economic growth.

But while very different, the two approaches are in no sense contradictory: One is long term and focuses on economic determinants, the other more immediate and focuses on political initiatives. Over time, they are likely to be mutually reinforcing.

Conclusion

The analysis above suggests, first that the risk that wars will start up again in post-conflict environments would be reduced if peacemaking were to be accorded far more prominence than CCH suggest. The argument for so doing is simple. Because peacemaking is now creating negotiated settlements that are much more stable (i.e. less likely to break down), increasing peacemaking efforts will mean more conflicts ending in stable peace agreements and fewer in the highly unstable "Other" category of terminations. Although estimating costs is beyond the scope of this paper it is clear that peacemaking is a very low-cost exercise compared with peacekeeping and peacebuilding.

Second, the assumptions that underpin CCH about the causes of war lead them to systematically ignore policy initiatives that address grievances as a means of reducing the incidents of war restarts. These include not just mediation, but all other attempts at conflict resolution, from power-sharing to regional autonomy (in the case of separatist conflicts), as well as peace and reconciliation commissions. This paper argues that the rejection of grievance is unwarranted, not least because Collier has himself argued that grievances can be an important cause of the resumption of conflict in post-conflict settings.

With respect to military coups this paper does not challenge CCH's finding that income levels and growth are important determinants of the risk of coups. But it argues that explanations that rely on these factors cannot account for the decline in coup numbers over the past decade and a half. A more compelling explanation is found in the sharp, though by no means consistent, increase in international political activism devoted to deterring coups and seeking to reverse those that have taken place.

Disease Control

DEAN T. JAMISON, PRABHAT JHA, AND DAVID E. BLOOM*

Introduction

This Challenge paper identifies priorities for disease control as an input into the 2008 Copenhagen Consensus project (hereafter, CC08). As such, it updates the evidence and differs somewhat in its conclusions from the communicable disease paper (Mills and Shilcutt 2004) prepared for the 2004 Copenhagen Consensus, which Lomborg (2006) summarizes.

Our analysis builds on the results of the Disease Control Priorities Project (DCPP).[1] The DCPP engaged over 350 authors and among its outputs were estimates of the cost-effectiveness of 315 interventions.[2] These estimates vary a good deal in their thoroughness and in the extent to which they provide region-specific estimates of both cost and effectiveness. Taken as a whole, however, they represent a comprehensive canvas of disease control opportunities. Some

interventions are clearly low priority. Others are attractive and worth doing, but either address only a relatively small proportion of disease burden or are simply not quite as attractive as a few key interventions. This chapter identifies seven priority interventions in terms of their cost-effectiveness, the size of the disease burden they address, and other criteria. Separate but related papers for CC08 deal with malnutrition (Horton *et al.* 2008, see chapter 6 in this volume), with water and sanitation (Hutton 2007), with air pollution (Larsen *et al.* 2008, see chapter 1 in this volume), and with education (Orazem *et al.*, 2008, see chapter 4 in this volume). It is worth listing our seven priorities at the outset:

- Tuberculosis treatment
- Heart attack treatment with generic drugs
- Malaria treatment and prevention package
- Increased coverage of childhood immunizations
- Tobacco taxation and regulation
- HIV/AIDS transmission interruption by a "combination prevention" package
- Improved surgical capacity at district hospitals to treat trauma and ensure safe childbirth

Before turning to the substance of the chapter, it is worth briefly stating our perspectives on the roles of the state and of international development assistance in financing health interventions. There are major externalities associated with control of many infections and there are important public goods aspects to health education and R&D. One view of the rationale for state finance is to address these market failures and to address needs of vulnerable groups. Our view is rather different.

* We are indebted to the following for helpful comments: David Canning, King Holmes, Christopher Murray, Ramanan Laxminarayan, Peter Piot, and Larry Rosenberg.

[1] The DCPP was a joint effort, extending over four years, of the Fogarty International Center of the US National Institutes of Health, the World Bank, and the WHO with financial support from the Bill and Melinda Gates Foundation. While the views and conclusions expressed in this chapter draw principally on the DCPP, others might reach different broad conclusions. In particular, views expressed in this chapter are not necessarily those of any of the sponsoring organizations.

[2] The DCPP resulted in two main volumes published in 2006. One deals with the *Global burden of disease and risk factors* (Lopez *et al.* 2006a). The other, *Disease control priorities in developing countries,* 2nd edn. (Jamison *et al.* 2006) discusses interventions to address diseases and risk factors and the health systems to deliver those interventions (the 1st edn. was published in 1993). This chapter will refer to these two volumes as DCP1 and DCP2, respectively.

Among the OECD countries only the USA focuses public finance on vulnerable groups – the poor and the elderly. Other OECD countries finance universal coverage for the (generally comprehensive) set of health interventions that they finance. Private finance is explicitly crowded out by public action, even for purely private clinical services – e.g. fixing broken legs, for which most individuals would be willing and able to pay for themselves (perhaps with privately financed insurance). Arrow's classic paper (1963) points to problems of asymmetric information and imperfect agency in clinical care and private insurance to which universal public finance is one policy response. At an empirical level the poor outcomes of the US system with respect both to health indicators and to total costs (and even with respect to public sector expenditures as a percent of GDP) are also suggestive of the merits of universal public finance (see Barr 2001 and Lindert 2004 for more extended discussions). The perspective of this chapter is, then, one of universal public finance as adopted by the non-US OECD countries. From this perspective, one is seeking to maximize health gains or a broader objective function subject to a public sector budget constraint without regard to the presence of externalities (except insofar as they affect aggregate health) and to address the needs of the poor through selecting interventions for universal finance that are of particular importance to them. No costs, then, accrue to targeting and no disincentives to work effort result from the potential loss of income-related health benefits. We further view the political economy of universalism as enhancing sustainability. Our perspective on public finance in health leads to less relative emphasis on infectious disease control in our short list of high priorities (although four of our seven priorities do deal with infection).

Our view of the role of international development assistance in health does, in contrast, centrally involve externalities and international public goods. Cross-border transmission of infection or drug resistance involves important negative externalities. R&D constitutes a public good that has been enormously impor-

tant in health. Likewise, facilitating diffusion of best practice through development assistance or price incentives can be viewed as correction of temporary price distortions and hence a reasonable purpose of aid. (Foreign direct investment (FDI) in the private sector is often viewed as an important vehicle for transferring technology and, hence, explicit incentives for appropriate technology transfer in health serve a similar purpose.) When we discuss the "best buys" in health we do so principally from the perspective of national authorities. But, for investments that may be of importance to development assistance beyond their importance from a national perspective – for example, for R&D – we point to the role of development assistance.

The first section of the chapter documents the enormous success in much of the world in the past forty-five years in improving health in low- and middle-income countries. Its conclusion is that future investments can build on past successes – increasing confidence in the practical feasibility of major additional gains in disease control. The second section summarizes evidence that health gains have had a major economic impact, and the third section uses this economic context to describe the methods used for the cost-benefit analyses reported. The fourth–sixth sections discuss problems and opportunities in child health, HIV/AIDS, and non-communicable disease (NCD), respectively. The seventh section concludes by identifying the few most attractive options and presenting (very approximate) cost-benefit analyses (CBAs) for them. This chapter emphasizes, although not exclusively, opportunities relevant to low-income countries in South Asia and SSA.

Progress and Challenges

Health conditions improved markedly throughout the world during most of the second half of the twentieth century, and this section begins by highlighting those achievements. Nonetheless, at the beginning of the twenty-first century, major problems remained. Parts of the world have simply not kept up with the remarkable

Table 3.1. Levels and changes in life expectancy, 1960–2005,

Region	Life expectancy (years)			Rate of change (years) per decade)	
	1960	1990	2005	1960–90	1990–2005
Low-and middle-income countries	44	63	65	6.3	1.7
East Asia and the Pacific	39	67	71	9.3	2.7
(China)	*36*	*69*	*72*	*11*	*2.0*
Europe and Central Asia	–	69	69	–	0.0
Latin America and the Caribbean	56	68	72	4.0	2.7
Middle East and North Africa	47	64	70	5.7	4.0
South Asia	44	59	63	4.7	2.7
(India)	*44*	*59*	*64*	*5*	*3.3*
SSA	40	49	47	3.3	-1.3
High-income countries	69	76	79	2.3	2.0
World	50	65	68	5.0	2.0

Source: World Bank, World Development Indicators, 2007.
Note: – = Not available.

progress in other areas; declines in mortality and fertility have led to an increasing importance of NCD; and the altogether new problem of HIV/AIDS has rapidly become prominent in many countries. Addressing these multiple problems within highly constrained budgets will require hard choices, even in the current era of expanding domestic health spending and overseas development assistance on health. This section concludes by reviewing these challenges.

Progress

Table 3.1 shows progress in life expectancy by World Bank region between 1960 and 2005. For the first three decades of this period, progress was remarkably fast – a gain of 6.3 years in life expectancy per decade on average, in the low- and middle-income countries, albeit with substantial regional variation. Progress continued between 1990 and 2005 but at a slower pace. SSA actually lost two years of life expectancy; Eastern Europe and Central Asia realized no gains.

In addition to overall progress, since 1950 life expectancy in the median country has steadily converged toward the (steadily growing)

maximum, and hence cross-country differences have decreased markedly (Oeppen and Vaupel 2002). This reduction in inequality in health contrasts with long-term *increases* in income inequality between and within countries. Yet despite the magnitude of global improvements in health, many countries and populations have failed to share in the overall gains or have even fallen behind. Some countries – for example, Sierra Leone – remain far behind. China's interior provinces lag behind the more advantaged coastal regions. A girl born in rural Madhya Pradesh state (in northern India) has six times the risk of dying before the age of one as that of a girl born in rural Kerala (in Southern India). Indigenous people everywhere probably lead far less healthy lives than do others in their respective countries, although confirmatory data are scant.

Much of the variation in country outcomes appears to result from the very substantial cross-country variation in the rate of diffusion of appropriate health technologies (or "technical progress"). Countries range from having essentially no decline in their infant mortality rates caused by technical progress to reductions of up to 5 percent per year (Jamison *et al.* 2004).

Measham *et al.* (2006) reached a similar conclusion concerning variation in infant mortality rate (IMR) decline across the states of India. Cutler *et al.* (2006) provide a complementary and extended discussion of the importance of technological diffusion for improvements in health. Consider for example the 10 million child deaths that occur currently each year. If child death rates were that seen in OECD countries, fewer than 1 million child deaths would occur each year. Conversely, if child death rates were those in OECD countries just 100 years ago, there would be 30 million child deaths a year. The key difference between now and then is not income but technical knowledge – about disease causation, interventions, and their application. Bloom and Canning (2007a) show that population health has tended to show continuous advancement among both high- and low-mortality countries over the past four–five decades, with some countries accelerating their progress and making a transition from the high-mortality cluster to the low-mortality cluster.

Consider the remarkable declines in infectious disease, except for HIV/AIDS worldwide and perhaps malaria in Africa (table 3.2). The development of vaccination, antimicrobial chemotherapy, and the ability to characterize new microbes have played key roles in the reduction of more than 90 percent in communicable disease mortality in Canada and the USA (US Centers for Disease Control and Prevention 1996). Today more than thirty common infectious diseases are controllable with live or killed viral or bacterial vaccines, or those based on bacterial sugars and proteins. In 1970, perhaps only 5 percent of the world's children under five were immunized against measles, tetanus, pertussis, diphtheria, and polio. The Expanded Program on Immunization raised this to about 75 percent of children by 1990, saving perhaps 3 million lives a year (England *et al.* 2001). The clearest success in immunization is the WHO-led campaign against smallpox, which culminated in the eradication of smallpox in human populations by 1979. More recently, WHO has been engaged in an on-going effort to eradicate poliomyelitis, which is more difficult technically

Table 3.2. Examples of science contribution to declines in infectious disease mortality in the twentieth century

Condition and intervention	Annual deaths prior to intervention in 000 (and ref. year)	Annual deaths after intervention in 000 (and ref. year)
Immunization services – against polio, diphtheria, pertussis, tetanus, and measles	~5000 (1960)	1,400 (2001)
Smallpox eradication campaign	~3000 (1950)	0 (1979)
Diarrhea – oral rehydration therapy	~4600 (1980)	1600 (2001)
Malaria outside Africa – indoor residual spray and acute management	~3500 (1930)	<50 (1990)
Malaria in Africa – limited use of indoor residual spray and acute management	~300 (1930)	1000 (1990)

Source: Jha *et al.* (2004).

than smallpox eradication. The effort has, nonetheless, reduced polio cases to zero in the large majority of countries and to a modest number in the rest. Prior to 1950, the only major antibiotics were sulfonamides and penicillin. Subsequently, there has been remarkable growth in discovery and use of antimicrobial agents effective against bacteria, fungi, viruses, protozoa, and helminths. Delivery of a combination of anti-tuberculosis drugs with direct observation (or DOTS, described below) has lowered case-fatality rates from well over 60 percent to 5 percent, and has also decreased transmission. The percentage of the world's TB cases treated with DOTS has risen from 11 percent to about 53 percent (Dye *et al.* 2006), which points to the practical possibility of still further gains.

Research into HIV/AIDS and related diseases is providing a better understanding of the internal structure of retroviruses and is accelerating the number of antiviral agents. Similarly, there is increasing knowledge of the modes of action of antifungal and antiparasitic agents (Weatherall *et al.* 2006). Large-scale studies have been able to identify smoking as a major cause of TB mortality worldwide (Bates *et al.* 2007) but especially in India (Jha *et al.* 2008). Finally, large-scale randomized trials have increasingly been used to establish widely practicable therapies, especially when modest, but important treatment benefits are sought (Peto and Baigent 1998). Advances in computing and statistics have led to more robust mathematical models of infectious disease spread (Nagelkerke *et al.* 2002). A new chapter is the development of molecular biology and recombinant DNA technology in the second half of the twentieth century. The benefits of DNA science to global health are as yet limited but could be extraordinary (see Weatherall *et al.* 2006). These technical advances enable major health improvements at low cost.

Factors from outside the health sector also affect the pace of health improvement: Education levels of populations appear quite important although the level and growth rate of income appear much less so (Jamison *et al.* 2004; Bloom 2005; Bloom and Canning 2007a). Hence, the importance of technical progress and diffusion should be viewed in a larger context. Expanded education facilitates diffusion of good practices, as in the case of maternal education improving child health. And, although rapid economic growth in many parts of the world, especially in coastal China and in urban India, might well mean that some can buy their way into better health, this chapter argues that there will be far more benefit if expanded public coffers are used on a relatively limited set of highly effective public health and clinical interventions. This point bears reiterating in a slightly different way: Income growth is neither necessary nor sufficient for sustained improvements in health. Today's tools for improving health are so powerful and inexpensive that health conditions can be reasonably good even in countries with low incomes.

Reasons for remaining health inequalities thus lie only partially in poverty or income inequality: The experiences of China, Costa Rica, Cuba, Sri Lanka, and Kerala state in India, among others, conclusively show that dramatic improvements in health can occur without high or rapidly growing incomes. The experiences of countries in Europe in the late nineteenth and early twentieth centuries similarly show that health conditions can improve without prior or concomitant increases in income (Easterlin 1996). A recent review has identified many specific examples of low-cost interventions leading to large and carefully documented health improvements (Levine and the What Works Working Group 2007). The public sector initiated and financed virtually all of these interventions. The goal of this chapter is to assist decision-makers – particularly those in the public sector – to identify the highest priority low-cost interventions to rapidly improve population health and welfare where the needs are greatest.

Remaining Challenges

Three central challenges for health policy ensue from the pace and unevenness of the progress just summarized and from the evolving nature of microbial threats to human health.

Unequal Progress

The initial challenge results from continued high levels of inequality in health conditions across and within countries. Bloom and Canning (2007a) have stressed that global inequalities are declining if one properly accounts for convergence across countries in health conditions, which more than compensates for income divergence. However, in far too many countries health conditions remain unacceptably – and unnecessarily – poor. This fact is a source of grief and misery, and it is a brake on economic growth and poverty reduction. From 1990 to 2001, for example, the under-five mortality rate remained stagnant or increased in twenty-three countries. In another fifty-three countries (including China), the rate of decline in under-five mortality in this period was less than half of the 4.3 percent per year required for each country to reach the fourth Millennium Development Goal (MDG-4). Meeting the

Table 3.3. Causes of under-five mortality, worldwide, 2001 Estimates from the GBD (000)

Cause	Total (stillbirths to 4)	Age 0–4	Neonatal (age 0–27 days)	Stillbirths
HIV/AIDS	340	340		
Diarrheal disease	1600	1600	116	
Measles	557	557		
Tetanus	187	187	187	
Malaria	1087	1087		
Respiratory infection (and sepsis)	1,945	1,945	1013	
Low birth weight	1301	1301	1098	
Birth asphyxia and birth trauma	739	739	739	
Congenital anomalies	439	439	321	
Injuries	310	310		
Other	5375	2101	446	3274
Total	13,874	10,600	3900	3274

Sources: Jamison *et al.* (2006); Mathers (2006)

Notes: 1. Of the estimated 13.9 million under-five deaths in 2001 only 0.9 percent occurred in high-income countries. Thus the cause distribution of deaths in this table is essentially that of low- and middle-income countries. 2. "Stillbirths" are defined as fetal loss in the third trimester of pregnancy.

About 33 percent of stillbirths occur after labor has begun – so-called intrapartum stillbirths. No good estimates exist for stillbirths by cause, but some of the cause categories (e.g. birth asphyxia, birth trauma, congenital anomalies) are the same as for age 0–4, so part of what is categorized as "other" in the total row will be distributed among the other existing rows when estimates are available.

MDG for under-five mortality reduction by 2015 is not remotely possible for these countries. (See Lopez *et al.* 2006 for country-specific estimates of child and adult mortality rates in 1990 and 2001 that were generated in a consistent way over time and across countries.) Yet the examples of many other countries, often quite poor, show that with the right policies dramatic reductions in mortality are possible. A major goal of this chapter is to identify strategies for implementing interventions that are known to be highly cost-effective for dealing with the health problems in children of countries lagging behind – for example, treatment for diarrhea, pneumonia, and malaria; immunization; and other preventive measures to reduce stillbirths and neonatal deaths.

About 10.6 million of the 49 million deaths in low- and middle-income countries occur in children between birth and the age of five. Table 3.3 summarizes what is known about the causes of deaths under the age of five, and under the age of twenty-eight days, in 2001. Table 3.3 also includes an estimate of the number of stillbirths.

It illustrates that about half of all deaths under the age of five (including stillbirths) occur in the first twenty-eight days, indicating the importance of addressing conditions important in this period.

Epidemiological Transition

A second challenge lies in NCD and injury. The next two decades will see the continuation of rising trends resulting from dramatic fertility declines (and consequent population aging) in recent years. The combination of an aging population with increases in smoking and other lifestyle changes mean that the major NCDs – circulatory system diseases, cancers, respiratory disease, and major psychiatric disorders – are fast replacing (or adding to) the traditional scourges – particularly infectious diseases and under-nutrition in children. Additionally, injuries resulting from road traffic accidents are replacing more traditional forms of injury. Responding to this epidemiological transition within sharply constrained resources is a key challenge. Table 3.4 provides cause-specific

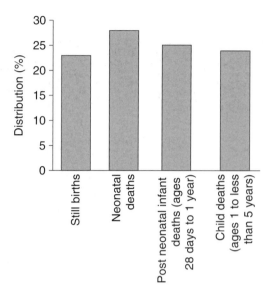

Figure 3.1 *Age distribution of deaths of children under five in low- and middle-income countries, 2001*
Source: Jamison et al. (2006).

Table 3.4. Causes of death in low- and middle-income countries, age five and older

Estimates from the GBD, 2001		
	Deaths (million)	percent of total
1. *Communicable, maternal, perinatal, and nutritional conditions*		
TB	1.5 million	4.0 percent
AIDS	2.2	5.8
Respiratory infections	1.5	4.0
Maternal conditions	0.5	1.3
Other	2.5	6.6
Sub-total	8.2	21.7
2. *Non-communicable disease*		
Cancers	4.9	13.0
Diabetes	0.7	1.9
Ischaemic and hypertensive heart disease	6.5	17.2
Stroke	4.6	12.2
Chronic obstructive pulmonary disease	2.4	6.3
Other	6.1	16.1
Sub-total	25.2	66.7
3. *Injuries*		
Road traffic accidents	1.0	2.6
Suicides	0.7	1.9
Other	2.7	7.1
Sub-total	4.4	11.6
Total	37.8 million	100

Source: Aggregated from Mathers *et al.* (2006: 126–31).

estimates of the number of deaths over the age of five due to major causes in low- and middle-income countries. This summary indicates that NCD already accounts for two-thirds of all deaths over the age of five in these countries, although nearly 22 percent of deaths continue to be from infection, under-nutrition, and maternal conditions, creating a "dual burden" to which Frenk and his colleagues have pointed (Barnum and Greenberg 1993).

HIV/AIDS Epidemic

A third key challenge is the HIV/AIDS epidemic. Control efforts and successes have been very real in high- and middle-income countries but are not yet widespread in low-income countries. As we outline below, the HIV/AIDS epidemic is best viewed as a set of diverse epidemics in regions or sub-regions. Each region's epidemic demands that we understand the reasons for HIV/AIDS growth, make appropriate interventions to decrease transmission to uninfected populations, and provide clinical care with life-prolonging drugs for those already infected. Recent data suggest that outside parts of Eastern and Southern Africa (including in large parts of Asia, Latin America, and elsewhere), growth of HIV/AIDS is slowing and that such reductions might be due to a (very uneven) increase in prevention programs.

The Economic Benefits of Better Health

The dramatic health improvements globally during the twentieth century arguably contributed as much or more to improvements in overall wellbeing as did the equally dramatic innovation in and expansion of the availability of material goods and services. To the substantial extent that appropriate investments in health can contribute to continued reductions in morbidity and mortality, the economic welfare returns to health investments are likely to be exceptional and positive – with previously unrecognized implications for public sector resource allocation. The purpose of this section is to explain the high values this chapter places on mortality reduction in its CBAs. Returns to better health go far beyond the contribution better health makes to per-person income, which itself appears substantial (see Bloom, Canning, and Jamison 2004; Lopez-Casasnovas *et al.* 2005). This section first summarizes the evidence concerning health's effect on per-person income and then turns to more recent literature concerning the effect of health changes on a broader measure of economic wellbeing than per-person income.

Health and Income

How does health influence income per person? One obvious linkage is that healthy workers are more productive than workers who are similar but not healthy. Supporting evidence for this plausible observation comes from studies that link investments in the health and nutrition of the young to adult wages (Strauss and Thomas 1998). Better health also raises per-person income through a number of other channels. One involves altering decisions about expenditures and savings over the lifecycle. The idea of planning for retirement occurs only when mortality rates become low enough for retirement to be a realistic prospect. Rising longevity in developing countries has opened a new incentive for the current generation to invest in physical capital and in education – an incentive that can dramatically affect national saving rates. Although a saving boom may be offset by the needs of the elderly after population aging occurs, it can substantially boost investment and economic growth rates while it lasts.

Encouraging FDI is another channel: Investors shun environments in which the labor force suffers a heavy disease burden and where they may themselves be at risk (Alsan *et al.* 2006). Endemic diseases can also deny humans access to land or other natural resources, as occurred in much of West Africa before the successful control of river blindness. Boosting education is yet another channel. Healthier children attend school and learn more while they are there.

Demographic channels also play an important role. Lower infant mortality initially creates a "baby-boom" cohort and leads to a subsequent reduction in the birth rate as families choose to have fewer children in the new low-mortality regime. A baby-boom cohort affects the economy profoundly as its members enter the educational system, find employment, save for retirement, leave the labor market, and finally become dependents again. The cohorts before and after a baby boom are much smaller; hence, for a substantial transition period, this cohort creates a large labor force relative to overall population size and the potential for accelerated economic growth (Bloom and Canning 2006; Bloom and Canning 2008).

If better health improves the productive potential of individuals, good health should accompany higher levels of national income in the long run. However, as Acemoglu and Johnson (2007) suggest, effects on per-person income may also be adversely affected by health-related population increases. How big a net contribution does better health make to economic growth? Evidence from cross-country growth regressions suggests the contribution is consistently substantial. Indeed, the initial health of a population has been identified as one of the most robust drivers of economic growth – among such well-established influences as the initial level of income *per capita* (negatively), geographic location, and institutional and economic policy environment. Bloom, Canning, and Sevilla (2004) find that one extra year of life expectancy raises GDP per person by about 4 percent in the long run. Jamison, Lau, and Wang (2005) estimate that reductions in adult mortality explain 10–15 percent of the economic growth that occurred from 1960 to 1990. Although attribution of causality is never unequivocal in analyses like these, household-level evidence also points consistently to a likely causal effect of health on income.

Health declines can precipitate downward spirals, setting off impoverishment and further ill health. For example, the effect of HIV/AIDS on *per capita* GDP could prove devastating in the long run. The International Monetary Fund (IMF) published a collection of important studies of the multiple mechanisms through which a major HIV/AIDS epidemic could be expected to affect national economies (Haacker 2004).

Health and Economic Welfare

Judging countries' economic performance by GDP per person fails to differentiate between situations in which health conditions differ: A country whose citizens enjoy long and healthy lives clearly outperforms another with the same GDP per person but whose citizens suffer much illness and die sooner. Schelling (1968) initiated efforts to assign economic value to changes in mortality probability and Johansson (1995) provides an up-to-date explication of the theory. Individual willingness to forgo income to work in safer environments and social willingness to pay for health-enhancing safety and environmental regulations provide measures, albeit approximate, of the value of differences in mortality rates. Many such willingness-to-pay (WTP) studies have been undertaken in recent decades, and their results are typically summarized as the *value of a statistical life* (VSL).

Although the national income and product accounts include the value of inputs into health care (such as drugs and physician time), standard procedures do not incorporate information on the value of changes in longevity. In a seminal paper, Usher (1973) first brought estimates of VSL into national income accounting. He did this by adding estimates of the value of changes in annual mortality rates (calculated using VSL figures) to changes in annual GDP per person. These estimates are conservative in

that they incorporate only the value of mortality changes and do not account for the total value of changes in health status. This chapter will later use a measure of 'disability-adjusted life years', or DALY, that includes disability as well as premature mortality in a way that calibrates disability weight in terms of mortality changes. (Valuation of changes in mortality, it should be noted, is only one element – albeit a quantitatively important one – of potentially feasible additions to national accounts to deal with outcomes for which there are not market prices. The US National Academy of Sciences has recently proposed broad changes for the USA that would include but go beyond valuation of mortality change (Abraham and Mackie 2005). Of specific relevance to this chapter is the economic welfare value of reductions in financial risk potentially associated either with a health intervention – typically prevention or early treatment – or with a risk-pooled way of financing it. Although we don't try to quantify this effect, we do provide a broad assessment of the impact of our priority interventions on financial risk.)

For many years, little further work was done on the effects of mortality change on full income, although, as Viscusi and Aldy (2003) document, the number of carefully constructed estimates of VSLs increased enormously. Bourguignon and Morrisson (2002) address the long-term evolution of inequality among world citizens, starting from the premise that a "comprehensive definition of economic wellbeing would consider individuals over their lifetime." Their conclusion is that rapid increases in life expectancy in poorer countries have resulted in declines in inequality (broadly defined) beginning some time after 1950, even though income inequality had continued to rise. In another important paper, Nordhaus (2003) assesses the growth of income plus the growth in the value of mortality change per capita in the USA in the twentieth century. He concludes that more than half of the growth in this indicator in the first half of the century – and somewhat less than half in the second half of the century – had resulted from mortality decline. In this period,

Annual changes as percentage of initial year GDP per capita

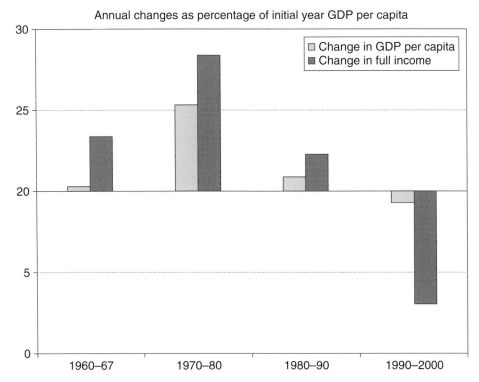

Figure 3.2 *Changes in GDP and full income per capita in Kenya, 1960–2000*
Source: Jamison et al. (2001).

real income in the USA increased six-fold and life expectancy increased by more than twenty-five years.

Three lines of more recent work extend those methods to the interpretation of the economic performance of developing countries. All reach conclusions that differ substantially from analyses based on GDP alone. Two of those studies – one undertaken for the Commission on Macroeconomics and Health (CMH) of the WHO (Jamison, Sachs, and Wang 2001) and the other at the IMF (Crafts and Haacker 2004) – assessed the impact of the HIV/AIDS epidemic. Both studies conclude that the epidemic in the 1990s had far more adverse economic consequences than previous estimates of effects on per-person GDP growth would suggest. The benefit estimates used in this chapter for successful interventions against HIV/AIDS are consistent with these findings from the CMH and IMF. Accounting for mortality decline in Africa before the 1990s, on the other hand, leads to estimates of much more favorable overall economic performance than does the trend in GDP per person. Figure 3.2 shows that in Kenya, for example, full income grew more rapidly than did GDP per person before 1990 (and far more rapidly in the 1960s). After 1990 the mounting death toll from AIDS appears to have only a modest effect on GDP per person but a dramatically adverse impact on changes in full income. Becker *et al.* (2003) confirm and extend the earlier work of Bourguignon and Morrisson (2002) in finding strong absolute convergence in full income across countries over time, in contrast to the standard finding of continued divergence (increased inequality) of GDP per person. Finally, Jamison, Jamison, and Sachs (2003) adapt standard cross-country growth regressions to model determinants of full income (rather than GDP per person). Like Bourguignon and Morrisson (2002), they conclude that inequalities have been decreasing.

The dramatic mortality declines of the past 150 years – and their reversal in Africa by HIV/AIDS after 1990 – have had major economic consequences. The effect of health on GDP is substantial. The intrinsic value of mortality changes – measured in terms of VSL – is even more substantial. What are the implications of these findings for development strategy and for CBAs of public sector investment options? Using full income in CBAs of investments in health (and in health-related sectors such as education, water supply and sanitation, and targeted food transfers) would markedly increase estimates of net benefits or rates of return. A major purpose of the Copenhagen Consensus project is to undertake intersectoral comparison of investment priorities by utilizing this "full-benefit" approach.

Cost-Benefit Methodology

The basic approach to cost-benefit analysis used in this chapter is to start with the cost-effectiveness (CE) results from the extensive comparative analyses reported in DCP2 (Jamison *et al.*, 2006; Laxminarayan *et al.* 2006). These results are expressed as the cost of averting a DALY, a summary measure involving mortality change and a valuation of disability change that can be considered to have been generated by calibration against mortality change.

The next sub-section describes an idealized version of our approach to CE – idealized in the sense that it seeks to explicitly call attention to the value of financial protection and non-financial costs (e.g. use of limited system capacity). The point is to serve as a reminder in drawing conclusions about some specific important considerations that go beyond the CE ratios reported. The following sub-section discusses DALYs and explicitly argues for a change in the way DALYs associated with deaths under the age of five are calculated. This change, which is adopted in our cost-benefit (C/B) analyses,

reduces the averted-DALY cost of a typical death under the age of five by about 50 percent while leaving the construction of DALYs for older ages unchanged. The third sub-section draws on the second main section of the chapter to assign, very conservatively, dollar values to DALYs for the subsequent C/B assessment. The final sub-section summarizes this chapter's approach to costing.

CE Analysis Broadly and Narrowly Construed

A starting point for CE analysis broadly construed is to observe that health systems have two main objectives: (a) to improve the level and distribution of health outcomes in the population and (b) to protect individuals from financial risks that are often very substantial and that are frequent causes of poverty (WHO 1999, 2000). Financial risk results from illness-related loss of income as well as expenditures on care; the loss can be ameliorated by preventing illness or its progression and by using appropriate financial architecture for the system.

We can also consider two classes of resources to be available: financial resources and health system capacity. To implement an intervention in a population, the system uses some of each resource. Just as some interventions have higher dollar costs than others, some interventions are more demanding of system capacity than others. In countries with limited health system capacity, it is clearly important to select interventions that require relatively little of such capacity. An implication is that in limited-capacity countries, interventions should sometimes be skewed toward the use of financial resources to conserve on system capacity. Human resource capacity constitutes a particularly important aspect of system capacity, discussed in a recent report of the Joint Learning Initiative (2004). Figure 3.3 illustrates this broadly construed vision of CE and, in its shaded region, the more narrow (standard) approach for which quantitative estimates are available. Jamison (2008) provides a more extended discussion.

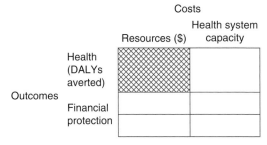

Figure 3.3 *Intervention costs and effects: a more general view*
Note: The shaded box represents the domain of traditional CE analysis.

Although in the very short run there may be little opportunity to substitute dollars for human resources or system capacity more generally, investing in the development of such capacity (which will often require foreign aid or investment) can help make more of that resource available in the future. Mills *et al.* (2006) discuss different types of health system capacity and intervention complexity and point to the potential for responding to low capacity by selecting interventions that are less demanding of capacity and by simplifying interventions. Mills *et al.* (2006) also explore the extent to which financial resources can substitute for different aspects of system capacity (see also Gericke *et al.* 2003). An important mechanism for strengthening capacity, inherent in highly outcome-oriented programs, may simply be to use it successfully – learning by doing.

The literature on economic evaluation of health projects typically reports the cost per unit of achieving some measure of health outcome – QALYs or DALYs, or deaths averted – and at times addresses how that cost varies with the level of intervention and other factors. Pritchard (2004) provides a valuable introduction to this literature. DCP1 reported such CE findings for about seventy interventions; DCP2 does so as well, in the end providing evidence on about 315 interventions. DCP2 authors were asked to use methods described in Jamison, Jamison and Sachs (2003). CE calculations provide important insights into the economic attractiveness of

an intervention, but other considerations – such as consequences for financial protection and demands on health system capacity – need to be borne in mind.

Defining and Redefining DALYs

The DALY family of indicators measures the disease burden from the age of onset of a condition by summing an indicator of years of life lost (YLL) due to the condition and an indicator of years of effective life lost due to disability (YLD) resulting from the condition. DALYs due to a condition are the sum of the relevant YLLs and YLDs.

DALYs generate a measure of the disease burden resulting from premature mortality by integrating a discounted, potentially age-weighted, disability-adjusted stream of life years from the age of incidence of the condition to infinity using a survival curve based on the otherwise expected age of death. The formulation within the family of DALYs previously used to empirically assess the global burden of disease specifies a constant discount rate of 3 percent per year and an age-weighting function that gives low weight to a year lived in early childhood and older ages and greater weight to middle ages. The current comprehensive volume on burden of disease reports global burden of disease estimates generated with the 3 percent discount rate but uniform age weights (Lopez *et al.* 2006a). Mathers *et al.* (2006) provide an extensive exploration of the uncertainty and sensitivity inherent in disease burden assessment, including the results of differing assumptions about age weighting and discount rates.

To be clear about the particular form of DALY being used, the terminology from Mathers *et al.* (2006) is employed. DALYs(r,K) are DALYs constructed using a discount rate of r percent per year and an amount of age weighting indexed by a parameter K. DALYs(3,1) are DALYs generated with a discount rate of 3 percent per year and with full age weighting – that is, $K = 1$. DALYs(3,0) are DALYs generated with a discount rate of 3 percent per year and with no

Table 3.5. Discounted YLL at different ages of death for several DALY formulations

Age group	Representative age of death (years)	YLL(3,1)	YLL(3,0)	YLLSB(3,0,1)	YLLSB(3,0, 0.54)
Antepartum	−0.080	0	0	30.42	4.95
Intrapartum	−0.001	0	0	30.42	9.13
Neonatal	0.020	33.09	30.42	30.42	9.40
Infant	0.300	33.36	30.40	30.40	12.95
Postneonatal infant	0.500	33.56	30.39	30.39	15.42
Child	2.000	34.81	30.28	30.28	26.40

Source: Jamison *et al.* (2006), table 6.6.
Note: YLL(3,1), YLL(3,0), and $YLL_{SB}(3,0,1)$ assume instantaneous acquisition of life potential, ALP ($A = 1$). YLL(3,1) assumes full age weighting ($K = 1$); the other three formulations assume uniform age weights ($K = 0$). $YLL_{SB}(3,0, 0.54)$ assumes gradual acquisition of life potential ($A = 0.54$). The subscript SB refers to formulations that do not give stillbirths zero weight.

age weighting – that is, $K = 0$. Mathers *et al.* (2006) present results concerning the burden of disease based on DALYs(3,0); Ezzati *et al.* (2006) present estimates of the burden of major risk factors. This chapter is based on DALYs (3,0), but slightly generalized.

This chapter uses an extension of the DALY family generated by modeling a concept of "acquisition of life potential," ALP. The intuition behind the ALP concept is that an infant (or fetus) only gradually acquires the full life potential reflected in a stream of life years – that is, ALP can be gradual, i.e. there is no single time point during gestation, or at birth, when the fetus makes an abrupt transition from zero to full life potential. Operationalizing this concept involves introducing a parameter, A, that indicates the speed of ALP (see Jamison *et al.* 2006 for precise definitions and assessments of the burden of disease that result). A is constructed so that for the fastest possible speed of ALP – namely, instantaneous ALP – $A = 1$. A is bounded below by 0. This chapter extends the notation DALYs(r,K) in two ways. First, it explicitly indicates the level of A by extending the DALY nomenclature to DALYs(r,K,A). Thus using this nomenclature, DALYs(3,0) become DALYs(3,0,1), because the standard DALY is the special case with instantaneous ALP. Second, when stillbirths are included in the range of events to be measured in the global

burden of disease, this is explicitly noted in the DALY nomenclature as $DALYs_{SB}(r,K,A)$. Notation around YLL is similarly extended.

Explicit modeling of ALP permits three instrumentally useful improvements to the previous formulation of DALYs:

- The DALY from a death seconds before birth is, in the previous formulation, 0; it jumps to more than thirty years at birth. The ALP formulation allows, but does not require, this discontinuity to be avoided.
- The ALP formulation allows, but does not require, DALYs to be associated with stillbirths.
- The ratio of the DALY from a death at age twenty, say, to that at birth is close to 1 for any reasonable set of parameter values in the previous DALY formulation. Many people's ethical judgments would give this ratio a value substantially greater than 1. The ALP formulation allows, but does not require, these judgments.

Only a limited number of empirical studies has attempted to assess directly the views of individuals concerning deaths at different ages. In an important early study, Crawford *et al.* (1989) relate grief from a death to the concept of reproductive potential as a function of age in population biology. (This is the expected number of offspring a person will have after a given age, given the fertility and mortality rates.) They conclude that for several diverse human groups the relationship shows grief to be closely related to reproductive value at the age of death when calculated for high mortality and high fertility populations for hunter-gatherer populations. An Institute of Medicine (1985) review of vaccine development priorities uses infant mortality equivalence in CE calculations. The committee members preparing the report collectively judged that the loss from a death at age twenty should be about twice that from an infant death. However, some preliminary trade-off studies suggest a value closer to three or four times. All three lines of evidence point to gradual rather than instantaneous ALP. What is clear, however, is that no completely defensible estimate (or even range) is currently available, and hence the numbers used in Jamison *et al.* (2006) should be viewed as only suggestive. Table 3.5 shows the YLLs associated with deaths at different young ages for alternative formulations of the DALY, including one with their preferred value of A = 0.54. This final column reports several estimates. (It is important to note that DALYs and YLLs for deaths above the age of five are unaffected by the introduction of ALP.) *Weighting the YLLs at different ages by the relative frequency of deaths at those ages gives a DALY$_{SB}$ (3,0, 0.54) loss of 16.4 DALYs for a typical under-five death, about half what is typically used. Our analyses use this figure.*

The Value of an Averted DALY

The VSL estimates yield a range of values for a statistical life – from around 100 to almost 200 times *per capita* income. Very approximately this can be translated to a value for a statistical life year (VSLY) in the range of 2–4 times *per capita* income. Tolley *et al.* (1994) provide a valuable overview of relevant estimates, including estimates of the value of preventing disability. The emphasis in this chapter is on low-income countries, defined by the World Bank for 2001 as countries with *per capita* incomes of less than $745 (exchange rate). The World Bank's

estimate of the average income of people living in low-income countries is $585 per year (World Bank 2007). Choosing a value for a VSLY at the low end of the range (a little below 2) would give a convenient value of $1,000, which is what this chapter uses in its main calculations as the value of a DALY. (Note that, for the reasons discussed, the DALY from a death under the age of five – and hence the benefit from preventing it – is about half that used in standard DALYs.) In appendix B we explore the sensitivity of our results to these assumptions by using a DALY value of $5,000 and by using standard DALYs (DALYs (3,0)) for child deaths. For some conditions – for example, anemia and the intestinal worm infections – the resulting loss in economic productivity is likely to be under-stated in the disability component of the DALY. In these cases, we will be under-estimating total benefits.

The Cost of an Averted DALY

The cost of buying an averted DALY with different interventions was calculated, in DCP2, by combining "typical" prices for a geographical region (Mulligan *et al.* 2003) with input quantities estimated from clinical and public health experience and case studies in the literature. For internationally traded inputs, prices were the same for all regions. (Because of tiered pricing, off-patent drugs were *not* considered to be internationally traded.) For local costs, regional estimates were used. Intervention costs, therefore, are *not* expressed in PPP dollars. The reason for this is that local costs present decision-makers with the appropriate numbers for budgeting and for comparing interventions in the context where they are working. (Regional costs are taken to be a better approximation of local costs than global costs would be.) On this point, the methods of this chapter differ from those of its predecessor (Mills and Shilcutt 2004).

Child Health

A small number of conditions accounts for most of the (large) differences in health between the poor and the not so poor. Almost 60 percent of the difference in DALY rates between low- and middle-income countries on the one hand and high-income countries on the other is due to the following conditions: Malaria, diarrhea, acute respiratory infections (ARI), vaccine-preventable diseases, and perinatal conditions. These are essentially childhood conditions.[3] Available technical options – exemplified by but going well beyond immunization – can address most of the conditions that affect children, and can do so with great efficacy and at modest cost. That short list of conditions, including micronutrient under-nutrition, relates directly to achieving the MDGs for health. Public expenditures to address those conditions have, in the past, benefited the relatively well off, albeit within poor countries (although global inequities in health have decreased because many poor countries have made much progress).

Under-Five Health Problems and Intervention Priorities

MDG-4 (reducing its level in 2015 by two-thirds relative to what it was in 1990) is highly ambitious. Yet in1990–2002, forty-six countries achieved rates of decline in under-five mortality greater than 4.3 percent per year (Lopez, Begg, and Bos 2006).

Basic knowledge about the power and the CE of interventions to address maternal and child health has been available since the 1980s. DCP2's work makes four important relatively new points. First, major declines in childhood mortality could well be accelerated with expanded case management of acutely ill children and with the addition of several new vaccines to the routine immunization schedule. These include those that protect against *Haemophilus influenza* type

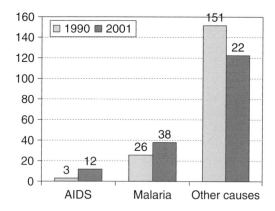

Figure 3.4 *Under-five deaths from HIV/AIDS, malaria, and other causes, per 000 births, 1990 and 2001, SSA*
Source: Lopez et al. (2006): table 2.4.

b (Hib) and *Streptococcus pneumoniae,* which are common causes of childhood pneumonia; hepatitis B, which tends to cause liver cancer; and rotavirus and shigella, which cause diarrhea (England *et al.* 2001). The Global Alliance for Vaccines and Immunization (GAVI) estimates that the addition of Hib and pneumococcal vaccines to vaccination programs could save 800,000 lives a year by 2010. Further GAVI estimates suggest that rotavirus and shigella vaccines might save 600,000 by 2010. Bloom, Canning, and Weston (2004) report rates of return to investment in basic vaccine packages of 12–21 percent

Second, as noted earlier, half of under-five deaths occur at ages less than twenty-eight days, when the substantial but usually neglected problem of stillbirth is considered. DCP2 identifies some highly cost-effective approaches to intervention against stillbirth and neonatal death (Lawn *et al.* 2006).

Third, there is a rapid spread of resistance of the malaria parasite to chloroquine and to sulfadoxine-pyrimethamine (SP). These inexpensive, highly effective, widely available drugs provide an important partial check on the high levels of malaria deaths in Africa, which are concentrated particularly in children. Their loss is leading to a rise in malaria mortality and morbidity that could be substantial. Figure 3.4

---

[3] By adding TB and AIDS to this list 75 percent of the difference would be accounted for.

illustrates increases in malaria death rates and decreases in death rates from other causes except AIDS in under-five children in SSA in the period from 1990 to 2001. (This increase in malaria mortality rates results in hundreds of thousands of deaths more than would otherwise have occurred.) The design of instruments for financing a rapid transition to appropriate treatments – in particular, artemisinin combination therapies (ACTs) – is a high priority (Institute of Medicine 2004; Arrow *et al.* 2005). The principal development assistance modality proposed – the Affordable Medicines Facility-malaria (AMFm) – aims to reduce the relative prices countries face for ACTs rather than to increase their budgets for purchasing them.

Fourth, although education interventions are considered separately (Orazem *et al.* 2008, see chapter 4 in this volume), it is worth noting in the context of considering alternatives for reducing child mortality that improvements in the quality of basic education can plausibly have benefit-cost ratios as high as for many health interventions – even if no benefits of education other than mortality reduction are included. (By "quality" of education, we refer narrowly to quality as reflected in scores on internationally standardized achievement tests, particularly those in mathematics.) Jamison *et al.* (2007) estimate that the effect of a 1 standard deviation improvement in quality would increase the annual rate of decline of infant mortality by about 0.6 percentage points – e.g. from a rate of decline of 2 percent to 2.6 percent per year, leading, after twenty years, to something over a 10 percent reduction in IMR relative to what it would otherwise have been. They estimate that this effect could be achieved for roughly 10 percent of the cost of a year of schooling, which is likely to be less than $100 per student per year in a low-income country. If the total fertility rate is 3 and the base level of IMR is 70 per 1,000, then education quality improvement is likely to result in a cost per (undiscounted) child death averted of around $1,000. Assuming, as this chapter does, a low DALY per child death of about 16 and the value of a DALY in low-income countries to be $1,000, then the B/C

ratio will be about 13. Discounting the benefits at 6 percent gives a B/C of 4, again ignoring any other benefits from the education. Increasing the value of averting a DALY from $1,000 to $5,000 would increase the B/C ratio to 20, even with 6 percent discounting. Using the estimated effects of a year of schooling from Jamison *et al.* 2007), the B/C for increasing the quantity of schooling by one year is 0.6 or (3 with $5,000 DALYs), ignoring other benefits.

In addition to the above, other intervention priorities for addressing under-five mortality are for the most part familiar:

- Maintain an emphasis on exclusive early breastfeeding, which has increased widely in all parts of the world over the last few years
- Expand immunization coverage of the current set of antigens in the Expanded Program on Immunization (EPI)
- Add new antigens – Hib, hepatitis B, rotavirus, and streptococcus – to the EPI schedule
- Expand the use of the simple and low-cost but highly effective treatments for diarrhea and child pneumonia through integrated management of childhood illness or other mechanisms
- Prevent transmission of and mortality from malaria by expanding coverage of insecticide-treated bednets, by expanding use of intermittent preventive treatment for pregnant women, and by use of indoor residual spraying with DDT and other insecticides
- Ensure widespread distribution of key micronutrients, most notably Vitamin A, zinc, and iron
- Expand the use of antiretrovirals (ARV) and breastfeeding substitutes to prevent mother-to-child transmission of HIV

In addition to interventions to reduce under-five mortality, one other priority is clear. The world's most prevalent infections are intestinal helminth (worm) infections, and children of all ages are the most heavily affected. Warren *et al.* (1993) review a range of experimental studies of the effectiveness of mass drug administration (in high-prevalence environments) and estimate quite attractive CE ratios. Hotez *et al.* (2006)

provide a more up-to-date discussion of these infections and related interventions. The discussion of school health services in Alderman *et al.* (2006) points to both the importance to children's school progress of taking albendazole where needed and the potential efficacy of school health programs as a vehicle for delivery. In the long run, improved sanitation and water supplies will prevent transmission. Use of albendazole is only an interim solution, but it is one that may be required for decades if the experience of the currently high-income countries is relevant, and its benefits relative to costs appear high.

Delivering Child Health Interventions

The list of potential interventions is far from exhaustive, and different regions, countries, and communities will face different mixes of the problems these interventions address. However, there can be little dispute that any short list of intervention priorities for under-five mortality in low- and middle-income countries would include many on the list in the preceding section. Why not, then, simply put money into scaling up these known interventions to a satisfactory level?

To greatly over-simplify – and these issues are discussed more substantially in Mills *et al.* (2006) – two schools of thought exist. One line of thinking – often ascribed to macroeconomist Jeffrey Sachs and his work as chair of the WHO CMH – concludes that more money and focused effort *are* the solutions. Although acknowledging dual constraints – of money and of health system capacity – Sachs and his colleagues (WHO CMH 2001; Sachs 2005) contend that money can buy (or develop, or both) relevant system capacity even over a period as short as five years. Major gains are affordable and health system capacity constraints can be overcome. Immunization provides an example of where, even in the short term, money can substitute for system capacity. Adding newer antigens to the immunization schedule is costly (although still cost-effective). In some environments, however, it proves less demanding of system capacity than

expanding coverage does. Money can be effectively spent by adding antigens at the same time as investing in the capacity to extend coverage. The newly established International Finance Facility (IFF), and the GAVI are institutional innovations to speed global immunization coverage.

A second school of thought acknowledges the need for more money, but asserts that health system capacity is often a binding short- to medium-term constraint on substantial scaling up of interventions. Van der Gaag (2004) emphasized this point in his critique of the 2004 Copenhagen Consensus Challenge paper on communicable diseases. Critical priorities are, therefore, system reform and strengthening while ensuring that such reforms focus clearly on achieving improved health outcomes and financial protection.

This chapter's perspective is closer to that of Sachs than of Van der Gaag while emphasizing the need to be explicit about intervention costs that are non-financial. This points to the need both to consider how to reduce such non-financial costs and to select interventions in part by the extent to which they are less demanding of non-financial inputs. Sepúlveda (2006) and others have described the "diagonal" approach being used in Mexico, where systems are strengthened while focusing on specific disease outcomes. Experience suggests that although such an approach demands considerable management, it is highly effective. Against a backdrop of low immunization coverage in Africa, Malawi, one of the poorest countries in the world, has succeeded in boosting immunization coverage against measles from only 50 percent in 1980 to almost 90 percent today. Malawi undertook a program to raise routine measles immunizations, including campaigns to catch children missed by routine efforts. As a result, the number of reported cases and deaths has fallen dramatically: During 1999, only two laboratory-confirmed cases were reported. And, for the first time ever, there were no measles deaths. Yet only two years earlier, almost 7,000 measles cases and 267 deaths (both of which are likely to be under-counts) were reported. This reduction was achieved despite 20 percent of the population not having access to health services, less than 50 percent having access to safe water, and only 3 percent having access to adequate sanitation. (Jha and Mills 2002).

Mills *et al.* (2006), as indicated, discussed these issues further in the context of all the problems facing a health system. From an individual country's perspective, however, if financial resources are available, the question is very much an empirical one: To what extent can those resources be effectively deployed in buying interventions, in buying out of prevailing system constraints, and in investing in relevant system capacity for the future? Accumulating experience suggests that to be successful, these choices will involve focused attention and sustained funding to achieve specific outcomes (Jha *et al.* 2002; Crogan 2006).

HIV/AIDS and TB

For dozens of countries around the world – including several of the most populous – the HIV/AIDS epidemics threaten every aspect of development. Most governments of affected low- and middle-income countries and most providers of development assistance have only recently begun to respond on more than a minimal level. Creation of the Global Fund to Fight AIDS, Tuberculosis, and Malaria can be viewed as an attempt by the world's top political leaders to improve on the records of existing institutions. The Fund's initial years have seen substantial success, but that success has been potentially undermined by constraints on resource availability (Bezanson 2005).

In contrast to the initially slow programmatic movement of most national leaders and international institutions, the R&D community – public and private – has made rapid progress in developing tools to control the HIV/AIDS epidemic, although both a vaccine and a curative drug remain distant objectives. Sensitive, specific, and inexpensive diagnostics are available; means of prevention have been developed and tested;

modes of transmission are well understood; and increasingly powerful drugs for controlling viral load allow radical slowing of disease progression. Tools for dealing with HIV/AIDS are thus available: Bertozzi *et al.* (2006) emphasize that a number of countries show by example that those tools can be put to effective use. Most of the high-income countries have done so, and Brazil, Mexico and Thailand provide examples of upper-middle-income countries that have forestalled potentially serious epidemics (del Rio and Sepúlveda 2002).

This section first discusses prevention and then antiretroviral therapy. It closes with a discussion of TB, as both an opportunistic infection of AIDS and a major global problem in itself.

Prevention of HIV Transmission

The HIV/AIDS pandemic is undoubtedly the most dramatic health challenge facing the world. HIV has reached every country in the world. In southern and eastern Africa, infection is running at unprecedented levels. However, the epidemic looks very different in different places. The dominant form of transmission worldwide is heterosexual, with other modes – the use of injected drugs and sex between men – being important in several regions. Three broad epidemiological patterns can be discerned. In eastern and southern Africa, the disease has spread quickly and widely throughout the population. HIV prevalence in antenatal clinic attendees doubled from 18 percent to 30 percent in Botswana from 1994 to 2005; in South Africa it increased from 3 percent to 15 percent over the same period. A few other countries in Africa have shown substantial but less dramatic increases to prevalence rates over 3 percent. The remaining African countries, and almost every other country in the world, have adult prevalence rates below 3 percent.

The reasons for the variations in prevalence between countries are not entirely clear and poorly researched. It is now clear that high levels of male circumcision protect against HIV/AIDS transmission at the population and individual level (Abdool Karim 2007). High levels of genital ulcer disease and low levels of male circumcision may help to explain the high HIV/AIDS levels seen in southern and eastern Africa. However, conditions rife for rapid growth exist in many places. These conditions include high levels of paid sex and partner change, high prevalence of sexually transmitted infections (STIs), low condom use rates, male mobility and migration, and low rates of male circumcision.

The key challenge for HIV/AIDS policy is to prevent transmission. In the absence of a vaccine, several interventions are of key importance. The most clearly effective preventive interventions are those targeting groups that – because of high rates of partner change, increased susceptibility to infection, or both – are highly vulnerable (Chen et al. 2007). Peer interventions among sex workers to teach them high levels of condom use, control of STIs, and client negotiation skills are effective. Less than one sex worker would need to be covered in a program for one year to prevent one infection (Jha et al. 2001).

A few countries in Asia with conditions for rapid growth in HIV-1 infections acted early by scaling up interventions in vulnerable groups. Their common principles were to work with the commercial sex industry, map where infection occurs, aim for high coverage, and base action on solid epidemiological information. The results are impressive. Thailand is the most famous example, where HIV-1 peaked in the early 1990s and has stayed at below 2 percent seroprevalence since. Less known are Mexico (del Rio and Sepúlveda 2002) and Cambodia, which copied the Thai "100 percent condom" program in commercial sex in 1997 in one state, and has shown impressive declines in HIV-1. More recent evidence from the four southern states of India suggest that new HIV infections might have dropped by 50 percent, probably due to changes in sex work (either the proportion using condoms or men going less often to sex workers; Dandona et al. 2006). Other interventions that complement vulnerable group interventions are effective. Despite controversy, STIs remain important as risk markers and risk factors for the spread of HIV. STI treatment for

vulnerable and general populations is probably effective for HIV control. Voluntary counseling and testing has led to some reduction in unsafe behavior in some studies, though the duration of the change is not clear. However, such testing is not necessarily a cost-effective form of prevention in all or even most settings, especially where prevalence is low. Voluntary testing is, however, a necessary prerequisite to some forms of treatment.

Although the transmission of HIV from mother to child is not of great epidemiological importance, since the infected children are very unlikely to transmit the disease, it is a mode of transmission that can be blocked, and which currently accounts for perhaps half a million deaths a year. Short courses of single ARV can halve transmission risk from about 40 percent to 20 percent. To be fully effective, replacement feeding is also required, given that breast milk is a source of transmission. Finally, needle exchange programs and blood safety programs can reduce these less common modes of transmission. More broadly, prevention efforts appear to work best when there is national leadership and simultaneous, sustained investment in multiple approaches to prevention, including efforts to reduce stigmatization of vulnerable groups. Increasing the availability of condoms for the wider population can enable more focused action. For example, the proportion of Senegalese women easily able to procure condoms rose from below 30 percent to 80 percent between 1992 and 1997. Focused information campaigns aimed at building public support and awareness are important, although these are not likely to change behavior in the absence of complementary preventive measures.

In those SSA countries with generalized epidemics that have spread far beyond vulnerable groups, a national approach is necessary. The reasons for the sharp decline in HIV/AIDS prevalence in Uganda, from about 20 percent in 1990 to 10 percent in 1999, are widely debated. It may be due, at least in part, to a broad-based prevention strategy addressed at the population as a whole, or simply to the fact that high death rates among those infected helped the epidemic to decline (James 2005). The replicability of the Ugandan experience to lower-prevalence settings is not established.

Bertozzi *et al.* (2006) point out that even by 2003 fewer than one in five people at high risk of infection had access to the most basic preventive services. In much of the world, little has been spent on prevention, and little has been achieved. In addition, the current US administration may be partially responsible for discouraging condom use in some countries and in stigmatizing and alienating commercial sex workers, who are particular priorities for prevention programs. Despite those problems, the potential for prevention is very real, and a number of successful countries have shown the possibility of using that potential well. Piot *et al.* (2008) summarize experience to date by observing that although evaluations of single interventions have often failed to find an impact, the countries that have mounted major programs of "combination prevention" have often achieved substantial success. The ingredients in the combination cocktail vary by location, but there is now reasonable evidence for its general success.

In addition to prevention, better management of patients with HIV/AIDS could avert much misery, both by treating opportunistic infections and by alleviating the often excruciating pain associated with many deaths. Medically inappropriate restrictions on the use of inexpensive but powerful opiates for pain control continue to deny dignity and comfort to millions of patients with HIV/AIDS and cancer in their final months (Foley *et al.* 2006).

Antiretroviral Treatment of AIDS

A primary focus on prevention strategies in the global response to HIV/AIDS reflects the fact that the future of the pandemic lies with those not yet infected. However, this cannot be taken as a reason to neglect the 35–40 million people currently living with the infection, 95 percent of them in low- and middle-income countries. Prophylaxis or treatments for some of the opportunistic infections that contrib-

ute to HIV/AIDS mortality are cost-effective (most notably antibiotics effective against TB). Since 1996, highly active antiretroviral therapy (HAART), which acts directly on the virus, has increased the life expectancy of people on treatment considerably. In developed countries, HAART has dramatically reduced but not eliminated HIV/AIDS mortality. Reduction in viral load slows or halts progression and can return individuals from serious illness to reasonable health. Available drugs leave a residual population of HIV/AIDS in the body, however, and this population grows if the drugs are stopped: At present, the drugs must be taken for life. Widespread use of these drugs in high-income (and some middle-income) countries has transformed the life prospects of infected individuals.

Early-generation antiretroviral drugs suffered notable shortcomings: They were enormously costly; regimens for their use were complicated, making adherence difficult; their use generated unpleasant side-effects; and rapid evolution of HIV/AIDS led to resistant mutants that undermined the efficacy of therapy. In a remarkably short time scientific advances have substantially attenuated those problems, making feasible, at least in principle, antiretroviral therapy in low-income settings. WHO's "3 by 5" program had as its objective, for example, to reach 3 million people in low- and middle-income countries with antiretroviral therapy by 2005. Although that goal was far from being met, the global effort to make treatment widely available is well under way. An important contributor has been the Clinton Foundation's effort to negotiate reductions in the prices of first-line and, more recently, second-line drugs.

Despite the indicated progress against the problems with antiretroviral drugs, challenges to their effective use in low-income environments remain formidable. The complexity of patient management is very real. Management requires high levels of human resources and other capacities in many of the countries where those capacities need to be most carefully rationed. Perhaps in consequence, achieving effective implementation has been difficult on even a limited scale. Bertozzi *et al.* (2006) review those problems and how they might be addressed.

Three points concerning widespread antiretroviral drug use are particularly noteworthy:

- *Poor implementation* (low adherence, development of resistance, interruptions in drug supplies) is likely to lead to very limited health gains, even for individuals on therapy. (This outcome is unlike that of a weak immunization program in which health gains still exist in the fraction of the population that is immunized.) Poorly implemented antiretroviral drug delivery programs could divert substantial resources from prevention or from other high-payoff activities in the health sector. Even worse, they could lead to a false sense of complacency in affected populations: Evidence from some countries suggests that treatment availability has led to riskier sexual behavior and increased HIV/AIDS transmission. The injunction to "do no harm" holds particular salience.
- Unless systematic efforts are made to acquire *hard knowledge about which approaches work and which do not*, the likelihood exists that unsuccessful implementation efforts will be continued without the appropriate reallocation of resources to successful approaches. Learning what works will require major variations in approach and careful evaluation of effects. Failing to learn will lead to large numbers of needless deaths. Most efforts to scale up antiretroviral therapy unconscionably fail to commit the substantial resources required for evaluation of effects. Such evaluations are essential if ineffective programs are to be halted or effective ones are to receive more resources.
- Many programs rely exclusively on the cheapest possible drugs, thereby risking problems with toxicity, adherence, and drug resistance. From the outset a *broader range of drug regimens* needs to be tested.

Use of ARV is likely to have a B/C ratio greater than 1 in many circumstances. However if such use competes with other highly attractive health investments in environments with limited human and financial resources, widespread adoption needs to be carefully sequenced.

Control of TB

TB is the leading cause of adult death from infectious disease after HIV/AIDS. Nearly 9 million new cases and perhaps 1.6 million deaths were caused by tuberculosis globally in 2003, with over 90 percent of these in low- and middle-income countries. TB, like HIV/AIDS, causes deaths during the productive working age, and can thus trigger household poverty. Only a small percentage of those infected with the TB bacillus go on to active disease such as pulmonary TB. Key risk factors for active tuberculosis include poverty, household crowding, and smoking (Bates *et al.* 2007).

TB can be controlled by preventing infection, by stopping progression from infection to active disease, and by treating active disease. The principal intervention is the "DOTS" strategy and its variations, centered on the diagnosis and treatment of the most severe and most infectious (smear-positive) forms of TB, but including treatment for smear-negative and extrapulmonary cases as well. Anti-TB drugs can also be used to treat latent M. tuberculosis infection and active TB in patients with HIV coinfection, and the widely used bacillus Calmette-Guérin (BCG) vaccine prevents (mainly) severe forms of TB in childhood (Dye *et al.* 2006). The cornerstone of TB control is the prompt treatment of active cases with short-course chemotherapy using first-line drugs, administered through the DOTS strategy, which has five elements: (i) political commitment; (ii) diagnosis primarily by sputum-smear microscopy among patients attending health facilities; (iii) short-course chemotherapy with three–four drugs including effective case management (including direct observation of treatment); (iv) a regular drug supply; and (v) systematic monitoring to evaluate the outcomes of every patient started on treatment.

The MDGs call for halting and beginning to

reverse new cases of TB by 2015 and the Stop TB Partnership calls for halving prevalence and deaths by 2015 relative to 1990 rates. It has been estimated that these goals can be reached if 70 percent of new infectious (smear-positive) cases worldwide are detected and 80 percent of those cases are treated successfully with the DOTS regime in "high-burden countries"; progress has been impressive. The case detection rate has increased from 11 percent globally in 1996 to 53 percent in 2004, and over 21 million TB patients were treated in DOTS programs in the decade after 1994. China and India have been noted as having particularly strong programs – although rigorous evaluation of the mortality impact of TB programs is still awaited. Key challenges remain the spread of HIV/AIDS infection in parts of Africa and drug resistance, especially in Eastern Europe. This suggests that DOTS alone might not be able to bring TB under control, especially in Africa and in the countries of the former Soviet Union.

The cost-effectiveness of TB control has been well established (summarized in Dye *et al.* 2006), but more recently Laxminarayan *et al.* (2007) have calculated the C/B of the WHO DOTS strategy at current levels relative to having no program in place. The ratio of marginal benefits to costs of implementing a global plan for DOTS is over 15 in the twenty-two "high-burden" countries, and 9 in the Africa region.

Non-Communicable Disease

At the same time that most low- and middle-income countries need to address health problems that are now effectively controlled in high-income countries, they are increasingly sharing the high-income countries' heavy burdens of cardiovascular system disease, cancers, respiratory diseases, psychiatric disorders, and automobile-related injuries. DCP2 has chapters addressing each of these NCDs and others. The public health research and policy community has been surprisingly silent about these epidemics even though, for example, cardiovascular disease (CVD) in low- and middle-income countries killed over twice as many people in 2001 as did HIV/AIDS, malaria, and TB combined (see table 3.4 for data on causes of deaths over the age of five). An important early exception was Feachem *et al.* (1992), who indicated approaches to treatment and prevention of these conditions that can be adapted to the tighter budget constraints of developing countries. WHO (2005) provides a valuable and more up-to-date discussion that emphasizes prevention. In addition, low-cost but effective approaches to long-term management of chronic conditions need to be developed and implemented, as was emphasized in a recent World Bank policy review (Adeyi *et al.* 2007). The challenge, as with so many other efforts to improve public health, is to identify approaches that provide genuine benefit in response to major sources of disease burden while costing sufficiently little that they can become (over time) universally available within the very tight public expenditure constraints of developing countries.

The remainder of this section briefly discusses, as examples, the prevention and management of CVD, and smoking as a risk factor for multiple NCDs.

Cardiovascular Disease

CVDs in low- and middle-income countries result in about 13 million deaths each year, over a quarter of all deaths in those countries. Most cardiovascular deaths result from ischemic heart disease (5.7 million) or cerebrovascular disease (4.6 million). (A potentially substantial fraction of the heart disease deaths may result from congestive heart failure.) In all countries, these deaths occur at older ages than do infectious conditions and thus account for a substantially smaller fraction of total disease burden in DALYs – 12.9 percent – than they do of deaths. However, a far greater proportion of the cardiovascular deaths in low- and middle-income countries occur in middle age (30–69) than they do in high-income countries, where they are concentrated at older ages.

The main risk factors for CVD account for

very large fractions of the deaths (and even more of the burden) from those diseases. For ischaemic heart disease, they collectively account for 78 percent of deaths in low- and middle-income countries; for stroke, they account for 61 percent (Ezzati *et al.* 2006). Measures to reduce the levels of those risk factors – high blood pressure, high intake of saturated animal fat, smoking, obesity, binge drinking of alcohol, physical inactivity, and low fruit and vegetable consumption – are the main means of prevention. Unlike the favorable experience with controlling tobacco use, attempts to change behaviors leading to obesity, hypertension, adverse lipid profiles, or physical activity appear to have had little success at a population level. A notable exception is the remarkable 25 percent decline in vascular mortality in the 1990s in Poland, which appears due to macroeconomic reforms that effectively removed the government subsidy for butter overnight, and simultaneously opened up markets from Western Europe of fresh fruits and vegetables, as well as products with lower amounts of saturated fat (Zatosnki *et al.* 2001). As Willett *et al.* (2006) document, many promising approaches remain to be tried. Common sense suggests that they should be initiated even while more systematic efforts to develop and evaluate behavior-change packages are ramped up.

Pharmaceutical interventions to manage two major components of cardiovascular risk – hypertension and high cholesterol levels – are well established and are highly cost-effective for individuals at high risk of a stroke or heart attack. Adding aspirin to the list of pharmaceutical interventions can reduce risk significantly further. From at least the time of publication of DCP1, researchers have recognized that the low cost and high effectiveness of drugs to prevent the reoccurrence of a cardiovascular event made their long-term use potentially cost-effective in low-income environments (Pearson *et al.* 1993). Even if sustained behavior change proves difficult to achieve, medications have the potential to reduce CVD risks by 50 percent or more. Simple combinations of cheap drugs can be

highly effective in reducing mortality among the millions of adults worldwide that already have some form of vascular disease or diabetes diagnosed. For example, among patients with a history of occlusive vascular disease such as stroke or heart attack, use of aspirin, a statin, and an antihypertensive drug could reduce the annual risk of major recurrence by about two-thirds; the ten-year risk of death or readmission to hospital is about 50 percent if people go untreated but only 16 percent if they receive daily treatment with three or four drugs.

All of these drugs are inexpensive and could easily be packaged into "polypills" or "generic-risk pills" for widespread use. Gaziano *et al.* (2006) develops the current evidence on that point. A key problem, however, concerns the health care personnel and systems requirements associated with the need for lifelong medication – a problem also faced with ARV therapy for AIDS and the use of medications to target several major psychiatric disorders. Adherence to drugs is a key issue, but unlike the challenge with HIV/AIDS drugs, resistance to use of polypill drugs is unlikely, and their costs are quite low. (These problems illustrate the importance of the non-financial costs discussed in the third and fourth sections and related issues of health system development.) How to achieve effective long-term management of lifesaving drugs is a key delivery and research challenge for health system reformers.

In contrast to the lifelong requirement for drug use associated with CVD risk reduction in high-risk individuals, treatment of acute heart attacks with inexpensive drugs is both less demanding of system resources and highly cost-effective (Gaziano *et al.* 2006). Given the high incidence of these problems, system-wide efforts to achieve high rates of appropriate drug use in response to acute heart disease are a high priority.

Tobacco Addiction

In most low-income countries, death in middle age increases in relative frequency as the effects of smoking increase. Most adult deaths worldwide involve vascular, neoplastic, and respira-

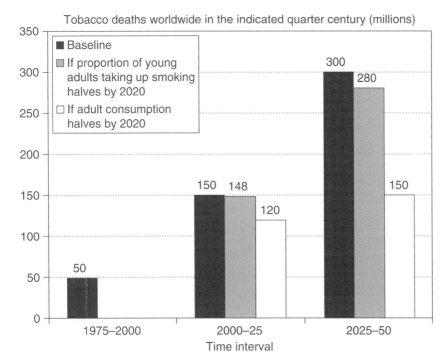

Figure 3.5 *Increase in tobacco-related deaths as populations age*
Source: Jha et al. (2006a).

tory disease, and smoking makes each of these more common. However, tobacco kills differently in different parts of the world. In China, the leading causes of death from smoking are chronic lung disease and lung cancer, with a noted excess also of TB deaths but relatively little heart disease (Liu *et al.* 1998). In India, the leading causes of death from smoking are TB in rural areas and acute heart attack in urban areas, with lung cancer less common (Jha *et al.* 2008).

In 2001, the number of tobacco-related deaths in developing countries was estimated to be 3.34 million or about 9 percent of deaths over the age of five in these countries (Lopez, Begg, and Bos 2006). However, extrapolating from current patterns, tobacco use may account for some 10 million deaths per year by 2030, with most of these occurring in low- and middle-income countries. In total, some 1 billion tobacco-related deaths might occur this century in contrast to 100 million in the twentieth

century. Unless there is widespread cessation of smoking, some 100 million of China's 200 million young male smokers and about 40 million of India's 100 million young male smokers will eventually die from tobacco-related causes. Smoking is already more common among poor or uneducated males than among richer or educated males, and smoking mortality accounts for about half of the difference in mortality risk between rich and poor men in Western countries (Jha *et al.* 2006b).

Preventing the initiation of smoking is important because addiction to tobacco makes smoking cessation very difficult, even for the numerous individuals who would like to do so. However, helping people quit smoking is at least as important as preventing initiation for there to be effects on mortality sooner than the very long run. Figure 3.5 portrays estimates showing that far more lives could be saved between now and 2050 with successful efforts to help people stop smoking than with efforts to keep them from starting. Reducing smoking levels is well demonstrated to be within the control of public policy. Indeed, many OECD countries have seen substantial declines in smoking deaths over the past two decades; for example, lung cancer deaths among young men between 30 and 44 years of age have fallen by nearly 80 percent in the UK (Peto *et al.* 2006), a change attributable chiefly to marked increases in cessation. Also, in OECD countries more than 30 percent of the adult population are ex-smokers, in contrast to only 2 percent in India, 9 percent in China, and 15 percent in Thailand (Jha *et al.* 2006b). Tobacco tax increases, dissemination of information about the health risks of smoking, restrictions on smoking in public and work places, comprehensive bans on advertising and promotion, and increased access to cessation therapies are effective in reducing tobacco use and its consequences (Jha *et al.* 2006a). Of these, taxing tobacco is particularly effective, with a 10 percent increase in price leading to a 4–8 percent drop in consumption (roughly equally split between cessation and initiation). Young people and the poor are particularly responsive to price (Jha and Chaloupka 2000).

Tobacco use is substantially different from other health challenges as it involves the use of a consumer good, with presumed economic benefits from that consumption. This has led to criticisms that tobacco control ignores the welfare benefits of smoking (Wolf 2006). This is no doubt to some extent correct, although measurement of welfare gains from an addictive substance is complex (Sen 2007). It is clear that among informed tobacco users there is a widespread desire to quit smoking, and willingness to pay for help with cessation at the same time that money is being spent on tobacco.

Of more importance is the widespread ignorance of risks. In China in 1996, 60 percent of adult smokers thought that smoking did little or no harm. Indeed, the recent increase in cessation in China might be related to new information on tobacco risks published in the late 1990s (Jha and Chen 2007). In most countries with good information on tobacco risks, over three-quarters of adult smokers regret ever having started as adolescents.

Putting addiction into a C/B framework is therefore tricky. Peck *et al.* (2000) built on an earlier framework by Barnum (1994) by comparing the consumer and producers surplus of tobacco (based on price and supply elasticities) to the VSL (conservatively valued as 1 times *per capita* GDP) weighted by tobacco-related mortality and the degree to which health smoking risks are known. They conclude that if a typical smoker underestimates his or her own health costs by 3–23 percent, then the net benefits of consumption are zero. Similarly, the marginal costs of a 10 percent higher price due to taxation have net welfare gains as long as 3 percent of smokers or more under-estimate their health risks of smoking.

While acknowledging the importance of attempts to estimate welfare losses associated with tobacco addiction, our approach in this chapter is simpler. We use published estimates of the costs of mounting a comprehensive tobacco control program (analogous to the "combination prevention" approach to HIV/AIDS transmission). CDC has recommended expenditures of $1–$4 *per capita*, but some US states have done well with less. DCP2 estimates expenditures for India of about $80 million per year. This figure includes costs of mobilizing public support, anti-smoking advertising and promotion, support for cessation programs and tax administration costs. Higher tobacco taxes raise net revenue, so with this perspective, tobacco taxation is cost savings. However, our B/C analysis is based on social costs, and treats the implementation costs of comprehensive tobacco control programs (of taxes and non-price interventions) like the implementation costs of other health programs.

In light of the range of published program cost, we use $1 billion per year as a reasonable estimate of the cost of comprehensive programs in the low- and middle-income countries. Our specific estimates of mortality reduction are

Table 3.6. Disease control: key investment priorities

Priority area	Indicative C/B ratio	Level of capacity required[a]	Financial risk protection provided[a]	Relevance for develop-ment assistance[a]	Increasedannual costs ($ billion)	Annual benefits[b]
1. TB: appropriate case finding and treatment	15:1	M	H	M	2	1 million adult deaths averted or 30 million DALYs averted
2. Heart attacks (AMI): acute management with low-cost drugs	25:1	M	H	H	0.2	300,000 heart attack deaths averted each year or 4.5 million DALYs averted
3. Malaria: prevention and ACT treatment package	20:1	M	L	M	0.5	500,000 (mostly child) deaths averted or 7.5 million DALYs averted
4. Childhood diseases: expanded immunization coverage	20:1	L	L	L	1	1 million child deaths averted or 20 million DALYs averted
5. Heart disease, respiratory disease, cancer, other: tobacco taxation and regulation	20:1	H	H	H	1	1 million adult deaths averted or 20 million DALYs averted
6. HIV: "combina-tion prevention"	12:1	M	H	H	2.5	2 million HIV infections averted or 22 million DALYs averted
7. Injury, difficult childbirth, other: surgical capacity at the district hospital	10:1	H	H	H	3	30 million "surgical" DALYs averted or about 20 percent of DALYs

Notes:
[a] Level of capacity required, extent of financial risk protection provided and relevance for development assistance are judged by the authors to be high (H), medium (M), or low (L).
[b] In the formulation of DALYs the benefits of averting a death in a given year all accrue in that year and are calculated as the present value (at a 3 percent discount rate) of the future stream of life years that would have occurred if the death had been prevented.

based on the effect of a 33 percent price increase (about a 50 percent increase in tax) on demand.

Opportunities for Disease Control

The preceding three sections identified a range of attractive options for disease control based, for the most part, on the 315 interventions that DCP2 reviewed (Jamison *et. al.* 2006). Laxminarayan, Chow, and Shahid-Salles (2006)

summarize the main findings on CE, which form the basis for the CBAs reported here. Appendix A, table 3A.1 provides highlights of those findings for South Asia and SSA. One thing that is clear in the summarization of the CE information is that there is a broad range of reasonable estimates for most interventions. This results partly from (often highly) incomplete information and uncertainty. It results also, and even more importantly, from the responsiveness of the CE function to variations in prices, in the scale of the intervention (and of its substitutes and complements), and in the epidemiological environment.

Given these often broad ranges in CE ratios, and hence in C/B ratios, it makes little sense to conclude with precise estimates or with attempts to quantify uncertainty. Rather we have identified seven major opportunities for investment in interventions that address a large disease burden highly cost effectively. Even valuing DALYs at a conservative $1,000 and, again conservatively, reducing by 50 percent the DALY associated with an under-five death (this affects the malaria and immunization numbers) the B/C ratios associated with investing in these opportunities is enormously high. (Appendix B provides a brief assessment of the sensitivity of our findings to key assumptions.) Overall this suggests that the conclusions we summarize in table 3.6 are conservative, principally because of the low value of $1,000 attached to DALYs for the computations reported in that table.

This summarizing table is not ranked on these seven interventions. First on the list in table 3.6 is case finding and treatment of tuberculosis (Dye and Floyd 2006). The seventh item – strengthening and expanding surgical capacity at the district hospital level (Debas *et al.* 2006) is an essentially systems-oriented intervention. Although the list of conditions that district hospital surgeons address is long, the most important in terms of benefits are dealing with difficult childbirths and with injury.

Table 3.6 includes information on B/C ratios and on total costs and benefits as well as judgments on other key parameters. Every opportunity in the table has not only a very high estimated B/C ratio but also, addresses the major disease burden. The interventions that would address the most DALYs are TB treatment and district hospital surgery. Each would provide a relatively high degree of financial protection to populations.

Experience with implementation of heart attack treatment – and, to a lesser extent, tobacco taxation and surgery – is much more limited in low-income countries than is experience with the other four interventions on the list. There is

a strong case for early, large-scale implementation trials in each of these three areas, and correspondingly strong arguments for international development assistance to finance these trials and learn from their results.

With the exception of surgery in the district hospital, the opportunities identified do not explicitly address the strengthening of health system capacity. It will be important to ensure that implementation includes related investments in manpower and institutions, with "related' broadly defined. One might consider there to be two broad approaches to strengthening health systems. One involves relatively non-specific investments in capacity and reforms of process. The second involves creating health system capacity to achieve specific measurable outcomes with high quality, a so-called "diagonal" approach (Sepúlveda 2006). In the second model capacity-strengthening spreads out from high-performing initial nodes. The approach that this chapter implicitly advocates is very much in the spirit of the latter.

From national perspectives the interventions on HIV/AIDS (combination prevention), on TB, on immunization, and on malaria prevention appear as very high priorities. Given that, for whatever reason, these interventions remain under-funded, there is a reasonable argument that development assistance funds should address these needs and to an important extent they do (through the very substantial resources of GAVI and the Global Fund Against AIDS, Tuberculosis, and Malaria). But most of these are familiar interventions with only modest international externalities. There is a reasonable argument that development assistance should deal with R&D, with reducing the risks of adopting new methods, and with cross-border externalities. By these criteria development assistance is doing less well in all but ignoring heart disease and surgical capacity. There is an initiative now being considered seriously by the international community to facilitate less expensive treatment with effective malaria drugs while preventing the development of resistance to the key drug artemisinin. The AMFm would operate by changing the prices countries face for drugs rather than supporting their purchase, and its support is a key priority.

All the interventions in table 3.6 have advantages and disadvantages relative to each other, and different individuals might well order them differently. The overwhelming general conclu-sion, however, is that even if all costs were increased by a factor of, say, 3 (appendix table 3B.1, row 3), there is a substantial and very specific list of major and highly attractive investment opportunities within the health sector.

Appendix A: Intervention Cost-Effectiveness in South Asia and SSA

DCP2 attempted to provide separate estimates of intervention CE for each of the World Bank's six regional groupings of low- and middle-income countries. The emphasis for the Copenhagen Consensus project, and for this chapter, is on low-income countries, which are concentrated in South Asia and SSA. Appendix table 3A.1 summarizes key DCP2 CE findings for these two regions.

Appendix table 3A.1. Neglected low-cost opportunities and high cost interventions in South Asia and SSA

	Cost per DALY averted ($)*	Thousands of DALYs averted*† per 20% increase in coverage	Burden of target diseases (millions of DALYs)*
Neglected low-cost opportunities in south Asia			
Childhood immunisation Increased coverage of traditional EPI programme	8	Not assessed	28.4

HIV/AIDS
  Voluntary counselling and testing
  Peer-based programmes for at-risk groups (eg commercial
    sex workers) to disseminate information, services (clean
    needles and condoms), and teach specific skills
  School-based interventions to disseminate information
  Prevention of mother-to-child transmission with
    antiretroviral therapy
	9–126	Not assessed	7.4

Surgical services and emergency care
  Surgical ward in district hospital, primarily for obstetrics,
    trauma, and injury
  Staffed community ambulance
  Training of lay first-responders and volunteer paramedics
	6–212	21.8	48.0–146.3

Tuberculosis
  Childhood vaccination against endemic disease
  Directly observed short-course chemotherapy
  Isoniazid treatment of epidemic disease
  Management of drug resistance
	8–263	Not assessed	13.9

Lower acute respiratory illnesses of children younger than age 5 years
  Community-based or facility-based case management of
    non-severe cases
  Case management package, including community-based
    and facility-based care for non-severe cases and hospital-
    based care for sever cases
	28–264	0.7–1.8	9.7–26.4

Cardiovascular diseases
  Management of acute myocardial infarction with aspirin
    and β blocker
  Primary prevention of coronary artery disease with
    legislation, substituting 2% of trans fat with
    polyunsaturated fat, at $0.50 per adult
	9–304	20.1	25.9–39.1

Appendix table 3A.1. (continued)

	Cost per DALY averted ($)*	Thousands of DALYs averted*† per 20% increase in coverage	Burden of target diseases (millions of DALYs)*
Cardiovascular diseases (*cont.*)			
Secondary prevention of congestive heart failure with ACE inhibitors and β blockers incremental to diuretics			
Secondary prevention of myocardial infarction and stroke with polypill, containing aspirin, β blocker, thiazide diuretic, ACE inhibitor, and statin			
Tobacco use and addiction	14–374	22.5	15.7
Tax policy to increase price of cigarettes by 33%			
Advertising bans, health information dissemination, tobacco supply reductions, and smoking restrictions			
Nicotine replacement therapy			
Maternal and neonatal care	127–394	21.3	37.7–47.8
Increased primary-care coverage			
Improved quality of comprehensive emergency obstetric care			
Improved overall quality and coverage of care			
Neonatal packages targeted at families, communities, and clinics			
Neglected low-cost opportunities in sub-Saharan Africa			
Childhood immunisation	1–5	Not assessed	Not assessed
Second opportunity measles vaccination‡			
Increased coverage of traditional EPI programme			
Traffic accidents	2–12	Not assessed	6.4
Increased speeding penalties, and media and law enforcement			
Speed bumps at most dangerous traffic intersections			
Malaria	2–24	20.8–37.6	35.4
Insecticide-treated bed nets‡			
Residual household spraying‡			
Intermittent preventive treatment during pregnancy‡			
Surgical services and emergency care	7–215	1.6–21.2	25–134.2
Surgical ward in a district hospital, primarily for obstetrics, trauma, and injury			
Staffed community ambulance			
Training of lay first-responders and volunteer paramedics			

Source: Table 3A.1 is based on chapters in DCP2 (Jamison *et al.* 2006), as summarized in Laxminarayan, Chow, and Shahid-Salles (2006), table 2.

Appendix B: Sensitivity Analysis

The analysis upon which we based the conclusions reported in table 3.6 was based on the following assumptions:

1 The DALY that was used was based on a 3 percent discount rate and *no age weighting*. These are the assumptions used in the most recent presentation of methods, data sources, and results on the global burden of disease (Lopez *et al.* 2006a, 2006b). Earlier tabulations of disease burden used age-weighted DALYs, which give broadly similar results except that somewhat more weight is given to conditions of middle age (TB, maternal deaths, trauma, psychiatric illness).

2 Jamison *et al.* (2006) (chapter 6 in Lopez 2006a) points to the mathematical impossibility, under plausible assumptions, of having the standard formulation of a DALY give a loss from a death at age 25 that would differ by more than 20 percent or so from the loss from a death at age 1 day. An alternative version of the DALY is proposed there (DALY (3,0, 0.54) and used in this chapter. The effect is to reduce the DALY of a death under the age of five by about 50 percent without changing the DALY from deaths at older ages.

3 In an attempt to include relevant health systems costs and to take a long-run view, cost estimates in this chapter are based on long-run average costs (at least in principle, as there is some variation in actual costing methods).

4 The chapter assumes zero deadweight loss from taxation.

5 The chapter assumes the value of a DALY to be $1,000.

Appendix table 3B.1 reports assessments of the robustness of our conclusions with respect to changes in these assumptions. On the most opti-

Appendix table 3B.1. Sensitivity analysis

Change in assumption	Consequence
1. Change the discount rate from 3 percent to 6 percent per year, i.e. change to DALYs (6,0, 0.54)	The number of DALYs averted from each of the interventions, and hence B/C, will decline by about 50 percent
2. Change from DALYs (3,0, 0.54) to DALYs (3,0)	The number of DALYs averted from immunization and from malaria control will approximately double, as will the B/C for the related interventions
3. Since *ex ante* costs are typically under-estimated, often substantially, multiply all costs by 3	B/C will decline to one-third of its otherwise estimated value for all interventions
4. The deadweight loss from taxation is increased from 0 to 50 percent of the revenue raised (Ballard *et al.* 1985 provide estimates in this range)	B/C value will decline by one-third
5. The value of a DALY averted is $5,000 rather than $1,000	B/C values go up by a factor of 5

mistic alternative assumption of appendix table 3B.1, the B/C for immunization and for malaria would increase by a factor of 10; for the other interventions, the factor is 5. Taking the least optimistic assumptions, the B/C of all interventions would decline by a factor of 10.

Bibliography

Abdool Karim, Q., 2007: Prevention of HIV by male circumcision, *BMJ*, **335**(7609): 4–5

Acemoglu, D. and Johnson, S., 2007: Disease and development: The effect of life expectancy on economic growth, *Journal of Political Economy*, **115**: 925–86

Adeyi, S., Smith, C., and Robles, S., 2007: *Public policy and the challenge of chronic noncommunicable diseases*, World Bank, Washington, DC

Alderman, H., Konde-Lute, J., Sebuliba, I., Bundy, D., and Hall, A., 2006: Effect on weight gain of routinely giving albendazole to preschool children during child health days in Uganda: Cluster randomised controlled trial, *BMJ*, **333**(122)

Alsan, M., Bloom, D.E., and Canning, D., 2006: The effect of population health on foreign direct investment inflows to low- and middle-income countries, *World Development*, **34**(4): 613–30

Aral, S.O., Over, M., Manhart, L., and Holmes, K.K., 2006: Sexually transmitted infections, in D.T. Jamison, J. Breman, A. Measham, G. Alleyne, M. Claeson, D. Evans, P. Jha, A. Mills, and P. Musgrove (eds.), *Disease control priorities in developing countries*, 2nd edn., Oxford University Press, Oxford and New York: 311–30

Arrow, K.J., 1963: Uncertainty and the welfare economics of medical care, *American Economic Review,* **53**: 851–83

Arrow, K.J., Gelband, H., and Jamison, D.T., 2005: Making antimalarial agents available in Africa, *New England Journal of Medicine*, **353**: 333–5

Ballard, C., Shoven, J., and Whalley, J., 1985: General equilibrium computations of the marginal welfare costs of taxes in the United States, *American Economic Review*, **74**: 128–38

Barnum, H., 1994: The economic burden of the global trade in tobacco, *Tobacco Control*, **3**: 358–61

Barnum, H. and Greenberg, E.R., 1993: Cancers, in D.T. Jamison, W.H. Mosley, A.R. Measham, and J.L. Bobadilla (eds.), *Disease control priorities in developing countries*, Oxford University Press, Oxford and New York: 529–59

Barr, N., 2001: *The welfare state as piggy bank: Information, risk, uncertainty, and the role of the state*, Oxford University Press, Oxford

Bates, M.N., Khalakdina, A., Pai, M., Chang, L., Lessa, F., and Smith, K.R., 2007: Risk of tuberculosis from exposure to tobacco smoke: A systematic review and meta-analysis. Archives of International Medicine, **167**(4): 335–42

Becker, G.S., Philipson, T.J., and Soares, R.R., 2003: The quantity and quality of life and the evolution of world inequality, *American Economic Review*, **95**: 277–91

Bertozzi, S., Padian, N.S., Wegbreit, J., DeMaria, L.M., Feldman, B., Gayle, H., Gold, J., Grant, R., and Isbell, M.T., 2006: HIV/AIDS prevention and treatment, in *Disease Control Priorities in* D.T. Jamison, J. Breman, A. Measham, G. Alleyne, M. Claeson, D. Evans, P. Jha, A. Mills, and P. Musgrove (eds.), *Developing countries*, 2nd edn., Oxford University Press, Oxford and New York: 331–70

Bezanson, K.A., 2006: Replenishing the global fund: an independent assessment – report for Global Fund

Bloom, D.E., 2005: Education and public health: Mutual challenges worldwide – Guest editor's overview, *Comparative Education Review*, **49**(4), 437–51

Bloom, D.E. and Canning, D., 2006: Booms, busts and echoes: How the biggest demographic upheaval in history is affecting global development, *Finance and Development*, **43**: 8–13

Bloom, D.E. and Canning, D., 2007a: The Preston Curve 30 years on: still sparking fires, *International Journal of Epidemiology*, **36**(3): 49–89

Bloom, D.E. and Canning. D., 2007b: Mortality traps and the dynamics of health transitions, *Proceedings of the National Academy of Sciences*, **104**: 16044–9

Bloom, D.E. Canning, D., 2008: Global demographic change: Dimensions and economic significance, in A. Prskawetz, D.E. Bloom, and W. Lutz (eds.), *Population aging, human capital accumulation, and productivity growth,* supplement to *Population and Development Review,* **33**, Population Council, New York: 17–51

Bloom, D.E., Canning, D., and Jamison, D.T., 2004: Health, wealth and welfare." *Finance and Development*, **41**(1): 10–15

Bloom, D.E., Canning, D., and Weston, M., 2004: The value of vaccination", *World Economics*, **6**(3): 15–39

Bourguignon, F. and Morrisson, C., 2002: Inequality among world citizens: 1820–1992, *American Economic Review*, **92**: 727–44

Breman, J.G., Mills, A., Snow, R.W., Mulligan, J., Lengeler, C., Mendis, K., Sharp, B., Morel, C., Marchesini, P., White, N.J., Steketee, R.W., and Doumbo, O.K., 2006: Conquering malaria, in D.T. Jamison, J. Breman, A. Measham, G. Alleyne, M. Claeson, D. Evans, P. Jha, A. Mills, and P. Musgrove (eds.), *Disease control priorities in developing countries*, 2nd edn., Oxford University Press, Oxford and New York: 413–32

Brenzel, L., Wolfson, L.J., Fox-Rushby, J., Miller, M., and Halsey.N.A., 2006: Vaccine-preventable diseases, in D.T. Jamison, J. Breman, A. Measham, G. Alleyne, M. Claeson, D. Evans, P. Jha, A. Mills, and P. Musgrove (eds.), *Disease control priorities in developing countries*, 2nd edn., Oxford University Press, Oxford and New York: 389–412

Chen, L., Jha, P., Stirling, B., Sgaier, S.K., Daid, T., 2007: Sexual risk factors for HIV infection in early and advanced HIV epidemics in Sub-Saharan Africa: Systematic overview of 68 epidemiological studies, *PLoS ONE*, **2**(10): e1001 doi:10.1371/journal.pone.0001001

Clemens, M., Radelet, S., and Bhavnani, R., 2004: Counting chickens when they hatch: The short-term effect of aid on growth, Working Paper, **44**, Center for Global Development, Washington, DC

Crafts, N. and Haacker, M., 2004: Welfare implications of HIV/AIDS, in M. Haacker (ed.), *The macroeconomics of HIV/AIDS*, International Monetary Fund, Washington, DC: 182–97

Crawford, C.B., Salter, B.E., and Jang, K.L., 1989: Human grief: Is its intensity related to the reproductive value of the deceased?, *Ethology and Sociobiology*, **10**(4): 29–307

Crogan, T.W., Beatty, A., and Ron, A., 2006: Routes to better health for children in four developing countries, *The Milbank Quarterly*, **84**(2): 333–58

Cutler, D., Deaton, A., and Lleras-Muney, A., 2006: The determinants of mortality, *Journal of Economic Perspectives*, **20**(3): 97–120

Dandona, L., Lakshmi, V., Sudha, T., Kumar, G.A., and Dandona, R., A population-based study of human immunodeficiency virus in South India reveals major differences from sentinel surveillance-based estimates, BMC Medicine, 4(31): 1–31

Davis, K., 1956: The amazing decline of mortality in underdeveloped areas, *American Economic Review*, Papers and Proceedings, **46**(2): 305–18

Debas, H.T., Gosselin, R., McCord, C., and Thind, A., 2006: Surgery, in D.T. Jamison, J. Breman, A. Measham, G. Alleyne, M. Claeson, D. Evans, P. Jha, A. Mills, and P. Musgrove (eds.), *Disease control priorities in developing countries*, 2nd edn., Oxford University Press, Oxford and New York: 1245–60

de Savigny, D., Kasale, H., Mbuya, C., and Reid, G., 2004: *Fixing health systems*, International Development Research Centre, Ottawa

del Rio, C. and Sepúlveda, J., 2002: AIDS in Mexico: Lessons learned and implications for developing countries, *AIDS*, **16**: 1445–57

Dye, C. and Floyd, K., 2006: Tuberculosis, in D.T. Jamison, J. Breman, A. Measham, G. Alleyne, M. Claeson, D. Evans, P. Jha, A. Mills, and P. Musgrove (eds.), *Disease control priorities in developing countries*, 2nd edn., Oxford University Press, Oxford and New York: 289–310

Easterlin, R.A., 1996: *Growth triumphant: the twenty-first century in historical perspective*, University of Michigan Press, Ann Arbor

England, S., Loevinsohn, B., Melgaard, B., Kou, U., and Jha, P., 2001: The evidence base for interventions to reduce mortality from vaccine-preventable diseases in low and middle-income countries, CMH Working Paper Series, **WG5:10**, www.cmhealth.org/docs/wg5_paper10.pdf

Ezzati, M. *et al.*, 2006: Role of smoking in global and regional cardiovascular mortality, *Journal of American College of Cardiology*, **48**(9): 1886–95

Feachem, R.G.A., Kjellstrom, T., Murray, C.J.L., Over, M., and Phillips, M. (eds.), 1992: *Health of adults in the developing world*, Oxford University Press, New York

Foley, K.M., Wagner, J.L., Joranson, D.E., and Gelband, H., 2006: Pain control for people with cancer and AIDS, in D.T. Jamison, J. Breman, A. Measham, G. Alleyne, M.

Claeson, D. Evans, P. Jha, A. Mills, and P. Musgrove (eds.), *Disease control priorities in developing countries*, 2nd edn., Oxford University Press, Oxford and New York: 981–94

Gajalakshmi, V. *et al.*, 2003: Smoking and mortality from tuberculosis and other diseases in India: Retrospective study of 43000 adult male deaths and 35000 controls, *Lancet*, **362**: 507–15

Gaziano, T., Reddy, K.S., Paccaud, F., Horton, S., and Chaturvedi, V., 2006: Cardiovascular disease, in D.T. Jamison, J. Breman, A. Measham, G. Alleyne, M. Claeson, D. Evans, P. Jha, A. Mills, and P. Musgrove (eds.), *Disease control priorities in developing countries*, 2nd edn., Oxford University Press, Oxford and New York: 645–62

Gericke, C.A., Kurowski, C., Ranson, M.K., and Mills, A., 2003: Feasibility of scaling-up interventions: The role of interventions design, Working Paper, **13**, Disease Control Priorities Project, Bethesda, MD

Graham, W.J., Cairns, J., Bhattacharya, S., Bullough, C.H.W., Quayyum, Z., and Rogo, K., 2006: Maternal and perinatal conditions, in D.T. Jamison, J. Breman, A. Measham, G. Alleyne, M. Claeson, D. Evans, P. Jha, A. Mills, and P. Musgrove (eds.), *Disease control priorities in developing countries*, 2nd edn., Oxford University Press, Oxford and New York: 499–530

Global IDEA Scientific Advisory Committee, 2004: Health and economic benefits of an accelerated program of research to combat global infectious diseases, *CMAJ*, **171**(10)

Haacker, M. (ed.), 2004: *The macroeconomics of HIV/AIDS*, International Monetary Fund, Washington, DC

Horton, S., Alderman, H., and Rivera, J.A., 2008: Malnutrition, see chapter 6 in this volume

Hotez, * *et al.*, 2006: Effect of albendazole treatments on the prevalence of atopy in children living in communities endemic with geohelminth parasites: A cluster-randomised trial, *Lancet*, **367**(9522): 1598–1603

Larsen, B., with Hutton, G., and Khanna, N., 2008: Air pollution, see chapter 1 in this volume

Hutton, G., 2007: Unsafe water and lack of sanitation, Paper prepared for CC08

Institute of Medicine, 1985: New vaccine

development: Establishing priorities, in *Diseases of importance in the United States*, I, National Academies Press, Washington, DC

James, J.S., 2005: Uganda study found that death reduced HIV prevalence; did the public take home the wrong message?, *AIDS Treat News*, **410**: 5–6

Jamison, D.T., 2006a: Investing in health, in D.T. Jamison, J. Breman, A. Measham, G. Alleyne, M. Claeson, D. Evans, P. Jha, A. Mills, and P. Musgrove (eds.), *Disease control priorities in developing countries*, 2nd edn., Oxford University, Oxford and New York: 3–34

Jamison, D.T., 2006b: The neglected problems of stillbirths and neonatal deaths, Paper prepared for the Global Forum on Health Research, 10th Meeting, Cairo

Jamison, D.T., 2008: Priority setting in health, Presentation at the Institution for Health Metrics and Evaluation–*Lancet* Conference on Global Metrics and Evaluation, Current State and Future Directions, Seattle and Washington, DC

Jamison, D.T., Breman, J., Measham, A.R., Alleyne, G., Claeson, M., Evans, D., Jha, P., Mills, A., and Musgrove, P. (eds.), 2006: *Disease control priorities in developing countries*, 2nd edn., Oxford University Press, Oxford and New York

Jamison, D.T., Jamison, E.A., and Sachs, J.D., 2003: Assessing the determinants of growth when health is explicitly included in the measure of economic welfare, Paper presented at the 4th World Congress of the International Health Economics Association, San Francisco, June

Jamison, D.T., Lau, and Wang, J., 2005: Health's contribution to economic growth in an environment of partially endogenous technical progress, in G. Lopez-Casanovas *et al.* (eds.), *Health and Economic Growth: Findings and Policy Implications*, MIT Press, Cambridge, MA

Jamison, D.T., and S. Radelet. 2005. "Making Aid Smarter." *Finance and Development* 42 (2): 42–46

Jamison, D.T., Sachs, J., and Wang, J., 2001: The effect of the AIDS epidemic on economic welfare in Sub-Saharan Africa, CMH Working Paper, **WG1:13**, Commission on

Macroeconomics and Health, World Health Organization, Geneva

Jamison, D.T., Sandbu, M., and Wang, J., 2004: Why has infant mortality decreased at such different rates in different countries?, Working Paper, **21**, Disease Control Priorities Project, Bethesda, MD

Jamison, D.T., Shahid-Salles, S., Jamison, J.S., Lawn, J., and Zupan, J., 2006: Incorporating deaths near the time of birth into estimates of the global burden of disease, in D. Lopez, C.D. Mathers, M. Ezzati, D.T. Jamison, and C.J.L. Murray (eds.), *Global burden of disease and risk factors*, Oxford University Press, New York: A427–62

Jamison, E.A., Jamison, D.T., and Hanushek, E.A., 2007: The effects of education quality on income growth and mortality decline, *Economics of Education Review*, **26**(6): 771–88

Jha, P., 2008: Sex, money and ideas: Twenty years of battling AIDS in India, *Commonwealth Health Ministers Book*, Hanley Press, London

Jha, P., Nagel, N.J.D., Ngugi, E., Wilbond, B., Prasada-Rao, J.V.R., Moses, S., and Plummer, F.A., 2001: Reducing HIV transmission in developing countries, *Science*, **292**(5515): 224–5

Jha, P. *et al.*, 2002: Improving the health of the global poor, *Science*, 295(5562): 2036–9

Jha, P. *et al.*, for Global IDEA Scientific Advisory Committee Health, 2004: Economic benefits of an accelerated program of research to combat global infectious diseases, *CMAJ*, 172(00): 1538–9

Jha, P. *et al.*, 2006a: Social inequalities in male mortality, and in male mortality from smoking: Indirect estimation from national death rates in England and Wales, Poland, and North America, *Lancet*, 368: 367–70

Jha, P. *et al.*, 2006b: Tobacco addiction, in D.T. Jamison, J. Breman, A. Measham, G. Alleyne, M. Claeson, D. Evans, P. Jha, A. Mills, and P. Musgrove (eds.), *Disease control priorities in developing countries*, 2nd edn., Oxford University Press, Oxford and New York: 869–86

Jha, P. *et al.*, 2008: A nationally representative case-control study of smoking and death in India, *New England Journal of Medicine*, February 13, Epub

Jha, **P**. and Chaloupka, F.J., 2000: The economics of global tobacco control, *BMJ*, 321: 358–61

Jha, P. and Mills, A., 2002: Improving health of the global poor, The Report of Working Group 5 of the Commission on Macroeconomics and Health, WHO, Geneva

Jha, P., Nagelkerke, N.J.D., Ngugi, E., Wilbond, B., Prasada-Rao, J.V.R., Moses, S., and Plummer, F.A., Reducing HIV transmission in developing countries, 2001: *Science*, 292(5515): 224–5

Jha, P. and Chen, Z., 2007: Poverty and chronic diseases in Asia: Challenges and opportunities, *CMAJ*, **177**(9): 1059

Johansson, P.O., 1995: Evaluating health risks, Cambridge University Press, Cambridge

Joint Learning Initiative, 2004: Human resources for health: Overcoming the crisis, Harvard University Press, Cambridge, MA

Kanbur, R., and Sandler, T., 1999: *The future of development assistance: Common pools and international public goods*, Overseas Development Council, Washington, DC

Keusch, G.T., Fontaine, O., Bhargava, A., Boschi-Pinto, C., Bhutta, Z.A., Gotuzzo, E., Rivera, J.A., Chow, J., Shahid-Salles, S.A., and Laxminarayan, R., 2006: Diarrheal diseases, in D.T. Jamison, J. Breman, A. Measham, G. Alleyne, M. Claeson, D. Evans, P. Jha, A. Mills, and P. Musgrove (eds.), *Disease control priorities in developing countries*, 2nd edn., Oxford University Press, Oxford and New York: 371–88

Lawn, J.E., Zupan, J., Begkoyian, G., and Knippenberg, R., 2006: Newborn survival, in D.T. Jamison, J. Breman, A. Measham, G. Alleyne, M. Claeson, D. Evans, P. Jha, A. Mills, and P. Musgrove (eds.), *Disease control priorities in developing countries*, 2nd edn., Oxford University Press, Oxford and New York: 531–50

Laxminarayan, R., Chow, J., and Shahid-Salles, S.A., 2006: Intervention cost-effectiveness: Overview of main messages, in D.T. Jamison, J. Breman, A. Measham, G. Alleyne, M. Claeson, D. Evans, P. Jha, A. Mills, and P. Musgrove (eds.), *Disease control priorities in developing countries*, 2nd edn., Oxford University Press, Oxford and New York: 35–86

Laxminarayan, R, Klein, E., Dye, C., Floyd, K.,

Darly, S., and Adeyi, O., 2007: Economic benefit of tuberculosis control, Resource for the Future, Policy Research Working Paper, **4295**, Human Development Network Health, Nutrition, and Population Team, World Bank, Washington, DC, August

Laxminarayan, R., Mills, A.J., Breman, J.G., Measham, A.R., Alleyne, G., Claeson, M., Jha, P., Musgrove, P., Chow, J.,Shahid-Salles, S.A., and Jamison, D.T., 2006: Advancement of global health: Key messages from the Disease Control Priorities Project, *The Lancet*, **367**: 1193–1208

Levine, R. and the What Works Working Group. 2007: *Millions saved: Proven successes in global health*, Jones and Bartlett, Sudbury, MA

Lindert, P.H., 2004: *Growing public: Social spending and economic growth since the eighteenth century, 1*, Cambridge University Press, Cambridge

Liu, B.Q. *et al.*, 1998: Emerging tobacco hazards in China, 1: Retrospective proportional mortality study of one million deaths, *BMJ*, 317: 1411–22

Lomborg, B. (ed.), 2004: *Global crises, global solutions*, Cambridge University Press, Cambridge

Lomborg, B. (ed.), 2006: *How to spend $50 billion to make the world a better place*, Cambridge University Press, Cambridge

Lopez, A.D., Begg, S., and Bos, E., 2006: Demographic and epidemiological characteristics of major regions of the world, 1990 and 2001, in A.D. Lopez, C.D. Mathers, M. Ezzati, D.T. Jamison, and C.J.L. Murray (eds.), *Global burden of disease and risk factors*, Oxford University Press, Oxford and New York: 17–44

Lopez, A.D., Mathers, C.D., Ezzati, M., Jamison, D.T., and Murray, C.J.L. (eds.), 2006a: *Global burden of disease and risk factors*, Oxford University Press, Oxford and New York

Lopez, A.D., Mathers, C.D., Ezzati, M., Jamison, D.T., and Murray, C.J.L., 2006b: Global and regional burden of disease and risk factors, 2001: Systematic analysis of population health data, *Lancet*, **367**: 1747–57

Lopez-Casasnovas, G., Rivera, B., and Currais, L. (eds.), 2005: *Health and economic growth: Findings and policy implications*, MIT Press, Cambridge, MA

Mathers, C.D., Murray, C.J.L., and Lopez, A.D., 2006: The burden of disease and mortality by condition: Data, methods and results for the year 2001, in A.D. Lopez, C.D. Mathers, M. Ezzati, D.T. Jamison, and C.J.L. Murray (eds.), *Global burden of disease and risk factors*: Oxford University Press, Oxford and New York: 45–240

Measham, A.R., 2006: Improving the health of populations: lessons of experience, Fogerty International Center of the US National Institutes

Measham, A.R., Rao, K.D., Jamison, D.T., Wang, J., and Singh, A., 1999: The performance of India and Indian states in reducing infant mortality and fertility, 1975–1990, *Economic and Political Weekly*, **34**(22): 1359–67

Meda, N., Ndoye, I,. M'Boup, S., Wade, A., Ndiaye, S., Niang, C., Sarr, F., Diop, I,. and Caraël, M., 1999: Low and stable HIV infection rates in Senegal: Natural course of the epidemic or evidence for success of prevention?, *AIDS*, **13**(11): 1397–1405

Meltzer, D., 2006: Economic approaches to valuing global health research, in D.T. Jamison, J. Breman, A. Measham, G. Alleyne, M. Claeson, D. Evans, P. Jha, A. Mills, and P. Musgrove (eds.), *Disease control priorities in developing countries*, 2nd edn., Oxford University Press, Oxford and New York: 157–64

Mills, A., and Shillcutt., S., 2004: Communicable diseases, chapter 2 in . B. Lomborg (ed.), *Global crises, global solutions*, Cambridge University Press, Cambridge: 62–114

Mulligan, J., Fox-Rushby, J.A., Adam, T., Johns, B., and Mills, A., 2003: Unit costs of health care inputs in low and middle income regions, Disease Control Priorities Project Working Paper, **9**, Fogarty International Center, National Institutes of Health, Bethesda, MD

Nagelkerke, N.J.D., Jha, P., de Vlas, S.J., Korenromp, E.L., Moses, S., Blanchard, J.F., Plummer, F.A., 2002: Modelling HIV/AIDS epidemics in Botswana and India: Impact of interventions to prevent transmission, *Bull World Health Organ*, **80**(2): 89–96

Nordhaus, W., 2003: The health of nations: The contributions of improved health to living standards, in K.M. Murphy and R.H. Topel (eds.), *Measuring the gains from health research: An economic approach*, University of Chicago Press, Chicago: 9–40

Oeppen, J., and Vaupel, J.W., 2002: Demography, broken limits to life expectancy, *Science*, **296** (5570): 1029–31

Orazem, P.F. *et al.*, 2008: *The benefits and costs of alternative strategies to improve education outcomes*, see chapter 4 in this volume

Peabody, J.W., Taguiwalo, M.M., Robalino, D.A., and Frenk, J., 2006: Improving the quality of care in developing countries, in D.T. Jamison, J. Breman, A. Measham, G. Alleyne, M. Claeson, D. Evans, P. Jha, A. Mills, and P. Musgrove (eds.), *Disease control priorities in developing countries*, 2nd edn., Oxford University Press, Oxford and New York: 1293–1308

Pearson, T., Jamison, D.T., and Trejo-Gutierrez, J., 1993: Cardiovascular disease, in Jamison, D.T., Mosley, W.H., Measham, A.R., and Bobadilla, J.A. (eds), *Disease control priorities in developing countries*, Oxford University Press, Oxford and New York: 577–94

Peck, R., Chaloupka, F.J., Jha, P., and Lightwood, J., 2000: Welfare analyses of tobacco, in P. Jha and F.J. Chaloupka (eds.), *Tobacco control in developing countries*, Oxford University Press, Oxford: 131–52

Peto, R. *et al.*, 1995: Cholesterol, diastolic blood pressure, and stroke: 13,000 strokes in 450,000 people in 45 prospective cohorts. Prospective studies collaboration, *Lancet*, **346**:1647–53

Peto, R. *et al.*, 2006: Mortality from smoking in developed countries, 1950–2000, 2nd edn., Clinical Trial Service Unit, Oxford, www.ctsu.ox.ac.uk/~tobacco, accessed September 24, 2007

Peto, R. and Baigent, C., 1998: Trials: The next 50 years. Large scale randomised evidence of moderate benefits, *BMJ*, **317**: 1170–1

Piot, P., Banton, M., Larson, H., Zewdie, D., and Mane, P., 2008: Coming to terms with complexity: A call to action for HIV prevention, *Lancet*, **372**(9641): 845–59

Preston, S.H., 1975: The changing relation between mortality and level of economic development, *Population Studies*, **29**(2): 231–48

Preston, S.H., 1980: Causes and consequences of mortality declines in less developed countries during the twentieth century, in R. Easterlin (ed.), *Population and economic change in developing countries*, University of Chicago Press, Chicago: 289–360

Pritchard, C., 2004: Developments in economic evaluation in health care: A review of HEED, OHE Briefing, **40**, Office of Health Economics, London, March

Radelet, S., 2003: *Challenging foreign aid*, Center for Global Development, Washington, DC

Sachs, J.D., 2005: The end of poverty: Economic possibilities for our times, Penguin, New York

Schelling, T., 1968: The life you save may be your own, in S.B. Chase, Jr. (ed.), *Problems in public expenditure analysis*, Brookings Institution, Washington, DC

Sen, A., 2007: Unrestrained smoking is a libertarian half-way house, *Financial Times*, February 12: 15

Sepúlveda, J., 2006: Foreword, in D.T. Jamison, J. Breman, A. Measham, G. Alleyne, M. Claeson, D. Evans, P. Jha, A. Mills, and P. Musgrove (eds.), *Disease control priorities in developing countries*, 2nd edn., Oxford University Press, Oxford and New York: xiii–xv

Simoes, E.A.F., Cherian, T., Chow, J., Shahid-Salles, S.A., Laxminarayan, R., and John, T.J., 2006: Acute respiratory infections in children, in D.T. Jamison, J. Breman, A. Measham, G. Alleyne, M. Claeson, D. Evans, P. Jha, A. Mills, and P. Musgrove (eds.), *Disease control priorities in developing countries*, 2nd edn., Oxford University Press, Oxford and New York: 483–98

Strauss, J. and Thomas, D., 1998: Health, nutrition, and economic development, *Journal of Economic Literature*, **36**(2): 766–817

Tolley, G., Kenkel, D., and Fabian, R., 1994: State of the art health values, in G. Tolley, D. Kenkel, and R. Fabian (eds.), *Valuing health for policy: An economic approach.* Chicago, University of Chicago Press: 323–44

US Centers for Disease Control, 1999: Achievements in public health, 1900–1999: Changes in the public health system, *MMWR*, 48(50): 1141, www.cdc.gov/mmwr/PDF/wk/mm4850.pdf

Usher, D., 1973: An imputation to the measure of economic growth for changes in life expectancy, in M. Moss (ed.), *The measurement of economic and social performance, NBER studies in income and wealth*, **38**, Conference on Research in Income and Wealth, Columbia University Press, New York

Van der Gaag, J., 2004: Perspective paper 2.2, in B. Lomborg (ed.), *Global crises, global solutions*, Cambridge University Press, Cambridge

Viscusi, W.K. and Aldy, J.E., 2003: The value of a statistical life: a critical review of market estimates throughout the world, *Journal of Risk and Uncertainty*, 27(1): 5–76

Warren, K. *et al.*, 1993: Helminth infection, in D.T. Jamison W.H. Mosley, A.R. Measham, and J.L. Bobadilla (eds.), *Disease control priorities in developing countries*, Oxford University Press, Oxford and New York: 131–60

Weatherall, D., Greenwood, B., Chee, H.L., Wasi, P., 2006: Science and technology for disease control: Past, present, and future, in D.T. Jamison, J. Breman, A. Measham, G. Alleyne, M. Claeson, D. Evans, P. Jha, A. Mills, and P. Musgrove (eds.), *Disease control priorities in developing countries*, 2nd edn., Oxford University Press, Oxford and New York: 119–38

WHO, 1999: *World Health Report 1999*, World Bank, Washington, DC

WHO, 2000: *World Health Report 2000*, World Bank, Washington, DC

WHO, 20005: *World Health Report 2005*, World Bank, Washington, DC

WHO CMH, 2001: *Macroeconomics and health: Investing in health for economic development*, WHO, Geneva

Wolf, M., 2006: The absurdities of a ban on smoking, *Financial Times*, June 22

World Bank, 1993; *World development report: investing in health*, Oxford University Press, New York

World Bank, 2007; *World Development Indicators*, World Bank, Washington, DC

World Economic Forum, 2008; Tackling tuberculosis: The business response, World Economic Forum, Davos

Yamey, G. on behalf of interviewees, 2007: Which single intervention would do the most to improve the health of those living on less than $1 per day?, *PLoS Med.*, **4**: 1557–60

Zatonski, A.W. and Jha, P., 2000: *The health transformation in eastern Europe after 1990: A second look*, The M. Sklodowska-Curie Memorial Cancer Center and Institute of Oncology, Cracow

Alternative Perspectives

Perspective Paper 3.1

DAVID CANNING

Introduction

The Challenge paper on disease control by Jamison, Jha, and Bloom (hereafter, JJB) puts forward a case for a high C/B ratio for a set of health interventions in developing countries. These are TB treatment, drug treatments to prevent CVD, the prevention and treatment of malaria, expanded coverage of immunization against childhood diseases, tobacco taxation, HIV/AIDS prevention, and an expansion in hospital surgical capacity to treat injuries and diseases and ensure safe childbirth.

Overall, my reading of the paper is that the high B/C ratios found for disease control are plausible. However, there are a number of issues and caveats that arise in the paper's estimates of B/C ratios for health interventions to which I would like to draw attention. The first is the estimation of benefit numbers where health is involved. After calculating the health benefits of the interventions, JJB use estimates of the value of a DALY to estimate the welfare benefits in money terms of all the health interventions. There is room for doubt over the simple rule of thumb used that in a poor country the value of a life year lived in good health is just over twice average *per capita* income per year. We will discuss some issues around this question – though it is difficult to resolve, and it may be that a higher rather than a lower figure is appropriate.

A second challenge to the analysis is the fact that in many developing countries most health

care spending is out of pocket. Given that these interventions have such high benefits, and low costs, why are people not already purchasing them? This speaks to a pervasive market failure. While market failures may exist for infectious disease, or in places where large costs mean that households need insurance but insurance markets fail, it is more difficult to make the case for an inherent market failure when the benefits to the intervention are private, and the costs per person treated are low. For preventive measures to control heart attacks, for example, the payoffs are private and the costs per person covered appear to be very low.

It may be that these market failures exist, but a case has to be made. If no market failure can be found, it is difficult to justify the large B/C ratios estimated in the paper. Even if market failures exist, there is an assumption that the appropriate solution is direct provision of the service. A better approach may be to tackle the market failure directly; for example if the market failure is informational, information campaigns as to the benefits of a health service may solve the problem at much lower public cost. The authors seem to assume that interventions will be funded through the public sector or international donors, while if the argument is that individual WTP far exceeds the costs, simply devising mechanisms to allow people to spend their own money on the intervention seems a more appropriate policy.

A related issue on the benefits of health

interventions is the lengthy discussion in the paper on the economic benefits of improved health – in the form, for example, of higher worker productivity. While much is made of this point in theory, when it comes to estimating the B/C ratios of the interventions only the direct health benefits are counted. There is also some discussion of financial risk protection as an additional benefit but this is not included in the calculations of B/C ratios. This may bias the resulting estimates downwards. More importantly, it may lead to overlooking some health interventions that have small health benefits but large economic benefits. Later, I will suggest that treatment and prevention of worm diseases and soil-born helminths fall into this category.

In terms of the costs, there is some doubt that the estimated costs reflect the actual costs that will be required in practice. Cost studies in health often focus on marginal costs and ignore the overhead and fixed costs that are required when a program is scaled up. Related to this is the issue of the appropriateness of a disease- or procedure-based intervention strategy vs. an emphasis on more broad-based care through the provision of the infrastructure for more comprehensive primary- and higher-level health care. It is sometimes unclear if the interventions are thought of as being costed at the margin, given the existence of, and working through, health care infrastructure, or if they are stand-alone programs. JJB are aware of this issue and discuss it at some length, but it is unclear if it has been satisfactorily resolved in their estimates.

One major challenge to the argument that these health interventions will lead to welfare gains is the fact that by saving lives the health programs envisioned will increase population numbers. This increase in population numbers will put pressure on the limited available resources, reducing income levels for everyone. This negative Malthusian externality may be large in an agricultural setting where a fixed factor – land – is a key resource. It would be interesting to see how much this crowding externality could affect the results.

While these issues around estimating the costs and benefits are important and should be addressed, the very high C/B ratios found imply that even if we reduce the money value of life and health substantially and increase the estimated costs of the interventions, the benefits of the interventions will still dramatically outweigh the costs.

In the second section, I briefly touch on some of the issues around putting money values on health benefits. In the third section, I discuss how including the productivity benefits of the health interventions being considered might add to the case for their implementation. In the fourth section, I discuss the cost side and argue that the interventions may be more expensive than estimated. In the fifth section, I investigate the market failures that have to form the basis of the argument for intervention. The sixth section looks at the issue of the economic consequences of the population boom that health interventions can engender through mortality reductions. The seventh section ends with an argument that intervention through de-worming may be considered a priority area on economic grounds, even if not in terms of its direct health benefits.

While I raise some methodological issues with the paper that make estimating the C/B ratios difficult, there is a reasonable case that a complete C/B calculation would increase the benefits relative to the costs over the estimates that have been reported. It may be that the estimates reported in the paper, though high, are conservative rather than extreme.

Money value of health benefits

CE analysis estimates the cost per unit of health benefit gained. These health benefits are then translated into money units by using estimates of the VSL and value of disability estimates. There are a number of technical difficulties with defining DALYs and age-adjusting life-span gains. These are discussed in the Challenge paper.

However, there are two issues concerning translating health improvements into money values that may have a bearing on the results found in the paper. The first is how the VSL varies with the level of income. The approach taken in the paper is to assume that the WTP for a statistical life is unit-elastic in income. This means that the value of health improvements is taken to be directly proportional to a country's income level. However Viscusi and Aldy (2003) report results from sixty VSL studies and forty studies of injury risk premiums. Viscusi and Aldy find an income elasticity of WTP for life and health of about 0.5. A low elasticity means that in poor countries people are more willing to pay a higher fraction of their income to avoid the risk of death and disability than in rich countries. This result may not be correct, but it needs discussion together with a more detailed argument for accepting unit elasticity in the WTP and the actual multiple of average income people in poor countries are willing to pay for a VSLY.

A second issue is that in C/B studies we usually add up the money value of the benefits to those who receive the intervention. In the health approach, we add up the health benefits, weighted equally across people with different income levels and WTP. JJB then translate the health benefits to money units, using average income in the countries in question to put a money value on life. This approach seems reasonable if the health gains are equally distributed over income groups. However, there are strong reasons to suspect that the health gains will be concentrated among the poor (in poor countries and the poor in richer countries), who typically have a much higher disease burden than the rich (as is indeed pointed out in the paper). The poor will typically have a lower WTP for health than the average person, making the reported B/C ratios too high.

The approach used by CE analysis is egalitarian: All gains to health within a country are weighted equally. This egalitarian flavor is maintained in the paper, where all health gains are translated to money units at the same rate. However in B/C calculations the key issue is efficiency. A low B/C ratio implies that the person would rather have the money than the intervention. The poor are less willing to pay for life, which is another way of saying they have a high value of money. For the poorest people

in the poorest countries, who have the worst health and the most to gain in health terms from the interventions being proposed, the value of money is high and the B/C ratios may be much lower than those that are being reported.

Productivity Benefits

There is a comprehensive review of the literature in the paper on the idea that health interventions have economic as well as health benefits. However, when it comes to estimating the B/C ratio for the health interventions, only health gains are included. Adding these economic benefits would give a clearer view of the overall gains from health interventions. To some extent this omission may be due to lack of data on the economic benefits of the interventions being assessed. There is certainly evidence for at least some of the interventions, and including this information might change the ranking of the interventions considered, and might raise other interventions above those currently being considered.

For example, suppose we focus on malaria. The loss of productive work time due to a bout of malaria has been estimated as 5.8 working days per bout of malaria in Zambia (Utzingerg et al. 2002). Other studies indicate that 4.0 days per bout are lost in Sri Lanka (Attanayake et al. 2000), and 10 days per bout in rural Colombia (Bonilla and Rodriguez 1993). Snow et al. (1999), estimate that in malaria-endemic areas (where natural immunity is common) adults on average suffer 0.4 bouts per year, though children aged between 0 and four suffer on average one bout of malaria per year.

The adult working days lost due to malaria fever will lead to a loss of income that is substantial, but not enormous. Larger effects may occur if malaria also affects productivity while in work. Early childhood exposure to malaria can retard physical and cognitive development in children, leading to poor outcomes in school and worse health, and low productivity, as an adult. A number of studies use national efforts to eradicate malaria in the 1950s and 1960s using

DDT spraying to estimate the long-term gains to children from avoiding early childhood exposure to malaria. Cutler *et al.* (2007) find that malaria eradication in India leads to significant gains in literacy in the areas in which malaria was initially endemic. Lucas (2005) finds that malaria had a substantial adverse effect on female literacy in Paraguay, Sri Lanka, and Trinidad and Tobago. Bleakley (2006), in an analysis of malaria eradication program in the USA, Mexico, Columbia, and Brazil shows that childhood exposure to malaria substantially depresses labor productivity in later life, lowering adult wages by as much as 50 percent.

These long-term economic effects of malaria on children are likely to dominate the cost of the working days lost due to malaria in adults. These economic gains have to be discounted since they come in adulthood, long after the health investment in reducing childhood exposure to malaria has been made; but even with discounting the economic benefits of malaria control may be a significant addition to the health benefits. In the paper the financial risk protection that comes from malaria control is rated as low, which presumably means that the cost of treatment and earnings forgone by adults when ill is not very substantial. The potential addition of the long-term economic consequences of childhood exposure might change these assessments.

Immunization against childhood disease has large effects on childhood mortality. These diseases may, like malaria, have a large morbidity burden in children affecting, in particular, their cognitive development. Bloom *et al.* (2005) estimate that the health gains that flow from childhood immunization will have a productivity benefit when these children become adults and that despite discounting the return on immunization as a purely economic investment (ignoring the direst health gains) is substantial and is comparable with investments in primary education.

A similar analysis could be applied to the other health interventions proposed. In particular, those that target morbidity, rather than mortality, such as the surgical treatment of injuries, are likely to have substantial benefits

in terms of worker productivity. In addition, interventions that affect childhood health – such as immunization – that have effects on their long-term physical and cognitive development are likely to have economic benefits once these children reach adulthood.

It may be that, due to uncertainty in the estimates of these economic benefits, JJB may be uncomfortable about including them in the calculations. However, it would still be useful to report estimates of the magnitude of the economic payoffs even if they are not ultimately used in the calculation of B/C ratios.

Costs

The Challenge paper discusses the issue of strengthening the health system as part of the intervention strategy. In addition to the financial constraints there are real resource constraints in terms of health sector infrastructure and personnel that may make the scaling up of interventions difficult. The vertical, disease-specific, approach does leave the question of how the overall health system will function in parallel. While attention is paid to this issue in the paper, and its importance is underlined, it is unclear how the vertical programs will be integrated with the health system in practice.

A related issue is the costing of the interventions. A recurrent problem in the health area is the costing of interventions at marginal cost, assuming the existence of health infrastructure, and sometimes even health workers. These costs can be wild under-estimates. It is recognized in the paper that these disease-specific interventions should go hand in hand with general increases in physical and human resources for the health sector. It is postulated in the paper that this will increase costs by a factor of 2 or 3, but this appears speculative. A better approach would be to distinguish costs from small-scale interventions to those found when scaling up interventions. There is the problem that many health interventions are joint products of a single health system, but more detailed evidence of the actual costs of large-scale interventions would be very helpful in making the case for these health initiatives.

Market Failure

The usual rationale for intervention in economics is some form of market failure. In a perfectly competitive market the price should be equal to both the marginal social cost of producing the good, and to the marginal welfare benefit to the consumer. This implies that, for market goods, under perfect competition, we should have B/C ratios of exactly 1. The C/B ratios given for the suggested interventions are very high, ranging from 10:1 up to 30:1. This speaks to widespread market failures in the provision of these health services. However there is no real discussion in the paper of what market failures are present, or how they might be overcome.

For infectious disease, the externality caused by infecting others gives a clear market failure that can justify intervention. This argument is applied to the prevention of HIV/AIDS, the prevention and treatment of TB, immunization against childhood diseases, and the prevention and treatment of malaria. Even in these cases, however, the private gain from prevention and treatment may be large relative to the social spill-over.

For example, in the case of the use of bednets against malaria, and the treatment of malaria, the estimates given in the paper are of a B/C ratio of 20:1. The major beneficiaries to the use of bednets and the treatment of malaria are those who directly avoid infection and receive treatment. There are spill-over effects through reduction in the malaria burden on others (Hii et al. 2001), but the vast majority of the benefits accrue to the household using the net and receiving the malaria treatment. However, despite having welfare gains whose money value is estimated to far outstrip the cost, households exhibit very low WTP for bednets, in both their observed purchases and stated contingent valuations (e.g. Guyatt et al. 2002 find low WTP for bednets in Kenya).

How are we to reconcile a household's fail-ure to purchase a bednet with the fact that the benefits are around twenty times the cost? There are, of course, possible explanations. It may be too poor – as pointed out above, the B/C ratios are calculated for an average person in the country, and the ratio for poor people may be lower. There may be information problems: People may not know or understand the health benefits. There may be capital market problems, so that the expenditures, while small, exceed current cash reserves and a loan is required, but not available. There are a host of possible explanations – but these explanations need to be made, and they also affect the nature of the intervention. If poverty is the problem, redistribution may be a better intervention than providing health services. If the problem is information, an advertising campaign may be better than direct provision. If it is credit market imperfections, this will affect many aspects of people's lives and the priority intervention may be micro-credit institutions rather than the direct provision of bednets.

Surgical interventions give essentially private benefits; there is no spill-over as with infectious disease. In this case, if the costs per person are high the issue may be the lack of health insurance. Presumably the high, but uncertain, cost of surgery is the reason that in table 3.6 its provision is assessed to give a high payoff in terms of alleviating financial risk. However, if lack of insurance is the key reason for the market failure in surgery provision, it raises the issue of why the right intervention is not the provision of health insurance, rather than direct provision of surgery.

The high B/C ratio for the acute management of heart attacks with low-cost drugs is perhaps the most difficult to explain, since the gains are private while the costs *per capita* are very low and should be affordable. This may be an information problem and the correct response is therefore to get the appropriate information to doctors and patients.

The issue of tobacco control has some special problems, as noted in the Challenge paper. More could be made of the issue of second-hand smoke and bans on smoking in public places.

The paper takes the view that there is an information problem which justifies intervention; I would give more weight to hyperbolic discounting and time inconsistency that lead people to start and continue smoking, despite the knowledge that in the long term the cost of the health risks outweigh the current benefits. This lack of rationality on the part of consumers can justify a paternalistic policy and may mean that simply providing information on the risks of smoking will be insufficient to change behavior.

Mortality Reduction and Population Growth

Mortality reductions that result from health interventions will lead to an increase in population numbers. While each individual who has a health improvement may see a welfare gain, in the aggregate population crowding can exert a negative externality through resource shortages. Acemoglu and Johnson (2006) suggest that this population pressure may explain why countries that undergo rapid improvements in health do not see simultaneous improvements in income *per capita*.

In its most extreme Malthusian form, this argument requires the existence of fixed resources – such as land – that become scarce as population expands. In a manufacturing economy the physical capital stock can adjust to match an increased population, but this adjustment may take time, leading to low capital–labor ratios during periods of rapid population growth.

Ashraf *et al.* (2007) undertake a simulation model of the Zambian economy and examine the economic effects of malaria eradication. This eradication lowers infant mortality, setting in progress a population boom. The authors assume a Cobb–Douglas production function and that rent on land amounts to 10 percent of national income. The importance of land, the slow adjustment of physical capital, and the delay in children reaching working age means that, over a twenty-year horizon income *per capita* falls after eradication. In the very long run the productivity gains from improved health

may increase income *per capita* above the initial baseline.

An important issue in thinking about the population response to health improvements is how reducing infant mortality can affect fertility decisions. Given that families care about the number of surviving children, reductions in infant mortality can reduce the desired number of births. Provided that family planning is available to achieve these lower fertility goals, the population boom due to lower infant mortality may be offset by a reduction in fertility. Indeed, fertility may fall more than one for one with infant mortality. Understanding the magnitude of this fertility response is therefore central to the question of the size of the crowding externality.

De-worming as an Additional Intervention

The parasitic infections, soil-transmitted helminths, and schistosomiasis have very high prevalence rates in developing countries. It is estimated that, worldwide, 2 billion people, almost one-third of the world's population, are infected with these diseases. Despite their high prevalence, these diseases have a low ranking in global estimates of the burden of disease, and are not a high priority on health grounds. The explanation of this low burden, given the high prevalence of these diseases, is their low mortality burden and the low disability weight given to these infections and their sequelae in the burden of disease estimates. King *et al.* (2005) focus on the 0.005 disability weight for schistosomiasis (where normal functioning has a weight of 0 and 1 corresponds to death) set by a panel of experts and used in Global Burden of Disease estimates. They argue that schistosomiasis infection produces a large disease burden in terms of anemia, diarrhea, low weight for height, and reduced physical fitness, and that a more accurate disability weight would be between 0.02 and 0.15, increasing the global DALY burden by a factor between 4 and 30. These "hidden" morbidities – which are difficult to ascribe to a disease at the individual level but are evident in population studies – are also likely to be present in other parasitic diseases.

The treatment of high-prevalence tropical diseases by mass chemotherapy, with general or school-based populations, is highly cost-effective. There exist cheap (or even free) drugs that can be administered safely to populations that have a large impact, curing the disease in the patient and interrupting transmission – for example, benzimidazole anthelmintics, and albendazole for soil-transmitted helminths and praziquantel for schistosomiasis. The high prevalence rates and absence of side-effects of these drugs means that it makes sense to avoid the costs of diagnosis and to treat everyone in the population at risk. However, when prevalence rates fall to very low levels after a successful level of intervention, it is eventually more cost-effective to carry out treatment only when the disease has been diagnosed in the primary health care clinic. Estimates of the cost of treatment per person range from $0.05 per drug to around $0.25 for combined therapy. De-worming needs to be repeated periodically since re-infection is common.

While the health benefits of this intervention may be substantial, the largest effect is likely to be seen in terms of economic gains. Iron-deficiency anemia, which can result from the parasitic diseases, has more insidious effects, lowering energy levels, worker productivity, and wages (Thomas *et al.* 2004)). The parasitic worm diseases are most common in children, where they have effects on school attendance, literacy, and physical development (Bleakley 2003; Miguel and Kremer 2004), though the potential for effects on cognitive development are less clear (Dickson *et al.* 2000). The combination of very low costs of treatment and large potential economic benefits mean that de-worming should be considered as an additional priority health intervention on economic grounds if not on health grounds alone (Molyneux *et al.* 2005; Canning 2006).

Bibliography

Acemoglu, D. and Johnson, S., 2006: Disease and development: The effect of life expectancy on economic growth, NBER Working Paper, **12269**

Ashraf, Q.H. *et al.*, 2007: Would curing malaria raise Zambian per capita GDP?, Brown University, mimeo

Attanayake, N., J. *et al.*, 2000: Household costs of "malaria" morbidity: A study in Matale district, Sri Lanka, *Tropical Medicine of International Health*, **5**(9): 595–606

Bleakley, H., 2003: Disease and development: Evidence from the American South, *Journal of the European Economic Association*, **1**: 376–86

Bleakley, H., 2006: Malaria in the Americas: A retrospective analysis of childhood exposure, University of Chicago, mimeo

Bloom, D.E., Canning, D., and Weston, M., 2005: The value of vaccination, *World Economics*, **6**(3): 15–39

Bonilla, E. and Rodriguez, A., 1993: Determining malaria effects in rural Columbia, *Social Science and Medicine*, **37**(9): 1109–1114

Canning, D., 2006: Priority setting and the "neglected" tropical diseases, *Transactions of the Royal Society of Tropical Medicine and Hygiene*, **100**(6): 499–504

Cutler, D., Fung, W., Kremer, M., and Singhal, M., 2007: Mosquitoes: The long-term effects of malaria eradication in India, NBER Working Papers, **13539**, National Bureau of Economic Research

Dickson, R., Awasthi, S., Williamson, P., Demellweek, C., Garner, P., 2000: Effects of treatment for intestinal helminth infection on growth and cognitive performance in children: Systematic review of randomised trials, *BMJ*, **320**: 1697–1701

Hii, J.L., Smith, T., Vounatsou, P., Alexander, N., Mai, A., Ibam, E., and Alpers, M.P., 2001: Area effects of bednet use in a malaria-endemic area in Papua New Guinea, *Transactions of the Royal Society of Tropical Medical* Hygiene, **95**(1): 7–13

Guyatt, H.L., Ochola, S.A., Snow, R.W., 2002: Too poor to pay: Charging for insecticide-treated bednets in highland Kenya, *Tropical Medicine & International Health*, **7**(10): 846–50

Jamison, D.T., Jha, P., and Bloom, D.E., 2007: Disease control, chapter 3 in this volume

King, C.H., Dickman, K., and Tisch, D.J., 2005: Reassessment of the cost of chronic helmintic infection: Meta-analysis of disability-related outcomes in endemic schistosomiasis, *Lancet*, **365**: 1561–9

Lucas, A., 2005: Economic effects of malaria eradication: Evidence from the malarial periphery, mimeo, https://editorialexpress. com/conference/NEUDC2005/program/ NEUDC2005.html

Miguel, E. and Kremer, M., 2004: Worms: Identifying impacts on education and health in the presence of treatment externalities, *Econometrica*, **72**(1): 159–217

Molyneux, D.H., Hotez, P.J., Fenwick, A., 2005: Rapid-impact interventions: How a policy of integrated control for Africa's neglected tropical diseases could benefit the poor, *Plos Medicine*, **2**(11), e336

Muela, S.H., Mushi, A.K., and Ribera, J.M., 2000: The paradox of the cost and affordability of traditional and government health services in Tanzania, *Health Policy and Planning*, **15**(3): 296–302

Snow, R.W. *et al.*, 1999: Estimating mortality, morbidity and disability due to malaria among Africa's non-pregnant population, *Bulletin of the World Health Organization*, **77**(8): 624–40

Thomas, D. *et al.*, 2004: Causal effect of health on labor market outcomes: Evidence from a random assignment iron supplementation intervention, California Center for Population Research, University of California Los Angeles

Utzinger, J. *et al.*, 2002: The economic payoffs of integrated malaria and control in the Zambia copperbelt between 1930 and 1950, *Tropical Medicine of International Health*, **7**(8): 657–77

Whittington D., Pinheiro, A.C., and Cropper, M., 2003: The economic benefits of malaria prevention: A contingent valuation study in Marracuene, Mozambique, *Journal of Health and Population in Developing Countries*

Perspective Paper 3.2

RAMANAN LAXMINARAYAN

Population health is a key to unlock economic wellbeing, but health interventions are not all equal in their ability to improve population health for a given level of spending. Recent efforts such as the Disease Control Priorities Project (DCPP) and the WHO Choice project have attempted to identify health interventions that are highly cost-effective but not being widely used, while also pointing out health interventions that are not cost-effective but are adopted nonetheless.

In the Challenge paper, Jamison, Jha, and Bloom (hereafter, JJB) draw on the accumulated knowledge of the DCPP to describe the ten health interventions with the greatest potential to improve health in low- and middle-income countries.[1] Their response focuses on the B/C ratios of the health interventions that offer the highest payoff and is appropriate given the constraints of the Copenhagen Consensus project. However, the challenges are not always "what" but sometimes "how." We know that CVD programs are cost-effective, yet why were CVD control programs successful in Poland but not in Russia? Similarly, why has vaccination against polio succeeded in so many countries yet failed in major states in India?

As JJB point out, country-level and regional efforts to increase the adoption of cost-effective interventions provide growing evidence that health can be improved substantially even in fairly poor countries with weak health systems. Yet the question of why these successes are not more broadly realized has not been satisfactorily answered, either by JJB or by projects such as

DCPP. It is important that future editions of DCPP and the Copenhagen Consensus project pay attention to how interventions are implemented.

Benefit-Cost Estimates

The starting point of improving delivery of health is to focus on priorities, and it is difficult to take issue with the priorities recommended by JJB. It is possible that JJB under-estimate the true cost of implementing the interventions, since no provision is made for uneven system efficiency, escalating marginal costs of implementation (because the easier-to-cover regions are already covered and existing personnel are already deployed), or marginal excess burden of tax revenues needed to pay for the interventions. However, even if one were to assume a cost that is two or three times the magnitude of what is estimated, the B/C ratios indicate extraordinarily good value for money. Moreover, it is likely that benefits are also under-estimated in these calculations, as discussed below.

Cost Estimates

JJB's cost estimates assume efficient health systems. Bringing health systems up to snuff is partly a matter of additional resources, but may be constrained by other factors, such as insufficient regulatory capacity, that cannot be solved in the short term. And in many countries, even when health care is provided largely by the private sector, health system capacity may exist in the cities but be poor or non-existent in rural areas. Figures 3.2.1 and 3.2.2 show percentages of primary health centers (PHCs)

---

[1] The author was part of the DCPP project and lead author on chapter 2, which synthesizes CE results from across the various chapters.

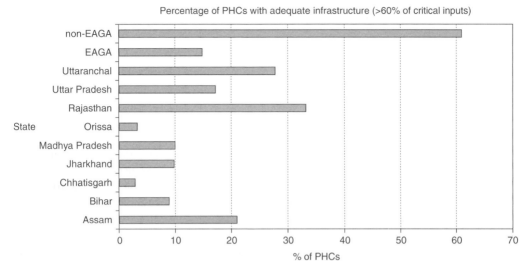

Figure 3.2.1 *PHC infrastructure*
Note: Empowered Action Group (EAGA) states designated by the Government of India are Bihar, Chhattisgarh, Jharkhand, Madhya Pradesh, Orissa, Rajasthan, Uttar Pradesh, and Uttaranchal. Our designation of EAGA refers to these states plus Assam.

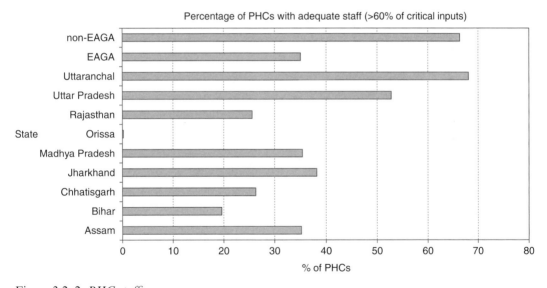

Figure 3.2. 2 *PHC staffing*

in India that have adequate infrastructure and staff in different states. In the poorly perform- ing states, less than a third of PHCs have at least 60 percent of the basic infrastructure. A relatively higher proportion has the requisite staff, but attendance is poor. Absenteeism is an issue not just in India but also in Bangladesh, Ecuador, Indonesia, Peru, and Uganda, where survey data has shown that 35 percent of health workers were absent (table 3.2.1) (Chaudhury *et al.* 2006). Another study has estimated the cost of improving health systems in India to be on

Table 3.2.1 Provider absence rates, by country and sector

	Absence rates (%) in:	
	Primary schools	Primary health centers
From this project:		
Bangladesh	16	35
Ecuador	14	–
India	25	40
Indonesia	19	40
Peru	11	25
Uganda	27	37
Unweighted average	19	35

Notes: (1) Providers were counted as absent if they could not be found in the facility for any reason at the time of a random unannounced spot check (see text for further detail). (2) In Uganda, the sampled districts were divided into sub-counties, and schools in sub-counties with level III health centers comprise the school sampling frame. This sampling strategy may have had the effect of understating slightly the national absence rate there, given that schools in more rural areas appear to have higher absence rates.

the order of US$1 billion–$1.5 billion per year (Chow *et al.* 2007).

Some of the cost estimates used in the Challenge paper have been updated since DCPP. For instance, one study estimates that US$47 billion is required for TB control during 2006–15 (94 percent for country-level implementation, 6 percent for international technical agencies), of which US$3 billion per year is for diagnosis and treatment for drug-susceptible TB in DOTS programs (Floyd and Pantoja 2007). The total resources required each year will be at least twice the $1.8 billion spent on TB control in 2005. The benefits of the additional $1.8 billion are estimated to exceed costs by a factor of 15 – impressive, yet markedly lower than what JJB report (Laxminarayan *et al.*, 2007).

Finally, costs may be under-estimated because no provision is made for the marginal excess burden of expenditures, which must apply whether the interventions are financed by national governments or by external donors. Warlters and Auriol (2005) estimate the marginal cost of $1 of public funds to be $1.17,

based on a sample of thirty-eight African countries. A more conservative figure would be a factor of 1.3, which is commonly used in developed countries where interventions are paid for through taxes (Ballard *et al.* 1985; Browning 1987).

Benefit Estimates

JJB are likely conservative in their estimates of the economic gains from the recommended interventions. They use a figure of $1,000 per DALY averted to estimate the benefits from health improvements. As they discuss, the VLSY offers a broader measure of the economic gain. Health improvements are unique because they extend the life span over which material gains from GDP growth can be enjoyed. A growing number of papers on the economic value of health improvements (Usher 1973; Nordhaus 2002; Becker *et al.* 2003; Murphy and Topel 2005) impute the value of increased life expectancy on economic well-being using revealed-preference approaches to value each year of longer life. As JJB describe, longevity gains can be quantitatively important when one is measuring welfare. Becker and his colleagues find that when longevity gains are taken into consideration, average yearly "full income" grew 4.1 percent between 1960 and 2000 for the poorest 50 percent of countries, of which 1.7 percentage points were due to health (Becker *et al.* 2003). The implication is that much of the welfare improvement in poorer countries over the past few decades has come in the form of improved health and that the economic contribution of these longevity increases is important.

What is the most reasonable value of a year of potential life gained? Viscusi and Aldy (2003) review more than sixty studies of mortality risk premiums from ten countries, and estimate an income elasticity of the VSL of about 0.5–0.6, but their elasticity estimates are influenced downward by three extreme observations for India. Dropping these observations yields an elasticity of roughly 1, and this is the value used in more recent studies (Becker *et al.* 2003). Using this elasticity estimate and starting from the US VSL of $4 million (associated with a US *per capita* GDP of roughly $30,000), we can compute the VSL of India (with *per capita* GDP of $660) to be $61,000. This roughly translates to $1,200–$3,000 per year of life saved, assuming a sixty-five-year life expectancy and a 0–3 percent discount rate. India likely ranks on the lower side of GDP for low- and middle-income countries. For a country like China, with a GDP *per capita* of $1,337, one can compute a VSLY that is between $2,500 and $6,400.

It is also important to consider the positive externalities of controlling communicable diseases. The benefits of TB control, as is the case with other communicable diseases, accrue not just to the patients but also to those around them who are at risk of infection. On average, each person with active and untreated TB will infect between ten and fifteen people every year, a few of whom will ultimately develop an active TB infection. The benefits of TB case detection and treatment therefore, include not just the productivity gains in the treated individual but also the averted productivity losses in individuals at risk of being infected. The chapter on TB in DCPP did use a dynamic model of infection to compute the external benefits of TB control, but this was an exception (Dye and Floyd 2006). If the benefits of control of other infectious diseases, such as malaria and vaccine-preventable diseases, include the effect of these averted losses, it is likely that the effects will be even larger than those reported in JJB.

An important consideration in future exercises of the kind attempted here is sensitivity to underlying model parameters, both economic and epidemiological. Giving policymakers a better sense of the confidence ranges using Monte Carlo or Latin hypercube sampling methods would inspire greater assurance at the time of application. For instance, a study examining the B/C ratios of TB interventions in the twenty-two high-burden endemic countries found that marginal benefits exceeded costs at baseline, but a sensitivity analysis showed that B/C ratios were unambiguously greater than 1 in only twelve of the twenty-two countries (Laxminarayan *et al.* 2007).

The Feasibility of Bringing Interventions to Scale

JJB point to specific successes described in "millions saved," a product of DCPP (Levine *et al.* 2004). These include interventions that also top the list in JJB, such as TB control, HIV/AIDS prevention, and tobacco control. CE indicates what policymakers should focus on, but does not explain why interventions succeed in some places and fail in others. One reason may be that national governments have not tried hard enough. However, this does not account for national constraints in program implementation that go beyond system capacity in the conventional sense. For instance, eliminating iodine deficiencies through salt iodization was possible in China because there were a few large manufacturers that could be easily regulated (Levine *et al.* 2004). In India, such a program would be difficult to implement because of the large number of small manufacturers and the lack of regulatory capacity to ensure effective iodization among them. Another example is Chagas disease control in South America, made possible by the region's economic prosperity (Levine *et al.* 2004). Although rising income does not necessarily mean that cost-effective disease interventions will be undertaken, it may ensure that interventions are more likely to succeed.

The scalability of local successes in malaria control is increasingly evident. Recent studies indicate that malaria can be rolled back across Africa using the tools that JJB identify – insecticide-treated bednets, indoor residual spraying, and provision of effective artemisinin-based antimalarials (Bhattarai *et al.* 2007; Sharp *et al.* 2007). The main concern continues to be the sustainability of reductions when donor attention is not replaced by national prioritization of disease control (D'Alessandro *et al.* 1995).

In the area of NCDs, JJB identify some clear priorities, such as increasing tobacco taxes, that may not necessarily require external assistance. In fact, there are good fiscal reasons for national governments to tax tobacco and alcohol – namely, to raise revenue – thereby reducing the burden on other taxes to pay for public spending (Parry *et al.* 2004). General equilibrium analyses from the Ramsey tax literature demonstrate that optimal commodity taxes exceed levels warranted on externality grounds for commodities that are relative leisure complements, the more so the more inelastic the own-price demand (e.g. Sandmo 1975).[2] Other priorities for controlling NCDs include managing heart attacks with low-cost drugs and improving surgical capacity at district hospitals. These are important to focus on because donors have traditionally been reluctant to engage in these areas. Donor assistance alone may not be enough to bring these interventions to scale, but they can serve an important demonstration role that may motivate national policymakers to do more.

Innovations in Health Financing

As JJB acknowledge, additional financial resources cannot by themselves achieve the desired health outcomes. Financial instruments used in the health sector must influence incentives for better performance, particularly within the public sector but also within the private sector where this is necessary. Financial approaches for improving public sector performance include making financial outlays conditional on performance and devolving more spending decisions to the local level. It may be worth quantifying the benefit of changes to alternative systems of financing health, since these could produce efficiency gains without necessarily requiring additional resources.

Local innovations in financing include risk pooling and community financing schemes, but the scalability of these innovations remains to proved (and they are outside the scope of the Copenhagen Consensus process). From a global perspective, remarkable returns on health investments have come in the form of new financing vehicles. Often, though not always, these have involved global financial arrangements: The same $10 billion for immunizations can be provided through multiple channels – UNICEF or GAVI or bilateral grants or loans.[3]

GAVI has proven to be a useful way of organizing the financing of childhood immunizations, but there have been no studies to show whether this approach has been more cost-effective than the alternatives. Although GAVI might have been even more cost-effective if it had excluded the Hep B antigen (Kumar and Puliyel 2007), it has made a difference in countries with poor immunization coverage (Lu *et al.* 2006). By making payments contingent on outcomes, GAVI has been able to rapidly deploy resources despite lingering implementation and monitoring problems (Brugha *et al.* 2002).

A second example is the proposed AMFm, an effort to make artemisinin-based combination therapies more affordable. The objectives of AMFm are multi-faceted and include displacement of artemisinin monotherapies that may expedite parasite resistance, saving at least a small fraction of the roughly 2 million lives lost to malaria each year, ensuring a stable demand for manufacturers that enter the antimalarial market, and ensuring a drug supply that is free of expired or counterfeit medicines. But the real innovation of AMFm is that it accomplishes several of these objectives by making artemisinin drugs less expensive than other drugs. Financing mechanisms that provide grants to countries to invest in the interventions of their choice do not necessarily alter relative prices; thus, a country using funds from the GAVI to buy antimalarials may still choose to buy cheaper, less-effective drugs because it can purchase more medicine for a given budget allocation. Changing relative prices is a particularly effective mechanism for influencing intervention choices within coun-

---

[2] The result does not apply if three conditions hold simultaneously: (i) there is an optimized non-linear income tax; (ii) leisure is weakly separable from consumption goods in utility; and (iii) preferences are identical across individuals (Atkinson and Stiglitz 1976; Saez 2002). However, all these conditions are unrealistic. For example, weak separability is rejected by empirical studies (see, e.g. Abbott and Ashenfelter 1976; Browning and Meghir 1991).

[3] See www.path.org/vaccineresources/files/gavi_briefcase_small.pdf for a full list of immunization financing options for national policymakers.

Table 3.2.2. Estimated B/C ratios of some other programs evaluated by the World Bank

Estimated B/C ratios of some investments in youth in selected countries

Investment	Estimated B/C ratio (assuming 5% annual discount rate)	Plausible ranges in estimated B/C ratio
Scholarship program (Colombia)	3.31	2.77–25.63
Adult basic education and literacy program (Colombia)	19.9	8.14–1.764
School-based reproductive health program to prevent HIV/AIDS (Honduras)	0.493	0.102–4.59
Iron supplementation administered to secondary school children (low-income country)	32.1	25.8–45.2
Tobacco tax (middle-income country)	11.34	6.96–38.56

Source: Knowles and Behrman (2003).

B/C ratios for selected development bank-supported investments

Project (year)	B/C ratio
Hill Forest Development Project, Nepal (1983)	1.18
Irrigation Systems Improvement Project, Philippines (1977)	1.48
Livestock Development Project, Uruguay (1970)	1.59
Livestock and Agricultural Development Project, Paraguay (1979)	1.62
Cotton Processing and Marketing Project, Kenya (1979)	1.80

Source: Gaag and Tan (1998).

tries while allowing for flexibility in national decisionmaking.

Closing Thoughts

The priority health interventions described in JJB are supported by the weight of evidence compiled in the DCPP, a recent global priority-setting exercise. The priorities rightly emphasize the importance of expanding interventions against TB, HIV/AIDS, and malaria while also engaging the growing challenge of NCDs. Each of these priorities, whether increasing coverage of DOTS for TB prevention and control or ramping up HIV/AIDS prevention programs, has been shown in specific contexts to improve health, but less is known about why these interventions take off in some places but fail in others. These priority interventions have the greatest B/C ratio within health and offer greater returns than others, such as investments

in youth in selected countries (Knowles and Behrman 2003) and selected development bank-supported investments (Gaag and Tan 1998) (see table 3.2.2).

This paper has summarized a few observations about such priority-setting exercises in general and how they can improve our ability to make better decisions on spending. In closing, I offer the following three points for the Copenhagen jury to consider:

1 There is great value in focusing on a few large interventions that have the greatest capacity to save lives and avert morbidity. Taking specific steps to generate and use clinical best practices, training service providers to do a few things frequently and well rather than many things poorly, and improving provider incentives by creating a legal and ethical environment where care providers do not profit personally from the sale of drugs, diagnostic procedures, or provision or referral of care

– all these approaches have merit and are described elsewhere (Peabody *et al.* 2006).

2 The issue of how the world should spend its money is important but relevant only if the proper financing and delivery mechanisms exist. Such mechanisms must not crowd out national health expenditures, excessively distort wages and resource allocations in the health sector, or inefficiently focus on some diseases to the exclusion of others (Halperin 2008). Therefore, whatever priorities are chosen, policymakers should recognize that the focus on certain interventions implies doing less well on other diseases and interventions.

3 To this end, the innovations needed are not just in technology but also in delivery systems. For instance, financing the global subsidy for ACTs, discussed by JJB, represents a novel approach to paying for a global public good, "antimalarial effectiveness," while also saving the lives of malaria-afflicted children.

Bibliography

Abbott, M. and Ashenfelter, O., 1976: Labour supply, commodity demand and the allocation of time, *Review of Economic Studies*, **43**: 389–411

Atkinson, A.B. and Stiglitz, J.E., 1976: The design of tax structure: Direct versus indirect taxation., *Journal of Public Economics*, **6**: 55–75

Ballard, C.L. *et al.*, 1985: General equilibrium computations of the marginal welfare costs of taxes in the United States, *American Economic Review*, **75**: 12838

Becker, G. *et al.*, 2003: The quantity and quality of life and the evolution of world inequality, *American Economic Review*, **95**(1): 277–91

Bhattarai, A. *et al.*, 2007: Impact of artemisinin-based combination therapy and insecticide-treated nets on malaria burden in Zanzibar, *Public Library of Science, Medicine*, **4**(11): e309

Browning, E.K., 1987: On the marginal welfare cost of taxation, *American Economic Review*, **77**: 11–23

Browning, M. and Meghir, C., 1991: The effects of male and female labor supply on commodity demands, *Econometrica*, **59**: 925–51

Brugha, R. *et al.*, 2002: GAVI, the first steps: Lessons for the Global Fund, *Lancet* **359**(9304): 435–8

Chaudhury, N. *et al.*, 2006. Missing in action: Teacher and health worker absence in developing countries, *Journal of Economic Perspectives*, **20**(1): 91–116

Chow, J. *et al.*, 2007: Cost-effectiveness of disease interventions in India, Discussion Paper, **07:53**, Resources for the Future, Washington DC

D'Alessandro, U. *et al.*, 1995: Mortality and morbidity from malaria in Gambian children after introduction of an impregnated bednet programme, *Lancet*, **345**(8948): 479–83

Dye, C. and Floyd, K., 2006: Tuberculosis, in D.T. Jamison (ed.), *Disease control priorities in developing countries*, 2nd edn., Oxford University Press, Oxford and New York: 289–312

Floyd, K. and Pantoja, A, 2007: Financial resources required for TB control to achieve global targets set for 2015, in *Stop TB Department Report*, WHO, Geneva

Gaag, J. v. d. and Tan, J.-P., 1998: The benefits of early child development programs: An economic analysis, World Bank, Washington, DC

Halperin, D., 2008: Putting a plague in perspective, Op-ed, *New York Times,* January 1

Knowles, J.C. and Behrman, J.R., 2003: Assessing the economic benefits of investing in youth in developing countries, World Bank, Washington, DC

Kumar, A. and Puliyel, J., 2007: GAVI funding and assessment of vaccine cost-effectiveness, *Lancet*, **369**(9557): 189; author reply: 189

Laxminarayan, R. *et al.*, 2007: Economic benefit of tuberculosis control, Policy Research Working Paper, **4295**, World Bank, Washington, DC

Levine, R. *et al.*, 2004: *Millions saved: Proven successes in global health*, Center for Global Development, Washington, DC

Lu, C. *et al.*, 2006: Effect of the Global Alliance for Vaccines and Immunisation on diphtheria, tetanus, and pertussis vaccine coverage: An independent assessment, *Lancet*, **368**(9541): 1088–95

Murphy, K.M. and Topel, R.H., 2005: The value of health and longevity, Working Paper, **11045**, National Bureau of Economic Research, Cambridge, MA

Nordhaus, W., 2002: The health of nations: The contribution of improved health to living standards, in K. Murphy and R. Topel (eds.), *The economic value of medical research,* University of Chicago Press, Chicago

Parry, I. *et al.*, 2004: The critical importance of fiscal considerations in evaluating alcohol policies, Resources for the Future, Washington, DC

Peabody, J.W. *et al.*, 2006: Improving the quality of care in developing countries, in D.T. Jamison (ed.), *Disease control priorities in developing countries*, 2nd edn., Oxford University Press, Oxford and New York: 1293–308

Saez, E., 2002: The desirability of commodity taxation under non-linear income taxation and heterogeneous tastes, *Journal of Public Economics*, **83**: 217–30

Sharp, B.L. *et al.*, 2007: Seven years of regional malaria control collaboration – Mozambique, South Africa, and Swaziland, *American Journal of Tropical Medicine and Hygiene*, **76**(1): 427

Usher, D., 1973: An imputation to the measure of economic growth for changes in life expectancy, in M. Moss (ed.), *The measurement of economic and social performance, studies in income and wealth: NBER Conference of Research in Income and Wealth,* Columbia University Press, New York: 193–225

Viscusi, W.K. and Aldy, J., 2003: The value of a statistical life: A critical review of market estimates throughout the world, *Journal of Risk and Uncertainty*, **27**(1): 5–76

Warlters, M. and Auriol, E., 2005: The marginal cost of public funds in developing countries: an application to 38 African countries, Policy Research Working Paper, **3679**, World Bank, Washington, DC

The Benefits and Costs of Alternative Strategies to Improve Educational Outcomes

PETER F. ORAZEM, PAUL GLEWWE, AND
HARRY PATRINOS

Benefits from Schooling

Few empirical relationships have been investigated more frequently than that between years of schooling and earnings. Hundreds of studies using a wide variety of datasets from developed countries, spanning many decades, and employing alternative specifications to correct for various potential sources of bias, have consistently found positive private returns per year of schooling.[1] Returns are frequently equal to or above long-run average market returns to other investments.

Estimated returns to schooling in developing countries have been comparable in magnitude to returns found in developed countries. Table 4.1 presents ordinary least squares (OLS) estimates of returns from a standard Mincerian earnings function applied to sixty-three household datasets from forty-two developing countries. The results are presented separately for males and females and for urban and rural residents. These

Table 4.1. Sample statistics of estimated returns per year of schooling in developing countries

Percentile	Male	Female	Urban	Rural
10	2.3	3.7	3.8	1.2
25	4.5	8.9	6.3	5.4
50	8.2	10.3	9.2	8
75	9.5	12.3	10.6	10.1
90	11.4	13.2	11.6	12.6
Average	7.2	9.8	8.3	7.5
Standard deviation	4.4	3.7	3.8	5
Skewness	−1.2	−1	−1.3	−0.9
Correlation		0.85		0.85

Note: Authors' compilations of estimated returns to schooling using a standard Mincerian earnings functions applied to sixty-three household datasets from forty-two developing countries. These are the same data sets used for figure 4.1, except that some datasets are dropped because they did not have separate information on urban, rural, male, and female earnings. We thank Claudio Montenegro for supplying these estimates.

datasets were selected because the variable definitions could be harmonized across countries and because separate returns could be estimated for men and women and for urban and rural residents.[2] The same model was estimated for all countries so that the variation is not due to specification choice. Several interesting results are apparent.

First, private returns, estimated as the percentage increase in annual earnings obtained from an additional year of schooling, are almost universally positive. In only one case for women, four cases for men, three for urban residents and two for rural residents did education fail to raise earnings. The interquartile range for estimated

* The opinions expressed are our own and not necessarily those of the World Bank. Amy Damon, Jean Fares, Deon Filmer, Sarojini Hirshberg, Manny Jimenez, Elizabeth King, Claudio Montenegro, Annette Richter, Ray Robertson, and T. Paul Schultz provided advice on topics, content and relevant literature as we prepared background materials for this paper. Shiva Sikdar provided able research assistance.

[1] Card (1999) contains an excellent review of the various estimation methods and biases associated with analysis of the returns to schooling. It appears that returns to schooling generated by OLS estimation tend to understate true returns, although the bias appears to be small.

[2] We are indebted to Claudio Montenegro for sharing these regressions results.

real returns across countries varies from 5 to 10 percent for men and from 9 to 12 percent for women. The interquartile range for both urban and rural residents lies between 5 and 11 percent. The median return ranges from 8 to 10 percent per year of schooling, depending upon the demographic group. This is quite consistent with the average return of 10.9 percent for low-income countries found in the Psacharopoulos and Patrinos (2004) literature survey of studies published in the 1990s. While there is considerable variation in the magnitude of the return, there does appear to be a positive reward to individual time spent in school.

A second generalization is that in all but a handful of countries, estimated returns to schooling are higher for women than for men. Estimated returns average 7.2 percent for men and 9.8 percent for women across the datasets. One might suspect that the difference in returns is due to a selection problem – a lower proportion of women than men are engaged in wage work, and so one might suspect that it is the most productive women that are disproportionately drawn into the labor market. However, the direction of bias is not obvious – women who opt not to enter the labor market will have a value of time in non-market activities that exceeds their market value, and so the bias could go in the opposite direction. However evidence presented by Schultz (1999) and Duraisamy (2002) suggests that selection has similar effects for men and women.[3]

A third notable finding is that in about two-thirds of the countries, returns to urban residents exceed those of rural residents, although the differences are smaller than those between men and women. Estimated returns average 8.3 percent for urban workers and 7.5 percent for rural workers. Again, one might suspect that the returns to rural workers are biased upward because a disproportionate share of rural workers will work without wages on home enterprises or farms. Again, the direction of bias is unclear, as those opting to work on a farm will have a higher value of time than their market opportunities. Additionally, higher wages in cities create an incentive to migrate from rural to urban markets, and so rural residents with the highest market skills will likely have moved to the cities.

Finally, the most telling result from the analysis of differences in returns to schooling across groups within countries is that the differences are so small. Estimated returns are very highly correlated across groups. The correlation in returns is 0.85 both between men and women and between urban and rural residents. Labor markets that reward education highly for men also reward education highly for women. Countries with high returns to education in their urban labor markets also have high returns to education in their rural labor market.

These returns suggest that across a wide array of countries at all stages of development, education consistently offers sizeable positive returns to wage earners – not only to urban male youths, but also to women and rural youths. Nevertheless, a year of schooling will be more productive in some environments than in others. All of the distributions of returns in table 4.1 are skewed downward, and so there is a tendency to have more extreme outliers at the bottom than the top. One reason that is quite plausible but is difficult to illustrate easily is that school quality differs across countries. However, if the economic environment rewards educational investments, then developing country parents have an incentive to seek private schools when the public schools are of low quality. Therefore, it is useful to examine other reasons why countries or their citizens may not capture the reward from schooling found in other countries.

Where Are Benefits from Schooling Greatest?

Schultz (1975) noted that human capital is most valuable in disequilibrium environments.

---

[3] One exception to this generalization that women have higher returns to schooling than men appears in transition economies. On average, women's rate of return to secondary education is 0.6 percentage points lower and their return to university education is 1.3 percentage points lower than estimated returns for men (Psacharopoulos and Patrinos 2004).

Writing from the perspective of agricultural economies, Schultz argued that in the absence of technological change, production shocks, or price shocks, traditional rules of thumb on how to efficiently manage a farm would be adequate. Consistent with that presumption, Fafchamps and Quisumbing (1999) and Godoy *et al.* (2005) found that schooling has a negligible effect on productivity on traditional farms, even though schooling raises earnings in the same locations for farmers engaged in wage work off the farm.

On the other hand, human capital has been shown to play a very important role in agricultural environments experiencing technological change. Huffman and Orazem (2006) show that the process of economic development almost universally requires an agricultural transition in which dramatic increases in the efficiency of food production simultaneously frees up labor for emerging industrial sectors while lowering the price of food (and hence raising real wages) in urban areas. The most educated farmers are the first to adopt improved varieties, equipment, and production practices (Huffman 1977; Besley and Case 1993; Foster and Rosenzweig 2004a; Abdulai and Huffman 2005). In India, returns to schooling were highest in areas where Green Revolution technologies were most complementary with local agriculture (Foster and Rosenzweig 1996).

In order for human capital to attain its highest returns, labor must be able to adapt to disequilibria, whether by moving to industries or areas with the strongest labor demand, adopting

or developing new technologies, or switching occupations to fulfill market needs. Good adaptive decisions require a reward, and so human capital will be most valuable when social or governmental institutions place few restrictions on mobility or trade, when wages and prices are flexible, and when property rights are enforced.[4] There is no stronger evidence of the role of freer markets in enhancing human capital productivity than in the rapid increase in returns to schooling observed in virtually all formerly planned economies as they made their transitions toward market systems (Fleisher *et al.* 2005).

Sen (1999) further stipulates that it is not so much any one economic institution as the combination of institutions that is important in defining economic freedom and the ability to seek rewards for skills. When we divide our countries into groups based on their relative ranking in the Heritage Foundation's Economic Freedom Index,[5] we get a picture of the importance of the overall economic environment in fostering returns to schooling (figure 4.1). Because higher index scores signify less economic freedom, countries whose index scores are in the lower half of the Economic Freedom Index have less regulated economies, fewer restrictions on trade, flexible wage and price adjustments, and government enforcement of property rights. Returns to schooling are, on average, just under 10 percent in these "economically free" countries. In contrast, countries in the more regulated half of the Index have returns to schooling averaging only 6.4 percent. The gap in average returns between more and less free countries is much larger than the gap in average returns between men and women or between urban and rural markets. More economically free countries have higher average returns at both high and low levels of average schooling, a proxy for the level of development in the country. This suggests that investments in schooling will be most valuable in countries that allow workers to find their highest returns across alternative sectors and occupations.[6]

There is considerable evidence that parents do respond to rising perceived returns to schooling. In India, Foster and Rosenzweig (1996) and

[4] Acemoglu *et al.* (2001); Acemoglu *et al.* (2002) have examined the role of institutions that constrain or enhance mobility and the exercise of property rights in retarding or fostering economic growth.

[5] Information on the Heritage Foundation Index is available at www.heritage.org/research/features/index/chapters/pdfs/Index2006_Chap5.pdf.

[6] The negative estimated returns to schooling came from Azerbaijan in 1995; Moldova in 1998; Cambodia in 1997; and Vietnam in 1992 although Moock *et al.* (2003) found small but positive returns for Vietnam in 1992–3. More recent surveys available for Cambodia and Vietnam have generated positive returns to schooling as those countries have liberalized their economies and improved the climate for protection of property.

% return

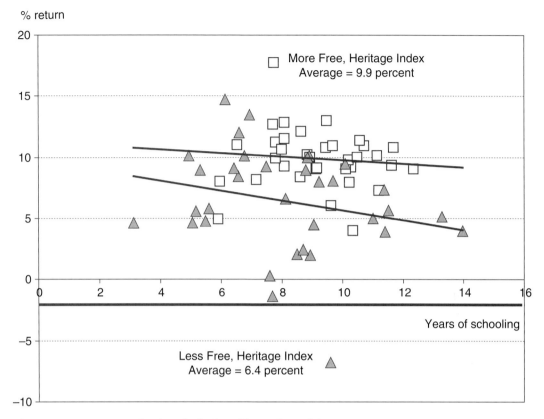

Figure 4.1 *Returns to schooling, by high and low values of the Heritage Economic Freedom Index: forty-six developing countries, various years, 1990–2004*
Note: Data used for table 4.1 are a sub-set of these datasets.
Source: Authors' compilation of sixty-nine earnings regressions provided by Claudio Montenegro, using household data from forty-six countries.

Kochar (2004) found that rural enrollments rise in areas with greater perceived returns to schooling due to technological innovations or rising urban demand for labor. Evidence from South Asia and Central America suggests that the rapidly growing export-oriented sectors disproportionately hired more educated youth, and that hiring has frequently targeted educated young women. This has helped to increase enrollment for girls even without an explicit program aimed at raising girls' enrollment (Gruben and McLeod 2006). Nevertheless, these responses are predicated on the ability of human capital to move to the area or sector where it can find its highest potential value in the economy, and

on parental ability to perceive those potential rewards.[7]

Of course, just spending time in school is not enough to generate a return. More important is what is learned during the time in school. Investments of time and money in a child's schooling that fail to produce basic cognitive skills such as literacy are almost surely wasted. In fact, studies that include both years of schooling

[7] Datt and Ravallion (2002) argue that economic growth in India has tended to benefit most those groups with more schooling. Sources of growth were complementary with skills. This is consistent with the recommendation that efforts to fight poverty through growth must include measures to raise the human capital of the poor.

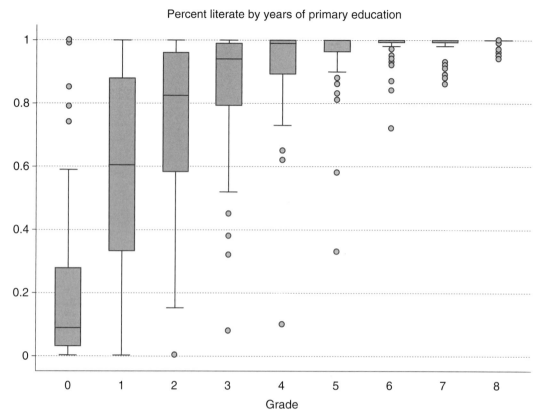

Percent literate by years of primary education

Figure 4.2 *Distribution of self-reported literacy by grade attainment for youth aged 15–24, various countries*
Source: authors' compilation of summary data from seventy-three household surveys spanning fifty-seven developing countries provided by Claudio Montenegro

and measures of cognitive skills find that it is the latter and not the former that drive earnings (Glewwe 2002). Similarly, Hanushek and Kimko (2000) found that it is average cognitive attainment and not average years of schooling that drives economic growth. More recently, Hanushek and Woessmann (2008) show that the cognitive skills of the population – rather than mere school attainment – are powerfully related to individual earnings, to the distribution of income, and to economic growth. Their empirical results show the importance of both minimal and high level skills, the complementarity of skills and the quality of economic institutions, and the robustness of the relationship between skills and growth.

While time in school does not guarantee the acquisition of cognitive skills, it is almost impossible to acquire those skills without formal schooling. As shown in figure 4.2, the probability of attaining self-reported literacy rises with years of schooling, although there is considerable variation in the pattern across countries. Children who complete the primary cycle, about six years of schooling, are almost certain to attain literacy in most countries. While it is theoretically possible that these children could have attained literacy without schooling, figure 4.2 shows that relatively few literate individuals never attended school. This presumption that schooling is needed for literacy underlies the Millennium Development Goal (MDG) of attaining universal primary education (UPE) by 2015.

Various estimates generated by UNESCO, UNICEF, and the World Bank place the annual additional cost of attaining UPE at between $9 billion and $34 billion. These estimates use various applications of procedures that apply current average costs of schooling to the fraction of children not in school. Even these high costs may be under-stated because the children who are currently not in school are disproportionately located in areas that are expensive to reach with schooling services or in households that are less keen to send children to school.[8] Others are not in school despite having access to local schools, and so adding more supply will not address the problem. We argue that in order to make efficient progress toward the UPE goal, we need to identify which illiterate populations can be served most economically.

Should Investments Concentrate on the Primary Level or Other Levels?

Much of our discussion will concentrate on raising the fraction of literate adults in the world, but for many developing countries that have already attained UPE, that level of schooling is no longer relevant. It is useful to comment briefly on why we focus on lower levels of schooling in identifying the highest benefit to cost interventions in the schooling arena.

It has commonly been presumed that schooling is subject to diminishing returns, so that the returns to primary schooling would exceed those for higher levels of schooling. Estimates of social returns to schooling reported by Psacharopoulos and Patrinos (2004) support that conjecture. Reported *per capita* schooling costs also suggest that the highest returns must be at the lowest levels: Government per pupil costs for secondary schools in low-income countries are more than double the costs for primary schools, and the per-pupil tertiary costs are nearly thirty-four times the primary costs. It is unlikely that any gains in relative private returns are large enough

to reverse the pattern of diminishing social returns to schooling.

Both theoretical arguments and empirical evidence support the view that interventions early in life have the highest returns. Carneiro and Heckman (2003) and Heckman and Masterov (2007) present a wealth of evidence that earlier investments in human capital, including those occurring before the start of formal schooling, are far more cost-effective than efforts to improve schooling later in life. It seems that because human capital development builds upon past accumulations of human capital, it is extremely important to develop a strong human capital base at an early age. Numerous pathologies including criminal activities, drug abuse, idleness, and chronic illnesses can be linked to a weak human capital foundation in the form of malnutrition, bad health, and poor schooling experienced at the youngest ages.

Nevertheless, in some settings, particularly those of more advanced developing countries, returns may be substantial at the secondary or even tertiary level. In industrialized economies, private returns to tertiary schooling rose relative to returns to secondary schooling as new technologies and investments in capital complemented the skills of college graduates (Schultz 2004b). One might suspect that similar changes are increasing the private returns to those with secondary or tertiary educations in developing countries.

This is particularly true in countries with strong growth in export trade. Xu (2000) argued that a developing country can expect to attract technology from multinational enterprises (MNEs) only if it has an adult population that meets a threshold level of education of roughly ten years of completed schooling. That assessment is consistent with findings that workers in foreign-owned enterprises in Indonesia, Vietnam, Malaysia, Guatemala, and elsewhere tend to be drawn from the upper tail of the schooling distribution in those countries (Goldberg and Pavcnik 2007), although the experience in Mexico appears to be in the opposite direction

---

[8] Glewwe and Zhao (2006) present a summary of these estimates and a critique of the methodologies employed.

(Robertson 2004). It is plausible that the rising returns to skill in the export sectors occur when there is insufficient migration toward growing sectors of the economy and/or because there is an insufficient supply of the types of skills exporters demand.

The OECD (2000) has revised the definition of literacy, going well beyond basic facility with reading and mathematics to incorporate functioning efficiently in the information age. This presents another illustration of the Schultz hypothesis: The level of minimal functional literacy rises with the level and complexity of the economic environment. As a country develops, the minimal level of schooling required to function effectively will increase. However, in those economies, many of the barriers to obtaining the requisite skills will be falling as the country progresses. The countries we will focus on here have not yet attained that level of development for a large portion of their citizenry.

If Parents Respond to Returns, What is the Public Role in Schooling Investments?

As argued above (p. 182) parents increase the intensity of their investments in schooling when expected returns rise. If this is true, then why don't parents select the efficient amount of time to send their children to school, the time at which the private rate of return to an additional year of schooling is equal to the market rate of return to other investments of comparable risk? Either there must be returns to schooling that are not captured by the households or there must be constraints on household schooling investments that prevent them from selecting the optimal investment.

Several external benefits are frequently

associated with women's schooling. The fertility transition, the common finding that the number of children per woman declines as economic growth occurs, has been tied to increases in women's value of time as their education increases (King and Mason 2001; Schultz 2002). Angrist et al. (2002) and Schultz (2004a) both found that increased schooling from randomly assigned vouchers and conditional cash transfers led to reduced fertility, although the evidence was somewhat weaker in the latter case. Increases in women's (and men's) schooling has also been associated with improvements in the health of their children and other family members, with improvements in the schooling of their children – and, as a consequence, a rising quality of life from one generation to the next (de Walque 2005; Oreopoulos et al. 2006; Paxson and Schady 2007). More schooling is associated with later age of marriage and lower teenage birth rates, which improves the health and schooling outcomes of the next generation (Black et al. 2004, 2005a; Cardoso and Verner 2006). Many of the most recent studies utilize changes in truancy laws to generate plausibly exogenous changes in years of schooling (e.g. Patrinos and Sakellariou 2005), increasing the confidence that these effects of parental schooling on children's welfare are causal. While in developed countries, some studies find only modest effects of parental schooling on their children (Black et al. 2005b), the effect appears to be stronger in developing countries.[9]

Markets are often credited with improving the allocation of resources in an economy, but those resource allocation decisions require agents who are able to absorb and react to information. Schooling is credited with lowering search costs and improving allocative efficiency, which has both private and social benefits. These efficiency gains will be spread broadly in the economy. For example, better-educated people are better able to migrate from rural to urban markets or from less-productive to more-productive sectors, helping those markets allocate labor efficiently. This implies that the economy will be producing more output from the same inputs, increasing the total size of the pie available. Not all of these benefits will be captured by the migrants themselves

[9] One could argue that to the extent that these transfers of schooling and health are confined within dynastic households, they are not really externalities. Parents will get utility from their children's health or future welfare. Nevertheless, there may still be external benefits to having healthier and more educated progeny that are not fully captured by the parents and their children.

(for example, labor that does not migrate will get higher wages as the migrants pursue their interests). Returns to capital are also enhanced by efficient allocations of labor.

Empirical studies have consistently found that it is the better educated who are the most likely to adopt new technologies. Of course these agents are acting in their own self-interest, but there will be benefits that accrue to others as well. For example, because food demand is relatively inelastic, improved productivity in the agricultural sector from newly adopted technologies or enhanced farming ability will lower food prices, which raises consumer surplus. Lower food prices will tend to raise the purchasing power of urban wages and will hasten the shift of labor out of agriculture and into the industrialized sector of the economy.

From Foster and Rosenzweig's (2004b) analysis of the distribution of benefits from India's Green Revolution, it is apparent that the technologies were first adopted by relatively skilled farmers in areas with complementary land and irrigation. The social or private returns to the technology would have been negligible without a group of farmers able to successfully implement the technologies. Falling food prices did displace some farmers, but the displaced agriculture labor fueled a rural industrialization. There was an expansion of manufacturing employment and increased wages and incomes in rural areas that were less suited to the Green Revolution; those areas benefited from the increased productivity of the farmers in the Green Revolution districts.[10]

Improved schooling opportunities can raise the quality of public servants and hence of public good provision. Indeed, improved human capital is believed to improve the quality of governance in democracies.[11]

Another reason why private schooling decisions may deviate from social optima is that parents may face borrowing costs that exceed the market interest rate. Becker and Tomes (1986) showed that if households are credit constrained, they will under-invest in their children's schooling, but all intergenerational transfers will be in the form of human capital and not wealth.

Households that are not credit constrained will invest optimally in their children's schooling and then make any additional transfers in physical wealth. This may be why there is a stronger apparent tie between parental and children's schooling in developing countries. In developed countries, credit constraints may not be important and so variation in children's schooling is not as strongly tied to parents' education or wealth (Carneiro and Heckman 2003; Cameron and Taber 2004). However, substantial segments of poorer countries are more likely to face credit constraints that will limit children's schooling opportunities.

The best evidence regarding these credit constraints is that child schooling appears to be atypically sensitive to unforeseen fluctuations in household income, positive or negative. Edmonds et al. (2006) found that unexpected pension income raised schooling of grandchildren in South Africa. In another setting, opening the Vietnam market to trade caused rapid increases in household income that increased child schooling in Vietnam (Edmonds and Pavcnik 2006). Negative income shocks from weather or national recessions cause poor households to reduce child time in school (Jacoby and Skoufias 1997, 1998; Funkhouser 1999; Glewwe and Jacoby 2004; Thomas et al. 2004). There is evidence that better educated parents can absorb these shocks more effectively (Glewwe and Hall 1998).

The existence of liquidity constraints creates a second role for government provision of schooling, even in the absence of external benefits. Under-investment in schooling by poor households means that the level of national skills will be lower than optimal. Furthermore, the under-investment will be concentrated among poor children who will then be consigned to poverty

---

[10] The need for educated farmers to adopt improved technologies that would raise food yields has become increasingly apparent with the run-up of food prices and their impact on poverty rates worldwide. This is one of the topics covered in the *World Development Report 2008: Agriculture for Development*.

[11] Haveman and Wolfe (1984) have a detailed review of the sources of private and social returns to schooling.

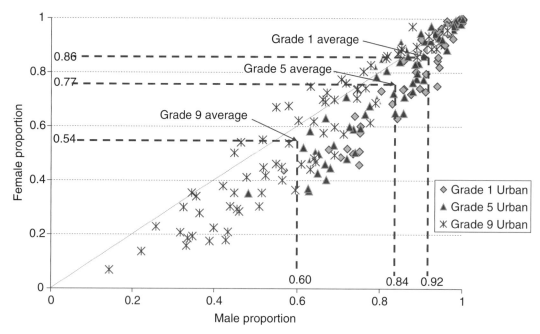

Figure 4.3A *Proportion of male and female urban population completing grades 1, 5, and 9 in seventy-two developing countries*

in the future due to their poor human capital endowments. Government provision of schooling can therefore also be justified as a means of equalizing the opportunity to escape poverty across households of varying economic status.

Where are the Most Serious Gaps in Enrollment Rates?

One of the MDGs is to attain universal primary education by 2015. Despite the consistency in estimated returns to schooling across countries, genders, and regions within countries, it is unlikely that this goal will be met. This section highlights which groups lag the furthest behind in attaining the goal, and which lagging groups can be aided in the most cost-effective manner.

To illustrate the magnitude of the problem, we make use of seventy-two household datasets on schooling attainment compiled by Deon Filmer of the World Bank. All the datasets were collected between 2000 and 2006. We computed the fraction of 20–29-year-olds who completed

grades 1, 5, and 9 in order to show how rapidly educational attainment drops off in these developing countries. The grade 5 information is of particular interest, in that completion of five years of schooling represents near assurance of lifetime literacy and numeracy. Separate estimates were generated for males and females and for urban and rural residents.

Figures 4.3a and 4.3b show the first illustration. Each point represents paired male and female proportions of the 20–29-year-old population that completed a given grade level in a country. Figure 4.3a shows the relationship for urban areas and figure 4.3b for rural areas. The dotted 45° line indicates combinations where males and females are equally likely to attain the grade level. Values on the axes range from 0 to 1, with 1 representing universal attainment. Larger deviations from the upper right-hand point (1,1) mean a greater gap from universal attainment of a given grade level.

The average schooling attainment combinations are also indicated for each grade level using dashed lines. Note that, by construction, the

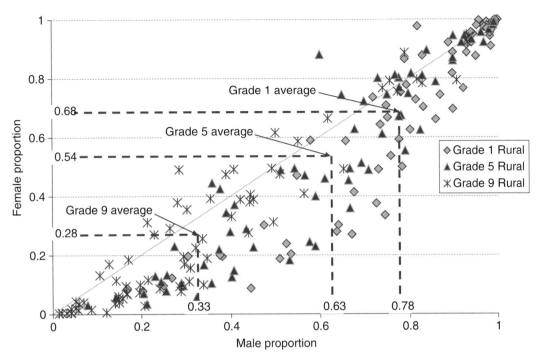

Figure 4.3B *Proportion of male and female rural population completing grades 1, 5, and 9 in seventy-two developing countries*

pattern of dots will move toward the origin as the level of schooling increases because the fraction completing grade 9 or more must be smaller than the fraction completing at least grade 5 which will, in turn, be smaller than the fraction completing grade 1.

Several facts emerge. First, most of the grade 5 points lie well below (1,1), and so most developing countries have yet to meet the goal of UPE. This is particularly true in rural areas. In urban areas, the norm is for 77 percent of women and 84 percent of men to complete grade 5. In rural areas, the norms are 54 percent and 63 percent, respectively. Aggregating across the seventy-two developing countries using population weights, 13 percent of urban residents and 28 percent of rural residents fail to complete five years of schooling. Second, in both urban and rural markets most combinations lie below the 45° line, indicating that, on average, males are more likely to reach each grade level than females. Women are farther away from UPE

than men. The population-weighted aggregates are that 20 percent of men and 26 percent of women fail to complete five years of schooling. Nevertheless, in some countries, girls do receive more schooling than boys. Third, rural points tend to be farther from the 45° line, and so male–female schooling gaps tend to be largest in rural areas. Fourth, there is a very high correlation in educational outcomes across demographic groups. Countries with high boys' enrollment rates also tend to have high girls' enrollment rates. Countries with high urban education rates have high rural rates as well. Finally, there is considerable heterogeneity across countries in schooling attainment levels, and so it is unlikely that the same strategy to raise enrollments would work in all countries. Some have yet to get a majority of children to complete grade 1 while others are approaching universal completion of grade 9, at least in their urban areas.

Figures 4.4a and 4.44b repeat the exercise, except that the points are combinations of urban

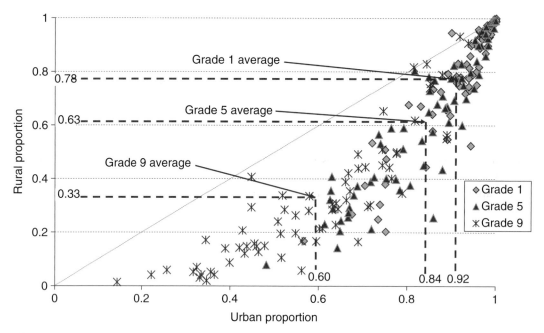

Figure 4.4A *Proportion of male urban and rural population completing grades 1, 5, and 9 in seventy-two developing countries*

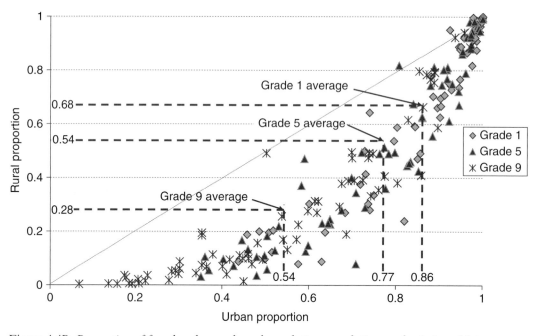

Figure 4.4B *Proportion of female urban and rural population completing grades 1, 5, and 9 in seventy-two developing countries*

Source: Authors' compilation of educational attainment data provided by Deon Filmer from seventy-two original household surveys collected from 2000 to 2006, www.worldbank.org/research/projects/edattain/.

and rural schooling attainment levels for males and females separately. Almost all combinations lie below the 45° line, indicating that urban residents get more schooling than rural residents. The degree of schooling inequality between urban and rural children, as indicated by the distance from the 45° line, increases with schooling level. Only 8 percent of urban males failed to complete grade 1, compared to 22 percent of rural male; 16 percent of urban males and 37 percent of rural males failed to complete grade 5, the gaps that must be filled to attain UPE. For both urban and rural males, there is a sharp drop off in attainment after grade 5. In only 60 percent of countries do a majority of male children complete grade 9, and only rarely do rural males reach that level.

Schooling levels are even lower for females. As shown in figure 4.4b, almost all combinations lie below the 45° line, indicating that urban females almost always get more schooling than their rural counterparts. A large advantage for urban females opens up immediately upon school entry. Just over two-thirds of rural females complete one year of schooling, but only 54 percent manage to complete grade 5. Of urban females, 86 percent complete at least one year of schooling and 77 percent complete grade 5. The UPE goal has not yet been satisfied for about one-quarter of urban girls and one-half of rural girls in developing countries. Consequently, while problems are not the same across countries, a significant proportion of developing countries have yet to attain the UPE goal.

Where and How can Schooling be Increased most Efficiently?

Given the substantial gap from UPE, our task is to identify where schooling attainment can be expanded most efficiently. In table 4.2, we present the stylized facts regarding the population of youth aged 15–19 that failed to complete grade 5 by region of the world. All youth in this age range should have been able to complete grade 5. We decompose the population failing

to complete grade 5 into two groups, those who never went to school and those who dropped out before completing grade 5. Our estimate of those who never went to school is given by the fraction of 14-year-olds who never attended. We present the data by population-weighted averages of geographic regions.

Our contention is that it is less expensive to get the children who have dropped out to complete the primary cycle than it is to get children who never attended school to attain literacy. We know that for children who at least started school, there exists school capacity that induced parents to send the child to school. In addition, these parents at least cared enough about their children's schooling to make an initial investment of child time. It is more difficult to induce parents who have not sent their children to school to enroll the child for the first time and to take the child through the primary cycle. The reason we focus on completing at least five grades is the result from figure 4.2 that five grades are sufficient to attain literacy. Investments that do not successfully carry the child through grade 5 are likely to be wasted.

The fraction of children not completing grade 5 varies from very small proportions in China and in Eastern Europe and Central Asia to over 40 percent of children in Africa. Worldwide, excluding China and the Eastern Europe and Central Asian countries, 30 percent of children in developing countries fail to complete grade 5. Of these, 55 percent started school but dropped out. To put these proportions into perspective, about 112 million children were born in developing countries in 2004. Assuming that current patterns do not change between 2004 and 2015, we estimate that 26 million of these children will fail to complete grade 5. Of these, 14.4 million will start school and drop out before attaining literacy and numeracy.[12] Those 14.4 million represent the most cost-effective target for raising literacy rates in the world. If these 14.4 million children were able to complete

---

[12] Our fraction of children not completing grade 5 is reasonably close to the UNESCO estimate of the fraction of children who are illiterate.

Table 4.2. Percentage of youth 15–19 years old not completing grade 5 and of 14 years old never starting school, by world region

Sample	Africa		Asia			Eastern Europe	Latin America		Middle East
	East-South	West-Middle	East-Pacifice	South	China	Central Asia	Central	South	North Africa
	[15]	[20]	[11]	[6]	[1]	[11]	[10]	[9]	[3]
All children									
Not completing[b]	40.9%	46.5%	12.6%	32.2%	1.3%	4.8%	17.5%	14.3%	19.1%
Never starting[c]	14.4%	24.6%	2.6%	17.1%	0.0%	3.5%	6.9%	0.8%	7.4%
Dropout[d]	26.5%	21.9%	10.0%	15.1%	1.3%	1.3%	10.6%	13.5%	11.7%
Males									
Not completing[b]	39.9%	40.9%	13.1%	25.0%	1.0%	3.3%	18.1%	16.5%	15.2%
Never starting[c]	12.5%	20.7%	2.4%	11.1%	0.0%	1.6%	7.8%	0.9%	4.2%
Dropout[d]	27.4%	20.2%	10.7%	13.9%	1.0%	1.7%	10.3%	15.6%	11.0%
Females									
Not completing[b]	41.9%	51.9%	11.9%	39.9%	1.8%	6.3%	16.8%	12.2%	22.9%
Never starting[c]	16.7%	28.5%	2.8%	23.5%	0.0%	5.0%	6.1%	0.7%	10.6%
Dropout[d]	25.2%	23.3%	9.2%	16.3%	1.8%	1.3%	10.7%	11.5%	12.3%
Urban									
Not completing[b]	20.4%	29.0%	7.3%	18.5%	1.2%	4.0%	11.4%	10.6%	10.6%
Never starting[c]	5.0%	13.2%	1.6%	8.1%	0.0%	2.2%	4.4%	0.6%	3.2%
Dropout[d]	15.4%	15.7%	5.7%	10.4%	1.2%	1.9%	7.0%	10.0%	7.4%
Rural									
Not completing[b]	46.6%	56.8%	15.1%	37.6%	1.4%	6.2%	23.9%	29.0%	27.9%
Never starting[c]	16.3%	30.6%	2.9%	20.6%	0.0%	5.4%	8.9%	1.7%	11.4%
Dropout[d]	30.3%	26.2%	12.1%	17.0%	1.4%	0.8%	15.0%	27.3%	16.5%
Bottom two household income quintiles									
Not completing[b]	55.0%	64.7%	24.0%	54.0%	1.8%	6.8%	44.6%	15.3%	35.2%
Never starting[c]	22.2%	36.8%	5.5%	27.8%	0.0%	5.7%	8.9%	1.7%	15.2%
Dropout[d]	32.9%	28.0%	18.5%	26.2%	1.8%	1.1%	35.8%	13.6%	20.0%

Source: Authors' compilation of data compiled by Deon Filmer from the most recently available household surveys conducted in each of the eighty-six developing countries between 1994 and 2005, *www.worldbank.org/research/projects/edattainl*.
[a] Population-share weighted averages of countries in the region. Number of countries included in the regional average is in brackets.
[b] The share of 15–19-year-olds who did not complete grade 5.
[c] The share of 14-year-olds who never attended school.
[c] The share of 14-year-olds who never attended school.
[d] Estimated share of 15–19-ear-olds who started school but dropped out before completing grade 5.
[e] Excluding China.

the primary cycle, the gap from UPE in these countries would decrease from 23 percent to 10 percent.

The other statistics in table 4.2 demonstrate that for almost all demographic groups, substantial progress toward UPE can be made by reducing dropouts. Aggregating across countries, 61 percent of males and 49 percent of females who failed to complete grade 5 did so because they dropped out. The corresponding ratios for urban and rural residents are 62 percent and 55 percent, respectively. We also show information on children in the lowest two quintiles of the income distribution.

We can also show the importance of household income as a factor influencing child schooling attainment. The bottom of table 4.2 includes the school entry, completion, and dropout rates for children living in households in the poorest two income quintiles. Children in the poorest households fail to complete grade 5 in higher proportions in every part of the world: 37 percent of the poorest children fail to complete grade 5, compared to 23 percent overall. Of these, 54 percent dropped out after starting school. For all these groups, therefore, reducing the incentives to drop out would generate substantial progress toward UPE for all demographic groups in all regions of the developing world.

Supply-Side Interventions

There are two avenues through which governments can influence parental schooling choices. Supply-side policies aim to improve the quantity or quality of schooling offered. These policies include direct provision of newly constructed schools or of school supplies by the central government, but they can also involve the decentralization of school control to local authorities who are believed to be able to allocate resources more efficiently to meet school needs. Demand-side policies attempt to directly influence parental incentives to allocate more of their children's time to school. We will argue that demand-side policies show more promise for cost-effective means of enhancing schooling outcomes, but we will first explain why we view supply-side mechanisms as less promising.

If you Build it, they May not Come

The biggest concern with new school construction is that most of the costs of new building and staffing are incurred before we find out if parents will send their children to the school. Duflo's (2001) analysis of Indonesia's massive public works project that doubled the number of primary schools in a six-year period resulted in a statistically significant but small 3 percent increase in average years of schooling. Similarly, Filmer's (2004) analysis of the relationship between distance and enrollments across twenty-one developing countries generally found very small marginal effects of lowering distance. Enrollment does not appear to be highly sensitive to the distance to the nearest school. This does not imply that school provision is unimportant – only that the existing supply is already located in the most dense child populations. New schools will be disproportionately located in relatively remote places where there are relatively few children to add to the rolls and relatively high costs of adding capacity.

Frequently forgotten in the analysis of new school construction projects is that they may cause some students currently going to private schools to switch to the new public schools. This is particularly true in urban areas of developing countries where private schools are more plentiful. As public school supply is expanded, some private school students are likely to switch to public schools and some private schools will close, diminishing the benefits of the supply expansion.[13] In rural areas, where private schools are frequently non-existent, there is no such crowding out effect of government school expansion.

Quality Matters, but we don't know how to Foster Quality

It is undoubtedly true that higher-quality schools enhance human capital production and raise the demand for education. However, research has failed to identify how to foster improved quality. For example, Rivkin et al. (2005) found that good teachers systematically produce better academic outcomes than do bad teachers. Unfortunately, good teachers and bad teachers look very much alike statistically – they have the same education levels, similar demographics, receive the same in-service training

[13] See Jimenez and Sawada (2001).

and are compensated similarly. In other words, teacher quality matters, but we don't know what matters for teacher quality. As teachers represent 74 percent of recurring school expenditures in developing countries (Bruns et al. 2003), it would seem that any policy aimed at improving school quality would have to confront teacher quality. The lack of agreement about how to foster teacher quality thwarts any general prescription regarding likely cost-effective avenues for improvement.

There have been many studies of the educational production process, with very inconsistent findings. Teacher or school attributes that appear critically important for student performance in one study prove unimportant or even detrimental in another. Experimental designs don't really resolve the problem because the value of one type of input (textbooks, say) may depend on what other assets the school has available (trained teachers, English-medium instruction). A particular experimental infusion of inputs may succeed in some settings and not others, complicating the applicability of the lessons to other schools and settings. As an example, Glewwe et al. (2009) found that making textbooks more available in Kenya benefited students in the upper tail of the ability distribution, who were prepared for the English-medium texts, but the texts had no impact on average and below-average students, most of whom could not read those textbooks.

Chaudhury et al. (2006) report that, in developing countries, teachers are absent about 20 percent of the time. Such absenteeism rates have a tremendous impact on the education sector. In terms of direct loss of financing, it is estimated that between 10 and 24 percent of recurrent primary education expenditures are currently lost to teacher absenteeism. Losses from teacher absenteeism range from $16 million per year in Ecuador to $2 billion per year in India (Patrinos and Kagia 2007). Many of the absences are perfectly legal as schools offer numerous ben-

efits for teachers, including many days of sick leave and annual leave. One might guess that simply removing these legal absences would help resolve the problem, except that comparisons of spot-check attendances with official attendance registries indicates that off-contract absences are rarely reported. Duflo and Hanna (2005) report on the effect of placing cameras with time indicators into remotely sited schools in India. Compared to schools without cameras, teacher attendance rises substantially. When teachers attend more regularly, their students attend more regularly as well, and the students appear to perform better on standardized tests. This experiment holds promise as a means of reducing shirking by teachers in a cost-effective manner, but we do not yet have enough information in other settings to know if these results generalize.

It is undoubtedly true that higher-quality schools enhance human capital production and raise school demand. However, our lack of clear rules of thumb regarding how to improve school quality suggest that we are not yet prepared to make general propositions regarding likely cost-effective avenues for improvement.

Are Better Managed Schools Better, or are Better Schools Better Managed?

International agencies have made decentralization of school management a central theme of new efforts to improve the efficiency of public service delivery in developing countries (Bardhan 2005). The clear attraction of the strategy is that it offers the potential of improving school outcomes without spending more on the schools – we simply "spend smarter and not harder," to modify the common aphorism. The available evidence, even that often used by proponents of decentralization, is really too uncertain to provide a high degree of confidence that local management can work in all settings, without complementary investments. Studies by Jimenez and Sawada (1999) of the EDUCO[14] schools in El Salvador and by King and Ozler (2001) of the autonomous schools in Nicaragua found that schools that exercised more local autonomy

---

[14] EDUCO comes from the Spanish acronym "Educacion con Participacion de la Comunidad," or "Community Managed Schools."

experienced gains in student attendance or test scores compared to other schools. However, participating schools are not randomly drawn – local authorities had to self-select into the programs and would be dropped if they did not fulfill their obligations. It is likely that the schools opting to accept local responsibility differ in ways that could vary school outcomes compared to communities that did not elect to participate in the program. In other words, a finding that autonomous schools outperform schools that are not autonomous does not imply that the non-autonomous schools would have had better outcomes if they, too, had become autonomous.

More recent papers continue to find that autonomous schools differ in important ways from those that do not exercise such authority. Gertler *et al.* (2006) find that Mexico's rural school-based management intervention resulted in a small but statistically significant reduction in repetition and failure rates for schools in poor areas. Galiani *et al.* (2005) found that early adopters of a school management program in Argentina experienced the largest improvements in schooling outcomes. Again, the sorting of schools into autonomous and non-autonomous groups is not random. In Mexico, schools choose to participate in the program. In Argentina, the early adopters were the wealthiest schools.

Even if decentralization were known to raise schooling outcomes using the same inputs, it is not clear how governments can best foster decentralization. Gunnarsson *et al.* (2007) found that most of the variation in the practice of local school autonomy occurs within and not between countries, suggesting that national policies to foster decentralized decision-making may have little effect on actual school autonomy.

We may eventually have a better grasp of how to foster local school management and how to generate the skills needed to manage schools in areas that do not already have those skills. At the current level of knowledge, it is premature to make a general recommendation that local school management will improve schooling outcomes.

Returns to Increased School Supply Come after a Long Lag

Supply-side interventions generally require the allocation of funds upfront with the hoped-for child or parental response becoming apparent only later. Once built, there is no economic return to a new school unless children enroll, but it may be five years before children attain permanent literacy. It may take some time for parents to perceive school quality improvements. Similarly, it may take some time for teachers and students to respond to better local school management. Perhaps even more important is that the returns to the parents will come in the form of increased child earnings that are far into the future and heavily discounted relative to the immediate direct and opportunity costs parents face in sending their children to school. The combination of upfront costs, uncertain response, and delayed benefits place supply-side interventions at a cost-benefit disadvantage compared to the demand-side alternatives discussed in the next section.

When conducting benefit-cost comparisons, efforts to shift the demand for schooling have some distinct advantages over efforts to influence supply. A demand-side stimulus can be targeted to the particular population currently not in school, whereas supply-side interventions will generally involve some redistribution of children who are already in school to new schools. Demand-side interventions can be made contingent on the child being in school, meaning that payment occurs only if the program is working. In contrast, as we have just seen, supply-side interventions generally require the allocation of funds upfront with the hoped-for child or parental response becoming apparent only later. Demand-side interventions have benefits to the household that are discounted less heavily because they can put money in the parents' pockets immediately, either by lowering schooling costs or providing transfer payments in exchange for the child being in school. The parents also see the benefits immediately rather than the less apparent return in the form of future income the child will earn as an adult.

Finally, from the societal perspective, demand-side interventions can influence behavior immediately and so have an advantage relative to the more heavily discounted benefits of supply-side interventions, at least in terms of increasing enrollment. Even so, some supply-side interventions may be justified by their impact on learning outcomes and by equity considerations, even though they could not yet be justified under strict comparisons of benefits against costs. Adding schools to rural areas is expensive, and there may be insufficient numbers of students to take advantage of the returns to scale needed to make the school cost-effective, even with 100 percent enrollment. Similarly, some reforms may be needed to shift the incentives for teachers or the aspirations of students, even if the reforms take hold only over a long time horizon.

Demand-Side Interventions

This section reviews three types of interventions: Interventions in child health or nutrition that attempt to improve the child's physical or mental ability to learn; efforts to lower the cost of public or private schooling that enhance households' ability to pay for schooling; and income transfers to households that are made conditional on the child's enrollment, which will make schooling more affordable and lower the opportunity cost of children's time in school.

Demand-side interventions will be most effective in settings with high income and price elasticities of demand for schooling and where the supply of schooling is also very elastic with respect to household willingness-to-pay (WTP) for schooling. Since stimulating demand in settings where

additional school space cannot accommodate more students will have little impact, demand-side strategies work best where there is excess capacity in existing schools, which allows more children to be added at a low marginal cost.

Health and Schooling

There is a high incidence of malnutrition in developing countries. UNICEF compilations indicate that 28 percent of children in developing countries are moderately or severely under-nourished. In areas where malnutrition is common, nutritional supplements and/or treatments for intestinal diseases or parasites offer an inexpensive way to raise school attendance and physical and mental capacity.

Numerous policies aimed at improving child health have been administered to children currently in school, including the distribution of nutrition supplements, provision of school lunches, school-based immunization programs, and delivery of health education for students. Programs have also been implemented to improve the health of infants and pre-school-age children, and these programs are the ones that have been most rigorously evaluated.

There is substantial evidence that malnutrition early in life compromises both cognitive and physical development in a way that may be difficult to reverse through better nutrition later in life. For example, Glewwe et al. (2001) found that controlling for other household background measures, children who were malnourished early in life start school later, complete fewer years of schooling, and learn less per year of schooling. Alderman et al. (2003) report similar findings for children who were malnourished because of exposure to civil war and drought in Zimbabwe. Evaluations of efforts to provide nutritional supplements to at-risk pre-school children in developed countries have shown permanent improvements in physical stature and cognitive development, both of which can raise lifetime earnings.[15]

Behrman et al. (2004) conducted an experimental evaluation of the Proyecto Integral de Desarrollo Infantil (PIDI) program in Bolivia.

---

[15] There have been several reviews of early childhood interventions that combine schooling and nutrition in developed countries. Reviews by Currie (2001), Carneiro and Heckman (2003), and Heckman and Masterove (2007) conclude that the benefits of these programs frequently exceed their costs and that the programs dominate interventions that occur later in life. Recipients of early childhood training are less likely to drop out of school or engage in criminal activities. Recipients of school breakfast programs have healthier diets (Bhattacharya et al. 2006) that can raise their cognitive development.

This program provides day care, nutritional inputs, and pre-school activities for low-income children aged 6–72 months. For children exposed to the program for periods exceeding one year, the authors report permanent gains in cognitive development and fine motor skills. Grantham-McGregor et al. (1991) report comparable findings for a similar program aimed at stunted infants in Jamaica, as do Armecin et al. (2005) for low-income rural households in the Philippines. Vermeersch and Kremer (2005) found that providing free breakfast to pre-schoolers raised attendance by 30 percent in Kenya, but did not raise average measured skills. An analysis of a program that combined de-worming medication with an iron supplement for pre-schoolers in India also raised attendance and physical stature (Bobonis et al. 2004).

Health programs have been shown to raise schooling investments for young school-aged children as well. Afridi (2007a, 2007b) found that a school lunch program in India increased attendance of girls but not of boys, but did lower the incidence of malnutrition for both boys and girls. This program costs just pennies per day. In a widely cited study, Miguel and Kremer (2004) examined the impact of a program that administered de-worming medicine to school children in Kenya. The treated children increased their attendance by 0.15 years per pupil, at an implicit cost of only $3.50 per child per year of schooling.

Nutritional programs can even have benefits at older ages. McGuire (1996) reports that giving iron supplements to secondary school-age children (13–15 years) in a low-income country can raise cognitive abilities by 5–25 percent or the equivalent of 0.5 years of schooling. Brown et al. (2006) found that the provision of iron supplements and treatments for intestinal parasites to adult apparel factory workers in India improved productivity. Even for these teenage or older recipients, nutritional supplements are inexpensive and can generate benefits well in excess of costs.

One reason these health interventions can be viewed as particularly cost-effective in raising schooling investments is that the schooling is a collateral benefit. The main aim for most of these programs is to improve child health, which is valuable in itself, and so raises the benefits side of the equation. On the cost side, expenses are incurred only if the children participate and so there is much less potential for wasted investments than is the case for supply-side interventions.

How generalizable are these studies to other developing country settings? Miguel and Kremer (2004) argue that the potential impact of de-worming on school attendance could be very large if expanded worldwide, in that 25 percent of children in developing countries are infected. However, it is useful to keep in mind that the impact is in raising the attendance of children already in school and not necessarily inducing children not in school to enroll. Secondly, their population of students had an infection rate of 92 percent and so the magnitude of the impact is likely related to fact that they selected sites most in need of the intervention – areas with more modest infection rates would have smaller program impacts. Demographic and health survey data suggest that health reasons are less often cited as a reason for children not being in school than are child work inside or outside the home, poverty, or lack of interest on the part of the child (table 4.3). Health is cited more often in Africa and in urban areas of Latin America, but is less often cited elsewhere.

Nevertheless, nutrition and health programs for pre-school age as well as school-age children will have particular relevance for the poorest households, who have a disproportionate share of the children who drop out before completing five grades. Many of these programs are relatively inexpensive to deliver. Most importantly, the benefits they offer from improved health alone may be much larger than the expense, even if they have little impact on schooling.

Lowering Schooling Costs

In many developing countries, parents face user fees for access to basic social services such as health care, sanitation, potable water, or schooling. These fees may discourage service utilization by the most vulnerable children: Girls, the poor, the rural, the disabled, and minority

Table 4.3. Reasons for not attending school in urban and rural populations, by world region

	All world regions		SSA		North Africa & Middle East		Central Asia & Europe		South & East Asia		Latin America & Caribbean	
	Urban	Rural	Urban	Rural	Urban	Rural	Urban	Rural	Urban	Rural	Urban	Rural
Work outside the home	7.4	4.2	3.3	1.8	0.7	0.7	9.3	7.8	8.7	4.4	18.3	10.0
Housework	7.3	11.5	5.3	7.9	5.6	9.9	6.3	9.3	10.7	19.7	11.7	17.9
Inadequate school supply	1.9	4.9	1.8	3.2	2.0	6.2	1.3	3.0	1.7	2.7	2.6	10.8
Poverty	18.2	18.1	24.1	23.9	4.6	3.4	1.3	0.8	24.2	26.3	11.9	11.3
Lack of interest	47.3	44.0	45.2	42.7	76.6	69.4	65.0	58.2	49.3	41.7	34.0	33.5
Health reasons	6.3	5.0	7.9	7.6	1.2	0.5	0.7	0.4	1.5	0.9	9.4	4.2
Others	11.5	12.3	12.4	12.9	9.3	9.9	16.0	20.5	4.0	4.3	12.1	12.3
Total	100.0	100.0	100.0	100.0	100.0	100.0	100.0	100.0	100.0	100.0	100.0	100.0

Source: Computations provided to the author by Elizabeth King based on data from Demographic 00.

Table 4.4. Percentage of developing countries charging primary school fees, by world region, 2005

	Africa	East Asia	South Asia	Eurasia	Latin America	Middle East North Africa	Total
Tuition fees	26%	25%	0%	20%	31%	40%	25%
Textbooks	17%	41%	0%	20%	31%	10%	25%
Uniforms	32%	41%	25%	10%	63%	20%	35%
Parent–Teacher Associations and Community Fees	67%	91%	50%	90%	73%	60%	69%
Other	35%	58%	37%	40%	36%	30%	36%
Official fees	65%	75%	50%	90%	63%	80%	63%
Unofficial fees	32%	58%	38%	30%	42%	40%	35%
Any fee	82%	92%	63%	100%	79%	90%	84%

Source: Author's compilation of data reported in Kattan (2006), annex 3. Original data taken from World Bank surveys conducted in 2005 in ninety-three developing countries.

ethnic or racial groups. If widespread, such user fees could be a significant barrier to the achievement of universal basic education and health care.

Primary School Fees are Commonly Charged in Developing Countries

In 2005, the World Bank commissioned a survey of primary school fees in developing ninety-three countries (Kattan 2006). The findings show a strong trend toward reducing the price of attending primary school in developing countries. Whereas only three countries offered free primary schools before 2000, sixteen had eliminated all school fees by 2005. The reduction or

elimination of universal fees for primary schooling has been particularly noticeable in Africa, where countries such as Cameroon, Ghana, Kenya, Lesotho, Tanzania, and Uganda have all reduced or eliminated fees since 2000. In fact, one could conclude that primary school fees do not represent a problem in that only 18 percent of the ninety-three developing countries officially charge tuition for primary schools.

Nevertheless, the vast majority of parents in developing countries still face private costs of sending their children to primary school, and these costs are often large relative to measures of household ability to pay. Even when government policy prohibits tuition, fees may be charged informally. Informal tuition is charged in 7 percent of the countries, raising the percentage charging primary school tuition to 25 percent. Even more important, as shown in table 4.4, countries charge a variety of fees associated with primary schooling, even when there is no tuition. Of the sixty-nine countries that have free primary school tuition, only sixteen actually offer free access to primary schools. The rest of the countries charge alternate fees for textbooks, uniforms, school support, or other mandated payments for accessing the school.

The most common of these is a fee charged by a Parent–Teacher Association or other community association that supports the school. While these fees may be voluntarily paid by households, failure to pay can lead to expulsion in other places. In addition, these fees tend to increase as tuition or other explicit fees are reduced. They are charged in 30 percent of the countries despite official policies stipulating that such fees should not be charged.

In at least one-quarter of the countries, parents are charged for textbooks. Over one-third of the countries charge for uniforms and for other fees associated with school activities. Overall, 63 percent of the developing countries have official policies to charge at least one of the five types of primary school fees considered. Fees are charged informally for at least one of the five fees in 35 percent of the countries. In total, parents in 84 percent of the developing countries have to pay either formal or informal fees to send their children to primary school. These fees are required in virtually all parts of the world including the two most populous, India and China. They are commonly charged in the poorest countries in the world: 82 percent of the countries in Africa, 63 percent of the South Asian countries, 79 percent of the Latin American countries, and 92 percent of the countries in East Asia. If these fees retard investments in primary education, then their impact is truly worldwide.

These fees can represent a significant burden to parents, particularly for the poorest households. Across thirty-four countries for which fee information was available, primary school fees represented over 10 percent of average household expenditures in six and between 5–10 percent in another six. The burden is greatest on the poor: A study by Oxfam (2001) found that the poorest two household income quintiles in developing countries average over 10 percent of their incomes on primary schooling. A study of household expenditure patterns in Bangladesh, Nepal, Uganda, and Zambia found that only food (and, in one case, clothing) takes a greater share of household expenditures in those poor countries (Boyle *et al.* 2002).

School Fees Adversely Affect Enrollments of Disadvantaged Groups

School fees will have an atypically large impact on enrollments of children that are particularly price-sensitive. Orazem and King (2008) argued that the most price-sensitive groups are likely to be rural residents, girls, and the poor. If true, programs that uniformly reduce the price of primary schooling for all children will disproportionately increase enrollments of girls, rural children, and the poor, the very groups that have been shown to lag in our education measure in table 4.2 and in figures 4.3 and 4.4. Kattan's (2006) review of the empirical record found large increases in enrollment in the countries that eliminated primary school fees. In the sub-set of countries where more detailed analysis was available, the most rapid increases in enrollments have been for poor, female, and rural children. Additionally, general fee reductions in Kenya, Lesotho, and Tanzania led to rising enrollments for orphans and children of parents with HIV/AIDS.

These findings of large enrollment responses to school fee reductions hold up in more careful evaluations that control for competing explanations. A rigorous evaluation is available of a program in Bogota, Colombia which was launched in 2004. The user fee reduction program, known as *Gratuidad*, was well targeted, using a proxy-mean index, such that the probability that households benefit from the fee reduction is a discontinuous function of their score. This fact allowed Barrera-Osorio *et al.* (2007) to implement a regression discontinuity design to estimate the program's effect. The results suggest that the program had a significant impact: The fee reductions offered to students from the poorest families had a positive effect on enrollment in primary and secondary schooling. The estimates suggest that the program raises the probability of enrollment for primary-aged students by about 3 percent and for secondary school-aged students by about 6 percent. These positive effects seem to be larger for at-risk students, and not to vary by gender.

Fafchamps and Minten (2007) took advantage of a unique political crisis to observe how parents respond to schooling costs. In Madagascar, supporters of a defeated presidential candidate imposed a blockade of the central highlands of Madagascar that disrupted the delivery of all public services, including education. Enrollment in rural primary schools was found to withstand the effect of the crisis. After the blockade was broken, the government suspended user fees for public services including school fees to help the communities recover from the economic consequences of the blockade. The fee suspensions were not applied immediately in all rural communes, and so the authors could compare enrollment changes in areas with and without user fees. They found that suspension of user fees resulted in significant increases in school enrollment.

Evaluations have found substantial increases in enrollment even from modest reductions in the costs parents face from sending their children to school. A program that cut household costs of uniforms and school materials in Kenya, at a cost of about $15 per child, increased years of schooling completed by 15 percent (Kremer et al. 2003). This is an important result in that it may not be necessary to eliminate all types of fees to get the desired behavioral response in terms of child time in school. Even places that eliminated fees officially often still have informal fees to help support school functions.

A case in point is the best-known and most-studied case of school user fee removal: That of Uganda, which removed user fees in 1997 as part of the effort to achieve UPE. Note that in Uganda, fees are still charged legally for textbooks, uniforms, and other school func-

tions. Nevertheless, Deininger (2003) found that elimination of primary school tuition lowered costs by 60 percent on average, or by about $16 per child. As a result, enrollments increased by 60 percent. Consistent with the presumption of larger price elasticities in rural areas, rural enrollments more than doubled while urban enrollments rose by only 16 percent. Using regression discontinuity and difference-in-difference estimation techniques, Grogan (2006) and Nishimura et al. (2008) found that the reduction in fees led to a reduction in delayed enrollments. The Nishimura et al. analysis concluded that grade completion rates up to grade 5 rose, with especially large effects among girls from poor households.

These very large responses to school price reductions are the best argument for demand-side efforts to improve literacy. The contrast with the very small increase in schooling that resulted from the doubling of the number of schools in Indonesia reported by Duflo (2001) is striking. For cost-benefit comparisons, we find that relatively low-cost fee reductions result in much large behavioral responses than has been obtained from supply-side interventions. Nevertheless, there is a significant concern that these large enrollment increases can over-tax the ability of the country to provide a productive school environment.

Reduction in User Fees Threatens School Quality

The Uganda case also points out a potential problem with reliance on user-fee reduction or elimination to attain UPE. The resulting enrollment expansion in Uganda came at the cost of considerable over-crowding, as school supplies did not keep up. Pupil–teacher ratios rose from 48:1 to 70:1 in rural areas and from 38:1 to 65:1 overall. Similarly, in the India school meal program, Afridi (2007a) reports that pupil teacher ratios were higher in participating classrooms because supply did not keep up with demand. This trade off between increased schooling demand and reductions in the quality of schooling appears to be a general characteristic of programs aimed at reducing user fees. Tiongson's (2005) review of twenty studies across ten countries found that, in all cases, enrollments rose. But, in the fifteen studies that considered the issue, measures of school quality fell in every case but one.

The loss in quality is not surprising – fees paid by parents can be a high fraction of the total financial support for a school. Private fees account for over half the resources available to primary schools in Cambodia, and for over half the revenues available to the schools in Uganda and Zambia before the elimination of fees; even after the elimination of legal school fees, informal fees still account for 80 percent of school expenditures in Malawi. In developing countries where the taxing authority is weak, charging fee for services rendered may be the only way for public agencies to recover costs. It is not surprising that the elimination or reduction of those fees creates a strain on service delivery and quality.

It is not clear how damaging this over-crowding is to student learning, but presumably children who were already in school may be negatively affected when these programs raise the number of students per teacher. Again, the Uganda case provides careful studies that address this issue. The Grogan (2006) study found that, following the fee reduction, there was a 10 percent fall in the probability that a publicly schooled child of a given age and socio-economic characteristics was able to complete a simple reading test contained in the 2001 Demographic and Health Survey Education Supplement. The Nishimura *et al.* (2008) study also found evidence of increased inefficiency: An increased likelihood that children who start school will drop out before completion.

We should emphasize that any program that increases enrollments atypically for the most disadvantaged groups would almost certainly result in a reduction in average measures of academic success. That is because the population of children in school will be weighted more heavily toward groups who would be expected to have more difficulty in school. The better measure of the net gain vs. loss from the program is whether the cognitive gains from increased enrollments

outweigh the losses attributable to over-crowding and reduced school quality. In the case of Uganda, it seems that the gains clearly outweigh the losses. A back-of-the-envelope computation suggests that even with a 10 percent increase in academic failure conditional on having entered school, the 60 percent increase in enrollments suggests that the fraction of children attaining literacy increased by 44 percent.

Ways to Reduce User Fees without Sacrificing School Quality

It is too simplistic to argue that cost reductions would be imposed only where there is excess school capacity and so we can avoid the added costs of hiring more teachers and building more schools. While we have demonstrated that the fraction of dropouts is large relative to the total number of children failing to complete the primary cycle and so potential capacity exists to meet their needs, in practice we know that some children will enter school that previously would not have enrolled at all. These first-time entrants will increase the number of children relative to teachers and will eventually necessitate additional resources in order to maintain quality.

Some have argued that the only way to reduce user fees in schooling is to have a coincident commitment to increase public support of the schools to replace lost revenues. The strongest advocacy for this view comes from the literature on user fees in health care. Removal of user fees increases usage, especially by the poor. A review of twenty-seven studies suggests that this policy has been most successful when supported by supply-side measures that remove other barriers to access (James *et al.* 2006). However, there are mechanisms by which demand-side measures can still increase utilization without sacrificing school resources.

The most obvious of these is to target the fee reduction to the most disadvantaged groups: The poor, female, rural, disabled, or minority children who are under-served by the for-fee service. These targeted scholarships maintain payments from those best able to pay who are already accessing schools while increasing enrollments of the most vulnerable. There is considerable experience with local targeting to identify those most deserving of public transfers at relatively low cost (Alderman 2001; Faguet 2004; Galasso and Ravallion 2005). Such efforts would lower the adverse impact of the demand response on school quality for those already in school.

The Private Sector may be Induced to Provide Some of the Necessary Supply

The most promising mechanisms to reduce schooling costs without sacrificing quality is to provide the targeted poor with the resources needed to pay for the costs of schooling. These vouchers could be used for support of public or quasi-public schools through the use of capitation grants, per-pupil payments that are made directly to the school. These could be used to induce new private suppliers of the service when local supply was insufficient. Finally, they could be directed to utilize existing excess capacity in private schools if the existing public schools are over-subscribed. There have been successful examples of each of these mechanisms in developing countries.

The availability of less expensive teaching and infrastructure inputs is a major reason to consider private rather than government school options to serve the expanding demand for schooling. James (1993) demonstrated that, in many developing countries, private schools are an important component of school supply: Private schools have excess capacity as measured by their relatively low numbers of students per teacher. In addition, private schools may have a lower marginal cost of adding additional capacity than government schools. In these circumstances, modest public subsidies that induce private school suppliers to contribute additional resources may increase enrollments at a fraction of the cost of pure public provision of schooling.

One way to accomplish this objective is through capitation grants to school operators. A program in Balochistan province in Pakistan attempted to spur both the demand for schooling among girls and to provide an incentive for private school entry by providing scholarships

to girls. Randomly selected neighborhoods were given the option of packaging up to 100 girls' scholarships of 100 rupees per month (equivalent to $3) to try to induce a school operator to open a school in the area. The scholarship offered declined over time, falling to zero after four years. In urban areas, even this modest subsidy was sufficient to induce new schools to open (Kim et al. 1999), and enrollments for both girls and boys rose relative to enrollments in control neighborhoods. A similar program in rural areas enabled schools to open, but the communities were too poor and the number of girls too few to allow the schools to become self-sustaining (Alderman et al. 2001). This raises an important lesson for the likely success of private school options to raise enrollments – invariably they will be most successful in areas that would have been able to support private schools in the absence of a subsidy: In other words, places with the greatest elasticity of supply for private schools.

In the Balochistan case, the privately managed scholarship schools were opened at one-quarter of the cost of a public school, in part because the schools were able to access property at a much lower cost than building a school and because the schools were able to hire teachers at well below the government pay scale. Despite that fact, school quality was sufficiently high that students in the newly formed scholarship schools outperformed students from similar backgrounds in government schools.

In areas where existing private schools are under-subscribed, vouchers may be an excellent mechanism by which governments can expand access less expensively than by building additional government schools. One example of this strategy was the Colombia PACES program that provided subsidies to municipalities to provide secondary school vouchers to poor children. There was ample evidence that the existing government school supply was insufficient to meet demand and that private schools could add additional students without requiring additional teachers or classrooms (King et al. 1999). Vouchers were offered only to children in the lowest socioeconomic strata in municipalities where private schools had committed to participate. The program cost of $193 (Knowles and Behrman 2005) is much higher than the cost of the primary school programs discussed above. Because the Colombia voucher aimed at secondary students, the opportunity cost of the children's time is much higher than would be the case if they were of primary school age.

Angrist *et al.* (2002, 2006) demonstrated that children who were randomly sorted into the program were 10 percent more likely to complete grade 8 and also scored 0.2 standard deviations higher on standardized tests, equivalent to adding an additional year of school. For those in doubt about the external benefits from education, it is interesting that voucher recipients also were less likely to marry young or cohabit, and were less likely to engage in child labor. A follow-up analysis confirmed that educational gains were permanent and not transitory.

A program in India provides a third mechanism to enable poor households to enroll their children in school. In many developing countries, students often participate in tutoring after school, with the tutoring often provided by the same teacher they have in class. Poor children cannot afford these services and may fall behind their peers. A program in India hired local women with high-school degrees to provide remedial tutoring to grade 3 and 4 children who had fallen behind in school (Banerjee *et al.* 2007). At a cost of $5 per child, the program raised the likelihood of a child achieving grade 1 math level by 11.9 percentage points and grade 2 language levels by 9.9 percentage points. By the end of the two-year program, children were performing on average 0.28 standard deviations higher on the test scores, roughly equivalent to having attained one additional year of schooling.

The reason the program is so inexpensive is that it hired less-qualified tutors at the market rate rather than requiring teaching certifications and paying the government rate. These tutors (called *balsakhis*, or children's friends) were paid only $10–$15 per month, roughly one-eighth of the government school teaching rate.[16]

Programs to reduce the costs of schooling to parents can have dramatic and immediate impacts on children's achievement and years of schooling completed. Moreover, they can take advantage of existing under-utilized capacity in the form of potential teachers and spaces in private schools at a fraction of the cost of building and staffing new schools. Finally, they have the additional advantage that they use resources only if the children use the services.

Conditional Cash Transfers

Latin American countries have moved rapidly to the use of conditional cash transfers to induce parents to send their children to school. These programs transfer income to a household in exchange for it sending their children to school, and many include other components, typically adding nutritional supplements and mandating health clinic visits for pre-school children and health training for mothers, so that they are not aimed solely at education outcomes. Programs have been or are being implemented in Argentina, Bangladesh, Brazil, Chile, Colombia, Costa Rica, Ecuador, Honduras, Jamaica, Mexico, Nicaragua, Peru, and Turkey.

As with other demand-side interventions, these programs will be most effective in environments in which schooling demand is highly income- and price-elastic and where large numbers of children are not in school. These circumstances typically prevail in poor communities. Indeed, these programs are usually aimed at the lowest income strata of society, and considerable attention has been paid to identifying which households truly deserve the program. Some of this effort seems misguided in that the poor often face transitory income streams that may make them appear poorer in some months and better off in others: A transitory nature that suggests that current income is a poor targeting mechanism. In urban areas, it can be costly for authorities to try to establish which households qualify on the basis of income and which do not,

---

[16] This should probably have been discussed as a supply-side intervention, except that it is virtually indistinguishable from the capitation and voucher systems discussed elsewhere. This system could have been designed as a voucher that would give households the resources to hire a tutor.

and such efforts lead to moral hazard problems in which households may take on activities that lower their earned income but increase their chance of getting the government transfer. There are significant advantages to using geographic targeting in populations where poverty is nearly universal, such as poor rural villages. In urban areas, targeting on parental education may be less expensive and is likely to be a better proxy for permanent income than is current income. In addition, parents cannot alter or conceal schooling as easily as they can alter or conceal their income, so the moral hazard problem and classification problems are less severe.

Conditional transfer programs will be most successful when they are aimed at populations not currently in school. In Brazil, where individual municipalities established their own programs until they were centralized under the federal Bolsa Familia program, some programs targeted children who were so young that the vast majority was already in school. Allowing self-selection into the program permitted families whose children would have been in school anyway to opt into the program and receive the transfer. Perhaps that is why the most careful evaluation of the Brazil program (Cardoso and Souza 2006) failed to show large benefits.

The Bangladesh Food for Education program transfers a grain ration instead of cash to poor households whose children regularly attend school. In other respects, this is similar to the Latin American programs discussed below. Meng and Ryan (2007) found that beneficiaries stay in school around one year longer than comparable eligible children who did not receive the transfer, with a larger effect for girls.

The most efficient targeting mechanism would be to focus on the ages at which school dropout occurs. In the least developed countries, the target would be children of primary school age. In middle-income developing countries, it would be more appropriate to target secondary school-aged children. Illustrating this point is the finding that in more-developed Mexico, conditional transfers had almost no impact on primary school enrollment (Schultz 2004a) while in less-developed Nicaragua, there were

substantial increases in primary school enrollment (Maluccio 2006). While most programs report positive impacts on enrollment, the gains are slight in some countries and substantial in others. For example, there was little impact in Honduras, where most of the targeted children were already in school and the transfer was considered too small to effectively move children away from child labor to schooling (Glewwe and Olinto 2004). On the other hand, enrollment rose by 23 percentage points in Nicaragua during the initial pilot phase, with most of the gains in the form of children exclusively spending time in school, rather than combining school and work.

Summarizing across programs, it appears that the largest effects from conditional transfers have been in rural areas and in areas that were particularly poor. The most efficient programs target transfers to groups that are not already in school so that households do not receive incentive payments for actions they would have undertaken even without the program.

Benefit-Cost Summary

Our primary task in this chapter has been to identify the low-hanging fruit for raising educational attainment in developing countries: What programs will raise education outcomes most per dollar spent? We argue that demand-side policies dominate supply-side policies because it is much less expensive to stimulate schooling demand and because the costs are incurred only when households fulfill the program's objectives. If households do not send their children to school, the government does not expend resources.

Estimated benefit-cost ratios for discount rates of 3 percent and 6 percent are reported in table 4.5. We report the estimates of other authors when we assess that they are more carefully done than anything we could do from reading the paper, although we make adjustments when the authors used other discount rates.

These estimates must be taken with a considerable grain of salt. First, while there are reliable

Table 4.5. Overview table of B/C ratios from various efforts to reduce Illiteracy

	Low discount (3%)			High discount (6%)		
	Benefit	Cost	BCR	Benefit	Cost	BCR
Health and nutrition programs						
Bolivia PIDI: pre-school and nutrition[a]	$5,107	$1,394	3.7	$2,832	$1,253	2.3
Kenya: dede-worming[b]	2246!	3.5!	642	1448!	3.5!	414
Kenya: pre-school and nutrition[c]	2246!	$29.13!	77	1448!	$28.6!	50.6
Iron supplements to secondary schoolers[d]	$474!	$10.49!	45.2	$289!	$10.29!	28.1
Scholarship/Voucher programs						
Pakistan urban girls' scholarship[e]	$3,924!	108!	36.3	$2,530!	$118!	21.4
Pakistan rural girls' scholarship[e]	$3,139!	$311!	10.1	$2,024!	$326!	6.2
India *balsakhis* tutorial program[f]	$7,002!	$9.85!	711	$4,515!	$9.76!	463
Uganda free primary school program[g]	3675!	$140!	26.3	2370!	$140!	16.9
Colombia: PACES secondary school urban voucher[h]	$476	$193	2.5	$205	$190	1.1
Conditional cash transfers						
Mexico Progressa[i]	$17,565!	$2585!	6.8	$12,923!	$2535!	5.1
Nicaragua: RED[j]	$5,920!	$1574!	3.8	$3,818!	$1574!	2.4

Sources: [a] Behrman *et al.* (2004).#
[b] Miguel and Kremer (2004).*
[c] Vermeersch and Kremer (2005).*
[d] Knowles and Behrman(2005).
[e] Alderman *et al.* (2003).***
[f] Banerjee *et al.* (2007).
[g] Deininger (2003).**
[h] Angrist *et al.* (2006).****
[i] Schultz (2004a).
[j] Maluccio (2006).
Notes: #Benefit-cost ratio computed in the paper with slight adjustments for differences in discount rate.
*Cost per year of schooling reported in Abdul Latif Jameel, Poverty Action Lab, MIT, Cambridge, MA (2005).
!Per year of schooling induced.
**Assumes that the government expands school space to accommodate additional students at the average cost per primary student
*** Cost does not include value of in kind donation of building.
**** Estimate does not include the value of reduced fertility behavior.

data on the costs of most of these programs, the benefits are based on the increase in projected lifetime earnings from the expected impact on years of schooling. Our review of returns to literacy and to years of schooling demonstrated considerable consistency across countries, genders, and urban and rural markets in the estimated returns to schooling. In the estimates we report, we assume that the return to schooling is an increase of 8 percent per year of schooling completed over an estimated average earning for labor in

the country. A modest variation in the returns to schooling will not be sufficient to reverse the conclusions regarding whether the benefits of the interventions outweigh the costs. On the other hand, we apply these expected returns to interventions that target young children who are not yet working, and so we do not have direct evidence of the impact of these interventions on their wages when they become adults.

Another reason why our calculations may be imprecise is that the returns to increased schooling will depend on labor market and schooling factors that will differ across countries. Returns will depend on the degree of economic freedom in the country – that is, on the ease with which human capital can move to its highest reward. The magnitude of the schooling increase will depend on how successfully the program can be targeted to those populations that will respond most elastically to the intervention. To maximize effectiveness, programs should focus on the grade level where dropouts are most prevalent: At the primary level in rural areas and in urban areas of the least developed countries, and at the secondary level for urban populations in middle-income countries. However, there is consistent evidence that the most productive interventions will be early in life because: (i) the costs of interventions increase with the age of the child; (ii) very early health and schooling interventions have been shown to be more productive than interventions later in life; and (iii) the earliest interventions have a longer lifetime left in which to recoup the benefits of the program. Generalizing across interventions, the most responsive populations to these interventions have been poor, rural, and female: The very groups that are currently furthest removed from universal primary education.

Skeptics may argue that the children who increase their schooling through these demand-side initiatives will receive below-average returns to that schooling, which will bias our benefits upwards. The rationale for these arguments is that adding more educated workers will crowd the market and lower wages for all educated workers, and that these children will over-crowd existing schools and lower quality for all students.

Yet the first of these arguments seems unlikely to hold. First, even if every dropout is induced to stay in school until grade 5, they will be a relatively small fraction of the literate workforce. The outward shift in the supply of literate workers will be modest. Second, in developing countries, returns to schooling have tended to be larger at the primary than at secondary levels of schooling, and so any adverse impact on returns will be starting from a higher base. Third, dropouts are disproportionately from households facing liquidity constraints, which means the returns to schooling are being equated to a higher than market rate of interest. Therefore, their current level of schooling is inefficiently low and the return to schooling artificially higher than the market rate. Fourth, returns to schooling in both developed and developing countries have remained remarkably stable over time despite very large increases in the supply of educated labor, potentially because there are external productive benefits from increasing fractions of educated workers that raise the efficiency of production.[17] Finally, even if the argument that raising the literacy rate would lower the return to literacy, a policy prescription that we keep some predominantly poor children illiterate so that we can raise the returns to schooling for literate children fails on almost any ethical dimension.

The second argument, that the children who are devoting more time to school will be spending that time in bad schools or else will be raising pupil–teacher ratios, is a more credible concern. If true, then perhaps increased time in school will not result in greater literacy. For example, the results of cognitive tests for the Kenya deworming experiment found that even though students spent more time in school, their performance on cognitive exams did not improve significantly, although follow-up surveys may yet find an impact. The increased enrollments in Uganda and India were apparently only modestly accommodated by increased school materials and so school quality may have suffered for all children. Nevertheless, there is no consistent finding that students perform more poorly in larger classrooms, especially in the range of pupil–teacher ratios observed in developing countries. Furthermore, our strategy begins with the group of students who started school, and so any increase in pupil–teacher ratios would occur because more students are staying in school and not because formerly absent students are now attending. Our view is that the

---

[17] See Kremer (1993) for an example of such a model and Acemoglu (2002) for a review of others.

tie between years of schooling and lifetime earnings is sufficiently strong that the benefits will yet become apparent as these children age, even if they do not appear immediately. It should be emphasized that, in most of the cases summarized in table 4.5, improved cognitive ability did accompany the increased time in school when both were measured.

In designing these programs, efforts to supplement existing supply by working outside the government school system are generally less expensive and subject to fewer regulatory constraints. Such private sector educational programs will be most effective in urban areas where the elasticity of educational supply is greatest. Health programs offer opportunities for collateral educational benefits while improving child welfare.

We should emphasize that where there are binding space constraints in school, stimulating demand will not be effective without a concomitant increase in supply. However, programs that require an increase in supply are much more expensive than programs that exploit existing excess school capacity. Secondly, programs that can make better use of existing resources such as those that reduce teacher absenteeism or enhance parental commitment to the school show promise but are still in preliminary testing. More work is needed to see how these programs can be generalized. Finally, we know teacher and school quality matter, but we do not know how to foster quality. Until we do, we cannot make a proposal focusing on quality enhancements.

In our estimates of the benefits of demand-side policy prescriptions, we assume a forty-five-year work career. In our projection of lifetime earnings, we implicitly assume that the value of time outside the market rises in value at the same rate as the value of time in the labor market. This assumption is particularly suspect in the cases where women are not commonly found in the labor market, as in the Pakistan example. On the other hand, we do not make any adjustments for possible external benefits of women's education such as healthier children and reduced fertility which would create a bias in the other direction, and note further that the literature has not demonstrated that returns to girls' schooling are substantially lower than are returns to boys' schooling. We also make no adjustments for any possible additional external benefits from better-functioning labor markets, more efficient use of capital and technology, or better-functioning government institutions. Finally, we assume that the benefits of the intervention are confined to the individual child who was the target of the intervention. It is plausible that benefits may cross generations, in that more-educated parents can better provide for their children, but such projections are even more speculative than the labor market earnings projections that underlie our current projections, and those benefits are occurring sufficiently far into the future that they will be heavily discounted. We expect that our more limited measure of the likely returns to schooling will counteract any upward bias in returns attributable to our ignoring any lower quality in the schools available to these children.

We provide summary information on benefit-cost ratios for many of the programs mentioned above. Our estimates concentrate narrowly on the returns from additional years schooling induced by the program. This can be misleading in either direction. The reported benefit-cost ratios will be biased downward in that they ignore external benefits and benefits from health improvements. These biases can be large. Adding the impact that increased years of schooling reduces the fertility rates of young women, as was found in the Colombia PACES case, raised benefit-cost ratios substantially, to 25.6, instead of 3.3 when only the earnings benefits of schooling are included (Knowles and Behrman 2005).

On the other hand, past returns to schooling may over-state the future earnings of previously marginalized children whose schooling is disproportionately rising as a result of these programs. Such groups may well face more difficulty finding employment and entry into higher-paying occupations than have groups who would finish schooling without public financial support.

Why Benefit-Cost Ratios Vary

It is immediately clear that many of these benefit-cost ratios are large, and some are extremely so. The largest tend to be very low-cost health interventions in areas with a very clearly defined need, such as 92 percent worm infestation in Kenya. Others are low-cost provision of private teachers or tutors for under-served poor children in urban Pakistan and in India. The very high benefit-cost ratios are attributable both to the selection of very low-cost interventions and to the placement of these interventions in settings where they would be disproportionately successful. The expansion of these programs more broadly would occur in less fruitful areas and at higher costs, implying that the benefit-cost ratios would fall. The key point is that even very substantial corrections for selection would still suggest that these programs were worthwhile.

The more broadly distributed interventions such as the conditional cash transfer programs or the voucher plans are less selective in terms of the places where the interventions are implemented, and as a result the benefits are more modest. In those cases, the largest benefits are found when they target populations that are initially out of school. For the Mexican Progresa intervention, cash transfers to younger children were almost certainly not cost-effective because most of the children were already in school. The cost per increased year of schooling at the primary level was roughly six times the cost of inducing an additional year of schooling at the secondary level.

Another generalization that is apparent in table 4.5 is that the largest benefit-cost ratios are interventions early in the child's life because the interventions cost less and the child's opportunity costs are small. Nevertheless, some programs targeted at older children can still be cost-effective if the costs are modest. The iron supplement aimed at secondary students had substantial benefits because the costs were so low. The benefits were more modest from the Colombia PACES program because the voucher was more costly, although recall that the benefits are more substantial when the collateral benefit

of reduced fertility was included. Importantly, neither the iron supplement program nor the voucher program required building more schools or adding capacity, a key to keeping their costs low relative to their benefits.

Conclusions

In examining the pattern of results in table 4.5, it seems clear that the most cost-effective interventions occur when children are dropping out for reasons of malnutrition or treatable illness. Often very low-cost interventions offered at the school site correct the health problems, improve the cognitive capacity of the child, and increase attendance. While this represents perhaps only 10 percent of the illiteracy problem according to the estimates in table 4.5, it is by far the most cost-effective solution. School dropout attributable to poverty or child labor is a more prevalent problem and requires more expensive interventions to correct. Nevertheless, the use of conditional cash transfers, capitation grants, or school vouchers can sufficiently increase literacy rates so that the benefits outweigh the costs.

Where possible, education and health interventions should be married, as each will enforce the other. It is cheaper to distribute health and nutrition services at the school site and, in so doing, parents are more likely to send their children to school. When the mechanism used to increase school demand involves transfers that improve a child's health and nutrition, we also improve the child's cognitive capabilities and school performance, raising the returns to the program. Any additional external benefits from individual schooling just add to the plus side of the ledger. These collateral benefits come at no added cost, lowering the risk and raising the expected return to the intervention.

To put our strategy in perspective, we estimate that every year approximately 14.4 million children could be induced to attain literacy in a cost-effective manner because they start schooling but drop out before completing grade 5. We take the fact that they start school as evidence that there is some source of school supply in close proximity to the home, and so it is the demand side that is constraining their completion of five years of schooling. Several modest-cost mechanisms have been tried to stimulate schooling demand for such children by lowering the cost of attending school or by tying the receipt of health services, nutritional supplements, or income to child attendance at school. Although some programs had higher costs, $250 would pay for all but the most expensive of the interventions summarized in table 4.5. That means that for $3.6 billion, and perhaps much less, we could significantly raise the schooling attainment of these 14.4 million children by one year. To raise their attainment by the 2.5 years on average needed to complete the primary cycle, the cost would come to $9 billion.

Bibliography

Abdulai, A. and Huffman, W.E., 2005: The diffusion of new agricultural technologies: The case of crossbreeding technology in Tanzania, *American Journal of Agricultural Economics*, **87**: 645–59

Acemoglu, D., 2002: Technical change, inequality, and the labor market, *Journal of Economic Literature*, **40**(1): 7–72

Acemoglu, D., Johnson, S., and Robinson, J.A., 2002: Reversal of fortune: Geography and institutions in the making of the modern world income distribution, *Quarterly Journal of Economics*, **117**: 1231–94

Acemoglu, D., Robinson, J.A., and Johnson, S., 2001: The colonial origins of comparative development: An empirical investigation, *American Economic Review*, **91**: 1369–1401

Afridi, F., 2007a: The impact of school meals on school participation: Evidence from rural India, Syracuse University, mimeo

Afridi, F., 2007b: Child welfare programs and child nutrition: Evidence from a mandated school meal program in India, Syracuse University, mimeo

Alderman, H., 2001: Multi-tier targeting of social assistance: The role of intergovernmental transfers, *World Bank Economic Review*, **15**: 3353

Alderman, H., Hoddinott, J., and Kinsey. B., 2003: Long-term consequences of early childhood malnutrition, IFPRI Discussion Paper, **168**, Washington, DC

Alderman, H., Kim, J., and Orazem, P.F., 2003: Design, evaluation, and sustainability of private schools for the poor: The Pakistan urban and rural fellowship school experiments, *Economics of Education Review*, **22**: 265–74

Alderman, H., Orazem, P.F., and Paterno, E.M., 2001: School quality, school cost and the public/private school choices of low-income households in Pakistan, *Journal of Human Resources*, **36**: 304–26

Angrist, J.D., Bettinger, E., Bloom, E., King, E.M., and Kremer, M., 2002: Vouchers for private schooling in Colombia: Evidence from a randomized natural experiment, *American Economic Review*, **92**(5): 1535–59

Angrist, J.D., Bettinger, E., and Kremer, M., 2006: Long-term educational consequences of secondary school vouchers: Evidence from administrative records in Colombia, *American Economic Review*, **96**: 847–62

Armecin, G., Behrman, J.R., Duazo, P., Ghuman, S., Gultiano, S., King, E.M., and Lee, N., 2005: Early childhood development programs and children's development: evidence from the Philippines, University of Pennsylvania, mimeo

Banerjee, A., Cole, S., Duflo, E., and Linden, L.L., 2007: Remedying education: Evidence from two randomized experiments in India, *Quarterly Journal of Economics*, **122**(3): 1235–64

Bardhan, P., 2002: Decentralization of governance and development, *Journal of Economic Perspectives*, **16**: 185–206

Bardhan, P., 2005: *Scarcity, conflicts and cooperation: Essays in the political and institutional economics of development*, MIT Press, Cambridge, MA

Barrera-Osorio, Felipe, Linden, L.L., and Urquiola, M., 2007: The effects of user fee reductions on enrollment: Evidence from a quasi-experiment, World Bank, Washington, DC, mimeo

Becker, G.S. and Tomes, N., 1986: Human capital and the rise and fall of families. *Journal of Labor Economics*, **4**: S12–S37

Behrman, J.R., Cheng, Y., and Todd, P., 2004:

Evaluating pre-school programs when length of exposure to the program varies: A nonparametric approach, *Review of Economics and Statistics*, **86**(1): 108–32

Besley, T. and Case, A., 1993: Modeling technology adoption in developing countries, *American Economic Review*, **83**: 396–402

Bhattacharya, J., Currie, J., and Haider, S.J., 2006: Breakfast of champions? The school breakfast program and the nutrition of children, *Journal of Human Resources*, **41**(3): 445–66

Bils, M. and Klenow, P.J., 2000: Does schooling cause growth?, *American Economic Review*, **90**(5): 1160–83

Black, S.E., Devereux, P.J., and Salvanes, K.J., 2004: Fast times at Ridgemont High? The effects of compulsory schooling laws on teenage births, IZA Discussion Paper, **1416**

Black, S.E., Devereux, P.J., and Salvanes, K.J., 2005a: From the cradle to the labor market? The effects of birth weight on adult outcomes, *Quarterly Journal of Economics*, forthcoming

Black, S.E., Devereux, P.J., and Salvanes, K.J., 2005b: Why the apple doesn't fall far: Understanding the intergenerational transmission of education, *American Economic Review*, **95**(1): 437–49

Bobonis, G., Miguel, E., and Sharma, C., 2004: Iron deficiency anemia and school participation, Poverty Action Lab Working Paper, 7

Boyle, S., Brock, A., Mace, J., and Sibbons, M., 2002: Reaching the poor: The "costs" of sending children to school, UK Department for International Development, London

Brown, D., Downes, T., Eggleston, K.N., and Kumari, R., 2006: Human resource management technology diffusion through global supply chains: Productivity and workplace based health care, Tufts University Department of Economics Discussion Papers, 616

Bruns, B., Mingat, A., and Rakotomalala, R., 2003: Achieving universal primary education by 2015: A chance for every child, World Bank, Washington, DC

Cameron, S.V. and Taber, C., 2004: Estimation of educational borrowing constraints using returns to schooling, *Journal of Political Economy*, **112**: 132–82

Card, D., 1999: The causal effect of education on earnings, in O. Ashenfelter and D. Card (eds.), *Handbook of labor economics, 3A*, Elsevier Science, Amsterdam

Cardoso, A.R. and Verner, D., 2006: School drop-out and push-out factors in Brazil: The role of early parenthood, child labor, and poverty, IZA Discussion Paper, **2515**

Cardoso, E. and Portela Souza, A., 2006: The impact of cash transfers on child labor and school enrollment in Brazil, in P.F. Orazem, G. Sedlacek, and P.Z. Tzannatos (eds.), *Child labor and education in Latin America*, InterAmerican Development Bank, Washington, DC, forthcoming

Carneiro, P. and Heckman, J.J. 2003: Human capital policy, in J.J. Heckman and A.J. Krueger, *Inequality in America: What role for human capital policies?* MIT Press, Cambridge, MA

Chaudhury, N., Hammer, J., Kremer, M., Muralidharan, K., Halsey Rogers, F., 2006: Missing in action: Teacher and health worker absence in developing countries, *Journal of Economic Perspectives*, **20**(l): 91–116

Currie, J., 2001. Early childhood education programs, *Journal of Economic Perspectives*,**15**(2): 213–38

Datt, G. and Ravallion, M., 2002: Is India's economic growth leaving the poor behind?, *Journal of Economic Perspectives*,**16**(3): 89–108

de Walque, D., 2005: Parental education and children's schooling outcomes: Is the effect nature, nurture, or both? Evidence from recomposed families in Rwanda, World Bank Policy Research Working Paper, **3483**

Deininger, K., 2003: Does cost of schooling affect enrollment by the poor? Universal primary education in Uganda, *Economics of Education Review*, **22**(3): 291–305

Duflo, E., 2001: Schooling and labor market consequences of school construction in Indonesia: Evidence from an unusual policy experiment, *American Economic Review*, **91**: 795–813

Duflo, E. and Hanna, R., 2005: Monitoring works: Getting teachers to come to school, NBER Working Paper, **11880**

Duraisamy, P., 2002: Changes in returns to education in India, 1983–94: By gender, age cohort and location, *Economics of Education Review*, **21**(6): 609–22

Edmonds, E.V., Mammen, K., and Miller, D.L., 2005: Rearranging the family? Household composition responses to large pension receipts, *Journal of Human Resources*, **40**(1): 186–207

Edmonds, E.V. and Pavcnik, N., 2006: The effect of trade liberalization on child labor, *Journal of International Economics*, **65**(2): 272–95

Fafchamps, M. and Minten, B., 2007: Public service provision, user fees and political turmoil, *Journal of African Economies*, **16**(3): 485–518

Fafchamps, M. and Quisumbing, A., 1999: Human capital, productivity, and labor allocation in rural Pakistan, *Journal of Human Resources*, **34**(2): 369–406

Faguet, J.-P., 2004: Does decentralization increase responsiveness to local needs? Evidence from Bolivia, *Journal of Public Economics*, **88**: 867–94

Filmer, D., 2004: If you build it, will they come? School availability and school enrollment in 21 poor countries, World Bank Policy Research Working Paper, **3340**

Filmer, D. and Pritchett, L., 1999: The effect of household wealth on educational attainment: Evidence from 35 countries, *Population and Development Review*, **25**(1)

Fleisher, B.M., Sabirianova, K., Wang, X., 2005: Returns to skills and the speed of reforms: Evidence from central and eastern Europe, China and Russia, *Journal of Comparative Economics*, **33**(2): 351–70

Foster, A.D. and Rosenzweig, M.R., 1996: Technical change and human-capital returns and investments: Evidence from the Green Revolution, *American Economic Review*

Foster, A.D. and Rosenzweig, M.R., 2004a: Technological change and the distribution of schooling: evidence from green-revolution India, *Journal of Development Economics*, **74**(1): 87–111

Foster, A.D. and Rosenzweig, M.R., 2004b: Agricultural productivity growth, rural economic diversity, and economic reforms: India, 1970–2000, *Economic Development and Cultural Change*, **54**(3): 509–42

Funkhouser, E., 1999: Cyclical economic conditions and school attendance in Costa Rica, *Economics of Education Review*, **18**: 31–50

Galasso, E. and Ravallion, M., 2005: Decentralized targeting of an anti-poverty program, *Journal of Public Economics*, **89**: 705–27

Galiani, S., Gertler, P., and Schargrodsky, E., 2005 School decentralization: helping the good get better, but leaving the poor behind, Working Paper, Universidad de San Andres, www.utdt.edu/congresos/pdf-sri/eee-691.pdf

Gertler, P., Patrinos, H.A., and Rubio-Codina, M., 2006: Empowering parents to improve education: Evidence from rural Mexico, World Bank, Policy Research Working Paper, **3935**, Impact Evaluation Series, **4**

Glewwe, P., 2002: Schools and skills in developing countries: Education policies and socioeconomic outcomes, *Journal of Economic Literature*, **40**: 436–83

Glewwe, P. and Hall, G., 1998: Are some groups more vulnerable to macroeconomic shocks than others? Hypothesis tests based on panel data from Peru, *Journal of Development Economics*, **56**: 181–206

Glewwe, P. and Jacoby, H.G., 2004: Economic growth and the demand for education: Is there a wealth effect?, *Journal of Development Economics*, **74**(1): 33–51

Glewwe, P., Jacoby, H.G., and King, E.M., 2001: Early childhood nutrition and academic achievement: a longitudinal analysis, *Journal of Public Economics*, **81**: 345–68

Glewwe, P. and Kremer, M., 2006: Schools, teachers and educational outcomes in developing countries, in E. Hanushek and F. Welch (eds.), *Handbook of economics of education*, Elsevier Science, Amsterdam

Glewwe, P., Kremer, M., and Moulin, S., 2009: Many children left behind? Textbooks and test scores in Kenya, *American Economic Journal: Applied Economics*, forthcoming

Glewwe, P. and Olinto, P., 2004: Evaluating of the impact of conditional cash transfers on schooling: An experimental analysis of Honduras' PRAF program, Final Report for USAID, International Food Policy Research Institute, Washington, DC

Glewwe, P. and Zhao, M., 2006: Attaining universal primary schooling by 2015: An evaluation of cost estimates, in J.E. Bloom, D.E. Cohen, and M.B. Malin (eds.), *Educating all children: A global agenda*, MIT Press, Cambridge, MA

Godoy, R., Karlan, D.S., Rabindran, S., and

Huanca, T., 2005: Do modern forms of human capital matter in primitive economies? Comparative evidence from Bolivia, *Economics of Education Review*, **24**(1): 45–53

Goldberg, P.K. and Pavcnik, N., 2007: Distributional effects of globalization in developing countries, *Journal of Economic Literature*, **45**(1): 39–82

Grantham-McGregor, S.M., Powell, C.A., Walker, S.P., and Himes, J.H., 1991: Nutritional supplementation, psychosocial stimulation, and mental development of stunted children: The Jamaican study, *Lancet*, **338**: 1–5

Grogan, L., 2006: Who benefits from universal primary education in Uganda?, University of Guelph, mimeo

Gruben, W.C. and McLeod, D., 2006: Apparel exports and education: How developing nations encourage women's schooling, *Federal Reserve Bank of Dallas Economic Letter*, **1**(3): 1–8

Gunnarsson, V., Orazem, P.F., Sánchez, M.A., and Verdisco, A., 2006: does school decentralization raise student outcomes?: Theory and evidence on the roles of school autonomy and community participation, Iowa State University Working Paper

Hanushek, E.A. and Woessmann, L., 2008: The role of cognitive skills in economic development, *Journal of Economic Literature*, **46**(3): 607–68

Hanushek, E.A., and Kimko, D.D., 2000: Schooling, labor force quality, and the growth of nations, *American Economic Review*, **90**(5): 1184–1208

Haveman, R.H., and Wolfe, B.L., 1984: Schooling and economic well-being: The role of nonmarket effects, *Journal of Human Resources*, **19**(3): 377–407

Heckman, J.J. and Masterov, D.M., 2007: The productivity argument for investing in young children, University of Chicago, mimeo

Huffman, W.E., 1977: Allocative efficiency: The role of human capital, *Quarterly Journal of Economics*, **91**: 59–79

Huffman, W.E. and Orazem, P.F., 2006: Agriculture and human capital in economic growth: Farmers, schooling and health, in R.E. Evenson, T.P. Schultz, and P. Pingali (eds.), *Handbook of agricultural economics*, 3, North-Holland, Amsterdam

Jacoby, H.G. and Skoufias, E., 1997: Risk, financial markets, and human capital in a developing country, *Review of Economic Studies*, **64**: 311–35

Jacoby, H.G. and Skoufias, E., 1998: Testing theories of consumption behavior using information on aggregate shocks: Income seasonality and rainfall in rural India, *American Journal of Agricultural Economics*, **80**: 1–14

James, C., Hanson, K., McPake, B., Balabanova, D., Gwatkin, D., Hopwood, I., Kirunga, C., Knippenberg, R., Meessen, B., Morris, S.S., Preker, A., Soucat, A., Souteyrand, Y., Tibouti, A., Villeneuve, P., and Xuh, K., 2006: To retain or remove user fees? Reflections on the current debate, *Applied Health Economics and Health Policy*, **5**(3): 137–53

James, E., 1993: Why do different countries choose a different public–private mix of educational services?, *Journal of Human Resources*, **28**(3): 571–92

Jimenez, E. and Sawada, Y., 1999: Do community-managed schools work? An evaluation of El Salvador's EDUCO program, *World Bank Economic Review*, **13**(3): 415–41

Jimenez, E. and Sawada, Y., 2001: Public for private: The relationship between public and private school enrollment in the Philippines, *Economics of Education Review*, **20**: 389–99

Kattan, R.B., 2006: Implementation of free basic education policy, Education Working Paper Series, 7, World Bank, Washington, DC

Kim, J., Alderman, H., and Orazem, P.F., 1999: Can private school subsidies increase enrollment for the poor? The Quetta urban fellowship program, *World Bank Economic Review*, **13**: 443–65

King, E.M. and Mason. A.D., 2001: *Engendering development through gender equality in rights, resources and voice*, Oxford University Press, New York

King, E.M., Orazem, P.F., and Wohlgemuth, D., 1999: Central mandates and local incentives: The Colombia education voucher program, *World Bank Economic Review*, **13**: 467–91

King, E.M. and Ozler, B., 2001: What's decentralization got to do with learning? The case of Nicaragua's school autonomy reform, Working Paper Series, Impact Evaluation of Education Reforms, **9**, Development Research Group, Poverty and Human Resources, World Bank, Washington, DC

Knowles, J.C. and Behrman, J.R., 2005: Assessing the economic returns to investing in youth in developing countries, in C.B. Lloyd, J.R. Behrman, N.P. Stromquist, and B. Cohen (eds.), *The changing transitions to adulthood in developing countries: Selected studies*, National Academies Press, Washington, DC

Kochar, A., 2004: Urban influences on rural schooling in India, *Journal of Development Economics*, **74**(1), 113–36

Kremer, M., 1993: The O-Ring theory of economic development, *Quarterly Journal of Economics*, **108**(3): 551–75

Kremer, M., Moulin, S., and Namunyu, R., 2003: Decentralization: A cautionary tale, Harvard University, mimeo, April

Maluccio, J., 2006: Education and child labor: Experimental evidence from a Nicaraguan conditional cash transfer program, in P.F. Orazem, G. Sedlacek, and P.Z. Tzannatos (eds.), *Child labor and education in Latin America*, InterAmerican Development Bank, Washington, DC

McGuire, J.S., 1996: *The payoff from improving nutrition*, Unpublished manuscript, World Bank, Washington, DC

Meng, X. and Ryan, J., 2007: Does a food for education program affect school outcomes? The Bangladesh case, IZA Discussion Paper, **2557**

MIT Abdul Latif Jameel Poverty Action Lab, 2005: Fighting poverty: What works?, www.povertyactionlab.com/research/Education percent20MDGs.pdf

Miguel, E. and Kremer, M., 2004: Worms: Identifying impacts on education and health in the presence of treatment externalities, *Econometrica*, **72**(1): 159–217

Moock, P.R., Patrinos, H.A., and Venkataraman, M., 2003: Education and earnings in a transition economy: the case of Vietnam, *Economics of Education Review*, **22**(5): 449–546

Nishimura, M., Yamano, T., and Sasaoka, Y., 2008: Impacts of the universal primary education policy on educational attainment and private costs in rural Uganda, *International Journal of Educational Development*, **28**: 161–75

OECD, 2000: *Literacy in the information age:*

Final report of the international adult literacy survey, Paris

Orazem, P.F. and King, E.M., 2008: Schooling in developing countries: The roles of supply, demand and government policy, in T.P. Schultz and John Strauss (eds.), *Handbook of development economics*, **4**

Oreopoulos, P., Page, M.E., and Huff Stevens, A., 2006: The intergenerational effects of compulsory schooling." *Journal of Labor Economics*, **24**(4): 729–60

Oxfam, 2001: Education charges: A tax on human development, *Oxfam Briefing Paper*, **3**

Patrinos, H.A. and Kagia, R., 2007: Maximizing the performance of education systems: The case of teacher absenteeism, in J.E. Campos and S. Pradhan (eds.), *The many faces of corruption: Tracking vulnerabilities at the sector level*, World Bank, Washington, DC

Patrinos, H.A. and Sakellariou, C.N., 2005: Schooling and labor market impacts of a natural policy experiment, *Labour*, **19**(4): 705–19

Paxson, C. and Schady, N., 2007: Cognitive development among young children in Ecuador: The roles of wealth, health and parenting, *Journal of Human Resources*, **42**(1): 49–84

Pitt, M., Rosenzweig, M.R., and Gibbons, D., 1993: Determinants and consequences of the placement of government programs in Indonesia, *World Bank Economic Review*, **7**(3): 319–48

Pritchett, L., 2004: Access to education, chapter 4 in B. Lomborg (ed.), *Global crises, global solutions*, Cambridge University Press, Cambridge

Psacharopoulos, G. and Patrinos, H.A., 2004: Returns to investment in education: A further update, *Education Economics*, **12**: 111–34

Reinikka, R. and Svensson, J., 2004: Local capture: Evidence from a central government transfer program in Uganda, *Quarterly Journal of Economics*, **119**(2): 679–705

Rivkin, S.G., Hanushek, E.A., and Kain, J.F., 2005: Teachers, schools, and academic achievement, *Econometrica*, **73**: 417–58

Robertson, R., 2004: Relative prices and wage inequality: Evidence from Mexico, *Journal of International Economics*, **64**(2): 387–409

Schultz, T.P., 1999: Health and schooling

investments in Africa, *Journal of Economic Perspectives*, **13**(3): 67–88

Schultz, T.P., 2002: Why governments should invest more to educate girls, *World Development*, **30**: 207–25

Schultz, T.P., 2004a: School subsidies for the poor: Evaluating the Mexican Progresa poverty program, *Journal of Development Economics*, **74**(1), 199–250

Schultz, T.P., 2004b: Perspective paper 4.1, in B. Lomborg (ed.), *Global crises, global solutions*, Cambridge University Press, Cambridge

Schultz, T.W., 1975: The value of the ability to deal with disequilibria, *Journal of Economic Literature*, **13**: 827–46

Sen, A., 1999: *Development as freedom*, Alfred. A. Knopf, New York

Thomas, D., Beegle, K., Frankenberg, E., Sikoki, B., Strauss, J., and Teruel, G., 2004: Education in a crisis, *Journal of Development Economics*, **74**: 53–85

Tiongson, E.R., 2005: Education policy reforms, in A. Coudouel and S. Paternostro (eds.), *Analyzing the distributional impact of reforms*, World Bank, Washington, DC

Vermeersch, C. and Kremer, M., 2005: School meals, educational achievement and school competition: Evidence from a randomized evaluation, Harvard University, mimeo

World Bank, 2008: *World Development Report 2008*, World Bank, Washington, DC

Xu, B., 2000: Multinational enterprises, technology diffusion, and host country productivity growth, *Journal of Development Economics*, **62**: 477–93

Alternative Perspectives

Perspective Paper 4.1

VICTOR LAVY

Introduction

The topic of the Challenge paper is education. The authors (Orazem, Glewwe, and Patrinos; hereafter, OGP) decided to focus their discussion on poorer countries of the developing world, and to address the challenge of identifying the most cost-effective way to make progress on the goal of Universal Primary Education (UPE). One of the Millennium Development Goals (MDGs) is to attain UPE by 2015 and OGP claim that under current educational policies it is unlikely that this goal will be met. In the search for various mechanisms that can be used to foster progress towards this goal, OGP suggest that mechanisms that stimulate schooling demand demonstrate the strongest indication of success to date, and are the most cost-effective.

In this Perspective paper I summarize the rationale and the solutions proposed in the Challenge paper, critically review some of the chapter's main underlying assumptions, and propose an alternative view with recommendations. I limit my discussion to the developing countries, as did OGP, although issues related to education and human capital accumulation are also currently under debate in most of the developed countries.

This paper is structured as follows. The second section presents a brief summary of the Challenge paper, the third presents comments on the Challenge paper's approach and methodology, the fourth outlines two alternative/additional components for improving educational attainment and learning outcomes in developing countries, the fifth offers some benefit-cost considerations and examples, and the sixth draws some brief conclusions.

Summary of the Challenge Paper

The first part of the chapter reviews the stylized facts regarding the levels of human capital investment and the returns to those investments in developing countries. The main reported findings and conclusions are:

1 Estimated rates of return in developing countries are comparable to the respective rates estimated in developed countries. The median return is in the range of 8–10 percent per year of schooling.
2 Estimated returns to schooling are higher for girls (mean of 9.8 percent) than for boys (mean of 7.2 percent), and are higher in urban areas (mean of 8.3 percent) than in rural (mean of 7.5 percent).
3 Rates of return are highly correlated across labor markets.
4 Given the high rate of return to schooling the *question* is why do so many children in developing countries do not even complete primary schooling?
5 The authors *claim* that the high rate of individuals who never attend school or drop

215

out in early grades is more puzzling given the presumption that schooling, or at least completion of primary education, is needed for literacy.

6 Based on their assessment of the empirical evidence, OGP *conclude* that the lower than optimal investment in schooling is due to constraints on household schooling investments, particularly credit constraints, that prevent them from selecting the optimal investment.

7 Various estimates from UNESCO, UNICEF, and the World Bank suggest that the cost of achieving universal primary education is between $9 and $34 billion. Against these high estimates, OGP *suggest* that a more cost-effective approach is to identify the illiterate populations that will respond more effectively to policy interventions rather than aim at achieving UPE.

8 The authors *suggest* that the interventions should concentrate on primary schooling because early childhood investment and primary schooling yield the highest returns.

9 The authors *calculate* that 20 percent of men and 26 percent of women in developing countries fail to complete five years of schooling (the threshold to literacy). The rates are higher in rural areas where half of all girls do not attain primary education and the gender gap is the largest. The authors *conclude* that the worldwide focus should be to maximize primary schooling attainment, although there is considerable heterogeneity across countries in schooling attainment levels and therefore different strategies should be used to raise school enrollments in different countries.

10 The authors *assume* that it is less expensive to educate school dropouts to the point of literacy than those who never attended school. This group amounts to 30 percent of children in developing countries (excluding China, Eastern Europe, and Central Asian countries) and the cost-effective policy should therefore focus on the 55 percent of these children who started school but dropped out. Based on 2004 data, this group

includes 14.4 million children per cohort. The authors *estimate* that interventions that will make these children literate will reduce the UPE gap in these countries from 23 to 10 percent.

Comparing Supply- and Demand-Side Interventions

The Challenge paper considers a series of supply- and demand-side policies that may improve the quantity and quality of schooling and conclude that demand-side policies are much more effective and cost-efficient as a means to achieve the goal of UPE in developing countries. The supply-side policies include the improvement of access through school construction, decentralization of school control to local authorities, and the reduction of teacher absenteeism. The authors discount the possibility of improving education outcomes because not much is known about policies to improve schooling quality. They also claim that returns to increased school supply are realized after a long lag while the cost is incurred upfront and that, unlike demand-side policies, supply-side interventions cannot be targeted to the population currently not in school.

The demand side policies that the Challenge paper recommends are focused on incentive programs that influence parental decisions regarding their children's enrollment in school. Reducing or eliminating school fees, providing school vouchers, and using conditional cash transfers to induce parents to send their children to school are the most prominent policies promoted. Also suggested are programs that improve child nutrition and health and that were shown to be effective in reducing schooling truancy.

The authors assume that demand-side policies are cheaper than other policies. They present the rates of return on many demand-side projects and show that they are very high (table 4.4), with benefit-cost ratios ranging from 1.2 to 528. The authors suggest that these results should be read with a considerable grain of salt, and I interpret them as meaning that the estimates have very large confidence intervals.

Comments on Approach and Methodology

OGP make two key decisions in terms of their preferred basic strategy to increase primary school completion rates in developing countries. The first is to focus on schooling attainment and to overlook the importance of school quality. The second is their decision to adopt demand-side policies as the only course of action and to completely overlook potentially cost-effective supply-side policies. I disagree with OGP about both of these decisions, and will explain why below.

Improving Schooling Quality and Education Outcomes other than Attainment

There is ample evidence from developed and developing countries that school quality is very important at both the micro level (determining individual earnings and income) and at the macro level (determining the economic growth of nations). Some studies have even shown that the quality of schooling dominates the effect of the quantity of schooling (Hanushek and Kimko 2000; Hanushek and Woessmann 2007). This evidence has led to major policy changes in developed and developing countries and in international organizations. For example, the World Bank, which has prioritized the achievement of universal primary education since the mid-1990s, has decided to shift some of its educational lending to encourage improvements in schooling quality.[1] Its past goals were to reach UPE enrollment and completion; equality of access for girls and other under-served groups; and improved learning outcomes. The Independent Evaluation Group (IEG) report (2006) concluded that access expansion was the most successfully met objective in Bank-supported primary education projects: 69 percent reached their expansion goals. In the twelve study countries where the Bank supported enrollment gains, gross enrollment ratios increased an average of 19 percentage points since 1995.[2]

However, these improvements in school access have not been accompanied by improvements in school quality. The more fundamental question is why so many children are not gaining any human capital even though they regularly attend school. For example, in India, a nationwide survey found that 65 percent of children enrolled in grades 2–5 in government primary schools could not read a simple paragraph, and 50 percent could not do simple subtraction or division (Pratham 2005). As a result in recent years there has been a shift in the World Bank lending priorities that emphasizes improvement in learning outcomes as an objective.

For these reasons, I think that OGP's decision not to include improvement in schooling quality as part of their recommended strategy is misguided. I also think that the claim that we still do not know much about how to improve school quality is not founded empirically since there is ample evidence, from both developing and developed countries, which can be used to design a cost-effective strategy to improve school quality and learning outcomes in poor countries. The following interventions are just

---

[1] The 2006 World Bank IEG report assessed the development effectiveness of assistance to countries to improve basic knowledge and skills through the provision of quality primary education to all children, particularly since the EFA movement began in 1990. The World Bank has invested $12.5 billion since 1995 years in developing countries to improve primary education. SSA, South Asia, and Latin America launched the most projects. The lending's objectives were to expand access to primary education and to improve learning outcomes. Based on the IEG's examination of loan documents, expansion goals were found to be met in every region.

[2] In countries such as Mali and Uganda, increases were explosive. Enrollment expansion has generally come through supply-side interventions. Only recently has the Bank begun to support demand-side policies, such as eliminating school fees (Uganda and Malawi), and providing girls' scholarships (Pakistan), or conditional cash transfers (Mexico). The IEG report also notes that the objectives of increasing the enrollment of girls and children from poor families were also generally reached; however, equity gaps did not always close. However, improving completion rates through reducing dropout and repetition was often under-emphasized, even in countries with very poor school completion records. Where it was an explicit objective, countries succeeded in only about a quarter of Bank-supported projects.

a sample of educational interventions that were shown to improve learning outcomes in poor and rich countries, and also to be cost-effective:

- Adding instruction time to under-achievers (Banerjee *et al.* 2007)
- Using computer-aided instruction (Banerjee *et al.* 2007)
- Combining class-size reduction with improved incentives to hire local teachers on short-term contracts or increasing parental oversight (Duflo *et al.* 2007a)
- Combining class-size reduction with tracking by initial achievement (Duflo *et al.* 2007a)
- Reducing class size (Angrist and Lavy 1999; Krueger 1999; Urquiola 2005)
- Reducing pupil–teacher ratios (Case and Deaton 1999)
- School choice through vouchers (Chang-Tai and Urquiola 2006)
- School competition (Hoxby 2000; Lavy 2006)
- On-the-job teacher training (Angrist and Lavy 2002)
- Targeted remedial education (Lavy and Schlosser 2005)
- Incentives to reduce teacher absenteeism (Duflo *et al.* 2007a)
- Conditional merit pay for teachers (Lavy 2002; Kremer and Glewwe 2003; Muralidharan and Sundararaman 2006; Lavy 2007a)
- Awards conditional on student performance (Lavy and Angrist 2007;

Additional Relevant Strategies

Demand vs. Supply-side Policies

Demand-side policies that are based on incentives to households, such as conditional cash transfers, or reduction or elimination of school fees, might be effective at increasing primary

school enrollment. OGP nicely summarize the current evidence, but my understanding of this literature is that the evidence on the effect of user-fee reduction is more robust and reliable than the evidence on conditional cash transfers. For example, a study (not cited by OPG) by Barrera-Osorio *et al.* (2007) evaluates the impact of a fee-reduction program launched by the city of Bogotá in 2004, and shows significant effects on enrollment in both primary and high school.[3] However, basing the strategy on demand-side policies only overlooks supply-side policies that have proven to be very effective and – perhaps even more crucially – it overlooks what may be one of the most important problems in education systems in poor countries, namely teacher absenteeism.

Supply-Side Policies based on Adding Teachers

In this section I review two similar educational programs that have been implemented in India. Both programs were based on adding para-teachers and both were very effective in achieving their objects, the first being to raise test scores of under-achievers in an urban setting and the second to increase school attendance, mainly of girls in rural areas. These programs demonstrate the potential of cost effective supply-side policies to increase attainment and learning of children from poor families.

Banerjee *et al.* (2007) studied a remedial education program in two cities that hired young women from the community to teach students lagging behind in basic literacy and numeracy skills. These children were taken out of the regular classroom to work with these young women for two hours per day (the school day is about four hours). This increased average test scores of all children in treatment schools by 0.28 standard deviations, mostly due to large gains experienced by children at the bottom of the test-score distribution. How can teachers who have less training than formal teachers be so effective? The authors provide two plausible explanations. First, teachers teach to the prescribed curriculum, and may not take the time to help those

[3] This program is targeted using a proxy-mean index, which allows the authors to implement a regression discontinuity design which yields rigorous and credible estimates of this program's effect. The results suggest that the program had a significant impact on enrollment in primary and high-school grades (3 and 6 percent, respectively). Importantly, these positive effects seem to be larger for at-risk students, and to not vary by gender.

students who are behind, and thus are completely ineffective as teachers for these students. Secondly, students share a common background with the young female teachers, but not with the formal teachers. If social attitudes and community prejudices limit teachers' effectiveness, this common background can explain the higher productivity of the para-teachers in this context. This program was remarkably cheap, as the salary of the young teacher was only a fraction of a teacher's salary. This study suggests that it may be possible to dramatically increase the quality of education in urban India, an encouraging result because a large fraction of Indian children cannot read when they leave school. The program is inexpensive and can easily be brought to scale: The remedial education program has already reached tens of thousands of children across India. An important unanswered question, however, given the evidence of decay in the gains a year after the program's end, is whether this effect is experienced only in the short term, or can be sustained several years after the program ends, to make a long-lasting difference in the lives of these children.

Banerjee et al. (2005) examine the cost of increasing attendance at non-formal schools in a tribal area of Rajasthan with low school attendance, particularly among girls. The study evaluates a program which provided a supplementary teacher, where possible female, in non-formal schools operated by an NGO. This program increased the average daily attendance of girls by 50 percent from a base of about four female students, but had no significant effect on the attendance of boys. The program cost per additional student attending school was 125 percent greater than the average cost of schooling. The study did not find compelling evidence of any change in test scores as a result of the intervention eighteen months after the program started. The study concludes that building new non-formal schools in unserviced areas would be a cheaper way of expanding enrollment than adding teachers, as long as average daily attendance in newly opened schools was at least two students. These results suggest that it is possible to raise primary school participation in India substantially above current levels, without a significant loss in the quality of teaching. However the cost of doing so will be substantially more than the current unit cost.

Teacher Absenteeism in Developing Countries

The poor learning outcomes of children in developing countries despite the significant improvement in access and attainment may be due, in part, to high non-attendance rates among teachers. Chaudhury et al. (2006) report results from surveys in which enumerators made unannounced visits to primary schools in Bangladesh, Ecuador, India, Indonesia, Peru, and Uganda and recorded whether they found teachers in schools. Averaging across the countries, about 19 percent of teachers were absent from school at this visit. These absence rates among teachers are high relative to those of both their counterparts in developed countries and other workers in developing countries.[4] The study found that absence rates are generally higher in poorer regions and absence is typically fairly widespread, even among school headmasters. Male teachers are absent more often than female. Teachers from the local area are absent less often.[5] In India's rural private schools and in locally managed non-formal education centers absence rates are high among these teachers as well, although private school teachers have lower absenteeism rates than public teachers in the same village. While official rules provide for the possibility of punitive action in the case of repeated absence, disciplinary actions for absences are rare. Teachers are almost never fired. Despite India's 25 percent teacher-absence rate, only one head teacher in the Chaudhury et al. (2006) sample of nearly 3,000 Indian gov-

[4] For example, in India, one-quarter of government primary school teachers were absent from school, but only about one-half of the teachers were actually teaching at enumerator visits.
[5] The study found some evidence that pay does not strongly affect absence, but that the quality of school facilities and working conditions does have an effect on the decision of teachers to come to work.

ernment-run schools reported a case in which a teacher was fired for repeated absence.

This state of affairs implies that developing countries are wasting considerable resources and missing opportunities to educate their children, because the vast bulk of education budgets go to pay salaries.[6] Even these figures may under-state the problem, since many teachers who come to work are not teaching. Improving teacher-attendance rates may be the first step

needed to make "UPE" a meaningful term.

Solving the absentee problem poses a significant challenge (see Banerjee and Duflo 2005 for a review). One solution suggested is to involve the community in teacher supervision, including the decisions to hire and fire teachers. However, in many developing countries, teachers are a powerful political force, and may resist attempts to curb their influence. Many governments have now begun to shift from hiring government teachers to hiring "para-teachers" instead. Para-teachers are hired on short, flexible contracts to work in primary schools and in non-formal education centers run by NGOs and local governments.[7] These flexible conditions represent an environment that may allow for policies that take into account high absenteeism rates, and aim to reduce its incidence and cost. Unlike government teachers, with para-teachers it may be feasible to implement incentive programs where salaries depend on actual days at work combined with effective monitoring. This may be effective, as para-teachers do not form an entrenched constituency, and are already subject to yearly renewal of their contracts, and there is a long queue of qualified job applicants. Thus, providing para-teachers with strong incentives may be an effective way to improve the quality of education, provided that they can teach effectively. Duflo, Dupas, and Kremer (2007a) present results that prove that such incentives effectively induce teachers to come to work more regularly, and to teach while at school. Technical approaches allowing objective monitoring of teacher attendance, such as the camera-monitoring system explored by this study, are very effective in this regard.[8] The program reduced teacher absenteeism by half and led to significant improvement in students' learning outcomes. The study shows that the benefits of this type of program, relative to its costs, are high, and are comparable to other successful education programs in developing countries that have been measured with randomized evaluations. Its estimated benefit-cost ratio was 1.83. The authors also show that the program's cost per year is very favorable in comparison to the Progresa program in primary

[6] Therefore many teachers receive substantial rents in the form of wages that are higher than their outside options. Teachers in low-income countries earn about four times GDP *per capita*, while those in rich countries earn only about twice GDP *per capita* GDP (Bruns *et al.* 2005).

[7] In some countries, informal teachers account for most of the growth in teaching staff over the last few years. In India alone, 21 million children attend NFEs. It is not clear that para-teachers are more motivated than other teachers. In India, Chaudhury *et al.* (2005b) found that locally hired para-teachers had significantly higher absence rates. In contrast, Duflo, Dupas, and Kremer (2007) found lower rates for para-teachers in Kenya.

[8] 9 Duflo, Hanna, and Ryan (2007) test whether direct monitoring of attendance, coupled with high-powered attendance-based incentives, improves school quality, in single-teacher NFEs in rural villages in Rajasthan, India. The NGO Seva Mandir implemented an innovative monitoring and incentive program in September 2003, which was tamper-proof. Each teacher was paid according to a non-linear function of the number of valid school days for which they were actually present. In comparison schools, teachers were paid a fixed monthly rate. The program resulted in an immediate and long-lasting improvement in teacher-attendance rates in treatment schools. Over the evaluation phase, program school teachers had an absence rate of 21 percent, much lower than the 44 percent baseline and the 42 percent rate in comparison schools. Absence rates stayed low after the proper evaluation phase, suggesting that teachers did not change their behavior only during evaluation. The study also shows that the teachers' response was almost entirely due to the financial incentives and not due to monitoring. When the school was open, teachers were as likely to be teaching in treatment as in comparison schools. Teachers at treatment schools taught a third more per month. A year in, test scores in the treatment schools were 0.17 standard deviations higher than in the comparison schools. Two and a half years into the program, treatment school students were also 10 percentage points (or 62 percent) more likely to transfer to formal primary schools, which required passing a competency test. The program's impact and cost are similar to other successful education programs.

schools in Mexico, which is primarily a transfer program to families. The authors acknowledge the difficulty of implementing such an incentive program in regular public schools. Based on their findings that para-teachers can be effective teachers, they conclude that if implementing strict monitoring within the government system turns out to be impossible, increasing teaching staff through the hiring of para-teachers is the preferred policy for many developing countries.

Supply-Side Policies based on Teacher Incentives

The evidence on ways to deal with teacher absence from work and the following evidence on incentive-based pay for teachers originate largely from experiments performed in India.[9] The external validity of these findings may of course be a concern, but it should be noted that perhaps a fourth of the children that the Challenge paper identified as the target for policies to achieve primary schooling are actually Indian. I therefore think that these and other related findings based on experiments performed in India should be carefully scrutinized.

Muralidharan and Sundararaman (2006) report the results from a randomized experiment in Andhra Pradesh, India, that tried alternative approaches to improving primary education. The first was to provide schools with additional para-teachers or with a cash grant and the second was to provide performance-based bonuses to teachers on the basis of the average improvement in their students' test scores. Both group incentives based on school performance and individual incentives based on teacher performance were considered. The additional spending in each of the four programs was calibrated to be slightly over 3 percent of a typical school's annual budget. The experiment randomly allocated the programs across a representative sample of 500 government-run schools in rural Andhra Pradesh, with 100 schools in each of the four treatment groups and 100 control schools serving as the comparison group. The results of this study suggest that performance-based bonuses to teachers had a significant

positive impact on test scores, with students in incentive schools scoring 0.19 and 0.12 standard deviations higher than students in control schools in math and language tests, respectively. The mean treatment effect of 0.15 standard deviations is equal to 6 percentile points at the median of a normal distribution. Incentive schools score higher in each of the five grades (1–5), across all quintiles of question difficulty, and in all the five districts where the project was conducted, with most of these differences being statistically significant.[10] Importantly, the study did not find any significant difference between the effectiveness of school-level group incentives and teacher-level individual incentives.[11]

The two input programs (an extra para-teacher and cash block grants) also had a positive and significant impact on test scores. Student test scores in input schools were 0.09 standard deviations higher than those in control schools. The input programs were around five times more cost-effective than the status quo but the incentive programs cost the same amount in bonuses paid, and students in incentive schools scored 0.06 standard deviations higher than students in input schools, with differences significant at the 10 percent level. Thus, performance-based bonus payments were more cost-effective, even when compared with effective inputs, and sub-

[9] The focus of primary education policy in India has typically been on access, enrollment, and retention; however, much less attention has been paid to low learning quality in schools. The Annual Status of Education Report found that 52 percent of children aged 7–14 in an all-India sample of nearly 200,000 rural households could not read a simple paragraph of second-grade difficulty, though over 93 percent of them were enrolled in school (Pratham 2005).

[10] The authors report that no adverse consequences were noticed as a result of the incentive programs. Incentive schools did significantly better on both the mechanical and conceptual test components, suggesting that the gains in test scores represent an actual increase in learning outcomes. Students in incentive schools also did significantly better in non-incentive subjects, suggesting positive spill-over effects.

[11] However, since the average government-run school in rural Andhra Pradesh is quite small with only three teachers, the authors admit that these results probably reflect a context of relatively easy peer monitoring.

stantially more so when compared with the status quo.[12]

The structure of these experiments follows closely the experiments studied by Lavy (2002, 2007), and the findings are also very similar. In these studies regression discontinuity and matching methods are used to show that both group and individual incentives for high-school teachers in Israel led to improvements in student outcomes.

Another analysis of a school-based teachers' incentive program, this time in Kenya, examined effects on both teacher behavior and test scores. The program randomly assigned fifty Kenyan primary schools to a treatment group eligible for monetary incentives (21–43 percent of monthly salary). The winning schools were determined by their average test score performance relative to other treatment schools in district-wide examinations; all teachers in the winning schools received awards. The program penalized schools for dropouts by assigning low scores to students who did not take the examination. Data were collected on many types of teacher effort – teacher attendance, homework assignments, pedagogical techniques, and holding extra test preparation sessions – and on student scores obtained after the program's conclusion.

During the two years the program was in place, student scores increased significantly in treatment schools (0.14 standard deviations above the control group). But the gain in scores was not attributable to the expected incentive-induced changes in teacher behavior. In fact, teacher attendance did not improve, and no changes were found in either homework assignment or pedagogy. Instead, teachers were more likely to conduct test-preparation sessions outside regular class hours. Data collected the year

after the program ended showed no lasting test-score gains, suggesting that the teachers focused on improving short-term rather than long-term learning. Consistent with this hypothesis, the program had no effect on dropout rates even though examination participation rose. The test score effect was also strongest in geography, history, and Christian religion, arguably subjects involving the most memorization.

Many other developing countries have developed and implemented system-wide teacher incentive programs. Since 1993, Mexican public school teachers have been eligible for large financial awards based on student test scores, among other factors. Under the Carrera Magisterial program, teachers participate in a year-long assessment process that awards 100 points for education, experience, and student test scores, among other factors. In recent years, teachers scoring above a nationally specified cutoff score (70) have enjoyed a sharply higher probability of receiving an award. The awards are substantial – more than 20 percent of the teacher's *annual* wage – and they persist for the teacher's entire career. Since 1993, over 600,000 teachers have been awarded the lowest level of award. Because it is so far-reaching, the Carrera Magisterial reform resembles an across-the-board wage increase for "good" teachers and may be expected to have led to an increase in the quality of new cohorts of teachers in the past decade. McEwan and Santibañez (2005) examined whether the incentives provided by Carrera Magisterial induced teachers to improve their students' test scores. A non-linear award structure introduced a discontinuity in the relationship between a teacher's initial point score and their classroom's test score and authors looked for the existence of such a discontinuity, which could be plausibly attributed to program-induced test-score improvements. The results suggested an effect on mean test scores of about 0.15–0.20 points in the vicinity of the discontinuity, equivalent to less than 10 percent of a standard deviation.

The National System for Assessing School Performance (Sistema Nacional de Evaluación del Desempeño de los Establecimientos Educacionales Subvencionados, SNED) has

---

[12] The evidence shows that there was broad-based support from teachers for the program. The study also revealed that the extent of teachers' *ex ante* support for performance pay was positively correlated with their *ex post* performance. The authors suggest that teachers are aware of their own effectiveness and that performance pay might not only increase existing teacher effort, but systematically draw more effective teachers into the profession over time.

been implemented in Chile since 1996. This policy is oriented toward all schools receiving government funding, whether administered by local government (municipal schools) or by the private sector (subsidized private schools). The schools that perform at high levels of excellence are chosen every two years and receive an incentive in the form of an excellence subsidy. Schools representing up to 25 percent of each region's enrollment receive awards. Program terms stipulate that 90 percent of the amounts assigned must go directly to the school's teachers, proportional to their hours of employment, with each school deciding the distribution of the remaining 10 percent. The SNED has been applied four times. In 2002, a parallel teaching-excellence bonus (Asignación de Excelencia Pedagógica) for those teaching grades 1–4 was added. This bonus consists of a monetary award (US$ 714 for ten years) linked to a voluntary, individual evaluation. To receive this award, teachers must successfully pass knowledge-based examinations, present their curricula, and a recording of a class in action. Of the 1,932 teachers who met the requirements, only 313 were considered excellent teachers.

Another known teachers' merit pay program in Latin America is Bolivia's comprehensive "merit wages" (salario al mérito) program, which was implemented from 1998. Its aim was to provide incentives and to improve teachers' performance, although no evidence is available of its efficiency. El Salvador has also implemented a school awards program (Plan de Estímulos a la Labor Educativa Institucional) to encourage public school teachers to work together to solve the problems affecting their schools and to improve the quality of education services offered to the community. The award consists of a monetary incentive for each teacher working at schools that meet objectives previously established by the Education Ministry (MINED). To assign this reward, all public schools at the pre-school, primary and secondary level were evaluated.

In most cases, the performance-based payment schemes are marginal additions which do not involve a complete revamping of the educational system. The evidence presented above and elsewhere[13] suggests that the respective performance and effectiveness gains can be considerable. It appears that teachers and schools are motivated by monetary incentives and respond to them by exerting more effort, applying more creativity, and modifying their pedagogical practices. Therefore, the measurement and reward of performance are potentially important elements in modernizing public school systems in developing countries. Such mechanisms also induce selection and sorting processes that discourage poor performers and attract better performers in the medium and longer term. Yet, notwithstanding their positive contribution, these incentives can also lead to unintended and undesired consequences growing out of their many inherent structural problems, such as measurement problems, or the possibility of teachers induced to direct their efforts exclusively to rewarded activities. Although there are unfortunately no magical cures for these problems, many lessons have already been drawn from the experience and evaluation of teachers' incentives programs.

Remarks on Cost and Benefit Considerations

Many of the supply-side policies discussed above are extremely efficient in terms of cost-benefit comparisons. For example, Duflo, Duopas, and Kremer (2007a) demonstrate that the *balsakhi* program in India is remarkably cheap, since the salary of the *balsakhi* (the main cost of the *balsakhi* program) is only a fraction of a teacher's salary (*balsakhis* were paid Rs 500–750 per month, or a little over $10–$15). Overall, the *balsakhi* program cost is approximately Rs 107 ($2.25) per student per year, while the computer-assisted learning program that was studied as well had a much higher cost, approximately Rs 722 ($15.18) per student per year, including the cost of computers and assuming a five-year depreciation cycle. The authors note that in terms of cost for a given improvement in test scores, scaling up the *balsakhi* program would

---

[13] See Lavy (2007).

be much more cost-effective than hiring new teachers and it would also be five–seven times more cost-effective than expanding computer-assisted learning. These authors also compared the cost-effectiveness of the *balsakhi* program to a range of programs that are analyzed in Kremer, Miguel, and Thornton (2004). The cost of the most cost-effective program they consider (an incentive program for children) was between $1.77 and $3.53 per 0.1 standard deviation (depending on the region). Using the same assumptions, the remedial education program cost between $0.67 and $1.77 per 0.1 standard deviations. The *balsakhi* program thus stands out as the most cost-effective program for learning improvement. The Challenge paper computes a benefit-cost ratio for this supply-side policy of 711 at a 3% discount rate and of 528 at a 4% discount rate.

Other examples of very cost-effective supply-side programs are the teachers' incentive programs studied in Muralidharan and Sundararaman (2006). Both the input and incentive interventions were highly cost-effective relative to the status quo. The study shows that the variable cost of running a typical government school in India is around Rs 300,000 a year. The input treatments added the equivalent of 16 percent of a normal year's learning for an additional cost of Rs 10,000 a year, and so 6.25 years of the programs would add an equivalent of a full year's learning at a cost of Rs 62,500 (or around 21 percent of the current variable cost of a year's schooling). Since a year of the incentive program added the equivalent of 26 percent of a normal year's learning, four years of such a program would add the equivalent of a full year's learning at a cost of Rs 36,000 (assuming the same program effects continue). OGP conclude that a teacher-incentive program could therefore add the equivalent of a full year of schooling at 12 percent of the current cost of a year's schooling, which would make it a very cost-effective program relative to the status quo with very high benefit-cost ratio.

As a third example, Duflo, Hanna, and Ryan (2007) discussed above show that a straightforward monitoring and incentive program can effectively reduce teacher truancy and that the benefits of this type of program, relative to its costs, are high, and comparable to other successful education programs in developing countries that have been evaluated with randomized evaluations. For example, expressed in terms of cost per outcome, this program cost approximately 11 cents for each additional instruction day per child, $60 per additional school year, and $3.58 per 0.10 standard deviations of increased test scores. OGP show that the cost per standard deviation increase in test scores in this program compares favorably to most education programs evaluated through randomized evaluation, but it is more expensive than the *balsakhi* remedial education program discussed above. The cost per additional year of schooling of the camera program is much higher than that of the de-worming program in Africa ($3.53 per additional year of schooling), but lower than that of any other programs evaluated in Africa, such as a child-incentive program ($90 per extra year) or a child-sponsorship program that delivered uniforms to children ($99 per extra year). Overall, the camera program is shown to be relatively cost-effective, in terms of both increasing instruction time and of increasing learning: We find a benefit-cost ratio of 1.83.

However, none of these programs and the other supply-side interventions discussed above allow for a full cost-benefit analysis (CBA), since their long-term effects on learning and on labor market outcomes are not known. The demand-side interventions discussed in the Challenge paper and its benefit-cost ratios do not escape this limitation, either.

Conclusions

The discussion presented in this paper suggests adding two major components to the education sector strategy in developing countries. The first is an effort to improve school quality by relying on interventions that have been shown to be effective in this regard, and the second is to use supply-side programs along demand-side programs in an attempt to increase primary school attainment and school quality. The supply-side policies share some of the benefits and shortcomings of the demand-side policies. For example, many of the quality interventions and the supply-side programs are also conditional, as are some of the demand-side policies that the Challenge paper recommends If teachers do not reduce their absence from work or do not improve education outcomes the government will not expand resources, as seen from the India camera and teacher-incentive experiments. But there is much symmetry on the negative side of both kinds of policies. For example, the external validity of some of the programs – namely, the possibility of implementing the experimental interventions in different settings and countries – is equally questionable for both demand- and the supply-side policies. The uncertainty of applying large-scale programs that were found to be effective in a small-scale experiment is a concern for both demand- and supply-side policies. Another concern for both types of policies is the unknown general equilibrium effects, and the longer-term effects of both demand- and supply-side policies.

Bibliography

Abhijit, V., Banerjee, S.J., and Kremer, M., with Lanjouw, J. and Lanjouw, P., 2005: Moving to universal primary education, costs and tradeoffs, Harvard University, March

Angrist, J. and Lavy, V., 1999: Using Maimonides' Rule to estimate the effect of class size on children's academic achievement, *Quarterly Journal of Economics*

Angrist , J. and Lavy, V., 2001: The effect of teachers' training on student achievements, *Journal of Labor Economics*, **19**(2): 343–69

Angrist, J. and Lavy, V., 2007: The effect of high-stakes high school achievement awards: Evidence from a group-randomized trial, *American Economic Review*, forthcoming

Atkinson, A., Burgess, S., Croxson, B., Gregg, P., Propper, C., Slater, H., and Wilson, D., 2004: Evaluating the impact of performance-related pay for teachers in England, The Centre for Market and Public Organisation, Department of Economics, University of Bristol, UK: 60

Banerjee, A. and Duflo, E., 2006: Addressing absence, *Journal of Economic Perspectives*, **20**(1): 117–32

Barrera-Osorio, F., Linden, L.L., and Urquiola, M., 2007: The effects of user fee reductions on enrollment evidence from a quasi-experiment, January

Case, A. and Deaton, A, 1999: School inputs and educational outcomes in South Africa, *Quarterly Journal of Economics*, **114**(3): 1047–84

Chang-Tai, H. and Urquiola, M., 2006: The effects of generalized school choice on achievement and stratification: Evidence from Chile's school voucher program, *Journal of Public Economics*, **90**: 1477–1503

Duflo, E., Dupas, P., and Kremer, M., 2007: Peer effects, pupil–teacher ratios, and teacher incentives: Evidence from a randomized evaluation in Kenya, September

Duflo, E., Dupas, P., and Kremer, M., 2007b: Peer effects and the impact of tracking: Evidence from a randomized evaluation in Kenya, Poverty Lab Working Paper, November

Duflo, E., Hanna, R., and Ryan, S., 2007: Monitoring works: Getting teachers to come to school, November

Figlio, D.N. and Kenny, L., 2006: Individual teacher incentives and student performance, National Bureau of Economic Research, Cambridge, MA

Glewwe, P., Ilias, N., and Kremer, M., 2003: Teacher incentives, National Bureau of Economic Research, Cambridge, MA

Gould, E., Lavy, V., and Paserman, D., 2004: Immigrating to opportunity: Estimating the effect of school quality using a natural experiment on Ethiopians in Israel, *Quarterly Journal of Economics*, **119**(2): 489–526

Habyarimana, J., 2004: Measuring and understanding teacher absence in Uganda, Georgetown University, unpublished paper

Hanushek, E., Woessman, E.A., and Kimko, D.D., The role of education quality for economic growth, World Bank Policy Research Paper, **4122**

Kremer, M., Muralidharan, K., Chaudhury, N., Hammer, J., Halsey Rogers, F., 2004: Teacher absence in India, World Bank, Washington, DC

Lavy, V., 2002: Evaluating the effect of teachers' group performance incentives on pupil achievement, *Journal of Political Economy*, **110**: 1286–1317

Lavy, V., 2005: Mechanisms and effects of free choice among public schools, NBER Working Paper (revised, 2007)

Lavy, V., 2007a: Performance pay and teachers' effort, productivity and grading ethics, *American Economic Review*, forthcoming

Lavy, V., 2007b: Using performance-based pay to improve the quality of teachers, *The Future of Children*, Spring: 87–110

Lavy, V. and Shlosser, A., 2005: Targeted remedial education for under-performing teenagers: Costs and benefits, *Journal of Labor Economics*, October

McEwan, P. and Santibañez, L., 2005: Teacher incentives and student achievement: Evidence from a large-scale reform, Wellesley College and RAND, unpublished ms

Muralidharan, K. and Sundararaman, V., 2006: Teacher incentives in developing countries: Experimental evidence from India, Department of Economics, Harvard University, November, mimeo

Pratham Mumbai Education Initiative, 2005: *Annual state of education report, 2005*, New Delhi

Rogers, F. Halsey, Lopez-Calix, J.R., Cordoba, N., Chaudhury, N., Hammer, J., Kremer, M., and Muralidharan, K., 2004: Teacher absence and incentives in primary education: Results from a new national teacher tracking survey in Ecuador, chapter 6, in World Bank, *Ecuador: Creating fiscal space for poverty reduction*, Washington, DC

Urquiola, M., 2006: Identifying class size effects in developing countries: Evidence from rural Bolivia, *Review of Economics and Statistics*, **88**(1): 171–7

Perspective Paper 4.2[1]

LANT PRITCHETT

As a development economist, I love the idea of the Copenhagen Consensus. As an economist, I naturally love the idea of comparing possible policy actions across domains to judge their attractiveness. Too often, public policies are discussed only by advocates/experts in particular sectors, so educators discuss education, doctors/public health experts discuss health, and transport engineers discuss highways. The result of this is what I find nearly every time I get my hair cut – the people who cut hair are more interested in my hair than I am and often recommend I "do more" with my hair. This is not as surprising as one would expect, for a variety of reasons: people who devote their careers to hair care, care about hair. So naturally if one gathers together experts in any field the discussion presumes "more should be done" in their sector and the only discussion is which of the many things in their sector are highest priority (and how to convince the rest of the world, mostly not true believers, to cough up the cash). Since economics is a theory about resource allocation (and since we are short on technical expertise in the specific sectors) a cross-sector comparison of allocations of public sector resources – weighing the gains to resources devoted to global warming against those devoted to disease eradication or improving nutrition – brings economics to the fore.

As a *development* economist, I love the idea because comparing alternatives, some of which affect poor people and some of which affect rich people, is the only way to highlight the stark consequences of the existing distribution of wealth, productivity, and income across the world. Spending (and of course imposing regulatory costs that reduce output is, for an economist, the equivalent of spending) a dollar of public resources has the effect of reducing the amount available for private consumption. In the richer countries of the world there might be the sense that reducing consumption to devote to public purposes has a low cost, because what would have been consumed is not that important – it would have been spent in crass materialistic, keep-up-with-the-Jones', advertising driven consumerism anyway, so "we" might as well take it away and spend it on what is truly important, like protection of the environment, or improving schools or raising the incomes of the poor.[2] In contrast, Banerjee and Duflo (2006) examined household surveys to create a statistical profile of "the poor." Among those living on $2/day around 66 cents of every dollar was spent on food. Roughly half of the population in poor countries is at this level of poverty. So, in thinking of devoting resources to global warming, or education, or health, if the alternative is a dollar's worth of private consumption for the typical poor-country citizen, at least half of this dollar would have gone to food (and the rest for things the household valued just as highly). The genius of the Copenhagen Consensus exercise is to create a feasible, evidence-based, alternative for the use of incremental resources that takes

[1] In fairness to the authors, I should point out that this is based on the first draft of their Challenge paper, and has, except for some minor editing remained substantially the same (which avoids rounds of responses and counter-responses in the perspective paper and comments, but might make these comments unfair to the current version).

[2] This view includes economists, and with evidence. Richard Layard's (2005) book *Happiness* emphasizes the evidence that above a threshold more income does not appear to produce more happiness and concludes, among other recommendations, that "We should spend more on helping the poor, especially in the Third World" (2005: 233).

into account the effectiveness of resources both across sectors and across the globe. This is a useful corrective to the confusion of small percentages – the costs of attacking global warming might be only 1 percent of GDP in a rich country. One percent sounds small, and one could easily think of ways to reduce consumption by 1 percent that just must have trivial consequences for wellbeing (although this is usually more of reducing one's neighbor's frivolous consumption than one's own – for instance, readers will point to the $100 billion spent annually in the USA on audio and visual equipment, non-smokers to the $38 billion spent on tobacco, and men perhaps to the $36 billion *more* spent on women's than men's apparel).[3]

But 1 percent of high-income country GDP is (in PPP$) roughly $320 billion dollars. That is a big number to poor people. The total poverty gap in the world (the difference between actual consumption of the poor and the "dollar-a-day standard" is roughly 35 billion dollars (in 2001 PPP)[4] – so 1 percent of rich country GDP is *ten times larger* than the global dollar-a-day poverty gap. Given the vast differences in wealth and consumption across the world, devoting 50 billion can seem trivial – just halve American purchases of DVDs for one year – or impossible – all of Ghana's or Kenya's GDP.

To preserve the logic of the exercise of comparisons across alternative uses of resources, one has to use the hard-headed logic of economics all the way through. That is, "beating something with nothing" – comparing the costs to an unspecified alternative – is difficult but maybe we want to compare forgone losses from attacking global warming, which generates a great deal of concern in rich countries, with something else that people can get a warm glow from – like programs to attack malnutrition or educate girls. But if we are to use economics to

compare these alternatives, we must *really* use economics. The essence of a normative "cost-effectiveness" exercise for public sector actions for an economist is to start from some objective function, usually an inequality averse (or at least neutral) aggregator of underlying utilities (self-assessed individual wellbeing) and from a model in which the choices of individual agents produce an equilibrium outcome. Then we ask, relative to the counter-factual of the existing equilibrium (which includes all existing public sector interventions) by how much does our objective function increase from public sector action A with cost (direct or indirect) P?

The problem with comparing *public sector* actions across two sectors – say, global warming and education – is that it is *not* the efficacy of "cost-effectiveness" of spending in the two sectors that should be compared, particularly of course if one is a pure public good (non-rival and non-excludable) and one is a pure private good (rival and excludable). We economists have two welfare theorems about that. Under a very stringent set of assumptions we know that governments cannot tax money away from people (and any regulatory imposition can be thought of as an equivalent) and give it back to them in private goods and make everyone better off – since if spending on private good X were a "priority" then that would have already been reflected in the choices of households. Of course the government could "improve" the distribution of income – but the second welfare theorem tells us that something like that this need not involve anything other than redistribution of cash. With private goods no sector-specific interventions are required.

Of course, this is not true when there are "market failures" – so it is possible for the government to tax money away from people and then spend that money in ways that makes everyone, by their own evaluation, better off. The classic examples are pure public goods, which are non-rival and non-excludable which means that no profit-maximizing producer will produce them.

It is with considerable trepidation I lay out this brief and simplistic account of normative

---

[3] All these figures are from the US Consumer Expenditure Survey (2006).
[4] These are just simple calculations from Chen and Ravallion (2004): there are 1089 "dollar-a-day" poor, the poverty gap is 6 percent of the poverty line, times 365 (to get to annual) times an adjustment for inflation to 2001 dollars; the total is 35,191 million.

public economics to an august Expert Panel of economists, but my key objections to this Challenge paper lay not so much in the empirical evidence it presents, but rather what to make of this evidence for policy. In my view, there are three fundamental issues with this chapter, and issues that are relevant to comparing the results to something like investing in global warming which is, at this stage of human history, something like the mother of all public goods (the quantitative magnitude of the economic returns can be debated but no one questions that greenhouse gas emissions are a global public good/bad and hence their reduction a legitimate matter for public policy).

First, it does not grapple sufficiently with the fact that education is predominantly a private good.

Second, it does not present a compelling positive theory of schooling that is consistent with a welfare theoretic interpretation of their results.

Third, it does not consider alternatives *at the margin* and *one by one*: the results which claim to be highly cost-effective with "demand-side" transfers mostly combine two policies – and it is the inessential one that actually produces all the gains.

Let me preface everything I am about to say with the comment that this is an excellent paper of its type. This paper is, if anything, atypically good, but these three issues are, more or less, endemic to this entire branch of the literature.

Education is Predominantly a Private Good

Bravely, the authors make things very hard for themselves right up front. Let's think of what I would want to demonstrate if I were to justify public sector spending on schooling. The optimal Pigovian tax/subsidy on a specific item depends on the *difference* between private returns and the public returns (which include the private returns). "Having an externality" is not like virginity, it is not a discrete, in fact, unless all markets are perfect then likely nearly all goods have *some* element of an externality – if

only in using a good which is a pure public good in production. The question is the *magnitude* of the externality compared to the *magnitude* of the private benefits.

Hence the authors make their life very difficult by starting with table 4.1 which shows there are very large *private* returns to schooling – on average, across the forty-two developing countries which they estimate, an additional year of schooling is associated with an 8.2 percent increase in wages for men and a 10.3 percent increases in wages for women, and a 9.2 percent increase in urban areas and 8 percent in rural areas. Why does this make their life difficult? Because if I really want to justify *public* spending on something I want the *private* gains to be small and the *public* gains to be large – say, a non-rival and non-excludable good. But what they show at the start is that the *private* gains are considerable, which means that, if, say, one were to justify public spending as a large proportion of the private spending then one needs not just some externalities, but very large externalities to education.

One way into that question is to ask: *If* the common policy of (near-) complete subsidization of all instructional costs of basic schooling *were* to be justified exclusively on the basis of externalities to schooling, how big do those externalities need to be (measured in a way consistent with the Mincer return)? [5] To calculate this, I assume the standard Mincer framework that wages are a function of labor market experience and its square, and years of schooling, a forty-five-year working life, 15 percent tax rate, and a discount rate of 11.5 percent. Why a discount rate of 11.5 percent? Because that is the discount rate at which a 15-year-old would choose to complete grade 9 at a Mincer wage increment of 9.9 percent if the only cost to the individual were the opportunity cost of the forgone wage. Now to calculate instructional

[5] These assumptions draw on Heckman and Klenow (1997) who do a similar calculation for college costs in the USA, with the result that the externality would need to be about 3 percentage points to justify the instructional cost subsidy at a typical public university; the calculations are reported in Pritchett (2006).

Table 4.2.1. What rate of excess social over private rate of return to schooling would rationalize full subsidization of instructional costs?

	I	II	III
Teacher years of schooling =	15	15	17
Teacher experience =	20	20	20
Primary class size = (secondary assumed half as large)	30	40	25
Age 6/ Schooling = 0	4.5	3.4	6.5
Age 10/ Schooling = 5	2.2	1.7	3.2
Age 15/Schooling =8	2.3	1.7	3.3

Note: The calculations assume the only private cost is wage forgone, a working life of forty-five years, 15 percent tax rate, and 11.5 percent discount rate. At these assumptions a 9.9 percent wage increment is sufficient to induce a 15-year-old to complete a ninth year of schooling at zero instructional cost. Source: Pritchett (2006).

costs of primary school we assume a teacher wage based on fifteen years of schooling (twelve plus three years' teacher training) at the Mincer return of 9.9 percent and twenty years' experience (with a 2.5 percent experience premium and a quadratic term such that experience premia peaks at twenty-five years). We explore a range of class sizes to get per-student cost and assume that teacher wages are only 60 percent of total instructional costs (as construction and maintenance costs of the buildings, plus administrative costs, plus all instructional materials need to be included). I assume secondary school instructional costs are 50 percent higher than primary. These assumptions give an estimate of instructional costs that has the main virtue of consistency, with a *patina* of plausibility.

In this simple framework the "externality-inclusive Mincer" – the impact of a year of schooling on aggregate wellbeing with all externalities monetized – should exceed the micro-Mincer – the impact of a year of schooling on an individual's wages – by between 3.5 to 6.5 percentage points at the primary level (because opportunity costs are low, instructional costs are a higher fraction of the total costs) and 1.7–3.3 percentage points at the secondary level (since opportunity costs are higher, instructional costs are a lower proportion of the total costs) (table 4.2.1).

Most of the discussions of the returns to education are like that in this Challenge paper, they assert: (a) there are *large private* returns to schooling and (b) there are plausibly *some* externalities to schooling (e.g. economic spillovers, health effects, reduced crime, etc.). But that there are *some* externalities to education only justifies *some* subsidy. It is already the case that most governments in the world offer highly subsidized schooling (at all levels, in fact) – usually free primary schooling. In fact, just taking the fact that *public* spending on education is roughly 4.1 percent of GDP in lower- and middle-income countries suggests that roughly 500 billion is already being spent on education in poor countries.

Therefore the question is not whether there are externalities or not, we are not looking for *some* externality, if one is talking about *expanding* the existing very large subsidies to schools then we must be looking for *huge* externalities. As just a simple example, suppose that in a country an unskilled worker, with zero years of schooling, supports a family of three (herself and two others) at the "two-dollar-a-day" standard and hence earns PPP$2,190 a year. With an 8 percent wage premium a worker with six years of school would make P$ 1,285 more and with ten years of schooling P$2,500 more. These differences should be glaringly obvious – and they are. As the authors show, the empirical fact that workers with more education on average have higher earnings must now rival Engel's curve for the best and most widely documented empirical regularity.

By the same token, if there were externalities of the equivalent to a 4.5 percent social return then *each* worker with a primary degree (five years of schooling) should contribute P$539 of benefits to the economy (over and above the wage returns) – 30 percent of the unskilled workers' total earnings. Each worker with junior secondary (nine years of schooling) at a 3.5 percent social return (weighted average of 4.5 and 2.3) should return P$794 of benefits to other people in the economy.

Effects of this magnitude should be easy to find. But in this section, there are just two arguments. One is credit constraints (on which, more below) and the other is "market failures" for which we get the usual suspects – educated women have fewer children (see n. 6),[6] they make markets more efficient – and a heartening acknowledgment from the authors that most of the benefits often cited as "externalities" are in fact internal to the household (e.g. healthier children) and so are not very "external." Again, no one doubts that there are *some* externalities. But do the externalities exceed the existing subsidies? This is important since on p. 196 the authors will argue for "demand-side" actions that *increase* the subsidy for enrollment. If the subsidy is already too large (e.g. crudely, the subsidy as a proportion of total costs already exceeds the externality as a proportion of total benefits) then these demand-side transfers – even if effective in raising enrollments – are welfare-worsening, as they exacerbate the welfare losses from the existing distortion. This would be like subsidizing driving when there are already net negative externalities to driving over other modes of transport.

No one likes to hear this, but there has never been a single case in which it was empirically demonstrated that the economic externality effects of schooling were sufficient to justify "free schooling" as optimal normative economics – much less free schooling plus. I have written a review of the evidence from aggregate output data on the evidence for a positive spill-over of education on aggregate output (over and above the private wage effect) for the *Handbook of Education Economics* and I fail to find any evidence at all for any positive externality to schooling in output/productivity – much less evidence of one of the magnitude needed to rationalize a full-cost subsidy.

Perhaps the authors could justify an excess of social over private returns of sufficient magnitude, but they have definitely laid out the hardest case – that private returns are universally high and external returns are not quantified at all.

Now, there are many other ways that spending on primary education can be justified – that education is a universal human right, that education

is a merit good, that the demands of political socialization demand universal education. I suspect that the actual positive theory of education has more to do with those arguments than with the economic return. But for the purposes of the present exercise of comparing alternative uses of public funds across sectors one cannot invoke "human rights" as a reason to spend on schooling without a counter of "intrinsic values" of an unchanged natural environment, the "right" to health, and so on, which immediately undermines the value of the exercise and returns the debate to non-quantifiable values and undermines the comparison.

Positive Theory of Schooling

The most interesting part of the most interesting table, table 4.3, in this chapter gets almost no mention. What do you think is the most important reason given for why children who are not in school are not attending school?

The "supply-side" view is that students lack access – cannot get to the buildings. While that may have been true many years ago, and probably remains true in some sparsely populated regions of some very poor countries, it is almost universally not the case now. Based on the survey evidence the authors cite, the average given for "access" is only 1.9 percent in urban areas and only 4.9 percent in rural. This is consistent with evidence from Filmer (2004) on the lack of importance of distance and with the importance of dropout as a cause of the lack of schooling completion (Pritchett 2004).

The "demand-side" view is that children drop out of school because they either (a) have very attractive alternatives or (b) are credit con-

---

[6] Since the authors return again and again to the example of lowered fertility as an external benefit, one has to make it clear that this depends on the view that children are like littering – private benefits which *impose net negative social costs.* I would be happy to see this "children are pollution" position defended as I do not believe it, nor do I believe there is any rigorous evidence for this view, and there are certainly counter-examples (e.g. positive externalities to economic agglomeration).

strained. Let's add up as reasons (saving for later how to parse these responses) the answers "work outside the home" "housework," and "poverty" – we get 32.9 percent in urban areas and 33.9 percent in rural areas. This is at least plausible. But those three *together* are not as big as the most common reason.

The most common reason given why children are not attending school is "lack of interest" – which is 47.3 percent of urban children and 44 percent of rural children not in school. This should set off alarm bells. Ten times as many children are out of school due to "lack of interest" than "lack of access."

Why do these children "lack interest"? This is hugely important to understand, as it also influences how we understand the other responses. If someone says the reason a child is not in school is because they "work outside the home" that may just be begging the question as the question is "why do they work outside the home and not go to school?" While it is obvious that children not in school work more, it is not so obvious how much is cause (children dropout of school in order to work) and how much is effect (once children have dropped out (for other reasons), they work more).

Here is my conjecture. Going to school reveals two things. First, it reveals your adeptness for formal schooling (not some catch-all like "intelligence" but just how good at school you are). Second, it reveals the quality of your school. By the time most children reach, say 14 or 15 years old, many of them "lack interest" in schooling because either (a) they have realized they are not adept at schooling (and hence do not like it) or (b) they realize the school they are in is miserable and/or no learning is going on or both (a) and (b). Rather than the model of parents pulling children out of school to work (in the market or at home) I would suspect the much more common phenomenon is children *pleading* with their parents to not have to go to school.

Just as one poignant historical example, Tyack (1974) tells that Helen Todd, a factory inspector in Chicago interviewed 500 children working in factories (often in dangerous and unpleasant conditions) and asked the question: "If your father had a good job and you didn't have to work, which would you rather do – go to school or work in a factory?" Of those 500 interviewed fully 412 said they would choose factory work – again under the explicitly made premise they did not have to for economic reasons. The researcher recounts asking one 14-year-old girl in one particularly unpleasant factory (lacquering canes, involving heat and turpentine) why she did not go to school and got the response "School is the fiercest thing you can come up against. Factories ain't no cinch, but schools is worst."

I think this is a much more plausible view of much of the dropout phenomena than is "credit constraints." First, strictly speaking, "credit constraints" is not a very good description of the problem. Let us take the authors' numbers seriously that the return to schooling is, say, 8–10 percent. Let us suppose that families in developing countries could borrow at the prime interest rate. The real interest rate in many countries in the world is around 8–10 percent. So given the opportunity to borrow at prime to finance schooling, many households would rationally decline the offer.

Second, if one is arguing that "credit constraints" are the culprit, imagine a pure relaxation of a household's credit constraint – would that money flow into education? Micro-credit programs typically have lending rates between 12 and 20 percent per annum and available returns on investments are profitable at those lending rates. One would need more research, but the range of investments for which households usually borrow when their credit constraint is relaxed have much higher returns (and quicker) returns than the 8–10 percent average return from schooling.

Third, one needs to be clear about the difference between a "credit constraint" and a "budget constraint." The fact that school enrollments are much lower to poorer people does not prove there is a "credit constraint" – consumption of all types of goods is lower for poor people than rich people because of a budget constraint. I would think evidence about the nature of a credit constraint could be inferred from a large temporary windfall. While there is some evidence of credit constraints from the South Africa evidence the authors cite, there is a much more widespread (non-experimental) evidence on the use of remittances of which my reading is that the marginal propensity to spend on education is about what we would expect if education decisions were budget constraint decisions not credit constraint decisions.

Kids who drop out can be classified into two types: (a) those who wish to drop out (and parents do not object) because their individually assessed returns to more schooling are low because either (a1) their personal adeptness is low and/or (a2) the quality of available schools is low (e.g. a flat learning profile, increment to achievement per year is low) and (b) those for whom anticipated returns to schooling are high (adeptness and school quality not the key issues) but (b1) they have very high marginal valuation of non-schooling goods because they are from poor households and/or (b2) they are credit constrained. Alternatively put, people drop out of school because marginal costs are higher than marginal benefits, which could be (a) because benefits are low or (b) costs are high.

The problem with assessing the implications of "demand-side transfers" – particularly conditional cash transfers – is that you are inducing people to return to school who have (or would have) chosen to drop out of school. If one does not distinguish between (a) and (b) reasons it is difficult to believe the returns to this are high, and certainly are not as high as alternative policies that make some attempt to differentiate – suppose by demanding high performance standards.

I realize there are some studies, cited by the authors, in which the returns to compulsory schooling appear to be as high as from chosen schooling, but this is actually a puzzle rather than something we would have expected from an underlying choice-based theory – and I suspect these type of results are quite context-specific to the schooling system (high average and uniform quality) and labor market (credential effects of having vs. not having a high school degree).

The results from Progresa – of impacts on attendance but not on measured learning outcomes – is consistent with the view that marginal students were forced back into marginal schools. If we really believe the returns to school are returns to skills it just cannot be the case that this has the same returns as a child choosing to attend. The argument in the chapter that "dropouts are disproportionately going to be in households facing liquidity constraints" is perhaps true, but dropouts are also likely to disproportionately weaker students and those disproportionately facing poor school options. Even if we add up "poverty" and "working outside the home" this is less than half of "lack of interest" in rural areas from their own "all world" column in table 4.3.

Analysis of Policy Options

A final quick point is that policy options that implicitly consist of a number of policies should be analyzed independently. This is particularly important for two of the demand-side issues considered.

First, with "conditional cash transfer" (CCT) programs it is vital to consider when the intervention is making an existing cash transfer conditional or a large new transfer that is also conditional. In the Progresa case, for instance, the cash transfer (in various forms) existed and hence the incremental step against which the incremental enrollment benefits are to be gauged was the making the transfer conditional – so the bulk of the resources were sunk costs in this calculation. If, however, one is launching a new program then the overall program needs to be justified on its entire range of benefits, of which increased schooling is only one part.

This consideration cuts both ways. For instance, the authors point out that giving a transfer at an age at which all children are in school has low marginal returns – but it may well be that the main objective of the *cash transfer* part of the scheme is to transfer income to poor households and hence excluding households with children in those ages from the design would defeat that purpose. On the other hand, it is going to be very hard to justify CCT on their education benefits alone unless they are very closely targeted to the ages and situations in which the enrollments are very low.

Second, one question with "demand-side" interventions is whether the costs of an additional school place (say, the average cost per child) is added to the cost of the program or not. If it is not, on the argument that class sizes are such that increases in class size have no effect so that the marginal cost of an additional student is zero and therefore only the incremental cost of the inducement need be included, this is essentially combining two policies. One is "increase class size" and one is "induce additional students to attend." If the assumptions that allow the exclusion of marginal costs from the demand-side calculations are correct (there is no net loss from increasing class size) then the "increase class size" reform has enormous economic returns – that, to scale, dwarf anything about the demand side. Perhaps one could argue that the bundle of the policies is cost-effective but we should at least be clear where the action is – if we include the full average cost of an additional school place it must be that these returns are considerably lower (as they have to be lower than for the marginal student who attends with no incentives).

Third, and returning somewhat to the two points above (about market failures and behavioral theories) combined with a sense of the evaluation of policy alternatives, the authors have an embarrassment of riches. According to them iron supplements to secondary school students have a benefit cost ratio of 32. What is the market failure? One can just buy iron supplements on the market, right? So if parents knew of these *private* benefits from a *private* action then they should willingly adopt, right? So consider the policy of "paying for iron supplements": why not a policy of "publicizing the benefits of iron supplements," from which one should get much higher uptake with less cost.

Similarly with something like *balsakhi* tutoring. There is a huge flourishing market for private schools in India (more than half of all children in urban areas are in private schools) and a huge market for tutoring (according to

ASER data even in rural areas roughly a quarter of all children do "tuitions" in addition to school). If you really believe the benefit-cost ratio is 528 – you can get 5,152 in benefits for only $9 – why not the policy of simply making parents aware of the potentially massive benefits of a particular type of tutoring? Is the behavioral model that parents will turn down a low-total-cost hugely *private* benefit intervention? If not, then spreading the information (the creation of which is a public good) should be enormously more cost-effective as a policy than scaling up the program. Alternatively if the essence is the particular model of *balsakhi* tutoring that has these enormous benefits, why not a private business scale-up of this model, as it should be an enormous cash cow?

Conclusion

This is an excellent chapter, laying out all the issues. But, if the game of normative public economics is to be played pitting one sector against another then all should have to play hard and by the same rigorous rules. Those rules are that the counter-factual for evaluating a public sector intervention has to be against the market equilibrium with a plausible behavioral model. On this score, education scores super-high on the *private benefits* which, perhaps paradoxically to most non-economists, actually makes *public policy* advocacy that much harder because one has to ask (a) what is the *magnitude* of the market failures that justify the intervention and (b) if there really are huge *private* benefits to feasible low-cost interventions, why have these not been (or could not have been) scaled up already?

Again, this is particularly relevant in comparisons across sectors when, in some sectors, like global warming, one is dealing *analytically* with an unambiguous pure global public bad (non-rival, non-excludable), in health there are unambiguous public goods (but also private goods), and so forth. So the *technological* cost effectiveness (output per unit input) is only the first step in *economic* cost-effectiveness.

Bibliography

Banerjee, A. and Duflo, E., 2006: Addressing absence, *Journal of Economic Perspectives*, 20(1): 117–32

Chen, S. and Ravallion, M., 2004:How have the world's poor fared since the early 1980s?, World Bank Policy Research Paper, **3340**

Filmer, D., 2004: If you build it, will they come? School availability and school enrollment in 21 poor countries, World Bank Policy Research Working Paper, **3340**

Heckman, J.P. and Klenow, P., 1997: *Human capital policy*, University of Chicago, Chicago

Layard, R., 2005: *Happiness: Lessons from a new science*, Penguin, London

Pritchett, L., 2004: Access to education, chapter 4 in B. Lomborg (ed.), *Global crises, global solutions*, Cambridge University Press, Cambridge

Pritchett, L., 2006: Does learning to add up add up: the returns to schooling in aggregate data, in R. Hanushek and F. Welch (eds.), *Handbook of the Economics of Education*, North-Holland, Amsterdam

Tyack, D.B. 1974: *The one best system: A history of American urban education*, Harvard University Press, Cambridge, MA

Climate Change

GARY W. YOHE, RICHARD S.J. TOL,
RICHARD G. RICHELS, AND
GEOFFREY J. BLANFORD

Multiple changes are occurring simultaneously around the globe at an increasing pace. Energy and resource scarcities have emerged or intensified. Different trade regimes have evolved. New communication and information technologies have exploded into daily life. New human health issues have appeared, and old health issues have, in some cases, been exacerbated. Changes in global climate and associated patterns of extreme weather events must be added to this list, especially for the global poor whose very livelihoods depend directly in many instances on the use of specific natural resources.

The Intergovernmental Panel on Climate Change (IPCC), in its Fourth Assessment Report (AR4, 2007), concluded that a portfolio of mitigation and adaptation will prove to be the best option for dealing with climate change; see IPCC (2007b, 2007c). In this Challenge paper, we provide some additional evidence in support of such a multi-faceted approach – a combination of mitigation, investment in research and development (R&D) on less-carbon-intensive technologies, and adaptation is found to be superior to adopting any single option at the expense of all others. In addition, it will become clear that ignoring climate change would mean that efforts which have been designed to ameliorate many of the other challenges contemplated in the Copenhagen Consensus exercise will ultimately be "swimming upstream" – i.e. expending effort unnecessarily simply to stay in place. We begin in the first section by offering a brief overview of the state of knowledge about the risks of climate change. We rely heavily in this overview on the IPCC's AR4 (IPCC 2007a, 2007b). This built on the second assessment where the observation that global mean temperature is rising was statistically confirmed (IPCC

1995). It also expands on the third assessment, in which increased concentrations of greenhouse gases (GHGs, most notably carbon dioxide) were seen with high confidence to be driving the warming and that climate impacts were beginning to be observed (IPCC 2001). Finally, in its fourth assessment, the IPCC attributed observed impacts to anthropogenic sources (IPCC 2007b) and they reported the statistical significance of anthropogenic sources of warming observed on continental scales (IPCC 2007a).

The second section provides some insight into how two integrated assessment models (MERGE and FUND) were combined to produce emissions and impacts scenarios along which four alternative policy approaches are examined; two appendices provide more detail about the models themselves. These four approaches are described in the third section, including a "Business as usual" baseline (alternatively viewed as a "No climate policy" approach) as well as three more proactive approaches. All are consistent with the Copenhagen Consensus budget constraint in both the near term (the next four years) and the future (in monetary equivalence that recognizes the very long time horizon for any climate policy). We ultimately favor the third pro-active alternative – a combination of R&D, mitigation, and adaptation – because it exploits the complementarity of (1) expanded adaptation to fight increases in infectious disease attributable to climate change combined with (2) straight mitigation efforts (enacted through market-based economic mechanisms) and (3) enhanced investment in R&D for emissions saving and carbon sequestration technologies that are harnessed most effectively by market-based mitigation.

Our results are presented in the fourth section, in terms of benefit-cost ratios that are derived using

236

standard discounting practices. We are pleased that our ultimate policy portfolio of R&D, adaptation, and mitigation produces a ratio that is well above the unity benchmark despite extraordinarily conservative representations of damages (because FUND includes endogenous adaptation in its damage functions) and the extraordinarily confining rules of the Copenhagen Consensus comparison exercise. The fifth section explores some caveats and extensions. Some note the significant value that would accrue if global policy over the next century or so could exploit cost-minimizing flexibility over the timing of mitigation and investment efforts rather than adhering to the Copenhagen Consensus budget constraint each year. Others speak to the implications of accommodating measures of risk aversion and more rapid participation by developing countries in the mitigation portion of our preferred policy approach. Concluding remarks in the sixth section bring our results into context with both the IPCC (2007a, 2007b, 2007c) assessments and the contribution of Cline (2004) to the Copenhagen Consensus exercise. A postscript records our reactions to the rankings that emerged in the spring of 2008 from the Expert Panel as well as subsequent portrayals of the results in the media.

Scoping the Problem

We begin by briefly summarizing the state of knowledge about observed and anticipated climate change and associated impacts as reported in IPCC (2007a, 2007b); observed impacts, anticipated climate trends, and major sources of risk across sectors and continents are all covered in some detail, with ample signposts so that interested readers can find the original sources. We finally conclude this section with a discussion of the value of pursuing mitigation and adaptation together in a portfolio approach designed to reduce risk.

Observed Climate Change through 2007

A robust signal of anthropogenic climate change (particularly warming) has now been detected with strong statistical significance in every continent except Australia; and, even there, the signal is quite evident. This is one of the signature conclusions of the Contribution of Working Group 1 to the AR4, and it is shown here in figure 5.1 (figure SPM.4, IPCC 2007a). The conclusion emerges when the bands of uncertainty from model simulations with and without anthropogenic forcing separate. Notice simply that it is the pink bands that track model trajectories derived from natural and anthropogenic forcing that straddle observed trends in continental average temperature. It follows immediately that thinking about mitigation makes sense for countries on every continent, especially in the long run, because they will all feel the effect of unabated climate change.

Manifestations of these observed and now attributed changes have also been noted across the globe. Tables 5.1 and 5.2, for example, provide, evidence with respect to transient trends in specific physical impacts as well as the incidence of extreme events (tables 10.2 and 10.3, IPCC 2007b). These tables focus on Asia, but they can easily be extended. The references listed can be tracked through chapter 10 of IPCC (2007b), and the take-home message for present purposes is that climate impacts have already been observed in regions where people are most vulnerable not only to climate-related stress, but also the other stresses captured in the Copenhagen Convention's list of challenges.

Anticipated Climate Change Impacts

Warming is generally anticipated across the globe, but it will be unevenly distributed. The general trajectory will depend on global emissions scenarios, to be sure, but impacts will depend critically on local manifestations. Most impact analyses authored since the turn of the century work from one of four alternative SRES development "storylines" that are differentiated along two dimensions (IPCC 2000). The A1 storyline and scenario family describes a future with rapid and globally integrated economic growth with population that peaks in the middle of the century. The A2 storyline envisions the same rapid growth across a

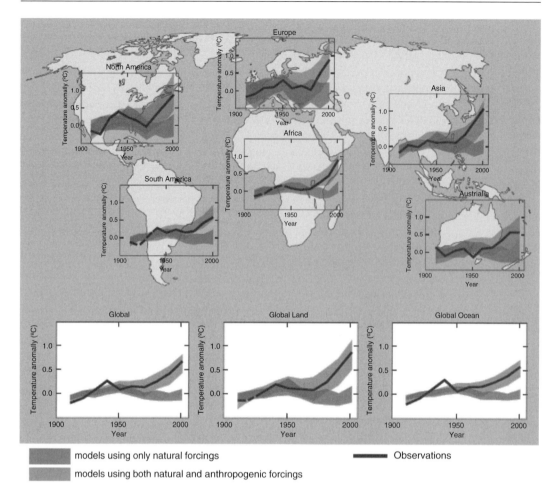

Figure 5.1 *Identifying the signal of anthropogenic warming on continental scales*
Source: Figure SPM.4. Comparison of observed continental- and global-scale changes in surface temperature with results simulated by climate models using natural and anthropogenic forcings. Decadal averages of observations are shown for the period 1906–2005 (black line) plotted against the centre of the decade and relative to the corresponding average for 1901–1950. Lines are dashed where spatial coverage is less than 50 percent. Blue shaded bands show the 5–95 percent range for nineteen simulations from five climate models using only the natural forcings due to solar activity and volcanoes. Red shaded bands show the 5–95 percent, range for fifty-eight simulations from fourteen models using both natural and anthropogenic forcings. (FAO 9.2, Figure 1).

heterogenous world where national and regional economies are self-reliant and preserve their local identities. The B1 and B2 storylines make the same contrasts in the integration dimension, but cast a future where economic activity moves rapidly toward service and information activities with reduced reliance on materials and the introduction of resource efficient technologies. Distributions of emissions scenarios derived from

six different integrated assessment models across the four storylines are displayed in Panel A of figure 5.2 (figure 3.8, IPCC 2007c).

Panel B of figure 5.2 shows results across a collection of global circulation models in terms of global averages and the associated global distributions for three SRES scenarios for the 2020s and the 2090s (figure SPM.6, IPCC 2007a). Significant warming is expected

Table 5.1. Observed past and present trends in climate and climate variability

Region	Country	Change in Temperature	Change in Precipitation	References
North Asia	Russia	2–3°C rise in past 90 years, more pronounced in spring and winter	Highly variable, decrease during 1951–95, increase in last decade	Saveliva, et al., 2000; Peterson et al., 2002; Gruza & Rankova, 2004
Central Asia	Mongolia	1.8°C rise in last 60 years, most pronounced in winter	7.5% decrease in summer and 9% increase in winter	
	Regional mean	1–2°C rise in temperature per century	No clear trend during 1900–96.	Peterson et al., 2002
	Northwest China	0.7°C increase in mean annual temperature from 1961 to 2000	Between 22% and 33% increase in rainfall	
Tibetan Plateau	Regional mean	0.16 and 0.32°C per decade increase in annual and winter temperatures, respectively	Generally increasing in northeast region	Liu and Chen, 2001; Liu et al., 1998; Zhao et al., 2004; Du and Ma, 2004
West Asia (Middle East)	Iran	During 1951–2003 several stations in different climatological zones of Iran reported significant decrease in frost days due to rise in surface temperature	Some stations show a decreasing trend in precipitation (Anzali, Tabriz, Zahedan) while others (Mashad, Shiraz) have reported increasing trends.	Rahimzadeh, 2006
East Asia	China	Warming during last 50 years, more pronounced in winter than summer, rate of increase pronounced in minimum than in maximum temperature	Annual rain declined in past decade in Northeast and North China, increase in Western China, Changjiang River and along southeast coast	Hu et al., 2003; Zhai et al., 1999; Zhai and Pan, 2003
	Japan	About 1.0°C rise in 20th century, 2 to 3°C rise in large cities	No significant trend in the 20th century although fluctuations increased	Japan Meteorological Agency, 2005; Ichikawa, 2004
	Korea	0.23°C rise in annual mean temperature per decade. Increase in diurnal range	More frequent heavy rain in recent years	Jung et al., 2002; Ho et al., 2003
South Asia	India	0.68°C increase per century, increasing trends in annual mean temperature, warming pronounced during post monsoon and winter	Increase in extreme rains in northwest during summer monsoon in recent decades, lower number of rainy days along east coast	Lal, 2003; Lal et al., 2001; Kripalani et al., 1996; Singh and Sontakke, 2002
	Nepal	0.09°C per year in Himalayas and 0.04°C in Terai region, more in winter	No distinct long-term trends in precipitation records for 1948–1994	Shrestha et al., 2000; Bhadra, 2002
	Pakistan	0.6 to 1.0°C rise in mean temperature in coastal areas since early 1900s	10 to 15% decrease in coastal belt and hyper arid plains, increase in summer and winter precipitation over the last 40 years in northern Pakistan	Farooq and Khan, 2004

Table 5.1. (continued)

Region	Country	Change in Temperature	Change in Precipitation	References
	Bangladesh	An increasing trend of about 1°C in May and 0.5°C in November during the 14-year period for 1985–1998	Decadal rain anomalies above long term averages since 1960s	Mirza and Dixit, 1997; Khan et al., 2000; Mirza, 2002
	Sri Lanka	0.016°C increase per year between 1961–90 over entire country, 2°C increase per year in central highlands	Increase trend in February and decrease trend in June	Chandrapala and Femando, 1995
SE Asia	General	0.1–0.3°C increase per decade reported between 1951–2000	Decreasing trend between 1961 and 1998; Number of rainy days have declined throughout SE Asia.	Manton et al., 2001
	Indonesia	Homogeneous temperature data were not available	Decline in rainfall in southern and increase in northern region.	Manton et al., 2001; Boer and Faqih, 2004
	Philippines	Increase in mean annual, maximum and minimum temperatures by 0.14°C between 1971–2000	Increase in annual mean rainfall since 1980s and in number of rainy days since 1990s; increase in inter-annual variability of onset of rainfall	Cruz et al., 2005, PAGASA, 2001.

Table 5.2. Observed changes in extreme events and severe climate anomalies

Country/Region	Key Trend	Reference
Intense Rains and Floods		
Russia	Increase in heavy rains in western Russia and decrease in Siberia; Increase in number of days with more than 10mm rain; 50 to 70% increase in surface runoff in Siberia	Gruza *et al.*, 1999; Gruza and Rankova, 2004; Izrael and Anokhin, 2001; Ruosteenoia *et al.*, 2003
China	Increasing frequency of extreme rains in western and southern parts including Changjiang river, and decrease in northern regions; More floods in Changjiang river in past decade; More frequent floods in Northeast China since 1990s; More intense summer rains in East China; Severe flood in 1999; 7-fold increase in frequency of floods since 1950s	Zhai and Pan, 2003; Zhai, 2004; Zhai *et al.*, 1999; Ding and Pan, 2002
Japan	Increasing frequency of extreme rains in past 100 years attributed to frontal systems and typhoons; Serious flood in 2004 due to heavy rains brought by 10 typhoons; Increase in maximum rainfall during 1961–2000 based on records from 120 stations	Kajiwara *et al.*, 2003; Isobe, 2002; Kawahara and Yamazaki 1999; Kanai *et al.*, 2004
South Asia	Serious and recurrent floods in Bangladesh, Nepal and Northeast states of India during 2002, 2003 and 2004; A record 944 mm of rainfall in Mumbai, India on 26–27 July 2005 led to loss of over 1000 lives with loss of more than US$250 millions; Floods in Surat, Barmer and in Srinagar during summer monsoon season of 2006; May 17, 2003 floods in southern province of Sri Lanka were triggered by 730 mm rain	India Meteorological Department, Reports, 2002–06; Department of Meteorology, Sri Lanka, 2003
Southeast Asia	Increased occurrence of extreme rains causing flash floods in Vietnam; landslides and floods in 1990 and 2004 in the Philippines, and floods in Cambodia in 2000	FAO, 2004a; Tran Viet Lien *et al.*, 2005; Cruz *et al.*, 2005; FAO/WFP, 2000; Environment News Service, 2002
Droughts		
Russia	Decreasing rain and increasing temperature by over 1°C have caused droughts; 27 major droughts in 20th century have been reported	Golubev and Dronin, 2003; Izrael and Sirotenko, 2003
Mongolia	Increase in frequency and intensity of droughts in recent years; Droughts in 1999–2002 affected 70% of grassland and killed 12 million livestocks	Batima, 2003
China	Increase in area affected by drought has exceeded 6.7 M ha since 2000 in Beijing, Hebei Province, Shanxi Province, inner Mongolia and North China; Increase in dust storms affected area	Zhou, 2003; Chan *et al.*, 2001; Yoshino, 2000, 2002
South Asia	50% of droughts associated with El Niño; Consecutive droughts in 1999 and 2000 in Pakistan and NW-India led to sharp decline in water tables; Consecutive droughts between 2000 and 2002 caused crop failures, mass starvation and affected ~11 million people in Orissa; Droughts in NE-India during summer monsoon of 2006	Webster *et al.*, 1998; Lal, 2003; India Meteorological Department Report, 2006
Southeast Asia	Droughts normally associated with ENSO years in Myanmar, Laos, Philippines, Indonesia and Vietnam; Droughts in 1997–98 caused massive crop failures and water shortages and forest fires in various parts of Philippines, Laos and Indonesia	Duong Lien Chau, 2000; PAGASA, 2001; Kelly *et al.*, 2000; Glantz, 2001
Cyclones/Typhoons		
Philippines	On an average 20 cyclones cross the Philippines Area of Responsibility with about 8–9 land fall each year; with an increase of 4.2 in the frequency of cyclones entering PAR during the period 1990–2003	PAGASA, 2001

Table 5.2. (continued)

Country/Region	Key Trend	Reference
China	Number and intensity of strong cyclones increased since 1950s; 21 extreme storm surges in 1950–2004 of which 14 occurred during 1986–2004	Fan and Li, 2005
South Asia	Frequency of monsoon depressions and cyclones formation in Bay of Bengal and Arabian Sea on the decline since 1970 but intensity is increasing causing severe floods in terms of damages to life and property	Lal, 2001; Lal, 2003
Japan	Number of tropical storms has two peaks, one in mid 1960s and another in early 1990s, average after 1990 and often lower than historical average	Japan Meteorological Agency, 2005

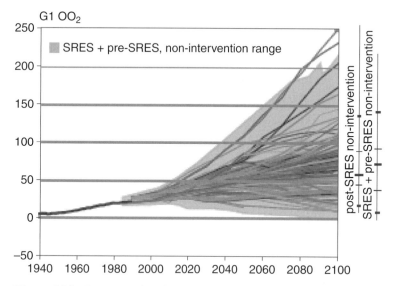

Figure 5.2A *Emissions distributions over time across the four SRES storylines of economic development*

Note: *The two vertical bars on the right extend from the minimum to the maximum of the distribution of scenarios: they also indicate the 5th, 25th, 50th, 75th, and 95th percentiles of the distributions for 2100 for post-SRES non-intervention runs as well as the full collection of runs available through 2007.*
Source: *Figure 3.8 (IPCC 2007c).*

everywhere, but especially in the northern latitudes. The 2–5° warming patterns expected across Asia and Africa by the 2080s along the higher-emissions scenarios A1B and A2 are, perhaps, most troubling because they will impact the very people who experience stress from the other challenges. Indeed, even the B1 scenario would push temperatures 2.5° higher toward the end of this century.

The discussion thus far has focused attention on what we know about the physical manifestations of climate change, with only passing mention to the activities that support human welfare. Tables 5.3 and 5.4 correct this omission by replicating the summary tables for major sectors and major regions, respectively, from AR4 (tables 20.8 and 20.9, IPCC 2007b). All of the entries in both tables were selected by the author teams of the respective chapters to illustrate key vulnerabilities selected by applying the criteria identi-

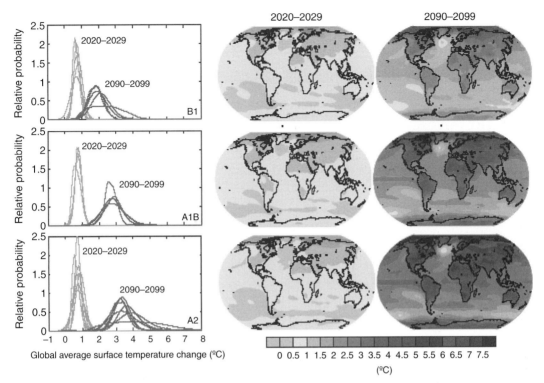

Figure 5.2B *Projections of surface temperatures for the 2020s and 2090s*
Source: Source: Figure SPM.6. Projected surface temperature changes for the early and late twenty-first century
relative to the period 1980–1999. The central and right panels show the AOGCM multi-model average projections
for the B1 (top). A1B (middle), and A2 (bottom) SRES scenarios averaged over the decades 2020–2029 (centre)
and 2090–2099 (right). The left panels show corresponding uncertainties as the relative probabilities of estimated
global average warming from several different AOGCM and Earth System Model, of Intermediate Complexity
studies for the same periods. Some studies present results for only a sub-set of the SRES scenarios, or for various
model versions. Therefore the difference in the number of curves shown in the left panels is due only to differences
in the availability of results [Figures 10.8 and 10.28].

fied in chapter 19 of IPCC (2007b). They are, in short, impacts that are important for human welfare, and references back to those chapters are indicated in the table notes.[1] The criteria used in the selection process included magnitude, rate, timing, and persistence. Where possible, the entries identify both a threshold calibrated to change in global mean temperature and a quantitative measure calibrated in the most appropriate metric. The time dimension along different scenarios, including mitigation scenarios, is reflected by the bars at the top of table 5.3.

The real message to be drawn from these data is one of uncertainty. No temperature threshold that might be subjectively judged as the lower bound of "dangerous climate change" can be guaranteed by even the most stringent of mitigation policies. It follows that adaptation designed to cope with the additional stress imposed by climate change (across many of the other challenge topics of the Copenhagen Consensus exercise) is an absolute imperative. Moreover, we are currently committed to roughly another 0.6°C of warming regardless of efforts to reduce future greenhouse gas emissions; speaking about

[1] The various chapters of the Working Group II report are available before their publication by Cambridge University Press on the IPCC website: www.ipcc-wg2. org/index.html.

Table 5.3. Examples of projected impacts, by sector

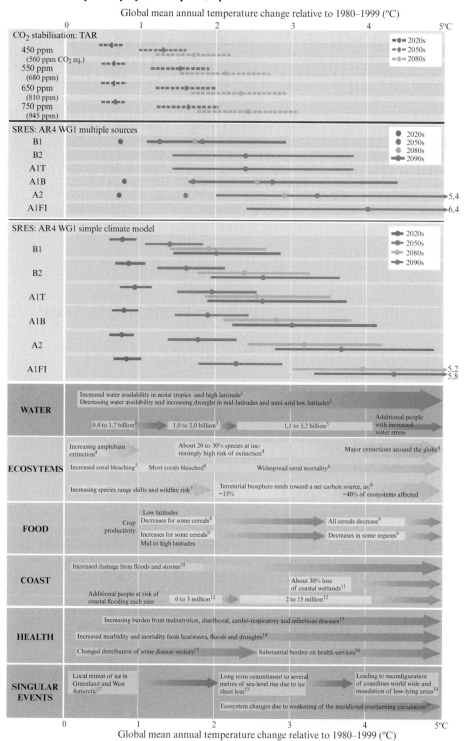

Examples of global impacts projected for changes in climate (and sea level and atmospheric CO₂ where relevant) associated with different amounts of increase in global average surface temperature in the 21st century. This is a selection of some estimates currently available. All entries are from published studies in the chapters of the Assessment. Edges of boxes and placing of text indicate the range of temperature change to which the impacts relate. Arrows between boxes indicate increasing levels of impacts between estimations. Other arrows indicate trends in impacts. All entries for water stress and flooding represent the additional impacts of climate change relative to the conditions projected across the range of SRES scenarios A1FI, A2, B1 and B2. Adaptation to climate change is not included in these estimations. For extinctions, "major" means ~40 to ~70% of assessed species.

The table also shows global temperature changes for selected time periods, relative to 1980–1999, projected for SRES and stabilisation scenarios. To express the temperature change relative to 1850–1899, add 0.5°C. More detail is provided in Chapter 2 [Box 2.8]. Estimates are for the 2020s, 2050s and 2080s, (the time periods used by the IPCC Data Distribution Centre and therefore in many impact studies) and for the 2090s. SRES-based projections are shown using two different approaches. Middle panel: projections from the WGI AR4 SPM based on multiple sources. Best estimates are based on AOGCMs (coloured dots). Uncertainty ranges, available only for the 2090s, are based on models, observational constraints and expert judgement. Lower panel: best estimates and uncertainty ranges based on a simple climate model (SCM), also from WGI AR4 (Chapter 10). Upper panel: best estimates and uncertainty ranges for four CO₂-stabilisation scenarios using an SCM. Results are from the TAR because comparable projections for the 21st century are not available in the AR4. However, estimates of equilibrium warming are reported in the WGI AR4 FOR CO₂-equivalent stabilisationᵃ. Note that equilibrium temperatures would not be reached until decades or centuries after greenhouse gas stabilisation.

Sources: 1, 3.4.1; 2, 3.4.1, 3.4.3; 3, 3.5.1; 4, 4.4.11; 5, 4.4.9, 4.4.11, 6.2.5, 6.4.1; 6, 4.4.9, 4.4.11, 6.4.1; 7, 4.2.2, 4.4.1, 4.4.4 to 4.4.6, 4.4.10; 8, 4.4.1, 4.4.11; 9, 5.4.2; 10, 6.3.2, 6.4.1, 6.4.2; 11, 6.4.1; 12, 6.4.2; 13, 8.4, 8.7; 14, 8.2, 8.4, 8.7; 15, 8.2, 8.4, 8.7; 16, 8.6.1; 17, 19.3.1; 18, 19.3.1, 19.3.5; 19, 19.3.5

ᵃ *Best estimate and likely range of equilibrium warming for seven levels of CO₂-equivalent stabilisation from WGI AR4 are: 350 ppm, 1.0°C [0.6–1.4]; 450 ppm, 2.1°C [1.4–3.1]; 550 ppm, 2.9°C [1.9–4.4]; 650 ppm, 3.6°C [2.4–5.5]; 750 ppm, 4.3°C [2.8–6.4]; 1,000 ppm, 5.5°C [3.7–8.3] and 1,200 ppm, 6.3°C [4.2–9.4].*

adaptation can therefore no longer be interpreted as "giving up on the problem."

Many of the bars in tables 5.3 and 5.4 highlight risks that will be born by the planet's most vulnerable – those who face declining opportunities to sustain subsistence born of higher temperatures and increased water stress. Tables 5.5 and 5.6 translate these vulnerabilities into global and regional estimates along representative scenarios for the 2080s; they replicate tables 20.4 and 20.5 in IPCC (2007b). While the precise numbers depend on climate futures and assumptions about adaptation and carbon dioxide fertilization (not to mention the specific global circulation model employed to represent future climate change), it is clear that future impacts depend most critically upon future development choices. For example, impacts calibrated in human lives are greatest along the A2 scenario, not because climate change would be most severe in that case, but because there would be more people on the planet.

Anticipated Climate Change Impacts on Agriculture

As can be gleaned from tables 5.3–5.6, vulnerability to climate risk is not uniform across the planet. Two explanations come to mind. On the one hand, as shown in figure 5.2, climate change itself is not uniformly distributed. In addition, vulnerability depends on socioeconomic factors that determine exposure, sensitivity, and adaptive capacity on a site-by site basis. To explore the ramifications of this diversity, consider the impact of climate change on cereals. Parry *et al.* (2005) superimposed these yield relationships onto geographically explicit representations of climate change to produce maps that show the relative changes in yield across the globe. Their findings for cereal yields in the 2080's are reflected here in figure 5.3 (figure 5, Parry, *et al.* 2005). Unabated climate change produces significant yield reductions across Africa and much of southern Asia even though gains are anticipated elsewhere. It follows that measures of global aggregates might show modest changes in overall productivity and thereby mask significant geographic dispersion. This disparity can, as well, be amplified by local climate factors that are not adequately captured in climate model outputs.

Comparing Adaptation and Mitigation

It is now widely accepted that mitigation alone is not enough to solve the climate problem; that was one of the major messages of tables 5.3 and 5.4. Nor will adaptation alone be sufficient. Even together, they may not be sufficient

Table 5.4. Examples of projected impacts, by region

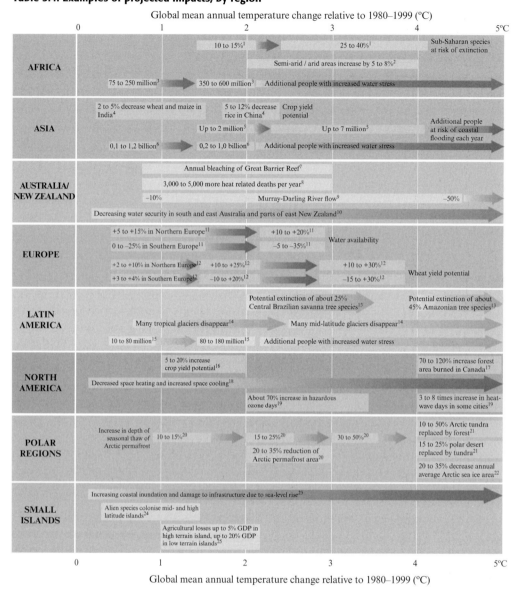

Global mean annual temperature change relative to 1980–1999 (°C)

Examples of regional impacts. See caption for Table 20.8.

Sources: **1**, 9.4.5; **2**, 9.4.4; **3**, 9.4.1; **4**, 10.4.1; **5**, 6.4.2; **6**, 10.4.2; **7**, 11.6; **8**, 11.4.12; **9**, 11.4.1, 11.4.12; **10**, 11.4.1, 11.4.12; **11**, 12.4.1; **12**, 12.4.7; **13**, 13.4.1; **14**, 13.2.4; **15**, 13.4.3; **16**, 14.4.4; **17**, 5.4.5, 14.4.4; **18**, 14.4.8; **19**, 14.4.5; **20**, 15.3.4, **21**, 15.4.2; **22**, 15.3.3; **23**, 16.4.7; **24**, 16.4.4; **25**, 16.4.3

to avoid dangerous interference and associated significant damages. These points are illustrated in Panels A and B of figure 5.4 for 2050 and 2100. Replicated from Yohe *et al.* (2006) and IPCC (2007b), both figures are based on

the intermediate A2 SRES emissions scenario assuming climate sensitivity turns out to be high. The regional distributions reflect climate impacts, calibrated in temperature change, for each country averaged across results derived

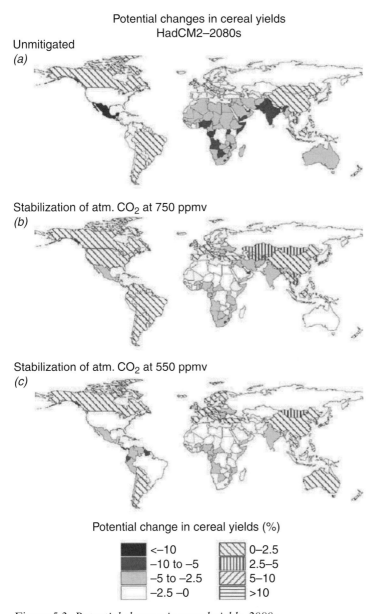

Figure 5.3 *Potential changes in cereal yields, 2080s*
Source: Changes in national cereal crop yields by the 2080s under three different emissions scenarios – (a)
unmitigated (IS92a), (b) S750 and (c) S550.

from a collection of global circulation models. The top left panels depict the global distribution of a vulnerability index without any specific climate policy intervention. The top right panels show the implications of improving adaptive capacity so that, by 2100, developing countries achieve levels that are typical of developed countries at the turn of the twenty-first century. Notice the improvement almost everywhere, but particularly in China, in 2050; notice, as well, that climate change overwhelms even enhanced adaptive capacity by 2100.

Table 5.5. Global-scale climate impacts by 2080

	Climate and socio-economic scenario			
	A1FI	A2	B1	B2
Global temperature change (°C difference from the 1961–1990 period)	3.97	3.21 to 3.32	2.06	2.34 to 2.4
Millions of people at increased risk of hunger (Parry et al., 2004); no CO_2 effect	263	551	34	151
Millions of people at increased risk of hunger (Parry et al., 2004); with maximum direct CO_2 effect	28	−28 to −8	12	−12 to +5
Millions of people exposed to increased water resources stress	1256	2583 to 3210	1135	1196 to 1535
Additional numbers of people (millions) flooded in coastal floods each year, with lagged evolving protection (Nicholls, 2004)	7	29	2	16

Note: change in climate derived from the HadCM3 climate model. Impacts are compared to the situation in 2080 with no climate change. The range of impacts under the SRES A2 and B2 scenarios represents the range between different climate simulations. The figures for additional millions of people flooded in coastal floods assumes a low rate of subsidence and a low rate of population concentration in the coastal zone.

Table 5.6. Regional-scale climate impacts by 2080

	Population living in watersheds with an increase in water-resources stress (Arnell, 2004)				Increase in average annual number of coastal flood victims (Nicholls, 2004)				Additional population at risk of hunger (Parry et al., 2004)[1] Figures in brackets assume maximum direct CO_2-enrichment effect			
	Climate and socio-economic scenario:											
	A1	A2	B1	B2	A1	A2	B1	B2	A1	A2	B1	B2
Europe	270	382–493	233	172–183	1.6	0.3	0.2	0.3	0	0	0	0
Asia	289	812–1197	302	327–608	1.3	14.7	0.5	1.4	78 (6)	266 (−21)	7 (2)	47 (−3)
North America	127	110–145	107	9–63	0.1	0.1	0	0	0	0	0	0
South America	163	430–469	97	130–186	0.6	0.4	0	0.1	27 (1)	85 (−4)	5 (2)	15 (−1)
Africa	408	691–909	397	492–559	2.8	12.8	0.6	13.6	157 (21)	200 (−2)	23 (8)	89 (−8)
Australasia	0	0	0	0	0	0	0	0	0	0	0	0

Note: change in climate derived from the HadCM3 climate model. Impacts are compared to the situation in 2080 with no climate change. The range of impacts under the SRES A2 and B2 scenarios represents the range between different climate simulations. The figures for additional millions of people flooded in coastal floods assumes a low rate of subsidence and a low rate of population concentration in the coastal zone.
[1] Analysis of project results carried out for this table.

The bottom two panels bring mitigation into the mix by tracing the implications of pursuing a least-cost path to limiting atmospheric concentrations of greenhouse gases to 550 parts per million (ppm) in carbon dioxide (and so less restrictive than restricting to 550 ppmv in carbon dioxide equivalents). The left panel captures only the effects of mitigation. Some improvement is observed in 2050, but the capacity to adapt is overwhelmed in most regions by 2100, despite mitigation effort. Comparing these results with the middle panel of figure 5.3 is also instructive. Parry et al. (2005) show mitigation having significant benefit for cereal yields in the 2080s. Their

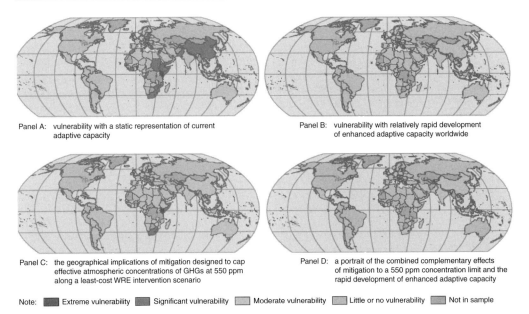

Panel A: vulnerability with a static representation of current
           adaptive capacity

Panel B: vulnerability with relatively rapid development
           of enhanced adaptive capacity worldwide

Panel C: the geographical implications of mitigation designed to cap
           effective atmospheric concentrations of GHGs at 550 ppm
           along a least-cost WRE intervention scenario

Panel D: a portrait of the combined complementary effects
           of mitigation to a 550 ppm concentration limit and the
           rapid development of enhanced adaptive capacity

Note: ■ Extreme vulnerability   ■ Significant vulnerability   ▨ Moderate vulnerability   □ Little or no vulnerability   ▦ Not in sample

Figure 5.4A *Geographical distribution of vulnerability, 2050 (A2 emissions: high climate sensitivity)*
Notes: Extreme vulnerability Significant vulnerability Moderate vulnerability Little or no vulnerability Not in sample
Source: Figure 1: Geographical distribution of vulnerability in 2050 along an A2 emissions scenario with a climate sensitivity of 5.5°C.

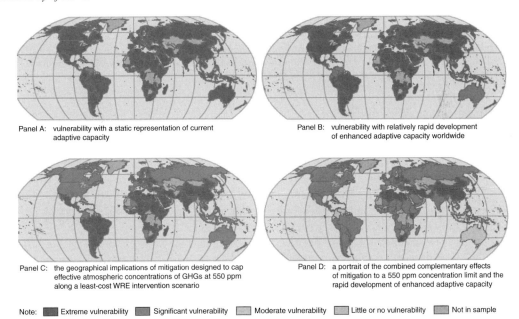

Panel A: vulnerability with a static representation of current
           adaptive capacity

Panel B: vulnerability with relatively rapid development
           of enhanced adaptive capacity worldwide

Panel C: the geographical implications of mitigation designed to cap
           effective atmospheric concentrations of GHGs at 550 ppm
           along a least-cost WRE intervention scenario

Panel D: a portrait of the combined complementary effects
           of mitigation to a 550 ppm concentration limit and the
           rapid development of enhanced adaptive capacity

Note: ■ Extreme vulnerability   ■ Significant vulnerability   ▨ Moderate vulnerability   □ Little or no vulnerability   ▦ Not in sample

Figure 5.4B *Geographical distribution of vulnerability, 2100 (A2 emissions: high climate sensitivity)*
Notes: Extreme vulnerability Significant vulnerability Moderate vulnerability Little or no vulnerability Not in sample
Source: Figure 3: Geographical distribution of vulnerability in 2100 along an A2 emissions scenario with a climate sensitivity of 5.5°C.

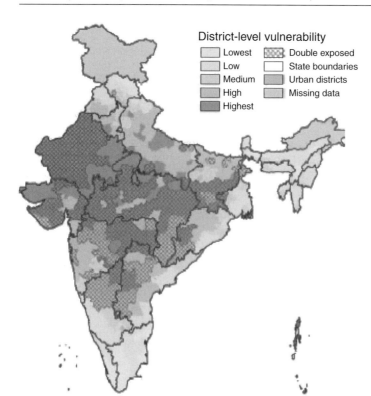

Figure 5.5A *Geographical distribution across India of stress from climate change and globalization*
Source: Figure 17.2. Districts in India that rank highest in terms of vulnerability to: (a) climate change and (b)
import competition associated with economic globalization, are considered to be double exposed (depicted with
hatching). Adapted from O'Brien et al. (2004).

results do not, however, reflect the high climate sensitivity embodied in the current figures. Nor do they aggregate multiple climate stresses felt across multiple sectors. Finally, the right panels of the two panels in figure 5.4 add enhanced adaptive capacity to the mix. Again, there is some additional improvement in 2050, and the combination of the two approaches is most effective. Unfortunately, vulnerability to climate change remains nearly everywhere by 2100.

Finally, it is important to note a widely held belief that communities are most vulnerable when they face multiple stresses (IPCC 2007b). In these cases, the sum of vulnerabilities from individual stresses falls short of total vulnerabilities because each source amplifies the risks associated with all of the others. Panel A of

figure 5.5 (from IPCC 2007b) illustrates this point explicitly for India; there are areas which feel stress not only from climate change but also from globalization. Panel B, derived from a close reading of chapter 9 of IPCC (2007b) shows that the multiple manifestations of climate change, itself, can be sources of multiple stress; it follows that vulnerability to climate risk, *per se*, can be amplified.

Modeling Emissions and Climate Impact Scenarios

Emissions Scenarios

Six emissions scenarios were constructed using the MERGE model (see appendix A, p. 270,

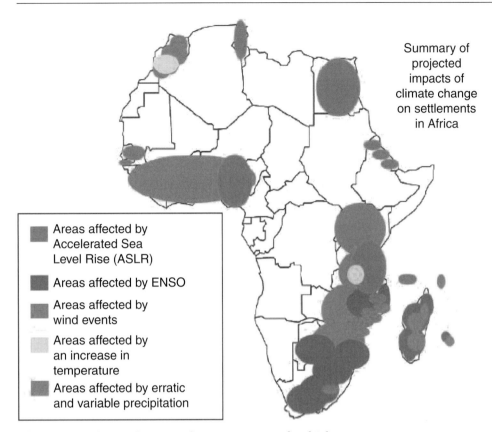

Figure 5.5B *Climate change can be its own source of multiple stress*

for a description of the model). In three scenarios, a pessimistic set of assumptions about new energy technology was applied, termed "technology as usual" (TAU). In the other three scenarios, an accelerated technology path (ATP) was applied to represent the results of a targeted R&D investment program. For each technology scenario, the model was used to evaluate three alternative emissions control strategies. The first is a reference case in which there is no price on carbon dioxide emissions. The reference scenario is used as a baseline for measurement of the costs and benefits of the emissions' mitigation effort entailed in the other two scenarios. However, note that there are two distinct reference cases, since the availability of new technology will affect deployment and emissions even in the absence of a carbon price.

Two mitigation scenarios were considered in which policy constraints place an implicit price on carbon emissions. Many mitigation studies assume full "where" and "when" flexibility to assure that a given stabilization target is achieved at least cost. That is, emissions are reduced where and when it is least costly to do so, subject to a long-term constraint on total greenhouse forcing in the atmosphere. Because this idealized framework would be very difficult to implement in reality given the current lack of

[2] Additional experiments could be conducted in which non-Annex B countries begin to participate in mitigation efforts by mid-century. Their participation would have little effect on the cost of meeting prescribed global emissions targets because, under the assumption that annual expenditure on climate policy is constrained by the annual budget imposed by this Copenhagen Consensus exercise, only modest mitigation effort would be undertaken. For deeper cuts in emissions, participation of rapidly growing developing countries will be crucial.

strong institutions for international and intergenerational cooperation, we conduct most of our analysis along a second-best mitigation scenario with much more limited flexibility. In this case, for example, only nations in annex B of the UNFCCC undertake emissions reductions (i.e. developing countries face a zero shadow price of carbon through 2100), and they do so according to annual emissions targets rather than toward a long-term stabilization goal.[2] Costs of mitigation are measured in terms of the deadweight loss in the economy as emissions reduction requirements force shifts to more expensive energy options. The discussion in this chapter focuses primarily on the limited mitigation scenario, but an understanding of the potential cost reductions of a flexible policy implementation is important nonetheless; a brief discussion of the difference is offered in the fifth section below.

In light of the Copenhagen Consensus project goal of measuring the benefits of a fixed expenditure, the specific targets for the mitigation scenarios were chosen heuristically so that the total cost of mitigation effort reached the desired amount. While the focus of the current exercise is the allocation of $75 billion over the next four years, coping with climate change will involve a long-term commitment to policy. Therefore the "budget" for this analysis assumes expenditure at an equivalent fraction of global GDP for the entire twenty-first century and beyond. Using the MERGE model's assumptions about economic growth and discounting, this amounts to a net present value of $800 billion, or roughly 0.05 percent of global GDP on an annual basis. It is our view that abandoning a four-year climate response program in 2012 is not an approach worth pursuing. That said, by focusing on the limited mitigation scenario, we do not assume an optimal allocation of these funds over time. We do not, therefore, commit future generations to underwriting decisions taken at the beginning of the twenty-first century. Instead, we

assume that the funds will be expended as they become available and thereby approximate, at least roughly, the muddling-through approach that would likely be forthcoming.

Because the emissions scenarios consider both mitigation effort and investment in R&D for new technology, the total budget is shared between these two activities. In the TAU scenarios, all $800 billion is allocated to the mitigation effort. Consistent with estimates from the Electric Power Research Institute (EPRI 2007), we assume an additional funding requirement of $50 billion, largely in the next few decades at a pace of $2.5 billion per year, for the R&D component. Thus in the ATP scenarios, only $750 billion is allocated to the mitigation effort. Note that in the optimal mitigation scenarios, most expenditure is delayed until future periods, whereas in the limited case, the annual emission targets necessitate an approximately constant annual rate of expenditure. Table 5.7 summarizes the six emissions scenarios.

Impacts Scenarios

Each emissions scenario was evaluated using the climate and impacts modules in the FUND model (see appendix B, p. 273, for a description of this model). First using a central, "best-guess" value for climate sensitivity (3.0°C) and later considering a range of values, FUND calculates a temperature trajectory associated with the given emissions path.[3] Market and non-market damages from climate impacts are calculated as a regional function of temperature increase. These calculations include economically efficient reactive adaptations, so they represent net impacts inclusive of the costs of adaptation. In addition to R&D investment and mitigation effort, we examine a third response activity – adaptation designed to confront specific health impacts more aggressively and proactively. This activity occurs *ex post* of climate changes and allows amelioration of their negative impact. Thus for selected emissions scenarios, damages are calculated with and without adaptation policies. The NPV cost of additional adaptation is $1 billion, much smaller than the cost of the other

[3] Climate sensitivity is a measure of the increase in equilibrium global mean temperature that would be associated with a doubling of the atmospheric concentration of carbon dioxide from pre-industrial levels – roughly 550–560 ppmv vs. 280 ppmv.

Table 5.7. MERGE emissions scenarios

Scenario	Policy description	Global emissions (billion tons CO2)		
		2000	2050	2100
TAU reference	No policy	24	44	67
TAU cost-effective mitigation	Global participation Stabilization at 5.2 W/m^2	24	43	20
TAU limited mitigation	Annex B only Emissions constant at 2010 levels	24	38	55
ATP reference	No policy	24	32	48
ATP cost-effective mitigation	Global participation Stabilization at 4.5 W/m^2	24	29	14
ATP limited mitigation	Annex B only Emissions reduced by 0.275 percent per year from 2010 levels	24	30	37

two activities. It is therefore not separated from the mitigation/R&D budget, but it is important to realize that it does not handle the wide range of impacts (particularly from extreme events and abrupt change) that are highlighted in the first section above.

Scoping the Proposed Responses

As suggested in the second section, we explore four responses within a synthesis of two integrated assessment models: FUND and MERGE. A review of the details of the models, as provided in the two appendixes, indicates that we thereby exploit the relative strengths of both (the technological detail of MERGE on the mitigation side and the geographic and sector diversity of FUND on the impacts and adaptation side). While the focus of the Copenhagen Consensus exercise is how to spend $75 billion over the next four years, it is also important to reiterate that coping with climate change will involve a long-term commitment to policy. We therefore examine a collection of approaches that builds toward a portfolio of adaptation and mitigation options that expend up to an equivalent proportion of global GDP over the next century. The present value (PV) of these expenditures, allocated either to fund a specific set of mitigation initiatives orchestrated over time to maintain

annual consistency with the Consensus budget constraint, or to underwrite the economic deadweight loss associated with those initiatives, amounts to $800 billion in constant 2000 dollars. This sum will always represent the cost side of our benefit-cost calculations.

The four responses that are the focus of our analysis are listed below; figure 5.6 shows their effects on emissions and temperature increases over time assuming a central climate sensitivity of 3°C.

(1) **"Business as usual" – the TAU reference case in table 5.7**
Inaction on the climate front is certainly an option that must be taken seriously. Climate change has never been favored in the Copenhagen Consensus process; moreover, global policy through the end of 2007 seems to have been long on rhetoric but short on action. Analyzing this case, in terms of both global aggregates and underlying regional and sectoral manifestations, also provides the baseline scenario against which potential benefits of the other policy options can be measured consistently and coherently.

(2) **"Mitigation only (annual)" – the TAU limited mitigation case in table 5.7**
Allocate the full budget each year from now until 2100 to underwriting the economic deadweight loss of mitigation with limited

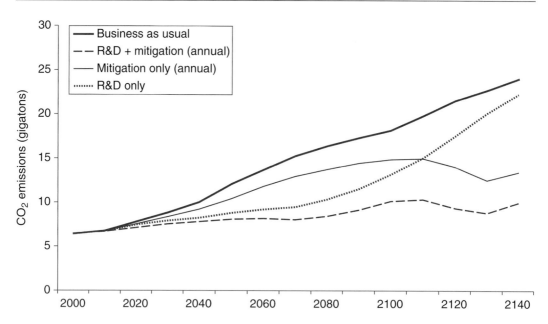

Figure 5.6 *Emissions (gigatons per year of CO₂) for alternative policies, 2000–2140*

flexibility. Economic instruments (e.g. a carbon tax) are employed to reduce emissions of greenhouse gases each year only up to the point where the annual economic cost matches the annual budget. In this option, there is no additional R&D investment in technology and no proactive adaptation (above the endogenous adaptation captured in FUND).

(3) **"R&D + mitigation (annual)" – the ATP Limited mitigation case in table 5.7**
Invest immediately in R&D to make new technologies for emission reduction and carbon sequestration available for commercialization and dissemination. These technologies complement near-term mitigation and eventually increase the efficiency of longer-term efforts to reduce emissions, but they are most effective only when offered in the context of market-based mitigation instruments. R&D investment into viable carbon capture and storage technologies would, for example, be useless if the price of carbon were zero; and the likelihood of significant market penetration of advanced solar technologies would be limited without

a carbon price signal that escalated over time. There is no additional adaptation, and mitigation is undertaken with limited flexibility (since annual expenditures for either R&D or deadweight loss coverage is limited annually to 0.05 percent of then-current global GDP).

(4) **"Adaptation + R&D + mitigation (annual)" – a portfolio approach**
This approach will be a combination of approach (3) with an additional focus on adaptations designed to ameliorate additional specific health impacts caused by climate change and related to some of the other Copenhagen Consensus Challenge topics. Additional expenditures covered within the specified budgetary limits underwrite responses to the likelihood that climate change will exacerbate health hunger problems worldwide. These expenditures cover only the increments attributed to climate change, but they are not inclusive (in the sense of covering all of the potential impacts laid out in the first section). Since these initiatives will not reduce the pace of climate change their cost, taken

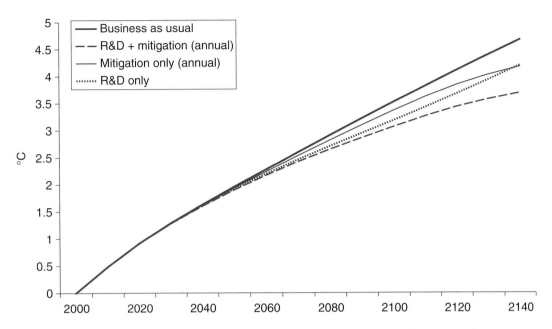

Figure 5.7 *Increases in global mean temperature °C above 2005 levels) for alternative policies, 2000–2140*
Note: The Adaptation only case is not shown because it has no effect on emissions and therefore tracks the Business as usual case.

in isolation, would reflect the degree to which the "Do-nothing" alternative would make it more difficult to make progress in other contexts. Comparisons with earlier approaches will illustrate the value of responding to the climate problem with a variety of approaches that simultaneously "fight the disease" and "treat the symptoms." As reported in the IPCC AR4, mitigation and adaptation should both be more effective given the complementary effects of the other, and we confirm this expectation.

Figure 5.6 shows the trajectories of CO_2 emissions for four cases. Figure 5.7 does the same for increases in global mean temperature, as derived from MERGE. Notice that the "Business as usual" trajectory puts the increase in global mean temperature at approximately 3.5°C in 2100 (relative to the 2007 level); we are, therefore, depicting a baseline that tracks roughly into the middle of the distribution of temperature increase reported in figure 5.2 for the A2 "storyline."

The first three correspond to options (1), (2), and (3) above. Adaptation is not depicted, since adaptation has no effect on emissions or temperature, so option (4) tracks along option "R&D + mitigation" trajectory. R&D alone is also depicted simply to show that enhanced technology produces a lower trajectory in the near to medium term even without other policy intervention (this is the "ATP Reference" case in table 5.7). It is included for reference, because enhanced technology will make any level of expenditure on mitigation more effective. It is not included as a stand-alone climate policy option, however, because emissions and temperatures rise at an increasing rate over the long term to the point that both eventually exceed the "Mitigation only" alternative.

For reference, it is important to note that mitigation constrained to the annual Copenhagen Consensus budget requires imposing a persistent

Table 5.8. Policies, costs, benefits, and B/C ratios (BCR)

Scenario	Description	NPV costs	NPV benefits	BCR
(2) Mitigation only (annual with partial "where flexibility")	Spend $18 billion per year (rising with economic growth) on mitigation	$800 billion	$685 billion	0.9
(3) R&D + Mitigation (annual with partial "where flexibility")	Accelerated phase-in of carbon-extensive energy technologies, followed by mitigation with a fixed annual budget	$800 billion	$1717 billion	2.1
(4) Adaptation + R&D + Mitigation (annual with partial "where flexibility")	As above plus purchase bednets and oral rehydration therapy for children in LDCs affected by climate change	$800 billion	$2129	2.7

real shadow price of $20 per ton of CO_2 (by some means – a carbon tax or a carbon permit market, for example) with or without R&D investment in enhanced carbon saving or sequestering technology. A more effective policy would show a real carbon price that increased over time at roughly the rate of interest. In either case, enhanced technology makes mitigation more effective in reducing emissions and slowing the rate of increase in global mean temperature.

Results

Table 5.8 shows the summary NPV statistics from our analysis of the three policy intervention alternatives described above, relative to the "do-nothing" alternative. Because of the long time horizon over which impacts from climate change will emerge, the choice of discount rate is critical for the cost-benefit calculus. In these calculations, the rate used to translate the benefits of avoided damages in the distant future to a present value is the same as the rate describing the return on a risk-free investment in the economic model, that is, the marginal productivity of capital. This symmetry implies that society is indifferent between incurring $1 million worth of damages in 2100 and losing an amount today that would be worth $1 million in 2100 if it were invested today.

Of course, many arguments have been made in support of a variety of alternative perspectives on the appropriate discounting approach for climate change. For a review of these arguments, see Portney and Weyant (1999). The discount

rate used here starts at 5 percent in 2007 and falls gradually to 4 percent by the end of the century. This choice is consistent with observed and anticipated market rates of return, where the decline reflects investors becoming more "patient" over longer time horizons. It is important to note, as well, that this discount rate is not based on the low pure rate of time preference employed by Cline (2004) in his contribution to the earlier Copenhagen Consensus exercise. Moreover, since this discount rate was used for computing optimal investments in energy technologies in MERGE and in adaptation in FUND, changing the discount rate would change the reference scenario as well as the various policy scenarios.

Figure 5.8 displays the underlying trajectories of climate damages, including the "Business as usual" option, in terms of percentage of global GDP. Figure 5.9 converts these estimates into benefits (damages forgone) for the three intervention alternatives. Notice that figure 5.8 shows the potential for beneficial climate change, at least as measured by global aggregate economic activity, through the first half of this century. This observation is one explanation for why the benefit-cost ratio reported in table 5.8 for "Mitigation only" can be less than unity (though the ratio climbs above unity for the "ATP cost-effective" case from table 5.7; this point will be discussed in the fifth section below). Conversely, the fact that our modeling allows for the possibility that modest climate change could be beneficial early in this century adds credibility to benefit-cost ratios of the three other interventions, especially the two which

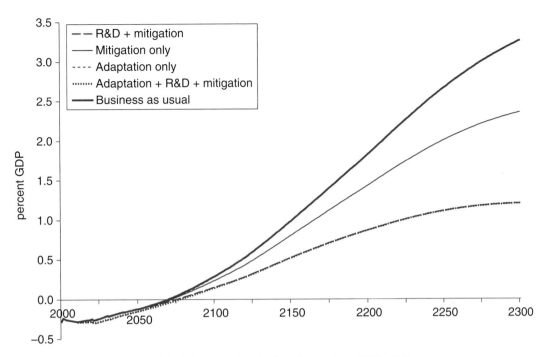

Figure 5.8 *Trajectories of global damages for the five alternatives, 2000–2300*

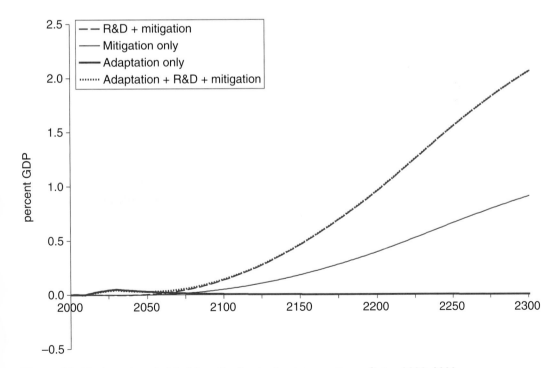

Figure 5.9 *Trajectories of global benefits for the five intervention policies, 2000–2300*

involve R&D-enhanced mitigation.

Turning now to options (3), and (4) ("R&D + mitigation (annual)" and "Adaptation + R&D + mitigation (annual)," respectively), notice that coupling mitigation constrained by an annual expenditure with early investment in R&D for enhanced carbon saving and carbon sequestering technology brings the benefit-cost ratio for mitigation up to 2.1, even with a discount rate set to mimic the return to private capital. The policy portfolio described in option (4) brings the power of enhanced R&D and expanded investment in adaptation together to raise the benefit-cost ratio of annual mitigation to 2.7. Both adaptation and R&D complement constrained mitigation efforts to such a degree that the associated benefit-cost ratio increases by a factor of 3 without spending an additional dime.

We do not consider adaptation alone as a response option, essentially because doing just adaptation addresses only the "symptoms" and not the "disease." We do, though, concentrate on the separable value of adaptation in the next section on caveats. We also do not address R&D as a stand-alone response, because mitigation policy and R&D go hand in hand. The smaller the cost differential is between the carbon-free technology and the carbon-venting technology, the smaller the tax (either implicit or explicit) needed to bring climate-friendly solutions into the marketplace. Put another way, R&D is most effective only when it is employed as a tool that complements mitigation efforts. It follows that the value of R&D cannot be calculated by manipulating the values recorded in table 5.8 for the policy portfolios recorded there.

Discussion and Caveats

We offer, in this section, brief discussions of three extensions to our analysis. In the first, we examine the implications of allowing mitigation policy designed in 2008 to be allocated over time so that it maximizes the efficacy of covering the deadweight loss of climate policy with a fund whose discounted value amounts to $800 billion.

This compensation over time is assumed to be financed by an annuity that derives its backing from annual contributions that are consistent with the Copenhagen Consensus budget constraint. Adding this "when flexibility" raises the benefit-cost ratio of "Mitigation only" to 3.3. A second subsection depicts some regional implications of all of the options; the third subsection adds uncertainty about climate sensitivity to the mix. In this case, the ratio of the expected net benefits of "Mitigation only" with "when flexibility" more than doubles to an extremely respectable 6.9.

Improved Cost Effectiveness with "When Flexibility"

All of the alternatives discussed above recognize, at least implicitly, the difficulty in imposing policies that would allocate mitigation efforts efficiently over time – "when flexibility" in the vernacular of the climate literature that is designed to minimize the discounted cost of achieving a given stabilization target. Achieving a concentration target imposes, at least to a first approximation, a limit on cumulative emissions over the very long term. Intuition born of the economics of exhaustible resources can, therefore, be applied to envision emissions trajectories that would minimize the discounted cost of achieving the target and thereby set an efficiency benchmark against which other, second-best approaches, can be judged. Again to a first approximation, the shadow price of carbon in this intertemporally optimal framework would be determined by an initial "scarcity rent" that increases roughly at the rate of interest over time.

Figure 5.10 offers insight into the significance of the optimal time path by adding the trajectory of global benefits for a "Mitigation only" option that allows for "when flexibility." As shown in the first row of table 5.9, cost-minimizing "when flexibility" financed over time by an $800 billion annuity, funded by the same expenditure pattern as in the budget-constrained case, would increase the benefit-cost ratio of "Mitigation only" from 0.9 to 3.3. Table 5.7 suggests how this dramatic effect is possible. Adding "when

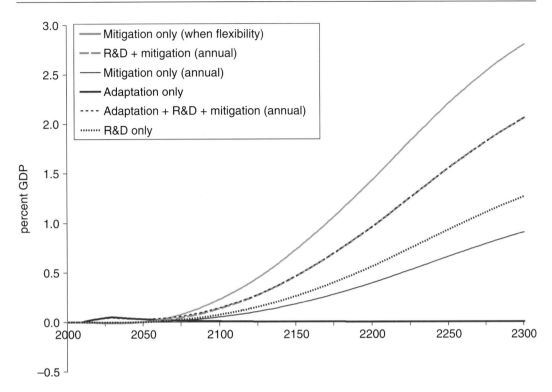

Figure 5.10 *Trajectories of global benefits for the alternative approaches, 2000–2300*

Table 5.9. Costs, benefits, and B/C ratios for dynamically flexible mitigation

Mitigation only (when flexibility added)	Spend an annuity of $18 billion (rising with economic growth) on mitigation	$800 billion	$2676 billion	3.3
Mitigation only (when flexibility added with uncertainty)	As above, but with uncertainty about the climate sensitivity	$800 billion	$5483 billion	6.9

flexibility" to the policy design means reducing emissions from 67 gigatons of CO_2 to 20 gigatons per year in 2100 (as compared with 55 gigatons for "Mitigation only" without intertemporal flexibility). This more stringent control late in the century is "financed" by savings generated from curtailed emissions reductions through the middle of the century (43 gigatons per year in 2050 is only a 2 percent reduction from 44 gigatons along the "Business as usual" alternative, while the 38 gigaton target for "Mitigation only (annual)" represents an almost 20 percent reduction).

While an optimal allocation of mitigation effort over time may be unrealistic, we emphasize that a mitigation scenario in which essentially no incremental effort is taken on over time is also unlikely. In order to achieve the stated UN goal of stabilizing GHG concentrations, at any meaningful level, emissions reductions far beyond those depicted in our annual expenditure budget scenarios must be realized. Moreover, as further mitigation becomes necessary, costs over time will inevitably rise, and it will become increasingly important to include the participation of developing countries.

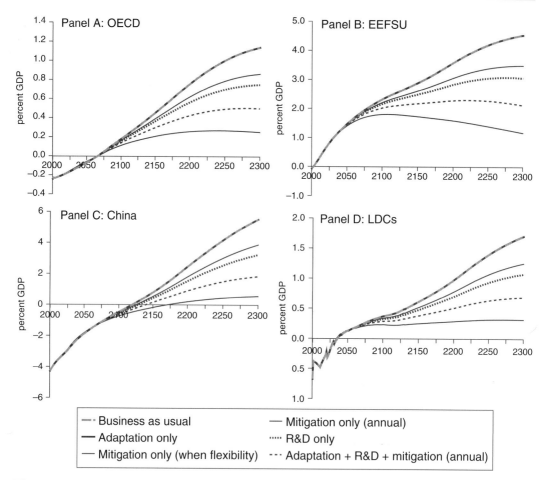

Figure 5.11 *Trajectories of estimated market damages, 2000–2300*

Regional Diversity

It is important to note that the impacts of climate change, and thus the benefits of any policy approach, are not evenly distributed across the globe. Figure 5.11 shows that market damages for four regional aggregates: The OECD, Eastern Europe and the Former Soviet Union, China, and the world's Least Developed Countries (LDCs). Notice that market damages are actually negative (i.e. modest climate change is beneficial) across much of the world early in this century for this level of regional disaggregation, at least. This does not mean that the market impacts of small increases in temperature are positive everywhere,

of course. Moreover, if the country-by-country impacts within each region were aggregated using population-based equity weights, then the positive aggregates would shrink quickly and turn negative earlier. Finally, it is also important to note that the trajectories of market impacts for our five policy options do not deviate significantly from one another until late in this century.

Non-market damages shown in Figure 5.12 for the same four regions show a decidedly different pattern. All begin with positive values (i.e. negative impacts). They continue higher almost immediately for China and the OECD, but they fall precipitously for Eastern Europe and the former Soviet Union and LDCs. This is again

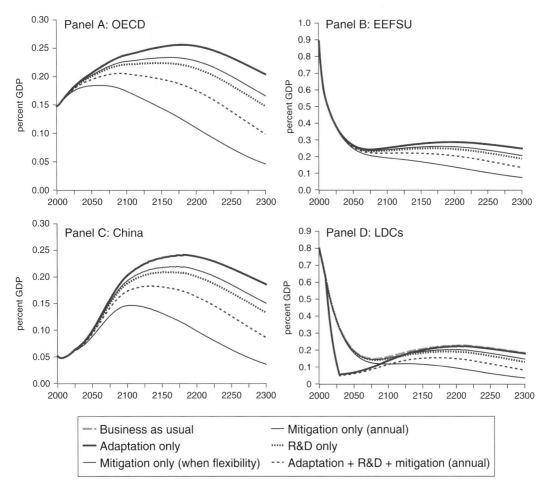

Figure 5.12 *Trajectories of estimated non-market damages, 2000–2300*

because development can diminish many non-market impacts (e.g. health impacts) by improving adaptive capacity. Notice, as well, that the implications for non-market impacts of our five alternative policies deviate from one another much earlier than for market impacts.

Adaptation

Our fourth option includes limited but proactive investment in adaptation designed to confront the marginal increase in vulnerability to infectious disease that could result from climate change. We do not, however, include adaptation as a stand-alone policy, because its scope is too limited. It does nothing to slow the pace of climate change, and so it does nothing to address the myriad of non-health impacts noted in the first section. Indeed, we included it in the final portfolio primarily to illustrate the cost (in terms of another topic of the Copenhagen Consensus exercise) of ignoring climate change.

Recall that figure 5.9 displayed the underlying trajectories of benefits (damages forgone) for the three intervention alternatives plus adaptation alone. Because adaptation has no effect on climate change, however, the trajectories for the options that include adaptation are difficult

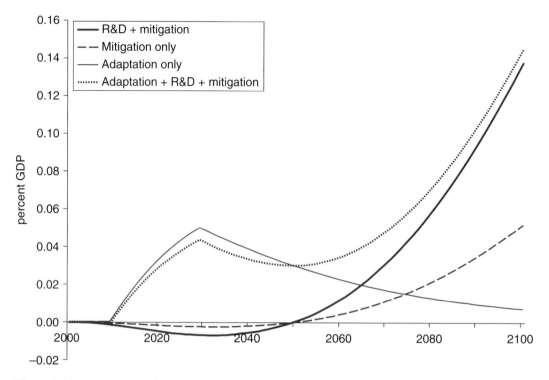

Figure 5.13 *Trajectories of global benefits for the four intervention policies, 2000–2100*

to distinguish from their baselines. Figure 5.13 shows that this observation is an artifact of the scale that defines the vertical axes of the earlier figures. Since the benefits for adaptation appear almost immediately (though they depreciate quickly over time as development overtakes the need for these specific adaptations in the health sector), focusing on a shorter time frame allows some differentiation of the cases with and without mitigation to emerge.

We calculated that efforts to promote global health would, if that course of inaction were chosen, see something on the order of $409 billion in additional disease-related cost and the alternative of spending additional $1 billion expenditure on bednets and oral rehydration therapy. We did, however, calculate the benefits of adaptation alone intervention. Finding that spending $1 billion on bednets and oral rehydration therapy would produce $409 billion, we produced a benefit-cost ratio that was an order of magnitude higher than that of Jamison *et al.*

(2008, see chapter 3 in this volume) This in itself is evidence that efforts to improve health worldwide in the absence of climate policy would, essentially, be "swimming upstream" against a current that was accelerating as the pace of climate change accelerated.

To be clear, an investment of $500 million per annum in malaria control would save 7.5 million DALYs. This amounts to $67/DALY, even though Jamison *et al.*'s table 3A.1 has a $2–$24/DALY ratio. We used $17/DALY, so we are in the latter range. We assume that a $10 bednet protects a family of four (two adults and two children) for four years (www.nothingbutnets.net), and that there are 15 DALYs per malaria death. If we had used $67/DALY, our benefit-cost ratio would fall from 300 to 200, because diarrhea dominates malaria in our analysis. Diarrhea kills more children (www.who.int/healthinfo/bod/en/index.html), and its worst consequences can be prevented with cheap, low-tech interventions (Laxminirayan *et al.* 2006). Note that Jamison *et al.* do not consider diarrhea. The difference between the high benefit-cost ratio of Jamison *et al.* and our very high benefit-cost ratio is therefore explained by the valuation of the benefits rather than the estimate of the costs. Jamison *et al.* assume a benefit of $1,000/DALY, or $15,000 per malaria death. In FUND, mortality is valued by the value of a statistical life rather than by the value of a year of life lost. The assumed value is 200 times *per capita* income, which in SSA implies $100,000 per malaria death. The survey of Viscusi and Aldy (2003) suggests that our US value of a statistical life is on the low side, while our income elasticity is too high; together, this argues for a value of statistical life in Africa that is decidedly higher than $100,000. Viscusi and Aldy (2003) also show that the value of a statistical life is not at all proportional to age (even when controlling for wealth differences) as implicitly assumed by putting a value on a DALY.

More to the point of the portfolio approach described in Option (4), however, it is important to note from table 5.8 that total net present benefits of mitigation, R&D investment, *and* this limited adaptation is $2,129 billion, while the comparable discounted sum for mitigation and R&D is only $1,717 billion. Even this limited adaptation adopted in the context of a complete portfolio adds more than it would, taken alone. Put another way, the sum of the PVs of mitigation, R&D, and limited adaptation taken individually is smaller than the PV of all three taken together, even when subjected to the constraints of the Copenhagen Consensus spending rules.

Uncertainty

All of our analysis was built upon the foundation of a deterministic baseline, and so it misses the uncertainties that cloud our ability to foresee precisely the consequences of climate change and climate policy. While we did not conduct a full investigation of the implications of all of the profound sources of uncertainty, we did examine the implications of one of the most important – the value assumed for climate sensitivity. Figure

5.14 provides an indication of the significance of this uncertainty by showing a cumulative distribution of NPV for the "Mitigation only" alternative with "when flexibility" (the TAU Cost-effective mitigation case in table 5.7) for climate sensitivities ranging from 0.5°C to 7.5°C. The probabilities assigned across this range are consistent with published estimates.[4]

It is clear that low sensitivities can produce negative NPVs for mitigation (i.e. the $800 billion discounted cost is higher than the discounted value of damages avoided) even assuming a cost-minimizing allocation over time in the implementation of climate policy. It is equally clear, though, that high climate sensitivities produce high damages (catastrophic damages for some regions at 7.5°C) and thus high benefits for the $800 billion investment in mitigation alone. The second row of table 5.9 shows that the expected PV of this option climbs to more than $5 trillion to support a benefit-cost ratio of nearly 7. Figure 5.15 shows the intertemporal distribution of benefits by depicting cumulative distributions of benefit estimates for selected periods across the range of climate sensitivities; the positive ranges essentially disappear as the future unfolds.

Geo-Engineering

As noted earlier, scientists and policymakers are beginning to appreciate that responding to climate change will require a portfolio of actions. The portfolio typically includes mitigation to slow the rate of climate change, adaptation to limit the damages that do occur, R&D on new and improved low carbon energy technologies to manage the costs of the transition to a low carbon world, and a reduction in scientific uncertainty so that we can make better-informed decisions in the future. This chapter has focused

---

[4] The probabilities assigned to climate sensitivities 0.5°C, 1.5°C, 2.5°C, 3.5°C, 4.5°C, 5.5°C, 6.5°C, and 7.5°C were 0.5 percent, 26.7 percent, 32 percent, 20.4 percent, 10.8 percent, 5.5 percent, 2.7 percent, and 1.4 percent, respectively. They are consistent with estimates drawn from IPCC (2007a) by Weitzman (2007) and characterized by a lognormal distribution with $\mu = 1.0$ and $\Sigma = 0.5$.

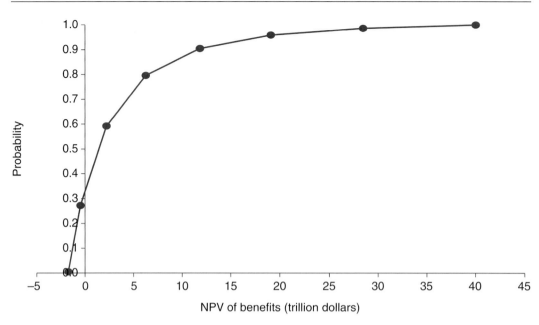

Figure 5.14 *Cumulative distribution of MPV of mitigation only for the "when flexibility" benchmark*

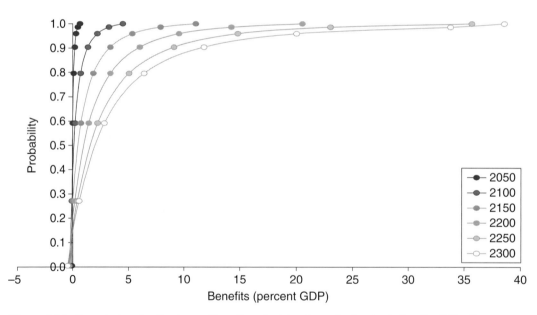

Figure 5.15 *Cumulative distributions of benefits of mitigation only for the "when flexibility" benchmark, 2050–2300*

on the first three. An oft-ignored, albeit controversial, alternative is geo-engineering – for example, changing the albedo of the atmosphere to reflect incoming light back into space to offset potential warming. This occurs naturally through volcanic eruptions or anthropogenically through the release of sulfur dioxide into the atmosphere when burning coal to generate electricity. Before policymakers can decide if geo-engineering should play a role along with other alternatives (for instance, if global warming occurs even more rapidly than the high end of the IPCC scenarios), a major research effort is needed to understand the efficacy, costs, and potential consequences and risks of the various geo-engineering strategies that have been proposed, and to identify other potential alternative strategies.

While there is a danger that some may interpret geo-engineering research as a "quick fix" to the climate problem that obviates critical adaptation and mitigation efforts, a failure to conduct careful research into different alternatives would be an even bigger risk. At present, it appears that geo-engineering could be simple, cheap, and effective, and that it could be unilaterally deployed by a medium-sized country. There is, however, the chance of unintended consequences which, if the geo-engineering project were designed to "make a dent" in the climate problem, could occur on very large scales. For instance, geo-engineering could reverse global or regional warming, but leave ocean acidification unaffected and accelerate changes in precipitation patterns. Articles on geo-engineering by well-respected researchers are beginning to appear in the literature, but a more extensive research program in this area is needed.

Concluding Remarks

Table 5.8 reports our summary results, and all but the "Mitigation only (annual)" option show benefit-cost ratios in excess of 1. In our assessment of the options, we conclude that the portfolio approach – option (5) that combines annual mitigation, investment in carbon-saving and carbon sequestering technology, and additional adaptation measures to combat potential increases in the incidence of some infectious disease – is the best choice. It has the highest benefit-cost ratio (a respectable 2.7), and it takes advantage of the complementarity noted in IPCC (2007b). To be more specific, calculations of the benefits derived from investing in R&D alone suggest that the total benefits of the portfolio approach that expends $50 billion on R&D (in PV) and $750 billion on "investment" in mitigation (also in PV) exceeds the sum of "Mitigation only" and "R&D only" by a discounted value of $50 billion. In other words, the complementarity works to allow R&D essentially to pay for itself when it is embedded (as it would be) in a more extensive mitigation program. Moreover, adding adaptation to the portfolio increases its discounted value (relative to adaptation alone) by another $3 billion. Clearly, each option makes the other options more effective i.e. the benefits of implementing the portfolio approach exceed the sum of their individual benefits.

Table 5.9 meanwhile shows that exploiting "when flexibility" and recognizing the uncertainty in our understanding of the climate system both significantly increase the value of climate policy. As noted above, implementing "when flexibility" is difficult. It implies committing future generations to intertemporal allocations in ways that could be very difficult to enforce. On the other hand, though, uncertainty about the climate system is profound, and the risk-reducing value of climate policy should not be ignored. Since table 5.9 suggests that the expected benefit of policy would double even if only current uncertainty about the climate sensitivity were included, we conclude that the true benefit-cost ratio of the portfolio approach described in option (5) is easily above 5.

While we certainly acknowledge that climate policy is a very long-term enterprise for which a four-year time horizon is virtually meaningless, it is important to recognize that our results are different from those reported to the 2004 Copenhagen Consensus exercise by Cline (2004) in many ways. We do not, for example, conduct an optimization exercise – i.e. we do not rely on "when flexibility" and we model only partial "where flexibility" in allocating expenditures that are fixed annually by the prescribed budget. Our mitigation policies do not, therefore, imply increasingly stringent interventions with carbon taxes that begin in the hundreds of dollars per ton and climb from there; ours climb quickly to a level near $20 per ton of CO_2 and stay there (in real terms) almost indefinitely. This is, of course, a manifestation of our interpretation of the Copenhagen Consensus budget constraint and our characterization of anticipated annual decisions to mitigate – i.e. the specific second-best world within which we chose to operate.

It is also important to emphasize that we did not employ a very low discount rate in an effort to produce acceptable benefit-cost ratios. Much like Stern *et al.* (2006), Cline (2004) used a pure rate of time preference that approximates zero. Both analyses thereby adopted a prescriptive approach that elevates the discounted value of future benefits significantly. Yohe (2006) reports that, as a result, almost 50 percent of the climate damages reported by Stern *et al.* (2006) lie in the post-2200 residual; and Nordhaus (2006) confirms the concerns raised by Manne (2004) when he demonstrates that applying such a discount rate across the economy would lead to a 10 percentage point increase in the saving rate (almost 50 percent increase) and reduce present consumption by about 13 percent (or $4 trillion). There are, of course, sound economic reasons for adopting a low discount rate for public investment when the private return to capital is taxed and public investment complements private investment (see Ogura and Yohe 1977, for example). Perhaps a case can be made that public investment in mitigation would complement private investment across a global economy, but that is beside the point here. By adopting a more conventional approach to discounting, we avoid all of this controversy.

We must admit, though, that none of our policies "solves the climate problem" in the sense of moving temperature increases significantly to the left in tables 5.3 and 5.4. Indeed, figure 5.7 shows that our portfolio option lowers the tempera-

ture increase from roughly 3.5°C to something slightly below 3.0°C in 2100. We do not, therefore, achieve the results reported for long-term stabilization at the top of table 5.3. Nor do we reduce significantly the risk of some profound impacts across all sectors and in all regions that many might consider "dangerous" in the parlance of the UN Framework Convention on Climate Change. Cast in that light, especially given the uneven distributions of impacts across regions and within specific populations, therefore, our portfolio proposal must be viewed more as a start that defines near-term policy in the context of a long-term discussion within which the expected benefits exceed tolerable costs by more than a factor of 5. It is, therefore, reassuring that the shadow price for carbon in the mitigation component of our portfolio is in line with estimates of expected cost-minimizing hedging policies reported in, for example, Yohe *et al.* (2004). There, an initial global carbon tax of roughly $10 per ton of CO_2 that would grow predictably and persistently at the rate of interest minimized the expected cost of achieving an as yet undetermined temperature target given a distribution over climate sensitivities of the sort described in the fifth section above. Our tax is twice that, but it remains constant over time; the hedging tax reaches $20 per ton within fifteen years and continues to rise.

In closing, therefore, our results are born of a mainstream economic analysis. They support climate policy with benefit-cost ratios in excess of unity, and they are consistent with responses supporting alternative risk-based approaches.

Postscript

The Copenhagen Consensus exercise asked eight of the world's top economists to examine research on the best ways to tackle ten major challenges that face the world in 2008: Air pollution, conflicts, disease, global warming, hunger and malnutrition, lack of education, gender inequity, lack of water and sanitation, terrorism, and trade barriers. According to the rules, these experts were to consider only the relative benefits and costs of different responses to each challenge proposed by authors of separate "Challenge papers," where estimates on both sides of the equation for each proposal were reported; the papers are collected here. The experts were then asked to create a prioritized list indicating how they thought that the world could most efficiently spend a limited amount of money and thereby do the most good. It is important to note that they were bound by a budget constraint that disallowed the normal conclusion for public investment – move forward as long as benefits exceed costs even if you have to borrow at the applicable rate of interest. As a result, many projects that would improve social welfare were "left on the cutting room floor."

This Challenge paper explored the benefits and costs of four responses to the climate problem: Doing nothing; investing only in mitigation; complementing investment in R&D into low-carbon energy technology with market-based mitigation; and investing in a portfolio of R&D into low-carbon energy, mitigation, and adaptation targeted on the additional stress caused by climate change. The Challenge paper did not recommend investing in R&D as a stand-alone option.

Table 5.8 and figure 5.13 showed comparative results for the last three options *vis-à-vis* doing nothing. As described throughout this chapter, they were all derived from analyses that were constrained severely by a conservative reading of the Copenhagen Consensus rules. To be specific, they involved allocating $800 billion in PV to covering program expense or economic cost through the year 2100; this is because $800 billion is the PV of extending the exercise's $75 billion over four years into something that made sense for a long-term problem like climate change. The mitigation-alone option, for example, would set up a fund from which the Expert Panel could compensate global citizens for economic costs of mitigation that summed to $800 billion in PV, but these compensations were timed to keep each year's cost estimate in line with a constant fraction (0.05%) of global GDP defined by the Consensus rules (that a

total of $75 billion could be expended over the next four years). The first line of table 5.8 shows that discounted benefits of annually constrained mitigation fell short of this cost.

The Expert Panel took note of this result, to be sure, when they ranked mitigation alone at the bottom of their priority list. They were, however, also privy to a set of alternative results for the mitigation-only option; these are the cases described in the fifth section where this initial policy intervention option was evaluated under slightly relaxed interpretations of the Copenhagen Consensus rules. These supplementary estimates are shown in table 5.9. There, for example, it becomes clear that allowing "when" flexibility" (i.e. intertemporal efficiency in the allocation of mitigation effort over time) and subsequently adding risk premia to the calculation of climate damages increased the benefit-cost ratio for an $800 billion investment in mitigation alone to more than 3 and nearly 7, respectively. When the experts rejected mitigation, *per se*, for no other reason than it has a sub-par benefit-cost ratio, they were clearly adopting a very strict and narrow interpretation of the rules.

The second and third rows of table 5.8 make this point, again, by showing the effect of allocating $50 billion of actual expenditure to research into greener technology over the next five or ten years. It follows that only $750 billon could be absorbed by the economic cost of adaptation (in the third row) and mitigation (similarly constrained in terms of annual contributions). The second row indicates how R&D into low-carbon technology increased the effectiveness of the market-based incentives (taxes) designed to mitigate emissions even without including intertemporal efficiency. In this option, R&D into low-carbon sources of energy essentially paid for itself, and total discounted benefits exceeded costs by a factor of about 2.1 under very conservative assumptions about developing country participation. Surprisingly, the Expert Panel ranked this alternative next to last.

It is important to note, in passing, that the difference between the benefits recorded in the first two lines is *not* the economic value of

R&D alone; the benefits recorded in the second line reflect the value of R&D projects when their *adoption, dispersion, and market penetration is encouraged and their relative efficacies are exploited by economic incentives provided by a mitigation policy.*

The last line in table 5.8 adds a modest program of adaptation program to the policy mix – one designed to ameliorate the additional health impacts imposed by climate change in many locations around the world by *taking actions above and beyond those suggested in the Challenge paper on health* (chapter 3 in this volume). This complete portfolio was favored because its benefit-cost ratio fell above 2.7 even with severely constrained mitigation. With this information to hand, the Expert Panel concluded that: "Mitigation only and a combination of mitigation and R&D were given the lowest two rankings by the Expert Panel, due to their very poor benefit/cost ratio. The option including adaptation was discarded, as the adaptation is essentially included in nearly every other option presented to the Copenhagen Consensus. An investment into R&D in low-carbon energy technologies was ranked 14th by the Expert Panel" (for details, see www.copenhagen consensus.com/Default.aspx?ID=788, 2008). The Director of the Consensus exercise has subsequently taken these words to a dangerous extreme in op-ed pieces published around the world (Lomborg 2008a, 2008b, 2008c, for example). He reports that the Expert Panel did not respond by concluding that the world should ignore the effects of climate change. He then builds on a misguided ranking of R&D alone to argue for dramatically increased R&D on low-carbon energy – such as solar panels and second-generation biofuels. He claims that this would solve the problem by 2050 without market-based intervention, and makes no mention of the other more favorable results that were at his and their disposal. He fails to acknowledge that the Challenge paper does not recommend a stand-alone R&D policy. He makes no reference to their unsupportable dismissal of adaptation. He is silent on the difficulty of casting climate change into a constrained benefit-cost structure.

In his words, "Attempts to curb carbon emissions along the lines of the bill now pending [a reference to Lieberman–Warner specifically that applies equally well to any of the alternative federal or regional proposals] are a poor answer compared with other options. The answer is to dramatically increase research and development so that solar panels become cheaper than fossil fuels sooner rather than later. Imagine if solar panels became cheaper than fossil fuels by 2050: We would have solved the problem of global warming, because switching to the environmentally friendly option wouldn't be the preserve of rich Westerners (Lomborg 2008a).

We are very unhappy that the Expert Panel would essentially invent their own policy and support it by inappropriately attributing the increased benefits of the mitigation and R&D portfolio to R&D alone; and we think that Lomborg's statements show how dangerous making such an error in public can be. There is no question that the appropriate policy portfolio will have to rely on developing new technologies to meet growing energy demands and protect the climate. There is no question that substantial investment will be required to develop those technologies and bring them to scale. But funding R&D alone is a non-starter. There is simply no guarantee that it would reduce emissions far enough and fast enough to avert runaway climate change. Our Challenge paper results clearly show what should be obvious: Market-based carbon pricing mechanisms designed to encourage private business to follow suit are an essential component for any climate policy, even one that begins with heavy investment in R&D. Lomborg and his experts, quite simply, ignored the necessity of including market-based systems such as cap and trade to deliver not only the funding, but also the economic incentive for R&D to pay off most effectively. Indeed, they ignored figures 5.6 and 5.7 which show how quickly the value of stand-alone R&D investments would depreciate over time if not complemented by market-based mitigation efforts.

It may be a little strange to see a response to op-ed pieces published in newspapers around the world in an academic publication, but we think that a public response somewhere is absolutely necessary. We admit that the Challenge paper did report that severely constrained mitigation alone would not cover the cost, but that was just the first step in a more thorough analysis that ultimately demonstrated how that fighting climate change can be a sound economic investment even though neither mitigation nor adaptation alone will be enough to "solve" the climate problem. R&D should be encouraged, but only as part of the world's climate change response portfolio to reduce carbon emissions significantly over the next century – i.e. only if applied in combination with other mitigation efforts.

The 2008 edition of the Copenhagen Consensus came at a critical time during the long preparatory run-up to the late 2009 negotiations for the next global warming treaty in Copenhagen. Instead of deliberate deception, discussions leading up to Copenhagen needed clear and accurate portraits of current research. They needed, as well, strong and well-informed political leadership from around the world so that the negotiations could craft emission reduction policies that are based on credible analyses, supported by scientific data and designed to meet the important scientific criteria. Since their acceptance of the Synthesis Report of the Fourth Assessment Report of the IPCC, governments have understood that they are looking for a portfolio of adaptation, mitigation, and research efforts to manage climate risk – an approach that is supported by our results in the Challenge paper.

Appendix A: The MERGE Model

The analysis is based in part on the MERGE model (a **M**odel for **E**valuating the **R**egional and **G**lobal **E**ffects of greenhouse gas reduction policies). MERGE is an intertemporal general equilibrium model. Like its predecessors, the current version is designed to be sufficiently transparent so that one can explore the implications of alternative viewpoints in the greenhouse debate. The current analysis utilizes those sub-models that provide a reduced-form description of the economy, the energy sector, and related emissions of carbon dioxide; the "handoff" to FUND occurs here.

MERGE provides a bottom-up representation of the energy-supply sector. For a particular scenario, a choice is made among specific activities for the generation of electricity and for the production of non-electric energy. Oil and gas are viewed as exhaustible resources. There are introduction constraints on new technologies and decline constraints on existing technologies. Mitigation effort can be simulated by applying constraints on annual emissions levels from participating countries, or by allowing optimal emissions reductions with respect to a long-term stabilization target.

Geographically, the world is divided into nine geopolitical regions: (1) the USA, (2) WEUR (Western Europe), (3) Japan, (4) CANZ (Canada, Australia, and New Zealand), (5) EEFSU (Eastern Europe and the Former Soviet Union), (6) China,

(7) India, (8) OILX (oil-exporting countries), and (9) ROW (the rest of world). Note the OECD (regions (1)–(4)), together with EEFSU, constitute annex B of the UN Framework Convention on Climate Change. The remaining four regions comprise non-annex B. MERGE is calibrated to 2000. Future periods are modeled in ten-year intervals. Hence, the Kyoto Protocol's first commitment period (2008–12) is represented as 2010.[1] All economic values, including technology costs, are reported in US $ of constant 2000 purchasing power.

Table 5A.1 identifies the alternative technologies available for future electricity supply.[2] We assume two electric-generation technology scenarios. The first is a "Technology as usual" (TAU) development path where investment in new technologies continues to follow the reduced-funding path observed over the past three decades. The second scenario involves an accelerated technology path (ATP), where an increased commitment to energy R&D leads to earlier breakthroughs, so that the introduction of advanced technologies occurs decades earlier than it would otherwise.

We assume that existing coal and nuclear power plants are retired during the first half of the twenty-first century according to a schedule consistent with sixty-year plant lifetimes. Existing natural gas assets are assumed to have twenty-year lifetimes, and hydroelectric power is constrained to existing levels. With respect to new fossil-based generation, the model does not distinguish between technologies within a given category, such as between different coal feedstocks, pulverized vs. gasified processes, or the means by which CO_2 is captured in carbon capture and sequestration (CCS) technologies. We assume that the cost of new nuclear generation

---

[1] Conference of the Parties, Kyoto Protocol to the United Nations Framework Convention on Climate Change, Report of the Conference of the Parties, Third Session Kyoto, December 1–10, FCCC/CP/1997/L.7/Add1. www.unfccc.de.

[2] Technology assumptions refer specifically to the USA. Assumptions for other regions are similar but vary in some cases.

Table 5A.1. Electric generation technology assumptions

Technology	ATP description	TAU description
Coal (without CCS)	LCOE* = $57 – $41/MWh Efficiency = 38 percent – 46 percent	*Same as ATP*
Coal with CCS	First available in 2020 LCOE* = $70 – $55/MWh Efficiency = 36 percent – 42 percent Capture rate = 90 percent	Not available until 2060 *Cost and performance as in ATP*
Natural gas (without CCS)	LCOE* = $50 – $70/MWh** Efficiency = 49 percent – 60 percent	*Same as ATP*
Natural gas with CCS	First available in 2020 LCOE* = $84 – $110/MWh** Efficiency = 39 percent – 42 percent Capture rate = 90 percent	Not available until 2060 *Cost and performance as in ATP*
Nuclear (new ALWR***)	First available in 2020 LCOE* = $40 $37/MWh Non-market cost = $10/MWh***	Limited to existing nuclear production levels until 2060 *Cost and availability as in ATP*
Hydroelectric	LCOE* = $40/MWh	*Same as ATP*
Wind	LCOE* = $86/MWh in 2010 LCOE* = $62/MWh in 2050	LCOE* = $86/MWh in 2010 LCOE* = $62/MWh in 2100
Biomass	LCOE* = $86/MWh in 2010 LCOE* = $69/MWh in 2050	LCOE* = $86/MWh in 2010 LCOE* = $69/MWh in 2100
Solar (thermal)	LCOE* = $144/MWh in 2010 LCOE* = $66/MWh in 2050	LCOE* = $144/MWh in 2010 LCOE* = $66/MWh in 2100
Solar (photovoltaic)	LCOE* = $225/MWh in 2010 LCOE* = $81/MWh in 2050	LCOE* = $225/MWh in 2010 LCOE* = $81/MWh in 2100

Notes:
* LCOE refers to full-levelized cost of electricity.
** Assumes reference path for natural gas fuel price. Actual price varies by scenario within the model.
*** ALWR refers to advanced light water reactor. Non-market cost rises with generation share.

has both a market and non-market component (see table 5A.1). The latter, which is calibrated to current usage, rises proportionally to market share and is intended to represent public concerns about environmental risks in the technology and associated nuclear fuel cycle.

MERGE includes three categories of renewable technologies: wind, biomass, and solar (thermal and photovoltaic). The final category of renewables represents the electric backstop technology. The distinguishing characteristics of the backstop category are (1) a zero GHG emissions rate and (2) that, once introduced, it is available at a constant marginal cost. It is intended to represent the fact that we will not run out of energy, but as conventional sources are exhausted there will be more expensive sources waiting in the wings.

Table 5A.2 identifies alternative sources of *non*-electric energy within the model. Oil and gas supplies for each region are divided into ten cost categories, where the higher-cost groups reflect the potential use of non-conventional sources. Coal may be used directly or converted into synthetic fuel liquids (at a large energy and emissions premium). In addition, plug-in hybrid electric vehicles (PHEVs) may be used to offset non-electric energy production for transportation with electric generation. With regard to carbon-free alternatives, the choices have been divided into two broad categories: biofuels refer to low-cost sources such as ethanol from biomass, while the backstop technology represents a high-cost option – for example, hydrogen produced via electrolysis using solar photovoltaics, or hydrogen from thermonuclear dissociation.

Table 5A.2. Non-electric energy technology assumptions

Technology	ATP description	TAU description
Coal (for direct use)	Cost = $2.50/GJ	*Same as ATP*
Petroleum (ten cost categories)	Cost = $5 – $7.25/GJ	*Same as ATP*
Natural gas (ten cost categories)	Cost = $6 – $8.25/GJ	*Same as ATP*
Synthetic (coal-based) liquids	Cost = $8.33/GJ	*Same as ATP*
Biofuels	Cost = $10/GJ	*Same as ATP*
Non-electric backstop	Cost = $25/GJ	*Same as ATP*
Plug-in hybrid electric vehicles	First available in 2010 Cost = $6 – $0/GJ (equivalent to $4000 – $0 per vehicle premium) Efficiency = 69 KWh/GJ (equivalent to 300 Wh/0.03 gallons per mile)	First available in 2050 *Cost and performance as in ATP*

Note: Typically, the energy-producing and energy-consuming capital stock is long lived. In MERGE, introduction and decline constraints are placed on *new* technologies. We assume that the production from new technologies in each region is constrained to 1 percent of total production in the year in which it is initially introduced and can increase by a factor of three for each decade thereafter. The decline rate is limited to 3.5 percent per year for new technologies, but there is no decline rate limit for existing technologies. This is to allow for the possibility that some emission ceilings may be sufficiently low to force premature retirement of the existing capital stock.

The key distinction is that biofuels are in limited supply, but the backstop is available in unlimited quantities at a constant but considerably higher marginal cost.

Turning from the supply to the demand side of the model, we use nested production functions to determine how aggregate economic output depends upon the inputs of capital, labor, electric, and non-electric energy. In this way, the model allows for both price-induced and autonomous (non-price) energy conservation and for interfuel substitution. Since there is a "putty-clay" formulation, short-run elasticities are smaller than long-run elasticities. This increases the costs of rapid short-run adjustments. The model also allows for macroeconomic feedbacks. Higher energy and/or environmental costs will lead to fewer resources available for current consumption and for investment in the accumulation of capital stocks.

Where international trade in emission rights is permitted, regions with high marginal abatement costs can purchase emission rights from regions with low marginal abatement costs.[3] There is also trade in oil and natural gas. Each of the model's nine regions maximizes the discounted utility of its consumption subject to an intertemporal budget constraint. Each region's wealth includes not only capital, labor, and exhaustible resources, but also its negotiated international share in global emission rights.

---

[3] In MERGE, emissions can be limited either directly in each region or by a carbon tax with "lump-sum" recycling of revenue. When the carbon taxes resulting from a particular cap and trade scheme are used as inputs to control emissions, they produce identical regional emissions that were inputs under cap and trade.

Appendix B: The FUND Model

This appendix uses version 2.9 of the *Climate Framework for Uncertainty, Negotiation and Distribution* (*FUND*). Version 2.9 of *FUND* corresponds to version 1.6, described and applied by Tol (1999, 2001, 2002a), except for the impact module, which is described by Tol (2002b, 2002c) and updated by Link and Tol (2004). A further difference is that the current version of the model distinguishes sixteen instead of nine regions. The model considers emission reduction of methane and nitrous oxide as well as carbon dioxide, as described by Tol (2006a). Finally, the model now has sulfur hexafluoride (SF_6) and a newly calibrated radiative forcing code. A full list of papers, the source code, and the technical documentation for the model can be found on line at ww.uni-hamburg.de/Wiss/FB/15/Sustainability/fund.html.

Essentially, *FUND* consists of a set of exogenous scenarios and endogenous perturbations. The model distinguishes sixteen major regions of the world – the USA, Canada, Western Europe, Japan and South Korea, Australia and New Zealand, Central and Eastern Europe, the former Soviet Union, the Middle East, Central America, South America, South Asia, Southeast Asia, China, North Africa, SSA, and Small Island States. The model runs from 1950 to 2300 in time steps of one year. The prime reason for starting in 1950 is to initialize the climate change impact module. In *FUND*, the impacts of climate change are assumed to depend on the impact of the previous year, thus reflecting the process of adjustment to climate change. Because the initial values to be used for the year 1950 cannot be approximated very well, both physical and monetized impacts of climate change tend to be misrepresented in the first few decades of the model runs. The twenty-second and twenty-third centuries are included to assess the long-term implications of climate change. Previous versions of the model stopped at 2200.

The period 1950–2000 is used for the calibration of the model, which is based on the *IMAGE* 100-year database (Batjes and Goldewijk 1994). The scenario for the period 2010–2100 is based on the MERGE scenario. The 2000–10 period is interpolated from the immediate past (http://earthtrends.wri.org), and the period 2100–2300 extrapolated.

The scenarios are defined by the rates of population growth, economic growth, and autonomous energy efficiency improvements as well as the rate of decarbonization of the energy use (autonomous carbon efficiency improvements), and emissions of carbon dioxide from land use change, methane, and nitrous oxide.

The scenarios of economic and population growth are perturbed by the impact of climatic change. Population decreases with increasing climate change-related deaths that result from changes in heat stress, cold stress, malaria, and tropical cyclones. Heat and cold stress are assumed to have an effect only on the elderly, non-reproductive population. In contrast, the other sources of mortality also affect the number of births. Heat stress affects only the urban population. The share of the urban population among the total population is based on the World Resources Databases (http://earthtrends.wri.org). It is extrapolated based on the statistical relationships between urbanization and *per capita* income, which are estimated from a cross-section of countries in 1995. Climate-induced migration between the regions of the world also causes population sizes to change. Immigrants are assumed to assimilate immediately and completely with the respective host population.

The tangible impacts are deadweight losses to the economy (cf. Fankhauser and Tol 2005). Consumption and investment are reduced without changing the savings rate. As a result, climate change reduces long-term economic growth, although consumption is particularly affected in the short term. Economic growth is also reduced by carbon dioxide abatement measures. The energy intensity of the economy and the carbon intensity of the energy supply autonomously decrease over time. This process can be accelerated by abatement policies, an option not considered in this appendix.

The endogenous parts of *FUND* consist of the atmospheric concentrations of carbon dioxide, methane, nitrous oxide and sulfur hexafluoride, the global mean temperature, the impact of carbon dioxide emission reductions on the economy and on emissions, and the impact of the damages to the economy and the population caused by climate change. Methane and nitrous oxide are taken up in the atmosphere, and then geometrically depleted. The atmospheric concentration of carbon dioxide, measured in ppm by volume, is represented by the five-box model of Maier-Reimer and Hasselmann (1987). Its parameters are taken from Hammitt *et al.* (1992). The model also contains sulfur emissions (Tol 2006a).

The radiative forcing of carbon dioxide, methane, nitrous oxide, sulfur hexafluoride, and sulfur aerosols is determined based on Ramaswamy *et al.* (2001). The global mean temperature T is governed by a geometric build-up to its equilibrium (determined by the radiative forcing RF), with a half-life of fifty years. In the base case, the global mean temperature rises in equilibrium by 2.5°C for a doubling of carbon dioxide equivalents. Regional temperature follows from multiplying the global mean temperature by a fixed factor, which corresponds to the spatial climate change pattern averaged over 14 GCMs (Mendelsohn *et al.* 2000). The global mean sea level is also geometric, with its equilibrium level determined by the temperature and a half-life of fifty years. Both temperature and sea level are calibrated to correspond to the best-guess temperature and sea level for the IS92a scenario of Kattenberg *et al.* (1996).

The climate impact module, based on Tol (2002b, 2002c) includes the following categories: agriculture, forestry, sea level rise, cardiovascular and respiratory disorders related to cold and heat stress, malaria, dengue fever, schistosomiasis, diarrhea, energy consumption, water resources, and unmanaged ecosystems. Climate change related damages can be attributed to either the rate of change (benchmarked at 0.04°C/yr) or the level of change (benchmarked at 1.0°C). Damages from the rate of temperature change slowly fade, reflecting adaptation (cf. Tol 2002c).

People can die prematurely due to temperature stress or vector-borne diseases, or they can migrate because of sea level rise. Like all impacts of climate change, these effects are monetized. The value of a statistical life is set to be 200 times the annual *per capita* income. The resulting value of a statistical life lies in the middle of the observed range of values in the literature (cf. Cline 1992). The value of emigration is set to be 3 times the *per capita* income (Tol 1995), the value of immigration is 40 per cent of the *per capita* income in the host region (Cline 1992). Losses of dryland and wetlands due to sea level rise are modelled explicitly. The monetary value of a loss of 1 km^2 of dryland was on average $4 million in OECD countries in 1990 (cf. Fankhauser 1994). Dryland value is assumed to be proportional to GDP per km^2. Wetland losses are valued at $2 million per km^2 on average in the OECD in 1990 (cf. Fankhauser 1994). The wetland value is assumed to have logistic relation to *per capita* income. Coastal protection is based on cost-benefit analysis (CBA), including the value of additional wetland lost due to the construction of dikes and subsequent coastal squeeze.

Other impact categories, such as agriculture, forestry, energy, water, and ecosystems, are directly expressed in monetary values without an intermediate layer of impacts measured in their "natural" units (cf. Tol 2002b). Impacts of climate change on energy consumption, agriculture, and cardiovascular and respiratory diseases explicitly recognize that there is a climatic optimum, which is determined by a variety of factors, including plant physiology and the behavior of farmers. Impacts are positive or negative depending on whether the actual climate conditions are moving closer to or away from that optimum climate. Impacts are larger if the initial climate conditions are further away from the optimum climate. The optimum climate is of importance with regard to the potential impacts. The actual impacts lag behind the potential impacts, depending on the speed of adaptation. The impacts of not being fully adapted to new climate conditions are always negative (cf. Tol 2002c).

The impacts of climate change on coastal zones, forestry, unmanaged ecosystems, water resources, diarrhea, malaria, dengue fever, and schistosomiasis are modeled as simple power functions. Impacts are either negative or positive, and they do not change sign (cf. Tol 2002c).

Vulnerability to climate change changes with population growth, economic growth, and technological progress. Some systems are expected to become more vulnerable, such as water resources (with population growth), heat-related disorders (with urbanization), and ecosystems and health (with higher *per capita* incomes). Other systems are projected to become less vulnerable, such as energy consumption (with technological progress), agriculture (with economic growth), and vector- and water-borne diseases (with improved health care) (cf. Tol 2002c).

Bibliography

ACIA (Arctic Climate Impact Assessment), 2004: *Impacts of a warming Arctic*, Synthesis Report of the Arctic Climate Impact Assessment, Policy Document prepared by the Arctic Council and presented at the Fourth Arctic Council Ministerial Meeting, Reykjavik, November 24

Batima, P., 2003: Climate change, Pasture-Livestock, Synthesis Report – Potential Impacts of Climate Change, Vulnerability and Adaptation Assessment for Grassland Ecosystem and Livestock Sector in Mongolia, ADMON publishing Ulaanbaatar: 36-47

Batjes, J.J. and Goldewijk, C.G.M., 1994: *The IMAGE 2 hundred year (1890–1990) database of the global environment (HYDE)*, RIVM, Bilthoven, **410100082**

Bhadra, B., 2002: Regional cooperation for sustainable development of Hindu Kush Himalaya region: Opportunities and challenges, Keynote paper presented at the Alpine Experience – An Approach for other Mountain Regions, Berchtesgaden, Germany, June 26–29

Blaikie, P.M., Cannon R., Davies I., and Wisner B., 1994: At *risk: Natural hazards, people's vulnerability, and disasters*. Routledge, New York

Boer, R. and Faqih, A., 2004: Current and future rainfall variability in Indonesia, AIACC Technical Report 021

Boo, K.O., Kwon, W.T., and Kim, J.K., 2005: Vegetation changes in regional surface climate over east Asia due to Global Warming using BIOME 4II, Nuovo Cimento, submitted

Chandrapala, L. and Fernando, T.K., 1995: Climate variability in Sri Lanka – a study of air temperature, rainfall and thunder activity, in *Proceedings of the International Symposium on Climate and Life in the Asia-Pacific*, University of Brunei, Darussalam, April 10–13

Chen, J., An, Z.S., and Liu, L.W., 2001: Variations in chemical compositions of the Aeolian dust in Chinese loess plateau over the past 2.5 Ma and chemical weathering in the Asian inland, *Science in China* (Series D), **44**(5): 403–13

Cline, W.R. (1992), *The economics of global warming*, Institute for International Economics, Washington, DC

Cline, W.R. (2004), Climate change, www.copenhagenconsensus.com/Default.aspx?ID=165

Cruz, R.V.O., Lasco, R.D., Pulhin, J.M., Pulhin, F.B., and Garcia, K.B., 2005: Climate change impact on water resources in Pantabangan Watershed, Philippines, AIACC Technical Report

CWC (Central Water Commission), 2001: Water and related statistics, Report of the Ministry of Water Resources, New Delhi

Ding, Z.Q. and Pan H.S., 2002: The causes and prediction of flood disaster in Heilongjiang Provinces, Heilongjiang Science and Technology of Water Conservancy, **3**: 5–7

Du, J. and Ma, Y.C., 2004: Climatic trend of rainfall over Tibetan Plateau from 1971 to 2000, *Acta Geographica Sinica*, **59**(3): 375–82

Duedall, I.W. and Maul, G.A., 2005: Demography of coastal populations, in M.L. Schwartz (ed.), *Encyclopedia of coastal science*, Springer, Dordrecht: 368–74

Duong, L.C., 2000: Lessons from severe tropical storm Linda, Workshop Report, The *impact of El Niño and La Niña on Southeast Asia*, February 21–23 Hanoi

Durkin, M.S., Khan, N., Davidson, L.L., Zaman, S.S., and Stein, Z.A., 1993: The effects of a natural disaster on child behaviour: Evidence for post-traumatic stress, *American Journal of Public Health*, **83**(11): 1522–4

Environment, News Service, 2002: Hungry Cambodians at the mercy of climate Change, Phnom Penh, November, 26, fttp://ens_news. xom/ens/nov2002/2002-11-26-02

EPRI (Electric Power Research Institute), 2007: the power to reduce CO_2 emissions: The full portfolio, Discussion Paper

Fan, D.D. and Li, C.X., 2006: Complexities of Chinese coast in response to climate change, *Advances in Climate Change Research*, **2** (Suppl. 1): 54–58 (in Chinese with an English abstract)

Fankhauser, S., 1994: Protection vs. retreat. The economic costs of sea level rise, *Environment and Planning A*, **27**: 299–319

Fankhauser, S. and Tol, R.S.J., 2005: On climate change and economic growth, *Resource and Energy Economics*, **27**: 1–17

FAO (Food and Agriculture Organization) 2000: *The state of food and agriculture 2000*, Rome

FAO (Food and Agriculture Organization), 2004a: *Yearbook of fishery statistics 2002, aquaculture production*, **94**/2, Food and Agriculture Organization of the United Nations, Rome

FAO (Food and Agriculture Organization), 2004b: *Data base, food and agriculture*, Organization of the United Nations, Rome

FAO (Food and Agriculture Organization)/**WFP** (World Food Program), 2000: *FAO/WFP Crop and food supply assessment mission to Cambodia*, Special Report, December 29, FAO Global Information and Early Warning System on Food and Agriculture/World Food Program

Farooq, A.B. and Khan, A.H., 2004: Climate change perspective in Pakistan, *Proceedings of the Capacity Building APN Workshop on Global Change Research*, Islamabad, June 8–10: 39–46

Glantz, M.H. (ed.), 2001: *Once burned, twice shy? Lessons learned from the 1997–98 El Niño*, United Nations University Press, Tokyo

Golubev, G. and Dronin, N., 2003: Geography of droughts and food problems in Russia of the twentieth century, Research Monograph of the Center for Environmental Systems Research, University of Kassel and Department of Geography, Moscow State University: 25–8

Gruza, G. and Rankova, E., 2004: Detection of changes in climate state, climate variability and climate extremity, *Proceedings of the World Climate Change Conference*, September 29–October 3, 2003, Moscow: 90–3

Hai, P.M., Sun, A., Ren, F., Liu, X., Gao, B., and Zhang, Q., 1999: Changes of climate extremes in China, *Climatic Change*, **42**: 203–18

Hammitt, J.K., Lempert, R.J., and Schlesinger, M.E., 1992: A sequential-decision strategy for abating climate change, *Nature*, **357**: 315–18

Ho, C.H., Lee, J.Y., Ahn, M.H., and Lee, H.S., 2003: A sudden change in summer rainfall characteristics in Korea during the late 1970s, *International Journal of Climatology*, **23**(1): 117–28

Hu, Z.Z., Yang, S., and Wu, R., 2003: Long-term climate variations in China and global warming signals, *Journal of Geophysical Research*, **108**(D19): 4614

IPCC (Intergovernmental Panel on Climate Change), 1995, *IPCC second assessment synthesis of scientific-technical information relevant to interpreting article 2 of the UNFCCC*, Cambridge University Press, Cambridge Ichikawa, 2004

IPCC (Intergovernmental Panel on Climate

Change), 2000, *Emissions scenarios, 2000*, Cambridge University Press, Cambridge

IPCC (Intergovernmental Panel on Climate Change), 2001, *Climate change 2001: synthesis report*, Cambridge University Press, Cambridge

IPCC (Intergovernmental Panel on Climate Change), 2007a, *Climate change 2007: The Science. Contribution of working group I to the fourth assessment report*, Cambridge University Press, Cambridge

IPCC (Intergovernmental Panel on Climate Change), 2007b, *Climate change 2007: Impacts, adaptation and vulnerability. Contribution of working group II to the fourth assessment report*, Cambridge University Press, Cambridge

IPCC (Intergovernmental Panel on Climate Change), 2007c, *Climate change 2007: Synthesis report,* Cambridge University Press, Cambridge

Isobe, H., 2002: Trends in precipitation over Japan, *Proceedings of the 6th Symposium on water resources*: 585–90

Izrael, Y.A. and Anokhin Y.A., 2000: Monitoring and assessment of the environment in the Lake Baikal region, *Aquatic Ecosystem Health & Management*, **3**: 199–202

Izrael, Y.A. and Sirotenko O.D., 2003: Modeling climate change impact on agriculture of Russia, *Meteorology and Hydrology*, **6**: 5–17

Jamison, D.T., Jha, P., and Bloom, D.E., 2008, Disease control, see chapter 3 in this volume

Japan Meteorological Agency, 2005: Global warming projection, **6**, with the RCM20 and UCM (in Japanese)

Jung, H.S., Choi, Y., Oh, J.-H., and Lim, G.H., 2002: Recent trends in temperature and precipitation over South Korea, *International Journal of Climatology*, **22**: 1327–37

Kajiwara, M., Oki, T., and Matsumoto, J., 2003: Inter-annual variability of the frequency of severe rainfall in the past 100 years over Japan, Extended abstract for a bi-annual meeting of the Meteorological Society of Japan (in Japanese)

Kanai, S., Oki, T., and Kashida, A., 2004: Changes in hourly precipitation at Tokyo from 1890 to 1999, *Journal of the Meteorological Society of Japan*, **82**: 241–7

Kattenberg, A., Giorgi, F., Grassl, H., Meehl, G.A., Mitchell, J.F.B., Stouffer, R.J.,

Tokioka, T., Weaver, A.J., and Wigley T.M.L., 1996: Climate models – projections of future climate, in *Climate change 1995: The science of climate change – contribution of working group I to the second assessment report of the intergovernmental panel on climate change*, first edn., J.T. Houghton *et al.* (eds.), Cambridge University Press, Cambridge: 285–357

Kawahara, M. and Yamazaki, N., 1999: Long-term trend of incidences of extreme high or low temperatures in Japan, Extended abstract (in Japanese) for a bi-annual meeting of the Meteorological Society of Japan

Kelly, P.M. and Adger, W.N., 2000: Theory and practice in assessing vulnerability to climate change and facilitating adaptation, *Climate Change*, **47**: 325–52

Khan, T.M.A., Singh, O.P., and Rahman, M.S., 2000: Recent sea level and sea surface temperature trends along the Bangladesh coast in relation to the frequency of intense cyclones, *Marine Geodesy*, **23**(2): 103–16

Kripalani, R.H., Inamdar, S.R., and Sontakke, N.A., 1996: Rainfall variability over Bangladesh and Nepal: Comparison and connection with features over India, *International Journal of Climatology*, **16**: 689–703

Lal, M., 2003: Global climate change: India's monsoon and its variability, *Journal of Environmental Studies and Policy*, **6**(1): 1–34

Lal, M., 2005: Implications of climate change on agricultural productivity and food security in South Asia, in *Key vulnerable regions and climate change – Identifying thresholds for impacts and adaptation in relation to Article 2 of the UNFCCC*, European Climate Forum, unpublished

Lal, M., Nozawa, T., Emori, S., Harasawa, H., Takahashi, K., Kimoto, M., Abe-Ouchi, A., Nakajima, T., Takemura , T., and Numaguti, A., 2001: Future climate change: implications for Indian summer monsoon and its variability, *Current Science*, **81**(9): 1196–1207

Laxminarayan, R., Mills, A.J., Breman, J.G., Measham, A.R., Alleyne, G., Claeson, M., Jha, P., Musgrove, P., Chow, J., Shahid-Salles, S., and Jamison, D.T., 2006: Advancement of Global health: Key messages from the disease control priorities project, *Lancet*, **367**: 1193–1208

Liu, C.M. and Chen, Z.K., 2001: *Assessment on water resources status and analysis on supply and demand growth in China*, China Water Conservancy and Hydropower Press, Beijing

Liu, S.R., Guo, Q.S., and Wang, B., 1998: Prediction of net primary productivity of forests in China in response to climate change, *Acta Ecologica Sinica*, **18**(5): 478–83

Lomborg, B., 2008a: A better way than cap and trade, *Washington Post*, www.washingtonpost.com/wpdyn/content/article/2008/06/25/AR2008062501946.html

Lomborg, B., 2008b: The black sheep, *Newsweek*, www.newsweek.com/id/144417

Lomborg, B., 2008c: McCain, Obama and hot air, *The Guardian*, www.guardian.co.uk/commentisfree/2008/jul/03/climatechange.usa/

Maier-Reimer, E. and Hasselmann, K., 1987: Transport and storage of carbon dioxide in the ocean: An inorganic ocean circulation carbon cycle model, *Climate Dynamics*, **2**: 63–90

Manne, A., 1999: The implications of prescriptive discounting, in P.R. Portney and J.P. Weyant, *Discounting and intergenerational equity*, RFF Press, Washington, DC

Manne, A., 2004: Response to the Challenge paper on Climate Change, www.copenhagenconsensus.com/Default.aspx?ID=165

Manton, M.J., Della-Marta, P.M., Haylock, M.R., Hennessy, K.J., Nicholls, N., Chambers, L.E., Collins, D.A., Daw, G., Finet, A., Gunawan, D., Inape, K., Isobe, H., Kestin, T.S., Lefale, P., Leyu, C.H., Lwin, T., Maitrepierre, L., Ouprasitwong, N., Page, C.M., Pahalad, J., Plummer, N., Salinger, M.J., Suppiah, R., Tran, V.L., Trewin, B., Tibig, I., and Lee, D., 2001: Trends in extreme daily rainfall and temperature in Southeast Asia and the South Pacific, 1961–1998, *International Journal of Climatology*, **21**: 269–84

Mendelsohn, R.O., Schlesinger, M.E., and Williams, L.J., 2000: Comparing impacts across climate models, *Integrated Assessment*, **1**: 37–48

Mirza, M.Q., 2002: Global warming and changes in the probability of occurrence of floods in Bangladesh and implications, *Global Environmental Change*, **12**, 127–38

Mirza, M.Q. and Dixit, A., 1997: Climate change and water management in the GBM Basins, *Water Nepal*, **5**: 71–100

Myoung-Han, A.H.N. and Lee, H.-S., 2003: A sudden change in summer rainfall characteristics in Korea during the late 1970s, *International Journal of Climatology*, **23**: 117–28

Nordhaus, W.D., 2006: *The Stern review on the economics of climate change*, http://nordhaus.econ.yale.edu/SternReviewD2.pdf

Ogura, S. and Yohe, G., 1977: The complementarity of public and private capital and the optimal rate of return to government investment, *Quarterly Journal of Economics*, **91**: 651–62

PAGASA (Philippine Atmospheric, Geophysical and Astronomical Services Administration), 2001: Documentation and analysis of impacts of and responses to extreme climate events, Climatology & Agrometeorology Branch Technical Paper, **2001–2**

Parry, M., Rosenzweig, C., and Livermore, M., 2005: Climate change, global food supply and risk of hunger, *Philosophical Transitions of the Royal Society*, **360**: 2125–38

Peterson, B.J., Holmes, R.M., McClelland, J.W., Vorosmarty, C.J., Lammers, R.B., Shiklomanov, A.I., Shiklomanov, I.A., and Rahmstorf, S., 2002, Increasing river discharge to the Arctic Ocean, *Science*, **298**: 137–43

Portney, P.R. and Weyant, J.P., 1999: *Discounting and Intergenerational Equity*, RFF Press, Washington, DC

Rahimzadeh, F., 2006: Study of precipitation variability in Iran, Research Climatology Institute, IRIMO

Ramaswamy, V., Boucher, O., Haigh, J., Hauglustaine, D., Haywood, J., Myhre, G., Nakajima, T., Shi, G.Y., and Solomon, S., 2001: Radiative forcing of climate change, in *Climate Change 2001: The scientific basis – Contribution of working group I to the third assessment report of the intergovernmental panel on climate change*, J.T. Houghton and Y. Ding (eds.), Cambridge University Press, Cambridge: 349–416

Ruosteenoja, K., Carter, T.R., Jylha, K., and Tuomenvirta, H., 2003: Future climate in world regions: An intercomparison of model based projections for the new IPCC emission scenarios, *The Finnish Environment Report*, **644**, Finnish Environment Institute, Helsinki

Savelieva, I.P., Semiletov, N.I., L.N., Vasilevskaya, and S.P. Pugach, 2000: A climate shift in seasonal values of meteorological and hydrological parameters for Northeastern Asia, *Progress Oceanography*, **47**: 279–97

Shi, L.Q., Li, J.F., Ying, M., Li, W.H., Chen, S.L., and Zhang, G.A., 2005, Advances in researches on the modern Huanghe Delta development and evolution, *Advance in Marine Science*, **23**(1): 96–104

Shrestha, A.B., Wake, C.P., Dibb, J.E., and Mayewski, P.A., 2000: Precipitation fluctuations in the Nepal Himalaya and its vicinity and relationship with some large scale climatological parameters, *International Journal of Climatology*, **20**: 317–27

Singh, N. and Sontakke, N.A., 2002: On climatic fluctuations and environmental changes of the Indo-Gangetic plains, India, *Climatic Change*, **52**, 287–313

Stern, N., Peters, S., Bakhshi, V., Bowen, A., Cameron, C., Catovsky, S., Crane, D., Cruickshank, S., Dietz, S., Edmonson, N., Garbett, S.-L., Hamid, L., Hoffman, G., Ingram, D., Jones, B., Patmore, N., Radcliffe, H., Sathiyarajah, R., Stock, M., Taylor, C., Vernon, T., Wanjie, H., and Zenghelis, D., 2006: *Stern review: The economics of climate change*, HM Treasury, London

Tol, R.S.J., 1995:The damage costs of climate change toward more comprehensive calculations, *Environmental and Resource Economics*, **5**: 353–74

Tol, R.S.J., 1999: The marginal costs of greenhouse gas emissions, *Energy Journal*, **20**(1): 61–81

Tol, R.S.J., 2001: Equitable cost-benefit analysis of climate change, *Ecological Economics*, **36**(1): 71–85

Tol, R.S.J., 2002a: Welfare specifications and optimal control of climate change: an application of fund, *Energy Economics*, **24**: 367–76

Tol, R.S.J., 2002b: Estimates of the damage costs of climate change – Part I: benchmark estimates, *Environmental and Resource Economics*, **21**: 47–73

Tol, R.S.J., 2002c: Estimates of the damage costs of climate change – Part II: dynamic estimates, *Environmental and Resource Economics*, **21**: 135–60

Tran, V.L., 2002: Climate change scenario for Red River Catchments, University of Twente

UNFCCC webpage, http://unfccc.int/methods_and_science/lulucf/items/1084.php

Viscusi, W.K. and Aldey, J., 2003: The value of a statistical life: A critical review of market estimates throughout the world, *Journal of Risk and Uncertainty*, **27**: 5–76

Webster, P.J., Magana, V.O., Palmer, T.N., Shukla, J., Tomas, R.A., Yanagi, M., and Yasunari, T., 1998: Monsoons: Processes, predictability and the prospects for prediction, *Journal of Geophysical. Research*, **103**: 14451–14510

Weitzman, M., 2007: The role of uncertainty in the economics of catastrophic climate change, Harvard University Working Paper, Cambridge, MA

Yohe, G., 2006: Some thoughts on the estimates presented in the *Stern Review* – An editorial, *Integrated Assessment Journal*, **6**: 66–72

Yohe, G., Andronova, N., and Schlesinger, M., 2004: To hedge or not against an uncertain climate future, *Science*, **306**: 415–17

Yohe, G., Malone, E., Brenkert, A., Schlesinger, M.E., Meij, H., Xing, X., and Lee, D., 2006: Global distributions of vulnerability to climate change, *Integrated Assessment Journal*, **6**: 35–44

Yoshino, M., 2002: Kosa (Asian dust) related to Asian monsoon system, *Korean Journal of Atmospheric Science*, **5**(S): 93–100

Yoshino, M., 2000: Problems in climatology of dust storm and its relation to human activities in Northwest China, *Journal of Arid Land Studies*, **10**: 171–81

Zhai, P.M., 2004: Climate change and meteorological disasters, *Science and Technology Review*, **193**(7): 11–14

Zhai, P.M. and Pan, X., 2003: Trends in temperature extremes during 1951–1999 in China, *Geophysical Research Letters*, **30**(17): 1913, doi:10.1029/2003GL018004

Zhao, L., Ping, C.L., Yang, D., Cheng, G., Ding, Y., and Liu, S., 2004: Changes of climate and seasonally frozen ground over the past 30 years in Qinghai–Xizang (Tibetan) Plateau, China, *Global and Planetary Change*, **43**: 19–31

Zhou, Y.H., 2003: Characteristics of weather and climate during drought periods in South China, *Journal of Applied Meteorological Science*, **14**, Supplement: 118–25

Alternative Perspectives

Perspective Paper 5.1

CHRIS GREEN*

Introduction

The Bali Conference concluded in mid-December 2007 with vague reference to a road map for a post-Kyoto climate policy. I, too, will begin with a "road map": to give the reader/listener some idea of my quite different "perspective" on climate policy. The following points are salient:

1 Greenhouse gas mitigation is first and foremost an energy technology problem.
2 Human-induced climate change is real, and, despite uncertainties, requires serious and priority attention.
3 The initiative that Yohe et al. (2008) in their Challenge paper find to have the highest benefit-cost ratio (a combination of mitigation, adaptation, and R&D) includes the right set of components. However, the mix, rationale, and methodological approach suggested in this Perspective paper are rather different.
4 Most important of all, stabilizing atmospheric concentrations of carbon dioxide at levels such as 450 or 550 ppm is a much bigger challenge than one would conclude from stabilization analyses that use so-called "no-climate policy" emissions scenarios as their reference points or "baselines." The implication: Stabilizing concentrations does not seem possible (or at best would be prohibitively costly) without directly addressing the difficult-to-solve energy technology problem.

How do these points mesh with the findings of Yohe et al. (2008). We are at one in maintaining that climate change needs to be taken seriously. We are also at one that there will be rising damages, evident even in Richard Tol's conservative *FUND* model with its adaptation-oriented approach, and in the work of Gary Yohe. The avoidable damages (benefits) exceed the paper's estimated mitigation costs, but this may reflect the existence of the Copenhagen Consensus budget constraint.

Because mitigation is budgetarily as well as benefit-cost limited, it is not clear by how much (or even whether) the Yohe et al. modeling results are also dependent on an assumed carbon-free "backstop" energy technology(ies). The MERGE model has sometimes employed such an assumption, in common with many (most?) economy–environment models. My approach is clearly at odds with a "backstop" assumption, whether carbon price-induced, or otherwise, because the backstop assumption essentially assumes away the problem by introducing unspecified carbon-neutral technologies with no assessment of their technological or economic feasibility. However, my views are consistent with a reported statement of one of the co-authors (Richels), who was quoted (by Andrew Revkin of the *New York Times,* May 4,

* The author is grateful for inputs from Peter King, John Watson, Manuel Cocco, Phil Sayeg Sarath Guttikunda, Tanyathon Phetmanee, and Poonyanuch Chockanapitaksa.

2007) as saying that "a carbon policy without an R&D policy is bankrupt."

I approach my task as follows. I take as established that climate scientists (IPCC WG (Working Group) I, and to some extent WG II), have made a compelling case that (i) humankind is altering the energy balance of the earth-atmosphere system; (ii) the impact of the altered balance on climate is likely to become substantial (the hope for a low and relatively benign "climate sensitivity" is rapidly fading), and (iii) the physical (glaciers, sea ice, etc.) and biological (corals, biodiversity, etc.) "tolerance" to substantial climate change may be lower than we might have hoped. (The jury is still out, it would seem, on the extent of the impact on humans, although predictable water stress, sea level rise and potential climate change-induced migrations suggest human impacts may be substantial, too.)

But I diverge substantially from the claims of IPCC WG III which conclude that the technologies needed to stabilize emissions are currently available or under development. I do not think the evidence indicates that we currently have the technological means to stabilize greenhouse gas (GHG) concentrations at a level sufficient to avoid an increasingly unpleasant climate change future. The issue of whether current technologies are adequate to climate stabilization has been a matter of vibrant debate that was almost entirely ignored by the IPCC (Hoffert *et al.* 1998, 2002; IPCC WG III 2001; Caldeira *et al.* 2003; Pacala and Socolow 2004; Edmonds *et al.* 2007; Wigley *et al.* 2007; Pielke *et al* 2008).

The debate is important! In my view, belief that the requisite technology(ies) is/are available and adequate to the challenge (IPCC 2001) has badly distorted climate policy for more than a decade. It has not only contributed to virtually single-minded focus on near-term mitigation, but to mitigation achieved by mandating emission-reduction targets. The commitments made not only lack credibility (Schelling 1992), but promote costly, and ultimately futile, attempts to achieve them. In what follows, I demonstrate why the technology challenge to GHG stabilization is huge (implying that there is a very large

energy technology gap), and that most assessments seriously understate the magnitude of that challenge.

Assessing the Challenge of GHG Stabilization

In this section, I assess the technology challenge to GHG stabilization with three rather different and impressionistic vignettes. One is the proposal that emanated from the G-8 meeting in May 2007. The second involves the move of energy-intensive industry to the Far East, particularly China. The third involves baselines against which the stabilization challenge is measured.

The G-8 Proposal

In 2007, the host of the G-8 meeting was Germany's Chancellor, Angela Merkel. Chancellor Merkel wanted the G-8 to sign up to an agreement to target a 50 percent reduction in *global* GHG emissions from *1990* levels. President Bush initially refused to go along, but under pressure appeared to agree that a 50 percent reduction from *current* (2007) levels could be seriously considered. (The final communiqué emphasized the apparent agreement on the 50 percent-by-2050 target, but failed to specify a reference year, nor define what is meant by net "GHG emissions" and so failed to address the relative importance of reductions in CO_2 vs. other GHGs.)

As is usual when discussions of targets come up, the emphasis is on what *ought* to be done, not on what *can* be done. The G-8 is apparently no exception. Had the appropriate arithmetic been done, it would have been clear that a reduction of *global* CO_2 emissions from an estimated 8 GtC in 2007 (emissions were 6 GtC in 1990) to 4 GtC in 2050 is for all intents and purposes out of the question. Why? Because it is tantamount to requiring a transformation of energy systems and economies sufficiently great that, on average, the world as a whole would have, in 2050, a lower carbon intensity (CO_2 emissions divided by GDP – i.e. C/GDP) than Switzerland had in 2005.

Let us put the implications of the G-8 proposal into perspective. Switzerland's economy, with its emphasis on high-valued, low-energy-using industries such as watches, banking, and finance, could not be more unrepresentative of the world's economy, especially the most rapidly growing and populous part. Not surprisingly, except for two or three exceedingly poor countries, including Chad and Cambodia, Switzerland has the lowest carbon intensity of output in the world.

Energy Intensity in Asia

The heightened concern over climate change is occurring at the same time as the *rate of increase* in global emissions of CO_2 is increasing, and momentous changes are taking place in the developing world. These developments are, of course, connected and probably account for much of the tripling in the annual rate of change in emissions from 1.1 percent/year in the 1990s to 3.1 percent/year in 2001–6. At the heart of these emission growth-rate changes is the development success story coming out of Asia. That story is increasingly associated with a huge shift in the location and relative importance of energy-intensive industries, which rely heavily on power generated from combusting coal.

The best example is China, which in 2006 accounted for 48 percent of the world's production of cement, 49 percent of the world's production of flat glass, 35 percent of its steel, and 28 percent of its aluminum (Rosen and Houser 2007). The list could go on, but it suffices to say that these are among the world's most energy-intensive industries with energy to output ratios ("energy intensities") about ten times higher than those of most other manufacturing industries. The important point is that as development proceeds, rural populations move to cities, but to an increasing extent no longer to shanties and slums but to high-rise buildings on broad streets that consume very energy-intensive materials. This is a process that is likely to continue for decades, not only in China, but all over populous southeast and south Asia, and eventually in Africa, until well beyond the middle of the century.

As a result, we have only begun to see the surge in global energy use that the transformational development process now implies. And with that development process and energy surge will come a GHG emissions surge that will terminate only with a transformation of the world's energy systems. Not only will that transformation be a slow process, but the required energy technologies, for the most part, are not yet both ready and *scalable*. And when they are ready and scalable, it will likely require a huge technology transfer to the developing world before there will be a substantial payoff in CO_2 emissions reductions.

Reference Scenarios and Baselines

In assessing what it will take to stabilize atmospheric GHG concentrations (in cost and technology terms), models usually employ no-climate-policy emission scenarios as references or baselines. However using such emission scenarios as baselines for assessing climate stabilization can mislead when it comes to assessing the amount of technological change needed (and, by extension, economic cost incurred) to stabilize climate (Pielke *et al.* 2008). The problem is that built into most emission scenarios are *assumptions* of very large amounts of emission reductions that will occur automatically due to technology change. In general, these "built-in" technologies require no attention to energy policies beyond following a "Business as usual" pathway and by definition do not include any future climate policies. Such assumed emission reductions appear to have been ignored by analysts (exceptions include Battelle Memorial Institute 2001, Edmonds and Smith 2006, and IPCC WGIII, chapter 3 2007a), most of whom implicitly assess the magnitude of the energy technology challenge by looking at what it takes to move from an emission scenario (with its "built-in" emission reductions) to an emissions path consistent with some stabilization level.

An illustration of these issues can be found by

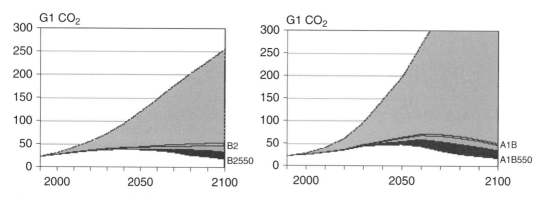

Figure 5.1.1 *Impact of technology on global carbon emissions, 2000–2100*
Note: Global carbon emissions (GIC) in four scenarios developed within the IPCC SRES and TAR (A2, B2 top and bottom of left panel; A1F1 and A1B top and bottom of right panel). The grey-shaded area indicates the difference in emissions between the original no-climate policy reference scenario compared with a hypothetical scenario assuming frozen 1990 energy efficiency and technology, illustrating the impact of technological change incorporated already into the reference scenario. Colour-shaded areas show the impact of various additional technology options deployed in imposing a 550 ppmv CO_2 stabilization constraint on the respective reference scenario, including energy conservation (blue), substitution of high-carbon by low- or zero-carbon technologies (orange), as well as carbon capture and sequestration (black). Of particular interest are the two A1 scenarios shown on the right-hand side of the panel that share identical (low) population and (high) economic growth assumptions, thus making differences in technology assumptions more directly comparable.
Adapted from Nakićenović et al. (2000); Riahi and Roehri (2001).
Source: Figure 3.3: Impact of technology on global carbon emission in reference and climate mitigation scenarios.

looking at the widely cited Pacala and Socolow (2004) paper. Pacala and Socolow (hereafter, PS) introduced the "wedge" concept and estimated that it would take 7 technology wedges, each equivalent to a cumulative emissions reduction of 25 GtC, to hold global emissions constant for the next fifty years. In conducting their analysis, however, PS used a baseline CO_2 emissions path (scenario) that already had 11 built-in wedges. Socolow (2006) subsequently acknowledged the existence of these built-in wedges, referring to them as "virtual" wedges. Thus the true number of PS wedges needed to maintain emission level constancy is 18 (7 + 11). About 60 percent of the technology challenge over the next fifty years, to say nothing of the challenge thereafter, had simply been assumed away.

To get around the problem of making assumptions about technology and a possible understatement of the future challenge, one can use a "frozen technology" baseline (Edmonds and Smith 2006; Pielke *et al.* 2008). A "frozen technology" baseline assumes that future emissions

will be the result of production using today's energy technology (hence the technology is "frozen"). While no one expects technology to be/remain "frozen", a hypothetical "frozen" technology baseline allows complete transparency in assumptions about future technologies, innovation, and the processes that will lead to such innovation, crucial issues that are obscured by emission scenario baselines.

Two "frozen" technology baselines" are illustrated (the dashed lines) in figure 5.1.1 (reproduced from IPCC AR4 WG III, chapter 3, 2007: 220), one each for the IPCC B2 and A1B scenarios. The built-in (assumed) emission reduction attributable to spontaneous technology change is, in each case, the large and increasing *tinted* area. The gray areas dwarf the "stabilization scenario" component – that is, the area that lies between the emission scenario pathway (the B2 and A1B lines in figure 5.1.1) and the 550 ppm stabilization pathway (B2 550 and A1B 550 in figure 5.1.1). Pielke *et al.* (2008) calculate the built-in component at from 50–90 percent of the cumulative emissions to be reduced via technology. While chapter 3 of IPCC WG III (Fisher and Nakićenović *et al.* 2007) recognizes the potential importance of built-in technologies, other chapters appear not to have incorporated the implications for that report's technology assessment or stabilization cost estimates.

Baseline Analysis

The vignettes in the preceding section, although different in character, have a common denominator: Enormous advances in energy technology will be needed to stabilize the atmospheric concentration of carbon dioxide. If much of these advances occur spontaneously, then the challenge of stabilization might be relatively simple and low-cost, as suggested by the IPCC. However if these advances require significant effort, then the challenge to stabilization could in fact be much, much larger than presented by the IPCC. The first two vignettes above allow us to view the energy technology challenge without the burden (yes, "burden," not benefit"!) of GHG emission scenarios. The third implies that most emissions scenarios – and this is certainly the case of most of the IPCC SRES scenarios – provide misleading baselines for assessing the energy technology challenge presented by climate stabilization – and, by extension, for estimating stabilization cost.

From an analytical standpoint it is the third vignette that needs pursuing. As indicated above, an alternative baseline for assessing the energy technology challenge to stabilization is the "frozen technology" baseline, as shown in figure 5.1.1. The advantage of a "frozen technology" baseline is that it allows the analyst to explicitly account for *all* technological changes required for stabilization. Failure to so account may lead to *double counting* of technologies: Once in the "gap" between the "frozen" technology baseline and the emissions scenario and again in the gap between the emissions scenario and the stabilization path.

I am not aware of any stabilization analyses that indicate which specific changes in technol-

Table 5.1.1. Emission-reduction wedges required to follow different WRE CO$_2$ concentration stabilization paths out to 2055

Scenario	Built-in wedges	450 ppm^a	550 ppm^a
A1B	24.8 (86%)	13.4	6.5
B2	14.7 (80%)	6.5	0.7

Note: "wedges" needed to move from the SRES emission scenario to the specified WRE stabilization path.

ogy are built into the reference or emissions scenario baselines and which are policy-induced. (Perhaps my knowledge of the relevant literature is too limited.) It is likely that stabilization models of the "top-down" variety, ones that invariably begin from a no-climate-policy (SRES-type) emissions scenario baseline, are particularly vulnerable to this problem. Although "bottom-up" models might, in principle, avoid this problem, the fact that most generate lower stabilization-cost estimates than top-down models is an indication that these, too, are not accounting for all required technological changes in their stabilization assessments.

That these methodological concerns are important is indicated by as yet unpublished work by Wigley *et al.* (2007). These authors used the PS concept of a "wedge" (i.e. a cumulative CO$_2$ emissions reduction of 25 GtC) to calculate the number of wedges built into the IPCC SRES scenarios, as compared to the number required to move from the SRES scenario to a range of stabilization scenarios – the WRE (Wigley *et al.* 1996) stabilization paths. If we confine ourselves to the A1B and B2 scenarios, and to stabilization at 450 and 550 ppm, table 5.1.1 provides interesting findings.

Table 5.1.1 demonstrates that even by mid-century technology "wedges" built into the SRES scenarios dominate the number of technology "wedges" required to move from a frozen technology baseline to a stabilization path. (As figure 5.1.1 indicates, the domination is much greater by 2100.) What is the nature of the built-in technology? In table 5.1.1, the numbers in parentheses indicate the percentage of built-in "wedges" attributable to energy intensity decline – that is, to a combination of energy efficiency improvements and sectoral shifts in output from energy-intensive industries to less-energy-intensity industries.

Several points can be made about energy-intensity decline in SRES emissions scenarios:

1 In general, the SRES scenarios build in high rates of energy-intensity decline. Of the forty scenarios (from four basic families, A1, A2, B1, and B2) thirty-two had 110-year (1990–2100) built-in energy-intensity declines greater than the 1.0 percent/year rate used in the BAU IS92a scenario. It is likely that, on balance, the energy-intensity declines in the SRES scenarios are unrealistic.

2 Baksi and Green (2007) have devised a method, using mathematically exact formulas, for computing aggregate energy-intensity decline from changes over time in the efficiency of different energy-using sectors and their relative contributions to GDP and energy use. They find that *even after applying stabilization policies*, it would be difficult to substantially exceed a 1.0 percent/year *global, average,* rate of energy-intensity decline over 1990–2100. Yet 80 percent of the *pre-policy* SRES scenarios build in 110-year global average annual rates of energy-intensity decline that exceed 1.0 percent/year.

3 The formulas generated by Baksi and Green (2007) can be used to demonstrate that only about 20 percent (bounds of 10 and 30 percent) of the *global* energy-intensity decline can possibly come from sectoral shifts. The rest must come from energy-efficiency improvement, which means technology change. While at the individual country level sectoral shifts can contribute considerably more than 20 percent of energy-intensity decline, at the global level there is a lot of cancelling out as energy-intensive industries move from one part of the world to another.

4 Baksi and Green (2007) also demonstrate that achieving very high, century-long, rates of energy-intensity decline (ones that would greatly reduce the amount of carbon-free energy required for stabilization) require improvements in energy efficiency that are almost surely physically impossible. For example, Baksi and Green show (table 4, 2007: 8) that a 2.0 percent rate of decline (the B1 marker scenario has a 2.13 percent average annual rate of decline, 1990–2100), requires sectoral energy-efficiency improvements ranging from 450 to 1100 percent.

5 Yohe *et al.* (2008) use the SRES A2 emissions scenario. It is not clear why the authors chose A2, because that scenario is the most pessimistic of all the SRES scenarios. A2 has by far the highest 2100 population (15.3 billion), lowest global GDP growth rate (2.1 percent average over 1990–2100), and *lowest technology change* (e.g. only a 0.57 percent rate of energy-intensity decline, 1990–2100) among the family of SRES scenarios. Fortuitously, the last characteristic implies that A2 has the least amount of built-in technology change. Wigley *et al.* (2007) calculate that out to 2055, only 4.7 wedges are built into the A2 scenario, while 12.7 and 6.9 additional wedges are required to stabilize at 450 and 550 ppm, respectively. (These numbers contrast starkly with the results for the A1B and B2 scenarios given in table 5.1.1.)

Implications for Climate Policy

If, as seems likely, the SRES emissions scenarios have made CO_2 stabilization appear much easier than it will be (Green and Lightfoot 2002; Pielke *et al.* 2008), then there are important implications for climate policy. First and foremost, a target-based climate policy that is focused on *ends* should give way to a technology-based policy that focuses on the *means* required to achieve stabilization. Further, there are implications for the relationship between a carbon-price policy and a technology policy. Instead of the carbon-price policy carrying the main load in the early stages, carbon prices should be viewed as playing two supportive roles: (a) as a means of raising revenues to finance the publicly financed component of the energy technology race without which stabilization is unachievable; and (b) as a way of sending a forward price signal that will be increasingly powerful as the carbon price slowly rises and as new technologies appear "on the shelf" (a form of what Yohe *et al.* 2008 term "when flexible" mitigation). These considerations suggest a carbon tax that starts low and rises gradually over time.

In thinking about climate policy, an important distinction should be made between technologies that are "on the shelf" and are therefore deployable now (if it were economically advantageous to do so), and those that either (a) require further development before deployment is possible; or (b) are still at the basic R&D stage; or (c) have not yet been thought of (Sanden and Azar 2005). Carbon prices are likely to be effective in inducing deployment of technologies that are "on the shelf", but may well be ineffective inducements to invest, long-term, in technologies that still require basic R&D. The value of such technologies is therefore quite uncertain. Even if R&D proves them to be viable, they must be decades away from deployment (Montgomery and Smith 2005).

As Montgomery and Smith (2005) have demonstrated, private funding of long-term R&D may run into a "dynamic" (time) inconsistency. Generally, current governments cannot tie the hands of future governments to cover the potentially large (as well as uncertain) *up-front* R&D investment costs for technologies that may or may not prove successful and deployable decades hence. The Montgomery and Smith and Sanden and Azar papers therefore imply that "induced technical change" may be less important than one might gather from IPCC WG III, chapter 11 (Barker *et al.* 2007). Further, to these considerations we may add a "political" time inconsistency between a four–five-year election cycle and the decades-long time scale for the development of deployable and scalable carbon-neutral energy technologies. These factors suggest that in choosing a carbon tax (and any artificially generated carbon price is and will be viewed as a "tax") one should focus on "political acceptability" rather than guess what effect such a tax might have on many decades' worth of innovation. (In other words, we cannot simply

rely solely on price mechanisms to stimulate the required technology R&D – or stimulate even a significant fraction of this R&D.)

An equally important question is the extent to which the technologies required for stabilization are already "on the shelf", or almost so. In 2001, in its Summary for Policy Makers (SPM) IPCC WG III argued that "most model results indicate that known technological options could achieve a broad range of atmospheric CO_2 stabilization levels, such as 550 ppmv, 450 ppmv, or below over the next 100 years, but implementation would require associated socio-economic and institutional changes" (IPCC 2001: 8). The IPCC defined "known technological options" as "technologies that exist in operation or pilot plant stage today" (2001: 8n.). In 2007, with only slightly more caution, the IPCC AR4 states in the SPM of its Synthesis Report (SYR) that "There is *high agreement* and *much evidence* that all stabilization levels assessed can be achieved by deployment of a portfolio of technologies that are currently available or expected to be commercialized in coming decades" (IPCC SYR 2007: 20). As indicated above, the earlier IPCC (2001) technology claims were contested by Hoffert *et al.* (2002). One possible reason for the difference between the IPCC and Hoffert *et al.* is that the former may be judging technological adequacy from the standpoint of moving from a SRES emissions scenario, with a considerable amount of technological change already built into it, to a stabilization path, rather than from a frozen technology baseline In contrast, the methodology developed by Hoffert *et al.* (1998) avoids this trap because it calculates carbon-neutral energy requirements from the equivalent of a "frozen" technology baseline, *given the explicitly accounted-for average annual rate of decline in energy intensity.*

There is another reason for the difference between IPCC WG III and the Hoffert *et al.* (1998, 2002) technology assessments. This revolves around the *scalability* of current carbon-neutral technologies. The scalability issue, emphasized by Hoffert *et al.* (2002), is more complex than may first appear. Some technologies are not yet scalable because they are still at the

R&D stage. In some cases, apparently "on the shelf" technologies are also not yet scalable. These technologies include some that are often touted as the future means of powering the planet in a carbon-neutral manner (e.g. solar and wind energy, carbon capture and storage (CCS), and reprocessed, closed-cycle, nuclear). An important limitation of these technologies is that they lack one or more of the "enabling" technologies required for scalability.

An example of an "enabling" technology is storage for intermittent and variable solar and wind power. These potentially large, but dilute energy sources are not only land-intensive (Lightfoot and Green 2002), but of limited use without storage. Electric utilities generally will not be able to meet any more than about 10 percent of non-peak electricity demand from directly supplied, intermittent, or variable sources. While pumped hydro, hydrogen, and compressed air energy storage can provide some storage potential, we are still very far from a good, reliable, and scalable means of storage for electricity generation and supply.

Similarly, CCS faces scalability issues on the storage side. While studies suggest that there is potentially plenty of storage capacity for CO_2 emissions captured and geologically sequestered in the foreseeable future (Herzog 2001; IPCC 2005), as a practical matter, each geological storage site needs to be checked for leakage potential. This will require a potentially time-consuming effort by a large number of geologists. Detailed examinations cannot be ignored: CO_2 leakage would not only limit the effectiveness of CCS, but create a public hazard because CO_2 in concentrated form is an asphixiant that disperses only slowly if a leak occurs. It is true that there are a number of small-scale examples of CCS, but there is nothing even remotely approaching the scale required for CCS to contribute significantly to reducing future net CO_2 emissions. Finally, "conventional," once-through, nuclear fission is not only limited by uranium 235 supplies, but faces limitations with respect to storage of the large amounts of radioactive waste that would be generated even if nuclear simply maintained

its current 17 percent share of global electricity generation.

Storage is not the only "enabling" technology that is required to make a number of carbon-neutral energy technologies viable. Other examples include retrofit technologies for the large and rising number of coal-fired plants, especially those in China, India and the USA, or for an alternative CO_2 capture from the air (Lackner 2003; Pielke 2007a). While nuclear electric generation is an obvious low carbon-emitting alternative to coal, large-scale expansion will greatly increase the incentive to reprocess nuclear "waste." However, doing so will require some means of "spiking" the resulting plutonium to make it too hot to handle by terrorists, and a means of preventing nuclear proliferation. While the latter clearly involves political ingenuity, it also involves science and engineering developments – as is indicated by the apparent technological as well as political hurdles ahead for the US-promoted Global Nuclear Energy Partnership (GNEP) (Tollefson 2008).

Once the scalability problem is understood, it is easier to see why there is still a large technology gap between usable carbon-neutral energy with current technologies and the amount required for climate stabilization. Green *et al.* (2007), build on Hoffert *et al.* (1998), in an attempt to measure the "advanced energy technology gap" (AETG), the gap between the carbon-neutral energy required for stabilization and the carbon-neutral energy that could be supplied from "conventional" carbon-neutral sources. "Conventional" carbon-neutral energy technologies include: Hydroelectricity (subject to site limitations); once-through nuclear fission (subject to uranium 235 supplies as well as security, political, and waste storage limitations); solar and wind without storage; some biomass, geothermal, tidal, and wave (ocean) energies. Green *et al.* found that "conventional" carbon-neutral energy sources might, at a stretch, supply 10–13 TW by 2100. Liberally assuming 13 TW from these "conventional" sources, we still need 15–25 TW of power from advanced technologies (the AETG) to reach the 28–38 TW of carbon emissions-free energy required by 2100 to stabilize at 550 ppm, assuming a 2.4 percent rate of growth of GDP (1990–2100). These findings support the Hoffert *et al.* (1998, 2002) claim that major breakthroughs in new as well as existing energy technologies and sources will be required for stabilization at 550ppm, and even more so for stabilization at 450 ppm.

Implications for Copenhagen Consensus Benefit-Cost Assessment

Yohe *et al.* (2008) demonstrate that moderate mitigation combined with energy R&D passes, by a substantial margin, a benefit-cost test, even when a "descriptive" rather than "prescriptively" low discount rate is employed. However, despite some explicitness on the technology side, their modeling does not, I think, capture just how difficult (and, in the absence of numerous technological breakthroughs, potentially costly) stabilizing CO_2 concentrations at any acceptable level will be.

Yohe, *et al.* express some frustration at the Copenhagen Consensus 2008 budgetary constraint. I share their frustration: A climate policy limited *globally* to $75 billion over four years seems to take climate change less seriously than it deserves. Climate change has a long time-scale dimension, global reach, and such huge complexity that it arguably should be set apart from other policies considered by the Copenhagen Consensus. There is, it seems, an "apple and oranges" problem with the budget – the issues considered do not seem directly comparable and so are difficult to consider under a single common set of budget constraints.

Nevertheless, given the technology-based approach that is central to any feasible attempt to stabilize climate, the budget constraint may not be too binding in the near future. If an average of $18.75 billion were spent each year (totaling $75 billion over the four years of the Copenhagen Consensus accounting period); if after four years the rate of spending increases at a rate of growth of GDP (assumed to be a modest 2.2 percent per annum); and, if the spending is devoted to

developing new energy technologies, especially those of an "enabling" sort, it would not take long before energy R&D would become a major global preoccupation. Substantial, scalable, "on the shelf" technologies could be expected to follow. (As this constitutes a separate proposal for the panel to consider, a benefit-cost analysis is found in the appendix, p. 291.)

If the R&D were funded by a carbon tax, then it would take a tax of only $1 per ton CO_2 on 60 percent of the approximately 30 $GtCO_2$/year (~8GtC/year) currently emitted to raise an average of $18.75 billion/year over the first four years. The tax rate would have to rise slowly thereafter, although at a rate slower than 2.2 percent, if emissions continue to rise and/or the base of the tax is expanded beyond 60 percent of global emissions. But frankly, if it were politically feasible, I cannot see why we cannot do better by starting with a more robust $5-10/tonne CO_2 tax, and then allow that tax to rise gradually over time. To keep within Copenhagen Consensus ground rules, the extra revenues could be used to reduce other taxes, especially ones with a high marginal cost of public funds.

Inconvenient Truths

Former Vice-President Gore was right that climate change is an "inconvenient truth." But there is more than one "inconvenient truth": A second "inconvenient truth" is that climate change is a difficult-to-solve energy-technology problem. That, of course, has been the main theme of this paper. Unfortunately, recognition (especially in climate policy circles) of the second "inconvenient truth" remains long overdue.

As a result, there is growing interest in "geo-engineering" climate (Crutzen 2006; Wigley 2006; Matthews and Caldeira 2007) to reduce the impact of rising concentrations of GHGs on climate, if not the emissions themselves. There are several rationales for the interest in geo-engineering. These include: (i) its apparently relatively low monetary cost; (ii) the belief that policymakers will not act quickly enough to reduce emissions sharply, and (iii) a perceived need to buy time for requisite new and scalable technologies to reach fruition. However, as Wigley (2006) stresses, geo-engineering cannot be used as a replacement for mitigation. Mitigation directed towards GHG (particularly CO_2) concentration stabilization is essential in order to keep ocean acidity from rising to levels that might seriously damage the ocean biosphere. In Wigley's view, geo-engineering should be seen as a way to gain time to develop and deploy appropriate mitigation technologies, or as an emergency response should climate changes occur more rapidly than currently projected.

While research on the possible use and practical feasibility of geo-engineering is important (including possible adverse consequences), priority should be given to mitigation research and the energy technology challenges that GHG stabilization presents. As indicated above, the annual cost of such a race could for the time being stay within very conservatively defined budget constraints. Such a research effort could make use of the huge amount of brainpower in an increasingly educated *global* population of 6.5+ billion. It would also give the next and following generations a large challenge (one that motivates because it is based on *creativity* rather

than on *sacrifice*). Moreover, a science-driven energy-technology program could have numerous beneficial *spill-overs* into other uses.

Still, there is legitimate concern that an R&D spending spree could be more wasteful than helpful. What is lacking is the design of an incentive-compatible (energy) technology program. Possibly, competing international consortia could do the trick (Green 1994) – but this idea requires more thought. While a few economists have given attention to the R&D process as it may apply to climate change (e.g. Blanford and Clarke 2003), it seems to me that more attention to (practical) mechanism design and incentive compatibility would be highly desirable.

There is a final matter. Failure to take a real shot at tackling the "second inconvenient truth" increases the likelihood that we will face still another "inconvenient truth." If for lack of technological focus we must turn to geo-engineering, we may have to make lose–lose choices between possibly deleterious side effects of geo-engineering and unavoidable GHG-induced climate change. That is a "third inconvenient truth," and probably not the last that climate change will throw at us.

Appendix: Benefit-Cost Analysis

The Copenhagen Consensus calls for applying benefit-cost analysis whenever a specific program or policy is proposed. This paper has accented the role of technology in "stabilizing climate," suggesting that the magnitude of the technology challenge is so large that stabilization is essentially unachievable without a successful energy-technology program/race. As a result, some attention to quantifying the relative benefits and costs of a technology-based climate policy is required.

Applying benefit-cost analysis to a technology-based program aimed at stabilizing climate is a dubious proposition. The results, timing, scalability of successful technologies, and success in reducing their costs on the one hand, and the climate change damages avoided (benefits) on the other are so uncertain as to make benefit-cost assessment little more than impressionistic. Of more concern is that benefit-cost ratios could easily distract from the message of the paper: That not only is the technology challenge to stabilization huge, but analyses that use emissions scenarios as baselines systematically under-state the magnitude of the challenge.

To partially avoid these pitfalls, I employ a very simple analytical framework, which could easily be adjusted by the (disbelieving) reader. I have placed the benefit-cost exercise in an appendix so that it may be less obtrusive to the main argument of the paper.

Assumptions

The framework that I employ assumes that:

(1) For a *fifty-year* period (say 2010–60), the accent is on an *incentive-compatible* technology race in which R&D spending begins at $17.2 billion dollars in year 1 and rises at a 2.2 percent rate for the next forty-nine years (totaling $75 billion in the first four years). Thus over a fifty-year period *cumulative*, global R&D spending on new energy technologies would total an undiscounted $1.539 trillion. (R&D expenditures would be financed by a low, slowly rising carbon tax, as explained in the main text above.)

(2) Over the course of the fifty-year period enough successful, deployable, and scalable technologies will appear that together they are capable of displacing carbon-emitting ones at a pace that makes possible the eventual stabilization of climate, even if for a time carbon concentrations "overshoot" the long-term level at which they must (to avoid mounting damages) be stabilized. (The methods associated with, inducing deployment of successful technologies once they reach the "shelf" are ignored in the benefit-cost analysis.)

(3) "Avoidable damages" (*d*) are assumed variously to constitute 3 percent, 5 percent, or 8 percent of gross world product (GWP) if no action other than adaptation to climate change is taken. Damages are assumed to be 1 percent of GWP if climate policy focuses first on technology development followed by deployment (and thereby emission abatement – a version of "when flexible", mitigation, to use Yohe *et al.*'s (2008) parlance) when scalable, cost-effective technologies reach the "shelf." "Avoidable damages" constitute the "benefits" in the analysis.

(4) The growth rate of GWP from 2010 to 2100 is assumed to be 2.2 percent, rising from an

estimated $41 trillion in 2010 to $290 trillion US $ in 2060.

(5) All values are discounted back to the present at a rate (r), variously assumed to be 4 percent, 3 percent, and 1.4 percent to provide some sensitivity analysis.

Benefit-Cost Ratios

I compare three pairs of policies. These are:

1 **"Stand-alone" adaptation** – essentially this is "no-policy" Business as usual (BAU), but with adaptation. That is, BAU climate change-related damages are net of damages avoided due to adaptation but are gross of adaptation costs

2 **"Brute-force" mitigation** – in which carbon dioxide emission abatement takes place at a *pace dictated by politically chosen or dictated emission reduction targets*. The ultimate target is to reduce global emissions to 4GtC in 2100, in order to stabilize atmospheric GHG concentration at about 550 ppmv CO_{2e}. The policy is carried out irrespective of the availability of effective, scalable, energy technologies, *and* with no long-term, funded R&D policy directed toward fundamental changes in energy technologies. Emission reduction under brute-force mitigation is achieved in good part via emission-constraint-induced reductions in economic growth). It is assumed (unrealistically) that the emissions reduction to obviate substantial avoidable climate change causes damages. While the damage avoidance assumption is undoubtedly unrealistic, it allows for conservative estimates of benefit-cost ratios for alternative policies when they are compared with "brute-force" mitigation. Thus, in the benefit-cost analysis below, it is assumed that additional, avoidable climate change-related damages are zero in the brute-force mitigation case.

3 **The R&D-based approach** proposed in this paper places the accent on energy technology R&D. The pace of mitigation (essentially a

form of "when flexibility") is tailored to the appearance "on the shelf" of effective, scalable, and reasonably competitive technologies. R&D expenditures start at $17.2 billion and grow at a 2.2 percent rate over fifty years. At the end of the first four years they total $75 billion, in line with the Copenhagen Consensus budget constraint. By the fiftieth year, R&D reaches an undiscounted $51 billion. It is further assumed that the new and improved technologies that result are sufficiently tested to avoid quickly becoming inferior technologies (such as is the case of first-generation ethanol and biodiesel production from corn, soybeans, and palm oil). To add realism, the R&D approach assumes: (a) some additional, avoidable climate damages (equaling 1.0 percent of cumulative, discounted GWP) are incurred due to delayed ("when flexible") mitigation, and (b) there are some "deployment costs" associated with the introduction and dispersion of new technologies. The deployment costs (which include such things as new CO_2 pipelines for CCS, more secure facilities for reprocessed (closed-cycle) nuclear plants, and DC power lines for distant transmission of wind energy) are assumed to be 0.5 percent of GWP. I have used the wildly high figure of 0.5 percent of GWP as a crude means of demonstrating how robust is the conclusion from the benefit-cost analysis below that there are substantial net benefits from adopting an R&D approach to climate policy. (In reality, I would be surprised if deployment costs, which will not begin immediately, were much in excess of 0.1 percent of GWP.)

The analysis is carried out for policies covering the period 2010–2100. The values of variables, designed to provide a range of benefit-cost ratios, are as follows:

(a) trend rate of GWP growth (g): 0.022 (2.2 percent)

(b) curtailed rate of growth of GWP growth due to *brute-force* mitigation (g'): 0.018; 0.020; 0.021

(c) discount rates (r): 0.04, 0.03, 0.014 (the last is the r used in Stern Review, 2006)

(d) climate damages (percent of GWP) under *stand-alone* adaptation (d): 0.03; 0.05, 0.08

(e) R&D program (as described above), but with:

    – deployment costs: 0.5 percent of GWP

    – climate damages due to slower rate of mitigation (d'): 1.0 percent of GWP

The pairs of policies, and the range of benefit-cost ratios calculated for each pair, are as follows (note that the GWP growth baseline or "trend" (g) is assumed to be 2.2 percent (0.022)):

	Low	Central	High
R&D vs. brute-force mitigation*	4.0[a]	11.7[b]	30.2[c]
R&D vs. stand-alone adaptation**	3.8[d]	7.6[e]	13.5[f]
Stand-alone adaptation vs. brute-force mitigation***	0.6[g]	1.4[h]	3.8[j]

Notes:

a) $g' = 0.021$; $r = 0.04$ f) $d = 0.08$; $r = 0.014$

b) $g' = 0.02$; $r = 0.03$ g) $g' = 0.021$; $d = 0.08$; $r = 0.014$

c) $g' = 0.018$; $r = 0.014$ h) $g' = 0.020$; $d = 0.05$; $r = 0.03$

d) $d = 0.03$; $r = 0.04$ j) $g' = 0.018$; $d = 0.03$; $r = 0.04$

e) $d = 0.05$; $r = .003$

B/C = benefit-cost

* B/C = GWP not lost + damages not avoided/ R&D + deployment costs

** B/C = (net) damages avoided/R&D + deployment cost

*** B/C = GWP not lost/climate damages

The most noteworthy findings are: (i) that the R&D approach, which implies a somewhat delayed pace of ("when") mitigation, substantial deployment costs, and modest climate damages *significantly beats* "brute-force" mitigation under even the most favorable assumptions for the latter; (ii) the R&D approach not surprisingly beats stand-alone mitigation; and (iii), what will be surprising to many, "brute-force" mitigation only beats BAU stand-alone adaptation under Stern Review-type assumptions of high climate damages, low discount rate, and very modest abatement (mitigation cost) .

One noteworthy finding (not shown) is that when the R&D approach is compared to "brute-force" mitigation, the benefit-cost ratio for R&D rises as the discount rate (r) falls, *for any given mitigation-curtailed rate of growth* (g'). For example, when $g' = 0.018$, the benefit-cost ratio is 30.2 when a Stern Review rate of discount, $r = .014$, is used (as shown in the table above), but only 22.2 when $r = 0.04$. When $g' = 0.02$, the benefit-cost ratio rises from 11.6 (when $r = 0.04$) to 17.1 (when $r = 0.014$). This suggests to me that critics of the Stern Review may have paid too much attention to its treatment of "benefits" (avoidable climate damages) and not enough to its treatment of mitigation costs, which are alleged to be only 1.0 percent of GWP. A 1.0 percent decline in GWP from what it would otherwise be in 2100 is equivalent to a reduction from a 2.2 percent to a 2.18 percent growth rate over the ninety-year period 2010–2100, assuming $r = 0.014$, and to a 2.17 percent growth rate when $r = 0.04$. These tiny reductions in growth rate are nothing like what can be expected from "brute-force" mitigation. Yet arguably the Stern Review's proposed mitigation policy is quintessentially "brute force."

Qualifications

While it might seem natural to qualify with respect to the model framework and parameters, I shall not pursue that course. (The reader is more than welcome to make modifications and see whether any of these upset the general conclusion that a successful energy-technology race would pass a benefit-cost test with flying colors.) Instead, I will (i) comment on the assumption that I believe most requires qualification: that the R&D program/race proves sufficiently successful over the fifty-year period to provide the means of displacing carbon-emitting energy technologies/sources to an extent sufficient to avoid major climate damages and (ii) explain why "brute-force" mitigation could substantially reduce the rate of growth of GWP by much more than any other analyses that I have seen.

Successful R&D

The reason why the "success" assumption requires attention is that even if the world's scientific/engineering talent (human capital) and its scientific facilities are up to the task (as I think they are or can be), and if funding is adequate (as it certainly could be with the very slightest of "political will"), success is not assured. The "program" could still generate more waste than results. Everything from (a) governments' attempting to "pick winners," to (b) "lock-in" to new technologies that could turn out to be inferior to those that come along later, to (c) bureaucratic overload, to (d) turf disputes, to (e) the influences of lobbyists and ideology could derail a technology race.

For this reason, I suggested in the concluding section of the paper that economists (and other social scientists, too) might do well to give attention to the design of an incentive-compatible energy technology race. Here one might think in terms of *practical* "mechanism design," which could potentially have very large (social) payoffs.

Growth-Rate Effects of "Brute-Force" Mitigation

Will "brute-force" mitigation be as costly as I suggest? Suppose that in order to avoid large GHG-related damages, policymakers decide that emissions must be cut more or less in half (from current levels) *by 2100*. (Some scientists think they need to be cut in half by 2050.) To do so would require emissions falling at something like an 0.8 percent *average annual* rate between now and 2100, although likely *rising* for the first few decades and then declining at a much faster (than 0.8 percent) rate later in the century. The reduction can be achieved either by (i) cutting the rate of growth of GWP, or (ii) technology change that allows for a dramatic decline in the carbon intensity of GWP (C/GWP).

For carbon emissions to *decline* at an *average annual* rate of 0.8 percent (2010–2100) while

GWP grows at an *average annual* rate of 2.2 percent (the rate implied by the values in the "central" case), requires the carbon intensity of GWP to decline at an *average annual* rate of 3.0 percent. (That is: –0.8 percent = 2.2 percent – 3.0 percent). What has been our actual experience? In the last few decades of the twentieth century, the average annual rate of *decline* in the carbon intensity of GWP was about 1.4 percent. In the first five years of the twenty-first century C/GWP has declined at a much slower rate (0.7 percent), and that is only when GWP is measured in purchasing power parity (PPP) terms. C/GWP has actually *increased* in the first years of the twenty-first century when GWP is calculated using market exchange rates (Pielke *et al.* 2008).

While the drop in the rate of decline in C/GWP may be temporary, there is certainly no reason to expect it to decline at a rate dramatically greater than the rate that prevailed in the latter part of the twentieth century. But even if we could achieve a century-long 2.0 percent rate of decline in the carbon intensity of GWP with "conventional" low-carbon-emitting technologies, we would still fall far short of the 3.0 percent rate of decline in C/GWP required if emissions are to be cut in half by 2100 while maintaining a 2.2 percent "trend" rate of growth in GWP.

Something has to give! *Either* we engineer a successful energy technology race, *or* dramatically reduce the growth of GWP, *or* we simply end up with accumulating atmospheric GHGs and climate damages. Consider what would happen in the absence of a successful energy-technology program. If "brute-force" mitigation is adopted to meet dictated emission reductions, it is altogether plausible (as demonstrated above) that the growth rate of GWP would be forced to decline from its 2.2 percent "trend" rate to, say, 1.8 percent for the period 2010–2100. That would cost (an undiscounted) $85 trillion in 2100 alone and an undiscounted $2280 trillion *cumulative* over the ninety-year interval. And that would not do the trick if we cannot push the rate of *decline* in C/GWP up to something close to 2.6 percent.

Finally, it is useful to show why a "brute-force" approach to mitigation could reduce the growth rate by much more than the 0.4 percentage points that it takes off the "trend" growth rate (from 2.2 percent to 1.8 percent) in the example above. Suppose that energy-intensity decline (2010–2100) is 1.1 percent and that over the same period "conventional" carbon-free energy is raised from the current 2+ TW to 13 TW (Green *et al.* 2007, and discussion in the paper). These assumptions imply a 1.5 percent/year rate of decline (2010–2100) in the carbon intensity of GWP (C/GWP). But if emissions are to be reduced to 4GtC by 2100 (that is, at a –0.8%/year rate), then the GWP growth rate would have to be limited to an average of 0.7 percent (–0.8 percent = 0.7 percent –1.5 percent). The cumulative undiscounted loss in GWP would be $6231 trillion. Enough said!

Bibliography

Baksi, S. and Green, C., 2007: Calculating economy-wide energy intensity decline rate: The role of sectoral output and energy shares, *Energy Policy*, **35**: 6457–66

Barker, T., Bashmakov, I., Althari, A., Amann, M., Chifuentes, L., Drexhage, J., Duan, M., Edenhofer, O., Flannery, B., Grubb, M., Hoogwijk., M., Ibitoye, F.I., Jepma, C.J., Pizer, W.A., and Yamaji, K., 2007: Mitigation from a cross-sectional perspective, in *Climate change 2007: Mitigation*, Contribution of Working Group III to the Fourth Assessment Report of the Intergovernmental Panel on Climate Change, B. Metz, O.R. Davidson, P.R. Bosch, R. Dave, and L.A. Meyer (eds.), Cambridge University Press, Cambridge

Battelle Memorial Institute, 2001: *Global energy technology strategy: Addressing climate change*, Joint Global Change Research Institute, College Park, MD

Blanford, G. and Clarke, L., 2003: On the optimal allocation of R&D resources for climate change technology development, Technical Report, UCRL–TR–200982, Lawrence Livermore National Laboratory, California

Caldeira, K., Jain, A.K., and Hoffert, M.I., 2003: Climate sensitivity, uncertainty and the need for energy without CO_2 emission, *Science*, 299: 2052–4

Crutzen, P., 2006: Albedo enhancement by stratospheric sulfur injections: A contribution to resolve a policy dilemma? *Climatic Change,* 77: 211–19

Edmonds, J.A. and Smith, S.J., 2006: The technology of two degrees, in H.J. Schnellnhuber *et al.* (eds.), *Avoiding dangerous climate change*, Cambridge University Press, Cambridge: 385–92

Edmonds, J.A., Wise, M.A., Dooley J.J., Kim, S.H., Smith, S.J., Runci, P.J., Clarke, L.E., Malone, E.L., and Stokes, GM., 2007: *Global energy technology strategy: Addressing climate change*, Global Energy Technology Strategy Program, Battelle Memorial Institute

Fisher, B.S., Nakićenović, N., Alfsen, K., Corfee Morlot, J., de la Chesnaye, F., Hourcade, J.-Ch., Jiang, K., La Rovere, E., Matysek, A., Rana, A., Riahi, K., Richels, R., Rose, S., van Vuuren, D., and Warren, R., 2007: Issues related to mitigation in the long term context, in *Climate change 2007: Mitigation*, Contribution of Working Group III to the Fourth Assessment Report of the Intergovernmental Panel on Climate Change, B. Metz, O.R. Davidson, P.R. Bosch, R. Dave, and L.A. Meyer (eds.), Cambridge University Press, Cambridge

Green, C., 1994: The greenhouse effect and environmentally induced technological change, in Y. Shionoya and M. Perlman, *Innovations in technology, industries, and institutions: Studies in Schumpeterian perspectives*, University of Michigan Press, Ann Arbor

Green, C., Baksi, S., and Dilmaghani, M., 2007: Challenges to a climate stabilizing energy future, *Energy Policy*, **35**, 616–26

Green, C. and Lightfoot, H.D., 2002: Making climate stabilization easier than it will be: The report of IPCC WG III, *C^2GCR Quarterly*, **2002–1**

Herzog, H.J., 2001: What future for carbon capture and sequestration?, *Environmental Science and Technology*, 35(7): 148–53

Hoffert, M.I., Caldeira, K., Jain, A.K., Haites,

E.F., Harvey, L.D.H., Potter, S.D., Schlesinger, M.E., Schneider, S.H., Watts, R.G., Wigley, T.M.L., and Weubbles, D.J., 1998: Energy implications of future stabilization of atmospheric CO_2 content, *Nature*, **395**: 881–4

Hoffert, M.I., Caldeira, K., Benford, G., Criswell, D.R., Green, C., Herzog, H., Jain, A.K., Kheshgi, H.S., Lackner, K.S., Lewis, J.S., Lightfoot, H.D., Manheimer, W., Mankins, J.C., Mauel, M.E., Perkins, J., Schlesinger, M.E., Volk, T., and Wigley, T.M.L., 2002: Advanced technology paths to global climate stability: Energy for a greenhouse planet, *Science*, **298**: 981–7

IPCC (Intergovernmental Panel on Climate Change), 2001: Contribution of WG III, *Climate change 2001: Mitigation*, Cambridge University Press, Cambridge

IPCC (Intergovernmental Panel on Climate Change), 2005: Special Report, *Carbon dioxide capture and storage*, Cambridge University Press, Cambridge

IPCC (Intergovernmental Panel on Climate Change), 2007a: Working Group III, *Climate change 2007: Mitigation of climate change*, Cambridge University Press, Cambridge

IPCC (Intergovernmental Panel on Climate Change), 2007b: Fourth Assessment Report, *Climate change 2007: Synthesis report,* Summary for Policy Makers, Cambridge University Press, Cambridge

Lackner, K.S., 2003: A guide to CO_2 sequestration, *Science*, **300**: 1677–8

Lightfoot, H.D. and Green, C., 2002: An assessment of IPCC Working Group III findings of the potential contribution of renewable energies to atmospheric carbon dioxide stabilization, McGill University, Centre for Climate and Global Change Research, Report **2002–5**, November

Matthews, H.D. and Caldeira, K., 2007: Transient climate-carbon simulations of planetary geoengineering, *Proceedings of National Academy of Sciences*, **104**: 9949–53

Metz, B., Davidson, O., Swart, R., and Pan, J., 2001: Intergovernmental Panel on Climate Change, Third Assessment Report, Working Group III, *Climate change 2001: Mitigation*, Cambridge University Press, Cambridge

Montgomery, D. and Smith, A., 2005: Price, quantity and technology strategies for climate change policy, *Human-induced climate change: An interdisciplinary assessment,* Cambridge University Press, Cambridge

Nakićenović, N. *et al.*, 2000: *Special report on emission scenarios*, Working Group III, IPCC, Cambridge University Press, Cambridge

Pacala, S. and Socolow, R., 2004: Stabilization wedges: Solving the climate problem for the next 50 years with current technologies, *Science*, **305**: 968–72

Pielke, R.A., Jr., 2005: Misdefining "climate change": Consequences for science and action, *Environmental Science and Policy,* **8**: 548–61

Pielke, R.A., Jr., 2007a: Air capture of carbon dioxide: Economic and political implications (under review at *Energy Policy*)

Pielke, R.A. Jr., 2007b: Future economic damages from tropical cyclones: Sensitivities to societal and climate changes, *Philosophical Transactions of the Royal Society A*, doi:10.1098/rsta.2007.2086: 1–13

Pielke, R.A., Jr., Wigley, T.M.L., and Green, C., 2008: Dangerous assumptions, *Nature*, **452**: 531–2

Riahi, K. and Roehri, R.A., 2001: Energy technology strategies for carbon dioxide mitigation and sustainable development, *Environmental Economics and Policy Studies*, 3(2): 89–123

Rosen, D.H. and Houser, T., 2007: China energy: A guide for the perplexed, Working Paper, Peterson Institute for International Economics, Washington, DC

Sanden, B.A. and Azar, C., 2005: Near-term technology policies for long-term climate targets: Economy wide versus technology specific approaches, *Energy Policy*, **33**:1557–76

Schelling, T.C., 1992: Some economics of global warming, *American Economic Review*, **82**(1): 1–14

Stern, N., 2006 *Stern review report on the economics of climate change,* HM Treasury, London

Tollefson, J., 2008: Nuclear fuel: keeping it civil, *Nature*, **451**: 380–1

Wigley, T.M.L., 2006: A combined mitigation/

geo-engineering approach to climate stabilization, *Science,* **314**: 452–4

Wigley, T.M.L., Caldeira, K., Green, C., and Hoffert.M.I., 2007: Climate, energy and CO_2 stabilization, March (unpublished)

Wigley, T.M.L., Richels, R., and Edmonds, J.A., 1996: Economic and environmental choices in the stabilization of atmospheric CO_2 concentrations, *Nature*, **379**: 240–3

Yohe, G.W., Tol, R.S.J., Richels, R.G. and Blanford, G.J, 2008: *Climate change*, see chapter 5 in this volume

Perspective Paper 5.2

ANIL MARKANDYA

Introduction

I find myself in agreement with much of the analysis of Yohe *et al.* in their Challenge paper (Yohe *et al.* 2008). To summarise, I think they are broadly correct when they say that:

- The consequences of climate change are serious, more so for developing countries than for developed ones. Indeed for some time to come climate change may well produce benefits in the more temperate zones, where most of the wealthier countries lie.
- The causes of climate change are to be found in the increased emissions of GHGs. Reductions in these gases will also reduce likely climatic impacts but mitigation will be expensive and the likely benefits may be small compared to the costs, *when the latter are measured using conventional discount rates of 4–5 per cent in real terms.*
- The benefits of action are enhanced when measures to reduce GHGs are accompanied by support for R&D in low-carbon technologies and when action is taken to adapt to climate change, especially by investing in measures to reduce the health impacts of such change.
- The ratio of benefits to costs rises further if mitigation policy is 'flexible', so that reductions are made when they are most effective.
- The same ratio goes up a great deal more if

we take account of uncertainty, where this uncertainty is measured in terms of the climate sensitivity parameter. This is true even when the benefits are still measured in terms of expectations – i.e. no account is taken of risk aversion.

In this Perspective paper I would like to make the following points. First, I believe the case for action on climate change is stronger than Yohe *et al.* (2008) have stated. They have gone for a minimalist approach, perhaps on the grounds that if the case can be made on the basis of the least controversial assumptions, it would be made, *a fortiori*, when these additional factors are taken into account. Notwithstanding this, I think the authors could have looked more closely at the *maximum potential* for GHG reduction that is justifiable given the parameters they have adopted. If a benefit-cost ratio of up to 7 is estimated for modest actions, a lower but still acceptable ratio may be justified for more severe actions.

Apart from this general point, I consider that four other factors need further attention. These are: (a) the estimation of benefits, (b) the issue of distributional effects, (c) the benefits of early action in opening up more options for the future and (d) a deeper treatment of uncertainty.[1] Each of these is now considered in turn.

Estimation of Benefits

The benefits estimated by Yohe *et al.* (2008) are most likely to be under-estimates of the damages of climate change. The *FUND* model, on which the Challenge paper is based, is well known for being conservative on the damages compared to

[1] I do not make any special comment on the choice of discount rate for discounting benefits. There is a substantial literature that argues for lower discount rates for programs with impacts over very long periods: see Stern (2006) for further details. If one took a lower discount rate as many suggest, the benefits of climate actions would exceed the costs by an even greater margin.

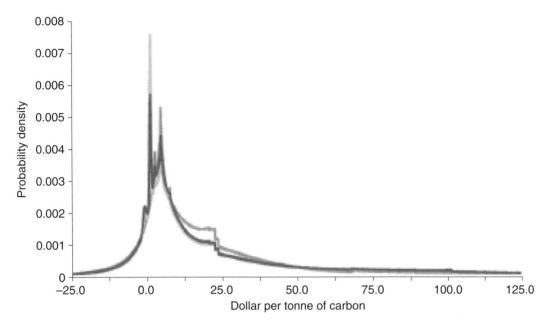

Figure 5.2.1 *Range of damage estimates in different studies*
Source: Tol (2005).

many other studies. Figure 5.2.1 shows the range of damage from studies as a density function, collected by one of the challenge authors (Tol 2005). Tol himself is very close to the modal value of this distribution, which is also the result of the *FUND* model with which he works. But there are others who have much higher estimates and the whole distribution is heavily positively skewed. Do we simply ignore them? That does not seem reasonable as several other models reported in the peer-reviewed literature are also credible. A mean value across all studies would be higher than that taken in the Challenge paper, even if one excluded some of the 'outliers'. Hence one can safely conclude that, based on the existing evidence, the Challenge paper is an under-estimate of the average damage costs in the literature.

Furthermore the literature itself needs to be recognised as incomplete. Many possible impacts have not been valued, because the nature of the impacts has not been fully characterized. Figure 5.2.2 shows the areas where there have been studies and where there have not. The

possible consequences of system change and surprise have not been evaluated in the literature. Nor have the 'socially contingent' impacts of climate-induced changes. These include migrations, social conflicts and the like. I accept that it is very difficult to include these at this stage, but that cannot be a reason for saying that they do not matter for policy purposes. If benefit estimation is unable to make progress in estimating such damages, we need other tools for making decisions in the area of climate change. That is the position taken by several people working the field, who argue that a notion of *acceptable risk* is a sounder approach in these circumstances.

Distributional Effects

Yohe *et al.* (2008) recognise that there are worrying distributional consequences to climate change, but they do not do anything about them in the reported cost-benefit analysis (CBA). The benefits are the simple sum of the reduced damages following a reduction in GHG emissions,

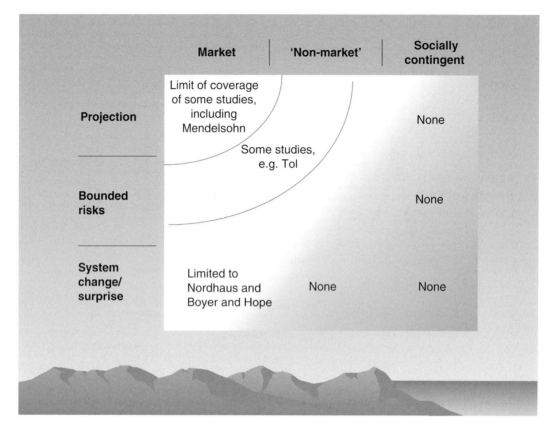

Figure 5.2.2 *Range of studies on climate impacts*

irrespective of where they occur. Yet no one seriously argues that decisions on investment of public funds between competing uses should be done without taking account of such distributional effects. In the case of climate change these regional differences are particularly egregious. If we look at figures 5.2 and 5.3 of the Challenge paper (pp. 241 and 244), the combined market and non-market damages in the LDCs (excluding China) are positive and significant throughout the period of analysis (to 2300) in the absence of climate change mitigation, while in the developed countries they are much smaller and possibly even negative for the next decade

[2] It is difficult to assess the total damages, as the market and non-market damages have not been added up in the Challenge paper. My comments are based on a visual examination of the two curves.

or two. China seems to be an exception, with negative damages (i.e. benefits) to about 2075.[2] Nevertheless it is clear that the 'Business as usual' (BAU) case implies higher damages to most poor countries and some benefits to the more developed countries.

From this starting point, any action taken generates greater benefits in the LDCs than it does in the developed (OECD) countries. At least that appears to be the case to 2100. This fact should be reflected in the final data looked at by those who make the decisions. Not to do so would be to ignore an important dimension of the problem.

Conversely not taking any action is tantamount to imposing higher costs on the poor than on the rich. Indeed, it could even be seen as providing benefits to the rich and imposing costs on the poor. At a discount rate of 5 per cent, most of the relevant costs and benefits are those over the next fifty years or so anyway, and, based on figures 5.2 and 5.3, up to 2050 the OECD countries have no damage costs while developing countries have costs of about 0.3 per cent of their GDP. Not acting on climate change is therefore a policy of transferring welfare from the poorer to the wealthier countries.

The Benefits of Early Action

The literature on climate change notes that there could be benefits to early action. The Stern Report, for example, makes this point on a number of occasions. Others have examined the problem of making decisions with irreversible consequences in other contexts from an options perspective (Dixit and Pindyck 1996; Mun 2005).

The issue here is that over time we will learn more about climate change and about the consequences of emissions generated today. If this process reveals that the situation is more benign than we thought, so much to the good. But if it reveals that the situation is more serious than our 'average' view, then it may be too late to take action, if previous action was based on an 'average' view of the seriousness of climate change.

I illustrate the problem with a simple example that captures many of the features of climate policy. Suppose we have three time periods in our horizon, one of which is the present. Suppose further that we can make decisions twice: once now and once at the end of the first period, when the true nature of the damages from emissions will be revealed. The costs of action are an increasing function of the level of emissions reductions. To provide a numerical illustration I have assumed that a 1 per cent reduction in emissions increases costs by 1.2 per cent. I assume furthermore that in any period the maximum reduction that is possible is 10 per cent from the BAU scenario. Of course the 'BAU scenario' will change as emissions are themselves altered by reductions in previous periods.

In period 1 we are told the precise nature of the climate change problem. The 'optimistic' scenario is that we discover there is no problem and associated damages are zero. The pessimistic scenario is that we discover the damages are twice the average we assumed in period 0. I assume that probabilities of each event are equal and that current expected values are correct. For such an example I consider two actions or programmes. The first is to reduce emissions in period 0 (i.e. today) by 10 per cent and then in period 2 to either take no action (if it is revealed that there is no problem), or to reduce them by a further 10 per cent if the problem is severe. The resulting figures show that the expected benefits from the programme are positive (equal to 2.87 in table 5.2.1), although if we look only at the costs and benefits of the period 0 to period 1 the net figure is zero.[3] Thus on benefit-cost ground the two-period decision would be marginal while a full three-period analysis is positive.

It is possible, however to think of a government as undertaking a bigger reduction in period 0 in view of the fact that future reductions are constrained and the situation may turn out to be more serious than anticipated. If the decision-maker chooses to make a reduction of 15 per cent on this basis instead of the 10 in period 1, the two-period net benefits are negative, but the three-period net benefits are both positive and greater than with action 1 (3.64 instead of 2.87).

The example makes two points. First, a short time-period analysis is misleading when the costs and benefits are linked over several periods. Second there can be a value to undertaking more emissions reductions today when future options are limited and when future knowledge will reveal information that may make it attractive to keep more options open in the future. In this simple example, the additional reduction of 5 per cent in emissions in period 0 can be seen as buying the option of making a bigger overall

---

[3] For the sake of simplicity I have not introduced any discounting. Doing so does not change the point being made.

Table 5.2.1. An example of the benefits of early action

Data	Period	Total	0	1	2
	Emissions BAU		0.00	150.00	200.00
	Damages (a)		0.00	0.00	0.00
	Damages (b)		0.00	30.00	40.00
Action 1					
	Controlled Emissions (a)	270.00	0.00	135.00	135.00
	Controlled Emissions (b)	297.00	0.00	135.00	162.00
	Damages (a)	0.00	0.00	0.00	0.00
	Damages (b)	59.40	0.00	27.00	32.40
	Costs (a)	1.50	0.00	1.50	0.00
	Costs (b)	3.37	0.00	1.50	1.87
	Benefits (a)	−1.50	0.00	−1.50	0.00
	Benefits (b)	7.23	0.00	1.50	5.73
	Expected Net Benefits	2.87	0.00	0.00	2.87
	Expected Benefits Period 0–1	0.00			
Action 2					
	Controlled Emissions (a)	255.00	0.00	127.50	127.50
	Controlled Emissions (b)	280.50	0.00	127.50	153.00
	Damages (a)	0.00	0.00	0.00	0.00
	Damages (b)	56.10	0.00	25.50	30.60
	Costs (a)	2.44	0.00	2.44	0.00
	Costs (b)	4.18	0.00	2.44	1.74
	Benefits (a)	−2.44	0.00	−2.44	0.00
	Benefits (b)	9.72	0.00	2.06	7.66
	Expected Net Benefits	3.64	0.00	−0.19	3.83
	Expected Benefits Period 0–1	−0.19			

reduction in emissions in period 1 in case it is discovered that the problem is more serious than was originally envisaged.

The analysis presented by Yohe *et al.* (2008) does not include the benefits of such options because it does not build-in *sequential learning*. Doing so will justify larger reductions today and will generate larger cost-benefit ratios for given reductions.

Uncertainty

Uncertainty is at the heart of the climate problem. Although Yohe *et al.* (2008) recognise its importance, I do not believe they give it the central role that it deserves.

In most applications of CBA, uncertainty is treated by replacing a range of possible costs and benefits by their expected values. This is what Yohe *et al.* (2008) have done and they show that the expected benefits increase sharply as account is taken of the more extreme outcomes. The result is a reflection of the substantially non-linear and convex damage function, where damages rise sharply and more than proportionally with climate sensitivity.

The authors could have gone further and added a risk premium to the damages, based on the willingness of people to pay (WTP) to reduce

the uncertainty associated with future developments.[4] Doing so is not difficult, and based on
the lognormal distributions they have taken, the
reductions in damages would then turn out to be
even greater, raising the benefit-cost ratio even
further beyond the 7 they obtain.

At a deeper level, however, one can question the use of benefit-cost analysis in these
circumstances. The problem is that we do not
know the probability distribution for the key
parameters that will determine the seriousness
of the climate impacts. Generally the discussion
is focused on the climate sensitivity parameter
and a lognormal distribution is taken. But the
variance of that distribution is not known. Nor
is the property of the tail of the distribution that
defines the likelihood of extreme events (e.g.
temperature increases of more than 6^0C with a
doubling of emissions, referred to in the literature as the climate sensitivity parameter S). All
we know is that it is not insignificant. Based on
IPCCIV (2007), the probability is that $S > 6^0$ is
about 5 per cent and the probability that it is
greater than 8^0C is about 2 per cent. These are
not insignificant probabilities, and they represent outcomes that would be catastrophic.

As Weitzman (2007) has shown, such extreme
events cause problems for decision-making
within the cost-benefit framework. One cannot
base decisions on expected utility theory, let
alone on expected value theory because the
relevant functions are unbounded. Moreover
knowledge about the parameters of the distribution cannot be learned from experience in
the usual Bayesian sense when the tails are so
'fat' to begin with. This is a dismal result in
many respects and Weitzman refers to it as the
'Dismal Theorem'. To quote from his paper, he
concludes:

> Perhaps in the end the economist can help most
> by not presenting a cost-benefit estimate for
> such situations as if it is accurate and objec-
> tive, and not even presenting the analysis as
> if it is an approximation to something that is
> accurate and objective, but by stressing the fact
> that such an estimate is arbitrarily inaccurate
> depending upon what is subjectively assumed
> about the tails and where they have been cut off.

This is unsatisfying and not what economists
are used to, but in situations where the Dismal
Theorem applies we may be deluding ourselves
and others if we think that we are able to deliver
anything much more precise than this with
even the biggest and most-detailed Integrated
Assessment Models.

This poses a more fundamental challenge to
the kind of exercise being undertaken under
the Copenhagen Consensus, where benefit-cost
ratios are the *sine qua non* on the basis of which
all decisions are made. We have to come to terms
with the fact that in some respects they are not,
and in the case of climate change we have to
include other supplementary or complementary
factors in deciding what actions are justified and
what are not. One such criterion is to ask what
the level of acceptable risk is that we can tolerate
and what are we willing to sacrifice to reduce the
actual level of risk to that acceptable level. Much
of the climate change debate is taking place in
such a framework, rather than a benefit-cost
framework.

Conclusions

This paper has made the following points:

- Climate change actions are justified on the
  basis provided in the Challenge paper, but
  the case can be made stronger if some other
  factors are taken into account. The Challenge
  paper could go further in seeing how much
  action is justified – it stops short of the most
  that can be supported on a cost-benefit basis.
- One reason to think that the Challenge paper
  errs too much on the low side is that the
  benefits of reducing emissions are under-
  estimated. The literature contains some much
  higher – and credible estimates.
- The second reason for arguing that action
  is justified is the distribution of the benefits.
  Climate action benefits most poor countries
  more than it does developed ones; conversely
  not taking action hurts poor countries more

[4] In a later version of their paper, Yohe *et al.* do discuss
this issue and recognise it.

than rich ones. Normally some weight is given to the distributional impacts of government investments when evaluating such measures. In our case such a weight would favour climate action (although it could also favour some of the other proposed actions being considered).

- The third reason for supporting more GHG reduction now is the benefits of early action. These buy the option of undertaking more reductions in the future if climate turns out to be a more serious problem than first thought.
- Finally there is the issue of uncertainty. Bringing in risk aversion would make the benefits larger than in the Challenge paper. But a more fundamental point is that with the kind of uncertainties we face the benefit estimation methods based on expected value and expected utility break down. We need to take account of the possibility of extreme events in a complementary framework, where governments decide on acceptable levels of risk and seek to minimise the costs of achieving those levels.

Bibliography

Dixit, A.K. and Pindyck, R.S., 1994: *Investment under uncertainty*, 2nd edn., Princeton University Press, Princeton

IPCC4, 2007: *Climate change, 2007: The physical science basis*, Contribution of Working Group I to the Fourth Assessment Report of the Intergovernmental Panel on Climate Change, Cambridge University Press, www.ipcc.ch

Mun, J., 2005: Real options analysis: Tools and techniques for valuing strategic investment and decisions, 2nd edn., Wiley Finance, New York

Stern, N., 2006: *Stern review on the economics of climate change*, Cambridge University Press, Cambridge, www.hmtreasury.gov.uk/independent_reviews/stern_review_economics_climate_change/sternreview_report.cfm

Tol, R.S.J., 2005, The marginal damage costs of carbon dioxide emissions: An assessment of the uncertainties, Energy Policy, **33**(16): 2064–74

Weitzman, M., 2007: The role of uncertainty in the economics of catastrophic climate change, Harvard University Working Paper, Cambridge, MA

Yohe, G.W., Tol, R.S.J., Richels, R.G., and Blanford, G.J., 2008: *Climate change*, see chapter 5 in this volume

Hunger and Malnutrition

SUE HORTON, HAROLD ALDERMAN, AND
JUAN A. RIVERA

Despite significant reductions in income poverty in recent years, under-nutrition remains widespread. Estimates published in the *Lancet* (Black *et al.* 2008) suggest that "maternal and child Under-nutrition is the underlying cause of 3.5 million deaths, 35 percent of the disease burden in children younger than 5 years, and 11 percent of total global DALYs." Under-nutrition can be indicated both by anthropometric indices (underweight, stunting, and wasting) and by missing micronutrients in poor-quality diets.

Under-nutrition in turn has negative effects on income and on economic growth. Under-nutrition leads to increased mortality and morbidity, which lead to loss of economic output and increased spending on health. Poor nutrition means that individuals are less productive (due to both physical and mental impairment), and that children benefit less from education. The 2004 Copenhagen Consensus paper on the topic discusses these mechanisms in detail (Behrman, Alderman, and Hoddinott 2004) (hereafter, BAH 2004). Reducing under-nutrition is one of the MDGs (Goal 1 aims to eradicate extreme poverty and hunger), and is also a key factor underpinning several others. Achieving goals in primary education, reducing child mortality, improving maternal health, and combating HIV/AIDS, malaria, and other diseases all depend crucially on nutrition.

There are cost-effective interventions for improving nutrition. The first section below discusses the challenge in more detail, the second describes selected priority solutions; the third section undertakes more detailed economic analysis of these solutions, and the fourth and final section discusses the implications of the analysis. This chapter builds on and updates previous detailed analysis from BAH 2004, and focuses on pushing the analysis for some solutions further than was possible at that time, adding analysis of some additional solutions, and incorporating what is new from the extensive research literature on nutrition interventions.

The Challenge

Available data tend to highlight nutritional deficiencies in the under-five population, where the consequences are very obvious (high mortality, losses in cognitive development) – but nutritional deficiencies are obviously also important in the other 88 percent of the developing world's population. Nutrition in the under-fives depends critically on nutrition of their mothers during pregnancy and lactation. Black *et al.* (2008) summarize the most up-to-date data on nutritional status. The data they use include anthropometric measurements expressed relative to expected body measurements in healthy populations, and estimates of micronutrient deficiencies based on serum determinations and food intake. The FAO provides regular updates on world hunger, in the *World food and state of food security in the world reports* (hunger is measured by data on aggregate food availability and patterns of distribution).

South Asia alone accounts for almost half of the world's population of stunted children under five (73.8 of the 177.7 million), and 10.3 of the 19.3 million severely wasted children. Africa accounts for another 56.9 million of the stunted and 5.6 million of the severely wasted (Black *et al.* 2008). ("Stunted" is defined as more than 2 standard deviations below the population standard for height-for-age, and "severely wasted" is more than 3 standard deviations below the standard for weight-for-height.) Underweight is declining in most regions, although in only a couple of regions (East Asia/Pacific, and Latin America/Caribbean) has it declined at a rate fast enough to meet the MDGs. Underweight is increasing in two regions (Eastern/Southern Africa; and Middle East/North Africa, where three large countries are experiencing conflict): UNICEF (2006). Underweight (weight-for-age) is a less precise measure of chronic nutritional status, but trends in stunting and wasting are less readily available.

Micronutrient under-nutrition is generally correlated with overall under-nutrition, since poverty limits both the quality as well as quantity of food in the diet. There are some exceptions, such as iodine deficiency, where iodine deficiency in the soil (dependent on geographic factors) has important impacts on dietary intake, if people rely mainly on local food:

- Prior to widespread salt iodization in the developing world, an estimated 633 million individuals suffered from goiter (WHO 2003): Currently 31 percent of developing-world households still do not consume iodized salt and are therefore not protected (UNICEF 2006). The lagging countries are in SSA, South Asia, and Central and Eastern Europe/ Commonwealth of Independent States (CIS).
- UNICEF (2006) estimates that 100–140 million children (mainly in South Asia and SSA) are still deficient in vitamin A, despite supplementation efforts in many countries.
- An estimated 2 billion individuals worldwide suffer from iron deficiency, of whom more than half are in South Asia. Progress has been very difficult, although policy efforts are intensifying. Age and reproductive status is at least as important as poverty in determining iron deficiency.
- Zinc deficiency is hard to measure but tends to be correlated with iron deficiency and low animal food intake. IZINCG (2004) estimates that 20 percent of the world's population is at risk for deficiency based on food intake patterns.
- Concern over folate is relatively new. Although diets based on unrefined grains and beans

(such as those in many rural areas of developing countries) tend to have good folate content, small studies for India and China find high incidence of birth defects, perhaps related to refined rice as the main staple. More work is needed.

The very significant societal and economic consequences of under-nutrition are categorized in an entire section of BAH 2004. They group the consequences into resource losses due to higher mortality and morbidity, direct links between nutrition and physical productivity, and indirect effects on productivity via cognitive development and schooling, and provide an extensive literature survey. Many studies provide estimates of the billions of dollars of economic losses attributable to under-nutrition, e.g. World Bank (2006) and Horton (2004).

Since the publication of the 2004 Copenhagen Consensus volume, there have been additional research studies extending our knowledge of the consequences of under-nutrition. Some of the more significant ones are longitudinal studies providing direct documentation of the effects in later life of under-nutrition in early childhood, rather than relying on inference. In inferential studies, for example, micronutrient supplementation in childhood is known to increase cognitive scores, and cognitive scores in adulthood are known to affect wages and hence productivity, so the effect of childhood supplementation on wages can be reliably inferred. BAH 2004 relied mainly on such studies, bolstered in some cases by comparison of twins or natural experiments. The new – and relatively few – longitudinal studies link data on childhood nutrition interventions directly to wages and other outcomes for those same individuals upon reaching adulthood. These studies confirm the general reliability of the inferential studies and also offer additional insights.

One important recent study tracks the consequences of an intervention supplying protein and micronutrients, originally undertaken between 1969 and 1977 in Guatemala. The individuals were re-surveyed in 2002–4, by which time the individuals were between twenty-five and forty-two years old, and had participated in the intervention for varying numbers of years at varying ages below the age of seven. The results in one paper (Hoddinott *et al.* 2008) show that wages for men who had received supplements below age three had wage rates which were 34–47 percent higher than those of the controls, and annual incomes 14–28 percent higher. Effects for women were not significant, which the authors attribute to women's paid labor market participation in this region being largely restricted to low-productivity activities such as agricultural processing.

Another paper from the same study documents that exposure to the supplement before the age of two was associated with increased schooling by 1.2 years for women, an increase in reading comprehension by 17 percent for men and women, and an increase in performance on Raven's test of Progressive Matrices of 8 percent (Maluccio *et al.* 2006). Even in the absence of direct wage benefits from schooling for women, plausibly there are benefits for the household from the increase in schooling of women.

Lozoff *et al.* (2006) provide a notable longitudinal study of iron supplementation in children of ages one and two, tracking the same individuals eighteen years later in Costa Rica. In the original intervention, anemia was corrected with iron supplements in the treatment group but not in the control. Results are reported for children without anemia at the end of the intervention as compared to those with anemia (hence this compares children in the treatment group and non-anemic children in the control group, with anemic children in the control group). Obviously the non-anemic group contained a higher proportion of higher socioeconomic status (SES) households, which is a possible confounding variable. Children received cognitive tests at five different points up to the age of nineteen.

The results are quite striking and suggest that in the middle SES group, those with adequate iron status scored 8–9 points above those who remained anemic in early childhood, a difference that was maintained up to the age of nineteen. In the lower SES group, those with adequate iron status scored 10 points higher in early child-

hood, which increased to 25 points at the age of nineteen. These differences generate significant differences in educational attainment and earnings that are being monitored (the Costa Rica study is still on-going).

Clearly, if improvement in nutrition can be achieved the benefits will be appreciable. But in order to assess the value of interventions as investments one also needs to know what resources are required to achieve a given improvement. Although poverty is a major underlying cause of malnutrition, programs to increase income or provide food to the poor are not necessarily the only (or the fastest) way to intervene. Environmental factors often adversely affect nutrition (for example, intestinal parasites and infections can lead to nutrient losses). Education also has important impacts. The mother's diet during pregnancy, her breastfeeding practices and weaning practices all have critical impacts on her baby, and nutritional deficiencies prior to about the age of two are crucial for nutritional status throughout the rest of life. Thus, in addition to interventions aimed at addressing poverty and low food intake, improvements in sanitation and in access to education can address underlying causes of malnutrition.

Technology can also be used to enhance nutrition. Developed countries have widely used food fortification (for the majority of the population) and supplementation (for specific groups) to improve nutrition, and developing countries have additional options with the advances in biotechnology. There are also circumstances where under-nutrition is related to special situations of the population, such as refugees, and HIV/AIDS. However, we are not addressing solutions for these special populations in this chapter, despite their importance.

To summarize, while there have been a number of key studies on the benefits of reducing malnutrition in terms of deaths averted, health care costs reduced, and productivity increased since BAH 2004, these largely confirm the estimates in that study. In contrast, new information on how to achieve results and improve delivery systems has substantial implications for program design. The next section focuses on a limited number of these promising solutions, based on some of the causal pathways identified above.

Solutions

We can group interventions to improve nutrition into at least three broad categories: Highly cost-effective interventions which involve or are similar to primary health interventions; cost-effective interventions which largely involve behavior change; and, finally, cost-effective but more costly interventions which transfer food and/or income to beneficiaries. In this section, because of the emphasis on costs and cost-effectiveness (CE) levels we focus on the first two categories only.

Highly cost-effective interventions improving nutrition include micronutrient interventions and the distribution of anthelminths over a wide range of age groups. A considerable amount of attention is currently being devoted to research on micronutrient interventions. Micronutrients were examined at length in the BAH 2004. The next sub-section updates that discussion, with extensions to some topics (zinc and folic acid) not previously treated at length. The following sub-section is devoted to anthelminths which were mentioned but not analyzed in detail in BAH 2004. Recent studies confirm that anthelminths are highly cost-effective ways to improve both nutritional status as measured anthropometrically, and iron/anemia status. Finally, antibacterial/antiparasitic measures to improve birthweight (for example treated bednets) were analyzed in BAH 2004, but insufficient new material was available to warrant discussion here.

Behavior change can be a cost-effective way to improve nutrition, with modest costs per beneficiary. Households may not be able to afford to increase the amount of food they can consume, but may be able to change the way it is allocated among household members, or the type of food that is consumed, or the way that it is prepared and served, in ways that can enhance nutrition. Education concerning the needs of pregnant and lactating women, of the impor-

tance of breastfeeding, and how to feed infants and young children, can have significant impacts on nutrition. Previous experience suggests that this education needs to be at the community level, which is discussed in the next sub-section. Although touched on in BAH 2004, it was not analyzed in detail. Our discussion in this sub-section focuses on nutrition education occurring in the community. Although nutrition messages delivered by the mass media may support other initiatives and are potentially a way to reach many people inexpensively, there is no recent literature suggesting that media messages alone can significantly change nutrition behavior.

These solutions (ranked by CE) are largely consistent with a recent authoritative survey of effectiveness in the *Lancet* (Bhutta *et al.* 2008), which states that "Of available interventions, counseling about breastfeeding and fortification or supplementation with vitamin A and zinc have the greatest potential to reduce the burden of child morbidity and mortality." They also conclude that "interventions for maternal nutrition (supplements of iron, folate, multiple micronutrients, calcium, and balanced energy and protein) can improve outcomes for maternal health and births" (2008: 417). Bhutta *et al.* are also very clear that all these interventions can tackle only a proportion of under-nutrition (around 30 percent). The larger proportion (the other 70 percent) requires provision of food and/or income to poor households. Although food and income transfers are also important development interventions, the benefit/cost (B/C) ratios are an order of magnitude lower than those considered here, and they are not discussed further here.

These three sub-sections describe the proposed solutions and provide references to the evidence base. A summary of CE and B/C data is collated from the literature (note that unless specified otherwise, in this discussion, the discount rate used is 3 percent, where a discount rate is appropriate; also, unless otherwise specified, an incidence rather than prevalence methodology is used: Methodology is discussed below). The detailed economic analysis of each solution is postponed until the third section, where sensitivity analysis (for example, to different discount rates) is also undertaken.

Micronutrient Interventions

A considerable amount of effort since the 1980s has been focused on reducing micronutrient deficiencies. This relies on a very extensive literature on the adverse effects of deficiencies in terms of mortality, morbidity, and economic costs, and the availability of inexpensive technologies to provide micronutrients.

International attention was first focused on iodine deficiency, which thanks to iodized salt has been considerably reduced as a global problem. Nevertheless, UNICEF (2006) estimates that 31 percent of developing-world households are still not consuming iodized salt, although efforts under way in lagging areas (particularly Eastern and Central Europe/CIS) are leading to improvements. Low coverage remains a problem, particularly in South Asia (India, Pakistan, and Bangladesh) and some SSA countries.

There has been relatively little significant new work on iodine interventions since BAH 2004. Salt iodization, costing around $0.05/person per year and averting significant cognitive losses, with a B/C ratio of the order of 30:1, remains a key priority (recalculated as incidence-based, from Horton 2006); no additional discussion is needed to reiterate the estimates of benefits and cost already available. For those areas where salt iodization is not currently feasible, recent recommendations are for a single annual large oral dose of iodized oil for children and pregnant and lactating women (de Benoist 2007). While more expensive than fortification, this is likely still very cost-effective, but few program data exist (areas requiring iodized oil are generally areas which are more remote and hard to reach, or where an inadequate regulatory environment makes commercial fortification patchy). We briefly discuss recent progress regarding iodine below.

In the early 1990s meta-analyses indicating the importance of vitamin A in reducing severity of infection and mortality led to concerted efforts to undertake mass-dose vitamin A supplementation of children from the ages of six to twenty-four months, often in conjunction with immunization campaigns. More recently, as vertical polio immunization campaigns are being phased out, there is a need to shift the mode of delivery for vitamin A either to the primary health care system (where this has good coverage) or Child health days. UNICEF (2006) estimates that there are still 100–140 million children (17–25 percent of children under five in developing countries) who are still deficient in vitamin A, mainly in South Asia and sub-Saharan Africa. We discuss below some new findings and policy implications

Iron is the third of the "big three" micronutrients, and progress has been harder to make than for the other two. Unlike these, single annual or semi-annual mass doses are not feasible. Iron supplementation programs have had mixed results, and although iron fortification is currently taking off in developing countries, coverage of many vulnerable populations remains problematic. We discuss below what is new since BAH 2004.

One possible reason that attention to zinc deficiency has only been more recent is that measuring zinc status in populations is difficult. Zinc deficiency in children is known to be associated with stunting, but the B/C ratios for increased adult productivity due to zinc supplementation in early childhood (higher wages/higher productivity are associated with increased stature) are considerably less than for iron. However, therapeutic treatment of diarrhea with zinc supplements below the age of one year is highly cost-effective, and recent work suggests that supplementation of young infants may also be cost-effective in reducing infection and hence mortality and morbidity. We discuss below results for zinc (mentioned, but not in much detail, in BAH 2004).

Work on folate is just beginning in developing countries. Chile, South Africa, and Mexico are among the first developing countries to use folic acid fortification in flour. This is discussed below, but work on benefits and costs in developing countries is still at a very early stage.

There are cross-cutting issues regarding the delivery of micronutrients. Fortification tends to have a lower unit cost than supplementation and hence is preferable if feasible, particularly if the deficiency is of importance across a wide range of population groups. Supplementation tends to be used if a sub-population is of particular interest and the micronutrient is more costly (vitamin A). Supplementation is also necessary if particular population groups (pregnant and lactating women, for example) have extraordinary needs which cannot be met by fortification alone (e.g. iron). If supplementation is the mode, then we need to consider the costs of distribution and of ensuring adherence to recommended frequency of intake, and in some cases (e.g. iron in malarial areas) the costs of screening the population prior to providing supplements. Of course, for many if not all micronutrients, a global cost-effective strategy likely requires a mix of fortification and supplementation.

Fortification of complementary foods (foods targeted to weaning age children) is an alternative to targeted supplementation. Commercially prepared complementary foods typically reach higher-income, more urbanized households, and this tends to have been left more to the market as an initiative. The Oportunidades Program in Mexico is an example where a fortified complementary food has been provided free to children below five in the poorest 5 million households. A less costly alternative has been development of "home fortification" – i.e. the provision of micronutrients which can be added to infant foods in the home. Examples are "Sprinkles" (a multiple-micronutrient sachet developed by Stan Zlotkin and his colleagues at the Hospital for Sick Children, Toronto), and "Plumpy" Nut (a ready-to-use-therapeutic food based on peanuts). Studies of Sprinkles suggest that they can be cost-effective when the effects of the iron and zinc components are analyzed (see p. 13). "Plumpy" Nut is very useful for special populations such as severely malnourished children needing nutritional rehabilitation

Finally, biofortification (through improved agricultural technology) is potentially very attractive, but its practical implementation has not progressed very far since BAH 2004. It is therefore covered but without much detail below.

Iodine

The success of salt iodization in eliminating deficiency in most countries has been an example to other micronutrient interventions. Iodide has been added to bread and salt for over eighty years (beginning in Western Europe), and iodate for fifty years. Since the 1980s, considerable progress has been made worldwide such that the number of countries where iodine is a public health problem has decreased from 110 in 2003 to 47 in 2007. Sixty countries have at least 70 percent of the population with access to iodized salt, and thirty-four have reached the Universal Salt Iodization goal of 90 percent (Iodine Network n.d.).

The remaining effort required is to reach countries where coverage is weak (many in the former Eastern Europe/CIS, and in SSA), as well as to raise coverage in those countries where it is incomplete. The efforts for iodine will also inform the success of other micronutrient interventions as to how to succeed in countries where infrastructure is weaker. They will also provide some guidance on how the marginal cost of increasing coverage may increase as the programs extend to cover harder-to-reach populations.

One method currently being used by the Micronutrient Initiative is to extend iodization to small salt producers. This requires innovative approaches, for example using GPS to locate these small, rural producers whose product often is consumed by poorer and more remote populations. These producers are then provided with the mobile equipment to use to iodize their product, and they often also need to be provided at no cost with the fortificant (otherwise their very poor customers might choose not to buy the fortified product). Further study of the costs of this technology will provide useful insights as to how costs increase as one tries to approach coverage goals (90 percent) (Venkatesh Mannar, Micronutrient Initiative, personal communication).

Other food products can be iodized (milk, water, and bread). Some countries have iodized the salt going into animal feed, since animals as well as humans suffer when the soils are deficient in iodine. This is also an indirect way indirectly to increase iodine in the human diet. In China, for example, iodine has been introduced into irrigation systems and can enter the food chain that way.

Vitamin A

Until recently, recommendations on the use of vitamin A focused on provision to lactating women up to eight weeks postpartum, and to children between six and seventy-two months old, which is estimated to reduce mortality below the age of three by 23 percent, with estimates of cost per death averted of $64–$294 (Ching *et al.* 2000), $289–$489 for Nepal through community health workers (Fiedler 2000: both Fiedler and Ching are cited in BAH 2004), and $100–$500 for eight low-income Asian countries (Horton 1999).

New evidence suggests that a comparable mortality reduction can be obtained by supplementation of neonates (Rahmathullah *et al.* 2003, where Indian infants were supplemented one or two days after delivery, and the benefits were observed from two weeks to three months). This may in future change the recommendations for vitamin A supplementation, although ensuring that neonates receive the vitamin A may be difficult, in countries with large rural populations and a low proportion of births occurring with trained birth attendants present. Neonatal supplementation is likely to be an attractive option only if it can be packaged with other postpartum care. Darmstadt *et al.* (2005) include neonatal vitamin A in the package of desirable add-ons to their evidence-based package for neonatal care.

Given that mortality rates in the first three months are typically higher than in the current age range covered (between six and thirty-six months), it is likely that supplementation of neonates will be even more cost-effective than supplementation of the older age groups – although this will depend heavily on how the cost of supplementation increases when targeting neonates.

New results on CE of programs include estimates from child health days in Ethiopia, where a package of interventions (vitamin A, de-worming, nutrition screening, and measles vaccinations) reach more than 10 million beneficiaries nationwide in the Enhanced Outreach Strategy, at an average cost per child per round of US$0.56 (Fiedler 2007a). The cost – which includes staff and training costs – increased to $1.04 per round per child if measles vaccine was included. There are two rounds per year. Fiedler estimates the cost per death averted (due to the vitamin A component) as $228 per life saved, or $9 per DALY saved, in the variant excluding measles vaccination. This is conservative and does not take into account benefits from the other components of the intervention, namely de-worming and nutrition screening. The results are likely replicable in other countries with mortality rates as comparably high as those in Ethiopia, in an environment where primary health care is sufficiently weak that the "campaign" strategy works well.

The cost data ($0.56 per round) above are consistent with estimates by Neidecker-Gonzalez (2007) for Africa for distribution of vitamin A capsules; they estimate that the costs are $1.00 per round for Asia and $1.50 per round for Latin America, and that the price of the capsule is a relatively small fraction of the cost, whereas personnel costs for training, distribution, etc. are larger.

The main mechanism for distribution of vitamin A capsules was previously through national immunization days for children in both Asia and Africa. In South Asia, this is now being integrated into primary health care as systems coverage develops, but in SSA Child health days remain the major vehicle for distribution. Likewise, coverage of mothers postpartum has often been when the mother brings the child in for BCG vaccination. Supplementation of mothers has to occur very quickly after the birth, such that there is no chance that they have become pregnant again, as the high-dose vitamin A is dangerous for the fetus, especially during the first trimester).

Currently about 71–73 percent of children are covered by the required two doses, in South Asia and SSA (UNICEF 2008). It has proven somewhat difficult to achieve further increases. In countries in SSA, periodic political crises or disruptions have prevented either the second round of coverage required in a year, or sometimes even both rounds. There are also children in most countries that are difficult to reach because of remote location, or because they are sick during the time when the child health days occur (and are therefore not brought to the site for vaccination). Ongoing work at the Micronutrient Initiative will estimate how costs increase in order to reach these hard-to-reach groups (Annie Wesley, personal communication).

Currently virtually all the capsules consumed have been provided by a single donor (Canada), and developing countries have not yet taken on the costs of sustaining the intervention: There has been no incentive to move to local procurement. It is conceivable that costs could fall if production were to shift to developing regions.

Iron

Shifting an individual from anemic to non-anemic status has strong productivity benefits. Horton and Ross (2003) summarize the productivity benefits for adults to be 5 percent in light manual work and 17 percent in heavy manual work. There are also effects attributable to cognitive benefits and associated schooling improvements of 4 percent in all other work.

Anemia and iron status, although correlated, are not synonymous (see, for example, the discussion in Horton and Ross 2003). The literature is also shifting to use hemoglobin levels as a continuous variable, rather than anemia cutoffs, as a better measure, since there are decrements in function and response to interventions even below the defined anemia cutoff.

New studies of effects since BAH 2004 include the longitudinal study in Costa Rica confirming the cognitive benefits already discussed (Lozoff et al. 2006). There have also been some useful new systematic literature surveys of the effects

of iron supplementation. Sachdev et al.'s (2005) survey concludes there are positive effects on mental development scores in children (particularly for children who were initially anemic or iron-deficient, and more strongly in children more than two years old). Similarly, Gera et al.'s (2007) survey shows that the effect of iron supplementation of children on hemoglobin is stronger where children were initially anemic. However, the effects of supplementation of iron on children's growth are not generally significant (Sachdev et al. 2006). These reviews confirm the value of early targeted interventions and reinforce the view that calculations of benefits should also include those attributable to cognitive development. Nevertheless, local conditions affect average response. For example, supplementation has a smaller impact in malaria hyperendemic areas, and where children already consume iron-fortified food (Gera et al. 2007).

There are ongoing studies of the effectiveness of supplementation programs at scale, trying to resolve why effects from efficacy studies prove elusive at broader scale. One finding is that using anemia status is a less sensitive indicator than hemoglobin status (Stoltzfus et al. 2004).

A new and extremely significant finding from a large-scale trial in a population with high rates of malaria is that iron supplementation of young children is associated with increased hospital admissions and mortality. Sazawal et al. 2006 recommend that iron supplementation in areas with high rates of malaria be given only to children who have been tested as iron-deficient, since the deleterious effects were for non-iron-deficient children. This has led to a change in the international guidelines (Stoltzfus 2007), which now suggest that iron fortification should still be a priority, as should iron supplementation of pregnant women and iron-deficient children, but universal iron supplementation (with tablets, syrups, or Sprinkles) should be avoided for young children at high risk of severe malaria. Testing, of course, increases costs in areas where it is necessary.

Some studies look at the costs and potential impacts of home fortification (Sprinkles) and conclude that the B/C ratio of Sprinkles' interventions (containing iron as well as other micronutrients) can be as high as 37:1 if one assumes that a course of intervention for four months between the ages of six months and one year largely protects an infant against anemia throughout childhood (Sharieff *et al.* 2006). Sprinkles are currently at the stage of use at program scale in several countries including Bangladesh, Mexico, and Mongolia, and were used at scale in the Indonesia province of Aceh following the tsunami.

Internationally considerable effort is being devoted to iron fortification, particularly of flour. The Flour Fortification Initiative has the goal of fortifying 70 percent of roller mill wheat flour with iron and folic acid by the end of 2008. The rate was 20 percent when the initiative started in 2004 and had reached 26 percent by 2006 (www.sph.emory.edu/wheatflour/progress. php, downloaded July 29, 2007). The Global Alliance for Improved Nutrition (GAIN) currently has projects for fortification of wheat flour in ten countries (in almost all, folic acid is included), and of maize flour in another three. GAIN is also supporting projects for iron fortification of soy sauce in China, and fish sauce in Vietnam (www.gainhealth.org/gain/ch/ en-en/index.cfm?page=/gain/home/about_gain/ progress_report2). The Micronutrient Initiative and WHO–EMRO has assisted thirteen countries in the Middle East to reach the current level of 7 million metric tons of flour being fortified with at least iron and folic acid (MI and WHO–EMRO 2007).

Although the fortification of cereal flour has received the greatest attention, other vehicles are also possible. One possibility is double-fortified salt (fortified with iodine and also encapsulated ferrous fumarate). The micronization process renders this more costly than simply fortifying flour, however it is an alternative where flour fortification is not an option. Although this is likely more costly than flour fortification, it compares favorably with other strategies such as supplementation alone, or anthelminth treatment alone, and is comparable in CE with supplementation combined with anthelminthics

(Annie Wesley, Micronutrient Initiative, personal communication).

Iron fortification has a very high B/C ratio, estimated as 8.7:1 (Horton and Ross 2003; Horton and Ross 2006: median for ten countries). The cost of iron fortification varies according to the iron compound used and the food vehicle, but can be $0.10–$0.12 per person per year. Fortification, however, requires that there exists a product that is purchased by a target population regularly and in sufficient quantities to convey the iron requirement. It also is administratively easier to the degree that processing is concentrated in a few mills or manufacturers. To offset the bias towards more refined or highly processed flours, trials using hammer mills at a village level are also under way.

While subsidies are often expensive and are not generally a cost-effective means of improving nutrition, where such programs are under way for other reasons – for example, school feeding – the marginal cost of adding fortificants is small and often achieves significant benefits. For example, in some districts iron fortification has been added to the flour provided in India's long-standing and controversial public distribution system, and in Mexico it is added to subsidized milk.

Iron supplementation also reduces maternal and neonatal mortality (although the reductions are not quite of the same magnitude as those for vitamin A and zinc, for example). Iron supplementation of pregnant women could reduce mortality for as little as $66–$115 per DALY in high-mortality regions of SSA and Southeast Asia (Baltussen *et al.* 2004) – although this particular study suggests caution since "evidence of intervention effectiveness predominantly relates to small-scale efficiency trials, which may not reflect the actual effect under expected conditions." Baltussen *et al.* (2004) use the cost of supplementation per pregnant woman as $10–$50 per year, including distribution and promotion costs, where the cost varies by region and wage cost of the personnel involved in distribution. BAH 2004 cite similar cost estimates for a program in Nepal.

Zinc

Work on zinc has been relatively recent, and many information gaps remain. There is strongest evidence in favour of therapeutic use of zinc for diarrhea, and WHO and UNICEF have incorporated this into their guidelines for treatment of diarrhea. There is no clear consensus on therapeutic use for respiratory and other infections. Efficacy trials of preventive use have shown benefits for mortality, morbidity, and growth but many gaps remain: There is little evidence from programs at scale, there is insufficient study of the proposed timing of preventive supplementation (age of child; daily vs. weekly dosage), and there needs to be more analysis of the effects of zinc as a component of multiple micronutrient supplementation, particularly where iron is included, rather than as a single supplement. Studies of zinc fortification have not yielded consistent results, but some of this could be attributable to methodological issues (This paragraph is drawn from a very useful short survey by Brown n.d.: ?2006).

There are on-going large-scale trials which should help to improve knowledge (Nepal, Zanzibar) as well as other trials (Peru, Ecuador, Bangladesh, Mexico), and these should lead to recommendations for the provision of zinc for both therapeutic and preventive uses. Although it is known that there are interactions when both iron and zinc are provided together in supplements, it is likely not desirable to provide only one if both are deficient. The adverse interactions are apparently less of an issue for iron and zinc fortification. GAIN is already funding combined zinc and iron (and other micronutrient) fortification of flour in three countries (wheat flour in all three countries, and maize flour in addition in one of the three).

CE results for zinc supplementation suggest that therapeutic use for diarrhea is highly cost-effective. Robberstad et al. (2004) suggest that the incremental cost of zinc as part of case management is $0.47 per course of treatment, leading to an average cost of $73 per DALY gained, and $2,100 per death averted. Sharieff et al. (2006) estimate the cost per DALY saved

as $12.20 ($8–$97) and the corresponding cost per death averted as $406 ($273–$248) for a preventive course of supplements. These results are for administration of a multiple micronutrient supplement including zinc, costing an estimated $1.20 per child (for sixty sachets consumed over a four-month period, between the ages of six and twelve months, in a country with high infant mortality levels and high diarrhea prevalence).

Although there can be effects on growth of preventive zinc supplementation, the effect of adult stature on wages is fairly modest and is unlikely to lead to a very high B/C ratio as a single nutrient. Preventive supplementation aimed at reducing morbidity and mortality is, however, potentially cost-effective at young ages, in environments where zinc is expected to be deficient and infant mortality rates are high. For example, a study by Sazawal et al. (2001) in India found that daily provision of a supplement including zinc from 30 to 284 days of age of small-for-gestational-age infants was associated with a 68 percent reduction in mortality as compared to the same supplement without zinc. Further study of the CE of this particular effect would be useful. It is too early to provide cost estimates for preventive zinc supplements until appropriate ages and dosage are better understood, as well as the interaction with iron, since it is unlikely that zinc would be provided as a preventive supplement without other micronutrients.

Work has been done to detail how therapeutic zinc supplements can be implemented (Zinc Task Force 2006). This includes sourcing the raw material, qualifying additional suppliers for international procurement (originally only one producer in a developed country was qualified), and adding zinc tablets and syrups to WHO's Essential Medicines List and the Interagency Emergency Health Kit. As of the end of 2006, only one country (Bangladesh) had taken all the national steps necessary for implementing a therapeutic zinc program (changing national policy, securing local supply, identifying financing strategies, training health workers, and educating caregivers, under the scaling up zinc for young children (SUZY) program). However, there are pilot schemes in several countries, and Helen Keller International distributed zinc following the tsunami during 2005 and 2006.

Studies suggest that zinc supplements are highly complementary to oral rehydration salts (ORS). Caregivers feel that ORS plus some kind of "medicine" is an appropriate treatment for diarrhea, and in a large trial in India, use of the combined therapy (ORS plus therapeutic zinc) had various advantages as compared to the control (ORS only). When zinc was also provided, use of other drugs decreased. (In most cases of diarrhea, use of other drugs such as antibiotics is not necessary and often not desirable.) The use of ORS also increased significantly when provided in combination with zinc. There were fewer reported cases of diarrhea and acute lower respiratory infections in the communities also using zinc, and hospitalizations from diarrhea, pneumonia, and all causes were lower (Bhandari *et al.* 2008).

Oral rehydration salts have been in use since the 1980s, and coverage rates in SSA were, using the latest information, on average 30 percent and 35 percent in South Asia, with the highest use being 61 percent in East Asia and the Pacific (UNICEF: www.childinfo.org/diarrhea_countrydata.php). The main obstacle to using therapeutic zinc at scale, in combination with ORS, is therefore financial. Unlike vitamin A, for example, no major donor has yet stepped up to underwrite implementation.

The Zinc Task Force has estimated what would be required for a Zinc Procurement Fund to provide a nine-year "bridge" to countries to take over the financing of supplies. There are fifty-six countries that they identify as eligible for the Fund (these consist of the sixty countries which are UNICEF's child survival priorities, but excluding China, India, Brazil, and Bangladesh under the assumption that these countries will be able to have their own production capabilities in the near future). The Fund would provide a 50 percent subsidy for zinc products for three years to the more developed countries in the group, and for the least developed countries would provide free supplies for

three years followed by three years of subsidized (50 percent) zinc.

The cost of the Fund over nine years would be $188 million (countries would fund the other 75 percent of the zinc costs in this scenario), and would save over 1.4 million child lives. This would have the potential to help considerably in achieving MDG 4 (which is to reduce by two-thirds the under-five mortality rate).

Folate

Interest in folate interventions in developing countries is quite new. Knowledge of the effects of folic acid intervention periconception on birth defects (particularly anencephaly and spina bifida, but also others) is not that new. Figures in Grosse *et al.* (2005) for the USA imply B/C ratios somewhere between 12:1 and 39:1 (the cost of folic acid fortificant for the USA was just a little over $0.01 per person per year; note that these are prevalence- rather than incidence-based estimates). These estimates are probably not too relevant for developing countries, which typically do not incur the large hospital costs that were saved in the USA, since babies in developing countries may not receive the same kind of treatment. Rather, the consequences for developing countries are likely to be better expressed in terms of the costs of the morbidity and mortality these babies suffer.

In South Africa, folic acid fortification of cereals began in 2003. The prevalence of neural tube defects fell by 30.5 percent (the rate decreased from 1.41 to 0.98 per 000 births), and the B/C ratio was estimated as 46:1 (Sayed *et al.* 2008). Perinatal mortality fell by 65.9 percent (from a rate of 0.419 to 0.143 per 000 births); typically the most severely affected infants die within the first week of life. Evidence for developed countries also links folic acid fortification to reductions in neuroblastoma (French *et al.* 2003). The effects of folic acid on coronary heart disease (CVD) are more debated, but there is no consensus on these results as yet.

Data for developing countries are scarce. However, studies for rural India and China find relatively high levels of neural tube defects at birth (Xiao *et al.* 1990; Cherian *et al.* 2005).

One possibility is that this is associated with consumption of rice, which when refined has low folate content.

The Flour Fortification Initiative lists only the USA, Canada, and Chile as currently mandating folic acid fortification of flour, although it is currently being used in a number of other countries. GAIN currently includes folic acid fortification in some, but not all, of its projects involving wheat and maize flour in developing countries. The Flour Fortification Initiative includes both iron and folic acid as the minimum fortificants that it aims to encourage countries to use.

Folate supplementation faces similar issues to iron supplementation in malarial areas. Some antimalarials (such as sulfadoxine and pyrimethamine) work by interfering with folate metabolism which inhibits the parasite. The Pemba study (Sazawal et al. 2006) exhibited adverse mortality consequences for children receiving iron and folic acid supplements in a high-malaria environment. A study of pregnant women in western Kenya provided iron and either a placebo, a low dose of folic acid, or the standard (national guidelines) dose (Ouma et al. 2006). The results suggest that use of the national standard (higher) dose of folic acid supplement compromised the efficacy of the antimalarials, as compared to placebo or a low dose, suggesting a need to revisit national guidelines. The levels of folic acid involved in fortification are less likely to be problematic, although this may require further trials for confirmation.

Since work on folate is relatively new, there has been no international technical/lobby group comparable to those which have done the work on vitamin A, iron, zinc, and iodine (IVACG, INACG, IZINCG, IDD Network). However, folate is explicitly included with the other four in the purview of the Micronutrient Forum (Micronutrient Forum 2007). Although little CE work has been done, it seems reasonable that folic acid fortification would be sufficiently cheap, and sufficiently beneficial, to be included in flour fortification programs when iron is used. More work is required: For example a formal international recommendation would be desirable, as would some examination of the feasibility of folic acid fortification of other foods for countries with rice-based diets. Some statement regarding folic acid in high-malaria areas might be desirable, confirming that fortification is not an issue but that higher-dose supplements might be.

Biofortification

BAH 2004 rated the potential for biofortification of staple crops as very high. Breeding efforts are on-going and there have already been a couple of efficacy studies of feeding trials for crops biofortified with iron and with vitamin A (cited in Meenakshi et al. 2007). The present value of estimated cost per crop, per country, range from $8million to $25million, over a thirty-year horizon. Meenakshi et al. (2007) estimate the median cost per DALY saved as about $10/DALY saved (optimistic scenario) and $120/DALY (pessimistic scenario). The corresponding B/C ratios are 50:1 and 4:1 (with $1000/DALY). Note that the current work on biofortification uses mainly conventional plant-breeding techniques, not GM ones.

Harvest Plus, the organization coordinating the breeding efforts, is currently focusing on six crops (rice, wheat, maize, cassava, beans, and orange-fleshed sweet potato) with ten other crops under review. One of those ten, pearl millet, has recently moved to the higher priority list. The three micronutrients under focus are iron, zinc, and vitamin A. Research is mostly focused on conventional breeding technology, with the exception of some work linked to Golden Rice (transgenic rice with enhanced vitamin A content). Harvest Plus is now partway through its ten-year plan (2003–13); it has largely completed the initial work required on screening for genes and is now moving into nutrition trials (Harvest Plus 2007).

The work is further advanced for vitamin A than for iron and zinc. Harvest Plus is at the stage of promoting orange-fleshed sweet potato in parts of Africa (typically the white-fleshed varieties have been preferred). Their research suggests that beta-carotene and provitamins A are controlled by fewer genes than for iron and zinc. One consequence is that the content of vitamin A is more stable across different environmental conditions, whereas iron and zinc content vary more by year (rice and pearl millet) and planting date (wheat) (Harvest Plus 2007).

The cost of biofortification includes up-front costs in identifying genetic material, followed by costs for each country of breeding locally appropriate varieties, with subsequent lower maintenance costs required to continue to keep the varieties appropriate. Meenakshi *et al.* (2007) suggest that the costs vary by crop and by country (obviously breeding costs tend to be larger in larger countries with more diverse growing conditions). Their estimates are that there are three main phases of costs, and the average PV that they use (for the first eighteen years, prior to the maintenance stage) is $0.75million per year per country (discounting future costs at 3 percent).

Anthelminths

Infection with soil-transmitted helminths is very high. Hotez *et al.* (2006) estimate that 1.2 billion people are infected with roundworm, 0.8 billion with whipworm, and 0.7 billion with hookworm. Many individuals have more than one infection, and over 2 billion people are estimated to be infected by some type of soil-transmitted helminths. These infections have adverse effects on nutritional status, and hookworm infections also have adverse effects on iron status.

Most existing treatment efforts are focused on school-age children, in part because data suggest that worm loads peak during these years – typically around the age of five for roundworms and whipworms, and in adolescence for hookworms. Additionally, in many countries, school settings provide a cost-effective means of reaching children.

The Partners for Parasite Control project based at WHO has as a goal to treat regularly at least 75 percent of school-age children at risk of illness from schistosomiasis and soil transmitted helminths by 2010 (www.who.org/wormcontrol/about_us/en). The 2005 global meeting (see WHO 2005) found that of the seventy-three

endemic countries, data on progress towards the goal were available for twenty-two for 2004. Of these, only three achieved coverage of more than 75 percent of the target population, and the median coverage was only 10 percent.

There are also benefits to treating other groups, particularly pre-school children and pregnant women. Although pre-school children typically have lower worm loads, one hypothesis is that worms interfere more with absorption of nutrients at younger ages: "helminth infections may stimulate inflammatory immune responses in young children with deleterious effects on protein metabolism and erythropoiesis" (Stoltzfus *et al.* 2004). Hotez *et al.* (2006) summarize the benefits from anthelmintic treatment. For preschool children, treatment is associated with motor and language development and reduced malnutrition. For school-age children, benefits include reduced anemia, and improved physical fitness, appetite, growth, and intellectual development. For pregnant women, benefits include improved maternal hemoglobin, birthweight, and child survival.

Studies since those surveyed by Hotez *et al.* (2006) include Alderman *et al.* (2006) which found higher weight gain for children below seven treated during child health days in Uganda, as compared to controls. In this program, a single dose of proprietary albendazole added $0.21 to the cost of child health days (attributing all the existing staff costs to vitamin A distribution and other activities at health days). Thus, the cost per child per year was $0.42 for two rounds of coverage, although bulk purchase of generic drugs could reduce these costs somewhat. Fiedler (2007a) estimates the costs for distribution on anthelmintics in Ethiopia at around $0.32 per child per year, including a share of the distribution costs (when the child health day is used to provide de-worming, vitamin A, and nutrition screening under five).

The CE of the school-age de-worming programs is very high. Miguel and Kremer (2004) estimate that treatment in Kenyan schools at a cost of $0.49 per child generated an NPV of wages of over $30 (prevalence rate of infection was 95 percent). De-worming was the most

cost-effective way to increase school participation in their study (and led to a 7.5 percentage
point increase in primary school participation
in treatment schools). If one allows for the fact
that additional teachers would have to be hired
to teach the increased number of children participating, the B/C ratio is still over 3:1.

There are apparently no previous CE or C/B
estimates in the literature for de-worming for
pre-school children and for pregnant women,
which appears to be a symptom of the neglect
of the topic of de-worming in the literature.
The Alderman et al. (2006) study in Uganda
looks at weight gain only, and not iron status
or vitamin A absorption and, thus, can not
form the basis of a B/C estimate. Moreover, the
comprehensive DCPP project does not include
CE estimates, although there is a chapter on
helminths (Hotez et al. 2006), nor is de-worming
included in the WHO–CHOICE CE estimates,
even for school-age children; de-worming is
aptly included by WHO under the Department
of Control of Neglected Tropical Diseases.
In a number of iron intervention studies (e.g.
Thomas et al. 2004; Beinner et al. 2005), de-
worming is included in the intervention (but not
in the title of the article), and yet a substantial
fraction of the outcomes attributed by the study
to the iron intervention may in fact be due to the
anthelminths.

We provide here estimates of the order of
magnitude involved for CE for de-worming
of pre-school children in areas with endemic
hookworm. Although de-worming has effects
on growth, these are relatively small (Bhutta et
al. 2008) and the economic effect is hence very
modest. The more important effect economically is the effect on anemia. Bhutta et al. (2008)
undertake a literature survey, and estimate that
the reduction in anemia in pre-school children
ranges from 4.4 percent to 21 percent. The
median of this range is 13 percent. Using Horton
and Ross (2006), the PV of the median cognitive loss attributable to anemia in a group of
developing countries was $1 per capita (the PV
of the loss per child in the relevant age range
ranged from $15 to $25). If we can assume
that de-worming children five times between

the ages of one and three can reduce anemia
by 13 percent and reduce the cognitive loss by
13 percent, and hence reduce future wages by
2.5 percent, then the PV of the loss potentially
avertable per person in the population is $0.13.
In Southeast Asia, the age group requiring coverage is approximately 4 percent of the population, and in SSA 6.5 percent. Accordingly, if
de-worming costs $0.50 per child per year, then
the B/C ratio is 7.5:1 in Southeast Asia and 4:1 in
SSA. (The assumption that these are the priority
areas is based on de Silva et al. 2003.)

Costs at this level are feasible as long as
de-worming is provided in combination with
another intervention (and hence shares distribution costs). De-worming as a single intervention
provided to pre-school children would likely
cost about twice as much and would have a correspondingly lower B/C ratio. These B/C ratios
are a little conservative (if reductions in stunting
also provide benefits in terms of adult productivity); the estimates are orders of magnitude only,
and require further verification.

Current WHO recommendations are that all
school-age children should be treated once a
year where the prevalence of worms is between
20 percent and 50 percent, and twice a year
where the prevalence is greater than or equal
to 50 percent. Hall et al. (2008) comment
on these recommendations and suggest that
where prevalence is at least 50 percent, then
treatment is desirable, for three reasons. First,
the disease probability (mean worm burden)
increases exponentially above this threshold.
Second, at this prevalence rate it is cheaper to
treat than to screen-and-treat. And finally, the
drugs are very safe. However Hall et al. (2008)
argue that at lower levels of prevalence (20–50
percent), it becomes less and less cost-effective
to treat everyone. Worldwide, treatment levels
are still far below the WHO recommendation.
It may therefore be cost-effective to prioritize
treatment to schoolchildren in the more highly
infected countries. Hall et al. (2008) advocate
that population sampling to determine prevalence levels is also sufficiently inexpensive, and
that this should be undertaken prior to deciding
to treat.

Nutrition Education at the Community Level

The previous discussion has considered a series of highly cost-effective interventions to improve nutrition, with B/C ratios similar to those of key primary health interventions such as immunization, prevention of malaria (using treated bed-nets, household spraying and preventive drug provision for pregnant women), and treatment of STDs to prevent HIV/AIDS. A key element of all these programs is that little behavior change on the part of beneficiaries is required beyond biannual participation in child health days or the purchase of fortified foods that look and taste identical to those previously consumed. In many cases, the gains come from inexpensive technological fixes provided to a population.

The limitation of the nutrition interventions discussed above is that they address only a modest component of overall under-nutrition. To make further progress, households may have to change their food practices. The key periods for such changes are during pregnancy, lactation, and weaning. Growth and cognitive deficits related to under-nutrition prior to the age of two are extremely difficult, if not impossible, to reverse.

The key messages involve the diet of pregnant and lactating women; breastfeeding; complementary feeding of infants and young children, particularly between six and twenty-four months; and identifying inadequate growth and weight gain particularly below the age of two. Delivering these messages effectively requires one-on-one discussion, typically with the mother. Weighing the mother-to-be, and weighing and measuring the baby, are very important tools with which to frame the educational messages, as long as it is recognized that the weighing is not an end in itself. The sessions can also be used to provide micronutrient supplements and anthelminths. Program experience suggests that such nutrition education can be provided cost-effectively on a par with many other attractive health investments, albeit at an order of magnitude more costly than nutrition interventions covered above.

We discuss below interventions grouped into three different types, which depend on the level of development of the country and the current level of development of health services. CE is typically higher when interventions are "packaged" with other interventions and the costs of personnel time are spread over multiple interventions. The three intervention types are: Incorporation of nutrition education into child health days; community nutrition promotion using volunteers; and nutrition education as part of the lowest tier of the health care system. Another way of thinking of this is as an integrated program of outreach and family–community care, where the relative weight of outreach and family–community care depends on the institutional background in individual countries (Darmstadt *et al.* 2005). Interestingly, Darmstadt *et al.* comment that for neonatal survival "Most of this benefit is derived from family–community care," which is consistent with our expectation for nutrition. The "package" of family–community care initiatives combined with nutrition education could be, for example, neonatal survival, or safe motherhood, or integrated management of child illness.

Outreach initiatives

Outreach initiatives play the greatest role in countries with the most limited coverage of primary health care services and are part of the legacy of vertical programs. Fiedler (2007b) cites UNICEF statistics that more than sixty countries have at least one child health day, with the vast majority having more than one. According to a Google search of the UNICEF website (August 1, 2007), the highest number of hits are for Africa, followed by Asia, with India running third. (Interestingly, there are also many references to the US child health day in October.) Most days include vitamin A, immunizations, and – increasingly – de-worming, with growth monitoring in about a quarter of the countries, and occasionally other interventions. Goodman *et al.* (2000) discuss the advantages of including vitamin A in immunization days.

Fiedler's (2007a) estimates for Ethiopia are that each round (of the two per year) costs

$0.56 per child, excluding measles vaccination and $1.04 including measles. The cost by component was 25 percent (vitamin A), 29 percent (de-worming), 15 percent (screening), and 31 percent (intensive education/other), in the model without measles immunization. Fiedler's CE estimates (attributing benefits only to the vitamin A component) were given on p. 311; if one redid the calculations to include benefits from de-worming, this would be an even more attractive investment. Ethiopia is an example of a country towards the lower extreme of the distribution of availability of primary health care facilities where the outreach format is likely to be particularly appropriate.

Community Nutrition Interventions

Community nutrition interventions incorporating growth promotion have a long history, and there are a number of surveys (see for example Allen and Gillespie 2001; World Bank 2006). Older success stories include Tamil Nadu state in India, Indonesia, and Thailand (see World Bank 2006 for references, and short descriptions for Tamil Nadu and Thailand), as well as Iringa, Tanzania (Pelletier and Jonsson 1994). Lessons from earlier programs have been synthesized by aid agencies (e.g. the BASICS program funded by USAID, with its six-component essential nutrition actions in health services). Many of these programs use community volunteers to mobilize the necessary large volume of personnel without concomitantly large personnel costs. However, successful programs need to maintain motivation of volunteers to maintain success, and to avoid the high training costs associated with high turnover.

Mason et al. (2001) describe Thailand's success in reducing underweight prevalence by about 3 percentage points per year in the 1980s (as compared to the usual 0.1–1.0 percentage point reduction per year in Asia in the absence of nationwide programs). The Tamil Nadu program was estimated to have a cost per death averted of $1492 (this program included highly targeted supplementary feeding: Ho 1985).

More recent programs include Bangladesh (BINP), Honduras, Madagascar, and Senegal

(World Bank 2006 contains brief descriptions for three of these, excluding Senegal). World Vision (2006) describes programs with impacts in four African countries (Ethiopia, Ghana, Malawi, and Tanzania) and is currently undertaking CE analysis (Siekmans, personal communication). Examples of careful impact studies include Galasso and Umapathi 2007: Madagascar – SEECALINE), Alderman et al. (2007: Senegal), and Alderman (2007: Uganda).

For Senegal, being in the treatment area reduced the probability of underweight by 17 percent as compared to the control (Alderman et al. 2007). For Madagascar (Galasso and Umapathi 2007) the program improved the average weight-for-age z-score by 7.6 percentage points as compared to the control, and height-for-age by 3.1 percentage points. For Uganda (Alderman 2007) the only consistent impacts were seen in the under-twelve-months age group, where the change in z-scores of weight-for-age were 0.22 standard deviations higher in the treatment than the control area (recumbent length was not measured for these youngest children, hence the effect on height-for-age is not known). For Bangladesh, there is no consistent evidence of differences in child nutritional status, maternal weight gain during pregnancy, or birthweight between project and non-project areas, although in project areas there was greater use of vitamin A and iron supplementation. There were also positive effects on weight in sub-groups such as among pregnant women who reported eating more (a key message from the nutrition education component), particularly destitute women (World Bank 2006).

Carefully done cost studies include Fiedler (2007b: RACHNA, CARE/India), and Fiedler (2003: Honduras, AINC). World Bank's (2006) survey suggests that the additional recurrent cost per recipient is about $1.60 to $10 ($11–$18 per person if food is included). This cost would be similar to the $5–$15 range recommended for such programs by Mason et al. (1999) without food (about double if food is also provided); Mason et al. argue that the programs below $5 in cost per person tend to have insufficient impact. The Honduras program fits into this same range

(Fiedler 2003 estimates the long-term, annual, recurrent cost per child participating as $6.82, and $4.0 as the incremental budget requirements per child participating, net of some shared costs such as personnel).

CE data still tend to be scarce. An older study for the Dominican Republic cost $493 per case of malnutrition averted (USAID 1988; this could be converted to cost per death averted, but the numbers would be relatively high; the cost per beneficiary at $23 is definitely in the higher range). Fiedler (2007b) estimates the cost per death averted from the RACHNA program as $1098, and the cost per DALY gained as $39. RACHNA is an add-on to the nationwide government interventions (in nutrition – ICDS and in reproductive health) and focuses on capacity-building and outreach to encourage women in particular to use available services. It is a somewhat unusual intervention (since it focuses on encouraging greater use of services, rather than providing a service), but the findings are interesting nonetheless.

The literature suggests that good program design is essential in interventions relying on behavior change. Immunization and fortification programs can fail – but this would be the exception rather than the rule. However, there are various behavior-change programs showing little or even no effect, and hence very poor CE. Country implementation capacity and program design are key. Thus, with the available data the CE of community nutrition programs is not well established. The measured benefits are often in terms of incremental growth; if these programs also enhance cognitive development then the benefits might appear higher. Moreover, if the community growth promotion also increases the utilization of micronutrients or anthelmintics then these benefits would also be used in the estimation of the B/C ratio.

Nutrition Components of Primary Health Care System

In middle-income countries and urban areas, coverage by existing primary health facilities tends to be better. One evaluation (Waters *et al.* 2006) estimates the CE of adding a health facility-based nutrition education program, including complementary feeding demonstrations, growth monitoring sessions and nutrition messages, and motivation for the personnel using an accreditation process combined with training. Waters *et al.* report that the marginal cost of the intervention was $6.12 per child reached, $55.16 per case of stunting prevented, and $1,952 per death averted. If one, however, costs out the staff time costs, this would increase costs to $15.37 per child reached, $138.50 per case of stunting prevented, and $4,900 per death averted. These cost levels indicate why poorer countries try to incorporate volunteers where possible.

Table 6.1 summarizes the basic CE and/or B/C data for the solutions advocated. All the proposed solutions have very attractive B/C ratios/CE. The following section undertakes a more detailed economic analysis and modeling.

Detailed economic analysis

This section presents the sensitivity analysis of the solutions, varying parameters such as the discount rate and the monetary equivalent of the DALY, and highlights some of the methodological issues. As per the Copenhagen Consensus guidelines, two different discount rates are used: The 3 percent social discount rate often used by international organizations such as the World Bank in social projects, and a higher rate of 6 percent closer to (although still far from equal to) the rate used on commercial projects.

Second, again following the Copenhagen Consensus guidelines, the DALY is assigned a monetary value in order to allow comparability with other investments, and the two alternatives used are $1,000/DALY and $5,000/DALY. There is no particular theoretical rationale for these numbers (other than a "rule of thumb" that health investments are good value if the cost is less than three times *per capita* GDP – and the $1,000 and $5,000 numbers would be reasonable for a poor country and a lower-middle-income country, respectively) (Mill and Shillcut 2004; Stokey 2004).

Table 6.1 Summary of CE and B/C estimates from the literature

Intervention	Cost/person/year[a]	CE	B/C ratio	Source
Micronutrient Supplementation				
Vitamin A Supplementation	$0.20	$3–16/DALY		Ching et al. (2000) Fiedler (2000) Horton (1999)
Zinc supplement (diarrhea therapy)	$0.47 (10 days)	$73/DALY		Robberstad et al. (2004)
Iron supplementation Pregnant women	$10–50	$66–115/DALY		Baltussen et al. (2004)
Micronutrient Fortification				
Salt iodization	$0.05		30:1	Authors' estimate[a]
Iron fortification	$0.10–12		7.8:1	Horton and Ross (2003)
Folate fortification	$0.01		12:1 to 39:1	Grosse et al. (2005) (USA)
Folate fortification	$0.01		46:1	Sayed et al. (2008) (South Africa)
Home fortification				
Iron home fortification	$1.20 (4 months)		37:1	Sharieff et al. (2006)
Zinc home fortification	$1.20 (4 months)	$12.20/DALY		Sharieff et al. (2006)
Biofortification	$0.–$1million/country/year	$10–120/DALY	4:1 to 50:1	Meenakshi et al. (2007)
Anthelminths, School age	$0.49 $0.32		3:1 to 60:1	Miguel and Kremer (2004) Fiedler (2007a) (cost)
Anthelminths, Pre-schoolers	$0.50		6:1	Authors' estimates
Community nutrition education				
Community nutrition	$5–10 no food $10–20 with food			Mason et al. (1999) World Bank (2006) (both surveys)
Community nutrition		$53/DALY[b]		Tamil Nadu, Ho (1985)
Community nutrition add-on		$39/DALY		India, Fiedler (2007a)
Community Nutrition		$61–153/DALY[c]		Peru, Waters et al. (2006)

Notes and sources:
[a] Authors' calculation; recalculates prevalence estimate using data and references from Horton (2006), to obtain incidence-based estimate. See also the appendix (p. 329).
[b] Assumes 28 DALYs saved are equivalent to one death averted, using Fiedler (2007a) number for India.
[c] Assumes 32 DALYs saved are equivalent to one death averted, for Peru.

For some readers, the cost per death averted may be a more familiar concept. A cost per DALY saved of $1,000 is approximately equal to a cost per death averted of about $30,000, and for a DALY saved of $5,000 the corresponding figure per death averted is about $150,000 (using a life expectancy of sixty and a discount rate of 3 percent). Note that the figures used for policy in developed countries would be considerably higher. The US EPA, for example, currently uses a "value of statistical life" (VSL) of $6.9 million.

We first discuss some methodological issues, then undertake some simulations. The reader is referred to BAH 2004 for a more detailed consideration of methodology.

Methodological Issues

In this section we discuss five issues regarding methodology, which affect the ranking of results and hence their policy implications. These issues are:

- the discount rate used, and how this changes the relative ranking of interventions which avert death, as compared to those which improve future productivity
- how CE or B/C ratios change across regions as costs and disease patterns vary
- the difference between incidence- and prevalence-based calculations
- the ethical concerns surrounding attaching a dollar value to the DALY
- the ethical concern as to whether a year of life saved is equally valuable at all ages.

Undertaking the calculations with different discount rates is not a trivial exercise. The effect depends on the time path of benefits, and may require going back to the original study data. Changing the discount rate for nutrition interventions has different effects on interventions which save lives and where benefits start to accrue immediately (DALYs saved), than where the outcome is cognitive improvement and where benefits accrue in the form of future productivity.

For example, an intervention that saves an infant life in a country where life expectancy is sixty years (assume for simplicity zero disability) saves 60 DALYs (undiscounted) or 28.5 DALYs (PV, discounted at 3 percent). If the DALY is valued at $1,000, this corresponds to $60,000 (undiscounted) or $28,505 (discounted). Similarly, an intervention that increases cognitive development in the first year of life, which increases productivity by an absolute amount of $2,000/year between the ages of twenty-one and fifty inclusive, also generates benefits of $60,000 (undiscounted), but only $22,356 (when discounted at 3 percent).

If we make the same comparison at a 6 percent discount rate, the PV of the DAL's saved for the life-saving intervention is $17,131, but the PV of the benefits from the cognitive intervention drops to only $9,207. With no discounting, the two projects yield the same outcome. Discounted at 3 percent, the cognitive project yields 78 percent of the value of the life-saving project; discounted at 6 percent, this drops to 54 percent. As discount rates increase, obviously interventions with returns further in the future become relatively less and less attractive.

Differences in costs and epidemiological profiles across countries matter. The CE and B/C data in table 6.1 are typically from individual studies in individual countries, and do not hold for all contexts. Even within countries, the average CE is not likely to remain the same as more and more of the population is covered. It is typically much more costly per person to cover the last 30 percent of the population than the first 70 percent.

Whereas data on epidemiological profiles across countries are readily available, data on health costs are less so. The relative price structures for different types of interventions differ across countries. In poor countries, interventions using tradables (such as higher-technology interventions in hospitals) are relatively more costly than interventions using non-tradables (such as nutrition education interventions intensive in salaries). Mulligan et al. (2005) provide carefully calculated templates of costs of selected health items in six different WHO regions. We use here the relative cost of a visit to a health center as an indicator of the kinds of nutrition interventions occurring at the community level. Their estimates are that the visit cost is approximately similar in South Asia and SSA, about 10 percent lower in East Asia, about 30 percent higher in Eastern Europe/Central Asia, about 112 percent higher in Middle East/North Africa, and about 150 percent higher in Latin America. Given also the epidemiological differences, this suggests that CE and B/C results for nutrition interventions in the low-income countries (many of which are in South Asia and SSA) are likely to be substantially different from those in the middle-income countries.

The difference between incidence- and prevalence-based estimates is another methodological issue. Incidence estimates compare the current cost of an intervention with the downstream benefits, all discounted to the present. These are preferred to prevalence estimates that simply compare the current costs of an intervention (for example, what it would cost to iodize salt throughout the developing world), with the current cost of the deficiency (e.g. the current losses attributable to IQ losses based on current patterns of goiter in mothers), using estimates as to what proportion of the costs could be averted by the intervention. Incidence-based calculations, however, involve more effort to undertake. Prevalence estimates should be regarded as rough estimates of the orders of magnitude involved, and they are less accurate as a measure of the incremental effect of a new intervention. In table 6.1, prevalence-based estimates from the literature have been recalculated as incidence-based, for comparability.

The conversion of DALYs to dollars raises ethical/conceptual issues. At the core, this requires assigning a monetary value to human life, a calculation that many find uncomfortable. Assigning different values to human life in different countries may be distasteful: Nevertheless, this is implicit in the "rule of thumb" statement that health spending to save one DALY is reasonable up to three times *per capita* GDP. Note that the values assigned in the Copenhagen Consensus project are as follows: With a life expectancy of sixty years, a 3 percent discount rate, and a DALY value of $1,000, a life saved (in infancy) is worth around $28,505; the same life saved is worth just $17,131 with a 6 percent discount rate. The same calculation at a DALY value of $5,000 implicitly values a human life saved at birth at $142,525 with a 3 percent discount rate, and $85,655 at a 6 percent discount rate.

Another related conceptual issue is the value of a year of human life at different ages. Current practice (in Jamison *et al.* 2006) is not to weight DALYs differentially at different ages, such that a healthy year of an infant's life is currently worth the same as a year of a prime-age adult's life and as a year of an elderly person's life. (This is of course different from the practice of discounting future benefits; for any individual, a future life year saved is worth less than an immediate life year saved.)

Thus saving an infant life in a country with a life expectancy of sixty, saves sixty years of life (which when discounted amounts to 28.5 life years saved if discounted at 3 percent). By contrast, saving a life at the age of fifty-nine saves only one life year (no discounting is necessary). This assigns a much greater benefit to interventions which save infant lives than those which save the lives of older adults. In the previous version of the DCPP (Jamison *et al.* 1993), this led to differential weighting of life years according to age, whereby life years saved of prime-age working adults were weighted more highly than life years saved of either children or the elderly. However, in the most recent version (Jamison *et al.* 2006) the differential weightings were not used. Obviously the relative weighting used changes the relative ranking of interventions, and hence has policy implications. In the more recent version, interventions affecting neonatal and infant survival were ranked higher as a result.

There are no easy solutions to these methodological issues. One needs to be aware of them when interpreting the results, and to treat the results as orders of magnitude rather than precise estimates.

Policy Simulations

In this section we undertake simulations to show the effect of varying the discount rate, and the dollar value assigned to a DALY. To simplify the exposition, we group those interventions with outcomes expressed in DALYs into two groups, using the CE magnitudes suggested from the literature and summarized in table 6.1. In one group the cost is approximately $20 (or less) per DALY saved, and in the other the CE is approximately $100 (or less) per DALY saved (calculated at a 3 percent discount rate). We also

Table 6.2. Sensitivity analysis: B/C ratios for nutrition interventions

Intervention	Discount rate 3% value of DALY $1,000	Discount rate 6% value of DALY $1,000	Discount rate 3% value of DALY $5,000	Discount rate 6% value of DALY $5,000
Highly effective vs. mortality (<$20/DALY)	50:1	30:1	250:1	150:1
Effective vs. mortality (<$100/DALY)	10:1	6:1	50:1	30:1
Salt iodization	30:1	12:1	Same as $1,000/DALY	Same as $1,000/DALY
Iron fortification	8:1	7:1	Same as $1,000/DALY	Same as $1,000/DALY
Anthelminths, preschool	6:1	2.4:1	Same as $1,000/DALY	Same as $1,000/DALY

Notes:
For sources and methods of calculation for salt iodization and iron fortification, see the appendix. Estimates for provision of anthelminths to school-age children at a 6% discount rate were made by present authors, based on Miguel and Kremer (2004) (who use a 3% discount rate). The "highly effective vs. mortality" group includes vitamin A supplementation. The "effective vs. mortality" group includes iron supplementation for pregnant women, therapeutic use of zinc for diarrhea, biofortification and community-based nutrition education.

undertake simulations for a few interventions where the outcome is calculated in dollars rather than DALYs.

We assume that the intervention costs and benefits are relevant for South Asia or SSA, where the large majority of undernourished people live. Costs in other regions would be higher, and health benefits would be smaller (since the incidence of under-nutrition is lower and mortality rates are usually higher, lower additional costs of targeting or screening would be necessary).

Table 6.2 then provides the sensitivity analysis, showing the effect of increasing the discount rate from 3 percent to 6 percent, as well as assigning the DALY a value of $1,000 or $5,000. For the countries in South Asia and SSA, the calculations with the DALY valued at $5,000 probably are less relevant. If *per capita* GNP is below $1,000, it likely does not make sense to value a DALY at $5,000. The higher DALY value is arguably more appropriate for middle-income countries (see the appendix, p. 329).

The results show that all the nutrition interventions described have very attractive B/C ratios at both 3 percent and 6 percent discount rates. Obviously, however, strong assumptions have been required to make these calculations.

The higher discount rate makes interventions benefitting children's cognitive development relatively less attractive, since the benefits are further in the future.

Table 6.3 provides very rough estimates of the total costs and total benefits involved in implementing these solutions at scale. A number of assumptions have been made, and the numbers should be regarded as orders of magnitude rather than precise. The estimates include scaling up in SSA and South and Asia only (unless otherwise indicated). This is where the majority of under-nourished children live, and from where the cost data are derived. It would likely be disproportionately more costly to scale up to address under-nutrition elsewhere. Moreover, the estimates are for scaling up most interventions to cover 80 percent of the population. We do not have good estimates as yet of the costs for scaling up to reach the last 20 percent, although we can surmise that the costs are higher, as are the benefits, on average.

Table 6.3 shows that investing about $120 million in micronutrient interventions in South Asia and SSA (zinc, vitamin A, and biofortification) could reduce DALY losses attributable to micronutrient malnutrition by 2 million DALYs (or about 5 percent of the total such

Table 6.3. Ballpark estimates of annual costs and benefits of scaling-up interventions

Intervention	Numbers Affected (millions)	Solution cost per person per year	CE and B/C used	DALYs aved/year (million)	Total cost/ year (million)	Total benefit/ year (million) at $1,000/DALY	BCR of Solutions $1000 per DALY
Solution 1: Micronutrient supplementation							17.3
Vitamin A Capsules <age two	11.8	$0.20	$10/ DALY	0.24	$2.4	$240	
Therapeutic zinc supplements, courses, infants Six to twelve months	58	$1.00	$73/ DALY	0.8	$58	$800	
Solution 2: Micronutrient fortification							9.5
Salt iodization	380	$0.05	30:1	Small	$19	$570	
Iron fortification	2,223	$0.12	8:1	Small	$267	$2,136	
Solution 3: Biofortification (Plant breeding)	36 countries	$0.75 million/ country	$55/ DALY	1.0	$60	$1,000	16.7
Solution 4: De-worming Pre-schoolers	53	$0.50	6:1	–	$26.5	$159	6.0
Solution 5: Community-based nutrition promotion	114	$7	$80/ DALY	10.0	$798	$10,000	12.5
Total all solutions	–	–	–	12.0	$1,171.5	$15,276	

Notes:
Salt iodization: assumes scale-up in the three more lagging regions (South Asia: current coverage 64 percent, SSA: current coverage 64 percent, and CEE/CIS: current coverage 50 percent), to 80 percent of households consuming iodized salt. Other developing regions have current coverage of 84–85 percent. Data on coverage from UNICEF (2008).
Vitamin A: assumes scale-up to full coverage (two doses) to 80 percent of children age two and below, in SSA (where coverage is currently 73 percent) and South Asia (where current coverage is 71 percent). For comparison, current coverage in East Asia is 82 percent. Data on coverage from UNICEF (2008).
Zinc supplements: assumes two courses of supplements per year for treatment of diarrhea OR a course of "Sprinkles" for children aged six–twelve months for approximately three months, reaching 80 percent of children in the six- to eighteen-month age group, in South Asia and SSA. Assumes that current coverage is essentially zero.
Iron fortification: assumes fortification reaching 80 percent of the population of SSA and South Asia, assuming negligible current coverage.
Biofortification: assumes spending on average on two staples per country for thirty-six countries in South Asia and SSA.
Anthelminths: assumes two treatments annually for 80 percent of children below between the ages of one and three, in Africa and Southeast Asia, assuming negligible current coverage.
Community nutrition: assumes program targeted to rural and poorer urban children in SSA and South Asia, reaching 80 percent of children below two.

losses attributable to micronutrient deficiencies, according to Bhutta *et al.* 2008). Investing about $800 million in nutrition education (focused on breastfeeding and complementary feeding) could reduce DALY losses attributable to stunting/wasting by 10 million DALYs (or about 12.5 percent of the losses attributable to stunting/ wasting, again using Bhutta *et al.* 2008). These interventions would by no means eliminate under-nutrition, but Bhutta *et al.* (2008) estimate that only about a third of stunting and a quarter of the mortality and morbidity associated with under-nutrition can be eliminated by these solutions. To eliminate the rest likely requires significant transfer of food and/or income, and longer-term changes in the status of women.

Additional investments in iron fortification and salt iodization would cost $286 million, with only small DALY gains but large returns in dollar terms. Although the resource cost is $286 million, the cost to governments could be considerably smaller, if consumers absorbed the modest per-person cost of the fortificant. De-worming pre-schoolers would cost $26.5 million, yielding $159 million in benefits.

Overall, implementing these solutions would cost $1.2 billion, yield benefits valued at $15.3 billion (using the $1,000/DALY value), and save 12.0 million DALYs. These DALYs saved represent about 3 percent of all DALYs lost in children below the age of five. The cost to governments and donors could be reduced to $0.9 billion if the costs of extending iron fortification and salt iodization were assumed by households. There is also the possibility of redirecting some existing spending, intended to improve nutrition, to these highly cost-effective solutions. Bhutta *et al.* (2008) comment that "supplementary feeding interventions beyond 36 months of age would probably not reduce stunting and might be inadvisable, since rapid weight gain in later childhood is associated with adverse long-term outcomes."

It should be noted that some of the benefits calculations rely heavily on the implicit value assigned to human life. Specifically, the calculations of the benefits for micronutrient supplements (vitamin A and zinc), for biofortification (new agricultural technology), and for nutrition education rely on the implicit assumption that saving an infant life is worth about $30,000 (if the DALY is worth $1,000, and the discount rate is 3 percent). The calculations for fortification (iodized salt, and iron fortification of cereals), and the calculations for de-worming, do not rely on this assumption and are robust to it.

Discussion

This chapter has revisited and updated previous estimates (BAH 2004) from the 2004 Copenhagen Consensus. In the previous study, micronutrient interventions were found to have among the highest B/C ratios of any development intervention. More recent research underscores this, and provides further guidance as to the type of interventions, as well as areas where additional work is needed. The current priorities are completing the coverage of under-two-year-olds with vitamin A capsules; extending vitamin A capsules to neonates; therapeutic zinc supplementation (with the six- to twelve-months group being likely the priority: Economic analysis has so far been restricted to therapeutic use for diarrhea); completion of universal salt iodization, and iron and folate fortification of staples. We have divided the solutions analyzed into supplementation and fortification. Biofortification (plant breeding for high-micronutrient content) remains promising but does not yet have widespread results.

Anthelminths (de-worming) have been examined in more detail than in the previous estimates. These are as attractive as some micronutrient interventions. Whereas current international guidelines and goals generally focus on school-age children, these should likely be extended to pre-school children in high-prevalence areas. We have not undertaken calculations for pregnant women in the second or third trimester, but it may also be cost-effective to provide de-worming for this group.

Nutrition education in the community, particularly focused on supporting breastfeeding and weaning practices, is also an attractive intervention when the program is implemented well. In SSA and South Asia this is likely to take the form of a community nutrition program, since few countries in these regions have good coverage of primary health care systems in which nutrition education can be included.

Finally, all these interventions address only a modest proportion of the overall under-nutrition problem. Bhutta *et al.* (2008) estimate that micronutrient interventions can reduce DALYs lost due to under-nutrition by 17 percent (reducing mortality prior to the age of three by 12 percent and stunting by 17 percent). Bhutta *et al.* (2008) estimate that a package (breastfeeding promotion and support, and promotion of complementary feeding and other support) could achieve a further reduction of 13 percent of DALYs lost due to under-nutrition (13 percent reduction in mortality, 16 percent reduction in stunting). To achieve a further reduction beyond this, one would have to consider broader programs such as food or cash transfers, enhancing the status of women, etc. It is not surprising that only a quarter to a third of under-nutrition can be removed by micronutrient interventions and nutrition education; the rest requires reduction of poverty, which is the major cause of children not having a diet adequate in quality and quantity.

The focus of interventions throughout this chapter has been on interventions in South Asia and SSA. These are the regions for which the CE and B/C data are drawn (B/C ratios are lower for other regions); and these are the regions where between 75 percent and 80 percent of the world's undernourished children live (75 percent of the stunted and 80 percent of the wasted).

The discussion has focused on nutritional outcomes; however, clearly nutritional improvements also have impacts on health and on educational achievement and hence other development outcomes, which have not been quantified here.

Appendix: Methods/Sources for Calculations in Table 6.2

Salt Iodization

Uses basic data described in Horton (2004). Assumes:

- cost of salt iodization, $0.05/person/year; iodization sufficient to remove threat of goiter
- goiter prevalence in pregnant women, 10 percent
- economic loss per birth to a woman with goiter averages, 15 percent
- future earnings accrue between the ages of twenty-one and fifty, and their PV at birth, *per capita* average, 11.18 times GDP/*per capita* (3 percent discount rate) or $4.61 (6 percent discount rate)
- life expectancy sixty years, no disability, and no mortality during working years twenty-one to fifty
- birth rate of 24 per 1,000 (similar to India)
- no real GDP growth
- GNI/*per capita*, $370 (similar to India in 2000, when costs obtained)
- Hence PV of benefits *per capita*, $1.47 (at 3 percent discount rate), and B/C approximately 30:1
- Present value of benefits *per capita*, $0.60 (at 6 percent discount rate) and B/C approximately 12:1

Iron Fortification

Uses data and methods from Horton and Ross (2003). Assumes:

- cost of iron fortification of flour, $0.12/*per capita*
- prevalence of anemia, about 60 percent
- iron fortification reduces anemia by 9 percentage points, or approximately 20 percent

- productivity losses in manual labour, 5 percent; in heavy manual labour, 17 percent; and in other work (cognitive effect), 4 percent
- future earnings accrue between the ages of twenty-one and fifty, and their PV at birth, *per capita* average, 11.18 times GDP/*per capita* (3 percent discount rate) or $4.61 (6 percent discount rate); but iron fortification must be maintained until adolescence to obtain future cognitive benefits (fifteen years of fortification)
- life expectancy, sixty years, no disability, and no mortality during working years twenty-one to fifty
- no real GDP growth
- GNI/*per capita*, $370 (India in 2000 at time of Horton and Ross, 2003, calculation)
- Benefits in terms of immediate impact on GDP, $3.78 (Horton and Ross 2003) (physical productivity)
- Benefits in terms of future GDP (cognitive gains), $1.03 (at 3 percent discount rate) and $0.38 (at 6 percent discount rate), based on labor share of GDP at 40 percent
- B/C ratio, 8:1 (3 percent discount rate) and 7:1 (6 percent discount rate)

Bibliography

Alderman, H., 2007: Longitudinal study of the nutrition and early child development program in Uganda, *World Development*, **35**(8): 1376–89

Alderman, H., Konde-Lule, J., Sebuliba, I., Bundy, D., and Hall, A., 2006: Effect on weight gain of routinely giving albendazole to preschool children during child health days in Uganda: Cluster randomized controlled trial, *British Medical Journal*, **333**: 122–6

Alderman, H., Nidiaye, B., Linnemayr, S., Ka, A., Rokx, C., Dieng, K., and Mulder-Sibanda, M., 2007: Effectiveness of a community-based intervention to improve nutrition in young children in Senegal: A difference in difference analysis, *Public Health Nutrition*, published online, June 18, 2008

Allen, L. and Gillespie, S., 2001: What works? A review of the efficacy and effectiveness of nutrition interventions, WHO ACC/SCN Nutrition Policy Paper, **19**, Geneva

Baltussen, R., Knai, C., and Sharan, M, 2004: Iron fortification and iron supplementation are cost-effective interventions to reduce iron deficiency in four subregions of the world, *Journal of Nutrition*, **134**: 2678–86

Beinner, M.A., Lamounier, J.A., and Tomaz, C., 2005: Effect of iron-fortified drinking water of daycare facilities on the hemoglobin status of young children, *Journal of the American College of Nutrition*, **24**(2), 107–14

Behrman, J., Alderman, H., and Hoddinott, J., 2004: Hunger and malnutrition, chapter 7 in B. Lomborg (ed.) *Global crises, global solutions*, Cambridge University Press, Cambridge

Bhandari, N., Mazumder, S., Taneja, S., Dube, B., Agarwal, R.C., Mahalanabis, D., Fontaine, O., Black, R.E., and Bhan, M.K., 2008: Effectiveness of zinc supplementation plus oral rehydration salts compared with oral rehydration salts alone as a treatment for acute diarrhea in a primary care setting: A cluster randomized trial, *Pediatrics*, **121**, e1279–e1285

Bhutta, Z.A., Ahmed, T., Black, R.E., Cousens, S., Dewey, K., Giugliani, E., Haider, B.A., Kirkwood, B., Morris, S.S., Sachdev, H.P.S., and Shekar, M., 2008: What works? Interventions for maternal and child under-nutrition and survival, *Lancet*, **371**: 417–40

Black, R.E., Allen, L.H., Bhutta, Z.A., Caulfield, L.E., de Onis, M., Essati, M., Mathers, C., and Rivera, 2008: Maternal and child under-nutrition: Global and regional exposures and health consequences, *Lancet* **371**: 243–60

Bobonis, G., Miguel, E., and Puri-Sharma, C., 2006: Anemia and school participation, *Journal of Human Resources*, **41**(4): 692–721

Brown, K., 2006: Information gaps for scaling-up programs to improve zinc nutrition, **A2Z** Technical Paper, www.a2zproject.org/resources.cfm, downloaded July 29, 2007

Cherian, A., Seena, S., Bullock, R.K., and Antony, A.C., 2005: Incidence of neural tube defects in the least-developed area of India: A population-based study, *Lancet*, **366**: 930–1

Ching, P., Birmingham, M., Goodman, T., Sutter, R., and Loevinsohn, B., 2000: Childhood mortality impact and costs of integrating vitamin A supplementation into immunization campaigns, *American Journal of Public Health*, **90**(10): 1526–9

Darmstadt, G.L., Butta, Z.A., Cousens, S., Adam, T., Walker, L., de Bernis, L., 2005: Neonatal survival 2: Evidence-based, cost-effective interventions: how many newborn babies can we save?, *Lancet*, **365**: 977–88

De Benoist, B., 2007: Control of iodine deficiency in pregnant and lactating women, and in children less than 2 years: Report of a WHO Technical Consultation, Presentation at Micronutrient Forum, Istanbul, April 16–18

De Silva, N.R., Brooker, S., Hotez, P.J., Montresor, A., Engels, D., and Savioli, L., 2003: Soil-transmitted helminth infections: Updating the global picture, *Trends in Parasitology*, **19**: 547–51

Fiedler, J.L., 2000: The Nepal national vitamin A program: Prototype to emulate or donor enclave?, *Health Policy and Planning*, **15**(2): 145–56

Fiedler, J.L., 2003: A cost analysis of the Honduras community-based integrated child care program, Washington, DC, World Bank HNP Discussion Paper, 408–27

Fiedler, J.L., 2007a: The cost of child health days: A case study of Ethiopia's enhanced outreach strategy, Social Sectors Development Strategies, Washington DC, draft, mimeo

Fiedler, J.L., 2007b: A cost analysis of the CARE/India RACHNA program, Social Sectors Development Strategies, Washington, DC, draft, mimeo

French, A., Grant, R., Weitzman, S., Ray, J.G., Vermeulen, M.J., Sung, L., Greenberg, M., and Koren, G., 2003: Folic acid food fortification is associated with a decline in neuroblastoma, *Clinical pharmacology & therapeutics*, **74**(3): 288–94

Galasso, E. and Umapathi, N., 2007: Improving nutritional status through behavioral change: Lessons from Madagascar?, Policy Research Working Paper, **4424**, World Bank, Washington, DC

Galasso, E. and Yau, J., 2006: Learning through monitoring: Lessons from a large-scale nutrition program in Madagascar, World Bank Policy Research Working Paper, **4058**, available at SSRN: http://ssrn.com/abstract=943915

Gera, T., Sachdev, H.P.S., Nestel, P., and Sachdev, S.S., 2007: Effect of iron supplementation on haemoglobin response in children: Systematic review of randomised controlled trials, *Journal of Pediatric Gastroenterology and Nutrition*, **44**: 468–86

Goodman, T., Dalmiya, N., de Benoist, B., and Schultink, W., 2000. Polio as a platform: using national immunization days to deliver vitamin A supplements. *Bulletin of the World Health Organization* 78(3), 305-314

Grosse, S.D., Waitzman, N.J., Romano, P.S., and Mulinare, J., 2005: Reevaluating the benefits of folic acid fortification in the United States: Economic analysis, regulation, and public health, *American Journal of Public Health*, **95**(11): 1917–22

Gulani, A., Nagpal, J., Osmond, C., Sachdev, H.P.S., 2007: Effect of administration of intestinal anthelmintic drugs on haemoglobin: Systematic review of randomized controlled trials, *BMJ*, doi:10.1136/bmj.39150.510475.AE

Hall, A., Hewitt, G., Tuffrey, V., and de Silva, N., 2008: A review and meta-analysis of the impact of intestinal worms on child growth and nutrition, *Maternal and Child Nutrition*, 4: 118–236

Harvest Plus, 2007: *Harvest plus medium term plan 2008–2010*, available at www.harvestplus/pdfs/hpmtp20082010.pdf, accessed July 31, 2008

Ho, T.J., 1985: Economic issues in assessing nutrition projects: Costs, affordability and cost-effectiveness, World Bank PHN Technical Note, 84:14, Washington, DC

Hoddinott, J., Behrman, J.R., Maluccio, J.A., Flores, R., and Martorell, R., 2008: Effect of a nutrition intervention during early childhood on economic productivity in Guatemalan adults, *Lancet*, **371**: 41–16

Horton, S. 1999: Opportunities for investments in nutrition in low-income Asia, *Asian Development Review*, **17**: 246–73

Horton, S., 2004: The economic impact of micronutrient deficiencies, in J.M. Pettifor and S. Zlotkin (eds.), *Micronutrient deficiencies during the weaning period and the first years of life. Nestle nutrition workshop series pediatric program*, **54**: 187–202, Karger AG, Basel

Horton, S., 2006: The economics of food fortification, *Journal of Nutrition*, **136**: 1068–71

Horton, S. and Ross, J., 2003: The economics of iron deficiency, *Food Policy*, **28**(1): 51–75; see also Horton, S. and Ross, J., 2006: Corrigendum, *Food Policy*, **32**: 141–3

Horton, S., Sanghvi, T., Phillips, M., Fiedler, J., Perez-Escamilla, R., Lutter, C., Rivera, A., and Segall-Correa, A.M., 1996: Breastfeeding promotion and priority setting in health, *Health Policy and Planning*, **11**(2): 156–68

Hotez, P.J., Bundy D.A.P., Beegle, K., Brooker, S., Drake, L., de Silva, N., Montresor, A., Engels, D., Jukes, M., Chitsulo, L., Chow, J., Laxminarayan, R., Michaud, C.M., Bethony, J., Correa-Oliveira, R., Xiao, S.H., Fenwick, A., and Savioli, 2006: Helminth infections: Soil-transmitted helminth infections and schistosomiasis, in D.T. Jamison, J.G. Breman, A.R. Measham, G. Alleyne, M. Claeson, D.B. Evans, P. Jha, A. Mills, and P. Musgrove, *Disease control priorities in developing countries*, 2nd edn., World Bank and Oxford University Press, Washington, DC and New York

Iodine Network, n.d.: Preventing brain damage from iodine deficiency, Secretariat, Network for Sustained Elimination of Iodine Deficiency, Ottawa

IZINCG, 2004. Assessment of the risk of zinc deficiency in populations and options for its control, in C. Hotz and K.H. Brown (eds.), *Food and Nutrition Bulletin*, **25**: S94–204

Jamison, D.T., Breman, J.G., Measham, A.R., Alleyne, G., Claeson, M., Evans, D.B., Jha, P., Mills, A., and Musgrove, P., 2006: *Disease control priorities in developing countries*, 2nd edn.,World Bank and Oxford University Press, Washington D,C and New York

Jamison, D.T., Mosley, W.H., Measham, A.R.

and Bobadilla, J.L. (eds.), 1993: *Disease control priorities in developing countries*, Oxford University Press, New York

Lozoff, B., Jimenez, E., and Smith, J.B., 2006: Double burden of iron deficiency in infancy and low socio-economic status: A longitudinal analysis of cognitive test scores to 19 years, *Archives of Pediatric and Adolescent Medicine*, **160**(11): 1108–13

Maluccio, J.A., Hoddinott, J., Behrman, J.R., Quisumbing, A., Martorell, R., and Stein, A.D., 2006: The impact of nutrition during early childhood on education among Guatemalan adults, University of Pennsylvania–IFPRI–Emory draft Philadelphia, Washington, DC, and Atlanta, mimeo

Mason, J., Hunt, J., Parker, D., and Jonsson, U., 1999: Investing in child nutrition in Asia, *Asian Development Review*, **17**(1, 2): 1–32

Mason, J., Hunt, J., Parker, D., and Jonsson, U., 2001: Improving child nutrition in Asia, *Food and Nutrition Bulletin*, **22**(3), supplement: 3–85

Meenakshi, J.V., Johnson, N., Manyong, V.M., Groote, H. De, Javelosa, J., Yanggen, D., Naher, F., Gonzalez, C., Garcia, J., and Meng, E., 2007: How cost-effective is biofortification in combating micronutrient malnutrition? An *ex ante* assessment, HarvestPlus Working Paper, **2**, IFPRI, Washington DC

Micronutrient Forum, 2007: News release, downloaded from www.micronutrientforum. org/newsRelease.pdf, July 29, 2007

Miguel, E. and Kremer, M., 2004: Worms: Identifying impacts on health and education in the presence of treatment externalities, *Econometrica*, **72**: 159–217

Mill, A. and Shillcut, S., 2004: Communicable disease, chapter 2 in B. Lomborg (ed.), *Global crises, global solutions*, Cambridge University Press, Cambridge

Mulligan, J.-A., Fox-Rushby, J.A., Adam, T., Johns, B., and Mills, A., 2005: Unit costs of health care inputs in low and middle income regions, DCPP Working Paper, **9**, available from www.dcpp.org

Neidecker-Gonzales, O., Bouis, H., and Nestel, P., 2007: Estimating the global costs of Vitamin A capsule distribution: A review of the literature and development of a country-level model, *Food and Nutrition Bulletin*, **28**(3): 307–16

Ouma, P., Parise, M.E., Hamel, M.J., ter Kuile, F.O., Otieno, K., Ayisi, J.G., Kager, P.A., Steketee, R.W., Slutsker, L., and van Eijk, A.M., 2006: A randomized controlled trial of folate supplementation when treating malaria in pregnancy with sulfadexine-pyrimethamine, PLoS Clinical Trials, **1**(6) e28

Pelletier, D.L. and Jonsson, U., 1994: The use of information in the Iringa Nutrition Program: Some global lessons for nutrition surveillance, *Food Policy*, **19**(3), 30–13

Rahmathullah, L., Tielsch, J.M., Thulasiraj, R.D., Katz, J., Coles, C., Devi, S., John, R., Prakash, K., Sadanand, A.V., Edwin, N., and Karamaraj, C., 2003: Impact of supplementing newborn infants with vitamin A on early infant mortality: Community based randomized trial in southern India, *BMJ*, **27**(7409): 254

Robberstad, B., Strand, T., Black, R.E., and Sommerfelt, H., 2004: Cost-effectiveness of zinc as adjunct therapy for acute childhood diarrhea in developing countries, *Bull. WHO*, **82**(7): 523–31

Sachdev, H.P.S., Gera, T., and Nestel, P., 2005: Effect of iron supplementation on mental and motor development in children: Systematic review of randomized controlled trials, *Public Health Nutrition*, **8**(2): 117–32

Sachdev, H.P.S., Gera, T., and Nestel, P., 2006: Effect of iron supplementation on physical growth in children: Systematic review of randomized controlled trials, *Public Health Nutrition*, **9**(7): 904–20

Sayed, A-R., Bourne, D., Pattinson, R., Nixon, J., and Henderson, B., 2008: Decline in the prevalence of neural tube defects following folic acid fortification and its cost-benefit in South Africa, *Birth Defects Research* (Part A), **82**: 211–16

Sazawal, S., Black, R.E., Menon, V.P., Dinghra, P., Caulfield, L.E., Dhingra, U., and Bagati, A., 2001: Zinc supplementation in infants born small for gestational age reduces mortality: A prospective, randomized, controlled trial, *Pediatrics*, **108**: 1280–6

Sazawal, S., Black, R.E., Ramsan, M., Chwaya, H.M., Stoltzfus, R.J., Dutta, A., Dhinga, U., Kabole, I., Deb, S., Othman, M.K., and Kabole, F.M., 2006: Effects of routine prophylactic supplementation with iron and folic acid on admission to hospital and mortality in preschool children in a high malaria transmission setting: Community-based, randomized, placebo-controlled trial, *Lancet*, **367**: 133–43

Sharieff, W., Horton, S., and Zlotkin, S., 2006: Economic gains of a home fortification program: Evaluation of "Sprinkles" from provider's perspective, *Canadian Journal of Public Health*, **97**(1): 20–3

Stokey, N., 2004: Expert Comments, in B. Lomborg (ed.), *Global crises, global solutions.* Cambridge University Press, Cambridge

Stoltzfus, R.J., 2007: Taking stock: Iron. Presentation at Istanbul, Turkey, Micronutrient Forum, April 16–18

Stoltzfus, R.J., Chway, H.M., Montresor, A., Tielsch, J.M., Jape, J.K., Albonico, M., and Savioli, 2004: Low dose daily iron supplementation improves iron status and appetite but not anemia, whereas quarterly anthelminthic treatment improves growth, appetite and anemia in Zanzibari preschool children, *Journal of Nutrition*, **134**: 348–56

Thomas, D., Frankenberg, E., Habicht, J.-P. *et al.*, 2004: Causal effect of health on labor market outcomes: Evidence from a random assignment iron supplementation intervention, Paper presented at Population Association of America Annual Meetings, Boston, April

UNICEF, 2006: *Progress for children: A report card on nutrition*, UNICEF, New York

UNICEF, 2008: *State of the world's children 2008*, UNICEF, New York

USAID, 1988: Growth monitoring and nutrition education: Impact evaluation of an effective applied nutrition program in the Dominican Republic, CRS/CARITAS, 1983–6, USAID Office of Nutrition, Washington, DC

Waters, H.R., Penny, M.E., Creed-Kanashiro, H.M., Robert, R.C., Narro, R., Willis, J., Caulfield, L.E., and Black, R.E., 2006: The cost-effectiveness of a child nutrition education program in Peru, *Health Policy and Planning*, **21**(4): 257–64

WHO, 2005: Report of the third global meeting of the partners for parasite control, Geneva, November 29–30 2004, WHO, Geneva

World Bank, 2006: *Repositioning nutrition as central to development: a strategy for large-scale action*, World Bank, Washington DC

World Vision 2006: *Improving nutrition of women and children: The MICAH program, final program report, 2005*, World Vision, Mississauga

Xiao, K.Z. *et al.*, 1990: Central nervous system congenital malformations, especially neural tube defects in 29 provinces, metropolitan cities and autonomous regions of China: Chinese Birth Defects Monitoring Program, *International Journal of Epidemiology*, **19**: 978–82

Zinc Task Force, 2006: *Integrated plan for accelerating zinc adoption for the management of diarrhea in developing countries*, Johns Hopkins University School of Public Health and others, draft, mimeo

Perspective Papers

Perspective Paper 6.1

REYNALDO MARTORELL

Introduction

Horton, Alderman, and Rivera (2008) (hereafter, HAR) address the challenge of hunger and malnutrition, as done earlier by Behrman, Alderman, and Hoddinott (2004) (hereafter, BAH) for the 2004 Copenhagen Consensus project. HAR state that their work "builds on and updates" the earlier work. There are differences in approach between these two analyses. Four opportunities are proposed by BAH (2004): (1) reducing the prevalence of low birthweight, (2) improving infant and child nutrition and promoting exclusive breastfeeding, (3) reducing the prevalence of iron deficiency anemia and of vitamin A, iodine, and zinc deficiencies, and (4) investing in technology in developing-country agriculture. HAR list four opportunities (or solutions): (1) micronutrient interventions, (2) antihelminths, (3) breastfeeding promotion – baby-friendly hospitals, and (4) nutrition education at the community level. While BAH describe the first three *opportunities* that address nutrition directly in terms of the intended goals (i.e. reducing the prevalence of low birthweight, child under-nutrition, and micronutrient deficiencies), HAR describe theirs in terms of the types of *interventions* to be implemented (i.e. micronutrient interventions, antihelminths, baby-friendly hospitals, and nutrition education), which makes them seem less compelling. Focusing on the interventions rather than the problems may narrow the mix of cost-effective

interventions that can address the problem and may expand the populations of interest beyond women and children under two years of age, the high priority groups for nutrition interventions.

The *Lancet* published a series of five papers dedicated to maternal and child under-nutrition and survival in early 2008 (Bhutta *et al.* 2008; Black *et al.* 2008; Bryce *et al.* 2008; Morris *et al.* 2008; Victora *et al.* 2008). This body of work represents the collective effort of many of the leaders of the nutrition scientific community. The first three papers are particularly relevant to HAR. Black *et al.* (2008) consider the extent of the problem of maternal and child under-nutrition and estimate the lost DALYs contributed by these problems; Victora *et al.* (2008) consider the long-term consequences of maternal and child under-nutrition for human capital and adult health; and Bhutta *et al.* (2008) consider the evidence about impact of the arsenal of interventions to improve maternal and child nutrition and end up with specific recommendations about which are "proven" interventions to recommend and which are not.

In this paper, attention is drawn to advances in research that are relevant to the challenge of eliminating hunger and malnutrition and which complement HAR's Challenge paper. In addition to what new research reveals about the efficacy and effectiveness of some nutrition interventions, we identify areas where HAR's conclusions may not be supported by the evidence or where they differ from those of the *Lancet* series.

Finally, we comment on the costs of implementing effective nutrition interventions at scale.

Limitations of Underweight as an Indicator of Nutritional Status

Underweight (<–2 SD below the reference mean) is the most widely used indicator of nutritional status in children less than five years of age and is the indicator emphasized by HAR. Underweight is also the indicator selected to assess progress in meeting MDG1, the Millennium Goal of eradicating extreme poverty and hunger. One of two targets of MDG1 to be achieved between 1990 and 2015 is to halve the proportion of people who suffer from hunger, and the indicator used by WHO and UNICEF to monitor progress is the underweight rate in children less than five years old (www.mdgmonitor.org/goal1.cfm). When time trends in underweight rates are examined, including projections to 2015, Eastern Asia (mainly driven by China), and Southeastern Asia along with Latin America and the Caribbean are regions of the developing world that are projected to meet MDG1 (de Onis *et al.* 2004) as HAR note.

Underweight is probably a very useful global indicator in populations where both stunting and wasting are common. However, childhood obesity is now increasingly common in many parts of the world, and in Latin America and the Caribbean in particular (de Onis and Blössner 2000; Martorell *et al.* 2000; Wang and Lobstein 2006). Childhood obesity can mask the problem of stunting and provide a false impression of progress in reducing hunger. National rates from Bolivia from the 2003 Demographic Health Survey (www.measuredhs.com) are presented in figure 6.1.1 for stunting, underweight, wasting, and obesity for children less than five years of age. Two reference populations are used, the 1978 WHO/NCHS reference (Dibley *et al.* 1987) and the 2006 WHO standards (de Onis *et al.* 2006). Regardless of the reference used, it is clear that the principal problem with impaired child growth in Bolivia is stunting; indeed about 30 percent of children were stunted in 2003. Wasting, on the other hand was as rare as in the reference population (by definition, fewer than 2.3 percent of the reference population is > –2 SDs). Underweight was much less common than stunting, as it is in countries in the region, and one reason for this is that childhood obesity, even in Bolivia, one of the poorest countries of the Western hemisphere, was more common than underweight in 2003. Use of the WHO 2006 standards, which are based on healthy children from around the world who were fed according to WHO's infant feeding recommendation and who grew up in environments that did not constrain growth (de Onis *et al.* 2006), yields higher rates of stunting and obesity and a slightly lower rate of underweight than obtained with the older reference.

The *Lancet* series has selected stunting as the indicator of choice to represent child undernutrition, complemented by indicators derived from comparisons of weight relative to height: wasting and obesity (Black *et al.* 2008). Stunting was the best predictor of long-term consequences for human capital (Victora *et al.* 2008).

The Copenhagen Consensus project should prefer stunting rather to underweight as the indicator of choice to track world progress over time as well as for use in evaluating the cost-effectiveness (CE) of interventions. Indeed, there is the danger that, in some settings, nutrition interventions may increase obesity (Uauy and Kain 2002; Gibson 2004, 2006) and thus over-estimate progress in reaching MDG1. The Copenhagen Consensus project should also use statistics about the extent of child under-nutrition that are based on the new WHO standards.

The Window of Vulnerability/ Opportunity: Pregnancy and the First Two Years of Life

HAR makes the point that emphasis should be placed, although not exclusively, on the first five years of life because of the serious consequences of malnutrition in children of this age. In fact, the consensus of the nutrition community is that one should focus even further on the vulnerable periods of intrauterine life and the first two

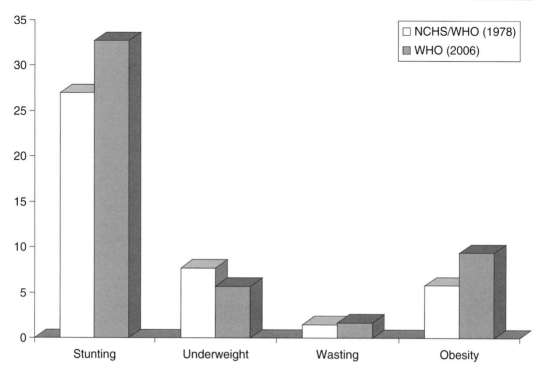

Figure 6.1.1 *Prevalence of stunting, underweight, wasting, and obesity in children (percentage below 2Z for all indicators except obesity, which is percentage above 2Z) <five years, using NCHS/WHO (1978) and WHO (2006) curves for Bolivia (DHS 2003)*

years of life. One of the central messages of the advocacy publication "Repositioning nutrition as central to development: A strategy for large scale action" is precisely the need to target this "window" in programs aimed at preventing under-nutrition and its consequences (World Bank 2006). BAH explicitly focused on women and young children, and did not include in their analysis of costs and benefits (C/B) interventions aimed at school children.

Figure 6.1.2 uses data from Peru to show that stunting is a phenomenon that develops in utero (i.e. growth retardation is observed at birth) and continues throughout the second year of life. By two years of age, z-scores are flat, implying that growth rates are similar to those in the reference population. While the pattern may vary somewhat, similar observations apply to all developing countries where stunting is observed (Shrimpton *et al.* 2001). Anemia, a marker of

mineral deficiencies, is also more common and its consequences more severe in children under two years of age (Lozoff *et al.* 2006).

We need to redefine the indicators of successful program delivery, impact, and costs in light of the need to focus on children under two. A good examples is growth promotion programs: Weighing children and promoting growth through counseling about health and nutrition in children older than two years of age is not the best use of resources, yet many such programs aimed at children under five reach more of the over-twos than the under-twos, who may be more likely to benefit (see discussion later about growth monitoring). It is likely that the effectiveness of programs measured through responses in either growth or micronutrient indicators of deficiency will be increased by reaching the more vulnerable, and thus more responsive, younger group.

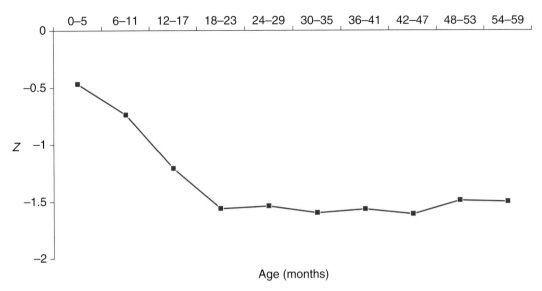

Figure 6.1.2 *Mean Z-scores for height-for-age relative to WHO standards in national data for Peru,*
2000

New Knowledge of the Consequences of Child Under-Nutrition

HAR make reference to new information since the 2004 Copenhagen Consensus project about the consequences of child under-nutrition, in particular evidence linking early childhood nutrition with human capital and economic productivity. Results from the 2002–4 follow-up study of the individuals who participated in the 1969–77 INCAP longitudinal study, which included a community-randomized, nutrition-supplementation intervention aimed at women and children less than seven years of age, are now published (Hoddinott *et al.* 2008). In the initial study, two villages were randomly assigned a nutritious supplement (atole) and two villages a less nutritious one (fresco). Economic data were obtained from 1,424 former participants in the supplementation trial (aged twenty-five to forty-two years) and used to estimate annual incomes, hours worked, and average hourly wages from all economic activities. Exposure to atole before, but not after, three years of age was associated with higher hourly wages, but only for men. For exposure to atole from 0 to two years, the

increase was US$ 0.67 per hour (95 percent C.I.: 0.16–1.17), which meant a 46 percent increase in average wages. There was a non-significant tendency for hours worked to be reduced and for annual incomes to be greater for those exposed to atole from 0 to two years.

The "Great Leap Forward" policies of Chairman Mao precipitated one of the worst famines in history, resulting in 15–30 million deaths. The long-term effects of the 1959–61 famine on the health and economic status of the survivors has been quantified (Chen and Zhou 2007). Exposure to the famine in early life (in people born between 1959 and 1962) was associated with a reduction in adult height of 3 cm and with lower incomes and wealth.

Information from five long-standing cohorts from Brazil, Guatemala, India, The Philippines, and South Africa show that poor fetal growth and stunting at two years of age is associated with shorter adult height, lower attained schooling, reduced adult income and decreased offspring birthweight (Victora *et al.* 2008). Also, children who are under-nourished in the first two years of life and who put on weight rapidly later in childhood and in adolescence are at higher risk of chronic diseases related to nutrition (Victora *et al.* 2008).

The results from Guatemala about the effects of improved nutrition prior to two years of age, of exposure to famine in the first two years of life, and of the consequences of poor fetal growth stunting at two years of age is the strongest evidence available indicating that investments in early childhood nutrition lead to improved adult health and greater economic wellbeing.

Interventions That Impact on Maternal and Birth Nutrition Outcomes

Improving maternal nutrition during pregnancy will lead to improved birth outcomes, an important step in improving child health and nutrition. However, the problem of intrauterine growth failure is often viewed as intractable. HAR did not comment on measures to improve birthweight and instead referred readers to BAR's previous work. Bhutta *et al.* (2008) review the pertinent literature to date, and provide summary estimates of impact for several interventions during pregnancy or delivery that are known to improve maternal and birth outcomes and that are recommended for implementation in all developing countries; these interventions and the intended outcome (in parenthesis) include iron folate and multiple micronutrient supplementation during pregnancy (reduced risk of anemia, improved birthweight), maternal iodine status through salt iodization (improved child survival and lower risk of cretinism), maternal calcium supplementation (reduced risk of preeclampsia), interventions to reduce smoking and indoor air pollution (outcomes not stated; these might include the prevention of respiratory infections, particularly in children and, possibly, the improvement of birth weight), and delayed cord clamping (improved neonatal iron status). This same review also recommended several interventions during pregnancy for implementation in specific contexts, that include: balanced energy protein supplementation during pregnancy (36 percent reduction in small-for-gestational-age newborns), maternal iodine

supplements (better survival of children and lower risk of cretinism), maternal de-worming in pregnancy (reduced risk of anemia), intermittent preventive treatment for malaria (reduced risk of anemia, 46 percent reduction in low birthweight), and insecticide treated bednets (23 percent reduction in risk of low birthweight). Several interventions during pregnancy were not recommended because the evidence shows little or no effect: nutrition education and advice and zinc, pyridoxine, and fish oil supplements.

Effect of Iron and Multiple Micronutrients on Birth Outcomes

Maternal anemia during pregnancy is associated with reduced birthweight (Rasmussen 2001) but evidence from randomized controlled trials of supplementation effects is limited, likely because the standard of care in many countries is to provide iron/folate supplements to women during pregnancy, making the inclusion of a placebo group often objectionable on ethical grounds. There are two US studies that were carried out in iron-replete, non-anemic women who were randomized early in pregnancy to receive iron until about twenty-eight weeks, when all women regardless of initial assignment began to receive iron (Cogswell *et al.* 2003; Siega-Riz *et al.* 2006). These studies found an average effect of iron supplementation to about twenty-eight weeks of 157g (table 6.1.1). This is presumably an underestimate of the impact of iron because all women began to receive iron at about twenty-eight weeks. Several studies from developing countries are also available that allow comparison between iron and placebo groups (Preziosi *et al.* 1997; Christian *et al.* 2003; Ziaei *et al.* 2007) or between iron *and* folic acid vs. a placebo (Agarwal *et al.* 1991; Christian *et al.* 2003). Overall, the average effect was 110g and 76g, respectively, in weighted and unweighted averages, equivalent to effects of 0.24 and 0.17, respectively (table 6.1.1). The difference between weighted and unweighted averages reflects the influence of larger studies, such as the one from Nepal.

The potential impact of iron supplementation during pregnancy should be explored

Table 6.1.1. Effects of iron supplementation during pregnancy on birthweight

Study	Birthweight differences (g)	Country	Effect size[a]	95 percent C.I.		P
Ziaei et al. (2007)	10	Iran	0.02	−0.12	0.17	0.75
Siega-Riz et al. (2006)	108	USA	0.19	0.00	0.38	0.04
Cogswell et al. (2003)	206	USA	0.36	0.09	0.64	0.01
Christian et al. (2003)	67	Nepal	0.15	0.04	0.27	0.01
Preziosi et al. (1997)	30	Niger	0.07	−0.21	0.35	0.63
Agarwal et al. (1991)[b]	290	India	0.77	0.51	1.02	0.00
Christian et al. (2003)[b]	60	Nepal	0.14	0.03	0.24	0.01
Overall[a] Unweighted	110		0.24	0.06	0.43	0.0111
Weighted	76		0.17	0.01	0.33	0.0355

Notes:
[a] Effect sizes were calculated for individual studies by dividing the difference between the mean change in treatment and control groups by the pooled SD. The overall mean effect size and 95 percent confidence were estimated using a random effects model. The overall mean effect size is reported for unweighted and weighted (weighted by the inverse of the intra-study variance) analyses.
[b] These two comparisons contrasted iron and folic acid supplementation to a placebo. All other comparisons were contrasts between iron alone and a placebo.

further in developing countries; a possible design that would meet ethical requirements would be one that contrasts the provision of iron and folic acid tablets, under regular program conditions and under enhanced conditions, with improved delivery and encouragement to consume the supplements. Folic acid has not been consistently shown to influence birthweight, so any differences would be attributed to iron. This design would under-estimate the impact of iron because, under regular program conditions, some women would ingest the supplements.

Several studies have been carried out to investigate whether multiple micronutrient supplementation during pregnancy leads to improved birthweight compared to supplementation with iron/folate (table 6.1.2). These studies suggest that there is a small effect attributed to multiple micronutrients of the order of 60g and 45g of birthweight in weighted and unweighted analyses, respectively, equivalent to effects of 0.14 and 0.10, respectively. It is not clear whether the effect of multiple micronutrients relative to a placebo would be the addition of the effect of iron relative to no iron *plus* the effect of multiple micronutrients relative to iron. This could be tested by adding a multiple micronutrient

supplementation group, under enhanced conditions, to the design just discussed.

All of the above suggests that successful implementation of iron folate supplementation during pregnancy will not only improve iron status but also have a small effect on birthweight. Multiple micronutrient programs may yield slightly greater effects on birthweight compared to just iron and folic acid.

Flour Fortification

Fortification of staples, such as wheat flour, is a promising intervention. If bioavailable fortificants are used and if the fortified product is consumed in adequate amounts by the target group, then the impact could be significant. Fortification has the potential to impact on women prior to pregnancy, whereas supplementation programs often begin several months into pregnancy for many women. Women who habitually consume fortified products may have improved folate intakes around the periconceptual period, and this will reduce the risk of neural tube defects. It is also advantageous to improve iron status prior to pregnancy. Children under two years of age will benefit less from fortification because they consume only small amounts of the staple and other

Table 6.1.2. Effects of multiple micronutrient supplementation vs. iron and folic acid on birthweight[a]

Study	Country	Absolute birthweight differences (g)	Effect size[b]	95 percent C.L.		P
Shankar (2008)	Indonesia	21.0	0.02	−0.02	0.05	0.36
Mardones et al. (2008)	Chile	65.4	0.14	0.01	0.26	0.03
Zagre et al. (2007)	Niger	67.0	0.34	0.26	0.42	<0.01
Gupta et al. (2007)	India	156	0.39	0.06	0.72	0.02
Fawzi et al. (2007)	Tanzania	67	0.13	0.08	0.17	<0.01
Osrin et al. (2005)	Nepal	77	0.18	0.05	0.30	0.00
Kaestel et al. (2005)[c]	Guinea-Bissau	53	0.10	−0.04	0.25	0.16
Kaestel et al. (2005)[c]	Guinea-Bissau	95	0.20	0.05	0.34	0.01
Friis et al. (2004)	Zimbabwe	49	0.08	−0.04	0.19	0.21
Christan et al. (2003)	Nepal	4	0.01	−0.10	0.12	0.87
Ramakrishnan et al. (2003)	Mexico	4	0.01	−0.15	0.17	0.90
Overall[1] Unweighted		60	0.14	0.07	0.21	0.0002
Weighted by sample size		45.0	0.098	−0.007	0.20	0.066
Weighted by inverse variance		44.9	0.097	−0.007	0.20	0.067

Notes:
[a] The treatment group received multiple micronutrients (MM) and the control group received iron except for the study by Mardones et al. (2008). In the Mardones et al. (2008) study, the treatment group received powder milk fortified with MM and omega-3 fatty acids while the control group received unfortified powder milk only; thus, differences found cannot be solely attributed to MM as they could also be due to essential fatty acids. Excluding the study by Mardones et al. (2008) has trivial effect on the estimate, 59g rather than 60g.
[b] Effect sizes were calculated for individual studies by dividing the difference between the mean change in treatment and control groups by the pooled standard deviation.
The overall mean effect size and 95 percent confidence interval across studies was then estimated assuming the random effects model.
Overall mean effect size is reported for unweighted and weighted (by sample size and by the inverse of the intra-study variance analysis).
[c] The study by Kaestel et al. (2005) allows contrasts between MM and supplementation at either 1 or 2 RDA versus iron.

measures may be required for them, such as supplementation, home fortification ("Sprinkles"), or fortified complementary foods.

Although a great deal of attention is being paid to fortification, particularly flour fortification, few sound evaluations of impact are available other than the case of Chile, where flour fortification has been shown to impact on folate status and to reduce neural tube defects (Castilla et al. 2003; Hertrampf et al. 2003). Imhoff-Kunsch et al. (2007) examined the potential contribution of flour fortification with iron and folic acid to the intakes of women of reproductive age in Guatemala, using national data on household purchases of wheat flour and products made from it. Assuming 5 percent availability for iron, wheat flour fortification met 6 percent of the estimated average requirement for iron and 33 percent of that for folic acid. For women living

under extreme poverty (mostly rural, indigenous households) the corresponding figures for iron and folic acid were 1 percent and 5 percent, respectively, whereas for women in non-poor households (mostly urban, non-indigenous), the corresponding figures were 12 percent and 71 percent, respectively. Thus, in Guatemala, where the traditional staple is corn but where bread is now consumed, particularly in urban areas, flour fortification has low potential for improving iron status but significant potential for improving folate status. However, rates of neural tube defects are high in the indigenous regions of Guatemala precisely where little fortified wheat flour is consumed. This analysis illustrates the need for careful evaluation of impact, which will obviously vary across countries by level of consumption of the fortified staple. The wheat belt around North Africa and the Middle

East would be an example of an area where wheat flour fortification can achieve a lot.

Neonatal Interventions

Bhutta *et al.* (2008) recommend breastfeeding promotion (provided individually or in groups to increase rates of exclusive breastfeeding in all countries and neonatal vitamin A supplementation in Asian populations (where it has been shown to improve survival). Neonatal vitamin K dosing and baby-friendly hospital initiatives were not recommended because of insufficient evidence, as were mass-media strategies for breastfeeding promotion because of evidence of little or no impact. HAR, on the other hand, highlight baby-friendly hospital initiatives as a particularly cost-effective intervention.

Interventions that Impact on Nutrition Outcomes in Infants and Children

Bhutta *et al.* (2008) have also identified interventions aimed at improving nutrition outcomes and survival in infants and children that are recommended for implementation in all developing countries, that are to be recommended only in specific contexts, and that are not recommended because of insufficient or no evidence of impact. Interventions that are recommended universally include, zinc fortification and supplementation (improved survival, prevention of diarrhea and pneumonia, reduced stunting), zinc supplementation in the management of diarrhea (reduced duration and severity of diarrhea), vitamin A fortification and supplementation (improved vitamin A status, improved survival), universal salt iodization (improved development), hand-washing and hygiene interventions (prevention of diarrhea), cooking in iron pots (improved iron status), and treatment of severe malnutrition (improved survival, reduced wasting). Interventions for specific contexts include conditional cash transfer programs (with nutrition education), behavioral change interventions to improve complementary feeding (reduced stunting), de-worming (improved iron status),

iron supplementation or fortification programs (improved iron status), and insecticide-treated bed-nets (reduced risk of malaria, improved iron status, improved survival).

The implementation of WHO guidelines for the treatment of severely malnourished children has been shown to be efficacious in reducing case-fatality rates when compared to conventional treatment (Bhutta *et al.* 2008). However, the treatment of severe malnutrition in a clinical setting is resource-intensive and requires skilled personnel; usually, the mother stays with the child and away from home, with disruptive consequences for the household and other children. Collins *et al.* (2006) argue that child-survival initiatives have ignored the problem of severe acute malnutrition that is estimated to kill 1.7 million children a year. According to Collins *et al.* (2006), where acute malnutrition is common, such as in conflict situations and in famine-stricken areas, the number of cases exceeds available inpatient capacity, case-fatality rates are 20–30 percent, and coverage is commonly under 10 percent. Moving the recuperation of those severely malnourished children without complications to the community and enabling the mother herself to treat the child is a promising alternative that appears to reduce case-fatality rates and increase coverage rates. This is possible through the use of new, ready-to-use, therapeutic foods that contain milk powder, sugar, vegetable oil, peanut butter, vitamins, and minerals; these energy-dense products need no water or cooking and are resistant to bacterial contamination. They have the potential to increase access to services, reduce costs, permit early initiation of treatment, and enhance compliance, and thus increase coverage and recovery rates. Collins *et al.* (2006) believe that this approach promises to be a successful and cost-effective treatment strategy. Bhutta *et al.* (2008) could not find any randomized controlled trials evaluating the impact on mortality reduction of community programs using ready-to-use therapeutic foods, and hence did not recommend this specific intervention.

Interventions not recommended for implementation anywhere include growth-monitoring and promotion and feeding of older pre-school children (Bhutta *et al.* 2008). The recommendation about growth-monitoring and promotion is likely to be controversial. Growth-monitoring (i.e. the act of weighing and plotting weights) is not an intervention but a tool, and in many programs this is all that is done. Growth-promotion implies using the information to counsel mothers about best practices in feeding and caring for children. At issue is whether the growth-monitoring part is needed; can the promotion part be done effectively without the monitoring part? Can growth-monitoring be an effective platform for anchoring other child health and nutrition interventions? These questions have not been answered with certainty, and good evaluations of growth-monitoring and promotion programs are needed. The lack of information, particularly from randomized controlled trials led Bhutta *et al.* (2008) not to recommend such programs. Not recommending the feeding of older children is clearly supported by the evidence; growth failure, as noted earlier, is confined to children less than two years old. What about feeding children less than two years of age? To what extent can complementary feeding be improved with behavior change communication and education alone? The evidence reviewed by Bhutta *et al.* (2008) is limited. In three studies in *food-secure* populations, nutrition education alone produced an increase in height-for-age *Z* of 0.25 (95 percent C.I. 0.01–0.49). The summary estimate from seven studies that provided complementary foods, with or without education, and that were carried out in *food-insecure* populations, had the highest impact on height-for-age *Z* of any type of intervention: 0.41 (95 percent C.I. 0.05–0.76). These results leave open the question whether nutrition education alone has an impact in food-insecure populations; until more evidence is presented, the interventions for improving complementary feeding in food-insecure populations should include nutrition education *and* fortified complementary foods.

Micronutrients and Stunting

Micronutrient programs have important effects on several outcomes such as survival (vitamin A, zinc), infection prevention (zinc), and cognitive development (iron, iodine); these effects provide ample rationale for programs that seek to correct micronutrient deficiencies. However, do micronutrient programs reduce stunting? Bhutta *et al.* (2008), as well as BAH and HAR, report that zinc interventions improve growth. In recent work (Ramakrishnan *et al.* forthcoming), we have been able to confirm the conclusions of Ramakrishnan *et al.* (2004) and find no effects on growth in height of interventions that provide iron or vitamin A. However, contrary to the current consensus, we do not find that zinc interventions improve growth in height. Bhutta *et al.* (2008) did not undertake a review of new literature but accepted results from a meta-analysis published by Brown *et al.* (2002) that found an average effect for change in height of 0.35 (95 percent C.I. 0.19–0.51). Our review was restricted to children under five years and included all previous studies included by Brown *et al.* (2002) for this age group, as well as numerous studies published since then. Based on forty studies involving 8,642 children, we found that the overall weighted mean effect was 0.07 (95 percent C.I. $-0.03, 0.17, p = 0.18$). We do not find a significant effect of zinc interventions on growth simply because most of the more recent studies report null findings. On the other hand, we find that providing multiple micronutrients has a weighted mean effect of 0.09 (95 percent C.I. $0.006, 0.17, p = 0.04$); this effect, while statistically significant, is small. Thus, micronutrient interventions have important effects that improve health and survival but do not prevent stunting.

Summary and Conclusions

HAR did not use the *Lancet* series on maternal and child under-nutrition in selecting their solutions. It is difficult to predict to what extent the series will be accepted as the consensus of the scientific community about effective interventions to address the problems of hunger and malnutrition, but the expectation is that the series will be seminal and influential. Not everything in this wide-ranging analysis will be accepted; for example, results from our recent meta-analysis indicate that zinc interventions are unlikely to prevent stunting, as claimed in the *Lancet* series.

The four solutions proposed by HAR include a sub-set of the interventions recommended by the *Lancet* series, and a few that have not been recommended:

1 HAR's first solution is to implement micronutrient programs, which would include salt iodization, vitamin A capsules for children less than two years old, therapeutic zinc supplements for children with diarrhea, iron fortification, and biofortification. Iron and folic acid as well as multiple micronutrient supplementation during pregnancy were not included. Salt iodization, vitamin A, and therapeutic zinc can reduce mortality and flour fortification with iron can improve iron status in school children and adults consuming appropriate amount of a bioavailable fortified product. Biofortification is a promising complement to flour fortification but is not yet an option to take to scale to address iron and zinc deficiencies. None of these micronutrient interventions, as we have noted above, will prevent stunting, with the possible exception of salt iodization.

2 HAR's second solution is de-worming for pre-school children, an intervention to be recommended where helminthic infection is a public health problem. In such settings, iron status will be improved, but stunting will not be prevented

3 The baby-friendly hospital initiative, HAR's third solution, is not effective in increasing appropriate breastfeeding practices, according to Bhutta *et al.* (2008). On the other hand, increasing rates of exclusive breastfeeding in children less than six months old through individual and group counseling of mothers will improve survival, but will not prevent stunting according to Bhutta *et al.* (2008).

4 HAR's fourth and last solution is nutrition education at the community level and including incorporation of nutrition education in child health days, community nutrition programs using volunteers, and nutrition education through the "lowest tier of the health system." While Bhutta *et al.* (2008) concluded that there was little or no evidence that nutrition education during pregnancy improved maternal and birth outcomes, nutrition education and counseling can improve rates of exclusive breastfeeding as well as complementary feeding patterns and linear growth. However, as noted earlier, it is not known, according to Bhutta *et al.* (2008), whether education alone will be effective in food-insecure populations.

While implementation at scale of HAR's four solutions will improve several dimensions of health and nutrition, it is unlikely that there would be much of a reduction in stunting. Bhutta *et al.* (2008) ran models to determine the potential impact of implementing "proven" interventions in the thirty-six countries with 90 percent of the burden of under-nutrition, and report that stunting at three years of age could be reduced by 30 percent, mortality between birth and three years by 25 percent, and DALYs associated with stunting, severe wasting, intrauterine growth retardation, and micronutrient deficiencies by 24 percent. These reductions are substantial, but would address only part of the problem. Other causes – such as poverty, education, and infection control – also need to be addressed. We must also continue to conduct research to identify new and better approaches to addressing the challenge of hunger and malnutrition.

What the *Lancet* series on maternal and child under-nutrition lacks is any explicit consideration of costs. What is needed is to take the work of the *Lancet* series and estimate the cost of recommended intervention packages for different regions of the world (packages will differ across regions, because some interventions are useful only for certain situations). Measures of impact are available from the *Lancet* series to estimate CE. For example, 71 million DALYs will be saved each year by implementing a package of effective interventions to reduce stunting and child mortality, to manage severe acute malnutrition, and to reduce anemia in pregnancy (Bhutta *et al.* 2008). Using the arbitrary benefit estimate of $1,000/DALY saved for poor countries, as done by HAR, the resulting annual benefit would be $71 billion. The cost of interventions to reduce one DALY is not well known. The figure of $100 per DALY is about twice the cost estimated in TINP, an effective nutrition program in Tamil Nadu (see HAR); this figure is also about the average cost of implementing HAR's solutions. Using the cost estimate of US $100 per DALY, the annual cost of saving 71 million DALYs through the above package of interventions would be $7.1 billion; if twice the cost per DALY saved is used, the cost of implementing the package of interventions to scale would be 14.2 billion per year, nearly the entire budget assigned to the Copenhagen Consensus Expert Panel to distribute among all challenges, not just nutrition. These estimates would yield C/B ratios between 5 and 10.

In summary, HAR do an excellent job of illustrating the high B/C ratio of nutrition interventions. However, their recommended package of solutions is too narrow and will fail to make much of a dent in terms of DALYs saved (12 million according to their own assumptions vs. 91 million just for the package of interventions noted above), and will not reduce stunting. A bolder choice would be to base the selection of solutions on the work presented in the *Lancet* series and to estimate the costs of implementing the recommended interventions to scale. The resulting annual budget, according to our back-of-an-envelope estimates, $7–$14, would be prohibitive for the Copenhagen Consensus project but is a fraction of the estimated annual cost of the Iraq war, $144 billion (Bilmes and Stiglitz 2008), see (www.washingtonpost.com/wpdyn/content/article/2008/03/07/AR2008030702846.html).

Bibliography

Agarwal, K.N., D.K. Agarwal, and K.P. Mishra, 1991: Impact of anaemia prophylaxis in pregnancy on maternal haemoglobin, serum ferritin & birth weight, *Indian Journal of Medical Research*, **94**: 277–80

Behrman, J., H. Alderman, and J. Hoddinott, 2004: Hunger and malnutrition, chapter 7 in B. Lomborg (ed.), *Global crises, global solutions*, Cambridge University Press, Cambridge

Bhutta, Z.A., T. Ahmad, R.E. Black, S. Cousens, K. Dewey, E. Giugliani, B.A. Haider, B. Kirwood, S.S. Morris, H.P.S. Sachdev, and M. Shekar, 2008: What works? Interventions for maternal and child under-nutrition and survival, *Maternal and child under-nutrition* (Series Paper 3), *Lancet*, **371**(9610): 412–40

Bilmes, L.J. and J.E. Stiglitz, 2008: The Iraq war will cost US $3 trillion, and much more, March 9, available from: www.washingtonpost.com/wp-dyn/content/article/2008/03/07/AR2008030702846.html41:64

Black, R.E., L.H. Allen, Z.A. Bhutta, L.E. Caulfield, M. de Onis, M. Ezzati, C. Mathers, and J. Rivera, 2008: Maternal and child under-nutrition: Global and regional exposures and health consequences, *Maternal and child under-nutrition* (Series Paper 1), *Lancet*, **5**: 22

Brown, K.H., J.M. Peerson, J. Rivera, and L.H. Allen, 2002: Effect of supplemental zinc on the growth and serum zinc concentrations of prepubertal children: A meta-analysis of randomized controlled trials, *American Journal of Clinical Nutrition*, **75**: 1062–71

Bryce, J., D. Coitinho, I. Darnton-Hill, D. Pelletier, and P. Pinstrup-Andersen, 2008: Maternal and child under-nutrition: effective action at national level, *Maternal and child under-nutrition* (Series Paper 4), *Lancet*, **65**: 82

Castilla, E.E., I.M. Orioli, J.S. Lopez-Camelo, M.G. Dutra, and J. Nazer-Herrera, 2003: Preliminary data on changes in neural tube defect prevalence rates after folic acid fortification in South America, *American Journal of Medical Genetics Part A*, **123A**: 123–8

Chen, Y. and L-A Zhou, 2007: The long-term health and economic consequences of the 1959–1961 famine in China, *Journal of Health Economics*, **26**: 659–81

Christian, P., S.K. Khatry, J. Katz, E.K. Pradhan, S.C. LeClerq, S.R. Shrestha, R.K. Adhikari, A. Sommer, and K.P. West, Jr., 2003: Effects of alternative maternal micronutrient supplements on low birth weight in rural

Nepal: Double blind randomised community trial, *British Medical Journal*, **326**: 571

Cogswell, M.E., I. Parvanta, L. Ickes, R. Yip, and G.M. Brittenham, 2003: Iron supplementation during pregnancy, anemia, and birth weight: A randomized controlled trial, *American Journal of Clinical Nutrition*, **78**: 773–81

Collins, S., N. Dent, P. Binns, P. Bahwere, K. Sadler, and A. Hallam, 2006: Management of severe acute malnutrition in children, *Lancet*, 2(368): 1992–2000

de Onis, M. and M. Blössner, 2000: Prevalence and trends of overweight among preschool children in developing countries, *American Journal of Clinical Nutrition*, **72**: 1032–9

de Onis, M., M. Blössner, E. Borghi, E.A. Frongillo, and R. Morris, 2004: Estimates of global prevalence of childhood underweight in 1990 and 2015, *Journal of the American Medical Association*, **291**: 2600–6

de Onis, M., C. Garza, A.W. Onyango, and R. Martorell (eds.), 2006: WHO child growth standards, *Acta Pædiatrica – International Journal of Pædiatrics*, **95**, Suppl. 450: 1–96

Dibley, M.J., J.B. Goldsby, N.W. Staehling, and F.L. Trowbridge, 1987: Development of normalized curves for the international growth reference: Historical and technical considerations, *American Journal of Clinical Nutrition*, **46**: 736–48

Fawzi, W.W., G.L. Msamanga, W. Urassa, E. Hertzmark, P. Petraro, W.C. Willett, and D. Spiegelman, 2007: Vitamins and perinatal outcomes among HIV-negative women in Tanzania, *New England Journal of Medicine*, **356**: 1423–31

Friis, H., E. Gomo, N. Nyazema, P. Ndhlovu, H. Krarup, P. Kaestel, and K.F. Michaelsen, 2004: Effect of multimicronutrient supplementation on gestational length and birth size: A randomized, placebo-controlled, double-blind effectiveness trial in Zimbabwe, *American Journal of Clinical Nutrition*, **80**: 178–84

Gibson, D., 2004: Long-term food stamp program participation is differentially related to overweight in young girls and boys, *Journal of Nutrition*, **134**: 372–9

Gibson, D., 2006: Long-term food stamp program participation is positively related to simultaneous overweight in young daughters

and obesity in mothers, *Journal of Nutrition*, **136**: 1081–5

Gupta, P., M. Ray, T. Dua, G. Radhakrishnan, R. Kumar, and H.P. Sachdev, 2007: Multimicronutrient supplementation for undernourished pregnant women and the birth size of their offspring: A double-blind, randomized, placebo-controlled trial, *Archives of Pediatrics and Adolescent Medicine*, **161**: 58–64

Hertrampf, E., F. Cortes, D. Erickson, M. Cayazzo, W. Freire, L. Bailey, C. Howson, G. Kauwell, and C. Pfeiffer, 2003: Consumption of folic acid-fortified bread improved folate status in women of reproductive age in Chile, *Journal of Nutrition*, **133**: 3166–9

Hoddinott, J., J.A. Maluccio, J.R. Behrman, R. Flores, and R. Martorell, 2008: Effect of a nutrition intervention during early childhood on economic productivity in Guatemalan adults, *Lancet*, **371**: 411–16

Horton, S., H. Alderman, and J.A. Rivera, 2008: Hunger and malnutrition, see chapter 6 in this volume

Imhoff-Kunsch, B., R. Flores, O. Dary, and R. Martorell, 2007: Wheat flour fortification is unlikely to benefit the neediest in Guatemala, *Journal of Nutrition*, **137**: 1017–22

Kaestel, P., K.F. Michaelsen, P. Aaby, and H. Friis, 2005: Effects of prenatal multimicronutrient supplements on birth weight and perinatal mortality: A randomised, controlled trial in Guinea-Bissau, *European Journal of Clinical Nutrition*, **59**: 1081–9

Lozoff, B., E. Jimenez, and J.B. Smith, 2006: Double burden of iron deficiency in infancy and low socio-economic status: A longitudinal analysis of cognitive test scores to 19 years, *Archives of Pediatrics and Adolescent Medicine*, **160**: 1108–13

Mardones, F., M.T. Urrutia, L. Villarroel, A. Rioseco, O. Castillo, J. Rozowski, J.L. Tapia, G. Bastias, J. Bacallao, and I. Rojas, 2008: Effects of a dairy product fortified with multiple micronutrients and omega-3 fatty acids on birth weight and gestation duration in pregnant Chilean women, *Public Health Nutrition*, **11**: 3040

Martorell, R., L. Kettel Khan, M.L. Hughes, and L.M. Grummer-Strawn, 2000: Overweight and obesity in preschool children from developing countries, *International Journal of Obesity*, **24**: 959–67

MDG Monitor (homepage on the Internet), 2007: New York: UN Development Programme, available from: www.mdgmonitor.org/goal1.cfm

MEASURE DHS (homepage on the Internet), 2007: Macro International, Inc., Calverton, MD, available from: www.measuredhs.com

Morris, S.S., B. Cogill, and R. Uauy, 2008: Effective international action against under-nutrition: Why has it proven so difficult and what can be done to accelerate progress?, *Maternal and child under-nutrition* (series paper 5). *Lancet*, **82**: 95

Osrin, D., A. Vaidya, Y. Shrestha, R.B. Baniya, D.S. Manandhar, R.K. Adhikari, S. Filteau, A. Tomkins, and A.M. Costello, 2005: Effects of antenatal multiple micronutrient supplementation on birthweight and gestational duration in Nepal: Double-blind, randomised controlled trial, *Lancet*, **365**: 955–62

Preziosi, P., A. Prual, P. Galan, H. Daouda, H. Boureima, and S. Hercberg, 1997: Effect of iron supplementation on the iron status of pregnant women: Consequences for newborns, *American Journal of Clinical Nutrition*, **66**: 1178–82

Ramakrishnan, U., N. Aburto, G. McCabe, R. Stoltzfus, and R. Martorell, 2004: Multi-micronutrient supplements but not vitamin A or iron supplements alone improve child growth: Results of three meta-analyses, *Journal of Nutrition*, **134**: 2592–2602

Ramakrishnan, U., T. Gonzalez-Cossio, L.M. Neufeld, J. Rivera, and R. Martorell, 2003: Multiple micronutrient supplementation during pregnancy does not lead to greater infant birth size than does iron-only supplementation: A randomized controlled trial in a semirural community in Mexico, *American Journal of Clinical Nutrition*, **77**: 720–5

Ramakrishnan, U., P. Nguyen, and R. Martorell, forthcoming: Meta-analyses of effects of micronutrient interventions on growth of children under 5 years of age

Rasmussen, K.M., 2001: Is there a causal relationship between iron deficiency or iron deficiency anemia and weight at birth, length of gestation and perinatal mortality? *Journal of Nutrition*, **131**: 590S–603S

Shrimpton, R., C.G. Victora, M. de Onis, R.C. Lima, M. Blossner, and G. Clulgston, 2001: Worldwide timing of growth faltering implications for nutritional interventions, *Pediatrics*, **107**: E75

Siega-Riz, A., A.G. Hartzema, C. Turnbull, J. Thorp, T. McDonald, and M.E. Cogswell, 2006: The effects of prophylactic iron given in prenatal supplements on iron status and birth outcomes: A randomized controlled trial, *American Journal of Obstetrics and Gynecology*, **194**: 512–19

Uauy, R. and J. Kain, 2002: The epidemiological transition: Need to incorporate obesity prevention into nutrition programmes review, *Public Health Nutrition*, **1A**: 223–9

Victora, C.G., L. Adair, C. Fall, P.C. Hallal, R. Martorell, L. Richter, and H.S. Sachdev, 2008: Maternal and child under-nutrition: Consequences for adult health and human capital, *Maternal and child under-nutrition* (series paper 2), *Lancet*, **23**: 40

Wang, Y. and T. Lobstein, 2006: Worldwide trends in childhood overweight and obesity, *International Journal of Pediatric Obesity*, **1**(1): 11–25

World Bank, 2006: *Repositioning nutrition as central to development: A strategy for large-scale action*, International Bank for Reconstruction and Development/World Bank, Washington, DC: 246

Zagre, N.M., G. Desplats, P. Adou, A. Mamadoultaibou, and V.M. Aguayo, 2007: Prenatal multiple micronutrient supplementation has greater impact on birthweight than supplementation with iron and folic acid: A cluster-randomized, double-blind, controlled programmatic study in rural Niger, *Food and Nutrition Bulletin*, **28**: 317–27

Ziaei, S., M. Norrozi, S. Faghihzadeh, and E. Jafarbegloo, 2007: A randomised placebo-controlled trial to determine the effect of iron supplementation on pregnancy outcome in pregnant women with haemoglobin > or = 13.2 g/dl, *British Journal of Obstetrics and Gynaecology*, **114**: 684–8

Perspective Paper 6.2

ANIL B. DEOLALIKAR

Introduction

The Challenge paper by Horton, Alderman, and Rivera (Horton *et al.* 2008) (hereafter, HAR) does a very good job of presenting the major malnutrition problems facing the developing world, and then discussing the different interventions that have been typically deployed to address these problems. The paper pulls together data on the cost-effectiveness (CE) of various nutritional interventions from the literature, and then calculates benefit-cost (B/C) ratios for these interventions under alternative assumptions about the discount rate and DALYs saved. It finds that interventions that target micronutrient deficiencies (through either supplementation or food fortification), as well as de-worming interventions, have the highest B/C ratios of any nutritional intervention, followed by breastfeeding promotion. The paper concludes that community nutrition interventions, which address protein-energy malnutrition (PEM) among children primarily via food supplementation, are cost-effective, but only when they are well designed and efficiently operated. In general, though, the paper concludes that these interventions are more expensive than micronutrient and deworming interventions.

HAR's paper is an impressive survey of the literature on the prevalence of malnutrition, the strategies to combat it, and the CE of these strategies. However, the paper provides little guidance to policy-makers interested in knowing how to allocate public spending on nutrition across different programs. Suppose that a low-income country has $100 million to spend on improving child nutrition; how should it best allocate this budget? Should the bulk of the money be spent on micronutrient interventions,

such as vitamin A supplementation and iron fortification, which have the highest B/C ratios, and relatively little on food supplementation or community nutrition programs which, according to the paper, are "cost-effective but more costly interventions" (HAR: 319)? These are tricky questions to address, but they are critical for a policy-maker facing competing challenges from a number of different nutritional interventions.

Micronutrient Deficiencies vs. Protein-Energy Malnutrition

HAR's paper reflects a broader trend that has been under way since the 1990s not only in the nutrition literature but also among nutrition workers and aid organizations – the tendency to view micronutrient deficiencies and protein-energy malnutrition as two separate sets of nutritional interventions. Further, there is an emerging bias in the development community in favor of programs that address micronutrient deficiencies relative to those that address PEM (Schuftan 1996, 1999). One wonders whether this is driven by the CE of micronutrient interventions, or whether it is determined by the technical nature and ease of implementation of micronutrient deficiencies (relative to PEM). Interventions that address PEM are complicated to plan and implement, and require community and household participation in order to be successful – unlike micronutrient interventions that can often be implemented top-down (e.g. via food fortification at source) (Aranceta 2003; Suarez-Herrera 2006). Indeed, relatively little is known about which interventions reduce PEM among children, and what the costs of these interventions are. In contrast, there is a good

347

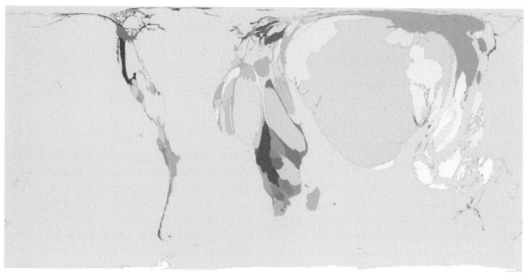

Figure 6.2.1 *The world's child malnutrition problem: South Asia and SSA*
Source: Worldmapper website, www.worldmapper.org.

deal of evidence on interventions that address micronutrient deficiencies.

The over-emphasis in the literature and in the development community on micronutrient interventions and the relative neglect of PEM interventions is unfortunate, for two reasons. First, while it is possible to deliver both micronutrients and calories in a properly designed community nutrition program, micronutrient deficiency programs are generally focused on the delivery of a single micronutrient (e.g. iron, folate, zinc, etc.).

Second, by almost any definition, the problem of child PEM, manifested primarily in the form of low child weight and height, is extremely severe in the poorest countries in Asia and Africa. Most recent estimates for India suggest that nearly one-half of all children aged 0–three years are underweight and about 40 percent are stunted. In Bangladesh, the incidence is comparable, with 48 percent of all children aged 0–three being underweight and 43 percent being stunted (2004 data). This means that these two countries alone account for over one-half of the world's underweight and stunted children. If the countries of SSA are included, this number rises to

three-quarters. Figure 6.2.1 illustrates the extent to which the world's child malnutrition problem is largely a South Asian and SSA problem.

Child malnutrition is so pervasive in South Asia that even a country such as Sri Lanka, which enjoys developed-country levels of school enrollment, adult male and female literacy, infant mortality, and life expectancy, faces a child malnutrition problem. Nearly one in three Sri Lankan children aged between three and fifty-nine months are underweight, and one in seven are stunted. The lack of match between Sri Lanka's performance on infant mortality and child malnutrition is difficult to understand since most factors that produce low rates of infant and child mortality (e.g. delivery and utilization of high-quality health services, high female literacy, good hygiene and health practices, etc.) are thought to result also in lower rates of child malnutrition.

An even more shocking fact about child malnutrition is that its prevalence has actually increased in SSA and not declined appreciably in South Asia. India, for instance, was able to reduce its child underweight rate merely to 46 percent in 2005–6 from a level of 52 percent

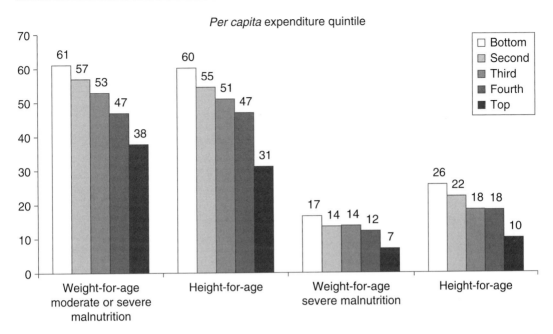

Figure 6.2.2 *Child nutrition rates (percent), by per capita expenditure quintile, ages 6–71 months, 2000*
Source: World Bank (2005).

in 1992–3 in spite of being one of the fastest-growing economies in the world (growing at an average annual rate of 6 percent over the period). The rate of stunting among children fell merely from 48 percent to 38 percent over the same period. If anything, India's (and, to some extent, Bangladesh's) experience indicates that the PEM problem is unlikely to be resolved by rapid economic growth. This highlights the need for additional, pro-active interventions to address PEM. It also challenges the notion that "poverty is a major underlying cause of malnutrition" (HAR: 307).

Interestingly, there is other evidence to suggest that malnutrition is, at best, weakly related to poverty. Data from Bangladesh show that even among the richest decile of households – a group that could not possibly be food-constrained – roughly a third of the children aged between six and seventy-one months are underweight or stunted (figure 6.2.2). The same pattern holds for India, Pakistan, and even Sri Lanka.

Thus, the development community cannot afford to waver in its attention to PEM among children and its commitment to reducing PEM levels in the poorest countries of the world. The prevalence of PEM among children is unacceptably high; the social and economic costs of PEM are very high and well documented; and focusing on micronutrient deficiencies alone, although extremely worthwhile, is unlikely to reduce PEM.

The Role of Non-Nutritional Interventions in Reducing PEM

HAR's paper focuses on a number of focused interventions that reduce child malnutrition, including micronutrient supplementation and fortification programs, hospital-based breast-feeding initiatives, and community nutrition programs. What is lost in this discussion is the fact that interventions outside the nutrition sector – indeed, even outside the health sector – can have profound effects on reducing child malnutrition. Indeed, it might be argued that, in the medium to long run, non-nutritional

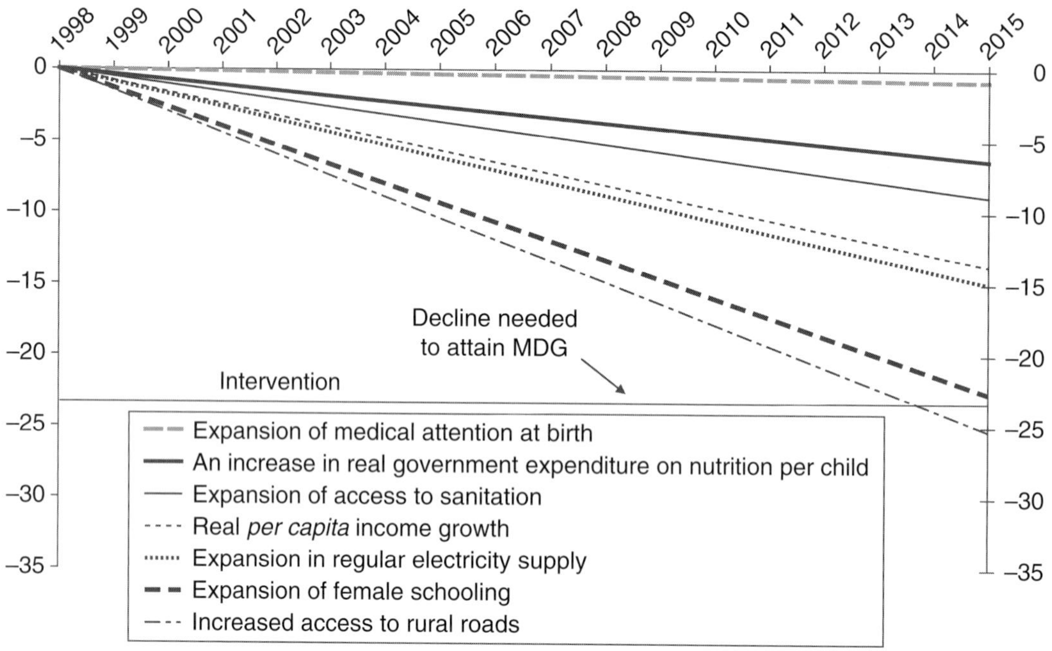

Figure 6.2.3 *Projected decline in percent of underweight children 0–3 years 1998–2015, India, under different intervention scenarios cumulative effect of each additional intervention)*
Source: Deolalikar (2005).

interventions, such as improving agricultural productivity, expanding female schooling, and bringing piped water and electricity to rural areas, might have larger effects on the reduction of child malnutrition than nutritional supplementation or fortification programs.

A study for India, which estimated the determinants of child malnutrition (weight-for-age) based on household survey data from the National Family Health Survey, and then simulated the likelihood of the country attaining the MDGs based on assumed changes in the "intervention" variables, found that a number of different interventions (including economic growth, increased public spending on nutrition programs, expansion of female schooling, and improved access to regular electricity and sanitation)[1] were together likely to enable the country to attain the nutrition-related MDG (Deolalikar 2005: see figure 6.2.3). However, an increase in

[1] The simulation assumed that all of these variables would increase at the same rate in the future as they had during the recent past.

public spending on nutrition alone was unlikely to help the country achieve that goal.

Another study for Bangladesh found that access to sanitation was associated with a 15 percent reduction in the prevalence of underweight children, even after controlling for land ownership, household consumption expenditure *per capita*, and maternal schooling (World Bank 2005). There are numerous other studies that have reported similar results (see Christiaensen and Alderman 2004). But a problem with nearly all of the studies of this genre is that the unit costs of the non-nutritional interventions (such as sanitation or electricity coverage) are not compiled, so it is not possible to know whether improved sanitation access or electricity coverage delivers more nutritional improvements per dollar of investment than community nutrition programs.

All of this points to a weakness in using the CE framework. There is a tendency in the CE literature to consider only those policy interventions for which unit costs have been calculated and B/C ratios worked out. As a result, many worthwhile interventions, such as infrastructural investments and expansion of female education, which have been shown to convincingly reduce child malnutrition but for which cost data have not been compiled and calculated, are ignored. Indeed, it is not clear that one can use the CE framework to evaluate such interventions since nutritional improvements are typically only one of several objectives and outcomes of these interventions (e.g. provision of electricity influences industrial and agricultural productivity, school attendance, child health, and child nutrition, among other things).

Using cross-country data, Smith and Haddad (2000) attempt to measure the relative contribution of different factors to the decline in the prevalence of child malnutrition (underweight rates) in developing countries between 1970 and 1995. The study's results, summarized in figure 6.2.4, are revealing; improvements in women's education contribute the most (43 percent) to the decline in child malnutrition, followed by improvements in food availability (26 percent), and in the health environment (as measured by access to safe water) (19 percent). Improvements in women's status (as proxied by changes in the female-to-male life expectancy ratio) contribute 12 percent to the total decline in child malnutrition between 1970 and 1995. Unfortunately, since consistent data across countries and over time were not available on nutritional intervention programs (indeed, many developing countries do not even have direct nutritional intervention programs), this variable was not included in the analysis. Hence, it is not possible to know the contribution of direct nutritional intervention programs relative to the contributions of female education, health improvements, and food availability. But the study does highlight the importance of interventions outside the nutrition sector in bringing about improvements in child nutritional status. HAR's paper does discuss a number of interventions that can reduce PEM among children. Among these are community nutrition projects incorporating growth promotion, nutrition outreach initiatives, and nutrition components of the health care system.

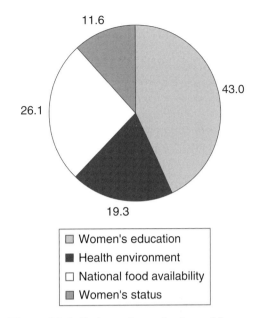

Figure 6.2.4 *Estimated contributions of factors to reductions in developing-country child malnutrition, 1970–95, percent*
Source: *Smith and Haddad (2000): 65.*

HAR's paper considers these as cost-effective but more expensive interventions relative to the micronutrient interventions. The paper correctly points out that good program design and implementation is essential for successful community nutrition interventions, and that CE data on these interventions are scarce. There would thus be a very high return to obtaining and calculating cost data on such interventions. There are a number of examples of successful community nutrition programs that have been effective in reducing child malnutrition in low-income settings (e.g., the Tamil Nadu Integrated Nutrition Program in India (TINP) and the programs in Indonesia and the Iringa region of Tanzania).

In recent years, Doctors Without Borders has successfully used a ready-to-eat paste preparation in alleviating starvation among children in countries such as Niger that have been hit hard by famine. The paste consists of powdered milk, ground peanuts, oil, sugar, vitamins, and minerals, and does not need water for preparation, which reduces the likelihood of food for infants and children being contaminated. Such ready-to-eat supplements have proven to be highly effective in producing rapid weight gain and reversing severe PEM among starving children. But there is no reason to wait until children are at a point of starvation to provide such supplements; the latter could be included in routine community nutrition programs or even be distributed through the same channels as micronutrient supplements are (Flax *et al.* 2008; Shepherd 2008). Unfortunately, cost data on the high-density paste supplement are not readily available, so it is not possible to calculate the CE of this intervention. However, it is unlikely that the CE of this supplement differs significantly from that of micronutrient interventions.

Role of Agricultural Productivity and Food Security in Reducing PEM

While it is obvious that child malnutrition has multiple causes, insufficient food availability at the individual or household level can nevertheless be an important contributing factor to under-nutrition. It is widely recognized that food security at an aggregate level (e.g. at the level of a district, state, or country) does not always translate into food security at the household level. India offers a telling example of this assertion; on average, the country produces more than enough food to feed its population, yet there are large numbers of people who are unable to meet their nutritional requirements. In SSA, the correlation between child malnutrition and food security is even stronger. This highlights the importance of agricultural productivity in reducing child malnutrition; low levels of agricultural productivity result in higher food prices, which in turn lead to malnutrition, especially among the most vulnerable children.

Large advances in biotechnology have taken place in recent years. There is tremendous scope for these technological advances to improve food security as well as promote environmental conservation (Tilman *et al.* 2001). Yet it is ironic that many countries with high child malnutrition rates have banned genetically modified (GM) foods owing to concerns about food safety and biodiversity.

Since the mid-2000s, many countries around the world have been facing food shortages and rising food prices. For instance, international wheat prices rose 123 percent in 2007 alone. Rice and maize prices increased by 40–50 percent in several developing countries. Unfortunately, because of a number of factors, including long-term climate change and the rising global demand for bio-fuels – caused by consumers in developed nations switching from fossil fuels to ethanol – these food shortages and price increases will become endemic. This will have serious repercussions for child malnutrition, especially in the poor countries of South Asia and SSA. This makes the case for biotechnology – to increase crop yields and thereby improve food security – even more compelling. Once again, it is not clear that the CE approach can be applied to interventions that increase agricultural productivity, since the latter typically have multiple goals (only one of which is the reduction in hunger and malnutrition).

Concluding Remarks

To summarize, while the B/C ratio estimates in HAR's Challenge paper are helpful in thinking about how to prioritize nutritional interventions, there are certain inherent limitations to these estimates. First, by ignoring the synergies among the various interventions (e.g., micronutrient supplementation and food supplementation), these estimates under-estimate the potential benefits that could be realized from integrating different nutritional interventions. For instance, there is some evidence that iron supplementation increases the capacity for physical growth among iron-deficient anemic children (Peragallo-Guarda 1984; Chwang *et al.* 1988; Lawless *et al.* 1994), so integrating iron supplementation into a community nutrition program could increase the benefits, and thereby the B/C ratio, of both iron supplementation and community nutrition programs. This points to a general problem with most such estimates – they assume a certain ("typical" or "ideal") mechanism for delivering a nutritional or micronutrient supplementation intervention. Changing the delivery mechanism (e.g. undertaking an intervention in isolation or integrating it with another intervention) can dramatically change the B/C ratio of an intervention.

A second related point is that HAR, and all other CE studies, assume the B/C ratios to be static. In fact, the CE of interventions is likely to be dynamic; the more experience a country has with a particular intervention, the lower will be the costs of that intervention (via learning-by-doing) and the higher will be the resulting B/C ratio. This means that if certain interventions are not chosen because they do not have the highest B/C ratio at a given point in time, a country may give up the opportunity to try these interventions out and reduce their costs (and increase their B/C ratio) in the long run via learning-by-doing. Community nutrition programs have low B/C ratios precisely because they rely on behavioral change and community organization and are significantly more difficult to implement than vertical micronutrient supplementation programs. However, over time, the B/C ratio would be expected to rise as communities become better at delivering nutritional programs.

Third, as Bhutta *et al.* (2008) argue, only about a third of stunting can be averted with available interventions in the short term, since maternal and antenatal factors have a powerful influence on stunting via low birthweight. For instance, the use of insecticide-treated bednets for pregnant women and prenatal care can have an important influence on birthweights and thereby on child nutrition and stunting. While HAR acknowledge the importance of these prenatal-based interventions, they do not consider them, either because "insufficient new material was not available to warrant discussion" or improved child nutrition is only one of many benefits of prenatal care or malaria prevention.

Fourth, a non-trivial portion of the world's malnutrition problem manifests itself in the form of what one might call "emergency malnutrition" – widespread protein-energy malnutrition brought about by civil conflict and natural disasters. Drought in the Sahel in the early 1980s affected tens of millions of children and adults in Mauritania, Mali, Chad, Niger, and Burkina Faso. More recently, the civil conflict in Darfur has brought about a humanitarian malnutrition crisis in Sudan. HAR's estimates provide little guidance on how to deal with such humanitarian nutritional crises. It would be useful to know the most cost-effective strategies for relieving acute malnutrition in emergency situations.

Finally, it is important to recognize that non-nutritional interventions, such as improved water, sanitation, transport and power infrastructure, as well as policies that enhance agricultural productivity and dietary diversification, might have larger effects on reducing malnutrition than nutritional interventions. The CE of these interventions is extremely difficult, if not impossible, to calculate, as nutritional improvements are only one of several objectives and outcomes of these interventions (e.g. provision of electricity influences industrial and agricultural productivity, school attendance, child health, and child nutrition, among other things). But that should not deter us from considering them as extremely worthwhile approaches to fighting malnutrition.

Bibliography

Aranceta, J., 2003: Community nutrition, *European Journal of Clinical Nutrition*, **57**, Suppl. 1: S79–S81

Arimond, M. and M.T. Ruel, 2004: Dietary diversity is associated with child nutritional status: Evidence from 11 demographic and health surveys, *Journal of Nutrition*, **134**: 2579–85

Baer, E.C., 1981: Promoting breastfeeding: A national responsibility, *Studies in Family Planning*, **12**(4): 198–206

Bhutta, Z.A., Ahmed, T., Black, R.E., Cousens, S., Dewey, K., Giugliani, E., Haider, B.A., Kirkwood, B., Morris, S.S., Sachdev, H.P.S., and Shekar, M., 2008: What works? Interventions for maternal and child under-nutrition and survival, *Lancet*, **371**: 417–40

Christiaensen, L. and H. Alderman, 2004:

Chwang, L., A.G. Soemantri, and E. Pollitt, 1988: Iron supplementation and physical growth of rural Indonesian children, *American Journal of Clinical Nutrition*, **47**: 496–501

Deolalikar, A.B., 2005: *Attaining the millennium development goals in India: Reducing infant mortality, child malnutrition, gender disparities and hunger-poverty and increasing school enrollment and completion?*, Oxford University Press, New Delhi

Flax, V.L., U. Ashorn, J. Phuka, K. Maleta, M.J. Manary, and P. Ashorn, 2008: Feeding patterns of underweight children in rural Malawi given supplementary fortified spread at home, *Maternal and Child Nutrition*, **4**(1): 65–73

Horton, S., H. Alderman, and J.A. Rivera, 2008: *Hunger and malnutrition*, see chapter 6 in this volume

Lawless, J.W., M.C. Latham, L.S. Stephenson, S.N. Kinoti, and A.M. Pertet, 1994: Iron supplementation improves appetite and growth in anemic Kenyan primary school children, *Journal of Nutrition*, **124**: 645–54

Peragallo-Guarda, N., 1984: Severity of iron deficiency anemia and its relationship to growth and morbidity in a population of pre-schoolers in Rural Guatemala, Doctoral dissertation presented to the faculty of the University of Texas Health Science Center, Houston, TX

Rouse, D.J., 2003: Potential cost-effectiveness of nutrition interventions to prevent adverse pregnancy outcomes in the developing world, *Journal of Nutrition*, **133**: 1640S–1644S

Schroeder, D.G., R. Martorell, J.A. Rivera, M.T. Ruel and J.-P. Habicht, 1995: Age differences in the impact of nutritional supplementation on growth, *Journal of Nutrition*, **125**: 1051–9

Schuftan, C., 1996: The community development dilemma: When are service delivery, capacity building, advocacy and social mobilization really empowering?, *Community Development Journal*, **31**(3): 260–4

Schuftan, C.,1999. "Different Challenges in Combating Micronutrient Deficiencies and Combating Protein Energy Malnutrition, or the Gap Between Nutrition Engineers and Nutrition Activists." *Ecology of Food and Nutrition* 37(6), December

Schuftan, C., 2003: Poverty and inequity in the era of globalization: Our need to change and to re-conceptualize, *International Journal of Equity Health*, **2**: 4–10

Shekar, M. and M.C. Latham, 1992: Growth monitoring can and does work: An example from the Tamil Nadu integrated nutrition project in rural South India, *Indian Journal of Pediatrics*, **59**(1): 00

Shepherd, S., 2008: Instant nutrition, Op-ed contribution, *New York Times*, January 30

Smith, L.C. and L. Haddad, 2000: Explaining child malnutrition in developing countries: A cross-country analysis, Research Report, **111**, International Food Policy Research Institute, Washington, DC

Suarez-Herrera, J.C., 2006: Community nutrition programmes, globalization and sustainable development, *British Journal of Nutrition*, **96**, Supp. 1: S23–S27

Tilman, D., P. Reich, J. Knops, D. Wedin, T. Mielke, and C. Lehman, 2001: Diversity and productivity in a long-term grassland experiment, *Science*, **294**: 843–5

World Bank, 2005: *Attaining the millennium development goals in Bangladesh: How likely and what will it take?*, Human Development Unit, South Asia Region, World Bank, Washington, DC

Water and Sanitation

DALE WHITTINGTON, W. MICHAEL HANEMANN, CLAUDIA SADOFF AND MARC JEULAND

Introduction

The 1980s were designated the International Water and Sanitation Decade, and the international community committed itself to ensuring that everyone in the world would have access to at least basic water and sanitation services by 1990. This target was not met. While hundreds of millions did receive access to new services, at the end of the decade well over 1.1 billion people still lacked improved water supplies, and more than 2.7 billion lacked sanitation services. By the year 2000, although another billion people had obtained access to improved water and sanitation services, population growth had left the number of those still unserved at roughly the same absolute level. In 2002, at the Johannesburg World Summit on Sustainable Development, the global community made a new commitment to a set of Millennium Development Goals (MDGs), including environmental sustainability. One of the targets under the environmental sustainability MDG is to cut by half the proportion of people in the world living without access to water and sanitation by 2015.

While we certainly hope that the global target for water and sanitation will be met this time, there are grounds for concern. Some important physical and economic features of water supply and sanitation make it inherently difficult to achieve broad-scale goals such as those of the International Water and Sanitation Decade and the MDG water and sanitation target – more difficult than for other MDG targets such as providing access to affordable essential drugs or communication and information technology. These features of water and sanitation have not been well recognized in the existing economics literature or in the policy literature.

Several factors are involved, but a key issue contributing to the difficulty of achieving improved access has been a fundamental misunderstanding of the economics of investment in the water and sanitation sector. The core problem is to ensure that the benefits of *improved* water and sanitation access will be large enough to cover or possibly exceed the costs for those who will bear them: yet surprisingly often, this need is overlooked. There are two aspects to this statement. One is distributional: those who pay the costs are not necessarily those who will receive the benefits. An additional complication is that large-scale water supply infrastructure investments often have multiple goals, such as flood and drought protection, hydropower generation, navigation, fisheries, and recreation, which further exacerbates the challenge of aligning beneficiaries and bill payers. The second issue is perhaps more surprising but, we believe, no less real. Even considering water supply alone (for which externalities are less significant than for sanitation, as most of the benefits accrue directly to those who consume the water), the incremental benefits of improved access to water and sanitation network infrastructure may simply not be large enough to cover the costs of improved access.

This happens for two reasons. First, for the network infrastructure technologies presently available, the cost of improved access to water is typically large. These high costs are due to the capital intensity of the investments associated with improved water supply, although the longevity of the capital means that it will provide benefits for many years into the future. Second, the incremental benefit can be small. This statement too may seem surprising – after all, we know that water is essential for life. Herein lies the paradox: precisely because water is essential for life, everybody does manage to have some sort of access to water, however inadequate and cumbersome. It is for this reason that the *incremental* benefit from *improved* access to water may not be so large. Contrast, for example, water supply with electrification. Because electricity is *not* essential for life, by no means everybody has access to electricity in their home. Without access in the home, there is no affordable or convenient way to use electricity because there is no way to carry electricity home. Therefore, when it becomes available, access to in-home electricity may be *perceived* as a greater boon than access to in-home piped water and sewerage. Consequently, users' willingness to pay for access to electricity may be greater than their willingness to pay for access to piped water and sewerage, even though water is essential for life and electricity is not.

The key to successful water and sanitation investments is to discover forms of service and payment mechanisms that will render the improvements worthwhile for those who must pay for them. In this chapter we argue that in many cases the conventional network technologies of water supply and sanitation will fail this test, and that poor households need alternative, non-network technologies. However, for some of these technologies, too, it will not necessarily be the case that improved water supply and/or sanitation will always be seen as worthwhile to those who must pay for it.

We argue that there is no easy panacea to resolve this situation. For any intervention, the outcome is likely to be context dependent. An intervention that works well in one locality may fail miserably in another. While it may be the same physical technology that is being applied, the outcome depends on economic and social conditions, including how it is implemented, by whom, and often the extent to which complementary changes – in behavior, in institutions, and sometimes in economic organization – also occur. For this reason, we warn against excessive generalization: one cannot, in our view, say that one intervention yields a rate of return of x% while another yields a return of y%, because

the economic returns are likely to vary with local circumstances. More important is to identify the circumstances under which an intervention is more or less likely to succeed. Also for this reason, when we analyze the selected water and sanitation interventions, we employ a probabilistic rather than a deterministic analysis to emphasize the variability of outcomes in the real world.

This chapter is organized in three parts. Part I focuses on conventional network technologies for water supply and sanitation. It opens with some general observations that are central to an understanding of the economics of municipal water and sanitation network infrastructure. We proceed from there to a focus on the costs of providing such infrastructure services, and then summarize some empirical evidence on the economic benefits derived from them. We then discuss the economic costs and the benefits involved and note the limitations of the analytical approach used in most such applications. Part I closes with some observations regarding the implications of these results.

Part II presents the probabilistic analytical approach that we use to analyze investments in the water and sanitation sector. We then illustrate this approach for the case of network infrastructure services.

In Part III we deploy this analytical framework to examine the costs and benefits of three specific low-cost, non-network water and sanitation interventions (deep boreholes with public hand pumps, total community-led sanitation campaigns, and biosand filters) and one high-cost intervention (large multipurpose dams in Africa).

Part I – Assessing the Costs and Benefits of Investments in Network Water and Sanitation Infrastructure

The Limits to Conventional Network Technologies

The conventional organization of water supply and sanitation services in industrialized countries typically involves centralized water supply sources and wastewater treatment facilities combined with relatively comprehensive pipe networks for water distribution and sewage collection. This system has the advantage of some economies of scale and cost efficiency.[1] It is a cheaper and more efficient way of delivering water to millions of water users in a given urban area than to have, say, thousands of water vendors each serving a small local area. This network infrastructure model for delivering water and sanitation services evolved in the United States and Europe roughly between the mid-19th century and the mid-20th century. It is an aspiration for most developing countries today.

However, in our view it may *not* be an appropriate medium-term aspiration in some low-income countries. As a system, it has significant weaknesses that make it hard to replicate in developing countries and may in fact make it hard to sustain in some industrialized countries.

Perhaps the single most important feature of the conventional networked water and sanitation infrastructure is that it is extremely capital intensive. Indeed, it is more capital intensive than any other utility service.[2] Moreover, the capital assets used in water supply cannot be moved to another location and are generally unusable for any other purpose; they represent an extreme type of fixed, non-malleable capital. Furthermore the physical capital in the water industry is very long-lived. The infrastructure associated with surface water storage and conveyance and the pipe network in the streets can have an economic life of one hundred years or more, far longer than that of capital employed in most manufacturing industry or in other public utility sectors.

The capital intensity, longevity, and economies of scale mean that water supply and sanitation costs are heavily dominated by fixed costs. In a conventional networked system the short-run marginal costs of water supply and sanitation are extremely small relative to the fixed costs. This has several important economic consequences. One consequence is a lumpiness of capital investment: there is a strong incentive to make a substantial expansion of capacity at a single point in time rather than to plan for a series of incremental changes spread out over time. The drawback is that it may take decades before the demand materializes to utilize this capacity. When fully utilized, the project provides water at a low cost; but there is uncertainty about whether and when it will be fully utilized, and meanwhile it ties up scarce capital.

Another consequence of the capital intensity is that the financing of water supply and sanitation infrastructure becomes a crucial constraint. Even though the facilities will provide benefits lasting for many decades, much of the cost must be paid upfront if the project is to succeed. Posterity may benefit, but it is not around to pay today's bill. A viable financing mechanism is the key to the successful implementation of conventional networked water and sanitation infrastructure.

If the financing of the substantial capital cost of this networked infrastructure is such a heavy burden, how was this overcome in the US and Europe in the past, and why should it not be handled similarly now in developing countries? People were not wealthy when the infrastructures were installed in the US and Europe in the 19th century. Why were people willing to pay the high upfront capital costs of water and sanitation then – why did they perceive the benefits to outweigh the costs then – but some people in developing countries are not willing to pay now? The answer lies with several peculiarities of history.

Throughout the 19th century and for the first half of the 20th century, the provision of urban water supply in the United States was financed mainly by property taxes paid by water users. There were two key requirements for this to be a viable mechanism. First, there had to be

---

[1] See Nauges and van den Berg (2008a) for an examination of the extent of economies of scale in operation and maintenance costs of network water and sanitation services in selected water utilities.

[2] In the US, for example, the ratio of capital investment to revenues in the water industry is double that in natural gas, and 70% higher than in electricity or telecommunications.

a well-developed system of local government finance based on universal assessment and payment of property taxes. Second, there had to be political acceptance of the use of property tax revenues for this purpose – property owners had to be willing to pay higher property taxes in return for access to piped water. That there was such a willingness to pay in the 19th-century United States is due to three somewhat idiosyncratic factors: (1) the fear of urban fires; (2) the misplaced belief in the miasma theory of disease; and (3) an abundance of raw water supplies.

Wood was widely used for buildings in American cities (unlike in developing countries today), and fire was a constant threat throughout much of the 19th century. Having a piped water supply in a street made it possible to install fire hydrants, which greatly increased protection against fire. This benefit was quickly reflected in improved property values and reduced fire insurance rates for properties served by a piped water supply.

Moreover, the miasma theory of disease was widely believed for much of the 19th century. Under this theory, it was held that "bad air" caused illness, including diseases such as cholera. Miasma was considered to be a poisonous vapor or mist filled with particles from decomposed matter that could cause illnesses and was identifiable by its foul smell. An obvious public health solution was to remove foul-smelling material from public access, and this could conveniently be accomplished by flushing the streets, washing away feces and other foul-smelling materials. This could only readily be done if the street was served by a piped water supply. The reduced health risk was also immediately reflected in improved property values. Thus, two of the main perceived benefits of piped water were conveniently reflected in improved property values and, given the existence of an effective system of property taxation, this provided a viable financing mechanism that did not require any information on the specific quantity of water consumed by each individual homeowner. This financing mechanism was technically feasible because raw water supplies were fortunately abundant in the eastern United States (and most of Europe), and

at low income levels and population densities, it was not necessary to use volumetric pricing to restrain or manage water use. This convenient set of circumstances does not exist today in many of the large metropolitan areas in developing countries.

Another distinctive feature of the evolution of water supply in the US involves sewage treatment. By 1900, over 80% of the urban population in the US was connected to sewers, but less than 4% of this population was served by sewage *treatment*. Most sewage was discharged raw (untreated) to water bodies, many of which were used for water supply intake by downstream communities. This created tremendous epidemics of water-borne disease. The failure to treat sewage was not due to a lack of technology, because the necessary technology for water purification had been known since the 1890s. In fact, there was a fierce debate among engineering and public health professionals in the US between 1900 and 1910 regarding how to deploy the new technology: public health experts argued for treating sewage prior to discharge, while engineers argued for treating water on intake from water bodies. The engineers won, based on the argument that treating drinking water was more cost effective and easier to finance: people would not be willing to pay to treat their own sewage because it did not benefit them directly – it benefited others, downstream – but they *would* be willing to pay to treat their drinking water. In the end, it took until about 1960 before 80% of the urban population in the US was served by (primary) sewage treatment.

The implications of the health benefits from the introduction of drinking-water treatment in the US after 1900 have, in our view, been somewhat misinterpreted. Using a careful and sophisticated econometric analysis, Cutler and Miller (2005) analyze mortality data for thirteen major US cities over the period 1900–1940 in relation to when they introduced drinking water treatment in the form of filtration or chlorination. They find that drinking-water treatment was responsible for nearly half the total mortality reduction, three quarters of the infant mortality reduction, and nearly two thirds of the child mortality reduction in these cities over this period. Their rough calculation suggests that the social rate of return to drinking-water treatment in these cities was greater than twenty-three to one, with a cost per person-year saved by clean water of about US$500 in 2003 dollars. They go on to infer from this that, in developing countries today, "inexpensive water-disinfection technologies can have enormous health returns—returns that reach beyond reductions in waterborne diseases—even in the absence of adequate sanitation services. . . . [If] only 1% of the roughly 1.7 million annual deaths from diarrheal diseases worldwide could be prevented by water disinfection, the corresponding social rate of return for one year alone would be about $160 billion."

To the extent that Cutler and Miller are extrapolating health benefits of drinking water treatment from networked to non-networked systems, we believe this is an unwarranted conclusion, for two reasons. First, drinking water treatment was so efficacious and economically beneficial in the United States precisely because a networked water supply system had already been in place for fifty years or more in these cities. Installing filtration or chlorination at the head of a pipe system is likely to be considerably more efficacious in reducing disease than, say, adding point-of-use treatment to a home in a slum where a tradition of hand washing is not well established and raw sewage drains directly into the street outside. Extrapolating the rate of disease reduction from the one water disinfection system and set of housing conditions to the other is highly problematic.

Second, there was a large payoff to drinking water treatment in these downstream cities precisely because *other* cities were upstream of their drinking water intake and these other cities had installed water and sewer networks and were disposing of their raw, untreated sewage into the surface water. In fact, the spread of sewage collection and large-scale discharge of untreated sewage in US cities in the last third of the 19th century created a major public health crisis, with a significant increase in the incidence of waterborne diseases. It was a major contributor to the "mortality penalty" of living in urban places.[3]

Both the increase in urban disease in the 19th century and the reduction in the decades after 1900 were consequences of the networked urban infrastructure. Given both a networked water supply system and a networked sewage collection system, but no sewage treatment, the addition of drinking water treatment to the network supply system was a highly profitable social investment. But, it would not have been nearly so profitable *without* networked water supply and/or networked sewage collection. Therefore, caution should be exercised before extrapolating Cutler and Miller's findings to areas in today's developing countries lacking one or both of these networked systems.

In summary, this brief review of the history of networked water supply and sanitation in the US leads to several conclusions. First, financing was the key factor determining the pace of water and sanitation provision in the US. Second, most of this infrastructure was paid for by the people who benefited from it: subsidies played a relatively minor role in the provision of urban water supply and sanitation, except for the provision of secondary treatment of sewage following the 1972 Clean Water Act.[4] Third, by the time drinking water supply networks were being established in most urban areas, the US was fortunate in having a well-developed system of local government finance based on universal assessment and payment of property taxes. Moreover, even though this was based, in part, on a misconception about the nature of the health benefits, there was a robust willingness

[3] As Cutler and Miller themselves note: "In seven states with good data before 1900, urban mortality was 30% higher in cities than in rural areas in 1890. The gradient was much steeper for infants and children. In 1880, infant mortality was 140% higher in cities, and in 1890, mortality among children 1–4 was 94% higher."

[4] For almost two decades following the passage of this act, the federal government subsidized approximately 75% of the capital cost of secondary treatment plants for sewage. But there was no major subsidy of primary sewage treatment in the preceding decades. And, while there was a major federal subsidy of irrigation water supply in the West following the creation of the Bureau of Reclamation in 1903, there never was any significant federal subsidy for urban water supply.

to pay for water supply that made local public finance politically viable. With sewage treatment, by contrast, there was no comparable willingness to pay, and this delayed the effective provision of sewage treatment for many decades – even in a country as rich as the United States.

Costs of Municipal Water and Sanitation Network Infrastructure

The preference for fresh, clean water supplies for drinking and washing lies deep in human consciousness and is reflected in all of the world's major religions (Priscoli, 2000). People may still long for a lost world in which wandering nomads could visit uncontaminated, refreshing springs, but in a world of more than 6 billion people such places are sadly few and remote. Even in areas with stringent water pollution control regulations, very few places remain where people can expect safely to drink untreated water from natural sources. The treatment and delivery of water to households, and the removal and treatment of their wastewater, cost serious money everywhere, but estimates of what it will cost to provide a certain level of service do vary widely in different locales. Also, most investments in this sector are incremental in nature. Only rarely would a community incur the costs of complete ("full service") piped water and sanitation systems at a single point in time.

In this section, we present some rough calculations in order to illustrate the magnitude of the costs of such investments. Our approach here is to estimate the average unit costs of providing an urban household with modern network water and sanitation services. We begin with representative unit costs per cubic meter for different components of water and sanitation services. Next we ascertain the typical quantities of water that households might use each month. We then multiply representative unit costs by typical monthly household water use to obtain estimates of the monthly economic costs of providing a household with full piped water and sanitation services.

The economic costs of providing a household with modern water and sanitation infrastructure

services are the sum of seven principal components:

1 Opportunity costs of diverting raw water from alternative uses to the household (resource rents).
2 Storage and transmission of untreated water to the urban area.
3 Treatment of raw water to drinking water standards.
4 Distribution of treated water within the urban area to the household.
5 Collection of wastewater from the household (sewerage collection).
6 Treatment of wastewater (sewage treatment).
7 Any remaining costs or damages imposed on others by the discharge of treated wastewater (negative externalities).

Table 7.1 presents some illustrative average unit costs for each of these seven components. The unit costs of these different elements could vary widely in different locations. For example, in a location with abundant fresh water supplies, item 1 (the opportunity cost of diverting water from existing or future users to our illustrative household) and item 7 (the damages imposed by the discharge of treated wastewater) may, in fact, be very low or even zero. In reality, however, in more and more places these opportunity costs are beginning to loom large.

Some cost components are typically subject to some economies of scale, particularly storage and transmission (item 2), treatment of raw water to drinking water standards (item 3), and treatment of sewage (item 6). This means that the larger the quantity of water or wastewater treated, the lower the per-unit cost. Other cost components are experiencing diseconomies of scale. As large cities go farther and farther away in search of additional fresh water supplies and good reservoir sites become harder to find, the unit cost of storing and transporting raw water (item 2) to a community can increase. There are also tradeoffs between different cost components: one can be reduced, but only at the expense of another. For example, wastewater can receive only primary treatment, which is much cheaper than secondary treatment, but

Table 7.1. Cost estimates: improved water and sanitation services (assuming 6% discount rate)[a]

No.	Cost component	US$ per m³[b]	% of total
1	Opportunity cost of raw water supply	0.05	3%
2	Storage and transmission to treatment plant	0.10	5%
3	Treatment to drinking water standards	0.10	5%
4	Distribution of water to households (including house connections)	0.60	30%
5	Collection of wastewater from home and conveyance to wastewater treatment plant	0.80	40%
6	Wastewater treatment	0.30	15%
7	Damages associated with discharge of treated wastewater	0.05	3%
	Total	2.00	100%

[a] Using a 3% discount rate, the total cost is US$1.80/m³.
[b] UNDP, 2006.

the negative externalities associated with wastewater discharge will then increase.[5]

The cost estimates in Table 7.1 include both capital expenses and operation and maintenance expenses. Annual capital costs are calculated using a capital recovery factor of 0.09, assuming a real discount rate of 6% and an average life of capital equipment and facilities of 20 years.[6] The opportunity costs of raw water supplies (item 1) are still quite low in most places, in the order of a few cents per cubic meter. Even in places where urban water supplies are diverted from irrigated agriculture or valuable environmental assets, the unit costs will rarely be above US$0.25 per cubic meter. Desalinization and wastewater reclamation costs will set an upper limit on opportunity costs of raw water of about US$0.50–1.00 per cubic meter for cities near the ocean, but the opportunity costs of raw water are nowhere near this level in most places.

Raw water storage and transmission and subsequent treatment (items 2 and 3) will typically cost about US$0.20 per cubic meter. Within a city the water distribution network and household connections to it (item 4) comprise a major

cost component, in many cases on the order of US$0.60 per cubic meter. The total cost of items 1–4, which essentially corresponds to water supply component of water and sewer services, comes to about US$0.85 per cubic

[5] Primary treatment of wastewater consists of physical operation only, such as screening and sedimentation. Secondary treatment includes biological and chemical processes that are used primarily to remove organic matter from water.

[6] Summary results also show total for a 3% discount rate. The capital recovery factor is defined as: $CR = r * (1 + r)^d / ((1 + r)^d - 1)$, where r is a real discount rate, and d is the duration of the capital. Our choice of a 3–6% range for a real discount rate was dictated by the organizers of the Copenhagen Consensus 2008 Project in order to ensure comparability across interventions in different sectors (e.g., water and sanitation services, health, global warming, etc.). The use of a single discount rate to account for both the social opportunity cost of capital and the social rate of time preference is appropriate when all of the funds for an investment or program displace alternative investments *and* the returns from displaced investments would have been reinvested in projects with the same rate of return. In this special case one can justify discounting by the social opportunity cost of capital, which is surely higher in developing countries than the 3–6% range proposed by the Copenhagen Consensus organizers. This is the rationale for the use by the World Bank of a 10% real discount rate for project evaluation, i.e., that investment capital in developing countries is scarce and the opportunity costs of the project being evaluated are high.

The lower end of the 3–6% range is a reasonable estimate for the social rate of time preference for use in discounting future benefits (and costs). An important economic question is, then, what investment and consumption are displaced by expenditures on the investment being evaluated, and how should these opportunity costs be valued? The use of a single, low real discount rate such as proposed by the Copenhagen Consensus organizers is in fact customary in the global health community, where a 3% real rate is used in the calculation of Disability-Adjusted Life Years (DALYs). But the implicit assumption is that funding will displace investment in rich countries, and the value of this displaced investment is low. If these donor funds could have been used by developing countries for alternative investments, the use of a 3% real discount rate without shadow pricing capital is theoretically incorrect.

The discount rate assumed has a significant effect on the monthly household costs of water and sanitation services. The use of a 3% real discount rate makes these costs appear significantly cheaper than they are likely to be in practice. This is one of the reasons that the costs of water and sanitation services in the global health literature appear so low.

meter.[7] The collection and conveyance of sewage to a wastewater treatment plant (item 5) is even more expensive than the water distribution; this removal will cost about US$0.80 per cubic meter, 40% of the total cost. Secondary wastewater treatment (item 6) will cost about US$0.30 per cubic meter. Damages resulting from the discharge of treated wastewater are very site-specific, but environmentalists correctly remind us that they can be significant, even for discharges of wastewater receiving secondary treatment. Let us assume for purposes of illustration that these costs are of the same order of magnitude as the opportunity costs of raw water supplies (US$0.05 per cubic meter).

As shown, total economic costs are about US$2.00 per cubic meter in many locations. We emphasize that costs shown here are not intended to represent an upper bound. For example, in small communities in the arid areas of the western United States costs of water and sanitation services can easily be double or triple these amounts per cubic meter. Note too that these cost estimates assume that financing is available at competitive international market rates and that countries do not pay a high default or risk premium. Using a real discount rate of 10% would result in monthly household costs about 25% higher.

Table 7.2 presents a reasonable lower-bound estimate of unit costs of piped water and sanitation services. Here the opportunity cost of raw water supplies and the damages from wastewater discharges are assumed to be zero. Only minimal storage is included and the only intake treatment is simple chlorination. Costs for the water distribution network assume the use of PVC pipes and shallow excavation. Wastewater

[7] Ideally one would look at the prices charged in developing countries to cross-check these unit cost estimates. However, the average prices that utilities charge for water in developing countries must be interpreted cautiously because very few utilities recover capital costs, and some achieve only partial recovery of operation and maintenance costs. Nonetheless, costs of US$0.85/m³ are consistent with some of the prices reported in a recent World Bank survey of water supply operators (Kariuki and Schwartz, 2005). See also Nauges and van den Berg (2008b).

Table 7.2. Cost estimates: improved water and sanitation services for low-cost option for private water and sewer connections (assuming 6% discount rate)[a]

No.	Cost component	US$ per m³
1	Opportunity cost of raw water supply (steal it)	0.00
2	Storage and transmission to treatment plant (minimal storage)	0.07
3	Treatment of drinking water standards (simple chlorination)	0.04
4	Distribution of water to households (PVC pipe)	0.24
5	Collection of wastewater from home and conveyance to wastewater treatment plant (condominial sewers)	0.30
6	Wastewater treatment (simple lagoon)	0.15
7	Damages associated with discharge of treated wastewater (someone else's problem)	0.00
	Total	0.80

[a] Using a 3% discount rate, the total cost is US$0.70/m³.

is collected with condominial sewers and the only wastewater treatment is provided by simple lagoons. Given all these assumptions, unit costs of piped water and sanitation services can be reduced to about US$0.80 per cubic meter.

How much water does a typical household in a developing country "need"? The quantity of water used by a household will be a function of the price charged, household income, and other factors. Currently most households in developing countries face very low prices for piped water and sanitation network infrastructure services. One can look at typical water use figures from households around the world to see how much water a household might be expected to use for a comfortable modern lifestyle. For households with an in-house piped water connection, in many locations residential indoor water use falls in the range of 110–220 liters per capita per day. For a household of six, this would amount to about 20–40 cubic meters per month. At the current low prices prevailing in many cities in developing countries, such levels of household

Table 7.3. Range of estimates of monthly water use (in-house, private connection)

Per capita daily water use	Persons per household	Days per month	Monthly household water use
55 liters	6 persons	30 days	10 m³
110 liters	6 persons	30 days	20 m³
220 liters	6 persons	30 days	40 m³

Table 7.4. Range of estimates of the full economic cost of providing improved water and sanitation services (in-house, private water connection; piped sewer)

Monthly household water use	Average cost US$0.80 per m³	Average cost US$2.00 per m³
10 m³	US$8	US$20
20 m³	US$16	US$40
40 m³	US$32	US$80

water use are common. Other things equal, households living in hot, tropical climates use more water for drinking, bathing, and washing than households in temperate or cold climates.

Assuming average unit costs of US$2.00 per cubic meter (Table 7.4), the full economic costs of providing 20–40 cubic meters of water to a household (and then dealing with the waste-water) would be US$40–80 per month (Table 7.4), more than most households in industrialized countries pay for the same services and far beyond the means of most households in developing countries.

One would expect poor households in developing countries with in-house water connections to respond negatively to high water and sanitation prices: they might curtail use to as little as 50–60 liters per capita per day. For a household with six members, at 55 liters per capita per day, total consumption would then amount to about 10 cubic meters per month. The full economic costs of this level of water and sanitation service at this reduced quantity of water use (assuming our unit costs of US$2.00 per cubic meter remained unchanged) would then be US$20.00 per month per household. With the unit costs of the low-cost system depicted in Table 7.2, the full economic cost of providing 10 cubic meters per month would be US$8 per household per month. This estimate should be regarded as a lower bound on the full economic costs of piped water and sanitation services in most locations.

In industrialized and developing countries alike, most people are unaware of the magnitude of the true economic costs of municipal water and sanitation network services. There are

several reasons why these economic costs are so poorly understood.

First, the capital costs are heavily subsidized by higher levels of government (and, in developing countries, by international donors), so that households with services do not see the true capital costs reflected in the volumetric prices they pay. Second, in many cities tariff structures are designed so that industrial water users subsidize residential users; households thus do not even see the full operation and maintenance costs in the prices they pay. Third, because many water utilities run financial deficits (in effect running down the value of their capital stock), water users in aggregate do not even see the full costs of supply. Fourth, most cities do not pay for their raw water supplies: typically the water is simply expropriated from any existing water sources (and their users) in outlying rural areas. Fifth, wastewater externalities are typically imposed on others (downstream) without compensation.

Sixth, the subsidies provided to consumers of water and sanitation services are not only huge but also regressive. It is often not politically desirable for the majority of people to understand that middle- and upper-income households, which generally use more water, are thus actually receiving the most benefit from subsidies. Tariff designs may in fact be made overly complicated in order to offset this reality and appear to be helping poorer households (Komives *et al.*, 2005). Most fundamentally, poor households are often not connected to the water and sanitation network at all and hence cannot receive the subsidized services. Even if they do have connections, the poor use less water than richer households, thus receiving lower absolute amounts of subsidy.

The estimates presented in Tables 7.1–7.4 are intended merely to suggest the likely magnitude of costs of water and sanitation services in many developing countries. A reasonable question to ask is whether costs differ much across countries in the developing world and between industrialized and developing countries. Labor costs are obviously lower in developing countries, but because water and sanitation projects are capital intensive, this cost component has less of an impact on total costs than for other goods and services. To our knowledge there are no publicly available international indices of water and sanitation project construction costs. To illustrate the magnitude of international cost differentials for some related goods and construction costs, Table 7.5 compares costs of rebar, cement, and industrial construction in 11 large cities in both industrialized and developing countries (in 2004 US dollars). Costs are indeed lower in cities such as New Delhi and Hanoi than in London and Boston, and lower costs for inputs such as cement and steel will translate into lower costs for water and sanitation projects.

It is, of course, less expensive to provide intermediate levels of water and sanitation services (such as public taps and communal sanitation facilities) than the costs in Table 7.5 would indicate. Monthly household costs for such services are, however, often quite considerable, roughly US$5 per month for much smaller quantities of water and lower levels of sanitation services. These costs are often reported to be as low as

US$1–2 per household per month, but such accounts often systematically underestimate key capital cost components and rarely reflect the real costs of financially sustainable systems.

Table 7.5. Comparison of costs of rebar, cement, and industrial facility construction in 11 cities

City	Rebar (US$/ton)	Cement (US$/ton)	Industrial construction (US$ per m²)
Boston	1100	85	915
Durban	1028	137	516
Los Angeles	992	135	699
London	981	96	850
Buenos Aires	765	82	n.a.
New Delhi	600	64	247
Jakarta	528	68	269
Bangkok	482	63	301
Shanghai	435	43	592
Hanoi	349	62	409
Nairobi	n.a.	n.a.	291

Source: Engineering News Record (2004).

Economic Benefits of Water and Sanitation Network Infrastructure Services: A Preliminary Overview of the Evidence

There are four main types of information sources where one can look for insight into the economic benefits that households receive from improved municipal water and sanitation services: (1) prices charged for vended water, (2) avertive expenditures (coping costs), (3) avoided costs of illness (COI), and (4) stated preference studies.[8] Of course, other water users – industries, small firms, government – also receive economic benefits from improved water sources, and their benefits should count in any benefit–cost analysis of investments to improve water and sanitation infrastructure. However, the majority of economic benefits from municipal water and sanitation network infrastructure investments in most cities will accrue to households, and we restrict our focus in the discussion below to household benefits in order to keep our task manageable.[9]

---

[8] Conceptually, a fifth source is hedonic property value studies. However, there are relatively few hedonic property value studies in the literature that provide convincing estimates of the capitalized value of water and sanitation network services, and we do not review them in this chapter.

[9] Note that although we have not counted the benefits of other water users, we have not included their costs either. Since the large majority of water use in most urban areas in developing countries is by households, the net benefits to other users would have to be very large to cancel out a net cost of providing households with network services.

Table 7.6. Examples of prices charged by water vendors – selected countries

Continent	Location	Type of water vendor	Price of water (dry season)
Africa	Ukunda, Kenya	Distributing vendor	US$9.40 per m^3
Central America	Tierra Nuevo, Guatemala	Tanker truck	US$2.00 per m^3
Asia	Delhi, India	Distributing vendor	US$6.00 per m^3
Asia	Jakarta, Indonesia	Tanker truck	US$1.80 per m^3

Market Data: Water Vending

The first source of information about the benefits of improved water services is evidence on what households in developing countries now pay to water vendors. Table 7.6, which shows some of the prices that vendors have charged households in selected cities, illustrates that many of these prices are in fact higher than our estimated costs of both improved water and sanitation services. Millions of households in developing countries are purchasing relatively small quantities of drinking and cooking water from vendors, and for many of these households the benefits of improved water services would typically exceed the costs of network water services.

The data on water vending must, however, be interpreted with caution. The vast majority of households in developing countries do *not* buy water from vendors. This fact tells us that for most people the perceived private benefits of vended water services (as measured by the household's willingness to pay) are *less* than the price a vendor would charge. Water vending data from selected World Bank Living Standards Measurement Surveys for Ghana, Nicaragua, and Pakistan show that less than 1% of the sample households were purchasing water from vendors. In Côte d'Ivoire 15% of sample households were purchasing from vendors. The average household purchasing from water vendors was spending US$4.40 per month in Ghana, US$6.00 in Nicaragua, and US$7.50 in Pakistan (Table 7.7) – substantial amounts no doubt, but still probably less than the full economic cost of piped services. Only in Côte d'Ivoire was the monthly expenditure of households purchasing from vendors (US$13.90) probably greater than

Table 7.7. Median monthly household expenditures on water (1998 US$)

	Households with in-house piped water connection	Households purchasing from water vendors
Côte d'Ivoire	US$12.40	US$13.90
Ghana	US$4.90	US$4.40
Nicaragua	US$4.60	US$6.00
Pakistan	US$1.00	US$7.50

Source: World Bank Living Standard Measurement Surveys, authors' calculations.

the full economic cost of improved piped water services. Of course, there are numerous places like Côte d'Ivoire where water vending is widespread, but in communities where vendors do not sell water, this is usually a clear signal that there is no market for such high-priced water services.[10]

Avertive Expenditures: Coping Costs

A second source of information on the benefits of improved water supplies is evidence about the amounts of money households in developing countries spend coping with unreliable, poor quality public supplies. In many

[10] For some households improved piped water services are not an unambiguously better service than purchasing vended water. Water vendors offer an important advantage over piped network water services: households have better (tighter) control over their water expenditures. If a child leaves a tap running, the household must pay for this water. There is no such financial risk if one purchases from vendors. Also, purchasing from vendors gives a household greater control over cash flow. If money is tight one month, the household can stop purchasing from vendors and perhaps collect water from a public tap at much less cost.

Table 7.8. Average monthly household coping costs of acquiring improved water, Kathmandu, Nepal (US$ per month)

Type of coping cost	Households with piped connection	Households without piped connection
Collection (time spent)	US$1.57	US$1.60
Pumping	US$0.50	US$0.46
In-house treatment	US$0.78	US$0.83
In-house storage	US$1.22	US$1.29
Total	US$4.07	US$4.18

Source: Pattanayak *et al.*, 2005. Averages are for 1,500 households in 2001.

developing countries households spend considerable amounts of both time and money trying to improve the poor services to which they currently have access. Many households incur expenses installing household storage capacity to ensure that they have water when the pipes run dry. Others undertake a wide variety of activities to treat contaminated water in their homes to make it safe to drink. These range from boiling, a common practice in many parts of Southeast Asia, to the installation of home filtration and disinfection systems. People expend time and effort walking to water sources outside their homes to collect water from public taps or unimproved, traditional water sources. Such coping costs should represent something close to a lower bound on the benefits households would receive from improved water and sanitation services; a household might well be willing to pay considerably more for improved water and sanitation services than it is spending now trying to deal with the deficiencies in the status quo.

A recent study by Pattanayak *et al.* (2005) attempts to quantify these coping costs for households in Kathmandu, Nepal. The existing public water system in Kathmandu is typical of the poor service in many Asian cities. About 70% of the population has a piped connection

and receives low-quality water one or two hours per day. Households pay US$1–2 per month for this poor water service. The other 30% of the population obtains its water from a combination of public taps, vendors, and private wells. Pattanayak and his colleagues estimated that the average monthly costs of coping with poor-quality, unreliable water supplies were about US$4 (Table 7.8). These estimates do not include the costs of coping with poor sanitation facilities, and coping costs may well be somewhat higher in other locations. However, neither these estimates nor others in the literature provide evidence that the costs of coping with poor quality water and sanitation services are generally in excess of our estimates of the full economic costs of piped water services.

Avoided Costs of Illness

The third source of data on the benefits of improved water and sanitation services is calculations of the avoided costs of illness from waterborne diseases. Many people become ill as a consequence of poor water and sanitation services, and as a result both the public sector health system and households incur a variety of costs, including (but not limited to) money spent on medicines, physicians' time treating these illnesses, and lost earnings due to absence from work, both for patients and for household members who must care for them. If water and sanitation services were improved, the incidence of such waterborne diseases would be reduced and this COI would be avoided. Thus, "avoided COI" is often cited as a component of the benefits of water and sanitation improvements.

In some respects calculations of avoided COI are the least useful source for insight into the benefits of improved water and sanitation improvements. It is widely understood by economists that estimates of avoided COI are lower-bound estimates of the health benefits of water and sanitation improvements; they do not include the economic value of the pain and suffering associated with an episode of illness, or the value of reduced risk of mortality. Nor do these estimates of avoided COI place any value on non-health-related benefits that come with improved water supplies, such as time savings and/or reduced coping costs. Moreover, avoided COI cannot easily be added to non-health-related coping costs, because the latter (e.g., boiling water, other disinfection methods) may also result in avoided COI.

Calculating the avoided COI that would result from improved water and sanitation services involves two further complications. First, for a given population, improved services result in a reduction in the number of infections from a variety of major diseases, including typhoid, cholera, shigellosis, and rotavirus. Because each of these has unique characteristics – duration, severity, treatment regimen, etc. – it can be very difficult to arrive at a single COI measure that is acceptable for analysis. Second, improved water and sanitation services only reduce and do not eradicate the risk of infection from these various diseases.[11] Esrey (1996) and Fewtrell *et al.* (2005) found that probably the best one could hope for from improved water and sanitation services would be a reduction in overall diarrheal incidence by 30–40%. The effect of improved services even on specific diseases in a specific location is still largely a matter of professional judgment and conjecture.

As a lower-bound estimate of benefits, the *ex-ante* COI estimate (i.e., the expected value of COI, taking into consideration the incidence of the disease) would not tell us much unless it were higher than the full economic costs of providing water and sanitation services. In fact, most *ex-ante* estimates of avoided COI are rather low. An example can be found in a recent study (Bahl *et al.*, 2004) reporting *ex-ante* estimates of COI for an outbreak of typhoid in one of the poorest slums in New Delhi, where the incidence of the disease is probably as high as almost anywhere in the world. The study estimated *ex-ante* private and public COI for individuals in different age groups, including children (Table 7.9).[12] For a typical household of five in this New Delhi slum, the total monthly *ex-ante* COI was about US$0.65 per month.

Because these *ex-ante* COI estimates are for a single disease (typhoid), they will be an underestimate of the total *ex-ante* COI avoided

Table 7.9. Average per capita *ex-ante* coi for typhoid fever, New Delhi slum (US$ per month)

Age group	Private	Government (public sector)	Total
0–2 yr	US$0.07	US$0.04	US$0.11
2–5 yr	US$0.13	US$0.42	US$0.55
5–19 yr	US$0.08	US$0.04	US$0.12
> 19 yr	US$0.03	US$0.03	US$0.06
All ages	US$0.06	US$0.07	US$0.13

Source: Bahl *et al.*, 2004.

from improved water and sanitation services. The World Health Organization estimates that roughly a quarter of the deaths due to poor water and sanitation in developing countries are due to typhoid fever. Assuming that COI estimates for other waterborne diseases would be similar in magnitude to those for typhoid, a rough estimate of total COI incurred from poor water and sanitation services might be made by increasing the *ex-ante* COI for typhoid by a factor of four (to US$2.60 monthly per household). But to obtain an estimate of the COI avoided due to improved water and sanitation, one would need to reduce this crude estimate to reflect the fact that improved services would reduce the incidence by only 35% (US$2.68 × 0.35 = US$0.94), or about US$1 per month per household.

This calculation is clearly inflated by the extremely high incidence of typhoid in the study area where data were gathered. In most locations

---

[11] This statement may be somewhat overoptimistic. Attempts to measure the health impacts of water and sanitation have had a long and checkered history, as Cairncross (1990) has noted. Cairncross argues for the importance of *behavioral change* as a key factor in health impacts from water and sanitation. He observes that in cases where a significant health impact was found, it was accompanied by improved hygienic behavior such as the washing of hands, food, and utensils. But the change in behavior did not always occur, and without it there was little health impact. Similar evidence that the provision of piped water is not a sufficient condition for improved child health is presented by Jalan and Ravallion (2003).

[12] When children were ill, the primary caregiver was interviewed about the costs of illness from the episode.

in developing countries the incidence of typhoid would be one or two orders of magnitude less than in this particular slum, and the *ex-ante* COI much lower than the estimates shown in Table 7.9.

However, our general point is that the empirical estimate of avoided COI is much less than the costs of improved water and sanitation services. Contrary to conventional wisdom in the sector, the COI estimate does not provide much economic justification for networked water and sanitation investments.

Stated Preferences: Household Willingness to Pay for Improved Water and Sanitation Services

A fourth source of evidence on the perceived household economic benefits of networked water and sanitation services in developing countries comes from numerous studies conducted over the past two decades in which households were asked directly whether improved water and sanitation services would be worth a specified amount per month – that is, whether the household would be willing to pay a specified monthly water bill if the residents could be assured of receiving higher-quality services.[13] One advantage of this type of evidence is that theoretically it includes all private benefits that accrue to the household, including time savings and other reduced coping costs, reduced morbidity and mortality from water-related diseases, and any aesthetic benefits derived from improved access to and convenience of the water source.

Before such contingent valuation surveys were conducted in developing countries during the mid-1980s, water and sanitation professionals commonly believed that households in developing countries were too poor to pay much

[13] Griffin *et al.* (1995) demonstrate that stated preference using the contingent valuation method can sometimes provide *ex-ante* predictions of household behavior that are quite similar to *ex-post* outcomes.

[14] In a recent paper, Whittington *et al.* (2008) compared the responses of husbands and wives in the same household to contingent valuation questions, and found that although the aggregate demand functions were not statistically different between husbands and wives, there were differences in some households in the intra-household allocation of the hypothetical good described in the survey (HIV/AIDS vaccine).

of anything for improved water and sanitation services. The contingent valuation (CV) surveys revealed that people were in fact often willing to pay considerably more for improved water and sanitation services than anyone then had expected. In some instances the results of these CV surveys were used for financial analysis of water utility operations, not for benefit–cost analysis of new investments. Some water and sanitation sector professionals were delighted to incorporate this evidence from contingent valuation surveys and from water-vending surveys into a new conventional wisdom that held that (1) people were willing and able to pay higher tariffs for improved water and sanitation services; (2) tariffs could be raised; and (3) private operators could recover the full costs of providing water and sanitation services.

Actually the contingent valuation surveys of household demand for improved water and sanitation services did not suggest that households' perceived economic benefits from improved water and sanitation services would commonly exceed the full economic costs of providing networked water and sanitation services. Indeed, as the results from selected contingent valuation studies for improved water services illustrate (Table 7.10), households' stated willingness to pay (WTP) varied a great deal from place to place and in many cases was far below the costs of providing networked water and sanitation services (note that the stated preference data reported in Table 7.10 come from both men and women respondents[14]).

Yet some CV studies revealed quite high household WTP for improved services. Table 7.10 shows that responses from a small market town in Uganda and from Kathmandu in Nepal revealed many households' expressed WTP for improved water services at rates close to US$10 per month, probably approaching the full economic costs of providing modest amounts of water using improved network services. CV studies for improved sanitation services conducted in Latin America (Russell *et al.*, 2001) revealed much higher WTP (e.g., US$10 per household per month) than CV studies in Africa and Asia (Whittington *et al.*, 1993; Choe *et al.*, 1996)

Table 7.10. Average household willingness to pay (WTP) for water services: a summary of eight contingent valuation studies

Author(s)	Study location	Date of study	Monthly WTP for public tap (unconnected hh)	Monthly WTP for new private connection	Monthly WTP for improved service
Whittington et al. (1990a)	Rural Haiti	1986	US$1.10	US$1.40	
Whittington et al. (1988)	Rural Tanzania	1987	US$0.32		
Briscoe et al. (1990)	Rural Brazil	1988		US$4.00	
Altaf et al. (1993)	Rural Pakistan	1989		US$1.50	
Whittington et al. (1993)	Kumasi, Ghana	1989		US$1.50	
Griffin et al. (1995)	Rural India	1989		US$1.38	
Whittington et al. (1998)	Lugazi, Uganda	1994	US$3.70	US$8.63	
Whittington et al. (2002)	Kathmandu, Nepal	2001	US$3.19	US$11.67	US$14.35

where WTP estimates often were extremely low (e.g., US$1–2 per household per month).

These estimates of households' willingness to pay for improved water and sanitation services from stated preference surveys require careful, nuanced interpretation. Ideally households should consider the mortality and morbidity risk reductions that their members and the community at large would receive. Conceptually they could provide a comprehensive measure of the economic benefits that incorporates both improved health outcomes and some of the external effects on the broader community. The vast majority of the criticism of stated preference surveys by economists has argued that such WTP estimates are inflated because respondents do not face an actual budget constraint (hypothetical bias) and because they are prone to say "Yes" too easily, perhaps just to please the interviewer ("yea saying").[15] From this perspective the low WTP estimates from stated preference reported in Table 7.10 should be even lower, reinforcing our argument that the benefits of networked water and sanitation services are in some cases less than the costs of services.

However, it is certainly plausible that some respondents may not have been aware of or may not have reflected carefully on the health benefits when they said whether or not they would pay the monthly charges offered in the CV survey. In

this case the WTP estimates in Table 7.10 would be underestimates of the total benefits from the water and sanitation investments because *ex-post*, after the infrastructure is installed, these households would learn more about the health benefits and value the services more.

These two possible effects would influence the WTP estimates in opposite directions, and it is difficult to say where the net effect might lie in any particular study. In their meta-analysis of 83 studies comparing stated and revealed preference WTP, Carson et al. (1996) conclude that there is no statistically significant difference between stated preference and revealed preference estimates for quasi-public goods such as water and sanitation investments. This finding is supported by comparisons of what respondents tell pollsters before elections and the results from actual referenda.[16]

[15] Evidence from the literature, however, suggests that hypothetical bias and "yea saying" are far from universal and can often be reduced by careful survey design (Carson et al., 2001; Johnston, 2006).

[16] There are two situations in which stated preference results do often differ from actual behavior. The first is the case of stated preference studies that ask for voluntary contributions. The second are comparisons of actual behavior versus stated preferences in laboratory experiments in which the stated preference questions are purely hypothetical. Neither of these cases applies to the WTP estimates in Table 7.10.

The economic goal of an investment project is not, of course, to have the benefits approach or be equal to the costs, but rather to have the benefits *exceed* the costs. We know of no CV studies from anywhere in the developing world that show that a majority of a city's population would be willing to pay substantially *more* than the full economic costs of supplying water and sanitation services.

A Simple Comparison of the Costs and Benefits of Network Infrastructure Services

Table 7.11 offers examples of some of the types of benefit and cost estimates discussed in the previous sections, using the actual data presented from Kathmandu. As can be seen from this example, there is little evidence in this particular case to suggest that the current monthly benefits *exceed* the monthly costs of a conventional water and sanitation network system.[17]

Another indication that the incremental cost of improved water supply may often exceed the perceived incremental benefit comes from the data shown in Figure 7.1, based on interviews with more than 55,000 households in 15 developing countries (Komives *et al.*, 2003). The data show that, at all income levels, more people have electricity than piped water or sewerage. Very few of the poorest households have piped water or sewerage, but almost a third of those households do have electrical service. As monthly household income increases from very low levels to US$300 per month, coverage of all of these infrastructure services increases rapidly; above US$300 coverage increases at a slower rate.

The fact that electricity coverage is higher than piped water and sewerage at all income levels does not necessarily mean that electricity is valued more than water and sewer infrastructure. It could be that electricity is cheaper than water and sanitation services, or that electricity

Table 7.11. Comparing monthly household costs and benefits of improved water and sanitation services: an example from Kathmandu, Nepal

Costs (from Table 7.4)	Estimate US$20
Benefits	
Reduced water vending expenditures	Minimal
Coping costs avoided	US$ 4
COI avoided	< US$ 1
CV estimate of WTP	US$11–$14

Note: Benefit estimates are overlapping and cannot be summed to obtain total benefits.

was simply available to households and water and sanitation infrastructure was not. However, in actuality electricity service is almost never cheaper than water or sewer services (unless a household's electricity connection is illegal), so this cannot be the explanation for the pattern shown in Figure 7.1. Komives *et al.* (2003) show that even in cases where households have access to piped water, sewers, and electricity, and electricity is more expensive, most households choose electricity first. This suggests that, although most households in developing countries would certainly like improved water and sanitation network services, it is *not* necessarily their most important priority. Given the choice, at least in some places, many households in developing countries appear to want electricity before an in-house piped water or sewer connection. In fact, it is unusual for a household in a developing country to have a piped water connection and *not* have electricity. That water itself is a necessity does not necessarily mean that people prefer piped water service over electrical service. Indeed, because it is a necessity, households must already have access to some source of water. The question thus becomes how much *improved access* to water (both quantity and quality) is worth to them.

Water and sanitation planners often present the need for improved services as a moral imperative or a basic human right, arguing that these services are "merit goods." The problem is that

---

[17] The results of such cost–benefit calculations may be quite different for other locations, but for many places they are likely to look much worse. WTP for improved services in Kathmandu is much higher than in similar CV studies elsewhere.

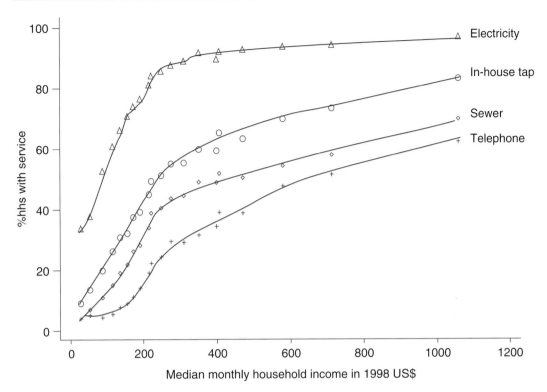

Figure 7.1 *Infrastructure coverage as a function of household income, from Komives et al. (2003)*

network water and sanitation services are very expensive to provide. If the beneficiaries do not themselves perceive the benefit as sufficiently large, financing will be a problem and, without a viable financing mechanism, provision will lag.

Proponents of increased investment in improved water and sanitation services in developing countries see five main problems or limitations with the kind of simple benefit–cost calculations presented in Table 7.11.

First, they argue that households' *perceived* economic benefits are not accurate reflections of the *actual* benefits people will receive from improved services. Many health professionals do not believe that people in areas that need such services (i.e. where health benefits would potentially be high) have an adequate understanding of the link between improved services and improved health, such that potential beneficiaries will tend to undervalue the water and sanitation services *ex ante*.[18] From this perspective,

ex-ante preferences, however they are measured, are not necessarily a sound guide to *ex-post* benefits. In effect, they contend that contingent valuation estimates of WTP for improved services are too low and are thus inclined to dismiss them in favor of other approaches to benefit estimation. To address such concerns, in Part II of this chapter we demonstrate an alternative approach to calculating the net benefits of network water and sanitation services, using a Monte Carlo simulation of the various components of costs and benefits associated with these investments.

A related concern is that poor people cannot clearly assess the value of *future* reductions in health risks. And because it has been observed that the poor typically have very high rates of

[18] But see our caveat in note 4 about whether there is actually solid empirical evidence that improved water and sanitation is a sufficient condition for an *ex-post* improvement in health.

time preference, indicating a focus on short-term concerns, it is also assumed that they will place little value on a stream of benefits provided by water and sanitation investments that may extend far into the future. The "misguided" priorities of beneficiaries are thus emphasized as a justification for decision makers overriding beneficiaries' preferences, in the interest of protecting the welfare of both existing and future generations.

A second argument is that there are positive health externalities associated with water and sanitation investments, and that estimates of individual households' benefits simply do not capture these spillover effects. This argument is much stronger for sanitation than for improved water services, but empirical evidence on the magnitude of the economic value of the positive health externalities associated with sanitation improvements is surprisingly quite limited. Even the private health benefits of improved water and sanitation investments are not as clear-cut or dramatic as is often assumed. There are numerous pathways for pathogens to infect people in a poor community besides contaminated drinking water, and in some situations bringing clean piped water but not improved sanitation to houses can even exacerbate the spread of infectious agents.

If sewerage infrastructure removes human wastes from a neighborhood, both homes that are connected to the network and those that are not connected may receive health benefits. In this case, the actions of those households that connect to the sewerage network confirm positive externalities on unconnected households. Estimates of diarrhea reduction in communities after the installation of such infrastructure should capture both the direct and indirect effects on health. Carefully designed stated preference surveys may also capture households' willingness to pay for such positive externalities.

Importantly, the argument for large positive health externalities within a given urban area is dependent on a substantial proportion of households not having improved water and sanitation services, and can thus benefit from the spillo-

vers. After a certain coverage level, the marginal benefit of positive spillovers will decrease (Cook et al., 2008). As coverage approaches 100%, the positive externalities within a given urban area will become negligible. Similarly, as more and more communities in a region install modern water intake treatment and wastewater treatment facilities, any positive health spillovers from investment in a specific city that are external to that urban agglomeration will also decrease.

There can also be positive environmental externalities associated with water and sanitation investments. A well-managed networked water and sanitation system can provide people with clean, potable water, and then return relatively clean wastewater to the environment. Investments in sewerage and wastewater treatment protect aquatic ecosystems and dependent biodiversity, and return flows from municipal water systems can contribute to rivers' environmental flow requirements. Under some hydrological situations municipal piped systems can help curtail unregulated groundwater exploitation, which often leads to falling water tables and risks of ecosystem degradation and saltwater intrusion.

Conversely, if wastewater is collected in sewers but discharged untreated (or only partially treated) to surface water bodies, these discharges may impose negative externalities either on the community itself or on communities downstream. These negative externalities typically include recreational and aesthetic losses, and may also (but not necessarily) cause human health problems. The aesthetic and recreational benefits of cleaning up surface waters are of course real, but these benefits are specific to locations and circumstances, and their values are typically difficult to ascertain. What empirical evidence exists suggests that they will be quite small in low-income countries, i.e., households in low-income countries are willing to pay very little to improve surface water quality for recreational and aesthetic reasons (see, for example, Choe et al., 1996).

Third, it is argued that the economic benefits of improved water and sanitation are not limited to households. Businesses and industries need piped water for many kinds of activities. Of particular importance to understanding the economic value of piped water and sanitation services is the macroeconomic risk that economies can face from outbreaks of diseases such as cholera. The emergence of SARS in 2003 and the recent cholera outbreak in Peru illustrate how epidemics can cause havoc with general macroeconomic conditions by curtailing travel, tourism, trade, and investment. Because improved water and sanitation services improve long-run health conditions, they represent a form of insurance against macroeconomic shocks. However, the evidence that improved water services greatly enhance business productivity and that business enterprises value improved water and sanitation services much more highly than households is largely a matter of conjecture. Davis *et al.* (2001) find that businesses in a small market town in Uganda actually place very little value on improved water services.

Fourth, it is argued that investments in improved water and sanitation investments benefit developing countries by serving as a kind of insurance against economic extremes. Water and sanitation investments are an important means of diversifying a development aid portfolio. A water supply reservoir and transmission line is likely to provide a city with raw water through both good economic times and bad. Unlike some forms of development assistance that deliver benefits only if economic growth is strong, water and sanitation supply projects tend to be less sensitive to cyclical changes in the business cycle. They thus provide households and businesses with a valuable service when they need it most.

All of these concerns may or may not apply in particular circumstances, and there is little in the literature on their empirical magnitude. Proponents argue that these, and other intangible benefits such as dignity and spirituality, easily tip the balance in favor of increased investment in improved water and sanitation services. But this presents hazards in both directions. On the one hand it invites policy makers to conjecture unsubstantiated benefits and forgo rigorous economic analysis, increasing the likelihood that valuable development dollars will be spent unwisely. On the other hand, dismissing these objections simply because it is not possible to attach robust economic values to them invites policy makers to discount potential social and environmental consequences of investing, or not investing, in water and sanitation.

Moreover, proponents of increased water and sanitation investment sometimes fail to address the risk that such projects may fail. In fact, in the past water and sanitation investments have been particularly prone to failure (Therkildsen, 1988). The benefit–cost comparison presented here is based on the assumption that water and sanitation investments will, in fact, deliver high-quality services and positive health outcomes. For example, the valuation estimates of households' WTP for improved water and sanitation services shown in Tables 7.10 and 7.11 were *contingent* on the proviso that a potable, 24-hour supply of water would actually reach the household. If a water and sanitation project does not deliver this level of service, such contingent valuation estimates of household benefits will be much too high. Sadly, experience has shown that many water and sanitation investments in developing countries do in fact fail by almost any measure of success. This risk of project failure must also be factored into any systematic assessment of costs and benefits.

Finally, proponents of increased investment in water and sanitation argue that lower service levels can result in much lower unit cost estimates. It is true, for example, that hand pumps and improved, ventilated pit latrines are considerably cheaper than network water and sewer services, and we explore lower-cost, non-network interventions in Part III of this chapter (using the same simulation methodology that we demonstrate in Part II). But it is also clear from the results of the contingent valuation surveys that the perceived benefits of such "intermediate" service levels are also much lower. People are willing to pay much less for access to public taps and hand pumps than they are for an in-house water and sewer connection. Thus both the benefits and the costs of simpler technologies are lower. As we show in Part III, lower service levels therefore may, or may not, increase the benefit–cost ratio.

Part II – The Economic Costs and Benefits of Investments in Network Water and Sanitation Services: A Monte Carlo Simulation Approach

Analytical Approach

In Parts II and III of this chapter we demonstrate a second, probabilistic approach to the evaluation of the costs and benefits of water and sanitation investments. In Part II we explain these calculations and then apply the approach to piped water and sewerage network infrastructure. In Part III we examine four water and sanitation interventions that we believe offer greater economic returns than network water and sewerage investments in many locations in developing countries – deep boreholes and hand pumps, total sanitation campaigns, biosand filters, and large multipurpose dams in Africa.

For all five interventions we present exploratory cost–benefit calculations for a range of conditions. There is inevitably some degree of uncertainty regarding the net benefits of a policy intervention in any arena, and water supply and sanitation investments are no exception. Both the benefits and the costs depend on circumstances that will vary with the specific locations and circumstances of implementation of the intervention. Estimates of net benefits for water and sanitation interventions, such as those we present in Parts II and III, are precisely that: estimates based on data from some specific instances that are being generalized for application to a broad range of circumstances. Our data still do not necessarily reflect the range of uncertainty associated with any specific implementation of a given water and sanitation intervention.

The question arises as to how to best conceptualize this uncertainty. One approach utilizes the concept of an additive error. The true benefits, B, may be thought of as the estimated benefits, $\bar{B}$, plus an additive error, ε_1; similarly, the true cost may be thought of as the estimated cost, $\bar{C}$, plus an additive error, ε_2. Consequently, the net benefit is

$$NB = \bar{B} - \bar{C} + \eta, \qquad (1)$$

where $\eta \equiv \varepsilon_1 - \varepsilon_2$. In this context, it would be natural to assume that $E\{\eta\} = 0$ and $\text{var}\{\eta\} = \sigma_\eta^2$, a constant. In that case, the estimate $(\bar{B} - \bar{C})$ can be taken as the expected value of the net benefit, around which there is a distribution. A modification would be to make σ_η^2 heteroskedastic, allowing it to vary with certain factors perhaps associated with circumstances relating to the specific application of the water and sanitation intervention.

The key feature of the approach just outlined is that, whatever the uncertainty, it does not affect the estimate of expected net benefit. However, this may be too benign an assumption. Specifically, it overlooks some of the real complications associated with the implementation of water and sanitation interventions. An alternative representation that captures the uncertainty of implementation has the following multiplicative error structure. One can think of the outcome of the intervention as dependent upon successfully surmounting a series of hurdles. There could, for example, be three hurdles. First, financing for the intervention project has to be found and the funds allocated. Second, the project has to be implemented on the ground. Third, project beneficiaries have to modify their behavior: for example, when a household is connected to a piped water supply system, household members must begin washing their hands after defecation. Only then are the health (and perhaps other) benefits realized.

It may well be the case that once a water and sanitation project is implemented, the benefits – or, at least, the full benefits – accrue only if the participants change their behavior. Consequently there are three possible outcomes. If the funds are not allocated or if the project is not implemented on the ground, there are no expenditures and no benefits: the net benefit is zero. If the funds are allocated and the project is implemented on the ground but there is only a partial change in behavior, the expected benefits are $\theta \bar{B}$, where θ is a fixed constant between 0 and 1, while the expected costs are $\bar{C}$; hence the expected net benefit in this case is $(\theta \bar{B} - \bar{C})$. Finally, if the funds are allocated and the project is implemented on the ground, and there is a complete change in behavior, the expected net benefit is $(\bar{B} - \bar{C})$.

Let γ denote the probability that the funds are allocated, and let λ denote the probability that the project is implemented on the ground, given that the funds are allocated. Finally, let π_1 denote the probability that there is only a partial behavior change given that the funds are allocated and the project is implemented on the ground, and let π_2 denote the probability that there is complete behavior change given that the funds are allocated and the project is implemented on the ground. Then the overall expected net benefits associated with the intervention are

$$\text{Expected net benefits} = \gamma \lambda [(\theta \pi_1 + \pi_2) \bar{B} - \bar{C}] < (\bar{B} - \bar{C}). \tag{2}$$

Equation (2) is a different representation of implementation uncertainty than (1), and it has different implications for how one might use information from the literature on the estimated benefits and costs of the water and sanitation intervention, $\bar{B}$ and $\bar{C}$. In the case of (1), while there is uncertainty, it does not have a meaningful impact on the estimate of expected net benefits. In the case of (2), the uncertainty significantly reduces the estimate of expected net benefits. If the data were confined to completed projects, one would observe only situations where $\gamma = \lambda = 1$, and one could not validly extrapolate these to situations where $\gamma < 1$ and/or $\lambda < 1$. Hence, one needs to account for implementation failure ($\gamma \lambda < 1$) as well as incomplete behavioral change ($\pi_1 > 0$). It should also be emphasized that γ, λ, π_1, and π_2 depend on the specific circumstances of the intervention. It may be possible to alter their value by planning or implementing the inter-vention differently. Accordingly, in designing the intervention, the goal should be to maximize γ, λ, and also π_2.

These issues surrounding the uncertainty in the benefits and costs of water and sanitation investments are rarely addressed adequately in the existing literature. It is a common, understandable wish to know the costs and benefits of water and sanitation investments all over the world, even if this is impractical. Because it is not feasible to conduct cost–benefit analyses of the millions of possible water and sanitation projects, the question arises as to how best to derive approximate measures.

There are several possible approaches; all involve positing a model for the cost–benefit calculations and then settling on a way to apply it to different locations. Most of the cost–benefit models available in the literature for evaluating water and sanitation investments involve at most a few dozen input parameters (Powers, 1978; Powers and Valencia, 1980; Lovei and Whittington, 1993; Whittington and Swarna, 1994; Hutton and Haller, 2004). The Powers and Lovei models were developed to analyze the costs and benefits of specific development projects under consideration for donor funding. The Hutton and Haller model, however, was never intended for analysis of specific invest-ment projects but rather to generate a global picture of costs and benefits of all potential water and sanitation investments.

Conceivably, one could randomly sample potential water and sanitation projects in devel-oping countries and apply the cost–benefit model to this sample of locations. To our knowledge, this has never been done, nor has it ever even been seriously considered by any multilateral donor organization, due to the expense and time required. A second approach to developing a global perspective on the array of possible water and sanitation investments would be to purposely select a number of representative locations and then collect site-specific, accurate information on the parameter values in the cost–benefit model. In fact, devel-opment economists are increasingly utilizing randomized controlled trials (RCTs) to obtain improved estimates of the effectiveness of program interventions such as improved water supplies (Pattanayak *et al.*, 2007a; Kremer *et al.*, 2007, 2008). The results of such RCTs provide site-specific estimates of program effectiveness that can be combined with the numerous other parameters and assumptions needed for benefit–cost analysis.

This movement in development economics toward more rigorous program evaluation is to be applauded, but transferring the results of RCTs from one site to other sites can be problematic. Also, the results from RCTs on program effectiveness are only one of many parameters in a cost–benefit calculation, and, as we show in Parts II and III, are often not the most important parameter affecting the benefit–cost results. Moreover, for certain types of interventions such as network water and sanitation services, it is not even possible to design RCTs.

A third approach is to calculate the benefits and costs for each country or region in the world, using country or region-specific information from global databases for those parameters for which such data are available. For parameters for which such secondary data are not available for each country or region, one would need to use evidence from a few site-specific studies or use professional judgment. One could then calculate the average benefits and costs of different types of water and sanitation interventions by country or region. This is the approach used by Hutton and Haller in their 2004 assessment of the global benefits of water and sanitation investments.

In this chapter, we use a fourth approach that constructs a probability distribution of a range of benefit–cost outcomes for the five water and sanitation interventions. As in Part I, except for the large dams in Africa intervention, our unit of analysis is the individual household (not commercial enterprises): we compare the costs of providing an improved water source or sanitation environment to a typical household in the community with the benefits that it would receive. For each intervention, we specify a simple cost–benefit model in which the monthly net benefits to a household are a function of about twenty different parameters.[19] Many (but not all) of the parameters are common to the models across the four household-based water and sanitation interventions. One way to compare the five interventions is then to consider the range of plausible cost–benefit outcomes as a ratio of benefits to costs, but we caution that this measure of comparison masks important differences in scale, and the financing requirements that these imply.

For each parameter in the cost–benefit model for each intervention except large dams in Africa, we make three types of assumptions. First, we specify a range of plausible values based on professional judgment and our reading of the literature. Second, we assume a specific probability distribution that determines the likelihood that a specific value within the specified range will occur. Third, we specify whether there is likely to be a correlation (association) between this parameter and other parameters in the cost–benefit model. For example, the cost of providing network infrastructure is likely to be higher in remote locations, which are also likely to be places where case fatality rates for diarrhea would be higher due to longer distances to health clinics. This approach thus follows the type of analysis described in equation (1) above rather than equation (2), as we are implicitly considering the likely parameter values that will occur in the field rather than a best-case scenario in which probabilities of success and failure must be explicitly included to yield realistic and expected outcomes. For the large dams intervention, our modeling approach is similar in practice, but there is a qualitative difference in the way it should be interpreted. Because the economic value of large dams is so dependent on context, we apply our cost–benefit model to only *one* illustrative situation and use the model and parameter ranges to represent our uncertainty about specific parameters, rather than the range these parameters can be thought to take in different locations.

---

[19] For large multipurpose dams in Africa, it is more sensible to consider costs and benefits on an aggregated basis.

We then conduct a Monte Carlo analysis that calculates the benefit–cost ratio for each of ten thousand different combinations of values for the parameters in the cost–benefit model for each of the five water and sanitation interventions. This yields a distribution of benefit–cost ratios for each intervention. For all of the interventions except large dams in Africa, the distribution of benefit–cost ratios for an intervention from the Monte Carlo calculations does not correspond to the distribution of actual situations in developing countries. Rather it is associated with the ranges of parameter values and other assumptions that we have made. Because we have used our best professional judgment to select the ranges for these parameters, in fact we expect to find water and sanitation projects in developing countries with a similar range of benefit–cost ratios. We do not know, however, the frequency with which any specific combination of parameter values – or benefit–cost ratios – would arise in the real world. Here, again, the distribution from the Monte Carlo simulation for the large dams intervention is qualitatively different; it represents plausible outcomes at only one *specific* dam location, informed by our uncertainty about model parameters.

There are three reasons why our approach is conceptually appealing. First, we specify ranges for all parameters in the cost–benefit model, not just a few selected parameters. We can thus easily identify which parameters have the largest effect on the cost–benefit ratio. Second, the Monte Carlo simulations allow us to incorporate into the model associations between selected parameters, and thus to reduce the occurrence of improbable combinations of parameter values. Third, we believe that probability distributions of cost–benefit ratios for the interventions are more useful than point estimates, because they allow us to focus on the policy-relevant question of where water and sanitation investments are likely to be most economically attractive.

With regard to the specific parameter values used in the cost–benefit models in Parts II and III, there is an important difference from the cal-culations presented in Part I, where we assumed the value of *ex-ante* mortality risk reductions from water and sanitation network investments was captured in the estimates of economic bene-fits from the available contingent valuation stud-ies. In Parts II and III, we do not rely on stated preference studies of households' willingness to pay for improved water and sanitation services for estimates of the benefits from mortality risk reduction, in part because such evidence is not available for the specific interventions we examine. Here we estimate the magnitude of the mortality risk reduction and multiply this by an assumed value of a statistical life (VSL).[20]

Evaluation of the Costs and Benefits of Network Water and Sanitation Services

We now explain in more detail how we use this second, probabilistic approach to calculate the costs and benefits associated with network water and sanitation services. The equations in our cost–benefit model are shown in Table 7.12 and our assumed ranges of parameter values in Table 7.13.

Costs

As discussed in Part I, the cost of full conven-tional network water and sanitation services is roughly US$2 per cubic meter (assuming the discount rate $r = 6\%$ and the life of capital is 20 years). In our simulations, we allow variation of a number of parameters that influence the cal-culation of costs: the real discount rate (3–6%) and the life of the investment (15–25 years) which influence the capital recovery factor, and the percentage of annual operation and main-tenance costs relative to annual capital costs (33–67%). In order to obtain the monthly cost per household, we multiply these adjusted unit costs by the monthly per capita consumption (obtained from an assumed daily consumption of 60–140 liters) and the number of household members (4–6 people). With parameters set at

[20] This approach might at first appear to be independent of stated preference methods, but in fact much of the literature on VSLs in developing countries uses stated preference methods.

Table 7.12. Equations for cost–benefit analysis of network water and sanitation services

Demand for water $Q = f(T)$	
Baseline demand	$Q_0 = 30 - (50/3) * T_{0w}$
Additional demand (demand curve)	For $T_{1w} > 0.1$, $Q_{1a} = 30 - (50/3) * T_{1w}$ For $0 \leq T_{1w} < 0.1$, $Q_{1b} = Q_{1b} - (2150/3) * T_{1w}$
Benefit type	
Time savings per trip collecting water (hours)	$T_{s1} = T_{0w}$
Time savings per trip to sanitation facility (hours)	$T_{s2} = T_{0s}$
Time savings per hh-month (hours)	$T_{s,m} = (T_{s1} * Q_0 + T_{s2} * Q_s) * 30 * S / 20$
Value of time savings per hh-month ($)	$V_{ts} = T_{s,m} * (w / 8) * v_t$
Avoided morbidity per hh-month ($)	$m = (I / 12) * E * S * COI$
Avoided mortality per hh-month ($)	$M = (I / 12) * E * S * CFR * VSL$
Total health per hh-month ($)	$V_H = M + m$
Aesthetic (quantity) per hh-month ($)	$V_A = [(w / 8) * v_t * 30 * S / 20] * [(T_{s1} * a_1 + 0.1) * (Q_{1a} - Q_0)$ $+ 0.1 * a_2 * (Q_{1b} - Q_{1a})] * (1 - h)$
Costs	
Capital recovery factor	$CR = r * (1 + r)^d / ((1 + r)^d - 1)$
Capital per hh-month ($)	$C_{c,m} = S * Q_{1b} * 30 * C_c * CR / (1000 * CR_{0.1, 20})$
O&M per hh-month ($)	$C_{o,m} = p_{om} * C_{c,m}$

their midpoint values, we obtain a monthly cost estimate of about US$25, which is consistent with the cost estimates presented in Part I.

Benefits

The economic benefits of improved water supply have three main components:

1 The value of any time savings that result from the installation of the new water source (see Table 7.14).
2 The value of lifestyle and aesthetic benefits from increased use of higher-quality and amounts of water obtained from the new source (see Table 7.14).
3 The monetary value of the health benefits.

These three components are considered in both the network water and sanitation intervention we consider here in Part II and the deep bore-hole and hand pump intervention examined in

Part III of this chapter. We assume on the structure of the demand curve shown in Figure 7.2 for both interventions, although the parameter values used to define the function vary, as shown in Tables 7.13 and 7.14).

In-house water and sewer connections provide a) a convenient source of water for households in a community, and b) a practical way to dispose of and eliminate human excreta from the house and neighborhood. Having a private water connection thus allows each household to eliminate completely the time expenses previously incurred collecting the original quantity of water it used from other sources. In some communities where in-house toilets or latrines are not available, household members will also no longer need to travel outside the house to defecate. We assume for simplicity that water tariffs are low (as is typical in most developing countries), so that there is an unambiguous fall

Table 7.13. Parameters used in cost–benefit analysis of network water and sanitation services[a]

Symbol	Parameter	Base case	Lower limit	Upper limit	Correlated parameters
C_c	Capital cost of network water and sanitation services, at $r = 0.1$, $d = 20$ yrs ($/m^3$)	2.5	2.0	3.0	Market wage (−0.5)
P_{om}	O&M expenditures, as a percent of monthly capital (%)	50	33	67	
d	Water project duration (yrs)	20	15	25	Capital cost (0.5)
r	Real (net of inflation) discount rate (%)	4.5%	3%	6%	
S	Household size	5	4	6	
T_{0w}	Status quo collection time (hrs/20L): traditional source	1.0	0.1	1.9	
T_{1w}	Collection time per liter (hrs/20L): improved	0	0	0	
T_{0s}	Time spent using sanitation facility (hrs/trip)	15	10	20	
Q_s	Round trips to defecation site per person per day	1	0.75	1.25	
w	Market wage for unskilled labor ($/day)	$1.25	$0.50	$2.00	
v_t	Value of time savings/market wage for unskilled labor	30%	10%	50%	
a_1	Ratio of aesthetic benefits to time savings benefits for demand curve segment 1	25%	0%	50%	
a_2	Ratio of aesthetic benefits to time savings benefits for demand curve segment 2	25%	0%	50%	
I	Diarrheal incidence (cases/person-yr)[b]	0.9	0.5	1.4	Capital cost (0.5)
E	% reduction in diarrhea incidence due to water project intervention	75%	60%	90%	
COI	Cost of illness ($/case)	$6	$2	$10	Market wage (0.5)
CFR	Diarrhea case fatality rate (%)[b]	0.08%	0.04%	0.12%	Capital cost (0.5)
VSL	Value of a statistical life ($)	$30,000	$10,000	$50,000	Market wage (0.7)
h	Percentage of aesthetic benefits that are actually health-related	25%	0%	50%	

[a] Our uncertainty analysis does not purport to use the real probability distributions associated with these parameters but instead is aimed at assessing the range of possible situations in poor developing countries; therefore we use uniform distributions of parameters.
[b] Revised Global Burden of Disease (GBD) Estimates (WHO, 2002). Available at www.who.int/healthinfo/bodgbd2002revised/en/index.html. Diarrhea incidence in developing country subregions ranges 0.6–1.29 case per capita per year (mean ~0.9) but may actually be higher or lower in some locations; CFR ranges 0.02–0.09, and is ~0.08% in Africa.

in the effective (shadow) price of water as a result of the new connection. One would expect that the household would use more water in response to this fall in price, and this is in fact what the available evidence suggests: households in communities with in-house connections increase the amount of water they use compared with the quantity collected when traditional sources are outside the home.

For purposes of illustration, we assume that before the installation of the in-house connection, the average household was collecting water from sources outside the home and using 13 liters per capita per day, that is, 65 liters per household per day, or about 2 cubic meters per household per month. Assume that before the new piped water system was installed, the household was spending about 1 hour to collect 20 liters, or 3.25 hours per day collecting the household's daily 65 liters. The monthly time

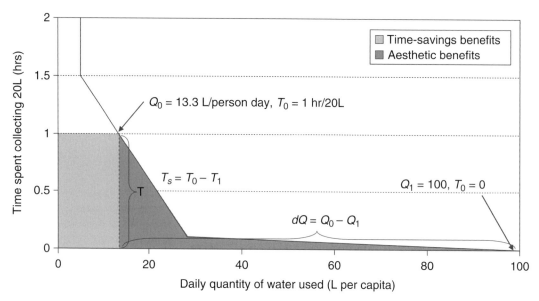

Figure 7.2 *Demand curve for water as a function of collection time, identifying two types of benefits obtained (time-savings and quantity-related benefits)*

savings for collection of 2 cubic meters of water would be 100 hours. Also assume that prior to the intervention, two adults in the household had to walk a 15-minute round trip per day to reach appropriate sanitation facilities, so that the additional time savings to household adults from having sanitation are about 15 hours per month.[21] The total time savings are thus about 115 hours.

The economic value of these time savings to households is likely to vary greatly depending on local labor market conditions and economic opportunities. In some small market towns the value of this time saving may approach the value of the unskilled market wage rate (Whittington et al., 1990b). In some places it may be essentially impossible to translate any of these time savings into cash. For example, in labor-surplus situations and in periods when the demand for agricultural labor is low, the value of time savings from an improved water source may be the

[21] Conservatively, we do not count time savings to children here because they 1) are not likely to travel far outside the house for sanitation purposes, and 2) probably have a low value of time.

value of leisure time. This does not mean that the household is indifferent to these time savings: women may much prefer devoting this time to child care and food preparation, for example, than to collecting water. But labor market opportunities will almost certainly affect how much the household is willing to pay to obtain these time savings.

Suppose that the local wage for unskilled labor in the community is $1.25 per day (US$0.16 per hour) and that the value of the time savings from the new water system is 30% of this market wage. The monetary value of the total time savings from the intervention (associated with not spending as much time to acquire the quantity of water collected elsewhere previously) would thus be US$5.40 per household per month. In our Monte Carlo calculations we vary (1) the market wage for unskilled labor (range $0.5–2/day), (2) the fraction of the value of unskilled wage rate used to estimate the value of time savings from the water project (range 0.1–0.5), (3) the time savings from not collecting water from existing sources (collection time from existing source varies from 0.1–1.9 hours/20 liters of

Table 7.14. Base case results for network water and sanitation services[a]

Benefits	Without new network	With new network	Change in physical units	Change in monetary units		
				3.0%	4.5%	6.0%
Time spent collecting initial quantity of water and accessing community sanitation (hrs per hh-month) [Value of time savings]	115	0	115	$5.39	$5.39	$5.39
Water use (L per hh-month) [Value of aesthetic and lifestyle benefits from increased water use]	2,000	15,000	13,000	$1.86	$1.86	$1.86
Number of non-fatal cases of diarrhea (per hh-month) [Value of reduction in morbidity]	0.38	0.09	(0.09)	$1.69	$1.69	$1.69
Risk of death from all diarrhea (per 1,000 hh-month) [Value of reduction in mortality]	0.30	0.08	(0.08)	$6.75	$6.75	$6.75
All benefits				$15.68	$15.68	$15.68
Costs						
CRF				0.067	0.077	0.087
Expenditures by all parties for new water system (per hh-month)	0			($19.03)	($24.54)	($30.99)
CB ratio				0.82	0.64	0.51
Net benefits				($3.34)	($8.86)	($15.30)

[a] For the results reported in this table, all parameters were set at their base case values as described in [TC]Table 7.13, except for the discount rate, which was varied between 3%, 4.5%, and 6%. The values in the cells in the three rightmost columns report the monetary value of the components of benefits and total costs on a per-household, per-month basis.

water, and (4) the time savings from having in-house sanitation facilities (10–20 minutes/trip, 0.75–1.25 trips/person-day for 1–3 adults/household).

The second component of the benefits from the network intervention is the consumer surplus on the increased water use that occurs because of the fall in the effective price of water. We can conceptualize this as the lifestyle and aesthetic benefits, as well as health benefits, that the household obtains from increased water use (Whittington and Swarna, 1994). In practice, when a household moves from a per-capita water use level of 10–15 liters per day to 100 liters per day, most of the increase in the quantity of water used is devoted to personal and household cleaning and washing. The consumer

surplus on this increased water use is difficult to estimate; the contingent valuation studies cited in Part I of this chapter would suggest that it is probably small. If these aesthetic and lifestyle benefits were 25% on a per-liter basis of the value of the time savings as shown in Table 7.13, they would then be about US$2.50 per household per month (note the kinked demand curve we use to account for the large increases in water consumption associated with in-house use). Because a portion of these benefits may actually be health-related, there is a risk of double-counting. To avoid that risk we apply a downward correction, assuming that 25% of aesthetic/lifestyle benefits are actually health benefits. In our Monte Carlo simulations we also vary the percentage of the value of the time savings used to estimate these aesthetic and lifestyle benefits (range 0–50%), the percentage of the aesthetic benefits that are actually health-related (range 0–50%), and, as mentioned previously, the consumption of water from the in-house connection (60–140 liter/capita-day).

The third component of the benefits is the economic value of the improved health of household members. It will probably come as a surprise to those unfamiliar with the literature on the relationship between improved water and sanitation services and health outcomes that this third component is both controversial and uncertain. It is difficult to know how an improved water system will affect health outcomes in a specific location, and it is also difficult to place a monetary value on the resulting health improvements. This stems in part from the limitations related to the cost of illness welfare measure, as discussed in Part I of this chapter. Specifically, in situations where households can engage in coping or averting behaviors that reduce the risk and/or impact of disease, it is difficult to estimate how an intervention will change health outcomes and impact welfare (Bockstael and McConnell, 2007). Furthermore, in some situations households may use multiple sources of water for various purposes, depending upon seasonal availability and quality considerations; in such situations they may engage in complicated tradeoffs between time savings and health benefits that can be understood only through careful field studies (Pattanayak *et al.*, 2007a, 2007b; Kremer *et al.*, 2007). We recognize these difficulties and introduce a number of parameters into our net benefit equation to attempt to characterize the various dimensions and uncertainties in health benefits.

Improved water systems are hypothesized to reduce a variety of diseases, including typhoid, cholera, and shigellosis. There are an estimated 2 million deaths annually due to such water-related diseases in developing countries, but in truth these estimates are subject to large uncertainty. Estimates of deaths from shigellosis are highly uncertain and vary between 250,000 and 1.2 million. Most health evaluations of water and sanitation interventions do not attempt to measure their effect on specific diseases or on mortality, but rather ask participants in the study about the diarrhea incidence in their households. Because most of the health intervention studies are not double-blinded, there is a risk of a placebo effect in these self-reported diarrhea data. The results of evaluations of water and sanitation interventions on diarrhea incidence vary widely in the literature.[22] In this section, for the purposes of illustration, we assume that the network water and sanitation intervention reduces the diarrheal incidence rate by 75% (range 60–90%). We also conduct a sensitivity analysis using a 100% reduction in diarrhea disease incidence to demonstrate the theoretical upper bound for health benefits within the urban area (i.e., total eradication of diarrheal disease in the target community), though we caution that this upper bound will in most cases either overestimate benefits (if other complementary investments such as improved housing do not accompany full network services) or understate costs (because the costs of such improvements are neglected).

A number of additional assumptions are necessary to measure the health benefits from in-house connections. First, one must know the baseline diarrhea incidence. In poor communities this can vary by more than an order of magnitude. Assume that diarrheal incidence is about 0.9 cases per person per year (range 0.5–1.4), or 4.5 cases per household.[23] The economically relevant question then becomes: "What would a typical household be willing to pay to reduce diarrhea incidence from 4.5 cases per year to 1.2 cases per year (i.e., the assumed 75% reduction

[22] For example, a recent meta-analysis by Fewtrell *et al.* (2005) reports a median reduction for a variety of intervention types of about 25–30% from baseline diarrhea incidence. Few of these studies, however, considered the effect of complete coverage of a community with in-house water and sanitation services. We thus use the 25% baseline reduction only for the low-cost intervention – boreholes and hand pumps – described in Part III.

[23] Incidence rates of 3–5 cases per year have been observed among high-risk population groups such as young children under the age of five (Kosek *et al.*, 2003). However, it is not appropriate to generalize these high incidence rates to the general population.

due to network water and sanitation services)?" We estimate the morbidity and mortality reduction benefits separately. We assume a case fatality rate (CFR) of 0.08% (range 0.04–0.12%), such that prior to the water intervention the annual risk of a household member dying from diarrhea is about 36/10,000. How much would reducing this risk of death to 9/10,000 be worth to a typical household?

One approach to estimating the value of this risk reduction is to multiply by the value of a statistical life. The literature on the value of mortality risk reductions in developing countries is growing, but still quite limited. Most of the studies have been conducted in large middle-income, urban areas in which many households have already gone through the demographic transition and now have small families and long lives (Vassandumrongdee and Matsuoka, 2005; Hammitt and Liu, 2004; Krupnick *et al.*, 2008). There are only two empirical studies of the value of mortality risk reductions in low-income rural areas of developing countries (Mahmud, 2007 and Maskery *et al.*, 2008). These two studies are from Bangladesh and both provide estimates of VSL that are much lower (US$2,000–25,000) than studies from middle-income urban areas. Bhattacharya *et al.* (2007) also report a VSL of similar magnitude for Delhi (US$30,000). These three recent studies suggest that transferring adjusted VSL estimates from industrialized countries, or using a rule of thumb that VSLs in developing countries should be 100 times per capita GDP, is ill advised. Although this literature must be considered preliminary, in our analysis we use this recent empirical evidence that suggests poor rural households put much less value on mortality risk reductions than households in industrialized countries or in middle-income, urban areas of developing countries. We assume a base case VSL of US$30,000 with a range from $10,000–50,000. The resulting value of the risk reduction due to the water supply and sanitation intervention would then be US$108 per year, or about US$9 per household per month.

In addition to the mortality benefits, individuals would receive the economic benefits of not suffering from non-fatal episodes of diarrhea.

We assume that the COI for a case of diarrhea is US$6 (range US$2–10). The annual cost of illness for the average household before the water supply intervention would be about US$27. The household would save about US$2.3 per month from reduced morbidity.

In these illustrative calculations, the two largest components of the benefits from the network services are time savings and mortality-reduction benefits; both aesthetic and morbidity-reduction benefits are considerably lower (Table 7.14).

Comparison of Costs and Benefits of Network Water and Sanitation Services

The costs and benefits for the base case parameters for network water and sanitation services are presented in Table 7.14 in terms of US$ per household per month. The total benefits are US$15.7 per household per month; the costs are US$24.5 per household per month. This implies a simple benefit–cost ratio (BCR) of 0.65. If we make the extreme assumption that this intervention leads to a 100% reduction in diarrheal disease incidence in the target community, the BCR increases to 0.75.

Figure 7.3 presents results of the Monte Carlo simulations for both the range of 60–90% (upper panel) and the upper bound (100%) reduction in diarrheal disease (lower panel). As shown, there are relatively few combinations of parameter values where investments in network water and sanitation are economically justified.

One limitation of these calculations is that they do not include benefits from potential production externalities from improved environmental conditions outside of the service area. For example, improved water quality in surface water bodies will lead to enhanced fisheries, improved recreation opportunities, lower treatment costs for users of downstream surface water, etc. Nonetheless, the calculations in Figure 7.4 and the distributions in Figure 7.5 suggest that these externalities would have to be very large to justify investments in network water and sanitation infrastructures. Such large externalities seem unlikely to us in most developing country locations.

Under what conditions would network water

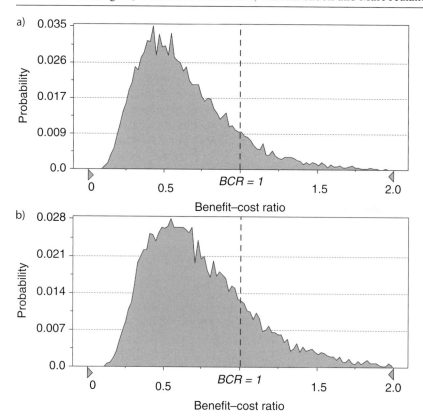

Figure 7.3 *Network water and sanitation services: distribution of benefit–cost ratio outcomes from Monte Carlo simulation (10,000 draws) with uniform parameter distributions, assuming a) 60–90% and b) 100% effectiveness against diarrheal disease*

and sanitation services be attractive economic investments? Figure 7.4 shows that the BCRs are most sensitive to variations in (1) per-capita consumption, (2) baseline diarrheal incidence, (3) value of a statistical life, and (4) assumptions about the value of time spent collecting water. The VSL is highly dependent on income (Mrozek and Taylor, 2002; Alberini and Chiabai, 2007); economic development will certainly lead to higher VSLs (Viscusi and Aldy, 2003; USEPA, 2000). Figure 7.5 demonstrates that if the assumed values of VSLs are higher, investments in network water and sanitation infrastructure become much more economically

attractive, though of course the challenges associated with financing remain.

Discussion

From our perspective, the biggest limitation of the kinds of benefit–cost calculations presented in Figure 7.4 and Part II of this chapter is that the benefit stream associated with capital-intensive water and sanitation network infrastructure is assumed to be static. In fact, the benefits that flow from water and sanitation investments may grow over time, due largely to economic growth and rising incomes. There is limited evidence that investments in municipal water and sanitation services actually *cause* economic growth.[24] At the same time, however, the sequencing of significant water investments could in theory set

[24] The available evidence for the United States is mixed but generally negative; for a summary, see Hanemann (2006).

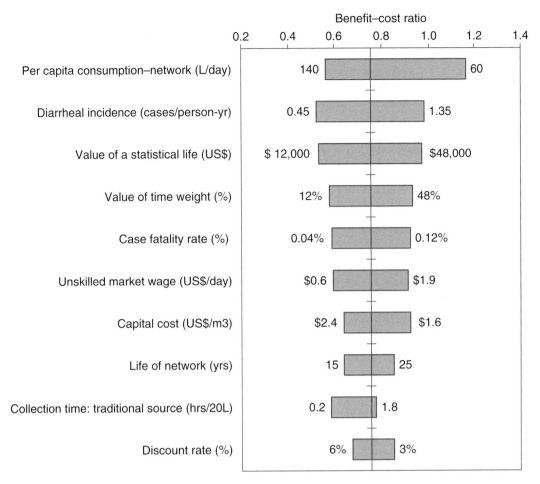

Figure 7.4 *Network water and sanitation intervention sensitivity analyses: effect of selected parameters on BCR (90% confidence intervals, holding other parameters at base case values)*

in motion path-dependent patterns of development (for example, by diminishing disease risks and providing reliable water inputs for potential industrial uses) that will change the expected returns to, and hence incentives for, subsequent investments in all sectors. Moreover, as illustrated in Figure 7.1 in Part I of this chapter, there is a strong association between household income and the provision of both piped water and sewer services. Higher-income households definitely want improved water and sanitation services, and, as incomes grow, the demand for such services grows. Thus even in the absence of a causal relationship, the benefit stream of water

and sanitation services becomes more valuable as economic growth proceeds.

Even though the benefits of improved water and sanitation services increase with economic growth, they must still be discounted back to the initial period to compare the present value of the benefit stream with the high initial capital costs and the present value of the operation and maintenance expenditures. For water and sanitation infrastructure, the magnitude of the present value of the benefit stream is very sensitive to the discount rate chosen because of the large up-front capital costs and the unusually long economic life of the assets. This is an old,

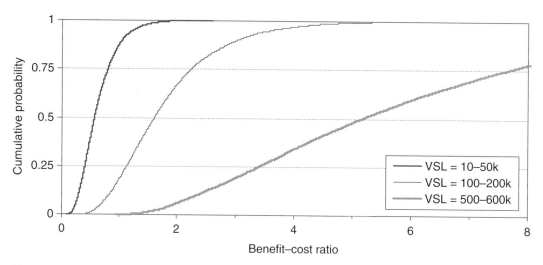

Figure 7.5 *Network water and sanitation intervention: the effect of the VSL parameter on the BCR simulation outcomes*

well-known problem in the economic appraisal of water resources projects. How growth in the demand for services affects the benefit–cost analysis of water and sanitation investments is largely determined by the relative magnitude of three parameters: (1) the rate of economic growth over the planning period, (2) the elasticity of WTP with respect to income, and (3) the discount rate (Whittington *et al.*, 2004).

In practice it has proven almost impossible for national governments or donor agencies to conduct rigorous economic appraisals of water and sanitation projects that address this level of complexity. As Hirschman pointed out half a century ago:

> The trouble with investment in social overhead capital (*e.g., water and sanitation investments*)... is that it is impervious to investment criteria.... As a result social overhead capital is largely a matter of faith in the development potential of a country or region.... Such a situation implies at least the possibility of wasteful mistakes.
> (1958, 84, emphasis added)

This is precisely what we have witnessed in

recent decades in the water and sanitation sector in developing countries, where "white elephants" and poorly performing projects have been a standard feature of the sector landscape (Therkildsen, 1988). Too often when it appears that a particular project might not pass a cost–benefit test, water professionals appeal to intangible benefits to argue that the investment will in fact pass the test.[25]

In conclusion, it is not our intention to imply that all investments in municipal water and sanitation network infrastructure will fail a rigorous economic test. We do believe it is the case, however, that not all investments will pass. In cities in rapidly growing economies, we expect the benefits of many projects, properly estimated, to exceed the costs. In other cases, however, the economic reality will be more nuanced and the attractiveness of specific water and sanitation investments in network infrastructure less clear-cut. Especially in situations where long-term economic growth prospects are uncertain, large capital investments in water and sanitation network infrastructure will often be problematic from an economic perspective, and preconceptions that seek to circumvent rigorous economic analysis should be viewed with considerable skepticism.

In Part III of this challenge chapter we look

[25] This is particularly the case in the evaluation of rural water and sanitation investments in developing countries, where neither donors nor national agencies attempt serious appraisal of such projects.

at three non-network water and sanitation interventions that we believe will have higher economic returns than network services for many developing country situations. We also consider multipurpose investments in major water resources infrastructure (large dams in Africa) that we show to be attractive economic development projects.

Part III – Analysis of Four Alternative Water and Sanitation Interventions

Introduction

In Part III of this chapter we shift our focus from piped water and sewerage network infrastructure, which we have argued is both expensive and difficult to finance, to look at four other water and sanitation interventions:

1 A rural water supply program for constructing deep boreholes with hand pumps in Africa.
2 A sanitation program designed to halt open defecation in South Asia.
3 Water-disinfection technology installed at the household level (point-of-use).
4 Large multipurpose dams in Africa.

In evaluating these four interventions, we use the same methodology employed in Part II to examine the case of network water and sanitation services. The first three interventions all seek to capture some of the potential benefits of network water or sanitation systems without incurring their large capital costs. Deep boreholes with hand pumps can be shared by many households, thus reducing the capital costs per household. The "total community sanitation" program is an intensive health-promotion campaign designed to stimulate demand for improved toilets without sewerage infrastructure (pour-flush toilets with drainage or improved sanitary pit latrines are used instead).

Point-of-use (POU) disinfection technologies can be conceptualized either as add-on, inexpensive but partial solutions to the unreliable, contaminated piped water supplies in many cities in developing countries, or as a stand-alone intervention to disinfect a contaminated traditional water source. In either case, the advantage of POU interventions is that capital costs are low. POU interventions are only a partial solution to water and sanitation problems because one must still manage to get water to the home. The last intervention, large multipurpose dams in Africa, takes us back to large, capital-intensive investments but expands the focus from household water and sanitation services to questions of regional water resources management.

Alternative Water and Sanitation Intervention 1 – A Rural Water Supply Program Providing Poor Rural Communities in Africa with Deep Boreholes and Public Hand Pumps

Description of the Intervention

A deep borehole with a public (non-motorized) hand pump is a commonly recommended improved water source for many poor rural communities in Africa and some other locations in the developing world. Many donors and national governments would consider this a low-cost, appropriate technology when households are too poor to afford individual household connections and when deep groundwater is the best available water source. When groundwater is shallow, a household can often afford its own private, hand-dug well and hand pump. When springs are available at higher elevations than the community, gravity-fed distribution systems with public taps and/or house connections will generally be preferred, because they enable households to avoid the effort associated with lifting water from the aquifer to the surface with a hand pump, and entail lower maintenance and repair costs.

Deep boreholes equipped with a public hand pump require the use of drilling rigs in potentially remote rural locations. It will often be necessary to transport drilling rigs on unpaved roads. Dry holes are not infrequent, so private contractors will either build into their pricing structure the cost of dry wells or simply charge by the depth of the well drilled without guaranteeing that the well will supply water. Public hand pumps need to be built to withstand heavy daily use.

Table 7.15. Equations for cost–benefit analysis of rural water supply project

Demand for water $Q = f(T)$	
Baseline demand	$Q_0 = 30 - (50/3) * T_0$
Additional demand	If $T_1 > T_0$, $dQ = 0$ $dQ = (50/3) * (T_0 - T_1)$ otherwise

Benefit type	
Time savings per trip (hours)	If $T_0 > T_1$, $T_s = (T_0 - T_1)$ $T_s = 0$ otherwise
Time savings per hh-month (hours)	$T_{s,m} = T_s * Q_0 * 30 * S / 20$
Value of time savings per hh-month ($)	$V_{ts} = T_{s,m} * (w/8) * v_t$
Avoided morbidity per hh-month ($)	$m = (I/12) * E * S * COI$
Avoided mortality per hh-month ($)	$M = (I/12) * E * S * CFR * VSL$
Total health per hh-month ($)	$V_H = M + m$
Aesthetic (quantity) per hh-month ($)	If $(dQ * S * 30/20) * T_s * (w/8) * v_t * a * (h) < V_H$, $V_A = (dQ * S * 30/20) * T_s * (w/8) * v_t * a * (1-h)$ $V_A = (dQ * S * 30/20) * T_s * (w/8) * v_t * a - V_H$

Costs	
Capital recovery factor	$CR = r * (1 + r)^d / ((1 + r)^d - 1)$
Capital per hh-month ($)	$C_{c,m} = (C_c + C_p) * CR / (n * 12)$
Other – O&M + non-pecuniary mgmt per hh-month ($)	$C_{o,m} = (C_o + C_m) / (n * 12)$

Rural water supply programs in developing countries have had a checkered history. In the 1980s sector professionals recognized that many rural water supply programs were in disarray (Churchill *et al.*, 1987; Briscoe and De Ferranti, 1988). Regardless of the type of technology utilized, rural water systems were not being repaired and many were simply abandoned. Sector professionals commenced a reexamination of the rural water sector to study why systems failed, and in the 1990s a new consensus emerged about how rural water supply programs should be planned and implemented. This new model for rural water supply programs, termed "demand-driven community management," sought to involve households in the choice both of technology and of institutional and governance arrangements, gave women a larger role in decision making, and aimed for households to pay all of the operation and maintenance costs of providing water services and at least some of the capital costs (Sara *et al.*, 1996; Sara and Katz, 1997; Whittington *et al.*, 1998).

New evidence suggests that this new planning model is working and that many of the problems associated with failed rural water projects can be overcome (Davis *et al.*, 2007; Komives *et al.*, 2007; Prokopy *et al.*, 2007; Thorsten, 2007; Whittington *et al.*, 2007). In three recent studies, a large majority of water projects that were part of demand-driven, community-managed rural water supply programs were found to be operational. Households were using the water from the improved sources and were satisfied with the improved water systems. Although numerous challenges remain, the rural water sector now has a set of planning and implementation procedures that promises much better results than were thought possible previously.

Clearly, rural water systems that are not being used and/or are broken will not pass a cost–benefit test. Now that there appears to be a strategy for delivering more sustainable improved water systems in rural areas, the question as to whether such investments would pass such a test becomes

Table 7.16. Parameters used in cost–benefit analysis of water supply project[a]

Symbol	Parameter	Base case	Lower limit	Upper limit	Correlated parameters
C_c	Capital cost ($) of borehole + hand pump	$6,500	$5,000	$8,000	O&M (0.5), Market wage (–0.5)
C_p	Program cost: capacity building and management ($/borehole)	$3,500	$2,000	$5,000	Market wage (–0.5)
C_o	O&M expenditures, repairs (annual)	$100	$50	$150	
C_m	Management costs (annual, non-pecuniary) – village + program	$500	$200	$800	
d	Water project duration (yrs)	15	10	20	Program costs (0.5)
r	Real (net of inflation) discount rate (%)	4.5%	3%	6%	
n	# households served by borehole	60	30	90	New source collection time (0.5)
S	Household size	5	4	6	
T_0	Status quo collection time (hrs/20L): traditional source	1.0	0.1	1.9	
T_1	Collection time per liter (hrs/20L) – improved	0.3	0.1	0.5	
w	Market wage for unskilled labor ($/day)	$1.25	$0.50	$2.00	
v_t	Value of time savings/market wage for unskilled labor	30%	10%	50%	
a	Ratio of aesthetic and lifestyle benefits to time savings benefits	25%	0%	50%	
I	Diarrheal incidence (cases/person-yr)[b]	0.9	0.5	1.4	Capital cost (0.5), Program costs (0.5)
E	% reduction in diarrhea incidence due to water project intervention	25%	10%	40%	
COI	Cost of illness ($/case)	$6	$2	$10	Market wage (0.5)
CFR	Diarrhea case fatality rate (%)[b]	0.08%	0.04%	0.12%	Capital cost (0.5), Program costs (0.5)
VSL	Value of a statistical life ($)	$30,000	$10,000	$50,000	Market wage (0.7)
h	Percentage of aesthetic benefits that are actually health-related	25%	0%	50%	

Notes:
[a] Our uncertainty analysis does not purport to use the real probability distributions associated with these parameters but instead is aimed at assessing the range of possible situations in poor developing countries; therefore we use uniform distributions of parameters.
[b] Revised Global Burden of Disease (GBD) Estimates (WHO, 2002). Available at www.who.int/healthinfo/bodgbd2002revised/en/index.html. Diarrhea incidence in developing country subregions ranges 0.6–1.29 case per capita per year (mean ~0.9) but may actually be higher or lower in some locations; CFR ranges 0.02–0.09, and is ~0.08% in Africa.

relevant.[26] We present here some preliminary cost–benefit calculations for investments in a demand-driven, community-managed rural water supply program that provides poor rural communities with deep boreholes and public hand pumps. Table 7.15 summarizes the equations used in the calculation of benefits and costs of this intervention. Table 7.16 presents the assumed parameter values and definitions.

The assumptions behind the equations and parameter values are described below.

[26] One can certainly question whether there is sufficient evidence to confidently posit a causal relationship between the demand-driven, community management planning model and project success. But for our purposes here the key point is that these rural water projects are working, not *why* they are working.

Discussion of Costs

Not only does it appear that the demand-driven, community management model for planning and implementing rural water supply programs is now contributing to improved delivery of water services in rural Africa, but additional help has come from another, unexpected quarter. Over the past decade increasing numbers of Chinese contractors have become active in many countries in Africa. The majority of their work has been in road and other construction projects, but increasingly they also bid for drilling contracts from national rural water supply agencies. Chinese contractors typically bring Chinese-made drilling rigs and their own drilling teams.

As a result of the increased competition for drilling contracts, often from these Chinese firms, prices of borehole drilling and hand-pump installation have fallen dramatically in Africa. Evidence shows that the price per borehole has dropped 50% in countries where small to medium-sized drilling contracts are regularly awarded – from about US$12,000 a decade ago to about US$6,000 today. This large drop in the real prices of boreholes, coupled with the success of new planning and implementation procedures, has changed the economic landscape of rural water programs in Africa.

There are of course additional costs associated with managing and administrating a national rural water program (UNEP, 1998). Real resource costs should include donor manpower, national agency administration, and community organization and health-promotion activities. We use a capital cost estimate for a borehole plus hand pump of US$6,500 (range US$5,000–8,000). Program overhead that includes these capacity-building and "software" costs for a large national rural water supply program is estimated at US$3,500 (range US$2,000–5,000), for a project total of US$10,000. The costs of stand-alone, "enclave" type donor-directed projects, common in the past, were substantially

[27] Note that this intervention is for water supply only and does not include new facilities for improved sanitation.

more (to the order of US$15,000–20,000 per borehole plus hand pump).

To obtain costs on a household basis per month, we annualize the capital costs of the borehole and hand pump. Assuming a capital recovery (CR) factor of 0.093 (interest rate = 4.5%, life of the capital = 15 years; see Table 7.16), the annual capital costs of this intervention come to about US$930 (the formula for the capital recovery factor is shown in Table 7.15 and in footnote 6). To obtain total annual costs, we add an estimate of the operation and maintenance costs. Recurrent expenditures of spare parts and minor repairs are assumed to be to the order of about US$100 per year (range $50–150), but this does not represent the full resource cost of running this water system. In the demand-driven, community management planning model, village water committees have assumed responsibility for management and oversight, and this entails the time and human capital of village leaders. A borehole attendant and/or caretaker is also typically assigned the tasks of keeping the borehole clean, making minor repairs, and collecting money from households which use the hand pump. Many times the borehole attendant and caretaker are unpaid, so assigning an opportunity cost to this labor is difficult. We assume for our calculations that these labor and management costs are about US$500 per year (range US$200–800), for a total annual cost of US$1,530, or about US$128 per month.

To determine the cost per household, we need to make an assumption about how many households will share the improved water source. Water sources such as this are typically designed for 250–500 people. In our experience, 500 people per borehole will lead to considerable crowding and longer queue times. We thus assume that 60 households (range 30–90) will share the borehole, given an average household size of 5 people (range 4–6). In the base case, 300 people share one borehole, and the monthly cost per household comes to about US$2.13. In the Monte Carlo simulations, we treat all of these costs and design parameters as unknowns and allow them to vary over the specified parameter ranges, shown in Table 7.16.[27]

Economic Benefits from the Installation of the Borehole and Public Hand Pump

We use the same framework for analysis of the borehole and hand-pump intervention as we did for the network water and sewer services in Part II. In the base case analysis, we again assume that the new hand pump provides a closer, more convenient source of water for households in the village. Having a hand pump in the village thus allows each household to spend less time collecting the same quantity of water from the improved source than from the original, traditional sources, and these households also increase their water consumption.

Specifically, as with the network intervention, we assume that before the installation of the new water project the average household was collecting water from traditional sources and using 13 liters per capita per day (or about 2 cubic meters per household per month), and spending about 1 hour to collect 20 liters (or 3.25 hours per day). Suppose that following installation of the new hand pump and borehole, collecting 20 liters takes only 20 minutes (or about 1 hour for 65 liters). The monthly time savings for collection of 2 cubic meters of water would be about 70 hours. We again assume that the local wage for unskilled labor in this rural community is $1.25 per day (range $0.5–2/day) and that the value of the time savings from the new water system is 30% of this market wage (range 0.1–0.5). In the base case, the monetary value of the 70 hours of monthly time savings from the water supply intervention would thus be US$3.28 per household per month. In our Monte Carlo calculations we further vary the extent of time savings (the range of collection time from traditional source is 0.1–1.9 hours/20L water, and of collection time from the improved source is 0.1–0.5 hours/20 liters of water). Our model therefore allows for the possibility of net time costs from using the improved water source, if the time spent by households collecting water from the borehole and hand pump exceeds the time spent collecting water from the original water source.

The aesthetic/lifestyle benefits from this water supply intervention are calculated in similar fashion to those found in Part II. These aesthetic and lifestyle benefits are assumed to be 25% of the value of the time savings described above (range 0–50%), of which 25% are assumed to be health benefits (range 0–50%); they are then about US$0.54 per household per month.

Finally, the third component of the benefits is the economic value of the improved health of household members. The reduction in diarrheal disease from the installation of a deep borehole and hand pump results from a combination of two causal relationships. The first is that moving a water source closer to the house will usually increase the quantities of water used by households. This increased water use enables better personal hygiene (e.g., handwashing and bathing). Based on a meta-analysis of 17 studies, Curtis and Caincross (2003) conclude that regular handwashing with soap reduces diarrhea incidence by 42–47%. Obviously handwashing with soap requires sufficient supplies of water.

The second cause of improved health is the use of source water of improved quality. In a study from the Philippines, VanDerslice and Briscoe (1993) found that source contamination poses a much more serious health risk than in-house contamination, in part because family members develop immunity to pathogens routinely encountered in the household environment. They conclude that contaminated water sources pose a serious risk of diarrhea while contamination of drinking water in the home usually does not. Nevertheless, we consider the magnitude of the causal relationship between the quality of water at the source and diarrhea risk to be uncertain and believe that it may be quite low in some instances. In a cross-section multicountry study, Esrey (1996) finds little association between intermediate water service (such as our proposed deep borehole and hand pump) and diarrhea incidence. Similarly, Kremer et al. (2007) find a reduction in diarrhea incidence of only 5% from spring improvements.[28] However, a recent meta-analysis by

[28] However, spring improvements will typically not provide the same water-quality improvement as deep boreholes and hand pumps because shallow groundwater is more easily contaminated by animal wastes and surface

Table 7.17. Base case results for borehole and public hand pump[a]

	Before hand pump + borehole intervention	After hand pump + borehole intervention	Change in physical units	Change in monetary units by discount rate		
Benefits				3%	4.5%	6%
Time spent collecting initial quantity of water (hrs per hh-month) [Value of time savings]	100	30	70	$3.28	$3.28	$3.28
Water use (L per hh-month) [Value of aesthetic and lifestyle benefits from increased water use]	2,000	3,750	1,750	$0.54	$0.54	$0.54
Number of non-fatal cases of diarrhea (per hh-month) [Value of reduction in morbidity]	0.38	0.28	(0.10)	$0.56	$0.56	$0.56
Risk of death from all diarrhea (per 1,000 hh-month) [Value of reduction in mortality]	0.30	0.23	(0.07)	$2.25	$2.25	$2.25
Total benefits				$6.63	$6.63	$6.63
Costs						
Expenditures by all parties for new water system (per hh-month)				$(2.00)	$(2.13)	$(2.26)
Benefit–cost ratio				3.3	3.1	2.9
Net benefits				$4.64	$4.51	$4.37

[a] For the results reported in this table, all parameters were set at their *base case* values as described in [TC]Table 7.16, except for the discount rate, which was varied between 3%, 4.5%, and 6%. The values in the cells in the three rightmost columns report the monetary value of the components of benefits and total costs on a per-household, per-month basis.

Fewtrell *et al.* (2005) mentioned in Part I reports a reduction of about 25% from baseline disease incidence due to water source interventions, similar to results for diarrheal disease discussed in Esrey *et al.* (1991). We therefore assume a wide range in possible diarrhea reduction due to the borehole intervention (10–40%). This reduction reflects the combined effect of both of these two (uncertain) causal relationships (increased quantity and improved water quality). For other parameters, we use the same ranges as before: diarrheal incidence (0.9 cases per person-year; range 0.5–1.4), case fatality rate

Footnote 28 (*cont.*)
runoff, and because the filling of containers at improved springs is often subject to more contamination than when vessels are filled from hand pumps. Also, improved springs do not offer the same reduction in time collection costs and the resulting increases in water use that can be used for personal hygiene as installing a deep borehole and hand pump within a village.

(0.08%; range 0.04–0.12%), VSL (US$30,000; range $10,000–50,000), and COI for a case of diarrhea (US$6; range US$2–10). As with the network water and sanitation services, the two largest components of the benefits from the borehole and public hand-pump intervention would be time savings and mortality-reduction benefits, with aesthetic and morbidity benefits being considerably lower.

Comparison of Costs and Benefits (Deep Borehole with Public Hand Pump)

We are now in a position to compare the costs of the borehole and hand-pump intervention with the estimated economic benefits, again using US$ per household per month as our unit of analysis. As shown in Table 7.17, the positive results from the new water system are the increases in household water use (US$0.54), time savings on the initial quantity of water used (US$3.28), the reduction in risk of death (US$2.25), and the

Table 7.18. Typology of sites for deep borehole with public handpump: categorized by benefit–cost ratio (BCR)

Prameter[a]	Unattractive sites (BCR < 1)		Attractive sites (BCR 1–2.99)		Very attractive sites (BCR > 3–4.99)		Extremely attractive sites (BCR > 5)	
# Households	55	(18)	57	(17)	64	(16)	72	(13)
Collection time: traditional (hrs/20L)	0.52	(0.46)	1.00	(0.49)	1.20	(0.43)	1.30	(0.39)
Value of time savings/market wage for unskilled labor (%)	27	(12)	28	(11)	32	(11)	36	(10)
Unskilled market wage ($/day)	1.08	(0.44)	1.17	(0.42)	1.40	(0.38)	1.58	(0.32)
Reduction in diarrhea (%)	22	(8)	25	(9)	26	(9)	28	(8)
Diarrheal incidence (cases/person-yr)	0.85	(0.28)	0.91	(0.29)	0.91	(0.29)	0.93	(0.29)
Value of a statistical life ($)	24,420	(11,448)	28,069	(11,254)	33,666	(10,194)	38,442	(8,711)
Annual management cost ($)	537	(166)	509	(173)	480	(173)	447	(164)
People per household	4.9	(0.6)	4.9	(0.6)	5.1	(0.6)	5.2	(0.6)
Collection time: improved (hrs/20L)	0.31	(0.12)	0.29	(0.12)	0.30	(0.11)	0.31	(0.11)
Case fatality rate (%)	0.08	(0.02)	0.08	(0.02)	0.08	(0.02)	0.08	(0.02)
Water project duration (yrs)	14.6	(3.1)	14.7	(3.2)	15.3	(3.2)	15.7	(3.0)
Capital cost ($)	6,625	(873)	6,589	(862)	6,348	(845)	6,172	(806)
Program cost ($)	3,631	(870)	3,585	(866)	3,381	(843)	3,189	(808)
Percent of simulations (%)	15.6		49.4		24.1		11.0	
BCR for "mean" of subgroup[b]	0.6		1.9		3.8		6.8	

[a] Mean parameter values in first row, standard deviations in parentheses.
[b] The BCR corresponding to the case with the "mean" parameter values reported in each column, and other parameters set to base levels; it is thus possible (as in column 2) for the "mean" result to thus fall outside the range of individual results.

savings in avoided cost of illness due to diarrhea (US$0.56), for a total benefit of US$6.63 per household per month. Total estimated costs of the water system are US$2.13 per household per month, which implies a BCR of about 3.1.

Applying the assumptions used here, it is easy to see that there will be situations in which this rural water supply intervention could be an extremely attractive economic investment (Table 7.18). The benefits of rural water supply projects will be highest in locations where diarrhea is high, where health-care facilities are poor (and thus CFRs from diarrhea are high), and where people are walking long distances for water from traditional sources. But such locations are also likely to have high capital costs, low values of time savings, and low VSLs. The economic value of this intervention is not particularly sensitive to changes in the discount rate in the 3–6% range.

Figure 7.7 presents the distribution of benefit–cost ratios from our Monte Carlo simulation and illustrates that there are also many combinations of realistic parameter values that result in BCRs less than 1. We also show in Figure 7.7 how this distribution changes when the parameter values shown in Table 7.1 are distributed normally (rather than uniformly) over the given ranges. Figure 7.8 shows that the BCRs are most sensitive to variations in (1) number of households using the new borehole, (2) the collection time from the traditional source, and (3) assumptions about the value of time spent collecting water. It follows that this intervention is most likely to be successful from an economic perspective in communities where:

1 Density is relatively high and many households utilize the new borehole.
2 Traditional water sources are distant and thus time savings are substantial, or labor market conditions create a high economic value for the time savings.

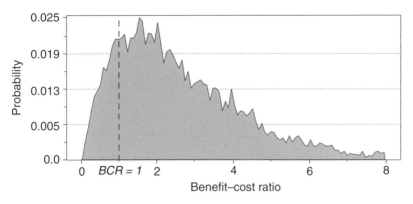

Figure 7.6 *Borehole with public hand pump: distribution of BCR outcomes from Monte Carlo simulation (10,000 draws) with uniform parameter distributions*

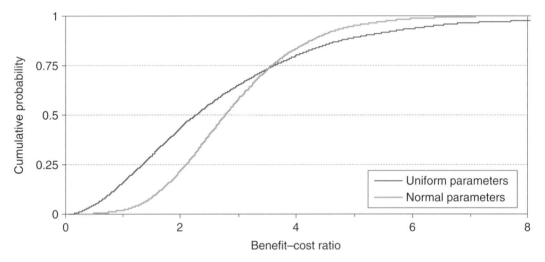

Figure 7.7 *Comparison of cumulative distribution of BCR outcomes for borehole and public hand pump given assumptions about parameter distributions (uniform or normal)*

Conversely, where these conditions fail to hold – for example, where density is low and few households utilize the new borehole, or where traditional water sources are close by and the value of time saved is low – the intervention is least likely to be successful.

[29] Limited uptake and use of improved water sources is the type of behavioral response by intended beneficiaries that has typically led to problems with supply-side interventions implemented by the international donor community in the water supply sector. The shift to demand-driven planning of water and sanitation interventions seeks to avoid low-priority projects from being selected.

In effect, these are the types of situations for which the valuation approach we use poses the most difficulties. Wherever some proportion of intended beneficiary households are able to and would continue to use alternative sources in preference to the "improved" one, economists would expect that behavioral responses to the project would be complicated. Households might choose to continue to use lesser-quality sources of water if they are more convenient or if there are other ways of coping with low-quality water (such as investment in in-house treatment technologies or other approaches).[29]

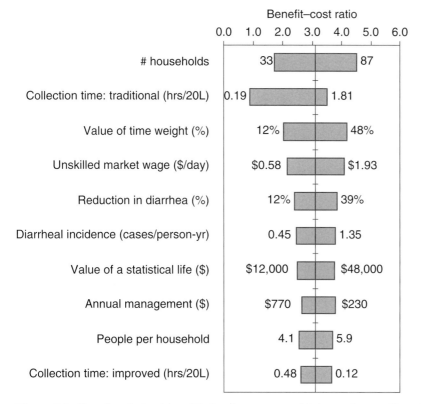

Benefit–cost ratio

Figure 7.8 *Deep borehole with public hand pump – sensitivity analyses: effect of selected parameters on BCR (90% confidence intervals, holding other parameters at base case values)*

Alternatively, households might use a variety of water sources for different purposes or depending on the performance of these alternatives as they change with time. In situations where numerous water supply alternatives exist, the criteria by which boreholes equipped with hand pumps are evaluated must be much more sophisticated than our simple model suggests.

Alternate Water and Sanitation Intervention 2 – Community-led Total Sanitation Campaigns to Achieve Open Defecation-Free Communities in South Asia

Description of the Intervention

The traditional approach to the sanitation challenge in developing countries has been to subsidize the construction of on-site latrines and also, when large subsidies from donors are available, sewerage systems and wastewater treatment plants. Yet the economic and health benefits from improved sanitation require not only improved technologies for excreta disposal but also important behavioral changes on the part of households. There are numerous innovative, low-cost technologies available for excreta disposal, virtually all of which can in theory be used hygienically. Feachem *et al.* (1983) note: "The greatest determinants of the efficacy of alternative facilities are, first, whether they are used by everyone all the time, and second, whether they are adequately maintained."[30]

Any effective sanitation solution must ensure that the needed behavioral changes occur.

---

[30] In Jamison *et al.* (2006), quoting a 1980s' World Bank Technologies Advisory Group on low-cost sanitation.

Surprisingly, a significant number of new, subsidized latrines are never actually used. In a recent assessment of newly provided household toilets in India, reported use rates ranged from 30% to 50%.[31] Simply providing access to improved sanitation facilities does not achieve the desired economic benefits. This type of disconnect can confound cost–benefit analyses where behavioral change is assumed but does not occur, such that returns are thus overestimated.

A community-led total sanitation (CLTS) approach has recently been developed in South Asia that focuses on mobilizing communities to achieve "total sanitation," that is, open-defecation-free environments. The CLTS approach was piloted in Bangladesh in 2001; it has been claimed that within five years more than 70 million people had achieved improved sanitation through CLTS programs (Sannan and Moulik, 2007), at a cost estimated to be roughly half that of comparable interventions (Allan, 2003).[32] CLTS is now being adapted and implemented at varying scales on India, Pakistan, Nepal, Cambodia, and Indonesia. Efforts to scale up this approach have met with varied success (Water and Sanitation Program, 2005; Pattanayak et al., 2007b).

The basic thrust of the CLTS model is to mobilize communities to change their behavior. Programs are designed to raise awareness of disease-transmission routes, health costs, and the social benefits of sanitation, emphasizing the communal costs of open defecation that are incurred if even a small number of people fail to comply. These interventions explicitly seek to change attitudes about the social acceptability of open defecation and the advantages of convenience, privacy, and dignity associated with

proper toilet usage. Banning open defecation becomes the goal, with the building of latrines treated as a means to that end. To trigger social and behavioral change, a variety of approaches has been used effectively, such as conducting "walks of shame" to open-defecation areas in the company of facilitators from local government or non-government organizations, or establishing children's brigades to promote and monitor the ban.

Once motivated, the community is provided with a menu of low-cost options and sometimes financial incentives to construct and maintain latrines appropriate to their circumstances and preferences. The approach is flexible and pragmatic with regard to technology choice. It emphasizes the construction of latrines from locally available, low-cost materials that meet very basic standards of safety – essentially they must be odor- and insect-free, and feces must not be visible. The "demand-driven" nature of the technological choice in this intervention is similar to that in intervention 1 (community-managed rural water supply), and turns out to be an important determinant of its cost-effectiveness.

CLTS programs have been implemented with a variety of cost-sharing arrangements and incentives. In some cases governments and/ or NGOs support awareness building, motivation, and training, while households pay all the costs of latrine construction. In other programs financial incentives are provided, such as direct household subsidies (sometimes targeted to families below the poverty line) or community-focused village-level awards conveyed once open-defecation-free status has been certified.

A key challenge for interventions that seek to change personal and community behavior is to adapt and implement context-appropriate mechanisms and incentives. This leads to a range of specialized implementation modalities that complicates the task of describing "typical" programs and results. It also leads to a broad range of observed results in terms of uptake (the percentage of households that actually build a latrine as a consequence of the program) and usage (the actual usage rate of latrines once they are built) that together have

---

[31] Usage rates of newly built toilets were estimated for programs in Andhra Pradesh (50%), Maharashtra (47%), and Himachal Pradesh (less than 30%). Use rates were reported to be higher in non-subsidized schemes where individuals were convinced to build toilets rather than being provided with them. See Sannan and Moulik (2007).

[32] Comparison is made between average costs of per family of CLTS programs in Bangladesh, relative to UNICEF estimates of average costs for pit latrines in Asia over the period 1990–2000.

a significant bearing on the benefits and costs of these interventions. Although CLTS programs are designed with the explicit goal of achieving 100% open-defecation-free villages, the best available evidence suggests that uptake rates are *on average* closer to 40%, and toilet usage rates (among "uptaking" households that have already built latrines) tend to be around 70%.[33] Highly successful interventions appear to have resulted in 100% open-defecation-free villages, but this has not been a typical result in scaling up CLTS interventions. Rather than focusing on best-case scenarios, the calculations below seek to reflect the range of plausible results that could be expected from large CLTS programs covering hundreds of villages.

Table 7.19 summarizes the equations used in the calculation of benefits and costs of our model CLTS intervention; Table 7.20 presents the assumed parameter values.

Discussion of Costs Associated with Community-Led Total Sanitation Programs

In this analysis we assume a CLTS program that includes low-cost latrine building and community mobilization. Costs are categorized as (1) costs of latrine construction, (2) the value of household time associated with participation in the CLTS, and (3) program-level costs to government and/or NGOs.

Latrine costs vary widely depending on the type of latrine chosen, the materials used, and whether outside labor must be hired. Typical CLTS programs have no or few subsidies for latrine building and instead promote low-cost toilet options. We do not specify whether a subsidy is made available for latrine building here, but instead use total capital costs for latrines whether paid for by households and/or governments. The Water and Sanitation Program (2005) found an average cost of US$4 for latrines built in total sanitation programs in Bangladesh, and US$12.80 in India (with a 68% subsidy). We assume a base cost of US$8 with a range of US$4–12 (Table 7.20). The annualized cost of the investment is calculated assuming a six-year infrastructure life and a 4.5% discount rate (for a capital cost recovery factor of 0.19),

Table 7.19. Equations for cost–benefit analysis of community-led total sanitation (CLTS) project

Benefits	
Time savings per hh-month (hours)	$T_{s,m} = 30 * T_s * Q * A * U * \mu / 60$
Value of time savings per hh-month ($)	$V_{ts} = T_{s,m} * (w / 8) * v_t$
Avoided morbidity per hh-month ($)	$m = (I / 12) * E * S * COI * U * \mu$
Avoided mortality per hh-month ($)	$M = (I / 12) * E * S * CFR * VSL * U * \mu$
Costs	
Capital recovery factor	$CR = r * (1 + r)^d / ((1 + r)^d - 1)$
Capital per hh-month ($)	$C_{c,m} = C_l * U * CR / 12$
Time costs per hh-month ($)	$C_{t,m} = v_t * [C_o * (w) * CR + C_t * (w / 8) * U] / 12$
Program costs per hh-month ($)	$C_{p,m} = [(C_{c,m} + C_{t,m}) / (1 - C_p)] - C_{c,m} - C_{t,m}$

and then adjusted to arrive at a monthly cost. To calculate the total monthly investment cost to an average household, we must also recognize that not all households will actually build a latrine as a consequence of the program. Assuming an average uptake rate of 40% (with a range of 20–60%), the cost of latrine construction per household per month is US$0.05.

Household time costs will include an upfront component, that is, the time spent in motivation and training meetings, as well as an ongoing time component to clean and maintain the latrine during its usable life. An upfront time commitment of ten days was assumed per participating ("uptaking") household – those who built toilets and attended education, training, and follow-up meetings. An up-front time commitment of three days was assumed for the remaining households which would have been exposed to the campaign but in the end chose not to participate fully. As in intervention 1, it was assumed that the local

[33] Pattanayak *et al.* (2007b). It should be noted that these findings were described by the authors as lower bounds due to the length of the survey period. At the time of the survey many respondents claimed that they had begun, or intended to begin shortly, the construction of in-house latrines.

Table 7.20. Parameters used in cost–benefit analysis of CLTS project[a]

Symbol	Parameter	Base case	Lower limit	Upper limit	Correlated parameters
C_l	Capital cost of one latrine ($)	$8	$4	$12	Incidence (0.5) Market wage (–0.5)
C_p	Program costs per household, upfront and ongoing (% of total costs/hh)	75	65	85	Incidence (0.5) Market wage (–0.5) Life of project (0.7)
C_t	Time expenses for initial training and construction (days/hh)	10	5	15	
C_o	Time expenses for ongoing training and maintenance (hrs/hh-yr)	10	5	15	
d	Life of project (yrs)	6	3	9	Latrine cost (0.5) Household size (–0.5)
r	Real, net of inflation, discount rate (%)	4.5%	3%	6%	
S	Household size	5	4	6	
A	Number of adults in household	2	1	3	Household size (0.7)
T_s	Round trip time spent traveling to site of open defecation – status quo (min)	15	10	20	Uptake (0.5) Usage (0.7)
Q	Round trips to defecation site per person per day	1	0.75	1.25	
U	Uptake of latrines (% of households)	40%	20%	60%	Reduction in diarrhea (0.5) Program costs (0.5)
μ	Usage of latrines by adults (%)	70%	50%	90%	Capital cost (0.5) Program costs (0.5) Ongoing time expenses (0.5)
w	Market wage for unskilled labor ($/day)	$1.25	$0.50	$2.00	
v_t	Value of time savings/market wage for unskilled labor	30%	10%	50%	
I	Diarrheal incidence (cases/pc-yr)[b]	0.9	0.5	1.4	
E	% Reduction of diarrhea due to CLTS intervention	30%	10%	50%	
COI	Cost of illness ($/case)	$6	$2	$10	Market wage (0.5)
CFR	Diarrhea case fatality rate (%)[b]	0.08%	0.04%	0.12%	Capital cost (0.5)
VSL	Value of a statistical life ($)	$30,000	$10,000	$50,000	Market wage (0.7)

[a] Our uncertainty analysis does not purport to use the real probability distributions associated with these parameters but instead is aimed at assessing the range of possible situations in poor developing countries; therefore we use uniform distributions of parameters.
[b] Revised Global Burden of Disease (GBD) Estimates (WHO, 2002). Available at www.who.int/healthinfo/bodgbd2002revised/en/index.html. Diarrhea incidence in developing country subregions ranges 0.6–1.29 case per capita per yr (mean ~0.9) but may actually be higher or lower in some locations; CFR ranges 0.02–0.09.

wage for unskilled labor is US$1.25 per day (US$0.15 per hour), and 30% of that amount was used as the monetary value of household time in the program. These up-front costs were spread over the duration of the project using the 0.19 capital recovery factor. For households that did build a latrine (40%), it was assumed that members spent an additional ten hours maintaining the latrine each year. The cost to an average household in terms of the value of time spent in the CLTS program was thus US$0.05 per household per month.

Program-level "software" costs were found to range roughly from 40% to 80% of total program costs (software plus latrine costs and household contributions) in CLTS-style interventions (Water and Sanitation Program, 2005). These overhead costs for CLTS are difficult to measure and likely to be underestimated as a consequence of undervaluing volunteer and NGO input, time from higher-level government officials in guidance and conceptualization of programs, or the use of temporarily diverted local staff to assist in intensive campaigns. Here we assume software costs are 75% of total program costs, with a range of 65–85%. Following these assumptions, the program cost per household per month is US$0.31.

Economic Benefits of Community-Led Total Sanitation Programs

The benefits of improved sanitation include health benefits and time savings associated with the convenience of an in-home latrine. Other important social benefits cited by participants in CLTS programs (but not incorporated in this analysis) include privacy, dignity, and security, particularly for women, who are often vulnerable when using secluded public areas. Aesthetic benefits might also be expected from limiting open-defecation practices within a village, but at the same time there may be aesthetic losses involved in having a latrine in the home, and in using an enclosed latrine. The value of changes in aesthetics is not addressed in this intervention.

The complexities associated with estimating the health benefits of water and sanitation investments were presented in the discussion of the conventional network water and sanitation investments and rural water supply interventions. Here we use comparable assumptions. We assume a 30% reduction in diarrhea incidence (with a 10–50% range) as the potential impact of the intervention, from a baseline of 7.5 cases per household per year to about 5 cases per household per year. Taking into account a 40% uptake rate and 70% usage rate (with a range of

50–90%) for latrines, we estimate that the benefit to the *average* household will be about an 8% ($0.3 \times 0.4 \times 0.7 = 0.084$) reduction in diarrhea incidence. For non-fatal diarrhea an average cost of US$6 per episode is again assumed, which would amount to a cost saving of US$0.19 per household per month. Assuming a case fatality rate of 8/10,000 and a VSL of US$30,000, the value of the averted mortality risk is US$0.78 per household per month.

Time savings for in-home sanitation were calculated by assuming that individuals otherwise walk a 15-minute round-trip (range 10–20) from their homes for this purpose each day (and make on average one such trip per day; range 0.75–1.25). Generally, the spaces used for open defecation are at the edge of villages, often near fields or railway lines. The monthly time savings for two adults with in-home sanitation would therefore be 15 hours per household per month. Given that on average only 40% of households will build latrines, and that of those which do only 70% on average will actually use them, we assumed 28% of the potential time savings as a benefit. Assuming again a local wage of US$1.25 per day and valuing the time savings at 30% of the market wage, the monetary value of the total expected time savings would be US$0.20 per household per month.

Comparison of Costs and Benefits of Community-Led Total Sanitation Programs

The costs and benefits of the total sanitation intervention are presented in Table 7.21, calculated in terms of US$ per household per month. The benefits of the program include averted mortality risks and reduced incidence of non-fatal diarrhea (US$0.95) as well as time savings associated with in-home latrines (US$0.20), for a total benefit of US$1.14 per household per month. Costs associated with the program include the capital costs of latrine construction (US$0.05), the value of household time participating in the program (US$0.05), and program-level "software" costs (US$0.31), for a total of US$0.41 per household per month. This implies a simple BCR of 2.8, suggesting that under circumstances similar to those assumed here,

Table 7.21. Base case results for CLTS program[a]

	Without CLTS intervention	With CLTS intervention[b]	Change in physical units[b]	Change in monetary units by discount rate[c]		
Benefits				3%	4.5%	6%
Time spent by adults walking to defecation site (hrs per hh-month) [Value of time savings]	15	0	15	$0.20	$0.20	$0.20
Number of non-fatal cases of diarrhea (per hh-month) [Value of reduction in morbidity]	0.38	0.26	(0.11)	$0.19	$0.19	$0.19
Risk of death from all diarrhea (per 1,000 hh-month) [Value of reduction in mortality]	0.30	0.21	(0.09)	$0.76	$0.76	$0.76
All benefits				$1.14	$1.14	$1.14
Costs						
Construction costs for latrines (per hh-month)				($0.05)	($0.05)	($0.05)
Time costs for households for CLTS (per hh-month)				($0.05)	($0.05)	($0.05)
Program-level costs for CLTS (per hh-month)				($0.29)	($0.31)	($0.32)
All costs				($0.39)	($0.41)	($0.43)
Benefit–cost ratio				3.0	2.8	2.7
Net benefits				$0.77	$0.73	$0.74

[a] For the results reported in this table, all parameters were set at their base case values as described in [TC]Table 7.20, except for the discount rate, which was varied between 3%, 4.5%, and 6%. The values in the cells in the three rightmost columns report the monetary value of the components of benefits and total costs on a per-household, per-month basis.
[b] Among participating households (i.e., households that build new latrines).
[c] For all households.

CLTS programs will very often be economically sound interventions.

A Monte Carlo simulation for this intervention (Figure 7.9) provides a distribution of BCRs resulting from 10,000 random draws on the parameters listed in Table 7.20, with a range of roughly 0–8. Figure 7.10 shows that for most combinations of parameter values CLTS interventions return favorable BCRs. Table 7.22 presents the average parameter values associated with four groups of outcomes from the Monte Carlo simulations. The mean parameter values in all categories are plausible, particularly in South Asia, although they are less typical in both the unattractive and extremely attractive categories.

A sensitivity analysis is presented to illustrate the influence of key parameters on the BCRs for this intervention (Table 7.10). Results are most sensitive to percentage reductions in diarrhea incidence, the value of a statistical life, absolute levels of diarrhea incidence, and rates of latrine uptake. As in the case of rural water supply (intervention 1), these investments will therefore be most beneficial where incidence of diarrhea and the value of a statistical life are both high. In contrast, the results for the CLTS are highly sensitive to the magnitude of the assumed reduction in diarrhea incidence. Unfortunately there is little robust evidence in the peer-reviewed literature on the correlation between sanitation-only investments and diarrheal disease reductions. Our assumptions are based on the best available evidence (Fewtrell et al., 2005), but other studies suggest that as villages approach open-defecation-free status the magnitude of disease

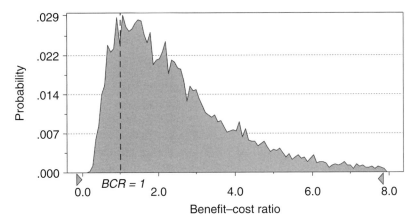

Figure 7.9 *Community-led total sanitation program: distribution of BCR outcomes from Monte Carlo simulation (10,000 draws) with uniform parameter distributions*

Table 7.22. Typology of community-led total sanitation program – sites categorized by benefit–cost ratio (BCR)[a]

Parameter	Unattractive sites (BCR < 1)		Attractive sites (BCR 1–2.99)		Very attractive sites (BCR 3–4.99)		Extremely attractive sites (BCR > 5)	
Reduction in diarrhea (%)	18	(7)	28	(10)	37	(9)	42	(7)
Diarrheal incidence (cases/person-yr)	0.72	(0.27)	0.87	(0.28)	1.01	(0.25)	1.13	(0.20)
Value of a statistical life ($)	28,290	(12,142)	29,304	(11,755)	30,651	(10,701)	34,171	(9,241)
CLTS project duration (yrs)	5.7	(2.1)	5.9	(2.0)	6.1	(1.9)	6.3	(1.8)
Uptake of latrines (% of hhs)	30	(9)	39	(11)	46	(10)	49	(8)
Program costs per household (% of total)	73	(6)	75	(6)	76	(5)	77	(5)
Case fatality rate (%)	0.07	(0.02)	0.08	(0.02)	0.09	(0.02)	0.10	(0.02)
Usage of latrines by adults (%)	62	(10)	69	(11)	75	(10)	77	(10)
People per household	4.9	(0.6)	5.0	(0.6)	5.1	(0.6)	5.1	(0.5)
Cost of illness ($/case)	5.7	(2.3)	6.0	(2.3)	6.2	(2.3)	6.7	(2.1)
Percent of simulations (%)	15.0		55.3		20.5		9.2	
BCR for "mean" of subgroup[b]	1.0		2.4		4.4		7.5	

[a] Mean parameter values in first row, standard deviations in parentheses.
[b] The benefit–cost ratio corresponding to the case with the "mean" parameter values reported in each column, and other parameters set to base levels.

reduction may rise sharply.[34] This relates to another key parameter in the sensitivity analysis: the level of uptake (percentage of households choosing to build latrines). Together this suggests that total sanitation interventions will be particularly attractive where uptake (behavior change) is highest, demonstrating the importance of the behavioral uncertainty that is embedded in benefit–cost analysis.

The success of CLTS programs depends heavily on tailoring project designs to specific

[34] Evidence from South Asia (Sannan and Moulik, 2007) suggests that significantly greater reductions in diarrhea incidence can be achieved in villages where all excreta is hygienically confined, because bacteriological contamination and disease transmission continue to be significant even when only a small percentage of the community practices open defecation.

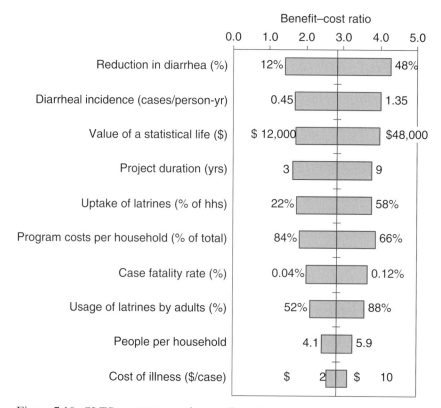

Figure 7.10 *CLTS sensitivity analyses: effect of selected parameters on BCR (90% confidence intervals, holding other parameters at base case values)*

social settings, recruiting and retaining effective "health motivators," and targeting communities that are open to change. This seems to have been the experience in scaling up CLTS-style interventions. Sharply tailored early pilot programs appear to have returned outstanding results. Yet as these programs were scaled up they did not achieve the same level of uptake and hence impact. Nonetheless, even at scale, many CLTS interventions will be economically beneficial. Where behavior can be radically changed, these interventions may be very economically attractive.

Alternate Water and Sanitation Intervention 3 – Biosand Filters for Point-of-Use Household Water Treatment

Description of the Intervention

Biosand filters are one of several possible technologies that households can use in-home to remove a wide variety of contaminants, including bacteria and viruses, from their drinking and cooking water. Other POU technologies include boiling, solar disinfection, chlorination, ceramic filters, and other types of filtration. POU technologies have gained support as a result of research highlighting the role of drinking-water contamination during collection, transport, and storage. POU technologies greatly reduce the first two of those problems (Clasen and Bastable, 2003) and compare favorably with other water and sanitation interventions in field trials (Fewtrell *et al.*, 2005; Clasen *et al.*, 2006; Stauber, 2007).

We selected the biosand filter for illustrative purposes; we do not argue that it is the "best" of the available POU technologies in every circumstance. Nonetheless, we do believe the biosand filter holds important advantages over other POU technologies. Globally, boiling is the most prevalent and accepted means of treating water in the household. Although boiling is highly effective at removing pathogens if done for a sufficient length of time (15–20 minutes), it is today infrequently promoted, because it is expensive in terms of fuel use, often inconvenient and unpleasant for household members, prone to recontamination, and in many places environmentally harmful in terms of indoor air pollution and as a contributor to deforestation. For chlorination, it has proven difficult to maintain high usage and/or compliance rates among households despite the very low cost of chlorine (Arnold and Colford, 2007). Solar disinfection and chlorination are also vulnerable to convenience and taste problems.

However, the biosand filter has been demonstrated in the field to be safe and effective under a wide variety of conditions, and close to 100,000 biosand filters are now being used by households in numerous developing countries (Kaiser *et al.*, 2002; Earwaker, 2006; Stauber, 2007). The biosand filter uses commonly available materials, is inexpensive to install, and is convenient and simple to use. Essentially all that is required is a concrete or plastic chamber, and sand, gravel, and a small section of PVC pipe (CAWST, 2007; Samaritan's Purse, 2007). Household members pour water into the top of the filter and allow time for the water to seep through the sand. Depending on the specific design of the device, biosand filters can typically provide a maximum of 30–60 liters per hour. Pathogens are removed by physical filtration and a biologically active slime layer (*Schmutzdecke*) that forms at the top of the sand column; suspended and some dissolved solids are removed by physical processes in the filter. Clean water is collected via an outlet tube at the top of the filter. The design of the filter thus ensures that there will always be water above the top of the sand bed, so that microbial activity in the *Schmutzdecke* is maintained. A biosand filter can easily provide hundreds of liters of clean water each day, more than enough for a household of typical size (about five members). The biosand filter can be installed inside or outside a house depending on site-specific conditions and household preferences.

Neither the biosand filter nor other household

POU technologies resolve the difficulties associated with getting adequate quantities of water to dwellings prior to treatment. They are thus only a partial solution to households' larger problem of securing safe, clean water for use at home. POU technologies could prove beneficial, however, in two very different situations. First, in rural areas, POU technologies such as the biosand filter could be used to improve the purity of water from traditional sources that household members carry back to their homes. It would also be possible to couple a POU technology with the rural water supply described above as intervention 1 (deep boreholes and hand pumps) in order to provide added assurance of clean drinking and cooking water. In these cases, the POU device helps solve the problem of both contaminated source water and contamination of water while in transit from the source to the household. In rural and in more urbanized areas, POU technologies could be used by households that depend on water from an unreliable, low-quality piped system (either from public taps or their own private connection).

There are three primary disadvantages of the biosand filter per se. First, the top of the filter traps silt and must be cleaned periodically. This involves adding water, stirring the top layer of sand, removing it, and then "restarting" the process of *Schmutzdecke* formation at the top of the sand column. While the new layer is forming, the filter is not as effective in removing pathogens.[35] For a period of a few days after cleaning, households need to use an alternative means of purifying their water, such as chlorination or boiling, or they must store previously filtered water over an extended period. The length of time between cleanings depends on the quality of the raw water that is used and local conditions. Typically filter cleaning is required a couple of times a year. In the worst case monthly cleanings may be necessary.

---

[35] Laboratory experiments suggest that immediately following cleaning, the biosand filter removes about 50% of viruses, 80–90% of bacteria, and >99% of parasites (Stauber, 2007).

Table 7.23. Equations for cost–benefit analysis of biosand filter

Benefits	
Avoided morbidity per hh-month ($)	$m = \sum_{t=1}^{d} \dfrac{\{(365 - b \cdot m)/365\} \cdot I \cdot E \cdot S \cdot COI}{12 \cdot (1 + \delta)^{t-1}}$
Avoided mortality per hh-month ($)	$M = \sum_{t=1}^{d} \dfrac{\{(365 - b \cdot m)/365\} \cdot I \cdot E \cdot S \cdot CFR \cdot VSL}{12 \cdot (1 + \delta)^{t-1}}$
Costs	
Capital recovery factor	$CR = r*(1 + r)^d / ((1 + r)^d - 1)$
Capital + program cost per hh-month ($)	$C_{c,m} = (C_c + C_s) * CR / 12$
Household time costs per month ($)	$C_{t,m} = v_t * (w / 8) * [T_t * CR + (T_m / 60) * m] / 12$
Community maintenance program cost per hh-month ($)	$C_{0,m} = 2 * (w/8) * T_o / 12$

Second, the biosand filter is large and takes up space in the house. In urban slums where space is at a premium, households will be reluctant to allocate the space needed for this technology. Third, once installed in a particular location, the biosand filter is very heavy (usually about 150 kg) and hard to move.[36] The biosand filter is thus most appropriate in rural or semi-rural areas, or in low-density urban neighborhoods.

Table 7.23 summarizes the equations used in the calculation of benefits and costs of the biosand filter intervention; Table 7.24 presents the assumed parameter values.

Discussion of Costs Associated with Programs for the Distribution of Biosand Filters

The biosand filter technology itself is extremely simple and easily scalable for use in different locations; essentially it simply requires a large container and sand. Manufacturing costs of a concrete biosand filter may be as low as US$20. However, a concrete container and sand are both heavy and bulky, and thus expensive to transport. Possible solutions to this problem include using plastic stacking containers instead of concrete ones, or on-site construction of concrete filters. Sand may be available locally, but typically filter-distribution programs prefer to

haul sand with the desirable size and properties to the household to ensure optimal performance of the filter (alternatively households themselves may be required to transport the filter and sand from a distribution point to their home). Solutions to the manufacturing and delivery of the filter and sand will be location-specific depending on transportation and other cost factors; there is no simple optimal solution that will be applicable everywhere.

As with the deep boreholes, with public hand pumps and community-led total sanitation programs, "software" costs for biosand filters can constitute a substantial portion of total resource costs. Typically a program to introduce biosand filters would entail meetings by program staff to explain the biosand filter technology to households in the community and the potential health benefits of its use. Households also need instruction in the procedures used to clean the filters. As with the rural water supply intervention, typically one individual in the community receives additional training in the biosand filter technology in order to provide back-up technical support to households when problems arise with their filters.

For this intervention we use a range of US$60–90 (base case $75) per biosand filter for the manufacturing and software costs, and US$15–35 (base case $25) for transportation and delivery costs of the filter and sand. We estimate the value of the opportunity costs to

---

[36] Moving the filter is also impractical because it causes compacting of the sand, such that reinstallation (emptying the filter and refilling with sand) may be necessary.

Table 7.24. Parameters used in cost–benefit analysis of biosand filter[a]

Symbol	Parameter	Base case	Lower limit	Upper limit	Correlated parameters
Cc	Cost of biosand filter + training + program ($)	75	60	90	Life of filter (0.5)
Cs	Transportation of filters ($)	25	15	35	CFR (0.5) Incidence (0.5) Market wage (−0.5)
Tt	Training time (hrs/hh)	8	4	12	
To	Operator's maintenance time (hr/hh-yr)	2	1	3	
Tm	Maintenance time (minutes/wash)	15	10	20	
m	Number of washes per year	6	2	10	
b	Days before Schmutzdecke regrowth	5	3	7	
r	Discount rate (%)	4.5%	3%	6%	
d	Life of filter (yr)	8	6	10	
n	# Households	60	30	90	
S	Household size	5	4	6	
w	Unskilled market wage ($/day)	1.25	0.50	2.00	
vt	Value of time/market wage for unskilled labor	0.3	0.1	0.5	
I	Diarrheal incidence (cases/pc-yr)[b]	0.9	0.5	1.4	
E	Reduction of diarrhea (%)	0.40	0.20	0.60	Training time (0.5)
δ	Rate of disuse (% of filters per year)	3	1	5	Operator maintenance time (−0.5) Training time (−0.5)
VSL	Value of a statistical life ($)	30000	10000	50000	Market wage (0.7)
CFR	Case fatality rate (%)[b]	0.08	0.04	0.12	
COI	Cost of illness ($/case)	6	2	10	Market wage (0.5)

[a] Our uncertainty analysis does not purport to use the real probability distributions associated with these parameters, but instead is aimed at assessing the range of possible situations in poor developing countries; therefore we use uniform distributions of parameters.
[b] Revised Global Burden of Disease (GBD) Estimates (WHO, 2002). Available at www.who.int/healthinfo/bodgbd2002revised/en/index.html. Diarrhea incidence in developing country sub-regions from 0.6–1.29 case per capita per yr (mean ~0.9), but may actually be higher or lower in some locations; CFR ranges 0.02–0.09.

the household of time spent in training and health-promotion activities (8 hours, range 4–12 hours). Operation and maintenance costs are only the time required by the household for filter cleaning, and an estimated 2 hours of the community manager's time per household per year (range 1–3 hours). We do not assign a cost to other filter-operation activities (e.g., pouring the water into the filter). We assume that the average filter lasts 8 years, with a range of 6–10 years.

Economic Benefits of Biosand Filter Dissemination Programs

Our estimates of the economic benefits of the biosand filter are based solely on the improved health outcomes from the intervention. Unlike the rural water supply and total community sanitation interventions, the biosand filter intervention provides no collection time savings benefits to the household. We calculate the mortality and morbidity consequences of the intervention and assign monetary values in precisely the same manner used for interventions 1 and 2.

Table 7.25. Base case results for biosand filters[a]

	Before biosand filter intervention	After biosand filter intervention	Change in physical units	Change in monetary units by discount rate		
Benefits				3%	4.5%	6%
Number of non-fatal cases of diarrhea (per hh-month) [Value of reduction in morbidity]	0.38	0.29	0.09	$0.75	$0.75	$0.75
Risk of death from all diarrhea (per 1,000 hh-month) [Value of reduction in mortality]	0.30	0.23	0.07	$2.99	$2.99	$2.99
All benefits				$3.73	$3.73	$3.73
Costs						
Capital, training and programs (per hh-month)				($1.19)	($1.26)	($1.34)
Community maintenance program (per hh-month)				($0.05)	($0.05)	($0.05)
Household time costs (per hh-month)				($0.01)	($0.01)	($0.01)
All costs				($1.25)	($1.33)	($1.40)
Benefit–cost ratio				3.0	2.8	2.7
Net benefits				$2.48	$2.41	$2.33

[a] For the results reported in this table, all parameters were set at their *base case* values as described except for the discount rate, which was varied between 3%, 4.5%, and 6%. The values in the cells in the three rightmost columns report the monetary value of the components of benefits and total costs on a per-household, per-month basis.

The key difference in the calculations is in the parameter value assumed for diarrhea reduction from the intervention. For the base case we assume a 40% reduction in diarrhea incidence for the biosand filter intervention (Fewtrell *et al.*, 2005; Clasen *et al.*, 2006), with a range of 20–60%. We assume conservatively that there are no health benefits for the five days required for regrowth of the *Schmutzdecke* (range 3–7 days) and assume an average of 6 cleanings per year (range 2–10).

Finally, as with intervention 2 (CLTS), behavior and usage are important; the rate at which households continue to use the filters determines the benefits obtained. Other POU interventions show that diarrhea reductions are significantly diminished due to noncompliance or breakage (Clasen *et al.*, 2006; Arnold and Colford, 2007; Brown, 2007), but research suggests that biosand usage rates remain relatively high over

[37] Christine Stauber, personal communication.

a number of years (Earwaker, 2006; Samaritan's Purse, 2007). We estimate that usage declines at a constant 3% rate (range 1–5%) each year, based on preliminary findings that 85–90% of filters remain in use after eight years in the field.[37]

Comparing the Costs and Benefits of Biosand Filter Dissemination Programs

As shown in Table 7.25, for our base case total household benefits from the biosand filter are about US$3.73 per month and costs are about US$1.33 per month, for a benefit–cost ratio of 2.9. Figure 7.11 shows that the BCR is most sensitive to the four parameters used to calculate the mortality reduction benefits: (1) the value of a statistical life, (2) percent diarrhea reduction achieved by the biosand filter, (3) the baseline diarrhea incidence, and (4) the case fatality rate from diarrhea. The morbidity-reduction benefits are much smaller, just over 50% of the total costs and 20% of the total benefits.

The distribution of benefit–cost ratios shown

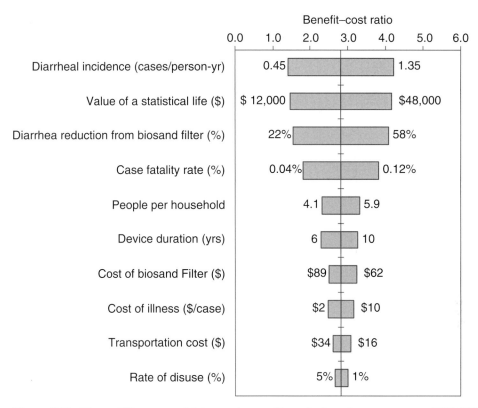

Figure 7.11 *Biosand filters – sensitivity analyses: effect of selected parameters on BCR (90% confidence intervals, holding other parameters at base case values)*

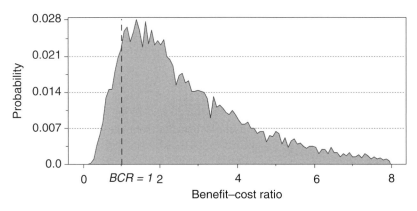

Figure 7.12 *Biosand filters: distribution of BCR outcomes from Monte Carlo simulation (10,000 draws) with uniform parameter distributions*

in Figure 7.12 is quite similar to those for boreholes with hand pumps and the total community-led sanitation campaign. Some combinations of parameter values yield BCRs of < 1, but many more show BCRs greater than 1. Table 7.26 shows that biosand filters will be extremely attractive investments where VSLs, diarrhea incidence, and the case fatality rate are all high.

Table 7.26. Typology of biosand filter project sites categorized by benefit–cost ratio (BCR)[a]

Parameter	Unattractive sites (BCR < 1)		Attractive sites (BCR 1–2.99)		Very attractive sites (BCR 3–4.99)		Extremely attractive sites (BCR > 5)	
Diarrheal incidence (cases/person-yr)	0.67	(0.24)	0.85	(0.28)	1.01	(0.24)	1.14	(0.18)
Value of a statistical life ($)	22,018	(10,052)	28,280	(11,560)	33,390	(10,133)	38,263	(7,960)
Diarrhea reduction from biosand filter (%)	31	(9)	38	(11)	44	(10)	49	(8)
Case fatality rate (%)	0.06	(0.02)	0.08	(0.02)	0.09	(0.02)	0.10	(0.01)
People per household	4.9	(0.6)	5.0	(0.6)	5.1	(0.6)	5.1	(0.6)
Filter duration (yrs)	7.5	(1.4)	7.9	(1.4)	8.2	(1.4)	8.4	(1.3)
Cost of biosand filter, training and program ($/hh)	76.6	(8.5)	75.5	(8.7)	74.5	(8.7)	72.5	(8.5)
Cost of illness ($/case)	4.9	(2.2)	5.9	(2.3)	6.4	(2.2)	6.9	(2.1)
Transportation cost ($/hh)	24.5	(5.8)	24.9	(5.9)	25.3	(5.6)	25.9	(5.3)
Rate of disuse (%/yr)	3.2	(1.1)	3.0	(1.2)	3.0	(1.2)	2.9	(1.1)
Percent of simulations (%)	11.1		53.7		22.6		12.5	
BCR for "mean" of subgroup[b]	0.7		1.9		3.8		6.8	

[a] Mean parameter values in first row, standard deviations in parentheses.
[b] The BCR corresponding to the case with the "mean" parameter values reported in each column, and other parameters set to base levels.

We would speculate, however, that locations with this combination of parameter values may be difficult to find. However, we would expect to find many locations in developing countries with parameter values similar to those shown for BCRs ranging from 1 to 3 ("attractive sites").

Alternate Water and Sanitation Intervention 4 – Large Multipurpose Dams in Africa

Description of the Intervention

In recent years large multipurpose dams have been among the most controversial infrastructure projects in both industrialized and developing countries (World Commission on Dams, 2000). Proponents cite several types of direct economic benefits: hydroelectric power generation, domestic and industrial water supply, drought mitigation, recreation, irrigation, and flood control. They also claim a variety of indirect benefits (e.g., increased employment, better

[38] Improved diplomatic relations and reduced conflict could result from cooperative international development of water-resources infrastructure. Unilateral construction of dams could have the opposite effect.

diplomatic relationships between riparians on international rivers, reduced risk of conflict over water resources, improved trade, and enhanced economic integration).[38] Critics, however, believe that these benefits are overstated or nonexistent, that the high construction and resettlement costs are underestimated, and that negative side effects, especially environmental and cultural losses, are high (Duflo and Pande, 2007). Table 7.27 presents a list of the types of costs and benefits typically associated with dam projects.

In the short space allotted to our discussion of this intervention, we cannot hope to explore all aspects of this debate – particularly the social and political dimensions. Nevertheless, we have selected large multipurpose dams in Africa as one of the water-related interventions for consideration in the Copenhagen Consensus 2008 because we believe that there are several compelling reasons why the construction of *some* new large dams in Africa should be part of this discussion. First, many countries in Africa are short of water storage to mitigate droughts and support economic development activities; the projections from the recent Intergovernmental

Table 7.27. Benefits and costs of large dam projects[a]

Benefits	Costs
Irrigation water demand*	Capital investment (Dam, energy transmission infrastructure, land) *
Municipal and industrial water demand	Operation and maintenance*
Hydropower generation*	Opportunity cost of flooded land*
Downstream hydropower and irrigation water due to regularization of flow*	Reduced water availability downstream for irrigation, municipal, industrial, hydropower (including transient costs)
Flood control*	Resettlement costs for flooded habitations*
Decrease in impacts of droughts	Economic rehabilitation costs for lost livelihoods*
Creation of fishery in reservoir	Lost river fisheries
Recreational benefits around reservoir	Lost river recreation
Carbon offsets*	Catastrophic risk*
Sediment control	Ecological costs (erosion, lost plant/animal habitats, salinization)
Navigation	Public health costs (increased waterborne disease)

[a] In general, a dam project will not entail all of the costs and benefits listed in this table. Benefits and costs that apply to the illustrative project considered in this section are indicated by an asterisk.

Panel on Climate Change suggest that this need will worsen during the century ahead as a consequence of climate change (IPCC, 2007). As shown in Figure 7.13, Ethiopia has almost two orders of magnitude less water storage per person than countries in North America; South Africa has almost one order of magnitude less. In the United States and Europe, welfare may be enhanced if citizens decide that their governments should halt the construction of large dams for environmental, recreational, and cultural reasons, and even decommission some dams that may have been poorly conceived. But countries like Ethiopia face an entirely different situation. They have essentially no water-storage facili-

ties and are confronted with great hydrological variability, which can take a significant toll on economic growth (World Bank, 2006).

Second, in countries where many large dams have already been built, the best sites are mostly gone: they were developed first. In such countries many of the remaining undeveloped sites have significant negative attributes. Some are in areas of great aesthetic or ecological value; some lie in earthquake-prone zones; and others would, if dammed, inundate areas with large populations and thus require massive resettlement. In contrast, dams have not yet been constructed at some of the best dam sites in Africa. This would suggest that at least some of these sites in Africa are worth careful consideration. We believe that cost–benefit analysis offers one important perspective from which to judge the wisdom of such investments.

Large multipurpose dams are the most capital-intensive of the water and sanitation interventions examined in this chapter, and their benefits and costs will extend much farther into the future than rural boreholes with hand pumps, biosand filters, or community-level sanitation campaigns. The majority of the costs of large dams will be incurred during construction, but the benefits, operation and maintenance costs, and some of the environmental and social costs will extend far into the future. The choice of the social rate of discount to use for valuing benefits (and costs) in the distant future is thus much more important than for the other three water and sanitation interventions reviewed above. Although this approach does not deal adequately with the shadow value of capital or the social opportunity cost of capital (see footnote 3, Part I), the objective of the cost–benefit calculations presented here is not to show the results of an in-depth, thorough project appraisal. Rather we want to direct the attention of the development community back to the economics of such large water-resources infrastructure. Real discount rates in the range of 3–6% will serve this purpose.

An additional complication associated with these calculations is that large dam projects in poor regions or countries can be the initial "anchor"

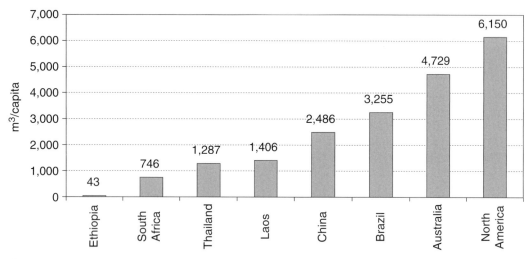

Figure 7.13 *Water storage per person in different countries*
Sources: Grey and Sadoffi 2007

investment of a strategic, transformational economic development plan that can affect many sectors of an economy. In effect the initial investment dictates one economic development path for a region instead of another. Such investments are the most difficult to assess with the partial equilibrium tools of cost–benefit analysis, because the relative prices of many goods and services may change as a result of the economic development initiatives and also because the opportunity cost of this water resources development "path" is the benefit of the development path not chosen, which is difficult to know.

To address these valuation challenges, historically many planners and engineers have proposed that the direct benefits of dam projects be increased by the use of a Keynesian "multiplier" so that the benefits that accrue to related, ancillary businesses – and to households in the form of increased income – can be included. Recently a major World Bank report has argued in support of the use of such multipliers to estimate the total benefits of dam projects (Bhatia *et al.*, 2005). In its simplest form, this "multiplier analysis" involves multiplying the direct economic benefits by an estimated multiplier (say 2.1) to obtain the total economic benefits of the investment.

The consensus of the economics profession

is that such use of multipliers to inflate the benefits of dam investment is conceptually incorrect (Boardman *et al.*, 2005), and we do not use this approach here. However, many of the benefits of a dam project do depend upon the completion of ancillary or associated capital investments. For example, hydropower generation from the dam will require transmission lines to carry the electricity to demand centers. If this transmission infrastructure has not yet been built, these costs will need to be incurred in addition to the costs of dam construction. Similarly, a dam may provide a controlled water supply that can be used to supply new irrigation schemes, but these irrigation schemes will need to be built, as will the infrastructure in the communities associated with them.

All of these attributes of investments in large dams serve to emphasize one of the main themes of this chapter: that the results of a cost–benefit analysis are highly contextual and site-specific. There are good and bad dam projects, and we do not attempt to reach any general conclusions about large dams. Rather we focus on a hypothetical investment in an authentic context in order to provide some illustrative calculations of the possible costs and benefits of a large dam in Africa, and to highlight some of the specific conditions that will influence these calculations.

For this intervention, we present the costs and benefits at the project level; we do not feel that it is conceptually or intuitively appealing to present the benefits and costs of this intervention on a per-household basis.

The context for this hypothetical intervention is the Blue Nile gorge in Ethiopia; Sudan and Egypt are downstream riparians. This mountainous region offers numerous dam sites that appear extremely attractive from several perspectives. First, the topography is favorable for hydroelectric power generation, since there is potential for sending water at high pressure (gravity head) through power turbines, thus producing large amounts of power that could provide electricity for Ethiopia where current usage is less than 25 kWh hours per capita – as well as for export to both Sudan and Egypt. Second, many sites have low surface-to-volume ratios, with corresponding low evaporation losses. Third, relatively few people live in the Blue Nile gorge, and thus resettlement costs and social impacts would be low. Fourth, the land is not used for other highly productive activities, and thus the land acquisition costs would be low.[39] Fifth, although there would certainly be ecological costs associated with flooding a portion of the Blue Nile gorge, this is not an area of especially high biological diversity. Sixth, earthquake risks have been judged to be low. Seventh, the benefits of regulation to downstream riparians are high. Regulation of Nile floods in Ethiopia would benefit Sudan in several important ways. Khartoum itself would be less at risk of flood damage. Hydropower generation could be increased at Sudanese reservoirs by regulation uplift. Storage in Ethiopia could mitigate droughts in Sudan, as well as enable some expansion of irrigation. Reduction in sediment loads could extend the economic lives of Sudanese reservoirs and enable the use of less restrictive operating rules. Eighth, the hydropower that could be generated is needed in the region. Egypt, Sudan, and Ethiopia are all growing rapidly, and there is a strong market demand for electricity.

For our benefit–cost calculations we consider a single hypothetical reservoir located in the Blue Nile gorge. The results of these calculations encourage us to believe that support for large multipurpose dams in such attractive sites should definitely be back on the agenda for consideration by the international development community. But we caution that this conclusion is not a general endorsement of large dams everywhere. The equations we use for the benefit–cost calculations relative to the dam project are shown in Table 7.28; our parameter assumptions are listed in Table 7.29 and explanation of the components of costs and benefits follows.

Discussion of Costs of a Large Multipurpose Dam in Africa

On the cost side we include the following components: direct construction costs of the dam and electricity-transmission infrastructure, operation and maintenance costs over the economic life of the project, land-acquisition costs, resettlement (compensation) costs to households currently living in the inundated area, risks of dam failure, and the cost of carbon emissions from construction and flooding of the reservoir area (with subsequent clearing of forested land, and decomposition of biomass). For the emissions from decomposition of biomass, we assume conservatively (in terms of the present value of the cost stream) that all carbon releases occur prior to the first year of reservoir filling, during construction, i.e., as land is cleared. We have not quantified costs associated with changes in ecosystem services.

We assume construction costs of US$2.5 billion over a seven-year construction period, plus an additional US$1 billion for transmission lines for electricity export. Many large construction projects experience both cost overruns and delays in completion. Only rarely do such projects finish under budget and ahead of schedule. For the purposes of the Monte Carlo simulations, we use an upper and lower bound on construction costs (US$2 billion and US$3 billion, respectively), just as we do on the other parameters in our cost–benefit calculations. In

---

[39] We assume that the land will not become relatively more valuable in the future, i.e., the future opportunity cost of the land remains low.

Table 7.28. Equations for cost–benefit analysis of large dam

Discounting factor in year t	$\delta_t = 1/(1+r)^{t-1}$	$\forall t = 1,...,D$
Benefits		
Value of hydropower (millions of US$ in year t)	$H_t = \eta_{b,t} * (H_p + H_d) * v_h * (1 + \Delta v_h)^{t-8}$	
Value of irrigation (millions of US$ in year t)	$I_t = \eta_{b,t} * (I_d * v_i) * (1 + \Delta v_i)^{t-8}$	
Flood control (millions of US$ in year t)	$F_t = \eta_{b,t} * F*\lambda$	
Value of carbon offsets (millions of US$ in year t)	$O_t = (\eta_{b,t} * (H_p + H_d) * p_o * \varepsilon) * (1 + \Delta v_O)^{t-8} / 10^6$	
Total benefits	$B = \Sigma_t [\delta_t * (H_t + I_t + F_t + O_t)]$	$\forall t = 1,...,D$
Costs		
Capital cost (US$ in year t)	$C_t = [\eta_{c,t} * (C_d + C_e)]$	
Resettlement and economic rehabilitation (millions of US$)	$R_t = n * C_r$ $R_t = 0$	if $t = 1$ otherwise
Operation and maintenance cost (US$ in year t)	$M_t = C_o*(C_d + C_e)/D$ $M_t = 0$	if $t > 7$ otherwise
Cost of carbon emissions from flooding + construction (millions of US$ in year t)	$C_{O,t} = \eta_{c,t} * E$	
Cost of catastrophic risk (US$ in year t)	Q_t = Cost of reconstructing dam + lost benefits	
Total costs	$C = \Sigma_t [\delta_t * (C_t + C_{O,t} + R_t + M_t + Q_t)]$	$\forall t = 1,...,D$

this case the lower- and upper-bound values establish a range from US$2 billion to $3 billion, and the base-case value of US$2.5 billion should be interpreted as including a "normal" cost over-run. We also allow for a construction delay of 0–4 years, with two years as the base case delay, for a total of nine years before any benefits begin to accrue from operation of the dam.

We assume that the annual operation and maintenance costs over the economic life of the project (75 years; range 50–100) would be 0.5% of the annual capital costs (range 0.35–0.65%). Land-acquisition costs are included in capital cost and are estimated to be about US$10 million. The compensation paid to displaced families is calculated as a multiple of average GDP per capita in Ethiopia based on costs observed in other locations around the world (Cernea, 1999). In the base case we use a multiple of 10 (range 5–15).

We include the risk of dam failure as an expected annual cost in every year over the economic life of the project, which we calculate by multiplying an estimate of the annual probability of failure (1 in 10,000 or 0.01%; range 0.005%–0.015%) by an estimate of the economic losses if dam failure were to occur. Our estimate of economic losses from dam failure is based on the cost of recon-struction plus the lost benefits over the period of reconstruction, and should be considered a lower bound since catastrophic damages from downstream flooding are not included.

Discussion of Benefits of a Large Multipurpose Dam in Africa

The main direct economic benefit of this hypo-thetical dam is the hydroelectric power gener-ated, assumed to be 8,000 gigawatt hours per year (range 7,000–9,000 GWh/yr). We assume that in the near and intermediate term these new electricity supplies will be exported to meet growing power demand in Sudan and Egypt. We thus value this hydropower generation at the cost of alternative supplies, which we estimate to be US$0.05 per kilowatt hour delivered to market (range US$0.03–0.07). We expect that the economic value of this hydropower will grow over time in real (net of inflation) terms. We thus include a parameter to reflect this increase in the relative value of hydropower (base case 0.5%, range 0 to +1%/yr).

Other benefits include the carbon offsets from

Table 7.29. Parameters used in cost–benefit analysis of large dam project[a]

Symbol	Parameter	Base case	Lower limit	Upper limit	Correlated parameters
H_p	Hydropower generated at dam (GW-hr/yr)	8000	7000	9000	
H_d	Net gain in hydropower generated in Sudan and Egypt (GW-hr/yr)	250	-100	600	
v_h	Value of hydropower ($US/kW-hr)	0.05	0.03	0.07	
Δv_h	Annual change in value of hydropower starting in first year of operation (%, net of inflation)	0.5	0	1	
I_d	Change in timely irrigation water downstream (bcm/yr)	1.5	1	2	
v_i	Net value of timely water downstream ($US/cm)	0.075	0.05	0.10	
Δv_i	Annual change in value of timely water starting in first year of operation (%, net of inflation)	0.5	0	1	
F	Change in expected annual flood damage (millions of US$)	12	4	20	
λ	Decrease in probability of flood (%)	50	25	75	GW-hr/yr generated –0.2)
p_o	Price of offsets (US$/ton CO_2)	20	15	25	
ε	Carbon offset factor	0.375	0.25	0.5	
Δv_O	Annual change in value of offsets starting in first year of operation (%, net of inflation)	0.5	0	1	
C_d	Capital cost of dam (millions of US$)	2500	2000	3000	
C_e	Capital cost of electrical transmission infrastructures (millions of US$)	1000	700	1300	Cost of infrastructure (0.5)
C_o	O&M expenditures (% annual capital cost)	50	35	65	Cost of infrastructure (0.5)
n	# households displaced	10000	8000	12000	
C_r	Economic loss per displaced household (US$)	2300	1150	3450	
μ	Risk of catastrophic failure (%)	0.01	0.005	0.015	
E	Project emissions (millions of tons of CO_2)	4.5	3.5	5.5	
D	Dam project duration (yrs)	75	50	100	
d	Project delay (yrs)	2	0	4	
r	Real (net of inflation) discount rate (%)	4.5%	3%	6%	

[a] Our uncertainty analysis does not purport to use the real probability distributions associated with these parameters, but instead is aimed at assessing a range of possibilities for the illustrative case we consider in this section.

generation of carbon-neutral hydropower, the delivery of timely irrigation water and hydropower uplift downstream due to enhanced flow regulation, and downstream flood-control benefits. For the carbon offsets, we assume the value to be US$20 (range US$15–25) and include the possibility of growth in the value of offsets (0.5%, range 0 to +1%/yr). In addition, hydropower generation in Sudan is estimated to

increase by 600 GWh/yr (range 400–800 GWh/yr) due to the improved regulation of downstream flows that would result from a dam in the Blue Nile gorge.

The flood-control benefits in Sudan are estimated as an annual benefit calculated as the expected value of reduced risk of floods times the anticipated flood damages. The reduction in the variability of flows that would result from a

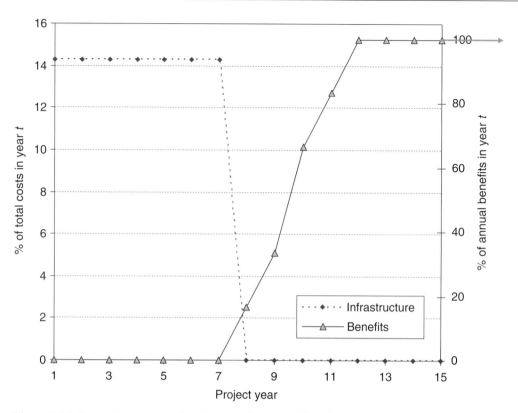

Figure 7.14 *Large dam project: distribution of costs and benefits in time (η function from Table 7.28)*

large hydroelectric dam in the Blue Nile gorge not only reduces flood damage in Sudan, it also increases flows during the summer, which benefit both navigation and irrigation. The value of this improved summer flow to irrigators is difficult to estimate, in part because increasing irrigation withdrawals in Sudan will correspond to some reduction in flows downstream. Determining upstream–downstream flow changes requires a system-wide analysis that takes account of the dynamics between changes in withdrawal patterns and evaporative losses, which is beyond the scope of these calculations. For purposes of illustration we assume that an additional 1.5 billion cubic meters of water would be used by Sudan annually as a result of this improved regulation (range 1–2 billion cubic meters (bcm)/ yr), and that the system-wide value of this improved supply is US$0.075 per cubic meter (range $0.05–0.10), or an annual benefit of

US$150 million. We expect the relative value of this water to increase over time in real terms (base case 0.5%, range 0 to +1%/yr) as Sudanese irrigation practices undergo modernization. We assume that hydropower in Egypt would decrease by 350 GWhr/yr (range 200–500 GWh/ yr) as a result of these upstream withdrawals.

We do not include in our benefit estimates such difficult-to-measure outcomes as better diplomatic relationships between riparians where cooperative transboundary development is achieved, reduced risk of conflict over water resources, improved trade, and enhanced economic integration. We also do not include the benefits of sediment control, which could be substantial.

Figure 7.14 summarizes our assumptions about the time profile of costs and benefits associated with this dam project. We assume that the benefits from dam operation do not immediately reach 100% once the construction

Table 7.30. Base case results for a large dam in Africa[a]

	Physical units	Present value of benefit and cost components ($US millions)		
Discount rate		3%	4.5%	6%
Benefits				
Hydropower at dam and downstream	+8250 GWhr/yr	$9643	$5958	$3907
Downstream irrigation in Sudan	+1.5 bcm/yr	$2630	$1625	$1066
Carbon offsets	3.1 million tons CO_2/yr	$1446	$894	$586
Flood benefits	50% flood reduction	$123	$77	$52
Total benefits		$13842	$8553	$5610
Costs				
Capital	N/A	$3115	$2946	$2791
O&M	N/A	$511	$330	$225
Carbon emissions	4.5 million tons CO_2	$80	$76	$72
Resettlement	10,000 households	$22	$22	$22
Catastrophic failure	0.01% risk of failure	$14	$10	$7
Total costs		$3743	$3384	$3117
Benefit–cost ratio		3.7	2.5	1.8
Net benefits		$10099	$5170	$2493

[a] For the results reported here, all parameters were set at their base case values as described in Table 7.29, except for the discount rate, which was varied between 3%, 4.5%, and 6%. The values in the cells in the three rightmost columns report the present value of the components of the benefit and cost streams over the life of the project.

project is complete but instead increase over time as the reservoir fills. Economic analysis of dam projects often does not correctly account for the partial benefits that accrue during the period after construction is completed while the reservoir is still filling. Ignoring the fact that benefits will be less while the reservoir is filling can substantially reduce the economic attractiveness of the investment (Block, 2006).[40]

Comparison of Costs and Benefits of a Large Multipurpose Dam in Africa

The results for the base case show a BCR for the hypothetical large dam of 2.5 using a discount rate of 4.5% (Table 7.30). Figure 7.15 shows that the results are most sensitive to changes in the real discount rate, the economic value of the hydropower generated, the capital costs of the dam, and the annual rate of increase in the relative price of the hydropower generated.

Figure 7.16 represents the frequency distribution of the BCRs from the Monte Carlo calculations. This frequency distribution suggests that

this hypothetical large dam is extremely attractive from an economic perspective, even without including many of the more difficult-to-measure benefits (e.g., reduced risk of conflict over water resources, increased trade, and economic cooperation). The frequency distribution in Figure 7.16 is conceptually different from those presented for the first three water and sanitation interventions in the sense that the spatial location of the investment is much more precisely specified: the large dam is located at a site with the characteristics of the Blue Nile gorge of Ethiopia. For the other interventions, we used ranges for parameter values that one would

[40] In fact, our calculations do not fully address the effect of filling a Blue Nile reservoir on the economic attractiveness of the investment. In order to adequately address this impact, a system-wide analysis similar to the one required for evaluating upstream–downstream changes in flow is necessary, because filling a large reservoir in Ethiopia would have impacts on dams and the water-release patterns of all the reservoirs downstream of a dam in the Blue Nile gorge.

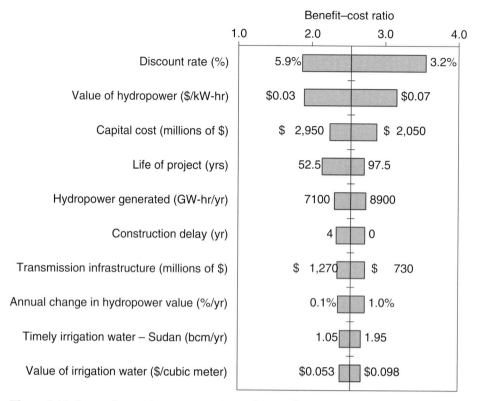

Figure 7.15 *Large dam project – sensitivity analyses: effect of selected parameters on BCR (90% confidence intervals, holding other parameters at base case values)*

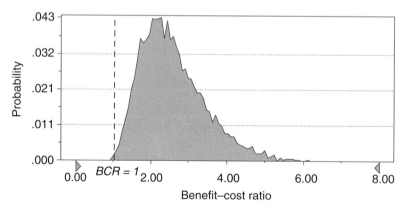

Figure 7.16 *Large dam project: distribution of BCR outcomes from Monte Carlo simulation (10,000 draws) with uniform parameter distributions*

expect to find throughout developing countries. The frequency distribution of BCRs in Figure 7.16 thus does not show such a wide range; almost all of the BCRs are positive. These eco-nomic results thus appear more attractive than those for the other three interventions because the mass of the distribution is centered on high benefit–cost ratios.

Table 7.31. Typology of dam project outcomes categorized by benefit–cost ratio (BCR)[a]

Parameter	Unattractive (BCR < 1)		Attractive (BCR 1–2.99)		Very attractive (BCR > 3–4.99)		Extremely attractive (BCR > 5)	
Real discount rate (%)	5.79	(0.21)	4.78	(0.79)	3.81	(0.59)	3.27	(0.25)
Value of hydropower (US$/kWh)	0.033	(0.003)	0.047	(0.011)	0.057	(0.009)	0.062	(0.006)
Capital cost (millions of US$)	2,835	(136)	2,547	(281)	2,392	(272)	2,203	(194)
Life of project (yr)	59.6	(7.6)	73.5	(14.5)	79.1	(13.4)	89.0	(8.6)
Hydropower generated (GWh/yr)	7692	(486)	7959	(574)	8103	(561)	8317	(530)
Construction delay (yr)	3.8	(0.6)	2.1	(1.4)	1.7	(1.4)	1.6	(1.5)
Transmission infrastructure cost (millions of US$)	1,155	(130)	1,022	(171)	944	(165)	862	(128)
Annual change in hydropower value (%/yr)	0.4	(0.3)	0.5	(0.3)	0.6	(0.3)	0.7	(0.3)
Percent of simulations (%)	0.1		72.2		26.3		1.3	
BCR for "mean" of subgroup[b]	0.92		1.88		3.42		4.92	

[a] Mean parameter values in first row, standard deviations in parentheses.
[b] The benefit–cost ratio corresponding to the case with the "mean" parameter values reported in each column, and other parameters set to base levels. The BCR can therefore lie outside the range predicted by the average values listed here, as in the extreme right column.

Table 7.31 presents the mean values of the most important parameters for four groups of outcomes from the Monte Carlo simulations: those with BCRs (a) < 1, (b) 1–2.99, (c) 3–4.99, and (d) ≥ 5. As shown, in order for the intervention to have a BCR of < 1, essentially everything would have to go wrong. The hydropower generated would have to be less than expected, and its value would have to be low and not increase in value over the economic life of the project. The dam construction would have to run over budget and experience delays in completion. Most importantly, the social rate of discount would have to be higher than in our base case. But the combinations of parameter values that result in a BCR of <1 occur in only 0.1% of outcomes from the Monte Carlo simulation.

Our cost–benefit results show that a large dam under conditions like those in the Blue Nile gorge of Ethiopia would be an extremely attractive economic investment. Although we did not quantify the costs associated with changes in ecosystem services, these would have to be high to change this conclusion. In presenting this analysis we do not comment on the political feasibility (and associated process costs) of such an investment. Nor have we touched on the distribution of benefits and costs. How the benefits and costs of large dam development can be shared is a matter for negotiation and ultimately requires trust and regional cooperation.

Our results suggest that there may be very good sites for large multipurpose dam investments in Africa, and that support for these interventions deserves the consideration and engagement of the international community.

Discussion of the Costs and Benefits of the Four Alternate Water and Sanitation Interventions

In the third part of this challenge chapter we have examined four alternate water and sanitation interventions: (1) rural water supply programs providing poor rural communities in Africa with deep boreholes and public hand pumps, (2) "total sanitation" (CLTS) campaigns to halt open defecation in South Asia, (3) the biosand filter, a specific point-of-use water-disinfection technology for household water treatment, and (4) a large, multipurpose dam in Africa. The first three interventions differ from the fourth in two related ways: they do not require the large capital cost of a network infrastructure, and they are best conceptualized as a prototype of a project that could be repeated in as many locations as needed. By contrast, the fourth intervention is a project that can be done once in a specific location, and financing issues will be paramount. The probabilistic simulation analysis that we have performed thus has a different interpretation for the first three interventions than for the fourth.

The difference in interpretation hinges on the distinction between uncertainty and variability. With every intervention, there is inevitably some uncertainty regarding the appropriate parameter values to be used in the cost–benefit assessment. But an additional consideration arises for the first three interventions, namely variability: these interventions are intended for application in many separate locations. The economic appraisal of such interventions depends on highly site-specific parameters such as disease incidence, the effectiveness of the intervention, and the case fatality rate, as was also the case with the network intervention. However, conducting the careful epidemiological studies that are needed for location-specific economic evaluations is expensive and time-consuming, and the value of the information will in many cases not be worth the cost of obtaining it unless the results can be generalized to other locations with confidence. One would hope that the parameters such as the effectiveness of the intervention could be transferred at least approximately from study sites to policy sites, but it is much less clear how to transfer critical parameters such as disease incidence and case fatality rates, which will be subject to substantial uncertainty unless epidemiological studies are conducted. Hence in these three cases our simulation analysis also characterizes the variability across applications in different locations. Another way of making this point is to say that if we knew the relevant parameter values with certainty, there would be a single estimate of net benefit for the fourth intervention, a large dam at a particular site in Africa, but there could not be a single global estimate of net benefits for the other interventions – boreholes, CLTS campaigns, and household treatment with biosand filters – because they each take place in many different locations

with potentially large differences in individual circumstances. Hence one cannot say that a sanitation campaign always has the same given net benefit regardless of the circumstances in which it is employed. The net benefit clearly depends on the specific circumstances.

Our simulation analysis for the first three interventions thus serves to identify the combination of circumstances – the combination of parameter values – that is conducive to a successful economic outcome and, also, the combination leading to an unsuccessful outcome. In this final section of Part III, we summarize and compare the results of the cost–benefit calculations of the three non-network water and sanitation interventions and then compare these three with large dams in Africa. Table 7.32 lists the eight parameters that (1) were used in the benefit–cost model for the three non-network water and sanitation interventions, and (2) were assumed to have the same values in each of the interventions. Table 7.33 lists ten parameters that had important effects on the BCRs of one or more of the interventions and varied over different ranges depending on the intervention (for example, reduction in diarrheal disease or duration of the intervention).

Table 7.33 illustrates some important differences between the interventions. The benefits from the rural water supply intervention are assumed to last longer (15 years) than those for the biosand filter intervention (8 years) or the CLTS intervention (6 years). However, annual operation and maintenance costs for the rural water intervention are significantly higher than for the biosand filter and CLTS interventions. The initial capital cost for the rural water supply intervention is also higher than for the biosand filter and CLTS interventions.

The three interventions also differ in important dimensions not shown in Table 7.33. The biosand filter intervention has the advantage that the benefits from household treatment are entirely under an individual household's control. Collective action by the community is not required. In contrast, the rural water supply intervention requires the active, continuing involvement of a village water committee

Table 7.32. Parameters with the same values in each of the three non-network water and sanitation interventions and base case assumptions

Parameter	Base case (range)		Units
Household size	5	(4–6)	people
Market wage for unskilled labor	1.25	(0.5–2.0)	US$/day
Value of time/market wage	0.3	(0.1–0.5)	None
Diarrhea incidence	0.9	(0.5–1.4)	cases/person-yr
Cost of illness	6	(2–10)	US$/case
Case fatality rate	0.08	(0.04–0.12)	%
Value of a statistical life	30,000	(10,000–50,000)	US$/statistical life
Discount rate	4.5	(3–6)	%

Table 7.33. Parameters with the greatest effects on the benefit–cost ratios: comparison of assumed values (with ranges) across the three community water and sanitation interventions

Parameter	Borehole + hand pump		CLTS		Biosand filter	
Reduction in diarrheal disease (%)	25	(10–40)	30	(10–50)	40	(20–60)
Duration of intervention (yrs)	15	(10–20)	6	(3–9)	8	(6–10)
Upfront investment: program + capital	$10,000	(7,000–13,000)	~$55/hh	(4–12)[a]	$100/hh	(75–125)[a]
Training time (hr/hh)	N/A		10	(5–15)[b]	8	(4–12)
Operation and maintenance costs (US$/yr)	600	(250–950)	0	(None)	0	(None)
Operation and maintenance time (hr/yr)	See above		10	(5–15)	3.5	(1.5–5.5)
Time spent, traditional situation	1 hr/20L	(0.1–1.9)	15 min/d	(10–20)	N/A	
Time spent, improved situation	0.3	(0.1–0.5)	0	(None)	N/A	
Usage	100		70	(50–90)	–3%/yr	(1–5)
Uptake	N/A		40	(20–60)	N/A	

[a] For both the CLTS and the biosand filter intervention, program costs represent the major fraction of the investment; the latrines and biosand filters cost roughly $8 and $20 per unit, respectively.
[b] Only for participating households; non-participating households assumed to spend 3 hours (range 2–4 hours).

in the management of the borehole and hand pump to ensure long-term successful performance. In fact, some proponents see this institutional aspect of the rural water intervention as an advantage rather than a limitation, because village water committees may learn to organize and work together to achieve other common goals. The CLTS intervention requires considerable collective action at the beginning of the program, but potentially less after household toilets are constructed. However, little is known about how latrine usage rates change over time in the absence of ongoing community management programs. Table 7.34 summarizes the compo-

nents of the benefits and costs in terms of US$ per household per month, and the BCRs for each of the three interventions for the base case parameter values (assuming a discount rate of 6%). As shown, all three interventions have very attractive BCRs.[41] These base case parameter

[41] Note that in Table 7.34 the household benefits for the borehole plus public hand-pump intervention are about US$6.6/month, and thus might be thought to approach the low end of the range of costs for network services (US$10/month). However, half of these benefits (US$3.3) come from time savings; therefore the borehole plus hand-pump intervention is most likely to be an economically attractive investment in places where time savings

Table 7.34. Comparison of the components of the benefits and costs of the four water and sanitation interventions (US$/hh-month)[a]

Benefit–cost category	Rural water	CLTS	Biosand filter	Large dam
Benefits				
Time savings	3.28	0.20	0	
Quantity/aesthetic	0.54	0	0	
Morbidity	0.56	0.19	0.75	
Mortality	2.25	0.76	2.99	
Total benefits	6.63	1.14	3.73	
Costs				
Capital, training and program	1.43	0.37	1.34	
Maintenance costs	0.83	0	0.05	
Household time costs	0	0.05	0.01	
Total costs	2.26	0.43	1.40	
Net benefits	4.37	0.72	2.33	
Benefit–cost ratio (BCR[b]	2.9	2.7	2.8	1.8

[a] Assuming 6% discount rate.
[b] BCRs for the first three water and sanitation interventions do not pertain to any specific location in developing countries; instead they represent outcomes given the average, base case parameter values described in Part II of this paper. In contrast, the BCR for the large dam intervention does pertain to one specific, illustrative project location.

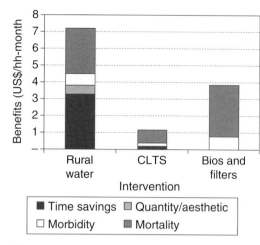

Figure 7.17 *Components of the benefits of the three water and sanitation interventions: base case parameter values*

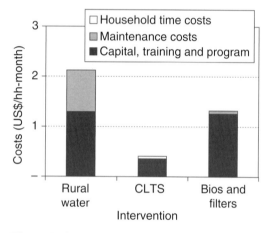

Figure 7.18 *Components of the costs of the three water and sanitation interventions: base case parameter values*

values simply correspond to the midpoints of the ranges that we believe to be plausible for these parameters in most developing country locations. We use these midpoint parameter values only to demonstrate the calculations for these interventions, and do not believe that they are sufficient to establish a prioritization or ranking of these three interventions. There are, however, important differences in the various components of benefits (Figure 7.17) and costs (Figure 7.18)

are substantial and people do not have easy access to alternative sources. In such remote, low-density rural locations, the costs of network infrastructure are also likely to be higher, and there would be few economies of scale in providing network services. In urban areas where economies of scale are possible, boreholes and hand pumps would yield few if any time savings, and health savings would be greatly diminished because people have access to other water options and nearby health services.

across the three interventions. This has implications for where these interventions will be most attractive.

The rural water supply intervention is the most expensive (US$2.26 per household per month), with larger up-front capital costs (Table 7.34) than the biosand filter or CLTS interventions. But it also yields the largest benefits (US$6.63 per household per month). Most of the benefits from rural water supply in the base case come from the value of time savings and the value of reduced mortality. Thus the rural water intervention is attractive from an economic perspective because it has the potential to deliver both health benefits and time savings. CLTS does result in some time savings, but not to the same extent as the rural water intervention in our base case. The BCR of the rural water intervention has been dramatically improved in the past decade by the presence of low-cost Chinese contractors operating in Africa.

The majority of the benefits of CLTS (67%) and the biosand filter (80%) are in the form of reduced mortality. As with the network water and sanitation services, for all three interventions the value of the reduced mortality benefits is heavily influenced by the assumed value of the VSL parameter. The economic value of reduced morbidity (avoided costs of illness) is a smaller percentage of the total benefits for all three interventions: 9% for rural water, 17% for CLTS, and 20% for the biosand filter (Figure 7.17). We emphasize, however, that the avoided COI measure of economic benefits does not account for pain and suffering, and that reliance on both COI and VSL measures suffers from shortcomings when behavioral responses to illness such as coping and averting expenditures reduce the risk of disease. Figure 7.19 shows frequency distributions of the benefit–cost ratios for all three water and sanitation interventions from the Monte Carlo simulations. These illustrate the apparent similarity of the three interventions. The rural water intervention has the fewest combinations of parameter values for which the BCR is < 1. The biosand filter intervention has the largest number of combinations of parameter values with high BCRs. However, it is again important to emphasize that these frequency distributions do not correspond with the frequency of outcomes for real locations (communities) in developing countries, but rather are the result of our assumed combinations of parameter values. The planning challenge is to find locations in the real world with high BCRs like those shown in Figure 7.19 for each of the three interventions, and to avoid locations with BCRs < 1. A location that is particularly favorable for one intervention may or may not be for another. It

may also be difficult to determine which sites are favorable or unfavorable due to a lack of site-specific data. Particularly for calculations of mortality benefits, there is great uncertainty surrounding the four key parameters (VSL, case fatality rates, diarrheal incidence, and percentage reduction in diarrheal incidence due to an intervention) for any specific location or region. But the large number of combinations of parameter values with positive BCRs should give planners wide latitude for action in the face of such uncertainty.

However, this large uncertainty on key parameters is a strong argument to maintain the demand-driven focus of the rural water intervention, and to extend it to both the biosand filter and the CLTS interventions. Sizeable community and household cash contributions to finance all three interventions can serve as important "demand filters" to ensure that after people receive the health education and other "software" messages designed by planners, the people themselves are convinced that these interventions will prove valuable in their local circumstances. Our benefit–cost calculations suggest that there will be places where each of the three water and sanitation interventions should not be undertaken. Demand filters are an important means of identifying such communities and avoiding investing in interventions where they are not needed or desired. The rural water supply intervention has the advantage that the distance households are walking to traditional sources to collect water and the time spent queuing at water points are much more easily observable than VSLs, case fatality rates, diarrheal incidence, and percentage reduction in diarrheal incidence due to an intervention. Yet, the economic value of these time savings is difficult to estimate. The presence of water vendors in an area with high water-collection times from traditional sources is tangible, compelling evidence that some households are willing to pay to avoid the time spent collecting water from traditional sources. Similarly the absence of widespread water vending can often be interpreted as evidence that households cannot pay much for such time savings.

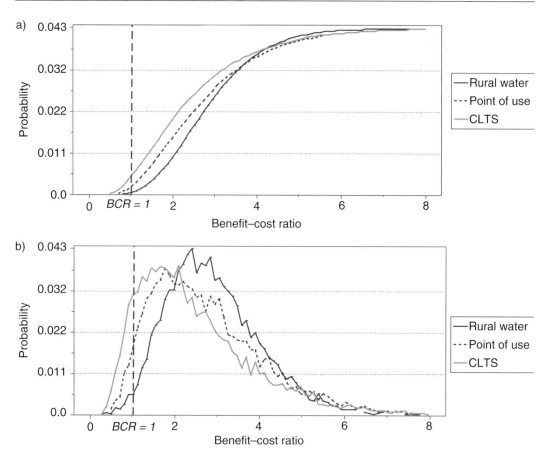

Figure 7.19 *a) Frequency and b) cumulative frequency distributions of the BCRs for the three non-network water and sanitation interventions*

Both the rural water and the biosand filter interventions appear to be scalable to large numbers of communities in developing countries. The biosand filter has the advantage that it can be used by households in both rural and (low-density) urban areas. Deep boreholes with hand pumps are not likely to be attractive in large urban settlements because of the risks of (1) contaminated groundwater, and (2) falling water tables (if large numbers of households in close proximity rely on wells). Even in rural areas, the use of deep boreholes is limited by groundwater and geologic (drilling) conditions. This is not true of the biosand filter, which can be used essentially anywhere except very high-density urban settlements (where finding space for the filters may be difficult).

The CLTS intervention has been shown to be scalable in South Asia. It is unclear how this intervention might work in Africa or Latin America, but there is no reason to be pessimistic in this regard. Sanitation and hygiene-promotion messages should be adaptable to local cultures. Table 7.34 also shows the BCR for the base case for the fourth intervention, a large multipurpose dam in the Blue Nile gorge in Ethiopia. Although in the base case the BCR of this large dam investment is less than for the first three interventions, it is still extremely attractive from an economic perspective. We would not conclude that this fourth intervention should receive a lower priority than the first three simply on the basis of this simple comparison of base case results in Table 7.34. The scalability of these investments is too different and the variability in the results too site-specific to make global statements about the desirability of one type of intervention over another.

Concluding Remarks

Our findings in Parts I and II suggest that the high costs and unique characteristics of conventional network water and sanitation investments make them especially challenging projects for many communities in developing countries. Some, but not all, water and sanitation network infrastructure projects will pass a rigorous economic test. In cities in rapidly growing economies, we expect the benefits of many projects, properly estimated, to exceed the costs. In other cases, however, the economic reality will be more nuanced and the attractiveness of specific water and sanitation investments in network infrastructure less clear-cut.

Policy makers in developing countries and donors in industrialized countries rightly have objectives in addition to economic efficiency (maximizing new benefits), such as alleviating poverty and furthering other political imperatives. Many people in industrialized countries would prefer to live in a world without extreme poverty and are willing to pay something for this. Policy makers and donors will make decisions about investments in the water and sanitation sector based on these multiple objectives, not on economic efficiency alone. The fact that the economic rationale for investment in water and sanitation network infrastructure is open to question in some situations will often not be a persuasive reason to delay. But when economists are asked for an economic (cost–benefit) analysis, in our view it is not helpful to include in the benefits of a water and sanitation investment a measure of the altruism that donors feel knowing that they may have improved the lives of people living without adequate water and sanitation conditions. This may be a reason to proceed with an investment, but it is not a calculation that policy makers have asked economists to include in a cost–benefit analysis. Policy makers and donors need to know what improved services are worth to people in developing countries not only to assess the wisdom of water and sanitation investments but also to thoughtfully address the financing challenge of constructing network water and sanitation systems in developing countries and to encourage the behavioral changes needed.

In this chapter we have argued that the key to successful water and sanitation investments is to discover forms of service and payment mechanisms that will render the improvements worthwhile for those who must pay for them. The plain truth is that international donors are simply not willing to pay the high capital costs of conventional water and sewer networks for the hundreds of millions of people in developing countries without these services, nor to assume the ongoing financial obligation to keep them operational. People in developing countries will have to pay the vast majority of these costs themselves, and careful cost–benefit and financial analyses are needed to accurately characterize the magnitude of this challenge.

We believe that all four of the interventions discussed in Part II (rural boreholes and hand pumps, community-led total sanitation, point-of-use treatment with biosand filters, and large dams in Africa) hold considerable promise for improving the economic livelihoods and health conditions of hundreds of millions of people in developing countries. None of these interventions, however, is a panacea. The success of each intervention will depend on the specific context in which it is implemented. The social context matters, as well as the physical and economic contexts, particularly where behavioral change is required for positive outcomes. We believe that the first three, non-network interventions discussed in Part III should be viewed as intermediate, not long-term, solutions to the water and sanitation problems of rapidly urbanizing societies in developing countries. Governments and donors should let people themselves decide whether such non-network options are preferable to waiting for network solutions to their water and sanitation problems. The fourth intervention, large dams in Africa, deserves renewed attention.

In communities where economic growth proceeds, we have little doubt that households and firms will ultimately want the advantages of large-scale, piped network infrastructure for the delivery of modern water and sanitation services, and they will struggle to finance these highly capital-intensive investments – a struggle that played out in the United States over much of the 19th century and beyond, as described above. With time the benefits of these water and sanitation investments will grow. There is limited evidence that investments in municipal water and sanitation services actually *cause* economic growth, but the sequencing of significant water investments could possibly set in motion path-dependent patterns of development that will change the expected returns to, and hence incentives for, subsequent investments in other sectors of the economy. Moreover, there is a strong association between household income and the provision of both piped water and sewer services. Higher-income households definitely want improved water and sanitation services, and, as incomes grow, the demand for such services grows. So even in the absence of a causal relationship, the benefit stream of water and sanitation services becomes more valuable as economic growth proceeds.

This chapter demonstrates the broad range of interventions that can be classified in the "water and sanitation" sector. The breadth of these options, the range of their potential returns, and the strong dependence on the specific circumstances of each project's design and implementation underscore the fact that there can be no single benefit–cost ratio for the water and sanitation sector. No sectoral-level analysis can replace rigorous, project-level economic analysis. Each water and sanitation investment is unique and must be designed for its specific context and judged on its merits.

Acknowledgments

We thank Robert Roche (World Bank), Mark Sobsey(UNC-CH),ChristineStauber(UNC-CH), Kaida-may Liang (UNC-CH), Benoit LaPlante (private consultant), Peter Rogers (Harvard University), Robert A. Young (Colorado State University), and Subhrendu Pattanayak (Duke University) for their advice and assistance during the preparation of this report.

Bibliography

Allan, S. (2003). *The WaterAid Bangladesh/VERC 100% Sanitation Approach; Cost, motivation and subsidy.* London: London School of Hygiene and Tropical Medicine

Alberini, A. and Chiabai, A. (2007). Urban environmental health and sensitive populations: How much are the Italians willing to pay to reduce their risks? *Regional Science and Urban Economics, 37*, 239–258

Altaf, A., Whittington, D., Smith, V.K., and Jamal, H. (1993). Rethinking rural water supply policy in the Punjab, Pakistan. *Water Resources Research, 29* (7), 1943–1954

Arnold, B.F. and Colford, J.M.J. (2007). Treating water with chlorine at point-of-use to improve water quality and reduce child diarrhea in developing countries: A systematic review and meta-analysis. *American Journal of Tropical Medical Hygiene, 76* (2), 354–364

Bahl, R., Sinha, A., Poulos, C., Whittington, D., Sazawal, S., *et al.* (2004). Costs of illness due to typhoid fever in an Indian urban slum community: Implications for vaccination policy. *Journal of Health Population and Nutrition, 22* (3), 304–310

Bhatia, R., Scatasta, M., Cestti, R., and Malik, R.P.S. (2005). *Indirect economic impacts of dams: Methodological issues and summary results of case studies in Brazil, India and Egypt.* Washington: The World Bank

Bhattacharya, S., Alberini, A., and Cropper, M.L. (2007). The value of mortality risk reductions in Delhi, India. *Journal of Risk and Uncertainty, 34*, 21–47

Block, P. (2006). Integrated management of the Blue Nile Basin in Ethiopia: Precipitation forecast, hydropower, and irrigation modeling. *PhD Dissertation.* Department of Civil, Environmental and Architectural Engineering. Boulder, Colorado, University of Colorado: 160pp.

Boardman, A.E., Greenberg, D., Vining, A., and Weimer, D. (2005). *Cost–benefit analysis: Concepts and practice.* Upper Saddle River, NJ: Prentice Hall

Bockstael, N.E. and McConnell, K.E. (2007). *Environmental and resource valuation with revealed preferences: A theoretical guide to empirical models.* Dordrecht, The Netherlands: Springer

Briscoe, J. and De Ferranti, D. (1988). *Water for rural communities: Helping people help themselves.* Washington, D.C.: The World Bank

Briscoe, J., di Castro, P.F., Griffin, C., North, J., and Olsen, O. (1990). Toward equitable and sustainable rural water supplies: A contingent valuation study in Brazil. *The World Bank Economic Review, 4* (2), 115–134

Brown, J. (2007). Effectiveness of ceramic filtration for drinking water treatment in Cambodia. *PhD Dissertation.* Department of Environmental Sciences and Engineering. Chapel Hill: University of North Carolina, 275pp.

Curtis, V. and Cairncross, S. (2003). Effect of washing hands with soap on diarrhea risk in the community: a systematic review. *The Lancet Infectious Diseases, 3* (5): 275–281

Carson, R.T., Flores, N.E., Martin, K.M., and Wright, J.L. (1996). Contingent Valuation and Revealed Preference Methodologies: Comparing the Estimates for Quasi-Public Goods. *Land Economics, 72* (1), 80–99

Carson, R., Flores, N.E., and Meade, N.F. (2001). Contingent valuation: Controversies and evidence. *Environmental and Resource Economics, 19*, 173–210

CAWST (2007). *Biosand filter description.* **Calgary**, Canada: Centre for Affordable Water and Sanitation Technology

Cernea, M. (1999). *The economics of involuntary resettlement: Questions and challenges.* Washington, D.C.: The World Bank

Choe, K., Whittington, D., and Lauria, D.T. (1996). The economic benefits of surface water quality improvements in developing countries: A case study of Davao, Philippines. *Land Economics, 72* (4), 519–537

Churchill, A., De Ferranti, D., Roche, R., Tager, C., Walters, A., *et al.* (1987). *Rural water supply and sanitation: Time for a change.*

World Bank Discussion Paper Series. Washington, D.C.: The World Bank

Clasen, T., Roberts, I., Rabie, T., Schmidt, W., and Cairncross, S. (2006). Interventions to improve water quality for preventing diarrhea (Cochrane Review). In: The Cochrane Library, Issue 3, 2006. Oxford, UK

Clasen, T.F. and Bastable, A. (2003). Faecal contamination of drinking water during collection and household storage: The need to extend protection to the point of use. *Journal of Water and Health, 1* (3), 109–115

Cook, J., Jeuland, M., Maskery, B., Lauria, D., Sur, D., Clemens, J., and Whittington, D. (2008). Re-visiting socially-optimal vaccine subsidies: An empirical application in Kolkata, India. *Journal of Policy Analysis and Management.* Under review

Curtis, V. and Cairncross, S. (2003). Effect of washing hands with soap on diarrhea risk in the community: A systematic review. *The Lancet Infectious Diseases, 3* (5), 275–281

Cutler, D. and Miller, G. (2005). The role of public health improvements in health advances: The 20th century United States. *Demography, 42* (1), 1–22

Davis, J. (2004). Corruption in public services delivery: Experience from South Asia's water and sanitation sector. *World Development, 32* (1), 53–71

Davis, J., Kang, A., Vincent, J., and Whittington, D. (2001). How important is improved water infrastructure to microenterprises? Evidence from Uganda. *World Development, 29* (10), 1753–1767

Davis, J., Lukacs, H., Jeuland, M., Alvestegui, A., Sotto, B., *et al.* (2007). Sustaining the benefits of rural water supply investments: Experience from Cochabamba and Chuquisaca, Bolivia. Submitted for publication

Duflo, E. and Pande, R. (2007). Dams. *Quarterly Journal of Economics, 122* (2), 601–646

Earwaker, P. (2006). Evaluation of household biosand filters in Ethiopia. Silsoe, UK: Department of Water Management, Cranfield University

Esrey, S. (1996). Water, waste, and well-being: A multicountry study. *American Journal of Epidemiology, 43* (6), 608–623

Esrey, S.A., Potash, J.B., Roberts, L., and Schiff, C. (1991). Effects of improved water supply and sanitation on ascariasis, diarrhoea, dracunculiasis, hookworm infection, schistosomiasis, and trachoma. *Bulletin of the World Health Organization*, 69, 609–621

Feacham, R.G., Bradley, D.J., Garelick, H., and Mara, D.D. (1983). *Sanitation and disease: Health aspects of excreta and wastewater management.* Chichester, UK: John Wiley and Sons

Fewtrell, L., Kaufmann, R., Kay, D., Enanoria, W., Haller, L., *et al.* (2005). Water, sanitation, and hygiene interventions to reduce diarrhoea in less developed countries: A systematic review and meta-analysis. *Lancet Infectious Diseases 2005*, 5 (1), 42–52

Grey, D. and Sadoff, C. (2007). Sink or swim? Water security for growth and development. *Water Policy 2007*, 9 (6), 545–571

Griffin, C., Briscoe, J., Singh, B., Ramasubban, R., and Bhatia, R. (1995). Contingent valuation and actual behavior: Predicting connections to new water systems in the State of Kerala, India. *World Bank Economic Review*, 9 (3), 373–395

Hammitt, J.K. and Liu, J. (2004). Effect of disease type and latency on the value of mortality risk. *Journal of Risk and Uncertainty*, 28, 73–95

Hanemann, W.M. (2006). The economic conception of water. In P.P. Rogers, M.R. Llamas, and L. Martinez-Cortina (Eds.), *Water crisis: Myth or reality?* (pp. 61–91). London and New York: Taylor and Francis

Hirschman, A. (1958). *The strategy of economic development.* New Haven: Yale University Press

Hutton, G. and Haller, L. (2004). *Evaluation of the costs and benefits of water and sanitation improvements at the global level.* Geneva: Water, Sanitation, and Health, Protection of the Human Environment, World Health Organization

IPCC (2007). *Climate change 2007: Impacts, adaptations and vulnerability: Scientific-technical analyses.* Contribution of Working Group II to the Second Assessment Report of the Intergovernmental Panel on Climate Change. Cambridge and New York: Cambridge University Press

Jalan, J. and Ravallion, M. (2003). Does piped water reduce diarrhea for children in rural India? *Journal of Econometrics, 112* (1), 153–173

Jamison, D., Breman, J., Measham, A., Alleyne, G., Claeson, M., *et al.* (2006). *Disease control priorities in developing countries.* New York: Oxford University Press

Johnston, R. (2006). Is hypothetical bias universal? Validating contingent valuation responses using a binding public referendum. *Journal of Environmental Economics and Management, 52*, 469–481

Kaiser, N., Liang, K., Maertens, M., and Snider, R. (2002). *BioSand household water filter evaluation 2001: A comprehensive evaluation of the Samaritan's Purse BioSand Filter (BSF) projects in Kenya, Mozambique, Cambodia, Vietnam, Honduras, and Nicaragua.* Calgary, Canada: Samaritan's Purse

Kariuki, M. and Schwartz, J. (2005). Small-scale private service providers of water supply and electricity: A review of incidence, structure, pricing and operating characteristics. *World Bank Policy Research Working Paper 3727.* Washington, D.C.: The World Bank

Katui-Kafui, M. (2002). *Drawers of water, vol. 2, Kenya country study.* London: International Institute for Environment and Development

Komives, K., Whittington, D., and Wu, X. (2003). Infrastructure coverage and the poor: A global perspective. In P. Brook and T. Irwin (Eds.), *Infrastructure for poor people: Public policy for private provision* (pp. 77–124). Washington, D.C.: The World Bank Public–Private Infrastructure Advisory Facility

Komives, K., Foster, V., Halpern, J., and Wodon, Q. (2005). *Water, electricity, and the poor: Who benefits from utility subsidies?* Washington, D.C.: The World Bank

Komives, K., Akanbang, B., Wakeman, W., Thorsten, R., Tuffuor, B., *et al.* (2007). Community management of rural water systems in Ghana: Post-construction support and water and sanitation committees in Brong Ahafo and Volta regions. *Water Resources Sustainability,* edited by Larry W. Mays, McGraw-Hill, New York

Kosek, M., Bern, C., and Guerrant, R.L. (2003). The global burden of diarrheal disease, as estimated from studies published between 1992 and 2000. *Bulletin of the World Health Organization, 81* (3), 197–204

Kremer, M., Leino, J., Miguel, E., and Zwane, A.P. (2007). *Spring cleaning: A randomized evaluation of source water quality improvement.* UC-Berkeley, Working Paper. http://elsa.berkeley.edu

Kremer, M., Null, C., Miguel, E., and Zwane, A.P. (2008). *Trickle down: Diffusion of chlorine for drinking water treatment in Kenya.* UC-Berkeley, Working Paper. http://elsa.berkeley.edu

Krupnick, A., Hoffman, S., Larsen, B., Peng, X., Yuan, C., *et al.* (2008). Willingness to pay for mortality risk reductions in Shanghai and Chongqing, China. World Bank, Washington, DC

Lovei, L. and Whittington, D. (1993). Rent-seeking in the water supply sector: A case study of Jakarta, Indonesia. *Water Resources Research*, 29 (7), 1965–1974

Mahmud, M. (2007). On the contingent valuation of mortality risk reduction in developing countries. *Applied Economics*, 1–11

Maskery, B., Islam, Z., Deen, J., and Whittington, D (2008). An estimate of parents' value of statistical life for their children in rural Bangladesh. Paper presented at the annual meetings of the European Association of Environmental and Resource Economists. 27 June, Gothenburg, Sweden

Mrozek, J.R. and Taylor, L.O. (2002). What determines the value of life? A meta-analysis. *Journal of Policy Analysis and Management, 21* (2), 253–270

Nauges, C. and van den Berg, C. (2008a). The impact of sector reform on the supply and demand for water supply services in Moldova. Working paper, Toulouse School of Economics (LERNA-INRA)

Nauges, C. and van den Berg, C. (2008b). Spatial heterogeneity in the cost structure of water and sanitation services: A cross-country comparison of conditions for scale economies. Working paper, Toulouse School of Economics (LERNA-INRA)

Pattanayak, S.K., Yang, J.C., Whittington, D., and Kumar, K.C.B. (2005). Coping with unreliable public water supplies: Averting expenditures by households in Kathmandu, Nepal. *Water Resources Research, 41* (2), W02012

Pattanayak, S., Blitstein, J.L., Yang, J.C., Dickinson, K.L., Patil, S.R., Poulos, C., and Wendland, K.M. (2007a). Promoting latrine use and improving child health: Design and baseline findings from a randomized evaluation of a community mobilization campaign in Bhadrak, Orissa. *RTI Working Paper 06-05*, Research Triangle Institute, North Carolina

Pattanayak, S.K., Dickinson, K.L., Yang, J.C., Patil, S.R., and Poulos, C. (2007b). Nature's call: Can social mobilization promote toilet use and improve welfare? Results from a field experiment in Orissa, India. Working paper, Research Triangle Institute

Powers, T. (1978). Benefit–cost analysis of urban water projects. *Water Supply and Management, 1*, 371–385

Powers, T. and Valencia, C.A. (1980). *SIMOP urban water model: Users' manual: A model for economic analysis of potable water projects in urban areas.* Inter-American Development Bank Papers on Project Analysis, No. 5. Washington, D.C.: Inter-American Development Bank, Economic and Social Development Department, Country Studies Division, Project Methodology Unit

Priscoli, J.D. (2000). Water and civilization: Using history to reframe water policy debates and to build a new ecological realism. *Water Policy, 1* (6), 623–636

Prokopy, L., Thorsten, R., Bakalian, A., and Wakeman, W. (2007). Evaluating the role of post-construction support in sustaining drinking water projects: Evidence from Peru. Submitted for publication

Russell, C., Vaughan, W.J., Clark, C.D., Rodriguez, D.J., and Darling, A. (2001). *Investing in water quality: Measuring benefits, costs and risk.* Washington, D.C.: Inter-American Development Bank

Samaritan's Purse (2007). *BioSand water filter: In depth.* Calgary, Canada: Samaritan's Purse

Sannan, D. and Moulik, S.G. (2007). *Community-led total sanitation in rural areas: An approach that works* (field note). New Delhi, India: Water and Sanitation Program – South Asia

Sara, J. and Katz, T. (1997). *Making rural water supply sustainable: Report on the impact of project rules.* Washington D.C.: UNDP–World Bank Water and Sanitation Program

Sara, J., Gross, A., and van den Berg, C. (1996). *Rural water supply and sanitation in Bolivia:*

From pilot to national program. Washington D.C.: UNDP–World Bank Water and Sanitation Program

Stauber, C.E. (2007). The microbiological and health impact of the BioSand filter in the Dominican Republic: A randomized controlled trial in Bonao. *PhD Dissertation.* Department of Environmental Sciences and Engineering. Chapel Hill: University of North Carolina, 213pp.

Therkildsen, O. (1988). *Watering white elephants? Lessons from donor-funded planning and implementation of rural water supplies in Tanzania.* Uppsala, Sweden: Centre for Development Research Publications, Scandinavian Institute of African Studies

Thorsten, R. (2007). *Predicting sustainable performance and household satisfaction of community-oriented rural water supply projects: A quantitative evaluation of evidence from Ghana and Peru.* Unpublished manuscript. Department of City and Regional Planning, UNC-CH, Chapel Hill, NC

UNDP (2006). *Beyond scarcity: Power, poverty and the global water crisis.* New York: United Nations Development Programme

UNEP (1998). *Sourcebook of alternative technologies for freshwater augmentation in Africa.* By J. Thornton. Nairobi, Kenya: International Environmental Technology Centre, United Nations Environment Program: 182pp.

US Environmental Protection Agency (2000). Guidelines for preparing economic analyses, EPA-R-00-003. Washington, DC

VanDerslice, J. and Briscoe, J. (1993). All coliforms are not created equal: A comparison of the effects of water source and in-house contamination on infantile diarrheal disease. *Water Resources Research, 29* (7), 1983–1995

Vassandumrongdee, S. and Matsuoka, S. (2005). Risk perceptions and value of a statistical life for air pollution and traffic accidents: Evidence from Bangkok, Thailand. *Journal of Risk and Uncertainty, 30* (3), 261–287

Viscusi, W., Kip, A., and Joseph, E. (2003). The value of a statistical life: a critical review of market estimates throughout the world. *Journal of Risk and Uncertainty, 27* (1), 5–76

Whittington, D., Mujwahuzi, M., McMahon, G., and Choe, K. (1988). *Willingness to pay for water in Newala District, Tanzania: Strategies for cost recovery.* WASH Field Report No. 246. Washington, D.C.: USAID Water and Sanitation for Health Project

Whittington, D., Briscoe, J., Mu, X., and Barron, W. (1990a). Estimating the willingness to pay for water services in developing countries: A case study of the use of contingent valuation surveys in southern Haiti. *Economic Development and Cultural Change, 38* (2), 293–311

Whittington, D., Mu, X., and Roche, R. (1990b). Calculating the value of time spent collecting water: Some estimates for Ukunda, Kenya. *World Development, 18* (2), 269–280

Whittington, D., Lauria, D.T., Wright, A.M., Choe, K., Hughes, J.A., *et al.* (1993). Household demand for improved sanitation services in Kumasi, Ghana: A contingent valuation study. *Water Resources Research, 29* (6), 1539–1560

Whittington, D. and Swarna, V. (1994). The economic appraisal of potable water supply projects. Working Paper, Asian Development Bank, Manila

Whittington, D., Davis, J., and McClelland, E. (1998). Implementing a demand-driven approach to community water supply planning: A case study of Lugazi, Uganda. *Water International, 23* (3), 134–145

Whittington, D., Pattanayak, S., Yang, J.C., and Kumar, B. (2002). Household demand for improved piped water services in Kathmandu, Nepal. *Water Policy, 4* (6), 531–556

Whittington, D., Lauria, D.T., Prabhu, V., and Cook, J. (2004). An economic reappraisal of the Melamchi water supply project, Kathmandu, Nepal. *Portuguese Economic Journal, 3* (2), 157–178

Whittington, D., Davis, J., Prokopy, L., Komives, K., Thorsten, R., *et al.* (2007). How well is the demand-driven, community management model for rural water supply systems doing? Evidence from Bolivia, Peru, and Ghana. Submitted for publication

Whittington, D., Suraratdecha, C., Poulos, C., Ainsworth, M., Prabhu, V., Tangcharoensathien, V. (2008). Household demand for preventive HIV/AIDS vaccines in Thailand: Do husbands' and

wives' preferences differ? *Value in Health.*
Forthcoming

WHO (2002). *Revised global burden of disease (GBD) 2002 estimates.* Geneva. Available at www.who.int/healthinfo/bodgbd2002revised/en/index.html

World Bank (2006). *Managing water resources to maximize sustainable growth: Country assistance strategy for the Federal Democratic Republic of Ethiopia.* Washington, D.C.: The World Bank

World Commission on Dams (2000). *Dams and development: A new framework for decision-making.* London: Earthscan Publications

Water and Sanitation Program (2005). *Scaling-up rural sanitation in South Asia: Lessons learned from Bangladesh, India and Pakistan.* Washington, D.C.: The World Bank, Water and Sanitation Program

Alternative Perspectives

Perspective Paper 7.1

JENNIFER DAVIS

1. Introduction

The principal messages found in Part I of the Challenge Paper by Whittington *et al.* – that water and sanitation services are expensive, and that conventional estimates of the value of economic benefits from household-level service provision in low-income countries are minimal – may strike some readers as provocative departures from the literature. Other recent papers dealing with the economic benefits of water and sanitation, many inspired by the Millennium Development process, have presented more sanguine conclusions regarding net benefits and cost effectiveness of water and sanitation investments (Stockholm International Water Institute; Sachs, 2005). Hutton and Haller (2004), for example, concluded that the return on each US$1 investment in a variety of water supply and sanitation improvements ranged between US$5 and US$28; these benefits were found "in all world regions" and none of the interventions considered yielded a benefit–cost ratio of less than 1. By contrast, the Challenge Paper authors conclude that in many cases "the incremental benefit of improved access to water and sanitation network infrastructure may simply not be large enough to cover the cost" of providing that access.

The apparent divergence of these conclusions is explained in large part by the fact that any number of interventions can be carried out under the guise of water and/or sanitation improvements. The first part of the Challenge Paper focuses on the costs and benefits of "top shelf" water and sanitation services, i.e., in-home piped water connections, toilets with sewer connections, and wastewater treatment. By contrast, international development organizations tend to focus on the more modest goals of ensuring access to "improved" water supply and "basic" sanitation *as per* the Joint Monitoring Programme definitions.[1] Disparities in both costs and benefits should be expected when latrines are compared with sewerage and wastewater treatment, and shared wells with in-home water network connections.

It is also the case, however, that the authors have understated the benefits of networked water and sanitation services. Discussion of investments in piped water and sewer networks is presented in the next section of the paper. The authors' analyses of three non-network water and sanitation interventions – deep borewells with hand pumps, community sanitation programs, and household water-treatment filters – are reviewed in section 3. A brief discussion of non-infrastructure investments designed to reduce water- and sanitation-related disease is provided in section 4, followed by a brief set of concluding remarks.

---

[1] www.wssinfo.org/en/122_definitions.html

430

2. Water and Sewer Networks

The Challenge Paper authors rightly point out that rigorous economic evaluation is rarely undertaken of water and sanitation interventions; one must rely on a literature that is replete with associative data and anecdotes. The authors use four types of data in order to estimate the economic benefits that accrue to households whose water supply and sanitation services are improved. Three of these – prices charged for vended water, household expenditures related to coping with poor services, and avoided costs of illness – are based on revealed preference (or, roughly, "market") data, while the fourth is grounded in stated preference information.

The authors do not consider the value of reduced risk of mortality from water- and sanitation-related illness. This omission is particularly egregious given that this parameter accounts for the majority (up to 80%) of the total economic benefits estimated for the non-network interventions evaluated in Part II of the Challenge Paper. Recent work suggests that mortality reductions resulting from the extension of piped water networks in urban areas can be substantial. Cutler and Miller (2005), for example, find that the provision of a treated, piped water supply was responsible for nearly half the total mortality reduction in major US cities between 1900 and 1940. The authors estimate a benefit–cost ratio of more than 23 (95% confidence interval of 7 to 40) for these investments.

With respect to the data that are presented in the Challenge Paper analysis, the limitations of stated preference ("willingness to pay" or contingent valuation) data for planning and policy decisions have been well documented (Diamond and Hausman, 1994; Davis,). Contingent valuation approaches suffer from hypothetical bias for several reasons. A structured, one-hour survey with an individual head of household bears little resemblance to households' decision-making process about major expenditure decisions such as infrastructure investment. Moreover, respondents do not face actual budget constraints when discussing "what if" scenarios, making the contingent valuation approach prone to "yea saying" and inflated valuation estimates (Boyle et al., 1993; Boyle et al., 1994; Kanninen, 1995).

The revealed preference (market) data used by the authors might thus be expected to be more reliable, assuming that prices of alternative services and avoided health care are reasonable proxies for the value of improved water and sanitation services. There are several reasons why this might not be the case, however. First, as noted by the Challenge Paper authors, the provision of these services generates external economic effects that are not fully reflected in market prices. In such circumstances the relevant question for economic analysis is not whether households themselves can or would pay the cost of improved services – which is how the authors have framed their analysis – but whether the expenditures required for such upgrades are greater than the value of the benefits they would generate, regardless of how those benefits are distributed.

When analysis is limited to a framework that excludes consideration of both reduced risk of mortality and external effects (as found in Part I of the Challenge Paper), the conclusion that the net benefits of providing piped water, sewerage, and wastewater treatment to unserved households are non-positive should not be surprising. In general the people who currently lack access to water supply and sanitation services are poor. About one third of the unserved live on less than US$1 per day, and another third on US$1–2 per day (United Nations Development Programme, 2006). Moreover, the individuals who would benefit most from the increased availability of time stemming from water and sanitation improvements are women and children. Using traditional cost–benefit approaches, it becomes quickly apparent that the economic value of the poorest segment of the world's poorest families will be meager. Their budget constraint precludes large (and meaningful) willingness-to-pay values, and their low earning potential translates into small foregone wage values.

The types of external effects that can arise from water and sanitation service improvements have been repeatedly enumerated but poorly quantified. Acknowledging the paucity of data on external benefits, the Challenge Paper authors do not attempt to incorporate them in the analysis. International development organizations have often made the same observations regarding the difficulty of measuring external benefits from investment in water and sanitation, but conclude instead that the magnitude of these benefits must exceed the costs of service improvements. Both of these approaches are unsatisfying: one ignores external effects (and concludes that costs often exceed benefits), while the other imputes unsubstantiated value to such effects (and concludes that benefits exceed costs).

Improving our understanding of the health benefits (both direct and spillover) of water and sanitation interventions is particularly important given the continued decline in mortality and rise in morbidity from water- and sanitation-related disease (Figure 7.1.1). That is, the percentage of person-days spent suffering from diarrhea is rising, but the case fatality rate continues to fall. The Challenge Paper authors argue that the benefits of reducing non-fatal episodes of diarrhea comprise a very small proportion of the total benefits derived from water and sanitation interventions. If true, and if trends in mortality and morbidity from water- and sanitation-related illness persist, we would expect the net benefits of water and sanitation investments to be decreasing over time, *ceteris paribus*.

It could be argued instead that the full costs of morbidity from water- and sanitation-related illness are poorly understood. For example, such morbidity impacts on savings, expenditures, and longer-term productivity of households, but the nature and magnitude of these effects are poorly understood (Kochar, 2004).

Similarly, few studies have attempted to quantify the contribution of water and sanitation services, mediated through health, to educational performance or productivity. Recently a body of work relating infectious disease to malnutrition – whose effects on long-term development are better studied – has begun to fill this gap (World Bank, 2008). Lack of access to safe water and sanitation has been associated

with increased prevalence of chronic diarrhea, which, in turn, is associated with malnutrition (Stephenson, 1999; Alderman *et al.*, 2006).

Children suffering from malnutrition have been shown to exhibit symptoms of diminished cognitive ability and lower educational attainment than healthy children (Berkman *et al.*, 2002; Alderman *et al.*, 2006). In addition, malnutrition is thought to cause the death of roughly half of the under-five children who die each year (World Bank, 2008; Fishman *et al.*, 2004; Caulfield *et al.*, 2006; Bryce *et al.*, 2005). Whereas the linkages between malnutrition and water and sanitation services have historically not been acknowledged, several recent analyses suggest that up to one half of the health consequences of malnutrition can be traced not to inadequate food supply but to inadequate water, sanitation, and hygiene services (Prüss-Üstün and Corvalán, 2006; World Bank, 2006; WHO, 2007).

A second set of reasons why market data may not accurately reflect the value of water supply and sanitation to households concerns the balance of power between men and women, both within the home and in the public arena. In most households of low-income countries, males have principal say over the family budget and expenditures. A considerable body of evidence in the practitioner or "grey" literature has suggested that women give relatively greater priority to water and sanitation services compared with men (Van Wijk, 1998). More rigorous academic work has also demonstrated that women prioritize child welfare and the provision of public goods relative to men (Miller, 2007). When women are given the opportunity to influence spending decisions, either directly or through democratic institutions, evidence suggests that allocations to water supply and sanitation increase (Chattopadhyay and Duflo, 2004). In short, men – from whom the sort of market data that the Challenge Paper authors draw upon for their analysis are typically generated – appear to be highly imperfect agents for members of the household who tend to benefit the most from water and sanitation improvements.

Third, the authors point to evidence that

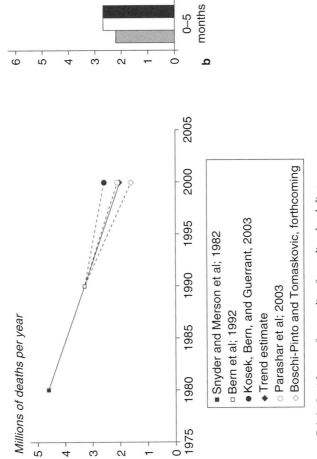

Figure 7.1.1 *Incidence of mortality from diarrheal disease*
Source: Keusch et al. (2006)

access to other public services such as electricity is higher than to improved water supply and sanitation services as indicative of the relatively lower demand for the latter. This reasoning assumes that the absence of evidence for demand for water and sanitation services equates to evidence of absence of that demand. It also presumes a well-functioning housing market that allows families to locate in dwellings with amenities that match their preferences. In some settings, however, plausible rival explanations exist on the supply side. For example, a substantial proportion of the hundreds of millions of people lacking access to water and sanitation services in urban areas are located in neighborhoods that are considered "unplanned" or "unregularized." These communities are often located beyond the reach of trunk infrastructure and/or are legally prohibited from receiving service improvements because of their tenure status.

An example from South Asia can help to illustrate this point. One well-known infrastructure upgrading scheme, the Slum Networking Project (SNP), was initiated in the Indian city of Ahmedabad in 1997. Municipal Corporation engineers worked together with NGOs to offer a bundle of infrastructure, environmental, and social services to slum households at affordable prices. The Ahmedabad Municipal Corporation was willing to allow unregularized slums located on city-owned land to participate; however, more than half of the unserved were located on state- or privately owned land. These communities were considered ineligible for participation in the project, regardless of residents' effective demand for service improvements.

In sum, the authors have done a service by raising awareness of the full economic costs of piped water, sewerage, and wastewater treatment services. Their omission of effects on mortality and reliance on market and revealed preference data in estimating benefits, however, clearly result in lower-bound values. Their analysis also brings into sharp focus the need for reliable evidence regarding spillover and longer-term effects of water and sanitation improvements on both health and productivity.

3. Non-network Water and Sanitation Interventions

The approach employed in Part II of the Challenge Paper is certainly innovative; it also responds to a chronic lack of nuance in the literature regarding the conditions under which particular water and sanitation investments are expected to yield positive net benefits. Any reasonable "solution" to deficient household water supply, sanitation, and hygiene will be successful in some settings and a failure in others. The authors' focus on generating distributions of benefit–cost ratios as opposed to point estimates, as well as their attention to characterizing the settings in which their chosen interventions appear most promising, are thus well appreciated.

That the authors' analytical approach is unique also gives rise to questions that cannot be answered with information provided in the Challenge Paper. The selection of a uniform distribution for all parameters in the model, for example, should be elaborated (e.g., whether alternative distributions affect results). In addition, the ranges of parameter values included in the models, as well as the standard deviation values, suggest less variation than some working in the water and sanitation field might expect. Finally, while acknowledging the authors' time and resource constraints, the analysis would be strengthened by some comparison of the model results with empirical data. For example, one could categorize available data for a particular intervention based on the authors' "site attractiveness" criteria, and evaluate the extent to which outcomes on the ground exhibit roughly the pattern implied by the simulation results.

The Value of Life

The Challenge Paper authors find that the majority (67–80%) of the benefits for the community sanitation and point-of-use treatment interventions are derived from reduced mortality, and that the economic value of mortality reductions is very sensitive to their assumed value of a statistical life (VSL). The authors' choice of US$30,000 for the base case is not well substantiated, and is considerably lower than the values reported in other recent work on this topic. For example, Viscusi and Aldy (2003) estimate the VSL for an individual in the US as US$7 million, with income elasticity of the VSL estimated to fall to 0.5–0.6. These findings have been used to argue that lives in developing countries should be valued at roughly 100 times per capita GDP (Simon, 1993). Setting aside possible moral objections regarding the calibration of the VSL for lower-income populations and using regional median values for *per capita* income, the implied values of a statistical life for Sub-Saharan Africa and South Asia range between four and sixteen times higher than those used in the Challenge Paper's analyses. Modest adjustments of the VSL would improve the (already attractive) interventions considered by the authors. More importantly, as noted above, inclusion of reduced mortality risk into the authors' piped network analysis might well lead to different substantive conclusions with respect to that level of service.

Incidence and Reduction of Diarrhea

The Challenge Paper authors' assumption of 0.9 cases of diarrhea per person per year is based on data from various developing regions and may understate regional incidence, particularly in Africa. Most incidence studies have restricted their focus to children less than five years old, whereas the Challenge Paper authors are apparently including all household members. Even considering the extrapolation required for comparison, the burden of diarrheal disease among the target population for the borehole intervention appears to be larger than that considered by the authors. World Health Organization data as well as literature reviews (Kirkwood, 1991) have found under-five diarrheal incidence in Sub-Saharan Africa to be in the order of five episodes per child per year. Adjusting this parameter value would thus improve the benefit–cost ratio of the borewell scenario in particular.

However, the authors' "base case" assumption of a 30% reduction in diarrheal incidence as

a result of a shared point source of water supply is probably optimistic (Zwane and Kremer, 2007). Even if the supply of water at the well is relatively safe, water quality often deteriorates during transport and storage (Wright *et al.*, 2004). At the same time, the increased quantity of water to which a typical household will have access provides an opportunity for improved hygiene (handwashing), which could reduce transmission of diarrhea-causing illness if concomitant investments are made in handwashing promotion (Curtis and Cairncross, 2003). The net effect of the implied adjustments to the benefit–cost analysis of the borewell intervention is unclear.

Decentralized Water Treatment

Water treatment at the point of use provides households with the opportunity to ensure that at least a minimal quantity of water needed for drinking and cooking is of good quality. As the Challenge Paper authors note, point-of-use treatment does not preclude the need to bring water to the dwelling. At the same time, POU approaches may have the effect of increasing the quantity of water available to a household for a given amount of time and/or effort, if adoption of POU allows the household to access (and treat) lower quality source water that is more convenient to the home. In such cases it would be appropriate to incorporate the consumer surplus on increased water use.

Correct, consistent use of POU technologies is critical to maintain the flow of health benefits they can generate. Whereas the literature on POU technologies such as the biosand filter suggests very high levels of efficacy in laboratory settings, field tests reveal a more mixed picture, as well as challenges in ensuring proper use (Baumgartner *et al.*, 2007). The Challenge Paper authors' assumption of a 2% decline annually in use of the household filter thus seems optimistic. For example, researchers from Cranfield University (Earwaker, 2006) found that 21% of a sample of Ethiopian households had ceased use of their biosand filters after five years (averaging a 4.5% annual decrease in usage). Brown and Sobsey (2007) found regular use of a ceramic filter – which admittedly requires more effort and recurrent investment on the part of users – fell by 2% per *month* among a sample of Cambodian households. Sensitivity analysis for this critical parameter is important for evaluating this intervention option, but is missing from the Challenge Paper. More generally, a better understanding of the settings in which sustained, correct use of household-level water-quality technologies is likely to be achieved is needed.

Threshold Effects in Sanitation

The community sanitation analysis requires an assumption regarding the relationship between rates of household latrine construction/use and health outcomes for both participating and non-participating families. The authors assume that, in a typical case, 28% of households will fully complete educational and motivational training and construct an improved sanitation facility such as a latrine. Partial participation, which is estimated at an additional 12% of households, entails completion of training and installation of improved sanitation infrastructure, but limited or no use of the sanitation facilities installed. The typical resulting health outcome for this level of full and partial participation is given as a 30% reduction in diarrheal incidence for the entire community.[2]

Two concerns arise regarding the conclusions of the total sanitation analysis. First, there is evidence to suggest the existence of threshold effects of sanitation coverage on health outcomes (Shuval *et al.*, 1981). There are very limited data on the relationship between changes in coverage with improved latrine facilities and health

[2] Research on Total Sanitation approaches is very limited; however, evidence from the processed literature suggests that participation rates higher than those assumed by the Challenge Paper authors are observed at least in some locations. One evaluation of thirteen communities in Nigeria, for example, found a median 80% participation rate in training and latrine construction, although data on consistency of latrine use were not provided (WaterAid, 2007).

outcomes (and even fewer regarding proper use of such facilities). Impacts are mediated by users' behavior to a greater extent than the other interventions considered, and will also vary with population density, topography, and source of water supply. Such uncertainties should be better reflected in the authors' model.

Second, given that community-led total sanitation is really a suite of activities and investments, it is difficult to discern the relative contribution of motivation and education *versus* improved sanitation infrastructure to health outcomes. Given that the ratio of "software" to "hardware" costs for the intervention is in the order of three to one, it would be helpful to know whether smaller investments in education and motivation could be made without diminishing the resulting benefits, or conversely if promotion of improved hygiene practices without concomitant hardware investments would reduce benefits substantially. This final point is discussed further in the following section.

4. Non-infrastructure Interventions

As the Challenge Paper authors note, it has been demonstrated in many settings that improvements in water supply and sanitation services may be necessary but insufficient to realize substantial improvements in health. Where reductions in diarrhea are not observed, a common explanation has been the lack of concomitant changes in behavior (Esrey *et al.*, 1991; Jalan and Ravallion, 2003). For water supply improvements that entail water transport and storage by household members – which characterize the majority of interventions occurring in developing countries today – safe water-management and hygiene practices are required to prevent re-contamination of supply (Zwane and Kremer, 2007). The benefits of sanitation infrastructure investments are maximized where households have the knowledge, ability, and motivation to use the facilities in a consistent and correct manner.

In recent years evidence has emerged regarding the potential for hygiene promotion programs to make substantial contributions to health, whether in parallel with infrastructure improvements or as stand-alone interventions. Historically hygiene promotion has received very limited attention in water and sanitation projects. For example, less than 1% of the US$5.5 billion in support for rural water and sanitation projects provided by the World Bank during the period 1978–2003 was spent on health education or behavior-change activities (Iyer *et al.*, 2006).

Evidence regarding the impacts of handwashing at critical times (e.g., after defecation, before eating) on diarrheal incidence is compelling, with typical impacts surpassing the median 30% reduction employed for analysis of the non-network interventions in the Challenge Paper. A meta-analysis by Curtis and Cairncross (Curtis and Cairncross, 2003), for example, found that handwashing with soap is associated with reductions in the risk of diarrhea of 42–47%. A randomized controlled trial in Pakistan found outcomes of this magnitude for both diarrhea and pneumonia incidence among children (Luby *et al.*, 2004). More recently, alcohol-based handrubs have been explored as an alternative method of hand hygiene in water-scarce locations of developing countries (Pickering *et al.*, 2008).

Limited information is available regarding the economic costs and benefits of hygiene-promotion programs. Hygiene promotion has been identified as a relatively cost-effective option for reducing child and infant mortality (Larsen, 2003; Varley *et al.*, 1998; Borghi *et al.*, 2002); however, evidence regarding full economic costs and benefits is too limited to enable direct comparison with the other interventions considered in the Challenge Paper. Just as the sustaining of benefits from improved water supply and sanitation services is dependent on adequate maintenance of installed infrastructure, the benefits of hygiene are realized only so long as households continue to practice handwashing at critical times. The period over which behavior change is sustained will have a major effect on the net benefits of a given program. Long-term compliance with hygiene regimens appears to be a challenge in at least some settings, and thus the

recurrent costs of effective hygiene programs may be substantial. With those caveats, it seems that hygiene promotion is deserving of greater consideration as a "water and sanitation" intervention in its own right.

5. Conclusions

Clearly there remains much to be learned about the impacts of water and sanitation improvements on health and welfare, at both the household and the national level. As demonstrated in the Challenge Paper, however, several types of investment have been shown to be economically attractive (within appropriate settings), even with an analytical approach that is restricted to localized and estimable benefits. Among the 1.2 billion and 2.6 billion persons lacking access to water supply and sanitation services, respectively, roughly 80% live in low-density ("rural") areas. The non-network interventions evaluated by the Challenge Paper authors appear particularly well suited for these types of communities.

The dangers of imputing unsubstantiated values to water and sanitation improvements were discussed above. Nevertheless, it is important to consider what is at stake in a world where two out of every five persons do not have even a basic pit for defecation, and two in ten cannot obtain safe drinking water. Certainly it is greater than current health care costs and lost earnings. Certainly the impacts of poor water and sanitation are felt by others than the potential "beneficiaries" who have been considered in this exercise. Many groups and individuals have committed substantial resources to extending services to poor households, often in other parts of the world. They are motivated in part by belief in the economic returns to such investments, but also by moral and religious imperatives that value human dignity, compassion, and solidarity. As Simon (1993) has noted, economic analysis which incorporates, rather than assumes away, the existence of such altruism and external effects would "have the merit of describing the world in which we actually live."

Bibliography

Alderman, H., Hoddinott, J., and Kinsey, B. (2006). Long term consequences of early childhood malnutrition. *Oxford Economic Papers*, *58*, 450–474

Baumgartner, J., Murcott, S., and Ezzati, M. (2007). Reconsidering 'appropriate technology': The effects of operating conditions on the bacterial removal performance of two household drinking-water filter systems. *Environmental Research Letters 2*, 1–6

Berkman, D., Lescano, A., Gilman, R., Lopez, S., and Black, M. (2002). Effects of stunting, diarrhoeal disease, and parasitic infection during infancy on cognition in late childhood: a follow-up study. *Lancet*, *359* (9306), 564–571

Borghi, J., Guinness, L., Ouedraogo, J., and Curtis, V. (2002). Is hygiene promotion cost-effective? A case study in Burkina Faso. *Tropical Medicine and International Health*, *7* (11), 960–969

Boyle, K., Walsh, M., and Bishop, R. (1993). The role of question order and respondent experience in contingent valuation studies. *Journal of Environmental Economics and Management*, *25* (1), 80–99

Boyle, K., Desvousges, W., Johnson, F., Dunford, R., and Hudson, S. (1994). An investigation of part-whole biases in contingent-valuation studies. *Journal of Environmental Economics and Management*, *27* (1), 64–83

Brown, J. and Sobsey, M. (2007). Use of ceramic water filters in Cambodia. Water and Sanitation Program Field Note. Jakarta: Water & Sanitation Program, Southeast Asia

Bryce, J., Boschi-Pinto, C., Shibuya, K., and Black, R. (2005). WHO estimates of the causes of death in children. *Lancet*, *365* (9465), 1147–1152

Caulfield, L.E., Richard, S.A., Rivera, J.A., Musgrove, P., and Black, R.E. (2006). Stunting, wasting, and micronutrient deficiency disorders. In Jamison, D.T. (ed.) *Disease control priorities in developing countries*. Washington D.C.: World Bank

Chattopadhyay, R. and Duflo, E. (2004). Women as policy makers: Evidence from a randomized policy experiment in India. *Econometrica*, *72* (5), 1409–1443

Curtis, V. and Cairncross, S. (2003). Effect of washing hands with soap on diarrhoea risk in the community: A systematic review. *The Lancet Infectious Diseases*, *3* (5), 275–281

Cutler, D. and Miller, G. (2005). The role of public health improvements in health advances: the 20th century United States. *Demography, 42* (1), 1–22

Davis, J. (2002) Assessing community preferences for development initiatives: Are willingness-to-pay studies robust to mode effects? *World Development*, *32* (4), 655–672

Davis, J. (2003) Scaling up slum upgrading: Where are the bottlenecks? *International Development Planning Review*, *26* (3), 301–319

Diamond, P.A. and Hausman, J.A. (1994). Contingent valuation: Is some number better than no number? *Journal of Economic Perspectives*, *8* (4), 45–64

Earwarker, P. (2006). Evaluation of household biosand filters in Ethiopia. MSc Water Management (Community Water Supply) thesis. Cranfield University, UK

Esrey, S., Potash, J., Roberts, L., and Shiff, C. (1991). Effects of improved water supply and sanitation on ascariasis, diarrhoea, dracunculiasis, hookworm infection, schistosomiasis, and trachoma. *Bulletin of the World Health Organization*, *69* (5), 609–621

Fishman, S., Caulfield, L.E., de Onis, M., Blossner, M., Hyder, A., Mullany, L., and Black, R.E. (2004). Childhood and maternal underweight. In Ezzati, M., Lopez, A.D., Rodgers, A. and Murray, C. (eds.) *Comparative quantification of health risks: Global and regional burden of disease attributable to selected major risk factors.* Geneva: World Health Organization

Hutton, G. and Haller, L. (2004). Evaluation of the non-health costs and benefits of water and sanitation improvements at global level. Report undertaken for the Evidence and Information for Policy Department, in collaboration with the Department for Protection of the Human Environment, World Health Organization. WHO/SDE/WSH/0404

Iyer, P., Davis, J., Yavuz, E., and Evans, B. (2006). Rural water supply, sanitation, and hygiene: A review of 25 years of World Bank lending (1978–2003). Washington, D.C.: The World Bank

Jalan, J. and Ravallion, M. (2003). Does piped water reduce diarrhea for children in rural India? *Journal of Econometrics*, *112*, 153–173

Kanninen, B. (1995). Bias in discrete response contingent valuation. *Journal of Environmental Economics and Management, 28* (1), 114–125

Keusch, G., Fontaine, O., Bhargava, A., Boschi-Pinto, C., Bhutta, Z.A., Gotuzzo, E., Rivera, J., Chow, J., Shahid-Salles, S.A., and Laxminarayan, R. (2006). Chapter 19: Diarrheal diseases. In D. Jamison *et al.* (eds.) *Disease control priorities in developing countries*, 2nd edition, Washington, D.C.: The World Bank

Kirkwood, B. (1991). Diarrhea. In Feachem R. and Jamison, D. (eds.) *Disease and mortality in Sub-Saharan Africa*. New York: Oxford University Press

Kochar, A. (2004). Ill-health, savings and portfolio choices in developing economies. *Journal of Development Economics, 73* (1), 257–285

Larsen, B. (2003). Hygiene and health in developing countries: Defining priorities through cost–benefit assessments. *International Journal of Environmental Health Research*, 13 (1), S37–S46

Luby, S., Agboatwalla, M., *et al.* (2004). Effect of intensive handwashing promotion on childhood diarrhea in high-risk communities in Pakistan: A randomized controlled trial. *JAMA, 291* (21), 2547–2554

Miller, G. (2007). Women's suffrage, political responsiveness, and child survival in American history. Unpublished manuscript, available at: www.ssc.wisc.edu/cde/demsem/suffrage.pdf

Pickering, A., Boehm, A., and Davis, J. (2008). Efficacy of alcohol-based rubs *versus* soap and water for hand hygiene: A field-based trial in Tanzania. Manuscript in preparation

Prüss-Üstün, A. and Corvalán, C. (2006). *Preventing disease through healthy environments: towards an estimate of the environmental burden of disease*. Geneva: World Health Organization

Sachs, J. (ed.) (2005). *Investing in development: A practical plan to achieve the Millennium Development Goals*. New York: The Millennium Development Project

Shuval, H.L., Tilden, R., Perry, B., and Grosse, R. (1981). Effect of investments in water supply and sanitation on health status: A threshold-saturation theory. *Bulletin of the World Health Organization, 59,* 243–248

Simon, H. (1993). Altruism and economics. *American Economic Review, 83* (2), 156–161

Stephensen, C. (1999). Burden of infection on growth failure. *Journal of Nutrition, 129,* 534–538

Stockholm International Water Institute. Securing sanitation: The compelling case to address the crisis. A report commissioned by the Government of Norway as input to the Commission on Sustainable Development (CSD) and its 2004–2005 focus on water, sanitation and related issues. Stockholm: Stockholm International Water Institute

United Nations Development Programme. Human Development Report 2006. New York: The United Nations

Van Wijk, C. (1998). *Gender in water resources management, water supply and sanitation: Roles and realities revisited*. The Hague: IRC

Varley, R.C., Tarvid, J., and Chao, D.N. (1998). A reassessment of the cost-effectiveness of water and sanitation interventions in programmes for controlling childhood diarrhoea. *Bulletin of the World Health Organization, 76* (6), 617–631

Viscusi, K. and Aldy, J. (2003). The value of a statistical life: A critical review of market estimates throughout the world. *Journal of Risk and Uncertainty, 27* (1), 5–76

WaterAid (2007). Community led total sanitation (CLTS): An evaluation of WaterAid's CLTS programme in Nigeria. London: WaterAid

WHO (2007). *The World Health Report 2007: A safer future global public health security in the 21st century*. Geneva: WHO

World Bank (2008). *Environmental health and child survival: Epidemiology, economics, experiences*. Environment and Development Series. Washington D.C.: The World Bank

World Bank (2006). *Repositioning nutrition as central to development: A strategy for large scale action*. Washington, D.C.: World Bank

Wright, J., Gundry, S., and Conroy, R. (2004). Household drinking water in developing countries: A systematic review of microbiological contamination between source and point-of-use. *Tropical Medicine & International Health, 9* (1), 106–117

Zwane, A. and Kremer, M. (2007). What works in fighting diarrheal diseases in developing countries? A critical review. *The World Bank Research Observer, 22,* 1–24

Perspective Paper 7.2

FRANK R. RIJSBERMAN AND
ALIX PETERSON ZWANE

1. Introduction

Access to some form of drinking water is a necessary condition for survival for all people, hence "water is life." Whittington *et al.* argue in the Challenge Paper that the *incremental* benefits of so-called "*improved water and sanitation*" may not be large enough to make investments in the sector attractive. The thorough and carefully constructed Challenge Paper argues that full, networked water and sanitation investments may likely be uneconomical, and that although low-cost technologies may be a better investment, the benefit–cost ratios of even these investments are low. Though Whittington *et al.* propose a somewhat cautious conclusion to their work, saying that "not all investments will pass [a rigorous economic test]," it is likely that, if their conclusions are accepted, the Copenhagen Consensus will be that water and sanitation is not a good investment for scarce donor or government funds. The Challenge Paper is important for its willingness to challenge received wisdom on this question and we welcome the chance to comment on it.

This Perspective Paper reviews the evidence and analysis provided by Whittington *et al.* and offers a complementary, and in some areas alternative, perspective on some key elements of the Challenge Paper. We argue that the balance of the rigorous economic evidence available suggests that Whittington *et al.* underestimate the benefits associated with water and sanitation investments and, as a result of the type of investments that they choose to study, also overstate the costs of these investments. Existing evidence based on actual behavior, as opposed to engineering estimates or stated preference reporting, does suggest that benefits of appro-

priate technologies can significantly exceed their costs. The challenge of making these beneficial investments sustainable should be researchers' and practitioners' central focus.

Whittington *et al.* focus in Part I of their paper on a discussion of the nature of "improved" water and sanitation services and the (economic and other) factors that make the rigorous economic analysis of water and sanitation services so complex. What constitutes "improved service" is indeed the subject of considerable debate in the literature and in the sector generally. Clearly, every human being does already have access to some form of water for drinking, or they would not be alive. The poor quality and limited quantity of water that is available to a large share of the world population, however, combined with a lack of access to sanitation and poor personal hygiene is indisputably linked to poor health. The global health burden of diarrheal disease is enormous and falls disproportionately on young children. Diarrheal illnesses account for perhaps 20% of deaths among children under age five (Bryce *et al.*, 2005). These diseases are transmitted via the fecal–oral route, meaning that they are passed by drinking or handling microbiologically unsafe water that has been in contact with human or animal waste, or because of insufficient water for washing and bathing.

The central question is perhaps not the link between water and health, but rather, *what level of improvement is required* to capture the lion's share of the improved health benefits, at minimal costs, for the underserved population, a large share of whom live on incomes of less than US$1/day, and virtually all on incomes of less than US$2/day. In the second half of Part I Whittington *et al.* choose to focus on only one form of improved services, described as "networked" water and sanitation services, to serve as the cornerstone for their benefit–cost analysis. This consists of a conventional system, as used around the world, which combines a centralized storage, centralized water-treatment plant, a piped network to provide water-supply connections to individual households, a piped sewer system to collect wastewater, and a centralized (minimal) sewage-treatment plant. This system of taps and flush toilets in homes has indeed been the conventional gold standard employed by water and sanitation utilities around the world for well over a century. Whittington *et al.* acknowledge the possibility to provide intermediate water and sanitation services at lower costs, but they appear to dismiss the possibility of significantly cheaper systems that still would provide a large share of the public health benefits. They select benefits estimates from the literature and compare these to illustrative cost estimates for the "networked" service and conclude that benefits do not exceed costs in likely scenarios. In short, in our view, the "gold-standard" opportunities chosen by Whittington *et al.* are not the most appropriate for the target group of beneficiaries; we believe that less costly (non-networked) options are available that would demonstrate significantly improved cost–benefit ratios.

In Part II of the Challenge Paper, Whittington *et al.* examine a limited set of alternative "non-networked" interventions, including source-water quality improvements (wells), a sanitation encouragement intervention, and point-of-use water treatment. In this case, they conclude that the benefits of each of these programs exceed their costs, but the benefit–cost ratios are fairly modest, in the range of two to four. Little discussion is given to the question of sustainability. In the case of wells, for example, Whittington *et al.* assert that community-based or demand-driven management models have solved many of the problems associated with maintaining rural water infrastructure. Sustained adoption of the other technologies in question, latrines and biosand filters, is not discussed.

In this paper we first discuss (in section 2) the health benefits estimated by Whittington *et al.* for the full-on networked services model – as we

believe there is compelling evidence that these are underestimated because of a failure to include an estimate of the benefits of avoided mortality and by failing to quantify the externalities associated with these investments, though they acknowledge that they may exist. We do not disagree with Whittington *et al.*'s cost estimates for the model they chose, but are of the opinion that the focus ought to be on different, innovative, decentralized, low-cost forms of services, with special emphasis on management and governance that reduces corruption, makes the service effective and sustainable, and capitalizes on linkages with other water sub-sectors, notably water used for livelihoods. A broader discussion of feasible and appropriate service levels beyond the "networked" approach would increase the relevance and value of the Challenge Paper. In section 3, we explore the potential for such systems in some detail. We summarize evidence that suggests that the net benefits of point-of-use water treatment products may be far above those estimated by Whittington *et al.*, and discuss the pressing challenge of ensuring sustainability in the rural sector.

Section 4 summarizes and concludes. Our perspective is that appropriately designed and managed low-cost water and sanitation systems, perhaps including point-of-use water treatment, and innovative information-based tools, can have significantly lower costs than the US$10 per household per month cost that is used by Whittington *et al.* as a low boundary, and that their estimates of benefits are a lower bound that underestimate the total value of the opportunity. Rigorous economic analysis of behavior change in randomized trials suggests, for example, that non-networked solutions can be extremely cost-effective investments. The challenge remains one of identifying ways to bring accountability and financial sustainability to the sector – to make water services work for the poor.

2. Networked Water and Sanitation Services

Part I of the Challenge Paper devotes a significant effort to comparing the costs and benefits of networked municipal water and sanitation infrastructure, providing the conventional "gold standard" of taps in homes and flush toilets. Whittington *et al.* review four possible sources of data on the benefits associated with improved water and sanitation. These are prices charged for vended water, avertive expenditures, avoided cost of illness, and stated preference studies. They add representative figures for WTP from these sources to conclude that the benefits of networked water and sanitation services cannot automatically be assumed to exceed the costs. We believe that there are significant gaps in this analysis that, while they may not be sufficient to reverse the authors' conclusions, certainly merit review.

The Challenge Paper concludes that it can easily be the case that piped water and sanitation investments will not be economical, despite the conventional wisdom that the benefits of improved water and sanitation service significantly exceed the costs. The authors also compare private willingness to pay to their estimate of the full economic costs of services to further emphasize that these investments may be inappropriate as cost-recovery may be difficult.

In this section, we discuss existing econometric evidence on the health benefits of water and sanitation service, and argue that there is substantial evidence that the benefits of this sort of investment are larger than estimated in the Challenge Paper. We also discuss the magnitude of the health externalities that have been identified for water-related illnesses as a further means of illustrating the point that benefits estimates that capture only private willingness to pay (like stated preference valuations, and avertive expenditures) may be inappropriately low. We choose

---

[1] This section draws on Zwane and Kremer (2007).
[2] The citation for this effect size chosen by Whittington *et al.* is Esrey (1996). While this is an oft-cited paper in the economics and policy literature on the impacts of water, sanitation, and hygiene investments, it is a cross-sectional analysis of country-level data and the results are subject to omitted variable bias (confounding) of unknown magnitude. However, recent randomized control trials of POU water-treatment technologies, as summarized by Fewtrell and others (2005), find similar impacts of water-quality improvements on diarrhea incidence.

---

to focus on the benefits side of the calculation made, as we believe that their cost calculations are reasonable, given their decision to focus on fully networked service provision. In the next section, we discuss alternatives to fully networked service that we believe are more appropriate for those currently underserved: the poor.

Econometric Evidence on the Avoided Mortality Benefits of Piped Water and Sanitation[1]

Contrary to Whittington *et al.*'s assertion, recent economic analysis has found that there are large health gains from networked water and sanitation, particularly in terms of child mortality. A failure to include an estimate of the benefits of avoided mortality, in addition to avoided illness, leads to an underestimation of the benefits associated with water related intervention. The cost-of-illness literature review presented by Whittington *et al.* is limited and appears to imply that a 30–40% reduction in diarrhea, "the best one could hope for," is disappointingly small.[2] In fact, randomized control trials have demonstrated that reductions in diarrheal incidence of this order of magnitude can be sufficient to reduce child mortality (Crump *et al.*, 2005) and there is a growing body of work Whittington *et al.* do not reference that uses rigorous econometric techniques to estimate large impacts of networked water and sanitation service on health outcomes.

Recent econometric evidence on the large benefits from piped water and sanitation service includes a study that exploits historical variation in the timing and location of water filtration and chlorination technology adoption across US cities to identify the contribution of improved water quality to the epidemiological transition in American cities (Cutler and Miller, 2005). This study finds that clean water was responsible for about half the observed decline in mortality and nearly two-thirds of the reduction in child mortality in cities.

In a less dense setting, Watson (2006) demonstrates similar mortality benefits. She exploits the fact that a series of water and sanitation interventions (including taps and flush toilets) introduced on Native American reservations in the United States during 1960–1998 were likely uncorrelated with other factors affecting infant health and were plausibly exogenous to local community characteristics (after accounting for country and year fixed effects). This research suggests that a 10% increase in the fraction of homes with improved water and sanitation services reduced infant mortality by 4%.

In a modern middle-income country setting, child mortality benefits have also been demonstrated. Galiani and others (2005) study a privatization reform that took place for about 30% of municipal water companies in Argentina in the 1990s to identify the impact of ownership on child health. They estimate that child mortality overall fell 5–7% in those that privatized their water services because in this context privatization improved service and expanded coverage, and that the effect was largest in the poorest areas, at around 24%.

External Benefits of Water and Sanitation Interventions

Whittington et al. also underestimate the health benefits associated with networked water and sanitation by failing to quantify the externalities associated with these investments, though they acknowledge that they may exist. In practice, there is evidence that externalities associated with sanitation-related programs are large, which has important implications for any discussion of how to pay for an investment. Watson (2006) quantifies the externalities associated with networked water and sanitation service by demonstrating that infant mortality rates fell among local residents not living on the reservation, just as they did among households that received new service. Miguel and Kremer (2004) quantify the externalities associated with providing deworming treatment to Kenyan school children as part of a randomized evaluation of the impacts of deworming on school attendance. They find that the program led to large reductions in worm infections that arise from poor sanitation conditions and increased school participation

among both treated and untreated children in the treatment schools and among children in neighboring schools. The external benefits of the program were qualitatively large; three quarters of the social benefit of treatment was in the form of externalities.

To the extent that private use of service affects the disease environment, private willingness to pay, the focus of Whittington et al.'s analysis, is only a partial indicator of the social value of an investment and should not determine whether a program or investment should go forward. Inefficiently low levels of demand can be expected even at subsidized service prices. In a companion study to the initial deworming evaluation, Kremer and Miguel (2007) find that drug take-up was extremely sensitive to cost and that even modest efforts at achieving project cost-sharing with parents resulted in large reductions (80%) in drug use relative to free treatment.

Additional work is needed to further understand the externalities associated with sanitation programs. The examples given here cannot describe fully the externalities associated with the sorts of programs that might be provided in many settings in developing countries today. The Bill and Melinda Gates Foundation's recent decision to fund a large randomized impact evaluation of the total sanitation campaign (a program that encourages communities to make their own investments to become open-defecation free) in several countries is a promising step in this direction. Nonetheless, existing evidence suggests that it is reasonable to begin from the assumption that externalities will be sufficiently large that on-going public support for sanitation programs is appropriate.

In contrast to the conclusions reached by Whittington et al., Cutler and Miller (2005) estimate that funds invested in US urban water systems between 1900 and 1940 produced a social rate of return of roughly $23 for every $1 spent. Whittington et al.'s failure to account for external benefits and mortality impacts leaves an incomplete picture of the cost-effectiveness of water and sanitation investments and focuses to too great an extent on the possibility of full cost recovery in this sector.

3. Water and Sanitation Services That Work for the Poor

The analysis in Part I of the Challenge Paper, and our comments in section 2 above, are based on a system that provides water through taps in homes and flush toilets with sewer systems. At estimated reasonable full costs of US$2.50 per cubic meter, per capita consumption in the range of 110–220 liter per capita per day results in monthly costs per household of US$50–100. This is a cost evidently unaffordable for the section of the population that needs service. Whittington *et al.* consider a lower cost of US$1 per cubic meter, and 55 liter per capita per day consumption, yielding a cost per household of about US$10 per month as a lower boundary on what service provision may require. They conclude that, particularly as there is a strong positive correlation between household income, the demand for water services, and the provision of water and sanitation services, networked water and sanitation services will be cost-beneficial (and will be built) only in cities in rapidly growing economies.

This conclusion, even if it were to hold with the larger health benefits that the economics literature has identified, has relatively few practical implications. Networked "gold standard" service is largely irrelevant for the rural poor in low-income countries (where low population densities make networked services uneconomical) and the urban poor in the informal settlements or slums that characterize the places where the underserved live. Whittington *et al.* rightly turn their attention to "non-networked" solutions in the second half of the Challenge Paper.

Part II of the paper uses Monte Carlo simulations to estimate the cost–benefit ratios associated with a limited set of "non-networked" solutions, including wells, sanitation campaigns

[3] Noting, at the same time, that in rapidly growing economies the Millennium Development Goals on water and sanitation are being met – underscoring the conclusion, also drawn by Whittington *et al.*, that in rapidly growing economies governments do invest successfully in water and sanitation services.

that result in partial coverage in a representative village, and one POU (in-home) water-treatment product, a biosand filter, but the paper does not consider in detail either how improved service may realistically be provided to the urban or peri-urban poor or key management and information barriers to implementation of either networked or non-networked solutions.

In the remainder of this section we discuss the potentially transformative role of information in the water and sanitation sector to make investments more useful and sustainable. We discuss institutional barriers to investment that we believe are underplayed by Whittington *et al.* and that must be solved for the benefits of source-water quality interventions to be realized. We also discuss alternative investments not considered by Whittington *et al.* that have a much higher rate of return than the alternative investments that they consider. We argue that a greater focus on a wider range of non-networked solutions and barriers to their implementation suggests that the net benefits of non-networked solution may be 4–12 times greater than the estimates presented by Whittington *et al.* A pressing policy and research need is direction on how to make these non-networked solutions sustainable.

Information for accountability

A key reason that public investments in water services for the poor have not been successful enough to meet the Millennium Development Goals (MDG) targets in the least developed countries,[3] particularly in Sub-Saharan Africa, is the same reason why other public services are failing the poor: a lack of accountability between providers, policymakers, and consumers has resulted in bad management and governance particularly (World Bank, 2004). The Challenge Paper would be richer for a discussion of innovative ways to deliver service and increase accountability in the system, in addition to the analysis undertaken for networked service.

Efforts to increase accountability in the system will likely directly affect the net benefits of networked and non-networked water and sanitation service. The water and sanitation sector, with its large and complex investments and its inherent need for service and maintenance, is particularly prone to corruption (Transparency International, 2008), directly affecting the attractiveness of investments in the sector. Curbing wastage and targeting investments will require improved information flows about how decisions are made and simply to make better decisions.

Accountability is linked to information quality and information flows. Citizens and civil society can hold governments accountable for investment levels and locations if informed accurately of what is being done. Governments can do a better job of improving coverage levels if they know better where need is greatest. Current data on need and coverage are largely based on information collected in health surveys administered for other purposes (e.g., the Demographic and Health Surveys). These data, as summarized and collated by the WHO/UNICEF Joint Monitoring Program,[4] are inappropriate for planning. They are insufficient because they are not locally representative and because they are based on engineering information about access rather than behavioral feedback on adequacy.

One example of a promising effort to generate the sort of data that can support data-driven planning is the recent work by UN-Habitat to measure water and sanitation service coverage, health, and socio-economic status in 15 towns around Lake Victoria in East Africa. Data-collection efforts like this, which are locally representative, hold the potential to inform investment decisions in a way that the JMP data cannot. Combining data of this sort with efforts to improve information flows to consumers and policy makers holds promise as a means of using information to make the system more accountable and efficient. The utility benchmarking efforts supported by the Water and Sanitation Program (a multi-donor partnership of the World Bank) and consumer report cards to solicit bottom-up feedback that are being implemented by NGOs like WaterAid (Government of Kenya, 2007) are other examples of the sort of

programs that could allow informed investment to be responsive and appropriately targeted, even if it does not reach "gold standard" levels. We need more information about the magnitude of the gains associated with new information-based approaches to increasing accountability, transparency, and efficiency, particularly in settings in which service provision is decentralized (such as Kenya and Ghana, for example).[5] Kariuki and Schwartz (2005) show that a new class of small-scale indigenous, private-sector water-service providers is emerging in developing countries that may also offer new opportunities for affordable water for low-income groups at market prices.[6]

Sustainability

The challenge of maintaining non-networked water infrastructure, and how this challenge may impact relative net benefit calculations, gets fairly little attention in the Challenge Paper. While acknowledging that wells and other improved sources were difficult to maintain in the past, Whittington *et al.* claim that "demand-driven" community management approaches that give local communities the responsibility for funding maintenance and a larger role for women constitute "a set of planning and implementation procedures that promises much better results than were previously thought possible."

We do not feel that the literature on community management warrants this conclusion. Instead, sustainability issues deserve more detailed treatment. In a recent comprehensive

---

[4] A discussion of the data sources can be found at: www.wssinfo.org/en/123_dataProcess.html

[5] Private-sector water companies are emerging in these settings that are willing and able to serve towns as small as five to ten thousand inhabitants (e.g. WaterHealth International: www.waterhealth.org). This is new in the sector where until recently private-sector service was equated with large multinational companies providing – highly controversial – services in major metropolitan areas.

[6] Kariuki and Schwartz conclude there are at least 10,000 such small private-sector water providers in 49 countries, while others conclude this is likely an underestimate in a rapidly growing industry.

review of community-based development projects, Mansuri and Rao (2004) note that existing research examining "successful" community-based projects does not compare these projects with centralized mechanisms for service delivery or infrastructure maintenance (for example, city or state financed). This makes it difficult to determine whether alternative project designs would have had different results. The limited empirical evidence suggests the impact of the community-based development approach on infrastructure maintenance is mixed at best.

Perhaps most importantly, neither retrospective analyses nor case studies like those cited in the Challenge Paper can establish a causal relationship between community participation and observed outcomes because this evidence is hampered by concerns about reverse causality. To take one example, it is difficult to determine whether the inclusion of women causes a particular outcome to occur, whether the fact that an outcome occurs encourages the participation and inclusion of women, or whether some other factors are driving these results.

Rather than dismissing sustainability as a largely settled issue, we believe that this remains a central challenge of non-networked water and sanitation interventions. We need to understand better how to sustain private behavior change, like the use of point-of-use water-treatment technologies, and maintain community-level infrastructure, perhaps via the creation of opportunities for income generation. Innovative solutions that allow for private service provision and/or income generation (e.g., multiple-use systems) should be rigorously evaluated, as well as other community-based interventions.

Alternative technologies

Point-of-Use Treatment

Using the simulation approach and avoided morbidity benefits estimates drawn from Fewtrell et al. (2005) and discussed in detail above, Whittington et al. conclude that source-water quality improvements are about twice as cost-beneficial as POU water-treatment products at preferred parameter values. This is in spite of an assumption that the health benefits associated with POU water treatment are slightly higher than those associated with source-water quality interventions. The conclusion about the relative cost-effectiveness of the alternative interventions is driven in large part by the decision to model a biosand filter as the POU technology, which is much more expensive than in-home chlorination but has not been established to be of greater cost-effectiveness. Contrary to the claim made in the Challenge Paper, there is evidence from randomized evaluations that, in fact, the cost-effectiveness of POU water treatment can dramatically exceed that of source-water quality interventions and, as such, that understanding how to get people to use these products and adopt them permanently is a central challenge for the sector.

As part of the Kenya Rural Water Project, Kremer et al. (2008a,b) evaluate the impact of source-water quality improvements achieved via *spring protection*, and estimate the valuation that people place on these improvements using a randomized evaluation approach, in which protection is phased in to springs over time in an order chosen at random. The source-water quality investment, in which natural springs are improved so that water flows through a pipe, gives access to uncontaminated ground water, just as wells do. The intervention improved child health: diarrhea among young children in treatment households falls by 4.7 percentage points, or one quarter on a base diarrhea prevalence of approximately 20%. Because of the methodology used, this benefit can confidently be ascribed to the program.

These revealed preference estimates have the advantage of being based on actual behavior changes observed in response to an exogenous change in the environment, and are not subject to the weakness that any particular parameter value chosen could be questioned. As with any empirical analysis, concerns about external validity, or the extent to which the results are generalizable, apply. However, we believe that more guidance from this sort of impact assessment is what should be used to inform investment decisions in the rural water sector, and the use of scarce resources for water and health more generally.

Relatively rigorous cost-effectiveness estimations that are derived from observing behavior may be higher or lower than those derived from simulation models. Kremer *et al.* (2008a) conclude that, at baseline levels of population density, the social returns to the source-water quality investment they study are in fact negative. However, if the springs had 60 users each, like the wells that Whittington *et al.* model, social returns would be modestly positive. WTP estimates are also similar in magnitude to the central benefits estimates that Whittington *et al.* use.

While the randomized impact evaluation evidence from Kenya presented by Kremer *et al.* (2008a,b) broadly supports the net benefit estimates from Whittington *et al.* for source-water quality interventions, it does not support the conclusion that POU water treatment is less cost beneficial than source-water interventions. Both interventions are highly cost effective by standard measures such as DALYs averted, and POU water treatment is likely to be more cost effective if distribution costs could be reduced from current levels. The greater challenge is reconciling the finding that willingness to pay for health and clean water is even lower than the cost of achieving it via the interventions that they study. Additional research is needed to identify alternative distribution mechanisms that confront this fact.

These conclusions differ from the Whittington *et al.* results for two reasons: the cost of the point-of-use product considered and the benefits of source-water quality interventions. Whittington *et al.* assume that there are significant non-health benefits associated with source water quality interventions (e.g., time savings) that are absent with POU products. Kremer *et al.* (2008a) find little empirical evidence of non-health benefits of spring protection – in terms of water appearance, taste or ease of water collection – could theoretically contribute to willingness to pay, we find no evidence that these have a significant effect on WTP in practice. The inclusion of terms for measured *E. coli*

contamination available at a subset of alternative water sources, as well as the household's perception of water quality at each source, reduces the coefficient estimate on the spring protection treatment indicator to near zero in discrete choice regression analysis. Because spring protection does not create a new water point, as well construction does, this finding may not hold for wells as it does for springs. However, even spring protection induces significant shifts in water-source choice, which suggests that it is possible that water-quality gains may account for a large portion of the gains associated with source-water quality improvement interventions.

On the cost side, the decision by Whittington *et al.* to focus on relatively expensive biosand filters instead of a chlorine product like WaterGuard significantly increases the cost of POU treatment in the Challenge Paper simulations relative to the figures used by Kremer *et al.* A wider analysis of alternative point-of-use treatment products with different costs would enhance the Challenge Paper analysis.

In sum, we do not agree with the conclusion drawn by Whittington *et al.* that source-water quality investments are more cost effective than point-of-use water treatment products. Rather, our reading of the literature is that additional work on the most effective and sustainable ways of increasing point-of-use technology adoption is needed as these may be very cost-effective technologies indeed if adoption can be sustained. Dissemination approaches currently being studied as part of the Kenya Rural Water Project include alternative distribution models such as the distribution of POU products at schools or clinics so that households with young children can be targeted, centralized treatment at water sources, and alternative marketing messages. Centralized treatment via simple dispensers located near water sources appears particularly popular and promising. In addition, we believe that the rapid emergence of a cottage industry of micro-utility providers that provides water services at market prices is a new phenomenon worth studying as a possible cost-effective alternative to the networked service provision analyzed by Whittington *et al.* in Part I of their paper.

Multiple-use Water Services

Whittington *et al.* discuss water-service systems that are designed, managed, and financed for a single use: drinking water. This is in line with the sectoral or silo approach in the water sector – and indeed with the request of the Copenhagen Consensus organizers – but not in line with the reality on the ground. In practice, poor people in rural and peri-urban areas use water available to them beyond the minimum required for drinking to generate income. Livelihood activities supported by water range from (vegetable) farming, livestock, and fishponds, to micro-enterprises. In the previous round of the Copenhagen Consensus exercise Rijsberman (2004) raised this issue as a separate opportunity and estimated a ballpark cost–benefit ratio for this opportunity of around 7 – admittedly without the benefit of the rigorous economic analysis that would be desirable. We offer no new evidence, but note that various publications document the dissemination and positive cost–benefit ratios of small-scale water technology for livelihoods – from treadle pumps to drip irrigation kits (e.g. Adetola *et al.*, 2007).

It is of particular interest to this discussion, however, that Renwick *et al.* (2007) recently completed a study for the Gates Foundation that aimed to assess the investment potential (costs, benefits, and poverty impacts) of multiple-use approaches. Multiple-use approaches involve integrated systems to provide water services for domestic or drinking as well as productive or livelihood uses. For new users this implies designing systems that can serve both needs; for existing users it means upgrading drinking-water systems to larger volumes that can generate income, or upgrading irrigation systems to provide better-quality water. Renwick *et al.* report that for new users, "intermediate multiple use systems" have a BCR range of 3.4–7.8 (at 10% discount rate); basic drinking water systems can be upgraded to intermediate multiple use systems at a BCR range of 4.7–8.6; and basic irrigation systems can be upgraded to interme-

diate multiple use systems at a BCR range of 2.9–6.8. The report estimates the potential users for this type of water services at about one billion people.

4. Conclusions

Whittington *et al.* provide a thorough and comprehensive overview of the complex issues associated with a rigorous economic analysis of the provision of water and sanitation services. Their analysis of the full costs of conventional, "gold standard" networked water and sanitation services, at a full economic cost of US$2.50 per cubic meter and monthly household costs of US$50–100, is complete and reasonable. However, it is not an appropriately designed opportunity for the target group, the unserved that have income levels at the $1–2-per-day range. These people are far more likely to be served by something less expensive if research can identify appropriate interventions.

The analysis of the benefits of this improved water and sanitation services is complete, but significantly underestimates the health benefits, in our view. This is because it fails to include an estimate of the benefits of avoided mortality or to quantify the positive externalities associated with the sector. We present recent evidence in the literature to support this argument.

We conclude that appropriate systems for the poor that currently lack water and sanitation services are unlikely to be of the full networked variety chosen by Whittington *et al.* Rather, a key question is how innovative low-cost systems can be designed and implemented to deliver services that work for the poor. In addition to innovative technology and engineering, a key focus of attention will need to be on effective management and governance systems. Transparent information on the services provided, and on the health impacts delivered, in a form that informs the managers in their pursuit of excellence and empowers the users to hold the service providers accountable, is likely to be a key element in the success of such systems. Point-of-use water treatment products are also likely to be an element of such systems; field evidence suggests that these technologies can be very cost-effective interventions if take-up rates can be sustained. Other innovative systems that deserve closer inspection – and from their rapid growth appear to offer attractive investment opportunities even at market rates – are the private micro-utilities springing up in (peri-)urban areas.

Early evidence from randomized field trials suggests that innovative water services such as point-of-use chlorination are likely to have health benefits that are significantly larger than those estimated by the Monte Carlo simulations presented by Whittington *et al.* Results from the Kenya Rural Water Project suggest that POU water treatment may be twice as cost effective as source water quality improvements, and extremely cost-effective relative to other health interventions, costing about $10 per DALY averted. Scaling up the benefit–cost ratios presented by Whittington *et al.* accordingly leads us to conclude that the benefit cost ratios for non-networked approaches may be in the order of magnitude of 6, an attractive investment, rather than in the more marginal range of around 2. More research to test these findings, and to ensure that benefits persist over time as a result of consistent product use, is needed.

Whittington *et al.* focus on drinking water and sanitation alone, as is indeed customary (but not helpful). A more realistic approach would be to address opportunities for water services to support income-generating activities in addition to providing health services. Renwick *et al.* (2007) conclude that intermediate multiple-use systems that provide water for drinking as well as support vegetable production, livestock rearing, fishponds or micro-enterprises have cost–benefit ratios of 3.4–7.8 (at a discount rate of 10%).

Our review leads us to believe that there are indeed significant opportunities for investments in water services that provide health benefits and have poverty-reducing impacts, potentially affecting one billion people, and with benefit–cost ratios in the range of 5–10 (at a discount rate of 5%).

Bibliography

Adetola, A., Barry, B., Namara, R., Kamara, A., and Titiati, A. (2007). Treadle pump irrigation and poverty in Ghana. Research Report 117. Colombo, Sri Lanka: International Water Management Institute

Bryce, J. *et al.* (2005). WHO estimates of the causes of death in children. *Lancet, 365,* 1147–1152

Crump, J.A., Otieno, P.O., Slutsker, L., Keswick, B., Rosen, D., Hoekstra, R., Vulule, J., and Luby, S. (2005). Household based treatment of drinking water with flocculant-disinfectant for preventing diarrhoea in areas with turbid source water in rural Western Kenya: Cluster randomised controlled trial. *British Medical Journal, 331,* 478–483

Cutler, D. and Miller, G. (2005). The role of public health improvements in health advances: the 20th century United States. *Demography, 42* (1), 1–22

Esrey, S.A. (1996). Waste, water and well-being: A multicountry study. *American Journal of Epidemiology, 143* (6), 608–622

Fewtrell, L. *et al.* (2005). Water, sanitation, and hygiene interventions to reduce diarrhoea in less developed countries: A systematic review and meta-analysis. *Lancet Infectious Diseases, 5,* 42–52

Galiani, S., Gertler, P., and Schargrodsky, E. (2005). Water for life: The impact of the privatization of water services on child mortality. *Journal of Political Economy, 113* (1), 83–120

Government of Kenya (2007). Citizens' report card on urban water, sanitation and solid waste services in Kenya. May, available: www-wds.worldbank.org/external/default/WDSContentServer/WDSP/IB/2008/11/05/000334955_20081105044559/Rendered/PDF/462830WP1Box331rd111Nairobi0Dec2008.pdf

Kariuki, M. and Schwartz, J. (2005). Small scale private service providers of water supply and electricity: a review of incidence, structure, pricing, and operating characteristics. World Bank Policy Research Working Paper 3727. Washington, DC: World Bank

Kremer, M. and Miguel, E. (2007). The illusion of sustainability. *The Quarterly Journal of Economics, 112* (3), 1007–1065

Kremer, M., Leino, J., Miguel, E., and Zwane, A.P. (2007). Spring cleaning: Rural water impacts, valuation, and institutions. Working paper, Berkeley, CA: UC Berkeley, available: http://elsa.berkeley.edu/~emiguel/research2.shtml

Kremer, M., Miguel, E., Null, C., and Zwane, A.P. (2008b). Trickle down: Diffusion of chlorine for drinking water treatment in Kenya. Working paper, Berkeley, CA: UC Berkeley, available: http://elsa.berkeley.edu/~emiguel/research2.shtml

Mansuri, G. and Rao, V. (2004). Community-based and -driven development: A critical review. *The World Bank Research Observer, 19* (1)

Miguel, E. and Kremer, M. (2004). Worms: Identifying impacts on education and health in the presence of treatment externalities. *Econometrica, 72* (1), 159–217

Renwick, M. *et al.* (2007). Multiple use water services for the poor: Assessing the state of knowledge. Arlington, VA: Winrock International

Rijsberman, F.R. (2004). Sanitation and access to clean water. In: Lomborg, B. (ed.), *Global Challenges, Global Solutions.* Cambridge University Press, 498–527

Transparency International (2008). *Global Corruption Report 2008.* Bonn, Germany

Watson, T. (2006). Public health investments and the infant mortality gap: Evidence from federal sanitation interventions and hospitals on U.S. Indian reservations. *Journal of Public Economics, 90* (8–9), 1537–1560

World Bank (2004). Making services work for the poor. Washington DC: World Bank

Zwane, A.P. and Kremer, M. (2007). What works in fighting diarrheal diseases in poor countries? A critical review. *World Bank Research Observer*, Spring, 1–24

The Challenge of Reducing International Trade and Migration Barriers

KYM ANDERSON AND L. ALAN WINTERS

The net economic and social benefits of reducing most government subsidies and opening economies to trade are enormous relative to the costs of adjustment to such policy reform. While barriers to trade in most goods and some services including capital flows have been reduced considerably over the past two decades, many remain. Such policies harm most the economies imposing them, but the worst of the merchandise barriers (in agriculture and textiles) are particularly harmful to the world's poorest people, as are barriers to worker migration across borders. Addressing this challenge would therefore also assist in meeting several of the other challenges identified in this project, including malnutrition, disease, poor education and air pollution.

This chapter focuses on how costly those anti-poor trade policies are, and examines possible strategies to reduce remaining distortions. Three opportunities in particular are addressed. The most beneficial prospect is the Doha Development Agenda of the World Trade Organization (WTO). If that proves to be too difficult politically to bring to a conclusion in the near future, the other two prospects we consider are sub-global preferential reforms such as the Free Trade Area of the Americas (FTAA) initiative, and the freeing up of the international movement of workers.

The chapter begins by defining the challenge. It then summarizes the arguments for removing trade and migration distortions, along with critiques by skeptics, before discussing the various opportunities for reducing subsidies and trade barriers and explaining why we chose to focus on the above-mentioned three. The core of the chapter is in the next two sections, which

review the economic benefits and adjustment costs associated with these three opportunities. That provides the foundation to undertake the benefit/cost analysis required to allow this set of opportunities to be ranked against those aimed at addressing the world's other key challenges. The chapter concludes with key caveats that suggest that taking up these opportunities could generate social benefit/cost ratios that are considerably higher than the direct economic ones quantified in this study, not least because they would also go some way toward addressing several of the other challenges identified by the Copenhagen Consensus project.

The Challenge

Despite the net economic and social benefits of reducing most government subsidies[1] and barriers to international trade and migration, almost every national government intervenes in markets for goods, services, capital and labor in ways that distort international commerce. To keep the task manageable, the policy instruments considered will be limited to those trade-related ones over which a government's international trade negotiators have some influence both at home and abroad, plus immigration numbers. That thereby excludes measures such as generic

[1] Not all subsidies are welfare-reducing, and in some cases a subsidy-cum-tax will be optimal to overcome a gap between private and social costs that cannot be bridged à la Coase (1960). Throughout this chapter all references to 'cutting subsidies' refer to bringing them back to their optimal level (which will be zero in all but those relatively few exceptional cases).

taxes on income, consumption and value added, government spending on mainstream public services, infrastructure and generic social safety nets in strong demand by the community, and subsidies (taxes) and related measures set optimally from the national viewpoint to overcome positive (negative) environmental or other externalities. Also excluded from consideration here are policies affecting markets for foreign exchange.

This challenge in its modern form has been with us for about 75 years. The latter part of the nineteenth century saw a strong movement toward laissez faire and widespread international migration, but that development was reversed following the first world war in ways that contributed to the Great Depression of the early 1930s and the conflict that followed (Kindleberger 1989). It was during the second world war, in 1944, that a conference at Bretton Woods proposed an International Trade Organization (ITO). An ITO charter was drawn up by 1947 along with a General Agreement on Tariffs and Trade (GATT), but the ITO idea died when the United States failed to progress it through Congress (Diebold 1952). Despite that, the GATT came into being from 1948 and during its 47-year history (before it was absorbed into the WTO on 1 January 1995) oversaw the gradual lowering of many tariffs on imports of most manufactured goods by governments of high-income countries. Manufacturing tariffs remained high in developing countries, however, and distortionary subsidies and trade policies affecting agricultural, textile, and services markets of both rich and poor countries, plus immigrations restrictions, continued to hamper efficient resource allocation, consumption choices, economic growth and poverty alleviation.

The GATT's Uruguay Round of multilateral trade negotiations led to agreements signed in 1994 that contributed to trade liberalization over the subsequent 10 years. But even when those agreements were fully implemented by early 2005, and despite additional unilateral trade liberalizations since the 1980s by a number of countries (particularly developing and transition economies), many subsidies and trade and migration restrictions remain. They include not just trade taxes-cum-subsidies but also contingent protection measures such as anti-dumping, regulatory standards that can be technical barriers to trade, and domestic producer subsidies (allegedly decoupled from production in the case of some farm support programs in high-income countries, but in fact only partially so). Insufficient or excessive taxation or quantitative regulations in the presence of externalities such as environmental or food safety risks also lead to inefficiencies and can be trade distorting. Furthermore, the on-going proliferation of preferential trading and bilateral or regional integration arrangements – for which there would be far less need in the absence of high barriers to trade and migration – is adding complexity to international economic relations. In some cases those arrangements are leading to trade and investment diversion rather than creation, changes that may be welfare reducing for some economies.

The reluctance to reduce trade distortions is almost never because such policy reform involves government treasury outlays. On the contrary, except in the case of a handful of low-income countries still heavily dependent on trade taxes for government revenue, such reform may well benefit the treasury (by raising income or consumption/value added tax revenues more than trade tax revenues fall, not to mention any payments foregone because of cuts to subsidy programs). Rather, trade distortions and barriers to immigration remain largely because further liberalization and subsidy cuts would redistribute jobs, income and wealth in ways that those in government fear would reduce their chances of remaining in power (and possibly their own wealth in countries where corruption is rife). The challenge involves finding politically attractive ways to phase out remaining distortions to world markets for goods and services, including for the capital and labor used to produce those products.

This challenge is even greater now than it was in the inaugural Copenhagen Consensus project four years ago. One reason is that the WTO membership is struggling to address the Doha

Development Agenda that was launched in the immediate aftermath of 11 September 2001 – a time when there was much more goodwill to cooperate multilaterally than seems to be the case now. Another reason is greater doubts about the wisdom in predominantly Christian western countries of allowing more immigrants from Moslem countries where recent global terrorism seems to have emerged. More generally, this is but part of a broader disenchantment with globalization that could result not just in a failure to reach agreement under the Doha Round to multilaterally liberalize trade but also in the *raising* of current trade and immigration barriers. Such a reversal of past reforms could do huge damage to the global trading system and raise global inequality. That suggests the counterfactual to opening markets is not the status quo but something potentially much worse than the present.

Evidence of anti-globalization sentiment abounds despite the lowered frequency and ferocity of public protests of the sort first seen at the WTO's Trade Ministerial Conference in Seattle in 1999 and annual meetings of the World Bank and IMF early this decade.[2] One recent example is a *Financial Times*/Harris poll in the United States and the five largest European countries, where those polled were nearly three times more likely to say globalization was having a negative rather than a positive effect on their countries (Giles 2007). Such attitudes contributed to the decision at the June 2007 Summit of EU leaders to bend to France's demand to drop the principle of free and undistorted competition from the treaty that, if ratified, will replace the EU constitution that was voted down by French and Dutch voters in 2005. Another example is the threat by members of the US congress to impose arbitrary trade barriers on products flooding in from China and to oppose liberal trade initiatives by the Bush Administration (e.g., for several bilateral free-trade agreements and for comprehensive immigration reform).

These and similar examples underscore the need to re-emphasize the virtues of a more open global trading system – a system to which around 70 additional developing and transition economies have subscribed since the WTO came into being in 1995, with a further 28 (including Russia) currently striving to join. The case needs to be made within the context of the on-going information and communication technology (ICT) revolution that is globalizing the world's economies ever more rapidly[3] and, via the internet, exposing differences in living standards to ever more people in developing countries and thereby raising demands for an easing of restrictions on international migration.

Arguments for Reducing Trade Distortions and Migration Barriers

Even before examining the empirical estimates of the benefits and costs of grasping various trade- and migration-liberalizing opportunities, the case can be made that such reform in principle is beneficial economically.[4] It then remains to examine whether particular reforms are also positive or negative in terms of net social and environmental outcomes. The latter cannot be

[2] That clash between the key international financial institutions and civil society groups is ironic since both seek the same outcome, namely a reduction in global poverty. As pointed out by Kanbur (2001), this common goal suggests there is much scope for the two groups to discuss their differences in views as to the best means to that end. Indeed, they have been in much closer dialogue in recent years, a result of which has been some convergence of views on the policy reforms needed to promote pro-poor economic development.

[3] So rapid is this phenomenon that one author has felt the need to revise his popular book on the subject three times in three years (Friedman 2007). Its influence on fragmenting the process of production has been sufficiently profound for economists to begin developing a theory of trade in 'tasks', to capture the fact that firms are offshoring an increasing array of their activities (e.g., Grossman and Rossi-Hansberg 2006).

[4] This survey does not pretend to provide a comprehensive coverage of the gains-from-trade theory, and is even more limited in covering the economics of international migration. For more trade theory, readers are referred to the handbooks by Grossman and Rogoff (1995) and Harrigan and Choi (2003) and the new textbook by Feenstra (2004). For a survey of the economics of migration, see for example Borjas (1994) and Faini, de Melo and Zimmermann (1999).

dealt with here in the same depth as the narrower economic analysis, but it is important because there are many who believe or assume the net social and environmental consequences are sufficiently negative as to outweigh the net economic benefits of market opening. We begin with the static and then dynamic gains from trade arguments before turning briefly to the economic effects of international migration of workers.

Static economic gains from own-country trade and subsidy reform

The standard comparative static analysis of national gains from international trade emphasizes the economic benefits from production specialization and exchange so as to exploit comparative advantage in situations where a nation's costs of production and/or preferences differ from those in the rest of the world. This is part of the more general theory of the welfare effects of distortions in a trading economy, as summarized by Bhagwati (1971). Domestic industries become more productive on average as those with a comparative advantage expand by drawing resources from those previously protected or subsidized industries that grow slower or contract following reform. The gains from opening an economy are larger, the greater the variance of rates of protection among industries – especially within a sector, insofar as resources are more mobile within than between sectors (Lloyd 1974). Likewise, the more productive domestic firms *within* industries expand by drawing resources from less productive firms that contract or go out of business. Indeed, theory and empirical studies suggest the shifting of resources within an industry may be more welfare-improving than shifts between industries.[5]

The static gains from trade tend to be greater as a share of national output the smaller the economy, particularly where economies of scale in production have not been fully exploited and where consumers (including firms importing intermediate inputs) value variety so that intra- as well as inter-industry trade can flourish. Less than full exploitation of scale economies is often the result of imperfect competition being allowed to prevail in the domestic marketplace, which again is more common in smaller and poorer economies where industries have commensurately smaller numbers of firms. This is especially the case in the service sector. One example is sub-sectors such as utilities, where governments have been inclined to sanction monopoly provision.[6] The gain comes from firms having to reduce their mark-ups in the face of greater competition.

Those gains from opening up will be even greater if accompanied by a freeing up of domestic markets and the market for currency exchange. The more stable is domestic macroeconomic policy, the more attractive will an economy be to capital inflows. And the more domestic microeconomic policies are friendly to markets and competition for goods, services and productive factors, the greater the likelihood that adjustments by firms and consumers to trade liberalization will lead to a more efficient utilization of national resources and greater economic welfare (Corden 1997). If domestic policy reforms included improving the government's capacity to redistribute income and wealth more efficiently and in ways that better matched society's wishes, concerns about the distributional consequences of trade liberalization also would be lessened.

With the vastly increased scope during the past decade to separate in time and space the various productive tasks along each value chain, thanks to the ICT revolution, firms are increasingly able to take advantage of factor cost differences across countries for specific tasks without having to sacrifice gains from product specialization or move the whole of their production operation offshore (Hanson, Mataloni and Slaughter 2005). Trade in many tasks (e.g.,

---

[5] See Melitz (2003) on the theory of this point and Trefler (2004) for an early empirical illustration.

[6] The argument for allowing such monopolies is that they could provide greater technical efficiency via their larger scale. The contrary argument is that, being sheltered from competition, they fall so short of that potential as to be less productive than two or more smaller-scale competing suppliers.

emailing data files) is not even recorded in official trade statistics and so is not directly subject to trade policies. That suggests the variance of import protection across all traded items is even greater than across just recorded trade in goods, so the welfare gains from reducing the latter could well be greater than that captured by conventional trade models.

Dynamic economic gains from own-country trade and subsidy reform

To the standard comparative static analysis needs to be added links between trade and economic growth. The mechanisms by which openness contributes to growth are gradually getting to be better understood by economists, thanks to the pioneering work of such theorists as Grossman and Helpman (1991), Rivera-Batiz and Romer (1991) and the literature those studies spawned, including econometric papers based on firm-level databases. Channels through which openness to trade can affect an economy's growth rate include the scale of the market when knowledge is embodied in the products traded, the degree of redundant knowledge creation that is avoided through openness, and the effect of knowledge spillovers (Romer 1994; Taylor 1999; Acharya and Keller 2007).

The dynamic gains from openness can be greater when accompanied by reductions in domestic distortions. As one example, Helpman and Itskhoki (2007) develop a two-country two-sector model of international trade in which one sector produces homogeneous products while the other, which produces differentiated products, has firm heterogeneity, monopolistic competition, search and matching in its labor market, and wage bargaining (so that some of the workers searching for jobs end up being unemployed). The two countries are similar except for frictions in their labor markets. They show that both countries gain from trade but that the country with lower labor market frictions gains proportionately more, and that its flexible labor market confers comparative advantage: the flexible country is a net exporter of differentiated products. Either country benefits by lowering

frictions in its labor market, but that harms the other country; but a simultaneous proportional lowering of labor market frictions in both countries benefits both of them. With trade integration both countries benefit (even though it may raise their rates of unemployment), but the flexible country has higher total factor productivity in this model.

When that trade reform includes financial markets, more is gained than just a lower cost of credit. The resulting financial deepening can stimulate growth too (Townsend and Ueda 2007). Prasad et al. (2006) add two other indirect growth-enhancing benefits of financial reform: they discipline firms to look after the interests of shareholders better and they discipline governments to provide greater macroeconomic stability.

Importantly from a policy maker's viewpoint, the available empirical evidence strongly supports the view that open economies grow faster (see the surveys by USITC 1997, Winters 2004, Billmeier and Nannicini 2007 and Francois and Martin 2007). Notable early macroeconometric studies of the linkage between trade reform and the rate of economic growth include those by Sachs and Warner (1995) and Frankel and Romer (1999). More recent studies also provide some indirect supportive econometric evidence. For example, freeing up the importation of intermediate and capital goods promotes investments that increase growth (Wacziarg 2001). Indeed, the higher the ratio of imported to domestically produced capital goods for a developing country, the faster it grows (Lee 1995; Mazumdar 2001). Greater openness to international financial markets also boosts growth via the stimulation to investment that more risk-sharing generates.

Rodrigeuz and Rodrik (2001) examine a number of such studies and claim the results they surveyed are not robust. However, in a more recent study that revisits the Sachs and Warner data and then provides new time-series evidence, Wacziarg and Welch (2003) show that dates of trade liberalization do characterize breaks in investment and GDP growth rates. Specifically, for the 1950–1998 period, countries that have liberalized their trade (raising their trade-to-GDP ratio by an average of 5 percentage points) have enjoyed on average 1.5 percentage points higher GDP growth compared with their pre-reform rate.

There have also been myriad case studies of liberalization episodes. In a survey of 36 of them, Greenaway (1993) reminds us that many things in addition to trade policies were changing during the studied cases, so ascribing causality is not easy. That, together with some econometric studies that fail to find that positive link, led Freeman (2004) to suggest the promise of raising the rate of economic growth through trade reform has been overstated. But the same could be (and has been) said about the contributions to growth of such things as investments in education, health, agricultural research, and so on (Easterly 2001). A more general and more robust conclusion that Easterly draws from empirical evidence, though, is that people respond to incentives. Hence getting incentives right in factor and product markets is crucial – and removing unwarranted subsidies and trade barriers is an important part of that process. Additional evidence from 13 new case studies reported in Wacziarg and Welch (2003) adds further empirical support to that view, as does the fact that there are no examples of autarkic economies that have enjoyed sustained economic growth, in contrast to the many examples since the 1960s of reformed economies that boomed after opening up.

Specifically, economies that commit to less market intervention tend to attract more investment funds, ceteris paribus, which raise their stocks of capital (through greater aggregate global savings or at the expense of other economies' capital stocks). This is consistent with the findings by Faini (2004) that trade liberalization

in the 1990s fostered inward foreign investment (and both had a positive impact on investment in education) while backtracking on trade reform had a negative impact on foreign investment. More open economies also tend to be more innovative, because of greater trade in intellectual capital (a greater quantity and variety of information, ideas and technologies, sometimes but not only in the form of purchasable intellectual property associated with product and process innovations), and because greater competition spurs innovation (Aghion and Griffith 2005; Aghion and Howitt 2006), leading to higher *rates* of capital accumulation and productivity growth (Lumenga-Neso, Olarreaga and Schiff 2005).[7]

A growing body of industry studies, including ones based on firm-level survey data that capture the reality of firm heterogeneity, provides additional support for the theory that trade reform boosts the rate of productivity growth.[8] It appears more productive firms are innately better at exporting, so opening an economy leads to their growth and the demise of the least-productive firms (Bernard et al. 2007). That leads to better exploitation of comparative advantage in terms not only of industries but also of firms within each industry. If those more productive firms are also foreign owned, as is clearly the case in China (Whalley 2006), then being open to FDI multiplies the gains from product trade openness. And if those foreign firms are involved in retailing, and they enter a country with suppliers whose productivity is below best-practice, they can put pressure on those suppliers to raise their productivity (and perhaps alert them as to ways to do that). Walmart's influence in Mexico provides one example of this force at work (Javorcik, Keller and Tybout 2006). Furthermore, if the foreign firms are supplying lower-cost service inputs into manufacturing, that can boost the productivity growth of local manufacturers using those service inputs, according to a recent study of the Czech Republic (Arnold, Javorcik and Mattoo 2006).[9]

It need not be just the most-productive firms that engage in exporting. For lower-productivity firms, incurring the fixed costs of investing in

[7] More open economies also tend to be less vulnerable to foreign shocks such as sudden stops in capital inflows, currency crashes and severe recessions (Frankel and Cavallo 2004).

[8] For an overview of this new theory, see Helpman, Marin and Verdier (2008).

[9] For a survey of the growth effects of opening to trade in services, see Hoekman (2006).

newly opened foreign markets may be justifiable if accompanied by the larger sales volumes that come with exporting. Lower foreign tariffs will induce these firms to simultaneously export and invest in productivity (while inducing higher-productivity firms to export without more investing, as in Melitz 2003). Lileeva and Trefler (2007) model this econometrically using a heterogeneous response model. Unique 'plant-specific tariff cuts serve as their instrument for the decision of Canadian plants to start exporting to the United States. They find that those lower-productivity Canadian plants that were induced by the tariff cuts to start exporting increased their labor productivity, engaged in more product innovation, and had high adoption rates of advanced manufacturing technologies. These new exporters also increased their domestic (Canadian) market share at the expense of non-exporters, which suggests that the labor productivity gains reflect underlying gains in total factor productivity.

In short, trade liberalization can lead not just to a larger capital stock and a one-off increase in productivity but also to higher *rates* of capital accumulation and productivity growth in the reforming economy because of the way reform energizes entrepreneurs. For those higher growth rates to be sustained, though, there is widespread agreement that governments also need to (a) have in place effective institutions to efficiently allocate and protect property rights, (b) allow domestic factor and product markets to function freely, and (c) maintain macroeconomic and political stability (Rodrik 2003; Wacziarg and Welch 2003; Baldwin 2004; Chang, Kaltani and Loayza 2005).

Perhaps the best single paper that brings these ideas together using a numerical open economy growth model is that by Rutherford and Tarr (2002). Their model allows for product variety, imperfect competition, economies of scale and international capital flows. It is dynamic, so the model can trace out an adjustment path to trade reform; and it is stochastic in that it draws randomly from uniform probability distributions for eight key parameters of the model. They simulate a halving of the only policy intervention (a 20 percent tariff on imports) and, in doing so, fully replace the government's lost tariff revenue with a lump-sum tax. That modest trade reform produces a welfare increase (in terms of Hicksian equivalent variation) of 10.6 percent of the present value of consumption in their central model. Systematic sensitivity analysis with 34,000 simulations showed that there is virtually no chance of a welfare gain of less than 3 percent, and a 7 percent chance of a welfare gain larger than 18 percent of consumption. Several modeling variants and sensitivity analysis on all the key parameters found that the welfare estimates for the same 10 percentage point tariff cut ranged up to 37 percent when international capital flows are allowed, and down to 4.7 percent when using the most inefficient replacement tax (a tax of capital). The latter result shows that even the very inefficient tax on capital is superior to the tariff as a revenue raiser. Increasing the size of the tariff cuts results in roughly proportional increases in the estimated welfare gains. Large welfare gains in the model arise because the economy benefits from increased varieties of foreign goods, which dominate the decrease in varieties of domestic goods. In order to assess the importance of variety gains, they then assume that one of the two sectors is subject to constant returns to scale and perfect competition (CRS/PC) – and find in that case that the additional varieties do not increase total factor productivity. Instead, a small welfare gain of about 0.5 percent of the present value of consumption emerges, which is of the same order of magnitude as in the many comparative static CRS/PC computable general equilibrium studies. Their results also illustrate the importance of complementary reforms to fully realize the potential gains from trade reform. In particular, with the ability to access international capital markets the gains are roughly tripled; and use of inefficient replacement taxes significantly reduce the gains. These combined results underscore the point that complementary macroeconomic, regulatory, and financial market reforms to allow capital flows and efficient alternate tax collection are crucial to realizing the potentially large gains from trade liberalization.

Economic consequences of international migration

Half a century ago it was shown, using the simplest of trade models, that trade in products could be a perfect substitute for trade in capital and labor (Mundell 1957). But increasingly it has become apparent that trade in factors of production can complement trade in goods, in which case freeing both would yield greater gains (Markusen 1983). Indeed, theory cannot predict whether that would result in factor trade increasing more or less than product trade (Michaely 2003), which suggests the greatest gains would come to those countries that open both. Certainly the two forces happened simultaneously in the later nineteenth century in what might be considered the first modern wave of globalization. And if product trade liberalization runs into political difficulties, there is all the more reason to expect gains from liberalizing international migration of workers, thereby bringing about greater wage equality across countries. By strengthening social and business networks across borders, migrants can lower the cost of and improve the quality of information on opportunities for trade and investment.

The economic consequences even at the country level are somewhat more complicated for worker flows than for product flows between nations, because the one-to-one correspondence between people and countries is disturbed. Perhaps the simplest way to deal with that is to consider the welfare of the new migrants separately from that of the host country's other residents and the remaining source country residents. But if new migrants repatriate a significant share of their earning from the host country to the source country, that will boost economic wel-fare of those remaining in the developing country. And if new migrant workers are more able to compete with earlier migrants than with locally born workers in the host country, those communities need to be separately identified too.

Opportunities for Reducing Barriers to Trade and Migration

Among the more feasible opportunities available today for encouraging trade negotiations to stimulate significant market opening and subsidy cuts, the most obvious is a non-preferential legally binding partial reform following the WTO's current round of multilateral trade negotiations, the Doha Development Agenda (DDA).

A second type of trade negotiating opportunity involving a subset of the world's economies is a reciprocal preferential agreement.[10] Efforts are also being made to negotiate a Free Trade Area of the Americas, which potentially would bring together all the economies of North, Central and South America. This is perhaps the largest reciprocal preferential agreement currently in prospect, and dwarfs the bilateral FTA negotiations and discussions the US and EU are each having with a range of other countries.[11] It is examined both without and with the prospect of an EU–Mercosur FTA.

There is also the opportunity for other high-income countries to follow the EU offer to least-developed countries (LDCs) and African, Caribbean and Pacific (ACP) small countries of duty-free access to their markets, but this opportunity involves only a very small volume of global trade (and may well cause losses for other poor countries that are not LDCs or ACPs, so could even worsen inequality among low-income countries), so estimates of its benefits are mentioned just in passing.

A more radical opportunity is considered instead, namely the freeing up of international flows of workers. Even though the WTO's current DDA could include it as part of the services (GATS Mode IV) negotiations (see Mattoo and Carzaniga 2002), it appears to have little

---

[10] Whether such preferential trade agreements are stepping stones or stumbling blocks to freer global trade is a much-debated point among economists. For a recent survey of the impact of regionalism on the multilateral trading system, see Baldwin (2008).

[11] A potentially larger FTA is that among members of APEC (the Asia Pacific Economic Cooperation forum). Currently referred to as FTAAP, it is embryonic and ill-formed at this stage.

prospect of being adopted multilaterally in this current round of negotiations. However, individual countries could adopt it unilaterally with the stroke of the legislators' pen. Hence it is considered separately from the first opportunity described above.

Economic Effects of Current Trade Barriers and Farm Subsidies

All the estimates considered below of the potential economic welfare gains from these opportunities are generated using computable general equilibrium (CGE) models of the global economy, the most common of which (GTAP) is described in the Appendix. The CGE welfare gains refer to the equivalent variation (EV) in income as a result of each of the shocks described.[12] While not without their shortcomings (see François 2000; Whalley 2000; Anderson 2003 and the caveats below), CGE models are far superior for current purposes to partial equilibrium models, which fail to capture the economy-wide nature of the adjustments to reform whereby some sectors expand when others contract and release capital and labor. They are also superior to macroeconometric models which typically lack sufficient sectoral detail and are based on time series analysis of the past which may no longer be relevant for the near future (François and Reinert 1997). CGE models were first used in multilateral trade reform analysis in ex post assessments of the Tokyo Round of GATT negotiations in the late 1970s/early 1980s (Cline *et al.* 1978; Deardorff and Stern 1979, 1986; Whalley 1985). Since then they have been used increasingly during and following the Uruguay Round, as well as for ex ante assessments of the Doha Round, of bilateral and other preferential economic integration agreements, and of unilateral reforms such as when a country considers acceding to the WTO.

Empirical comparative static economy-wide CGE model simulations of the potential economic welfare gains from prospective multilateral trade liberalization typically generate positive gains for the world and for most partici-pating countries. In the case of sub-global preferential trade reform studies, the estimated gains to the countries involved are always smaller, and some excluded countries – and even some participating ones – may lose. When increasing returns to scale and monopolistic competition (IRS/MC) are assumed instead of constant returns to scale and perfect competition (CRS/PC), and firms are assumed to be heterogeneous rather than homogeneous, and when trade is liberalized not just in goods but also in services and investment flows, the estimates of potential gains can increase several fold. Economy-wide modelers have also begun to examine the effects of lowering barriers to temporary labor movements across national borders. Virtually all such studies are in comparative static mode, however, and so are unable to capture the crucially important growth-enhancing dynamic effects of trade reform described in the previous section. It is therefore not surprising that they generate results for gains from trade reform that are only a small fraction of GDP.

Such low estimated gains seem to fly in the face of casual empiricism. Irwin (2002), for example, notes that three different countries in three different regions chose to liberalize in three different decades (Korea from 1965, Chile from 1974 and India from 1991 – see Irwin 2002, Figures 2.3 to 2.5), and per capita GDP growth in each of those countries accelerated markedly thereafter by several percentage points per year. Admittedly those historical liberalization experiences involved also complementary reforms to other domestic policies and institutions that would have contributed significantly to the observed boosts in economic growth. Even so, they support the point made in the previous section that trade can generate not only static efficiency gains but also dynamic gains.

Some CGE modellers have tried to proxy that dynamic effect by adding an additional one-off total factor productivity shock to their trade

---

[12] EV is defined as the income that consumers would be willing to forgo and still have the same level of well-being after as before the reform. For a discussion of the merits of EV versus other measures of change in economic welfare, see for example Just, Hueth and Schmitz (2004).

Table 8.1. Comparative static estimates of economic welfare gains from full global liberalization of goods and services trade

Study	Market assumptions[a]	Sectors liberalized	Baseline year (of EV welfare measure)	Welfare gain, non-OECD (US$ billions)	Welfare gain, global (US$ billions)[b]	Year of currency (US dollars)[b]
AMV (2006)	CRS/PC	Goods only	2015	142	287	2001
BKS (2005)	IRS/MC	Goods, services and FDI	1997	na	2417 {2616}	1997 {2001}
HRT (2002)	CRS/PC	Goods only	1995	100 {113}	456 {514}	1995 {2001}
WBGEP (2002)	CRS/PC plus productivity boost	Goods only	2015	539 {583}	832 {901}	1997 {2001}

[a] Constant returns to scale/perfect competition and increasing returns to scale/monopolistic competition/firm-level differentiated products.
[b] In cases where the year of currency is pre-2001, welfare values shown below the reported numbers, in {}, have been inflated to 2001 assuming 2 percent inflation per year (the change in the United States' GDP Deflator).
Sources: Anderson, Martin, and van der Mensbrugghe (2006a, Table 12.4); Brown, Kiyota, and Stern (2005, Table 4); Harrison, Rutherford, and Tarr (2002, Table 5); and World Bank (2002, Table 6.1).

reform scenarios. But reform may also raise the *rate* of factor productivity growth and/or of capital accumulation. Such endogenous growth has yet to be satisfactorily introduced into CGE models, and in any case it is unclear how to interpret a model's estimated welfare effects if households are reducing current consumption in order to boost their or their descendants' future consumption by investing more.

It should be kept in mind that all the experiments in the comparative static CGE studies surveyed below reduce only trade barriers plus agricultural production and export subsidies. The reasons for including subsidies only in agriculture are that they are the key subsidies explicitly being negotiated at the WTO (where non-agricultural export subsidies are illegal), they represented an estimated two-fifths of all government expenditure on subsidies globally during 1994–8 (van Beers and de Moor 2001, Table 3.1), and they are fully represented in the GTAP database whereas subsidies for most other sectors are not included so it is not possible to estimate their welfare cost within the same framework. And the reason for not also

[13] Full opening of borders to immigration would be such a huge shock, and so unlikely politically relative to opening product and capital markets, as to be not worth considering.

explicitly estimating the welfare impacts of other domestic policies and institutions (even though, because of their complementarity, they can affect the payoff from opening up) is that typically they are beyond the sphere of influence of international trade negotiators.

With this as background, we first consider estimates of the economic benefits associated with freeing global trade completely, before turning to each of the three opportunities for politically more feasible partial reforms. The reasons for reviewing gains from full trade reform are twofold: because it provides a benchmark against which to compare the benefits of lesser reforms; and because several models have generated full global trade reform results,[13] making it possible to see the range of outcomes that emerge from these different models.

Global cost of current distortions to international trade

Estimates of the global cost of current trade distortions are obtained by simulating the removal of those policies as represented in a global CGE model. Table 8.1 reports a selection of estimates of the economic benefits associated with complete removal of goods trade barriers and agricultural production and export subsidies.

The first one listed in Table 8.1 is by Anderson, Martin and van der Mensbrugghe (2006a,b). The AMV study provides the simplest scenario: full global liberalization of just merchandise trade and farm subsidies. It uses the latest version of the World Bank's Linkage model, assuming constant returns to scale and perfect competition in all product and factor markets.[14] The GTAP Version 6 database, which provides trade and protection data for 2001 (see Dimaranan 2006), is employed in that study to generate a new baseline for 2005 (allowing for recent policy changes including the completion of implementation of the Uruguay Round, the EU expansion to 25 members, and the accession of new members such as China and Taiwan to WTO), and then to project the world economy forward a decade assuming no further trade policy reforms. This baseline for 2015 is then compared with how it would look after full adjustment following the phased removal of all countries' trade barriers and agricultural subsidies from 2005. The economic welfare gain is estimated to be US$287 billion per year in 2001 dollars as of 2015 (and hence slightly more each year thereafter as the global economy expands). Of that, $86 billion p.a. is estimated to accrue to developing countries.

These AMV results are the lowest of the estimates summarized in Table 8.1, and so should be considered as very much lower-bound estimates of the current cost of global distortions to international trade. But they have been widely used in the WTO's Doha Round as a measure of what is on the table for negotiation in the DDA's agricultural and NAMA (non-agricultural market access) talks, in part because they have also been carefully decomposed in various ways to illuminate the relative importance of the various issues under discussion (see below).

The second study listed in Table 8.1, BKS, is by Brown, Kiyota and Stern (2005). It uses the Version 5 GTAP data base projected from its 1997 base to 2005, but they embed it in the authors' static Michigan Model of World Production and Trade (www.ssp.umich.edu/rsie/model) to produce the highest of the surveyed estimates of global welfare gains from complete removal of trade barriers and agricultural subsidies: $2,616 billion p.a. when converted in 2001 US dollars. This much larger estimate is the result of several features of the BKS study: having China and Taiwan's implementation of their WTO accession commitments in the experiment rather than in the baseline; the inclusion of IRS/MC for non-agricultural sectors and therefore product heterogeneity at the level of the firm rather than the national industry; liberalization of services in addition to goods trade (with IRS/MC assumed for the huge services sector); and the inclusion in services liberalization of the opening to foreign direct investment. The latter boosts substantially the gains from services liberalization, which account for nearly two-thirds of this study's estimated total gains.

The other two estimates in Table 8.1 of the gains from complete trade liberalization are between these two extremes. The HRT study (Harrison, Rutherford and Tarr 2002) uses much larger trade elasticities than other models and so gets a considerable gain for goods trade reform ($514 billion compared with AMV's $287 billion) even though it refers to 1995 when the world economy was somewhat smaller.

The WBGEP study (World Bank 2002) uses the World Bank's Linkage model but the Version 5 GTAP protection levels as of 1997, before projecting the world economy to 2015. That WBGEP study differs from the AMV study not only in using an older protection database (as do the BKS and HRT studies) but also in assuming liberalization boosts factor productivity in each industry according to the extent of growth in the share of production exported by the industry. The case presented suggests the gains would be $901 billion p.a. when converted in 2001 US dollars. By way of comparison, AMV re-ran their more recent model with that same factor productivity multiplier, and it boosted their total global gains from $287 billion to $461 billion (Anderson, Martin and van der Mensbrugghe

[14] The Linkage model is fully described by its creator (van der Mensbrugghe 2005). It is more of a long-run model than GTAP, having higher supply and trade elasticities, and it is recursive dynamic and so is readily projected forward.

2006a, Table 12.20). The fact that this is barely half as large as the number in the WBGEP study has been the subject of much discussion, and led to a detailed explanation being provided by van der Mensbrugghe (2006). The explanation involves a mixture of factors, including a new source of data on tariffs (which incorporated tariff preferences more comprehensively and hence lowered the average bilateral tariff) and on agricultural assistance (which on average implied less agricultural protectionism, and the incorporation of major reforms between 1997 and 2005 (most notably implementation of the Uruguay Round agreements, including the phase-out of the Multifibre Arrangement, EU expansion, and the reforms in China that accompanied its accession to WTO). On the one hand, the fact that this drop in the cost of remaining trade distortions was so large is worth celebrating, as it indicates the extent to which distortions in the world's markets for goods have been reduced in less than one decade. On the other hand, the cost of policies still in place remains huge, hence this chapter's search for opportunities to bring about further liberalization.

Which Countries Bear the Cost, and Which Sectoral Policies Impose the Cost?

The AMV study has laid out how its estimated global cost of current policies affecting merchandise trade is distributed across countries and from which sectoral policies they originate. The basis of that is the estimated tariff structure of 2005, summarized in Table 8.2. It shows agricultural products are subject to much higher tariffs than manufactures, especially in high-income countries which also provide large subsidies to farmers. It also shows that tariffs in developing countries are much higher than in high-income countries for manufactures, and almost as high for farm products. From that one would expect developing countries to be imposing a high cost on themselves from their own policies, and agricultural policies to be a significant contributor to the global cost of merchandise trade distortions.

The detailed country distribution of AMV's estimated welfare costs is provided in Table 8.3, where it is expressed as a gain from full liberalization. The real value in 2001 US dollars is shown in column 1, and it is subdivided in columns 2 and 3 into that part due to the terms of trade effects of current policies (which for small countries in a homogeneous-products model would be equivalent to the effect of other countries' policies, but not in models using Armington trade elasticities that distinguish products by country of origin and so give each country some degree of market power internationally), and to the rest (which is predominantly due to own-country policies). The bold rows towards the bottom of the table indicate for high-income countries that one-seventh of the cost to them comes from the adverse terms of trade effects of global distortions, whereas for developing countries the opposite is true: global reform would worsen their terms of trade. Hence the difference between the two country groups in absolute cost of own-country policies is closer than the overall cost, although still higher for high-income countries. When expressed as a percentage of baseline income, however, the loss is greater for the developing country group, at 0.8 percent compared with 0.6 percent for high-income countries; and insofar as column 2 proxies the cost contribution of other countries' policies, then the final numbers in parentheses suggest developing countries' losses from policies of that country group are proportionately more than twice those of the much larger high-income economies (1.1 compared with 0.5 percent) – which is consistent with the differences in average tariffs reported in Table 8.2.

Table 8.4 summarizes how those costs are attributable to different sectors of the two country groups. Row 9 suggests that agricultural and food policies are responsible for 63 percent of the cost of merchandise trade distortions to both developing and high-income countries. That is, even though that sector represents only about one-twelfth of global production and trade, its policies contribute nearly two-thirds of the welfare loss from trade and subsidies affecting goods markets. Also, columns 4 and 5 show that for developing countries the cost is split equally between policies of high-income countries and

Table 8.2. Import-weighted average applied tariffs, by sector and country, 2005 (percent)

Importing region	Agriculture and processed food	(Primary agriculture only)	(Processed food only)	Textiles and clothing	Other manufacturing
World	15.2			9.3	3.1
High-income	15.9			7.3	1.2
Australia & NZ	2.6	0.3	3.3	13.9	4.1
EU25 + EFTA	13.9	13.2	14.7	5.1	1.7
United States	2.4	2.3	2.5	9.6	0.9
Canada	9.0	1.2	14.1	8.7	0.5
Japan	29.3	48.0	20.8	9.0	0.4
S. Korea & Taiwan	53.0	84.5	22.4	9.2	3.6
Hong Kong & Sing.	0.1	0.0	0.2	0.0	0.0
Developing countries	14.2			14.3	7.1
Middle-income	12.1			13.6	6.0
Argentina	7.1	5.6	7.8	11.1	10.1
Brazil	5.0	2.4	9.0	14.7	9.7
China	10.3	9.9	11.0	9.6	5.5
Mexico	10.3	10.8	9.7	7.8	4.3
Russia	13.5	14.6	12.8	15.8	7.8
South Africa	8.6	5.9	10.6	21.9	5.4
Thailand	16.7	12.7	19.2	16.4	7.6
Turkey	16.6	16.4	17.0	3.8	1.2
Rest of East Asia	13.4	18.6	9.0	8.7	3.5
Rest of LAC	10.8	9.2	11.8	12.9	8.4
Rest of ECA	15.7	10.4	19.5	9.3	3.2
M. East & N. Africa	13.1	8.2	18.3	23.9	7.2
Low-income	22.0			17.9	14.1
Bangladesh	12.7	7.4	21.2	29.9	16.2
India	49.9	25.7	75.6	26.5	24.2
Indonesia	5.0	4.3	6.2	8.0	4.3
Vietnam	37.1	13.1	44.8	29.1	12.3
Rest of South Asia	21.1	14.2	32.0	6.6	14.3
Selected SSAfrica[a]	11.8	10.2	13.0	12.5	7.5
Rest of SSAfrica	21.2	18.0	23.6	26.2	14.0
Rest of the world	11.8	1.9	18.7	5.6	8.9

[a] The selected Sub-Saharan African countries (for which national modules are available in the Linkage model) include Botswana, Madagascar, Malawi, Mozambique, Tanzania, Uganda, Zambia, Zimbabwe.
Source: Projections from the GTAP database Version 6.05 using the World Bank's Linkage model, by Anderson, Martin, and van der Mensbrugghe (2006a, Table 12.3).

those of developing countries, whereas for rich countries 58 percent of the cost is from own-country and other rich countries' policies.

Despite the large cost of agricultural poli-cies to developing countries as a group, an important question was raised during and following the Copenhagen Consensus process in 2004 (Panagariya 2004). It was: wouldn't that

Table 8.3. Impacts on real income from full liberalization of global merchandise trade, by country/region, 2015

(relative to the baseline, in 2001 dollars and percent)	Total real income gain p.a. ($ billion)	Change in income due just to change in terms of trade ($ billion)	Gain due to improved efficiency of resource use net of terms of trade effect ($ billion)	Total real gain as percentage of baseline income in 2015a
Australia and New Zealand	6.1	3.5	2.6	1.0 (0.4)
EU 25 plus EFTA	65.2	0.5	64.7	0.6 (0.6)
United States	16.2	10.7	6.5	0.1 (0.0)
Canada	3.8	−0.3	4.1	0.4 (0.4)
Japan	54.6	7.5	47.1	1.1 (1.0)
Korea and Taiwan	44.6	0.4	44.2	3.5 (3.5)
Hong Kong and Singapore	11.2	7.9	3.3	2.6 (0.8)
Argentina	4.9	1.2	3.7	1.2 (0.9)
Bangladesh	0.1	−1.1	1.2	0.2 (2.4)
Brazil	9.9	4.6	5.3	1.5 (0.8)
China	5.6	−8.3	13.9	0.2 (0.5)
India	3.4	−9.4	12.8	0.4 (1.5)
Indonesia	1.9	0.2	1.7	0.7 (0.7)
Thailand	7.7	0.7	7.0	3.8 (3.4)
Vietnam	3.0	−0.2	3.2	5.2 (5.5)
Russia	2.7	−2.7	5.4	0.6 (1.2)
Mexico	3.6	−3.6	7.2	0.4 (0.8)
South Africa	1.3	0.0	1.3	0.9 (0.9)
Turkey	3.3	0.2	3.1	1.3 (1.2)
Rest of South Asia	1.0	−0.8	1.8	0.5 (0.9)
Rest of East Asia	5.3	−0.9	6.2	1.9 (2.2)
Rest of LAC	10.3	0.0	10.3	1.2 (1.2)
Rest of ECA	1.0	−1.6	2.6	0.3 (0.8)
Middle East and North Africa	14.0	−6.4	20.4	1.2 (1.7)
Selected SSA countries[b]	1.0	0.5	0.5	1.5 (0.8)
Rest of Sub-Saharan Africa	2.5	−2.3	4.8	1.1 (2.2)
Rest of the World	3.4	0.1	3.3	1.5 (1.5)
High-income countries	201.6	30.3	171.3	0.6 (0.5)
Developing countries	85.7	−29.7	115.4	0.8 (1.1)
Middle-income countries	69.5	−16.7	86.2	0.8 (1.0)
Low-income countries	16.2	−12.9	29.1	0.8 (1.4)
East Asia and Pacific	23.5	−8.5	32.0	0.7 (1.0)
South Asia	4.5	−11.2	15.7	0.4 (1.4)
Europe and Central Asia	7.0	−4.0	11.0	0.7 (1.1)
Sub-Saharan Africa	4.8	−1.8	6.6	1.1 (1.5)
Latin America and the Carib	28.7	2.2	26.5	1.0 (0.9)
World total	287.3	0.6	286.7	0.7 (0.7)

[a] Numbers in parentheses refer to that due to efficiency gains net of terms of trade effects.
[b] Selected Sub-Saharan African countries include Botswana, Madagascar, Malawi, Mozambique, Tanzania, Uganda, Zambia, Zimbabwe.
Source: Anderson, Martin and van der Mensbrugghe (2006a, Table 12.4).

Table 8.4. Regional and sectoral source of gains from full liberalization of global merchandise trade, developing and high-income countries, 2015 (relative to the baseline scenario)

	Gains by region in $ billion			Percent of regional gain		
	Developing	High-income	World	Developing	High-income	World
Developing countries liberalize:						
Agriculture and food	28	19	47	33	9	17
Textiles and clothing	9	14	23	10	7	8
Other merchandise	6	52	58	7	26	20
All sectors	43	85	128	50	42	45
High-income countries liberalize:						
Agriculture and food	26	109	135	30	54	47
Textiles and clothing	13	2	15	15	1	5
Other merchandise	4	5	9	5	3	3
All sectors	43	116	159	50	58	55
All countries liberalize:						
Agriculture and food	54	128	182	63	63	63
Textiles and clothing	22	16	38	25	8	14
Other merchandise	10	57	67	12	29	23
All sectors	86	201	287	100	100	100

[a] Small interaction effects are distributed proportionately and numbers are rounded to sum to 100 percent.
Source: Anderson, Martin, and van der Mensbrugghe (2006a, Table 12.6).

cost be borne predominantly by relatively affluent agricultural exporters such as Argentina, Brazil and Thailand, while poorer developing countries such as in Sub-Saharan Africa (SSA) would be beneficiaries of current agricultural protection policies of high-income countries? SSA countries would be benefiting, so Panagariya's argument went, either as net food importers (since international food prices are depressed by rich-country agricultural protection) or as net agricultural exporters accessing (duty-free and often quota-free) those protected markets via preferential trade agreements such as enjoyed by former colonies or least-developed countries. The first part of the argument seems to be supported by column 2 of Table 8.3, which shows that Argentina, Brazil and Thailand – along with Australia and New Zealand – are the main losers from the terms of trade effects of current policies. But so too is the southern Africa region, while the rest of SSA benefits (i.e., would lose from full merchandise liberalization).

Table 8.5. Impact of full liberalization of high-income countries' food and agriculture import barriers and subsidies on indexes of real[a] export and import prices, Sub-Saharan Africa, 2015 (percent)

	Export prices		Import prices	
	Agric & food	Other products	Agric & food	Other products
Sub-Saharan Africa	2.5	1.2	4.3	0.4
South Africa	1.0	0.7	3.5	0.4
Other Southern Africa	4.1	3.2	2.8	0.5
Rest of Sub-Saharan Africa	2.2	1.1	4.8	0.3

[a] Relative to the numeraire which in this version of the Linkage model is the price of high-income countries' exports of manufactures.
Source: Anderson, Martin, and van der Mensbrugghe (2006c).

To address Panagariya's question more fully requires restricting the experiment to just agricultural policies and of just high-income countries, and to decomposing the effects to see

Table 8.6. Terms of trade's contribution to real income changes from full liberalization of high-income countries' food and agriculture import barriers and subsidies, Sub-Saharan Africa, 2015 (in 2001 US$ billion)

	Change in regional welfare due to:		
	Change in export prices	Change in import prices[a]	Sum of export and import price effects
Agric and food products – all SSA	0.94	−0.38	0.56
South Africa	0.05	−0.09	−0.04
Other Southern Africa	0.36	−0.03	0.33
Rest of Sub-Saharan Africa	0.53	−0.25	0.28
Non-agricultural products – all SSA	1.45	−0.53	0.92
South Africa	0.35	−0.15	0.20
Other Southern Africa	0.37	−0.10	0.27
Rest of Sub-Saharan Africa	0.72	−0.29	0.43

[a] The numbers in this column have the opposite sign to the import price indexes in Table 8.5 because an import price rise reduces real income (whereas numbers in the export columns have the same sign).
Source: Anderson, Martin, and van der Mensbrugghe (2006c).

the contributions of agricultural versus non-agricultural prices of imports versus exports. That has since been done in a paper by the same AMV authors and reported in Tables 8.5 (see previous page) and 8.6. Table 8.5 reveals that indeed SSA's agricultural and food import price index rises, but so too does the export price index. Evidently the rise in demand for SSA exports enjoying little or no preferential access more than outweighs the reduced earnings from their exports that have been enjoying substantial preferences. But that is only half the story. The other half has to do with changes in prices of non-agricultural products. Table 8.5 shows that while the price of other imported goods rises slightly, because of growth in demand for them relative to their supply in high-income countries as their incomes rise, the price of SSA's exports of non-agricultural goods rises even more. The relative importance of each of these sets of price changes in contributing to the changes in regional economic welfare is summarized in Table 8.6, which reveals two things. First, the negative contribu-

tion to SSA welfare from higher import prices is more than offset by the positive contribution from higher export prices (except for farm products in South Africa where they almost cancel out). And second, the contributions on both the export and import side are larger from non-agricultural than from agricultural price changes. So even though the price changes shown in Table 8.5 for SSA from high-income country agricultural liberalization are smaller for non-farm than farm products, the greater weight of non-farm products means their net positive welfare contribution to SSA via the terms of trade effect is greater.[15]

Within Agriculture, Which Policy Instruments Reduce Welfare Most?

As the WTO's Doha negotiations on agriculture got under way from late 2001, developing countries initially put most emphasis on the need to reduce agricultural subsidies. So when an early draft of the Anderson and Martin (2006) book presented results suggesting those subsidies contributed little to the global welfare cost of agricultural policies relative to restrictions on market access (just 7 percent, compared with the 93 percent contribution of import tariffs), those CGE modeling results were treated with

[15] This is very similar to the result found by the OECD Secretariat using their version of the GTAP model known as GTAPEM, which is almost the same as the GTAP model referred to in the Appendix (Tangermann 2005).

some scepticism.[16] To convince sceptics required examining the issue from first principles, to show that the 93 percent result – which is supported by the modeling studies of two other institutions (USDA 2001 and OECD 2006) – is not just an artifact of the computable general equilibrium models they use.[17] A study by Anderson, Martin and Valenzuela (2006) was designed to provide more intuition for this repeated research finding. To ensure transparency, it used widely available data and focused on a simple back-of-the-envelope model rather than a computable general equilibrium (CGE) model with its inherent complexities. Its results confirmed the overwhelming importance of market access found in the studies using CGE models.

Despite these results, domestic support should not be ignored in the Doha negotiations, not least because it is extremely important for some products of great interest to developing countries. This is particularly so for cotton, where Anderson and Valenzuela (2007) estimate that abolishing domestic subsidies on cotton would provide almost 80 percent of the $147 million in total welfare gains to Sub-Saharan Africa from cotton market reform. There is also a systemic risk that restraints on market access barriers, if unaccompanied by restraints on domestic support, could lead some high-income countries to replace market access barriers with distorting domestic support. The key policy message to draw from these results, though, is that reductions in domestic support cannot, alone, be expected to realize very much of the potential global trade and welfare gains sought from the Doha agricultural negotiations, and that achieving improvements in market access is extremely important for a successful outcome in these negotiations.

Quantifying Economic Benefits of Reducing Barriers to International Trade and Migration

In the light of the above modeling results showing the costs of current policies, we focus now on assessing in turn the benefits from the three

opportunities identified earlier in the chapter to reduce those distortions, namely via the Doha Development Agenda of the WTO, via sub-global preferential trade reforms such as the FTAA initiative, and via allowing more international movement of workers.

Prospective Benefits from the Doha Development Agenda

Anderson, Martin and van der Mensbrugghe (2006a,b) examine in great detail the comparative static consequences of the main options that have been canvassed in the Doha Round. They show a range of global welfare gain estimates via partial goods trade liberalization from less than $20 billion to as much as $120 billion per year. In their 'Pessimistic', minimalist-reform scenario, little more is achieved other than the phase out of farm export subsidies, a modest reduction in agricultural domestic support and, for agricultural and non-agricultural tariffs, a reduction only in 'binding overhang' (the gap between each legally bound tariff and the typically much lower actual tariffs being applied to imports from different trading partners). The key aspect of this scenario is the inclusion of 'sensitive' and 'special' farm product exceptions in the tariff cutting formula, whereby virtually all the items with peak applied tariffs would avoid being cut in both high-income and developing countries. The first column of Table 8.7 shows that with such a minimalist outcome, developing countries

---

[16] One reason countries put different emphases on the three pillars, and perhaps a reason the EU seeks to downplay the importance of market access, is that a large share of support for its farmers – and most of its food processors – comes from market access barriers. By contrast, domestic support measures are much more important in the United States.

[17] Hoekman, Ng and Olarreaga (2004), using a simpler partial equilibrium framework and extremely detailed information on tariffs plus official WTO data on domestic subsidies, also established the importance of agricultural market access barriers. Their findings were even stronger than the 93 percent result cited above. They found that reductions in domestic support would yield less than one percent of the gains obtainable from reductions in market access barriers.

Table 8.7. Comparative static estimates of economic welfare gains from partial trade and subsidy reform under the Doha Development Agenda, 2015 (in 2001 US$ billion)

	Scenarios:		
	"Pessimistic":	"Central":	"Optimistic":
	Agric-only reform, with sensitive products exceptions and with SDT	Agric and non-agric reforms, without sensitive products but with SDT	Agric and non-agric reforms, without sensitive products and no SDT
Low-income countries	0.1	12.5	17.1
Middle-income countries	−0.5	16.1	22.7
High-income countries	18.1	79.2	96.4
Total, world	17.7	96.1	119.3
		(= 0.2% of GDP)	

[a] For specifics of scenarios, see text (SDT = special and differential treatment: two-thirds cuts by developing countries and none by least developed countries).
Source: Anderson, Martin, and van der Mensbrugghe (2006a, Table 12.14).

as a group would gain nothing and high-income countries would gain just $18 billion per year by 2015 (in US 2001 dollars). This assumes also that special and differential treatment (SDT) is invoked, whereby developing countries cut their bound rates by only two-thirds as much as high-income countries (hence their applied rates by very little, given their high degree of 'binding overhang'), and UN-designated LDCs do not liberalize at all.

Having exposed the importance of 'sensitive' and 'special' farm product exception in this way, the hope is that negotiators will be more ambitious in the final agreement on agriculture, which in turn would allow a more ambitious outcome for non-agriculture. When that exceptional treatment for agricultural tariffs is dropped and a 50 percent cut in non-agricultural tariffs is included, the projected developing country gain rises to almost $30 billion per year, and the high-income country gain quadruples (mainly because rich countries would be lowering their applied tariffs on their most protected items such as rice, sugar and dairy products). In this 'central' scenario, the projected global gain is $96 billion per year in 2015, which is 0.2 percent of global GDP.

If developing countries were to not invoke SDT, the probability of reaching a Doha agreement would rise substantially – and developing

countries would gain much more, because of greater own-country reform. The final column of Table 8.7 shows that if developing countries (including LDCs) fully engaged in the sense of cutting their tariffs by the same proportion as high-income countries, their gain in this 'Optimistic' scenario would rise by more than a third above that from the second ('Central') scenario, and the global gains would be almost $120 billion per year (compare columns 2 and 3 of Table 8.7).

The 'Central' scenario is about mid-way between the various proposals that were on the table before the Doha Round went quiet (Martin and Anderson 2006), so it is that one which is chosen as one around which we do benefit/cost analysis below. In July 2007 the Chairs of the Agricultural and the NAMA negotiations provided new texts for members to consider as they try to narrow their differences. True, many developing countries remained cautious about undertaking more liberalization commitments, and the fast track authority for the US President expired on 30 June 2007, so agreement may yet prove elusive or still be some years away. But if a fair compromise between those current positions is reached, it would represent a substantial agreement—much more so than the Uruguay Round Agreement on Agriculture in terms of cuts both in bound tariffs and subsidies and in actual delivered levels of farm protection and support. The potential Doha agreement on non-agriculture in that scenario is substantial too. Moreover, such an outcome on goods trade reform is likely to be accompanied by an as-yet unknown degree of commitment to reform policies affecting markets for services, which would multiply the gains, possibly by several orders of magnitude based on the earlier discussion of results reported in Table 8.1. With that in mind, together with the fact that the numbers in Table 8.2 are generated from a model that does not include increasing returns to scale, imperfect competition, productivity enhancement or dynamics, the 'Central' scenario's benefits (equal to 0.2 percent globally and 0.28 percent for developing countries) should be considered very much lower-bound estimates.

As for an upper bound on comparative static gains, the results in Table 8.1 suggest it could be as much as nine times greater, depending on the extent to which services trade and investment are also liberalized, on the strength of influence of imperfect competition and economies of scale, and on the extent to which the appropriate counterfactual in 2015 is not just current policies but rather more protectionist ones in the absence of a robust Doha agreement. To err on the conservative side, we choose an upper bound of five times the lower bound, or 1.0 percent of GDP globally (1.4 percent for developing countries). We also assume that those gains will accrue fully after an eight-year phase-in period from 2008, prior to which the gains will begin in 2008 at one-eighth the full amount as of 2015 and rise by a further one-eighth each year until 2015.

There are dynamic gains from trade to consider in addition to the above comparative static ones. The past experiences of successful reformers such as Korea, China, India and Chile suggest trade opening immediately boosts GDP growth rates by several percentage points per year for many years. A conservative estimate might be that reform boosts GDP growth rates – projected to 2015 by the World Bank (2006) to be 2.7 percent for high-income countries and 4.6 percent for developing countries and so 3.2

percent globally – by one-sixth or 0.45 of a percentage point for high-income countries and by one-third or 1.53 percentage points for developing countries, that is, to 3.15 and 6.13 percent, respectively, and hence from 3.2 to 3.73 percent globally through to 2015.[18,19] For the period after 2015, we assume the boost to growth rates diminishes linearly over time, petering out by 2025 in the low-gain case and by 2050 in the high-gain case. Thereafter there would be no further dynamic benefit in the absence of further reforms, just the continuing comparative static gain of 0.2 percent globally and 0.28 percent for developing countries. This is in line with the summary of the literature provided by Winters (2004), who argues that while the growth increments due to trade liberalization will be temporary, they could last several decades.

In addition to these contributions to net global benefits, multilateral trade opening also can contribute to reducing inequality and poverty both between and within countries (Hertel and Winters 2006; Hertel et al. 2007). While those are benefits that cannot be incorporated in the standard benefit-cost metric used in this project, they can be thought of as positive externalities that reduce such things as inter- and intra-national social tensions, environmental degradation, malnutrition, and disease, thereby addressing several of the other challenges being considered by the Copenhagen Consensus project.

---

[18] For years beyond 2015, we assume the developing country real GDP growth rate converges lineally from 4.6 percent to the current global average of 3.2 percent p.a. over the remaining 85 years (while high-income countries continue to grow at 2.7 percent).

[19] Econometric support for the claim that this assumed increase in GDP growth rates is conservative is provided by Romalis (2007), who estimates that the elimination of just import tariffs, and only by high-income countries, would boost annual GDP growth in developing countries by up to 1.6 percentage points. In the model by Rutherford and Tarr (2002), their 10 percentage point cut in tariffs led to a rise in the steady-state growth rate of 2 percent p.a. to 2.6 percent over the first decade and 2.2 percent over the first five decades (and even after fifty years their annual growth rate is 2.1 percent).

Table 8.8. Comparative static estimates of economic welfare gains from an FTAA compared with global liberalization of goods and services trade (in 2001 US$ billion)

(a) BKS study (goods and services reform)[a]

	FTAA	Unilateral free trade by the Americas	Global full trade liberalization (by 100%)
United States and Canada	79	403	641
Latin America and Caribbean	49	113	172
Total, Americas	128	516	813
Rest of world	−10	364	1803
Total, world	118	880	2616

(b) HRTG study (goods reform only)[b]

	FTAA	FTAA plus EU-Mercosur FTA	Global trade liberalization by 50%	Doha scenario, lower-bound partial reform[c]
United States and Canada	3	2	4	6
Latin America and Caribbean	11	31	15	8
Total, Americas	14	33	19	14
European Union	−3	23	43	31
Japan	−1	−1	50	24
Other countries	−5	−5	93	27
Total, world	5	50	205	96

[a] Values shown have been inflated from their reported 1995 values to 2001 values assuming 2 percent inflation per year (the change in the United States' GDP Deflator).
[b] Values shown have been inflated from their reported 1996 values to 2001 values assuming 2 percent inflation per year (the change in the United States' GDP Deflator).
[c] Taken from Scenario 7 in Anderson, Martin, and van der Mensbrugghe (2006a, Table 12.14), as discussed in the text.
Sources: Brown, Kiyota, and Stern (2005, Table 4) and Harrison *et al.* (2004, Table 6).

Prospective Benefits of Just Removing Intra-American Trade Barriers

The negotiations to create a Free Trade Area of the Americas – the largest such FTA negotiation currently under way – have run into political problems, so it is not clear if/when they might conclude. The same is true of the negotiations to create an FTA between the European Union and the Southern American countries that are members of Mercosur (see http://ec.europa.eu/external_relations/mercosur/intro/index.htm). It is nonetheless worth considering that type of opportunity so as to point out that the potential global gains from such sub-global FTAs are only a small fraction of those obtainable from multilateral liberalization. Two studies that examine both multilateral reform and the FTAA are the BKS study and a follow-on to the HRT one, by

Harrison *et al.* (2004). BKS estimate the gains from the FTAA to be just one-twenty-fourth that from a full multilateral trade liberalization, and for the HRTG study the difference is even greater. The North and Latin American economies are projected to gain (Table 8.8), although the estimated magnitudes differ considerably between the two FTAA studies – just as they do in Table 8.1, and for the same reasons. Note, however, that both studies suggest excluded economies in aggregate would be worse off if the FTAA went ahead, as is always possible with sub-global reforms because of trade diversion.

Table 8.8 also reports broader liberalizations, so as to be able to compare their estimated welfare effects on the Americas and the rest of the world with those that might result from an FTAA. The BKS study shows how much greater would be the gains to the North and Latin American countries if each of them were instead just to adopt free trade unilaterally: North America would be five times better off, and Latin America 2.3 times better off. Even more striking is the effect on the rest of the world: instead of losing slightly as in the FTAA scenario, other regions would gain substantially from unilateral trade reform in the Americas. And then if the unilateral reform extended to the rest of the world (i.e., a move to global free trade), the Americas would be better off by a further 50+ percent (because of also gaining from other regions' reform), while the rest of the world would be five times better off (Table 8.8(a)).

The HRTG study reported two other variants of broader reform. The first involves adding an EU–Mercosur FTA on top of the FTAA. That reduces substantially the welfare-reducing aspects of the FTAA for Latin America and the EU, but the rest of the world still loses slightly in aggregate. If instead all countries were to liberalize even by just halving their tariffs, the rest of the world would be far better off but Latin America would benefit only half as much because of greater competition/ the loss of preferences into the markets of North America and the EU. The final column of Table 8.8(b) reports the results from the lower-bound Doha scenario described above. That scenario would involve considerably less liberalization than a 50 percent across the board global reform, especially for developing countries because of the Special and Differential Treatment they have demanded in the form of lesser tariff cuts under the Doha Round, so not surprisingly they are lower than the global 50 percent case. Note, though, that they generate much bigger gains than the FTAA plus EU–Mercosur scenario for all but Latin America – and Latin America could alter that simply by committing to open up somewhat more under Doha than may be required of them (e.g., to match the degree of opening up involved in joining FTAs with North America and the EU).

Even if several such large FTAs were to be agreed, their potential contribution to world economic welfare would remain only a fraction of what is potentially achievable via a similar degree of tariff cuts under a multilateral agreement. Furthermore, these FTA studies take no account of the dampening effect of the rules of origin that almost invariably constrain the extent to which firms can take advantage of any FTA's removal of bilateral tariffs (Krueger 1999).

Similarly, studies of Europe's proposed Economic Partnership Agreements (EPAs) with the poor countries of the African, Caribbean and Pacific (ACP) Group almost all anticipate zero gains or actual economic losses from them, at least in static terms.[20] In those studies their authors felt the effects on economic growth generally were too difficult to model formally. One of the very few studies that does offer empirical estimates of the effects of FTAs on economic growth, by Vamvakidis (1999), finds either zero or negative effects.

Of course there is more motivation to forming preferential FTAs than just economic welfare, but that is also true of multilateral agreements. Moreover, the latter have the virtue of being non-discriminatory, of involving much less negotiating cost per dollar of benefit, and of having a far higher probability of no country, nor any significant group of households within each participating country, losing from the agreement – in part because multilateral reform encourages each country to move resources to activities in which the country has its strongest comparative advantages, whereas preferential FTAs may encourage resources to move to now more profitable activities which subsequently become uncompetitive following the next FTA or WTO agreement. All this implies the costs of adjusting to an FTA per dollar gained is likely to be far lower for a WTO agreement than for an FTA. And since the probability of an FTAA forming looks even less promising than for concluding a DDA agreement during the next few years, there is no point in formally calculating a benefit/cost ratio for this opportunity.

---

[20] A small selection of the literature includes: Gasiorek and Winters (2004), Milner, Morrissey and McKay (2005), and UNECA (2007). All find fault with specific aspects of the EPAs but none suggests that correcting these faults would make a dramatic difference to the conclusions.

Removing Developed Country Barriers to Exports from Least-Developed Countries

The EU's initiative to extend market access preferences to LDCs provides duty- and quota-free access to the EU for exports of 'everything but arms' (EBA). That initiative received in-principle, best-endeavours endorsement at the WTO Ministerial in Doha in November 2001, but without any specific timetable. A similar initiative has been put forward for providing free market access for all African products (Collier 2007).

Liberal though that proposal sounds, note that it does not include trade in services (of which the most important for LDCs would be movement of natural persons, that is, freedom for LDC laborers to work on temporary visas in the EU or other high-wage countries). Also, a number of safeguard provisions are included in addition to the EU's normal anti-dumping measures. Furthermore, access to three politically sensitive agricultural markets, bananas, rice and sugar, is being phased in by the EU only gradually over this decade – and they are subject to stricter safeguards.

Several empirical studies of the initiative have already appeared. A World Bank study by Ianchovichina, Mattoo and Olarreaga (2001) compares the EU proposal, from the viewpoint of Sub-Saharan Africa (SSA), with recent initiatives of the United States and Japan. Its GTAP modelling results suggest that even the most generous interpretation of the United States' Africa Growth and Opportunity Act (which they model as unrestricted access to the US for all SSA exports) would benefit SSA very little because the US economy is already very open and, in the products where it is not (e.g. textiles and clothing), SSA countries have little comparative advantage[21]. By contrast, the EU proposal, especially if it were to apply to all Quad countries (the EU, the US, Canada and Japan), would have a sizeable effect on SSA trade and welfare – provided agriculture is included in the deal. Just from EU access alone, SSA exports would be raised by more than US$0.5 billion and SSA economic welfare would increase by $0.3 billion per year (a 0.2 percent boost).[22] The results overstate the benefits of the EU proposal, however, as this World Bank study assumes all SSA countries (excluding relatively wealthy South Africa and Mauritius), not just the LDCs amongst them, would get duty- and quota-free access.

Another World Bank study, by Hoekman, Ng and Olarreaga (2002), uses a partial equilibrium approach and looks at the benefit of the EU initiative for LDCs not just in SSA but globally. It finds that trade of LDCs would increase by US$2.5 billion per year if all Quad countries provided LDCs with duty- and quota-free access on all merchandise.[23] However, almost half of that increase would come as a result of trade diversion from other developing countries. The authors suggest this is trivial because it represents less than 0.1 percent of other developing countries' exports (about $1.1 billion), but precisely because the diversion will be in simple goods that can be produced in LDCs, it will mostly fall on people in other poor countries whose circumstances are hardly better than those in the LDCs.[24] Moreover, if the 48 LDCs are given such preferences, they will become advocates *for* rather than *against* the continuation of MFN tariff peaks for agriculture and textiles – diminishing considerably the number of WTO members negotiating for their reduction. It may be true that MFN reductions in agricultural and

---

[21] A more recent *ex post* study of AGOA declares it to have been a success – Frazer and van Biesebroeck (2007). It raised Africa's exports by 0.15% of GDP. As the authors note, this is not insignificant, but, especially for an arrangement whose virtues are much proclaimed, it is a drop in the bucket.

[22] This is very similar to the estimate by UNCTAD/ Commonwealth Secretariat (2001, Ch. 3).

[23] This and other estimates of gains from preferential market access provisions need to be discounted to the extent that such things as rules of origin, anti-dumping duties, and sanitary, phytosanitary and other technical barriers limit the actual trade allowed. For a detailed analysis of these types of restrictions on EU imports from Bangladesh in recent years, see UNCTAD/ Commonwealth Secretariat (2001, Ch. 5).

[24] The impact outside the LDC group would be far from trivial for Mauritius, however, since the vast bulk of its exports are quota-restricted sales of clothing and sugar to the EU and US. See the discussion in UNCTAD/ Commonwealth Secretariat (2001, Ch. 6).

textile tariffs would help LDCs much less than it would help other developing countries, as the study by Hoekman, Ng and Olarreaga (2002) finds; but the gains to consumers in the QUAD would be more than sufficient to allow them to increase their aid to LDCs to compensate many times over for the loss of LDC income from the preference erosion that necessarily accompanies MFN reform.

Another cause for concern is that most estimates of the effects of preferences do not take into account that firms are heterogeneous. When preferences and their accompanying rules of origin (ROOs) encourage more capital-intensive production (e.g., to take advantage of volumetric import quotas), they may raise investment and exports but they also bias exports away from less capital intensive activities in which the LDCs have a comparative advantage, and in the process lower average productivity of exporters. Evidence of this in Bangladesh's exports to the US and EU is provided by Demidova, Kee and Krishna (2006). That study finds the firms that take advantage of the less restrictive ROOs of the EU (as compared with the US) are less productive than the firms that export to the US.

These results suggest the gains from this opportunity for developing countries as a group – or even for just the LDCs amongst them – are meagre at best,[25] and possibly negative in aggregate for developing countries. And as with preferential FTAs, the costs associated with this opportunity are likely to be relatively high because it would encourage resources to move to activities which subsequently become uncompetitive following the next FTA or WTO agreement. Hence this opportunity does not warrant a formal benefit/cost calculus.

Prospective Benefits of Freeing up International Labor Movements

The challenge in high-income countries of a shortage of low-skilled workers has been eased by merchandise trade with and FDI flows to labor-abundant developing countries, most notably China in the past two decades. But that has been far from sufficient to equalize wages across countries. Historical experience in the 50 years to the First World War showed that by far the fastest way to bring about a convergence in living standards is through international migration (Williamson 2002). Notwithstanding the liberalization of much merchandise trade post the Second World War, and the opportunity through the WTO's Doha Round to reduce services trade barriers further, the CGE analyses by Winters *et al.* (2003) suggest that this will still be the case in the foreseeable future. When coupled with an aging population in high-income countries, there is a compelling case for them to expand their quotas on immigrants from developing countries. Indeed Mattoo and Subramanian (2003) argue that this would be essential if the Doha Round is to deliver on its promise of being development-friendly.

None of the studies listed in Table 8.1 considers the possibility of the services negotiations including provision for more temporary movement of labor (Mode IV in the WTO's General Agreement on Trade in Services, GATS). Yet if trade liberalization in goods and other services proves too difficult politically to achieve in the next few years, the benefits of formally liberalizing international labor flows as a possible substitute for goods trade is worth contemplating – not least because otherwise illegal migration is likely to increase (Hanson 2006). Current immigration laws are very strict, such that labor flows are much less significant across borders than flows of goods, other services and financial capital. Presumably this helps explain why the dispersion of pay for similarly skilled workers across the globe so greatly exceeds the dispersion of prices for goods and financial capital (Freeman 2007). This in turn signals an additional opportunity for reducing inequality and poverty. Freeman discusses some radical policy options for making such a commitment more palatable in receiving countries (e.g., auctioning off visas and using the revenue to compensate any losers among current residents), as does

[25] To any such generalizations there is always the possibility of exceptions. Collier and Venables (2007) argue the non-reciprocal preferential access to the EU market was no less than transformational for Mauritius.

Table 8.9. Global labor force structure, 2001 and projected to 2025 without and with assumed extra migration (millions)

	Base 2001	Base 2025	2025 with extra migrants	Number of extra migrants, 2001–25	Difference in 2025 labor force (%)
Developing countries (DCs):					
Unskilled labor	2396	3294	3284	−9.8	−0.3
Skilled labor	200	267	263	−4.5	−1.7
TOTAL, DC LABOR	2596	3561	3547	−14.2	−0.4
High-income countries (HICs):					
DC migrant workers:					
Unskilled labor	24.7	25.3	35.1	9.8	39
Skilled labor	3.1	3.2	7.7	4.5	138
Total DC migrant workers	27.8	28.5	14.3	14.2	50
TOTAL, HIC LABOR	480.8	474.0	488.2	14.2	3

Source: World Bank (2006, Table 2.2).

Pritchett (2007) in his provocative book *Let Their People Come.* Meanwhile, Schiff (2007) explores which policy measure might be optimal among the three options of permanent, guest-worker or GATS Mode IV flows.[26]

An early attempt to measure the gains from freeing international migration was made more than two decades ago by Hamilton and Whalley (1984). Moses and Letnes (2004) have updated that study, and find a reduction in international migration controls sufficient to reduce the difference between developing country and global wage rates by 10 percent generates a welfare gain of the order of $774 billion per year, in 1998 US dollars (assuming unitary elasticities of substitution in production in all regions).

More recently, the Linkage model used for the above Doha analysis has been used by the World Bank in a study of the potential gains from a one-off expansion over a 25-year period in international migration (World Bank 2006, Ch. 2). That study builds on earlier work by Winters *et al.* (2003) and draws on a new bilateral migration and remittances database involving no less than 226 countries (Parsons *et al.* 2007), thereby capturing the past patterns of

migration between different countries (including the profile of accompanying family members if any). It simulates the impacts of an increase in migrants per year from developing to high-income countries that accumulates to a 3 percent boost in the latter's labor force (both skilled and unskilled) by 2025, a total of 14.2 million workers and their families coming at the rate of 568,000 extra migrant workers per year over the 25 years beginning in 2001. To put that in context, in 2000 a net total of 2.4 million people migrated from developing to high-income countries (UN Population Division 2002, Table 1). That extra 3 percent gain in the high-income countries' workforce by 2025 represents a loss of merely 0.4 percent to the developing countries' workforce, and even in the developing countries' skilled category it represents only a 1.7 percent loss of workers (final column of Table 8.9).

That comparative static migration study estimates the global gains by 2025 would amount to $674 billion per year in 2001 US dollars. Of that, $624 billion would be enjoyed by current citizens of developing countries. That includes those who migrate, whose share is estimated to be $481 billion in after-tax income (net of what the model assumes they remit back to their country or origin, based on past bilateral remittance patterns of existing migrants, the average of

[26] See also the contribution on migration to the first Copenhagen Consensus Project, by Martin (2004).

which is 17 percent of the migrant's earnings).[27] The small residual gain to the host country comprises a non-trivial gain to natives ($138 billion), but a loss to earlier migrants (of $88 billion or 6 percent) because they would face stronger competition in the workplace from the new migrants than would natives (even though the proportional increase in skilled migrant workers is much higher than in unskilled migrants to get the same 3 percent increase in both groups of workers in host countries). That is, their good fortune from being an earlier migrant would be shared somewhat with the newest migrants as the stock of migrants grows (see Table 8.10).

That comparative static aggregate global gain of $674 billion per year represents just over 1 percent of the projected global income for 2025. We assume the annual migration numbers return to normal after 2025, and that the on-going comparative static gain for the rest of this century from this accelerated program remains at just over 1 percent of global GDP. It is difficult to say how those gains would be shared between groups over a whole century (four generations), but if they were shared in the same proportions between migrants and natives as in 2025 (see final column of Table 8.10) then most would go to current citizens of developing countries, particularly the migrants themselves. To err on the conservative side, we also assume there are no additional dynamic gains from migration, even though they may well be a similar order of magnitude to those from product trade reform.

That proportional comparative static global gain in 2025 is more than five times the proportional gain reported above for the 'Central' Scenario of the Doha Round as of 2015 (both expressed in 2001 US dollars). Or to put it another way, if the extent of increased migration was only one-fifth as large (a 0.5 instead of 3.0 percent increase in the recipient countries' labor force by 2025) it could generate the same proportional comparative static global gain as the Doha Round might achieve via goods trade liberalization – but with more of the gain going to current citizens of developing countries.

The migration opportunity is of course not necessarily an alternative to the Doha oppor-

Table 8.10. Comparative static estimates of economic welfare effects of a boost to international worker migration, 2025 (in 2001 US$ billion)

	$ billion	Share (percent)
New migrants	481	*71*
Natives (non-migrants) in developing countries	143	*21*
Total, current DC citizens	624	*92*
Natives in high-income countries	138	*21*
Recent migrants in high-income countries	−88	*−13*
Total, current HIC citizens	50	*8*
World total	674	*100*

Source: World Bank (2006, Table 2.3).

tunity. Indeed, if Doha were to also embrace (as part of a GATS Mode IV agreement) the migration scenario described above, the resulting greater international economic integration would boost the gains from Doha enormously. The additional gains from Doha may not be exactly the sum of the two scenarios, as the net effect would depend on the degree to which product trade is a substitute for this form of 'trade' in labor services. But given the smallness of the proportional changes in the aggregate size and skill composition of the workforce involved in that extra migration shown in Table 8.9, and the expected complementarity between trade in products and trade in such productive factors (Markusen 1983), adding those net benefits would be a reasonable approximation.[28]

[27] Remittances since 1995 have become more important than official development assistance flows to developing countries and were equal to inflows of foreign direct investment in 2003. They have risen as a share of developing country GDP from 0.1 percent in 1970 to 0.9 percent by 1990, 1.4 percent by 2000 and 1.9 percent by 2005 (Spence *et al.* 2008).

[28] In a recent econometric study of migration to OECD countries, Dolman (2008) finds that countries tend to trade and invest more with countries from which they have received more migrants, especially if there are large language and other characteristics that distance those countries – and those greater trade and especially investment flows are not at the expense of flows with other countries.

Quantifying Economic Costs of Reducing Trade and Migration Barriers

The above benefits from reform are not costless, of course. And the costs associated with trade reform differ from those associated with migration, so they are considered in turn.

Costs Associated with Doha Trade Reform

Expenditure on trade negotiating, and on supporting policy think tanks and the like to develop and disseminate a convincing case for trade reform, could be expanded many fold before running into declining returns. But even with a substantial expansion in those activities, the overall cost would be trivial compared with the global gains from trade reform (a fraction of 1 percent of the benefits).

Of much more significance are the private costs of adjustment for firms and workers as reform forces some industries to downsize or close to allow others to expand (Matusz and Tarr 2000; François 2003). Those costs are ignored in the global CGE models discussed above, where the aggregate employment rate is held constant in each economy.[29]

There are also social costs to consider. They include social safety net provisions insofar as such schemes are developed/drawn on by losers from reform (e.g., unemployment payments plus training grants to build up new skills so displaced workers can earn the same wage as before).

All three types are one-off costs to weigh against the non-stop flow of economic benefits from reform. The private and social costs of adjustment tend to be smaller, the longer the phase-in period or smaller the tariff or subsidy cut per year (Furusawa and Lai 1999). Also, CGE simulation studies suggest that the annual change in an industry's terms of trade due to phased trade reform is typically very minor

[29] Incorporating adjustment activities, such as worker retraining, appears to be of small, second-order importance in CGE modeling if the government is able to make credible policy commitments (Karp and Paul 2005) – which it is in the case of multilateral reform agreements under the WTO.

relative to changes due to exchange rate fluctuations, technological improvements, preference shifts and other economic shocks and structural developments associated with normal economic growth (Anderson et al. 1997).

Estimates of the magnitude of those costs are difficult to generate, but all available estimates suggest they are minor relative to the benefits from reform. An early study by Magee (1972) for the United States estimated the cost of job changes including temporary unemployment to be one-eighth of the benefits from tariff and quota elimination initially. Even assuming that transition took as many as five years, he estimated a benefit/cost ratio of 25. A subsequent study which examined a 50 percent cut in US tariffs (but not quotas) came up with a similar benefit/cost estimate (Baldwin, Mutti and Richardson 1980). In more recent debates about trade and labor, analysts have had difficulty finding a strong link between import expansion and increased unemployment (see Greenaway and Nelson 2002). One example is a study of the four largest EU economies' imports from East Asia (Bentivogli and Pagano 1999). Another European example is a study of the UK footwear industry: liberalizing that market would incur unemployment costs only in the first year, because of the high job turnover in that industry, and those estimated costs are less than 1.5 percent of the benefits from cutting that protection (Winters and Takacs 1991). A similar-sized estimate is provided by de Melo and Tarr (1990) using a CGE model that focuses just on US textile, steel and auto protection cuts and drawing on estimates of the cost of earnings lost by displaced workers (later reported by Jacobson, LaLonde and Sullivan 1993).

For developing countries also the evidence seems to suggest low costs of adjustment, not least because trade reform typically causes a growth spurt (Krueger 1983). In a study of 13 liberalization efforts for nine developing countries, Michaely, Papageorgiou and Choksi (1991) found only one example where employment was not higher within a year. A similar study for Mauritius by Milner and Wright (1998) also found trade opening to be associated with employment growth rather than decline.[30] A survey of 18 Latin American countries for the period 1970 to 1996, by Marquez and Pages (1998), found some increases in short-term unemployment, but mainly in countries where the real exchange rate appreciated as a result of capital inflows that had accompanied the reforms. That small short-term negative effect soon reversed as production became more labor intensive following reform, according to studies by Moreira and Najberg (2000) for Brazil and de Ferranti *et al.* (2001) for a wide range of Latin American and Caribbean countries over the 1990s.

If the adjustment costs are so small and may lead to more rather than fewer jobs even during the adjustment period, why are governments so reluctant to open their economies? The reason is because the anticipated losses in jobs and asset values are very obvious and concentrated whereas the gains in terms of new job and investment opportunities are thinly spread, are less easily attributed to the trade reform, and are taken up often by people other than those losing from the reform.[31] Moreover, there is considerable uncertainty as to who in fact will end up bearing the costs or reaping net benefits, leading all groups to be less enthusiastic about reform (Fernadez and Rodrik 1991). As discussed above, the few losers are prepared to support politicians who resist protection cuts, while the gains are sufficiently small per consumer and unassisted firm as to make it not worthwhile for those many potential gainers to get together to lobby for reform, particularly given their greater free-rider problem in acting collectively (Olsen 1965). Thus reform has political, and possibly employment, costs for politicians and one should not underestimate the difficulties of political action to reduce/eliminate trade protection measures. We do not factor these into the economic cost/benefit analysis for society as a whole, however, because they are not of a comparable form and the purpose of the Copenhagen Consensus process is to contribute to their erosion. Nor do we count the transfers among people within each country as part of the gross benefits and costs of reform, since they are clearly transfers rather than net costs or benefits to each national society. Rather, we implicitly assume society costlessly compensates the losers using the extra tax revenue from those whose incomes rise.

A prime example of the role analysis can play has to do with effects on developing countries

---

[30] A further impact of trade policy reform about which concern is often expressed is the loss of tariff revenue for the government. This is of trivial importance to developed and upper middle-income countries where trade taxes account for only 1 and 3 percent of government revenue, respectively. For lower middle-income countries that share is 9 percent, and it is more than 20 percent for more than a dozen low-income countries for which data are available, so how concerned should those poorer countries be? The answer depends on whether/how much that revenue would fall and, if it does fall, on whether/how much more costly would be the next best alternative means of raising government revenue. On the first of those two points, government revenue from import taxes will rise rather than fall with reform if the reform involves replacing, with less prohibitive tariffs, any of the import quotas or bans, or tariffs that are prohibitive (or nearly so) or which encourage smuggling or under-invoicing or corruption by customs officials. It is possible even in a tariff-only regime that lower tariffs lead to a sufficiently higher volume and value of trade and that the aggregate tariff collection rises. Examples of recent trade policy reforms that led to increased tariff revenue are Chile and Mexico (Bacchetta and Jansen 2003, p. 15) and Kenya (Glenday 2002). See also Greenaway and Milner (1993) and Nash and Takacs (1998). Since the economy is enlarged by opening up, income and consumption tax collections will automatically rise too. On the second point, about the cost of raising government revenue by other means if tax revenue does fall, Corden (1997, Ch. 4) makes it clear that in all but the poorest of countries it will be more rather than less efficient to collect tax revenue in other ways. Even countries as poor as Cambodia have managed to introduce a value added tax. Hence from a global viewpoint there is no significant cost that needs to be included in response to this concern. To the extent subsidies are also cut as part of the reform, the chances of government revenue rising are even greater. Income and consumption tax revenue also will rise as the economy expands following reform. In any case CGE modellers typically alter those other tax rates when trade tax revenues change so as to keep the overall government budget unchanged.

[31] In the Australian context of high unemployment in the latter 1970s, Max Corden was prompted to write a deliberately non-technical paper called 'Tell us where the new jobs will come from?' because he knew the answer was not obvious to non-economists (Corden 1979). The paper proved so popular that thousands of offprints were distributed and in 1985 it was reprinted in *The World Economy*.

in reforms to support for agriculture in OECD economies. The primary channel for such effects is through the terms of trade, which in turn depend in part on whether a country is a net exporter or importer of the affected OECD products. Long-term support for agriculture in OECD countries, coupled with often-negative assistance to farmers in many developing countries, has left developing countries as a group dependent on imports of these subsidized products. As a result, an across-the-board cut in all domestic support for OECD agriculture leads to welfare losses for many developing countries and to declines in farm incomes in Europe, Japan and North America. Such a reform package is therefore unlikely to be implemented on its own. An alternative approach is to focus on broad-based reductions in market price support, as has begun occurring in the EU where domestic support has increasingly replaced border measures. As Dimaranan, Hertel and Keeney (2004) show, a shift from market price support to land-based payments could generate a win-win-win outcome whereby OECD farm incomes are maintained and yet world price distortions are reduced and economic welfare rises for most developing countries and globally. Provided these increased domestic support payments are not linked to output or variable inputs, the trade-distorting and welfare-reducing effects are likely to be small, thereby providing an effective way of offsetting the potential losses that would otherwise be sustained by OECD farmers. This type of policy re-instrumentation increases the probability that such reforms are politically acceptable in the reforming economies while simultaneously increasing the likelihood that they will be beneficial to developing countries.

The existing estimates of the adjustment costs to trade reform are very small, but they are concentrated on particular individuals and so perhaps deserve large weight socially. It is cer-

tainly possible that those estimates omit some elements too, such as the disutility of one-off uncertainty and disruption experienced by everyone in adjusting to policy changes.[32] Hence, so as not to exaggerate the net gains from a Doha trade reform, it is assumed here that there would be an adjustment period of eight years following the beginning of liberalization (assumed to be 2008), and that in each of those years the adjustment costs would be 15 percent of the annual comparative static benefits as of 2015 (and zero thereafter) in the high case, and 5 percent in the lower-bound case when much less adjustment would be needed. For the high case that amounts to $71 billion per year during 2008 to 2015 globally, of which $24 billion is expended in developing countries, when expressed in 2005 US dollars by using the projection to 2015 of global GDP provided by the World Bank (2006). For the lower-bound case the costs would be one-third of those values.

Costs Associated with Increased International Migration

The migration opportunity also would involve costs. There are the direct one-off costs to migrants of obtaining visas and work permits, transport and transitional expenses, costs of searching for housing, schooling, employment, etc. upon arrival, as well as the emotional cost of separating from extended family and in some cases temporarily breaking up the nuclear family. There are also one-off costs to the host-country government of processing applications and providing initial help with housing, welfare payments and the like.

In terms of adjustment costs in the workplace, insofar as migrants are attracted or recruited to positions for which there is excess demand, they will be reducing underemployment of capital in those industries. Since that is a significant part of the motivation for host countries seeking migrants, especially as their native population is aging rapidly, this may well offset the other costs associated with migration – especially if the skill mix and timing of immigration flows are designed to alleviate such labor shortages. However, to err

---

[32] We should be explicit that we cannot take the distributional dimensions into account more formally in this aggregate analysis, but they obviously matter in the real world. A detailed discussion of the effects of trade liberalization on poverty is given by Winters (2002) and Winters, McCulloch and McKay (2004).

on the conservative side for the purpose of calculating benefit/cost ratios, it is assumed here there are net costs involved for both the migrants and the host governments' taxpayers.

Fees charged by private recruitment agencies offer evidence of part of the direct cost of migration to migrants. The World Bank (2006, Table 3.1) cites several studies within the range $700 to $1,700, but one for Thai emigrants to Japan of more than $8,000. Such studies may overstate the true cost of the services actually offered, however, insofar as the agency is able to capture also some of the lifetime benefits expected by the migrant (Abella 2004).

For present purposes, in the absence of reliable estimates of overall costs, it is necessary to rely on using a range of guesses. Our low guesstimate is that each migrant worker (and his family) spends on average $7,000 in 2001 US dollars to migrate in the year of migration. To err on the conservative side and allow for significant social costs associated with increased immigration and emigration we have chosen, for the high-cost case, combined costs of three times the low-cost ones, or $21,000 per worker and family in the year of migration. The same-sized average costs are assumed also to be borne by the host country government (a low of $7,000 and a high of $21,000 in the year of migration). These are generous cost estimates, to allow for the fact that some migrants may draw social welfare benefits beyond their first year. But we assume that after the first year migrants subsequently become fiscally neutral on average in the sense that the cost of public services they receive after settling is just equal to the income tax they pay.

Net Benefits and Benefit/Cost Analysis

With these numbers fed into a spreadsheet, it is possible to graph the flow of annual net benefits from the various scenarios. A sample of these from 2008 through to 2100 is presented in Figures 8.1 and 8.2 in terms of annual increments to GDP (not the difference in levels). In each case we refer to the 'high net gains' scenarios. Figure 8.1 shows the Doha scenario and the scenario with extra migration, as well as the undiscounted base projection of GDP increments each year in the world and in developing countries (the dark lines). Were the Doha partial reforms to be phased in over an eight-year period beginning in 2008, our 'central' scenario including dynamic gains projects those GDP increments in the world and in developing countries to follow the higher dashed lines in Figure 8.1. Given the higher GDP growth rate assumed for developing rather than developed countries over this century, it is not surprising that by 2100 those countries would be enjoying an even larger share of those global gains from trade reform than in the earlier years – although many of them would by then have joined the 'high-income country' club. The net benefits in Figure 8.1 are not discounted back to present-value terms. To see the impact that discounting has, Figure 8.2 reports the net present value data using the higher (6 percent) discount factor to express it in 2008 present-value terms.

Three key points are worth stressing about the depicted numerical simulation results. First, from a global viewpoint the gains from extra migration exceed those from trade reform in the early years, but over the long term the comparative static gains from a Doha trade reform are similar in magnitude to those from the extra migration scenario.

Second, the dynamic gains from trade reform can be seen clearly from Figure 8.2 to be many times greater than the comparative static gains. There may well be dynamic gains from extra migration too, although to err on the conservative side we have not included them in this simulation exercise.

Third, from the viewpoint of current citizens of just developing countries (including its extra-emigrants-to-be), they would reap the vast majority of the global gains from extra migration and those gains to them would far exceed at least the comparative static gains to them from a Doha trade reform that excluded greater temporary migration of labor. That suggests an extra flow of migrants to today's high-income countries probably would have a stronger egalitarian, pro-poor distributional outcome in favour

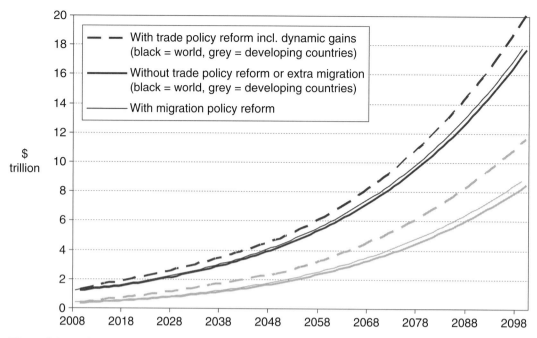

Figure 8.1 *Undiscounted increments through to 2100 of world and developing country incomes without reform, with a Doha trade policy reform (without extra migration) and with extra migration (without Doha)*
Source: Authors' estimates underlying Table 8.11's high net gains cases

of current developing country citizens than just allowing more products to be traded.

The range of present-value benefits and costs for the low- and high-gain cases, using both 3 and 6 percent as the discount rate to bring the net benefit flows back to the present (2008), is summarized in Table 8.11. In all cases the benefits are estimated through to the year 2100, and they and the up-front costs continue to be expressed in 2001 US dollars.

In the Doha trade reform scenarios, the 'low gains' case refers to global comparative static gains of just 0.2 percent of GDP while the 'high gains' case refers to global gains five times that lower benefit. In present value terms the net benefit of a 'central' Doha outcome ranges from $42 trillion to $113 trillion at the higher discount rate and about four times that at the lower discount rate. The costs range from $50 billion to $450 billion in present value terms, but they are mostly private rather than government costs and are

dwarfed by the gross benefits. Today's developing countries reap the majority of those net gains, as their share of the global economy is assumed to grow throughout this century (although at a progressively slower rate after 2015). Their benefit/cost ratios from the trade reform opportunity offered by the Doha Round are between 690 and 900 in the higher discount rate case and between 2700 and 3100 in the lower discount rate case. This is clearly an extremely high payoff activity, if only the political will to bring about a successful conclusion to the Doha Round can be found.

If for political reasons the Doha Round cannot be brought to a successful conclusion, high-income country governments still have the opportunity to boost their intakes of migrant workers from developing countries. In the migration scenarios, the low-cost ('high net gains') case refers to one-off costs of just $14,000 per worker and family (shared equally by the migrants and the host government). For the high-cost ('low net

(a) NPV of world GDP increments

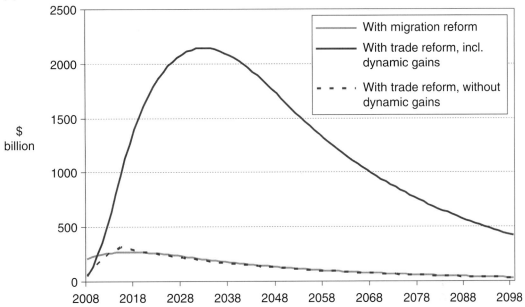

(b) NPV of increments to incomes of developing country citizens (including emigrants)

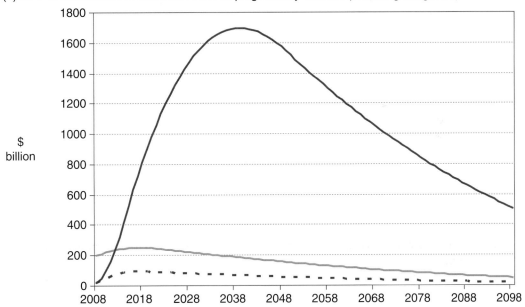

Figure 8.2 *Net present value of discounted annual increments to world and developing country incomes to 2100 from migration reform and from trade policy reform (with and without dynamic gains)*
Source: *Authors' estimates underlying Table 8.11's high net gains cases*

Table 8.11. Net present value of benefits and costs to 2100, and benefit–cost ratios, from liberalizing subsidies and trade barriers globally under the WTO's Doha Development Agenda, and liberalizing migration (in 2001 US$ billion)

	Trade reform benefit–cost ratio including dynamic gains			
	3% discount rate		6% discount rate	
	Low	High	Low	High
Global	1121	932	363	269
Developing	3147	2724	895	692

	Trade reform costs and benefits including dynamic gains (NPV 2008)											
	3% discount rate						6% discount rate					
	Low			High			Low			High		
	GB	C	NB	GB	C	NB	GB	C	NB	GB	C	NB
Global	172666	154	172512	424495	456	424039	51485	142	51343	113028	420	112607
Developing	161583	51	161532	419477	154	419323	42355	47	42308	98215	142	98073

	Migration reform benefit–cost ratio without dynamic gains			
	3% discount rate		6% discount rate	
	Low	High	Low	High
Global	336	112	137	45
Developing	838	279	299	100

	Migration reform costs and benefits without dynamic gains (NPV 2008)											
	3% discount rate						6% discount rate					
	Low			High			Low			High		
	GB	C	NB	GB	C	NB	GB	C	NB	GB	C	NB
Global	37852	113	37739	37852	338	37514	12456	91	12365	12456	274	12182
Developing	47197	56	47141	47197	169	47028	13628	46	13582	13628	137	13491

	Trade reform benefit–cost ratio without dynamic gains			
	3% discount rate		6% discount rate	
	Low	High	Low	High
Global	47	80	17	28
Developing	68	113	21	35

	Trade reform costs and benefits without dynamic gains (NPV 2008)											
	3% discount rate						6% discount rate					
	Low			High			Low			High		
	GB	C	NB	GB	C	NB	GB	C	NB	GB	C	NB
Global	7260	154	7106	36298	456	35842	2371	142	2229	11856	420	11436
Developing	3473	51	3422	17367	154	17212	981	47	933	4903	142	4761

	Trade and migration reform benefit–cost ratio without dynamic gains			
	3% discount rate		6% discount rate	
	Low	High	Low	High
Global	169	93	64	35
Developing	471	200	157	66

Table 8.11. (continued)

	Trade and migration reform costs and benefits without dynamic gains (NPV 2008)											
	3% discount rate						6% discount rate					
	Low			High			Low			High		
	GB	C	NB	GB	C	NB	GB	C	NB	GB	C	NB
Global	45112	267	44845	74150	794	73356	14827	233	14594	24312	694	23618
Developing	50670	108	50562	64563	323	64240	14609	93	14516	18531	279	18252

Source: Authors' calculations based on assumptions in text.

gains') case, combined costs of three times the low-cost ones are assumed, or $42,000 per worker and family in the year of migration. In present value terms the global net benefit of that increased flow of migrants for 25 years is shown in Table 8.11 to be $13 trillion at the higher discount rate and $38 trillion at the lower discount rate. Since costs are so small compared with benefits, the benefit/cost ratios for developing country citizens are again very high, ranging between 100 and 840. This too is without doubt a very high payoff, and one that does not even require multilateral agreement – it simply requires greater benevolence on the part of developed country citizens and their national governments.

Social and Environmental Benefits and Costs of Reducing Trade and Migration Barriers

Because trade reform generates large and ongoing economic gains while incurring comparatively minor one-off adjustment costs, it would allow individuals and governments the freedom to spend more on other pressing problems, thereby *indirectly* contributing to the alleviation of other challenges facing society.[33] But in addition, trade reform would also *directly* alleviate some of those challenges. This section first focuses on the impact of trade reform on poverty alleviation, since that is the solution to many of the world's problems. It then turns to trade reform's impact on the environment, before briefly commenting on its impact on several of the other specific challenges being addressed in this project, namely, communi-

cable diseases, conflicts, under-investment in education, corruption, and malnutrition and hunger. The social impacts of migration are briefly canvassed also.

Poverty Alleviation

Evidence presented by Dollar and Kraay (2002), Sala-i-Martin (2006) and others, and carefully surveyed in Ravallion (2006), suggests aggregate economic growth differences have been largely responsible for the differences in poverty alleviation across regions. Initiatives that boost economic growth are therefore likely to be helpful in the fight against poverty, and trade liberalization is such an initiative. But cuts to subsidies and trade barriers also alter relative product prices domestically and in international markets, which in turn affect factor prices. Hence the net effect on poverty depends also on the way those price changes affect poor households' expenditure and their earnings net of remittances. If the consumer and producer price changes (whether due to own-country reforms and/or those of other countries) are pro-poor, then they will tend to reinforce any positive growth effects of trade reform on the poor.

The effects of trade reform on global poverty can be thought of at two levels: on the income gap between developed and developing countries, and on poor households within developing countries. On the first, the CGE estimates surveyed above suggest that current developing

[33] On the intrinsic benefits of freedom of opportunity and action that freer markets provide people, apart from their positive impact in boosting income and wealth, see Sen (1999).

countries, which produce just one-fifth of global GDP, would enjoy nearly half of the net present value of the global static plus dynamic gains from reducing trade barriers. Clearly that will lower substantially the income gap between developed and poorer countries on average.

How poor households *within* developing countries are affected is more difficult to say (Winters 2002; Winters, McCulloch and McKay 2004). What is clear from Table 8.4 is that the agricultural policies of developed countries provide a major source of developing country gains from reform, and lowering barriers to textiles and clothing trade also is important. Both would boost the demand for unskilled labor and for farm products produced in poor countries. Since two-thirds of the world's poor live in rural areas and, in least-developed countries, the proportion is as high as 90 percent (OECD 2003a, p. 3), and since most poor rural households are net sellers of farm labor and/or food, one would expect such reforms to reduce the number in absolute poverty. A set of analyses reported in Hertel and Winters (2006), in which GTAP and national CGE model results are carefully combined with household income and expenditure survey data for more than a dozen developing countries, tests this hypothesis and finds strong support for it in most of the country case studies considered.

The evidence on international migration's impact on global poverty is overwhelmingly positive. That is not to say that every small developing country will have less poverty if migration is freed up, because it will depend on the skill mix of the migrants and the extent of remittances they send back, among other things; but in most cases the findings are unequivocal (World Bank 2006, Ch. 3).

The Environment

The effects of trade reform on the environment have been the focus of much theoretical and empirical analysis since the 1970s and especially in the past dozen or so years (Copland and

Taylor 2003; Beghin *et al.* 2002). Until recently environmentalists have tended to focus mainly on the *direct* environmental costs they perceive from trade reform, just as they have with other areas of economic change.[34] That approach does not acknowledge areas where the environment might have been *improved,* albeit indirectly, as a result of trade reform (e.g., from less production by pollutive industries that were previously protected). Nor does it weigh the costs of any net worsening of the environment against the economic benefits of policy reform of the sort described above.

The reality is that while the environmental effects of reform will differ across sectors and regions of the world, some positive and some negative, there are many examples where cuts to subsidies and trade barriers would reduce environmental damage (Anderson 1992; Irwin 2002, pp. 48–54). For some time the OECD has been encouraging analysis of these opportunities (OECD 1996, 1997, 1998, 2003b). Environmental NGOs are increasingly recognizing them too. They and the better-informed development NGOs seem to be coming to the view that the net social and environmental benefits from reducing subsidies and at least some trade barriers may indeed be positive rather than negative, and that the best hope of reducing environmentally harmful subsidies and trade barriers is via the WTO's multi-issue, multilateral trade negotiations process (see, e.g., Cameron 2007).

If there remains a concern that the net effect of trade reform on the environment may be negative nationally or globally, that should be a stimulus to check whether first-best environmental policy measures are in place and set at the optimal level of intervention, rather than a reason for not reducing trade distortions. This is because if they are so set, we would then know that the direct economic gains from opening to trade would exceed society's evaluation of any extra environmental damage, other things equal (Corden 1997, Ch. 13).

Much environmental damage in developing countries is a direct consequence of poverty (e.g., the slash-and-burn shifting agriculture

---

[34] See the critique by Lomborg (2001).

of landless unemployed squatters). Insofar as trade reform reduces poverty, so it will reduce such damage. More generally, the relationships between per capita income and a wide range of environmental indicators have been studied extensively. Because richer people have a greater demand for a clean environment, income rises tend to be associated with better environmental outcomes once incomes rise above certain levels.[35] Even though more pollutive products are being consumed as incomes rise, many abatement practices have been spreading fast enough to more than compensate. And openness to trade accelerates that spread of abatement ideas and technologies, making their implementation in developing countries affordable at ever-earlier stages of development.

Estimating the global cost to society of all environmental damage that might accompany a reduction in subsidies and trade barriers, net of all environmental gains, is extraordinarily difficult both conceptually and empirically.[36] In the absence of any sufficiently comprehensive estimates it will be assumed that the net effect of reform on the environment would be zero.

When the environmental impact is global rather than local, as with greenhouse gases and their apparent impact on climate change, international environmental agreements may be required (see Cline 2004b). When developing countries are not party to such agreements, however, it is difficult to prevent 'leakage' through a re-location of carbon-intensive activities to those non-signatories. An alternative or supplementary approach that is likely to achieve at least some emission reductions, and at the same time generate national and global economic benefits rather than costs, involves lowering coal subsidies and trade barriers. Past coal policies have encouraged excessive production of coal in a number of industrial countries and excessive coal consumption in numerous developing countries including transition economies. Phasing out those distortionary policies has both improved the economy and lowered greenhouse gas emissions globally – a 'no regrets' outcome or win-win Pareto improvement for the economy and the environment (Anderson

and McKibbin 2000). Additional opportunities for reducing greenhouse gases through cutting energy subsidies are pointed to in the UNEP study by von Moltke, McKee and Morgan (2004).

Communicable Diseases

Communicable diseases are more common among the poor, so again trade reform's contribution to poverty alleviation will in turn impact on human health in general and the reduced incidence of diseases in particular. Furthermore, the greater openness of economies ensures medicines and prevention technologies are more widespread and cheaper, particularly following the Doha WTO conference of trade ministers and the subsequent Decision of 30 August 2003 on the TRIPS Agreement and Public Health. That Decision by the WTO General Council ensures developing country governments can issue compulsory licenses to allow other companies to make a patented product or use a patented process under licence without the consent of the patent owner, while developing countries unable to produce pharmaceuticals domestically can now import generic copies of patented drugs made under compulsory licensing by other developing countries.

---

[35] This is the theme of the recent book by Hollander (2003). For statistical evidence of the extent to which different environmental indicators first worsen and then improve as incomes rise (sometimes called the environmental Kuznets curve), see the special issue of the journal *Environment and Development Economics*, Volume 2, Issue 4 in 1997 and the more recent papers by and cited in Harbaugh, Levinson and Wilson (2002) and Cole (2003).

[36] A beginning nonetheless is being made, with several governments funding ex ante evaluations of the WTO Doha Round's potential impact on the environment. The EU's efforts include a workshop on methodological issues which are laid out in CEPII (2003), and further work has been contracted to the University of Manchester whose progress can be traced at http://idpm.man.ac.uk/sia-trade/Consultation.htm. Ex post analyses are also being undertaken by NGOs. See, for example, Bermudez (2004) for WWF's sustainability impact assessment of trade policies during 2001–3.

Conflicts

Openness tends to break down the common prejudices that accompany insularity, and to broaden mutual understanding between people with different cultures and customs. It also expands economic interdependence among countries, which raises the opportunity cost of entering into conflicts with trading partners. Insofar as it reduces income inequality across countries, then that too may diffuse tension between nations – a point that has even greater significance following the terrorist attacks of 11 September 2001. Indeed, there is now statistical support for Immanuel Kant's hypothesis that durable peace is supported by representative democracy, trade, and membership of international organizations: Oneal and Russett (2000) find that all three contribute independently to more peaceful relationships with other countries.[37] And casual observation suggests that more autarkic economies tend to be less democratic.

Where openness involves also greater international migration, there tends to be less intercultural conflict and more social gains from multiculturalism. Conversely, it is in societies that resent immigrants and impose strict migration quotas where cultural clashes seem to be more common. Clashes between ethnic groups are also more common where a minority prospers greatly relative to the majority or other significant minorities (Chua 2003). Such income and wealth inequality within a country tends to be less common the more open is the economy, at least after the initial adjustments to reform (Williamson 2002).

While many of these types of empirical studies struggle to clarify the direction of causation, and so their results need to be treated with caution, the weight of evidence nonetheless lends support to the view that greater openness can contribute to lessening conflict.

[37] A recent survey of the evidence did not find a significant direct link between poverty and terrorism, however. Rather, Krueger and Maleckova (2003) concluded that terrorism was more a response to political conditions and long-standing feelings of indignity and frustration.

Education Under-investment

Parents and governments are less likely to under-invest in education the higher their incomes, other things equal. So to the extent that trade reform raises incomes, it contributes to better educational outcomes. That is especially so for the very poorest who cannot afford even primary education: a slight increase in the cash income of poor farm families, for example following a reform-induced increase in international prices of farm products, can make it possible to pay the (often relatively high) school fees that are otherwise unaffordable.

If immigration restrictions are eased, the private incentive to invest in education in developing countries would increase even more. This offsets – at least partially but possibly more than fully – the brain drain concern often raised about emigration. It also would help to offset any reduction in the skill premium in wages in developing countries that may follow from liberalization of trade in goods.

Poor Governance and Corruption

A tolerance for subsidies and trade barriers breeds rent-seeking by special interests seeking protectionist policies for their industry. If those policies include import licensing, that breeds corruption through encouraging bureaucrats responsible for allocating licences to accept bribes from would-be importers. Together those activities ensure that the welfare costs of trade barriers are higher than is typically measured, since a share of the private rents they generate is wasted in these lobbying activities. Tax-avoiding corruption is also encouraged in the case of import tariffs, for example through bribing customs officers or through smuggling. For these reasons it is not surprising that statistical analysis has found less open economies to be more corrupt (Ades and di Tella 1999).

Malnutrition and Hunger

Food security is always a great concern in poor countries, especially those dependent on food imports where there are fears that reducing agricultural subsidies and protectionism globally will raise the price of those imports. But food security is defined as always having access to the minimum supply of basic food necessary for survival, so enhancing food security is mainly about alleviating poverty. That suggests this issue needs to be considered from a household rather than national perspective. And the discussion above argues that poverty is more likely than not to be alleviated by cuts to trade and immigration barriers.

Hunger and under-nutrition can be eased by trade not only in goods but also in agricultural technologies, in particular newly bred varieties of staple crops. The introduction of high-yielding dwarf wheat and rice varieties during the Green Revolution that began in Asia in the 1960s is a previous case in point, whereby producers and consumers shared the benefits in terms of higher farm profits and lower consumer prices for cereals. A prospective case in point is the possibility of breeding crop varieties that are not only less costly to grow but are 'nutriceuticals' in the sense they contain vitamin and mineral supplements. The most promising is so-called 'golden rice'. Consumers in many poor countries suffer from chronic vitamin A deficiency that can lead to blindness, weakened immune systems, and increased morbidity and mortality for children and pregnant and lactating women. Golden rice has been genetically engineered to contain a higher level of beta-carotene in the endosperm of the grain and thereby provide a vitamin A supplement. By being cheaper and/or more nutritionally beneficial, it would improve the health of poor people and thereby also boost their labor productivity. Anderson, Jackson and Nielsen (2005) estimate that the latter economic benefit from this new technology could be as much as 10 times greater than just the traditional benefits of lower production costs – not to mention that poor people would live longer and healthier lives. This new technology has yet to be adopted, however, because the European Union and some other countries will not import food from countries that may contain genetically modified organisms (GMOs) – even though there is no evidence that GM foods are a danger to human health (see, e.g., King 2003). The cost of that trade barrier to developing countries – which is not included in the estimates in Table 8.1 – has been very considerable (Anderson and Jackson 2005).

Social Aspects of Migration

Notwithstanding the economic gains that could result from more international migration, and the desire by millions more people in developing countries to migrate (as witnessed by the huge queues of applicants in embassies, the rise in illegal immigration, the increase in asylum seekers, and the high fees paid by recruiters and people smugglers), governments of rich countries are reluctant to open up greatly. Migration has much broader implications for society than opening up to trade in products or financial capital. While many of those implications are positive for both sending and receiving countries, others are perceived as negative. The implications of increased diversity in the destination countries are especially complex and virtually impossible to include adequately in an economic benefit/cost calculus. Cooperation between the two sets of countries can ease some of the concerns, though, especially if they result in agreements that provide for temporary migration and the enforcement of laws that protect migrants from exploitation and abuse.

Caveats

Measuring both the benefits and the costs of liberalizing subsidies and barriers to trade and migration is still an inexact science, despite the huge amount of progress that has been made over the past two decades in global CGE modelling.[38] We have tried to accommodate shortcomings by providing a range of estimates and by erring on the conservative side in the above analysis. Nonetheless, it is worth reviewing the key areas where analytical improvements are still needed. On the cost side, more empirical research on the

[38] Parts of this section draw on the survey by François and Martin (2007).

real costs of adjustments to trade policy changes and of international migration, and how they are spread over time for different groups, would be helpful. On the benefit side, economists have made more progress but plenty of scope remains for further improvements, particularly on the size and longevity of dynamic gains from trade reform. Key areas, discussed in turn below, are the assumed policy counterfactual, the tariff aggregation issue, product quality differences, new products, measurement of distortions in markets for service products, and behaviour of labor markets particularly in response to changes in restrictive immigration policies.

The Protection Counterfactual

The standard approach used in evaluating the consequences of international trade agreements is to compare the agreed tariff binding with the previously applied tariff rate, and to treat the post-agreement tariff rate as the lesser of the two rates. This essentially involves treating the current applied rate as a deterministic forecast of future protection rates in the absence of the agreement.

There are two potentially serious problems with this specification of the counterfactual. One is that the trend rate of protection responds systematically to underlying determinants that evolve over time. The second is that annual protection rates fluctuate substantially around that trend. Taking account of either or both of these counterfactuals can have large impacts on the estimated benefits of international trade liberalization agreements.

Anderson and Hayami (1986) and Lindert (1991) provide insights into the likely evolution of agricultural trade policies in the absence of international agreements. Key findings include a strong tendency for agricultural protection to rise with economic development because of fundamental changes in the structure of the economy. In particular, there is a tendency for agricultural protection to be low or negative in very poor countries because the number of farmers is large and it is difficult for them to organize to apply pressure on governments. Because

farmers are mainly subsisting at that stage, their real incomes are not greatly affected by increases in farm output prices. By contrast, the urban population in a poor country is far smaller and easier to organize, and food is an important part of consumer budgets.

As economies develop, however, all of these economic factors change in ways that shift the political-economy balance more towards agricultural protection. Farmers become fewer in number and find it easier to organize themselves. They also become more commercial in orientation, so that their real incomes are more strongly influenced by agricultural output prices. At the same time, the urban population becomes larger and hence harder to organize, and the importance of food in consumer budgets and hence in real wage determinations declines. The end result can be a very rapid increase in agricultural protection rates in high-growth economies. Without the new discipline of the Uruguay Round's Agreement on Agriculture, agricultural protection rates in Europe and Northeast Asia may well have kept rising over the past 15 years, and may continue to rise in fast-growing middle-income countries whose tariff and subsidy bindings in WTO are still well above applied rates (Anderson 2006).

Also striking is the large variation in national rates of agricultural protection over time. This is because trade and subsidy policies are frequently used also to stabilize domestic agricultural prices in the face of variations in world prices (Tyers and Anderson 1992). The value of legal bindings on those policies via trade agreements, even when the bindings are well above applied rates at the time of the agreement, is non-trivial and yet is not captured in most models because those models are not stochastic. As François and Martin (2004) show, even bindings that are set well above average rates of protection may greatly diminish the costs of protection when international prices peak. They estimate, for example, that the European tariff binding on wheat, at 82 percent, reduced the cost of protection to this commodity by almost a third, despite being substantially above the average rate of protection prevailing during the preceding 15 years for which data were available. This suggests our current CGE models are understating the gains from tariff and subsidy bindings, particularly for farm products.

Aggregation of Protection

Trade barriers vary enormously across commodities, and frequently also across suppliers thanks to regional and other preferential trade agreements. This variation in rates of protection increases the cost of any given 'average' level of protection, since the cost of protection increases with the square of the rate of protection. Necessarily, some degree of aggregation is unavoidable in modeling the real world because the available information on the structure of production and consumption is at a higher level of aggregation than information on tariffs and trade. Further aggregation is employed for computational reasons in a world of more than 225 countries, thousands of product tariff lines, many different occupations and skill levels in labor markets, etc. And additional problems are introduced by the typical approach to aggregation of trade barriers, namely, using averages weighted by external trade: as protection rates rise, the weights associated with these measures decline, which means that a tariff that completely blocks trade has the same measured impact as a zero tariff.

The modern approach to tariff aggregation provides a possible means of dealing with the aggregation problem. Anderson and Neary (1992) have developed a single tariff aggregator that captures the welfare impacts of a non-uniform tariff. Building on this approach, Bach and Martin (2001) use a tariff aggregator to capture the impacts of changes in the tariff regime on the expenditure required to achieve a given level of utility, and another to capture the impact on tariff revenues. Manole and Martin (2005) provide closed-form measures of these aggregators for the widely used constant-elasticity-of-substitution functional form. Applying these procedures to a sample of seven developing countries, they find that appropriate aggregation increases the estimated cost of protection

on average twenty-fold relative to the cost estimated using a weighted average tariff.

The problems of aggregation are particularly intense in agriculture because of the enormous variation in rates of protection across countries and commodities, especially among the industrial countries. Simple solutions, such as the representative-weighting approach used in some versions of the MAcMAP database (Bouët et al. 2004), deal with the weighting problem without addressing the aggregation bias problem associated with nonlinearity in the costs of individual tariffs. In a recent paper, Anderson (2006) proposes a new aggregation method that deals with both the aggregation bias and weighting problems while maintaining global payment balances, allowing it to be applied in future global CGE models.

Product Quality and Variety Differences

A separate aggregation issue has to do with the fact that, within any product classification, there is a wide range of qualities and varieties available. The only way product quality or variety differences enter most CGE models is by distinguishing between a product's country of origin. This is done using so-called Armington elasticities which can ensure domestically produced goods are imperfect substitutes for imported goods in aggregate, and imports from one country are an imperfect substitute for goods imported from any other country (Armington 1969).

In the real world, however, there is an ever-increasing array of qualities and varieties available for any product from each supplying country. It appears consumers (including producers using those products as intermediate inputs) are willing to pay for a greater variety of different quality products, even though that product differentiation may be costly in terms of shorter production runs and more advertising. Hummels and Klenow (2005) suggest that these improvements in quality are sufficiently rapid that the prices received by countries for the products that they continue to export – as distinct from their new exports – actually rise by 0.09 percent for each increase of 1 percent in national income. This result is strikingly at variance with traditional Armington models, which generate a reduction in export prices when economies grow and exports expand.

Feenstra, Markusen and Zeile (1992) suggest the welfare cost of tariff protection can be underestimated by as much as a factor of 10 when this consideration is not included in the analysis. Further evidence of the importance of this issue is provided by Broda and Weinstein (2006). In a study of US import data from 1972 to 2001, they find that the upward bias in the conventional import price index, because of not accounting for the growth in varieties of products, is approximately 1.2 percent per year, and estimate that the welfare gain from variety growth in US imports is 2.8 percent of GDP. Both computational capability and data improvements are needed before this issue can be dealt with comprehensively in global CGE models.

The Emergence of New Products

Standard models used to assess the implications of trade reforms are based on the assumption that expansion of exports following liberalization involves increasing the volume of the products initially being exported, but not of any other products. The Armington assumption also rules out expanding the markets to which goods are being supplied: if exports to a particular country are initially zero, then in most CGE models they remain zero following reform.

Recent research, however, highlights the key role of the 'extensive' margin, where export expansion involves increases in the range of products exported (Hummels and Klenow 2005) and expansion in the range of markets supplied (Evenett and Venables 2002). Hummels and Klenow conclude that only about one-third of the export expansion associated with economic growth comes from the 'intensive margin' where greater quantities of the same products are exported. And Evenett and Venables find that about one-third of the expansion of exports from developing countries was obtained by exporting products to countries to which they had not previously exported.

In a world where importers exhibit a preference for variety in the goods they purchase, these observations on the importance of extensive-margin growth have major implications. Increasing the volumes of the same products, as under the Armington assumption, has the inevitable consequence of driving down the price of exports and causing income losses to the exporter from deterioration in the terms of trade. Where exports are characterized by an expansion in the range of products supplied, the preference for variety exerts a counteracting force—helping to increase the demand for exports. In simulations introducing the Hummels–Klenow preference for variety in exports from China and India, Dimaranan, Ianchovichina and Martin (2007) found that the terms of trade for these exporters need not deteriorate significantly, despite very high projected rates of export growth.

Some traditional treatments of new varieties, such as those based on monopolistic competition and a love-of-variety inspired by Krugman (1980), are typically implemented with agriculture and services as perfectly competitive sectors and the rest of the economy characterized as monopolistically competitive. However, as Rodrik (2004) notes, the process of discovering efficient new exports is just as important and difficult in agriculture and services as in manufacturing. Models developed by Melitz (2003), with a fixed cost of entry into export markets, provide a basis for modeling the endogenous emergence of new products. Again this is an area for future data and CGE model development.

Distortions in Markets for Services

The potential gains from trade liberalization in services are rarely considered in CGE models, or at best are included only in rather rudimentary ways. This is because of a lack of good data on bilateral services trade, and methodological difficulties in modeling distortions in services markets. This is a serious omission, since there are indications that the costs of barriers to trade in services may be much larger than the barriers presented by conventional trade measures such as tariffs and subsidies (Dee, Hanslow and Pham 2003).

Konan and Maskus (2006) point out that the costs of services distortions are likely to be larger than those of merchandize trade because they typically involve restrictions not only on cross-border trade (Mode 1 of GATS), but also on supply by establishing enterprises in the country or by the movement of service suppliers (Modes 3 and 4 of GATS). Jensen, Rutherford and Tarr (2007) find that the benefits of reform in services trade, when allowing for productivity growth in trading a wider range of qualities of goods as the quality of business services rises (following Markusen, Rutherford and Tarr 2006), completely dominate as a source of benefits from likely reforms following Russia's accession to the WTO. These methodological developments have begun to find their way into global CGE models, as reflected in the BKS study cited in Table 8.1, but much scope remains to improve services trade data and the measurement and modelling representation of services market distortions.

CGE models typically ignore the dynamics of financial capital markets. Trade expands the demand for international financial services to transfer the required payments and often to provide temporary credit. Trade reform thereby 'thickens' international markets by raising not only the share of global goods production that passes through them, which reduces the variation across time in prices for traded products, but also markets for international financial services to transfer the required payments and to provide temporary credit. Together these forces contribute to the long-term stability of financial markets. Openness also tends to reduce inflation. It can do so by increasing competition in domestic markets, which drives down prices and reduces political pressure on the central bank to inflate, and by providing more options for people to hold savings in foreign currencies, which reduces the ability of governments to inflate savings (Rogoff 2003).

Productivity-enhancing Impacts of Reform

Economists have long been convinced that participation in international trade provides a bonus through improvements in productivity. Most of the investigation of these gains has been empirical, based loosely on Arrow's (1962) concept of learning-by-doing. Major contributions to this literature include Feder (1983), Dollar (1992) and Sachs and Warner (1995), all of whom find strong links between export performance and economic growth. Rodriguez and Rodrik (2001) raise concerns about the robustness of the estimated relationship between aggregate exports and productivity growth. During the same period, Clerides, Lach and Tybout (1998) questioned the learning-by-doing framework based on firm-level findings that exporting firms were more efficient before entering export markets, rather than because of learning-by-doing after entering these markets.

More recent research on the aggregate links between exports and productivity growth has more carefully examined the potential endogeneity of the relationship, and continues to find an aggregate relationship (Frankel and Romer 1999). A number of subsequent firm-level studies have re-examined the relationship between exporting and growth, and have found evidence of productivity growth associated with learning-by-doing after firms enter exporting. Blalock and Gertler (2004) find an increase in firm productivity of between 2 and 5 percent after Indonesian firms enter export markets. Fernandes and Isgut (2006) find evidence of an increase in productivity from learning-by-exporting when Colombian firms entered export markets. Van Biesebrock (2005) finds that African exporting firms had higher productivity before entering export markets, and that their productivity levels, and their subsequent rates of productivity growth, increased after entering export markets. Girma, Greenaway and Kneller (2004) also find both higher initial levels of productivity and higher productivity growth rates after entry into exporting.

To date the econometric literature on the growth benefits of trade liberalization provides little guidance on how long the dynamic effects from a one-off trade reform will last. This is yet another area requiring further empirical research.

Modeling Labor Market and Migration Responses to Immigrations Restrictions

Labor markets are very crudely modeled in global CGE models, partly for simplicity but also because of the difficulties in compiling internationally comparable data on skill levels and occupations. This problem is compounded when one abandons the assumption of no international labor flows and seeks to model the effects of altering restrictions on immigration. The approach adopted in the World Bank (2006) study cited above is but a start to addressing this issue, and much scope remains for further work in this area. More empirical research is needed also on the costs associated with international migration to both the migrants and to (particularly host country) governments.

Conclusion

The theory and available evidence surveyed above show that subsidies and trade barriers, including restrictions on the international movement of labor, are wasteful. Pre-announced, gradual reductions in them, especially if done multilaterally, would yield huge economic benefits and relatively little economic cost, and hence extremely high benefit/cost ratios. Moreover, such reforms would contribute enormously to reducing global inequality and poverty. Furthermore, while some social and environmental effects may be perceived as negative, many more will be positive. Even where some of those effects are harmful, there are almost always cheaper ways of obtaining better social and environmental outcomes than via trade and subsidy measures. The reasons these inefficient measures persist is partly lack of understanding of the benefits being foregone, but mostly it is because a small number of vested interests lobby for their retention (although in the case of immigration restrictions there is also opposition from some long-time citizens in high-income countries who believe their country is already at or beyond the optimal degree of cultural diversity).

The challenge is to find politically feasible opportunities for ridding the world of subsidies and trade barriers and lowering immigration restrictions. This chapter suggests the most obvious way is currently before us in the form of the Doha Development Agenda of multilateral trade negotiations under the World Trade Organization. Seizing that opportunity for reform could reduce government outlays by hundreds of millions of dollars, and make it less attractive to seek preferential trade agreements which are prone to making excluded countries worse off. A successful Doha outcome would also make it less pressing to lower immigration barriers insofar as trade in products is a substitute for international labor movements – although the estimated global gains and inequality-reducing consequences of more migration are so large as to make this worthwhile in addition (or at least as part of a Doha outcome under Mode IV of the services component). Cuts in subsidies and trade barriers also would provide a means for citizens to spend more on other pressing problems (because under freer trade the world's resources would be allocated more efficiently), thereby *indirectly* contributing to opportunities to alleviate other challenges facing the world; and they could also *directly* alleviate poverty and thereby reduce environmental degradation and address other challenges such as communicable diseases, conflicts and arms proliferation, education under-investment, and hunger and malnutrition. All that is needed is the political will to agree to and implement such reforms. If that is not found for concluding the global Doha Round soon, and given that far lower net benefits will flow from sub-global preferential trade agreements (especially for citizens of left-out countries) and the potentially huge benefits from migration (especially for citizens of today's developing countries), it would not be surprising if demands for visas and work permits intensifies along with increased irregular immigration.

Appendix: The Global, Economy-wide GTAP Database and the GTAP and Linkage CGE Models

To estimate the potential economy-wide effects of regional and multilateral trade liberalizations, by far the most common methodology since the 1980s has involved global computable general equilibrium (CGE) models and databases.[39] It is a daunting task to compile and periodically update all the necessary data for such a model so, under the direction of Professor Tom Hertel of Purdue University, a consortium was established more than a decade ago for this purpose. Known as GTAP (the Global Trade Analysis Project), it is currently providing Version 6 of its database publicly (with a pre-release of Version 7 now under review by consortium members). That database provides reconciled production, consumption and bilateral goods and services trade data plus subsidies and trade distortion estimates[40] (including developing country preferences) as of 2001 for more than 80 countries or country groups spanning the world, each divided into 57 sectors spanning the entire economy (see www.gtap.org). Earlier versions based on 1997 or 1995 data had less country and product disaggregation and did not include tariff preferences. This database is the foundation of most global CGE trade models in use today. Version 6 is described in detail in Dimaranan (2006).

In addition, the GTAP Center at Purdue University has developed its own family of applied general equilibrium models (Hertel 1997). The core GTAP model is a standard, multi-region CGE model that is currently being used by more than one thousand researchers in scores of countries on five continents. (The GTAP database builds on contributions from many of these individuals, as well as the national and international agencies in the GTAP Consortium.) Perfect competition and constant returns to scale are assumed for all sectors of each economy in the core comparative static version.

The GTAP model utilizes a sophisticated representation of consumer demands that allows for differences in both the price and income responsiveness of demand in different regions depending upon both the level of development of the region and the particular consumption patterns observed in that region. On the supply-side, differences in factor endowments within and between countries interact with different sectoral factor intensities to drive changes in the sectoral composition of output in response to structural or policy shocks. The GTAP production system distinguishes sectors by their intensities in five primary factors of production: agricultural land, other natural resources, unskilled labor time, skilled labor time, and physical capital. Thus in a region where physical capital is accumulating rapidly relative to other factors, for example, that region's relatively capital-intensive sectors tend to expand at the expense of other sectors. In addition to differences in intermediate input intensities, import intensities are also permitted to vary across uses. Since much trade is in intermediate inputs, the distinction between sales to final consumers and sales to other firms can be important. Lowering the cost of imported goods to consumers is quite different from lowering the cost of intermediate inputs to domestic firms that may be competing with imports in the final product market.

---

[39] On the need for adopting a general rather than partial equilibrium methodology, see Anderson (2002).

[40] Estimating the height of trade barriers is a non-trivial task in itself, even for merchandise (Evans 2003) but especially for services (Findlay and Warren 2001) and if technical barriers to trade are involved (Maskus and Wilson 2001).

As well, products are differentiated by place of production. The linkage between the different prices of a product is typically quite strong, but will depend on the degree of substitutability in consumption. In addition to matching up more effectively with reality, this approach has the advantage of permitting bilateral trade to be tracked, as opposed to simply reporting total exports net of imports.

The Linkage model has been developed for use by the World Bank's global economic projections team (van der Mensbrugghe 2005). It is a relatively straightforward CGE model but with some characteristics that distinguish it from standard comparative static models such as the GTAP model. A key difference is that it is recursive, so while it starts with 2001 as its base year it can be solved annually through to 2015. The dynamics are driven by exogenous population and labor supply growth, savings-driven capital accumulation, and labor-augmenting techno- logical progress (as assumed for the World Bank's global economic prospects exercise, see World Bank 2004, 2005). In any given year, factor stocks are fixed. Producers minimize costs subject to constant returns to scale production technology, consumers maximize utility, and all markets – including for labor – are cleared with flexible prices. There are three types of production structures. Crop sectors reflect the substitution possibility between extensive and intensive farming. Livestock sectors reflect the substitution possibility between intensive versus pasture feeding. And all other sectors reflect standard capital/labor substitution (with two types of labor: skilled and unskilled). As in the GTAP model there is a single representa- tive household per modeled region, allocat- ing income to consumption using the extended linear expenditure system. Trade is modeled using a nested Armington structure for each product, in which aggregate import demand is the outcome of allocating domestic absorption between the domestically produced good and aggregate imports of that product, and then that aggregate import demand is allocated across source countries to determine the pattern of bilateral trade flows. Government fiscal balances

are fixed in any given year, with the fiscal objec- tive being met by changing the level of lump sum taxes on households. This implies that losses of tariff revenues are replaced frictionlessly by higher direct taxes on households. The current account balance also is fixed. For example, if import tariffs are reduced, the propensity to import increases and additional imports are financed by increasing export revenues. The latter typically is achieved by a real exchange rate depreciation. Finally, investment is driven by savings. With fixed public and foreign saving, investment comes from changes in the savings behavior of the domestic household and from changes in the unit cost of investment. The latter can play an important role in a dynamic model if imported capital goods are taxed. Because the capital account is exogenous, rates of return across countries can differ over time and across simulations. The model only solves for relative prices, with the numéraire, or price anchor, being the export price index of manufactured exports from high-income countries. This price is fixed at unity in the base year and throughout the projection period to 2015.

Bibliography

Abella, M. (2004), 'The Role of Recruiters in Labor Migration', in D.S. Massey and J.E. Taylor (eds.), *International Migration: Prospects and Policies in a Global Market,* Oxford: Oxford University Press

Acharya, R.C. and W. Keller (2007), 'Technology Transfers Through Imports', NBER Working Paper 13086, Cambridge MA, May

Ades, A. and R. di Tella (1999), 'Rents, Competition, and Corruption', *American Economic Review* 89(4): 982–93, September

Aghion, P. and R. Griffith (2005), *Competition and Growth: Reconciling Theory and Evidence,* Cambridge MA: MIT Press

Aghion, P. and P. Howitt (2006), 'Appropriate Growth Policy: A Unified Framework', *Journal of the European Economic Association* 4: 269–314

Anderson, J. (2006), 'Consistent Policy Aggregation', mimeo, Boston College, Boston MA

Anderson, J. and J.P. Neary (1992), 'Trade Reform with Quotas, Partial Rent Retention, and Tariffs', *Econometrica* 60(1): 57–76

Anderson, K. (1992), 'Effects on the Environment and Welfare of Liberalising World Trade: The Cases of Coal and Food', Ch. 8 in *The Greening of World Trade Issues*, edited by K. Anderson and R. Blackhurst, London: Harvester-Wheatsheaf and Ann Arbor MI: University of Michigan

Anderson, K. (2002), 'Economy-wide Dimensions of Trade Policy Reform', Ch. 2 in *Development, Trade and the WTO: A Handbook*, edited by B. Hoekman, A. Matoo and P. English, Washington D.C.: The World Bank

Anderson, K. (2003), 'Measuring Effects of Trade Policy Distortions: How Far Have We Come?', *The World Economy* 26(4): 413–40, April

Anderson, K. (2006), 'Reducing Distortions to Agricultural Incentives: Progress, Pitfalls and Prospects', *American Journal of Agricultural Economics* 88(5): 1135–46, December

Anderson, K., B. Dimaranan, T. Hertel and W. Martin (1997), 'Economic Growth and Policy Reforms in the APEC Region: Trade and Welfare Implications by 2005', *Asia-Pacific Economic Review* 3(1): 1–18, April

Anderson, K. and Y. Hayami (1986), *The Political Economy of Agricultural Protection: East Asia in International Perspective,* London: Allen and Unwin

Anderson, K. and L.A. Jackson (2005), 'Some Implications of GM Food Technology Policies for Sub-Saharan Africa', *Journal of African Economies* 14(3): 385–410, September

Anderson, K., L.A. Jackson and C.P. Nielsen (2005), 'GM Rice Adoption: Implications for Welfare and Poverty Alleviation', *Journal of Economic Integration* 20(4): 771–88, December

Anderson, K., W. Martin and D. van der Mensbrugghe (2006a), 'Market and Welfare Implications of the Doha Reform Scenarios', Ch. 12 in *Agricultural Trade Reform and the Doha Development Agenda*, edited by K. Anderson and W. Martin, London: Palgrave Macmillan (co-published with the World Bank)

Anderson, K., W. Martin and D. van der Mensbrugghe (2006b), 'Doha Merchandise Trade Reform: What's at Stake for Developing Countries?', *World Bank Economic Review* 20(2): 169–95, July

Anderson, K., W. Martin and D. van der Mensbrugghe (2006c), 'Would Multilateral Trade Reform Benefit Sub-Saharan Africa?', *Journal of African Economies* 15(4): 626–70, December

Anderson, K., W. Martin and E. Valenzuela (2006), 'The Relative Importance of Global Agricultural Subsidies and Market Access', *World Trade Review* 5(3): 357–76, November

Anderson, K. and W. McKibbin (2000), 'Reducing Coal Subsidies and Trade Barriers: Their Contribution to Greenhouse Gas Abatement', *Environment and Development Economics* 5(4): 457–81, October

Anderson, K. and E. Valenzuela (2007), 'The World Trade Organization's Doha Cotton Initiative: A Tale of Two Issues', *The World Economy* 30(8): 1281–1304, August

Armington, P. (1969), 'A Theory of Demand for Products Distinguished by Place of Production', *IMF Staff Papers* 16(1): 159–78, March

Arnold, M., B. Javorcik and A. Mattoo (2006), 'The Productivity Effects of Services Liberalization: Evidence from the Czech Republic', mimeo, World Bank

Arrow, K. (1962) 'The Economic Implications of Learning by Doing', *Review of Economic Studies* 29(3): 155–173, June

Bacchetta, M. and M. Jansen (2003), 'Adjusting to Trade Liberalization: The Role of Policy, Institutions and WTO Disciplines', Special Studies 7, Geneva: World Trade Organization, April

Bach, C. and W. Martin (2001), 'Would the Right Tariff Aggregator for Policy Analysis Please Stand Up?', *Journal of Policy Modeling* 23: 621–35

Baldwin, R.E. (2004), 'Openness and Growth: What's the Empirical Relationship?' in *Challenges to Globalization: Analysing the Economics*, edited by R.E. Baldwin and L.A. Winters, Chicago: University of Chicago Press for NBER and CEPR

Baldwin, R. (2008), 'Big-Think Regionalism: A Critical Survey', NBER Working Paper 14056, Cambridge MA, June

Baldwin, R.E., J. Mutti and J.D. Richardson (1980), 'Welfare Effects on the United

States of a Significant Multilateral Trade Reduction', *Journal of International Economics* 6: 405–23

Beghin, J., D. van der Mensbrugghe and D. Roland-Holst (2002), *Trade and the Environment in General Equilibrium: Evidence from Developing Economies*, Norwell MA: Kluwer Academic Publishers

Bentivogli, C. and P. Pagano (1999), 'Trade, Job Destruction and Job Creation in European Manufacturing', *Open Economies Review* 10: 156–84

Bermudez, E. (2004), *Sustainability Assessments of Trade Policies and Programmes,* Gland, Switzerland: WWF International, January

Bernard, A.B., J.B. Jensen, S.J. Redding and P.K. Schott (2007), 'Firms in International Trade', NBER Working Paper 13054, Cambridge MA, April

Bhagwati, J.N. (1971), 'The Generalized Theory of Distortions and Welfare', in *Trade, Balance of Payments and Growth,* edited by J.N. Bhagwati *et al.*, Amsterdam: North-Holland

Billmeier, A. and T. Nannicini (2007), 'Trade Openness and Growth: Pursuing Empirical Glasnost', IMF Working Paper 07/156, Washington D.C., July

Blalock, G. and P. Gertler (2004), 'Learning from Exporting Revisited in a Less Developed Setting', *Journal of Development Economics* 75: 397–416

Borjas, G.J. (1994), 'The Economics of Immigration', *Journal of Economics Literature* 32(4): 1167–77

Bouët, A., Y. Decreux, L. Fontagné, S. Jean and D. Laborde (2004), 'A Consistent, *Ad Valorem* Equivalent Measure of Applied Protection Across the World: the MAcMaps-HS6 Database', CEPII Working Paper 2004-22, CEPII, Paris

Broda, C.M. and D.E. Weinstein (2006), 'Globalization and the Gains from Variety', *Quarterly Journal of Economics* 121(2): 541–85

Brown, D.K., K. Kiyota and R.M. Stern (2005), 'Computational Analysis of the Free Trade Area of the Americas (FTAA)', *North American Journal of Economics and Finance* 16: 153–85

Cameron, H. (2007), 'The Evolution of the Trade and Environment Debate at the WTO', Ch.

1 in *Trade and Environment: A Resource Book*, edited by A. Najam, M. Halle and R. Melendez-Ortiz, Geneva: International Centre for Trade and Sustainable Development (ICTSD), see www.trade-environment.org

CEPII (2003), *Methodological Tools for SIA: Report of the CEPII workshop held on 7–8 November 2002 in Brussels*, Paris: CEPII Working Paper No. 2003-19. Download at www.cepii.fr/anglaisgraph/workpap/pdf/2003/wp03-19.pdf

Chang, R., L. Kaltani and N. Loayza (2005), 'Openness Can be Good for Growth: The Role of Policy Complementarity', Policy Research Working Paper 3763, World Bank, Washington D.C., November

Chua, A. (2003), *World on Fire: How Exporting Free Market Democracy Breeds Ethnic Hatred and Global Instability,* New York: Random House

Clerides, S., S. Lach and J. Tybout (1998), 'Is Learning By Exporting Important? Micro-dynamic Evidence from Colombia, Mexico and Morocco', *Quarterly Journal of Economics* 113(3): 903–47

Cline, W.R. (2004a), *Trade Policy and Global Poverty,* Washington D.C.: Center for Global Development

Cline, W.R. (2004b), 'Climate Change', Ch. 1 in *Global Crises, Global Solutions*, edited by B. Lomborg, Cambridge: Cambridge University Press

Cline, W.R., T.O. Kawanabe, M. Kronsjo and T. Williams (1978), *Trade Negotiations in the Tokyo Round: A Quantitative Assessment*, Washington D.C.: Brookings Institution

Coase, R. (1960), 'The Problem of Social Cost', *Journal of Law and Economics* 3: 1–44

Cole, M.A. (2003), 'Development, Trade, and the Environment: How Robust is the Environmental Kuznets Curve?', *Environment and Development Economics* 8(4): 557–80

Collier, P. (2007), *The Bottom Billion: Why the Poorest Countries are Failing and What Can Be Done About It*, London: Oxford University Press

Collier, P. and A.J. Venables (2007), 'Rethinking Trade Preferences: How Africa Can Diversify Its Exports', *The World Economy* 30(8): 1326–45, August

Copland, B. and M.S. Taylor (2003), *Trade and the Environment: Theory and Evidence*, Princeton NJ: Princeton University Press

Corden, W.M. (1979), 'Tell Us Where the New Jobs Will Come From', *Bank of New South Wales Review* Vol. 30, October. Reprinted in *The World Economy* 8(2): 183–88, June 1985, and as Ch. 7 in the author's *The Road to Reform: Essays on Australian Economic Policy,* Melbourne: Addison-Wesley, 1997

Corden, W.M. (1997), *Trade Policy and Economic Welfare* (second edition), Oxford: Clarendon Press

de Ferranti, D., G.E. Perry, D. Lederman and W. Maloney (2001), *From Natural Resources to the Knowledge Economy: Trade and Job Quality,* Latin American and Caribbean Studies, Washington D.C.: World Bank

de Melo, J. and D. Tarr (1990), 'Welfare Costs of US Quotas on Textiles, Steel and Autos', *Review of Economics and Statistics* 72: 489–97

Deardorff, A.V. and R.M. Stern (1979), *An Economic Analysis of the Effects of the Tokyo Round of Multilateral Trade Negotiations on the United States and Other Major Industrial Countries*, MTN Studies 5, Washington D.C.: U.S. Government Printing Office

Deardorff, A.V. and R.M. Stern (1986), *The Michigan Model of World Production and Trade: Theory and Applications*, Cambridge MA: MIT Press

Dee, P., K. Hanslow and D.T. Pham (2003), 'Measuring the Cost of Barriers to Trade in Services', in *Services Trade in the Asia-Pacific Region*, edited by T. Ito and A.O. Krueger, Chicago: University of Chicago Press for the NBER

Demidova, S., H.L. Kee and K. Krishna (2006), 'Do Trade Policy Differences Induce Sorting? Theory and Evidence from Bangladeshi Apparel Exporters', NBER Working Paper 12725, Cambridge MA, December

Diebold, W., Jr. (1952), *The End of the ITO,* International Finance Section, Essays in International Finance No. 16, Princeton NJ: Princeton University Press

Dimaranan, B.V. (ed.) (2006), *Global Trade, Assistance, and Protection: The GTAP 6 Data Base,* Center for Global Trade Analysis, Purdue University, West Lafayette

Dimaranan, B.V., T. Hertel and R. Keeney (2004), 'OECD Domestic Support and the Developing Countries', in *The WTO, Developing Countries and the Doha Development Agenda*, edited by B. Kuha-Gasnobis, New York: Palgrave Macmillan

Dimaranan, B.V., E. Ianchovichina and W. Martin (2007), 'Competing uIT Giants: Who Wins? Who Loses?', Ch. 3 in *Dancing with Giants: China, India and the Global Economy*, edited by L.A. Winters and S. Yusef, Washington D.C.: World Bank

Dollar, D. (1992), 'Outward-oriented Developing Economies Really Do Grow More Rapidly: Evidence from 95 LDCs, 1976–1985', *Economic Development and Cultural Change* 40(3): 523–44

Dollar, D. and A. Kraay (2002), 'Growth is Good for the Poor', *Journal of Economic Growth* 7(3): 195–225, September

Dolman, B. (2008), 'Migration, Trade and Investment', Staff Working Paper, Productivity Commission, Canberra, February

Easterly, W. (2001), *The Elusive Quest for Growth,* Cambridge MA: MIT Press

Evans, C. (2003), 'The Economic Significance of National Border Effects', *American Economic Review* 93(4): 1291–312, September

Evenett, S. and A. Venables (2002), 'Export Growth in Developing Countries: Market Entry and Bilateral Trade Flows', www.alexandria.unisg.ch/Publikationen/22177

Faini, R. (2004), 'Trade Liberalization in a Globalizing World', CEPR Discussion Paper No. 4665, London, October

Faini, R., J. de Melo and K.F. Zimmermann (1999), *Migration: The Controversies and the Evidence,* Cambridge: Cambridge University Press

Feder, G. (1983), 'On Exports and Economic Growth', *Journal of Development Economics* 12: 59–73

Feenstra, R.C. (2004), *Advanced International Trade: Theory and Evidence*, Princeton NJ: Princeton University Press

Feenstra, R.C., J.R. Markusen and W. Zeile (1992), 'Accounting for Growth with New Inputs', *American Economic Review* 82(2): 415–21, May

Fernandes, A. and A. Isgut (2006), 'Learning-by-Exporting Effects: Are They for Real?', mimeo, Washington D.C.: World Bank

Fernandez, R. and D. Rodrik (1991), 'Resistance to Reform: Status Quo Bias and the Presence of Individual Specific Uncertainty', *American Economic Review* 81: 1146–55

Findlay, C. and T. Warren (2001), *Impediments to Trade in Services: Measurement and Policy Implications,* London and New York: Routledge

François, J.F. (2000), 'Assessing the Results of General Equilibrium Studies of Multilateral Trade Negotiations', Policy Issues in International Trade and Commodities Study Series No. 3, Geneva: UNCTAD

François, J.F. (2003), 'Assessing the Impact of Trade Policy on Labour Markets and Production', pp. 61–88 in *Methodological Tools for SIA*, CEPII Working Paper No. 2003-19, Paris: CEPII

François, J. and W. Martin (2004), 'Commercial Policy, Bindings and Market Access', *European Economic Review* 48: 665–79, June

François, J.F. and W. Martin (2007), 'Great Expectations: Ex Ante Assessments of the Welfare Impacts of Trade Reforms', mimeo, Erasmus University, Rotterdam, January

François, J.F. and K.A. Reinert (eds.) (1997), *Applied Methods for Trade Policy Analysis: A Handbook*, Cambridge and New York: Cambridge University Press

Frankel, J.A. and E.A. Cavallo (2004), 'Does Openness to Trade Make Countries More Vulnerable to Sudden Stops, Or Less? Using Gravity to Establish Causality', NBER Working Paper 10957, Cambridge MA, December

Frankel, J.A. and D. Romer (1999), 'Does Trade Cause Growth?', *American Economic Review* 89(3): 379–99, June

Frazer G., and J van Biesebroeck (2007), 'Trade Growth Under the African Growth and Opportunity Act', NBER Working Paper No. 13222, July

Freeman, R.B. (2004), 'Trade Wars: The Exaggerated Impact of Trade in Economic Debate', *The World Economy* 27(1): 1–23, January

Freeman, R.B. (2007), 'People Flows in Globalization', NBER Working Paper 12315, Cambridge MA, June

Friedman, T.L. (2007), *The World is Flat: The Globalized World in the Twenty-First Century,* London: Penguin

Furusawa, T. and E.L.C. Lai (1999), 'Adjustment Costs and Gradual Trade Liberalization', *Journal of International Economics* 49: 333–61

Gasiorek, M., and L.A. Winters (2004) 'What Role for the EPAs in the Caribbean?', *The World Economy* 27(9): 1335–62

Giles, C. (2007), 'Backlash in Rich Nations Against Globalization', *The Financial Times,* London, 22 July

Girma, S., D. Greenaway and R. Kneller (2004), 'Does Exporting Increase Productivity? A Microeconometric Analysis of Matched Firms', *Review of International Economics* 12(5): 855–66

Glenday, G. (2002), 'Trade Liberalization and Customs Revenue: Does Trade Liberalization Lead to Lower Customs Revenue? The Case of Kenya', *Journal of African Finance and Economic Development* 5(2): 89–125

Greenaway, D. (1993), 'Liberalizing Foreign Trade Through Rose-Tinted Glasses', *Economic Journal* 103: 208–22

Greenaway, D. and C. Milner (1993), 'The Fiscal Implication of Trade Policy Reform: Theory and Evidence', UNDP/World Bank Trade Expansion Program Occasional Paper 9, Washington D.C.: World Bank

Greenaway, D. and D.R. Nelson (eds.) (2002), *Globalization and Labour Markets*, (two volumes), London: Edward Elgar Publishers

Grossman, G.M. and E. Helpman (1991), *Innovation and Growth in the Global Economy*, Cambridge MA: MIT Press

Grossman, G.M. and K. Rogoff (eds.) (1995), *Handbook of International Economics Volume III*, Amsterdam: North-Holland

Grossman, G.M. and E. Rossi-Hansberg (2006), 'Trading Tasks: A Simple Theory of Offshoring', NBER Working Paper 12721, Cambridge MA, December

Hamilton, B. and J. Whalley (1984), 'Efficiency and Distributional Implications of Global Restrictions on Labor Mobility', *Journal of Development Economics* 14: 61–75

Hanson, G.H. (2006), 'Illegal Migration from Mexico to the United States', *Journal of Economic Literature* 44: 869–924

Hanson, G.H., R.J. Mataloni and M.J. Slaughter (2005), 'Vertical Production Networks in Multinational Firms', *Review of Economics and Statistics* 87(4): 664–78

Harbaugh, W.T., A. Levinson and D.M. Wilson (2002), 'Re-examining the Empirical Evidence for an Environmental Kuznets Curve', *Review of Economics and Statistics* 84(3): 541–51, August

Harrigan, J. and E.K. Choi (eds.) (2003), *Handbook of International Trade*, Oxford: Blackwell

Harrison, G.W., T.F. Rutherford and D.G. Tarr (2002), 'Trade Policy Options for Chile: The importance of Market Access', *World Bank Economic Review* 16(1): 49–79

Harrison, G.W., T.F. Rutherford, D.G. Tarr and A. Gurgel (2004), 'Trade Policy and Poverty Reduction in Brazil', *World Bank Economic Review* 18(3): 289–317

Helpman, E. and O. Itskhoki (2007), 'Labor Market Rigidities, Trade and Unemployment', NBER Working Paper 13365, Cambridge MA, October

Helpman, E., D. Marin and T. Verdier (eds.) (2008), *The Organization of Firms in a Global Economy*, Cambridge MA: Harvard University Press

Hertel, T.W. (ed.) (1997), *Global Trade Analysis: Modeling and Applications*, Cambridge and New York: Cambridge University Press

Hertel, T.W. and L.A. Winters (eds.) (2006), *Poverty and the WTO: Impacts of the Doha Development Agenda*, New York: Palgrave Macmillan and World Bank

Hertel, T.W., R. Keeney, M. Ivanic and L.A. Winters (2007), 'Distributional Effects of WTO Agricultural Reforms in Rich and Poor Countries', *Economic Policy*, 22: 289–337, April

Hoekman, B. (2006), 'Trade in Services, Economic Growth and Development, and International Cooperation: A Survey of the Literature', mimeo, World Bank, May

Hoekman, B., F. Ng and M. Olarreaga (2002), 'Eliminating Excess Tariffs on Exports of Least Developed Countries', *World Bank Economic Review* 16: 1–21, January

Hoekman, B., F. Ng and M. Olarreaga (2004), 'Agricultural Tariffs Versus Subsidies: What's More Important for Developing Countries?' *World Bank Economic Review* 18(2): 175–204

Hollander, J. (2003), *The Real Environmental Crisis: Why Poverty, Not Affluence, is the Environment's Number One Enemy,* Berkeley CA: University of California Press

Hummels, D. and P. Klenow (2005), 'The Variety and Quality of a Nation's Exports', *American Economic Review* 95(3): 704–23

Ianchovichina, E., A. Mattoo and M. Olarreaga (2001), 'Unrestricted Market Access for Sub-Saharan Africa: How Much is it Worth and Who Pays?', *Journal of African Economies* 10: 410–32

Irwin, D.A. (2002), *Free Trade Under Fire*, Princeton NJ: Princeton University Press

Jacobson, L.S., R.J. LaLonde and D.G. Sullivan (1993), 'Earnings Losses of Displaced Workers', *American Economic Review* 83(4): 685–709, September

Javorcik, B., W. Keller and J. Tybout (2006), 'Openness and Industrial Responses in a Walmart World', NBER Working Paper 12457, Cambridge MA, August

Jensen, J., T. Rutherford and D. Tarr (2007), 'The Impact of Liberalizing Barriers to Foreign Direct Investment in Services: The Case of Russian Accession to the World Trade Organization', *Review of Development Economics* 11(3): 482–506, August

Just, R.E., D.L. Hueth and A. Schmitz (2004), *The Welfare Economics of Public Policy*, London: Edward Elgar

Kanbur, R. (2001), 'Economic Policy, Distribution, and Poverty: The Nature of Disagreements', *World Development* 29(6): 1083–94

Karp, L. and T. Paul (2005), 'Intersectoral Adjustments and Policy Interventions: The Importance of General Equilibrium Effects', *Review of International Economics* 13(2): 330–55, May

Kindleberger, C.P. (1989), 'Commercial Policy Between the Wars', in Peter Mathias and Sidney Pollard (eds.), *The Cambridge Economic History of Europe, Vol. 8*, Cambridge: Cambridge University Press

King, D.K. (2003), *GM Science Review: First Report*, prepared by the GM Science Review Panel under the chairmanship of Sir David King for the UK government, July

Konan, D. and K. Maskus (2006), 'Quantifying the Impact of Services Liberalization in a Developing Country', *Journal of Development Economics* 81(1): 142–62

Krueger, A.B. and J. Maleckova (2003), 'Education, Poverty, Political Violence and Terrorism: Is There a Causal Connection?', *The Journal of Economic Perspectives* 17(4): 119–44

Krueger, A.O. (1983), *Trade and Employment in Developing Countries, Volume 3: Synthesis and Conclusions,* Chicago: University of Chicago Press for NBER

Krueger, A.O. (1999), 'Free Trade Agreements as Protectionist Devices: Rules of Origin', pp. 91–102 in *Trade Theory and Econometrics: Essays in Honour of John S. Chipman,* edited by J. Melvin, J. Moore and R. Riezman, London: Routledge

Krugman, P. (1980), 'Scale Economies, Product Differentiation, and the Pattern of Trade', *American Economic Review* 70(5): 950–9

Lee, J.-W. (1995), 'Capital Goods Imports and Long-Run Growth', *Journal of Development Economics* 48: 91–110, October

Lileeva, A. and D. Trefler (2007), 'Improved Access to Foreign Markets Raises Plant-Level Productivity . . . For Some Plants', NBER Working Paper No. W13297, Cambridge MA, September

Lindert, P. (1991), 'Historical Patterns of Agricultural Protection', in P. Timmer (ed.), *Agriculture and the State,* Ithaca NY: Cornell University Press

Lloyd, P.J. (1974), 'A More General Theory of Price Distortions in an Open Economy', *Journal of International Economics* 4(4): 365–86, November

Lomborg, B. (2001), *The Skeptical Environmentalist: Measuring the Real State of the World,* Cambridge and New York: Cambridge University Press

Lumenga-Neso, O., M. Olarreaga and M. Schiff (2005), 'On "Indirect" Trade-Related R&D Spillovers', *European Economic Review* 49(7): 1785–98, October

Magee, S.P. (1972), 'The Welfare Effects of Restrictions on US Trade', *Brookings Papers on Economic Activity* 3: 645–701

Manole, V. and W. Martin (2005), 'Keeping the Devil in the Details: A Feasible Approach to Aggregating Trade Distortions', Paper presented to the European Trade Study Group meetings, Dublin, September

Markusen, J.R. (1983), 'Factor Movements and Commodity Trade as Complements', *Journal of International Economics* 13: 341–56

Markusen, J., T. Rutherford and D. Tarr (2006), 'Foreign Direct Investment in Service and the Domestic Market for Expertise', *Canadian Journal of Economics*

Marques, G. and C. Pages (1998), 'Trade and Employment: Evidence from Latin America and the Caribbean', IDB Working Paper No. 366, Inter-American Development Bank, Washington D.C., January

Martin, P. (2004), 'Migration', Ch. 8 in *Global Crises, Global Solutions,* edited by B. Lomborg, Cambridge: Cambridge University Press

Martin, W. and Anderson, K. (2006). 'The Doha Agenda Negotiations on Agriculture: What Could They Deliver?', *American Journal of Agricultural Economics* 88(5): 1211–18, December

Maskus, K. and J. Wilson (eds.) (2001), *Quantifying the Impact of Technical Barriers to Trade: Can it be Done?* Ann Arbor MI: University of Michigan Press

Mattoo, A. and A. Subramanian (2003), 'What Would a Development-Friendly WTO Architecture Really Look Like?', IMF Working Paper WP/03/153, Washington D.C., August

Mattoo, A. and A. Carzaniga (eds.) (2002), *Moving People to Deliver Services: Labour Mobility and the WTO,* London: Oxford University Press

Matusz, S. and D. Tarr (2000), 'Adjusting to Trade Policy Reform', in *Economic Policy Reform: The Second Stage,* edited by A.O. Krueger, Chicago: University of Chicago Press

Mazumdar, J. (2001), 'Imported Machinery and Growth in LDCs', *Journal of Development Economics* 65: 209–24, June

McCulloch, N., L.A. Winters and X. Cirera (2001), *Trade Liberalization and Poverty: A Handbook,* London: Centre for Economic Policy Research

Melitz, M. (2003), 'The Impact of Trade on Intra-industry Reallocations and Aggregate Industry Productivity', *Econometrica* 71(6): 1692–725

Michaely, M. (2003), 'Goods Versus Factors: When Borders Open, Who Moves?', *The World Economy* 26(4): 533–54, April

Michaely, M., D. Papageorgiou and A. Choksi (eds.) (1991), *Liberalizing Foreign Trade, 7: Lessons of Experience in the Developing World*, Cambridge MA and Oxford: Basil Blackwell

Milner, C., O. Morrissey and A. McKay (2005), 'Some Simple Analytics of the Trade and Welfare Effects of Economic Partnership Agreements', *Journal of the African Economies* 14(3): 327–58

Milner, C. and P. Wright (1998), 'Modelling Labour Market Adjustment to Trade Liberalization in an Industrializing Country', *Economic Journal* 108: 509–28, March

Moreira, M. and S. Najberg (2000), 'Trade Liberalization in Brazil: Creating of Exporting Jobs?', *Journal of Development Studies* 36(3): 78–99, February

Moses, J.W. and B. Letnes (2004), 'The Economic Costs to International Labor Restrictions: Revisiting the Empirical Discussion', *World Development* 32(10): 1609–26

Mundell, R.A. (1957), 'International Trade and Factor Mobility', *American Economic Review* 47: 321–35

Nash, J. and W. Takacs (1998), 'Lessons from the Trade Expansion Program', Ch. 1 in *Trade Policy Reform: Lessons and Implications*, edited by J. Nash and W. Takacs, Washington D.C.: World Bank

OECD (1996), *Subsidies and the Environment: Exploring the Linkages*, Paris: OECD

OECD (1997), *Reforming Energy and Transport Subsidies: Environmental and Economic Implications*, Paris: OECD

OECD (1998), *Improving the Environment Through Reducing Subsidies*, Paris: OECD

OECD (2003a), *Agricultural Trade and Poverty: Making Policy Analysis Count*, Paris: OECD

OECD (2003b), *Environmentally Harmful Subsidies: Policy Issues and Challenges*, Paris: OECD

OECD (2006), *Agricultural Policy and Trade Reform: Potential Effects at Global, National and Household Levels*, Paris: OECD

Olsen, M. (1965), *The Logic of Collective Action*, Cambridge MA: Harvard University Press

Oneal, J. and B. Russett (2000), *Triangulating Peace: Democracy, Interdependence and International Organizations*, New York: Norton

Panagariya, A. (2004), 'Subsidies and Trade Barriers: Alternative Perspective 10.2', pp. 592–601 in *Global Crises, Global Solutions*, edited by B. Lomborg, Cambridge and New York: Cambridge University Press

Parsons, C.R., R. Skeldon, T.L. Walmsley and L.A. Winters (2007), 'Quantifying International Migration: a Database of Bilateral Migrant Stocks', World Bank Policy Research Working Paper 4165, Washington D.C., March

Prasad, E., K. Rogoff, S. Wei and A. Khose (2006), 'Effects of Financial Globalization on Developing Countries', IMF Occasional Paper 220, Washington D.C.

Pritchett, L. (2007), *Let Their People Come: Breaking the Gridlock on Global Labor Mobility*, Washington D.C.: Center for Global Development

Ravallion, M. (2006), 'Looking Beyond Averages in the Trade and Policy Debate', *World Development* 34(8): 1374–92, August

Rivera-Batiz, L. and P. Romer (1991), 'International Integration and Endogenous Growth', *Quarterly Journal of Economics* 106: 531–56

Rodrigeuz, F. and D. Rodrik (2001), 'Trade Policy and Economic Growth: A Skeptic's Guide to Cross-National Evidence', in *NBER Macroeconomics Annual 2000*, edited by B.S. Bernanke and K. Rogoff, Cambridge MA: MIT Press

Rodrik, D. (2003), 'Growth Strategies', NBER Working Paper 10050, Cambridge MA, October

Rodrik, D. (2004), 'Industrial Policy for the Twenty-first Century', mimeo, Harvard University, Cambridge MA. http://ksghome.harvard.edu/~drodrik/UNIDOSep.pdf

Rogoff, K.S. (2003), 'Disinflation: An Unsung Benefit of Globalization', *Finance and Development* 40(4): 54–5, December

Romalis, J. (2007), 'Market Access, Openness and Growth', NBER Working Paper 13048, Cambridge MA, July

Romer, P. (1994), 'New Goods, Old Theory, and the Welfare Costs of Trade Restrictions', *Journal of Development Economics* 43(1): 5–38

Rutherford, T.F. and D.G. Tarr (2002). 'Trade Liberalization, Product Variety and Growth in a Small Open Economy: A Quantitative

Assessment', *Journal of International Economics* 56(2): 247–72

Sachs, J.D. and A. Warner (1995), 'Economic Reform and the Process of Global Integration', *Brookings Papers on Economic Activity* 1: 1–95

Sala-i-Martin, X. (2006), 'The World Distribution of Income: Falling Poverty and . . . Convergence, Period', *Quarterly Journal of Economics* 121(2): 351–97

Schiff, M. (2007), 'Optimal Immigration Policy: Permanent, Guest-Worker, or Mode IV?' mimeo, Washington D.C.: World Bank, June

Sen, A. (1999), *Development as Freedom,* New York: Anchor Books

Spence, M. *et al.* (2008), *The Growth Report: Strategies For Sustained Growth and Inclusive Development* (Report of the Commission on Growth and Development, chaired by Michael Spence), Washington D.C.: World Bank

Tangermann, S. (2005), 'OECD Area Agricultural Policies and the Interests of Developing Countries', *American Journal of Agricultural Economics* 87(5): 1128–44, December

Taylor, M.S. (1999), 'Trade and Trade Policy in Endogenous Growth Models', Ch. 15 in *International Trade Policy and the Pacific Rim*, edited by J. Piggott and A. Woodland, London: Macmillan for the IAE

Townsend, R.M. and K. Ueda (2007), 'Welfare Gains from Financial Globalization', IMF Working Paper 07/154, Washington D.C., July

Trefler, D. (2004), 'The Long and Short of the Canada–US Free Trade Agreement', *American Economic Review* 94(4): 870–95, September

Tyers, R. and Anderson, K. (1992), *Disarray in World Food Markets: a Quantitative Assessment*, Cambridge and New York: Cambridge University Press

UN Population Division (2002), *International Migration Report 2002*, New York: United Nations

UNECA (2007), *The Economic and Welfare Impacts of EU–Africa Economic partnership Agreements,* ATPC, Briefing Note No. 6, UNECA, Addis Ababa

UNCTAD/Commonwealth Secretariat (2001), *Duty and Quota Free Market Access for LDCs: An Analysis of Quad Initiatives,* Geneva: UNCTAD and London: Commonwealth Secretariat

USDA (2001), *Agricultural Policy Reform in the WTO: The Road Ahead*, Economic Research Service, Agricultural Economic Report 802, US Department of Agriculture, Washington D.C.

USITC (1997), *The Dynamic Effects of Trade Liberalization: An Empirical Analysis,* Publication 3069, US International Trade Commission, Washington D.C., October

Vamvakidis, A. (1999), 'Regional Trade Agreements or Broad Liberalization: Which Path Leads to Faster Growth?', *IMF Staff Papers* 46(1): 42–69

van Beers, C. and A. de Moor (2001), *Public Subsidies and Policy Failures: How Subsidies Distort the Natural Environment, Equity and Trade and How to Reform Them,* Cheltenham: Edward Elgar

van Biesebrock, J. (2005), 'Exporting Raises Productivity in Sub-Saharan African Manufacturing Firms', *Journal of International Economics* 67: 373–91

van der Mensbrugghe, D. (2005), 'Linkage Technical Reference Document: Version 6.0', mimeo, World Bank, Washington D.C., January and at www.worldbank.org/ prospects/linkagemodel

van der Mensbrugghe, D. (2006), 'Estimating the Benefits: Why Numbers Change', Ch. 4 in *Trade, Doha and Development: A Window into the Issues,* edited by R. Newfarmer, Washington D.C.: World Bank

Ventura, J. (2005), 'A Global View of Economic Growth', in P. Aghion and S. Durlauf (eds.), *Handbook of Economic Growth*, Amsterdam: Elsevier

von Moltke, A., C. McKee and T. Morgan (2004), *Energy Subsidies: Lessons Learned in Assessing Their Impact and Designing Policy Reforms,* London: Greenleaf Books for UNEP

Wacziarg, R. (2001), 'Measuring the Dynamic Gains From Trade', *World Bank Economic Review* 15(3): 393–429, October

Wacziarg, R. and K.H. Welch (2003), 'Trade Liberalization and Growth: New Evidence', NBER Working Paper 10152, Cambridge MA, December

Whalley, J. (1985), *Trade Liberalization Among Major World Trading Areas*, Cambridge MA: MIT Press

Whalley, J. (2000), 'What Can the Developing Countries Infer from the Uruguay Round Models for Future Negotiations?', Policy Issues in International Trade and Commodities Study Series No. 4, Geneva: UNCTAD

Whalley, J. (2004), 'Assessing the Benefits to Developing Countries of Liberalization in Services Trade', *The World Economy* 27(8): 1223–53, August

Whalley, J. (2006), 'China's FDI and Non-FDI Economies and the Sustainability of Future High Chinese Growth', NBER Working Paper No. 12249, Cambridge MA, May

Williamson, J.G. (2002), 'Winners and Losers Over Two Centuries of Globalization', WIDER Annual Lecture 6, United Nations University, Helsinki, reprinted in pp. 136–74 of *Wider Perspectives on Global Development,* London: Palgrave Macmillan, 2006

Winters, L.A. (2002), 'Trade Liberalisation and Poverty: What Are The Links?', *The World Economy* 25(9): 1339–68, September

Winters, L.A. (2004), 'Trade Liberalization and Economic Performance: An Overview', *Economic Journal* 114: F4–F21, February

Winters, L.A., N. McCulloch and A. McKay (2004), 'Trade Liberalization and Poverty: The Empirical Evidence', *Journal of Economic Literature* 62(1): 72–115, March

Winters, L.A. and W.E. Takacs (1991), 'Labour Adjustment Costs and British Footwear Protection', *Oxford Economic Papers* 43: 479–501

Winters, L.A., T. Walmsley, Z.K. Wang and R. Grynberg (2003), 'Liberalizing Temporary Movement of Natural Persons: An Agenda for the Development Round', *The World Economy* 26(8): 1137–61, August

World Bank (2002), *Global Economic Prospects 2002: Making Trade World for the World's Poor,* Washington D.C.: The World Bank

World Bank (2004), *Global Economic Prospects 2004: Realizing the Development Promise of the Doha Agenda,* Washington D.C.: The World Bank

World Bank (2005), *Global Economic Prospects 2005: Trade, Regionalism, and Development,* Washington D.C.: The World Bank

World Bank (2006), *Global Economic Prospects 2006: Economic Implications of Remittances and Migration,* Washington D.C.: The World Bank

Alternative Perspectives

Perspective Paper 8.1

ALAN V. DEARDORFF

Introduction

Kym Anderson and Alan Winters, in their Challenge Paper on trade and migration, have done a fine job of marshaling the evidence on the net benefits of liberalization. Their message is the familiar one that developing countries, especially, stand to gain from further liberalization of barriers to trade and migration, and therefore that such liberalization should play a central role in any list of initiatives to address the challenges posed in the current round of the Copenhagen Consensus. Like most if not all economists who deal with these issues in their research and teaching, I agree with their conclusion. I also agree that the studies they cite in their paper provide the best evidence that we have of what the costs and benefits of this liberalization might be.

To put their arguments and findings into perspective, therefore, I will make just a few points. First, their use of a benefit-cost ratio as a means of quantifying the desirability of liberalization is misleading, if not inappropriate, especially given their use of CGE models for that purpose. Second, I would prefer that they not look just at the net economic benefits from liberalization and compare them to costs associated with implementation. Rather, it would be preferable to quantify both the gross economic benefits and gross economic costs separately, and in particular to give more attention than they do to the gross costs.

Finally, I will note that the real challenge

with regard to trade and migration is not to know what to do, but rather to find a way to do it. Recent experience with the Doha Round of trade negotiations, as well as with efforts, in the United States at least, to liberalize migration, has been depressingly unsuccessful. I will conclude with some very tentative thoughts about how the world might move forward in the direction that the Challenge Paper shows convincingly to be desirable.

Pros and Cons of Benefit-Cost Ratios

A few years ago I was asked by the dean of our policy school to teach the course on benefit-cost analysis. I objected that I knew nothing about this subject and was told that of course I did, as I had been practicing benefit-cost analysis for most of my career in my work on tariffs and other international trade barriers. Sure enough, when I read the textbook that my dean, Ned Gramlich, had himself written (Gramlich 1990), I found much of it very familiar. However, there was one point that would have been unfamiliar to me, had it been included in his text: the use of benefit-cost ratios as a criterion for selecting policies. In fact, this tool was mentioned by Gramlich only to dismiss it as misleading. Better, he said, to use the net benefits of a policy or project – that is, total benefits minus total costs – as a guide to choosing among alternatives. That will yield the maximum improvement in social welfare, whereas the choice with the highest benefit-cost ratio might not, if costs of various choices differ.[1]

As I recall reading about the first Copenhagen Consensus, the exercise then was to consider alternative ways of spending a fixed sum of resources, and in that context the use of a benefit-cost ratio versus a measure of net benefit from that given cost is equivalent. But in general, if the costs of alternatives are not the same, then the choice of one with the largest benefit-cost ratio may be far from optimal.

Of course, a benefit-cost ratio of less than one is nonetheless very meaningful, since it indicates that the net benefit from the choice is negative. Thus calculating benefit-cost ratios in order to check that they exceed one is worth doing in many contexts. However, in the context of trade policy, the models that we normally use actually guarantee that benefit-cost ratios will always be larger than one, at least for the world as a whole. That is the message of the large theoretical literature on the gains from trade, which shows that under certain assumptions aggregate economic welfare of the world as a whole is increased by reducing trade barriers to zero. The same is true for individual countries except for the possibility of terms-of-trade effects that may in addition divert welfare from some countries to others. The assumptions under which these gains from trade exist may be implausible, but they are routinely made in the computable general equilibrium (CGE) models that Anderson and Winters cite. Therefore the positive net benefits from moving to free trade, and thus the result that benefit-cost ratios exceed one, are true by assumption.

Still, one might argue, one might not have expected these ratios to be as large as Anderson and Winters find them to be. In their Table 8.11, they report benefit-cost ratios from complete trade liberalization ranging from a low of 17 to a high of 3147. This means that the benefits from liberalization are at least seventeen times their costs, and probably much, much higher. Surely that is a strong indication not only that liberalization is beneficial but that the costs of liberalization are negligible.

In fact, however, the costs that are included in the denominator of this benefit-cost ratio are far from being the total costs imposed by liberalization. Anderson and Winters treat as costs only the costs that are, as they note, ignored in CGE models: administrative costs of changing policies, adjustment costs of firms and workers moving from one equilibrium to another, and social costs of programs to assist those displaced by liberalization. These, they note, are indeed small compared to the net benefits that the CGE models do quantify as arising from liberalization, largely because they are transitory while the net economic gains persist over time.

But these net benefits are themselves a difference between benefits and costs, the latter being the fall in wages and returns to specific assets (including both physical and human capital) in import-competing industries. As is familiar from partial equilibrium analysis of tariffs, trade liberalization creates a net benefit that is the difference between, on the one hand, a much larger benefit to buyers of an imported product and, on the other, a loss, often substantial, to domestic sellers. How these losses appear in a CGE model depends on its structure, perhaps being a fall in returns to specific factors or perhaps being a fall in the wage of the country's scarce factor. But either way, these are costs that, if they were included together with their matching benefits in both the denominator and the numerator of the benefit-cost ratio, would make that ratio much smaller.

To illustrate, see Figure 8.1.1, which shows the very standard partial equilibrium analysis of a specific tariff, $t=\$4$, on supply, demand, and welfare of a small country facing a world price $P^W=\$8$ for a good that it imports. In the presence of the tariff, the domestic price is the world price plus the tariff, $12; domestic supply is 100 units; domestic demand is 170 units; and therefore the country imports 70 units, generating a tariff revenue of $280. When the tariff is removed, domestic price falls to the world price, $8; quantity supplied falls to 60; quantity demanded rises to 190; and imports increase to

---

[1] See Gramlich (1990, p. 42).

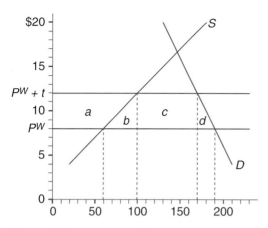

Figure 8.1.1 *Economic effects of a tariff*

130 units. This static equilibrium analysis does not tell us the costs of implementing the tariff cut, such as administrative cost or adjustment costs of suppliers moving into another industry. It does, however, tell us the net economic gain from the tariff cut aside from these transitory costs, which is the elimination of the "dead weight loss" due to the tariff and is measured in the figure by the areas of the two triangles b and d. Adding the areas of the two triangles together, the dead weight loss in this example is $120. Suppose that the implementation costs are as small as Anderson and Winters find them to be, say $2. Then the benefit-cost ratio is 60.

But the economic losses caused by the tariff cut include much more than just these implementation costs, and indeed the gross economic gain is also much larger than this forgone dead weight loss. Removal of the tariff causes demanders of this good to gain the change in consumer surplus, which is the full area to the left of the demand curve between the two prices, and thus $4×180 = $720. At the same time, suppliers lose producer surplus equal to $4×80 = $320, while

the government loses the entire tariff revenue, $280. If we include these gains and losses in the calculation of the benefit-cost ratio, then benefits are $720 while costs are $2+320+280 = $602, and the benefit-cost ratio is only 720/602 = 1.2

One might object that the figure shows quite a large tariff (50 percent), and the tariff revenue is therefore much larger than we usually see, at least in developed countries. But with a little manipulation of the figure you can see that, as the tariff being eliminated becomes smaller, the benefit-cost ratio becomes even smaller and closer to one.[2]

Gross Benefits and Gross Costs

I would prefer, therefore, that the analysis of liberalization of both trade and migration report separately both the gross benefits and the gross costs that these liberalizations entail. That might not be easy to do, since CGE modelers (including myself) do not routinely provide this information. They may report changes in wages and returns to capital, which could in principle capture Stolper-Samuelson-driven changes in returns to scarce and abundant factors. But much more relevant would be industry-specific changes in wages, employment, and asset values that impact the lifetime earnings of those who have invested in industry-specific skills and assets.

Anderson and Winters acknowledge these costs, but they treat them as minor and transitory. They are indeed transitory, but only in the sense that many of those affected will eventually retire and die, being replaced by others who have invested their physical and human capital in other industries. Anderson and Winters mention them primarily in order to note the ability of those who will bear these costs to use political action to resist cuts in protection. In fact, however, the costs to them as human beings should also be acknowledged in a full analysis of liberalization.

This is especially true in countries where policies do a poor job of providing safety nets for those impacted by economic change. This is per-

[2] In Figure 8.1.1, for example, if the tariff had been only $1 instead of $4, with the same world price and supply and demand curves, the demander benefit of eliminating it would become only $187.5, the supplier cost of eliminating it would be $65, and the tariff revenue lost would be $115. Then even if the implementation cost were now zero, the benefit-cost ratio for tariff elimination would be only $187.5/$180 = 1.04.

haps least true in Europe, but it is certainly true in the most developing countries, and it is arguably true in the United States as well. The economic arguments of economists in favor of trade liberalization, as embodied in CGE models, are based on the result that the gains from trade are larger than the losses. But advocates of trade liberalization are often criticized for ignoring those losses entirely. I have often defended our discipline by insisting that we certainly do not ignore the losses, and I point to both the Stolper-Samuelson Theorem and the specific factors model as part of the evidence in our favor. But quantitative analyses of trade liberalization, as exemplified here by Anderson and Winters, too easily feed that criticism by giving only minimal attention to those losses.

Anderson and Winters mention these costs primarily in the context of explaining protection. The costs are sufficiently concentrated and identifiable, they say, that 'the few losers are prepared to support politicians who resist protection cuts' (p. 24). That may well be true. But one does not need explicit or costly lobbying activities, or politicians 'selling' protection as suggested by Grossman and Helpman (1994), for representatives of trade-impacted legislative districts to seek protection for their constituents.[3] On the contrary, many societies and their governments view it as quite appropriate to resist economic harm to significant parts of their populations, even if that means foregoing or delaying aggregate economic gain. Corden (1974) called this the Conservative Social Welfare Function, and he used it to explain protection without the explanation resorting to manipulation of self-interested politicians.[4]

The human costs of trade liberalization are particularly important when they are borne by the poor in developing countries. Fortunately, that is not always, or perhaps not even often, the case. The benefits from protection in developing countries often accrue to the highest-income urban elites, which is why protection is particularly hard politically to eliminate. But there are also plenty of cases in which the poor stand to lose from freer trade. In those cases trade liberalization will run counter to poverty reduction unless

deliberate steps are taken to prevent that. An example that comes to mind is peasant farmers who grow maize in Mexico, and who have been unable to compete with the large mechanized farms of the United States as NAFTA removed their protection. Other examples undoubtedly exist and need to be identified as part of the preparation for any move to liberalize trade. CGE modelers should ideally seek not only to identify those poor who will be displaced by trade, but also to model policy initiatives that might ameliorate the harm that will be done to them. These policy initiatives would certainly include the slow phasing in of tariff reductions, and hopefully they would also include other policies such as relocation and retraining programs to assist displaced populations to transition into expanding sectors of the economy.

Subsidies and Migration

I have been talking explicitly about international trade, and about trade policies such as tariffs. The Anderson and Winters paper also deals explicitly and extensively with migration. In addition, the topic of this Challenge includes subsidies, although these get less attention than barriers to trade and migration in the Anderson and Winters paper. The points I have raised here, however, apply as well to migration and to subsidies as they do to trade and tariffs.

Benefit-cost ratios are no better as a guide to migration policy, or to dealing with subsidies, than they are to trade liberalization. Instead, as Gramlich (1990) stressed and I echo, in both cases one should look at overall net benefits from a policy change, not worry about how large a multiple benefits may be of costs. Just as importantly, however, one needs to acknowledge what the gross costs are, and to confront them with additional policies wherever possible.

Anderson and Winters do that implicitly in

---

[3] See Hall and Deardorff (2006) for an analysis of legislative lobbying that does not involve persuading legislators to support actions that they would not otherwise favor.
[4] See also Deardorff (1987) for use of the Conservative Social Welfare Function to motivate safeguard policies.

dealing with migration. In terms of economic effects, it is clear that net benefits would be maximized by allowing migration to be, like trade, perfectly free. But they do not for a moment entertain free migration as a candidate for policy. Their choice instead is to model an arbitrary 3 percent increase in the labor force of developed countries through migration. That is presumably far less than would occur with free migration, for reasons that remain unmodeled.

Subsidies are handled by Anderson and Winters along with trade barriers as just another distortion of international trade, and not a terribly important one at that, except for a few particular industries and countries (e.g., cotton, and the developing country cotton producers). Quantitatively and in terms of net benefits from liberalization, I am prepared to believe that they are right. In that sense, subsidies probably do not deserve the attention that they have received in the Doha Round negotiations. But if we look, again, at the gross benefits and costs of removing subsidies, which are very different than they are for tariffs, then the attention they are getting and the resistance to removing them may become more understandable.

The Real Challenge: Making Liberalization Happen

One might hope that – once economists make the case that reducing barriers to international trade and migration will be beneficial for the world overall, and especially for the poor – then the liberalization itself will happen naturally. But economists have been making this case in various forms and forums for over two centuries. Trade barriers have indeed come down occasionally, especially during the last half of the twentieth century. But it took the institution

of the GATT to make that happen, and in recent years further reductions on a multilateral basis have been elusive. Making the economic case for reducing barriers is certainly worth doing, but it will never be enough.

The problem today takes two forms: the impasse that has been reached in the Doha Round of multilateral trade negotiations within the WTO; and the proliferation of preferential trading arrangements (PTAs) outside of the WTO. These two problems are mutually reinforcing, the Doha impasse both prompting, and being prompted by, the PTAs. Together these two problems mean that while trade barriers are still being reduced, they have become more discriminatory. It is therefore unclear whether the world trading system is becoming less distorted, or more.

The Doha Round, dubbed the Doha Development Agenda, began in 2001, not long after the events of September 11 focused the world's attention on achieving greater harmony in the world, especially with regard to developing countries. In the years since 2001, however, progress in the negotiations has repeatedly stalled. The reason has been the usual reluctance of each negotiating party to give up its own protective policies while continuing to demand such concessions from others. This reluctance is not new, having nearly derailed the Uruguay Round negotiations repeatedly during the 1980s and 1990s. However, it seems to make negotiations this time around even more intractable than before, for at least two reasons.[5]

One is that the larger developing countries are, for the first time, negotiating in concert under the name of the Group of Twenty.[6] This is a positive development, in that developing countries are finally having a more meaningful voice in the negotiations. But it also means that success of the negotiations requires not just agreement between the United States and the European Union, as in the past, but also between them and the developing countries. The fact that the differences between developed and developing countries are much larger than among developed countries alone, means both that the benefits from further liberalization are

---

[5] A third reason is the proliferation of PTAs, which give the participants some of the gains in market access that they might have pursued multilaterally. This reduces their incentive to participate in the multilateral negotiations and to offer meaningful concessions when they do.

[6] Membership has fluctuated and it currently includes 23 developing countries.

arguably larger than in previous rounds, but also that agreement on liberalization is even harder to achieve.

A second reason for the impasse, since 2006, is the inability of the United States to play a credible leadership role. President Bush lost control of the U.S. Congress in 2006. Then, in 2007, his Fast Track Authority, to bring trade agreements to Congress for approval without amendment, expired. Both events undermine the confidence that other negotiating countries have that the United States will be able to deliver on any trade agreement that it signs. Without the United States leading, or even credibly participating in, the negotiations, there is little reason for other groups of countries to make concessions.

Perhaps anticipating this conundrum, or perhaps contributing to it, the Bush administration has pursued since its inception an agenda of bilateral negotiations with a long list of partners. The European Union, after doing the same in the 1990s, abstained from further PTAs for a few years. But the EU is now renewing its push for such agreements even as the United States has had to pull back with the expiry of Fast Track.[7] Many other countries, too, have negotiated PTAs, so that today the web of overlapping preferential arrangements – Bhagwati's "spaghetti bowl" – encompasses almost every country in the WTO.

On its face this might suggest that barriers to trade have been substantially reduced well below their most favored nation (MFN) levels negotiated in the Uruguay Round. In terms of simple average tariffs, this is true. However, these preferential tariffs both "create" and "divert" trade, as Viner (1950) taught us years ago. Trade diversion is surely harmful to the countries diverted from, while also being harmful to the country doing the discriminating. Furthermore, these preferential tariff cuts apply only to imported goods that satisfy often very stringent rules of origin. The need to document the history of traded goods for this purpose, and to engineer supply chains so as to conform to these rules, means that distortions of trade have arguably increased rather than decreased.

How, then, can multilateral progress toward reducing trade barriers be achieved? The only answer that I can see is leadership. That is, somebody in authority has to lead the way. They must lead the way, but not out of self-interest, because the political forces resisting trade liberalization today are as strong as ever, making it unlikely that a political figure can gain by openly advocating free trade. In the past, the forces of protectionism have sometimes been countered by those who stood to gain by exporting, working quietly in the background, since their interests are often identified with corporations which are unlikely to excite public sympathy. But export interests no longer seem to be playing as vigorous a role as they once did, perhaps because the most bothersome trade barriers from their perspective have already been eliminated, or perhaps because they stand to gain almost as much from PTAs as from multilateral free trade.

Therefore, we must hope for a leader who will push for liberalization simply because it is the right thing to do. To be able to accomplish anything, that leader must probably come from a country or group of countries that is large and rich, presumably the United States or the European Union. But those economic powerhouses actually stand to gain only a little from further liberalization, since their own markets are already quite large and open, and since they have already gained preferential access to many markets elsewhere. Therefore, while economic analysis such as that cited by Anderson and Winters can show that liberalization is the right thing to do from the perspective of their own aggregate constituencies, the political resistance by those who stand to lose (the gross economic costs, again) will make this hard to sell.

Rather, what we need are leaders who are willing and able to make the moral case for liberalization as an essential piece of helping the poor in developing countries. The case for free trade to help ourselves is no longer compelling in rich countries, if it ever was, even though in the aggregate it is valid. But the case for free trade to help the poor around the world could, I believe, be made much more convincingly to the public

---

[7] See Evenett (2007).

than it now is.

Globalization has had many effects, some positive and some negative. One that should be taken advantage of is that people today are much more aware than they once were of how others around the world are able to live. Poverty abroad is seen regularly in the media, along with the violence that so often accompanies it. In addition, if alleviating poverty is not a worthy enough goal for its own sake, then the spill of both poverty-induced violence and poverty-induced disease across borders has also become much more visible in recent years. Therefore, the public in the rich world may be better placed than ever before to understand the need to take steps, and even to bear some cost, to solve these problems. If leaders could understand and talk about the importance of trade liberalization for poverty alleviation abroad, then I believe that much of the public in the rich world would be eager to help.

That, of course, is where the Copenhagen Consensus comes in. There are many problems that need to be solved for the good of humanity at large, not for the self-interested benefit of individual countries. Trade liberalization is only one tool for solving these problems, but it is one that has been touted as a tool to benefit ourselves. It is indeed that, in the aggregate. But we may be more successful, as well as more honest, if we sell it as a tool to help others.

Bibliography

Corden, W.M. (1974), *Trade Policy and Economic Welfare*, Oxford: Clarendon Press

Deardorff, A.V. (1987), 'Safeguards Policy and the Conservative Social Welfare Function', in *Protection and Competition in International Trade*, edited by H. Kierzkowski, Oxford: Blackwell, 22–40

Evenett, S.J. (2007), 'The US Exits, the EU Enters: What Prospects for Western FTA Initiatives in the Asia-Pacific?', Working Paper, University of St Gallen and CEPR, October

Gramlich, E.M. (1990), *A Guide to Benefit-Cost Analysis* (second edition), Long Grove IL: Waveland Press

Grossman, G.M. and E. Helpman (1994), 'Protection for Sale', *American Economic Review* 84: 833–50

Hall, R.L. and A.V. Deardorff (2006), 'Lobbying as Legislative Subsidy', *American Political Science Review* 100: 69–84

Viner, J. (1950), *The Customs Union Issue*, New York: Carnegie Endowment for International Peace

Perspective Paper 8.2

ANTHONY J. VENABLES

Introduction

Most people – or most economists at least – will agree that there are enormous potential gains from a better integrated world economy. International wage differentials of 100:1 are not compatible with economic efficiency, let alone equity. Rapidly growing exports have accompanied virtually all successful growth experiences. The analytical arguments for gains (static and dynamic) from trade are well established, and there are many empirical studies supporting the case. But even if we agree with these broad messages, the challenge of quantifying the gains from a change in trade or migration policy is difficult. There is no automatic policy lever that can trigger rapid export expansion, and trade liberalization does not automatically foster growth. The mechanisms linking trade policy instruments to economic outcomes are highly conditional – under one set of other circumstances a trade policy change might have a transformative impact on economic performance, under another set of circumstances the same policy change might have a minimal effect. And just as the benefits of policy reform are hard to predict, so the obstacles to reform are hard to overcome. There are deep and complex reasons why migration and trade liberalizations are hard to implement.

Can the benefits and costs of reducing barriers to trade be quantified? It is certainly worth the effort, but this note argues for caution. Quantification that is too mechanical, that downplays real obstacles to change, that is too speculative (or alternatively offers a spurious degree of precision), may not be a useful approach for promoting economic reform. Asking a series of smaller questions – what reforms are feasible, which are most beneficial, how should they be prioritized – is more insightful than seeking to put a number on a policy change, the outcome of which is conditional on myriad other policy changes.

Reducing Barriers to Trade

The challenge paper covers both international trade and migration and I look first at the arguments to do with trade, and then discuss migration briefly in section 3 of this note. The challenge paper (Anderson and Winters 2008) provides a useful summary of the literature in these areas, and I focus in this note on the quantification exercises that it contains. Each of the main elements of quantification are discussed in turn; the benefits of trade reform; the costs of trade reform; their combination in a present value calculation. The first task is of course to specify the trade policy change being considered. I follow the authors in focusing on the Doha Development Agenda (DDA), although return to discussion of some alternative policy measures in conclusions (section 4).

Conditional Benefits

The authors' approach involves three main steps. The first is to take a standard computable general equilibrium (CGE) model and use this to produce 'central' estimates of the comparative static effects of the DDA. These effects are very small – around 0.2 percent of GDP. The second step is to argue that different specifications both of the model and of the breadth of the policy change being investigated can produce results that vary by a factor of 9:1. They therefore keep the 'central' case as the basis for the reported 'lower net gains' and multiply by 5 to provide the basis for their 'high net gains' case. The third step is to assume that a one-off trade reform also has a long run growth effect, making world economic growth more than 0.5 percent per annum faster than it otherwise would have been in each year out to 2015, with this growth increment tailing off by 2025 in the low gain case or 2050 in the high gain case.

What numbers come out of this analysis? We can get a sense of the order of magnitudes by comparing the present value (at 6 percent discount rate) of the income gains from these alternative cases. For example, in the 'lower net gain case', while the CGE effects are small, adding the growth effects yields a present value of benefits which is around 25 times larger globally and 40 times larger for developing countries, than is the present value of benefits from the CGE alone. For the high net gains case they are multiplied by a further factor of 5. The CGE modelling effects are therefore just a tiny fraction of the aggregate gains presented.

What is good and what is bad about this process? Let us consider each of the steps in turn.

Starting with a CGE model provides a sound and micro-founded basis for analysis. CGE models allow detailed analysis of sectoral impacts of policy change, but their analysis is, at the simplest level, based on all sectors being perfectly competitive and operating under non-increasing returns to scale. Extended versions of such models contain simple forms of increasing returns to scale, often combined with product differentiation, thereby creating additional sources of gains from trade. In these models a policy change typically produces quite small changes in volumes of output in different sectors and countries, and there are real income gains (losses) where volumes increase in activities operating with price greater (less than) marginal cost due to imperfections such as trade barriers. This in turn yields small real income gains – the central case DDA gains of 0.2 percent of world GDP, noted above, with a wide band of variation created by different model specifications.

There is general recognition that CGE models provide a very incomplete picture of the effects of trade. Essentially, they may be good for economies in which there is very little opportunity for productivity improvement, but they provide extremely poor guides to changes in economies (or sectors) where trade can have a 'transformative' and productivity-enhancing effect. There is then a need to take into account the growth effects of trade, as the authors attempt to do. As noted above, the authors make assumptions about growth effects which end up yielding benefits which overwhelm the estimates from the CGE modelling; their dynamic effects are at least 25 times larger than those from the CGE model.

What do we know about the growth effects of trade? While this is not the place to undertake a full review of this hotly contested area of research, certain facts stand out. The first is that there is a strong association between trade and growth. For example, Hausmann, Pritchett and Rodrik (2005) identify 80 growth accelerations, and find that the export to GDP ratio is around 10 percentage points higher at the beginning of an acceleration than previously, and 15 percentage points higher eight years into the acceleration. Jones and Olken (2007) identify 30 'up-breaks' in the growth of 125 countries over 40 years. Up-breaks are strongly associated with increased trade, and during an average up-break the share of exports in GDP increases by 12.2 percentage points. Patillo and Gupta (2005) study 34 sub-Saharan African growth accelerations and find that export growth is around 5–14 percentage points higher during acceleration than otherwise.

Second, the causal relationships underlying this association are not well understood. I doubt that any researcher would make a claim like 'successful completion of the Doha round will cause my country to have a growth and trade acceleration'. It takes complex sets of reforms to bring about sustained growth, and to attribute an acceleration of growth of income or trade to a single policy lever is not correct. Even in the simple world of economic theory, we know that there are threshold effects involved in growing export sectors. Success depends on raising productivity, and there are increasing returns such that small initial differences between countries can translate into large differences in outcomes.

In view of this, how should we assess the authors' approach of assuming that growth is 0.5 percent higher in all countries for some number of years? I think we can say with some confidence that in countries lacking supporting policy measures the growth effect will be smaller. But at the same time, in countries that are enabled to grow new export sectors (such as labor-intensive manufacturing) the growth effects will be many times larger. The point is that when the wider economic environment is appropriate the growth effects of trade liberalization can be hugely larger than those used by the authors, but when the economic environment is not supportive the effects can be absent. This conventional wisdom is summarized by World Bank (2005); '. . . trade protection is not good for economic growth . . .. trade openness by itself is not sufficient for growth. . .'

Is 0.5 percent extra growth for the next several decades a good average across these cases? I don't think that the paper provides evidence for this claim, thus raising serious doubts about the usefulness of the numbers presented. Furthermore, since outcomes are conditional on other policy measures, what policies should the researcher condition on in undertaking this averaging? Trade reform coupled with 'optimal' domestic circumstances and reform may have a transformative effect, bringing about Asian growth rates, but such domestic policies and circumstances, while to some extent endogenous, are not directly controllable.

The difficulty of modelling the dynamic and transformative effects of trade together with the conditional nature of the effects of trade policy, make for a challenging research agenda for trade researchers and for those, such as the Copenhagen consensus, who seek to quantify the relationship between policy actions and outcomes. This is not a call to abandon attempts to quantify the effects of trade reform. But it suggests that it may be better to break investigation up into detailed analyses of what we think actually happens, rather than undertake such highly conditional aggregate calculations.

Complex Costs

The authors attribute two main sources of cost to removing trade barriers. One is the cost of international negotiation, and the other the adjustment costs faced by factors of production that become redundant in one sector and need to relocate to another. The authors admit to the difficulty of this task, and work with estimates based on the adjustment costs of sectoral trade reforms. They place these at 15 percent (high case) or 5 percent (low case) of the comparative static gains, lasting for just eight years.

In my view the political economy of reform raises a wide range of issues that go beyond the simple costs of negotiation and adjustment. To see why, it is worth recalling one of the most basic (and the most widely cited) models of the political economy of reform, due to Fernandez and Rodrik (1991). Following reform, one sector of the economy will expand and its workers will gain. The other sector contracts, and some of its workers will lose (they will find it hard to be re-employed) while others will gain (they are re-employed in the expanding sector). Before the reform, workers in the contracting sector do not know whether they will be re-employed or not, and their expectation (knowing the probabilities of re-employment) is of a loss. It is then easy to find an example in which reform is blocked (e.g., the contracting sector employs more workers than the expanding one), even though there would be aggregate gains from the reform and, *ex post*, a majority of workers would gain. Can the losers be offered compensation, so that their opposition to reform would be bought off? In this example there are enough resources for compensation to be paid and a Pareto improvement to be made, but there is also a fundamental problem. Once the trade reform has happened and some of the workers have been re-employed (and the uncertainty about who is re-employed has been resolved), those remaining in the contracting sector may now be a minority of the population. It will not be in the interest of the majority to pay whatever compensation was previously offered. Whereas the *ex ante* median voter was in the contracting sector, *ex post* the median voter is in the sector that expands. In short, the offer of compensation was incredible – and workers, knowing this, oppose the original reform. Society has no credible way of committing to compensate the losers.

This is just one argument of many that can be made about the political economy of reform, but it illustrates clearly that simply saying compensation is cheap, fails to capture the obstacles to reform. Without suitable commitment mechanisms government may simply find it impossible to implement reform. Any government seeking to implement a reform package will come under pressure from lobby groups, in particular those who see the reform as undermining their influence or their well-being at future stages of the reform process. Political capital has to be expended in a reform process, and we should be asking, what is the opportunity cost of this political capital? If quantification is the imperative, then the authors should be looking at the shadow price of reform and of political capital, not simply assuming that the nominal cost is equal to the full opportunity cost. In short, there are quite deep reasons why reforms have not already been undertaken, and to simply ignore these is not very helpful.

Present Value Calculations

Combining costs and benefits, the authors find that the effect of the DDA is to cause income in 2098 to be around 10 percent greater (in the high case) than it otherwise would have been. The associated net present values range from $50 trillion (low case, 6 percent discount rate) to $424 trillion (high case, 3 percent discount rate), i.e., from somewhat larger than current annual world GDP to approximately ten times current GDP. Global benefit cost ratios range from 269:1 to 1121:1.

Two observations are worth making. One is a reminder that gains grow with GDP, assumed to be growing at least 3.5 percent p.a. Discounting at 3 percent therefore places us in the looking

glass world where gains would be unbounded but for the assumed fixed time horizon, and where postponing reform (and shifting the time horizon accordingly) raises the present value of net benefits. Second, the counterfactual to the policy change being considered is that the DDA, or something like it, will not happen in the next 100 years. Put at its simplest, this says that we are evaluating DDA now or never. I do not find this a very helpful thought experiment. It would be better to allow for a probability that trade reform will occur at some date, perhaps by working with a higher discount rate.

Both these observations point to the fact that it would be much better to express net gains as an annual flow, telling us what we are foregoing because a trade reform has not yet happened, than it is to compute a present value and associated benefit-cost ratio.

International Migration

The migration experiment is probably on more secure ground in its estimate of economic benefits, if not of costs. The experiment is well defined, and draws on a recent World Bank Study (World Bank 2006). 14.2 million additional workers, plus their families, move from developing to high-income countries over a given time period. The gains are estimated at an annual flow of $674 billion, or $48,000 per worker. This is a comparative static gain, essentially coming from the difference in the marginal value product of workers before and after migration. Some fuller discussion of assumptions underlying this figure would have been helpful (what is assumed about cost of living differences, skill levels, training incentives, future convergence or divergence of international wage differences and so on). The estimate nevertheless provides a good reflection of the massive inefficiency burden imposed on the world economy by immobility of labor.

The cost side is vulnerable to criticisms along the same lines as those made above for the authors' handling of trade liberalization. The costs on which the authors focus are simply those of administration, travel, and some labor market adjustment. Once again, this underestimates – or ignores – the social and political economy costs of migration. These may be difficult to quantify, and may be politically sensitive. But to ignore them is surely wrong.

Feasible Reform Alternatives: A Targeted Challenge

I am skeptical about the value of the exercise undertaken in this paper – while at the same time thinking that expanded trade would bring very large gains for many countries, and also believing in the value of quantification.

Advocacy carries several dangers – such as the 'let's use the largest numbers that seem plausible' syndrome. The fact is that the gains from economic growth associated with exporting that have actually occurred in some countries would have seemed, ex ante, to be implausibly large. But, as we have argued, they are conditional gains and have only been achieved after surmounting complex obstacles.

It would be more insightful – and perhaps also more influential – to focus the challenge on particular sets of actions that would enable countries to participate more effectively in the world trading system. A liberal world trading environment is one aspect of this, but so too are measures such as aid for trade, domestic reform agendas, or policies that enable trade reform to move forwards. Regional integration is also important. It is dismissed far too quickly in the present paper, largely on the basis of calculations from CGE models which, according to the authors' own method, are a guide to less than 5 percent of the gains from trade liberalization. The same is true of the treatment of trade preferences for developing countries, where prospects for transformative export growth and associated productivity improvements and changing comparative advantage are simply ignored.

In conclusion, study of a well-defined problem – for example, how to formulate policy and quantify the gains of diversifying Africa's exports – would be a more targeted and useful challenge.

Bibliography

Anderson, K. and L.A. Winters (2008), 'The Challenge of Reducing International Trade and Migration Barriers', processed, University of Adelaide

Fernandez, R. and D. Rodrik (1991), 'Resistance to Reform: Status Quo Bias and the Presence of Individual Specific Uncertainty', *American Economic Review* 81: 1146–55

Hausmann, R., L. Pritchett, and D. Rodrik (2005), 'Growth Accelerations', *Journal of Economic Growth* 10: 303–29

Jones, B. and B. Olken (2007), 'The Anatomy of Start-Stop Growth', *Review of Economics and Statistics* 90(3): 582–7

Patillo, C.A. and S. Gupta (2005), 'Sustaining Growth Accelerations and Pro-Poor Growth in Africa', IMF Working Paper 05/195

World Bank (2005), *Economic Growth in the 1990s: Learning From a Decade of Reforms'*, Washington D.C.

World Bank (2006), *Global Economic Prospects 2006: Economic Implications of Remittances and Migration*, Washington D.C.

Transnational Terrorism

TODD SANDLER, DANIEL G. ARCE AND WALTER ENDERS*

Introduction

Major terrorist campaigns date back to the Jewish Zealots' struggle against the Roman Empire from 48 AD to 70 AD, the Hindu Thugs' brutal attacks against innocent travelers in India from 600 AD to 1836 AD, and the Assassins' actions against the Christian crusaders in the Middle East from 1090 AD to 1956 AD (Bloom, 2005; Rapoport, 1984). In fact, the Thugs may have murdered more than 800 people a year during their twelve-century existence (Hoffman, 2006, 82–83), making them twice as deadly on an annual basis as the modern era of terrorism (1968–2006). Some form of terrorism has characterized civilization for the last 2,000 years. Each of the two recent globalization periods has been associated with transnational terrorism that has international implications. In the earlier era of globalization starting in 1878 and ending in 1914, the anarchists waged a terrorist campaign that culminated in World War I. More recently, leftists and fundamentalists utilized transnational terrorism to capture headlines during the current era of globalization from the last third of the twentieth century to the present day.

During the modern era of transnational terrorism, terrorists crossed borders and, in some instances, staged incidents in foreign capitals to focus world attention on their cause or grievance. Some high-profile attacks – e.g., Black September's abduction of Israeli athletes during

the 1972 Munich Olympics, Hezbollah's suicide bombing of the US Marine barracks in Beirut on 23 October 1983, Hindu extremists' downing of Air India flight 182 on June 23, 1985, the downing of Pan Am flight 103 on 21 December 1988, the truck bombing of the World Trade Center on February 26, 1993, and the near-simultaneous hijackings on 11 September 2001 (henceforth, 9/11) – made the world acutely aware of the potential threats posed by today's resourceful terrorists. The attacks on 9/11 struck at the financial and security symbols of America and, in so doing, highlighted the vulnerability to terrorism of even the most powerful nation on earth. Because it is human nature to overspend on unlikely catastrophic events, it is likely that terrorists have succeeded in getting the world to overspend on counterterrorism, while ignoring much more pressing problems for a world besieged with exigencies involving health, the environment, conflict, and governance. Terrorism is a tactic of asymmetric conflict, deployed by the weak for a strategic advantage against a strong opponent.

Transnational terrorism presents a unique challenge that differs fundamentally from the other global crises studied by the Copenhagen Consensus. First, the number of lives lost or ruined by transnational terrorism is rather minor compared with other challenges considered by the Copenhagen Consensus. On average only 420 people are killed and another 1,249 are injured each year from transnational terrorist attacks. Nevertheless, the public in rich countries views transnational terrorism as one of the greatest threats. This is rather ironic since over 30,000 people die on US highways annually, yet highway safety is not as much of a public concern. Second, protective or defensive counterterrorism measures may merely deflect attacks to softer targets.

* Sandler's research was partially supported by the US Department of Homeland Security (DHS) through the Center for Risk and Economic Analysis of Terrorism Events (CREATE) at the University of Southern California, grant no. 2007-ST-061-000001. However, any opinions, findings, and conclusions or recommendations are solely those of the authors and do not necessarily reflect the views of the DHS.

For example, the installation of metal detectors in airports in January 1973 decreased skyjackings, but increased kidnappings and other hostage missions; the fortifications of US embassies reduced embassy assaults, but increased assassinations of diplomatic officials (Enders and Sandler, 1993, 2006a). Unlike other challenges, countermeasures may have unintended harmful consequences: strong offensive measures against terrorists can lead to backlash attacks as new grievances are created. Third, guarding against transnational terrorism can utilize resources at an alarming rate without greatly reducing the risks. In contrast, terrorists require moderate resources to create great anxiety in a targeted public. Fourth, transnational terrorism poses a real dilemma for liberal democracies: responding too fully compromises democratic principles and gains support for the terrorists, whereas responding too meekly loses constituency support and exposes the government's failure to protect lives and property (Wilkinson, 1986, 2001). Thus, government actions can become the root of future attacks. Fifth, terrorism can assume more deadly forms involving chemical, biological, radiological, and nuclear attacks. The signs of such threats are beginning to emerge (Ivanova and Sandler, 2006, 2007). Sixth, evaluating solutions or actions against terrorism is particularly difficult owing to counterfactuals – e.g., the incidence of terrorism without these actions – that are hard to identify. Typically, only the benefit or cost side of a solution is readily known.

Basic Messages

This chapter has a number of basic messages that are troublesome and, perhaps, surprising. Unlike many challenges, there is no solution to transnational terrorism because it is a cost-effective tactic of the weak against a more formidable opponent. Very cheap terrorist attacks can create significant anxiety – the material cost of a suicide attack may be as little as $150 and on average kills twelve people (Hoffman, 2006; Pape, 2006). Some rogue nations utilize terrorism as an inexpensive means to destabilize or harm other nations. Even effective antiterrorism campaigns will temporarily work only until the terrorists either find new leaders or sources of resources. Even if a terrorist group is annihilated, a new group may surface for some other cause. Thus, terrorism can be put into remission but it cannot be eliminated. Granting terrorist concessions will signal to future terrorists that terrorism pays, so that compromise may fuel future terrorist campaigns (Sandler and Arce, 2003).

Three of the five "solutions" proposed here – business as usual, increased proactive responses, and enhanced defensive measures – have very adverse benefit–cost ratios (BCRs) under a wide range of scenarios, *even when the most promising assumptions are invoked*. The most effective solutions are the cheapest, but they must overcome the greatest obstacles that require either greater international cooperation or more sensitive and farsighted policymaking. Such qualities seldom characterize rich countries' actions. When it comes to security, nations are especially loath to sacrifice much autonomy. The BCRs associated with some of our solutions are driven by two primary considerations: the costs of counterterrorism and the losses in the gross domestic product (GDP) in countries experiencing terrorist attacks. Estimates of both of these factors are in the billions of US dollars. Unlike many challenges, lives lost and damaged by transnational terrorism – though tragic – are relatively modest in number. Thus, our Disability-Adjusted Life Years (DALYs) values for annual terrorism-related deaths and injuries under various solutions are in the millions of US dollars. As a consequence, expenditures on counterterrorism on the cost side and saved GDP on the benefit side become the essential determinants of the BCRs of some solutions.

Both of these determinants are exceedingly difficult to calculate. Most countries do not publish counterterrorism spending, because this information may be of strategic value to the terrorists – the United States is an exception. Moreover, relevant expenditures may be in myriad places in a government's budget and difficult to allocate to antiterrorism per se. We must, therefore, devise a means to estimate these expenditures based on what is observable. Because the application of analytical techniques to the study of terrorism is still in its infancy, there are only a few studies that have tried to estimate GDP consequences of terrorism (Blomberg, Hess, and Orphanides, 2004; Gaibulloev and Sandler, 2008; Tavares, 2004). The Blomberg, Hess, and Orphanides (2004) and Tavares (2004) study allows us to estimate the consequences of transnational terrorism on reduced per capita GDP growth, which can then be translated into GDP losses. Although today's terrorists are bent on causing great economic harm, the past influence of transnational terrorist attacks on economic growth has been fortunately small. While this may not be true of a terrorism-ridden region (the Basque Country in Spain) or a small country (Israel) experiencing a sustained campaign (Abadie and Gardeazabal, 2003; Eckstein and Tsiddon, 2004), it is generally true of most diversified countries where economic activities from terrorism-prone sectors shift to more secure sectors (Sandler and Enders, 2008). Given this limited influence of terrorism on GDP, homeland security costs of some solutions swamp GDP savings from fewer attacks, thus resulting in adverse BCRs. We demonstrate that the "war on terror" following 9/11 did reduce transnational terrorism during the ensuing two years as the al-Qaida network was greatly stressed; nevertheless, the associated BCR is much less than one.

A study like this one requires many heroic assumptions that obviously affect the BCRs attached to the solutions. At every decision juncture when estimating the benefits and costs for our enhanced security solutions, we chose calculation methods that placed greater weights to benefits and smaller weights to costs so as to keep the BCRs as high as possible. This practice makes our adverse BCRs for the three security solutions robust to alternative assumptions. Even the use of value of life calculations, which are more in keeping with rich countries' practices, does not alter our qualitative conclusions.

Primer

Terrorism is the premeditated use or threat to use violence by individuals or subnational groups

against noncombatants in order to obtain a political or social objective through the intimidation of a large audience beyond that of the immediate victim. Two essential constituents of the definition are violence and the presence of a political or social motive. Violent acts for extortion purposes are crimes but are not terrorism. Similarly, violence for revenge or sociopathic reasons, such as the shootings at Columbine High School or Virginia Tech, are crimes that create much fear and anguish, but are not terrorism since there is no political motive. Without violence or its threat, terrorists cannot induce a political decision maker to respond to their demands. Even with the violence, concessions are often not granted. Terrorists broaden their audience beyond their immediate victims by making their attacks appear to be random, so that everyone feels at risk. Unlike some criminal acts in large cities, terrorist incidents are not random but well-planned and often well-executed attacks, where terrorists weigh carefully the risks, costs, and payoffs.

Terrorism definitions contain at least three other key ingredients: the victim, the perpetrator, and the audience. The identity of the victims is the most controversial. Some definitions require the victim to be a noncombatant, so that an attack against a soldier of an occupying force is not considered to be terrorism even when the attackers are asking for political change – e.g., the pullout of occupying forces. However, the US Department of Defense's definition of terrorism drops the noncombatant distinction. Virtually all definitions consider politically motivated attacks against civilians as terrorism. The data set International Terrorism: Attributes of Terrorist Event (ITERATE) includes terrorist actions against peacekeepers, but not against an occupying army, as acts of terrorism (Mickolus et al., 2006).[1] Though less controversial, the identity of the perpetrator also presents difficulty. Most definitions exclude state terror where a state or government uses terror tactics against its own citizens (e.g., China's actions during the Cultural Revolution). Our definition follows this practice by characterizing the perpetrators as individuals or subnational groups but

[1] On ITERATE, see Mickolus (1980, 1982) and Mickolus, Sandler, and Murdock (1989).

not the state itself. States can, however, sponsor terrorists through funding, training, intelligence, equipment, safe haven, freedom from prosecution, or other means (Mickolus, 1989). State-assisted terrorism is known as state-sponsored terrorism and is included in ITERATE. The downing of Pan Am flight 103 is considered to have been state sponsored by Libya, since a Libyan intelligence agent was found guilty of the attack. Evidence gathered following the La Belle discotheque bombing in West Berlin on 4 April 1986 pointed to Libyan sponsorship. In reaction, the United States launched a retaliatory raid on Libya on 15 April 1986. The US Department of State (2003) included Cuba, Iran, Iraq, Libya, North Korea, Sudan, and Syria on a list of state sponsors of terrorism. More recently, Iraq and Libya have been removed from the list (US Department of State, 2007). Finally, the audience refers to the target group that the terrorist campaign is meant to intimidate. The 9/11 attacks were intended to cause anxiety in the flying public and people who work in large cities. Thus, the audience extended beyond those killed and injured on 9/11. In many ways, 9/11 had a global audience.

Terrorists desire the widest possible audience so that their demands and horrific events become known. Their campaign seeks to circumvent the normal political process through threats and violence. By intimidating a target population, terrorists want this audience to feel sufficiently vulnerable to apply pressure on decision makers to give into terrorist demands. Political decision makers must weigh the anticipated costs of conceding, including possible countergrievances from other interests, against the expected costs of future attacks. When the consequences of future incidents outweigh the costs of concessions, the government may grant the terrorist demands. Traditionally, terrorists pose a greater problem for liberal democracies than for autocracies (Eubank and Weinberg, 1994, 2001; Weinberg and Eubank, 1998). This follows because liberal democracies must be restrained in their reaction, while autocracies can be unrestrained. Many characteristics of liberal democracies – freedom of association, rights of the accused, freedom of

movement, funding opportunities, periodic elections, and information availability – provide the perfect environment for terrorists to plan and execute their actions. Most important, liberal democracies have press freedoms that allow terrorists to seek the media attention that they crave. Eubank and Weinberg (1994) showed that incipient democracies, as in some developing countries, are especially prone to terrorist events.

Domestic Versus Transnational Terrorism

Another crucial distinction is between domestic and transnational terrorism. Domestic terrorism is homegrown and has consequences for just the host country, its institutions, citizens, property, and policies. In a domestic incident, the perpetrators, victims, and audience are all from the host country. Moreover, there is no foreign sponsorship or involvement in a domestic terrorist event. Timothy McVeigh's bombing of the Alfred P. Murrah Building in Oklahoma City in April 1995 was the deadliest domestic terrorist event in US history. Civil wars are often associated with domestic terrorism that an insurgency can direct at the ruling government or general population. The government may respond with state terror (e.g., death squads) against a population of potential supporters of the insurgency.

Targeted liberal democracies have frequently employed the right balance of defensive and proactive policies against *domestic* terrorist threats. In Italy, the Red Brigades were brought to justice; in France, Action Direct members were captured; in Belgium, Combatant Communist Cells members were also apprehended. Although these groups engaged in some transnational terrorist attacks, their biggest threat was to the host country. When confronted with domestic terrorism, a country cannot sit back and hope that another country will dispose of the threat, since no other country is at risk. A targeted country has no choice but to confront the threat with appropriate counterterrorism measures.

Transnational terrorism involves incidents where the perpetrators, victims, or audience are from two or more countries. If an incident begins

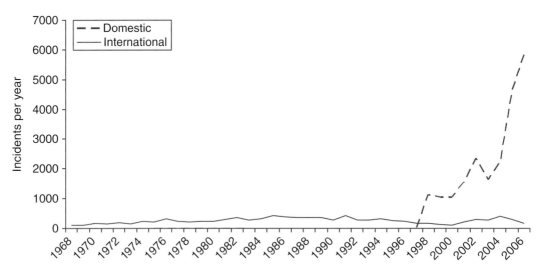

Figure 9.1 *Domestic and transnational incidents*

in one country but terminates in another, then the incident is a transnational terrorist event, as in the case of a midair hijacking of a plane that leaves Athens bound for Cairo and is made to fly to Algiers. The kidnappings of foreign workers in Iraq in 2004 were transnational terrorist events. The toppling of the World Trade Center towers on 9/11 was a transnational terrorist incident because the victims were from ninety different countries, the mission had been planned and financed abroad, the terrorists were foreigners, and the targeted audience was global. An attack against a multilateral organization is a transnational terrorist incident owing to its multi-country impact and victims, as in the case of the suicide car bombing of the UN headquarters in Baghdad on 19 August 2003. The Popular Front for the Liberation of Palestine (PFLP) seizure of eleven Organization of Petroleum Exporting Countries (OPEC) ministers in Vienna on 21 December 1975 is another instance of transnational terrorism. Most terrorist events directed against the United States and its people and property do not occur on US soil and, hence, are transnational terrorist events. In fact, 40 percent of all transnational terrorism is directed at US interests (Enders and Sandler, 2006a).

Based on data from the (National) Memorial Institute for the Prevention of Terrorism (MIPT)

(2006), Figure 9.1 displays annual amounts of domestic and transnational terrorism. The domestic terrorism time series starts in 1998 because MIPT began gathering statistics on such incidents only at that time. The rise in domestic terrorist events is due, in part, to MIPT's augmented capability over time in collecting the data. Domestic terrorism is much more prevalent than transnational terrorism; nevertheless, we focus on transnational terrorism as the challenge since we are interested in putting this transfrontier problem into perspective with respect to the other transfrontier challenges studied by the Copenhagen Consensus. Moreover, the civil war chapter indirectly includes the consequences of domestic terrorism in its casualty and economic consequences. Transnational terrorism is a global concern because grievances or issues in one country can cause a terrorist attack in another country as the perpetrators seek the maximum media coverage. As rich countries institute tighter security measures at home, this action can alter the geographical distribution of these events so that prime-target countries' assets are hit at softer foreign venues (Enders and Sandler, 2006b).

Terrorism must also be distinguished from some related concepts, such as war, guerrilla warfare, and insurgencies. War is generally more discriminating than terrorism in its targeting. In a war, civilians are typically not taken hostage or targeted.[2] War also abides by certain conventions with respect to the treatment of prisoners and the observance of diplomatic immunity (Hoffman, 2006). In contrast, terrorists make their own rules and go after civilians because they are easy targets that create maximum anxiety for the population. War is on a much grander scale than terrorism and involves much greater casualties and damages. In many wars, especially guerrilla wars, terrorism is one tactic of many that is deployed by adversaries to weaken the enemy. Guerrilla warfare involves large paramilitary groups that control territory from which to launch attacks against targets that often include the host country's military. In Colombia, Fuerza Armadas Revolucionarias de Colombia (FARC) is a paramilitary force that numbers in the thousands and employs terrorism and other methods (e.g., armed attacks) in its confrontation with the government. Although FARC has conducted some transnational terrorist attacks in Colombia on foreign interests, FARC relies on domestic terrorism and other operations. Finally, an insurgency intends to overthrow a government through the use of irregular military operations that may include terrorism (Hoffman, 2006). Insurgencies are used against occupying forces and unpopular governments. As a winning strategy, insurgencies try to gain popular support through propaganda aimed at exposing the alleged injustices of the government. Civil wars are often associated with insurgencies and guerrilla warfare.

On Terrorist Rationality

From an economist's viewpoint, rationality is not determined on the basis of the desirability of an agent's objective or tactics. We consider terrorists to be rational actors who respond in an appropriate and predictable fashion to changes in their constraints as they optimize their objective while confronting an adversary who is trying to outwit and defeat them. Consequently, we must anticipate that terrorists will try to minimize the impact of counterterrorism actions of the government. Thus, actions by govern-

ments to protect their officials shift attacks to business people and others – tourists and ordinary citizens – as the terrorists account for the augmented security afforded to officials. Such reactions underscore terrorist rationality. As shown below, terrorists are more adept at making collective decisions than targeted governments, which often work at cross-purposes with one another (Enders and Sandler, 2006a; Sandler, 2005). For the analysis of this challenge, terrorist rationality and anticipated reactions are crucial in evaluating the stream of benefits and costs associated with the solutions later offered to this challenge.

Causes of Transnational Terrorism

Terrorism can stem from various causes that include ethno-nationalism, separatism, social injustice, nihilism, single issues (e.g., animal rights), fundamentalist beliefs, religious freedom, anticapitalism, and leftist ideology. Often, terrorist campaigns, fueled by ethno-nationalism or separatism, are domestic in orientation as attacks are directed at weakening the government or at forcing it to overreact so as to lose popular support. David Rapoport (2004) characterizes four waves of terrorism since the late 1870s. The first wave involved the anarchists, whose campaign had a strong transnational orientation as they tried to internationalize their struggle by exporting it to other countries including the labor movement in the United States. During the second wave, the anticolonialists were active in gaining independence during the 1950s and 1960s – e.g., Algeria and Cyprus. Some of these anticolonial campaigns had transnational implications through the use of the foreign press to make their grievances known more broadly. The left-wing terrorists were the dominant influence during the third wave from the late 1960s. This wave marked the emergence of modern transnational terrorism

---

[2] The bombing of London, Tokyo, and Dresden in World War II are clear exceptions to the general rule since civilians were the target in these attacks. Other exceptions include the US atomic bombs dropped on Hiroshima and Nagasaki.

Table 9.1. Leftist terrorists versus fundamentalist terrorists

Left-wing terrorists	Fundamentalists
• Secular, speaks for group	• Religious, speaks for God
• Selective targets, minimal collateral damage	• General targets, maximal collateral damage
• Often give advanced warning of bombings	• Any advanced warning is of a generalized threat
• No use of suicide bombing	• Some use of suicide bombings
• Interested in a constituency	• Less interested in a constituency
• Rely on bank robberies, kidnappings, and assassinations	• Rely on bombings, armed attacks, and kidnappings
• No interest in using chemical, biological, radiological, or nuclear attacks	• Interest in using chemical, biological, radiological, or nuclear attacks
• The attack must further its goal	The attack may be warranted if it kills nonbelievers

as terrorists routinely took their attacks to foreign airports and capitals to get noticed. This was particularly true of the left-wing Palestine Liberation Organization (PLO) and its offshoots such as the PFLP that sought an independent Palestinian state. To get the attention of Israel and its supporters, Palestinian terrorist groups staged some spectacular incidents abroad. Within Europe, leftist terrorist groups attacked symbols of capitalism and imperialism, which at times included foreign corporations, foreign military personnel, and multilateral organizations. The fourth, and current, wave consists of fundamentalist terrorism, which began with the Soviet invasion of Afghanistan and the Iranian students' takeover of the US embassy in Tehran in November 1979.[3] Currently, half of the active transnational terrorist groups are fundamentalist in orientation (Hoffman, 2006). Elements of past waves remain as a new wave ensues. Although the fundamentalists are the main influence today, representative groups from the first three waves – especially, the leftists – are present (Hoffman, 2006). Today's leftists carry on antiglobalization campaigns that attack multilateral and capitalist institutions.

Fundamentalist terrorism has foundations in all of the major religions – for example, Hindu extremists brought down Air India flight 182 on 23 June 1985, and a Jewish extremist assassinated Israeli Prime Minister Yitzhak Rabin.

[3] In a statistical analysis, Enders and Sandler (2000) trace the start of fundamentalist terrorism to the fourth quarter of 1979 when these two events took place.

Nevertheless, Islamic fundamentalists are by far the main influence on transnational terrorism today. Their demands range from an Islamic fundamentalist state to the United States leaving the Gulf States. In other instances, Islamic fundamentalists call for the destruction of Israel. An al-Qaida loosely affiliated network includes groups such as al-Qaida Iraq, Abu Sayyaf, Jemaah Islamiyah, al Jihad (Egyptian Islamic Jihad), al-Qaida Saudi Arabia, and others in many countries such as Tunisia, Pakistan, Jordan, Egypt, Indonesia, Kuwait, the Philippines, Yemen, Kenya, and Saudi Arabia (Hoffman, 2003; US Department of State, 2003).

Table 9.1 indicates some primary contrasts between the two main terrorist influences today. Obviously, the fundamentalists present the much greater threat as they target more indiscriminately and consider nonbelievers, even women and children, as legitimate targets. Indeed, even the unintentional death of Muslim bystanders can be tolerated (Wright, 2006, 174–175). The attacks on 9/11 demonstrate that some of these groups will go to extreme measures to maximize carnage. Those attacks are estimated to have caused $80–90 billion in costs (Kunreuther, Michel-Kerjan, and Porter, 2003). Faced with such destructive attacks and the desire of al-Qaida to employ chemical, biological, radiological, and nuclear attacks (Hoffman, 2006), the huge increases in homeland security expenditures following 9/11 may be easily understood from the viewpoint of a prime-target nation such as the United States. Moreover, Scheuer (2006, 20–21) contends that al-Qaida is unique because it poses a direct national security threat to America, has more growth potential, and is more religiously motivated than any other organization associated with the current wave of terrorism. The contrasts in Table 9.1 underscore that the fundamentalists are bent on killing people and can be anticipated to escalate the carnage by employing ever more deadly means of attacks. Their use of suicide bombing has proven deadly – twelve times more deadly than conventional terrorism (Pape, 2006).

In contrast to left-wing terrorists, Michael Scheuer (2006, 5) states that "the United States and the West have little useful context in which to try to understand Osama bin Laden." Scheuer blames the rise of fundamentalist terrorism on failed US foreign policy, including the stationing of troops in Saudi Arabia, economic sanctions against Iraq, and other actions in the Middle East and the Muslim world. Scheuer and others (see, e.g., Bloom, 2005) argue that the Islamic world hates US foreign policy (e.g., support of the Muslim world's absolutist kings and denial of Palestinian human rights). Bin Laden is able to tap into this hatred in his fatwa and call to arms. Scheuer's message is that the United States and its allies can do much to defuse the terrorism threat by applying a different mindset to its policy that impacts Islamic countries so as to minimize the humiliation that some of their citizens feel. For starters, the United States must realize that ideas and values must be exploited to US advantage to stem the current wave of fundamentalist terrorism. Western values do not apply universally and may import poorly to countries with little experience of democracy. In addition, the war on terror must eschew overly harsh proactive measures, such as the excesses of Abu Ghraib Prison, which initiated a kidnapping campaign against foreigners in Iraq (Brandt and Sandler, 2009). Detentions without trials in Guantánamo Bay tarnish the principles of American liberty and justice, and create new grievances that can result in future terrorist attacks. This is a lesson that should have been learned from the French experience in Algeria and Indochina.

Statistical Overview

We now present a brief statistical overview of terrorism drawing data from ITERATE, MIPT, and the now defunct US Department of State (1989–2004) *Patterns of Global Terrorism.*[4] The available data are events data that are coded from media accounts of terrorist events. For example, ITERATE relies on a host of sources for its information, including the Associated Press, United Press International, Reuters tickers, the Foreign Broadcast Information Services (FBIS) *Daily Reports*, and major US newspapers. Mickolus (1982) first developed ITERATE for the period running from 1968 through 1977. The data set now covers 1968–2005 (Mickolus *et al.*, 2006). Coders use the descriptions of the various terrorist events to construct time-series data for forty key variables common to all transnational terrorist incidents. Coding consistency for the data is achieved by applying identical criteria and maintaining continuity among coders through the use of overlapping coders and monitors. ITERATE excludes guerrilla attacks on military targets of an occupying force and all terrorist incidents associated with wars or major military interventions. MIPT also uses these conventions and is jointly gathered by RAND and researchers at St. Andrews University, Scotland. US Department of State data also apply a nearly identical operational definition for transnational terrorism.

In Table 9.2, the number of transnational terrorist incidents per year is listed for 1968 through 2006, complete with the number of deaths and injuries. The primary source of this data is the US Department of State (various years), with figures for 2004–2006 coming from MIPT (2006). There are some things to note about the data – e.g., on average only 420 persons are

[4] The US Department of State's *Patterns of Global Terrorism* was replaced by annual reports on terrorism by the National Counterterrorism Center (NCTC), which does not distinguish between domestic and transnational incidents. Moreover, it includes insurgent attacks against an occupying military force. Thus, recent NCTC reports give the false impression that transnational terrorism is worsening in terms of the number of events.

Table 9.2. Transnational terrorist incidents: casualties 2006–1968

Year	Number of events	Deaths	Wounded
2006	161	283	423
2005	308	550	864
2004	395	732	2,023
2003	208	625	3,646
2002	202	725	2,013
2001	355	3,296	2,283
2000	426	405	791
1999	395	233	706
1998	274	741	5,952
1997	304	221	693
1996	296	314	2,652
1995	440	163	6,291
1994	322	314	663
1993	431	109	1,393
1992	363	93	636
1991	565	102	233
1990	437	200	675
1989	375	193	397
1988	605	407	1,131
1987	665	612	2,272
1986	612	604	1,717
1985	635	825	1,217
1984	565	312	967
1983	497	637	1,267
1982	487	128	755
1981	489	168	804
1980	499	507	1,062
1979	434	697	542
1978	530	435	629
1977	419	230	404
1976	457	409	806
1975	382	266	516
1974	394	311	879
1973	345	121	199
1972	558	151	390
1971	264	36	225
1970	309	127	209
1969	193	56	190
1968	125	34	207

Sources: Data for 2004–2006 come from Memorial Institute for the Prevention of Terrorism (MIPT) at www.mipt.org; data for 1988–2003 come from US Department of State (various years), *Patterns of Global Terrorism*; data for 1968–1987 come from tables provided to Todd Sandler in 1988 by the US Department of State, Office of the Ambassador at Large for Counterterrorism.

Table 9.3. Domestic terrorist incidents: casualties 2006–1998

Year	Number of events	Deaths	Wounded
2006	5,824	10,969	18,788
2005	4,654	7,641	14,395
2004	2,251	4,334	8,837
2003	1,621	1,876	4,434
2002	2,350	1,793	4,392
2001	1,527	1,387	3,030
2000	1,044	736	2,475
1999	1,047	809	2,413
1998	1,124	1,794	2,851

Source: MIPT.

killed and another 1,249 are injured annually by transnational terrorism. Thus, transnational terrorism is associated with relatively few casualties compared with other challenges studied by the Copenhagen Consensus. Regarding the number of incidents, the peak of transnational terrorism occurred in the 1980s, which was the era of state sponsorship. The number of deaths and injuries varies by year, with some years displaying greater totals. Except for 2001, injuries illustrate more variability than deaths. Enders and Sandler (1995) show that transnational terrorism goes through cycles. The figures in Table 9.2 prove important for our counterfactual exercise, since they will enable us to identify likely influences of increases in either proactive or defensive measures that followed 9/11. The variability in casualty totals is due in part to the presence of large-scale attacks (i.e., "spectaculars") that can greatly affect yearly totals. In 2001, 9/11 had the main influence on deaths, while, in 1998, the simultaneous bombings of the US embassies in Kenya and Tanzania had the primary influence on deaths and injuries. Compared with everyday events such as automobile accidents, transnational terrorism kills and maims relatively few individuals.

In Table 9.3, domestic incidents and their casualty values are indicated for 1998 and beyond. The much higher totals in 2005 and 2006 are due to two factors: the insurgency in Iraq and

Table 9.4. Select spectacular transnational terrorist attacks

Date	Event	Perpetrator	Deaths
22 July 1946	Bombing of local British military headquarters at King David Hotel, Jerusalem	Irgun Zvai Leumi	91
2 Aug 1980	Bombing of Bologna railway station	Armed Revolutionary Nuclei	84
23 Oct 1983	Suicide truck bombing of US Marines' barracks in Beirut	Hezbollah	241
23 June 1985	Downing of Air India Boeing 747, en route from Montreal to London	Sikh extremists	329
21 Dec 1988	Downing of Pan Am flight 103, en route from London to New York	Libyan intelligence agent	270
19 Sept 1989	Downing of Union des Transports (UTA) flight 772, en route from Brazzaville to Paris	Hezbollah	171
12 March 1993	Thirteen bombings in Bombay	Pakistani agents	317
7 Aug 1998	Simultaneous bombings of US embassies in Nairobi, Kenya, and Dar es Salaam, Tanzania	al-Qaida	223
11 Sept 2001	Four suicide hijackings that crashed into the World Trade Center towers, the Pentagon, and a field in rural Pennsylvania	al-Qaida	2,974*
12 Oct 2002	Two bombs outside two Bali nightclubs	Jemaah Islamiyah	202
11 March 2004	Bombing of commuter trains and stations during morning rush hour in Madrid	al-Qaida	190
1 Sept 2004	Barricade hostage seizure of school children and parents in Beslan	Chechen rebels	344

* Not counting the 19 hijackers.
Source: Quillen (2002a, 2002b) and ITERATE.

its many car bombings and MIPT's improved capability in recording these events over time. Domestic events are also tabulated by the National Counterterrorism Center, established after 9/11. Table 9.4 lists some spectacular terrorist events. The date, the event, the perpetrator, and the number of deaths are indicated in the four columns beginning with the Zionist bombing of the King David Hotel, which housed the British military headquarters in Jerusalem. This event was a large factor in the British deciding to give Israel its independence. With the exception of the Beslan school seizure, bombings and the downing of airplanes are the primary spectacular events. Fundamentalist terrorists have figured prominently in the spectaculars, thus concurring with the lessons drawn from Table 9.1. Moreover, Table 9.4 shows that conventional attacks are capable of killing relatively large numbers of people. Nonetheless, with the exception of 9/11, the death tolls tend to be in the hundreds for such large-scale incidents.

To give a fuller picture of transnational terrorism, Figure 9.2 indicates the time series plots of incidents per quarter for bombings and all transnational terrorist incidents, based on ITERATE data for 1968–2005. A number of features are worth highlighting. First, both series display peaks and troughs, indicative of cycles. Some large peaks followed key events such as the peak in the middle of 1986 after the US retaliatory raid on Libya or the peak in early 1991 after the US-led Gulf War. US foreign policy can instigate waves of terrorist attacks. Second, bombings are the favorite tactic of terrorists, accounting for about half of all attacks. The bombing series imparts its general shape to the all-incident series. Third, from the early 1990s to about 2002, there is a downward trend to both series owing to less state sponsorship during the post-Cold War era (Enders and Sandler, 2000, 2002; Hoffman, 1998). The fall of the communist regimes also meant that left-wing ideology lost some of its appeal to potential terrorists and their

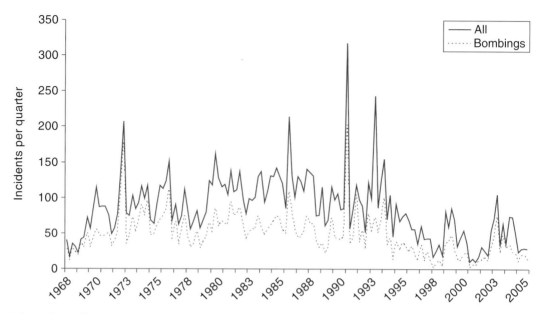

Figure 9.2 *All incidents and bombings*

supporters. Fourth, there has been some upward drift in attacks in the last couple of years, following a lull after the war on terror began. Figure 9.3 displays the proportion of transnational terrorist incidents with casualties – i.e., attacks with a death or an injury – on a quarterly basis. This time series also displays peaks and troughs. The key feature is the clear upward drift from the early 1990s – the time at which fundamentalist terrorists became the dominant force. As Table 9.1 implies, the rise of fundamentalist terrorists resulted in more carnage, which came at a time when transnational terrorist attacks were fewer in numbers. This increase in lethality of transnational terrorism is what worries the world, particularly prime-target rich nations. The use of domestic terrorism in large-scale car bombings in the emerging civil war in Iraq also feeds this anxiety as some countries fear that such attacks may be eventually employed in transnational terrorist incidents in major capitals.

Economic Consequences of Terrorism

Terrorists are intent on causing economic hardship in targeted economies. Terrorism can impose costs on a targeted country through a number of avenues. Terrorist incidents have economic consequences by diverting foreign direct investment (FDI), redirecting public and private funds to security, or limiting international trade. If a developing country loses sufficient FDI – an important source of savings – from terrorism, then it may experience reduced economic growth. Just as capital may take flight from a country plagued by a civil war (see Collier *et al.*, 2003), a sufficiently intense terrorist campaign may greatly reduce capital inflows (Abadie and Gardeazabal, 2008; Blomberg and Mody, 2005; Enders and Sandler, 1996; Enders, Sachsida, and Sandler, 2006). In some instances, terrorism may impact specific industries as 9/11 did on airlines and tourism (Drakos, 2004; Enders, Sandler, and Parise, 1992; Ito and Lee, 2005). Other growth-reducing impacts from terrorism can come from investment being redirected to government expenditure in terms of homeland security (Blomberg, Hess, and Orphanides, 2004). In general, transnational terrorism increases the costs of doing business in a country and this can have economic ramifications.

Although the study of the economic conse-

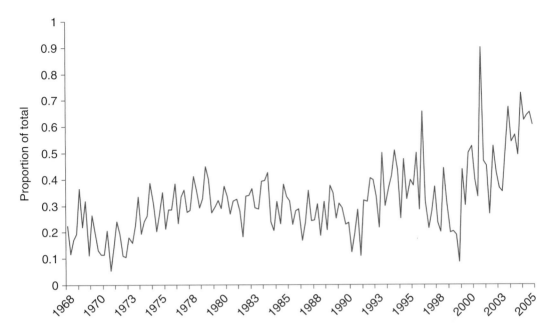

Figure 9.3 *Proportion of casualty incidents*

quences of terrorism is not well-researched, some general principles are emerging from recent studies.[5] Given the low intensity of most transnational terrorist campaigns in a given country, the macroeconomic consequences of terrorism are generally modest and short-lived. Transnational terrorism is not on par with civil or guerrilla wars and, in general, has fairly localized economic effects. The likely candidate countries for discernible GDP losses are either developing or small countries that experience a protracted terrorist campaign. A spectacular attack like 9/11 can affect GDP in any country. Generally, rich diversified economies are able to endure terrorism with limited GDP influences because activities will shift to less risky sectors. Moreover, rich countries can apply monetary and fiscal policies to ameliorate the impact. Such countries can regain citizens' confidence by augmenting homeland security, which has some GDP implications. Most of the impact of transnational terrorism will be to specific sectors that confront enhanced terrorism risks. Surprisingly, most large-scale terrorist incidents have had little effect on stock markets. The noteworthy exception is 9/11 where

stock market took 30–40 days to recover from the initial and large sell-off (Chen and Siems, 2004).

Why Is Transnational Terrorism So Difficult to Eradicate?

Transnational terrorism is so difficult to eradicate because it is so cheap and effective in capturing the world's attention. In essence, terrorists require minimal resources to mount attacks. A terrorist group can, at times, be annihilated, but new groups will surface, lured by the power of taking actions against a much more formidable enemy. Moreover, actions to kill a group's leaders may result in more ruthless leaders replacing them, as the Israelis discovered with respect to Black September and Hamas. In Table 9.5, the size of some of the primary terrorist groups is listed, based on figures from the US Department of State (2003). A couple of observations are noteworthy. Despite its huge expenditures on intelligence, governments are ill-informed about

[5] This paragraph draws from Sandler and Enders (2008).

Table 9.5. Select terrorist groups' sizes (April 2003)

Group	Estimated number of operatives
Abu Sayyaf	200–500
al-Jihad	unknown – 100s
al-Qaida	unknown – 1000s
Armed Islamic Group (GIA)	<100
Euzkadi ta Askatasuna (ETA)	unknown – 100s
Fuerza Armadas Revolucionarias de Colombia (FARC)	9,000– 12,000
Hezbollah	unknown – 100s
Jemaah Islamiyah	unknown – 100s
Mujahedin-e Khalq Organization	1000s
Palestine Islamic Jihad	unknown
Palestine Liberation Front (PLO)	unknown
Popular Front for the Liberation of Palestine (PFLP)	unknown
Popular Front for the Liberation of Palestine – General Command	100s

Source: US Department of State (2003)

the strength of terrorists. In April 2001, the US Department of State (2001, 69) estimated al-Qaida numbers as "several hundreds to several thousands" – far below subsequent estimates following the US-led invasion of the Taliban in Afghanistan on 7 October 2001. Although some countries' armies number in the hundreds of thousands, most terrorist groups are small and number in the hundreds. An insurgent group, such as FARC, numbers in the thousands, but this is very unusual.

The operational budget of al-Qaida was put at $30 million prior to 9/11 (National Commission on Terrorist Attacks upon the United States, henceforth 9/11 Commission, 2004, 170) with much of the money going into training camps and infrastructure. Generally, terrorist attacks are inexpensive and create

[6] This terminology is from Shubik, Zelinsky, and Krstic (2006).

much more damage to the targeted society than they cost. In Table 9.6, we present the damage inflicted compared to the material costs of operation for seven major terrorist attacks. The right-hand column gives the "damage exchange ratio,"[6] which indicates the payback per dollar of operation. These ratios range from 3,200:1 (African embassies bombings) to 1,270,000:1 (London transportation bombing), thus showing that some terrorist incidents have an amazing payback in damages relative to the costs of the operation. Of course, such ratios only include the variable costs of the action and do not put a value on the lives of any terrorists killed. Even if fixed costs are proportioned to an operation and the terrorists' lives are valued, the damage exchange ratios are still huge. In a recent study, Enders, Sachsida, and Sandler (2006) show that on average each US-directed transnational terrorist incident in OECD countries reduced US foreign direct investment stock in the targeted country by $1 million, yet cost very little to execute.

Given the small costs of such operations, targeted countries have a difficult time in doing away with transnational terrorism, because terrorists need to shift very little money to fund a particular operation. Thus, terrorists can transfer their money in small transactions – less than $5,000 – because only transfers above this ceiling must be reported under current guidelines. In addition, terrorists can use the *hawala* system of informal cash transfers, where bookkeeping balances are held and settled among a network of balance holders at a later time through a wire transfer or an exchange of commodities. Terrorists have engineered means – e.g., trade in precious commodities – to transfer funds following efforts after 9/11 to limit the funding of missions. Transnational terrorism is virtually impossible to eradicate because terrorists need minimal resources and little manpower to set up shop.

Asymmetries between Terrorists and Targeted Governments

There are many asymmetries between transnational terrorists and their targeted governments

Table 9.6. Asymmetry of damages versus costs of terrorist operations

Terrorist incident	Damages inflicted	Costs of operation	Damage exchange ratio
World Trade Center bombing, 1993[1]	$500,000,000	<$2,000	250,000:1
African Embassy bombings, 1998	$161,000,000	<$50,000	3,200:1
USS *Cole* suicide bombing, 2000	$240,000,000	$50,000[3]	4,800:1
9/11 hijackings, 2001	$85,000,000,000[2]	$400,000[3]	212,500:1
Bali nightclub bombings, 2002	$3,000,000,000	$35,000[3]	85,714:1
Madrid train bombings, 2004	$269,000,000	$10,000	26,900:1
London transport bombings, 2005	$2,540,000,000	$2,000	1,270,000:1

[1] Mickolus and Simmons (1997).
[2] We took the average of the $80–90 billion figure given by Kunreuther, Michel-Kerjan, and Porter (2003).
[3] Cronin (2006).
Source: Shubik, Zelinsky, and Krstic (2006), unless otherwise indicated.

that, unfortunately, work to the terrorists' advantage. Perhaps the most essential asymmetry involves how the terrorists are able to cooperate, thereby solving their collective action problem, while governments are less able to cooperate. Dating back to the late 1960s, transnational terrorist groups have collaborated in loose networks (Hoffman, 1998). Terrorist cooperation assumes many forms, including training, intelligence, safe haven, financial support, logistical assistance, weapon acquisition, and exchange of personnel (Alexander and Pluchinsky, 1992). By contrast, governments place a huge value on their autonomy over security matters and this limits their cooperation, except following an exigency such as 9/11. What other factors explain this difference in achieving collective action by terrorists and targeted governments? Sandler (2005) attributes this difference to three asymmetries. First, governments' strength provides a false sense of security, thereby blindsiding them to their need for cooperation to be more effective against the transnational terrorist threat. By contrast, terrorists' relative weakness, compared with the formidable governments that they attack, means that terrorists must pool resources to augment their modest arsenals. Second, governments often do not agree on which groups are terrorists – e.g., until recently, the European Union (EU) did not view Hamas as terrorists. Despite different agendas, supporters, and goals, many groups agree on similar

opponents – the United States and Israel. The Palestinian terrorists and European left-wing terrorists shared similar ideologies and enemies. Third, governments and terrorists make decisions with different time horizons. In liberal democracies, government officials display interests that only extend to the next election period unless they are certain of re-election. Because governments turn over, past agreements to combat terrorism may not be honored by new leaders, thus limiting the anticipated gains from such agreements. For example, in reaction to the 3/11 Madrid train bombings, Spanish Prime Minister Zapatero withdrew his country's strong support of Bush's war on terror following Zapatero's win in the 2004 national elections. Government officials tend to show little patience when making counterterrorism policies – i.e., they display a high discount rate. Terrorist leaders demonstrate much greater patience because they are usually tenured for life, so they view intergroup cooperative arrangements as continual. As such, terrorists place more weight on future benefits than targeted governments. Terrorist groups know that reneging on pledged cooperation with another group will not only lead to retribution with that group withholding support in the future, but it also tarnishes the group's reputation, thus jeopardizing its ability to cooperate with other groups.

Through successful collective action, terrorists gain an advantage over governments. With

Table 9.7. Asymmetries between targeted governments and terrorists

Targeted governments	Terrorists
• Target rich	• Target poor
• Strong relative to adversary	• Weak relative to adversary
• Take a short-term viewpoint when interacting with other governments	• Take a long-term viewpoint when interacting with other terrorist groups
• Do not agree on common enemies	• Agree on common enemies
• Do not address their collective action concerns	• Address their collective action concerns
• Restrained in their response, except to large-scale attacks such as 9/11	• Can be restrained or unrestrained in their response, depending on group
• Hierarchical organization	• Nonhierarchical organization
• Not well informed about terrorists' strength	• Reasonably well informed about government's strength
• First-mover disadvantage	• Second-mover advantage
• Impatience	• Patience

Source: Modification of Enders and Sandler (2006a, Table 6.1).

the formation of global networks, terrorists can identify and exploit softer targets wherever they appear. Given the smaller cooperation among governments, softer targets or weak links are ever present for terrorists to exploit. Moreover, terrorists can dispatch their best-equipped cell to the most opportune target.

Other asymmetries work to the terrorists' advantage. Liberal democracies present terrorists with target-rich environments. In contrast, terrorists take a low profile and hide among the general population, thus they offer a target-poor environment to the government. Governments have to protect everywhere, while terrorists can focus on vulnerable targets. Another asymmetry involves the adversaries' responses: liberal democracies must typically be restrained in their response, while terrorists – especially, fundamentalists – can be unrestrained. A targeted government can be less restrained when faced with an incident such as 9/11 where thousands die. Governments utilize a hierarchical structure, while terrorists employ a nonhierarchical structure. Enders and Su (2007) show that rational terrorist groups will select a loosely linked cell structure so that infiltrating one cell may yield little useful intelligence on the organization. While a cellular structure limits terrorist groups' vulnerability, it also inhibits their ability to acquire chemical,

biological, radiological, and nuclear substances. Governments are not well-informed about terrorist groups' strength as Table 9.5 illustrated, while terrorists are reasonably knowledgeable about the government's strength as some parts of a government budgets are often a matter of public record. Terrorists have a second-mover advantage, while the governments have a first-mover disadvantage, because terrorists can observe how governments harden potential targets and then attack accordingly. This was true of 9/11 where Logan, Newark, and Dulles airports were viewed as poorly screened. In Table 9.7, crucial asymmetries are summarized. These asymmetries give terrorists an advantage that makes eradicating terrorism very difficult.

Other Considerations

There are numerous factors other than asymmetries that make it difficult to either eradicate transnational terrorism or address it effectively. For instance, "weakest-link" countermeasures represent major impediments to international cooperation when target nations differ greatly by income. Counterterrorism policies abide by the weakest link when the overall level of security attained depends on the smallest effort expended by targeted countries. Consider actions to eliminate a transnational terrorist group's safe haven, where it trains, plans missions, recruits operatives, and dispatches teams. If all but a single country denies terrorists a safe haven on their soil, the one holdout undercuts the efforts of the others. For international airports, the airport instituting the most lax security essentially determines the overall safety of the flying public, insofar as a vulnerable airport is apt to attract the terrorists. Measures to freeze terrorist assets also represent weakest-link countermeasures, since the least vigilant countries influence disproportionately the ability of terrorists to maintain their assets. There is, thus, a need to "shore up" the weakest link – i.e., bring their effort level up to an acceptable standard. This shoring-up process faces a collective action problem as nations wait for others to augment the efforts of the weakest link(s). Consequently, free riding characterizes steps taken to bring up effort levels in weakest links. A prime-target country typically does not have sufficient means to shore up all weakest links so that cooperation is necessary.

Transnational terrorism offers rogue nations, which operate outside of acceptable norms, a means to destabilize another nation while hiding behind a cloak of secrecy as they sponsor terrorist attacks abroad. Such actions can be cost effective, with a large damage-exchange ratio. Even if the state sponsor is discovered, countries confront a collective action problem in retaliating against the sponsor. This follows because countries are inclined to hold back their response so as to benefit from any response by the country enduring the terrorist incident. Why put one's soldiers in harm's way when some other nation may do so? Retaliation also runs the risk of condemnation by the world community if the proof of sponsorship is not completely convincing or else the retaliation kills some innocent people. The latter is likely when terrorists purposely live within the general population.

Technological advances are also providing terrorists with means that they tailor and exploit for new atrocities. Thus, terrorists use the internet to augment anxiety with videos of beheadings. It also allows them to spread propaganda, while communicating with other operatives, and to claim credit for events by posting videos. Since the late 1960s, terrorists have been quick to adopt advances in explosive devices – e.g., plastic explosives, novel timing devices, and innovative detonators. Authorities must view terrorism as a dynamic threat whose forms and methods are ever morphing. Anticipating novel forms of attacks can be more challenging than stopping planned conventional attacks.

Another factor promoting terrorism is past success. In 1983, the departure of the multinational forces (MNF) from Beirut following the near-simultaneous suicide bombing of the US Marine barracks and the French Paratroopers' sleeping quarters encouraged future terrorist campaigns. These two suicide truck/car bombings became the prototype for suicide truck bombings in Sri Lanka, Iraq, Turkey, Saudi Arabia, and elsewhere. Proven methods create a demonstration effect, copied by terrorists worldwide. The news media unwittingly disperse terrorist innovations globally in a short period of time. The so-called "Blackhawk down" al-Qaida attack on US forces in Somalia gave the terrorists a victory as the United States left in defeat. Any concessions, including withdrawing forces or paying ransoms to kidnapping, encourage future terrorism. This poses a real weakest-link problem as the country least able to resist making concessions or paying ransoms changes the terrorists' priors about how resistant other nations will be. As nations cave in, terrorists become more optimistic that others will follow suit if the right hostage is abducted or spectacular event is executed.

Transference of Terrorist Attacks

Transference is policy-induced changes in terrorist behavior and represents another impediment in limiting transnational terrorism. This phenomenon again highlights that terrorists are rational actors who respond to changes in risks in an appropriate manner that, unfortunately, may limit gains from counterterrorism policies. Actions by governments to guard one venue cause the terrorists to shift to another venue.

Following 9/11, there was an increase in homeland security in the United States, Canada, and European countries. A recent study shows that since 9/11 there has been a clear transference of attacks against US interests to the Middle East and Asia (Enders and Sandler, 2006b). Today's fundamentalist terrorism is shifting to those countries, where large support populations exist and terrorists do not have to transcend fortified borders to attack US and Western assets. With transference, a counterterrorism policy that raises the price of one mode of attack will induce terrorists to switch to now relatively cheaper modes of attack. Based on ITERATE data and statistical analyses, Enders and Sandler (2006a) show that the installation of metal detectors in airports on January 5, 1973 led to an immediate and prolonged drop in skyjackings. At the same time, there was a significant and large increase in hostage and other incidents. Unfortunately, metal detectors also resulted in a diversion into more deadly incidents, an unintended consequence of the policy (Enders and Sandler, 2006a, 81–82). In another transference, Enders and Sandler (1993) find that securing embassies led to more assassinations and attacks against embassy officials in nonsecure venues. The policy message is simple: counterterrorism measures must either make all modes of attack more difficult or else reduce terrorist resources if transference is to be avoided. The latter require *proactive measures* in which terrorists and their assets are targeted, as the United States and its allies did in Afghanistan in October 2001.

Transference can also have a temporal nature in response to terror alerts or temporarily enhanced security. If these actions are announced or visible, then the terrorists will merely shift an intended attack from the present to the future once the authority's guard is down. The homeland security alert system provides terrorists with information that is to their advantage. Moreover, terrorists can manipulate the system by increasing internet "chatter" or threats to cause wasteful security enhancements and decreasing chatter or threats when they really intend to strike. Repressive actions by a targeted government that closes off political means – rallies and election of representatives – will cause terrorists to rely more on violent attacks. Thus, the policy message is not to close off legitimate political channels of expression owing to an undesirable transference (also see Frey, 2004). Very harsh proactive measures can either cause a backlash attack by sympathetic groups or greater recruitment of terrorists (Rosendorff and Sandler, 2004; Siqueira and Sandler, 2007). This recruitment can result in a spectacular incident where greater manpower and resources are needed. The Madrid train bombings on 11 March 2007 and the London transport bombings on July 7, 2005 are backlash attacks by groups sympathetic to al-Qaida.

Thus, proactive responses have a downside that must be weighed against the likely fall in terrorism. We show later that the war on terror at the end of 2001 not only decreased the number of incidents but also resulted in incidents with more casualties on average. Terrorists responded to the higher risks by going after incidents with potentially greater payoffs, which is a rational response. Moreover, such antiterrorism campaigns lead to a short-term lull in attacks as terrorists find new hiding places and regroup. Quite simply, transnational terrorism is not so easy to address.

Geographical Transference

Transference of terrorist attacks can also be geographical, in which heightened security in one part of the world transfers transnational terrorist incidents to less secure countries. To show the pattern of transnational terrorist attacks over time, we apply the regional classifications given in the US Department of State (2003) *Patterns of Global Terrorism*, where six regions are characterized. These regions are the Western Hemisphere (North, Central, and South America), Africa (excluding North Africa), Asia (South and East Asia, Australia, and New Zealand), Eurasia (Central Asia, Russia, and the Ukraine), Europe (West and East Europe), and the Middle East (including North Africa). This partition of countries puts most of the Islamic population into the Middle East, Eurasia, and Asia.

In Figure 9.4, we utilize ITERATE data to

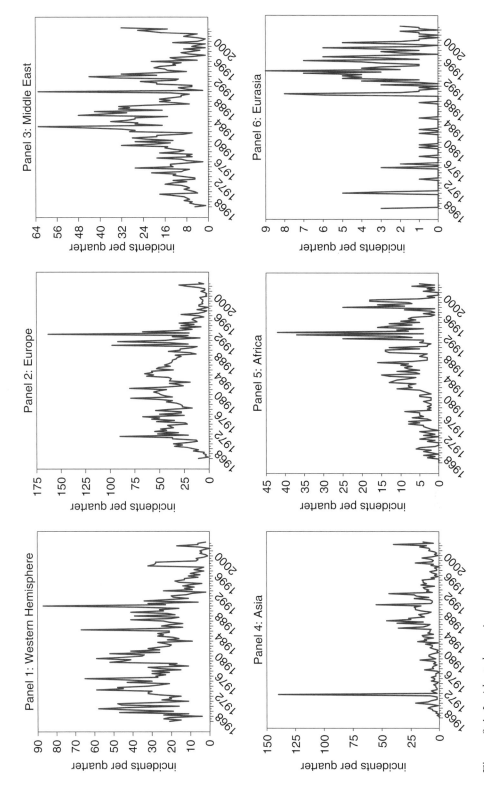

Figure 9.4 *Incidents by region*

show the changing pattern over time of transnational terrorism by region. Panels 1 and 2 display a sustained decrease in transnational terrorist attacks, beginning in the early 1990s for the Western Hemisphere and Europe, respectively. From 1968 to 1992, there was a lot of spillover terrorism from the Middle East, staged in Western Europe. In panel 3, the Middle East is associated with an increase in transnational terrorism for the start of the 1990s, followed by a fall around 1993, and then an increase after 9/11. This same post-9/11 rise characterizes Asia and Eurasia. In a recent paper, Enders and Sandler (2006b) show statistically that heightened homeland security in parts of the Western Hemisphere and Europe induced terrorists to shift their attacks on Western interests to regions where Islamic fundamentalists can rely on indigenous populations for support. This can be seen in panels 3 and 4. Eurasia experienced an increase in transnational terrorism at the time when the Western Hemisphere and Europe experienced a decrease. Nevertheless, the number of transnational terrorist attacks is small in Eurasia compared to the Middle East, Asia, and elsewhere.

Measurement and Other Problems

Coming up with five solutions and their benefit–cost ratios is particularly difficult for transnational terrorism. Before we indicate how we circumvented this obstacle, we briefly describe why transnational terrorism is more problematic to do benefit and cost analysis on than many other challenges. First, there are no real solutions

[7] For example, we can regress the number of tourists in period t against past values of tourists and the current (and past) value(s) of terrorist attacks. Once this equation is estimated, we can determine the level of tourism with current and past levels of terrorism. Next, we set the coefficients on the terrorism terms in the estimated equation equal to zero (i.e., the counterfactual) and again ascertain the level of tourism. The difference in tourism with and without terrorism for the estimated equation indicates terrorism's influence on tourism (Enders, Sandler, and Parise, 1992).

to transnational terrorism owing to transference and the other considerations given earlier. The best hope is for action that ameliorates terrorism in the immediate term. Any stream of benefits and costs from solutions or policies is limited in time and lasts for two to five years before some new related or unrelated threat surfaces. Second, there is the *counterfactual* problem, because there is no true way to know what terrorism would have been had certain policies not been taken, once they are imposed. If, for example, nations had cooperated more prior to 9/11, would 9/11 have been avoided? No one can know for sure. Sometimes, a researcher can apply econometric techniques to identify the counterfactual – e.g., the use of a transfer function in time series analysis.[7] This requires estimating the level of a variable – say, the number of tourists – with terrorism present and then using the estimating equation to ascertain what would happen if terrorism had been zero. When estimating benefits and costs for solutions, the counterfactual is relevant for at least one side of the calculation. Suppose the solution involves greater proactive measures against the terrorists, then the counterfactual is on the benefit side, since we do not know the reduction in terrorism in light of these measures. If, instead, we hypothesize augmented international cooperation, then the counterfactual involves both the cost and benefit sides, because we have never experienced such levels of cooperation.

Third, policy cost information is often difficult to ascertain. Most countries do not reveal how much is spent on some components of counterterrorism or homeland security, since it may be in a country's strategic interest to keep this information secret. This is particularly true of the intelligence budget. Even when this information is available, there is still the problem as to what counts and what does not count as counterterrorism actions. That is, does the US-led invasion of Afghanistan against the Taliban and al-Qaida count? Most researchers classify this war as a proactive response to a terrorist threat. Similarly, does the US-led invasion of Iraq on March 20, 2003 count when there was no clear indication that Iraq, at the time, supported or harbored al-Qaida? Some researchers exclude this war as a proactive response to terrorism.[8] In computing costs, there is also the joint-cost problem when funds are used for multiple activities, because costs must then be assigned. For example, disaster relief in the United States goes to responding to both natural and terrorist disasters. In general, the costs of many "solutions" do not lend themselves to easy calculation. This means that the costs of augmented cooperation must be proxied. Even the costs of enhanced defensive measures are difficult to ascertain, since we do not know the costs of current measures in most countries. Thus, a procedure must be devised for ascertaining these costs. The same is true about the expense of foreign policy changes by prime-target countries.

Other measurement problems exist for our study. There are no records kept of the degree of injuries from terrorist attacks. As seen earlier in Table 9.2, there is just a tally on the number of injuries. This then presents an issue when we compute the DALYs associated with transnational terrorism; however, we are able to address this problem in the next section. Additionally, the damage inflicted by most terrorist attacks is not readily available, except for a few spectacular incidents (see Table 9.6). The best way to address this lacuna is to rely on a method that calibrates losses in GDP. The alternative is to measure the losses associated with various sectors of the economy (such as the airlines and tourism industries) and add them to the losses associated with terrorism-induced reductions in international trade and foreign direct investment. These losses can then be reduced by benefits accruing to those sectors of the economy that expand as a result of terrorism (such as law enforcement). However, it is exceedingly difficult to measure the overall sectoral losses and gains. If, for example, international trade declines as a result of terrorism, intranational trade should expand as domestic firms replace international firms as suppliers of goods. Instead of using this indirect method, we find it to be far easier to compute the net losses from terrorism as manifested in overall GDP levels.

The Building Blocks to Benefit–Cost Analysis

To calculate the benefits and costs for various solutions, we must first be able to assign a cost to transnational terrorism in terms of lives lost and injuries sustained, security expense, and GDP losses. These three building blocks allow us to do counterfactual analyses so as to measure benefits for the proposed solutions that ameliorate, in the short term, the level of transnational terrorism.

Human Costs: Computing DALYs

To establish the human costs, we must compute the DALYs associated with terrorism for either a given or representative year using casualty figures for transnational terrorism, previously presented in Table 9.2 for 1968–2006. This table gives the casualties in terms of deaths and injuries on an annual basis. In order to calculate the DALYs associated with terrorism, we must categorize the wounded into their respective injury components (i.e., disability D weights). Unfortunately, data on the nature of terrorist-induced injuries sustained are unavailable. We can, however, derive a suitable proxy by appealing to a study conducted by Abenhaim, Dab, and Salmi (1992) of the physical and psychological injuries associated with a terrorist campaign involving twenty-one attacks (twenty bombings and one machine gun attack) that occurred in France during 1982–1987. This campaign resulted from spillover terrorism related to the political situation in the Middle East. These authors sent surveys to the population of 324 civilian victims, who were registered by the police. There was 86 percent participation rate to the survey with 78 percent returning the completed survey and another 8 percent responding to a phone interview. Psychological symptoms were identified from assessing self-reporting on a diagnostic portion of the survey. Although a few studies exist that document the injuries corresponding to an *isolated* terrorist incident, this French study is the most recent longitudinal data

---

[8] Terrorism became a problem in Iraq in 2004 after the ouster of Saddam Hussein and the insurgency began.

Table 9.8. Terrorism DALYs: base year 2005 (5% discount rate)

	% of Subjects[1]	Number of injuries[2] N	Disability weight[3] D	YLD for East Mediterranean life expectancy ($1,000)	YLD for European life expectancy ($1,000)	YLD for US life expectancy ($1,000)
Distribution of lesions						
Hearing loss	46.9	405.22	0.12	768.667	815.731	832.414
Severe burns	15.4	133.06	0.26	536.346	569.186	580.826
Head trauma	15.0	129.60	0.35	717.041	760.943	776.505
Eye injury	13.0	112.32	0.11	191.757	203.498	207.660
Respiratory impairment	6.7	57.89	0.28	255.307	270.939	276.480
Fracture(s) and/or amputations	4.5	38.88	0.35	215.112	228.283	232.952
Psychological symptoms						
PTSD	18.1	156.38	0.11	259.569	275.461	281.095
Major depression	13.3	114.91	0.76	1380.542	1465.070	1495.032
Total YLD[4]				4324.342	4589.112	4682.964
YLL[5] (550 deaths)				8694.275	9226.606	9415.300
DALYs = YLD + YLL				13018.617	13815.718	14098.264
DALYs @ $5,000				65093.083	69078.588	70491.318

[1] Source: Abenhaim, Dab, and Salmi (1992).
[2] $N = 864 \times$ (% of subjects).
[3] Source: Mathers, Lopez, and Murray (2003).
[4] $YLD = 1000 \times N \times D\,[1 - \exp(-0.05 \times L)]/0.05$.
[5] $YLL = 1000 \times N[1 - \exp(-0.05 \times L)]/0.05$.

set on injuries stemming from terrorist incidents that we could find. We, therefore, use this study to interpolate injury categories from wounded tallies in Table 9.2. Even though transnational terrorism includes more than bombings, the French study on assessing injuries is an excellent proxy because over half of all transnational terrorist attacks are bombings, which are the most likely attacks to result in injuries.

We employ the distribution of injuries given in the French study to compute DALYs for transnational terrorist attacks in Table 9.8 for 2005 as the base or representative year, when 550 people died and 864 were wounded. In the left-most column, the type of lesion and psychological symptoms are indicated, in which PTSD stands for posttraumatic stress disorder. The next column lists the percentage of injured that displayed these consequences, where the injury total is greater than 100 percent because victims may experience multiple injuries. In the third column, the number of each type of injury is determined by multiplying the corresponding

percentage by 864 – the number of wounded in 2005. The associated calculation then provides the number of injuries, N, for ascertaining the years lost to disability (YLD). In the fourth column, the disability weights, D, for these injuries are taken from Mathers, Lopez, and Murray (2003). When a complete correspondence between the disability weight and the lesion does not exist, the following interpretations are applied. The disability weight for hearing loss is that assigned to a severe or profound treated loss. Head trauma is given the weight for a fractured skull or an intracranial injury, both of which have the same disability weight. For respiratory impairment, we use the largest respiratory weight, associated with lower respiratory infection episodes. Bombings are known to have significant impact on internal organs: shock waves from the blast induce significant tissue disruption at air-liquid interfaces, a process known as "spalling" (Frykberg, 2002). For fracture(s) and amputation(s), we equate the loss to a fractured femur, which is the highest

Table 9.9. Terrorism DALYs: using average yearly deaths and wounds 1968–2006 (5% discount rate)

	% of Subjects[1]	Number of injuries[2] N	Disability weight[3] D	YLD for East Mediterranean life expectancy ($1,000)	YLD for European life expectancy ($1,000)	YLD for US life expectancy ($1,000)
Distribution of lesions						
Hearing loss	46.9	585.91	0.12	1111.436	1179.487	1203.609
Severe burns	15.4	192.39	0.26	775.517	823.000	839.831
Head trauma	15.0	187.39	0.35	1036.788	1100.268	1122.769
Eye injury	13.0	162.41	0.11	277.267	294.243	300.261
Respiratory impairment	6.7	83.70	0.28	369.156	391.758	399.770
Fracture(s) and/or amputations	4.5	56.22	0.35	311.036	330.080	336.831
Psychological symptoms						
PTSD	18.1	226.12	0.11	375.317	398.297	406.443
Major depression	13.3	166.15	0.76	1996.162	2118.382	2161.705
Total YLD[4]				6252.678	6635.516	6771.219
YLL[5] (419.79 deaths)				6639.264	7045.772	7189.865
DALYs = YLD + YLL				12891.942	13681.287	13961.084
DALYs @ $5,000				64459.711	68406.437	69805.421

[1] Source: Abenhaim, Dab, and Salmi (1992).
[2] $N = 1249.28 \times$ (% of subjects).
[3] Source: Mathers, Lopez, and Murray (2003).
[4] $YLD = 1000 \times N \times D [1 - \exp(-0.05 \times L)]/0.05$.
[5] $YLL = 1000 \times N[1 - \exp(-0.05 \times L)]/0.05$.

among fractures and exceeds all amputations except foot or leg. We consistently use the higher weights for ambiguous cases to give injuries the highest possible monetary consequences. The rather low DALYs later associated with transnational terrorism cannot be blamed on us taking a conservative approach.

The duration, L, of each injury is treated as permanent for the victim's remaining life span. Given that terrorist attacks rarely target children, we assume that a representative victim has reached his or her mean life expectancy, averaged across males and females. Consequently, the duration of the injury is for half of the victim's life expectancy. For the purpose of sensitivity analysis, we conduct the analysis for the life expectancy in three geographical regions: Eastern Mediterranean, European, and the United States, as reported in the World Health Organization's mortality tables for each region. The duration is as follows: Eastern Mediterranean, 31.25 years; Europe, 36.5 years; and the United States, 38.75 years.

Assuming a discount rate of 5 percent and a value of $1,000 per DALY, we calculate the YLD for each injury or symptom using the following formula:

$$YLD = \$1000 \times N \times D \times [1 - \exp(-0.05 \times L)]/0.05. \tag{1}$$

For deaths, the years of life lost (YLL) calculations are performed in a similar fashion, except that death has a disability weight of one. This calculation is applied to the 550 deaths in 2005. The three right-hand columns in Table 9.8 aggregate the YLD and YLL for the three different life spans to derive the DALYs. For 2005, YLD is almost half the value of YLL. This would not be true had more people been injured. At a value of $1,000 per DALY, the human cost of terrorism ranges from $13 to $14.1 million in 2005, which is very modest. When a DALY is valued at $5,000, the human cost of terrorism ranges from $65.1 to $70.5 million in 2005. In Table 9.9, we conduct an analogous exercise but use the *average annual* terrorism deaths (419.79)

Table 9.10. Relative values of terrorism DALYs compared with other challenges

Terrorism DALYs[1] as a percent of:	Percent
World perinatal DALYs (2001)	0.02
World HIV/AIDS DALYs (2001)	0.02
World malaria DALYs (2001)	0.03
World tuberculosis DALYs (2001)	0.04
World road traffic accidents DALYs (2001)	0.04

[1] These ratios are the same for $1,000 and $5,000 DALYs. We use terrorism DALYs in terms of US life expectancy.

and injuries (1249.28) for the 1968–2006 period from Table 9.2. As shown in Table 9.9, there is little change in the range or values of DALYs using an average year, thus indicating a robust analysis. The sole difference is that YLD and YLL are close in value. Henceforth, we use values from Table 9.9 associated with the $5,000 DALY.

As a basis of comparison, we calculate terrorism DALYs for US life expectancy (which is the highest) as a percentage of the world DALYs for a selection of the 20 leading global challenges for 2001. The rankings for these challenges in terms of DALYs are perinatal conditions (No. 1), HIV/AIDS (No. 5), malaria (No. 8), tuberculosis (No. 10), and road traffic accidents (No. 11). In Table 9.10, the transnational terrorism DALYs percentages range from a mere 0.02 for perinatal conditions and HIV/AIDS to 0.04 for tuberculosis and traffic accidents.[9] When measured in terms of DALYs, transnational terrorism is a minor problem because relatively few people die or are injured each year. If we include deaths and wounds from domestic terrorism, the percentages would increase by over tenfold since 7,641 persons died and 14,395 were wounded in domestic terrorism during 2005 (see Table 9.3). Nevertheless, terrorism DALYs percentages are still relatively small when compared with these other challenges, where much larger numbers of people die or are injured.

[9] These ratios are the same for $1,000 and $5,000 DALYs.

Homeland Security Costs

The second building block concerns the amount spent on homeland security worldwide. This is a difficult figure to compute since most countries do not display a line item in their budget for homeland security. Moreover, homeland security involves many activities including control of immigration, inspection of imports, hardening of targets, gathering of intelligence, guarding of borders, security at airports, and other activities. A decision must be made whether to include just defensive actions or to also include proactive measures such as the US-led invasions of Afghanistan in October 2001 and Iraq in March 2003.

We address these difficulties in a number of ways. There are reliable figures for the United States and the United Kingdom that we can use to proxy estimates for other countries. This proxy is based on the *percentage of GDP* devoted to homeland security in the United States and the United Kingdom following 9/11. The dilemma involves going from US and UK estimates to a worldwide calculation when such figures are not available. Nine alternative calculation methods are used, some of which include just defensive measures while others include defensive and proactive measures. When a proactive response is included, the invasion and occupation of Iraq is included in two of the calculations and left out of one of the calculations. Prior to the US invasion in 2003, Iraq had supplied monetary inducements to some suicide terrorists in Israel and there was some terrorist presence on Iraqi soil (e.g., safe haven to an ailing Abu Nidal). The invasion of Afghanistan is, however, included in all three of our calculations involving proactive measures owing to the safe haven given by the Taliban to Osama bin Laden and al-Qaida. These nine alternative calculations provide both the annual costs and the capitalized costs (over five years) of homeland security. Even with the most conservative estimates, we will discover that homeland security is the dominant consideration in the benefit–cost ratios for some of our proposed solutions.

Our alternative procedures – numbered M1 through M9 – are best understood in conjunction with Table 9.11. We identify sixty-six countries,

Table 9.11. Worldwide homeland security estimates under nine alternative methods (in $ billions)

Country	GDP 2005 (current US$)	M1	M2	M3	M4	M5	M6	M7	M8	M9
Afghanistan	7.2	0.025	0.010	0.025	0.025	0.023	0.007	0.010	0.007	0.004
Algeria	102.3	0.358	0.149	0.358	0.358	0.327	0.102	0.149	0.102	0.051
Argentina	183.3	0.642	0.268	0.642	0.642	0.587	0.183	0.268	0.183	0.092
Australia	700.7	2.452	1.023	2.452	2.452	2.242	0.701	1.023	0.701	0.350
Austria	304.5	1.066	0.445	1.066	1.066	0.974	0.305	0.445	0.305	0.152
Bahrain	13.0	0.045	0.019	0.045	0.045	0.042	0.013	0.019	0.013	0.006
Belgium	364.7	1.277	0.533	1.277	1.277	1.167	0.365	0.533	0.365	0.182
Bosnia and Herzegovina	9.4	0.033	0.014	0.033	0.033	0.030	0.009	0.014	0.009	0.005
Brazil	794.1	2.779	1.159	2.779	2.779	2.541	0.794	1.159	0.794	0.397
Canada	1115.2	3.903	1.628	3.903	3.903	3.569	1.115	1.628	1.115	0.558
China	2228.9	7.801	3.254	7.801	7.801	7.132	2.229	3.254	2.229	1.114
Colombia	122.3	0.428	0.179	0.428	0.428	0.391	0.122	0.179	0.122	0.061
Cyprus	15.7	0.055	0.023	0.055	0.055	0.050	0.016	0.023	0.016	0.008
Czech Republic	122.3	0.428	0.179	0.428	0.428	0.392	0.122	0.179	0.122	0.061
Denmark	254.4	0.890	0.371	0.890	0.890	0.814	0.254	0.371	0.254	0.127
Egypt, Arab Rep.	89.3	0.313	0.130	0.313	0.313	0.286	0.089	0.130	0.089	0.045
Finland	193.2	0.676	0.282	0.676	0.676	0.618	0.193	0.282	0.193	0.097
France	2110.2	7.386	3.081	7.386	7.386	6.753	2.110	3.081	2.110	1.055
Georgia	6.4	0.022	0.009	0.022	0.022	0.020	0.006	0.009	0.006	0.003
Germany	2781.9	9.737	4.062	9.737	9.737	8.902	2.782	4.062	2.782	1.391
Greece	213.7	0.748	0.312	0.748	0.748	0.684	0.214	0.312	0.214	0.107
Haiti	4.2	0.015	0.006	0.015	0.015	0.014	0.004	0.006	0.004	0.002
Hungary	109.2	0.382	0.159	0.382	0.382	0.349	0.109	0.159	0.109	0.055
India	785.5	2.749	1.147	2.749	2.749	2.513	0.785	1.147	0.785	0.393
Indonesia	287.2	1.005	0.419	1.005	1.005	0.919	0.287	0.419	0.287	0.144
Ireland	196.4	0.687	0.287	0.687	0.687	0.628	0.196	0.287	0.196	0.098
Israel	123.4	0.432	0.180	0.913	0.469	0.395	0.432	0.913	0.432	0.432
Italy	1723.0	6.031	2.516	6.031	6.031	5.514	1.723	2.516	1.723	0.862
Japan	4505.9	15.771	6.579	15.771	15.771	14.419	4.506	6.579	4.506	2.253
Jordan	12.9	0.045	0.019	0.045	0.045	0.041	0.013	0.019	0.013	0.006
Kenya	18.0	0.063	0.026	0.063	0.063	0.058	0.018	0.026	0.018	0.009
Korea, Rep.	787.6	2.757	1.150	2.757	2.757	2.520	0.788	1.150	0.788	0.394
Kuwait	74.7	0.261	0.109	0.261	0.261	0.239	0.075	0.109	0.075	0.037
Lebanon	22.2	0.078	0.032	0.078	0.078	0.071	0.022	0.032	0.022	0.011
Luxembourg	33.8	0.118	0.049	0.118	0.118	0.108	0.034	0.049	0.034	0.017
Malaysia	130.1	0.456	0.190	0.456	0.456	0.416	0.130	0.190	0.130	0.065
Mexico	768.4	2.690	1.122	2.690	2.690	2.459	0.768	1.122	0.768	0.384
Morocco	51.7	0.181	0.076	0.181	0.181	0.166	0.052	0.076	0.052	0.026
Netherlands	594.8	2.082	0.868	2.082	2.082	1.903	0.595	0.868	0.595	0.297

Table 9.11. (continued)

Country	GDP 2005 (current US$)	M1	M2	M3	M4	M5	M6	M7	M8	M9
New Zealand	109.0	0.382	0.159	0.382	0.382	0.349	0.109	0.159	0.109	0.055
Norway	283.9	0.994	0.415	0.994	0.994	0.909	0.284	0.415	0.284	0.142
Pakistan	110.7	0.388	0.162	0.388	0.388	0.354	0.111	0.162	0.111	0.055
Peru	78.4	0.275	0.115	0.275	0.275	0.251	0.078	0.115	0.078	0.039
Philippines	98.3	0.344	0.144	0.344	0.344	0.315	0.098	0.144	0.098	0.049
Poland	299.2	1.047	0.437	1.047	1.047	0.957	0.299	0.437	0.299	0.150
Portugal	173.1	0.606	0.253	0.606	0.606	0.554	0.173	0.253	0.173	0.087
Qatar	29.0	0.102	0.042	0.102	0.102	0.093	0.029	0.042	0.029	0.015
Romania	98.6	0.345	0.144	0.345	0.345	0.315	0.099	0.144	0.099	0.049
Russian Fed.	763.7	2.673	1.115	5.652	2.902	2.444	2.673	5.652	2.673	2.673
Saudi Arabia	309.8	1.084	0.452	1.084	1.084	0.991	0.310	0.452	0.310	0.155
Singapore	116.8	0.409	0.170	0.409	0.409	0.374	0.117	0.170	0.117	0.058
Slovak Republic	46.4	0.162	0.068	0.162	0.162	0.149	0.046	0.068	0.046	0.023
Slovenia	34.0	0.119	0.050	0.119	0.119	0.109	0.034	0.050	0.034	0.017
South Africa	240.2	0.841	0.351	0.841	0.841	0.768	0.240	0.351	0.240	0.120
Spain	1123.7	3.933	1.641	3.933	3.933	3.596	1.124	1.641	1.124	0.562
Sri Lanka	23.5	0.082	0.034	0.082	0.082	0.075	0.023	0.034	0.023	0.012
Sweden	354.1	1.239	0.517	1.239	1.239	1.133	0.354	0.517	0.354	0.177
Switzerland	365.9	1.281	0.534	1.281	1.281	1.171	0.366	0.534	0.366	0.183
Tanzania	12.1	0.042	0.018	0.042	0.042	0.039	0.012	0.018	0.012	0.006
Thailand	176.6	0.618	0.258	0.618	0.618	0.565	0.177	0.258	0.177	0.088
Turkey	363.3	1.272	0.530	1.272	1.272	1.163	0.363	0.530	0.363	0.182
Ukraine	81.7	0.286	0.119	0.286	0.286	0.261	0.082	0.119	0.082	0.041
United Kingdom	2192.6	7.674	3.201	16.225	8.332	7.016	7.674	16.225	3.201	3.201
United States	12455.1	43.593	43.593	92.168	47.329	39.856	43.593	92.168	43.593	43.593
Venezuela, RB	138.9	0.486	0.203	0.486	0.486	0.444	0.139	0.203	0.139	0.069
Yemen, Rep.	14.5	0.051	0.021	0.051	0.051	0.046	0.014	0.021	0.014	0.007
Total		147.19	86.81	207.78	151.85	134.57	80.89	153.68	76.42	63.16
FV2005		147.19	86.81	207.78	151.85	134.57	80.89	153.68	76.42	63.16
FV2006		150.14	88.54	211.93	154.89	137.27	82.51	156.75	77.95	64.42
FV2007		153.14	90.32	216.17	157.99	140.01	84.16	159.88	79.51	65.71
FV2008		156.20	92.12	220.49	161.15	142.81	85.84	163.08	81.10	67.02
FV2009		159.32	93.96	224.90	164.37	145.67	87.56	166.34	82.72	68.37
PV in billions of US$		695.09	409.94	981.19	717.09	635.51	382.00	725.71	360.87	298.26

Method 1 (M1): US homeland security percentage of 0.35 of GDP is applied to all sample countries.
Method 2 (M2): US homeland security percentage of 0.35 of GDP is applied to just the United States; UK homeland security percentage of 0.146 of GDP is applied to other sample countries.
Method 3 (M3): US homeland security plus Afghanistan/Iraq campaigns percentage of 0.74 of GDP is applied to United States, United Kingdom, Israel, and Russia; US homeland security percentage of 0.35 of GDP is applied to other sample countries.
Method 4 (M4): US homeland security percentage of 0.38 of GDP without Iraq campaign is applied to United States, United Kingdom, Israel, and Russia; US homeland security percentage of 0.35 of GDP is applied to other sample countries.
Method 5 (M5): US homeland security percentage of 0.32 of GDP is applied to all sample countries. This percentage equals the share of GDP that consists of 61 percent of US DHS budget plus $10 billion for private security.

Table 9.11. (continued)

Method 6 (M6): US homeland security of 0.35 of GDP is applied to the United States, United Kingdom, Israel, and Russia; 0.10 percent of GDP is applied to other sample countries.
Method 7 (M7): US homeland security percentage of 0.74 of GDP is applied to the United States, Israel, and Russia; UK homeland security percentage of 0.146 of GDP is applied to all other sample countries.
Method 8 (M8): US homeland security percentage of 0.35 of GDP is applied to the United States, Israel, and Russia; UK homeland security percentage of 0.146 of GDP is applied to United Kingdom; and 0.10 percent of GDP is applied to all other sample countries.
Method 9 (M9): US homeland security percentage of 0.35 of GDP is applied to the United States, Israel, and Russia; UK homeland security percentage of 0.146 of GDP is applied to the United Kingdom; and 0.05 percent of GDP is applied to other sample countries.

listed in the left-hand column of Table 9.11, that have experienced transnational terrorism in recent years. All major industrial countries are included in the sample, so that excluded countries, whose GDP are small, would not change totals by much. The second column displays GDP amounts for 2005 in billions of current US dollars for each sample country, taken from the World Bank (2007). The next nine columns provide homeland security estimates for each of our methods in billions of US dollars.

To illustrate the methods, we first indicate how we assign homeland security expenditures in the United States and the United Kingdom for the calculations. For the United States, we appeal to the careful study by Hobijn and Sager (2007) on the increase in homeland security in 2005, compared with 2001. These authors compute both federal and private sector augmented homeland security expenditures and put the annual amount at $43.6 billion in 2005, which is 0.35 percent of US GDP. This first calculation includes no proactive spending. For the United Kingdom, we use Treverton *et al.* (2008, 73) figure for British counterterrorism and domestic security, which averages to $3.2 billion per year for two recent snapshots in time. This latter figure is 0.146 percent of UK GDP in 2005.

In Table 9.11, Method 1 (M1) applies the US GDP percentage to all sample countries for a total of $147.19 billion in 2005. To capitalize this value (see column 3), we allow for GDP growth of 2 percent to give the future value in 2006 (FV2006). Similar FV values are calculated through 2009. To get the present value, we apply the appropriate discount factor to each FV – e.g., we divide FV2006 by $(1 + .05)$

and FV2007 by $(1 + .05)^2$ – and then sum the five discounted FV terms. Thus, the capitalized value of M1 is $695.09 billion over five years. Method 1 is a high-end estimate because most sample countries will not have allocated over a third of 1 percent of their GDP on enhanced homeland security since 9/11. Method 2 is more realistic by applying the US percentage to just the United States and the UK homeland security percentage of 0.146 percent of GDP to the other sixty-five sample countries. For M2, the annual value is $86.81 billion and the five-year capitalized value is $409.94 billion, with the United States accounting for half of all homeland security spending. This seems to be a realistic share for the prime-target country, whose interests are attacked on average 40 percent of the time.

Method 3 is more controversial because we include the annualized expenditure associated with the Afghanistan and Iraq Wars, based on figures given in Treverton *et al.* (2008, 67–68). These authors provide an educated guess on the annual cost of US federal spending on homeland security, Afghanistan/Iraq, and associated activities (e.g., foreign assistance to at-risk countries). They also include state and local spending on homeland security along with private-sector spending of $10 billion, which is close to private spending amounts in Hobijn and Sager (2007). According to Treverton *et al.* (2008), the United States annually has spent $92 billion on defensive and proactive measures since 9/11, which amounts to 0.74 percent of US GDP in 2005. The authors offer a smaller figure to augmented homeland security than Hobijn and Sager (2007). M3 applies the 0.74 percent to the four prime-target nations – the United States, the United Kingdom, Israel, and Russia

– and applies the earlier 0.35 percent to the other sample countries. Our justification is that these four countries have proactive campaigns that support the higher percentage. M3 gives an annual costs of $207.78 billion and a capitalized five-year costs of $981.19; M3 represents our top-level estimate and provides an upper bound. Method 4 excludes the Iraq campaign, since the al-Qaida connection in Iraq prior to the US invasion was not clear-cut in contrast to Taliban-ruled Afghanistan. According to calculations in Treverton *et al.* (2008), $47.2 billion or 0.38 percent of US GDP in 2005 was spent on augmented homeland security if Iraq costs are excluded. M4 applies this percentage to the GDP of the four prime-target countries and uses the smaller 0.35 percent for the other sample countries. This results in annual costs of $151.85 billion and capitalized five-year costs of $717.09.

Method 5 takes a radically different approach by taking 61 percent of the US Department of Homeland Security (DHS) budget for 2005. We use this percentage because officials classify 61 percent of the DHS budget as going to terrorism-related homeland security activities (DHS, 2004). We also add $10 billion of private spending on homeland security to $29.6 billion (= 0.61 × $48.5 billion) for a total US spending figure of $39.6 billion or 0.32 percent of US GDP in 2005. M5 applies this percentage to all sample countries to give annual costs of $134.57 billion and capitalized five-year costs of $635.51 billion.

Methods 6–9 are variations on the themes thus far introduced. M6 is a conservative estimate that applies the US defensive spending of 0.35 percent of GDP to just the four prime-target countries and applies 0.10 percent of GDP to all other sample countries for annual costs of $80.89 billion and capitalized five-year costs of $382 billion – estimates similar to M2. Method 7 is more conservative than M3 because the UK percentage of 0.146 is applied to the United Kingdom and to all nonprime-target countries. M7 provides a more measured valuation of defensive and proactive efforts than M3 and is not too different than M4. Method 8 is a

conservative variant of M1 since the US defensive percentage of 0.35 of GDP is only applied to the United States, Israel, and Russia; the UK percentage of 0.146 of GDP is applied to the United Kingdom; and a percentage of just 0.10 of GDP is applied to the other 62 sample countries. Finally, M9 is a variant of M8 where a very conservative 0.05 percent of GDP is used for the 62 nonprime-target countries. With M9, we have the smallest homeland security cost thus far of $63.16 billion in 2005 and $298.26 billion when capitalized for five years. The United States accounts for 68 percent of these totals.

For our solutions below, we favor two of the above methods – M7 and M9. Since homeland security is the dominant factor in three of our subsequent benefit–cost calculations, we intentionally choose the method M9 that offers the smallest defensive expenditures, so that the adverse ratios cannot later be attributed to our discretion or alleged bias. Given the annual costs on US homeland security, M9's worldwide spending of $63.36 billion is a highly restrained estimate of augmented defensive measures. For an estimate involving proactive and defensive efforts, we favor M7 which applies a fairly conservative defensive effort to nonprime-target countries. Of course, myriad other variants can be examined, but M7 and M9 are reasonable upper and lower bounds on these estimates. Even though we utilize just two methods, we provide nine calculations so that the reader can get a feel for how alternative assumptions could affect our BCR calculations, which we leave to the interested reader. As shown by M7, the inclusion of proactive measures can greatly augment security spending estimates.

Lost GDP

The third building block involves estimating the annual and capitalized five-year losses in GDP associated with transnational terrorist incidents on a country's soil. At the outset, we should expect such losses to be rather modest unless a country is plagued with transnational terrorism or else experiences a spectacular terrorist event such as 9/11 (Sandler and Enders, 2008). Most transnational terrorist incidents kill on average less than one person and have limited economic consequences (Enders and Sandler, 2006a). We utilize the findings from a study by Blomberg, Hess, and Orphanides (henceforth BHO) (2004) that estimates the losses in per capita income growth for countries experiencing one or more transnational terrorist events in that year.[10] BHO (2004) present a panel study of 177 countries for the 1968–2000 sample period. These authors show that each year of transnational terrorism results, on average, in a fall in income per capita growth of just 0.048 percent, which is similar to the findings of Tavares (2004), who puts this loss at 0.038 percent. To be able to use BHO's findings to compute terrorism-induced GDP losses, we need the population (Pop), the per capita GDP in 2005, and the growth rate of per capita GDP between 2004 and 2005 in percent (denoted by 2005 growth/100) for all countries experiencing transnational terrorism during 2001–2005.

The results of our computations are indicated in Table 9.12. In the left-hand column, we list all countries experiencing one or more terrorist attacks during 2001–2005. Population in thousands is indicated in the second column, and the number of years of transnational terrorist events (T_i) in country i during 2001–2005 is listed in the third column. Thus, Algeria experiences transnational terrorist attacks in two years during 2001–2005, while Bosnia-Herzegovina experiences such attacks in four of five years. The terrorism data come from ITERATE, while the Pop and GDP data come from the World Bank (2007). Per capita GDP for 2005 is displayed in the fourth column, while 2005 per capita GDP growth is given in the fifth column.

The sixth column indicates the cost of transnational terrorism in terms of lost GDP for 2005 for just those countries experiencing an attack in 2005. The entry in this column is computed as follows:

$$(\text{Pop} \times \text{per capita GDP}) \times (2005 \text{ growth}/100) \times 0.048.$$

These figures are in thousands so that the total GDP lost in 2005 is approximately $19.412

billion. In the seventh column, we compute an "average yearly cost" in lost GDP for each country based on the fraction of years ($T_i/5$) during 2001–2005 that a country experiences one or more transnational terrorist attacks. The entry is now computed as:

$$(T_i/5)(\text{Pop} \times \text{per capita GDP}) \times (2005 \text{ growth}/100) \times 0.048.$$

This latter computation gives a better average picture that is not as dependent on which countries are attacked during the base year. Thus, a rich nation, such as the United States, cannot have such a disproportionate influence when the latter method is utilized. In Table 9.12, the losses in GDP for this averaging procedure are $17.363 billion in 2005. We favor this latter technique since it provides a more country-balanced approach; however, there is not a large difference between the two calculations in Table 9.12.

To capitalize the losses over five years, we compute the present value entries associated with the seventh column for each of the following four years, discounted by a 5 percent interest rate. For each year after 2005, we also allow GDP to grow at the respective country's 2005 growth rate. The five present value terms for 2005–2009 are then summed for the countries' entries in the right-hand column displaying the "5-year cost in growth." The sum over all countries finally gives the capitalized five-year GDP costs of $83.407 billion. If we had used Tavares' (2004) calculations, these GDP losses would be even smaller. An important insight emerges: homeland security is much more expensive than average estimated losses in GDP tied to the impact of transnational terrorism. This situation very much favors the terrorists, whose actions not only cause harm to targeted economies but also force countries to allocate large amounts of resources to security.

---

[10] These authors measure transnational terrorism as a dummy variable equal to 1 if there are one or more attacks in a given year and zero otherwise. They do not include the level of terrorism – i.e., number or severity of transnational terrorist incidents as an independent variable.

Table 9.12. Lost GDP due to transnational terrorism attacks[1]

Country	Pop (000)	T_i	per capita GDP	2005 growth (%)	2005 cost[2]	2005 cost (average)[3]	5-year cost in (growth)[4]
Algeria	32,854	2	$2,066	3.65		$47,625	$229,081
Angola	15,941	1	891	10.90		14,889	87,969
Argentina	38,747	2	8,096	7.87		475,126	2,577,941
Australia	20,321	1	22,423	1.53		66,962	303,025
Bahrain	727	1	14,588	5.18		5,278	26,524
Bangladesh	141,822	1	415	3.43		19,427	92,866
Belgium	10,471	1	23,381	0.72		16,980	75,069
Bosnia-Herzegovina	3,907	4	1,486	5.25	$14,658	11,726	59,052
Brazil	186,405	2	3,597	0.92		118,876	528,604
Burundi	7,548	2	105	−1.89		288	1,179
Cambodia	14,071	1	356	4.89		2,357	11,751
Chad	9,749	1	267	2.27		569	2,631
Chile	16,295	1	5,747	5.09		45,813	229,633
Colombia	45,600	3	2,174	3.51		100,425	481,162
Congo-Brazzaville	57,549	4	997	5.89	162,441	129,952	666,418
Czech Republic	10,196	1	6,515	5.98		38,190	196,345
Denmark	5,418	1	31,607	2.80		46,082	216,312
Ecuador	13,228	1	1,534	2.37		4,635	21,494
Egypt	74,033	3	1,662	2.87	169,746	101,848	479,055
El Salvador	6,881	1	2,127	0.99		1,397	6,224
Eritrea	4,401	1	176	1.14		85	381
Germany	82,485	3	23,928	0.94		533,246	2,372,185
France	60,743	4	23,641	0.89		490,591	2,179,380
Georgia	4,474	3	23,928	0.94		28,926	128,679
Greece	11,089	2	12,367	3.35		88,280	420,980
Haiti	8,528	2	428	0.70	1,235	494	2,182
Hong Kong	6,944	1	29,945	6.14		122,699	633,683
India	1,094,583	4	586	6.70	2,068,104	1,654,484	8,684,099
Indonesia	220,558	4	942	4.12	411,415	329,132	1,604,632
Iran	67,700	2	1,962	4.75		121,346	602,393
Israel	6,909	4	18,406	3.42		167,090	798,377
Italy	57,471	4	19,387	0.18		77,457	337,112
Jordan	5,411	3	2,091	4.45	24,211	14,527	71,500
Kenya	34,256	2	428	0.23		660	2,876
Kuwait	2,535	4	20,578	5.12	128,457	102,766	515,586
Kyrgyzstan	5,156	2	319	−1.56		492	2,036
Lebanon	3,577	3	5,627	−0.02	172	103	447
Libya	5,853	1	7,517	1.53		6,467	29,267
Macedonia	2,034	1	1,889	3.72		1,375	6,629

Table 9.12. (continued)

Country	Pop (000)	T_i	per capita GDP	2005 growth (%)	2005 cost[2]	2005 cost (average)[3]	5-year cost in (growth)[4]
Madagascar	18,606	1	233	1.73		722	3,287
Malaysia	25,347	3	4,434	3.30		107,068	509,914
Mauritania	3,069	1	447	2.26	1,493	299	1,380
Mexico	103,089	1	6,172	1.90		116,112	531,078
Morocco	30,168	2	1,354	0.37		2,907	12,722
Netherlands	16,329	1	23,535	0.80		29,646	131,369
Nigeria	131,530	1	420	4.38	116,369	23,274	114,324
Norway	4,618	1	39,666	1.68		29,610	134,585
Pakistan	155,772	4	596	5.16	230,590	184,472	926,708
Peru	27,968	2	2,319	5.00		62,326	311,590
Philippines	83,054	3	1,124	3.26		87,686	417,052
Saudi Arabia	24,573	4	9,323	3.78		333,331	1,609,538
Sierra Leone	5,525	1	218	3.74		433	2,089
Singapore	4,351	1	25,443	3.60		38,306	183,991
Solomon Islands	478	1	647	1.71		51	232
Spain	43,389	3	15,610	1.73		337,165	1,534,497
Sri Lanka	19,582	3	1,004	4.27		24,242	118,717
Sudan	36,233	4	462	5.56	44,785	35,828	182,042
Sweden	9,024	1	29,532	2.31		59,178	273,899
Syria	19,043	1	1,161	1.65		3,509	15,935
Tajikistan	6,507	1	237	6.09		903	4,658
Thailand	64,233	3	2,440	3.50		158,429	758,908
Tunisia	10,022	1	2,418	3.24		7,543	35,856
Turkey	72,636	5	3,390	5.86	694,126	694,126	3,557,020
United Kingdom	60,203	4	26,688	1.23	946,715	757,372	3,397,505
United States	296,497	3	37,574	2.48	13,266,740	7,960,044	37,020,669
Russia	143,151	5	2,444	6.68	1,124,468	1,124,468	5,898,583
Uzbekistan	26,593	1	673	5.18		8,924	44,854
Venezuela	26,577	2	4,939	7.20		181,743	967,393
Yemen	20,975	4	590	1.02	6,083	4,867	21,703
Totals					$19,411,808	$17,363,247	$83,406,855

[1] Pop = population in 2005 in thousands; T_i = number of years during 2001–2005 in which there was at least one terrorist event; per capita GDP = per capita GDP in thousands of real 2000 US dollars; 2005 growth = growth rate of per capita GDP between 2004 and 2005 (in percent); 2005 cost = estimated real GDP cost of terrorism (in thousands) using the 2005 measure of terrorist incidents; 2005 cost (average) = estimated real GDP cost of terrorism (in thousands) using the average level of terrorism over the 2001–2005 period; 5-year cost = real present value of 2005 cost (average) (in thousands) over the next five years using a 5 percent discount rate.
[2] If a country had at least one terrorist in 2005, the entry for 2005 cost is measured as (Pop × per capita GDP) × (2005 growth/100) × 0.048.
[3] The entries for 2005 cost (average) is computed as: $(T_i/5)$(Pop × per capita GDP) × (2005 growth/100) × 0.048.
[4] 5-year cost is the present value of the entry for 2005 cost (average) for each of the next four years discounted at a 5 percent real interest rate. The 'growth' entries project that per capita GDP levels continue at their 2005 growth rates.

Our calculations suggest that this second impact is worse than the economic impact. As countries competitively harden potential targets in the hopes of transferring attacks abroad, the security cost worsens (Sandler and Siqueira, 2006). The $17.363 billion average annual loss in GDP is, however, small compared with the losses of 9/11, valued at $80–90 billion. But one must remember that there had never been a terrorist attack remotely as costly as 9/11.

Solutions

We reiterate that there is no true solution to transnational terrorism because this tactic empowers the weak. Our solutions are in terms of policy choices that may ameliorate the problem in the short run with fewer attacks. Even the most clever defenses will be outwitted with time and so we typically work with a five-year time horizon, unless stated otherwise. Similarly, proactive measures do not have permanent influences because new generations of terrorists may surface or the terrorists can replenish lost resources with time. In calculating the associated benefits and costs for each policy option, we must confront a counterfactual on either the benefit or cost side as to what would have happened in the absence or presence of the policy. This requires assumptions that may be controversial.

Solution 1: Business as Usual

"Business as usual" involves doing nothing different than the post-9/11 actions that were instituted by the United States and other target countries following the unprecedented hijackings in September 2001. We construct the counterfactual by calculating the average annual attacks for 2002–2006, compared with those for 1990–2001. This comparison indicates that there are on average 129 fewer incidents per year for the post-9/11 period when compared with the pre-9/11 twelve years, which is a 34 percent drop in transnational terrorism (see Table 9.2). In terms of casualties in the post-9/11 period, there is both good and bad news. The good news

is that there are 120 fewer injuries per year; the bad news is that there are 67 more deaths per year. The latter follows because the terrorists performed more deadly incidents to make fewer incidents have a larger payoff. Also, augmented defensive and proactive measures meant that only the more determined terrorist groups continued their attacks.

Benefits come, in part, from the reduced GDP losses from the 34 percent drop in transnational terrorist incidents. If this fall is assumed to be evenly distributed across target incidents, then this results in a capitalized five-year GDP savings of $28.358 billion ($= 0.34 \times \$83.406$ billion). In principle, additional benefits should also stem from reduced casualties from fewer deaths and injuries; but, in fact, these anticipated benefits are negative based on $5,000 DALYs. The 67 more deaths per year give a capitalized five-year loss of $26.1 million, while the 120 fewer injuries per year give a capitalized five-year gain of $11.3 million, which, in turn, lowers the benefit of this solution to $28.343 billion.

Costs are associated with security expenditures. To compute these costs, we first use the most conservative capitalized five-year value of $298.3 billion associated with M9 that includes just defensive increases following 9/11. This then provides a BCR of 0.095, so that less than ten cents on a dollar is returned. Next, we use the less conservative capitalized five-year cost of $725.7 billion associated with M7 that includes proactive and defensive augmentation following 9/11. This higher cost yields a BCR of 0.039 or a return of just under four cents on a dollar. Given that the two drivers of the BCR calculation – i.e., saved GDP and security expenditures – are in the billions of dollars while casualty consequences are in the millions of dollars, little would change with a $1,000 DALY, except that the BCR would be slightly higher since net casualty costs are reduced to about $2.2 million.

An obvious criticism of our computation is that many target countries value lives and injuries by more than the $5,000 DALY, used to investigate the human consequences of challenges in developing countries. Thus, our procedure may undervalue casualties. To respond to this criticism, we apply a $2 million value of life – the average compensation paid to the families of victims of 9/11 (Enders and Sandler, 2006a, 207) – for the 67 additional lives loss per year with Solution 1 and capitalize this value over five years. This gives a present value loss of $609 million. Next, we modify the YLD calculations to be based on a $2 million value of life.[11] This gives a saving for the 120 reduced injuries of $345 million when capitalized. With this higher value of life, our corresponding BCRs are now 0.094 for M9 and 0.039 for M7. The bottom line is that not much changes, since saved GDP and security costs remain the drivers. Our BCRs – though potentially controversial – are robust.

Why do countries invest in a policy option that apparently has such an adverse BCR? For the United States and other prime-target countries, politics and extreme risk aversion surely play a role. Government officials realize that a single terrorist incident – like 9/11 – could result in $80–90 billion loss. If such losses are not weighted by the appropriately small likelihood, then overspending on security follows. People often overrespond to very low probability catastrophic events when compared with more certain events with small losses. Moreover, target nations are in a security race to deflect terrorist attacks onto foreign soil. Consequently, overspending may result. With reports in July 2007 that al-Qaida has regrouped (US News & World Report, 2007), the United States will likely raise spending on defensive and proactive measures.

Solution 2: Greater International Cooperation

Solution 2 involves greater cooperation in freezing assets and cutting off terrorists' resources, which may come from charitable contributions, drug trafficking, counterfeit goods, commodity trading, and illicit activities. This solution also concerns extraditing suspected terrorists to face prosecution and punishment if guilty. Additionally, this solution is tied to increased police cooperation among countries so that major plots – e.g., the August 2006 plan to blow up transatlantic flights leaving London

with liquid explosives – are foiled. Although this is a relatively cheap solution that can have a permanent impact if links are maintained, it is a difficult solution to consummate because nations do not like to sacrifice autonomy over security and judicial affairs. Moreover, a single noncooperator – say, a nation that harbors terrorist assets – can undo much of the efforts of others. This is a particularly difficult solution to evaluate because benefits *and* costs involve counterfactuals.

On the cost side, we give high-end and low-end estimates by drawing on the 2005 budget of Interpol and the 2006 budget of the International Monetary Fund (IMF). In 2005, the entire operating budget of Interpol was just $58 million (€42.8 million) (Interpol, 2005), 88 percent of which was contributed by member states. Interpol fosters interstate police cooperation. This increased cooperation could involve doubling this budget to $116 million in perpetuity, whose present value is $2.32 billion if the discount rate is 5 percent. For monitoring of terrorist funds, we allocate *one tenth* of IMF's monitoring (global, regional, and country), governance, and capacity-building budget of $709.7 million to enhanced counterterrorism (Committee to Study Sustainable Long-Term Financing of the IMF, 2007). This $71 million expenditure is an educated guess that is 55 percent of IMF global monitoring spending. Most IMF activities are country-specific monitoring, technical assistance, external training, and bilateral surveillance that have little to do with counterterrorism so that allocating 10 percent of IMF administrative spending is surely on the high side. At a 5 percent discount rate, the perpetual stream of $71 million has present value of $1.42 billion. In total, our high-end cost estimate is a perpetual expenditure stream valued at $3.74 billion (= $2.32 billion + $1.42 billion). Throughout, we assume that extradition

---

[11] This modification is to multiply $\Sigma_i N_i D_i$ (see Tables 9.8–9.9) where i denotes the various injury classifications by $2 million. (Remember that $D_i < 1$ for injuries.) The resulting figure is then capitalized over a five-year period at a discount rate of 5 percent. Note that deaths mean that $\Sigma_i N_i D_i$ equals the number of deaths since $D_i = 1$ and $\Sigma_i N_i$ sums those who have died.

is virtually costless, since countries are merely utilizing the capacity built into their judicial and executive branches. The low-end estimate for augmented cooperation is to assign just half of the Interpol budget ($29 million) and 5 percent of the IMF administrative budget ($35.5 million) to supporting greater cooperation for an annual spending stream of $64.5 million. At a 5 percent discount rate, this perpetual stream is valued at $1.29 billion.

Because most terrorist acts do not cost very much, increased police and monetary cooperation is not aimed at curbing small events, such as routine bombings or political assassinations. Rather, this enhanced cooperation is likely to stop a spectacular event that involves a great deal of planning and dedicated resources by the terrorists. Conservatively, we suppose that such actions are able to halt one spectacular terrorist event per year, such as the August 2006 plot against transatlantic flights or the recent plot to hold members of the Canadian parliament hostage. The associated yearly benefit would be the average losses associated with a spectacular terrorist event which can vary from $500 million for the 1993 World Trade Center bombing to $80–90 billion for 9/11. We conservatively place a value of $1 billion on the damages saved from one less spectacular incident. As a perpetual income stream, this results in a saving of $20 billion. Similar remarks can be made for enhanced intelligence expenditures. Antiterrorism intelligence efforts are credited with preventing several potentially spectacular incidents such as the one to blow up fuel supply tanks at New York's JFK airport, revealed in June 2007.

Based on the high-end cost estimate, the BCR is then 5.348; based on the low-end cost estimate, the BCR is then 15.504. We have clearly made some heroic assumptions. Nevertheless, the BCR should be greater than one, because police cooperation is very cheap owing to economies of scope and other considerations, while any large terrorist event avoided can save hundreds of millions of dollars if not billions. Since our benefits and costs are perpetual streams, the BCR is independent of the discount rate, which cancels out in the numerator and denominator.

Surely police forces are cooperating internationally to some extent. What we have tried to show is that the payback per dollar from additional cooperation is apt to be high given how costly spectacular terrorist events can be. To engage in such events, terrorists must take extra risks owing to the greater manpower, resources, training, and planning that must support such attacks. Internationally linked police operations are better able to spot such large-scale terrorist efforts. Although such cooperation has favorable BCRs, countries have jealously guarded their autonomy over police and security matters.

Solution 3: Increased Proactive Response

This solution calls for increased proactive measures along the lines of the invasion of Afghanistan and other offensive actions against terrorists and their supporters taken by the United States and its allies. These actions ranged from the Philippines to Djibouti and immediately followed 9/11. They are known as Operation Enduring Freedom and do not include the invasion and occupation of Iraq, which began in 2003 (Belasco, 2007). Thus, we use the experience of the US-led proactive campaign as a role model for what an increased proactive response might achieve in terms of BCRs. In some of our cost estimates, we also include Operation Noble Eagle, which secured US military bases abroad from which to plan and launch proactive counterterrorism measures.

In order to get a counterfactual, we contrast the level of transnational terrorism in the first two years following 9/11 when there was the greatest proactive antiterrorist campaign with the levels in 2002–2006 and 1990–2001. We use only a two-year horizon for this solution, since al-Qaida and other terrorists had rebounded by 2004 with transnational terrorism back up to pre-9/11 levels. Moreover, many nations supporting such efforts had dropped out after two years. The war on terror put transnational terrorism into partial remission for two years but did not cure it.

The annual number of transnational terrorist

attacks for 2002–2003 is 205 incidents compared with 255 incidents per year for the post-9/11 period through 2006. We use this comparison for the counterfactual so as to adjust for the continued presence of defensive measures throughout the post-9/11 period. Thus, there are 50 fewer attacks per year or a decline of 13 percent in attacks over the 1990–2001 period that we attribute to the larger offensive measures. This translates into $2.257 billion (= 0.13 × $17.363 billion) saving in world GDP for one year. With 5 percent discounting and a two-year time horizon, this gives a benefit of $4.41 billion from saved GDP. Unfortunately, these two years saw violent terrorist events that killed 675 people and injured 2830 others per year. Compared with 1990–2001, there are 159 more deaths and 916 more injuries per year, which is a negative benefit of $75.04 million when evaluated for two years at a 5 percent discount rate and a $5,000 DALY. When the human losses are deducted from the GDP savings, we have net benefits of $4.335 billion associated with the third solution.

Next, we turn to costs which have been computed by the Congressional Research Service (Belasco, 2007). For the relevant two years, Operation Enduring Freedom costs $35.5 billion, while Operation Noble Eagle costs $21 billion for a total of $56.5 billion. This figure drops to $35.5 billion if we leave out Operation Noble Eagle on the grounds that it was only indirectly of a proactive nature. The BCR for the higher costs is 0.077, giving back less than eight cents on a dollar, while the BCR for the lower costs is 0.122, giving back just over twelve cents on a dollar. Given the short-term fix of such proactive campaigns and their great expense, the adverse ratios are not so surprising. It does not help that terrorists tend to respond with more deadly events to make their fewer operations have a greater anxiety consequence. If we use the $2 million value of life calculations, the BCR falls to 0.047 for the high-cost estimate and to 0.075 for the low-cost estimate. The ratios are even more adverse because the casualties that rose with proactive measures now have a greater value. In fact, if we were to include expenditures

by US allies, the BCRs would be even more adverse.

A proactive campaign would pay better if there is a way to eliminate the terrorist threat long term as some European nations did with left-wing terrorists – e.g., Italy with the Red Brigades, France with Direct Action, and Germany with Red Army Faction. But this assumes that terrorist groups in one country do not inspire groups in other countries to take up the cause. Unfortunately, the al-Qaida network encourages groups to take up the holy war. To limit the negative consequences from a proactive campaign, actions must be measured and properly justified to the world audience to maintain the high moral ground.

Solution 4: Augmented Defensive Measures

Our fourth solution is to harden targets globally in order to decrease terrorists' success and to limit their gains when they are logistically successful. This solution is fraught with difficulties because there will always be softer targets somewhere so that such actions will cause some transference of attacks. Transference is, however, not necessarily all bad if the terrorists are forced to attack a less valuable venue. To begin this thought experiment, we must choose a percentage increase for defensive measures. In fact, the percentage really does not make much difference to the BCRs and so we choose a 25 percent increase for illustration.

Since the increase is only in defensive measures, costs must be based on one of the methods in Table 9.11 that includes no proactive response. To be as conservative as possible, we choose M9 which gives the smallest cost estimate. The capitalized five-year costs of this solution are easy to calculate and equal $74.6 billion (= 0.25 × $298.3 billion). Benefits are far more difficult to compute because of transference; thus, we should anticipate that the number of attacks will *not* fall by 25 percent. To make the strongest possible case for the adverse BCR to follow, we assume the very best (but unlikely) scenario – that attacks drop by 25 percent. This assumption means that our benefits are an upper bound on the true benefits. With this assumption, the capitalized five-year benefits in saved GDP are $20.852 billion. To these benefits, we must add the estimated gains from fewer casualties. Again, we allow for the best possible scenario where the annual average number of deaths and wounds (for the 1968–2006 period) fall by 25 percent. This means 313 fewer wounded and 105 fewer dead per year for capitalized five-year benefits of $76.31 million and $40.86 million, respectively, when based on a $5,000 DALY and 5 percent discount rate. Thus, total benefits are $20.969 billion so that BCR equals 0.281 or a return of about 28 cents on a dollar. In fact, benefits are less than this best-case scenario, thus implying a smaller BCR. The ratio will improve if we use a $2 million value of life, because the best-case benefits from reduced casualties are $1.854 billion – i.e., $899.58 million from wounded and $954.65 million from deaths. Now, BCR equals 0.304, which is still adverse.

Virtually, any percentage increase in defensive measures will yield similar BCRs. The driver of this result is that security costs far outweigh the counterfactual benefits in terms of lower casualties and saved GDP. Such a solution can be more attractive if transnational terrorism becomes more deadly or more harmful to the economy. For this to happen, we must envision chemical, biological, radiological, or nuclear terrorist attacks, which we address later. Based on current threats, it is not surprising that enhanced security is not an ideal solution, because nations probably already spend too much on security in strategic actions to shift attacks abroad.

Solution 5: More Sensitive Foreign Policies on the Part of a Prime-Target Nation

The last solution is the most difficult to evaluate on either a cost or benefit basis. This solution is motivated, in part, by Michael Scheuer's (2006) *Through Our Enemies' Eyes*, in which he explains that fundamentalist-based transnational terrorism has been a reaction to insensitive US foreign policy.

This solution requires projecting a more positive US image, negating terrorist propaganda, identifying terrorist hypocrisy (e.g., when they murder Muslims in Jordan and Egypt), and showing a more humane side of US foreign policy. This may be achieved, in part, by being more evenhanded by recognizing Israeli and Palestinian rights to exist and prosper. In other instances, more sensitive foreign policy can be promoted by reallocating and/or increasing foreign assistance. Currently, the United States gives only 0.17 percent of gross net income as official development assistance – some $22.7 billion in 2006 (OECD, 2007). Next to Greece, the United States allocates the smallest share of national income among OECD countries to foreign assistance. Moreover, US aid is highly skewed to countries that support the United States in its foreign policy agenda. Currently, the larger shares of US foreign assistance goes to Iraq, Sudan, Afghanistan, Pakistan, Colombia, Israel, Jordan, and Ethiopia – countries that the United States deem important in its war on terror. Such aid is not necessarily looked upon as being altruistic, given that the United States is pursuing policy goals with its gifts. Some redistribution of foreign aid may be a costless way of winning favor with the world community through efforts to direct aid to helping people without reciprocity.

Given its ability to move people and supplies, the United States is in an excellent position to bring relief to disaster areas. US efforts in Indonesia after the December 2004 tsunami were an effective way to display a humane side of the United States to a country with a large Muslim population. Efforts by the United States to expand its humanitarian aid in terms of greater foreign assistance with no strings attached will gain respect for the United States within the world community. Certainly, the United States has the capacity to do more to address hunger, diseases, and poverty.

Terrorists have been adept in winning over people with ideas and values. The United States and other target countries must also learn to gain the high moral ground through culture-sensitive policies that do not impose Western values. In this regard, democracy cannot be rapidly introduced into countries that have had little or no experience with democracy. US administrations must choose their words carefully, not to insult or humiliate other countries whose policy goals differ with those of the United States. The United States must also ensure that its treatment of prisoners maintains the rights and liberties, embodied by international law. Ill-treatment of prisoners may result in an outbreak of terrorist actions as hostage-taking events showed following the April 2004 revelations about US abuses at Abu Ghraib. Instead of seeking military bases in the Middle East, the United States could rely on its aircraft carriers to position troops and materiel as required. Land bases have led to clashes of culture in the past that have angered people against the United States.

Although it is difficult, we try to estimate the magnitude of the benefits from a more sensitive US foreign policy. Suppose that this policy solution decreases attacks against US interests by 25 percent a year. This would reduce transnational terrorism by 10 percent since 40 percent of all transnational terrorist attacks are on average directed against US interests, mostly abroad. This would then save $8.34 billion in GDP when capitalized over five years. If, moreover, homeland security could be reduced worldwide by 10 percent owing to the lessened threat, then this would save at least another $29.83 billion over five years. These two benefits total $38.17 billion. Reduced casualties (42 fewer fatalities and 125 fewer wounded) from 10 percent fewer attacks provide additional benefits of $46.868 million over five years at a $5,000 DALY. In total, benefits are estimated at $38.217 billion if a quarter of attacks against US interests are curbed.

With the exception of increased foreign aid, this solution is virtually costless since foreign assistance can be redistributed among recipients with little or no costs to the US budget. Ensuring that the United States respects human rights in its handling of prisoners of war is also costless. If the 25 percent reduction in US-oriented attacks is a reasonable assumption, then foreign aid can be increased by $7–8 billion a year and still give a BCR that is 1 or larger. This is about a 33 percent increase in US-funded official development assistance. Even if US attacks drop by less than 25 percent, this solution has much to offer because any fall in such attacks has a payback with little expense. The United States needs to understand what it can do through its rhetoric and policy stance to reduce transnational terrorist attacks against its interests that have negative consequences for countries where attacks are staged.

Of course, it is very difficult to know what type of foreign assistance will do the most to win favor with people worldwide and to curb transnational terrorism. We believe that assistance that responds to dire needs and has no reciprocity implied holds the best chances in this regard. A recent study indicates that regimes with greater civil liberties are better able to curb transnational terrorism (Krueger and Maleckova, 2003). Tavares (2004) shows that regimes with more civil liberties sustain smaller GDP losses from terrorism.

Solution Summary

Table 9.13 provides a summary of the five solutions and their basic variants in terms of benefits, costs, and BCRs. For four of the solutions (all except Solution 2), we calculate the consequences of casualties in terms of $5,000 DALY and a $2 million value of life. There would be little change to the BCRs if we used $1,000 DALY since savings in GDP and spending on security are driving our results. If we were to use a discount rate of 3 percent instead of 5 percent, then this will have little effect on the BCRs for Solutions 1, 3, and 4. For example, the BCRs for Solution 1 rise slightly to 0.098 and 0.040 as benefits increase slightly relative to costs. A lower discount rate will leave the ratios for the two variants of Solution 2 unaffected owing to our long time horizon. For Solution 5, a lower discount rate will make the benefits more favorable. In the Appendix, Table 9.1.3 indicates benefits, costs, and BCRs for our solutions using a 3 percent discount rate. The Appendix also gives the calculations for the cost of homeland security (Table 9.1.1) and lost GDP

Table 9.13. Solutions: benefits, costs, and benefit–cost ratios based on 5% discount rate (benefits and costs are in billions of US$)

Solutions	$5,000 DALY			$2 million value of life		
	Benefits	Costs	BCR	Benefits	Costs	BCR
Solution 1 (M9)[1]	28.343	298.3	0.095	28.094	298.3	0.094
Solution 1 (M7)[1]	28.343	727.7	0.039	28.094	727.7	0.039
Solution 2A[2]	20.000	3.74	5.348	–	–	–
Solution 2B[2]	20.000	1.29	15.504	–	–	–
Solution 3A[3]	4.335	56.5	0.077	2.657	56.5	0.047
Solution 3B[3]	4.335	35.5	0.122	2.657	35.5	0.075
Solution 4	20.969	74.6	0.281	22.706	74.6	0.304
Solution 5	38.217	–	–	38.930	–	–

[1] Solution 1 (M9) is based on Method 9 in Table 11 for calculating homeland security expense; Solution 1 (M7) is based on Method 7 in Table 11 for calculating homeland security expense.
[2] Solution 2A uses a higher costs for police cooperation and IMF monitoring than Solution 2B. DALY and Value of Life do not figure into the calculations of benefits for Solution 2A and 2B.
[3] Solution 3A is based on the cost of Operation Enduring Freedom (Afghanistan) and Operation Noble Eagle, while Solution 3B is only based on the cost of Operation Enduring Freedom.

due to terrorism using a 3 percent discount rate. Regardless of the discount rate, our basic message remains the same: security-based solutions display adverse BCRs. We favor low-cost solutions that either augment international cooperation of target governments or else put forward a more sensitive foreign policy stance. Neither of these solutions are easy to implement.

Prognosis for the Future and Conclusions

The biggest unknown is what types of attacks may be used by terrorists in the future. Our adverse BCRs for costly Solutions 1, 3, and 4 are because transnational terrorism has not killed or injured many people and has done relatively little damage to economies. But more deadly and damaging attacks in the future may eventually justify the high cost of defensive and proactive expenditures. Surely, this fear drives US expenditure on homeland security and its global war on terrorism. As al-Qaida strengthens, the United States has good reason to be vigilant and proactive against new terrorist attacks that can be very costly.

For the future, the most worrying terrorist attacks are chemical, biological, radiological, or nuclear (CBRN) in nature. Table 9.14 lists examples of each kind of CBRN terrorist attacks. Chemical attacks may involve nerve, blood, choking, or blistering agents, which if dispersed in confined areas can murder large numbers of people. The March 1995 sarin attack on the Tokyo subway had this potential but fortunately did not disperse as planned and so only twelve people died. For biological terrorist attacks, viruses and bacteria pose the greatest concern because once deployed they can replicate themselves and be passed among the victims. Fortunately, bacteria, such as anthrax, are difficult to "weaponize" so that the bacteria will be inhaled in sufficient quantity by the victims. The optimal aerosol particle size is one to five microns, which is sufficiently tiny to remain airborne for hours and sufficiently light to be readily dispersed through air-exchange systems in buildings and other closed spaces. The most worrisome radiological attack is a dirty bomb, which is an explosive device used to disperse highly radioactive substances. A dirty bomb in Manhattan or Los Angeles can create huge economic consequences by making parts of the

Table 9.14. Types of chemical, biological, radiological, and nuclear attacks

* *Chemical attacks*
    * Nerve agents (for example, sarin, VX)
    * Blood agents (for example, hydrogen cyanide)
    * Choking agents (for example, chlorine)
    * Blistering agents (for example, mustard gas)
* *Biological attacks*
    * Poison (for example, ricin, botulinum toxin)
    * Viruses (for example, smallpox, viral hemorrhagic fevers, flu)
    * Bacteria (for example, anthrax)
    * Plagues (for example, black plague, tularemia)
* *Radiological attacks*
    * Radiological dispersement device (for example, dirty bomb)
    * Spread radioactive contaminants without a bomb or device
* *Nuclear terrorism*
    * Attack against a nuclear facility
    * Exploding a nuclear bomb
    * Stealing a bomb and blackmail

Source: Enders and Sandler (2006a, Table 11.1), Institute of Medicine (2002), and White (2003).

city uninhabitable if plutonium has been used. Nuclear terrorist attacks are the most unlikely.

In recent papers, Ivanova and Sandler (2006, 2007) investigate the likely nature of future CBRN terrorist attacks, based on data on past CBRN terrorist incidents, gathered by the Monterey Institute of International Studies. On average, past CBRN incidents killed a half of a person, thus making them only half as deadly as conventional terrorist attacks (Ivanova and Sandler, 2006). This does not mean that future CBRN terrorist attack will kill few people; rather, it means that conventional terrorism has, until now, posed a greater threat. As a potential hazard, CBRN terrorism presents a great potential risk that justifies vigilance and security precautions. In past incidents, the most common CBRN agent was chemical substances (205 incidents), which account for almost two-thirds of all sample incidents.[12] Biological events are second with forty-two instances. There were relatively few radiological events (twenty-six) and even fewer nuclear incidents (eight). Ivanova and Sandler (2006, 2007) demonstrate that religious cults and terrorist groups with a transnational orientation pose the largest threat. Moreover, groups that engaged in a past CBRN incident are more likely to participate in future CBRN incidents. Rich democratic countries are the likely venue for future CBRN attacks.

When CBRN terrorism becomes a greater possibility, the BCRs for Solutions 1, 3, and 4 will become much larger as benefits grow relative to costs. Fortunately, there are some inhibitors for this disturbing scenario. The cellular structure of today's terrorist groups makes it difficult for them to surmount acquisition and weaponization barriers. CBRN agents pose a handling risk that many terrorists are reluctant to assume. A deadly CBRN terrorist attack is apt to alienate supporters of some terrorist groups. Moreover, such attacks will induce a target country to unleash an unrestrained retaliation that many groups cannot survive – e.g., Aum Shinrikyo following the sarin attack on the Tokyo subway. Finally, a conventional attack like 9/11 is sufficiently deadly to limit the need for CBRN terrorist attacks.

We conclude with some basic insights. First, there is no panacea for transnational terrorism – effective action buys a government some time until a new group surfaces or terrorists discover novel ways to circumvent barriers. Transnational terrorism favors terrorists over a more capable government. Second, solutions that rely on massive defensive and/or proactive measures have adverse BCRs, primarily because such actions are very expensive. Third, transnational terrorism has, in the past, been associated with relatively few casualties and small economic consequences. Fourth, the best remedies are the cheap ones that either foster international cooperation or make prime-target nations think through foreign policy choices.

[12] The statistics in this paragraph come from Ivanova and Sandler (2007)

These solutions are the most difficult to achieve. We do *not* advocate that governments concede to terrorists' demands; rather, we recommend that foreign policy be evenhanded, farsighted, and respectful of other cultures.

We fully recognize that many people will fault our efforts as "making up numbers." Based on calibrated losses of GDP, past casualties, and expenditures on homeland security, we devise counterfactuals to ascertain the payback per dollar for certain solutions to transnational ter-

rorism. Our BCRs are very robust to alternative assumptions. We hope that our study motivates others to ask: are current policy choices with respect to transnational terrorism worth the expenditures? This question needs to be asked and answered. Also, the global community must consider expenditures on transnational terrorism relative to other challenges such as disease, hunger, and the environment. This study is a first step to addressing such questions.

Appendix

The following tables relate to the use of a 3 percent discount rate when computing the cost of homeland security (Table 9.1.1) and lost GDP due to transnational terrorism (Table 9.1.2). Table 9.1.3 replicates Table 13 but based on a 3 percent discount rate.

Table 9A.1. Worldwide homeland security estimates under nine alternative methods (in $ billions): 3% discount rate

Country	GDP 2005 (current US$)	M1	M2	M3	M4	M5	M6	M7	M8	M9
Afghanistan	7.2	0.025	0.010	0.025	0.025	0.023	0.007	0.010	0.007	0.004
Algeria	102.3	0.358	0.149	0.358	0.358	0.327	0.102	0.149	0.102	0.051
Argentina	183.3	0.642	0.268	0.642	0.642	0.587	0.183	0.268	0.183	0.092
Australia	700.7	2.452	1.023	2.452	2.452	2.242	0.701	1.023	0.701	0.350
Austria	304.5	1.066	0.445	1.066	1.066	0.974	0.305	0.445	0.305	0.152
Bahrain	13.0	0.045	0.019	0.045	0.045	0.042	0.013	0.019	0.013	0.006
Belgium	364.7	1.277	0.533	1.277	1.277	1.167	0.365	0.533	0.365	0.182
Bosnia and Herzegovina	9.4	0.033	0.014	0.033	0.033	0.030	0.009	0.014	0.009	0.005
Brazil	794.1	2.779	1.159	2.779	2.779	2.541	0.794	1.159	0.794	0.397
Canada	1115.2	3.903	1.628	3.903	3.903	3.569	1.115	1.628	1.115	0.558
China	2228.9	7.801	3.254	7.801	7.801	7.132	2.229	3.254	2.229	1.114
Colombia	122.3	0.428	0.179	0.428	0.428	0.391	0.122	0.179	0.122	0.061
Cyprus	15.7	0.055	0.023	0.055	0.055	0.050	0.016	0.023	0.016	0.008
Czech Republic	122.3	0.428	0.179	0.428	0.428	0.392	0.122	0.179	0.122	0.061
Denmark	254.4	0.890	0.371	0.890	0.890	0.814	0.254	0.371	0.254	0.127
Egypt, Arab Rep.	89.3	0.313	0.130	0.313	0.313	0.286	0.089	0.130	0.089	0.045
Finland	193.2	0.676	0.282	0.676	0.676	0.618	0.193	0.282	0.193	0.097
France	2110.2	7.386	3.081	7.386	7.386	6.753	2.110	3.081	2.110	1.055
Georgia	6.4	0.022	0.009	0.022	0.022	0.020	0.006	0.009	0.006	0.003
Germany	2781.9	9.737	4.062	9.737	9.737	8.902	2.782	4.062	2.782	1.391
Greece	213.7	0.748	0.312	0.748	0.748	0.684	0.214	0.312	0.214	0.107
Haiti	4.2	0.015	0.006	0.015	0.015	0.014	0.004	0.006	0.004	0.002
Hungary	109.2	0.382	0.159	0.382	0.382	0.349	0.109	0.159	0.109	0.055
India	785.5	2.749	1.147	2.749	2.749	2.513	0.785	1.147	0.785	0.393
Indonesia	287.2	1.005	0.419	1.005	1.005	0.919	0.287	0.419	0.287	0.144

Table 9A.1. (continued)

Country	GDP 2005 (current US$)	M1	M2	M3	M4	M5	M6	M7	M8	M9
Ireland	196.4	0.687	0.287	0.687	0.687	0.628	0.196	0.287	0.196	0.098
Israel	123.4	0.432	0.180	0.913	0.469	0.395	0.432	0.913	0.432	0.432
Italy	1723.0	6.031	2.516	6.031	6.031	5.514	1.723	2.516	1.723	0.862
Japan	4505.9	15.771	6.579	15.771	15.771	14.419	4.506	6.579	4.506	2.253
Jordan	12.9	0.045	0.019	0.045	0.045	0.041	0.013	0.019	0.013	0.006
Kenya	18.0	0.063	0.026	0.063	0.063	0.058	0.018	0.026	0.018	0.009
Korea, Rep.	787.6	2.757	1.150	2.757	2.757	2.520	0.788	1.150	0.788	0.394
Kuwait	74.7	0.261	0.109	0.261	0.261	0.239	0.075	0.109	0.075	0.037
Lebanon	22.2	0.078	0.032	0.078	0.078	0.071	0.022	0.032	0.022	0.011
Luxembourg	33.8	0.118	0.049	0.118	0.118	0.108	0.034	0.049	0.034	0.017
Malaysia	130.1	0.456	0.190	0.456	0.456	0.416	0.130	0.190	0.130	0.065
Mexico	768.4	2.690	1.122	2.690	2.690	2.459	0.768	1.122	0.768	0.384
Morocco	51.7	0.181	0.076	0.181	0.181	0.166	0.052	0.076	0.052	0.026
Netherlands	594.8	2.082	0.868	2.082	2.082	1.903	0.595	0.868	0.595	0.297
New Zealand	109.0	0.382	0.159	0.382	0.382	0.349	0.109	0.159	0.109	0.055
Norway	283.9	0.994	0.415	0.994	0.994	0.909	0.284	0.415	0.284	0.142
Pakistan	110.7	0.388	0.162	0.388	0.388	0.354	0.111	0.162	0.111	0.055
Peru	78.4	0.275	0.115	0.275	0.275	0.251	0.078	0.115	0.078	0.039
Philippines	98.3	0.344	0.144	0.344	0.344	0.315	0.098	0.144	0.098	0.049
Poland	299.2	1.047	0.437	1.047	1.047	0.957	0.299	0.437	0.299	0.150
Portugal	173.1	0.606	0.253	0.606	0.606	0.554	0.173	0.253	0.173	0.087
Qatar	29.0	0.102	0.042	0.102	0.102	0.093	0.029	0.042	0.029	0.015
Romania	98.6	0.345	0.144	0.345	0.345	0.315	0.099	0.144	0.099	0.049
Russian Fed.	763.7	2.673	1.115	5.652	2.902	2.444	2.673	5.652	2.673	2.673
Saudi Arabia	309.8	1.084	0.452	1.084	1.084	0.991	0.310	0.452	0.310	0.155
Singapore	116.8	0.409	0.170	0.409	0.409	0.374	0.117	0.170	0.117	0.058
Slovak Republic	46.4	0.162	0.068	0.162	0.162	0.149	0.046	0.068	0.046	0.023
Slovenia	34.0	0.119	0.050	0.119	0.119	0.109	0.034	0.050	0.034	0.017
South Africa	240.2	0.841	0.351	0.841	0.841	0.768	0.240	0.351	0.240	0.120
Spain	1123.7	3.933	1.641	3.933	3.933	3.596	1.124	1.641	1.124	0.562
Sri Lanka	23.5	0.082	0.034	0.082	0.082	0.075	0.023	0.034	0.023	0.012
Sweden	354.1	1.239	0.517	1.239	1.239	1.133	0.354	0.517	0.354	0.177
Switzerland	365.9	1.281	0.534	1.281	1.281	1.171	0.366	0.534	0.366	0.183
Tanzania	12.1	0.042	0.018	0.042	0.042	0.039	0.012	0.018	0.012	0.006
Thailand	176.6	0.618	0.258	0.618	0.618	0.565	0.177	0.258	0.177	0.088
Turkey	363.3	1.272	0.530	1.272	1.272	1.163	0.363	0.530	0.363	0.182
Ukraine	81.7	0.286	0.119	0.286	0.286	0.261	0.082	0.119	0.082	0.041
United Kingdom	2192.6	7.674	3.201	16.225	8.332	7.016	7.674	16.225	3.201	3.201
United States	12455.1	43.593	43.593	92.168	47.329	39.856	43.593	92.168	43.593	43.593

Table 9A.1. (continued)

Country	GDP 2005 (current US$)	M1	M2	M3	M4	M5	M6	M7	M8	M9
Venezuela, RB	138.9	0.486	0.203	0.486	0.486	0.444	0.139	0.203	0.139	0.069
Yemen, Rep.	14.5	0.051	0.021	0.051	0.051	0.046	0.014	0.021	0.014	0.007
Total		147.19	86.81	207.78	151.85	134.57	80.89	153.68	76.42	63.16
FV2005		147.19	86.81	207.78	151.85	134.57	80.89	153.68	76.42	63.16
FV2006		150.14	88.54	211.93	154.89	137.27	82.51	156.75	77.95	64.42
FV2007		153.14	90.32	216.17	157.99	140.01	84.16	159.88	79.51	65.71
FV2008		156.20	92.12	220.49	161.15	142.81	85.84	163.08	81.10	67.02
FV2009		159.32	93.96	224.90	164.37	145.67	87.56	166.34	82.72	68.37
PV in billions of US$		721.8	425.7	1018.9	744.7	659.9	396.7	753.6	374.7	309.7

Method 1 (M1): US homeland security percentage of 0.35 of GDP is applied to all sample countries.
Method 2 (M2): US homeland security percentage of 0.35 of GDP is applied to just the United States; UK homeland security percentage of 0.146 of GDP is applied to other sample countries.
Method 3 (M3): US homeland security plus Afghanistan/Iraq campaigns percentage of 0.74 of GDP is applied to United States, United Kingdom, Israel, and Russia; US homeland security percentage of 0.35 of GDP is applied to other sample countries.
Method 4 (M4): US homeland security percentage of 0.38 of GDP without Iraq campaign is applied to United States, United Kingdom, Israel, and Russia; US homeland security percentage of 0.35 of GDP is applied to other sample countries.
Method 5 (M5): US homeland security percentage of 0.32 of GDP is applied to all sample countries. This percentage equals the share of GDP that consists of 61 percent of US DHS budget plus $10 billion for private security.
Method 6 (M6): US homeland security of 0.35 of GDP is applied to the United States, United Kingdom, Israel, and Russia; 0.10 percent of GDP is applied to other sample countries.
Method 7 (M7): US homeland security percentage of 0.74 of GDP is applied to the United States, Israel, and Russia; UK homeland security percentage of 0.146 of GDP is applied to all other sample countries.
Method 8 (M8): US homeland security percentage of 0.35 of GDP is applied to the United States, Israel, and Russia; UK homeland security percentage of 0.146 of GDP is applied to United Kingdom; and 0.10 percent of GDP is applied to all other sample countries.
Method 9 (M9): US homeland security percentage of 0.35 of GDP is applied to the United States, Israel, and Russia; UK homeland security percentage of 0.146 of GDP is applied to the United Kingdom; and 0.05 percent of GDP is applied to other sample countries.

Table 9A.2. Lost GDP due to transnational terrorism attacks (3% discount rate)

Country	Pop (000)	T_i	per capita GDP	2005 growth (%)	2005 cost[2]	2005 cost (average)[3]	5-year cost in (growth)[4]
Algeria	32,854	2	$2,066	3.65		$47,625	$242,655
Angola	15,941	1	891	10.90		14,889	93,424
Argentina	38,747	2	8,096	7.87		475,126	2,734,894
Australia	20,321	1	22,423	1.53		66,962	320,725
Bahrain	727	1	14,588	5.18		5,278	28,111
Bangladesh	141,822	1	415	3.43		19,427	98,361
Belgium	10,471	1	23,381	0.72		16,980	79,430
Bosnia-Herzegovina	3,907	4	1,486	5.25	$14,658	11,726	62,588
Brazil	186,405	2	3,597	0.92		118,876	559,353
Burundi	7,548	2	105	−1.89		288	1,246
Cambodia	14,071	1	356	4.89		2,357	12,454
Chad	9,749	1	267	2.27		569	2,785
Chile	16,295	1	5,747	5.09		45,813	243,368
Colombia	45,600	3	2,174	3.51		100,425	509,647

Table 9A.2. (continued)

Country	Pop (000)	T_i	per capita GDP	2005 growth (%)	2005 cost[2]	2005 cost (average)[3]	5-year cost in (growth)[4]
Congo-Brazzaville	57,549	4	997	5.89	162,441	129,952	706,486
Czech Republic	10,196	1	6,515	5.98		38,190	208,157
Denmark	5,418	1	31,607	2.80		46,082	229,057
Ecuador	13,228	1	1,534	2.37		4,635	22,756
Egypt	74,033	3	1,662	2.87	169,746	101,848	507,294
El Salvador	6,881	1	2,127	0.99		1,397	6,586
Eritrea	4,401	1	176	1.14		85	403
Germany	82,485	3	23,928	0.94		533,246	2,510,188
France	60,743	4	23,641	0.89		490,591	2,306,124
Georgia	4,474	3	23,928	0.94		28,926	136,165
Greece	11,089	2	12,367	3.35		88,280	445,875
Haiti	8,528	2	428	0.70	1,235	494	2,309
Hong Kong	6,944	1	29,945	6.14		122,699	671,844
India	1,094,583	4	586	6.70	2,068,104	1,654,484	9,208,957
Indonesia	220,558	4	942	4.12	411,415	329,132	1,700,009
Iran	67,700	2	1,962	4.75		121,346	638,347
Israel	6,909	4	18,406	3.42		167,090	845,612
Italy	57,471	4	19,387	0.18		77,457	356,621
Jordan	5,411	3	2,091	4.45	24,211	14,527	75,759
Kenya	34,256	2	428	0.23		660	3,042
Kuwait	2,535	4	20,578	5.12	128,457	102,766	546,433
Kyrgyzstan	5,156	2	319	-1.56		492	2,153
Lebanon	3,577	3	5,627	-0.02	172	103	472
Libya	5,853	1	7,517	1.53		6,467	30,976
Macedonia	2,034	1	1,889	3.72		1,375	7,022
Madagascar	18,606	1	233	1.73		722	3,479
Malaysia	25,347	3	4,434	3.30		107,068	540,059
Mauritania	3,069	1	447	2.26	1,493	299	1,461
Mexico	103,089	1	6,172	1.90		116,112	562,179
Morocco	30,168	2	1,354	0.37		2,907	13,459
Netherlands	16,329	1	23,535	0.80		29,646	139,004
Nigeria	131,530	1	420	4.38	116,369	23,274	121,131
Norway	4,618	1	39,666	1.68		29,610	142,455
Pakistan	155,772	4	596	5.16	230,590	184,472	982,168
Peru	27,968	2	2,319	5.00		62,326	330,217
Philippines	83,054	3	1,124	3.26		87,686	441,699
Saudi Arabia	24,573	4	9,323	3.78		333,331	1,704,995
Sierra Leone	5,525	1	218	3.74		433	2,213
Singapore	4,351	1	25,443	3.60		38,306	194,889

Table 9A.2. (continued)

Country	Pop (000)	T_i	per capita GDP	2005 growth (%)	2005 cost[2]	2005 cost (average)[3]	5-year cost in (growth)[4]
Solomon Islands	478	1	647	1.71		51	246
Spain	43,389	3	15,610	1.73		337,165	1,624,253
Sri Lanka	19,582	3	1,004	4.27		24,242	125,781
Sudan	36,233	4	462	5.56	44,785	35,828	192,965
Sweden	9,024	1	29,532	2.31		59,178	289,984
Syria	19,043	1	1,161	1.65		3,509	16,867
Tajikistan	6,507	1	237	6.09		903	4,939
Thailand	64,233	3	2,440	3.50		158,429	803,834
Tunisia	10,022	1	2,418	3.24		7,543	37,975
Turkey	72,636	5	3,390	5.86	694,126	694,126	3,770,854
United Kingdom	60,203	4	26,688	1.23	946,715	757,372	3,595,552
United States	296,497	3	37,574	2.48	13,266,740	7,960,044	39,197,172
Russia	143,151	5	2,444	6.68	1,124,468	1,124,468	6,255,039
Uzbekistan	26,593	1	673	5.18		8,924	47,539
Venezuela	26,577	2	4,939	7.20		181,743	1,026,043
Yemen	20,975	4	590	1.02	6,083	4,867	22,966
Totals					$19,411,808	$17,363,247	$88,349,106

[1] Pop = population in 2005 in thousands; T_i = number of years during 2001–2005 in which there was at least one terrorist event; per capita GDP = per capita GDP in thousands of real 2000 US dollars; 2005 growth = growth rate of per capita GDP between 2004 and 2005 (in percent); 2005 cost = estimated real GDP cost of terrorism (in thousands) using the 2005 measure of terrorist incidents; 2005 cost (average) = estimated real GDP cost of terrorism (in thousands) using the average level of terrorism over the 2001–2005 period; 5-year cost = real present value of 2005 cost (average) (in thousands) over the next five years using a 3% discount rate.
[2] If a country had at least one terrorist in 2005, the entry for 2005 cost is measured as (Pop × per capita GDP) × (2005 growth/100) × 0.048.
[3] The entries for 2005 cost (average) is computed as: $(T/5)$(Pop × per capita GDP) × (2005 growth/100) × 0.048.
[4] 5-year cost is the present value of the entry for 2005 cost (average) for each of the next four years discounted at a 3 percent real interest rate. The "growth" entries project that per capita GDP levels continue at their 2005 growth rates.

Table 9A.3. Solutions: benefits, costs, and benefit–cost ratios based on 3% discount rate (benefits and costs are in billions of US$)

Solutions	$5,000 DALY			$2 million value of life		
	Benefits	Costs	BCR	Benefits	Costs	BCR
Solution 1 (M9)[1]	30.032	309.7	0.097	30.326	309.7	0.098
Solution 1 (M7)[1]	30.032	753.6	0.040	30.326	753.6	0.040
Solution 2A[2]	33.333	6.23	5.348	–	–	–
Solution 2B[2]	33.333	2.15	15.504	–	–	–
Solution 3A[3]	4.373	56.5	0.077	2.678	56.5	0.047
Solution 3B[3]	4.373	35.5	0.123	2.678	35.5	0.075
Solution 4	22.185	77.425	0.287	24.928	77.425	0.321
Solution 5	40.843	–	–	41.550	–	–

[1] Solution 1 (M9) is based on Method 9 in Table 11 for calculating homeland security expense; Solution 1 (M7) is based on Method 7 in Table 11 for calculating homeland security expense.
[2] Solution 2A uses higher costs for police cooperation and IMF monitoring than Solution 2B. DALY and Value of Life do not figure into the calculations of benefits for Solution 2A and 2B.
[3] Solution 3A is based on the cost of Operation Enduring Freedom (Afghanistan) and Operation Noble Eagle, while Solution 3B is only based on the cost of Operation Enduring Freedom.

Bibliography

Abadie, A., and J. Gardeazabal, 2003: The economic cost of conflict: a case study of the Basque country, *American Economic Review*, 93(1), 113–132

2008: Terrorism and the world economy, *European Economic Review*, 52(1), 1–27

Abenhaim, L., W. Dab, and L.R. Salmi, 1992: Study of civilian victims of terrorist attacks (France 1982–1987), *Journal of Clinical Epidemiology*, 45(2), 103–109

Alexander, Y., and D. Pluchinsky, 1992: *Europe's red terrorists: the fighting communist organizations*, Frank Cass, London

Belasco, A., 2007: The cost of Iraq, Afghanistan, and other global war on terror operations since 9/11, Congressional Research Service (CRS) Report for Congress, Code RL33110, CRS, Washington, DC

Blomberg, S.B., and A. Mody, 2005: How severely does violence deter international investment?, mimeo, Department of Economics, Claremont McKenna College, Claremont, CA

Blomberg, S.B., G.D. Hess, and A. Orphanides, 2004: The macroeconomic consequences of terrorism, *Journal of Monetary Economics*, 51(5), 1007–1032

Bloom, M., 2005: *Dying to kill: the allure of suicide terror*, Columbia University Press, New York

Brandt, P., and T. Sandler, 2009: Hostage taking: understanding terrorism event dynamics, *Journal of Policy Modeling*, 31, forthcoming

Chen, A.H., and T.F. Siems, 2004: The effects of terrorism on global capital markets, *European Journal of Political Economy*, 20(2), 249–266

Collier, P., L. Elliot, H. Hegre, A. Hoeffler, M. Reynal-Querol, and N. Sambanis, 2003: *Breaking the conflict trap: civil war and development policy*, Oxford University Press, Oxford

Committee to Study Sustainable Long-Term Financing of the IMF, 2007: *Final report* (Crockett Report), International Monetary Fund, Washington, DC

Cronin, A.K., 2006: How al-Qaida ends: the decline and demise of terrorist groups, *International Security*, 31(1), 7–48

Department of Homeland Security (DHS), 2004: *Budget in brief*, DHS, Washington, DC, www.dhs.gov/interweb/assetlibrary/FY_2005_BIB_4.pdf

Drakos, K., 2004: Terrorism-induced structural shifts in financial risk: airline stocks in the aftermath of the September 11th terror attacks, *European Journal of Political Economy*, 20(2), 436–446

Eckstein, Z., and D. Tsiddon, 2004: Macroeconomic consequences of terror: theory and the case of Israel, *Journal of Monetary Economics*, 51(5), 971–1002

Enders, W., and T. Sandler, 1993: The effectiveness of anti-terrorism policies: a vector-autoregression-intervention analysis, *American Political Science Review*, 87(4), 829–844

1995: Terrorism: theory and applications. In K. Hartley and T. Sandler (eds.), *Handbook of defense economics, vol. 1*, North-Holland, Amsterdam, 213–249

1996: Terrorism and foreign direct investment in Spain and Greece, *Kyklos*, 49(3), 331–352

2000: Is transnational terrorism becoming more threatening? A time-series investigation, *Journal of Conflict Resolution*, 44(3), 307–322

2002: Patterns of transnational terrorism, 1970-1999: alternative time-series estimates, *International Studies Quarterly*, 46(2), 145–165

2006a: *The political economy of terrorism*, Cambridge University Press, Cambridge

2006b: Distribution of transnational terrorism among countries by income class and geography after 9/11, *International Studies Quarterly*, 50(2), 367–393

Enders, W., and X. Su, 2007: Rational terrorists and optimal network structure, *Journal of Conflict Resolution*, 51(1), 33–57

Enders, W., A. Sachsida, and T. Sandler, 2006: The impact of transnational terrorism on US foreign direct investment, *Political Research Quarterly*, 59(4), 517–531

Enders, W., T. Sandler, and G.F. Parise, 1992: An econometric analysis of the impact of terrorism on tourism, *Kyklos*, 45(4), 531–554

Eubank, W.L., and L.B. Weinberg, 1994: Does democracy encourage terrorism?, *Terrorism and Political Violence*, 6(4), 417–435

2001: Terrorism and democracy: perpetrators and victims, *Terrorism and Political Violence*, 13(1), 155–164

Frey, B.S., 2004: *Dealing with terrorism – stick or carrot?*, Edward Elgar, Cheltenham, UK

Frykberg, E.R., 2002: Medical management of disasters and mass casualties from terrorist bombings: how can we cope?, *Journal of TRAUMA, Injury, Infections, and Critical Care*, 53(2), 201–212

Gaibulloev, K., and T. Sandler, 2008: Growth consequences of terrorism in Western Europe, *Kyklos*, 61(3), 411–424

Hobijn, B., and E. Sager, 2007: What has homeland security cost? An assessment: 2001–2005, *Current Issues in Economics and Finance*, 13(2), 1–7, www.newyorkfed.org/research/current_issues

Hoffman, B., 1998: *Inside terrorism*, Columbia University Press, New York

2003: Al Qaeda, trends in terrorism, and future potentialities: an assessment, *Studies in Conflict and Terrorism*, 26(6), 429–442

2006: *Inside terrorism*, revised ed., Columbia University Press, New York

Institute of Medicine, 2002: *Biological threats and terrorism: assessing the science and response capabilities*, National Academy Press, Washington, DC

Interpol, 2005: *Interpol at work, finances*, 30–31, www.interpol.int/Public/ICPO/InterpolAtWork/iaw2005.pdf

Ito, H., and D. Lee, 2005: Assessing the impact of the September 11th terrorist attacks on US airline demand, *Journal of Economics and Business*, 57(1), 75–95

Ivanova, K., and T. Sandler, 2006: CBRN incidents: political regimes, perpetrators, and targets, *Terrorism and Political Violence*, 18(3), 423–448

2007: CBRN attack perpetrators: an empirical study, *Foreign Policy Analysis*, 3(4), 273–294

Krueger, A.B., and J. Maleckova, 2003: Education, poverty, and terrorism: is there a causal connection?, *Journal of Economic Perspective*, 17(4), 119–144

Kunreuther, H., E. Michel-Kerjan, and B. Porter, 2003: Assessing, managing and financing extreme events: dealing with terrorism, Working Paper 10179, National Bureau of Economic Research, Cambridge, MA

Mathers, C.D., A.D. Lopez, and C.J.L. Murray, 2003: The burden of disease and mortality by condition: data, methods and results for 2001, http://files.dcp2.org/pdf/GBD/GBD03.pdf

Memorial Institute for the Prevention of Terrorism (MIPT), 2006: *Countering terrorism and knowledge*, www.mipt.org

Mickolus, E.F., 1980: *Transnational terrorism: a chronology of events 1968–1979*, Greenwood Press, Westport, CT

1982: *International terrorism: attributes of terrorist events, 1968–1977* (ITERATE 2), Inter-University Consortium for Political and Social Research, Ann Arbor, MI

1989: What constitutes state support of terrorism? *Terrorism and Political Violence*, 1(3), 287–293

Mickolus, E.F., and S.L. Simmons, 1997: *Terrorism, 1992–1995: a chronology of events and a selectively annotated bibliography*, Greenwood Press, Westport, CT

Mickolus, E.F., T. Sandler, and J.M. Murdock, 1989: *International terrorism in the 1980s: a chronology of events*, 2 vols., Iowa State University Press, Ames, IA

Mickolus, E.F., T. Sandler, J.M. Murdock, and P. Flemming, 2006: *International terrorism: attributes of terrorist events, 1968–2005* (ITERATE), Vinyard Software, Dunn Loring, VA

National Commission on Terrorist Attacks upon the United States, 2004: *The 9/11 Commission Report*, Norton, New York

Organization of Economic Cooperation and Development (OECD), 2007: Table 1: net official development assistance in 2006 (preliminary data for 2006), www.oecd.org/dataoed/14/5/38354517.pdf

Pape, R.A., 2006: *Dying to win: the strategic logic of suicide terrorism*, Random House, New York

Quillen, C., 2002a: A historical analysis of mass casualty bombers, *Studies in Conflict and Terrorism*, 25(5), 279–292

2002b: Mass casualty bombings chronology, *Studies in Conflict and Terrorism*, 25(5), 293–302

Rapoport, D.C., 1984: Fear and trembling: terrorism in three religious traditions, *American Political Science Review*, 78(3), 658–677

2004: Modern terror: the four waves. In A.K. Cronin and J.M. Ludes (eds.), *Attacking terrorism: elements of a grand strategy*,

Georgetown University Press, Washington, DC, 46–73

Rosendorff, B.P., and T. Sandler, 2004: Too much of a good thing? The proactive response dilemma, *Journal of Conflict Resolution*, 48(5), 657–671

Sandler, T., 2005: Collective versus unilateral responses to terrorism, *Public Choice*, 124(1–2), 75–93

Sandler, T., and D.G. Arce, 2003: Terrorism and game theory, *Simulation and Gaming*, 34(3), 319–337

Sandler, T., and W. Enders, 2008: Economic consequences of terrorism in developed and developing countries: an overview. In P. Keefer and N. Loayza (eds.), *Terrorism, economic development, and political openness,* Cambridge University Press, Cambridge, 17–47

Sandler, T., and K. Siqueira, 2006: Global terrorism: deterrence versus pre-emption, *Canadian Journal of Economics*, 39(4), 1370–1387

Scheuer, M., 2006: *Through our enemies' eyes*, revised ed., Potomac Books, Washington, DC

Shubik, M., A. Zelinsky, and L. Krstic, 2006: Terrorism: who pays?, Social Science Research Network, Working Paper Series, http://ssrn.com/abstract=956403

Siqueira, K., and T. Sandler, 2007: Terrorist backlash, terrorism mitigation, and policy delegation, *Journal of Public Economics*, 91(9), 1800–1815

Tavares, J., 2004: The open society assesses its enemies: shocks, disaster and terrorist attacks, *Journal of Monetary Economics*, 51(5), 1039–1070

Treverton, G.F., J.L. Adams, J. Dertouzos, A. Dutta, S.S. Everingham, and E.V. Larson, 2008: The costs of responding to the terror threat: the US case. In P. Keefer and N. Loayza (eds.), *Terrorism, economic development, and political openness*, Cambridge University Press, Cambridge, 48–80

United States Department of State, various years: *Patterns of global terrorism*, US Department of State, Washington, DC
   2007: *Country reports on terrorism*, www.state. gov/s/ct/rls/2006

US News & World Reports, 2007: Al Qaeda regroups, News desk, July 16, www.usnews. com/blogs/news-desk/2007/7/12/al-qaeda-regroups.html

Weinberg, L.B., and W.L. Eubank, 1998: Terrorism and democracy: what recent events disclose, *Terrorism and Political Violence*, 10(1), 108–118

White, J.R., 2003: Terrorism: 2002 update, 4th ed., Wadsworth/Thomson Learning, Belmont, CA

Wilkinson, P., 1986: *Terrorism and the liberal state*, revised ed., Macmillan, London
   2001: *Terrorism versus democracy: the liberal state response*, Frank Cass, London

World Bank, 2007: *World development indicators*, http://devdata.worldbank.org/dataonline

Wright, L., 2006: *The looming tower. Al-Qaeda and the road to 9/11*, Knoft, New York

Alternative Perspectives

Perspective Paper 9.1

S. BROCK BLOMBERG

1. Introduction

The guidelines for writing a Perspective Paper for the Copenhagen Consensus are well articulated. "The purpose of the Perspective Paper is to balance the Challenge Paper indicating important issues of the challenge not sufficiently dealt with in the paper. If there are several different views upon the particular challenge and the solutions solving it, the Perspective Paper Author should emphasize this and provide necessary information not sufficiently reported in the Challenge Paper. Thus, the paper shall review published research that might have been left out in the Challenge Paper; indicate alternate interpretations of the estimates; and/or point out other strengths, weaknesses and omissions in the Challenge Paper."

Sandler, Arce and Enders (2007) (henceforth SAE) have written a thorough and thoughtful Challenge Paper. It proposes five different policy alternatives, and using Benefit–cost ratio calculations, shows that most of the alternative policies to stem terrorism are not worth the effort, economically speaking. In fact, the only policy SAE find worthwhile is increasing international cooperation. The methodology is solid and the execution is top notch.

Therefore, our Perspective Paper is going to take a slightly different approach than suggested in the opening paragraph. Rather than spend the majority of the paper quibbling over the various assumptions of the Challenge Paper, we offer a more productive strategy. We provide an alternative modeling strategy to SAE. We do not presume that one approach is preferred over the other but rather provide a menu of approaches from which the reader may select, depending on his or her preferences. Our alternative model attempts to estimate the welfare cost of terrorism by exploring only the forgone consumption from being mired in a world of conflict. Following the approach by Lucas (1987), we demonstrate how one can theoretically "price" the effect that war has on consumption's growth and volatility. Intuitively, these consumption growth costs from war would be avoided in a perpetually peaceful world, which allows us to calculate the equivalent variation of how much individuals would be willing to give up in order to live in a peaceful world.

For the most part, our results dovetail with what was found in SAE. Using both the baseline GDP approach and the welfare approach, we show that business as usual (BAU) is not very cost effective, yielding 7–15 cents on the dollar. Interestingly, even though we come at the problem from a very different angle, these results are similar to what is shown by SAE, who found a return of 4–10 cents on the dollar. This may mean that these results are robust to various strategies for estimating the benefits and costs associated with the current policy environment. In addition, we show that increased proactive measures is also an ineffective policy, yielding 8–19 cents on the dollar. These values are somewhat larger than those found in SAE, though the conclusion is the same. We also show that the least cost-effective policy is the option described by SAE as "more sensitive foreign policy." In this case, we assume the more sensitive foreign policy entails increased economic aid and calculate a yield of 5–10 cents on the dollar. SAE do not actually do a formal calculation so we do not compare our results. Still, the return is not terribly different from the BAU result, implying that it would not be much worse than employing the current policy.

The one area in which we find slightly different results than SAE is the international cooperation alternative. The differences are probably because we adopt a slightly different experimental design than SAE. Instead of assuming certain returns to international cooperation, our policy experiment assumes that the international community has already been cooperating to prevent UN-targeted organizations, e.g. al-Qaida and the Taliban. Using the welfare cost approach, we find that increased international cooperation is not cost effective, yielding a return of 26 cents on the dollar. When employing the GDP cost approach, however, we find our only cost-effective result with a BCR of 1.06.

2. Experimental Design

We employ myriad candidate policies to investigate the optimal strategy to prevent transnational terrorism. Our candidate strategies follow SAE and are business as usual, increased international cooperation, increased proactive responses, enhanced defensive measures, and a more sensitive foreign policy alternative or increased economic aid. We do not consider augmenting defense measures as it is a linear projection of other alternatives. In each case, we estimate a BCR by using history and its associated counterfactual.

To conduct the policy experiment, we need to consider an environment that allows us to compare control and experimental groups. In this case, we consider that there has been a change in attitudes and policies toward terrorism pre- and post-September 11 2001. We assume the dynamics of transnational terrorism and counterterror-

ism policies were different after 2001. Obviously, conducting such an exercise requires assumptions on the causal impacts of terrorism that are almost surely overstated and in some cases problematic. With this caveat, we proceed by giving an overview of how we consider each candidate policy.

First, we investigate the impact of current counterterrorism policy by comparing the cost of increased expenditure on homeland security to the increased benefit associated with the change in incidence and severity of transnational terrorism in 2002–2006 as compared with the previous period. Second, we consider the impact of increased international cooperation by comparing the cost of increased expenditure by IMF, INTERPOL, and other international organizations versus the change in incidence and severity of transnational terrorist groups targeted by the UN (al-Qaida and the Taliban) in 2002–2006 as compared with the previous period. Third, we analyze the effect of increased proactive measures by calculating the cost of increased military intervention in the early part of the war in Afghanistan and Iraq versus the change in incidence and severity of transnational terrorism in those locales as compared with the previous period. Finally, we estimate the effect of increased economic aid by comparing the cost of the United States' economic aid to Afghanistan and the new development initiative, the Millennium Challenge Account, versus the change in incidence and severity of transnational terrorism in low-income countries as compared with the previous period.

SAE include an additional option, to augment defense measures. As this is a linear projection of other options, we felt there was little more to be gained from this option that was not already addressed in SAE. Hence, we do not consider it as an alternative.

3. Methodology

In the following subsections, we describe our approach to assessing the relative merits of a variety of policy alternatives. We first present the costs of terrorism, followed by an explanation of the value of the policy alternatives. As the experiment will be to investigate the BCR of the alternatives, we will assume the cost to society is the expenditure for each policy alternative and the benefit is the reduction in the cost to terrorism.

Estimating Human Cost of Terrorism

In this subsection, we follow the methodology of SAE exactly. Rather than repeat a detailed description of how one calculates the economic cost due to fatalities and injuries, we refer the reader to SAE. As they show, the DALYs associated with terrorism are small when compared with these other global challenges, where much larger numbers of people die or are injured.

Estimating GDP Cost of Terrorism: Baseline Approach

To estimate the GDP loss due to transnational terrorism, we begin with the approach described in SAE, with one small wrinkle – we add in the conflict complementarity associated with the transference to other forms of conflict. In other words, Blomberg, Hess, and Orphanides (2004) (henceforth BHO) demonstrated that the incidence of terrorism is associated with the incidence of other forms of conflict. These costs should also be included as an indirect cost of terrorism.

BHO also found that there was an important conflict complementarity between terrorism and internal conflicts such as civil war. Over a five-year time period, we estimate this amount to be approximately equivalent to the effect of a one-year cost associated with a terrorist event. We calculate this as follows: BHO estimate that the presence of one form of conflict increases the other by 7.7 percent. Taken over a five-year period with a 5 percent discount rate, we estimate that a terrorist event increases the likelihood of an internal conflict of 35 percent. Since the impact of internal conflict on growth on average is –1.27 percent, then the impact from this conflict complementarity on growth is approximately 5 percentage points or equivalent to a one-year impact from terrorism. Therefore, to calculate the additional response due to transference in other forms of conflict, we

add an additional loss in GDP growth to the five-year loss above that is equivalent to the one-year loss when an internal conflict occurs. Otherwise our results are identical to those of SAE.

Estimating the Cost of Terrorism: Welfare Approach

In this section, we provide an alternative approach to estimating the cost associated with terrorism using a technique first suggested by Lucas (1987) to estimate the potential gains from removing business cycles to welfare in a society. The approach uses utility measures rather than baseline GDP cost approach. A formal description is included in the technical appendix. We provide a condensed description below.

Lucas' approach asks us to consider two consumption paths – the path where there is some positive probability of entering into adverse or beneficial states and a synthetic path where the probabilities of entering into such states are zero. Since Lucas is concerned only with business cycle effects, he does not allow the average rate of consumption growth to differ between these two welfare paths. By equating the two consumption paths, one can "price" the amount an individual would be willing to give up on an annual basis to attain the latter path – i.e., its equivalent variation. Lucas' insight hinges on the observation that the average person (or representative agent) would be willing to give up some portion of their current consumption to reduce or eliminate the uncertainty or variance of consumption over their lifetime. Formally, we construct utility-based measures and compare the expected welfare from each country remaining in its realized path of consumption to another synthetic path of consumption where there is no state of transnational terrorism.

To implement the welfare calculations, we need to provide parameter values for the discount rate (θ) and the coefficient of relative risk aversion (ρ), in addition to the consumption growth and volatility measures calculated in the appendix. Clearly, changes in θ and ρ will affect growth. Four important issues in the selection of these parameters should be kept in mind. First, the parameter values should be plausible. Second, the parameters are constrained such that the model's restrictions are satisfied. Third, the parameter values selected should be suggestive of a lower bound for growth. Fourth, the reader should get an indication of the robustness of growth to changes in the values chosen for θ and ρ. We provide results for the welfare measures using θ = .08 and ρ = 2. These values were chosen for these reasons, based on the criteria just discussed (see Blomberg (2008) for more discussion).

Estimating the Cost of Implementing Policies

In this subsection, we describe how we calculate the cost of the alternative policies. We measure the cost of these policies directly by the change in expenditures during the policy window (e.g. 2002–2006) as compared with the previous period. As most of these costs are taken directly from budget reports, we devote less attention to explaining the manner in which they are constructed.

First, we estimate the cost of increased expenditure on homeland security in 2002–2006 as compared with the previous period. We consider two approaches. As there are reliable figures for only the United States and the United Kingdom, we use these to proxy estimates for other countries. We first adopt the methodology of SAE and base the proxy on the percentage of GDP devoted to homeland security in the United States and the United Kingdom following 9/11. However, this will most surely overstate global expenditure as the United States and the United Kingdom are outliers (the top two) in terms of their military expenditure. To adjust for this, we then adopt a methodology that bases the proxy on the percentage of world military spending in the United States and the United Kingdom following 9/11 and adjust global homeland security accordingly.

Second, we consider the impact of increased international cooperation by comparing the cost of increased expenditure by IMF, INTERPOL, and other international organizations in 2002–2006 as compared with the previous period. To be consistent, we first adopt the methodology of SAE, who estimate the portion of IMF and INTERPOL budgets related to enhanced counterterrorism. Next, we employ actual expenditure by a variety of international agencies working to stem terrorism following 9/11. This is the first serious departure from SAE, as we do not estimate portions of the budget, but instead take actual spending devoted to counterterrorism from IMF, INTERPOL, and other counterterrorist agencies such as International Atomic Energy Agency's (IAEA) Nuclear Security Action Plan, the G-8's Financial Action Task Force (FATF), the United Nations, and the Egmont group. We also include the cost of freezing funds devoted to terrorism.

Third, we analyze the effect of increased proactive measures by calculating the cost of greater military intervention in the early part of the war in Afghanistan and Iraq. We employ the same estimates reported by SAE.

Finally, we estimate the effect of increased economic aid by comparing the cost of the United States' new development initiative, the Millennium Challenge Account, and its increased economic aid to Afghanistan.

4.   Results

Policy Alternative One: Business as Usual

Our experimental design allows us to construct the counterfactual by calculating the average annual attacks for 2002–2006, compared with those for 1990–2001, exactly as in SAE. In this case, SAE show that there is a 34 percent drop in transnational incidents but there are 67 more deaths and 120 fewer injuries.

To calculate the economic benefits associated with the increased expenditure on homeland security, we provide SAE estimates on the reduced GDP losses capitalized over the sixty-six impact countries over the five-year period which is $28.358 billion or 0.34 × $83.406 billion. (See Table 1A-B in Blomberg (2008).) The benefit is reduced, however, due to the net loss in human costs, so that SAE lower the benefit of this solution to $28.347 billion. We add an additional benefit to increase in expenditure on homeland security, by including the reduced GDP losses due to transference of internal conflict. We estimate the reduced GDP losses capitalized over the sixty-six impact countries over the five-year period to be $1.618 billion or 0.34 × $4.758 billion. (See Table 1A-B in Blomberg (2008).) Hence, once we include conflict complementarities, we estimate the total benefit to business as usual policies to be $29.961 billion.

To calculate the economic benefits using the alternative approach, we take the estimated welfare benefits over the sixty-six aforementioned impact countries. To do this, we calculate each country's optimal growth with our assumed parameter values, and add up the increased dollar value associated with such a rise in consumption growth.[1] In this case, we estimate the average loss in consumption growth to be approximately 1 percent, which computed across the impact countries is $132.569 billion. Therefore, we estimate the benefit of business as usual to be $45.073 billion as our experiment presumes that there is a 34 percent decline in the bottom-line number reported in SAE. The total benefit also includes the added human cost, which therefore reduces the benefit to $45.062 billion.

It it instructive to note that the alternative approach using the Lucas (1987) technique yields a higher estimate on the benefits associated with decreased terrorism, in the order of a 50 percent increase over the baseline approach. Experimenting with different parameter values can go very far in explaining the difference. For example, we assume the constant relative risk-aversion parameter ρ is 2, which is around the conventionally accepted upper bound. If we lower our estimate for ρ, then the difference between the estimates widens. If we assume that individuals are excessively risk-averse when it comes to terrorism, we may investigate how high ρ would need to be in order to obtain similar estimates to the baseline. We consider the possibility that $\rho = 4$, which would be significantly higher than is typically assumed. If $\rho = 4$, then the total benefit is estimated to be $28.767 billion. Research by Becker and Rubenstein (2005) suggests that ρ should not be significantly greater than 4 when understanding the economic behavior associated with terrorism.

Another explanation for the difference in the estimates may be in how the different approaches model the welfare loss associated with terrorism. In the baseline approach, we assume there is a direct dollar for dollar loss to individual welfare from lost income. In the welfare-based approach, we assume there may be greater losses due to the onset of greater risk and individuals would pay more to prevent such uncertainty in the future. Hence, if one believes that the economic costs of such uncertainty are important and should be directly modeled, then the benefits of the BAU policies may be as much as $45.062 billion, otherwise they may be as low as $29.951 billion.

To calculate the economic costs associated with increased expenditure on homeland security, we begin by employing the estimate of spending from SAE by applying the US GDP percentage to all sample countries for a total of $147.19 billion in 2005. When capitalized over a five-year period, the present discounted value is $695.09 billion. As this number is almost assuredly too high, SAE adopt eleven different alternatives to settle on their low estimate (M9), which requires an assumption of a low constant percentage of worldwide GDP to be devoted to homeland security, or about $298.3 billion.

Given the challenges associated with estimating worldwide homeland security expenditure based on only having accurate measures for the United States and the United Kingdom, we are sympathetic to employing this naive estimate. However, we adopt a slightly different approach that assumes homeland security costs are a constant fraction of military expenditure. This approach may help to correct for the fact that the United States and the United Kingdom are outliers.

Table 9.1.1 provides the estimates from both approaches. In the table, we provide estimates from countries that spend the most on the military according to the Stockholm International Peace Research Institute (SIPRI).[2] These fifteen countries make up approximately 83 percent of all military expenditure, with the United States

---

[1] In Blomberg (2008), we provide these estimates in Table 2A-B that is analogous to Table 1A-B.
[2] www.sipri.org\contents\milap\milex\mex_trends.html

Table 9.1.1. Estimates of homeland security

	Country	Using UK Est	Using US Est	SAE Est (M1)	SAE Est (M9)
1	USA	28.5	43.6	43.6	43.6
2	UK	3.2	4.9	7.7	3.2
3	France	2.9	4.4	7.4	1.1
4	China	2.7	4.1	7.8	1.1
5	Japan	2.4	3.6	15.8	2.3
Top 5		39.6	60.6	82.3	51.2
6	Germany	2	3.1	9.7	1.4
7	Russia	1.9	2.9	2.7	2.7
8	Italy	1.6	2.5	6	0.9
9	Saudi Arabia	1.6	2.4	1	0.2
10	India	1.3	2	2.7	0.4
Top 10		48	73.3	104.4	56.7
11	South Korea	1.2	1.8	2.7	0.4
12	Australia	0.7	1.1	2.5	0.1
13	Canada	0.7	1.1	3.9	0.6
14	Brazil	0.7	1.1	2.8	0.4
15	Spain	0.7	1	3.9	0.6
Top 15		53.3	81.5	122.9	58.7
FV2005		64	94.8	147.2	63.2
FY2006		65.3	96.7	150.1	64.4
FY2007		66.6	98.6	153.1	65.7
FY2008		67.9	100.6	156.2	67
FY2009		69.3	102.6	159.3	68.4
PV in US$ bn		302.2	447.7	695.1	298.3

and the United Kingdom making up 51 percent. Our approach requires that a greater share of homeland security spending is paid for by the United States and the United Kingdom. Our homeland spending estimates for the top fifteen countries is 50 percent lower than SAE (M1) estimate when using the US rate and significantly smaller when using the UK rate. When capitalized over a five-year period, the present discounted value is between $427.7 billion and $302.2 billion. In summary, the approach is more directly constructed by data and therefore yields a result more in line with expectations than when using the (M1) estimate. Interestingly though, our low estimate is not that different to the low estimate (M9) in SAE, even though SAE employ a more ad hoc approach.

Policy Alternative Two: Increased International Cooperation

The policy alternative investigates the impact of greater cooperation in freezing assets and cutting off terrorists' resources, drug trafficking, and illicit activities. To investigate this policy alternative, our experimental design again allows us to construct the counterfactual by comparing the pre-sample period to the post-sample period. However, in this case it is more challenging to devise a scheme that tests the impact of international cooperation independently from other policy alternatives.

SAE tackle this issue by making as they say "some heroic assumptions." They compare the cost of monitoring, assumed to be one tenth of IMF's monitoring, and a doubling of

INTERPOL's budget to the benefit of eliminating one major catastrophic event, assumed to be $1 billion. We take a very different approach, but still make some restrictive assumptions.

Our experiment is to investigate the costs and benefits of international cooperation in the post-9/11 period relative to the pre-sample period. We will compare the benefits of reduced welfare loss of the main terrorist organizations specifically targeted by international agencies versus the increased budgetary costs of these international agencies.

Our experiment begins with the United Nations Security Council Resolution 1373, which raised the issue of global awareness and encouraged global counterterrorism capability, cooperation, and effectiveness. The UN initially added only al-Qaida and the Taliban regime of Afghanistan to the sanctions list. Since then, several international groups have stepped forward.

- The United Nations Security Council constructed a working group called the Counterterrorism Committee (CTC) to handle the issue of global awareness and global counterterrorism capability, cooperation, and effectiveness.
- The International Atomic Energy Agency's Nuclear Security Action Plan provides advice, training, and equipment to its 136 Member States to combat nuclear terrorism. The United States has contributed $15.9 million since the Action Plan's inception in March 2002. The IAEA coordinates its nuclear security activities with the United States and other donor states to mutually reinforce nuclear security goals.
- The Financial Action Task Force is an intergovernmental body whose purpose is the development and promotion of national and international policies to combat money laundering and terrorist financing. The FATF is therefore a "policy-making body" created in 1989 that works to generate the necessary political will to bring about legislative and regulatory reforms in these areas. The FATF has published 40 + 9 Recommendations in order to meet this objective.
- In 2002, the boards of the IMF and World Bank approved a pilot program of assessments under anti-money laundering and combating the financing of terrorism (AML/CFT). An important element of the AML/CFT program is the provision of related technical assistance (TA).[3]
- INTERPOL is the world's largest international police organization, with 186 member countries. Created in 1923, it facilitates cross-border police cooperation, and supports and assists all organizations, authorities, and services whose mission is to prevent or combat international crime.
- Egmont Group is an international body created in 1995 for the purpose of financial intelligence sharing (and named for the Egmont-Arenberg palace in Belgium where it was established). Although created to fight money laundering, in the fall of 2005 the group broadened its mandate to include tracking and freezing assets and blocking transactions of entities and persons engaged in proliferation activities and support.

Our experiment is to compare the activity of the UN-targeted groups, al-Qaida and the Taliban, in the pre- and post-time samples. There are two challenges when trying to isolate the impacts of terrorist organizations. First, not all attacks are claimed by the organizations themselves. In fact, a significant portion of attacks is not attributed to any organization. Second, we do not have access to the ITERATE data for the entire sample period.

To combat these concerns, we first gather data that employs similar methodology, the MIPT, then we use it to estimate the incidents attributed to al-Qaida and the Taliban relative to those in which there is an associated aggressor, and weight the impact of the aggregate attacks in ITERATE accordingly. Table 9.1.2 shows the relative change in the percentage of attributable al-Qaida and Taliban incidents, deaths, and injuries pre- and post-sample using the MIPT data. The table shows that in the pre-sample

---

[3] See "Twelve-Month Pilot Program of Anti-Money Laundering and Combating the Financing of Terrorism (AML/CFT) Assessment-Joint Report on the Review of the Pilot Program," 11 March 2004, available on the IMF external website: www.imf.org

Table 9.1.2. Activity recorded for the Taliban and al-Qaida

	Incidents	Fatalities	Injuries
1996–2001	8	3223	7453
2002–2006	14	162	874
Difference	6	−3061	−6579

period, al-Qaida and the Taliban accounted for eight attacks with 7,453 injuries and 3,223 fatalities. This is not surprising given the damage associated with September 11 in the pre-sample period and the lack of such a catastrophic event in the post-sample period.

However, Table 9.1.2 also shows an increased activity by al-Qaida and the Taliban in the experimental period. In the pre-sample, these two terrorist groups accounted for eight different attacks in six different countries. In the experimental period, they accounted for fourteen attacks in seven countries. One explanation for the rise in the number of attacks is that international cooperation may have led to a transference to more frequent strikes, each with smaller magnitude.

To estimate the benefit in the reduction of human cost associated with international cooperation, we employ a similar methodology to SAE. This calculation is applied to the 3,061 fewer deaths and 6,579 fewer injuries, due almost entirely to the one-year difference between 2001 and 2002. At a value of $5,000 per DALY, the benefit for reducing the human cost of terrorism ranges from $472 million to $486 million.

To estimate the relative economic benefits associated with enhanced international cooperation, we then isolate the seven impact countries over the five-year post-sample period (see Table 9.1.3a). The lost GDP associated with the attacks actually rose during the experimental period and is estimated to be $444 million. In addition to increases in terrorism, there were increases in internal conflicts in the experimental period. These increases are included in column 7 and are estimated to be $86 million. Taken together, the loss in GDP cost associated with

al-Qaida and the Taliban is therefore $531 million. As the number of attacks per country actually rose during the experimental period from six to eight, we estimate that one third of this loss in GDP is due to transference, or about $177 million. In summary, when taken together, the net benefit from international cooperation is $486 million – $177 million = $3109 million.

To calculate the economic benefits using the alternative approach, we take the estimated welfare benefits over the seven aforementioned impact countries using our assumed parameter estimates, and add up the increased dollar value associated with such a rise in consumption growth. We provide these estimates in Table 9.1.3b. In this case, we estimate the average loss in consumption growth to be approximately less than 1 percent, which computed across the impact countries is $1.231 billion. We estimate a loss in benefits due to international cooperation to be a one-third rise in this number, or $410 million. Of course, the total benefit also includes the reduction in human cost, so when taken together, the net benefit from international cooperation is $486 million – $410 million = $76 million.

To calculate the economic cost associated with greater international coordination, we simply add up the increased budget costs associated with the expansion of the aforementioned agencies and include the lost economic efficiency associated with freezing capital of suspected terrorist financiers. These economic and budgetary costs are provided in Table 9.1.4. To estimate the cost of frozen capital, we assume lost returns commensurate with what actually occurred. As approximately $100 million in assets have been frozen, this means an opportunity cost of $78 million using average returns from the S&P 500.[4] In each case, we assume an annual increase of 2 percent and then sum the total value over a five-year horizon. The aggregate sum of all these costs over the five-year horizon is $293 million.

Policy Alternative Three: Increased Proactive Measures

This solution calls for increased proactive measures such as Operation Enduring Freedom. In

---

[4] seekingalpha.com/article/35520-investing-for-yield-total-return-implications

Table 9.1.3. The seven impact countries over the five-year post-sample period

(a) Lost GDP due to al-Qaida and the Taliban in the post-sample period

Country	Pop (000)	Ti	per capita GDP	2005 growth (%)	2005 cost (average)	Conflict complementarity
Indonesia	220558	1	942	4.12	82,175	16435
Kenya	34256	1	428	0.23	324	
Pakistan	155772	1	596	5.16	45,989	9198
Saudi Arabia	24573	2	9323	3.78	166,267	33253
Syria	19043	1	1161	1.65	3,502	
Tunisia	10022	1	2418	3.24	7,537	
Turkey	72636	1	3390	5.86	138,523	27705
Total					$444,318	$86,591

(b) Welfare loss due to al-Qaida and the Taliban in the post-sample period

Country	Pop (000)	Ti	per capita GDP	GDP	Final consumption % of GDP	Welfare cost growth
Indonesia	220558	1	942	63.89	7.40	316,957
Kenya	34256	1	428	74.26	10.04	23,089
Pakistan	155772	1	596	77.97	13.12	138,216
Saudi Arabia	24573	2	9323	26.33	4.89	333,578
Syria	19043	1	1161	63.30	9.93	29,808
Tunisia	10022	1	2418	57.85	4.76	39,124
Turkey	72636	1	3390	63.75	8.86	349,740
Total						$1,230,513

order to get a counterfactual, we contrast the level of transnational terrorism in the first two years following 9/11 when there were the greatest proactive measures and compare it with the previous period. As we have already done the calculations associated with the benefits of a reduction in lost GDP and the welfare cost over the five-year horizon, calculating the benefits over a two-year horizon is straightforward.

In a previous section we showed that the GDP cost over the longer horizon is $83.406 billion. We also demonstrated that this cost increases the likelihood of other conflicts and this conflict complementarity is $4.758 billion. Taken together, we estimate a loss in GDP of $88.164 billion over the five-year period. We also employed an alternative methodology and estimated the welfare benefit associated with an

elimination in terrorism to be $132.569 billion over the five-year period. On an annual basis, the value for GDP is $18.320 billion and the value for welfare is $26.514 billion. To estimate the impact in increased proactive measures, it only requires us to scale these values by the change in incidents over the smaller horizon.

The annual number of transnational terrorist attacks for 2002–2003 is 205 incidents compared with 255 incidents per year for the post-9/11 period through 2006. This means that there are fifty fewer attacks per year, or a decline of 13 percent over the 1990–2001 period, that we attribute to the larger offensive measures. This translates into a $2.381 billion (= 0.13 × $18.320 billion) saving in world GDP for one year. With 5 percent discounting over a two-year time horizon, this gives a benefit of $4.649 billion from

Table 9.1.4. Economic cost of international cooperation

Year	INTERPOL	IMF	IAEA	FROZEN ASSET	FAFT G8	UN	EGMONT	Total
1	8.0	3.5	20	15.6	2.61	5	1.8	45.9
2	8.2	3.6	20.4	15.6	2.7	5.1	1.8	46.8
3	8.3	3.6	20.8	15.6	2.7	5.2	1.9	47.8
4	8.5	3.7	21.2	15.6	2.8	5.3	1.9	48.7
5	8.7	3.8	21.6	15.6	2.8	5.4	1.9	49.7
	37.8	16.5	94.4	78	12.3	23.6	8.5	293.3

Notes: Each budget number begins in year one and is increased by 2 percent per annum and discounted at a 5 percent rate over a five-year period. INTERPOL's budget increase is found by comparing the 2005 budget ($58 million (€42.8 million) (SAE, 2007) with the previous year's budget of $50 million or €36.9 million (see www.interpol.int/Public/ICPO/PressReleases/PR2003/PR200330.asp). Hence, the budget increase is assumed to be $8 million per annum. IMF's budget on AMF/CFT for FY2005 is $3.5 million and is found in box 5, page 28 in "INTERNATIONAL MONETARY FUND: The FY 2005 Budget and the Medium-Term Expenditure Framework," prepared by the Office of Budget and Planning, approved by Barry H. Potter, 1 April 2004. The IAEA has calculated its annual funding needs at $12 million for its programs and an additional $20 million per year to enable the Agency to respond to urgent situations that require immediate security upgrades (see www.iaea.org/NewsCenter/Features/Nuclear_Terrorism/index.shtml). We only use the upgrade number for which the United States has pledged $15.9 million. The cost of frozen assets is assumed to be actual loss in opportunity cost of $100 million (see www.whitehouse.gov/news/releases/2001/12/100dayreport.html and seekingalpha.com/article/35520-investing-for-yield-total-return-implications). The UN budget is based primarily on its Global Programme Against Terrorism (GPAT), which budgeted $5 million in 2004 (see www.unodc.org/pdf/brochure_gpt_may2000/20.pdf), and on the UN action on counterterrorism (see www.un.org/terrorism/cttaskforce.shtml). The G8 FAFT budget is primarily based on the FAFT-GAFI, which in 2004 (assuming a dollar/euro rate of 1.5) was $2.61 million (see www.faft-gafi.org/dataoecd/41/25/34988062.pdf). The Egmont Group's budget is primarily driven by the establishment of the secretariat in Toronto, which is currently estimated at $1.8 million (see www.fintrac.gc.ca/publications/presentations/2007-03-29-eng.asp).

saved GDP. In terms of welfare benefits, this translates into a $3.447 billion ($= 0.13 \times \$26.514$ billion) saving in world GDP for one year. With 5 percent discounting over a two-year time horizon, this gives a benefit of $6.729 billion.

Unfortunately, these two years had violent terrorist events that killed 675 people and injured 2,830 others per year. Using SAE's estimate this amounts to a negative benefit of $75.04 million when evaluated for two years at a 5 percent discount rate and a $5,000 DALY. Subtracting this from the benefits above, we find a benefit of $4.576 billion in GDP and a benefit of $6.656 billion in welfare.

For the relevant two years, SAE show that Operation Enduring Freedom costs $35.5 billion, while Operation Noble Eagle costs $21 billion for a total of $56.5 billion. This figure drops to $35.5 billion if we leave out Operation Noble Eagle.

Policy Alternative Five: Increased Economic Aid

The final policy alternative involves an increased sensitivity in foreign policy. Our experimental design looks at the increased funding to low-

income countries and to Afghanistan in particular, which means considering two initiatives. The first, the Millennium Challenge Corporation (MCC), is a United States government corporation designed to work with some of the poorest countries in the world. Established in January 2004, MCC is based on the principle that aid is most effective when it reinforces good governance, economic freedom, and investments in people. The initiative that created the MCC, the Millennium Challenge Account, has authorized $3 billion so far, so that the change in policy of increased economic aid fits squarely in our policy window. The second initiative is the Afghanistan Freedom Support Act, which authorizes $3.47 billion for Afghanistan over fiscal years 2003–2006 for humanitarian purposes.

To estimate the benefits associated with increased aid to poorer countries including Afghanistan, we continue to conduct exercises comparing pre-sample to experimental periods. To calculate the economic benefits associated with the increased economic aid to possible problem regions, we estimate the reduced GDP losses of low-income countries which may be eligible for economic aid. Table 9.1.5 reports the results

Table 9.1.5. The thirty-nine impact low-income countries

(a) Lost GDP due to transnational terrorism attacks in low-income countries

Country	Pop (000)	T_i	Per capita GDP	2005 growth (%)	2005 cost (average)	5 year cost in (growth)	Conflict comple-mentarity
Algeria	32,854	2	$2,066	3.65	47,568	231,801	$47,625
Angola	15,941	1	891	10.9	14,862	83,146	14,889
Bangladesh	141,822	1	415	3.43	19,380	94,046	
Bosnia-Herzegovina	3,907	4	1,486	5.25	11,704	58,802	
Burundi	7,548	2	105	−1.89	−288	−1,261	−288
Cambodia	14,071	1	356	4.89	2,352	11,733	
Chad	9,749	1	267	2.27	567	2,693	569
Colombia	45,600	3	2,174	3.51	100,213	487,045	100,425
Congo-Brazzaville	57,549	4	997	5.89	129,772	659,951	129,952
Ecuador	13,228	1	1,534	2.37	4,617	21,956	
Egypt	74,033	3	1,662	2.87	101,702	488,295	
El Salvador	6,881	1	2,127	0.99	1,391	6,444	
Eritrea	4,401	1	176	1.14	85	394	
Georgia	4,474	3	971	10	12,908	71,422	
Haiti	8,528	2	428	0.7	491	2,260	
India	1,094,583	4	586	6.7	1,650,260	8,522,845	1,654,484
Indonesia	220,558	4	942	4.12	328,702	1,616,191	329,132
Iran	67,700	2	1,962	4.75	121,139	602,816	
Jordan	5,411	3	2,091	4.45	14,501	71,747	
Kenya	34,256	2	428	0.23	647	2,956	
Kyrgyzstan	5,156	2	319	−1.56	−493	−2,174	
Macedonia	2,034	1	1,889	3.72	1,372	6,695	
Madagascar	18,606	1	233	1.73	720	3,383	
Mauritania	3,069	1	447	2.26	298	1,413	
Morocco	30,168	2	1,354	0.37	2,902	13,285	
Nigeria	131,530	1	420	4.38	23,228	114,779	
Pakistan	155,772	4	596	5.16	183,957	922,593	184,472
Peru	27,968	2	2,319	5	62,263	311,317	
Philippines	83,054	3	1,124	3.26	87,647	423,949	87,686
Sierra Leone	5,525	1	218	3.74	432	2,111	
Solomon Islands	478	1	647	1.71	51	238	51
Sri Lanka	19,582	3	1,004	4.27	24,177	119,218	24,242
Sudan	36,233	4	462	5.56	35,740	180,615	35,828
Syria	19,043	1	1,161	1.65	3,502	16,428	
Tajikistan	6,507	1	237	6.09	902	4,603	
Thailand	64,233	3	2,440	3.5	157,982	767,663	158,429
Tunisia	10,022	1	2,418	3.24	7,537	36,445	
Uzbekistan	26,593	1	673	5.18	8,900	44,652	
Yemen	20,975	4	590	1.02	4,847	22,467	4,867
Total					$3,168,538	$16,024,960	$2,772,363

Table 9.1.5. (continued)

(b) Welfare cost of terrorism in low-income countries

Country	Pop (000)	T_i	Per capita GDP	2005 growth (%)	2005 cost (average)	5 year cost in (growth)	Conflict comple-mentarity
Algeria	32854	2	2066	67876364	33.42	4.55	128,408
Angola	15941	1	891	14203431	67.00	4.89	26,326
Bangladesh	141822	1	415	58856130	76.40	5.10	122,688
Bosnia-Herzegovina	3907	4	1486	5805802	99.18	4.97	63,280
Burundi	7548	2	105	792540	87.34	4.89	3,828
Cambodia	14071	1	356	5009276	84.99	12.19	8,363
Chad	9749	1	267	2602983	59.85	−7.88	−58,253
Colombia	45600	3	2174	99134400	61.92	4.72	514,666
Congo-Brazzaville	57549	4	997	57376353	85.21	4.89	540,093
Ecuador	13228	1	1534	20291752	65.98	6.43	33,681
Egypt	74033	3	1662	123042846	71.55	3.03	838,827
El Salvador	6881	1	2127	14635887	93.08	2.56	45,109
Eritrea	4401	1	176	774576	82.24	−26.16	−1,554
Georgia	4474	3	971	4342562	77.05	1.54	36,563
Haiti	8528	2	428	3649984	67.00	4.89	13,523
India	1094583	4	586	641425638	58.27	5.67	3,927,836
Indonesia	220558	4	942	207765636	63.89	7.40	1,265,718
Iran	67700	2	1962	132827400	45.88	1.28	456,112
Jordan	5411	3	2091	11314401	102.62	22.67	55,865
Kenya	34256	2	428	14661568	74.26	10.04	46,153
Kyrgyzstan	5156	2	319	1644764	84.54	8.32	6,345
Macedonia	2034	1	1889	3842226	78.42	3.44	9,268
Madagascar	18606	1	233	4335198	83.15	2.57	11,926
Mauritania	3069	1	447	1371843	92.35	27.18	1,981
Morocco	30168	2	1354	40847472	59.84	0.69	195,304
Nigeria	131530	1	420	55242600	38.93	−10.79	−203,988
Pakistan	155772	4	596	92840112	77.97	13.12	551,980
Peru	27968	2	2319	64857792	65.73	4.40	243,848
Philippines	83054	3	1124	93352696	79.80	6.52	558,788
Sierra Leone	5525	1	218	1204450	89.96	4.89	2,997
Solomon Islands	478	1	647	309266	67.00	4.89	573
Sri Lanka	19582	3	1004	19660328	76.95	4.89	125,423
Sudan	36233	4	462	16739646	69.39	4.89	128,324
Syria	19043	1	1161	22108923	63.30	9.93	29,808
Tajikistan	6507	1	237	1542159	95.43	4.89	4,071
Thailand	64233	3	2440	156728520	58.24	4.87	757,949
Tunisia	10022	1	2418	24233196	57.85	4.76	39,124
Uzbekistan	26593	1	673	17897089	73.19	4.89	36,237
Yemen	20975	4	590	12375250	61.36	4.89	83,890
Total							$10,651,082

Table 9.1.6. Solutions: benefits, costs, and benefit–cost ratios

| | Challenge approach | | | Perspectives approach | | |
| | $5000 DALY | | | $5000 DALY | | |
Solutions	Benefits	Costs	BCR	Benefits	Costs	BCR
Solution 1 (M7)[1]	28.343	727.7	0.039	29.951	427.7	0.070
Solution 1 (M9)[1]	28.343	298.3	0.095	45.062	302.2	0.149
Solution 2A[2]	20.000	3.74	5.348	0.076	0.293	0.259
Solution 2B[2]	20.000	1.29	15.504	0.311	0.293	1.061
Solution 3A[3]	4.335	56.5	0.077	4.576	56.5	0.081
Solution 3B[3]	4.335	35.5	0.122	6.656	35.5	0.187
Solution 4[4]	20.969	74.6	0.281	20.969	74.6	0.281
Solution 5A[5]	38.217			0.362	6.47	0.056
Solution 5B[5]	38.217			0.639	6.47	0.099

Notes:
[1] For Challenge approach: solution 1A is based on Method 7 in SAE (2007) Table 11 for calculating homeland security expense; solution 1B is based on Method 9 in Table 11 for calculating homeland security expense. For Perspectives approach: solution 1A employs the GDP cost approach with conflict complementarities; solution 1B employs the welfare approach. See Table 3 for calculating homeland security expense.
[2] For Challenge approach: solution 2A uses higher costs for police cooperation and IMF monitoring than solution 2B. DALY and Value of Life do not figure into the calculations of benefits for solutions 2A and 2B. For Perspectives approach: solution 2A employs the welfare approach; solution 2B employs the GDP cost approach with conflict complementarities.
[3] For Challenge approach: solution 3A is based on the cost of Operation Enduring Freedom (Afghanistan) and Operation Noble Eagle, while solution 3B is based only on the cost of Operation Enduring Freedom. For Perspectives approach: solution 3A employs the GDP cost approach with conflict complementarities; solution 3B employs the welfare approach.
[4] Taken directly from SAE (2007).
[5] For Challenge approach: taken directly from SAE (2007). For Perspectives approach: solution 5A employs the GDP cost approach with conflict complementarities; solution 5B employs the welfare approach.

for the thirty-nine impact low-income countries. As there were eighty-two episodes, each country experienced an average of 2.16 incidents. This number is 3.5 percent lower than the pre-sample average of 2.24, suggesting a slight decrease in terrorism during the experimental period. The direct impact of terrorism capitalized over the five-year period is $16.024 billion and the indirect cost due to the conflict complementarities is an additional $2.772 billion, making the entire loss in GDP cost $18.796 billion. We therefore estimate the reduced GDP losses capitalized over the low-income impact countries over the five-year period to be $657 million, or 0.035 × $18.796 billion. As we do not have access to fatalities rates for low-income countries in the experimental period, we assume the human cost to be similar to the estimate in policy alternative one, such that the benefit falls by $11 million, lowering the reduction in GDP loss to $639 million.

To find the estimate using our welfare-based methodology, we conduct the same experiment as alternative one, though we restrict our analysis to the eligible low-income countries. In this case, we estimate a welfare loss of $10.651 billion, which when interacted with the 3.5 percent decline in terrorist activity is $373 million, or 0.035 × $10.651 billion. Finally, we reduce this by $11 million due to human costs, making the final number $362 million.

The cost of the policy is simply the budgetary allocations for MCC and Afghanistan over the five-year time span. In this case the combination of the two programs amounts to $6.47 billion.

5.   And the Winner is. . .

Our Perspective Paper takes the approach by estimating two types of models – a GDP cost approach similar to the Challenge Paper and one based on a welfare model – to see which, if any, of the policy alternatives is most cost effective.

Table 9.1.6 provides a summary of these results and compares them to the challenge results. The first column provides the five different policy alternatives described above. Note that policy alternative 4 is not discussed here as it is a linear projection of policy 1. In each case, the various alternatives are ordered with the smaller BCR above the larger BCR. Columns 2–4 provide the results from SAE and columns 5–7 provide the results from our models.

For the most part, our results dovetail with what was found in SAE (2007). Using both approaches, we show that BAU is not cost effective, yielding 7–15 cents on the dollar. We also show that increased proactive measures is also an ineffective policy, yielding 8–19 cents on the dollar. Both of these findings are somewhat larger than those found by SAE, though the conclusion is the same. We also show that the least cost-effective policy is increased economic aid and we calculate a yield of 5–10 cents on the dollar. Still, the returns on each of these policies are not terribly different and not at all cost effective.

The one alternative in which we find a slightly different result is when evaluating the international cooperation alternative. Using the welfare cost approach, we find that increased international cooperation is not cost effective, yielding a return of 26 cents on the dollar. When employing the GDP cost, we estimate a BCR of 1.06. Hence, the results are sensitive to the model employed. However, international cooperation still has the highest yields.

Bibliography

Becker, G., and Y. Rubenstein, 2005. Fear and the response to terrorism: an economic analysis, mimeo

Blomberg, S.B., 2008. The Copenhagen Consensus 2008 Working Paper: Perspective Paper on transnational terrorism policies, mimeo

Blomberg, S.B., G. Hess, and A. Orphanides, 2004: The macroeconomic consequences of terrorism, Journal of Monetary Economics, 51(5), 1007–32

Lucas, R., 1987: Models of business cycles, Basil Blackwell, New York

Mathers, C., A. Lopez, and C. Murray, 2003: The burden of disease and mortality by condition: data, methods and results for 2001, mimeo (files.dcp2.org/pdf/GBD/GBD03.pdf)

Sandler, T., D. Arce, and W. Enders, 2007: Transnational terrorism, *Challenge Paper* prepared for Copenhagen Consensus

Perspective Paper 9.2

MICHAEL D. INTRILIGATOR

Introduction and Overview

The Sandler, Arce, and Enders (2007) paper (henceforth SAE) on transnational terrorism for the May 2008 Copenhagen Consensus provides an excellent overview of the general nature, background, and history of the subject of terrorism and its modern variant in the current globalized world, transnational terrorism. (See also Enders and Sandler, 2005 for a comprehensive overview of economic analyses of terrorism.) This Perspective Paper provides a supplement to and extension of this paper, discussing some important issues related to the future of transnational terrorism that were not covered in the SAE paper. First, it treats some of the devastating consequences of the potential for transnational terrorist acquisition and use of weapons of mass destruction (WMD), including nuclear, biological, and chemical weapons. Second, it discusses some important ways of preventing or treating the consequences of transnational terrorism through international cooperation and mutual support among national governments, international public and private organizations, and global business. Such cooperation and mutual support represent important ways of dealing with the major challenges to the world community stemming from transnational terrorism.

The Evolving Nature of Transnational Terrorism

Transnational terrorism has become a powerful and growing force in the current globalized world system. It has manifold dimensions: security, economic, political, environmental, and others that can affect the future of the planet. Terrorism is "the premeditated use or threat to use violence by individuals or subnational groups in order to obtain a political or social objective through the intimidation of a large audience beyond that of the immediate victims" (Enders and Sandler, 2005). Terrorism has become a global phenomenon in what amounts to yet another manifestation of globalization. What was formerly a phenomenon of nations, such as Ireland, Sri Lanka, and Israel, and, earlier, a tactic used in the developing world's struggle for independence from the colonial empires of Britain, France, Holland, Belgium, Portugal, and other great powers, has evolved from a regional to a multinational and now global phenomenon. For example, the transnational terrorist organization responsible for the 11 September 2001 (9/11) attacks on the US in New York and Washington, DC, al-Qaida ("the base" in Arabic), which had earlier operated in Sudan and then in Afghanistan and Pakistan, is now a global organization, with branches in Great Britain, Morocco, Iraq, Indonesia, the Philippines, and elsewhere. It has, in fact, learned from global business entities such as McDonald's and Starbucks the value of franchising, setting up franchise operations in many nations. By contrast, the US after the 9/11 attacks set up a hierarchical organization, the Department of Homeland Security (DHS), to counter al-Qaida and other transnational terrorist organizations. DHS was later shown to be dysfunctional in the aftermath of Hurricanes Katrina and Rita in New Orleans and the US Gulf coast. Transnational terrorists have created dispersed and flat organizations, while DHS, the main US antiterrorist organization, is one that is concentrated and top heavy, attempting to

577

pull together many prior agencies and operations that do not fit together and cannot work together. Transnational terrorist organizations, including al-Qaida, have also borrowed from global business the value of modern technology, making extensive use of the web, the internet, cell phones, etc. for purposes of communication, recruitment, training, fund raising, planning, identification of targets (e.g. via Google World), etc.

The phenomenon of transnational terrorism has made most industrialized countries highly vulnerable to terrorist attacks due to the globalization of communications, the development of international transport (notably air transport), the concentration of populations and resources in urban zones, etc. For many reasons, including the growth of grievances, particularly those toward the US and Europe as a result of the Iraq and Afghan wars; religious fanaticism; the advent of weak or failed transitional states; the diffusion of technology; the composition of the population, with more single young men that may become recruits for the terrorists; extremist ideologies; global funding; the growth of transnational crime organizations; and other factors, there will in all likelihood be a continuation of high levels or even a growth of transnational terrorism in the foreseeable future. These issues are discussed in detail by the Norwegian expert on terrorism Brynjar Lia in his authoritative book, *Globalisation and the Future of Terrorism: Patterns and Predictions.* This book concludes by stating that there are ". . .important structural factors in today's world creating more propitious conditions for terrorism. . . [leading to a] sustained, if not higher, level of transnational terrorism." Lia ends his book by stating that "Regrettably, high levels of terrorism are going to be with us for a very long time" (Lia, 2005).

The SAE paper notes the long history of terrorism, dating back at least 2,000 years, as well as its current nature. (See also Rapoport, 2004 on four waves of terrorism.) It also correctly asserts that transnational terrorism often occurs during periods of globalization such as the current one that began in the 1960s, after the world started to recover from the devastation of World War

II, as well as the previous period of globalization over the 100-year period from the end of the Napoleonic Wars with the Congress of Vienna in 1815 to the outbreak of World War I in 1914. (The SAE paper suggests that this prior wave of globalization started in 1878, presumably with the Congress of Berlin, but elements of this earlier epoch of globalization, that was based on the colonial system, were in place after 1815.) The SAE paper, however, in my view, understates how transnational terrorism has been evolving in recent years and its potential global impacts in the near future. As one important example of this evolution, transnational terrorism has adopted some approaches of global business, as already noted, such as the extensive use of franchising and the web and its use of worldwide publicity and recruitment, all of which make it a *transnational* threat, representing a newer development. Another important aspect of its evolution that is understated in the SAE paper lies in the attempt of transnational terrorists to obtain weapons of mass destruction that they may well acquire in the medium-term future, over the next 5–15 years. This significant threat is underestimated in the SAE paper, leading them to conclude that ". . . it is likely that terrorists have succeeded in getting the world to overspend on counterterrorism, while ignoring much more pressing problems for a world besieged with exigencies involving health, the environment, conflict, and governance." There is no doubt that these other challenges to the world do exist, some of which are explicitly treated in the Copenhagen Consensus, but the threat of transnational terrorists obtaining and using weapons of mass destruction, whether biological, chemical, or radiological represents an enormous challenge to the world. The SAE paper correctly states that the number of lives lost due to terrorist acts in the recent past has been small by comparison with the lives lost from other causes, but this can change dramatically if the transnational terrorists obtain and use a nuclear weapon as they are intent on doing. (The SAE paper does note, however, that such threats are beginning to emerge, citing the 2006 and 2007 papers by Ivanova and Sandler.)

The Threat of Transnational Terrorist Use of WMD

Transnational terrorism and the potential acquisition by terrorists of weapons of mass destruction are part of the "asymmetric" dynamics of the various unexpected and newer types of threats that have thrust the international community into a new and highly uncertain situation. These dynamics have included not only the 9/11 (2001) al-Qaida terrorist attacks on New York and Washington but also the 10/12 (2002) attack on Bali, the 3/11 (2004) terrorist attacks on Madrid and the 7/11 (2005) terrorist attacks on London. Transnational terrorist acquisition of nuclear weapons is the logical next step in these dynamics, representing an extremely serious problem that must not be dismissed or minimized. Indeed, the US casualties and losses on 9/11 would be seen as relatively minor in comparison to a possible terrorist strike using nuclear weapons that could involve not thousands of casualties, as in the 9/11 attacks but rather hundreds of thousands or even potentially millions. One of the only things that both candidates in the US presidential election in 2004 agreed on was that this is the most serious threat the country faces.

Graham Allison (2004, 2005, 2006) discusses the issue of a possible terrorist strike using nuclear weapons in his 2004 book, *Nuclear Terrorism*. He emphasizes that, as he puts it in the subtitle, nuclear terrorism is the "ultimate preventable catastrophe." Unfortunately, his conclusion, much as that of the SAE paper on this issue, may be overly optimistic. Allison's proposals for strict control over fissile material and the prevention of the acquisition of nuclear weapons by additional nations, while excellent policies, are being proposed some fifty years too late, have not yet been adopted, and may not work perfectly even if adopted, as seen in the only partially successful nonproliferation regime. It is even possible that transnational terrorist groups have already obtained enough fissile material to produce a nuclear weapon, given the large amount of the fissile material existing worldwide. They may even already possess such a weapon, perhaps one obtained through the A.Q. Khan network based in Pakistan that sold nuclear weapons technology to various nations and perhaps also to transnational terrorists. They may have also obtained such weapons from the poorly protected stockpiles of tactical nuclear weapons in Russia, including nuclear land mines, nuclear torpedoes, and nuclear "suitcase" bombs.

Of various possible "nightmare scenarios," most devastating would be a repeat of the earlier terrorist attacks against the US, Spain, or Britain, or other nations, but this time with nuclear weapons. If a terrorist group gained access to a nuclear weapon, it could use it or at least threaten to do so. If Osama bin Laden had even a crude nuclear weapon he could have used it on 9/11 or in other al-Qaida attacks. Some information exists about terrorists' intentions to obtain nuclear weapons. Osama bin Laden has specifically referred to the acquisition of nuclear weapons by the al-Qaida transnational terrorist network as a "religious duty," and documents were found in their caves in Afghanistan regarding their intent to obtain and use WMD that even included a schematic diagram of a nuclear weapon. After the 9/11 attacks, al-Qaida spokesman Abu Gheith wrote (2002):

> We have not reached parity with them. We have the right to kill 4 million Americans – 2 million of them children – and to exile twice as many and wound and cripple hundreds of thousands. Furthermore, it is our right to fight them with chemical and biological weapons, so as to afflict them with the fatal maladies that have afflicted the Muslims because of the [Americans'] chemical and biological weapons.

If this stated goal of retribution were true, the only way that al-Qaida could attain this objective would be to use nuclear weapons or highly destructive and sophisticated chemical or biological agents. It would be impossible for them to repeat their 9/11 scenario of highjacked airliners flown into buildings enough times to kill 4 million Americans, including 2 million children.

Other nightmare scenarios involving transnational terrorist use of WMD include a strike with conventional weapons against a nuclear power plant near a major city such as the Indian Point plant, which is just 24 miles north of New York City and has 20 million people living within a 50-mile radius. Another such scenario would involve transnational terrorists placing a nuclear weapon in a container on a freighter entering a major port, such as the Los Angeles/Long Beach port complex, by far the largest in the US. Transnational terrorists could place such a bomb in one of the many containers entering US ports as almost none of them is inspected. The Los Angeles/Long Beach port complex represents an important potential target for terrorists since it accounts for over 40 percent of all US foreign trade. Thus, knocking it out of commission would have an enormous impact on the economies not only of the US but also of all its trading partners, potentially disrupting much of world trade (Intriligator and Toukan, 2006). Yet another such nightmare scenario would involve transnational terrorists placing a nuclear weapon on a large cruise ship set to detonate when it reaches a major port, such as New York City. (See also Lake, 2000 and Garwin, 2002.) Some acts of transnational terrorism, including 9/11, were foreseen by the US Commission on National Security in the 21st Century (the Hart-Rudman Commission) in its 1999 report, which stated: "Terrorism will appeal to many weak states as an attractive option to blunt the influence of major powers. . .[but] there will be a greater incidence of ad hoc cells and individuals, often moved by religious zeal, seemingly irrational cultist beliefs, or seething resentment. . .The growing resentment against Western culture and values. . .is breeding a backlash. . .Therefore, the United States should assume that it will be a target of terrorist attacks against its homeland using weapons of mass destruction. The United States will be vulnerable to such strikes" (US Commission on National Security in the 21st Century, 1999). A similar conclusion involving transnational terrorist use of WMD should be reached today.

It is customary to classify nuclear, biological, chemical, radiological weapons as WMD, but there are important differences among these

weapons. In fact, it is misleading or even mistaken to lump together all of these weapons as one category of WMD since nuclear weapons are in a class all to themselves in view of their tremendous destructive potential. While nuclear weapons are not now, as far as we know, in the hands of transnational terrorists, they could be some time in the future, given that this is an old technology that is well understood worldwide and given that there has recently been a proliferation of WMD-related technologies and materiel. Furthermore, recent trends in terrorist incidents indicate a tendency toward mass-casualty attacks for which WMD are ideally suited. There is even a type of rivalry between various transnational terrorist groups to have the largest impact and the greatest publicity, topping the actions of rival groups and driving them ultimately and inexorably to the acquisition and use of WMD, given that they have the means, motive, and opportunity to do so.

The terrorist attacks on the World Trade Center (1993), the Tokyo subway (1995), and the Murrah Federal Building in Oklahoma (1995) clearly signaled the emergence of this new trend in terrorism mass casualty attacks. Terrorists who seek to maximize both damage and political impact by using larger devices and who try to cause more casualties have characterized this new pattern of terrorism. There have also been the revelations that A.Q. Khan, the "father" of Pakistan's nuclear weapon, provided nuclear weapons technology to several nations, suggesting the emergence of a type of nuclear weapons "bazaar" that will sell components, technology, fissile material, etc. to the highest bidder, including another nation such as North Korea, or Iran, or possibly even a well-financed terrorist group. If terrorists had access to the necessary funding they could probably find with another such expert or middleman to provide them the detailed plans or even the components for a nuclear weapon.

There are many different types of terrorist groups or networks worldwide; and they are not all fundamentalist Muslim or based in the Middle East or South and Southeast Asia. Two types of terrorist groups that might resort to the use of

WMD against the US are non state-sponsored terrorists and state-sponsored terrorists. Non state-sponsored terrorists are those that operate autonomously, receiving no significant support from any government. These groups may be transnational; they do not see themselves as citizens of any one country and they operate without regard for national boundaries. Typical of such groups is al-Qaida. Most present perceptions in the US are that the primary goal of al-Qaida is to attack the American people based upon what they think and believe rather than what the US foreign policy is and how it is implemented. This is a narrow view, however, for one should look more closely at the strategic aims of al-Qaida and other radical extremists. Their aims include stopping all US aid to Israel with the ultimate aim of eliminating Israel; removing the presence of US and other western forces from the Middle East region (from Morocco to Iran and from Syria to Yemen); stopping the US protection of oppressive Middle Eastern regimes; the overthrow of the House of Saud and the establishment of a fundamentalist radical regime in Saudi Arabia (bringing all of its energy resources – about 60 percent of the world's proven oil reserves – under their version of Islamic control); and the eventual establishment of a Pan-Islamic state stretching across the Middle East and Asia.

State-sponsored terrorists are international groups that generally operate independently but are supported and controlled by one or more nation-states as part of waging asymmetric surrogate war against their enemies. The US State Department has labeled Cuba, Iran, Libya, North Korea, Sudan, and Syria as state sponsors of terrorism. The common motive between the two groups is to undermine US policy and influence, and for the US to change its policy. Their motivation is probably not merely poverty and ignorance, as is often alleged, but rather revenge for past humiliations and retribution as stated in the above quote from Abu Gheith. As Friedman (2003) states: "The single most underappreciated force in international relations is humiliation." (See also Stern, 2000, 2003.) Of course, different terrorist groups have different motivations and ideologies, so there

is no such thing as a "stereotypical terrorist." Furthermore, a terrorist network would not be able to operate in the capacity that they do in the absence of other components that engage in fundraising, recruitment, and social support. In contrast to previous forms of transnational terrorism, the support base of transnational terrorist groups has spread throughout the globe rather than in any distinct geographical cluster.

One important consequence of the US invasion of Afghanistan was to eliminate the main base of al-Qaida, destroying its central command structure. In the absence of this central command structure, individual networks appear to have gained greater freedom and independence in tactical decisions than the traditional terrorist cells of the past. This particular trend in terrorism represents a different and potentially far more lethal one than that posed by the more familiar, traditional, terrorist adversaries. The 9/11 attacks demonstrated that transnational terrorism is now more lethal and that it can have a fundamental political and strategic impact. The threat of terrorist use of WMD is still possible and perhaps inevitable given the goals of al-Qaida, which is probably now rebuilding its central command structure.

There has been to date only one example of a terrorist group using WMD. This historic example is the release of sarin nerve gas on the Tokyo subway by the Japanese terrorist group Aum Shinrikyo on 20 March 1995. This attack represented the crossing of a threshold and demonstrated that certain types of WMD are within the reach of some terrorist groups. The attack came at the peak of the Monday morning rush hour, right under police headquarters, in one of the busiest commuter systems in the world and resulted in 12 deaths and over 5,000 injuries. While the number of deaths was relatively small, this was the largest number of casualties of any terrorist attacks up to that time. This number of casualties is exceeded only by the 9/11 attacks on the World Trade Center in New York and the Pentagon in Virginia as well as in Pennsylvania, which resulted in about 3,000 deaths and almost 9,000 nonfatal casualties. Even before their attack on the Tokyo subway Aum Shinrikyo had conducted attacks using sarin and anthrax. Following this 1995 attack in Japan, President Clinton issued Presidential Decision Directive 39 stating that the prevention of WMD from becoming available to terrorists is the highest priority of the US government.

Countering Transnational Terrorism: The Role of Mutual Support

Just as transnational terrorism has been evolving in recent years, the approaches to countering it must also evolve, but they have not done so. It is starting to be recognized that transnational terrorism cannot be treated by government's action alone and certainly not by a single government's action, as for example in the rhetoric of US President George W. Bush after the 9/11 attacks. President Bush ultimately realized that the US alone could not counter transnational terrorism and declared a "global war on terror" (GWOT) to enlist the support of other nations.

Both national governments and international public and private organizations could play an important role in helping counter transnational terrorism, in two ways. First, national governments and international organizations, including global businesses, can provide more extensive mutual support to counter transnational terrorism. Second, the same organizations could play a key role in preventing transnational terrorists from acquiring resources of fissile material (particularly highly enriched uranium, for which a bomb design is straightforward and well understood, in contrast to plutonium) funding, recruits, weapons, information, etc. The first is essential to deal with potential transnational terrorist strikes using WMD, while the second is one of the most important ways of preventing such strikes.

Transnational terrorism and global business are two important aspects of the current wave of globalization, and mutual support could be a highly important means to counter transnational terrorism, ranging from local law enforcement agencies and first responders, to corporations, states and regions, up to and including nations

and international organizations. A historical example of such mutual support is the aid from over a century ago that the citizens of Los Angeles provided to San Francisco after the 1906 earthquake and fire. They sent a train filled with relief supplies of food, medicine, tents, blankets, etc. that arrived just one day after the disaster. Local jurisdictions like Los Angeles have mutual aid agreements with other jurisdictions, but it is not clear how well they will work in a major disaster such as a terrorist strike using WMD, including nuclear weapons, which may happen. (See Katona, Sullivan, and Intriligator, Eds. 2006, especially Intriligator and Toukan, 2006.) Also illustrative of such mutual support are the examples in Sheffi (2005) of companies helping each other in emergency situations, whether natural disasters or terrorist strikes. (See also Alexander and Alexander, 2002; Auerswald *et al.*, 2006; and Lia, 2005.) Current antiterrorism entities, whether at the national level, such as the US DHS, or at the international level could well learn the value of augmenting their use of such mutual support from the experience of local first responders as well as that of business entities. In addition, global business could play an important role in depriving global terrorist organizations, such as al-Qaida of resources needed to conduct terrorist acts. Unfortunately the DHS, while publicly emphasizing such cooperation and mutual support with other public and private entities at both the national and international level, does not adequately act in this way, remaining aloof of other entities with which it might well cooperate and remains focused on preventing a repeat of 9/11.

Mutual Support Among Nations

Nations must rely on mutual support to deal with the threat of transnational terrorism. There must be joint production of intelligence to combine and collate information about potential terrorist strikes and the capabilities of terrorist organizations.

It should also be recognized that the most effective way to defeat transnational terrorism is not to try to protect vulnerable assets. That is the principal approach of the US DHS, which concentrates on protecting airplanes and airports, ignoring other potential targets. Such an approach is like generals fighting the last war, in this case, the 9/11 attacks. Many other types of terrorist attack are possible, however, as seen in the Bali, Madrid, London, and other terrorist attacks since 2001 on nightclubs, trains, buses, and subways. In fact, there are an enormous number of potential targets for terrorists, including railroads, seaports, chemical plants, nuclear power plants, bridges, tunnels, and high-rise buildings, just to name a few. If certain potential targets are protected, such as airplanes and airports that will not solve the problem of terrorism since the terrorists will simply substitute other targets, following the path of least resistance. An economist, William Landes, recognized the importance of such *substitution* many years ago in his 1978 article, where he noted that in a period of airplane hijackings, simply improving the safety of the airplanes would lead the terrorists to substitute other targets for airplanes (Landes, 1978). He noted as one possibility terrorist strikes on embassies, which actually occurred many years later in East Africa in the al-Qaida strikes on US embassies in Kenya and Tanzania.

A much more effective strategy to deal with transnational terrorism is to deprive terrorist organizations of resources of funding, recruits, weapons, information, etc. and particularly fissile material that could be used to manufacture a nuclear weapon through joint actions of nations in collaboration with international organizations, private and public. That would be an appropriate part of President George W. Bush's "global war on terror." It should also include directly confronting the terrorists in their bases and training camps, such as those of al-Qaida in the tribal areas of Pakistan.

Conclusions and Recommendations

Transnational terrorism is a new phenomenon that clearly represents a serious threat today, the most dangerous aspect of which is the threat of such terrorists acquiring and using WMD. Equally clearly, the current US and other national systems to defend against transnational terrorism as well as current global institutions are not prepared to deal with this threat. Both national and international systems must learn how these threats can be addressed through mutual support, following the example of global business as well as local police, fire, and other first responders. Both local safety agencies and global businesses have learned the value of cooperation and mutual support from experience. This experience could be applied at other levels, whether at the national or international level to address the threat of transnational terrorism.

Overall, we are probably not any safer now than we were before the implementation of the post 9/11 strategies and the situation is even worse given the avowed goal of some transnational terrorist groups to obtain and use WMD (see Intriligator, 2006). The major question is, how can we prevent a terrorist attack using WMD, such as a nuclear 9/11? We should recognize and avoid the denial syndrome and begin thinking about "worst case scenarios" and working on ways to prevent them from happening. We should not ignore the possibility that these horrific events could ever happen, as the US did before 9/11. It is important to study how terrorists think and the nature of their motivation. Terrorists will likely be using the path of least resistance, so tightening up airport security, for example, will mean that they will substitute other vulnerable targets, such as ports, nuclear power plants, chemical plants, bridges, high-rise office buildings, and other critical infrastructure. Clearly any protection should have a net benefit after taking into account its direct and indirect consequences.

Bibliography

Alexander, D.C., and A. Yonah, 2002: *Terrorism and business*, Transnational Publishers, Inc., Ardsley, New York

Allison, G., 2004: *Nuclear terrorism: the ultimate preventable catastrophe*, Times Books (paperback edition, Henry Holt & Co., New York, 2005)

Allison, G. (ed.), 2006: *Confronting the specter of nuclear terrorism*, The ANNALS of the American Academy of Political and Social Science Series, Sage Publications, Thousand Oaks, CA

Auerswald, P.E., L.M. Branscomb, T.M. LaPorte, and E.O. Michel-Kerjan (eds.), 2006: *Seeds of disaster, roots of response; how private action can reduce public vulnerability*, Cambridge University Press, New York

Enders, W., and T. Sandler, 2005: *The political economy of terrorism*, Cambridge University Press, New York

Friedman, T.L., 2003: The humiliation factor, *The New York Times*, 9 November

Garwin, R.L., 2002: Nuclear and biological megaterrorism, 27th Session of the International Seminars on Planetary Emergencies, 21 August 21, www.fas.org/rlg/020821-terrorism.htm, part of which appears as The technology of megaterror, *Technology Review*, 1 September 2002

Gheith, A., 2002: "Why we fight America": Al-Qa'ida spokesman explains September 11 and declares intentions to kill 4 million Americans with weapons of mass destruction, MEMRI No. 388, 12 June, memri.org/bin/articles.cgi?Area=jihad&ID=SP38802

Intriligator, M.D., 2006: The threat of insecurity: are we meeting the challenge? in *Beyond the Millennium Declaration: embracing democracy and good governance*, the Global Governance Group and the Municipality of Athens Development Agency, Athens, Greece, June

Intriligator, M.D., and A. Toukan, 2006: Terrorism and weapons of mass destruction, Chapter 4 in Katona, Sullivan, and Intriligator (eds.), 2006

Katona, P., Sullivan, J.P., and Intriligator, M.D. (eds.), 2006: *Countering terrorism and WMD: creating a global counter-terrorism network*, Routledge, London

Lake, A., 2000: *Six nightmares: real threats in a dangerous world and how America can meet them*, Little Brown, Boston

Landes, W., 1978: An economic study of U.S. aircraft hijacking, 1961–1976, *Journal of Law and Economics*, 21, April

Lia, B., 2005: *Globalisation and the future of terrorism: patterns and predictions*, Routledge

Rapoport, D., 2004: Modern terror: the four waves, in A.K. Cronin and J.M. Ludes (eds.), *Attacking terrorism: elements of a grand strategy*, Georgetown University Press, Washington, DC, 46–73

Sandler, T., D.G. Arce, and W. Enders, 2007: Transnational terrorism, Paper prepared for the 2008 Copenhagen Consensus, July

Sheffi, Y., 2005: *The resilient enterprise*, MIT Press

Stern, J., 2000: *The ultimate terrorists*, Harvard University Press

2003. *Terror in the name of God: why religious militants kill*, Ecco, New York

US Commission on National Security in the 21st Century (chaired by former US Senators Gary Hart and Warren Rudman), 1999: *New world coming: American security in the 21st century*, September, http://govinfo.library.unt.edu/nssg/Reports/reports.htm

Women and Development

CHAPTER 10

ELIZABETH M. KING, STEPHAN KLASEN, AND
MARIA PORTER

Introduction

Gender shapes one's role at home, in society, and in the economy. All cultures interpret and translate men's and women's biological differences into expectations about what behaviors and activities are appropriate for them and what rights, resources, and power they possess. Over the past three decades, these gender differences have increasingly gained prominence in the development agenda. More attention is being given to the plight of poor and disadvantaged women in developing countries, as well as to the unfinished gender agenda in more developed countries. Recognizing the importance of ensuring equal opportunities for females and males on grounds of both fairness and efficiency and as an instrument for achieving poverty reduction and economic growth, the international development community has included gender equality among the Millennium Development Goals (MDGs).

MDG3 reflects the strong belief by the development community that starkly unequal access to assets and opportunities between men and women produce further inequalities, harming not only women but also their families, and their communities. For example, disparities in education, employment, and wages hurt the women affected and also reduce the overall efficiency of the economy. Gender disparities that begin at a young age have significant long-term effects and are more costly to overcome later. Restricting the pool of educated people to boys reduces the overall talent pool. Disparities in rights constrain the choices available to women in many aspects of life – the right to marry, to divorce, to determine family size, to inherit and manage property, to allocate one's labor to household enterprises, to undertake income-earning activities outside the home, and to travel independently.

In this Challenge Paper we identify and elaborate four key policies that address fundamental disadvantages that women face. These policy choices are informed by the concept that equality means having equal ability to have a life of one's choosing and that this depends on having equal rights, equal opportunity – in access to markets (e.g., labor, land, credit) and to resources or public services – and equal voice. To illustrate, unequal access to education and health services, to productive assets, markets and to employment affects power relations between women and men, starting with their relative ability to make decisions within their households. These inequalities also lead to unequal capacity to take advantage of economic and other opportunities or to participate in public policy debates and formulation. We stop short of defining gender equality in terms of *equality of outcomes* because people might choose different paths in their pursuit of wealth and happiness, and because an intrinsic aspect of equality is to let women and men choose different (or similar) roles and different (or similar) outcomes according to their preferences and goals. Even in an environment of equal opportunity women and men may choose to pursue different goals and outcomes.

The next section describes the scope of the challenge in achieving gender equality, focusing on selected measurable disparities in rights, resources, and voice. Section 3 presents a conceptual framework for understanding gender disparities; it underpins our choice of the key policies for reducing women's disadvantages. The body of empirical evidence that supports our selection is reviewed under the discussion of each policy in Section 4. This evidence is used to inform our estimates of the benefits and costs of each policy. By comparing the benefit–cost ratios of the selected policies, Section 5 summarizes the menu of policies that we believe are critical to improving women's status and reducing gender inequalities.

Scope of the challenges

While there are exceptions with respect to some indicators, women are at a disadvantage relative to men with respect to rights, opportunities and voice; this is substantiated by data from across the developing world. The premise of our paper is that empowering women in key aspects of their lives will overcome this disadvantage and help achieve broader development goals. In this section we illustrate a few indicators of gender disparities and women's disadvantage that pertain to the policy options that we then present in the next section. We do not attempt to be comprehensive in this review because excellent recent reports, such as *The State of the World's Children 2007: Women and Children* (UNICEF 2006) and the Global Monitoring Report 2007 (World Bank 2007), already provide such a review.

Investments in girls' schooling

The push to achieve universal primary education has yielded higher girls' enrollments at all levels of schooling, and many countries have achieved or are close to achieving gender parity in primary enrollments. This progress has been remarkable,

[1] This is measured using the gross enrollment rate. Following UNESCO (2005) parity is defined as a female-to-male ratio exceeding 0.97. A ratio below 0.97 indicates significant female disadvantage. In 35 countries (of the 83 that achieved the 2005 target) there was significant *male* disadvantage, with boys' gross enrollment rate lagging behind girls' (the female-to-male ratio exceeded 1.03). In these countries, mostly countries of East Asia and the Pacific, Europe and Central Asia and Latin America and the Caribbean, boys' enrollment exceeds 90 percent. Thus a male disadvantage tends to occur in education systems with overall high participation in schooling.

showing that pro-poor but gender-neutral education policies such as more schools in rural areas and lower fees for all can overcome the barriers that have kept girls from schools. In addition, some countries have also established programs that aim to remove stronger obstacles for girls in poorer, more remote, or more disadvantaged families. Examples are stipends (e.g., Bangladesh), conditional cash transfers (e.g., Mexico), and vouchers (e.g., Pakistan) targeted to girls.

Between 1990 and 2005, girls' enrollment in primary education increased in virtually all regions of the developing world; the sole exception was East Asia and the Pacific where girls' gross enrollment rate already exceeded 100 percent in the early 1990s. Girls' enrollment in secondary school rose as well, especially in East Asia, Latin America and the Caribbean, and the Middle East and North Africa regions. By 2005, 83 developing countries (out of 140 with data) had met the intermediate MDG3 target of gender parity in primary and secondary enrollment rates (World Bank 2007).[1] Most of these countries are in regions where enrollment historically has been high – East Asia and the Pacific, Europe and Central Asia, and Latin America and the Caribbean. In the Middle East and North Africa, most countries met the target by 2005, but this region also included three countries (out of 13 with data) with significant female disadvantages in enrollment. In Sub-Saharan Africa, less than one-quarter of all countries met the target by 2005, but reliable data are scarcer in these countries. In South Asia, Bangladesh and Sri Lanka are notable for achieving parity, but the others have failed to meet the target of parity in secondary school enrollment. Of the 57 countries that failed to meet the MDG in 2005, 35 countries – most in Sub-Saharan Africa – are on track to attain the target by 2015, leaving 22 countries (again predominantly in Sub-Saharan Africa and South Asia) seriously off track.

At the tertiary education level, female enrollment does better relative to male enrollment. In 2005 the female tertiary enrollment rate lagged behind the male rate in 63 countries (of 130 countries with data) but exceeded the male rate in 65 countries.[2] This overall reversal in relative enrollment rates is largely due to more boys leaving school for jobs during or after the secondary level, whereas girls of the same age do not have similar work opportunities. In some countries, the principal draw for teenage girls would instead be early marriage and parenthood.

Despite the progress in enrollment rates, it is estimated that of the nearly 137 million illiterate youths in the world, three-fifths are girls (UNESCO 2005). Not surprisingly, the female-to-male literacy ratio is lowest in Sub-Saharan Africa, Middle East and North Africa, and South Asia, as these are the regions that also have more unequal primary and secondary enrollment rates. In 25 of the countries in these regions, the ratio is fewer than 80 literate young women for every 100 literate young men. The ratio is lowest in Yemen and Afghanistan, where only 36 young women are literate for every 100 literate young men.

Country-level statistics hide significant gender disparities within countries, such as those between urban and rural populations. The graphs in Figure 10.1 of data from the demographic and health surveys illustrate vastly different enrollment profiles between urban and rural people. Disaggregation by income, race, ethnicity, and caste can also reveal substantial gender gaps even in countries that do well at the national level. These gender gaps between urban and rural areas, among ethnic or racial groups, or between rich and poor people explain why some countries have not reached the gender parity target (e.g, Bolivia, Cambodia, Ecuador, Guatemala, Laos PDR, Morocco, and Pakistan) (Lewis and Lockheed 2006). For education and literacy, the female disadvantage is always larger in rural areas and among lower-income households. This is further accentuated in countries that have not reached overall gender parity in school enrollments (largely in Sub-Saharan Africa, the Middle East and North Africa).

Safe motherhood

A country's population growth rate and the age structure of its population affect its ability to address issues such as hunger, housing shortages, large dependency burdens and environmental degradation which are all intensified by rapid population growth. They also affect the welfare of individuals and families in the current as well as succeeding generations (see, for example, Bloom and Williamson 1998). Fertility rates have declined in developing countries from over 6 children per woman in the 1950s to 2.8 children per woman, but fertility rates remain at 5.46 children per woman in the 49 least developed countries, mostly in Sub-Saharan Africa (Levine et al. 2006). Bearing many children is hard on women who do not have access to good prenatal or postnatal care or safe delivery services. Around eight million women suffer life-threatening pregnancy-related complications each year; over 529,000 women die, of whom 99 percent are from developing countries (UNFPA 2004). South Asia and Sub-Saharan Africa account for 74 percent of the global burden of maternal conditions (Graham et al. 2006). In the developing world, one-third of all pregnant women receive no health care during pregnancy, and 60 percent of deliveries take place outside of health facilities, with skilled personnel assisting only half of all deliveries (UNFPA 2004).

In developing countries, 61 percent of maternal deaths occur 23–48 hours after delivery because of problems such as postpartum hemorrhage and hypertensive disorders or after 48 hours because of sepsis. Complications from unsafe abortions account for 13 percent of maternal deaths, though this is probably an underestimate (Table 10.1). Direct obstetric conditions (those that specifically arise from pregnancy) account for 80 percent of maternal deaths, most caused by uncontrolled hemorrhaging, while indirect obstetric conditions (those aggravated

[2] Female disadvantage was evident mainly in Sub-Saharan Africa and South Asia. Male disadvantage was notable in Middle East and North Africa (Algeria, Iran, Jordan, and Libya), East Asia and the Pacific (the Philippines and Thailand), Latin America and the Caribbean (Honduras, Nicaragua, Panama), and Europe and Central Asia. Reflecting the legacy of the Soviet Union and historically high enrollment rates in Europe and Central Asia, countries there had high female tertiary enrollment rates that exceeded male enrollment rates.

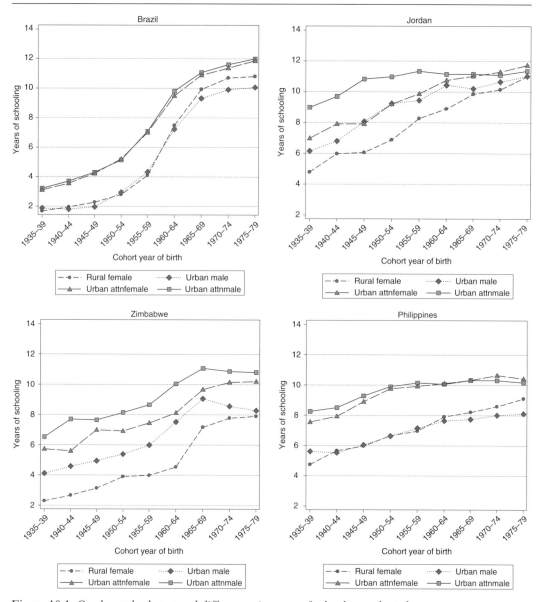

Figure 10.1 *Gender and urban–rural differences in years of schooling, selected countries*
Source: Demographic and health surveys, latest years

by or threatening pregnancy) account for the remainder and include diseases such as HIV/AIDS and malaria (Graham *et al.* 2006).

Women's risk of pregnancy-related death or disability depends on the number of and spacing between pregnancies, mother's age, and whether the birth was an unwanted one. Family plan-

ning programs have aimed to influence each of these factors through more information, education, and communication interventions, as well as through services that offer contraception methods. Since 1994, family planning use has increased globally from 55 per cent of married couples to 61 per cent. Use varies regionally, ranging from about 25 per cent in Africa to nearly 65 per cent in Asia (where high use in China raises the average)[3], and 70 percent in Latin America, the Caribbean, and industrialized regions (UNFPA 2004). The official indicator for MDG6, contraceptive prevalence rate, considers all methods of contraception, computed as the percentage of women who are practicing, or whose sexual partners are practicing, any form of contraception, traditional or modern (UNDP 2003). Compared to traditional methods, however, modern methods offer women and their partners a more reliable way to control their fertility and to prevent the spread of sexually transmitted diseases.

Of particular note is the situation of teenage girls. Teenage pregnancy rates are still high in many countries, especially in Africa (Table 10.2). Childbearing at such a young age is associated with disproportionate health risks to the mother and baby (maternal mortality, delivery complications, premature delivery, and low birth weights). Adolescent motherhood is also associated with early departure from school, lower human capital accumulation, lower earnings, and a higher probability of living in poverty as an adult.

Financial autonomy and economic empowerment

Studies from a diverse set of countries, including Bangladesh, Brazil, Canada, Côte d'Ivoire, Ethiopia, France, Indonesia, South Africa, Taiwan (China), and the United Kingdom, indicate that women's and men's unequal control of resources has significant – and different – impacts on household consumption and expenditure (e.g., Duflo 2000; Pitt and Khandker 1998; Pitt et al. 2003; Porter 2007; Thomas 1990). While the precise effects of female and male resource control differ from place to place, results suggest that increases in the relative resources controlled by women result in a relatively larger share of household resources going to family welfare, especially to expenditures on children – even after controlling for per capita income and demographic characteristics of the household. Thus, there are considerable positive externali-

Table 10.1. Causes of maternal mortality and morbidity (%)

	Mortality	Morbidity
Hemorrhage	28	18
Sepsis	15	16
Hypertensive disorders	14	9
Obstructed labor	8	9
Unsafe abortion	13	26
Other maternal	22	22
	100	100

Nonobstetric (indirect) causes of death and morbidity, such as tuberculosis and malaria, have been excluded.
Source: Graham et al. (2006).

ties to women having more control over household resources.

Age patterns of labor force participation, however, show that in all regions of the world, women have significantly lower probabilities of working than men. Three distinct patterns emerge across regions. First, in some regions, male labor force participation rates are 1.5–2 times the female labor force participation rates, as in the Middle East and North Africa, South Asia, and Latin America and the Caribbean regions. Among women aged 20–24, the average labor force participation rate ranges from 37 percent to 49 percent, below the average of 55 percent or higher for the remaining regions. Among those aged 25–49, the average participation rate is 37–60 percent, again much lower than that in the remaining regions. Other countries have much higher female participation rates, although women remain concentrated in low-paying, small-scale agriculture or self employment in the nonagricultural sector (Table 10.3). During the period 1990–2003 women's share in nonagricultural wage employment increased in all regions – but the increase was modest and uneven across regions and countries (World Bank 2007). Particularly in formal sector employment, large gender gaps persist,

[3] When China (with a large population and high prevalence) is left out of the calculations, only 46 per cent of married women in Asia are using contraception.

Table 10.2. Fertility rates, teenage pregnancy and family planning

	Total fertility rate	Percentage who had children or are currently pregnant	Unmet need for family planning
Sub-Saharan Africa			
Benin 2001	5.6	21.5	27.2
Burkina Faso 2003	5.9	23.2	28.8
Cameroon 2004	5.0	28.4	20.2
Chad 2004	6.3	36.6	20.7
Congo (Brazzaville) 2005	4.8	27.3	16.2
Eritrea 2002	4.8	14.0	27.0
Ethiopia 2005	5.4	16.6	33.8
Ghana 2003	4.4	13.8	34.0
Guinea 2005	5.7	31.8	21.2
Kenya 2003	4.9	23.0	24.5
Lesotho 2004	3.5	20.2	31.0
Madagascar 2003/2004	5.2	34.0	23.6
Malawi 2004	6.0	34.1	27.6
Mali 2001	6.8	40.4	28.5
Mozambique 2003	5.5	41.0	18.4
Nigeria 2003	5.7	25.2	16.9
Rwanda 2005	6.1	4.1	37.9
Senegal 2005	5.3	18.9	31.6
Tanzania 2004	5.7	26.0	21.8
Zambia 2001/02	5.9	31.6	27.4
North Africa/West Asia/Europe			
Armenia 2005	1.7	4.7	13.3
Egypt 2005	3.1	9.4	10.3
Jordan 2002	3.7	4.3	11.0
Moldova Republic of 2005	1.7	6.1	6.7
Morocco 2003–2004[2]	2.5	6.5	10.0
South & Southeast Asia			
Bangladesh 2004[3]	3.0	32.7	11.2
Indonesia 2002/2003	2.6	10.4	8.6
Nepal 2001	4.1	21.4	27.8
Philippines 2003	3.5	8.0	17.3
Vietnam 2002	1.9	3.4	4.8
Latin America & Caribbean			
Bolivia 2003	3.8	15.7	22.7
Colombia 2005	2.4	20.5	5.8
Dominican Republic 2002	3.0	23.3	10.9
Honduras 2005	3.3	21.5	-
Nicaragua 2001	3.2	24.7	14.6

Source: ORC Macro, 2007. MEASURE DHS STATcompiler. www.measuredhs.com

(1) Total fertility rate and proportion of women pregnant: Total fertility rate for the three years preceding the survey and the percentage of women 15–49 currently pregnant, by selected background characteristics.

(2) Teenage pregnancy and motherhood: Percentage of women 15–19 who are mothers or pregnant with their first child by selected background characteristics.

(3) Unmet need for family planning services: Percentage of currently married women with unmet need for family planning, met need for family planning, and the total demand for family planning services.

Table 10.3. Women's participation in the informal sector

	Percentage of non-agricultural labor force that is in the informal sector 1991/1997		Women's share of the informal sector in the non-agricultural labor force 1991/1997
	Women	Men	
Africa			
Benin	97	83	62
Chad	97	59	53
Guinea	84	61	37
Kenya	83	59	60
Mali	96	91	59
South Africa	30	14	61
Tunisia	39	52	18
Latin America			
Bolivia	74	55	51
Brazil	67	55	47
Chile	44	31	46
Colombia	44	42	50
Costa Rica	48	46	40
El Salvador	69	47	58
Honduras	65	51	56
Mexico	55	44	44
Panama	41	35	44
Venezuela	47	47	38
Asia			
India	91	70	23
Indonesia	88	69	43
Philippines	64	66	46
Thailand	54	49	47

Source: The World's Women 2000: Trends and Statistics, United Nations, Chart 5.13.

particularly in Sub-Saharan Africa and South Asia (e.g. Klasen 2006; Klasen and Lamanna 2007). In a third group of countries, female participation rates are high and women's share in nonagricultural paid work is closer to men's. In these countries (predominantly in East and South-East Asia), the gender wage gap continues to be large, however, with much of the gap persisting even after controlling for worker characteristics (Klasen 2006).

There are many reasons why women's labor force participation and earnings are lower than men's. These reasons include the division of responsibilities at home which results in women's marginal product of time spent in child care and home production being higher than the marginal product of their time in the labor market, which might feed back into lower investments in their schooling. The calculus of these decisions within the home has been the topic of numerous theoretical and empirical studies in economics (led by the seminal work by Becker 1965). The reasons also include implicit or explicit gender discrimination in wage employment, and statutory or customary laws preventing equal access to land or property.

Where wage or formal employment is a relatively small part of the labor market or where women are effectively excluded from such employment due to its incompatibility with childbearing and childrearing tasks, women's lack of access to land and capital for self employment is an important barrier to women's economic autonomy or empowerment (see Estudillo, Quisumbing and Otsuka 2001). Farm or nonfarm, female-run enterprises tend to have poorer access to credit and related financial services, machinery, and information (Saito *et al.* 1994). Udry (1996) and Udry *et al.* (1995) show that production could potentially increase by 6–15 percent if the quality of land and inputs are reallocated across farm plots in Burkina Faso, specifically between those farmed by women and those farmed by men.

There are several reasons why women lack access to financial capital, land, and other productive inputs. In some countries, such as Bangladesh, women are restricted by laws of purdah from participating in market activities and interacting with men outside their families. They typically lack the collateral necessary to access credit, because property is often inherited by men, and women are precluded from buying or owning land or capital. Such market imperfections provide a strong case for the need to target women when providing financial services to the poor. Besides opening up work opportunities for women, giving women access to credit improves their bargaining position within the household, with second-round benefits that include better health status of children. Improving women's access to productive capital is one of the four policy options we present in this paper, so we return to this topic in section 4.

Political participation and voice

National constitutions around the world affirm the principle of basic human rights, and many of them contain an explicit reference to non-

discrimination between women and men with respect to those rights. But in many countries, men and women still do not have equal rights. Many women are still treated as minors in family law; for instance, they cannot pass on citizenship to a child, or they need a male relative's permission to travel outside their locality, or they cannot inherit land (World Bank 2001, 2007). Moreover, they have little voice in formulating laws or policies that directly and profoundly affect them. To illustrate: although collecting water and firewood is largely the responsibility of women and girls in many rural areas,[4] new rules are being formulated by men without involving the women in proposing viable alternatives following forest closure (Cornwall 2003). Women are often excluded from forest committees that frame these new rules about forest protection.

Legal reforms can redress gender inequalities in rights – and recently several countries have adopted legislation affirming the equality of men and women and explicitly outlawing discrimination based on sex. For example, Timor-Leste's post-independence constitution affirms equal rights for women and men in marriage and the family and within social, economic and political life. Rwanda's 2003 constitution guarantees equal rights of spouses in marriage and divorce, outlaws discrimination based on sex, guarantees the right of women and men to vote and run for office, calls for equal pay for equal work, and establishes the right to education. In Azerbaijan, a presidential decree in 2000 instructed the government to ensure women and men are represented equally in the state administration and have equal opportunities under ongoing reforms (UNFPA 2004). Similarly, some countries (including Belgium, the Dominican Republic, Portugal, Spain, and Uruguay) have passed laws increasing penalties for gender-based violence. In Pakistan, a bill was passed in 2006 removing rape from the jurisdiction of Islamic laws and making it a crime punishable under the country's penal code.

But equal rights on paper do not necessarily translate into practice. For example, many countries have introduced mandatory education laws recognizing basic schooling as a human right – but the way education is delivered deters girls

---

[4] In Ghana, Tanzania, and Zambia women account for no less than two-thirds of household time devoted to water and fuel collection, while children – mostly girls – account for between 5 and 28 percent of household time spent on these activities (Malmberg Calvo 1994). In rural Nepal and Pakistan poor access to firewood means women spend more hours collecting firewood and fewer hours generating income (Cooke 1998; Ilahi and Jafarey 1999).

Table 10.4. Percent share of women in parliament, January 1997 and January 2007

	Single House or lower House		Upper House or Senate		Both Houses combined	
	1997	2007	1997	2007	1997	2007
Nordic countries	36.4	40.8	–	–	36.4	40.8
Americas	12.9	20.0	11.5	19.3	12.7	19.9
Sub-Saharan Africa	10.1	16.6	13.6	18.5	10.4	16.8
Asia	13.4	16.5	9.9	15.7	13.1	16.4
Pacific	9.8	12.4	21.8	31.8	11.6	14.5
Arab States	3.3	9.5	2.1	6.3	3.3	8.8
Total number of female ministers	3956	6462	556	1074	4512	7436
Total number of ministers	34839	37174	5914	6708	40753	43882

Source: www.ipu.org/wmn-e/world.htm

more than boys from going to school in some settings. Many constitutions now give women and men the right to vote and to be elected to public office – but gender disparities in literacy and access to information and cultural norms restrict women's mobility outside the home and limit their participation in political forums.

One way to achieve more equal rights for men and women is to change the composition of the official bodies that make and enforce laws granting those rights. Increasing the number of women in politics is thought to be one way of doing so. The right to engage in public debate, the right to vote, and the right to run for public office are rights that many people take for granted, but there are few measures of these political rights that are comparable across countries. The MDG indicator of gender equality in the political sphere is the share of women in national parliaments.[5] This share varies widely from 9.6 percent in the Arab countries to 17.8 percent in Sub-Saharan African countries and to 41.6 percent in Nordic countries (Table 10.4).

In truth, this indicator is a visible but essentially limited measure of women's political participation. Women who succeed in winning national elections may be extremely effective leaders and perceived as such, but the performance of this select group of women is hardly an accurate indicator of women's political participation in general.[6] Women's opportunities to influence decision-making rest not only on women who are elected into national office but also on how and whether those women represent women's interests, whether they raise their voices and, when they do, whether anyone listens. Agarwal (1997) draws attention to familiar constraints: time; official male bias; social constraints about women's capabilities and roles; the absence of a "critical mass" of women politicians; and lack of public speaking experience.

Indicators of women's voice as citizens may be at least as important as women's share in parliaments. One very basic indicator is the number and share of women and men with citizenship documents, starting with birth registrations (and ending with death registries). Recent research by the Inter-American Development Bank showed under-registration of births in six Latin American countries, varying from 8.4 percent in Peru to 25.8 percent in the Dominican Republic. Characteristics associated with the risk of a child being undocumented from birth to age 5 include poverty, rural residence, and teen motherhood (Duryea et al. 2006). As citizens,

[5] This is also the political component of the gender empowerment index first developed by the United Nations Development Program for its 1995 Human Development Report (UNDP 1995, Bardhan and Klasen 1999).

[6] For instance, South Asia, noted for its large gender disparities, is also known for having had a relatively large number of women presidents and prime ministers – from Indira Gandhi of India, Chandrika Kumaratunga and Sirimavo Bandaranaike of Sri Lanka, Benazir Bhutto of Pakistan, and Khaleda Zia and Sheikh Hasina of Bangladesh.

women can join political organizations and participate in political action. Data from the World Values Survey indicate that they do, although at a lower level than men.

With more political power, women can work to establish equal rights for women and men, especially in family law, laws about gender-related violence, property rights, and political rights – and especially for the enforcement of these rights and laws. Gender-based violence perpetrated on women is a reflection of women's lack of power at home, in the streets and before the law. While male to male violence can be interpreted as men's way of handling conflict, male to female violence can be interpreted as the expression of men's need to reinforce well-entrenched, rigid gender roles, exacerbated by grossly unequal power (physical and otherwise) between men and women.[7] For example, men in Bangladesh view wife-beating as a right and as a normal way to keep women's "unruly nature" in check (Narayan *et al.* 2000). The *machismo* culture in some Latin American and Caribbean countries is characterized by chronic domestic violence, infidelity, and desertion within a structure of consensual unions, and by aggressive and highly intransigent male to male relations (Sara-Lafosse 1998). In wartime, rape and other abuse against women have been widely used weapons of terrorism and humiliation (Goldblatt and Meintjes 1998; Pedersen 2002; Rehn and Sirleaf 2002).

A Framework for Choosing Policy Options to Achieve Gender Equality

Choosing priority options

There is a wide-ranging set of policy options or strategies that potentially can reduce gender inequalities and women's disadvantage, so it

would be an immense task to compare the relative costs and benefits of all or most of them in order to identify what should be development priorities. To illustrate the immensity of this task, consider that the challenge of improving education, the topic of another Copenhagen Consensus Challenge Paper, can be addressed by several options having to do with expanding school supply, improving the quality of education, or promoting demand for education (Pritchett 2004). All are within the realm of education. In contrast, the strategies for addressing gender inequalities pertain to any number of development sectors, such as education, health, land reform, microfinance, pension reform, and so on. Given this multisectoral nature of the gender challenge, in fact, each Challenge Paper for the Copenhagen Consensus initiative could have ranked policy options according to their impact on gender inequalities!

In this paper we present estimates of the costs and benefits implied by just four policy options. We chose these options not so much on the basis of estimated relative costs and benefits for a large number of options as on the basis of a familiar conceptual model of individual and household behavior and the rich empirical literature associated with that model. The model as elaborated by a generation of economists starting with Gary Becker's seminal work (1965) emphasizes the life cycle of investments in males and females that may lead to unequal opportunities and outcomes in schools and labor markets.[8] According to this model, from childhood, households shape gender roles and expectations in the way they allocate resources to sons and daughters, such as through decisions about boys' or girls' education or about sons working in the farm and other market work while daughters work in home and care-giving activities. This gender-based allocation implies that by the time girls and boys become adults and form new households, women typically have fewer years of education, work longer hours than men, and yet have less experience in the labor force, earn lower wages, and have less say in community politics.

Informed by this model (and its variants) and the related body of empirical work, we selected

---

[7] Men do not have a monopoly on violence, however. Historical evidence shows that women are capable of perpetrating or condoning violence against both men and women. For example, in South Africa many women supported apartheid, firmly convinced that racial divisions and violence were necessary to ensure order (Goldblatt and Meintjes 1998).

[8] For a survey of this large literature, see for example Schultz (1995, 2001) and Haddad, Hoddinott and Alderman (1997).

four policy options that correspond to critical stages in a woman's life – or the critical roles that she plays – with a view to increasing women's *agency*, that is, a woman's ability or power to make choices and exercise those choices. The four policy options are to increase and improve girls' schooling, provide support for women's reproductive roles, improve women's access to financial services, and increase women's political participation. These policies have the potential to improve greatly women's well-being. A large empirical literature also indicates that they can contribute to overall development. For each policy option we identify specific approaches for implementation. For example, to increase girls' schooling levels, we have considered alternative demand and supply strategies and have chosen to focus on the demand-side intervention of conditional cash transfers. We discuss the arguments and evidence for each of the policy options and the specific approaches in the respective sections below.

Assessing the options

In line with the framework of the Copenhagen Consensus Project, we quantify the benefits from each policy option in terms of the resulting higher incomes or disability-adjusted life-years (DALYs) gained (Lomborg 2004). DALYs are estimated from the potential years of life lost due to premature death, poor health, or disability for all age groups. It was used as a measure of adult morbidity and mortality by the Global Burden of Disease project, a worldwide collaboration of over 100 researchers, sponsored by the World Health Organization and the World Bank.[9] The study used information from a number of countries to estimate the costs of individual causes of morbidity and mortality to healthy life. In this paper, each DALY gained is set to be equivalent to either $1,000 (used in our *low-value* scenario) or $5,000 (*high-value* scenario), and both sets of estimates are presented for each option. Finally, because each option is associated with a stream of costs and benefits over time, we compute present values using two discount rates – 3 percent for the *low-discount* scenario and 6 percent for the *high-discount* scenario – to compare the predicted costs and benefits across the options. These are the parameters used in the Copenhagen Consensus Challenge Papers.

Two caveats are noteworthy. First, there are significant cross-country or regional differences in the costs and benefits of each option. That is, one policy option that would be greatly needed in one country or region may not be as beneficial in another setting, or one policy may be more costly to implement in one context than another. The existing literature is not large enough to provide specific guidance on this point. Due to the limited availability of data and findings that are comparable across countries, we ignore most of these across- and within-country differences in projecting the benefits and costs of the global solutions. However, those options that are relatively pro-poor carry more weight in our estimates. Thus, most of our policy options are thus geared towards implementation in the two developing regions where gender inequality and poverty are greatest, Sub-Saharan Africa and South Asia.

This focus on poor people is chosen partly for equity reasons and partly because the potential benefits from policies that lift the barriers to economic or political participation are likely to be largest for them. The studies that have estimated differential price responses (elasticities) to interventions find a larger response among poorer people (e.g., Orazem and King 2008 for a review). At the same time, the costs of reaching some poor people could be very high (for example, costs could increase with remoteness of residence), precluding interventions on the basis of cost–benefit analysis. Unfortunately, cost estimates are often missing from (or at least not reported in) studies that have assessed the impact of programs.

In principle, we could choose options that are gender-neutral in terms of design (such as lifting the user fees for all schoolchildren) or those that are gender-targeted (such as lifting user fees only for girls). Gender-neutral initiatives may be more costly to implement. For example, eliminating secondary school fees as applied to all students

---

[9] See Anand and Hanson (1996) for a critical view of the implicit value-judgments included in the calculation of DALYs.

would have a larger marginal impact on girls if the price elasticity of demand is higher for girls but the cost of such a universal (gender-neutral or non-targeted) initiative would also be far greater than a targeted scholarship program, even net of implementation and monitoring costs of a targeted program. On the other hand, for political reasons, non-targeted programs might also be easier to implement because their universal coverage would not attract resistance from non-beneficiaries. With these considerations, we have chosen to propose gender-targeted interventions in areas where such targeting has already proved to be politically feasible, at least in some contexts.

A second caveat has to do with the costs of the policy options. In measuring these costs, we include estimates of the direct and indirect costs of implementation, enforcement, targeting and monitoring as comprehensively as possible. Some costs are incurred at the level of individuals and households, and some are incurred by a government agency or a non-government organization. Costs are incurred over a period of time for each of the options, but the duration of the period varies according to the alternative scenarios we consider. We obtain cost data from a variety of sources, including past studies and policy or program documents. Overall, we find that cost data on specific interventions across different settings are generally missing from published sources; we patch together the best information available to us.

Each option implies both short-run and long-run benefits. As requested in the framework for Copenhagen Consensus Challenge papers, we make projections about benefits over a period of 100 years. For such a long period, it makes sense to trace not only obvious direct benefits but also more indirect, "second-round" or "second-generation" benefits. As with costs, benefits accrue to individuals, to households, and to communities and society as a whole. For example, more schooling for girls today will confer long-run benefits to those girls in terms of their health and employment, as well as to their children's well-being in the future. At the same time, studies have found a positive association between female education and measures of aggregate economic growth.

The next sections present the four policy options for improving the status and welfare of women in developing countries. The discussion of each option begins with the justification for choosing the option, and then presents the benefit and cost estimates associated with the option, and finally alternative benefit–cost ratios corresponding to a range of scenarios. We begin with the option that pertains to schooling which are investments in the earlier years of life of a woman and then proceed to options that relate to three later aspects of a woman's life – as worker, mother, and citizen and leader.

Option 1 – Increase and Improve Girls' Schooling

While there has been considerable progress in reducing the gender gap in schooling enrollments and achievements across the developing world, significant gender gaps remain in particular regions and at particular levels of education. Specifically, in parts of South Asia (most notably Northern India and Pakistan) and many poorer countries in Sub-Saharan Africa (especially in West Africa), there remain large gender gaps in primary enrollments. In a larger group of countries across the developing world, there are sizable gender gaps in secondary enrollments. They are particularly large in countries in South Asia and Sub-Saharan Africa (see World Bank 2007). As a result, women still have more than two fewer years of schooling than men in South Asia, and about 1.5 fewer years in Sub-Saharan Africa, on average (the gap is larger in individual countries; see Barro and Lee 2001).

This inequality in schooling is not only an issue of gender inequity that demands rectification, but also an issue of efficiency because it lowers the development opportunities of the countries involved. The growth, fertility, and mortality impacts of female education have been examined extensively in the empirical literature (for a review, see e.g., Klasen 2006, World Bank 2001, and Abu-Ghaida and Klasen 2004). In particular, the positive impact of female education on growth has been well documented with estimates in a relatively tight range (surveyed in Abu-Ghaida and Klasen 2004; individual studies include Dollar and Gatti 1999; Klasen 2002; Yamarik and Ghosh 2003; Knowles *et al.* 2002). Similarly, there is an even larger literature documenting the impact of female education on lower fertility, better nutrition, lower mortality, and better education of children (e.g. Behrman *et al.* 1999; Galor and Weil 1996; Holmes 2003; Lagerlöf 2003; Schultz 1997; Orazem and King 2008; Smith and Haddad 2002; Summers 1994). Some of the benefits found are:

- Higher overall human capital of the population by removing the sex-specific distortion (under the assumption of an equal distribution of talents, a discriminatory policy will mean that the education system is not educating the most talented);
- Higher average returns to education under the assumption that the marginal returns to female education are higher;
- More female employment which would reduce a similar distortion in employment opportunities and allow countries to promote export-led pro-poor growth that is often heavily reliant on female-intensive manufacturing industries; this also increases female bargaining power, and improves economic and political governance, each with positive effects for economic growth and reductions in mortality;
- Later marriage which reduces fertility and population growth, thereby allowing greater investment in each child, which in turn promotes economic growth;
- Lower undernutrition and mortality rates in families as educated women have healthier children through more health knowledge, more income, and more bargaining power; and
- More education for the next generation (as female education has a large impact on the inter-generational transmission of education); moreover, mother's education can exert a larger impact on daughters' education than father's education.

An important analytical issue is why education gaps persist despite the benefits from female education. The implication is that a range of externalities play a central role. In the regions where girls' schooling are lower relative to boys', parents do not typically reap the full benefits of educating girls as daughters are expected to leave the household upon marriage and will, in contrast to sons, not be responsible for the old age support of the parents (see models in Hill and King 1995; Rosenzweig and Schultz 1982), nor carry the family's name. The benefits to the next generation that accrue via the mortality, education, and fertility effects are also not usually captured by the parents making the schooling choices. As in other instances of external effects, there is therefore a clear case for a public intervention to internalize these externalities.

The critical question is what type of policy would be able to increase girls' schooling effectively, particularly in the two regions where gender gaps remain pervasive, namely, South Asia and Sub-Saharan Africa. Policies can weaken the incentives for parents to favor sons. For example, by developing formal old-age security mechanisms that reduce the need felt by parents to self-insure and eventually change perceptions about the role of sons and daughters for old-age support of parents. These are long-term societal changes, but they can sometimes be hastened by policy changes or by economic growth (e.g., Dollar and Gatti 1999). In the short to medium-term, a more direct approach might be for public policy to provide special incentives to send girls to school to balance the existing incentives favoring boys. Policies could improve the opportunities for schooling available to girls (i.e., increasing the supply of schools for them) or increase the demand for more female education.

The rapid increase in enrollment rates in developing countries today was made possible by large expansions in school supply, so supply is now unlikely to be the primary cause of existing large gaps. This has not always been the case, of course,[10] and even today, there are exceptions. In Pakistan single-sex schooling is still the norm and the supply of schools for girls (particularly at the

[10] For example, Duflo (2001) finds that the school building program in Indonesia about 30 years ago had a significant effect on enrollments, achievements, and earnings (unfortunately, only males are examined).

secondary level in rural areas) is much more limited than for boys. As estimated by Alderman *et al.* (1996), about half of the difference in schooling outcomes of boys and girls might be due to the simple unavailability of school for girls. In such circumstances, building schools could be the most cost-effective policy to increase girls' schooling. In addition, there is some evidence that parental reluctance to send a child to school in these circumstances also relates to the lack of a culturally appropriate learning environment for girls, which includes ensuring girls' safety on the way to school, provision for latrines, and female teachers (e.g. World Bank 2001).[11] In general, however, the enrollment response to a school building program, while statistically significant, has been found to be small as the average distances to primary schools have declined (Pritchett 2004; Filmer 2004).[12]

A different supply-related intervention is to improve the quality of schooling, a challenge facing most developing countries. To the extent that such reforms equally improve the schools available to both boys and girls, however, they may not be critical to reducing gender gaps in schooling. We do not focus on these reforms here but should note that such reforms could be an important complement to the measures proposed below.

Demand-side interventions seek to increase female schooling by increasing parental demand to send their daughters to school. They can address other direct and opportunity costs of schooling that might be significantly higher for girls than boys. Direct costs (such as school fees, uniforms, textbooks, supplies) could be sizable (as a share of per capita income) in many developing countries (estimates are that these are 22 percent of per-capita income in poor African countries, according to the ILO/UNCTAD Advisory Group (2001)); opportunity costs could also be large as children in school are not available for child labor, household production, or sibling care. Lowering these direct and/or opportunity costs would likely increase enrollments. In many sub-Saharan African countries, the easiest way to accomplish this is to lift user fees as has been done recently in Uganda, Lesotho, Malawi, and Tanzania. In each case, the enrollment response was large although the effect of these larger enrollments on years of schooling completed or on productive skills is not clear as the enrollment expansion might have been achieved at the expense of the quality of learning (see Deininger 2003). If school crowding were an issue due to higher enrollments, one would have to budget additional funds to pay for more teachers and more classrooms, although not necessarily in proportion to the increase in enrollments as class sizes can increase somewhat without a large impact on quality (e.g., double shifts can be used to save on construction costs).

What policy tools raise household demand for girls' schooling? If the aim is to increase female schooling in particular, one option would be to lift user fees for girls only although this might be politically difficult to implement (but surely not impossible). Several countries have tried different interventions. One option would be to hand out cash to families where girls are out of school in the form of an unconditional cash transfer, with the expectation that the income elasticity of girls' schooling exceeds that of boys' (e.g., Tansel 2002, for Turkey). A careful analysis by Todd and Wolpin (2006), however, finds that the response would be about 20 percent lower than if the cash transfer were conditioned on school attendance. This suggests that conditional cash transfer (CCT) programs in which households receive funds should be tied to children attending school.

[11] The supply of a close and culturally appropriate school for girls can have sizable impacts on enrollments in some contexts provided that the school is quite close (not necessitating girls to travel more than half a kilometer on their own), a female teacher is present, and there are adequate sanitary facilities for girls (e.g. Hill and King 1995; Alderman, Orazem and Paterno 2001; Orazem and King 2008; Herz and Sperling 2004). In these contexts, specific supply-side interventions could help.

[12] However, the impact of supply interventions could still be large at the secondary level. The impact of the supply-side interventions of Mexico's PROGRESA program suggests that a cohort of 1,000 girls who have completed the primary cycle will receive 27 more years of schooling in lower secondary school as a result of a decrease in the average distance to such schools; the corresponding number for boys is 25 more years of schooling (Coady and Parker 2004).

Principally, there have been two types of CCT programs. One type refers to programs in which households receive stipends for direct and indirect schooling costs of girls, which cease when the girl drops out or misses too many classes. A prime example is the Bangladesh secondary education stipend program for girls. This program and similar ones in Pakistan and Cambodia have been found to increase enrollment rates significantly (see Kim, Alderman and Orazem 1999, on Pakistan; Khandker, Pitt and Fuwa 2003 on Bangladesh; Filmer and Schady 2006 on Cambodia). A second type is a transfer of resources to households (typically to mothers) with the condition that children within a certain age range attend school. The Latin American CCT programs, pioneered by Mexico's PROGRESA (now called Oportunidades) program, are the classic examples of such programs. They are particularly useful as points of reference as they have been rigorously evaluated using randomized methods. Following these programs, we propose a CCT program that transfers resources to mothers conditional on girls of schooling age actually attending school as the most feasible and cost-effective way to increase female education.

Benefits and costs

Benefits

The benefits of female schooling have been discussed above. Here we want to discuss the benefits of the CCT program as a specific tool to increase female education. We base our discussion on several rigorous evaluations of Mexico's PROGRESA program. Schultz (2004) finds that the program raised schooling enrollments of girls in such a way that their expected years of schooling was 0.7 years higher in program areas than in non-program areas. Examining the medium-term impacts of the program, Behrman, Parker, and Todd (2008) find that it has increased female education by about 1 year in the medium-term. Todd and Wolpin (2006) find that one could generate larger effects if the CCT was focused on the transition from primary to secondary schooling, or just focused on secondary education.

Targeting girls through programs such as CCTs not only has the obvious advantage of preventing leakage but also appears to generate a larger enrollment response (than the effects of targeting boys) in most of the studies that have evaluated such programs. In the case of PROGRESA, from an average secondary enrollment rate of 65 percent for boys, the rate increased by 8 percentage points in 1998 and by 5 percentage points a year later. Girls' baseline enrollment was lower at 53 percent, and the program raised this by 11–12 percentage points in both years, about double the impact on boys (Coady and Parker 2004). This type of intervention also has the added benefit over a policy of lifting user fees of ensuring that beneficiary children attend school regularly.

More specifically our empirical assessment of this policy option will be based on a CCT program paid to mothers and linked to girls' education in a typical Sub-Saharan African or South Asian country (average per capita income of \$450 in exchange rates).[13] In this option, this sum is paid out to mothers over 7 years to a cohort of girls, following them from the 3rd to the 9th grade of basic education.[14] Taking the entire eligible population of the three regions

[13] The precise scale of the program is hard to assess and given the imprecision of the calculations we present here it is hard to determine an "optimal" scale. In the calculations, we thus imagine a program that would attempt payout transfers to all households with girls in Sub-Saharan Africa and South Asia, conditional on them attending school But one should keep in mind that a program that would try to reach all girls via such a conditional cash transfer program would be much more costly (on a per girl term) as the costs to get hard-to-reach girls into school (who are out of school due to extreme remoteness or extreme cultural and economic barriers to schooling) would be higher and might not be achievable with the conditional cash transfer. Conversely, if the program is targeted towards the majority of the poor, the cost effectiveness is likely to be higher. See Glewwe and Zhao (2005) on costs of universal primary education (UPE).

[14] By bringing additional cash in the hands of women, the program would strengthen women's influence in household decision-making. Studies by Thomas (1990, 1997) and others (e.g., Haddad and Hoddinott 1994) have found that the greater the influence of women in the household, the greater the household's expenditures related to the nutrition and health of children.

and using UN population data and projections would amount to about 70 million (118 million) potential beneficiaries in Sub-Saharan Africa (South Asia) in 2005, rising (falling) to about 115 million (112 million) by 2050.

In our assessment of this approach to raising girls' schooling options, we assume that the intervention would increase girls' schooling by 0.7–1 years, which are benefit estimates derived from PROGRESA. As significant as this benefit is, it underestimates what we expect to be the full benefits of the option for two reasons. First, PROGRESA was applied in a situation where school enrollments were already relatively high, and certainly much higher than in our target countries. Second, CCT programs have benefits beyond improving educational outcomes and have been found to also improve health and nutrition outcomes and women's status in households, as well as to reduce child labor, as mentioned earlier. These additional benefits are ignored in our baseline empirical assessment, thus providing a stricter test for the program. In a sensitivity analysis we will consider these additional benefits.

For estimates of the benefits of female education, we use the results from Knowles et al. (2002) who found the elasticity of per-capita income with respect to years of female schooling to be 0.37, i.e. a 1 percent increase of female schooling would increase per-capita income by 0.37 percent. This estimate is relatively low, considering the findings of a range of related studies (e.g., Klasen 2002; Klasen and Lamanna 2007; Forbes 2000; Abu-Ghaida and Klasen 2004). This estimate is also lower than one we would obtain from using a typical rate of return calculation as done by Schultz (2004), who uses a 12 percent rate of return. We choose to use the estimates of the macro returns to education as there has been some question about the micro returns overestimating the social returns to education (see Pritchett 2001). We apply the macro elasticity with the assumption that per-capita income is $450 over the working life of a woman, on average. We also take account of the beneficial intergenerational transmission of education by adding one-half of that benefit

for the remainder of the 100 years. This assumption is within the range of typical findings in the literature (see, for example, Gaviria 2007, and Bourguignon et al. 2007).

In addition, we consider one of the many external benefits of female education discussed above. Specifically, we assume that increasing average female education by one year would reduce under-five mortality by 13/1000. This is based on Schultz (1997) and is again lower than other estimates (see Abu-Ghaida and Klasen 2004 for a discussion). We will not separately estimate nutrition benefits or the benefits that would accrue through fertility decline associated with female education. These effects might be partly accounted for in our reduced form estimates. In a sensitivity analysis we additionally consider the benefits of the cash transfer given to the mother on mortality of her children. We assume that about half of the cash transfer will be a pure windfall and use the estimates from Thomas (1990) on the impact of unearned incomes of mothers on the survival rate of their children in Brazil.

Costs

As for cost estimates, we will use the average amount of the PROGRESA transfer, which is about 6 percent of per-capita income per child in Mexico per year. Applying this percentage to an average poor South Asian or Sub-Saharan African country, we obtain an average per-child transfer of $27 per year. To this we add 20 percent to cover administrative costs (although they were only 9 percent of program costs for PROGRESA, and 18 percent in the case of the Bangladesh stipend program), bringing the per-pupil yearly cost to $32.

If aid agencies were to spend $1 billion for this policy option, they could fund the schooling of 4.4 million additional girls for seven years. Alternatively, if the goal is to cover the entire eligible population of girls in South Asian and Sub-Saharan African countries, the annual cost of the program would be $6 billion in 2005, rising to $7.3 billion in 2050 (in real terms). In a sensitivity analysis we also consider the additional costs of supplying the education at another 20 percent of the costs of the transfer.

Table 10.5. Option 1 – assumptions used for estimating benefit–cost ratios

Basic assumptions	
Initial income at exchange rates (World Development Indicators)	$450
Initial female schooling (Abu-Ghaida and Klasen, 2004)	3 years
Total fertility rate (World Development Indicators)	3
Cost assumptions	
Costs of grants in relation to per-capita income (derived from Schultz 2004)	6%
Additional administrative costs share (derived from IFPRI 2004)	20%
Additional costs to ensure supply for increased demand	20%
Annual costs per student (CCT plus administrative cost)	$32
Duration of grant receipt	7 years
Number of students supported per $ billion spent	4.4 million
Benefit assumptions	
Increase in schooling attainment (Behrman, Parker, Todd 2008)	1 year
Increase in schooling attainment (Schultz 2004)	0.7 year
Increase of schooling attainment of next generation	50% of initial effect
Increase in income (elasticity with respect to schooling years, Knowles, Lorgelly, and Owen 2002)	0.37
Reduction in child mortality per year of schooling (Schultz 1997), phased in over 10 years after girls complete schooling	13/1000
Reduction in child mortality per $ of cash transfer for 50% of population and duration of program (Thomas 1990)	0.007/1000
Increase in DALYs for every death under 5 averted (based on average life expectancy in region)	47

Table 10.5 summarizes our full set of assumptions on costs and benefits.[15]

Benefit–cost ratios

Table 10.6 shows the results for various scenarios of this policy option. We apply high and low values of a DALY to the mortality benefit (after translating the reduction in child mortality into DALYs), for high and low discount rates, and for impacts of an additional 0.7 year and one year. We see benefit cost-ratios that range from 3.1 to 23.2. Predictably, the effects are larger when the education effect is presumed larger. More interesting is that the highest effect always happens to be highest when a high DALY and a low discount rate are applied. This is due to the very large and relatively constant mortality effect. As the results in the bottom of Table 10.6 show, allowing for an additional 20 percent increase in costs for increasing the supply while assuming that the

cash transfer will have an immediate windfall effect in reducing mortality slightly lowers the benefit–cost ratios as the cost increase is larger than the benefit increase. But in all cases, the benefit–cost ratios remain very large.

Design and implementation issues

It is hard to imagine that such a program would immediately be implemented at a national scale in all countries. It would instead be prudent to roll out the program slowly, while constantly monitoring the effects on schooling quantity and quality, as well as other side-effects. For this reason, it might be best if initially the program would focus

[15] Coady and Parker (2004) estimate much larger costs in Mexico of both supply- and demand-side interventions at the secondary level. They estimate that achieving an extra completed year of secondary schooling for boys would cost 12,000 pesos for boys and 7,000 pesos for girls.

Table 10.6. Option 1 – estimates of benefits and benefit–cost ratios for conditional cash transfer (cct) program to promote female education per $ billion spent

	Low discount rate		High discount rate	
	DALY (low value)	DALY (high value)	DALY (low value)	DALY (high value)
Assuming CCT program will achieve 1 more year of female schooling ('000 $)				
Income benefit	5786163	5786163	2936553	2936553
Mortality benefit	3483236	17416182	1609963	8049814
Total benefit	9269399	23202345	4546516	10986367
Benefit–cost ratio	9.27	23.20	4.55	10.99
Assuming CCT program will achieve 0.7 more years of schooling ('000$)				
Income benefit	4050314	4050314	2055587	2055587
Mortality benefit	2438265	12191327	1126974	5634869
Total benefit	6488579	16241641	3182561	7690457
Benefit–cost ratio	6.49	16.24	3.18	7.69
Assuming 1 more year of schooling, additional supply costs and direct mortality benefit of cash transfer				
Income benefit	4959568	4959568	2517045	2517045
Mortality benefit	2992070	14960348	1385905	6929525
Total benefit	7951638	19919916	3902950	10446571
Benefit–cost ratio	7.95	19.92	3.90	10.45

on population groups for which girls' enrollment rates are particularly low (basically the rural poor). This would mean focusing on the "average" rural poor for whom female enrollments in primary and secondary education are still low. As the program is expanded, it could include harder-to-reach groups (where both costs as well as benefits may well be larger), such as girls living in remote areas or in extremely poor families.

Clearly, the administrative challenge of effectively monitoring the conditions attached to the cash transfer can be significant, particularly in poorer countries. There is a wealth of experience from the Latin American programs on the costs and challenges of monitoring which would need to be incorporated. Interestingly, there is evidence from Ecuador where a cash transfer program had the desired effect even though the conditionality was only announced but never enforced (Araujo and Schady 2008).

One way to increase the cost-effectiveness of the program would be to never make these programs national, but always keep them focused on those groups that initially had low enrollment rates. One way to do that would be to limit the program to rural areas. While this might increase the cost-effectiveness, such a limit might generate distortions and political resistance so that this has to be carefully assessed in a particular country circumstance. There are several ways in which one might be able to further enhance the cost-effectiveness of the program. First, one might extend the program just to groups and phases in education where enrollment rates are still low. This might mean that the program will begin with primary school girls in rural West Africa and only focuses on the last 3 years of secondary school in urban South Asia. Second, another way to enhance the effectiveness would be to focus the grants on difficult transitions such as the transition from primary to secondary schooling or to pay it out as a prize for secondary completion (Todd and Wolpin 2006). Third, one might want to allow the program to vary depending on economic circumstances. For example, the program could be expanded in times of economic crises to prevent girls from then being taken out of school. Conversely, it could be curtailed during "normal" times. Evidence from de Janvry *et al.* (2006) suggests that this might be an important function of such programs and they could be re-designed to strengthen this insurance function. Lastly, one might want to link the amount of the conditional cash transfer to performance at school. Evidence from a randomized evaluation in Kenya suggests that merit scholarships can lead to significantly improved test scores (Kremer, Miguel, and Thornton 2004).

A last issue to investigate is whether and to what extent it would be necessary to pay funds to the schools to have an incentive to monitor attendance and to respond with expansion of the educational programs as a result of increased enrollments. The importance of such an accompanying intervention would probably depend on country circumstances and is hard to predict. The level of expenditures required will depend greatly on the institutional set-up chosen. Duflo, Dupas, and Kremer (2007) show evidence that the hiring of substitute teachers on contracts in Kenya is not only much cheaper but also more effective in terms of educational outcomes than simply expanding the existing teacher pool at current conditions. This points to the need to examine carefully the institutional set-up for such interventions, as the cost–benefit ratios may greatly depend on improving them in the process of implementing these interventions.

Option 2 – Provide Support for Women's Reproductive Role

Women's reproductive role is broad, encompassing childbirth and a multitude of activities associated with infant and child care, and spanning 15–25 years of a woman's life. As we discussed above, motherhood is associated with serious risks to women's health, especially among the poorest populations. We choose to define this option as focusing on programs that reduce risks associated with fertility – preventing pregnancy, complications, and deaths due to these complications in pregnancy or childbirth (Graham *et al.* 2006). Its three components are family planning programs for young women, support for safe births, and emergency contraception and related services.[16]

In this option, we make no assumptions about women's desired fertility levels, only that women should be able to access the reproductive services they need in order to have safer pregnancies and safer births. However, economic development is itself a potent factor in fertility decisions because it increases the value of women's labor supply and raises demand for human capital investments in children (Schultz 1994). In Indonesia, Gertler and Molyneaux (1994) conclude that increased contraceptive use accounted for three-fourths of the fertility decline in Indonesia during the period 1982–1987, but that this was mainly due to the fast rate of economic growth at that time which opened up new jobs for young women in the labor market, not the increase in the supply of family planning services.[17]

Estimates suggest that more than 130 million women or 17 percent of all married women in developing countries would prefer to avoid a pregnancy but are not using any form of family planning; 64 million women are using less effective methods. Demographers refer to these women as having an "unmet need" for family planning, a concept that has influenced the development of family planning programs for more than 20 years (Casterline and Sinding 2000).[18] Demographic and Health Survey data

[16] A growing number of countries have introduced emergency contraception since the ICPD; some have made it easier for women to access it, for example, by ending restrictions on over-the-counter sales. India, Iran, and Nepal provide it through the national family planning program. In the Dominican Republic, emergency contraception can be obtained through private pharmacies, while in Malaysia and Pakistan, NGOs are supplying it (UNFPA 2004). Programs addressing sexual violence often offer emergency contraceptive pills along with counseling to women who have been raped. In Chile, doctors and emergency rooms can distribute the pills to women who have been raped (UNFPA 2004).

[17] This is similar to Pritchett's (1994) conclusion that contraceptive use is an obvious proximate determinant of fertility and hence an important correlate of fertility, but contraceptive prevalence has no effect on excess fertility (or the fraction of births that are unwanted) and little independent effect on fertility, after controlling for fertility desires.

[18] Unmet need refers to women and couples who do not want another birth within the next two years, or ever, but are not using a method of contraception. Unmet need results from growing demand, service delivery constraints, lack of support from communities and spouses, misinformation, financial costs and transportation restrictions (UNFPA 2004).

in 53 countries reveal that in 16 of 25 countries outside of Sub-Saharan Africa, "unmet need" among married women is 15 percent or lower (Ashford 2003). In Sub-Saharan African countries, 16–38 percent of women say their need for family planning is not met, and current contraceptive use is lower than elsewhere. Thus, the total demand for family planning – defined as the sum of "unmet need" and current contraceptive use – averages 44 percent in Sub-Saharan Africa, compared with an average of 70 percent in Asia, the Middle East and North Africa, and Latin America and the Caribbean.

What are the barriers to contraceptive use among women who might want the services? In addition to the lack of accessible services, and shortages of equipment, commodities and personnel, other barriers are (Casterline and Sinding 2000, UNFPA 2004):

- Lack of method choices appropriate to the situation of the woman and her family. This can include shortages of support for and supply of temporary methods for birth spacing, and the need to address cultural sensitivities (e.g., bleeding or spotting side effects where blood taboos are prevalent).
- Lack of knowledge about the safety, effectiveness and availability of choices; many women do not know the full range of available contraceptive methods that allow them to choose the method that best matches their circumstances and intention;
- Lack of community or spousal support;
- Side-effects for some, and insufficient follow-up to promote method switching and lack of knowledge on how to manage these side-effects; and

[19] Villar et al. (2003), found limited evidence supporting large-scale interventions providing multivitamins, minerals, or protein-energy supplements, but found that iron and folic acid are effective against anemia.

[20] These are similar to the recommendations made in Maternal Mortality 2005 to achieve the fifth MDG of reducing maternal mortality by 75 percent between 1990 and 2015 (WHO, 2007).

[21] Graham et al. (2006) identified necessary resources and costs using the WHO mother-baby package costing tool (WHO 1999). Other studies of cost-effectiveness of maternal health care programs also rely on this package.

- Financial constraints.

During pregnancy, maternal problems arise from malnutrition. Appropriate interventions could include the provision of multivitamins, minerals, or macronutrient supplements, such as protein-energy supplements as well as iron and folic acid to combat anemia. While evidence of the impacts of such policies has been limited,[19] Graham et al. (2006) find that interventions in addressing maternal health are more cost-effective if nutritional supplementation is included. This is particularly true for South Asia, where low birthweight contributes significantly to the burden of disease.

The greatest risk to mother and child, however, occurs during childbirth, and various support services are needed then. Experts recommend the best way to combat such risk is to prevent unplanned pregnancies and unsafe abortions and to ensure that delivery services are provided by professionals skilled in obstetrics, both in health facilities and in homes.[20] Health centers for primary care are needed to provide prenatal care (including managing abortion complications), postpartum care, and care of newborns (Graham et al. 2006). Routine prenatal care includes screening and treatment of syphilis, immunization with tetanus toxoid, prevention and treatment of anemia, and prophylaxis or bed nets for preventing and treating malaria. Basic emergency obstetric care (BEmOC) should also be available but is highly dependent on the availability of supplies, drugs, infrastructure, and skilled health care providers. In case of need, a rapid referral communication chain is needed between district-level hospitals and the primary-care level. District hospitals must be able to provide surgical interventions and blood bank services. Lastly, routine physical examinations of postpartum women are critical.

For the maternal health programs of this policy option, we consider a number of specific program options following the analysis by Graham et al. (2006).[21] These are:

- Routine maternity care: 50 percent of pregnant women would attend prenatal care,[22] 50 percent receive professional intrapartum care, 20 percent of the complicated cases being referred to the secondary level of care,[23] of whom 50 percent receive needed CEmOC (comprehensive emergency obstetric care).[24]

- Increased primary level coverage: coverage increases to 70 percent of women receiving prenatal care and 70 percent receiving care during delivery, plus 50 percent of the complicated cases are referred to the secondary level of care, of whom 90 percent receive needed CEmOC, including interventions for high-risk babies.
- Improved overall quality of care[25] and coverage consists of the same increased coverage as above, but provides enhanced prenatal and delivery care (BEmOC), as well as nutritional supplementation.

Additional benefits accrue from increasing primary coverage from 50–70 percent under the assumption that women who access professional delivery care also receive prenatal care (Graham *et al.* 2006). Prenatal care is thus a crucial entry point into the maternal health care system, and a 20 percent increase in prenatal care coverage would result in many more women also accessing the other components of the maternal health care program, including obstetric first aid and CEmOC. One limitation of the study is that the authors do not take into consideration the degree to which socioeconomic differentials influence women's willingness and ability to access secondary levels of care in case of complications. In a study of a facility-based maternity care strategy in Matlab, Bangladesh, Anwar *et al.* (2004) found that women from poorer households used the delivery facilities significantly less than those who were better off. The wealthiest 20 percent of the population were three times more likely to access these services than the poorest 20 percent. In addition, although overall facility utilization increased during the study period, this inequality in use persisted.

Benefits and costs

Benefits

There are significant health benefits for women and their infants and the rest of their families from fewer unwanted pregnancies, fewer abortions, longer birth intervals, lower exposure to sexually transmitted infections and mother-to-child transmission of these diseases, and protection against ovarian cancer using certain contraceptives (see Figure 10.2). Women who give birth in their 20s rather than in their teens and who space their births farther apart are less likely to have complications during pregnancy or delivery. They are better able to care for their infants, assume their home responsibilities or return to work more quickly. Moreover, costs associated with a health crisis are averted.

It has been estimated that meeting the needs of women for family planning programs would avert some 52 million pregnancies each year (half of which would be delayed to a later time, in accordance with stated desires) for an estimated annual cost of $3.9 billion (UNFPA 2004). Preventing or delaying these unintended

---

[22] Components of prenatal care include: clinical examination for severe anemia, height, weight, and blood pressure; obstetric examination for gestational age estimation and uterine height, fetal heart, detection of malpresentation and position, and referral; gynecological examination; urine test; laboratory tests for hemoglobin, blood type and rhesus status, syphilis and other symptomatic testing for STDs; advice on emergencies, delivery, lactation, and contraception; education on clean delivery, warning signs, and premature rupture of membranes; iron and folic acid supplements; multivitamins; tetanus toxoid immunization; HIV voluntary testing and counseling; screening and treatment for syphilis; and balanced protein-energy supplements (Graham *et al.* 2006, Table 26.5).

[23] This includes: clean delivery technique, clean cord cutting, clean delivery of baby and placenta; active management of the third stage of labor; episiotomy if appropriate; recognition and management of delivery complications and referral; intraveneous fluid and uterotonics if bleeding occurs; partograph; essential newborn care; and intraveneous antibiotics (Graham *et al.* 2006, Table 26.5).

[24] The CEmOC package at the secondary level addresses the following issues: postpartum hemorrhage; antepartum hemorrhage; sepsis; pregnancy-induced hypertension; obstructed labor; abortion; ectopic pregnancy; and high-risk infants (Graham *et al.* 2006, Table 26.5).

[25] This includes the above components, in addition to: magnesium sulfate; forceps or vacuum extraction; manual removal of placenta; removal of retained products of conception; corticosteroids for preterm labor; antiretrovirals for prevention of mother-to-child transmission of HIV; and antibiotics for premature rupture of membranes (Graham *et al.* 2006, Table 26.5).

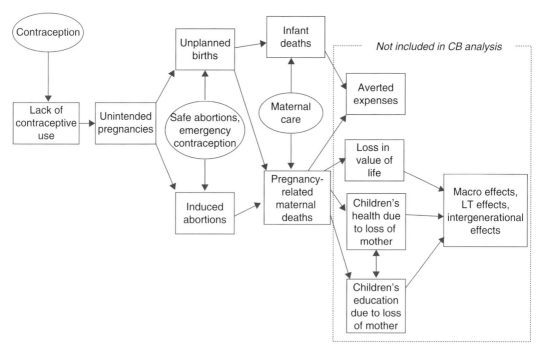

Figure 10.2 *Option 2 – flowchart of benefits from improved women's reproductive choices*

pregnancies would also prevent 23 million unplanned births (a 72 per cent reduction); 22 million induced abortions (a 64 per cent reduction); 1.4 million infant deaths; 142,000 pregnancy related-deaths (including 53,000 from unsafe abortions);[26] 505,000 children losing their mothers due to pregnancy related deaths.

These estimates are obtained using specific assumptions about the availability of technical processes, and are likely to overstate some of

the benefits that poor countries are likely to see. However, even if we were to consider only one of these benefits, the impact on mortality would still be large.

Besides these health-related benefits, there are other benefits for increasing women's agency over their reproductive roles. Early, unplanned childbearing is generally negatively associated with girls' educational attainment. Whether or not this is a causal relationship is the subject of debate among researchers, but it is reasonable to assume that limited access to family planning services limits the ability of young women to exercise their reproductive choices, typically with direct consequences for their educational attainment, labor force participation, and earnings.[27] Just as changes in the opportunity cost of women's time influences desired fertility, fertility influences women's ability to work or find work: a woman's capacity to perform physical labor is diminished during the period surrounding childbirth and child care; these intermittent or prolonged absences from the labor force reduce her cumulative work experience and thus also her earning power.

[26] According to a joint study by the World Health Organization, UNICEF, UNFPA and the World Bank (WHO 2007), of an estimated total of 536,000 maternal deaths worldwide, developing countries accounted for 99 percent (533,000) of the deaths. Slightly more than half of the maternal deaths (270,000) occurred in the Sub-Saharan Africa region alone, followed by South Asia (188,000). In all, Sub-Saharan Africa and South Asia accounted for 86 percent of global maternal deaths.

[27] It is also the case that early pregnancies matter most in countries where the average schooling levels extend into later adolescence (Eloundou-Enyegue and Stokes 2004). In contrast, in countries where the average duration of schooling is short or where reproductive norms prescribe early marriage and childbearing for girls, the absence of family planning programs would not be a binding constraint to fertility behavior.

Table 10.7. Option 2 – assumptions used for estimating benefit–cost ratios

	South Asia	Sub-Saharan Africa
Benefits		
DALYs lost due to unwanted fertility and unsafe abortions in year 0 (Levine *et al.* 2006, Table 57.2)	1,669,727	1,821,721
Number of women with an unmet need for contraception (Levine *et al.* 2006)	89,375,000	66,445,000
Number of years to eliminate unwanted fertility and unsafe abortions*	14	43
Number of DALYs gained per million population** from maternal health programs (Graham *et al.* 2006):		
Routine maternity care	3,273	6,969
Increased primary-level coverage	4,582	9,757
Improved overall quality of care and coverage with nutritional supplements	9,354	20,664
Costs		
Average cost of family planning program per DALY gained (2001 US$) (Levine *et al.* 2006)	30	34
Cost of maternal health programs per DALY saved per million population (million US$) (Graham *et al.* 2006):		
Routine maternity care	25	86
Increased primary-level coverage	148	92
Improved overall quality of care and coverage with nutritional supplements	144	86

* This is based on a total percent decline in the fertility rate in developing countries over the past 50 years of 53% (from 6 to 2.8 children per woman), implying an annual decline in the fertility rate of roughly 1.07%. Taking the fertility rates in South Asia and sub-Saharan Africa of 3.3 and 5.2 respectively, if these rates were to decline annually by 1.07%, it would take around 14 years to do so in South Asia and 43 years in sub-Saharan Africa.
** Total population in 2001 (millions) for South Asia and sub-Saharan Africa respectively are 1,375 and 685 (WDI Indicators).

There are consequences for children's future education and welfare as well. Healthier mothers are less likely to have infants of low birth weight, one factor that is significantly associated with child survival and illness as well as with later adult outcomes. For example, Behrman and Rosenzweig (2004) conclude that in the United States birth weight is positively related to a person's schooling attainment and adult height.

To derive our estimates of the benefits from this policy option, we use Levine *et al.*'s (2006) estimates of DALYs gained from family planning programs in developing regions, and those by Graham *et al.* (2006) from maternal health programs.[28] Their estimates reflect only the direct health benefits of these programs for women and children. While this policy option also has non-health-related effects, we limit our benefit estimates to health gains and therefore understate the benefit–cost ratios for the option.

Lastly, we focus the analysis on countries in South Asia and Sub-Saharan Africa in recognition of the large gender-related challenges in the two regions (Table 10.7).

Costs

To cost this policy option, we have to assign costs for its two components – family planning programs and maternal health programs. Types of family planning programs themselves are associated with different costs (Levine *et al.* 2006). For example, IUDs and voluntary sterilization have the lowest cost per CYP (couple-year of protection), but the highest fixed costs. Oral contracep-

[28] Unfortunately, because of the high degree of uncertainty and dearth of reliable data on specific costs and benefits of the various components included within this option, we must rely on the point estimates derived by Graham *et al.* (2006), which makes it impossible to evaluate the relative cost-effectiveness of the different components because of overlapping confidence intervals.

tives are generally the least costly, and implants are the most costly. In general, costs per CYP are considerably higher in Africa than in other countries ($14 compared to $4 to $5), but the marginal benefits are also deemed to be higher because of the significant unmet need in the region. And while marginal costs decline as the number of contraceptive users increases, so may the marginal returns to increasingly mature programs.

One limitation of estimating the cost-effectiveness of family planning programs using results from previous studies is that most studies estimate average costs rather than marginal costs. Experimental studies in Matlab, Bangladesh have estimated costs per averted birth ranging from $95 (Attanayake *et al.* 1993) to $296 (Simmons *et al.* 1991). In comparison, Levine *et al.* (2006) estimate the cost per averted birth in South Asia to be $113.

The costs per DALY saved due to family planning programs in South Asia and Sub-Saharan Africa as estimated by Levine *et al.* (2006) are on the low end of previous estimates for low-income countries. The 1993 World Development Report (World Bank 1993) estimated costs were between $40 and $60 per DALY for low-income countries. Jamison (1993) estimated costs to run between $20 and $100 per DALY, depending on child and maternal mortality rates. Since costs are lowest in high mortality countries, the Levine *et al.* (2006) estimates for South Asia and Sub-Saharan Africa are comparable to these previous estimates.

Graham *et al.* (2006) also make a number of assumptions to derive their cost-effectiveness estimates. These included but were not limited to: excess capacity, so that increase in prenatal care coverage does not require an increase in the number of or capacity of existing health care facilities; increase in expenditure on educa-

tion, information, and communication when increasing prenatal care coverage; and improved quality in prenatal care and CEmOC require increased expenditure on training (10 percent of personnel cost).

In our estimates, we assume that the number of years needed to eliminate unwanted fertility and unsafe abortions would be 14 years in South Asia and 43 years in Sub-Saharan Africa. This is based on applying the total percent decline of 53 percent (from 6 to 2.8 children per woman)[29] in the fertility rate in developing countries over the past 50 years – which translates to an annual decline in the fertility rate of 1.07 percent – from the fertility rates in South Asia and Sub-Saharan Africa, 3.3 and 5.2 respectively. Over the course of 14 years in South Asia and 43 years in Sub-Saharan Africa, we assume that family planning programs would be implemented along with maternal health programs, and that the benefits would take place in the same year as the intervention. Thus all estimates were discounted and summed up over the course of these years.

Benefit–cost ratios

Table 10.8 shows a wide range in the benefit–cost ratio for alternative forms of this option. Combining the benefits and costs of the family planning program with maternal health programs, the benefit–cost ratio varies from 10.20 for the program that offers increased primary coverage, to 11.75 for the routine maternity care program (both using the lower value of DALYs and the lower discount rate of 3 percent).

The effectiveness of many of the programs considered depends crucially upon the degree to which several design and implementation issues can be addressed, including availability of skilled personnel, effectiveness of referral systems, surveillance, and better access to the poorest women (Graham *et al.* 2006). The cost-benefit analysis relies heavily on the results of the cost-effectiveness analysis done by experts of the Disease Control Priorities Project (2006). The cost-effectiveness of the provision of maternal care services and family planning programs were estimated separately. However, integrating the two types of services is likely to be more

---

[29] We assume that an appropriate goal of a fertility rate of 2.8 births per woman is more reasonable in this case than the much lower average fertility rate for developed countries. Since family planning programs such as those proposed here have proven successful in other developing countries, but only insofar as reaching the 2.8 TFR, a lower rate would perhaps be too unrealistic as a goal for South Asia and Sub-Saharan Africa.

Table 10.8. Option 3 – estimates of benefits and costs for support for women's reproductive role (US$ million)

	Low discount rate		High discount rate	
	DALY (Low value)	DALY (High value)	DALY (Low value)	DALY (High value)
Total benefits to family planning	38,982	194,911	30,802	154,010
Benefits to maternal care				
Routine maternity care	174,595	872,973	124,173	620,866
Increased primary-level coverage	244,436	1,222,180	173,844	869,220
Improved overall quality of care* and coverage	511,764	2,558,819	363,223	1,816,114
Total benefits				
Routine maternity care	213,577	1,067,884	154,975	774,875
Increased primary-level coverage	283,418	1,417,091	204,646	1,023,230
Improved overall quality of care* and coverage	550,746	2,753,730	394,025	1,970,124
Cost of implementing family planning program	956	956	717	717
Costs of maternal care				
Routine maternity care	17,227	17,227	12,521	12,521
Increased primary-level coverage	26,826	26,826	19,626	19,626
Improved overall quality of care* and coverage	49,592	49,592	35,909	35,909
Total costs				
Routine maternity care	18,183	18,183	13,237	13,237
Increased primary-level coverage	27,782	27,782	20,343	20,343
Improved overall quality of care* and coverage	50,547	50,547	36,626	36,626
Benefit–cost ratio				
Routine maternity care	11.75	58.73	11.71	58.54
Increased primary-level coverage	10.20	51.01	10.06	50.30
Improved overall quality of care* and coverage	10.90	54.48	10.76	53.79

* Improved overall quality of care includes nutritional supplementation.

efficient than offering separate programs, since costs would be distributed jointly across services (Levine *et al.* 2006). For example, less profitable contraceptive services can be cross-subsidized by clinics that also provide services such as Papanicolaou smears, ultrasounds, pregnancy tests, abortions, and post-abortion care.

In order to reduce maternal risk factors, the aforementioned health system improvements will not be sufficient. Social, cultural, and economic factors also play an important role, as do reproductive rights (Graham *et al.*

2006). Ten countries have adopted family laws and legislation to make men more responsible for reproductive health. For example, the Lao People's Democratic Republic has adopted a national birth-spacing policy, reversing a pro-natalist policy adopted in the 1990s. Under the new policy, contraception is provided for free and without coercion. Belize's National Health Policy outlines reproductive rights, including voluntary counseling and testing for HIV infection; ensures tax exemption for NGOs that provide health services; and sets protocols for family planning services. As mentioned earlier, in Papua New Guinea the requirement for a "husband's consent" for contraceptive use has been removed. These legislative reforms remove some of the social barriers that stand in the way of women making choices that are good for them and their families.

Option 3 – Reduce Women's Financial Vulnerability Through Microfinance

The aim of this option is to improve women's ability to earn income as needed or desired and thus reduce their financial vulnerability. As mentioned earlier in the paper, removing legislative and regulatory barriers to women's employment or legislating measures that would allow more women to work can be a powerful tool – and one that has been used by many countries. In poorer developing countries, however, this tool has a much more limited scope for impact than in developed countries because the size of the formal or regulated sector is much smaller than the rest of the labor market. We thus focus on a policy option for self-employment. A significant number of women are employed in the informal sector, but most lack access to formal credit markets. Formal sector commercial banks focus on lending to larger business, while microfinance institutions (MFIs) cater to the informal sector and to women in particular. In general, three different types of lending services are provided by MFIs (Cull, Demirgûç-Kunt, and Morduch, 2007):

[30] All values were derived using official exchange rates.
[31] These are also termed joint-liability lending institutions (JLLIs).
[32] While individual-based microlending institutions show higher average loan sizes than MFIs using joint-liability lending, these larger average loan sizes imply lower costs and lower interest rates. Thus, on average, larger loan sizes are as profitable as smaller ones (Cull, Demirgûç-Kunt, and Morduch 2007). However, while individual-based loans average $1,220, village banks provide group loans averaging $148. The latter are most dependent upon subsidies of the three aforementioned categories of institutions. The majority (88 percent) of village banks' clients are women, whereas 46 percent of borrowers of individual-based loans are women.

In individual-based lending, a loan contract involves one lender and one borrower who is liable for the loan (another individual may serve as a guarantor). These loans often require collateral, although borrowers who have a history of successfully repaying their loans often do not need collateral. In such cases, the promise of future loans (and often of greater amounts) provides sufficient incentive to the borrower to repay. MFIs, such as the Grameen Bank in Bangladesh, which have a significant number of members with successful repayment histories, are increasingly turning to this form of lending. Their average loan size is $1,220, and the average subsidized share of funding is 11.0 percent.[30]

Group-based lending[31] allows members to choose a group of peers with whom to join the program, so each borrower is responsible not only for her own loan, but also for the loans of the other group members. If any one group member defaults, all members become ineligible for further loans. Thus, collateral is replaced by group pressure in ensuring repayment. Examples include the Grameen Bank in Bangladesh and BancoSol in Bolivia. Their average loan size is $431, and average subsidized share of funding is 27.7 percent.

In village-based lending, every branch of the MFI forms a single, large group which establishes its own form of governance. Examples include FINCA, Pro Mujer, and Freedom from Hunger. Their average loan size is $149, and average subsidized share of funding is 35.5 percent.[32]

The diversity of MFI programs makes it difficult to determine precisely how many programs exist, and how many borrowers they have. Depending on the definition, estimates of the number of MFIs operating today range from 300 to 25,000. The Microfinance Information eXchange (MIX), known as the "Bloomberg" of microfinance, reports nearly 1,000 MFIs worldwide, nearly half of which are self-sustainable. Estimates of the number of borrowers range from 30 million to 500 million, and millions more save with these MFIs. The Microcredit Summit Campaign reports over 64 million borrowers worldwide in 2006, up from more than 9 million borrowers in 2000 (Daley-Harris 2006). As the number of borrowers has rapidly increased, MFIs have received more attention from the international community, and microfinance is increasingly viewed as an important tool for alleviating poverty. Indeed, the year 2005 was designated the "International Year of Microcredit" by the UN General Assembly (see www.yearofmicrocredit.org), and Muhammad Yunus received the Nobel Peace Prize in 2006 for founding the Grameen Bank, one of the first microfinance institutions.

There are a number of reasons why the Grameen Bank and many other MFIs have focused on women. Firstly, they recognize that women who receive credit may command greater bargaining power in the household. A number of studies on Bangladesh have found this to be the case (Khandker 2005; Pitt and Khandker 1998; Pitt et al. 2003; Porter 2007). And since women tend to be responsible for children's health and education, this increased bargaining position for women within the household translates into a larger share of the household's limited resources being devoted to children's human capital.

Secondly, by supporting women's entrepreneurial activities, women's access to credit resources tends to also increase their labor force participation (Pitt and Khandker 1998). Under standard neoclassical assumptions about the production function, if women have less access to capital than men, then the returns to capital for women should be higher than for men, and this higher return to capital could mean faster economic growth.[33] This holds true if women do not pass their loan funds on to their husbands (commonly referred to as "pipelining"), and provided that the loan funds are not regarded as perfectly fungible within the household.

Thirdly, there is considerable evidence that women have better repayment records than men. Khandker, Khalily, and Khan (1995) find that 15.3 percent of male borrowers in 1991 missed payments before the final due date, while only 1.3 percent of women did. Women may be more reliable in repaying loans because

they are often less mobile, and as a result, may fear social sanctions more than men, may be more risk-averse, and therefore more conservative in their investment strategies. Due to inexperience in this area, women may also be more easily swayed by pressure from peers and loan officers.

Benefit and cost estimates

The cost–benefit estimates discussed below are calculated based on microfinance programs that provide both credit and savings services. While studies have shown the importance of providing savings services to women clients, further study is needed to estimate the benefits that accrue to savers. Since the services were bundled together, it is not possible to determine the benefits or costs of each individually.

Benefits

Although there have been numerous studies of the impact of MFIs, relatively few of them have employed techniques to address selection bias. While targeting the poor may result in underestimated effects, results can also be overestimated since many microfinance clients already have initial advantages over their neighbors (Coleman 2002, Alexander 2001).[34] In order to estimate the returns to microfinance, we use the results of a number of different studies which estimate the impact of MFIs on households and take considerable measures to control for selection bias. In particular, we use a number of estimates from a study on the effects of microcredit in Bangladesh which was conducted by the World Bank and the Bangladesh Institute for Development Studies (BIDS). Household

[33] For example, Udry (1996) finds that productivity differentials in agricultural productivity in Burkina Faso are attributed to the intensity of production between plots cultivated by men and women, rather than to inherent skills differentials. This outcome is inefficient because of diminishing returns to fertilizer. Therefore, by providing women with credit, they would be able to purchase additional inputs.

[34] McKernan (2002) showed that not controlling for selection bias can result in the effect of participation on profits to be overestimated by as much as 100 percent.

Table 10.9. Option 3 – assumptions used for estimating benefit–cost ratios

Annual growth in number of new poor women borrowers (Khandker *et al.* 1995, Table 3.4)	35%
Number of new borrowers in initial year of program (Khandker *et al.* 1995, Table 3.4)	348,000
Average loan per new borrower (Cull, Demirgûç-Kunt and Morduch 2007)	285
Benefits	
First year return to credit for household (increase in consumption) (Khandker 2005)	9.45%
Average annual increase in household expenditure from old loans (Khandker 2005)	0.98%
Number of years borrower accrues increased expenditure from old loans in lifetime	30
Elasticity of intergenerational transmission of income and health	0.50%
Number of generations whose expenditures increase due to old credit (not including self)	2
Number of generations of children whose health is improved (including own children)	4
Increase in DALYs, Lower Bound:	
Increase in DALYs per $ loaned to women (first year of loan) (Duflo 2000)	0.000030
Increase in DALYs per $ loaned to women (2nd & 3rd years after loan) (Duflo 2000)	0.000003
Increase in DALYs, Upper Bound (Pitt *et al.* 2003)	0.000686
Costs	
Cost for Grameen Bank (1991/92) (Khandker 1998)	0.172
Cost for BRAC (1991/92) (Khandker 1998)	0.444
Weighted average of above two costs based on loans disbursed (Khandker 1998)	0.204

[35] It is important to note, however, that Bangladesh is one of the poorest countries where most rural women are subject to Islamic purdah laws and are often precluded from engaging in market activities and prevented from conversing with men who are not relatives. Nonetheless, Bangladesh has had a long history of microfinance directed towards women. One of the first microcredit programs ever established was the Grameen Bank in Bangladesh, and more recently, the microfinance market has become quite saturated, particularly in targeting the poor.

[36] Khandker (2005) estimated significantly lower program effects than those found originally by Pitt and Khandker (1998). Pitt and Khandker (1998) addressed the causality issue using fixed effects and a quasi-natural experimental design to control for heterogeneity and selection bias at the household, individual, and village levels. However, Morduch (1998, 1999) was critical of some key assumptions used in this study. For example, as a source of variation, Pitt and Khandker used the eligibility criterion of borrowers owning no more than half an acre of arable land, which Morduch argued was not strictly followed. Pitt applied robustness checks to show that any possible mistargeting did not change the results much from those found in Pitt and Khandker's 1998 paper (Pitt 1999). Morduch also suggested an alternative method for estimating credit effects using the same survey data. While he estimated significantly lower credit effects, Pitt suggested Morduch was under-estimating the true effects (Pitt 1999).

[37] This is the average of 14.7 percent and 4.2 percent.

panel survey data was collected in 1991/92 and 1998/99. We use the most recently available results in our calculations. The assumptions that underpin our estimates are given in Table 10.9.

Due to lack of similar information on other countries, we must make a significant leap in assuming that the results for Bangladesh hold also for other countries and for the next 100 years.[35] For Bangladesh, Khandker (2005) finds that a 100 taka loan in 1991/92 increased household expenditures by 14.7 taka in 1991/92, and by 16.3 taka in 1998/99, while a 100 taka loan in 1998/1999 increased household expenditure by only 4.2 taka in 1998/9.[36] These findings may indicate diminishing marginal returns to borrowing. Using these results, we estimate that every new dollar loaned per year will raise household expenditures by 9.45 percent[37] in the first year. Women who receive a loan in year 0 will continue to accrue benefits from this loan for the remainder of their life spans (assumed to be approximately 30 years), with an average annual increase in household expenditure of 0.98

Upper bound estimate: 0.000686 increase in DALYs per $ loaned;
Lower bound estimate: 0.00003 increase in DALYs per $ loaned in 1st year, 0.000003 increase in
subsequent 2 years

9.45% 1st year; 0.98%
in subsequent years

```
┌─────────────┐      ┌─────────────────────┐          ┌─────────────────────┐
│   Micro-    │ ───> │ Increased           │ ───────> │ Improved health     │
│   finance   │      │ expenditures,       │          │ of children         │
└─────────────┘      │ particularly on     │          └─────────────────────┘
                     │ children            │                    │
                     │ (via women's        │          0.5% of prior generation's
                     │ increased           │                    │  health
                     │ household           │          ┌─────────────────────┐
                     │ bargaining power)   │ ──────>  │ Improved health of  │
                     └─────────────────────┘          │ future generations  │
                              │                        └─────────────────────┘
0.005% for 1st generation;    │                                 │
0.00002% for 2nd              ▼                                 ▼
                     ┌────────────────────────────────────────────────┐
                     │    Increased income of future generations      │
                     └────────────────────────────────────────────────┘
```

Figure 10.3 *Option 3 – flowchart of benefits from microfinance program*

percent.[38] This will hold for women who borrow in subsequent years as well. Thus, the benefits will accumulate considerably (see Figure 10.3). We assume these benefits will continue to accrue for future generations and will reflect a permanent increase in household wealth as a result of this access to credit.

Borrowing by women has been shown not only to raise household expenditures, but also to improve women's bargaining position within the household. As women invest more in their children, this increased bargaining can be seen in the improved health outcomes of their children. Pitt *et al.* (2003) find that credit to women increased height-for-age of girls and boys in Bangladesh. Duflo (2000) also finds that pension payments received by grandmothers in South Africa significantly improved the height-for-age z-scores of their granddaughters. Since height-for-age is a measure of malnutrition, we use the results from these studies to estimate a lower and an upper bound of the number of DALYs gained by a reduced number of malnourished children resulting from credit provided to women (see Appendix Tables 10.A1 and 10.A2 for details).

There are a number of additional benefits that we did not include in our estimates but which deserve some mention here. One such benefit relates to effects on children's schooling. Pitt and Khandker (1998) find that both male and female credit participation in Bangladesh increase boys'

school enrollment by similar magnitudes, while only female participation in the Grameen Bank seems to affect girls' enrollment. In contrast, a study on SEWA finds no effect on girls' schooling (Chen and Snodgrass 2001). Because of the contradictory evidence regarding the effect of microfinance on children's schooling, we exclude them from our estimates; if there were a positive effect, then our benefit–cost ratios would be underestimates.

Another potential benefit pertains to spillover effects to non-participating households. Since MFIs target the poorest or most vulnerable members of the population, the effects on non-participants may be considerably lower. Although there have been some attempts to estimate these effects, it would be difficult to generalize results to non-participants without an appropriate method for addressing the high selectivity of participation.

As we move up the income ladder and the enterprise size scale, borrowers show divergent characteristics and borrowing needs.[39] Coleman

---

[38] This is calculated as 16.3 minus 9.45, divided by 7 years between the two survey years.

[39] Cull, Demirgüç-Kunt, and Morduch (2007) study a sample of 124 MFIs in 49 countries representing around 50 percent of all microfinance clients around the globe. While these are perhaps the more profitable and cost-efficient institutions, even in this select group, only half of the institutions were profitable and financially self-sustainable. One of the reasons for lack of self-sustainability might be lack of scale; only in eight countries do

(1999, 2002) finds that wealthier borrowers in Northeast Thailand experience greater effects and he notes that this may be because they are less credit-constrained. One reason wealthier borrowers may have experienced larger impacts was because they could commandeer larger loans. Thailand is relatively wealthy, and villagers have access to credit from a range of sources. Village banks' loans may be too small to make a notable average difference in the welfare of households. In fact, Coleman reported that complaints about small loans led some women to leave the banks.

Thus, an important limitation of microfinance lies in scaling up to non-poor customers, and in particular, in the ability of MFIs to accompany their customers as they grow richer. Joint-liability lending relies on groups of borrowers with similar borrowing needs and the profitability of the approach relies on large numbers of borrowers and groups. As clients become wealthier, they will find they are limited by constraints other than credit, such as property rights and labor regulations. These issues will need to be addressed, as microfinance will not completely address poverty and gender inequality on its own.

Supply of loans

Again for want of more studies, we use the results for Bangladesh as parameters to estimate ben-

Footnote 39 (*continued*)
microfinance borrowers account for more than 2 percent of the population (Honohan 2004). While a mature microfinance industry may be more self-sustainable, as MFIs grow and mature, they seem to focus less on the poor (Cull, Demirgûç-Kunt, and Morduch 2007), which could be interpreted either as a success story for their borrowers or as mission drift. Targeting the poorest is more costly, but innovative program designs have combated this (e.g., ASA in Bangladesh; Banco do Nordeste in Brazil channels many of its transactions through post office networks, reducing its costs and borrowers' transaction costs) (Littlefield, Morduch, and Hashemi 2003).

[40] We have also examined data from 757 MFIs which have submitted their information on MIX (as of July 2007). All available data from 1998 through 2006 were used to approximate the costs of lending to women. Approximately, the average cost per dollar loaned is about $0.20. Similar costs were also reported in the Spring 2007 MicroBanking Bulletin published by Microfinance Information Exchange, Inc.

efits. It is important, however, to keep in mind the scale of these programs, as there are different returns at different levels of lending. The average number of members reached by the Grameen Bank was 1.066 million in 1991, of whom 0.986 million were women, and 1.424 million in 1992, of whom 1.334 million were women (Khandker *et al.* 1995). To project the annual increase in borrowers in our estimates, we use the annual rate of increase in Bangladesh, 35 percent.

We assume that $285 will be the average loan of every new borrower, based on the average loan size of village-based lending programs ($149) and of group-based lending ($431) (Cull, Demirgûç-Kunt, and Morduch 2007)). This loan size is comparable to the average amount obtained by the World Bank/BIDS 1991/92 survey and used to estimate the benefits cited above ($254.63).

Costs

While microfinance programs increase their members' access to financial services, they are very costly to operate and typically require extensive subsidies (Robinson 2001; Armendariz de Aghion and Morduch 2005). The full costs of these programs are partially recovered by the organizations themselves through interest income from loan disbursement and deposits with other banks and income from investments. Therefore, the social cost of a subsidized microcredit program can be measured by its negative economic profit, or the net subsidy allocated to the program. This is also equal to the accounting profit net of the market cost of subsidized resources, including grants provided for training, research and monitoring (Khandker 1998, Khandker *et al.* 1995). Khandker (1998) estimates that the economic cost per dollar of a disbursed loan is $0.172 for the Grameen Bank and $0.444 for BRAC. While BRAC's costs are over 2.5 times greater than those of Grameen, the Grameen Bank disbursed nearly six times more in loans than BRAC. These differing costs may reflect different economies of scale, but also may be partly explained by BRAC's emphasis on providing training to its borrowers.[40]

Bringing together our benefit and cost

Table 10.10. Option 3 –estimates of benefits and costs for microfinance (US$ million)

	Low discount rate		High discount rate	
	DALY			
	(Low value)	(High value)	(Low value)	(High value)
Assuming the lower bound increase in DALYs from microcredit				
Income benefit	1,296	1,296	862	862
Mortality benefit	165	825	136	680
Total benefits	1,461	2,121	998	1,543
Total costs				
Constant average costs scenario	922	922	767	767
Constant high costs scenario	2,007	2,007	1,669	1,669
Constant low costs scenario	778	778	647	647
Declining costs scenario	817	817	682	682
Benefit–cost ratio				
Constant average costs scenario	1.59	2.30	1.30	2.01
Constant high costs scenario	0.73	1.06	0.60	0.92
Constant low costs scenario	1.88	2.73	1.54	2.39
Declining costs scenario	1.79	2.59	1.46	2.26
Assuming the upper bound increase in DALYs from microcredit				
Income benefit	1,296	1,296	862	862
Mortality benefit	3,105	15,526	2,579	12,896
Total benefits	4,401	16,822	3,441	13,758
Total costs				
Constant average costs scenario	922	922	767	767
Constant high costs scenario	2,007	2,007	1,669	1,669
Constant low costs scenario	778	778	647	647
Declining costs scenario	817	817	682	682
Benefit–cost ratio				
Constant average costs scenario	4.78	18.25	4.49	17.95
Constant high costs scenario	2.19	8.38	2.06	8.24
Constant low costs scenario	5.66	21.64	5.32	21.28
Declining costs scenario	5.38	20.58	5.05	20.17

estimates, we obtain benefit–cost ratios that vary between 0.6 and 21.64, depending on the assumptions made (Table 10.10). The average benefit–cost ratio is 6.21. When we include the mortality benefits from improved children's health, and calculate estimates based on Duflo (2000), the benefit–cost ratio varies between 0.6 and 2.73, with an average of 1.70. This would be a lower bound. We also estimate an upper bound based on the results estimated by Pitt *et* *al.* (2003), where the benefit–cost ratios range from 2.06 to 21.64, with an average of 10.71.

Design and implementation issues

The impact of microfinance programs depends greatly on how they are designed, as well as the extent to which women have access to other forms of credit. For example, there are a number of different incentive-schemes for encouraging repayment which may affect men and women borrowers differently. Screening group members ex-ante, as well as monitoring ex-post, have been shown to play an important role in the success of joint-liability lending. Communication between group members raises default rates resulting from more risky projects. In contrast, repeat loans reduce both the borrowers' incentives to engage in more risky activities, and raise repayment rates (Gine *et al.* 2006). Progressive lending, that is, increasing loan amounts over time, can also increase repayment by further raising the opportunity costs of default for borrowers (Armendariz de Aghion and Morduch 2005).[41]

In addition to repayment schemes, MFIs also differ in the training and other extension services they provide. While some MFIs such as the Grameen Bank focus primarily on providing financial services, others such as BRAC (also in Bangladesh) provide extensive training to borrowers. The evidence on whether such services are beneficial or cost-effective is scant. However, in a randomized control trial Karlan and Valdivia (2006) find that adding business training (about business knowledge, marketing strategies, use of profits, record-keeping) to a group lending program in Peru for female microentrepreneurs improved repayment and client retention rates. It is important that the clients find the training useful enough to outweigh its time costs.

As the microfinance industry grows, MFIs are increasingly competing with each other. During the industry's early days, MFIs avoided direct competition with each other, often dividing up their clientele instead in order to maximize

outreach with limited resources. With informal moneylenders as their primary competitors, MFIs could rely on repeat and progressive lending to ensure repayment, as borrowers did not have good alternatives. More recently, however, in countries with more mature MFI sectors, such as Bangladesh, Bolivia and Uganda, MFIs are competing directly with each other. McIntosh, de Janvry, and Sadoulet (2005) find that an MFI in Uganda experiencing more competition faces declining repayment rates, although participation is still rising. This suggests that many clients are borrowing from competing MFIs simultaneously. McIntosh and Wydick (2005) find that such competition can be bad for borrowers who become over-indebted and subsequently receive less favorable loan terms. This tendency for clients to be over-indebted may be mitigated through effective information sharing among lenders about clients' default behavior. A credit information sharing system can also make MFIs themselves more cost-effective. For example, Luoto, McIntosh, and Wydick (2007) found that the introduction of a credit information system in Guatemala allowed MFIs to lower their break-even interest rate by more than 2.5 percentage points.

While MFIs have focused primarily on providing credit services to the poor, savings services have also been proven to be equally important in alleviating financial constraints of poor people. Non-formal financial savings instruments generally provide either security or returns, but not both, and poor people may even accept a negative return to ensure security.[42] Because of liquidity constraints, MFI clients in Indonesia use credit as much for consumption as for investment purposes (Johnston and Morduch 2007). SEWA bank members in India also hold significant outstanding debt, in some cases far greater than their annual household income. This may be an additional cost to MFIs, and a reason for other risk-coping mechanisms besides loans, such as savings and insurance (Chen *et al.* 2005).

Ashraf, Karlan, and Yin (2006a, 2006b) use a random experiment in the Philippines to assess the effect of a new product in which savers commit to restrict access to savings accounts

[41] Using household data across members of more than 262 Thai joint-liability groups, Ahlin and Townsend (2007) find that informal sanctioning, or ex-post reductions in moral hazard, reduce repayment in poor rural areas, while ex-ante screening, which reduces the risk of adverse selection, reduces repayment in wealthier regions of the country. Where borrowers have stronger social ties, or increasingly share information with unrelated group members and relatives, they are less likely to repay their loans.

[42] For example, Anderson and Baland (2002) surveyed hundreds of women in Kenya, an overwhelming majority of whom indicated that their primary reason for joining a ROSCA was to save.

until a specific self-set date or until they have reached a pre-committed savings balance. Only 28 percent of clients decided to use this product, but those who did saw an 81 percent increase in their average savings balances over a 12-month period. While this effect was not sustained,[43] the commitment product led to greater investment in durable goods preferred by women, such as washing and sewing machines, and kitchen appliances. The effect on decision-making power was strongest for married women who had below-median household decision-making power prior to the intervention, according to a survey instrument used in the study. For women above the baseline median, the positive effect was greatest for non-market goods such as children's schooling and the number of children.

In another study, Ashraf, Karlan, and Yin (2006c) assess a program which provided door-to-door savings collection. The authors find that among those who used this service (15 percent of clients to whom it was offered), savings increased by 25 percent, while borrowing declined. This suggests that some borrowers do use savings for consumption smoothing rather than investment. Households which accepted the service tended to live farther away from the nearest branch, thus indicating the deterrent effect of travel costs, and were more likely to be married, again showing the importance of the time pressure in these households.

Option 4 – Strengthen Women's Political Voice Through Affirmative Action

Legal, social, and economic rights provide an enabling environment in which women and men can participate productively in society, attain a basic quality of life, and take advantage of the new opportunities that development affords. Institutional reform is important to promote gender equality in many areas, but five areas stand out – family law,[44] protection against violence,[45] land rights,[46] labor laws,[47] and political rights. Social, legal, and economic institutions together underlie observed gender inequalities and are barriers to reducing those disparities.

Institutional reform that promotes gender equality must be the first element of a strategy to engender broad-based, sustainable development. In the short run societal institutions are difficult and slow to change; yet, even dramatic transformation is possible – though often in the face of great resistance and at high cost. Gender-related institutional reform can have a profound impact on the decisions and behaviors of individuals and households. Our fourth option focuses on reforms that would expand women's political voice in society. Most countries' statutory codes give women the right to vote and to

[43] After 30 months the average balance was only 33 percent higher compared to that of non-participants and the difference was not significant any more; many clients did not use the account repeatedly.

[44] *Family law*, whether based on statutory, customary, or religious law, establishes the level of autonomy and control women and men have in family matters, including marriage, divorce, child custody, control of conjugal property, and inheritance of property. Inequalities in family law directly affect women's welfare; they weaken women's bargaining power in the household which can have important second-round effects on family welfare.

[45] In many countries laws that ostensibly protect women from gender-related violence contain biases that discriminate against the victims or that render the laws ineffective. Often these laws define violence in very narrow terms or impose burdensome evidentiary requirements. The first goal of legal reform would be to identify and correct gender biases in existing laws, such that violent behavior becomes more costly to the abuser.

[46] As discussed earlier, equal access to and control of land resources is important for several reasons. Insecure land rights can reduce female farmers' productivity and inhibit women's access to credit, since land is an important form of collateral. Land reforms that provide for joint titling of husband and spouse or that enable women to hold independent land titles can increase women's control of land where statutory law predominates. Where customary and statutory laws operate side by side, their interactions must be taken into account if efforts to strengthen female access to land are to succeed.

[47] Labor laws that restrict the types of work women can do or limit the hours they can work, even when couched as "special protection," restrict women's access to the labor market. Such legal restrictions should be eliminated. At the same time, equal employment and equal pay legislation can help form the basis for equal rights and equal protection in the labor market. But such legislation may have limited impact in the short run – both because large numbers of female workers remain in informal sector jobs and because adequate enforcement may be lacking.

hold political office, but the numbers discussed earlier indicate that gender inequalities in political representation are large.

Legal reform is a necessary step in improving gender equality in rights – and in establishing a supportive institutional environment more broadly. In many cases, the cost entailed by these reforms is often largely of a political or social nature, rather than a fiscal or financial one. In many cases too, appropriate laws already exist; what are lacking is implementation and enforcement which do have cost implications, both political as well as financial. The state clearly has a role to play in giving a strong mandate through reform of laws and regulations. But the effectiveness of statutory reform depends largely on the state's capacity to implement and enforce – and on the leadership and action of other groups in society.

This policy option consists of three components. The first is to legislate political reservation for elected executive and legislative positions in government, especially at subnational or local levels. Gender quotas are a fast-track approach to expanding women's presence in the political arena. In general, political selection in many countries is based on economic advantage and political connections – politicians are more likely to be educated, own land, and have family political connections (Besley, Pande, and Rao 2005). At the national level, even in the most gender-unequal countries, a few women are able to ascend to high political positions, but typically by virtue of their elite socioeconomic class and relationship to male politicians. It is important, however, to begin at subnational levels where novice female politicians can acquire relevant experience and build their constituency at a more realistic scope and pace.

There are other reasons for a focus on women's participation in subnational or local governments, instead of MDG5's focus on the share of women in national parliaments. One is that over the last two decades, decentralization has been a major institutional reform in a large number of countries in Latin America, Asia, and Africa, including the two most populous countries of the world, China and India. These reforms have shifted major decision-making responsibilities about revenue collection and public services to local governments and communities, so more is at stake at the local level. For example, China's decentralization policy stipulates multiple layers of service supervision involving national agencies with oversight functions as well as corresponding agencies in country and village governments. India's decentralization law in 1993 gave the Gram Panchayat (GP) [48] primary responsibility in allocating government funds to development schemes it defines and implements, including welfare programs (such as antenatal care and childcare for pre-school children) and public works (drinking water, roads, housing, electricity, irrigation, education) (Ghatak and Ghatak 2002; Besley, Pande, and Rao 2005). In principle, India's GPs have complete flexibility in allocating these funds and make decisions by majority voting.

In addition, there are more opportunities for leadership by women at the community level. Self-help women's groups have mushroomed throughout the developing world, constituting a good training ground for female leaders and a potent political base for women who decide to enter politics. According to the 2005 Afrobarometer data on the participation of men and women in various types of organization, rural women are at least as likely to be active members or leaders in such organizations, suggesting that in Sub-Saharan African countries rural women are accumulating experience as organizational leaders (Table 10.11).

Lastly, many governments have already taken steps to mandate minority representation in legislatures, including quotas for women in parliaments or in local governments or quotas for parties' candidate lists for legislatures. For example, Argentina pioneered a candidate quota law in 1991. Though the law was initially ridiculed, the current female membership in the National Congress is the highest ever attained – 42 percent in the Senate and 33 percent in the House, and the country has elected its first female president.

---

[48] Gram Panchayats, or GPs, are village councils which encompass 10,000 people and serve as India's vehicle for decentralized provision of public goods in rural areas.

Table 10.11. Participation rate of men and women in organizations (%)

	Rural men N = 9,885		Rural women N = 9,917	
	Active member	Official leader	Active member	Official leader
Religious group	41.82	5.95	41.67	5.58
Trade union or farmers' association	11.47	1.75	10.44	1.97
Professional or business association	6.76	1.05	7.6	1.29
Community development or self-help association	14.32	2.75	13.39	2.51

Source: Afrobarometer (2005), Sub-Saharan Africa, Round 3 data.

The policy spread across the region, and by the end of the decade, ten other Latin American countries had adopted legislative quotas, and an eleventh, Colombia, introduced them for senior executive appointments.

In India, political representation was mandated for women in the GPs through the 73rd amendment to the federal Constitution in 1993. The amendment established the framework of a three-tiered local government system, with regular elections every five years, devolving power over rural public works and welfare services from the states to the GPs throughout India. Reservation has drastically increased the number of women in the village councils: In two states, West Bengal and Rajasthan, in reserved GPs, 100 percent of the Pradhans are female, while in unreserved GPs the percentage of women Pradhans is much smaller – only 6.5 percent in West Bengal and 1.7 percent in Rajasthan (Chattopadhyay and Duflo 2004). In Bangladesh, in 1997 women received the mandate to be directly elected to the Union Parishad (UP), local government institutions, through three reserved seats in each UP. This was the culmination of a groundbreaking initiative in 1978 to include two women as nominated members of the UP; this number was raised to three in 1983. In 2002 there were over 12,800 elected women members in 4,198 UPs throughout the country (World Bank 2007). Under the current government, Pakistan reserved one-third of seats for women in all three tiers of local government and 17 percent in the national and provincial legislatures. These reserved seats are filled through direct election at the union council level and indirect election at the tehsil and district level. At the national and

provincial level, a proportional representation system has been adopted to fill the reserved seats for women. The reserved seats brought more than 40,000 women to local governments and 205 to the national and provincial legislatures.

In Uganda, the 1997 Local Government Act provided for one-third reservation for women on all Local Councils (previously Resistance Councils). Namibia also adopted quota laws for parliamentary and municipal elections in the mid-1990s; as a result, women's representation in parliament rose from single digits to 28 percent during 1990–2003. And in 2000 the French parliament approved a law requiring that parties field an equal number of male and female candidates in legislative elections. In cities of more than 3,500 inhabitants where the parity law was applied, women's presence on municipal councils rose to 48 percent.

A second component of this option is to launch and maintain for at least 30 years a nation-wide, systematic public information or advocacy campaign in support of the above policy, not unlike the information campaigns in many countries about family planning, HIV/AIDS prevention, the use of seatbelts in cars, and smoking. It is hard for women to win elections, partly because voters believe female politicians are less effective, and partly because women do not have the experience to win elections. Affirmative action opens up some very real threats to women; conflicts emerge between men and women and possibly even between older and younger women who have different expectations and understanding of gender roles. Because women sometimes face a backlash, social and economic reprisals for violating stereotypes regarding the role of women (Rudman 1998), reservation and public information campaigns should remain in place for a long time.

There is evidence of the need for a sustained public information campaign. In Bangladesh, the women members of the UPs faced serious problems in carrying out their functions due to resistance by the chairman and other members. In Pakistan, women councilors across the three tiers of local government faced similar institutional and social constraints to perform their roles effectively. They were ignored, treated with contempt, denied development funds and expected to confine themselves to "women's issues". In India, respondents in a survey were systematically less likely to declare satisfaction with the public goods they were receiving in villages with female *pradhans* (Beaman *et al.* 2006).[49] Particularly striking is the fact that individuals were less satisfied with water service, even though both the quality and quantity of drinking water facilities were deemed higher in reserved villages. This performance assessment of female leaders is similar to the results

of laboratory experiments in the United States and Western Europe which suggest that women leaders are often evaluated more negatively than male leaders, holding performance constant (see Eagly and Karau 2002 for a survey). Women are typically judged to have less leadership abilities than men with similar characteristics, and the same actions performed by men and women in leadership situations are evaluated more negatively when women are the leaders.

A sustained public information campaign has the potential to reach and motivate substantial numbers of audiences in developing countries. Nationally representative Demographic and Health Survey data from various countries reveal that men and women are already exposed to different communication channels. They are more likely to listen to the radio or watch television once a week than to read a newspaper, so broadcast media are potentially the most effective communication channels for a public information campaign in a wide range of settings (Table 10.12). Evidence from evaluations of different media campaigns demonstrates the power of communication media in changing social behaviors.[50] For example, a newspaper campaign in Uganda was used to reduce corruption of public funds by providing more information to schools and to parents about the government's school grant program (Reinikka and Svensson 2005). A review of studies that measure the effectiveness of 24 mass media interventions in developing countries on changing HIV-related knowledge, attitudes, and behaviors (published from 1990 through 2004) showed effects on a variety of outcomes (Bertrand *et al.* 2006).

One example of such a campaign for women's political participation is India's experience with the Society for Participatory Research in Asia (PRIA), a non-profit development organization in New Delhi. PRIA launched a Pre-Election Voter's Awareness Campaign in 16 districts of Rajasthan with the objective of creating an enabling environment for free and fair elections and advocate for women representatives. It used a large variety of communication methods such as folk theatre, puppet shows, slogan writing, participatory videos, audio cassettes, distribu-

---

[49] In India, a proposed amendment that would ensure a 33 percent quota for women in parliament has not been passed. Despite constitutional guarantees of gender equality, the women's reservation bill has failed to become law; though female parliamentarians seem united in their support for the bill, male parliamentarians have united against the bill. Gender as a cohesive force exists, among women politicians, but is weak because they are, as a group, small in number.

[50] The public information campaign could use a communication model similar to that described by Figueroa *et al.* (2002). In this model a catalyst (i.e., a particular trigger, such as a political reservation law) starts the community dialogue about a specific issue of concern or interest to the community. If effective, this dialogue leads to collective action and the resolution of a common problem. The catalyst is necessary because the community does not *spontaneously* initiate dialogue and action. An alternative approach to a public information campaign is the use of opinion leaders as change agents through diffusion (see review by Valente and Davis 1999), but this interpersonal approach is also often aided by mass media and other communication strategies. This approach uses the existing information dissemination network within the community. Rotating credit associations in developing countries are an example of a community group that follows this approach.

Table 10.12. Mass media exposure, by gender

	Men	Women
No mass media exposure	15.0	24.5
Reads newspaper weekly	32.1	27.9
Watches television weekly	42.6	49.9
Listens to radio weekly	69.2	55.5
All three media	20.3	18.6

Source: DHS, latest year; population-weighted shares.

tion of pamphlets and manuals, a bicycle rally, a march, and small group meetings. On the whole, popular communication methods (pamphlets, posters, and pictures) and group meetings were found to be more effective for reaching women than the mass media (PRIA 2000; IDS 2001).

The third component of this option is to invest in leadership and management training programs for female politicians and political aspirants at the subnational or local level. The objectives are to help female local politicians be better able and more confident to fulfill their responsibilities. A majority of women who enter government for the first time often lack sufficient understanding of laws and formal bureaucratic procedures, do not have experience engaging in political discussions, and do not have a ready network of colleagues. In many cultures the long-held norm is that men, not women, attend community meetings, and if women do attend, they do so without speaking. It is not surprising that the female pradhans in India who hold reserved positions had little political experience prior to the 1998 election. Eighty-nine percent of them (as compared with 57 percent of male pradhans) had never been elected to a panchayat position and most had not even participated in any panchayat activity (Chattopadhyay and Duflo 2004). But increasing the probability that a woman enters politics raises also the personal returns of investing in political skills, so this program need not fund experienced female politicians. Many countries have training programs for government officials and managers, but a training program that is targeted to help women who are less educated, who belong to disadvantaged groups, or who are in local politics for the

first time would be more suited to these novice politicians.

Benefits and costs

Benefits

The first direct effect of political reservation is to give voters the opportunity to assess the ability of women as political leaders, thereby helping to change male and female attitudes towards women leaders. Indeed, early successes by women as policymakers and political players will not only improve their own abilities but likely also motivate other women to vie for political positions in the future, thus making for a sustainable reform. We have already mentioned above the increase in the number of women politicians in the countries that adopted laws mandating political reservation. In addition to women holding more political positions, the reform has also increased the general participation of women in political activities or events. For example, reserved GPs with women pradhans in West Bengal have on average 21 percent higher women attendance at the biannual general assemblies relative to the unreserved GPs (Chattopadhyay and Duflo 2004). In addition, the share of women speaking at these assemblies is 13 percentage points higher in GPs reserved for women (Beaman et al. 2005). And while on average, a woman speaking at these meetings is 14 percentage points more likely to receive a negative response than a man speaking, in unreserved GPs this likelihood is higher (at 25 percentage points).

Besides giving women greater voice in government (a "rights-based" view), does greater political representation by women change the content of policy decision-making? If yes, what are the consequences of the change? Some studies conclude that men and women have different policy preferences, with women more likely to support women's policy preferences. In the United States, for example, women legislators are said to be more likely than men to take liberal positions across a number of social issues, particularly spending on childcare and other child-related expenses (Edlund, Haider, and Pande 2003). Not surprisingly, some research also finds that a higher proportion of female representation within a legislature increases the amount of legislative attention to female policy priorities, though not necessarily to policy outputs (Crowley 2004; Schwindt-Bayer and Mishler 2005). In Uganda, women parliamentarians at the national level showed their capacity to promote gender-equity legislation by passing an amendment to the penal code in 1990 that made rape a capital offence. Similar findings are probably forthcoming from developing countries that have mandated political representation by women, but for now our discussion is limited to the empirical evidence provided by several studies of India's reform at the panchayat level (Pande 2003; Banerjee et al. 2004; Chattopadhyay and Duflo 2004; Beaman et al. 2006). Because of the randomized way in which the rotation of reserved GPs had been designed, India's reform constitutes a large social experiment that can be evaluated rigorously. Specifically, a comparison of the reserved and unreserved GPs provides direct evidence of a causal relationship between political reservation for women and development indicators.

To predict the total benefits from this option, we combine the India-specific results about the (first-order) impacts of political reservation with findings from other published studies about the second-order effects of the reform in terms of income growth and DALYs gained. Admittedly, applying the India results to the developing world as a whole is a far-reaching assumption, but one that we take because of the absence of better data in developing countries. Our estimates should then be interpreted as an illustration at best, keeping in mind that the few other studies we have cited provide corroborative, though largely qualitative, evidence. Our assumptions about the channels of the benefits are contained in Figure 10.4.

With respect to the development benefits from an increase in women's political participation, the evaluation studies of India's policy experiment (already cited above) indicates the following:

- *Water supply and public health*. In West Bengal, there are significantly more public drinking water taps and hand-pumps when the GP pradhan position is reserved for a woman, and there is also evidence that the drinking water facilities are in better condition (though this coefficient is not significant at the 5 percent level) (Chattopadhyay and Duflo 2004). The supply of safe drinking water is higher in reserved GPs than in unreserved GPs by 0.95 percent. A meta-analysis of the literature on the impact of safe water supply, sanitation, and hygiene promotion estimates the resulting reduction in the burden of diarrheal disease to be in the range of 43,992–51,358 DALYs gained (Caincross and Valdmanis 2006). We use the lower number which the authors regard as the realistic estimate for estimating the benefit from more investments in water supply.[51]

- *Child immunization*. A child between the ages of 1 and 5 residing in a village reserved for a female pradhan has 2 percentage-points higher probability of having completed all five vaccinations in an immunization program (Beaman et al. 2005). This could be the result of an improvement in the quality of service of health workers in reserved GPs. In Rajasthan, health care providers are less likely to be absent from work in health facilities in villages reserved for women, and they are more likely to have visited villages in reserved GPs (Banerjee, Deaton and Duflo 2004). In West Bengal, teams of mobile health workers are more likely to visit the villages in reserved GPs than in unreserved GPs (Chattopadhyay and Duflo 2004). Moreover, better public service does not seem to come at a higher price: both men and women are significantly less likely to have to pay a bribe to obtain a service if they live in a GP where the position of pradhan is reserved for a woman (Beaman et al. 2005).

---

[51] For example, in India, diarrhea prevalence amongst infants in families with piped water is twice as high for those in the poorest quintile than the richest. Access to piped water significantly reduces diarrhea prevalence and duration. Disease prevalence amongst those with piped water would be 21 percent higher without it. Illness duration would be 29 percent higher. Safe water supply is defined as a household with access to piped water either via a tap in the premises of the household or from a public tap nearby (Jalan and Ravallion 2003).

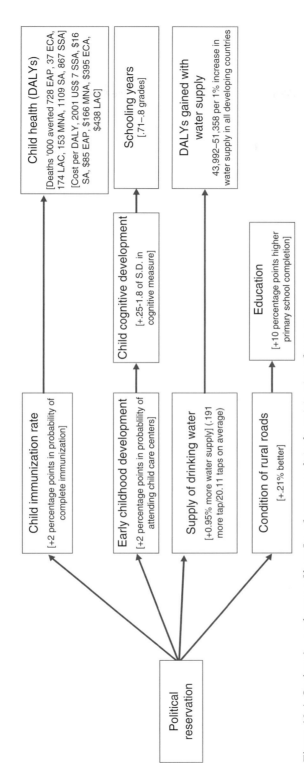

Figure 10.4 Option 4 – pathways of benefits of greater political participation of women
Source: Brenzel et al. (2006), Cairncross and Valdmanis (2006), Chattopadhyay and Duflo (2004), and Mu and van de Walle (2007)

- *Early childhood development.* In reserved GPs preschool children are 2 percentage-points more likely to attend an *anganwadi* (community child care center) which provides child feeding and care (Beaman *et al.* 2006). From a review of the impact of different ECD programs, community-based child centers would seem to have the following effect on the cognitive development of very young children: 0.37 of a standard deviation in Bangladesh, 0.4–1.5 in Bolivia, 0.66 in Guinea, 0.5–1.8 in the Philippines, and 0.25 in Vietnam (Engle *et al.* 2007).
- *Roads.* In reserved GPs, the condition of rural roads has been found to be 0.21 percent better (Beaman *et al.* 2006). To assess the implication of this impact, we use the results of an evaluation of a rural road rehabilitation project in Vietnam. We note that improving roads raised the availability of employment opportunities for unskilled labor by 11 percent, the number of upper secondary schools by 17 percent, and the primary school completion rate by 15–25 percent (Mu and van de Walle 2007). The results change when impacts are measured after another two years; only those on the primary completion rate are sustained through to the medium term, so we include only the benefits on schooling. A number of new outcome indicators reveal significant impacts in the longer run, such as markets becoming newly available, but we ignore these potential second-round benefits.

We use the above results to estimate the expected benefits from this option. We focus only on selected benefits, ignoring additional benefits the studies have suggested. For example, because the effect of reservation on spending on other public goods, including the supply of informal education centers and transportation, is either insignificant or opposite in sign in West Bengal and Rajasthan, the two states evaluated, we attempt to offset these losses by including only the benefits from more drinking water taps and assume that the benefits from more hand-pumps and better water quality fully offset the losses to the community of a negative (even when insignificant) impact on education centers and transportation.

We also exclude all second-round benefits, such as the gains from improvements in cognitive development raising the educational attainment of the next generation. Thus, we opt for a more conservative estimate of benefits. Table 10.13 provides a summary of these assumptions.

Costs

The introduction and implementation of political reservation has social costs. There will be costs to male politicians who will have fewer seats to compete for in each election. There will be costs to people who hold beliefs contrary to the reform and they might actively or passively resist the reform. We presented evidence above that female politicians tend to receive a more negative assessment than men for the same level of performance. Lastly, as with affirmative action policies in the labor market, there may be short-to-medium-run productivity losses associated with electing women into office who have little or no knowledge or experience with policy decision-making and government functions (this assumes that the productivity loss is actually significant). Estimating these costs directly is a difficult task; the evaluations of affirmative action policies such as India's social experiment with reserved seats do not provide cost estimates of the successful passage and implementation of legislative reforms.

To derive the costs associated with this option, we estimate what it would take to reduce the costs to the "losers" (e.g., male politicians) under political reservation. We include two types of cost – the cost of dissolving the resistance of the "losers" through public information campaigns, and the cost of improving the productivity of new women politicians through training programs. With respect to the former, we assume that the legislation instituting the political reservation requires preparation, including lobbying politicians to initiate and pass the legislation and persuading citizens through 5 years of a public information campaign. Moreover, we assume that the advocacy campaign, in various forms, should not stop with the passage of the law but should be sustained over a period of 30 years or more. If the historical experience of the industrial countries with respect to electing

Table 10.13. Option 4 – assumptions used for estimates of benefit–cost ratios

% share of women politicians (based on mean % share in parliament, 2005)	12.83
% annual growth in share of women politicians	
High scenario: 20 years to reach 30% share, 30 years to reach 50%	0.045
Low scenario: 30 years to reach 30% share, 45 years to reach 50%	0.03
Benefits	
Immunization rates, 2005 (mean; but used population-weighted, region-specific rates)	69.32
Total DALYs gained per % increase in immunization (DCPP, 2006)	10485395
Estimated impact of political reservation on immunization rates (Beaman *et al.* 2006)	+2 percentage points
% population with access to safe water supply, 2004	Missing #
DALYs gained per 1% increase in safe water supply (Cairncross and Valdmanis 2006)	
Low scenario	43,993?
High scenario	51,358
Estimated impact of political reservation on water supply (Beaman *et al.* 2006)	Missing #
Estimated impact of political reservation on road quality (Beaman *et al.* 2006)	0.21% better
Estimated impact of better roads on primary schooling completion (Mu and van de Walle 2007) [same as 15–25% increase noted in text?]	+10 percentage points
Average primary school completion rate (World Bank 2007), range of 58–98%	84%
Wage premia for completed primary education (Pritchett), 1.97–2.44	2%
Costs	
Adult population in less developed countries, 15–64 (2005) (http://esa.un.org/unpp/index.asp?) Missing #	
% population, ages 25–59	40%
% population female	49%
% population rural (mean; but used region-specific rate) (http://esa.un.org/unpp/index.asp?)	57.1
Average % women who are official leaders in organizations (e.g., community development) (Afrobarometer data, 2005)	2.62–5.6%
Average (per person) annual cost of public information campaign, $US 2007	
Low (for high-density or urban populations)	1
High (for low-density or rural populations)	1.5
Average annual cost per trainee in management/leadership course [2007 US$?]	
Same as basic education expenditure	27

women into political positions is a good indication of what it would take to change the hearts and minds of citizens, including women, then it would take at least a generation to approach gender equality in local government positions.

A public information campaign would include the development of campaign material, publicist costs (for arranging media coverage), and publication costs. There will be choices made about which mass media network to use – print, radio, television, Internet/new media delivery. Studies suggest that radio communication may be the most cost-effective, where cost-effectiveness is defined here as the cost per number of women and men reached by the campaign whose perception and behavior is changed by the campaign.[52]

[52] For example, in Tanzania, women who recalled radio messages about family planning were 1.7 times as likely as women who reported no exposure through radio programs to have discussed family planning with their spouse and were 1.9 times as likely to have been currently using family planning (Jato *et al.* 1999).

Media experts indicate that television production costs 4–10 times more per minute than radio (Booz Allen Hamilton 2006). To estimate costs, we consider information about costs and results from large public information campaigns related to family planning programs and health programs.

In addition to the cost of a public advocacy campaign, costs include the costs of training potential women leaders. To derive these estimates, we assume that only women who are between the ages of 25 and 59 will be eligible for training and that only roughly 2–5 percent of them would be interested in being elected, based on the Afrobarometer data on the percent of women who were active as leaders in community organizations. We also assume that of these women, only one-fifth can be given training each year, that any woman can attend more than one training spell, and (tentatively for now) at the same average annual cost as providing basic education, without specifying the duration of the training or the opportunity cost of attendance. Table 10.13 summarizes these cost assumptions.

Benefit–cost ratios

We estimate benefit–cost ratios for two principal scenarios. In one scenario, a 30-percent share of women in local political positions would be achieved in 20 years and gender parity, defined as a 50 percent share, in 30 years. In a second scenario, it would take longer to raise women's political representation – 30 years to reach 30 percent and 45 years to reach gender parity. We note that at least in terms of national parliaments the Nordic countries are at just under gender parity, whereas other countries are at a far lower percentage.

Because of the generally long horizon in achieving the goals for this option, our benefit–cost ratio estimates are quite sensitive to our choice of discount rate. The estimated ratios range from a low of 2.3 to a high of 17.7 for the "fast" scenario and from a low of 1.7 to a high of 12.0 for the "slow" scenario. These estimates are presented in Table 10.14.

Design and implementation issues

How might this option work? Below we examine key features of the reforms in India and Uganda in order to illustrate some of the design and implementation issues that reformers will need to address.

The setting up of the Committee on the Status of Women in India (CSWI) marked the start of a movement for greater representation of women in politics in India. Its 1976 report suggested that women's representation in political institutions, especially at the grass-roots level, needed to be increased through a policy of reservation of seats for women. In 1988, the National Perspective Plan for Women suggested that a 30 percent quota for women be introduced at all levels of elective bodies. Women's groups insisted that reservation be restricted to the *panchayat* (village council) level to encourage grass-roots participation in politics. The consensus around this demand resulted in the adoption of the 73rd and 74th amendments to the Indian Constitution in 1993.

The 1993 amendment included mandates to ensure that GP budget decisions were representative of the preferences of the community. First, GPs must hold a general assembly every six months to report on activities and submit the proposed budget to voters for ratification, and pradhans must have regular office hours to allow villagers to formally request services and lodge complaints. Second, states are required to reserve one third of all council seats and pradhan positions for women. Since electoral rules ensure that GPs reserved for women are selected at random and that reserved seats cycle among GPs evenly, any difference in outcomes in reserved and unreserved GPs can be confidently attributed to the reservation policy. Reservations for women have been implemented in all major states except Bihar and Uttar Pradesh (which have only reserved 25 percent of the seats for women in the 1995/96 elections).

In 1995, the question of quotas in parliament was raised again. Initially, most political parties agreed to this proposition, but when the

Table 10.14. Option 4 – estimates of benefits and costs for political affirmative action

	Low discount rate		High discount rate	
	DALY (Low value)	DALY (High value)	DALY (Low value)	DALY (High value)
Assuming women's share in local government takes 20 years to reach 30% and 30 years to reach 50%				
Income benefit	13092042	13092042	7157200	7157200
Mortality benefit	79028735	477823691	41157806	248948077
Total benefits	92120777	490915734	48315005	256105276
Total costs				
Low cost scenario	27686210	27686210	19095849	19095849
High cost scenario	34908690	34908690	21226741	21226741
Benefit–cost ratio				
Low cost scenario	3.33	17.73	2.53	13.41
High cost scenario	2.64	14.06	2.28	12.07
Assuming women's share in local government takes 30 years to reach 30% and 45 years to reach 50%				
Income benefit	13092042	13092042	7157200	7157200
Mortality benefit	55406842	319568790	28950683	167022327
Total benefits	68498884	332660832	36107882	174179526
Total costs				
Low cost scenario	27686210	27686210	19095849	19095849
High cost scenario	34908690	34908690	21226741	21226741
Benefit–cost ratio				
Low cost scenario	2.47	12.02	1.89	9.12
High cost scenario	1.96	9.53	1.70	8.21

bill addressing this issue was introduced in the Eleventh Parliament in 1997, several parties and groups raised objections. The objections focused on two main issues: the issue of overlapping quotas for women in general and those for women of the lower castes; and the issue of elitism because most women's groups felt uneasy about giving special privileges to elite women by ensuring seats for them in the parliament. Most women MPs have supported the 81st Amendment, which would ensure a 33 percent quota for women in parliament, even though party discipline has not allowed them to vote for this (Rai 2002; Narasimhan 2002).

In Uganda, the way the one-third reservation for women was implemented in the 1997 Local Government Act implies ambiguities about the constituencies they are supposed to represent. The one-third reservation has not been applied to existing seats in local government councils.

Rather, except at the village level, the number of seats on all local councils has been expanded by a third to accommodate women. In effect, the reserved seats do not disturb established competitions for ward seats; instead, these reserved seats represent clusters of two to three wards, in effect at least doubling the constituency that women are meant to represent, compared to regular ward representatives. Until 2002 these elections were not by secret ballot but by voters physically queuing up behind the candidate they support; this was finally changed to a secret ballot at the district level in time for the 2002 local council elections. In addition, the elections for the women's seats are held separately, a good two weeks after the ward elections, reinforcing the sense that they are outside regular politics. In the 1998 local government elections, this system failed to attract enough voters for the women's elections all over the country, putting in question the perceived legitimacy of the elected women (Ahikire 2001).

Similar ambiguities and constraints afflict the women in the 53 reserved district-level parliamentary seats (Goetz 2002). The Constitution makes a subtle distinction between women representatives and other categories of special representatives (for whom there are simply a few national seats, not district seats), such as youth, workers, and disabled people. Representatives of other special interest groups are elected directly by their national organizations, but women are elected through an electoral college composed of local government politicians from the district.

Conclusions

In this Challenge Paper we identify and elaborate four key policies that address fundamental disadvantages that women face and prevent them from having a life of their own choosing and simultaneously limit the development potential of entire societies. These policy choices are informed by a framework of gender equality that is based on equality in rights, equality of opportunity, access to markets (e.g., labor, land, credit) and to resources, and equality of voice. It is also informed by research on the damage caused by such gender inequalities on overall economic growth and human development.

We review the scope of challenges regarding gender equality and the welfare of women, with a focus on developing countries. Since large gender disparities are present in so many different aspects of life, it is not easy to limit the options to such a small number of specific policies without appearing overly simplistic. It is not sufficiently helpful to recommend broad swaths of policy, such as to recommend an increase in women's employment and earnings, since there are a multitude of ways by which to achieve that, including a wide range of legislative reforms. Thus, while we include as our first option to increase and improve girls' schooling, a relatively general recommendation, in particular we lend our support to the use of a demand-side approach – specifically, cash transfers to households that are conditioned on girls attending school – that has proved effective in raising girls' enrollment rate and completed years of schooling. This would be especially effective in settings where government programs to expand school spaces have been successful.

From a long list of possible policy reforms in different sectors, we have chosen those that we believe would most increase women's agency, that is, women's ability and power to act on their choices in life, and those that correspond to the different roles that women are expected to play or do play the world over – mother, worker, and citizen. The option of (1) increasing and improving girls' schooling is an obvious choice, as indicated by the evidence on its importance and by the fact that it occurs early in a woman's life and therefore can provide benefits to the entire society for many years. We also put forward the options of (2) supporting women's reproductive roles through services that ensure greater access to family planning programs, safer pregnancies, safer births, and safer abortions; (3) expanding women's access to financial services in order to improve their access to household resources and to reduce their financial vulnerability, which reduced poverty and mortality of all in the household; and (4) strengthening women's voice in policy through greater political representation in local governments with positive effects on the development choices made by local leaders. Our selection is admittedly not based on a comparison of the benefit–cost ratios for a complete list of possible options, but it is based on our review of the economic literature on gender issues and the conceptual framework summarized in the paper. We have discussed the evidence from previous studies that justifies the choice of these four options.

We summarize our main estimates in Table 10.15. Using the lower value of DALYs, the benefit–cost ratios range widely from 0.73 to 11.75 using a discount rate of 3 percent and from 0.60 to 11.71 using a discount rate of 6 percent. Using the higher value of DALYs yields benefit–cost ratios that range from 1.06 to 58.73 using the lower discount rate and from 0.92 to 58.54 using the higher discount rate.

Table 10.15. Summary of benefit–cost ratios for four options and selected scenarios

Option	Alternative scenarios	Low discount rate DALY (Low value)	Low discount rate DALY (High value)	High discount rate DALY (Low value)	High discount rate DALY (High value)
1a	High return scenario	9.27	23.20	4.55	10.99
1b	Low return scenario	6.49	16.24	3.18	7.69
1c	High return-high cost scenario	7.95	19.92	3.90	10.45
2a	FP + Routine maternity care	11.75	58.73	11.71	58.54
2b	FP + Increased primary-level coverage	10.20	51.01	10.06	50.30
2c	FP + Improved overall quality of care & coverage + nutritional supplements	10.90	54.48	10.76	53.79
3a	Constant average costs scenario	1.59	2.30	1.30	2.01
	Constant high costs scenario	0.73	1.06	0.60	0.92
	Constant low costs scenario	1.88	2.73	1.54	2.39
	Declining costs scenario	1.79	2.59	1.46	2.26
3b	Constant average costs scenario	4.78	18.25	4.49	17.95
	Constant high costs scenario	2.19	8.38	2.06	8.24
	Constant low costs scenario	5.66	21.64	5.32	21.28
	Declining costs scenario	5.38	20.58	5.05	20.17
4a	Low cost scenario	3.33	17.73	2.53	13.41
	High cost scenario	2.64	14.06	2.28	12.07
4b	Low cost scenario	2.47	12.02	1.89	9.12
	High cost scenario	1.96	9.53	1.70	8.21

Note: These are extracted from Tables 6, 8, 10, 14.

This table suggests that some versions of the microcredit option have the lowest benefit cost-ratio while versions of the option to support the reproductive role of women have the highest. In interpreting these ratios, it is important to keep in mind that they depend greatly on the availability of reliable and comparable data across countries; due to severe data scarcity, some of these estimates are based only on thin empirical evidence. With increased availability of data, the estimates will likely change; nonetheless, while the absolute values of the estimates may change, the relative ranking of these options may not.

We analyzed the benefit–cost ratios of the four policy options individually, and yet it is clear that they potentially interconnect. For example, better educated girls become mothers who would have fewer, healthier, more educated children, tend to engage in their own business activities and therefore have greater demand for access to loans and other financial services, and would be more likely to enter politics. Similarly, women who have greater access to financial services have more bargaining power within the household and would probably have greater demand for family planning services and better maternal and child care services. Because it is impossible to trace all the indirect benefits of each option, our estimates miss many of these important synergies. It follows that the policy options would be more potent if they are implemented together or at least at about the same time. Moreover, taking into account these synergies could result in a different ranking of the options.

At the same time, we raise some caveats about our benefit–cost estimates. In particular, we calculate benefits on the basis of parameter estimates of just a few empirical studies on developing countries and we apply those estimates generally in our calculations. For example, not many microcredit programs have been evaluated like the Grameen Bank in Bangladesh; similarly, few political representation reforms have been evaluated rigorously outside India. For this reason, we use the results of the studies of these programs to predict the benefits from a widespread application. While we consider low and high scenarios with respect to benefits if estimates range widely, we are clearly not able to capture the heterogeneity among the countries, much less within countries. Our estimates would have to be interpreted in this light, and they would have to be adjusted as more evidence becomes available from various settings. In addition, our estimates will also have to be adjusted even for Bangladesh or India because the long-run impact of the Grameen Bank or of mandated political representation might be significantly different from its short-run impact; and there is even some controversy on the accuracy of the reported short-run impacts in the literature as these estimates inevitably are partly influenced by the preferred empirical strategy, data selection issues, and the like.

We find very few cost or benefit–cost estimates of programs, especially ones that are calculated alongside an assessment of their benefits. This makes the costing of the options difficult. It is hardly ever clear what items are included in the cost estimates and therefore how much of the cost is fixed or variable, whether existing infrastructure or personnel have been included or excluded from the cost of a program, and so on. Programs are implemented with different levels of administrative efficiency which will affect program costs and/or benefits independently of other factors; this is one aspect of available cost numbers that we are not able to discern for lack of published information. Finally, as with benefits, we do also consider low- and high-cost scenarios when estimates range widely, but we are not able to address heterogeneity in costs across countries, much less within countries. Thus precise magnitudes of the benefit–cost ratios should be treated as indicative. Nonetheless, overall they show that investments in women not only promote gender equity, but can be highly cost-effective interventions to promote overall development.

Bibliography

Abu-Ghaida, D., and S. Klasen, 2004: The costs of missing the Millennium Development Goal on gender equity, *World Development* 32(7), 1075–1107

Agarwal, B., 1997: "Bargaining" and gender relations: within and beyond the household, *Feminist Economics*, 3(1), 1–51

Ahikire, J., 2001: Gender equity and local democracy in contemporary Uganda: addressing the challenge of women's political effectiveness in local government, Working Paper, 58, Centre for Basic Research: Kampala, Uganda

Ahlin, C., and R.M. Townsend, 2007: Using repayment data to test across models of joint liability lending, *Economic Journal* 117, F11–F51

Alderman, H., J.R. Behrman, D.R. Ross, and R. Sabot, 1996: Decomposing the gender gap in cognitive skills in a poor rural economy, *Journal of Human Resources* 31(1), 229–254

Alderman, H., P.F. Orazem, and E.M. Paterno, 2001: School quality, school cost and the public/private school choices of low-income households in Pakistan, *Journal of Human Resources*, 36(2): 304–26

Alexander, G., 2001: An empirical analysis of microfinance: Who are the clients? *Paper presented at 2001 Northeastern Universities Development Consortium Conference*

Anand, S. and K. Hanson, 1997: Disability-adjusted life years: a critical review, *Journal of Health Economics*, 16(6): 685–702

Anderson, S., and J. Baland, 2002: The economics of ROSCAs and intra-household allocation, *Quarterly Journal of Economics* 117(3), 983–995

Angrist, J., E. Bettinger, E. Bloom, E. King, and M. Kremer, 2002: Vouchers for private schooling in Colombia: Evidence from a randomized natural experiment, *The American Economic Review* 92(5), 1535–1558

Anwar, A.T.M *et al.*, 2004: Bangladesh: inequalities in utilization of maternal health care services – evidence from MATLAB, Health, Nutrition, and Population (HNP) Discussion Paper, World Bank, Washington, DC

Araujo, M.C., and N. Schady, 2008: Cash transfers, conditions, and school enrollment in Ecuador, *Economía* 8(2), 43–70

Armendariz de Aghion, B., and J. Morduch, 2005: *The Economics of Microfinance*, MIT Press: Cambridge, MA

Ashford, L., 2003: Unmet need for family planning: recent trends and their implications for programs, Measure Communication Policy Brief, Population Reference Bureau: Washington, DC

Ashraf, N., D. Karlan, and W. Yin, 2006a: Tying Odysseus to the mast: Evidence from a savings commitment product in the Philippines, *Quarterly Journal of Economics* 121(2), 635–672

Ashraf, N., D. Karlan, and W. Yin, 2006b: Female empowerment: Further evidence from a commitment savings product in the Philippines, Yale University Working Papers, 949

Ashraf, N., D. Karlan, and W. Yin, 2006c: Deposit collectors, *Advances in Economic Analysis and Policy* 6(2), Article 5, www.bepress.com/bejeap/advances/vol6/iss2/art5

Attanayake, N., V. Fauveau, and J. Chakraborty, 1993: Cost-effectiveness of the Matlab MCH-FP Project in Bangladesh, *Health Policy and Planning*, 8(4), 327–38

Banerjee, A., A. Deaton, and E. Duflo, 2004: Health care delivery in rural Rajasthan, *Economic and Political Weekly*, 39(9), 944–949

Bardhan, K., and S. Klasen, 1999: UNDP's gender-related indices: A critical review, *World Development* 27(6), 985–1010

Barro, R.J., and J.W. Lee, 2001: International data on educational attainment: Updates and implications, *Oxford Economic Papers, Special Issue on Skills Measurement and Economic Analysis* 53(3), 541–563

Beaman, L., E. Duflo, R. Pande, and P. Topalova, 2005: Women politicians, gender bias, and policy-making in rural India, Background Paper for *The State of the World's Children 2007*, UNICEF, New York, NY

Behrman, J.R., and M.R. Rosenzweig, 2004: Returns to birthweight, *Review of Economics and Statistics* 86(2), 586–601

Behrman, J.R., A. Foster, M.R. Rosenzweig, and P. Vashishtha, 1999: Women's schooling, home teaching, and economic growth, *Journal of Political Economy* 107(4), 682–714

Behrman, J.R., S. Parker, and P.E. Todd, 2008: Medium term impact of the Oportunidades Program, in Klasen, S., and F.D. Nowak-Lehman, *Poverty, Inequality, and Policy in Latin America*, MIT Press: Cambridge, MA

Behrman, J.R., and M.R. Rosenzweig, 2002: Does increasing women's schooling raise the schooling of the next generation? *American Economic Review* 92(1), 323–334

Bertrand, J.T., K. O'Reilly, J. Denison, R. Anhang, and M. Sweat, 2006: Systematic review of the effectiveness of mass communication programs to change HIV/AIDS-related behaviors in developing countries, *Health Education Review* 21(4), 567–597

Besley, T., R. Pande, and V. Rao, 2005: Political selection and the quality of government: evidence from South India, Economic Growth Center Discussion Paper, 921, Yale University: New Haven, CT

Bloom, D., and J. Williamson, 1998: Demographic change and economic miracles, *World Bank Economic Review*, 12(3), 419–55

Booz Allen Hamilton, 2006: *Review of the Voice of America and the International Broadcasting Bureau*, Washington DC

Bourguignon, F.F. Ferreira, and M. Menendez, 2007: Inequality of opportunity in Brazil, *Review of Income and Wealth*, 53(4), 585–618

Buvinic, M., A. Medici, E. Fernández, and A.C. Torres, 2006: Gender differentials in health, Chapter 10 in *Disease Control Priorities in Developing Countries*, second edition, edited by D.T. Jamison, J.G. Breman, A.R. Measham, G. Alleyne, M. Claeson, D.B. Evans, P. Jha, A. Mills, and P. Musgrove, Oxford University Press and The World Bank: New York, NY

Cairncross, S. and V. Valdmanis, 2006: Water supply, sanitation and hygiene promotion, chapter 41 in *Disease Control Priorities in Developing Countries*, edited by D. Jamison *et al.*, 2nd edn., Oxford University Press and World Bank, Washington, DC, 771–92

Casterline, J.B., and S.W. Sinding, 2000: Unmet need for family planning in developing countries and implications for population policy, *Population and Development Review* 26(4), 691–723

Caulfield, L.E., S.A. Richard, J.A. Rivera, P. Musgrove, and R.E. Black, 2006: Stunting, wasting and micronutrient deficiency disorders, Chapter 28 in *Disease Control Priorities in Developing Countries*, second edition, edited by D.T. Jamison, J.G. Breman, A.R. Measham, G. Alleyne, M. Claeson, D.B. Evans, P. Jha, A. Mills, and P. Musgrove, Oxford University Press and The World Bank: New York, NY

Chattopadhyay, R., and E. Duflo, 2004: Women as policy makers: evidence from a randomized policy experiment in India, *Econometrica* 72(5), 1409–1443

Chen, M.A., R. Khurana and N. Mirani, 2005: *Towards Economic Freedom: The Impact of SEWA*, Self Employed Women's Association (SEWA): Ahmedabad, India

Chen, M.A. and D. Snodgrass, 2001: Managing resources, activities and risk in urban India, Management Systems International, http://pdf.dec.org/pdf_docs/Pnacn571/.pdf

The Impact of SEWA Bank, Assessing the impact of microenterprise services (AIMS): Washington, DC

Coady, D., and S. Parker, 2004: Cost-effectiveness analysis of demand- and supply-side education interventions: The case of PROGRESA in Mexico, *Review of Development Economics* 8(3), 440–451

Coleman, B.E., 1999: The impact of group lending in Northeast Thailand, *Journal of Development Economics* 60, 105–141

Coleman, B.E., 2002: Microfinance in northeast Thailand: Who benefits and how much?, *Economics and Research Department Working Paper No. 9*, Asian Development Bank

Collins, D.B., and E.F. Holton III, 2004: The effectiveness of managerial leadership development programs: A meta-analysis of studies from 1982 to 2001, *Human Resource Development Quarterly* 15(2), 217–248

Cornwall, A., 2003: Whose voices? Whose choices? Reflections on gender and participatory development, *World Development*, 31(8), 1325–42

Crowley, J.E., 2004: When tokens matter, *Legislative Studies Quarterly*. 29(1), 109–36

Cull, R., A. Demirgüç-Kunt, and J. Morduch, 2007: Financial performance and outreach: A global analysis of leading microbanks, *Economic Journal* 117, F107–F133

Daley-Harris, S., 2006: State of the Microcredit Summit Campaign Report 2006, www.microcreditsummit.org/Pubs/reports/socr/2006/ExecutiveSummarySOCR.pdf; www.microcreditsummit.org/Pubs/reports/socr

de Janvry, A., E. Finan, E. Sadoulet, and R. Vakis, 2006: Can conditional cash transfer programs work as safety nets in keeping children at school and from working when exposed to shocks?, *Journal of Development Economics* 79, 349–373

Deininger, K., 2003: Causes and consequences of civil strife: Micro-level evidence from Uganda, *Oxford Economic Papers* 55(4), 579–606

Disease Control Priorities Project, 2006: Maternal deaths: An unacceptable lack of progress,

Disease Control Priorities Project, www.dcp2.org, March

Dollar, D., and R. Gatti, 1999: Gender inequality, income, and growth: Are good times good for women?, *Policy Research Report on Gender and Development, Working Paper Series No. 1*, World Bank: Washington, DC

Duflo, E., 2000: Child health and household resources in South Africa: Evidence from the old age pension program, *American Economic Review Papers and Proceedings* 90(2), 393–398

Duflo, E., 2001: Schooling and labor market consequences of school construction in Indonesia: Evidence from an unusual policy experiment, *American Economic Review* 91(4), 795–813

Duflo, E.P. Dupas, and M. Kremer, 2007: Peer effects, pupil-teacher ratios, and teacher incentives: Evidence from a randomized evaluation in Kenya, MIT: Poverty Action Lab, www.povertyactionlab.com/papers/peer%20pupil.pdf

Duryea, S., A. Olgrati, and L. Stone, 2006: The under-registration of births in Latin America, Working Paper 551, Research Department, Inter-American Development Bank, Washington, DC

Eagly, A.H. and S.J. Karau, 2002: Role congruity theory of prejudice toward female leaders, *Psychological Review*, 109, 573–98

Edlund, L., L. Haider, and R. Pande, 2003: Unmarried parenthood and redistributive politics, *Journal of the European Economic Association*, 3(1), 95–119

Engle, P.L., M.M. Black, J.R. Behrman, M. Cabral de Mello, P.J. Gertler, L. Kapiriri, R. Martorell, M.E. Young, and the International Child Development Steering Group, 2007: Strategies to avoid the loss of developmental potential in more than 200 million children in the developing world, *Lancet*, 369, 229–42

Eloundou-Enyegue, P.M., and C.S. Stokes, 2004: Teen fertility and gender inequality in education: A contextual hypothesis, *Demographic Research* 11(11), 305–334

Figueroa, M.E., D.L. Kincaid, M. Rani, and G. Lewis, 2002: Communication for social change: An integrated model for measuring the process and its outcomes, *The Communication for Social Change Working Paper Series 1*, Rockefeller Foundation and Johns Hopkins University Center for Communication Programs: New York

Filmer, D., 2004: If you build it, will they come? School availability and school enrollment in 21 poor countries, *World Bank Policy Research Working Paper 3340*, World Bank: Washington, DC

Filmer, D. and N. Schady, 2006: Getting girls into school: Evidence from a scholarship program in Cambodia, World Bank Policy Research Working Paper WP3910

Filmer, D. and N. Schady, 2008: Getting girls into school: evidence from a Scholarship Program in Cambodia, *Economic Development and Cultural Change*, 56(3): 581–617, www.journals.uchicago.edu/doi/abs/10.1086/533548 - fn1

Forbes, K.J., 2000: A reassessment of the relationship between inequality and growth, *American Economic Review* 90(4), 869–887

Foreit, K.G., M.P.P. de Castro, and E.F. Duarte Franco, 1989: The impact of mass media advertising on a voluntary sterilization program in Brazil, *Studies in Family Planning* 20(2), 107–116

Galor, O., and D.N. Weil, 1996: The gender gap, fertility, and growth, *The American Economic Review* 86(3), 374–387

Gaviria, A., 2007: Intergenerational transmission of education in Latin America. *Economia*

Gertler, P.J., and J.W. Molyneaux, 1994: How economic development and family planning programs combined to reduce Indonesian Fertility, *Demography* 31(1), 33–63

Ghatak, M., and M. Ghatak, 2002: Recent reforms in the Panchayat System in West Bengal: Toward greater participatory governance, *Economic and Political Weekly* 37(1), 45–58

Gine, X., P. Jakiela, D. Karlan, and J. Morduch, 2006: Microfinance games, *Policy Research Working Paper 3959*, World Bank: Washington, DC

Glewwe, P. and M. Zhao, 2005: Attaining universal primary completion by 2015: How much will it cost? *American Academy of Arts and Sciences Working Paper*, American Academy of Arts and Sciences: Cambridge, MA

Goetz, A.M., and R.S. Gupta, 1996: Who takes the credit? Gender, power and control over loan use in rural credit programs in Bangladesh, *World Development* 24(1), 45–63

Goetz, A.M., 2002: No shortcuts to power: constraints on women's political effectiveness in Uganda, *Journal of Modern African Studies*, 40(4), 549–75

Goldblatt, B., and S. Meintjes, 1998: South African women demand the truth, in *What Women Do in Wartime: Gender and Conflict in Africa*, edited by M. Turshen, and C. Twagiramariya, Zed Books: London and New York

Graham, W.J., J. Cairns, S. Bhattacharya, C.H.W. Bullough, Z. Quayyum, and K. Rogo, 2006: Maternal and perinatal conditions, Chapter 26 in *Disease Control Priorities in Developing Countries*, second edition, edited by D.T. Jamison, J.G. Breman, A.R. Measham, G. Alleyne, M. Claeson, D.B. Evans, P. Jha, A. Mills, and P. Musgrove, Oxford University Press and The World Bank: New York

Haddad, L., and J. Hoddinott, 1994: Women's income and boy–girl anthropometric status in the Cote d'Ivoire, *World Development* 22, 543–554

Haddad, L., J. Hoddinott, and H. Alderman, 1997: *Intrahouse Resource Allocation in Developing Countries*, Johns Hopkins University Press, Baltimore, MD

Herz, B., and G.B. Sperling, 2004: *What Works in Girls' Education? Evidence and Policies from the Developing World*, Council on Foreign Relations: New York, NY

Hill, M.A., and E.M. King, 1995: Women's education and economic well-being, *Feminist Economics* 1(2), 21–46

Holmes, J., 2003: Measuring the determinants of school completion in Pakistan: analysis of censoring and selection bias, *Economics of Education Review*, 22(3): 249–64

Honohan, P., 2004: Financial sector policy and the poor, Working Paper No. 43, World Bank: Washington, DC

IDS, 2001: Gender and participation, *Development and Gender Brief* 9, PRIA

Ilahi, N. and S. Jafarey, 1998: Markets, deforestation and female time allocation in rural Pakistan, Department of Economics, McGill University, Montreal, Ontario

ILO/UNCTAD Advisory Group, 2001: *The Minimum Income for School Attendance (MISA) Initiative: Achieving International Development Goals in African Least Developed Countries*, ILO/UNCTAD: Geneva, Switzerland

Jalan, J., and M. Ravallion, 2003: Does piped water reduce diarrhea for children in rural India?, *Journal of Econometrics* 112, 153–173

Jamison, D.T., 1993: Investing in health, *Finance and Development*, 30(2), 2–5

Jato, M.N., C. Simbakalia, J.M. Tarasevich, D.N. Awasum, C.N.B. Kihinga, and E. Ngirwamungu, 1999: The impact of multimedia family planning promotion on the contraceptive behavior of women in Tanzania, *International Family Planning Perspectives* 25(2), 60–67

Johnston, D., and J. Morduch, 2007: Microcredit vs. microsaving: Evidence from Indonesia, Paper presented at the World Bank/World Bank Economic Review Conference on Access to Finance, 15–16 March 2007

Karlan, D., and M. Valdivia, 2006: Teaching entrepreneurship: impact of business training on microfinance clients and institutions, Yale University: New Haven, CT

Karlan, D., and J. Zinman, 2006: Expanding credit access: using randomized supply decisions to estimate the impacts, Yale University: New Haven, CT

Khandker, S.R., 1998: *Fighting Poverty with Microcredit: Experience in Bangladesh*, Oxford University Press, Oxford

Khandker, S.R., 2005: Micro-finance and poverty: Evidence using panel data from Bangladesh, *World Bank Economic Review* 19, 263–286

Khandker, S.R., B. Khalily, and Z. Khan, 1995: Grameen Bank: Performance and sustainability, Discussion Paper 306, The World Bank: Washington, DC

Khandker, S.R., M.M. Pitt, and N. Fuwa, 2003: Subsidy to promote girls' secondary education: The female stipend program in Bangladesh, Working Paper, The World Bank: Washington, DC

Kim, J., H. Alderman, and P.F. Orazem, 1999: Can private school subsidies increase enrollment for the poor? The Quetta Urban Fellowship Program, *World Bank Economic Review* 13(3), 443–465

Klasen, S., 2002: Low schooling for girls, slower growth for all? Cross-country evidence on the effect of gender inequality in education on economic development, *World Bank Economic Review* 16(3), 345–373

Klasen, S., 2006: Pro-poor growth and gender inequality, Discussion Paper 151, Ibero-America Institute for Economic Research: Göttingen, Germany

Klasen, S., and F. Lamanna, 2007: The impact of gender inequality in education and employment on economic growth: updates and extensions, mimeo, University of Göttingen: Göttingen, Germany

Knowles, S., P.K. Lorgelly, and P.D. Owen, 2002: Are educational gender gaps a brake on economic development? Some cross-country empirical evidence, *Oxford Economic Papers* 54(1), 118–149

Kremer, M., E. Miguel, and R. Thornton, 2004: Incentives to learn. CID Working Paper No. 109, Center for International Development, Harvard University: Cambridge, MA

Lagerlöf, N.P., 2003: Gender equality and long-run growth, *Journal of Economic Growth* 8(4), 403–426

Levine, R., A. Langer, N. Birdsall, G. Matheny, M. Wright, and A. Bayer, 2006: Contraception, Chapter 57 in *Disease Control Priorities in Developing Countries*, second edition, edited by D.T. Jamison, J.G. Breman, A.R. Measham, G. Alleyne, M. Claeson, D.B. Evans, P. Jha, A. Mills, and P. Musgrove, Oxford University Press and The World Bank: New York

Lewis, M. and M. Lockheed, 2006: Inexcusable Absence: Why 60 million girls still aren't in school and what to do about it, Center for Global Development: Washington, DC, 31–40

Littlefield, E., J. Morduch, and S. Hashemi, 2003: Is microfinance an effective strategy to reach the Millennium Development Goals?, www. idlo.int/texts/IDLO/mis7533.pdf (accessed 22 August 2007)

Lomborg, B. (ed.), 2004: *Global Crises, Global Solutions*, Cambridge University Press

Lundberg, S., and R.D. Plotnick, 1995: Adolescent premarital childbearing: do economic incentives matter? *Journal of Labor Economics* 13(2), 177–200

Luoto, J., C. McIntosh, and B. Wydick, 2007: Credit information systems in less-developed countries: A test with microfinance in Guatemala, *Economic Development and Cultural Change* 55(2), 313–334

Malmberg Calvo, C., 1994: Case study on access of women to domestic facilities, SSATP Working Paper, 11, World Bank, Washington, DC

Matheny, G., 2004: Family planning programs: Getting the most for the money, *International Family Planning Perspectives* 30(3), 134–138

Maurer, K., 1999: Bank Rakyat Indonesia (BRI), Indonesia, in *Challenges of Microsavings Mobilization: Concepts and Views from the Field,* Deutsche Gesellschaft fur Technische Zusammenarbeit (GTZ), Eschborn, Germany, A. Hannig, and S. Wisniwski

McIntosh, C., A. de Janvry, and E. Sadoulet, 2005: How rising competition among microfinance lenders affects incumbent village banks, *Economic Journal* 115, 987–1004

McIntosh, C., and B. Wydick, 2005: Competition and microfinance, *Journal of Development Economics* 78(2), 271–298

McKernan, S., 2002: The impact of microcredit programs on self-employment profits: Do noncredit program aspects matter?, *Review of Economics and Statistics* 84(1), 93–115

Morduch, J., 1998: Does microfinance really help the poor? New evidence from flagship programs in Bangladesh, Harvard University mimeo: Cambridge, MA

Morduch, J., 1999: The microfinance promise, *Journal of Economic Literature* 37(4), 1569–1614

Mu, R., and D. van de Walle, 2007: Rural roads and poor area development in Vietnam, Policy Research Working Paper Series No. 4340, The World Bank: Washington, DC

Narasimhan, S., 2002: Gender, class, and caste schisms in affirmative action policies: The curious case of India's Women's Reservation Bill, *Feminist Economics* 8(2), 183–190

Narayan, D. *et al.*, 2000: *Can Anyone Hear Us? Voices of the Poor*, Oxford University Press, New York

Orazem, P., and E.M. King, 2008: Schooling in developing countries: The roles of supply, demand and government policy, in *Handbook of Development Economics, Volume 4*, Elsevier B.V. Press, Oxford, edited by T.P. Schultz and J. Strauss

Pande, R., 2003: Can mandated political representation provide disadvantaged minorities policy influence? Theory and evidence from India, *American Economic Review* 93(4), 1132–1151

Pedersen, D., 2002: Political violence, ethnic conflict, and contemporary wars: Broad implications for health and social well-being, *Social Science & Medicine* 55, 175–190

Piotrow, P.T., J.G. Rimon, K. Winnard, D.L. Kincaid, D. Huntington, and J. Convisser, 1990: Mass media family planning promotion in three Nigerian cities, *Studies in Family Planning* 21(5), 265–274

Pitt, M., 1999: Reply to Jonathan Morduch's "Does Microfinance Really Help the Poor?" New evidence from flagship programs in Bangladesh, mimeo, Brown University: Providence, RI

Pitt, M., and S.R. Khandker, 1998: The impact of group-based credit programs on poor households in Bangladesh: Does the gender of participants matter?, *Journal of Political Economy* 106(5), 958–996

Pitt, M., S.R. Khandker, O.H. Chowdhury, and D. Millimet, 2003: Credit programs for the poor and the health status of children in rural Bangladesh, *International Economic Review* 44(1), 87–118

Porter, M., 2007: Empirical essays on household bargaining in developing countries, Chapter 2, University of Chicago, Department of Economics, Doctoral Dissertation

PRIA (Society for Participatory Research in Asia), 2000: Pre-election voters' awareness campaign, Rajasthan, PRIA, New Delhi

Pritchett, L., 2004: Access to education, in *Global Crises, Global Solutions*, edited by B. Lomborg, Chapter 4, 175-23

Pritchett, L., 2001: Where has all the education gone, *World Bank Economic Review* 15(3), 367–391

Rai, S.M., 2002: *Gender and the Political Economy of Development*, Polity Press, Cambridge

Rehn, E., and E.J Sirleaf, 2002: *Women, War and Peace: The Independent Experts' Assessment on the Impact of Armed Conflict on Women and Women's Role in Peace-building*, United Nations Development Fund for Women, New York

Reinikka, R. and J. Svensson, 2005: Fighting corruption to improve schooling: evidence from a newspaper campaign in Uganda, *Journal of the European Economic Association*, 3(2), 259–67

Robinson, M., 2001: *The Microfinance Revolution: Sustainable Banking for the Poor*, World Bank: Washington, DC

Robinson, W.C., and G.L. Lewis, 2003: Cost-effectiveness analysis of behavior change interventions: a proposed new approach and an application to Egypt, *Journal of Biosocial Science* 35(4), 499–512

Rosenzweig, M.R., and T.P. Schultz, 1982: Market opportunities, genetic endowments, and intrafamily resource distribution: Child survival in rural India, *American Economic Review* 72(4), 803–815

Rudman, L., 1998: Self-promotion as a risk factor for women: The costs and benefits of counterstereotypical impression management, *Journal of Personality and Social Psychology* 74(3), 629–645

Saito, K.A., with contributions from H. Mekonnen and D. Spurling, 1994: Raising the productivity of women farmers in sub-Saharan Africa, World Bank Discussion Papers, 230, World Bank, Washington, DC

Sara-Lafosse, N., 1998: Machismo in America Latina and the Caribbean, in *Women in the Third World: An Encyclopedia of Contemporary Issues*, edited by N.P. Stromquist, Garland Publishing, New York

Schultz, T.P., 1994: Human capital, family planning, and their effects on population growth, *American Economic Review* 84(2), 255–260

Schultz, T.P. (ed.), 1995: *Investment in Women's Human Capital*, University of Chicago Press, Chicago, IL

Schultz, T.P., 1997: Demand for children in low income countries, in *Handbook of Population and Family Economics*, edited by M.R. Rosenzweig, and O. Stark, Volume 1A, North-Holland

Schultz, T.P., 2001: Why governments should invest more to educate girls, Center Discussion Paper, 836, Yale University Economic Growth Center, New Haven, CT

Schultz, T.P., 2004: School subsidies for the poor: Evaluating the Mexican PROGRESA poverty program, *Journal of Development Economics* 74(1), 199–250

Schwindt-Bayer, L.A. and W. Mishler, 2005: An integrated model of women's representation, *Journal of Politics*, 67(2), 407–28

Simmons, G.B., D. Balk, and K.K. Faiz, 1991: Cost-effectiveness analysis of family planning programs in rural Bangladesh: evidence from Matlab, *Studies in Family Planning*, 22(2), 83–101

Strauss, J., and D. Thomas, 1995: Human resources: empirical modeling of household and family decisions, in *Handbook of Development Economics*, edited by J.R. Behrman, and T.N. Srinivasan, North-Holland, Amsterdam, Vol. 3A, 1883–2024

Shirin, R., 2002: *Class, Caste and Gender, Women in Parliament in India*, International IDEA 2002, Women in Parliament, Stockholm (www.idea.int)

Skoufias, E., 2005: PROGRESA and its impacts on the human capital and welfare of households in rural Mexico: A synthesis of the results of an evaluation by IFPRI, Research Report 139, International Food Policy Research Institute: Washington, DC

Smith, L.C., and L. Haddad, 2002: How potent is economic growth in reducing undernutrition? What are the pathways of impact? New Cross-Country Evidence, *Economic Development and Cultural Change* 51(1), 55–76

Sood, S., and D. Nambiar, 2006: Comparative cost-effectiveness of the components of a behavior change communication campaign on HIV/AIDS in North India, *Journal of Health Communication* 11(1), 143–162

Summers, L.H., 1994: *Investing in all the People, Educating Women in Developing Countries*, EDI Seminar Paper No. 45, Economic Development Institute of The World Bank: Washington, DC

Tansel, A., 2002: Determinants of school attainment of boys and girls in Turkey: Individual, household and community factors, *Economics of Education Review* 21, 455–470

Thomas, D., 1990: Intrahousehold resource allocation: An inferential approach, *Journal of Human Resources* 25, 635–664

Thomas, D., 1997: Incomes, expenditures, and health outcomes: evidence on intrahousehold resource allocation, *Intrahousehold Resource Allocation in Developing Countries*, edited by L. Haddad, J. Hoddinott, and H. Alderman, Johns Hopkins University, Baltimore, MD

Todd, P.E., and K.I. Wolpin, 2006: Assessing the impact of a school subsidy program in Mexico: Using a social experiment to validate a dynamic behavioral model of child schooling and fertility, *American Economic Review* 96(5), 1384

Udry, C., 1996: Gender, agricultural production and the theory of the household, *Journal of Political Economy* 104(5), 1010–1046

Udry, C., J. Hoddinott, H. Alderman, and L. Haddad, 1995: Gender differentials in farm productivity: Implications for household efficiency and agricultural policy, *Food Policy* 20(5), 407–423

UNESCO, 2005: *Education for All Global Monitoring Report*, UNESCO: Paris

UNICEF, 2006: *The State of the World's Children 2007: Women and Children*, UNICEF, New York, NY

United Nations, 2000: *The World's Women 2000: Trends and Statistics*, United Nations: New York

United Nations Development Programme (UNDP), 1995: *Human Development Report*, UNDP: New York

United Nations Development Programme (UNDP), 2003: *Indicators for Monitoring the Millennium Development Goals: Definitions, Rationale, Concepts and Sources*, UNDP: New York, NY

UNFPA, 2004: *State of World Population 2004, The Cairo Consensus at Ten: Population, Reproductive Health, and the Global Effort to End Poverty*, UNFPA: New York

Valente, T.W., and R.L. Davis, 1999: Accelerating the diffusion of innovations using opinion leaders, *Annals of the American Academy of Political and Social Science* 566, 55–67

Villar, J., M. Merialdi, A.M. Gulmezoglu, E. Abalos, G. Carroli, R. Kulier, and M. de Oni, 2003: Nutritional interventions during pregnancy for the prevention or treatment of maternal morbidity and preterm delivery: an overview of randomized controlled trials, *Journal of Nutrition*, 133: 5, 1606S–1625S

WHO, 1999: Mother–baby package costing spreadsheet, *WHO/FCH/RHR/99.17.* Geneva: WHO

World Bank, 1993: *World Development Report: Investing in Health*, Oxford University Press: New York, NY

World Bank, 2000: *China National Development and Sub-National Finance: A Review of Provincial Expenditures*, The World Bank: Washington, DC

World Bank, 2001: *Engendering Development (Through Gender Equality in Rights, Research, and Voice)*, Oxford University Press and The World Bank: Washington, DC

World Bank, 2007: *Global Monitoring Report: Millennium Development Goals, Confronting the Challenges of Gender Equality and Fragile States*, World Bank: Washington, DC

World Health Organization (WHO), 2007: *Maternal Mortality in 2005: estimates developed by WHO, UNICEF, UNFPA, and the World Bank*, WHO Press: Geneva, Switzerland

Yamarik, S., and S. Ghosh, 2003: *Is Female Education Productive? A Reassessment*, Tufts University: Medford, MA; www.csulb.edu/~syamarik/Papers/FemaleEd/.pdf

Yunus, M., 2003: *Banker to the Poor*, Public Affairs: New York

Alternative Perspectives

Perspective Paper 10.1

LAWRENCE HADDAD

In many parts of the world, one of the most unfortunate things that can happen to a person is to be born female. Women and girls are subject to norms that treat them as objects, are denied rights as basic as the freedom to leave their village, and are excluded from opportunities that many take as a given.

Although much worse in some regions than others, women's relative powerlessness is a global phenomenon – witness many feminists in the United States agonizing over whether to vote for Hillary Clinton or to vote for the person who best represents their positions on the issues.

Women's relative lack of power means that they are unable to influence the framing of the norms, values, laws, and institutions that, in turn, may reinforce their relative powerlessness. The reasons for this powerlessness are wrapped up in biological and cultural evolutions which often reinforce each other. They have been laid down and reinforced and enforced over hundreds and thousands of years. Is it difficult for public policy to break this cycle of powerlessness? Surprisingly, the evidence says "no." The authors highlight three options where interventions have successfully broken through the cultural barriers in a ruthlessly pragmatic fashion: microfinance targeted to women, cash transfers targeted to women conditional on girls' attendance at school, and the reservation of positions for women in legislative bodies. Credible evaluations have shown that within a short period of time, women have been empowered

by these interventions – directly and in terms of indirect or second-round effects. The fourth option selected by the authors for intervention – reproductive health – is also an area where good evaluations show large returns. It is a bit disappointing that this option is the only one that is not treated within an implicit power framework – it is framed as a shortage of services, a lack of knowledge, financial constraints, and lack of spousal support. No mention is made of the make-up of the institutions prioritizing health spending needs.

It is difficult to argue with the four options selected by the authors. They are all sensible in that they build on fundamental research and more operational evidence. They have all been evaluated well, at least on the impacts side. Given the options outlined, the key literatures, by and large, have been done justice. Costs are difficult to categorize and delineate and, in part because of this, are chronically badly measured in development interventions and I am very dubious – as are the authors – of the numbers presented here, despite the authors' best efforts. All the options outlined are politically thinkable in most contexts. As to the cost-benefit ratios, I am pretty sceptical of them, again, as are the authors, because of the cost data, and hence cannot take the rankings of the options too seriously, even if some of the ratios are 10–20 times larger than others. But if the outcome of this paper were greater priority of and support to some or all of these options then I would be very happy.

Nevertheless, the paper represents somewhat of a lost opportunity to think outside the box. What do I mean?

First it is a shame that the authoring team is composed entirely of economists. They are fine economists, but gender is essentially about power. And most economists are not terribly good at recognising power within their work and incorporating it into their models and empirics, even armed with bargaining models. Furthermore, the authors are steeped in the US microeconometric approach to economics (if in doubt check the preponderance of such papers cited in the references). I myself am embedded in this tradition, and have a lot of time for it, but it is not the only tradition, and certainly not always the most important. It is a tradition that is very apolitical and is loath to draw upon literatures that do not speak in the same probabilistic languages (i.e., it is very comfortable with, say, epidemiology and demography). But there are vast literatures out there about how power relations are shifted through the creation of invited spaces for negotiation and contestation and how further such spaces can be carved out through social mobilization (Eyben, Harris, and Pettit 2006).

The main consequence of this self-imposed straitjacket is that the authors do not give sufficient consideration to issues of voice, representation and recognition in terms of the capacity of citizens to claim rights and the obligation of states to deliver on those claims. In short, the authors do not do justice to the political, anthropological, and sociological literatures – feminist or not – that deal with the power relations between men and women, how they are shaped, and how they can be re-shaped. How do institutions shape these power relations? How malleable are they? Where are the points of maximum leverage? There seems to be an implicit assumption that individual agency is the best way to effect change. Is this based on a consideration of how change happens? Is this how things changed have changed for women in the rich countries? Where is a consideration of different forms of collective action and social mobilization? There are calls for a public information or advocacy campaign and for leadership and management training, but these are essentially apolitical interventions, and gender is about rebalancing power – it will involve contestation and negotiation – it will not yield to management training. As cited in Coyle (2007), economists based in the United States have very different political orientations to anthropologists and political scientists based there. These differences will tell in terms of how the Copenhagen Challenge is framed and answered – our authors should guard against this unipolar view by building in more safeguards of plurality.

The author's institutional centre of gravity might also be a hindrance to a more contested and political perspective. The World Bank finds it difficult to explicitly define its political role, despite having a very significant implicit role. It would have been very refreshing to witness such a critical self-reflection, perhaps in the context of why King's excellent work on gender at the World Bank appears – to this outsider – to have found such lukewarm support from Bank senior management when push comes to shove. When will we see a World Development Report on the scandal of how women are discriminated against in nearly all countries?

Second, the very nature of the exercise is to focus on "what works". What works is a subset of what has been tried and evaluated. What about promising initiatives that have not been evaluated in a probabilistic sense? What about visionary ideas that have not even been tried? Ten years ago conditional cash transfers would not have made it into the list of options. The same could have been said about microfinance thirty years ago. It would have been useful to have a "venture capital" section in the paper – what might work, given half a chance? Drawing on a more diverse literature would have been one way to avoid the purely pragmatic consolidation of a particular subset of knowledge and interventions well-known to the authors. For example, work led by Andrea Cornwall at IDS is focusing on how women actually seek to empower themselves through their everyday activities (www.pathwaysofempowerment.org; Cornwall, Harrison, and Whitehead 2004). Often these

Table 10.1.1. Option 3: Calculation of DALYs averted per dollar loaned to women (Upper Bound)

	Girls	Boys	Source
(1) Women's credit elasticity of children's height-for-age (cm per age-year)	1.14	1.53	Pitt *et al.* 2003
(2) % increase in cm per age-year needed to move child out of malnourishment (at average age in Pitt *et al.* (2003) sample	11.97	11.45	Est. from WHO Child Growth Standards www.who.int/childgrowth/standards/
(3) % increase in credit needed to move child out of malnourishment	10.50	7.48	(2) / (1)
(4) Average amount women borrowed (taka)	9,675.95	9,675.95	Pitt *et al.* 2003
(5) 1991–92 average exchange rate (taka/dollar)	38.00	38.00	World Development Indicators Database
(6) Average amount women borrowed (US$)	254.63	254.63	(4) / (5)
(7) $ needed (in loans) to save one child from malnourishment (on average)	2,927.41	2,160.13	(6) x [1 + (3)]
(8) Average DALYs saved per undernourished child averted	2.13	2.13	Caulfield *et al.* 2006 Table 28.4
(9) $ needed in loans to women to avert one DALY due to undernourishment	1,374.26	1,014.06	(7) / (8)
(10) DALYs averted per $ loaned to women	0.000728	0.000986	1 / (9)

do not correspond to the donor superhighways constructed for women's empowerment – superhighways that often place more emphasis on speed than destination.

So, have the authors missed any opportunities? Who knows? If I had written the paper I would have focused on some related literatures that may have generated different or additional options. For example, I am struck by the power of Chattopadhyay and Duflo's (2004) work on how female representation on village councils in India significantly affects spending priorities for the same budget constraint. We need more work that looks at these links. There is very little in the paper drawing on social capital literatures – from economics or elsewhere that shows how the composition of social networks can advance women's rights. There is little from the communications technology literature about how mobile phones may have shifted power balances. There is very little about how nondemocratic political choices (the one-child policy in China) profoundly affect female to male survival ratios. Work on how important the relative size of assets brought to marriage by men and women is

for determining future bargaining within households is barely touched upon (Quisumbing and Maluccio 2003). The work on registration and identity (one example of recognition I referred to earlier) cited in the paper is a promising example of how to potentially change fundamental norms, although the authors do not actually tell us the male-female disaggregated results of this work. All of these issues may appear tangential to the challenges. They may be. They also may appear to be less amenable to policy change in any single instance. But if they can be shaped, they may have very profound impacts. In short, the confidence intervals will be very wide, but the expected value of their impacts could dwarf the benefit-cost ratios outlined in this paper.

In conclusion, the options identified are sensible and will prove to be good investments. They are difficult to rank and choices about which to act on will have to be made according to the policy space available to support them. In a given context, when the problem, political and solution streams come together, then there will be space for pushing one or more of these four options.

Table 10.1.2. Option 3: Calculation of DALYs averted per dollar loaned to women (Lower Bound)

		1st year of loan	2nd & 3rd years after loan	Source
(1)	Increase in height-for-age z-score per dollar increase in income to women (standard deviations)	0.000226	0.000226	Duflo
(2)	% increase in household expenditure per dollar loaned to women	9.450000	0.980000	Khandker (2005)
(3)	Increase in height-for-age z-score per dollar loaned to women	0.000021	0.000002	(2) / 100 x (1)
(4)	Increase in z-score needed to move child out of malnourishment	1.500000	1.500000	WHO
(5)	$ needed (in loans) to save one child from malnourishment (on average)	70,084.49	675,814.68	(4) / (3)
(6)	Average DALYs saved per undernourished child averted	2.13	2.13	Caulfield *et al.* 2006 Table 28.4
(7)	$ needed in loans to women to avert one DALY due to undernourishment	32,900.90	317,258.66	(5) / (6)
(8)	DALYs averted per $ loaned to women	0.000030	0.000003	1 / (7)

But there are few surprises in the options outlined. That would be fine, if such surprises had been entertained. But more lateral (as opposed to unilateral) thinking is necessary to ensure we are not foregoing other more profound–and risky – options, at the individual, organizational, and institutional levels. Much more economics research needs to be focused on institutional and representational issues and how these affect outcomes – direct and indirect, quantifiable and qualitative. That can occur sensibly only if economists recognize that gender relations are about power and politics, and that means economists reading outside their discipline of comfort and working with those who will challenge their explicit and implicit assumptions about the power relations between women and men.

Bibliography

Chattopadhyay, R. and E. Duflo, 2004: Women as Policymakers: Evidence from a Randomised Policy Experiment in India. *Econometrica* 72(5)

Cornwall, A., E. Harrison, and A. Whitehead, 2004: Repositioning Feminisms in Gender and Development, *IDS Bulletin* 35(4)

Coyle, D., 2007: *The Soulful Science: What Economists Really Do and Why it Matters*, Princeton University Press, Princeton NJ

Eyben, R., C. Harris, and J. Pettit, 2006: Exploring Power for Change, *IDS Bulletin* 37(6)

Quisumbing, A., and J. Maluccio, 2003: Resources at Marriage and Intrahousehold Resource Allocation, *Oxford Bulletin of Economics and Statistics* 65(3)

Perspective Paper 10.2

AYSIT TANSEL

Introduction

The Third Millenium Development Goal is to promote gender equality and empowerment of women, which is one of the important and legitimate policy goals of the international development community. Gender equality is the basis for the well-being of women and the society in several dimensions. This goal is desirable not only for intrinsic reasons such as fairness, but also for such reasons as attaining efficiency, reducing poverty, and generating social and economic growth in individual countries as well as the international community.

The gender agenda of the international organizations includes women in both the developed and developing countries. There are issues yet to be addressed in the developed countries. However, the issues in the developing countries are considered to be urgent. Since the 1970s the sad and dangerous conditions of the poor and under-privileged women lacking opportunities in developing countries have become an increasingly prominent issue on the agenda of the international development community. For this reason, this Challenge Paper by King, Klasen, and Porter (KKP henceforth) focuses on women in developing countries.

This Challenge Paper by KKP identifies and develops in detail four essential challenges about the disadvantages to which women are subject. The challenges identified are women's human capital, and women's access to financial services, supporting women's reproductive roles, and enabling women's voice to be heard in policy. The Challenge Paper suggests four corresponding solutions to these areas of policy options. These solutions are cash transfers to women conditional on girls attending school (CCT), microfinance programs, family planning programs, and increasing the representation of women in local governments. As a result of careful computations of benefits, costs, and the benefit–cost ratios, KKP find that the solution of providing family planning programs and related services has the highest benefit–cost ratio and that the microcredit program has the lowest benefit–cost ratio.

Several issues I raise in this Perspective Paper include the following. First, the resulting ranking of the solutions in the Challenge Paper was a surprise for me. I attribute the resulting ranking to the fact that the indirect benefits of the policy options considered are ignored. I would have expected to find the solution of CCT to rank first. The most important and unique function of education is that it affects women's ability to make choices. If women could get more schooling this would translate into their improved health and nutrition, improved access to credit, improved control of fertility, and increased political voice. When girls become mothers, the benefits of a mother's education include reduced child mortality and morbidity and increased child schooling. I claim that to stop with the wage returns to schooling is to ignore the household productivity effects and empowerment effects on the allocation of household resources. However, many of these indirect effects also have longer time frames than completing school and entering work before marriage, followed probably by family rearing for a decade and then half of the women will eventually return to the labor force as their children enter school. These indirect repercussions are also relevant for other options but especially important for women's schooling. CCT may be a cost-effective instrument to accomplish a targeted program of schooling for girls, regardless of the causes for girls receiving less schooling without the programs. However, family planning programs at much lower cost could have wide repercussions on the woman's productivity over a lifetime and family health, and thus the decline in fertility is only the opening wedge of returns from family planning and is targeted at those who need the services. Similar arguments are relevant for other policy options and solutions which are elaborated under "Ignoring the Indirect Benefits and Interconnections". For these reasons, the benefit estimates are underestimates of the true benefits. Their inclusion may well lead to a different ranking than the one provided in the Challenge Paper.

Second, one of the common grounds for all of the four options suggested is empowerment of women, whether in private life or public life. Empowering women improves not only their living conditions, but also their participation in the social and economic life of a country, which results in long-term sustainable development. CCT, microfinance and family planning programs all empower women in their private life, which increases their bargaining power and allows them to play an active role in decision making within the household. The last option of increasing representation of women in local governments empowers women in public life. Therefore, the empowerment of women with their improved bargaining power and decision making may be taken as the departure point for evaluating the solutions suggested by KKP. There are a number of benefits accruing from empowerment and improved decision making of women, such as beneficial human capital outcomes for children and the family, reduced fertility, increased labor force participation and increased political participation of women. For instance, Schady and Rosero (2007) provide evidence that unconditional cash transfers to poor women in rural Ecuador increase their bargaining power in the household. Swain and Wallentin (2007) provide evidence from India that microfinance programs not only increase income, but also empower women and increase their self-confidence, respect, and esteem.

Roushdy (2004) provides evidence that women's empowerment leads to greater investment in children in Egypt.

Third, although gender inequality and the disadvantages women face are sometimes rooted in formal, legal, and regulatory institutions, they are more often rooted in informal, social, and cultural institutions and prevent women's participation in private as well as public life. For this reason, it is of great importance that the four solutions be accompanied by gender-sensitive education given to girls and boys as well as women and men together through awareness-raising programs. This will enhance the empowerment process of women, increase the impact of the solutions, and create positive synergies for each of the solutions suggested.

Fourth, the four solutions are interrelated in terms of their outcomes. I would recommend that they are put into practice at the same time. This would reinforce their benefits. There are significant synergies to be gained by the simultaneous implementation of the four policy options.

Summary of the Challenge Paper

This Challenge Paper by KKP on women concentrates on the welfare of women in developing countries, hence the title "Women and Development". The authors consider the disadvantages that women face in developing countries. These disadvantages are thought to limit women's choices in private and public life. The resulting gender disparities appear in many aspects of life. One could suggest as many challenges and solutions as there are gender disparities.

Rather than recommending broad and general policies which could be achieved by a range of competing or complementary solutions, KKP prefer to present four specific challenges within a framework of gender equality. This framework includes equality in rights, equality of opportunity, equality in access to (land, labor, and credit) markets and resources, and equality of voice in public life. The challenges chosen are in conformity with the roles women play or are expected to play in private and public life, such as that of mother, worker, and citizen. The choices are justified with evidence from a wide range of previous studies. The worldwide evidence confirms that the policy options chosen are expected to most increase women's ability and power to exercise their life choices in private and public life.

The first challenge is increasing and improving girls schooling. There is vast evidence on the importance and benefits of this option in the literature. Admittedly, this is a somewhat general recommendation which could be approached in a variety of ways, such as from demand-side or supply-side policies, or both. The authors propose the specific demand-side solution of cash transfers to mothers conditional on girls attending school. This solution has already been successfully implemented in several developing countries and has proven to be effective in increasing both the enrollment rates and the completed years of schooling of girls. Further, the authors call attention to targeting this policy to the poorest and the disadvantaged girls since the standard procedures already address the issue of raising enrollments of both boys and girls in many developing countries.

The second challenge is expanding women's access to financial services. This is expected to improve women's claim to household resources and diminish their financial vulnerability. The solution suggested and evaluated is the microfinance program. Although there are many implementations of microfinance programs in the developing world, very few of them are evaluated in terms of their benefits, such as the Grameen Bank in Bangladesh.

The third challenge is supporting women in their reproductive roles. The solution to achieve this goal includes ensuring access to family planning programs, safer pregnancies and births, and safer abortions. There are many implementations of such programs throughout the developing world. Furthermore, they are widely evaluated in their various aspects.

The fourth challenge is enabling women's voice to be heard in public policy. The solution suggested and evaluated is greater political representation of women in local governments.

Such political representation reforms are very few in the developing world and the only rigorous evaluation available of a program for women's greater representation in local governments is that for India.

Each of the four challenges and the suggested solutions are evaluated in terms of their benefits and costs. The benefit–cost ratios computed suggest that supporting the reproductive role of women by ensuring access to family planning programs and the associated services has the highest benefit–cost ratio. The policy option of expanding women's access to financial services through microfinance has the lowest benefit–cost ratio.

Strengths of the Challenge Paper

The most important strength of the Challenge Paper by KKP is the meaningful selection of the challenges which are specific but fundamental. These are increasing and improving girls' education, expanding women's access to financial services, supporting women in their reproductive roles, and allowing women's voice to be heard in policy. The solutions suggested are also specific: these are cash transfers to mothers conditional on girls attending school, microfinance programs for women, ensuring access to family planning programs, safe pre-natal and birth services, and, finally, greater political representation of women in local governments, corresponding to the challenges. Careful and comprehensive review of the literature is another strength of the Challenge Paper. KKP use the best available empirical estimates in the literature for the evaluation of each of the solutions considered. Finally, the benefit and cost estimates provided constitute the first comprehensive and detailed evaluation of the solutions suggested in terms of their benefits and costs.

Weaknesses of the Challenge Paper

The first and the most important weakness in the evaluation of the solutions is that the benefit computations take into account mainly the direct benefits (with some exceptions), but ignore the indirect benefits of the solutions. The second important weakness is that the Challenge Paper is not clear about the time frames to fruition of the solutions suggested. There needs to be further discussion and clarification of this issue separately for the direct and indirect benefits of the solutions. The third important weakness of the Challenge Paper is that it ignores the possibilities of economies of scale in costs in the provision of the solutions, with the exception of the declining costs scheme in the solution of microfinance. These are further discussed below.

Ignoring the Indirect Benefits and Interconnections

The four policy options suggested by KKP are interconnected and have indirect benefits. For example, better education of girls could lead to better control of fertility, better nutrition and health of the family, and fewer, healthier and more educated children. Better-educated girls in adult life are more likely to enter wage work or own business and have greater claim and easier access to all financial services including loans. Finally, better-educated girls would be more likely to take part in politics and public life in the future. Thus, it appears that more and better education of girls may be at the heart of many other beneficial and desirable outcomes. As such, increasing and improving girls' education does in fact encompass the three other policy options considered in the Challenge Paper.

The Challenge Paper takes into account the indirect benefits of movements out of malnutrition in the benefit computation of the solution of microfinance, but not in the benefit computation of other solutions. Reduced child mortality is taken into account in the benefit computations for the CCT program, but not the other external benefits. The evaluation of the microcredit program does not include the benefits from improved child schooling. Similarly, there is evidence that women's greater access to finance leads to greater bargaining power within the household, with the result of greater demand for family planning services, better prenatal and birth care, and improved nutrition, health, and education for children. Another interconnection could be traced to supporting women's reproductive roles through family planning services, improved pre-natal care, and safer abortions, which will mean reduced maternal and infant mortality and morbidity. This will also translate into healthier women with fewer children, which in turn will enable women to participate in the labor force and to be involved in politics. Further indirect benefits will follow with fewer but better qualified children. As is demonstrated in the quantity-quality trade-off literature, fewer children imply better health and better educational outcomes for children in less developed country settings (Schultz 2008a). Another example of an ignored indirect benefit is the impact of reduced fertility on child health and schooling. Glick, Marini, and Sahn (2007) provide evidence from the natural experiment of twins that fertility control has significant positive impacts on child health and schooling. Further, Bloom et al. (2007) estimate a large negative effect of fertility on women's labor force participation. Their simulations show that fertility reduction affords a 47 percent increase in income and that the increased labor force participation of women generates a further gain of 21 percent income. For all these reasons, the ranking of the solutions may change when indirect benefits are taken into account.

The estimates in KKP do not take into account most of the indirect benefits of the solutions, due to the lack of such data. Therefore, the benefit estimates of each solution are in fact an underestimate or a lower bound of the true benefits. Among the four policy options, the set of indirect benefits is the largest in the case of the first policy option of increasing and improving girls' education. At this point I reiterate my belief that the policy option of increasing and improving girls' education would rank number one if indirect benefits were taken into account.

Time Frames to Fruition

The time frame or gestational period for investments in women is important for the evaluation of the solutions. Although differences among the four solutions in terms of the time frames to fruition are taken into account in the calculation of benefits in the Challenge Paper, they are not emphasized. The fruits of increasing and improving girls' education would be reaped when the girl reaches adulthood and beyond. This would mean a time frame of at least 9–12 years assuming a girl starts school at six, employment at 16 and reaches adulthood at 18 years of age. In view of the long years to fruition for this option, it could be considered as a long-term option. In contrast, the policy option of expanding women's access to financial services is expected to reach fruition within a year in its direct benefits. However, if the microfinance schemes have a pay-off, it is in the longer term. Once the women are connected with the market and credit system, they can borrow repeatedly and eventually have a good credit record and collateral to enter the formal credit system if they need to expand their business. Yet the evidence from many fragmentary sources suggests that few of these home handicraft and livestock type activities that women become engaged in due to microfinance expand beyond a home-scale operation. If this is true, then the pay-off is for an initial credit round only. However, it is possible to think that it can achieve a more sustained return and expansion in the women's productive career. Similarly, the third policy option of supporting women in their reproductive roles is expected to reach fruition within a short period of time, like a few years, while the fourth policy option of allowing women's voice in policy to be heard would require only a few years to fruition. Therefore, the third and the fourth solutions could be considered to be short-term or medium-term projects.

Economies of Scale in Costs

The most important strength of the Challenge Paper is its contribution to the estimation of the costs of the four solutions considered because in the solution evaluation literature, the estimation of costs has received much less attention than that of the benefits and therefore, in the literature, evidence on various cost components of the solutions is scanty. However, an important weakness related to the cost estimates is that the authors were not able to separate out the fixed administrative costs from the variable costs. Thus, it is not possible to evaluate if there are economies of scale from the operation of a solution. Economies of scale would reduce the variable costs once the infrastructure is put into place. So the cost of these solutions may be lower than the actual used estimates. This reasoning may even be behind the low cost, and therefore, high benefit–cost ratio and eventual ranking as first of the solutions of supporting reproductive role of women.

Comparison of Benefits

KKP does not bring out a comprehensive discussion of benefits and costs of each of the solutions, rather it concentrates on a discussion of benefit–cost ratios. The presentation of the benefit–cost ratios implies that the solution of family planning programs has the highest benefit–cost ratio and the microcredit program the lowest. In order to give an idea about the benefits involved behind the benefit–cost ratios, I present the following discussion based on benefit estimates compiled from the various tables in the Challenge Paper corresponding to the evaluations with "Low Discount Rate and High Value of DALY" with the highest return and/or lowest cost scenarios for each of the policy instruments. KKP reports income benefits, mortality benefits, and total benefits for each of the solutions except for the family planning programs, for which only the total benefits are available. Highest income benefits accrue with the policy instrument of "political voice." More importantly, enormous mortality benefits occur again with the policy instrument of political voice. The second highest income, mortality and total benefits are with the CCT program. The total benefits, in terms of millions of dollars, are in the order of 300-400 for the political voice; 20–30 for the CCT; 2–15 for the Microfinance and 2–3 for the family planning programs. These benefits of political voice are 10–20 times more than that of the CCT and 100–150 times more than that of the family planning programs. Accordingly, in terms of total benefits, the policy instrument of political voice ranks first, the CCT program ranks second, Microcredit ranks third, and the family planning program ranks the last, and the differences among these rankings are vast. However, in terms of benefit–cost ratio, the family planning program, which is a policy option that has the lowest benefits, ranks first. This finding is somewhat disturbing because it is the least benefit option. The benefit–cost ratio for the family planning program is around 50 which is at least twice more than that of CCT.

The main problem with the tables in the Challenge Paper is that the origin of some of the numbers is not clear and that they lack defined units and they would require much more detail in their derivation to evaluate them as a serious basis for comparing the solutions, such as those in Tables 10.7, 10.9 and 10.13. Some of the cost figures with nutritional supplements are lower than those without them, as in Tables 10.9 and 10.13. It would be most beneficial for the authors to document clearly the sources of each table and number, and if they are mere guesses of the authors, that must be stated in the footnotes. It would be instructive to work out an example in an appendix illustrating the step-by-step computation of benefits and costs for each solution.

Increasing Education level and Conditional Cash Transfers

In terms of increasing the educational level of women, KKP focus on the single policy of CCT over a range of other demand-side and supply-side policies. KKP argue convincingly for a demand-side policy of conditional cash transfers targeted at girls as a better option than improvements on the supply side. This is reasonable as there is important evidence of efficacy of targeted demand-side interventions, such as the girls' stipend program in Bangladesh (Khandker *et al.* 2003). KKP also note that

supply-side improvements are much harder to implement when the government is not very competent and when institutional reforms are needed, as is the case in the poorest countries in focus. Furthermore, school quality is currently rather low in Africa. This would be one reason why reliance on demand-side policies would be more effective in such settings. For instance, African governments in recent years instituted the (not gender targeted) demand-side policy of eliminating school fees for both boys and girls. The enrollment response to this policy has been very large. As a result, the systems have been stretched and there is real concern of decline in quality all the more. Thus, no really successful demand-side policy can ignore supply inadequacies which could be met either by the public or private sector. However, the private sector would not be feasible as it would need to charge families for tuition.

In contexts such as that of Africa, boys' schooling is also much too low, especially beyond primary school, although it is better than that of girls. Under these circumstances, a policy only to help girls may be difficult to implement when boys are also very inadequately educated. Perhaps a higher level of subsidy for girls as in the PROGRESSA program of Mexico would be politically acceptable. Then, if boys are included, it could lead to a very large demand response and result in supply and quality problems.

In this regard, alternative ways to increase female schooling include lifting user fees for girls only, or distributing vouchers to girls that would cover the user fees. However, such proposals may prove to be hard to implement due to political reasons. In order to be able to implement such laws, an article that allows for special temporary measures, such as positive discrimination, should be included within a country's law. The UN Convention on the Elimination of All Forms of Discrimination against Women (CEDAW) signed by over 180 countries, which are members of the UN, urges in its Article 4, Paragraph 1 that the governments take these special temporary measures to eliminate the long-standing inequalities faced by women and girls.

Less obvious factors may also have a positive effect on schooling. Even providing nutritious meals at school is an important factor for families, especially the poor ones, to send their daughters and sons to school. Dreze and Kingdon (2001) report that provision of midday meals are particularly effective in increasing girls' enrollment in schooling in India. School participation of girls was about 15 percentage points higher when local schools provided a midday meal than when they did not.

As another alternative policy to increase girls' schooling, KKP suggest unconditional cash transfers with the expectation that income elasticity for girls' schooling is higher than that for boys'. An example given for this expectation is the case in Turkey given by Tansel (2002). I would like to point out a similar situation in the West African country of Cote d'Ivoire by Tansel (1997), where statistically significant income elasticity for girls' schooling but not for boys' schooling is found.

One supply-side policy that is disregarded by KKP is school construction. The literature provides evidence on the significant but small impact of distance for girls' enrollment. Tansel (1997) finds that while the primary school distances are not significant, middle and secondary school distances reduce primary school attendance and the middle and post-middle schooling years attained in the West African country of Ghana. These effects are larger for girls than for boys, which implies that distance is a greater deterrent for girls' enrollment in education than that for boys' in Ghana. Furthermore, in Cote d'Ivoire, distance effects for girls and boys are equivalent. KKP note that distance may be more important at the secondary level. However, the educational gaps, at least in Africa, occur not at school entry but at progression, including the period beyond primary education. Therefore, it is possible that reducing the distance barrier is more important to gender equity than is generally recognized. Parents may be reluctant either to let girls travel long distances to lower or upper secondary schools which are much more sparsely distributed, or to have them live away from home, near where these schools are located. Both of

these reasons may be a result of security concerns but at the same time may be related to the high opportunity cost of time of girls who are needed for work at home. So, school construction addresses not only the supply constraint but the demand constraint as well.

Indirect costs of schooling that keep girls away from school, for example their being needed to help their mothers in household chores and care of their siblings, need to be addressed. Provision of affordable or free child care centers could be a solution to such issues and increase girls' enrollments by freeing up girls' time from sibling care and household production. Empirical evidence supports the notion that girls' access to education is constrained by their household production obligations (Glick and Shahn 2000). Thus, policies of provision of childcare services would reduce the demand for girls' labor at home and thus the opportunity cost of their attending school. Lokshin et al. (2004) found that lower local childcare costs in Kenya increase both girls' schooling and mothers' employment. Flexible school schedules may help girls balance school and domestic work obligations and increase their school attendance (Herz and Sperling 2004).

In this context, family planning programs resulting in reductions in fertility may also help increase girls' school attendance, since fewer siblings means a smaller burden of childcare obligations on older sisters. Childcare would also raise the earnings returns to women's schooling since it would enable them to expect to enter formal work as is discussed by Glick (2007). There is no empirical evidence on the return on childcare services or flexible school shifts as there is on that of CCT. Although KKP indicate recognition of many of these factors in their discussion, it is somewhat unsatisfactory to ignore complementary solutions.

Differences between girls' and boys' education are also observed at tertiary level. In about half of the 130 countries with data, at the tertiary education level, the female enrollment rate exceeded the male rate in 2005. KKP suggest that this is due to the fact that boys leave school for jobs after secondary school whereas girls do not because they do not have the same work opportunities. Here, it could be clarified that girls need comparatively higher qualifications to enter the same job as men. Furthermore, cultural factors may be at play also. For example, girls are "protected" from the "dangers and hardships" of working life (security concerns) and seen fit only for jobs that are considered not to include these hardships (which are usually jobs that require good or higher education) and if the family needs money, boys are called on to find a job and contribute to the budget, not girls. Consequently, they continue further education (Lyon 1996). KKP emphasize that average national gender parity ratios tend to conceal rural/urban differences in educational indicators. It is very true that substantial gender disparities could be concealed not only by the rural/urban difference, but also by differences in social and economic classes.

There is a concern regarding a possible increase in the fertility rates among participant families in the CCT program. However, this can be prevented with possible awareness-raising activities for families with the aim of explaining the targets of CCT and possible risks of increased fertility rates within their communities. Therefore, CCT should be accompanied by awareness-raising programs.

In the discussion of the policy option of "increasing and improving girls' schooling," KKP point out that "(daughters should) not be responsible for old age support of parents. . . ." Interestingly enough, especially in today's urban populations, the daughters turn out to be the ones taking care of elderly parents, as this fits into their gender roles (Medical News Today, 2004). Furthermore, in the rural areas, although sons may be responsible for the old-age support of their parents, in practice it is the son's wife who shoulders this responsibility. Therefore, while a woman is not expected to care for her aging parents, she is expected to take care of her husband's aging parents. Migration into cities may not change this situation.

The success of the conditional cash transfer program depends on the assumption that lack of girls' enrollment is a result of poor economic conditions. However, there may be multiple forms of discrimination and cultural factors at play in this process. Often parents with traditional beliefs are reluctant to send their daughters to school because they are ignorant of the benefits of girls' education. Under these circumstances "sensitization interventions" (Glick 2007) of supplying public information on the benefits of girls' schooling would be inexpensive solutions.

Financial Vulnerability and Microfinance Programs

The second challenge considered by KKP is reducing women's financial vulnerability through microfinance. Microfinance programs are designed to address the disadvantages women face in the credit market. There are a number of reasons why micro-institutions focus on women. First, this will increase bargaining power of women, who are usually responsible for children's education and health expenditures, which results in increased expenditures on children's human capital. Studies summarized in Schultz (2002) indicate that women's preference for investing in children's human capital is stronger than that of men. Second, this will increase labor force participation of women, which will benefit the economy of the country, and third, women will have better repayment records. There is considerable discussion on increased feminization of poverty due to globalization (Sen and Sen 1985; Medeiros and Costa 2007). Therefore, I suggest that feminization of poverty is also another important reason for microfinance institutions to focus on women.

Microfinance institutions focus on women in order to provide economic benefits to women. This cannot be the sole method to include women in the labor market because it ignores the fact that not all women want to be entrepreneurs or want to take risks and open up businesses. In such cases women should be counseled and supported to search for wage employment. One benefit of self-employment (as opposed to full-time wage employment) may be that women may be able to combine market work and domestic chores. Morrison *et al.* (2007) present evidence on the impact of women's access to markets not only on poverty reduction, but also on productivity at the individual and household level.

In addition, there is evidence that microfinance institutions' focusing on women does not necessarily result in formal sector activities. It is more likely that resulting activities will be in the informal sector. For this reason, the Self-Employed Women's Association (SEWA) underlines the importance of institutional change while organizing poor self-employed women aiming to secure reliable employment as well as self reliance (Bhatt 2006).

Evidence from all over the world shows that the largest gender gap in labor force participation occurs between the ages of 25–49. This is the age interval when women are expected to be taking care of children and the elderly. This information shows the importance and the necessity of social care services that will take the burden of care away from women and enable them to participate in the labor market. There are regional differences in the world with respect to women's labor force participation rates. In both the regions with high and low women's participation rates, the difference between the sectors that employ women and those that employ men continues to be a problem where women are concentrated in sectors mainly characterized by low productivity, lower quality, and more precarious forms of paid work (Heintz 2006).

In the light of the above, I am skeptical about the idea that microfinance for self-employed women is a perfect solution when getting women out of the home and into the wage labor force may have greater long-term promise for their career paths, and may also raise the opportunity cost of more children, thereby lowering fertility. However, it is not necessarily the best option to enter the wage labor force when there are productive activities for the women to expand in the home at little cost to their family. In Matlab Bangladesh, as women reduce their fertility in the program-treated villages, they tend to earn more when they work in the wage labor force.

However, actually, fewer women work in the wage labor force, and more work at home. Estimates with data fit to a Heckman-type model in Schultz (2008b) demonstrate this pattern. One would surmise that entry into the wage labor force is a major barrier for rural women in South Asia or West Asia, whereas entry into wage labor is more readily accomplished by women in the urban settings. However, not enough careful econometric study of these issues is available.

Reproductive Support and Family Planning Programs

Fertility affects the welfare of women, children, and men and the well-being of families and the society. Access to reproductive health is critical to the promotion of gender equality and empowerment of women. Thus, the third challenge considered by KKP is support for women's reproductive role. The solution suggested is to provide family planning programs, pre-natal care, safe childbirth, and safe abortion services. At this point I suggest that post-natal services should not be forgotton since women's vulnerable position continues while still breast feeding and she could make use of supplements and services available.

Women with fewer children may reallocate more of their time to more productive activities outside the family. Their children enjoy more schooling and better nutrition and health care. Joshi and Schultz (2007) find gains from family planning programs in terms of child survival and child schooling in Matlab Bangladesh. The trade-off between quantity and quality of children is a commonly accepted stylized fact which has been challenged recently in different developmental contexts.

Women with fewer children have a higher propensity to allocate more of their time to labor force participation. Thus, fertility decline may increase both labor force participation and hours worked. The decline in fertility is associated with fewer risks of maternal mortality and morbidity, and increased ability to bargain more effectively over the allocation of household resources. Women's improved bargaining power in the household may lead to an increase in their human capabilities and they may invest a greater amount in their children's human capital. However, the use of family planning program services depends on their acceptability by women and their husbands. Therefore, men and women need to be educated about the benefits of reproductive control and health for women and their children.

Political Voice of Women in Local Governments

The fourth challenge considered is strengthening the political voice of women by increasing the participation of women in local governments. Chattopadhyay and Duflo (2004), who provide evidence on women's voice in local governments in India, emphasize different spending priorities of women in public life than those of men. As part of this project, investment in leadership and management training programs for the political aspirants of such positions is suggested. I think one problem with this policy option might be that women can become divided over party politics and may not have solidarity among themselves and therefore not give enough support to gender issues. Another problem is that in many countries standing for election to a public office requires significant financial investment. Since women in general have less accumulated wealth than men all over the world, they may not be able to make the necessary financial investment although by law there may be a quota for them.

In the section on "Political Participation and Voice," it is mentioned that one summary indicator of women's voice in public life is the "gender empowerment measure." It combines political participation, economic participation, and economic power. I would like to add that there is also the important notion of "political power". Women may become parliamentarians, but can be given very powerless ministries or may never be given any titles to affect policy. This notion is called "the token representation of women" (Beckwith 2007). Thus, women may remain marginalized in the political process.

What has been Left Out?

There are two issues that could be considered complementary to the solutions proposed to the challenges by KKP. The first issue I raise is the issue of "gender mainstreaming and gender budgeting" to be adopted by the governments and other organizations. Gender mainstreaming is a process of assessing the implications for women and men of legislation, policies, or programs in all areas, such as political, economic, and societal spheres, and at all levels in order to eliminate inequalities and achieve gender equality. Gender budgeting is the budgetary component of gender mainstreaming practices. It includes incorporation of not only a gender perspective into the design, development, adoption, and execution of all policies, but also budgetary processes with appropriate resource allocation to support gender equality and enhance women's empowerment.

The second issue I raise is violence against women. Violence against women mostly takes place in the private sphere and was, until recently, considered beyond the responsibility of governments. It was at the 1993 UN Vienna Conference that violence against women was defined and declared as an integral and inseparable violation of human rights. Violence against women could result in physical, sexual, or psychological harm or suffering by women as well as their children. It is also defined to include threats of such acts, coercion, or arbitrary deprivation of liberty whether occurring in public or in private life with the aim of controlling and oppressing women. In some parts of the developing world, violence against women takes the form of female circumcision and homicide for not conforming to the cultural norms, and occurs frequently. Or empowerment of women at home may create tensions leading to domestic violence. Some forms of domestic violence do not even have a solution that could be addressed with education since evidence shows that they are widespread even among the educated. Moreover, in many countries, the laws discriminate against the victims of gender-related violence. Often violence is defined in very narrow terms and the proof of evidence is not only burdensome but also on the victim. Therefore, this is an area in which institutional reform is needed. The reform could focus on four main areas such as prevention, protection, prosecution, and compensation. The prevention approach should not only include legislation to punish gender-based violence but also open up discussion of cultural norms. The protection approach should include access to healthcare and legal advice as well as provision of shelter. The prosecution approach should ensure the necessary legislation for the prosecution of violence perpetrators. Lawyers, the police, and judges should be given the necessary training for appreciation of this kind of crime and its threats. Special attention is needed to make it more costly to the offender. The compensation approach should include various ways to compensate for the harm women suffer due to the violence they have experienced.

Conclusions

This Perspective Paper evaluates the four challenges and the solutions presented in the Challenge Paper. Several conclusions emerge.

Each of the four solutions, CCT, microfinance, family planning programs, and increasing representation of women in local governments would be more effective if they were complemented by educational programs and awareness raising programs for girls, boys, women, and men with a focus on women's rights. Such public programs could also help break cultural traditions, social norms, informal family and social laws that have implications for gender inequality. They could be incorporated into each solution or they could be realized separately under an overall program.

The Challenge Paper concludes that family planning programs and associated services have the highest benefit–cost ratio and that the microfinance program has the lowest benefit–cost ratio. A closer look at the benefits shows that greater political representation of women in local governments has extremely large benefits. As a result of this, one wonders if and how this

solution could be provided in a cost-effective way. This point needs further investigation.

Child and elderly care services emerge as an essential factor for labor market participation of women and school attendance of older girls by reducing time burdens.

There are indirect benefits to each of the solutions. Because only a few and not all of the indirect benefits are taken into account, the resulting benefits are underestimations of the true benefits. Thus, the benefit–cost ratios computed may be misleading. The family planning program and associated services are identified as the solution with the highest benefit–cost ratio by a large margin which may change if full benefits are considered.

Because of the indirect benefits, there are interconnections between the four solutions. I would recommend their joint implementation. This would reinforce their benefits and allow great synergies to be achieved. Such a multiple intervention would also reflect a strong commitment on the part of the government and institutions involved.

Bibliography

Beckwith, K., 2007: Numbers and Newness: The Descriptive and Substantive Representation of Women, *Canadian Journal of Political Science* 40(1): 27–49

Bhatt, E., 2006: *We Are Poor But So Many: The Story of Self-Employed Women in India*, Oxford University Press, New York/New Delhi

Bloom, D.E., D. Canning, G. Fink, and J.E. Finlay, 2007: Fertility, Female Labor Force Participation and the Demographic Dividend, National Bureau of Economic Research Working Paper 13583. Cambridge, MA: NBER

Chattopadhyay, R., and E. Duflo, 2004: Women as Policy Makers: Evidence from a Randomized Policy Experiment in India, *Econometrica* 72(5): 1409–1443

Dreze, J., and G.G. Kingdon, 2001: School Participation in Rural India, *Review of Development Economics* 5(1): 1–24

Glick, J.P., 2007: Policy Impacts on Schooling Gender Gaps in Developing Countries:

The Evidence and a Framework for Interpretation, Ithaca, NY: Cornell University

Glick, P., and D.E. Sahn, 2000: Schooling of Girls and Boys in a West African Country: The Effects of Parental Education, Income and Household Structure, *Economics of Education Review* 19(1): 63–87

Glick, J.P., A. Marini, and D.E. Sahn, 2007: Estimating the Consequences of Unintended Fertility for Child Health and Education in Romania: An Analysis Using Twins Data, *Oxford Bulletin of Economics and Statistics* 69(5): 667–691

Heintz, J., 2006: *Globalization, Economic Policy and Employment: Poverty and Gender Implications,* Geneva: ILO Employment Strategy Papers

Herz, B., and G.B. Sperling, 2004: What Works in Girls' Education: Evidence and Policies from the Developing World, Council on Foreign Relations: New York

Joshi, S., and T.P. Schultz, 2007: Family Planning as an Investment in Development: Evaluation of a Program's Consequences in Matlab, Bangladesh, Economic Growth Center Discussion Paper No. 894, Yale University, New Haven, CT

Khandker, S., M. Pitt, and N. Fawa, 2003: Subsidy to Promote Girls' Secondary Education: The Female Stipend Program in Bangladesh, Washington, DC: The World Bank

Lokshin, M., E. Glinskaya, and M. Garcia, 2004: The Effect of Early Childhood Development Programs on Women's Labor Force Participation and Older Children's Schooling in Kenya, *Journal of African Economies* 13(2): 111–137

Lyon, E.S., 1996: Success with Qualifications, Comparative Perspectives on Women Graduates in the Labor Market, *Higher Education* 31(3): 301–323

Medical News Today, 2004: Women Who Early in Life Care for Elderly Parents Are at Higher Risk of Poverty Later, 14 August (www.medicalnewstoday.com/articles/12069.php)

Medeiros, M., and J. Costa, 2007: Is There a Feminization of Poverty in Latin America?, *World Development* 36(1), 115–127

Morrison, A., D. Raju, and N. Sinha, 2007: Gender Equality, Poverty and Economic Growth, Policy Research Working Paper 4349. Washington, DC: World Bank

Roushdy, R., 2004: Intrahousehold Resource Allocation in Egypt: Does Women's Empowerment Lead to Greater Investments in Children?, Cairo, Egypt: Economic Research Forum (ERF) Working Paper 0410

Schady, N., and J. Rosero, 2007: Are Cash Transfers Made to Women Spent Like other Sources of Income?, Policy, Research Working Paper WPS 4282, Impact Evaluation Series no. IE 17. Washington, DC: The World Bank

Sen, G., and C. Sen, 1985: Women's Domestic Work and Economic Activity: Results from National Sample Survey, *Economic and Political Weekly* 27 April, WS49–55

Schultz, T.P., 1997: Demand for Children in Low Income Countries, in M. Rosenzweig and O. Stark (eds.) *Handbook of Population and Family Economics*, Volume lA, Amsterdam: North-Holland Publishing Co.

Schultz, T.P., 2002: Why Governments Should Invest More to Educate Girls, *World Development* 30(2): 207–225

Schultz, T.P., 2008a: Population Policies, Fertility, Women's Human Capital and Child Quality, in T.P. Schultz, and John Strauss (eds.) *Handbook of Development Economics*, Vol. 4. Amsterdam: Elsevier Publishing Co.

Schultz, T.P., 2008b: Beyond Fertility Reduction, Can Family Planning Programs Promote Development? Evidence from a Long-Term Social Experiment – 1977–1996, Paper presented at the AEA meeting in New Orleans, 3–5 January 2008

Swain, R.B., and F.Y.Wallentin, 2007: Does Microfinance Empower Women? Evidence from Self Help Groups in India, Upsala, Sweden: Upsala University, Department of Economics Working Paper 24

Tansel, A., 1997: Schooling Attainment, Parental Education and Gender in Cote d'Ivoire and Ghana, *Economic Development and Cultural Change* 45(4): 825–856

Tansel, A., 2002: Determinants of School Attainment of Boys and Girls in Turkey: Individual, Household and Community Factors, *Economics of Education Review* 21: 455–470

PART II
Ranking the opportunities

Expert Panel Ranking

JAGDISH N. BHAGWATI,
FRANÇOIS BOURGUIGNON, FINN E. KYDLAND, ROBERT
MUNDELL, DOUGLASS C. NORTH, THOMAS SCHELLING,
VERNON L. SMITH,
NANCY L. STOKEY

The Goal of the Project

The goal of Copenhagen Consensus 2008 project was to set priorities among a series of proposals for confronting ten great global challenges: Air pollution, Conflicts, Diseases, Education, Global Warming, Malnutrition and Hunger, Sanitation and Water, Subsidies and Trade Barriers, Terrorism, and Women and Development.

Ranking the Proposals

A Panel of economic experts, comprising eight of the world's most distinguished economists, was invited to consider these issues. The Panel members were: Jagdish N. Bhagwati of Columbia University, François Bourguignon of Paris School of Economics and former World Bank chief economist, Finn E. Kydland of University of California, Santa Barbara (Nobel laureate), Robert Mundell of Columbia University in New York (Nobel laureate), Douglass C. North of Washington University in St. Louis (Nobel laureate), Thomas C. Schelling of University of Maryland (Nobel laureate), Vernon L. Smith of Chapman University (Nobel laureate), and Nancy L. Stokey of University of Chicago.

The Panel was asked to address the ten challenge areas and to answer the question: "What would be the best ways of advancing global welfare, and particularly the welfare of the developing countries, illustrated by supposing that an additional $75 billion of resources were at their disposal over a four-year initial period?"

Ten Challenge papers, commissioned from acknowledged authorities in each area of policy (chapters 1–10 in this volume), set out more than thirty proposals for the Panel's consideration. During the week-long conference, the Panel examined these proposals in detail. Each paper was discussed at length with its principal author and with two other specialists who had been commissioned to write critical appraisals, and then the experts met in private session. Based on the costs and benefits of the solutions, the Panel ranked thirty proposals, in descending order of desirability.

Final Overall Ranking

	Solution	Challenge
1	Micronutrient supplements for children (vitamin A and zinc)	Malnutrition
2	The Doha development agenda	Trade
3	Micronutrient fortification (iron and salt iodization)	Malnutrition
4	Expanded immunization coverage for children	Diseases
5	Biofortification	Malnutrition
6	De-worming and other nutrition programs at school	Malnutrition & Education
7	Lowering the price of schooling	Education
8	Increase and improve girls' schooling	Women
9	Community-based nutrition promotion	Malnutrition
10	Provide support for women's reproductive role	Women
11	Heart attack acute management	Diseases
12	Malaria prevention and treatment	Diseases

	Solution	Challenge
13	Tuberculosis case finding and treatment	Diseases
14	R&D in low-carbon energy technologies	Global Warming
15	Bio-sand filters for household water treatment	Water
16	Rural water supply	Water
17	Conditional cash transfers	Education
18	Peace-keeping in post-conflict situations	Conflicts
19	HIV/AIDS combination prevention	Diseases
20	Total sanitation campaign	Water
21	Improving surgical capacity at district hospital level	Diseases
22	Microfinance	Women
23	Improved stove intervention	Air Pollution
24	Large, multi-purpose dam in Africa	Water
25	Inspection and maintenance of diesel vehicles	Air Pollution
26	Low-sulfur diesel for urban road vehicles	Air Pollution
27	Diesel vehicle particulate control technology	Air Pollution
28	Tobacco tax	Diseases
29	R&D and mitigation	Global Warming
30	Mitigation only	Global Warming

In ordering the proposals, the Panel was guided predominantly by consideration of economic costs and benefits. The Panel acknowledged the difficulties that cost-benefit analysis (CBA) must overcome, both in principle and as a practical matter, but agreed that the cost-benefit approach was an indispensable organizing method. In setting priorities, the Panel took account of the strengths and weaknesses of the specific cost-benefit appraisals under review, and gave weight both to the institutional preconditions for success and to the demands of ethical or humanitarian urgency. As a general matter, the Panel noted that higher standards of governance and improvements in the institutions required to support development in the world's poor countries were of paramount importance.

For some of the proposals, the panel found that information was too sparse to allow a judgment to be made. These proposals, some of which may prove after further study to be valuable, were therefore excluded from the ranking.

Each expert assigned his or her own ranking to the proposals. The Panel's ranking was calculated by taking the median of individual rankings. The Panel jointly endorses the median ordering shown above as representing their agreed view.

Malnutrition and Hunger

The Expert Panel examined the following solutions to this challenge: micronutrient supplementation (Vitamin A and zinc), micronutrient fortification (iron and salt iodization), biofortification (agricultural improvements through R&D), de-worming (which also improves education), and nutritional education campaigns. The Panel ranked solutions to this challenge very highly, because of the exceptionally high ratio of benefits to costs. Micronutrient supplements were ranked at 1 and fortification was ranked at 3, with tremendously high benefits compared to costs; biofortification was ranked at 5.

Trade and Subsidies

In this area, the Expert Panel considered the following solutions: a high-quality outcome to the Doha international trade round; and increasing the rate of migration to boost the labor force in high-income countries. In the case of trade reform, lives are not directly and immediately at risk, and the biggest barrier is political, not financial. However, as a group, the Expert Panel concluded that a comprehensive conclusion to the Doha development agenda would yield such exceptionally large benefits, in relation to comparatively modest adjustment costs, that this solution was ranked at 2.

Diseases

Under this topic, the Expert Panel examined solutions to the challenge of both communicable and non-communicable disease. The solutions examined were: fighting tuberculosis through drugs and improved case identification; making cheap drugs that treat acute heart disease available to developing countries; combining a malaria prevention package (mosquito nets, DDT spray, etc.) with subsidies on new treatments; expanding immunization and micronutrient coverage for children in developing nations; implementing tobacco taxes in developing nations; a multiple-intervention approach to preventing and treating HIV/AIDS; and making investments in hospitals. Several disease solutions were ranked very highly by the Expert Panel, where the benefits significantly exceeded the costs. These options included expanded immunization coverage for children (ranked at 4); heart attack acute management (ranked at 11); malaria prevention and treatment (ranked at 12); and tuberculosis case finding and treatment (ranked at 13).

Education

The research the Expert Panel considered focused on targeting children who had already attended some school and then dropped out. The solutions examined were: providing nutritional supplements or treatments for intestinal parasites to raise school attendance and increase physical and mental capacity; reducing the cost of schooling; and conditional cash transfers (where parents are paid in exchange for sending their children to school regularly). The first of these solutions was combined with a proposed solution from the Diseases Challenge paper, because both largely dealt with de-worming and its benefits. This combined solution was ranked at 6. Lowering the price of schooling was ranked at 7, with an investment of $5.4 billion yearly for an added three years of schooling covering in total 12.6 million elementary school dropouts.

Women and Development

Under this heading, the Expert Panel considered measures to increase and improve girls' schooling; providing support for women's reproductive role; microfinance to poor women borrowers; and affirmative action. Measures to improve and increase girls' schooling, through conditional cash transfers to mothers, was ranked at 8 by the Panel, providing excellent benefits to costs; support for women's reproductive role was ranked at 10.

Climate Change

The Expert Panel considered four solutions in this area: investing only in mitigation; investing in mitigation and R&D into low-carbon energy technology; investing only in R&D into low-carbon energy technology; and investing in a combination of mitigation, R&D, and adaptation. Mitigation only and a combination of mitigation and R&D were given the lowest two rankings by the Expert Panel (at 29 and 30, respectively), due to their very poor benefit-cost ratio (BCR). The option including adaptation was discarded, as adaptation is essentially included in nearly every other option presented to the Copenhagen Consensus. An investment in R&D in low-carbon energy technologies was ranked at 14 by the Panel.

Sanitation and Water

Under this heading, the Expert Panel considered interventions that would improve access to clean drinking water and/or sanitation. The solutions they considered were: setting up a rural water supply program providing poor communities in Africa with deep boreholes and public hand pumps; developing campaigns that raise awareness of disease transmission, health costs, and the social benefits of sanitation; ensuring that affected communities have access to technology to remove contaminants in raw water supplies; and building reservoirs in some parts of Africa, such as the sparsely inhabited Blue Nile Gorge in Ethiopia. The Expert Panel considered that bio-sand filters and the rural water supply program offered some promising benefits as intermediate solutions to this problem, and ranked them at 15 and 16, respectively.

Conflicts

The main focus of the research that the Expert Panel examined was on reducing the risk of conflict re-emerging in a country after civil war. It used the provision of aid as a benchmark solution, and then suggested the following: linking aid to limits on military spending; sending significant military forces into nations emerging from conflict to reduce the risk of a relapse into violence; and providing (and having the ability to back up) a promise that a military force would intervene when a democratically elected government was threatened by violence. The Expert Panel found that peace-keeping forces in post-conflict situations could provide fair benefits for the cost, and ranked the solution at 18.

Air Pollution

The Expert Panel examined research that explored solutions to both indoor and outdoor air pollution. The solutions considered were: providing a chimneyless rocket stove to those using unhealthy, old-fashioned stoves; switching to low- and ultra-low sulfur vehicle fuels (diesel and gasoline) for urban vehicles; retrofitting diesel-fueled buses and delivery trucks with filters that reduce urban pollution and its health effects; and introducing exhaust emission limits for diesel vehicles and checking tailpipe emissions in a bid to curb pollution. The solution to indoor pollution was ranked at 23, higher than the outdoor air pollution solutions (ranked at 25 and 26, respectively), whose very high costs outweighed the benefits in a developing nation context.

Terrorism

The Expert Panel chose not to include any of the proposed solutions to the challenge of terrorism in the overall ranking. Though the Challenge paper presented innovative and new work on the economic costs and benefit of terror prevention, the Panel found that there was not sufficient evidence regarding the proposed options.

Solution	Yearly cost (million USD)
1 Micronutrient supplements for children (vitamin A and zinc)	60
2 The Doha development agenda	0
3 Micronutrient fortification (iron and salt iodization)	286
4 Expanded immunization coverage for children	1,000
5 Biofortification	60
6 De-worming and other nutrition programs at school	27
7 Lowering the price of schooling	5,400
8 Increase and improve girls' schooling	6,000
9 Community-based nutrition promotion	798
10 Provide support for women's reproductive role	4,000
11 Heart attack acute management	200
12 Malaria prevention and treatment	500
13 Tuberculosis case finding and treatment	419
Total	18,750

Note: All costs are based on the Challenge paper authors' estimates. In the case of Solution 13 (Tuberculosis case finding and treatment), the author estimates the total costs of the intervention to be $1 billion. However, owing to the annual budgetary restriction of $18.75 billion, only $419 million can be allocated.

How to spend $75 billion over four years

When the budgetary constraints of the Copenhagen Consensus framework are applied to the Expert Panel's prioritized list, money can be allocated to thirteen of the solutions. The yearly budget is $18.75 billion (4 years x $18.75 billion = $75 billion), and provides for a broad range of investments.

Individual Rankings

JAGDISH N. BHAGWATI

I would like to explain why I put the Doha development agenda into the ranking and ranked it at 1. First, the passage of Doha does require resources: e.g. for financing "aid for trade" programs such as adjustment assistance programs in developing countries (without which they cannot liberalize politically). Doha already delivers sufficient stimulus in regard to gains from trade liberalization (even though they could have been larger), for the social returns relative to the cost of aid to be very high, compared to all the other alternatives before us.

I did not rank the environmental R&D expenditure so highly because the funds necessary to make any impact are far greater than those we were dealing with, and I have argued in the *Financial Times* for a substantial Superfund to be set up to finance such R&D and other measures aimed at the victims of global warming. The other rankings are somewhat weak, in my view, and could have been slightly adjusted after even more debate.

Ranking the Opportunities:
Jagdish N. Bhagwati

1	The Doha development agenda
2	De-worming and other nutrition programs at school
3	Lowering the price of schooling
4	Increase and improve girls' schooling
5	Micronutrient supplements for children (vitamin A and zinc)
6	Micronutrient fortification (iron and salt iodization)
7	Improved stove intervention
8	Improving surgical capacity at district hospital level
9	Expanded immunization coverage for children
10	Large, multi-purpose dam in Africa
11	Community-based nutrition promotion
12	Peace-keeping in post-conflict situations
13	Heart attack acute management
14	Malaria prevention and treatment
15	Tuberculosis case finding and treatment
16	Low-sulfur diesel for urban road vehicles
17	Inspection and maintenance of diesel vehicles
18	Diesel vehicle particulate control technology
19	Affirmative action
20	Provide support for women's reproductive role
21	Biofortification

22	Conditional cash transfers
23	Package of trade and migration reform
24	Migration reform
25	R&D in low-carbon energy technologies
26	Rich nations drop barriers to poor nations
27	HIV/AIDS combination prevention
28	Mitigation only
29	Package of adaptation, R&D and mitigation
30	R&D and mitigation
31	Tobacco tax
32	Removing intra-American trade barriers
33	Microfinance

FRANÇOIS BOURGIGNON

One of the difficulties faced by the experts of the Copenhagen Consensus committee was how to rank "development solutions" which were sometimes hardly comparable. The way to calculate the benefit-cost ratio (BCR) of micro-oriented interventions such as providing micronutrients to children, or providing improved stoves to poor families in order to reduce indoor air pollution, is fairly clear. Data to estimate the precise costs and benefits of these interventions may be hard to gather, but the methodology is conceptually simple. Things are less straightforward when dealing with more macroeconomic interventions such as liberalizing trade, as in the Doha agenda, or dealing with global warming. With these interventions, there is no clear spending involved; instead, costs correspond to missed income opportunities in the future, as compared to the status quo, whereas benefits are more difficult to evaluate and to allocate across individuals. The order of magnitude of the two types of interventions is also quite different. Several micro-oriented interventions undertaken at the global level would fit the $18.75 billion virtual annual budget of the Copenhagen Consensus. But a more macro-intervention, such as mitigation or R&D policies to reduce global warming risks, would easily absorb the whole Copenhagen Consensus budget every year during the twenty-first century. This difficulty in comparing these two kinds of intervention means that any ranking that includes both must be made with care. Whereas two interventions of the micro-type may be ranked without too much ambiguity, the same does not seem to be true for two interventions of the macro-type, and a fortiori when comparing micro and macro interventions.

Climate Change (Chapter 5)

Having said this, I have personally ranked global warming interventions at the top of my list (at 1 and 2). This is because of my strong feeling about the urgency of action in this area. It is true that, using the discount rates (3–5 percent per annum) recommended by the Copenhagen Consensus team, the estimated BCRs of mitigation, adaptation, and R&D in the field of global warming are not that impressive (i.e. between 2 and 3). At the same time, however, a major issue in the analysis of anti-global warming policies is precisely that of the discount rate. The view that deaths caused by some dramatic natural disaster, itself due to global warming a century from now, are 50 or 100 times less important than deaths occurring today (as implied by a 3–5 percent discount rate) is shocking, and suggests that reference to an implicit "market" discount rate may be irrelevant with a very distant time horizon. The discount rate also has a very strong impact on the size of benefits to be expected from measures aimed at controlling global warming. The BCRs of such interventions would be larger by an order of magnitude with lower discount rates – a rate of 0.1 percent is used in the Stern Review. Note also that the issue behind the value of the discount rate is not only ethical or philosophical. As shown by Weitzman, a discount rate much lower than observed "market" rates may be justified by taking into account the uncertainty of future outcomes of global warming and the non-zero probability of truly catastrophic events.

A last point contributes to a dramatic under-evaluation of the damage of global warming. It has to do with the fact that the poorest regions of the world are most likely to be hit much harder by climate change, with very few resources to adapt to that change; the impact on their welfare will be very great. If the marginal welfare loss of poor people matters more than that of the rest of the global population, the standard evaluation of climate change damage at the global level is largely under-estimated.

Among the global warming challenges, I ranked the "mitigation only" option (at 25) well below the two options involving R&D-related spending. Technological innovation is clearly key here, and the incentives provided by "mitigation only" interventions may not be enough to quickly generate a major break-through.

Malnutrition (Chapter 6)

The benefits of any intervention that would permit improved malnutrition are measured rather precisely through experimentation. They are enormous in comparison with the costs of some interventions, in both absolute and relative terms – i.e. BCRs. Benefits consist mostly of saved lives or DALYs and increases in economic performances.

From my point of view, the "De-worming and other nutrition programs at school" (ranked at 3) intervention belongs as much to nutrition as to education interventions. The cost of these measures is extremely low and leads to BCRs that are really huge – i.e. above 100. Moreover, it is important to stress that experimentation with these interventions has been conducted in a very rigorous way so that estimates of BCRs can be considered to be reasonably precise.

The same kind of argument applies to "Micronutrient supplements for children (Vitamin A and zinc)" and "Micronutrient fortification (iron and salt iodization)" (ranked at 4 and 5). These are low (absolute) cost interventions – $60 and $286 million at the global level, respectively – with high benefits in both DALYs and economic performances. For the lowest evaluation of a DALY ($1,000), BCRs are between 10 and 30, depending on the kind of intervention and the discount rate being used. Not undertaking such programs where they can work would be both extremely bad economics and essentially unethical. "Biofortification" yields slightly less favorable results (ranked at 9).

Programs of "Community-based nutrition promotion" could compare with the previous interventions. However, there is much less precision in evaluating the impact of a promotion campaign as compared with experimenting with specific treatments. I ranked that option below the other interventions in malnutrition (at 14).

Education (Chapter 4)

Accumulation and effective use of human capital includes better nutrition and better and broader school coverage. I ranked some of the educational interventions just after nutrition programs, although they sometimes have comparable BCRs. I ranked "Conditional cash transfer" above "Increase and improve girls' schooling" (at 6 and 7, respectively), as the second is essentially a conditional cash transfer targeted at a specific population – as, for instance, in Bangladesh. BCRs for these interventions are high and, from my point of view, under-estimated because they ignore the impact of cash transfers on present poverty and nutrition in the families that receive the transfer, and also the impact of more education on governance (and indirectly on growth), in a given country. At the same time, these interventions are definitely more expensive – in terms of total cost – than those geared at improving nutrition.

I ranked the "Lowering the price of schooling" intervention behind or at the same level as the two previous ones (at 8). All these interventions are comparable as they include a compensation for the opportunity cost of schooling for parents and therefore lower the cost of schooling. Note, however, that the elasticity of schooling with respect to schooling costs is very imperfectly known as it relies on only a few experiences. Also, some important dimensions are often ignored in evaluating such policies. This is the case in particular with the quality of schooling and cognitive achievements of students. The Ugandan experience of making primary schooling free had an immediate impact on school enrollment (a doubling), but the potential effect on school quality and educational achievements has not been evaluated.

Disease (Chapter 3)

As with malnutrition, there are relatively low-cost interventions that can save a large number of lives. Both treatments and costs are well defined, whereas results are generally based on experimentation that may not always be wide enough to grant great precision. The three interventions dealing with specific diseases: "Expanded immunization coverage for children," "Malaria prevention and treatment," "Tuberculosis case finding and treatment" all lead to BCRs equal to 20 or more. They are comparable in terms of DALYs saved. In all cases, $1 billion permits us to avert 1 million deaths annually, and to save 15–30 million DALYs. The relative imprecision of existing analyses, as well as some possible arbitrariness in the calculation of DALYs depending on the age of the potential victim of a disease – the issue of the cost of under-five vs. adult death – does not permit a clear ranking of these interventions, which I actually ranked at 10, 11, and 12, respectively. They rank high among all interventions analyzed by the committee, although the issue of the capacity required from local health systems is generally not well taken into account.

I included "Provide support for women's reproductive role" in these health-related interventions (at 13) because most of the benefits usually taken into account when evaluating these policies refer to the health of the women and their children. Yet, there also are non-health benefits arising from this type of intervention, such as longer schooling for young girls, higher labor force participation, or more care given to existing children. BCRs based on health benefits are around 10. They would probably be much higher if those non-health benefits were taken into account, but no precise estimate is available.

Compared to those previously discussed, other interventions ("Heart attack acute management," "Improving surgical capacity at district health level") belonging to the Disease challenge seem to have limited effects, or effects that benefited broader segments of the population than only poor people. They are accordingly ranked at a lower level (at 17 and 20, respectively). It must be recognized, however, that there is probably more uncertainty about their costs and their impact than for better-known treatments. Note also that the "Tobacco tax" raises some conceptual issues for the measurement of the BCR. How should the cost be measured? Should it be the cost of the tax for the consumers? But, then, what should be done with the proceeds of the tax? Or should it be the distortion and deadweight loss created by the tax? But, then, how should it be measured? Presumably, the BCR would be much higher in the second case. Conceptual ambiguity in this case made me rank that intervention at a low level (at 29).

Peace-Keeping (Chapter 2)

This is an original intervention with potentially huge benefits. Indeed, it is now well known that conflicts (past, present, and latent) are one of the most negative factors for development. At the same time, peace-keeping operations are expensive and are not always successful. Both the cost and the impact of this kind of intervention are variable and can be estimated only in a very imprecise way. Given our knowledge in the area of conflicts and development, a standard BCR calculation has to be based on rather strong assumptions and can be indicative only of some kind of "average" peace-keeping intervention. Experts mention BCRs around 10:1, which is a high number, but incorporates assumptions that may be debatable. Yet, the idea seemed original enough and focused on a major cause for the slow development of part of the world. Accordingly, I ranked it at the middle of the list (at 15).

Water and Sanitation (Chapter 7)

Water and sanitation is part of a Millennium Development Goal, which may be taken as broadly complementary with those dealing with health, education, and nutrition. Yet, a thorough analysis of the cost and benefits of the water and sanitation interventions seems to indicate that BCRs are lower than with other interventions. The experts in charge of that analysis took the precaution of accounting for the wide variety of project contexts and the resulting dispersion of BCRs. (This is an excellent initiative, which should be applied more systematically.) They estimate that around 10 per cent of basic "access to water" projects have a BCR above 5:1, but the mean of the whole distribution in only 3:1. My ranking (at 16) of these "Rural water supply" interventions reflects the mean rather than the top of the distribution, which seems natural for comparing them with the other interventions. However, there clearly are circumstances where the development contribution of water projects may be much higher. Other interventions under the water and sanitation heading ("Bio-sand filters for household water treatment," "Total sanitation campaign," "Large, multi-purpose dam in Africa") are ranked at the same level (at 18, 19, 22, respectively).

Microfinance (Chapter 10)

Among the various types of interventions reviewed for the Copenhagen Consensus 2008 process, microfinance was considered, as part of the solutions to address the issue of the role of women in development. (Presumably, microfinance operations may also target men.) It follows that the analysis made of microfinance for women gives only a partial view of what can be achieved. A further restriction in the expert analysis conducted for the Copenhagen Consensus is the fact that it essentially relies on Bangladeshi experience (Grameen Bank and BRAC). How these experiences would work in other contexts is therefore unclear. It is similarly unclear whether extending microfinance beyond its present limits in Bangladesh would yield the same results as those observed in the past because it would necessarily have to address new groups of borrowers. With all these restrictions, the estimated BCR of women-targeted microfinance operations in Bangladesh is only slightly larger than 2:1 when it is assumed that microfinance has a low impact on DALYs, which seems to me the most reasonable assumption.

Although I am not sure those figures are precise enough to make a judgment, they explain why I ranked microfinance at a relatively low level (at 23).

Air Pollution (Chapter 1)

Indoor air pollution from using cooking fuels is known to cause serious health damage in many poor countries, particularly in SSA. A priori, the "Improved stove intervention" which reduces the quantity of solid fuels being used, and therefore the quantity of pollution, seems attractive. It is a low-cost intervention in both absolute and per capita terms. However, benefits seem to be very imprecisely estimated because of the lack of experimentation. In effect, experimentation itself is difficult to conduct since a considerable period of trials would be necessary to be able to calculate the actual impact of indoor air pollution on health. As a result, there is considerable divergence among the available estimates of BCRs coming from different studies. It is this uncertainty rather than the characteristics of this intervention that led me to rank it at a low level (at 24). The same argument applies still more strongly to interventions dealing with outdoor air pollution.

The Doha Development Agenda (Chapter 8)

I have deliberately not ranked the trade liberalization or Doha development trade agenda. Essentially, I find it very difficult to compare such an intervention with the others in the list because both the costs and the benefits seem difficult to measure. Of course, one can always say that the cost of this measure is essentially nil since it consists of governments reducing tariffs and agricultural subsidies by the stroke of a pen. As efficiency

gains are being obtained from such a measure, the overall BCR would simply be infinite!

Things are not that simple, however. Some countries are bound to gain with the measures considered in the Doha round and others are bound to lose – for instance, the net food importers facing higher international prices of agricultural commodities. In the absence of redistribution instruments that would compensate the losers and distribute equitably the overall gain, some correction should be made in the measurement of the overall benefit – or, equivalently, a cost in terms of social welfare should be introduced in the evaluation of the reform. The same applies to distributional effects within countries. Trade liberalization is highly desirable: It is essential that all efforts be made for an agreement to be obtained on the Doha agenda. I fully share the view that this should be a priority for the international development community, and I would tend to rank it at the top of the list. I preferred to handle it separately, however, because of the total lack of comparability with other interventions. The same line of argument would apply to all interventions that essentially rely on international agreements aimed at facilitating the development of the poorer nations, such as greater international cooperation or making foreign policies in developed countries more development-oriented.

Ranking the Opportunities: François Bourgignon

1	R&D and mitigation
2	R&D in low-carbon energy technologies
3	De-worming and other nutrition programs at school
4	Micronutrient supplements for children (vitamin A and zinc)
5	Micronutrient fortification (iron and salt iodization)
6	Conditional cash transfers
7	Increase and improve girls' schooling
8	Lowering the price of schooling
9	Biofortification
10	Expanded immunization coverage for children
11	Malaria prevention and treatment

12	Tuberculosis case finding and treatment
13	Provide support for women's reproductive role
14	Community-based nutrition promotion
15	Peace-keeping in post-conflict situations
16	Rural water supply
17	Heart attack acute management
18	Bio-sand filters for household water treatment
19	Total sanitation campaign
20	Improving surgical capacity at district hospital level
21	HIV/AIDS combination prevention
22	Large, multi-purpose dam in Africa
23	Microfinance
24	Improved stove intervention
25	Mitigation only
26	Diesel vehicle particulate control technology
27	Inspection and maintenance of diesel vehicles
28	Low-sulfur diesel for urban road vehicles
29	Tobacco tax
30	Target nations changing foreign policies
31	Greater international cooperation
32	Increased proactive response
33	Business as usual
34	Augmented defensive measures

FINN E. KYDLAND

I was not a member of the Copenhagen Consensus 2004 panel, but did participate on the panel in a similar event, the Consulta de San José in Costa Rica in October 2007, which focused on only Latin America. It is interesting to compare the solutions considered in the two events, along with their ultimate rankings. Although parts of Latin America are in dire need of welfare-improving solutions, clearly many of the areas considered were those of nations much further along in their development than those in, say, SSA and in parts of Asia. This characteristic is reflected in the nature of some of the highest-ranking solutions.

In San José, improving fiscal rules was seen as a great opportunity to enhance the budget process within many countries in Latin America and to realign incentives in ways that might potentially increase nations' growth rates substantially. This solution was ranked at 2. Ranked at 3 on the panel's list was increased investment in infrastructure, including maintenance. Ranked at 4 was the idea of establishing independent policy and program evaluation agencies. An independent (public or private), and possibly international, agency should provide evaluation or monitor government programs and policies over time. Between nations, the agencies should share information on effective policies.

In contrast, in the Copenhagen Consensus 2008 process, the high-ranking solutions reflected the needs of extremely poor nations (some with per capita incomes of perhaps one-fiftieth, or less, of those of the richest nations), and it may not always be so obvious what the long-term benefits of these solutions would be for the nation as a whole. Still, the needs were judged by the experts to be so profound – and, in some cases, the costs so low – that the BCRs were estimated to be extremely high, placing these solutions at or near the top of our rankings. We concluded that there would be extraordinarily high benefits from providing micronutrients – particularly vitamin A and zinc – to undernourished children in South Asia and SSA (ranked at 2). These measures help prevent neonatal death. The cost is tiny: Reaching 80 percent of the 140 million or so undernourished children in the world would require a commitment of around $60 million annually, and the economic gains would eventually clear $1 billion a year. Similarly, providing iron and iodized salt is another top investment (ranked at 4). Fortifying products with iron costs as little as 12 cents per person per year. We know that iron deficiency leads to stunting and cognitive and developmental problems. For $286 million we could get iodized salt and fortified basic food items to 80 percent of those in the worst-affected areas. The benefits are estimated to be somewhere around nine times higher than the costs.

Among other top-ranked solutions in the health area were interventions such as de-worming and other nutritional programs in school, which would allow children to be better nourished (at 3), and expanded immunization coverage for children (at 5). One can make a case that these solutions promote education as well, making the children healthier and better fit to learn. Moreover, alleviating these health problems may free up time for the parents, especially for the mothers, to potentially engage in gainful pursuits. I suppose because of my weight on this potential, my rankings of both of these proposals ended up three to four places above the Expert Panel's overall rankings. In this respect, of course, focusing on direct measures to further education is likely to be more effective strictly from that perspective. For that reason, after the health-related solutions came solutions such as lowering the price of schooling (ranked at 7), and increasing and improving girls' schooling by paying mothers to send their children to school (ranked at 6).

I have already mentioned some health solutions that must be regarded as rather short-run in nature. They are "short-run" in the sense that if we were to return five years after a country had implemented them, the chances are that the needs in the next cohort of children would be almost as great. Some solutions have benefits in terms of raising, primarily through better education, the nation's stock of human capital, with sizeable potential benefits in the longer run. A solution that really emphasizes the long run is the removal of trade barriers (ranked 1 by me, 2 overall). Even if one were to factor in the costs to those who may lose in the short run (say, particular industries or workers with certain skills), a large and convincing body of theoretical and empirical economics, as summarized to the Panel by the experts, supports the idea that the long-run benefits to the nation as a whole can be very large. Unless the economies of developing nations grow, they will still be mired in the same problems of poverty five or ten years down the road. By reducing trade barriers, income per capita will grow, enabling the currently poor countries to take care of some of these other problems, such as health and education, for themselves. Perhaps the ultimate long-run worry is the issue of global warming.

It may surprise some that two solution proposals to combat global warming ended up near the bottom of our ranking list (at 21 and 25, respectively). These proposals were found by the experts to be simply too expensive in relation to their benefits. The proposal in this vein that ended up reasonably high (ranked at 11 on my list, 14 overall) was R&D in low-carbon energy technologies to combat global warming. I would like to emphasize that any policies to encourage a move in that direction have to make sense in terms of the incentives they provide. My fellow Nobel laureate at University of California at Santa Barbara, Walter Kohn, who worries a lot about the speed of technological progress in producing solar panels and about their eventual adoption, once recounted to me the following: Some time ago, the government decided to provide temporary subsidies for installing such panels. This policy had the predictable result (to an economist with some understanding of dynamics, at least) of creating shortages of solar panels at the same time that, because of the temporary nature of the subsidies, producers had no additional incentive to increase the pace of their efforts to advance technology and thus reduce the cost of the panels.

Ranking the Opportunities: Finn E. Kydland

1	The Doha development agenda
2	Micronutrient supplements for children (vitamin A and zinc)
3	De-worming and other nutrition programs at school
4	Micronutrient fortification (iron and salt iodization)
5	Expanded immunization coverage for children
6	Increase and improve girls' schooling
7	Lowering the price of schooling
8	Malaria prevention and treatment
9	Peace-keeping in post-conflict situations
10	Provide support for women's reproductive role
11	R&D in low-carbon energy technologies

12	Heart attack acute management
13	Community-based nutrition promotion
14	Biofortification
15	Tuberculosis case finding and treatment
16	Rural water supply
17	Bio-sand filters for household water treatment
18	HIV/AIDS combination prevention
19	Total sanitation campaign
20	Conditional cash transfers
21	R&D and mitigation
22	Microfinance
23	Improving surgical capacity at district hospital level
24	Improved stove intervention
25	Mitigation only
26	Greater international cooperation
27	Tobacco tax

ROBERT MUNDELL

Ranking the Opportunities: Robert Mundell

1	Rural water supply
2	Micronutrient supplements for children (vitamin A and zinc)
3	Micronutrient fortification (iron and salt iodization)
4	Biofortification
5	Tuberculosis case finding and treatment
6	Expanded immunization coverage for children
7	Malaria prevention and treatment
8	Increase and improve girls' schooling
9	Community-based nutrition promotion
10	De-worming and other nutrition programs at school
11	Total sanitation campaign
12	Provide support for women's reproductive role
13	HIV/AIDS combination prevention
14	Lowering the price of schooling
15	R&D in low-carbon energy technologies
16	Bio-sand filters for household water treatment
17	The Doha development agenda
18	Low-sulfur diesel for urban road vehicles

19	Inspection and maintenance of diesel vehicles
20	Peace-keeping in post-conflict situations
21	Improved stove intervention
22	Microfinance
23	Heart attack acute management
24	Improving surgical capacity at district hospital level
25	Removing intra-American trade barriers
26	Greater international cooperation
27	R&D and mitigation
28	Conditional cash transfers
29	Mitigation only

DOUGLASS C. NORTH

Because issues that involve institutional change have very uncertain cost estimates, I have tended to rank higher issues that did not entail institutional change but simply involved expenditure of money. We simply do not know enough about the costs of political change to make sensible cost estimates that can be compared with other kinds of costs. Also some of the issues, such as malaria, have become so "popular" that I did not believe they needed any push from us.

Ranking the Opportunities: Douglass C. North

1	Micronutrient supplements for children (vitamin A and zinc)
2	Micronutrient fortification (iron and salt iodization)
3	Rural water supply
4	Bio-sand filters for household water treatment
5	Total sanitation campaign
6	Biofortification
7	De-worming and other nutrition programs at school
8	Community-based nutrition promotion
9	Expanded immunization coverage for children
10	Tuberculosis case finding and treatment
11	HIV/AIDS combination prevention
12	Heart attack acute management

13	R&D in low-carbon energy technologies
14	Microfinance
15	Provide support for women's reproductive role
16	Increase and improve girls' schooling
17	Lowering the price of schooling
18	Conditional cash transfers
19	Improved stove intervention
20	Improving surgical capacity at district hospital level
21	Malaria prevention and treatment
22	Diesel vehicle particulate control technology
23	Low-sulfur diesel for urban road vehicles
24	Inspection and maintenance of diesel vehicles
25	Peace-keeping in post-conflict situations
26	Tobacco tax
27	Large, multipurpose dam in Africa
28	R&D and mitigation
29	Mitigation only
30	Affirmative action

THOMAS C. SCHELLING

The strongest impression I bring from the Copenhagen Consensus 2008 process is of the complementarity among some of the most effective programs. The provision of nutrients – vitamin A, iodine, iron, zinc, and a few others – has not only powerful endorsement under the heading of "nutrition," where its ratio of benefits to costs is spectacular. It is almost equally potent in averting the most lethal and morbid effects of the vector-borne or water-borne diseases. It is also a potent influence on education: Undernourished children do not benefit from schooling as better-fed children do. Closely related is the effect of intestinal worms on health, even education; worms can be classed as attacks on nutrition or as illness itself. The delivery of nutrients, of anti-worm pills, or vaccines should be viewed as a composite; a common infrastructure should underpin them all. Their costs need not be additive; their benefits should be. And perhaps educational institutions should be recognized as a crucial part of the infrastructure for delivery of vaccines and anti-worm pills, perhaps even nutrients.

Dealing with nutrition, disease, and education as separate issues or programs misses this synergy. It misses the combined benefits and neglects the potential common costs. And it dilutes the argument for a public health infrastructure that includes both nutrition and disease but also the school system. If there is a third Copenhagen Consensus, I recommend that a public health infrastructure, combining these related health effects, be consolidated into a single program and its benefits be summed and its costs estimated but not separately summed, and schools should be part of that infrastructure. This is my basis for putting nutrients, vaccines, worm pills, and other highly cost-effective programs at the very top of the list (ranked at 1–4). My judgment is not based only on their separate benefits and costs but what those benefits will be, in relation to costs, when the programs are appropriately consolidated into a public-health delivery system

I emphasize two features of this exercise. The main one is that this is supposed to be a budget process: How to distribute a modest increment in some kind of internationally sponsored foreign aid to the program areas where an infusion of money can make a significant difference. Two of the proposed programs to which I attach great significance, global warming and free trade, simply do not lend themselves to this issue of additional aid money. Global warming could, of course, use more funds for R&D; current R&D programs for energy are disgracefully meager in both Europe and the USA; but it would have to be part of a determined effort to take carbon emissions seriously, and there is no sign that such a decision or such decisions have been made. And I see no way that a modest injection of money might clear the way for freer trade.

This Copenhagen Consensus process is primarily a public relations game. The purpose is, or should be, to identify and promote, with careful analysis, possibilities in relation to poverty and its ramifications that have not received the identification and attention that their benefits in relation to costs merit. In 2004 we felt that HIV/AIDS, especially in Africa and other poor countries, was an enormous challenge not being properly met; in 2008, HIV/AIDS appeared to be an enormous challenge that was being met, on a scale that did not need another push from our Consensus. Free trade, I believe, receives all the attention it can absorb, and nothing our Consensus says can have any impact.

I believe the influence of any further Copenhagen Consensus will depend on the identification of opportunities to further the development of health and productivity in poor countries that have not been sufficiently identified and appreciated. I believe we have done this with nutrition, worms, vaccines, etc. I thought we did it with some clean-water programs in 2004. With the assumption of very limited resources, as in 2008, we cannot afford to dilute our recommendations with issues that have adequate momentum, or issues that a little money cannot advance.

Ranking the Opportunities: Thomas C. Schelling

1	Micronutrient supplements for children (vitamin A and zinc)
2	Micronutrient fortification (iron and salt iodization)
3	De-worming and other nutrition programs at school
4	Community-based nutrition promotion
5	Expanded immunization coverage for children
6	Heart attack acute management
7	Biofortification
8	Bio-sand filters for household water treatment
9	Provide support for women's reproductive role
10	Lowering the price of schooling
11	Conditional cash transfers
12	Increase and improve girls' schooling
13	R&D in low-carbon energy technologies
14	Tuberculosis case finding and treatment
15	Malaria prevention and treatment
16	Improving surgical capacity at district hospital level
17	Rural water supply
18	Total sanitation campaign

19	HIV/AIDS combination prevention
20	Microfinance
21	Improved stove intervention
22	Peace-keeping in post-conflict situations

VERNON L. SMITH

Introduction

All forms of human socio-economic betterment depend upon wealth created by the growth of knowledge and skill specialization, which depends vitally on the scope of market development. These principles have informed my judgment in evaluating the Copenhagen Consensus world issues and the solutions offered. In this reckoning, policies that appear most likely to promote freedom, self-development, improve health, and expand the individual's capacity to produce, adapt, and choose a personal lifestyle, all commend high priority. Such policies are also most likely to pay for themselves, especially where the Challenge papers estimate high benefits relative to cost.

An important component of "cost" that was persistently emphasized by the Expert Panel concerned the difficulties and practical problems of actually delivering and implementing any given solution. This barrier includes the problem of dysfunctional and corrupt governments in many areas of the world, whose peoples are precisely the ones most in need of investment in human economic development. Regrettably, in such cases, it can be preferable to do nothing than to take action that strengthens the abusive power of such governments.

Hunger and Malnutrition (Chapter 6)

I ranked all the micronutrient solutions very highly because of their astonishing ability to deliver better health and cognitive ability to young children. Moreover, these nutrients positively interact with the development of immunity to many diseases:

- "Biofortification" (ranked at 4): This solution refers to research and investment in the development of genetically modified seeds that yield increased micronutrients directly in the grain. $60 million/year invested in biofortification carries the potential of replacing the need for more extensive and expensive programs for micronutrient supplements, or the fortification of staple foods such as flour. The latter programs must overcome cultural and distributional barriers, particularly in the poorest and most remote regions.
- "Micronutrient supplements for children (vitamin A and zinc)" (ranked at 9) and "Micronutrient fortification (iron and salt iodization)" (ranked at 13): I see both of these solutions as bridge programs to be supported – where they can actually be delivered – until they can be replaced by the biofortification of seeds that produce the enriched grains.

Trade and Subsidies (Chapter 8)

My highest priority, and the related "solutions" were:

- "Package of trade and migration reform" (ranked at 1), "Migration reform" (ranked at 2), and "The Doha development agenda" (ranked at 3): Essentially, I would strongly support any of these initiatives, however politically challenging. Liberalized migration has enormous potential for freeing people and their descendants from those political and cultural circumstances that deny opportunity for self-betterment. The five leading countries in the Economic Freedom Index were significantly defined and created by past migration: Singapore, Hong Kong, Australia, New Zealand, and the USA. Even a small amount of trade liberalization and subsidy reduction would generate new income that would more than pay for the entire cost of all the Copenhagen Consensus solutions.

Disease Control (Chapter 3)

Here, my rank ordering of individual disease solutions was:

- "Malaria prevention and treatment" (ranked at 5): Malaria is a largely preventable disease that can be brought under control with countermeasures such as indoor residual spraying with DDT, but control has slipped away from the public health reach in Africa. Since interventions began there have been substantial world-wide reductions in mortality because of immunization services (for polio, diphtheria, pertussis, tetanus, and measles), the eradication campaign for smallpox, and malaria control outside Africa. This progress contrasts with deaths from malaria inside Africa, which have more than tripled because of the limited use of indoor residual spraying that has been part of the acute management programs applied elsewhere (see Jamison et al., chapter 3 in this volume, table 3.2, and figure 3.4). The Copenhagen Consensus meeting in 2004 also assigned high priority to malaria control; subsequently, The WHO announced (September 15, 2006) approval of indoor residual spraying with DDT, a practice the organization stopped promoting in the early 1980s when health concerns were raised. (See: "WHO gives indoor use of DDT a clean bill of health for controlling malaria," and "WHO promotes indoor spraying with insecticides as one of three main interventions to fight malaria," Washington, DC, September 15, 2006.) Malaria prevention and treatment is low-cost compared with its benefits, and is relatively practical to deliver.
- "Expanded immunization coverage for children" (ranked at 6): A single visit to schools enables this relatively low-cost program to yield immense long-term benefits.
- "Tuberculosis case finding and treatment" (ranked at 10): Tuberculosis is second only to HIV/AIDS in causes of death from infectious diseases, but presents case management challenges and requires patient attendance at health facilities, making delivery more difficult than malaria control and one-time immunization programs. HIV/AIDS is the most difficult to prevent and treat of the communicable diseases. It is primarily a disease

of the poorest developing regions, which also present the most difficult problems of access. A recent assessment of progress states that "it is clear that treatment alone will never end the AIDS pandemic. New infections far outstrip our ability to treat everyone infected with the virus: around three people are newly infected for every person put on therapy – and current therapy is a lifelong commitment" ("25 years of HIV," *Nature*, May 15, 2008, p. 290). Sadly, I believe that the best hope for control of this disease where it is most needed, must await fundamental new understanding from basic research. Therefore, I concur with my Expert Panel colleagues in not listing the HIV/AIDS combination solution high enough to be within our $75 billion budget constraint.

Education (Chapter 4)

The Expert Panel discussion centered on reducing school cost to the parents (family). The issue is not well described as only "Lowering the price of schooling." "Lowering the price" and "lowering the cost" to parents are not equivalent. The Challenge paper discussed several strategies each effective in some subset of countries:

– Lowering government education fees (price) by subsidy: This was effective in some countries.
– Capitation grants: In many developing countries, private schools are important and their costs are lower than those of public schools. These grants have been successful as a means of encouraging the opening of new schools.
– Vouchers for low-income families have been effective in some countries.
– Subsidies for tutors have been effective in increasing the performance of children from low-income families in India.

For all these reasons, I assigned a high rating to "Lowering the cost (not only "price") of schooling" (ranked at 8).

Women and Development (Chapter 10)

"Increase and improve girls' schooling" (ranked at 11): I ranked this solution highest in this category. The evidence favoring this solution is reinforced by the Challenge paper, which showed that the rate of return on investment in girls' schooling is 36 percent higher (the return increases from 7.2 percent to 9.8 percent) than the comparable return on boys' schooling. The solutions the Expert Panel ranked at 7 ("Lowering the price of schooling") and at 8 ("Increase and improve girls' schooling") provide a combined expenditure total of $11.4 billion per year on education. A focus on girls' schooling, as well as general schooling, is clearly justified by economic fundamentals, and does not depend on affirmative action.

Climate Change (Chapter 5)

Climate change science is inherently limited by its inability to make controlled experiments that enable the predictions of climate change models to be tested against observations, as in physics, biology and the social sciences, for example: Its primary tools are computer simulation models. Some of the isolated components of these models (for example, infrared absorption by carbon dioxide) are better understood than how to weigh them in models of complex physical interaction among the components. These complex theoretical models are testable only by calibrating them on historical climate observations, and reserving some of the historical data to determine how accurate the models are in predicting the "out-of-sample" observations. To represent an accurate test, the data reserved for testing must be unbiased – i.e. represent a sample generated under the same environmental conditions as the data used for calibrating (estimating the parameters of) the model. Under these ideal conditions, subject only to random sampling variation, the model can be tested by using it to "predict" the independent data not used in the baseline calibration. This is a large order, trumped by the simple fact that the recent period during which it is thought that warming has had significant anthropogenic causes is the period beginning with 1972 (temperatures fell, 1940–72; rose, 1815–1940; fell, 1750–1815). This means, of course, that only part of the data for calibration from the past thirty-five years can be used to test predicatively the rest of the data; this results in very large standard errors of prediction, severely diminishes the reliability of the test exercise, and even implies a respectable probability of climate cooling, not warming. These limitations and uncertainties have been ignored in much of the public debate on climate change. These methodological problems do not reflect negatively on the dedication or competence of climate modelers, but refer only to the immense fundamental problem that confronts the science of climate change. In view of the monumental possible damage from warming, these realities are frustrating, but extreme possibility does not provide justification for mitigation actions.

Within the budget constraints of the Copenhagen Consensus process, the most attractive of the Challenge paper solutions would reduce expected temperatures from 3.5C to only 3C. Clearly, to make very much difference (assuming reduced carbon emissions will be effective) we need to know far more about low-carbon energy technologies than now exists. For this reason I rated R&D investment in this area at 25 among the 42 solutions I ranked. If it should turn out that we face a cooling rather than a warming problem, the resulting inventory of low-carbon technologies would not be implemented.

My view is that we should continue to monitor and study climate change; that we should not incur the draconian mitigation costs now being championed in some quarters, which would endanger our rapid global growth in income, human betterment, and knowledge. Such action would be counterproductive by reducing our capacity to deal with alternative challenges that have far more certainty of delivering huge short-run benefits, while weakening our ability to adapt to climate change in the event that the more dismal, untested, computer model predictions turn out to be realized. And if the extreme predictions are not realized, we have avoided wastefully diverting those resources from alleviating far more certain and immediate human harm.

Sanitation and Water (Chapter 7)

Based on my reading of their relative effectiveness and value in delivering tangible benefits, my ranking of the three solutions was: "Rural water supply" (at 12), "Bio-sand filters for household water treatment" (at 15), and "Total sanitation campaign" (at 23). Rural water quality and supply programs complement health, nutrition, and disease control, and deserve high-priority support.

Conflicts (Chapter 2)

In my judgment, the best of the alternatives considered – "Peace-keeping in post-conflict situations" (ranked at 32) – had a high opportunity cost relative to other uses of the funds.

Air Pollution (Chapter 1)

I regarded the best of the options considered to be "Improved stove intervention" (ranked at 24).

Terrorism (Chapter 9)

Interesting and imaginative as was this expert investigation, the evidence seemed inadequate to justify the funding for any solution.

Conclusions

Overall, the primary Copenhagen Consensus issues have not changed substantially since the 2004 process, although new studies have modified specific elements in setting priorities. Thus, relatively high benefits per unit cost are realizable in malaria control, nutrition, children's immunization programs, education (including special attention to girls' schooling), and sanitation and water supply. HIV/AIDS treatment continues to present formidable problems of delivery: The immense progress in treatment requires a lifelong commitment and access to clinics. Climate change as a predictive science is severely constrained by data and methodological limitations that argue strongly against incurring draconian costs with uncertain benefits in the absence of major improvements in low-carbon technology. Liberalizing trade and migration, and reducing subsidies, easily dominates all the challenges and more than pays its way.

Ranking the Opportunities: Vernon L. Smith

1	Package of trade and migration reform
2	Migration reform
3	The Doha development agenda
4	Biofortification
5	Malaria prevention and treatment
6	Expanded immunization coverage for children
7	De-worming and other nutrition programs at school
8	Lowering the price of schooling
9	Micronutrient supplements for children (vitamin A and zinc)
10	Tuberculosis case finding and treatment
11	Increase and improve girls' schooling
12	Rural water supply
13	Micronutrient fortification (iron and salt iodization)
14	Provide support for women's reproductive role
15	Bio-sand filters for household water treatment
16	Conditional cash transfers
17	Heart attack acute management
18	Tobacco tax
19	HIV/AIDS combination prevention
20	Community-based nutrition promotion
21	Improving surgical capacity at district hospital level
22	Microfinance
23	Total sanitation campaign
24	Improved stove intervention
25	R&D in low-carbon energy technologies
26	Large, multipurpose dam in Africa
27	Health and nutrition programs
28	Affirmative action
29	Inspection and maintenance of diesel vehicles
30	Low-sulfur diesel for urban road vehicles
31	Diesel vehicle particulate control technology
32	Peace-keeping in post-conflict situations
33	Greater international cooperation
34	Removing intra-American trade barriers
35	Rich nations drop barriers to poor nations
36	Increased proactive response
37	Target nations changing foreign policies
38	Augmented defensive measures
39	Business as usual
40	Package of adaptation, R&D and mitigation
41	R&D and mitigation
42	Mitigation only

NANCY L. STOKEY

Limiting Factors

The proposals I have ranked 1–20 have BCRs significantly above unity, and in this sense all are "worthwhile." The proposals I have ranked 21–29 are "not worthwhile," either because they have BCRs below unity or for other reasons.

The decision problem before the Expert Panel involved spending an incremental $75 billion spread over four years. Although this is a substantial sum, note by way of comparison that the direct US budget authority for the war in Iraq has been about $100 billion per year for each of the last five years. Note, too, that the goal is to consider incremental funding. A number of important health problems – for example, HIV/AIDS, malaria, and tuberculosis – are already receiving substantial funding from various sources. This reduces to some extent their priority for additional funding.

The design of the 2008 Copenhagen Consensus process implemented several improvements over that of 2004. Authors of the 2008 Perspective papers used a common discount rate (3 percent and 6 percent) for valuing future benefits, and common methods for valuing lives saved – $1,000 and $5,000 per DALY. As a consequence the BCRs reported in the various

Perspective papers are much more comparable. The method for valuing lives saved could be further improved, however. As Tom Schelling noted during the discussion, using the discounted value of DALYs probably over-values infants relative to older children and adults. The loss of the primary wage-earner in a household with dependents is probably much more serious than the loss of an infant. Similarly, the death of an older child, in whom time and education has been invested and who has stronger emotional and social connections to the family, may be a greater loss than the death of an infant.

For some of the proposals – providing nutritional supplements, expanding immunization, and conditional cash transfers for schooling – the limiting factor is direct financial cost. For other proposals – implementing the Doha development agenda of tariff reductions, adopting affirmative action legislation for women, levying a tobacco tax – the limiting factor is political resistance. For projects in the first category, computing BCRs is straightforward, at least in principle, and comparing ratios is appropriate. For proposals in the second category, the "costs" are not financial, so BCRs are not well defined. For example, implementing a tobacco tax has no direct costs: Indeed, the tax would generate revenues. Improving the political status of women may be a good idea, but it is not an outcome that can be "purchased" in the way that malaria treatment can be. The same can be said of implementing the Doha agenda, which involves tariff and subsidy reductions. The loss of tariff revenue is not the important barrier: It is the consequences for trade flows and for prices faced by domestic producers and consumers. The exercise would be more consistent if proposals of the second type were excluded. In the end, most of them were unrated by the Expert Panel; the Doha agenda got barely enough votes to stay on the final overall list.

The cost and benefit figures in these proposals are rough calculations, made on the basis of available information. In most cases the available information is sparse, to put it mildly. Thus, a high priority should be to develop better data. Specifically, it would be extremely useful – and

not very expensive – to fund field trials for some of the top-ranking projects, to get better estimates of both costs and benefits.

Subsidies and Trade Barriers (Chapter 8)

Among all the proposals considered here, the largest gains would come from implementing the Doha round of trade reforms. It is important here to be clear about magnitudes, however. It is easy when talking about large numbers to get confused. Was that US$ measured in millions, or billions, or trillions? The Copenhagen Consensus 2008 budget is $75 billion. If this sum were spent on projects with an average BCR of 20 (an optimistic assumption), it would produce total benefits of $1.5 trillion. The direct gains from trade reform, from the more efficient use of resources, are huge and would be enjoyed every year. Implementing the Doha reforms would produce gains in the range of $300 billion–$2.6 trillion per year, depending on the extent of the liberalization.

In addition, evidence is growing that international trade stimulates productivity growth in developing countries. For example, China, India, and Chile have all enjoyed rapid growth in productivity and in per capita income as they have become more export-oriented. Depending on the extent of the liberalization, the estimate of the productivity effect, and the discount rate, the total gains from trade reform are in the range $100 trillion–$400 trillion: Yes, these are trillions. Moreover, implementing trade reform has trivial out-of-pocket costs. Lowering barriers to international trade is perhaps the only policy issue with broad support from economists across the political spectrum. Unfortunately, after seven years of negotiation, the Doha talks collapsed in July 2008. Political considerations mean that this enormous free lunch will remain out of reach. World leaders should hang their heads in shame.

I ranked this proposal in the middle (at 9) only because it does not really fit the budgetary nature of this exercise and political considerations make it unlikely to be adopted in the foreseeable future.

Hunger and Malnutrition (Chapter 6)

The proposals in this category are exceptional, with some of the highest BCRs among the expenditure-based programs. The total cost for all of the proposals in this area is about $1.2 billion, and the overall BCR is 13. All should have high priority for funding. In particular, providing micronutrients to infants and children seems to offer a cheap way to improve both physical and mental capacity. These two proposals offer an opportunity to do enormous good at very low cost. Eliminating hunger is a noble goal but an expensive one: calories (rice, wheat, corn, and so on) are costly. But some of the worst side-effects of overall malnutrition can be avoided by providing key micronutrients. The most effective means of delivery depends on the nutrient. "Micronutrients (vitamin A and zinc)" – both of which the body can absorb in large quantities and store – can be provided in the form of periodic supplemental tablets, and the target group – young children – can be reached in school. "Micronutrient fortification (iron and salt iodization)" – which the body cannot store – can be provided by fortifying basic foods. These programs (ranked at 1 and 2, respectively) offer very high BCRs, and their total costs – $60 million for supplements and $286 million for fortification – are low.

The proposal for "Biofortification" (ranked at 3) involves developing strains of rice and other staple crops that are biofortified with iron and vitamin A. Funding research to accelerate the development of these crops looks very worthwhile. The proposal for "De-worming and other nutrition programs at school" (ranked at 8) overlaps one of the Education proposals: The model is a very successful program in Kenya, and the BCR is quite high.

"Community-based nutrition promotion" (ranked at 4) involves educating people – mainly women – about both overall nutritional issues and the special needs of pregnant women,

lactating women, infants, and small children. Education is difficult, and changing behavior even more so. Nevertheless, the potential benefits are large, so this proposal seems like a good candidate for field trials.

The proposals in this area are based on relatively good evidence about the benefits and costs, and the Perspective papers talked explicitly about the ease and difficulty of implementing various types of proposals. For example, policies that involve changing behavior are more difficult (more expensive) to implement. There are always questions about expanding coverage to a higher fraction of the population or extending it to new regions or countries, but there seems to be relatively strong experience in this area.

Conflicts (Chapter 2)

Some deaths are more horrible than others, for both victim and bystander. Although it is hard to say exactly how BCRs should be adjusted to reflect this view, it is nevertheless worth noting. The world stood by as atrocities were committed in Rwanda, and it is now doing little for Darfur. The proposal to provide "Peace-keeping in post-conflict situations" (ranked at 5) seems very worthwhile. In my opinion, the Perspective papers under-state the benefits.

Women and Development (Chapter 10)

The proposals here are quite diverse. Programs to "Provide support for women's reproductive role" (ranked at 6) have several different kinds of benefits, and taken together they make this a worthwhile program. Women's health clinics would deal with complications during pregnancy and reduce the risk of maternal and fetal death during delivery. In addition, allowing women access to better family planning technologies would allow them to better control the timing of pregnancies, delaying first pregnancies and increasing birth spacing. This would reduce the incidence of low birthweight, the cause of many development problems in infants. The beneficiaries would be mothers, infants, and siblings.

Programs to improve access to and quality of education in developing countries offer high BCRs. The ratios are high for boys as well as for girls, however. Thus, even though educational attainment for girls lags attainment for boys in many countries, at this point it seems difficult to support programs that "Increase and improve girls' schooling" but exclude boys. Thus, I ranked this proposal much lower (at 24) than the proposal offering "Conditional cash transfers" for keeping children (of either sex) in school (ranked at 12).

Strengthening the political voice of women is a laudable goal, but it is unclear how it is to be achieved, and in any case it seems less urgent than other issues.

The overall evidence on microfinance seems mixed. Some of its advocates claim that it is economically viable on its own, so no subsidies should be needed. Some of its detractors claim that its benefits per dollar of subsidy are similar to other cash transfer programs. I find it difficult to assess claims about the value of subsidies delivered in this form.

Disease Control (Chapter 3)

Many of the proposals in this area have impressive BCRs. "Expanded immunization coverage for children" (ranked at 7) has been effective in the past, reducing infant and child mortality rates dramatically over the last four decades. As vaccines against additional diseases become available, expanding these programs seems very worthwhile.Providing inexpensive medications for problems such as "Heart disease acute management" (ranked at 11) is a novel and intriguing idea. This project is an excellent candidate for field trials, to determine if attractive BCRs can be realized in practise. Substantial funding for "HIV/ AIDS combination prevention," "Malaria prevention and treatment," and "Tuberculosis case finding and treatment" is already being provided by various international organizations and private foundations. These problems deserve high priority

in an overall sense; in terms of additional funding they are still attractive, but are not at the top of the list (ranked at 14, 15, and 13, respectively).

Building hospitals in areas that lack provision has a number of benefits. For example, "Improving surgical capacity at district hospital level" would mean that traumatic injuries such as broken limbs could be treated more effectively. But the cost of provision is high. Thus, while this proposal has a BCR over unity, it ranks lower than the others in this area (at 19).

Increasing the "Tobacco tax" in developing countries does not seem like a high priority (ranked at 25).

Education (Chapter 4)

Better education raises earnings for market work and also improves productivity in various kinds of "home work" such as child rearing. Several issues are involved in improving education: getting kids to enroll in school, getting them to attend once enrolled, preventing them from dropping out, and getting them to learn while they are in school. An added benefit of school attendance is that schools provide a convenient forum for implementing various health and nutrition programs, and school age children are an important target group for such programs. The proposal for providing nutritional supplements and treatment for intestinal parasites ("De-worming and other nutrition programs at school") is very similar to one of the Malnutrition proposals. De-worming (ranked at 8) is especially important for school age children, since they are more vulnerable than adults to the adverse consequences of parasites. School age children are also a target group for micronutrient supplements (vitamin A and zinc). In both cases, schools offer a convenient forum for distributing the appropriate tablets. This is an outstanding proposal, as discussed above.

In many developing countries public schools are not free: Fees are common. In addition, for many families in these countries children can work and contribute to family income from an early age, so sending a child to school entails a reduction in family income. It is no surprise that eliminating school fees raises attendance. Paying compensation to low-income families for keeping children in school – conditional cash transfers – raises attendance even further. This proposal looked more attractive than a similar Women and Development proposal targeted at girls only, as discussed above.

Climate Change (Chapter 5)

The world cannot ignore the problem of global warming. The question is: What is to be done? More specifically, what should be done immediately and what should be planned for the near and more distant future? In the very short run (the next few years), a moderate amount of global warming is already "locked in" as a result of past emissions, even if current and future emissions were to drop (magically) to zero. Nothing can be done to prevent this warming, but some measures may be useful to help the most affected populations deal with its consequences. In the medium run (the next decade or so), emissions of greenhouse gases can be reduced dramatically only by significantly reducing the use of fossil fuels. This would exact a heavy economic toll: The recent steep rise in gasoline prices illustrates this very clearly. A tax on carbon emissions would act in precisely the same way, except that it would apply to coal and natural gas as well as gasoline. The costs in terms of forgone GDP would be substantial. It is worth noting, however, that Europeans have long been living quite comfortably with high gasoline prices. In the longer run, the world will need both cleaner technologies for using fossil fuels and alternative sources of energy – solar, wind, and water. These alternatives exist at present mainly as high-cost experiments and less-than-reliable secondary sources.

What does this mean for policy? The first priority is public support for basic "R&D in low-carbon energy technologies" (ranked at 10). The private sector can be relied on to fund more applied R&D but in this area, as in others, there is a role for public funding of basic research.

Immediate adoption of a very modest (global) carbon tax would probably also be desirable, with a tentative timetable for future increases. An immediate tax would provide useful information about how much emissions could be reduced at low cost, and would signal to markets that the global community was serious about reducing emissions. It would also allow time to develop the institutions that would eventually be needed to implement more serious emissions controls. The failure of the Doha trade talks makes one gloomy about the prospects for global cooperation on carbon emissions, however.

Sanitation and Water (Chapter 7)

The proposals for "Bio-sand filters for household water treatment," "Rural water supply," and a "Total sanitation campaign" (ranked at 16, 17, and 18, respectively) are all worthwhile, with BCRs of 2.7–3.2. But these ratios, while respectable, are considerably lower than some of the others. The proposal for a "Large multipurpose dam in Africa" on the Blue Nile (ranked at 23) looks like an attractive project for a consortium of governments from the relevant countries. The hydroelectric power produced by such a dam should generate sufficient revenues to make the project economically viable, even without subsidies.

Air Pollution (Chapter 1)

The figures here make a convincing case that this is an area that deserves no attention from the international community. The three proposals related to diesel fuel vehicles ("Inspection and maintenance of diesel vehicles," "Low-sulfur diesel for urban road vehicles," and "Diesel vehicle particulate control technology") (ranked at 26, 28, and 27, respectively) all have BCRs well below unity if DALYs are evaluated at $1,000. These technologies may have merit in rich countries, but in low-income regions they are not worthwhile. The proposal for "Improved stove intervention" (ranked at 22) has a BCR of 1.7–7.5, but it is suspect on other grounds. One of the largest benefits is supposed to be savings in fuel costs. If the figures are correct, it is surprising that there is not a private market for these stoves. Moreover, in field trials the recipients did not apparently bother to maintain and repair the stoves, so they fell out of use. The stoves do not seem to appeal to their target customer base: Perhaps the designers need input from a focus group.

Terrorism (Chapter 9)

The proposal for better international cooperation is certainly worthwhile, but political factors rather than lack of funds seem to be the main stumbling block.

Final Remarks

Many of the top-rated proposals, in my individual ranking and in the Expert Panel ranking as well, are targeted at increasing "human capital," broadly defined, by improving nutrition, health, and education. Programs in these areas have excellent track records for success, in the sense of delivering high benefits per dollar expended. Although the specific proposals considered here are new, these past successes make one optimistic that much more can be done.

Ranking the Opportunities: Nancy L. Stokey

1	Micronutrient supplements for children (vitamin A and zinc)
2	Micronutrient fortification (iron and salt iodization)
3	Biofortification
4	Community-based nutrition promotion
4	Community-based nutrition promotion
5	Peace-keeping in post-conflict situations
6	Provide support for women's reproductive role
7	Expanded immunization coverage for children
8	De-worming and other nutrition programs at school
9	The Doha development agenda
10	R&D in low-carbon energy technologies
11	Heart attack acute management
12	Conditional cash transfers
13	Tuberculosis case finding and treatment
14	HIV/AIDS combination prevention
15	Malaria prevention and treatment
16	Bio-sand filters for household water treatment
17	Rural water supply
18	Total sanitation campaign
19	Improving surgical capacity at district hospital level
20	Lowering the price of schooling
21	R&D and mitigation
22	Improved stove intervention
23	Large, multi-purpose dam in Africa
24	Increase and improve girls' schooling
25	Tobacco tax
26	Inspection and maintenance of diesel vehicles
27	Diesel vehicle particulate control technology
28	Low-sulfur diesel for urban road vehicles
29	Mitigation only

Conclusion

This book represents the end of two years of work, since we last started approaching the experts who fill these chapters and asked them to identify the best ways to solve the world's biggest problems.

They have provided us with the ultimate overview of how global decision makers can best put their money to use when they intend to improve the state of the world. The next part is up to you, the reader. Which of these projects do you think deserves attention first? Where do you think additional money should be spent? Where will you donate your money?

Prioritization is hard. It is much easier to say that we want to do everything. It's much easier to say that every global problem is important and we should solve them all, right now.

It is important not just to talk about what is the best thing to do right now, but also to acknowledge that some things should not be our top priority.

When the expert panel of economists made their findings in Copenhagen in 2008, they ranked lowest the proposal of combating climate change policies with mitigation only. The benefits of mitigation alone would be lower than the costs. Spending a dollar would get back less than a dollar worth of good.

Similarly, solutions to the problem of outdoor pollution have very low cost–benefit ratios when seen in a developing nation context because they are so expensive. It does not make sense for scarce resources to go to these investments first.

Since the first Copenhagen Consensus exercise was held in 2004, it is heartening to see things getting better in some areas. It is important to acknowledge and celebrate this progress.

One thing that stands out for me is that during the last four years, there has been a great increase in interventions and funding for HIV/ Aids prevention and treatment programs. Some of this growth in spending came as a result of the 2004 Copenhagen Consensus identifying HIV/ Aids initiatives as the best investments that the planet could make.

Because of that extra work, in 2008 the expert panel concluded that additional funds could achieve more in other areas. That tells me why it is vital that we continue to fund this research, and to promote the idea of prioritization of extra resources to achieve the most possible. Problems will change and evolve, and so will our knowledge about the best ways to respond.

I know that this book is sobering reading. It is eye-opening to realize the scale and spread of the planet's biggest challenges. It is tragic that the world's poorest billion people suffer the heaviest burden of the big problems.

Vitally, though, this is a book of solutions, not of problems. To me, one of the most remarkable features of the Copenhagen Consensus is that – twice now – we have had groups of the world's top economists agree to produce a prioritized list of solutions to the big problems.

The research papers we commissioned from specialist scholars show that we have the knowledge to do tremendous amounts of good in each of these areas.

Looking at the 'top ten' solutions identified by the expert panel, there are some fantastic ways to spend money to achieve good.

Paying mothers to send their daughters to school (the 10th best investment identified by the Copenhagen Consensus 2008) doesn't just improve the chances of girls staying in school – which we know is important – but it also puts money into the hands of women. That gives women more power in the home and increases the chances that that money will be spent on other children.

To me, one of the amazing things about the Copenhagen Consensus and this book is that they bring attention to important issues that are far from sexy. Take the sixth best investment: de-worming. Experts in the fields of both education and disease argue that de-worming would dramatically improve the life of afflicted children. As Sue Horton, the malnutrition and hunger scholar, said in Copenhagen, we would rather have kids benefiting from nutrition than the worms benefiting.

The top three investments offer staggering rewards for their expense. The third-highest investment, micronutrient fortification, is effectively iodizing salt and fortifying flour and staples with iron.

Salt iodization prevents goitre. This has been all but eradicated in the developed world, yet three-in-ten families in the developing world don't have this protection. Iodizing salt costs just five cents per person, per year.

Fortifying products with iron costs as little as twelve cents per person, per year. We know that iron deficiency leads to stunting and cognitive and developmental problems.

For $286 million, we could get iodized salt and fortified basic food items to 80 percent of the populations in the worst-affected areas. The benefits are estimated to be somewhere around nine times higher than the costs. This is a very, very good investment.

Next up the list we see the Doha Round where a comprehensive deal would have very positive results. The costs are obviously comparatively low, yet the potential benefits are very large.

If developing countries cut their tariffs by the same proportion as high-income countries, and services and investment are also liberalized, the global annual gains could climb to $120 billion, with $17 billion going to the world's poorest countries by 2015.

Politicians should be ashamed to have allowed the Doha Round to collapse in disarray. Global fear about free trade leaves the planet at risk of missing out on the extraordinary benefits it offers. Free trade is not just good for big corporations, or for job growth. It is plain good.

The top-ranked solution by the experts this year was providing micronutrients – particularly vitamin A and zinc – to 80 percent of the 140 million or so undernourished children in the world. This would require a commitment of just $60 million annually, a small fraction of the billions spent each year battling terrorism or combating climate change. The economic gains from improved productivity and a lower burden on the health system would eventually clear $1 billion a year. In effect, this means that each dollar brings benefits worth more than $17. This is an astonishingly good investment and I hope it is one that policy makers take note of.

Finding the most cost-effective ways to tackle the world's problems is no simple challenge and should not be left to professional economists alone. This research was years in the making. I now leave it in your hands to make your own decisions about the investments that would be greatest for humanity.

Bjørn Lomborg
2008